INTELLECTUAL PROPERTY:
LAW & THE INFORMATION SOCIETY

Cases & Materials

Fifth Edition, 2021

James Boyle
William Neal Reynolds Professor of Law
Duke Law School

Jennifer Jenkins
Clinical Professor of Law (Teaching) & Director,
Center for the Study of the Public Domain
Duke Law School

Center for the Study of the Public Domain

Table of Contents

Chapter Eleven
COPYRIGHTABLE SUBJECT MATTER

Chapter Twelve
COPYRIGHT'S "REACH": INFRINGEMENT

A Preface: Lessons from the Pandemic

This edition was written during a pandemic. COVID-19 spread around the world, causing death and illness and changing bits of our lives forever. We saw friends and relatives lose their loved ones or fall sick themselves. We saw global tragedy, exacerbated by global inequality. We saw heroes and fools, brilliant innovation and blundering idiocy. Most of all, we sat in our houses, staring at our little screens, whether they were bringing us law school classes over Zoom, Queen's Gambit, or the latest scientific research.

Something else remarkable happened during that interminable and tragic year. Beyond the *pathos* of loss and the *bathos* of the trivia with which we distracted ourselves, there was an intellectual sea-change. For much of 2020, a large percentage of the world's population focused on the kinds of issues that intellectual property scholars obsess about every day. How do we incentivize research into, and production of, vaccines against this disease? Remember that the incentives may range from the pursuit of scientific fame or the urgings of the conscience, to the politician's desire to give voters what they want, or the drug company's pursuit of future profits.

What is the role of the public or private sector? Will research, manufacture and delivery—shots into arms—go fastest if it is fueled by "push" or "pull"? *Ex ante* grants from governments and philanthropists or *post hoc* property rights over discoveries? More specifically, what aspects of knowledge and discovery should be available to all, "free as the air to common use," so that an entire global community can build upon them? What aspects must be fenced off, covered by exclusive rights such as patents, protected as trade secrets, or merely sequestered in copyrighted scientific journal articles, sitting behind paywalls? Will exclusive rights lure biotech startups and drug companies to focus on this problem, enticed by the promise of a lucrative monopoly were they to succeed? The central issue of intellectual property is the balance between open and closed, public domain and private right. The pandemic added the pressing humanitarian issues of global public health to the technocratic questions of optimum innovation policy. What is the right balance between encouraging innovation through exclusion and spreading its results cheaply to the world? This question was particularly acute in a context where leaving a significant proportion of the world unvaccinated is a threat to everyone, even the vaccinated, because of the possibility of mutation.

Should we have a global moratorium over the enforcement of patents over COVID vaccines and therapies? Or will that actually slow down the very process it is supposed to help, either because it scrambles the incentive system or because the know-how and tacit knowledge required to make the new vaccines goes far beyond the patents and is almost impossible to pass on, even if its possessors were willing to do so? If that were true, then the ability effectively to make the vaccine will remain in Europe and the US whatever the legal status of the patent rights. But is it true? And how can we know when much of that technology is secret? The more one knows, the more numerous the questions become.

Today's struggles do not take place in a vacuum; they are shaped by earlier decisions, inflection points and design choices about institutions and architecture. Intellectual property law and policy played a major role in those choices. The incredibly rapid sharing of the COVID-19 genome, which jump-started the vaccine development process, took place against the background of the earlier sequencing of the human genome. At the time, efforts were made to "privatize" aspects of that genomic map. Those efforts were rebuffed, for reasons that you will study in this class, and the eventual public-private partnership that released the first draft of the human genome did so openly. Both the map and the tools used to draw it were widely shared. That would turn out to be vital in the vaccine development process, but so would the long-pursued private efforts to create mRNA vaccines, which overcame daunting technical obstacles to produce an incredibly promising new technology, the uses for which go far beyond COVID. To pick another example, we take for granted the existence of a network—the internet—and the law and custom of open access to scientific literature, particularly when it lays out the results of government funded research. Both were vital in the accelerated process of scientific development but, as you will learn, neither was inevitable and both faced (and still face) considerable opposition.

These questions are exactly the types of issues intellectual property scholars study. They are not the *only* issues you will focus on in this course—far from it, and this should be reassuring to those of you who have been (falsely) told that intellectual property law requires a technical or scientific background.

You will be addressing whether a satirical mashup infringes the copyright over a song and whether a parodic website attacking a corporation or public figure commits trademark infringement. Does the United States Olympic Committee get to prohibit the holding of a "Gay Olympic games"? Is it legal to "jailbreak" your iPhone, so that you can use apps that Apple did not approve? You will learn about attempts to claim property rights over the text of the law, human genes, and the shape and color of a banana costume. On the other end of the spectrum, you will learn about the creation of privately constructed commons where the creators have chosen to grant their users rights to copy and even modify the work; using private intellectual property rights to create a space of public freedom. These include free and open source software such as Android, Chrome, and Linux. The authors of that software may range from scientists employed by major corporations to private individuals contributing to the project for the love of creation or the hope of professional recognition. But this intellectual shared space also includes Creative Commons licensed content, from Wikipedia and open access scientific literature to the textbook you are reading at this moment. You will see fights over intellectual property rules significantly shape the architecture of the Internet that is such a central and unquestioned feature of your lives. You will see the Mattel corporation attempt to stop a conceptual artist from taking pictures of Barbie "being attacked by various vintage household appliances," and work out whether it is legal to use bots to play the early levels of World of Warcraft. You will read Mark Twain arguing for perpetual copyright, Macaulay describing copyright as a tax on readers for the benefit of writers and Victor Hugo explaining how the rights of authors are central to free speech and to an intelligentsia that is not dependent on the state. Free speech, transgressive art, innovation and economic growth, the ecologies of creativity from cooking and stand-up to software, literature and music. All of this will be grist to our mill.

Our point here is simple. The pandemic shows us how vital these questions are and how important it is to get them right. But we also hope you can get a hint of how *fascinating* they can be. We feel privileged to study them. We hope this book gives you some sense of why, and how, that might be.

Introduction

This is an introduction to intellectual property law, the set of private legal rights that allows individuals and corporations to control intangible creations and marks—from logos to novels to drug formulæ—and the exceptions and limitations that define those rights. It focuses on the three main forms of US federal intellectual property—trademark, copyright and patent, with a chapter on trade secret protection—both Federal and state. Despite that central focus, many of the ideas discussed here apply far beyond those legal areas and far beyond the law of the United States. The cases and materials will discuss the lines that the law of the United States draws; when an intellectual property right is needed, how far it should extend and what exceptions there should be to its reach. But those questions are closely linked to others. How should a society set up its systems for encouraging innovation? How should citizens and policy makers think about disputes over the control of culture and innovation? How do businesses re-imagine their business plans in a world of instantaneous, nearly free, access to many forms of information? How should they do so? And those questions, of course, are not limited to this country or this set of rules. They should not be limited to the law or lawyers, though sadly they often are.

A word on coverage: An introductory class on intellectual property simply does not have time or space to cover everything. This course is designed to teach you basic principles, the broad architectural framework of the system, the conflicting policies and analytical tools that will be useful no matter what technological change or cultural shift tomorrow brings. Imagine the lawyer who started practicing in the late 1970s and had to deal with the rise of cable TV, a global internet, digital media, peer to peer systems, genetic engineering, synthetic biology . . . but also with viral marketing, the culture of "superbrand" identity, cybersquatting and social media. You will be that lawyer, or that citizen. Your world will change that much and you will need the tools to adapt.

To achieve this goal—a "future-proofed" grasp of the basic principles and tensions of the system—the book has to omit large swaths of detail. For example, standard form, "click to accept," contracts and licenses are extremely important in the world of digital commerce, but will be covered only to the (important) extent they intersect with intellectual property law. Even within the topics that are covered, the approach of the class is highly selective. We will cover the basic requirements for getting a trademark, and the actions that might—or might not—infringe that right. But we will not cover the complexities of trademark damages and injunctions, international trademark practice or the fine detail of the ways that Federal and state trademark law interact. Copyright law is full of highly specialized provisions—applying special rules to cable television stations or music licenses, for example. We will be mentioning these only in passing. Similarly, patent law is an enormously complex field; there are entire courses just on the details of patent drafting, for example, and there is a separate "patent bar" exam for registered patent attorneys and agents. This class will touch only on the basics of patentable subject matter, and the requirements of utility, novelty, and non-obviousness.

As we will explain in a minute, one feature of this book makes this selectivity less of a problem. Because this is an "open" casebook, an instructor can take only those chapters that he or she finds of interest and can supplement, delete or edit as she wishes.

Comparison of the Three Main Forms of Federal Intellectual Property

	TRADEMARK	COPYRIGHT	PATENT
Constitutional and Statutory Basis	Commerce clause, Lanham Act. (There are also state trademarks.)	IP Clause, Copyright Act	IP clause, Patent Act
Subject Matter	Word, phrase, symbol, logo, design etc. used in commerce to identify the source of goods and services	Creative works—for example, books, songs, music, photos, movies, computer programs	Inventions—new and useful processes, machines, manufactured articles, compositions of matter. Not abstract ideas or products/laws of nature
Requirements for Eligibility	Not generic (or merely descriptive without secondary meaning), identifies source of product or service, used in commerce	Original expression, fixed in material form	Useful, novel and non-obvious to a person having ordinary skill in the art (PHOSITA)
Rights	Basic trademark right only *vis a vis* a particular good or service. Bass for beer, not ownership of word "Bass." Prevent others from using confusingly similar trademarks; for famous marks, prevent others from "diluting" the mark. Also prohibitions against false or misleading advertising.	Exclusive rights to copy, distribute, make "derivative works", publicly perform and publicly display. Possibly new right to stop circumvention of digital 'fence' protected © works.	Exclude others from making, using, selling or importing invention
Duration	*If* renewed and continually used in commerce, can be perpetual.	Life plus 70 years; 95 years after publication for corporate works	20 years for utility patents
How Rights are Procured	USPTO trademark registration process for ® status, though common law rights are recognized absent registration	Creation and fixation in a tangible medium; registration is not required to get copyright (but is required for suit to enforce)	USPTO patent application process
Examples of Limitations and Exceptions	Genericity, nominative fair use, parodic use	Idea and fact/expression distinction, scènes à faire, fair use, first sale	Abstract knowledge in patent application disclosed freely. Subsequent inventors can "build on" patented invention and patent result without permission. Both inventors must consent to market resulting compound invention.

Basic Themes: Three Public Goods, Six Perspectives

This book is organized around a debatable premise; that it is useful to group together the three very different types of property relations that comprise Federal intellectual property law—trademark, copyright and patent. A chart that summarizes their main features is on the previous page. Obviously, trademarks over logos are very different from copyrights over songs or patents over "purified" gene sequences. The rules are different, the constitutional basis changes, the exceptions are different and there is variation in everything from the length of time the right lasts to the behavior required to violate or trigger it. Why group them together then? The answer we will develop depends on a core similarity—the existence of a "good"—an invention, a creative work, a logo—that multiple people can use at once and that it is hard to exclude others from. (Economists refer to these as "public goods" though they have more technical definitions of what those are.) Lots of people can copy the song, the formula of the drug, or the name Dove for soap. But the approach in this book also depends on the *differences* between the goals of these three regimes and the rules they use to cabin and limit the right so as to achieve those goals. The idea is that one gains insight by comparing the strategies these very different legal regimes adopt. The proof of that pudding will be in the eating. Our readings will also deal with the claim that the term "intellectual property" actually causes more harm than good.

This book is built around six perspectives. Some are introduced as separate chapters, while others are woven into the materials and the problems throughout the entire class. The first deals with the main rationales for (and against) intellectual property. The second focuses on the constitutional basis for, and limitations on, that property in the United States. The third is the substance of the course; the basic doctrinal details of trademark, copyright and patent, and the broad outlines of trade secrecy, which is protected both by state rules and a new Federal cause of action. The fourth concentrates on the way that intellectual property law reacts dynamically to changes in technology. We will focus on what happens when trademark law has to accommodate domain names, when copyright—a legal regime developed for books—is expanded to cover software and when patent law's subject matter requirements meet the networked computer on the one hand and genetic engineering on the other. In particular, the copyright portion of the course, which makes up the largest portion of the book, will detail extensively how judges and legislators used the limitations and exceptions inside copyright law to grant legal protection to those who create software, while trying to minimize anti-competitive or monopolistic tendencies in the market. The fifth deals with the metaphors, analogies, similes and cognitive "typing" we apply to information issues. This is an obviously artificial property right created over an intangible creation; the way that the issue is framed—the baselines from which we proceed, the tangible analogies we use—will have a huge influence on the result. Finally, the conclusion of the course tries to synthesize all of these perspectives to point out prospects, and guiding principles, for the future.

An Open Course Book?

This book is made available under a Creative Commons Attribution, Non-Commercial, Share-Alike 3.0 Unported License. Later in the semester, you will be able to engage in learned discussion of this arrangement. You will be able to work out what the copyright on the book does and does not cover (hint, Federal legal materials are in the public domain), why and how the license is enforceable, and what rights you would have even in the absence of a license (such as the right to quote or criticize). At the moment, all you need to know is this. You are free to copy, reprint or reproduce this book in whole or part, so long as you attribute it correctly (directions are given on the copyright page) and so long as you do not do so commercially, which we interpret to mean "for a profit." In other words, you can print copies and distribute them to your students or your friends, who apparently have very geeky interests, at the cost of reproduction, but you may not make a competing commercial edition and sell it for a profit or use it as a draw to promote your own commercial textbook business. You can also modify this book, adding other material, or customizing it for your own class, for example. But if you do modify the book, you must license the new work you have created under the same license so that a future user will receive your version with the same freedoms that you were granted when you received this version.

Why do we do this? Partly, we do it because we think the price of legal casebooks and materials is obscene. Law students, who are already facing large debt burdens, are required to buy casebooks that cost $150–$200, and "statutory supplements" that consist mainly of unedited, public domain, Federal statutes for $40 or $50. This is not a criticism of casebook authors, but rather of the casebook publishing system. We know that putting together a casebook is a lot of work and can represent considerable scholarship and pedagogic innovation. We just put together this one and we are proud of it. But we think that the cost is disproportionate and that the benefit flows disproportionately to conventional legal publishers. Some of those costs might have been justifiable when we did not have mechanisms for free worldwide and almost costless distribution. Some might have been justifiable when we did not have fast, cheap and accurate print on demand services. Now we have both. Legal education is already expensive; we want to play a small part in diminishing the costs of the materials involved.

We make this casebook available in two forms. First, it can be digitally downloaded for free. No digital rights management. Second, it is available in a low cost but high quality paperback version for about $35—which given the possibility of resale, might make it an environmentally attractive alternative to printing out chapters and then throwing them away. The companion statutory supplement is available under a similar arrangement— though under a license that is even more open. We also hope both of these options are useful for those who might want to use the books outside the law school setting. The casebook and the statutory supplement will be available for a combined price around $50. Those who do not want, or cannot afford, to pay that price can use the free digital versions.

The price of this book is intended to be a demonstration of how unreasonable casebook costs are. We are making the digital version freely available and trying to price the paper version inexpensively, but we entirely support those authors who wish a financial reward. We calculate that they could actually set the price of an 825 page book *$100 cheaper* than the average casebook today (albeit in paperback) and still earn a comparable royalty per book to what they currently earn. For example, in 2016, Professors Mark Lemley, Peter Menell, and Robert Merges began self-publishing their excellent casebook on intellectual property, *Intellectual Property in the New Technological Age*, which allowed them to make it far less expensive.

Authors could even make the digital version freely available and do nicely on print sales, while benefiting in terms of greater access and influence. Our point is simply that the current textbook market equilibrium is both unjust and inefficient. Students are not the only ones being treated unfairly, nor is the market producing the variety or pedagogical inventiveness one would want. One practical example: using current print on demand technology, images are as cheap as words on the page. This book has many of them—from comic book pages illustrating the doctrine, to flow charts, to pictures that give context to the cases. It is *useful* to see the *Lotus v. Borland* menus, the "food-chain Barbie" pictures, the actual article from *Harper & Row v. Nation Enterprises*, to see the logos at stake in the trademark cases, the allegedly copyrighted sculptures on which people park their bikes, or a graphic novel version of the *de minimis* controversy in musical sampling. Our point is that standard casebooks are not just vastly overpriced, they are awkward, inflexible, lacking visual stimulus, incapable of customization and hard to preview and search on the open web.

Personally, we do not merely wish to lower the costs of educational materials but, where possible, to make those materials open—a different thing. Open licenses and freely downloadable digital versions make the digital version of educational materials freely available to the world, not just in terms of zero price, but in terms of legal freedoms to customize, translate, edit and combine. We are not the first to try and make open source educational material or even casebooks. We would like to thank the good folk at Creative Commons and MIT Open Courseware, Barton Beebe, Bryan Frye, Lydia Loren, CALI's eLangdell, Jordi Weinstock, Jonathan Zittrain, and the H20 project at Harvard for giving us ideas and inspiration.

We also hope that the inexorable multiplication of projects such as these will be an aid to those still publishing with *conventional* textbook publishers. To the casebook author trapped in contracts with an existing publishing house: remember when you said you needed an argument to convince them to price your casebook and your supplement more reasonably? Or an argument to convince them to give you more options in making digital versions available to your students in addition to their print copies, but without taking away their first sale rights? Here is that argument. Traditional textbook publishers *can* compete with free. But they have to try harder. We will all benefit when they do.

We have another goal, one that resonates nicely with the themes of the course. Most authors who write a casebook feel duty-bound to put in a series of chapters that make its coverage far more comprehensive than any one teacher or class could use. Jane Scholar might not actually teach the fine details of statutory damages in copyright, and whether they have any constitutional limit, but feels she has to include that chapter because some other professor might think it vital. As a result, the casebook you buy contains chapters that will never be assigned or read by any individual instructor. It is like the world of the pre-digital vinyl record. (Trust us on this.) You wanted the three great songs, but you had to buy the 15 song album with the 9 minute self-indulgent drum solo. This book contains the material *we* think vital. For example, it has introductory sections on theoretical and rhetorical assumptions that we think are actually of great practical use. It spends more time on constitutional law's intersection with intellectual property or the importance of limitations and exceptions to technological innovation than some other books, and less on many other worthy topics. Because of the license, however, other teachers are free to treat the casebook in a modular fashion, only using—or printing—the chapters, cases and problems they want, adding in their own, and making their own "remix" available online as well, so long as they comply with the terms of the license.

Structure and Organization

A word about the organization of the book: First, each chapter has a series of problems. The problems bring up issues that we want you to think about as you read the materials. Some are intended to "frame" the discussion, others to allow you to measure your mastery of the concepts and information developed, or to deepen your understanding of the analytical and argumentative techniques the book sets forth. The problems are covered under the same license—you should feel free to extract them, even if you do not use the book. Second, in the copyright section, we draw on material from our educational graphic novel *Theft!: A History of Music* to present some of the doctrinal material in a memorable and visually interesting manner. Third, each major section of the book—trademark, copyright, patent—is preceded by a flow chart to show students how the whole jigsaw puzzle fits together. The flow charts can also be used to work through the materials in the problems. Then, at the end of the section, we provide a checklist of issues that the casebook has dealt with; students can use these for outlining or simply refreshing their memories.

The open licensing arrangement of the book means that we include little material that is not either public domain, written by the authors themselves, or available under a Creative Commons license. But since that same licensing arrangement allows for near infinite customization by users, we hope that is not too much of a problem. We include short excerpts from *The Public Domain*—also Creative Commons licensed and freely downloadable—with hyperlinks to the full versions of those readings. We use it as a companion text in the course. The excerpts provide historical and theoretical background keyed to the discussion and the problems. Instructors and readers who wish to omit those readings, or to insert other secondary materials, should just ignore them.

Some acknowledgements: We would like to thank Mr. Balfour Smith, the coordinator of the Center for the Study of the Public Domain at Duke Law School for his tireless editorial efforts, for navigating the publishing process and for his nifty cover designs.

We would like to thank generations of students—not only at Duke—for patiently teaching their teachers what works and what does not. We would like to thank our predecessors for teaching us how hard it is to make a good casebook and how important one can be. Particular thanks in that regard go out to Julie Cohen, Rochelle Dreyfuss, Paul Goldstein, Edmund Kitch, Roberta Kwall, David Lange, Mark Lemley, Jessica Litman, Robert Merges, and Peter Menell. Special thanks to Dana Remus, Joseph Blocher, James Grimmelman, Kathy Strandburg, Amy Kapczynski, Josh Walton, and David Dame-Boyle for being test readers or intrepid early adopters. Finally, James thanks Jennifer and Jennifer thanks James. Aww.

If you adopt the book, or any part of it, please let us know! Comments to boyle [AT] law.duke.edu are always welcome, particularly if you can tell us why certain chapters or exercises were helpful or not helpful to you as an instructor or student, or describe a particular customization. Free digital versions of the latest edition will be available at https://law.duke .edu/cspd/openip/.

Note on the Fifth Edition: This edition introduces a new set of tools for teachers and students; flowcharts before and checklists after each doctrinal subject. Teaching remotely during the pandemic, we found that this helped the students structure their analysis and get beyond the elements of a cause of action to more sophisticated topics. Substantively, we have added the landmark *Google v. Oracle* decision and notes on recent appellate fair use decisions. There are new notes on *Georgia v. PRO,* dealing with the copyrightability of state law, and *PTO v. Booking.com* on genericity in trademarks. We explained the recently-passed CASE Act, which introduces a small claims procedure for copyright infringement, and updated the empirical analysis of the patent system. We added many images and comic book pages to illustrate the material. Finally, and perhaps most importantly, we added a preface explaining how the pandemic showed the importance—but also the intellectual fascination—of the questions this course covers.

James Boyle and Jennifer Jenkins
Durham, NC, July 2021

CHAPTER ONE

The Theories Behind Intellectual Property

Every student is familiar with the theoretical throat-clearing that often appears at the beginning of a course—"what do we really mean by inorganic chemistry?"—never to reappear in either the student's understanding of the materials or on the exam. It needs to be stressed that this chapter is not like that at all. The theories that explain the justifications for and limitations on intellectual property get applied every day in intellectual property disputes. The parties themselves have to decide whether or not to object to a particular use or benefit that flows from their creations. They have to decide how to structure their activities so as to make a profit or achieve some social goal. In both cases, the analysis of the costs and benefits of exclusion and the economics of information covered in the first section of the course are central to the activity. And finally, if a legal dispute arises, the theoretical ideas behind intellectual property are very much part of the picture. As a result, this chapter is devoted to the theories behind intellectual property and the ways those theories play out in practice.

Framing: The first theme is the way that intellectual property issues are "framed," the analogies, metaphors and moral baselines that define the discussion. Social, regulatory or legal disputes about information issues do not arrive in popular consciousness or courtroom automatically "preformatted." We have many strong, and sometimes contradictory, sets of normative assumptions about information. It plays a vital role in:

- our conception of privacy, a term we assume to begin with informational control, the ability to control the flow of information about ourselves, for reasons both dignitary and instrumental.

- our conception of the public sphere of speech, free expression and debate; from "sunlight is the best disinfectant" to "the marketplace of ideas," our baseline when thinking about issues we frame as "speech issues" is that the free flow of information is both right and good.

- our conception of the efficient, competitive market. Precisely because individual informed choice is what leads to aggregate overall efficiency, in the perfect market, information is free, instantaneous and perfect.

- our conception of information property—the intangible information or innovation goods that I should be able to own and control, either because that property right will encourage others to socially useful innovative activities, or because we think that in some deontological—duty-based—sense, the information is simply *mine*—for example, because I worked hard to generate it.

Notice how these implicit normative frames are (often) at odds with each other. Privacy is a value that will not always further the goal of free expression, and *vice versa*. Think of the European "right to be forgotten" on search engines. (Though privacy may also reinforce free speech—the anonymous whistleblower, the secret ballot.) The search for costless instantaneous information-flow will conflict fundamentally with the postulate that someone has to be paid for generating that information in the first place, perhaps by being granted a property right to control that information—a contradiction that you will find to be central in this course. And the conflicts are not just binary, or between those pairs alone.

It would be one thing if we conducted our debates by saying "should we think of this with our 'information property,' or our 'costless information' glasses on?" "Speech or privacy?" But the rhetorical frames are often implicit rather than explicit. We characterize some new issue or technology using similes and metaphors that hark back to the past, each of which is freighted with normative associations that conjure up one or other of these frames. Is an online social network a *private* mall, a local *newspaper*, a *public* park or a *common carrier* like the phone company? Is a search engine just like the *travel guide book* that maps the city—good neighborhoods and bad—or like the guy who *takes a cut* for steering you towards the man with the illegal drugs? Speech? Property? Privacy? Competition? By being aware of the implicit messages and associations that come with our metaphors and our framings, we can challenge our unreflective way of classifying the issue, alerting ourselves to nuances we might otherwise have missed. But these framings can also be used as a matter of advocacy, whether in court or in the media, thoroughly transforming the way a question is perceived, regulated or decided.

Justifying Intellectual Property: The second theme goes to the 'why,' 'when,' and 'how much' of intellectual property.

Can a scriptwriter get a copyright on the stock plot themes used in spy movies—spies with silenced pistols, car chases, glamorous assassins in tight clothing? What if he were the first person to come up with those particular plot lines? Does the answer to that question have to do with how detailed the plot line is, or does it have to do with the effect that copyrighting stock plot lines would have on film? Or both?

Does ownership of a copyright in software give you the right to forbid another person from "decompiling" that software—reverse engineering it so that he can build a compatible or "interoperable" program? Should it give you the right to forbid that activity? Does the answer to those questions depend on whether an unauthorized *copy* is created while the program is being reverse engineered? Or does it depend on the effect that prohibiting reverse engineering would have on the software market? Or both?

Trademark gives you the exclusive right to use a name or symbol in connection with a particular kind of commercial activity—Delta for airlines (or Delta for faucets, or coffee—at least in Europe.) Bass for ale (or Bass for electronics.) Prius for hybrid cars. Should you be able to prohibit a competitor from using your trademarked name in comparative advertising? "Toyota Prius owners will find that the Nissan Leaf is superior to their existing hybrid. It is 100% electric! Say 'no' to the gas guzzling Prius and 'yes' to Leaf!"

Can you patent an algorithm that can be used to "hedge" or guard against risk in the energy market? Does that depend, should that depend, on whether the algorithm is implemented in a computer or does it depend on some theory about leaving free certain raw material for the next generation of inventors? On whether or not we need patents to encourage the development of new business methods?

We cannot answer all those questions here—that will take the entire course. But discussing them would be hard without some grasp of the ideas we will discuss in the first section.

Three linked questions will come up as we consider these issues.

- If I put my labor into gathering some information or developing some innovation, do I presumptively gain a right over that information or innovation? (And if so, how extensive a right?)
- Should we view intellectual property rights in terms of their utilitarian effects rather than on some notion of labor and value? In other words, should we grant rights when that is necessary to produce more innovation and information, or to facilitate signaling between producers and consumers, but only then and

only to that extent?

- Every day our activities produce effects on others. When we are not forced to internalize those effects, we call them externalities. Some of those externalities are negative (pollution, for which the factory does not have to pay) and others positive (the great TV chef who starts a cooking craze that ends up making most food served in a culture better, including food served by and to people who never watched the show). Many intellectual property claims have to do with positive externalities. Someone says "you have benefited from what I did! Therefore I should be able to control your activity, or at least get paid!" When do we find these arguments convincing and when not? Why?

Those are our three basic questions about intellectual property.

Let us now turn back to the preliminary step, the framing of information issues in the first place.

PROBLEM 1-1
FRAMING.

Every time someone uses a phone, the phone company necessarily ends up with a lot of information: what number was called, when it was called, how long the call lasted. In the eloquent regulatory parlance of telecommunications law this data is called Customer Proprietary Network Information or CPNI.

This data accretes over time, so that the phone company can see how often a particular customer calls a particular number, and when he or she typically does so and so on. What's more, this information can be cross-indexed with other sources of information or other databases. On the macro level, calls can be grouped by area code, which gives a rough guide to the geographical location of the person called, though less so in the era of cell phones. On the micro level, numbers can be identified by reverse lookup, so that the company—or the entity it provides this information to—can identify exactly who or what is being called: your mother, your local market, your hairdresser.

CPNI is important for another reason. By having unrestricted ability to use their own existing customer data, incumbent telephone companies have an advantage over startups that want to break into the market. The advantage comes in two related areas. First, marketing. Because they have the CPNI of their own customers, telephone companies know precisely the people to whom they might market a "friends and family plan", or a long distance plan, a big data plan, or an international calling plan with unlimited talk time. Caller data identifies the chatty out-of-stater, the lonely expatriate, or the small town queen bee. It is a treasure trove for the marketing of the plans that would appeal to each—rather than a confusing welter of options broadcast to the world at large. Studies have shown that consumers respond much more positively to this kind of targeted advertising rather than the "shotgun" approach that those seeking to enter the market must use. Second, CPNI is also (though telephone companies do not typically stress this fact) extremely valuable in *pricing* such offerings. Willingness to pay is best gleaned from past behavior and CPNI reveals past behavior. For these two reasons, new telephone companies have claimed incumbents' ability to mine their own customers' data is a significant barrier to market-entry.

We have mentioned four "frames" into which information issues can be placed.
i.) Information as that which must be controlled to protect privacy.

ii.) Perfect information—free, instant and available to all—as a necessary condition of a competitive market.

iii.) Information as something that can be owned, as property.

iv.) Information as that which must circulate freely in the service of freedom of expression and free speech—both political and commercial.

Assume that Congress gave the FCC authority to regulate telephone companies' use of CPNI. What framings would you suggest in order to make the strongest case for regulating use of CPNI tightly? (For example, requiring that consumers "opt in" to having their information used for any purpose other than billing and solving technical problems.) What kinds of anecdotes or analogies might you use to strengthen the salience and appeal of those ways of framing the problem? If you were a lawyer or strategist for the telephone companies, how would you respond? What alternative framings, or moral "baselines" could you provide? What analogies or anecdotes would you use to strengthen *these* frames or baselines? Without getting into the details of administrative law, how might you frame the broad outlines of a court challenge to any such regulations?

James Boyle, *The Apple of Forbidden Knowledge*
Financial Times, *August 12, 2004*

You could tell it was a bizarre feud by the statement Apple issued, one strangely at odds with the Palo Alto Zen-chic the company normally projects. "We are stunned that Real-Networks has adopted the tactics and ethics of a hacker to break into the iPod, and we are investigating the implications of their actions under the DMCA [Digital Millennium Copyright Act] and other laws." What vile thing had RealNetworks done? They had developed a program called Harmony that would allow iPod owners to buy songs from Real's Music Store and play them on their own iPods. That's it. So why all the outrage? It turns out that this little controversy has a lot to teach us about the New Economy.

Apple iPods can be used to store all kinds of material, from word processing documents to MP3 files. If you want to use these popular digital music players to download copy-protected music, though, you have only one source: Apple's iTunes service, which offers songs at 99 cents a pop in the US, 79p in the UK. If you try to download copy-protected material from any other service, the iPod will refuse to play it. That has been the case until now. Real's actions would mean that consumers had two sources of copy-protected music for their iPods. Presumably all the virtues of competition, including improved variety and lowered prices, would follow. iPod owners would be happy. But Apple was not.

The first lesson of the story is how strangely people use the metaphors of tangible property in new economy disputes. How exactly had Real "broken into" the iPod? It hadn't broken into my iPod, which is after all my iPod. If I want to use Real's service to download music to my own device, where's the breaking and entering? What Real had done was make the iPod "interoperable" with another format. If Boyle's word processing program can convert Microsoft Word files into Boyle's format, allowing Word users to switch programs, am I "breaking into Word"? Well, Microsoft might think so, but most of us do not. So leaving aside the legal claim for a moment, where is the ethical foul? Apple was saying (and apparently believed) that Real had broken into something different from my iPod or your iPod. They had broken into the idea of an iPod. (I imagine a small, Platonic white rectangle, presumably imbued with the spirit of Steve Jobs.)

Their true sin was trying to understand the iPod so that they could make it do things that Apple did not want it to do. As an ethical matter, is figuring out how things work, in order to compete with the original manufacturers, breaking and entering? In the strange nether land between hardware and software, device and product, the answer is often a morally heartfelt "yes!" I would stress "morally heartfelt". It is true manufacturers want to make lots of money, and would rather not have competitors. Bob Young of Red Hat claims "every business person wakes up in the morning and says 'how can I become a monopolist?'" Beyond that, though, innovators actually come to believe that they have the moral right to control the uses of their goods after they are sold. This isn't your iPod, it's Apple's iPod. Yet even if they believe this, we don't have to agree.

In the material world, when a razor manufacturer claims that a generic razor blade maker is "stealing my customers" by making compatible blades, we simply laugh. The "hacking" there consists of looking at the razor and manufacturing a blade that will fit. But when information about compatibility is inscribed in binary code and silicon circuits, rather than the molded plastic of a razor cartridge, our moral intuitions are a little less confident. And all kinds of bad policy can flourish in that area of moral uncertainty.

This leads us to the law. Surely Apple's legal claim is as baseless as their moral one? Probably, but it is a closer call than you would think. And that is where the iPod war provides its second new economy lesson. In a competitive market, Apple would choose whether to make the iPod an open platform, able to work with everyone's music service, or to try to keep it closed, hoping to extract more money by using consumers' loyalty to the hardware to drive them to the tied music service. If they attempted to keep it closed, competitors would try to make compatible products, acting like the manufacturers of generic razor blades, or printer cartridges. The war would be fought out on the hardware (and software) level, with the manufacturer of the platform constantly seeking to make the competing products incompatible, to badmouth their quality, and to use "fear, uncertainty and doubt" to stop consumers switching. (Apple's actual words were: "When we update our iPod software from time to time, it is highly likely that Real's Harmony technology will cease to work with current and future iPods.") Meanwhile the competitors would race to untangle the knots as fast as the platform manufacturer could tie them. If the consumers got irritated enough they could give up their sunk costs, and switch to another product altogether. All of this seems fine, even if it represents the kind of socially wasteful arms race that led critics of capitalism to prophesy its inevitable doom. Competition is good, and competition will often require interoperability.

But thanks to some rules passed to protect digital "content" (such as copyrighted songs and software) the constant arms race over interoperability now has a new legal dimension. The Digital Millennium Copyright Act and equivalent laws worldwide were supposed to allow copyright owners to protect their content with state-backed digital fences that it would be illegal to cut. They were not supposed to make interoperability illegal, still less to give device manufacturers a monopoly over tied products, but that is exactly how they are being used. Manufacturers of printers are claiming that generic ink cartridges violate the DMCA. Makers of garage door openers portray generic replacements as "pirates" of their copyrighted codes. And now we have Apple claiming that RealNetworks is engaged in a little digital breaking and entering. In each case the argument equates the actions required to make one machine or program work with another to the actions required to break into an encrypted music file. For a lot of reasons this is a very bad legal argument. Will it be recognised as such?

There the answer is less certain. In the United States, there are exceptions for reverse engineering, but the European copyright directive bobbled the issue badly, and some of the efforts at national implementation have the same problem. In the legitimate attempt to protect an existing legal monopoly over copyrighted content, these "technological measure" provisions run the risk of giving device and software manufacturers an entirely new legal monopoly over tied products, undercutting the EU's software directive and its competition policy in the process. Pity the poor razor manufacturers. Stuck in the analogue world, they will still have to compete to make a living, unable to make claims that the generic sellers are "breaking into our razors."

Though this is an entirely unnecessary, legally created mess there is one nicely ironic note. About 20 years ago, a stylish technology company with a clearly superior hardware and software system had to choose whether to make its hardware platform open, and sell more of its superior software, or whether to make it closed, and tie the two tightly together. It chose closed. Its name: Apple. Its market share, now? About 5 per cent. [In 2020 it was 9.6%.] Of course, back then competition was legal. One wishes that the new generation of copyright laws made it clearer that it still is.

Questions:

1.) What are the differences in the way that Boyle and Apple frame the Apple/Real Networks controversy? Do any of the arguments they use apply to Problem 1-1?

2.) Boyle uses as an example the manufacturer of a razor or a printer trying to prevent competing companies from offering generic versions of the blade or the toner cartridge. The razor company and printer company produced this market—in that sense they provide a "benefit" to the generic companies which did nothing to develop either product. Why do we commonly assume nevertheless that the original companies do not have the right to control complementary products? Does that assumption apply with information age goods? Why? Why not?

3.) Might there be socially negative effects if Apple and other providers of "platform technologies" like phones and game consoles are not allowed to exclude a competitor from its ecosystem? What would they be?

4.) Three different ways of seeing intellectual property issues are posed on pages 2–3; as rightful rewards to labor, as incentives to innovation and facilitators of market signals between producers and consumers, and finally as claims that arise whenever an activity yields a positive externality to a third party. Can Apple make any or all of these claims? What is Boyle's response?

PROBLEM 1-2

JUSTIFYING AND LIMITING.

It is early in the days of the Internet and you and your friends have just had a great idea. You are avid football fans, fond of late night conversations about which team is really the best, which player the most productive at a particular position. Statistics are thrown about. Bragging is compulsory. Unlike other casual fans, you do not spend all your time rooting for a particular *team*. Your enjoyment comes from displaying your knowledge of *all* the players and *all* the teams, using statistics to back up your claims of superiority and inferiority. You find these conversations pleasant, but frustrating. How can one determine definitively who wins or loses these debates? Then you have a collective epiphany. With a computer, the raft of statistics available on football players could be harvested to create imaginary teams of players, "drafted" from every team in the league, that would be matched against each other each week according to a formula that combined all the statistics into a single measure of whether your team "won" or "lost" as against all your friends' choices. By adding in prices that reflected how "expensive" it was to choose a particular player, one could impose limits on the tendency to pick a team composed only of superstars. Instead, the game would reward those who can find the diamond in the rough, available on the cheap, who know to avoid the fabled player who is actually past his best and prone to injury.

At first, you gather at the home of the computer-nerd in your group, who has managed to write the software to make all this happen. Then you have a second epiphany. Put this online and *everyone* could have their own team—you decide to call them FANtasy Football Teams, to stress both their imaginary nature and the intensity of the football-love that motivates those who play. Multiple news and sports sites already provide all the basic facts required: the statistics of yardage gained, sacks, completed passes and so on. The NFL offers an "official" statistics site, but many news outlets collect their own statistics. It is trivial to write a computer program to look up those statistics automatically and drop them into the FANtasy game. Even better, the nature of a global network makes the markets for players more efficient while allowing national and even global competition among those playing the game. The global network means that the players never need to meet in reality. FANtasy Football Leagues can be organized for each workplace or group of former college friends. Because the football players you draft come from so many teams, there is always a game to keep track of and bragging to be done on email or around the water cooler.

FANtasy Football is an enormous success. You and your friends are in the middle of negotiations with Yahoo! to make it the exclusive FANtasy Football League network, when you receive a threatening letter from the NFL. They claim that you are "stealing" results and statistics from NFL games, unfairly enriching yourself from an activity that the league stages at the cost of millions of dollars. They say they are investigating their legal options and, if current law provides them no recourse, that they will ask Congress to pass a law prohibiting unlicensed fantasy sports leagues. (Later we will discuss the specific legal claims that might actually be made against you under current law.) As this drama is playing out, you discover that other groups of fans have adapted the FANtasy Football idea to baseball and basketball and that those leagues are also hugely popular.

i.) Your mission now is to lay out the ethical, utilitarian or economic arguments that you might make in support of your position that what you are doing should not be something the NFL can control or limit—whether they seek to prohibit you, or merely demand that you pay for a license. What might the NFL say in support of its position or its proposed law?

ii.) Should you be able to stop the "copycat" fantasy leagues in baseball and basketball? To demand royalties from them? Why? Are these arguments consistent with those you made in answer to question i.)?

John Locke, Of Property
Two Treatises on Government

§ 26. Though the earth and all inferior creatures be common to all men, yet every man has a "property" in his own "person." This nobody has any right to but himself. The "labour" of his body and the "work" of his hands, we may say, are properly his. Whatsoever, then, he removes out of the state that Nature hath provided and left it in, he hath mixed his labour with it, and joined to it something that is his own, and thereby makes it his property. It being by him removed from the common state Nature placed it in, it hath by this labour something annexed to it that excludes the common right of other men. For this "labour" being the unquestionable property of the labourer, no man but he can have a right to what that is once joined to, at least where there is enough, and as good left in common for others.

§ 27. He that is nourished by the acorns he picked up under an oak, or the apples he gathered from the trees in the wood, has certainly appropriated them to himself. Nobody can deny but the nourishment is his. I ask, then, when did they begin to be his? when he digested? or when he ate? or when he boiled? or when he brought them home? or when he picked them up? And it is plain, if the first gathering made them not his, nothing else could. That labour put a distinction between them and common. That added something to them more than Nature, the common mother of all, had done, and so they became his private right. And will any one say he had no right to those acorns or apples he thus appropriated because he had not the consent of all mankind to make them his? Was it a robbery thus to assume to himself what belonged to all in common? If such a consent as that was necessary, man had starved, notwithstanding the plenty God had given him. We see in commons, which remain so by compact, that it is the taking any part of what is common, and removing it out of the state Nature leaves it in, which begins the property, without which the common is of no use. And the taking of this or that part does not depend on the express consent of all the commoners. Thus, the grass my horse has bit, the turfs my servant has cut, and the ore I have digged in any place, where I have a right to them in common with others, become my property without the assignation or consent of anybody. The labour that was mine, removing them out of that common state they were in, hath fixed my property in them. . . .

§ 29. Thus this law of reason makes the deer that Indian's who hath killed it; it is allowed to be his goods who hath bestowed his labour upon it, though, before, it was the common right of every one. And amongst those who are counted the civilised part of mankind, who have made and multiplied positive laws to determine property, this original law of Nature for the beginning of property, in what was before common, still takes place, and by virtue thereof, what fish any one catches in the ocean, that great and still remaining common of mankind; or what amber-gris any one takes up here is by the labour that removes it out of that common state Nature left it in, made his property who takes that pains about it. And even amongst us, the hare that any one is hunting is thought his who pursues her during the chase. For being a beast that is still looked upon as common, and no man's private possession, whoever has employed so much labour about any of that kind as to find and pursue her has thereby removed her from the state of Nature wherein she was common, and hath begun a property.

§ 30. It will, perhaps, be objected to this, that if gathering the acorns or other fruits of the earth, etc., makes a right to them, then any one may engross as much as he will. To which I answer, Not so. The same law of Nature that does by this means give us property, does also bound that property too. "God has given us all things richly." Is the voice of reason confirmed by inspiration? But how far has He given it us "to enjoy"? As much as any one can make use of to any advantage of life before it spoils, so much he may by his labour fix a property in. Whatever is beyond this is more than his share, and belongs to others. Nothing was made by God for man to spoil or destroy. And thus considering the plenty of natural provisions there was a long time in the world, and the few spenders, and to how small a part of that provision the industry of one man could extend itself and engross it to the prejudice of others, especially keeping within the bounds set by reason of what might serve for his use, there could be then little room for quarrels or contentions about property so established.

§ 31. But the chief matter of property being now not the fruits of the earth and the beasts that subsist on it, but the earth itself, as that which takes in and carries with it all the rest, I think it is plain that property in that too is acquired as the former. As much land as a man tills, plants, improves, cultivates, and can use the product of, so much is his property. He by his labour does, as it were, enclose it from the common. Nor will it invalidate his right to say everybody else has an equal title to it, and therefore he cannot appropriate, he cannot enclose, without the consent of all his fellow-commoners, all mankind. God, when He gave the world in common to all mankind, commanded man also to labour, and the penury of his condition required it of him. God and his reason commanded him to subdue the earth—i.e., improve it for the benefit of life and therein lay out something upon it that was his own, his labour. He that, in obedience to this command of God, subdued, tilled, and sowed any part of it, thereby annexed to it something that was his property, which another had no title to, nor could without injury take from him.

§ 32. Nor was this appropriation of any parcel of land, by improving it, any prejudice to any other man, since there was still enough and as good left, and more than the yet unprovided could use. So that, in effect, there was never the less left for others because of his enclosure for himself. For he that leaves as much as another can make use of does as good as take nothing at all. Nobody could think himself injured by the drinking of another man, though he took a good draught, who had a whole river of the same water left him to quench his thirst. And the case of land and water, where there is enough of both, is perfectly the same.

§ 33. God gave the world to men in common, but since He gave it them for their benefit and the greatest conveniencies of life they were capable to draw from it, it cannot be supposed He meant it should always remain common and uncultivated. He gave it to the use of the industrious and rational (and labour was to be his title to it); not to the fancy or covetousness of the quarrelsome and contentious. He that had as good left for his improvement as was already taken up needed not complain, ought not to meddle with what was already improved by another's labour; if he did it is plain he desired the benefit of another's pains, which he had no right to, and not the ground which God had given him, in common with others, to labour on, and whereof there was as good left as that already possessed, and more than he knew what to do with, or his industry could reach to.

§ 34. It is true, in land that is common in England or any other country, where there are plenty of people under government who have money and commerce, no one can enclose or appropriate any part without the consent of all his fellow commoners; because this is left common by compact—i.e., by the law of the land, which is not to be violated. And, though it be common in respect of some men, it is not so to all mankind, but is the joint propriety of this country, or this parish. Besides, the remainder, after such enclosure, would not be as good to the rest of the commoners as the whole was, when they could all make use of the whole; whereas in the beginning and first peopling of the great common of the world it was quite otherwise. The law man was under was rather for appropriating. God commanded, and his wants forced him to labour. That was his property, which could not be taken from him wherever he had fixed it. And hence subduing or cultivating the earth and having dominion, we see, are joined together. The one gave title to the other. So that God, by commanding to subdue, gave authority so far to appropriate. And the condition of human life, which requires labour and materials to work on, necessarily introduce private possessions.

Questions:

1.) Which side in Problem 1-2 can appeal to Locke's arguments? The NFL? The FANtasy Football Players? Both? Find the passage that supports your answers.

2.) Should Locke's argument apply to information goods? Why? Why not?

3.) Locke talks about a realm that is "left common by compact." What does this consist of in the realm of information? Would Locke imagine that private property needs to be introduced to the "great common" of the information world, just as it was to the wilderness?

James Boyle, Why Intellectual Property?
Please read <u>The Public Domain</u> *pp 1–16*

Imagine yourself starting a society from scratch. Perhaps you fought a revolution, or perhaps you led a party of adventurers into some empty land, conveniently free of indigenous peoples. Now your task is to make the society work. You have a preference for democracy and liberty and you want a vibrant culture: a culture with a little chunk of everything, one that offers hundreds of ways to live and thousands of ideals of beauty. You don't want everything to be high culture; you want beer and skittles and trashy delights as well as brilliant news reporting, avant-garde theater, and shocking sculpture. You can see a role for highbrow, state-supported media or publicly financed artworks, but your initial working assumption is that the final arbiter of culture should be the people who watch, read, and listen to it, and who remake it every day. And even if you are dubious about the way popular choice gets formed, you prefer it to some government funding body or coterie of art mavens.

At the same time as you are developing your culture, you want a flourishing economy—and not just in literature or film. You want innovation and invention. You want drugs that cure terrible diseases, and designs for more fuel-efficient stoves, and useful little doodads, like mousetraps, or Post-it notes, or solar-powered backscratchers. To be exact, you want lots of innovation but you do not know exactly what innovation or even what types of innovation you want. . . . *Read the rest*[1]

Note:

1.) The Locke and Boyle excerpts present perhaps the central question of intellectual property policy: the balance between the incentives provided by exclusive property rights and the preservation of the commons, the raw material for future creativity and competition.

---

[1] These are optional additional readings, keyed to the discussions in the book. *The Public Domain* is also available under a Creative Commons license. Ask your teacher if this is required.

Selling Wine Without Bottles
The Economy of Mind on the Global Net
John Perry Barlow, 1992

"If nature has made any one thing less susceptible than all others of exclusive property, it is the action of the thinking power called an idea, which an individual may exclusively possess as long as he keeps it to himself; but the moment it is divulged, it forces itself into the possession of everyone, and the receiver cannot dispossess himself of it. Its peculiar character, too, is that no one possesses the less, because every other possesses the whole of it. He who receives an idea from me, receives instruction himself without lessening mine; as he who lights his taper at mine, receives light without darkening me. That ideas should freely spread from one to another over the globe, for the moral and mutual instruction of man, and improvement of his condition, seems to have been peculiarly and benevolently designed by nature, when she made them, like fire, expansible over all space, without lessening their density at any point, and like the air in which we breathe, move, and have our physical being, incapable of confinement or exclusive appropriation. Inventions then cannot, in nature, be a subject of property. . . ."

—Thomas Jefferson

Throughout the time I've been groping around Cyberspace, there has remained unsolved an immense conundrum which seems to be at the root of nearly every legal, ethical, governmental, and social vexation to be found in the Virtual World. I refer to the problem of digitized property. The riddle is this: if our property can be infinitely reproduced and instantaneously distributed all over the planet without cost, without our knowledge, without its even leaving our possession, how can we protect it? How are we going to get paid for the work we do with our minds? And, if we can't get paid, what will assure the continued creation and distribution of such work?

Since we don't have a solution to what is a profoundly new kind of challenge, and are apparently unable to delay the galloping digitization of everything not obstinately physical, we are sailing into the future on a sinking ship. This vessel, the accumulated canon of copyright and patent law, was developed to convey forms and methods of expression entirely different from the vaporous cargo it is now being asked to carry. It is leaking as much from within as without.

Legal efforts to keep the old boat floating are taking three forms: a frenzy of deck chair rearrangement, stern warnings to the passengers that if she goes down, they will face harsh criminal penalties, and serene, glassy-eyed denial.

Intellectual property law cannot be patched, retrofitted, or expanded to contain the gasses of digitized expression any more than real estate law might be revised to cover the allocation of broadcasting spectrum. (Which, in fact, rather resembles what is being attempted here.) We will need to develop an entirely new set of methods as befits this entirely new set of circumstances.

Most of the people who actually create soft property—the programmers, hackers, and Net surfers—already know this. Unfortunately, neither the companies they work for nor the lawyers these companies hire have enough direct experience with immaterial goods to understand why they are so problematic. They are proceeding as though the old laws can somehow be made to work, either by grotesque expansion or by force. They are wrong.

The source of this conundrum is as simple as its solution is complex. Digital technology is detaching information from the physical plane, where property law of all sorts has always found definition.

Throughout the history of copyrights and patents, the proprietary assertions of thinkers have been focused not on their ideas but on the expression of those ideas. The ideas themselves, as well as facts about the phenomena of the world, were considered to be the collective property of humanity. One could claim franchise, in the case of copyright, on the precise turn of phrase used to convey a particular idea or the order in which facts were presented.

The point at which this franchise was imposed was that moment when the "word became flesh" by departing the mind of its originator and entering some physical object, whether book or widget. The subsequent arrival of other commercial media besides books didn't alter the legal importance of this moment. Law protected expression and, with few (and recent) exceptions, to express was to make physical.

Protecting physical expression had the force of convenience on its side. Copyright worked well because, Gutenberg notwithstanding, it was hard to make a book. Furthermore, books froze their contents into a condition which was as challenging to alter as it was to reproduce. Counterfeiting or distributing counterfeit volumes were obvious and visible activities, easy enough to catch somebody in the act of doing. Finally, unlike unbounded words or images, books had material surfaces to which one could attach copyright notices, publisher's marques, and price tags.

Mental to physical conversion was even more central to patent. A patent, until recently, was either a description of the form into which materials were to be rendered in the service of some purpose or a description of the process by which rendition occurred. In either case, the conceptual heart of patent was the material result. If no purposeful object could be rendered due to some material limitation, the patent was rejected. Neither a Klein bottle nor a shovel made of silk could be patented. It had to be a thing and the thing had to work.

Thus the rights of invention and authorship adhered to activities in the physical world. One didn't get paid for ideas but for the ability to deliver them into reality. For all practical purposes, the value was in the conveyance and not the thought conveyed.

In other words, the bottle was protected, not the wine.

Now, as information enters Cyberspace, the native home of Mind, these bottles are vanishing. With the advent of digitization, it is now possible to replace all previous information storage forms with one meta-bottle: complex—and highly liquid—patterns of ones and zeros.

Even the physical/digital bottles to which we've become accustomed, floppy disks, CD-ROM's, and other discrete, shrink-wrappable bit-packages, will disappear as all computers jack in to the global Net. While the Internet may never include every single CPU on the planet, it is more than doubling every year and can be expected to become the principal medium of information conveyance if [not], eventually, the only one.

Once that has happened, all the goods of the Information Age—all of the expressions once contained in books or film strips or records or newsletters—will exist either as pure thought or something very much like thought: voltage conditions darting around the Net at the speed of light, in conditions which one might behold in effect, as glowing pixels or transmitted sounds, but never touch or claim to "own" in the old sense of the word.

Some might argue that information will still require some physical manifestation, such as its magnetic existence on the titanic hard disks of distant servers, but these are bottles which have no macroscopically discrete or personally meaningful form.

Some will also argue that we have been dealing with unbottled expression since the advent of radio, and they would be right. But for most of the history of broadcast, there was no convenient way to capture soft goods from the electromagnetic ether and reproduce them in anything like the quality available in commercial packages. Only recently has this changed and little has been done legally or technically to address the change.

Generally, the issue of consumer payment for broadcast products was irrelevant. The consumers themselves were the product. Broadcast media were supported either by selling the attention of their audience to advertisers, using government to assess payment through taxes, or the whining mendicancy of annual donor drives.

All of the broadcast support models are flawed. Support either by advertisers or government has almost invariably tainted the purity of the goods delivered. Besides, direct marketing is gradually killing the advertiser support model anyway.

Broadcast media gave us another payment method for a virtual product in the royalties which broadcasters pay songwriters through such organizations as ASCAP and BMI. But, as a member of ASCAP, I can assure you this is not a model which we should emulate. The monitoring methods are wildly approximate. There is no parallel system of accounting in the revenue stream. It doesn't really work. Honest.

In any case, without our old methods of physically defining the expression of ideas, and in the absence of successful new models for non-physical transaction, we simply don't know how to assure reliable payment for mental works. To make matters worse, this comes at a time when the human mind is replacing sunlight and mineral deposits as the principal source of new wealth.

Furthermore, the increasing difficulty of enforcing existing copyright and patent laws is already placing in peril the ultimate source of intellectual property, the free exchange of ideas.

That is, when the primary articles of commerce in a society look so much like speech as to be indistinguishable from it, and when the traditional methods of protecting their ownership have become ineffectual, attempting to fix the problem with broader and more vigorous enforcement will inevitably threaten freedom of speech.

The greatest constraint on your future liberties may come not from government but from corporate legal departments laboring to protect by force what can no longer be protected by practical efficiency or general social consent.

Furthermore, when Jefferson and his fellow creatures of The Enlightenment designed the system which became American copyright law, their primary objective was assuring the widespread distribution of thought, not profit. Profit was the fuel which would carry ideas into the libraries and minds of their new republic. Libraries would purchase books, thus rewarding the authors for their work in assembling ideas, which otherwise "incapable of confinement" would then become freely available to the public. But what is the role of libraries in the absence of books? How does society now pay for the distribution of ideas if not by charging for the ideas themselves?

Additionally complicating the matter is the fact that along with the physical bottles in which intellectual property protection has resided, digital technology is also erasing the legal jurisdictions of the physical world, and replacing them with the unbounded and perhaps permanently lawless seas of Cyberspace.

In Cyberspace, there are not only no national or local boundaries to contain the scene of a crime and determine the method of its prosecution, there are no clear cultural agreements on what a crime might be. Unresolved and basic differences between European and Asian cultural assumptions about intellectual property can only be exacerbated in a region where many transactions are taking place in both hemispheres and yet, somehow, in neither.

Notions of property, value, ownership, and the nature of wealth itself are changing more fundamentally than at any time since the Sumerians first poked cuneiform into wet clay and called it stored grain. Only a very few people are aware of the enormity of this shift and fewer of them are lawyers or public officials.

Those who do see these changes must prepare responses for the legal and social confusion which will erupt as efforts to protect new forms of property with old methods become more obviously futile, and, as a consequence, more adamant.

From Swords to Writs to Bits

Humanity now seems bent on creating a world economy primarily based on goods which take no material form. In doing so, we may be eliminating any predictable connection between creators and a fair reward for the utility or pleasure others may find in their works.

Without that connection, and without a fundamental change in consciousness to accommodate its loss, we are building our future on furor, litigation, and institutionalized evasion of payment except in response to raw force. We may return to the Bad Old Days of property.

Throughout the darker parts of human history, the possession and distribution of property was a largely military matter. "Ownership" was assured those with the nastiest tools, whether fists or armies, and the most resolute will to use them. Property was the divine right of thugs. By the turn of the First Millennium A.D., the emergence of merchant classes and landed gentry forced the development of ethical understandings for the resolution of property disputes. In the late Middle Ages, enlightened rulers like England's Henry II began to codify this unwritten "common law" into recorded canons. These laws were local, but this didn't matter much as they were primarily directed at real estate, a form of property which is local by definition. And which, as the name implied, was very real.

This continued to be the case as long as the origin of wealth was agricultural, but with dawning of the Industrial Revolution, humanity began to focus as much on means as ends. Tools acquired a new social value and, thanks to their own development, it became possible to duplicate and distribute them in quantity.

To encourage their invention, copyright and patent law were developed in most western countries. These laws were devoted to the delicate task of getting mental creations into the world where they could be used—and enter the minds of others—while assuring their inventors compensation for the value of their use. And, as previously stated, the systems of both law and practice which grew up around that task were based on physical expression.

Since it is now possible to convey ideas from one mind to another without ever making them physical, we are now claiming to own ideas themselves and not merely their expression. And since it is likewise now possible to create useful tools which never take physical form, we have taken to patenting abstractions, sequences of virtual events, and mathematical formulae—the most un-real estate imaginable.

In certain areas, this leaves rights of ownership in such an ambiguous condition that once again property adheres to those who can muster the largest armies. The only difference is that this time the armies consist of lawyers.

Threatening their opponents with the endless Purgatory of litigation, over which some might prefer death itself, they assert claim to any thought which might have entered another cranium within the collective body of the corporations they serve. They act as though these ideas appeared in splendid detachment from all previous human thought. And they pretend that thinking about a product is somehow as good as manufacturing, distributing, and selling it.

What was previously considered a common human resource, distributed among the minds and libraries of the world, as well as the phenomena of nature herself, is now being fenced and deeded. It is as though a new class of enterprise had arisen which claimed to own air and water.

What is to be done? While there is a certain grim fun to be had in it, dancing on the grave of copyright and patent will solve little, especially when so few are willing to admit that the occupant of this grave is even deceased and are trying to up by force what can no longer be upheld by popular consent.

In a more perfect world, we'd be wise to declare a moratorium on litigation, legislation, and international treaties in this area until we had a clearer sense of the terms and conditions of enterprise in Cyberspace. Ideally, laws ratify already developed social consensus. They are less the Social Contract itself than a series of memoranda expressing a collective intent which has emerged out of many millions of human interactions.

Humans have not inhabited Cyberspace long enough or in sufficient diversity to have developed a Social Contract which conforms to the strange new conditions of that world. Laws developed prior to consensus usually serve the already established few who can get them passed and not society as a whole.

To the extent that either law or established social practice exists in this area, they are already in dangerous disagreement. The laws regarding unlicensed reproduction of commercial software are clear and stern . . . and rarely observed. Software piracy laws are so practically unenforceable and breaking them has become so socially acceptable that only a thin minority appears compelled, either by fear or conscience, to obey them.

I sometimes give speeches on this subject, and I always ask how many people in the audience can honestly claim to have no unauthorized software on their hard disks. I've never seen more than ten percent of the hands go up.

Whenever there is such profound divergence between the law and social practice, it is not society that adapts. And, against the swift tide of custom, the Software Publishers' current practice of hanging a few visible scapegoats is so obviously capricious as to only further diminish respect for the law.

Part of the widespread popular disregard for commercial software copyrights stems from a legislative failure to understand the conditions into which it was inserted. To assume that systems of law based in the physical world will serve in an environment which is as fundamentally different as Cyberspace is a folly for which everyone doing business in the future will pay.

As I will discuss in the next segment, unbounded intellectual property is very different from physical property and can no longer be protected as though these differences did not exist. For example, if we continue to assume that value is based on scarcity, as it is with regard to physical objects, we will create laws which are precisely contrary to the nature of information, which may, in many cases, increase in value with distribution.

The large, legally risk-averse institutions most likely to play by the old rules will suffer for their compliance. The more lawyers, guns, and money they invest in either protecting their rights or subverting those of their opponents, the more commercial competition will resemble the Kwakiutl Potlatch Ceremony, in which adversaries competed by destroying their own possessions. Their ability to produce new technology will simply grind to a halt as every move they make drives them deeper into a tar pit of courtroom warfare.

Faith in law will not be an effective strategy for high tech companies. Law adapts by continuous increments and at a pace second only to geology in its stateliness. Technology advances in the lunging jerks, like the punctuation of biological evolution grotesquely accelerated. Real world conditions will continue to change at a blinding pace, and the law will get further behind, more profoundly confused. This mismatch is permanent.

Promising economies based on purely digital products will either be born in a state of paralysis, as appears to be the case with multimedia, or continue in a brave and willful refusal by their owners to play the ownership game at all.

In the United States one can already see a parallel economy developing, mostly among small fast moving enterprises who protect their ideas by getting into the marketplace quicker than their larger competitors who base their protection on fear and litigation.

Perhaps those who are part of the problem will simply quarantine themselves in court while those who are part of the solution will create a new society based, at first, on piracy and freebooting. It may well be that when the current system of intellectual property law has collapsed, as seems inevitable, that no new legal structure will arise in its place.

But something will happen. After all, people do business. When a currency becomes meaningless, business is done in barter. When societies develop outside the law, they develop their own unwritten codes, practices, and ethical systems. While technology may undo law, technology offers methods for restoring creative rights.

A Taxonomy of Information

It seems to me that the most productive thing to do now is to look hard into the true nature of what we're trying to protect. How much do we really know about information and its natural behaviors?

What are the essential characteristics of unbounded creation? How does it differ from previous forms of property? How many of our assumptions about it have actually been about its containers rather than their mysterious contents? What are its different species and how does each of them lend itself to control? What technologies will be useful in creating new virtual bottles to replace the old physical ones?

Of course, information is, by its nature, intangible and hard to define. Like other such deep phenomena as light or matter, it is a natural host to paradox. And as it is most helpful to understand light as being both a particle and a wave, an understanding of information may emerge in the abstract congruence of its several different properties which might be described by the following three statements:

- Information is an activity.
- Information is a life form.
- Information is a relationship.

In the following section, I will examine each of these.

I. INFORMATION IS AN ACTIVITY

Information Is a Verb, Not a Noun.

Freed of its containers, information is obviously not a thing. In fact, it is something which happens in the field of interaction between minds or objects or other pieces of information. . . .

The central economic distinction between information and physical property is the ability of information to be transferred without leaving the possession of the original owner. If I sell you my horse, I can't ride him after that. If I sell you what I know, we both know it.

II. INFORMATION IS A LIFE FORM

Information Wants To Be Free.

Stewart Brand is generally credited with this elegant statement of the obvious, recognizing both the natural desire of secrets to be told and the fact that they might be capable of possessing something like a "desire" in the first place.

English Biologist and Philosopher Richard Dawkins proposed the idea of "memes," self-replicating, patterns of information which propagate themselves across the ecologies of mind, saying they were like life forms.

I believe they are life forms in every respect but a basis in the carbon atom. They self-reproduce, they interact with their surroundings and adapt to them, they mutate, they persist. Like any other life form they evolve to fill the possibility spaces of their local environments, which are, in this case the surrounding belief systems and cultures of their hosts, namely, us. . . .

Like DNA helices, ideas are relentless expansionists, always seeking new opportunities for lebensraum. And, as in carbon-based nature, the more robust organisms are extremely adept at finding new places to live. Thus, just as the common housefly has insinuated itself into practically every ecosystem on the planet, so has the meme of "life after death" found a niche in most minds, or psycho-ecologies.

The more universally resonant an idea or image or song, the more minds it will enter and remain within. Trying to stop the spread of a really robust piece of information is about as easy as keeping killer bees South of the Border. The stuff just leaks.

Information Wants To Change

If ideas and other interactive patterns of information are indeed life forms, they can be expected to evolve constantly into forms which will be more perfectly adapted to their surroundings. And, as we see, they are doing this all the time.

But for a long time, our static media, whether carvings in stone, ink on paper, or dye on celluloid, have strongly resisted the evolutionary impulse, exalting as a consequence the author's ability to determine the finished product. But, as in an oral tradition, digitized information has no "final cut."

Digital information, unconstrained by packaging, is a continuing process more like the metamorphosing tales of prehistory than anything which will fit in shrink wrap. From the Neolithic to Gutenberg, information was passed on, mouth to ear, changing with every re-telling (or re-singing). The stories which once shaped our sense of the world didn't have authoritative versions. They adapted to each culture in which they found themselves being told.

Because there was never a moment when the story was frozen in print, the so-called "moral" right of storytellers to keep the tale their own was neither protected nor recognized. The story simply passed through each of them on its way to the next, where it would assume a different form. As we return to continuous information, we can expect the importance of authorship to diminish. Creative people may have to renew their acquaintance with humility.

But our system of copyright makes no accommodation whatever for expressions which don't at some point become "fixed" nor for cultural expressions which lack a specific author or inventor.

Jazz improvisations, standup comedy routines, mime performances, developing monologues, and unrecorded broadcast transmissions all lack the Constitutional requirement of fixation as a "writing." Without being fixed by a point of publication the liquid works of the future will all look more like these continuously adapting and changing forms and will therefore exist beyond the reach of copyright.

Copyright expert Pamela Samuelson tells of having attended a conference last year convened around the fact that Western countries may legally appropriate the music, designs, and biomedical lore of aboriginal people without compensation to their tribe of origin since that tribe is not an "author" or "inventor."

But soon most information will be generated collaboratively by the cyber-tribal hunter-gatherers of Cyberspace. Our arrogant legal dismissal of the rights of "primitives" will be back to haunt us soon.

Information Is Perishable

With the exception of the rare classic, most information is like farm produce. Its quality degrades rapidly both over time and in distance from the source of production. But even here, value is highly subjective and conditional. Yesterday's papers are quite valuable to the historian. In fact, the older they are, the more valuable they become. On the other hand, a commodities broker might consider news of an event which is more than an hour old to have lost any relevance.

III. INFORMATION IS A RELATIONSHIP

Meaning Has Value and Is Unique to Each Case

In most cases, we assign value to information based on its meaningfulness. The place where information dwells, the holy moment where transmission becomes reception, is a region which has many shifting characteristics and flavors depending on the relationship of sender and receiver, the depth of their interactivity.

Each such relationship is unique. Even in cases where the sender is a broadcast medium, and no response is returned, the receiver is hardly passive. Receiving information is often as creative an act as generating it. . . .

Familiarity Has More Value than Scarcity

With physical goods, there is a direct correlation between scarcity and value. Gold is more valuable than wheat, even though you can't eat it. While this is not always the case, the situation with information is usually precisely the reverse. Most soft goods increase in value as they become more common. Familiarity is an important asset in the world of information. It may often be the case that the best thing you can do to raise the demand for your product is to give it away.

While this has not always worked with shareware, it could be argued that there is a connection between the extent to which commercial software is pirated and the amount which gets sold. Broadly pirated software, such as Lotus 1-2-3 or WordPerfect, becomes a standard and benefits from Law of Increasing Returns based on familiarity.

In regard to my own soft product, rock and roll songs, there is no question that the band I write them for, the Grateful Dead, has increased its popularity enormously by giving them away. We have been letting people tape our concerts since the early seventies, but instead of reducing the demand for our product, we are now the largest concert draw in America, a fact which is at least in part attributable to the popularity generated by those tapes.

True, I don't get any royalties on the millions of copies of my songs which have been extracted from concerts, but I see no reason to complain. The fact is, no one but the Grateful Dead can perform a Grateful Dead song, so if you want the experience and not its thin projection, you have to buy a ticket from us. In other words, our intellectual property protection derives from our being the only real-time source of it.

Exclusivity Has Value

The problem with a model which turns the physical scarcity/value ratio on its head is that sometimes the value of information is very much based on its scarcity. Exclusive possession of certain facts makes them more useful. If everyone knows about conditions which might drive a stock price up, the information is valueless.

But again, the critical factor is usually time. It doesn't matter if this kind of information eventually becomes ubiquitous. What matters is being among the first who possess it and act on it. While potent secrets usually don't stay secret, they may remain so long enough to advance the cause of their original holders.

Point of View and Authority Have Value

In a world of floating realities and contradictory maps, rewards will accrue to those commentators whose maps seem to fit their territory snugly, based on their ability to yield predictable results for those who use them.

In aesthetic information, whether poetry or rock 'n' roll, people are willing to buy the new product of an artist, sight-unseen, based on their having been delivered a pleasurable experience by previous work.

Reality is an edit. People are willing to pay for the authority of those editors whose filtering point of view seems to fit best. And again, point of view is an asset which cannot be stolen or duplicated. No one but Esther Dyson sees the world as she does and the handsome fee she charges for her newsletter is actually for the privilege of looking at the world through her unique eyes.

Time Replaces Space

In the physical world, value depends heavily on possession, or proximity in space. One owns that material which falls inside certain dimensional boundaries and the ability to act directly, exclusively, and as one wishes upon what falls inside those boundaries is the principal right of ownership. And of course there is the relationship between value and scarcity, a limitation in space.

In the virtual world, proximity in time is a value determinant. An informational product is generally more valuable the closer the purchaser can place himself to the moment of its expression, a limitation in time. Many kinds of information degrade rapidly with either time or reproduction. Relevance fades as the territory they map changes. Noise is introduced and bandwidth lost with passage away from the point where the information is first produced.

Thus, listening to a Grateful Dead tape is hardly the same experience as attending a Grateful Dead concert. The closer one can get to the headwaters of an informational stream, the better his chances of finding an accurate picture of reality in it. In an era of easy reproduction, the informational abstractions of popular experiences will propagate out from their source moments to reach anyone who's interested. But it's easy enough to restrict the real experience of the desirable event, whether knock-out punch or guitar lick, to those willing to pay for being there.

The Protection of Execution

In the hick town I come from, they don't give you much credit for just having ideas. You are judged by what you can make of them. As things continue to speed up, I think we see that execution is the best protection for those designs which become physical products. Or, as Steve Jobs once put it, "Real artists ship." The big winner is usually the one who gets to the market first (and with enough organizational force to keep the lead).

Information as Its Own Reward

It is now a commonplace to say that money is information. With the exception of Krugerands, crumpled cab-fare, and the contents of those suitcases which drug lords are reputed to carry, most of the money in the informatized world is in ones and zeros. The global money supply sloshes around the Net, as fluid as weather. It is also obvious, as I have discussed, that information has become as fundamental to the creation of modern wealth as land and sunlight once were.

What is less obvious is the extent to which information is acquiring intrinsic value, not as a means to acquisition but as the object to be acquired. I suppose this has always been less explicitly the case. In politics and academia, potency and information have always been closely related.

However, as we increasingly buy information with money, we begin to see that buying information with other information is simple economic exchange without the necessity of converting the product into and out of currency. This is somewhat challenging for those who like clean accounting, since, information theory aside, informational exchange rates are too squishy to quantify to the decimal point.

Nevertheless, most of what a middle class American purchases has little to do with survival. We buy beauty, prestige, experience, education, and all the obscure pleasures of owning. Many of these things can not only be expressed in non-material terms, they can be acquired by non-material means.

And then there are the inexplicable pleasures of information itself, the joys of learning, knowing, and teaching. The strange good feeling of information coming into and out of oneself. Playing with ideas is a recreation which people must be willing to pay a lot for, given the market for books and elective seminars. We'd likely spend even more money for such pleasures if there weren't so many opportunities to pay for ideas with other ideas.

This explains much of the collective "volunteer" work which fills the archives, newsgroups, and databases of the Internet. Its denizens are not working for "nothing," as is widely believed. Rather they are getting paid in something besides money. It is an economy which consists almost entirely of information.

This may become the dominant form of human trade, and if we persist in modeling economics on a strictly monetary basis, we may be gravely misled.

Getting Paid in Cyberspace

How all the foregoing relates to solutions to the crisis in intellectual property is something I've barely started to wrap my mind around. It's fairly paradigm-warping to look at information through fresh eyes—to see how very little it is like pig iron or pork bellies, to imagine the tottering travesties of case law we will stack up if we go on treating it legally as though it were.

As I've said, I believe these towers of outmoded boilerplate will be a smoking heap sometime in the next decade and we mind miners will have no choice but to cast our lot with new systems that work.

I'm not really so gloomy about our prospects as readers of this jeremiad so far might conclude. Solutions will emerge. Nature abhors a vacuum and so does commerce.

Indeed, one of the aspects of the electronic frontier which I have always found most appealing—and the reason Mitch Kapor and I used that phrase in naming our foundation—is the degree to which it resembles the 19th Century American West in its natural preference for social devices which emerge from it conditions rather than those which are imposed from the outside.

Until the west was fully settled and "civilized" in this century, order was established according to an unwritten Code of the West which had the fluidity of etiquette rather than the rigidity of law. Ethics were more important than rules. Understandings were preferred over laws, which were, in any event, largely unenforceable.

I believe that law, as we understand it, was developed to protect the interests which arose in the two economic "waves" which Alvin Toffler accurately identified in The Third Wave. The First Wave was agriculturally based and required law to order ownership of the principal source of production, land. In the Second Wave, manufacturing became the economic mainspring, and the structure of modern law grew around the centralized institutions which needed protection for their reserves of capital, manpower, and hardware.

Both of these economic systems required stability. Their laws were designed to resist change and to assure some equability of distribution within a fairly static social framework. The possibility spaces had to be constrained to preserve the predictability necessary to either land stewardship or capital formation.

In the Third Wave we have now entered, information to a large extent replaces land, capital, and hardware, and as I have detailed in the preceding section, information is most at home in a much more fluid and adaptable environment. The Third Wave is likely to bring a fundamental shift in the purposes and methods of law which will affect far more than simply those statutes which govern intellectual property.

The "terrain" itself—the architecture of the Net—may come to serve many of the purposes which could only be maintained in the past by legal imposition. For example, it may be unnecessary to constitutionally assure freedom of expression in an environment which, in the words of my fellow EFF co-founder John Gilmore, "treats censorship as a malfunction" and re-routes proscribed ideas around it.

And, despite their fierce grip on the old legal structure, companies which trade in information are likely to find that in their increasing inability to deal sensibly with technological issues, the courts will not produce results which are predictable enough to be supportive of long-term enterprise. Every litigation becomes like a game of Russian roulette, depending on the depth the presiding judge's clue-impairment.

Uncodified or adaptive "law," while as "fast, loose, and out of control" as other emergent forms, is probably more likely to yield something like justice at this point. In fact, one can already see in development new practices to suit the conditions of virtual commerce. The life forms of information are evolving methods to protect their continued reproduction.

While I believe that the failure of law will almost certainly result in a compensating re-emergence of ethics as the ordering template of society, this is a belief I don't have room to support here.

Instead, I think that, as in the case cited above, compensation for soft products will be driven primarily by practical considerations, all of them consistent with the true properties of digital information, where the value lies in it, and how it can be both manipulated and protected by technology.

Relationship and Its Tools

I believe one idea is central to understanding liquid commerce: Information economics, in the absence of objects, will be based more on relationship than possession.

One existing model for the future conveyance of intellectual property is real time performance, a medium currently used only in theater, music, lectures, stand-up comedy and pedagogy. I believe the concept of performance will expand to include most of the information economy from multi-casted soap operas to stock analysis. In these instances, commercial exchange will be more like ticket sales to a continuous show than the purchase of discrete bundles of that which is being shown.

The other model, of course, is service. The entire professional class—doctors, lawyers, consultants, architects, etc.—are already being paid directly for their intellectual property. Who needs copyright when you're on a retainer?

In fact, this model was applied to much of what is now copyrighted until the late 18th Century. Before the industrialization of creation, writers, composers, artists, and the like produced their products in the private service of patrons. Without objects to distribute in a mass market, creative people will return to a condition somewhat like this, except that they will serve many patrons, rather than one.

We can already see the emergence of companies which base their existence on supporting and enhancing the soft property they create rather than selling it by the shrink-wrapped piece or embedding it in widgets. . . .

Interaction and Protection

Direct interaction will provide a lot of intellectual property protection in the future, and, indeed, it already has. No one knows how many software pirates have bought legitimate copies of a program after calling its publisher for technical support and being asked for some proof of purchase, but I would guess the number is very high.

The same kind of controls will be applicable to "question and answer" relationships between authorities (or artists) and those who seek their expertise. Newsletters, magazines, and books will be supplemented by the ability of their subscribers to ask direct questions of authors.

Interactivity will be a billable commodity even in the absence of authorship. As people move into the Net and increasingly get their information directly from its point of production, unfiltered by centralized media, they will attempt to develop the same interactive ability to probe reality which only experience has provided them in the past. Live access to these distant "eyes and ears" will be much easier to cordon than access to static bundles of stored but easily reproducible information.

In most cases, control will be based on restricting access to the freshest, highest bandwidth information. It will be a matter of defining the ticket, the venue, the performer, and the identity of the ticket holder, definitions which I believe will take their forms from technology, not law.

In most cases, the defining technology will be cryptography.

Crypto Bottling

Cryptography, as I've said perhaps too many times, is the "material" from which the walls, boundaries—and bottles—of Cyberspace will be fashioned.

Of course there are problems with cryptography or any other purely technical method of property protection. It has always appeared to me that the more security you hide your goods behind, the more likely you are to turn your sanctuary into a target. Having come from a place where people leave their keys in their cars and don't even have keys to their houses, I remain convinced that the best obstacle to crime is a society with its ethics intact.

While I admit that this is not the kind of society most of us live in, I also believe that a social over-reliance on protection by barricades rather than conscience will eventually wither the latter by turning intrusion and theft into a sport, rather than a crime. This is already occurring in the digital domain as is evident in the activities of computer crackers.

Furthermore, I would argue that initial efforts to protect digital copyright by copy protection contributed to the current condition in which most otherwise ethical computer users seem morally untroubled by their possession of pirated software.

Instead of cultivating among the newly computerized a sense of respect for the work of their fellows, early reliance on copy protection led to the subliminal notion that cracking into a software package somehow "earned" one the right to use it. Limited not by conscience but by technical skill, many soon felt free to do whatever they could get away with. This will continue to be a potential liability of the encryption of digitized commerce.

Furthermore, it's cautionary to remember that copy protection was rejected by the market in most areas. Many of the upcoming efforts to use cryptography-based protection schemes will probably suffer the same fate. People are not going to tolerate much which makes computers harder to use than they already are without any benefit to the user.

Nevertheless, encryption has already demonstrated a certain blunt utility. New subscriptions to various commercial satellite TV services sky-rocketed recently after their deployment of more robust encryption of their feeds. This, despite a booming backwoods trade in black decoder chips conducted by folks who'd look more at home running moonshine than cracking code.

Even in cases such as images, where the information is expected to remain fixed, the unencrypted file could still be interwoven with code which could continue to protect it by a wide variety of means.

In most of the schemes I can project, the file would be "alive" with permanently embedded software which could "sense" the surrounding conditions and interact with them. For example, it might contain code which could detect the process of duplication and cause it to self-destruct. Other methods might give the file the ability to "phone home" through the Net to its original owner. The continued integrity of some files might require periodic "feeding" with digital cash from their host, which they would then relay back to their authors.

Of course files which possess the independent ability to communicate upstream sound uncomfortably like the Morris Internet Worm. "Live" files do have a certain viral quality. And serious privacy issues would arise if everyone's computer were packed with digital spies.

The point is that cryptography will enable a lot of protection technologies which will develop rapidly in the obsessive competition which has always existed between lock-makers and lock-breakers. But cryptography will not be used simply for making locks. It is also at the heart of both digital signatures and the afore-mentioned digital cash, both of which I believe will be central to the future protection of intellectual property.

An Economy of Verbs

The future forms and protections of intellectual property are densely obscured from the entrance to the Virtual Age. Nevertheless, I can make (or reiterate) a few flat statements which I earnestly believe won't look too silly in fifty years.

In the absence of the old containers, almost everything we think we know about intellectual property is wrong. We are going to have to unlearn it. We are going to have to look at information as though we'd never seen the stuff before.

The protections which we will develop will rely far more on ethics and technology than on law. Encryption will be the technical basis for most intellectual property protection. (And should, for this and other reasons, be made more widely available.) The economy of the future will be based on relationship rather than possession. It will be continuous rather than sequential. And finally, in the years to come, most human exchange will be virtual rather than physical, consisting not of stuff but the stuff of which dreams are made. Our future business will be conducted in a world made more of verbs than nouns.

John Perry Barlow: 1947–2018

John Perry Barlow was a friend of ours. He was also a lyricist for the Grateful Dead, wordsmith, cowboy, co-founder of the Electronic Frontier Foundation, Burning Man regular and *bon vivant* extraordinaire. We could go on. John Perry was known not just for the essay you have just read but for his extraordinary 1996 *Declaration of the Independence of Cyberspace*. This is how it begins.

> Governments of the Industrial World, you weary giants of flesh and steel, I come from Cyberspace, the new home of Mind. On behalf of the future, I ask you of the past to leave us alone. You are not welcome among us. You have no sovereignty where we gather. We have no elected government, nor are we likely to have one, so I address you with no greater authority than that with which liberty itself always speaks.

> I declare the global social space we are building to be naturally independent of the tyrannies you seek to impose on us. You have no moral right to rule us nor do you possess any methods of enforcement we have true reason to fear. Governments derive their just powers from the consent of the governed. You have neither solicited nor received ours. We did not invite you. You do not know us, nor do you know our world. Cyberspace does not lie within your borders. Do not think that you can build it, as though it were a public construction project. You cannot. It is an act of nature and it grows itself through our collective actions.

> You have not engaged in our great and gathering conversation, nor did you create the wealth of our marketplaces. You do not know our culture, our ethics, or the unwritten codes that already provide our society more order than could be obtained by any of your impositions. You claim there are problems among us that you need to solve. You use this claim as an excuse to invade our precincts. Many of these problems don't exist. Where there are real conflicts, where there are wrongs, we will identify them and address them by our means. We are forming our own Social Contract. This governance will arise according to the conditions of our world, not yours.

> Our world is different. Cyberspace consists of transactions, relationships, and thought itself, arrayed like a standing wave in the web of our communications. Ours is a world that is both everywhere and nowhere, but it is not where bodies live. We are creating a world that all may enter without privilege or prejudice accorded by race, economic power, military force, or station of birth. We are creating a world where anyone, anywhere may express his or her beliefs, no matter how singular, without fear of being coerced into silence or conformity. Your legal concepts of property, expression, identity, movement, and context do not apply to us. They are all based on matter, and there is no matter here.

Recent events—the manipulation of social media and elections, the attack on net neutrality, the invasions of privacy by spam, phishing, and big data commercialism—might lead many to see these words as hopelessly naïve. Since the future of intellectual property depends in so many ways on the future of the internet, that is a question we will discuss. But here is a contrary view from Cindy Cohn, the Executive Director of EFF.

> Barlow was sometimes held up as a straw man for a kind of naïve techno-utopianism that believed that the Internet could solve all of humanity's

problems without causing any more. As someone who spent the past 27 years working with him at EFF, I can say that nothing could be further from the truth. Barlow knew that new technology could create and empower evil as much as it could create and empower good. He made a conscious decision to focus the former: "I knew it's also true that a good way to invent the future is to predict it. So I predicted Utopia, hoping to give Liberty a running start before the laws of Moore and Metcalfe delivered up what Ed Snowden now correctly calls 'turn-key totalitarianism.'" Barlow's lasting legacy is that he devoted his life to making the Internet into "a world that all may enter without privilege or prejudice accorded by race, economic power, military force, or station of birth . . . a world where anyone, anywhere may express his or her beliefs, no matter how singular, without fear of being coerced into silence or conformity."

Requiescat in pace, dude. The words will never be quite as elegant, the civil rights activism so good-humored, the vision of the future so all-encompassing. And the parties? The parties will definitely suffer. We are all the poorer for your loss.

Questions:

Selling Wine Without Bottles was written from 1992 to 1993, right at the birth of the World Wide Web. You live in the world John Perry Barlow was trying to predict.

1.) What are his essential points?

2.) What did he get right? Wrong? What struck you with the force of the new?

3.) Which of his predictions are still up for grabs? Does the Declaration of the Independence of Cyberspace still sound a chord, or is it both obsolete and hopelessly naïve?

4.) Focus on music. Judging by your own behavior and that of your peers, is he right about the efficacy or lack of efficacy of the law? About ethics? About the new business models of the music industry?

International News Service v. The Associated Press
248 U.S. 215 (1918)

Mr. Justice PITNEY delivered the opinion of the court.

The parties are competitors in the gathering and distribution of news and its publication for profit in newspapers throughout the United States. The Associated Press, which was complainant in the District Court, is a cooperative organization, incorporated under the Membership Corporations Law of the State of New York, its members being individuals who are either proprietors or representatives of about 950 daily newspapers published in all parts of the United States. Complainant gathers in all parts of the world, by means of various instrumentalities of its own, by exchange with its members, and by other appropriate means, news and intelligence of current and recent events of interest to newspaper readers and distributes it daily to its members for publication in their newspapers. The cost of the service, amounting approximately to $ 3,500,000 per annum, is assessed upon the members and becomes a part of their costs of operation, to be recouped, presumably with profit, through the publication of their several newspapers. Under complainant's by-laws each member agrees upon assuming membership that news received through complainant's service is received exclusively for publication in a particular newspaper, language, and place specified in the certificate of membership, that no other use of it shall be permitted, and that no member shall furnish or permit anyone in his employ or connected with his newspaper to furnish any of complainant's news in advance of publication to any person not a member. And each member is required to gather the local news of his district and supply it to the Associated Press and to no one else.

Defendant is a corporation organized under the laws of the State of New Jersey, whose business is the gathering and selling of news to its customers and clients, consisting of newspapers published throughout the United States, under contracts by which they pay certain amounts at stated times for defendant's service. It has wide-spread news-gathering agencies; the cost of its operations amounts, it is said, to more than $ 2,000,000 per annum; and it serves about 400 newspapers located in the various cities of the United States and abroad, a few of which are represented, also, in the membership of the Associated Press.

The parties are in the keenest competition between themselves in the distribution of news throughout the United States; and so, as a rule, are the newspapers that they serve, in their several districts.

Complainant in its bill, defendant in its answer, have set forth in almost identical terms the rather obvious circumstances and conditions under which their business is conducted. The value of the service, and of the news furnished, depends upon the promptness of transmission, as well as upon the accuracy and impartiality of the news; it being essential that the news be transmitted to members or subscribers as early or earlier than similar information can be furnished to competing newspapers by other news services, and that the news furnished by each agency shall not be furnished to newspapers which do not contribute to the expense of gathering it. And further, to quote from the answer: "Prompt knowledge and publication of world-wide news is essential to the conduct of a modern newspaper, and by reason of the enormous expense incident to the gathering and distribution of such news, the only practical way in which a proprietor of a newspaper can obtain the same is, either through cooperation with a considerable number of other newspaper proprietors in the work of collecting and distributing such news, and the equitable division with them of the expenses thereof, or by the purchase of such news from some existing agency engaged in that business."

The bill was filed to restrain the pirating of complainant's news by defendant in three ways: First, by bribing employees of newspapers published by complainant's members to furnish Associated Press news to defendant before publication, for transmission by telegraph and telephone to defendant's clients for publication by them; Second, by inducing Associated Press members to violate its by-laws and permit defendant to obtain news before publication; and Third, by copying news from bulletin boards and from early editions of complainant's newspapers and selling this, either bodily or after rewriting it, to defendant's customers. . . .

The only matter that has been argued before us is whether defendant may lawfully be restrained from appropriating news taken from bulletins issued by complainant or any of its members, or from newspapers published by them, for the purpose of selling it to defendant's clients. Complainant asserts that defendant's admitted course of conduct in this regard both violates complainant's property right in the news and constitutes unfair competition in business. And notwithstanding the case has proceeded only to the stage of a preliminary injunction, we have deemed it proper to consider the underlying questions, since they go to the very merits of the action and are presented upon facts that are not in dispute. As presented in argument, these questions are: 1. Whether there is any property in news; 2. Whether, if there be property in news collected for the purpose of being published, it survives the instant of its publication in the first newspaper to which it is communicated by the news-gatherer; and 3. Whether defendant's admitted course of conduct in appropriating for commercial use matter taken from bulletins or early editions of Associated Press publications constitutes unfair competition in trade.

Complainant's news matter is not copyrighted. It is said that it could not, in practice, be copyrighted, because of the large number of dispatches that are sent daily; and, according to complainant's contention, news is not within the operation of the copyright act. Defendant, while apparently conceding this, nevertheless invokes the analogies of the law of literary property and copyright, insisting as its principal contention that, assuming complainant has a right of property in its news, it can be maintained (unless the copyright act be complied with) only by being kept secret and confidential, and that upon the publication with complainant's consent of uncopyrighted news by any of complainant's members in a newspaper or upon a bulletin board, the right of property is lost, and the subsequent use of the news by the public or by defendant for any purpose whatever becomes lawful. . . .

In considering the general question of property in news matter, it is necessary to recognize its dual character, distinguishing between the substance of the information and the particular form or collocation of words in which the writer has communicated it.

No doubt news articles often possess a literary quality, and are the subject of literary property at the common law; nor do we question that such an article, as a literary production, is the subject of copyright by the terms of the act as it now stands.

But the news element—the information respecting current events contained in the literary production—is not the creation of the writer, but is a report of matters that ordinarily are publici juris; it is the history of the day. It is not to be supposed that the framers of the Constitution, when they empowered Congress "to promote the progress of science and useful arts, by securing for limited times to authors and inventors the exclusive right to their respective writings and discoveries" (Const., Art I, § 8, par. 8), intended to confer upon one who might happen to be the first to report a historic event the exclusive right for any period to spread the knowledge of it.

We need spend no time, however, upon the general question of property in news matter at common law, or the application of the copyright act, since it seems to us the case must turn upon the question of unfair competition in business. And, in our opinion, this does not depend upon any general right of property analogous to the common-law right of the proprietor of an unpublished work to prevent its publication without his consent; nor is it foreclosed by showing that the benefits of the copyright act have been waived. We are dealing here not with restrictions upon publication but with the very facilities and processes of publication. The peculiar value of news is in the spreading of it while it is fresh; and it is evident that a valuable property interest in the news, as news, cannot be maintained by keeping it secret. Besides, except for matters improperly disclosed, or published in breach of trust or confidence, or in violation of law, none of which is involved in this branch of the case, the news of current events may be regarded as common property. What we are concerned with is the business of making it known to the world, in which both parties to the present suit are engaged. That business consists in maintaining a prompt, sure, steady, and reliable service designed to place the daily events of the world at the breakfast table of the millions at a price that, while of trifling moment to each reader, is sufficient in the aggregate to afford compensation for the cost of gathering and distributing it, with the added profit so necessary as an incentive to effective action in the commercial world. The service thus performed for newspaper readers is not only innocent but extremely useful in itself, and indubitably constitutes a legitimate business. The parties are competitors in this field; and, on fundamental principles, applicable here as elsewhere, when the rights or privileges of the one are liable to conflict with those of the other, each party is under a duty so to conduct its own business as not unnecessarily or unfairly to injure that of the other. *Hitchman Coal & Coke Co. v. Mitchell.*

Obviously, the question of what is unfair competition in business must be determined with particular reference to the character and circumstances of the business. The question here is not so much the rights of either party as against the public but their rights as between themselves. See *Morison v. Moat.* And although we may and do assume that neither party has any remaining property interest as against the public in uncopyrighted news matter after the moment of its first publication, it by no means follows that there is no remaining property interest in it as between themselves. For, to both of them alike, news matter, however little susceptible of ownership or dominion in the absolute sense, is stock in trade, to be gathered at the cost of enterprise, organization, skill, labor, and money, and to be distributed and sold to those who will pay money for it, as for any other merchandise. Regarding the news, therefore, as but the material out of which both parties are seeking to make profits at the same time and in the same field, we hardly can fail to recognize that for this purpose, and as between them, it must be regarded as quasi property, irrespective of the rights of either as against the public. . . .

Not only do the acquisition and transmission of news require elaborate organization and a large expenditure of money, skill, and effort; not only has it an exchange value to the gatherer, dependent chiefly upon its novelty and freshness, the regularity of the service, its reputed reliability and thoroughness, and its adaptability to the public needs; but also, as is evident, the news has an exchange value to one who can misappropriate it.

The peculiar features of the case arise from the fact that, while novelty and freshness form so important an element in the success of the business, the very processes of distribution and publication necessarily occupy a good deal of time. Complainant's service, as well as defendant's, is a daily service to daily newspapers; most of the foreign news reaches this country at the Atlantic seaboard, principally at the City of New York, and because of this, and of time differentials due to the earth's rotation, the distribution of news matter throughout the country is principally from east to west; and, since in speed the telegraph and telephone easily outstrip the rotation of the earth, it is a simple matter for defendant to take complainant's news from bulletins or early editions of complainant's members in the eastern cities and at the mere cost of telegraphic transmission cause it to be published in western papers issued at least as early as those served by complainant. Besides this, and irrespective of time differentials, irregularities in telegraphic transmission on different lines, and the normal consumption of time in printing and distributing the newspaper, result in permitting pirated news to be placed in the hands of defendant's readers sometimes simultaneously with the service of competing Associated Press papers, occasionally even earlier.

Defendant insists that when, with the sanction and approval of complainant, and as the result of the use of its news for the very purpose for which it is distributed, a portion of complainant's members communicate it to the general public by posting it upon bulletin boards so that all may read, or by issuing it to newspapers and distributing it indiscriminately, complainant no longer has the right to control the use to be made of it; that when it thus reaches the light of day it becomes the common possession of all to whom it is accessible; and that any purchaser of a news-paper has the right to communicate the intelligence which it contains to anybody and for any purpose, even for the purpose of selling it for profit to newspapers published for profit in competition with complainant's members.

The fault in the reasoning lies in applying as a test the right of the complainant as against the public, instead of considering the rights of complainant and defendant, competitors in business, as between themselves. The right of the purchaser of a single newspaper to spread knowledge of its contents gratuitously, for any legitimate purpose not unreasonably interfering with complainant's right to make merchandise of it, may be admitted; but to transmit that news for commercial use, in competition with complainant—which is what defendant has done and seeks to justify—is a very different matter. In doing this defendant, by its very act, admits that it is taking material that has been acquired by complainant as the result of organization and the expenditure of labor, skill, and money, and which is salable by complainant for money, and that defendant in appropriating it and selling it as its own is endeavoring to reap where it has not sown, and by disposing of it to newspapers that are competitors of complainant's members is appropriating to itself the harvest of those who have sown. Stripped of all disguises, the process amounts to an unauthorized interference with the normal operation of complainant's legitimate business precisely at the point where the profit is to be reaped, in order to divert a material portion of the profit from those who have earned it to those who have not; with special advantage to defendant in the competition because of the fact that it is not burdened with any part of the expense of gathering the news. The transaction speaks for itself, and a court of equity ought not to hesitate long in characterizing it as unfair competition in business. . . .

It is to be observed that the view we adopt does not result in giving to complainant the right to monopolize either the gathering or the distribution of the news, or, without complying with the copyright act, to prevent the reproduction of its news articles; but only postpones participation by complainant's competitor in the processes of distribution and reproduction of news that it has not gathered, and only to the extent necessary to prevent that competitor from reaping the fruits of complainant's efforts and expenditure, to the partial exclusion of complainant, and in violation of the principle that underlies the maxim sic utere tuo, etc. . . .

The decree of the Circuit Court of Appeals will be

Affirmed.

Mr. Justice CLARKE took no part in the consideration or decision of this case.

Mr. Justice HOLMES, dissenting.

When an uncopyrighted combination of words is published there is no general right to forbid other people repeating them—in other words there is no property in the combination or in the thoughts or facts that the words express. Property, a creation of law, does not arise from value, although exchangeable—a matter of fact. Many exchangeable values may be destroyed intentionally without compensation. Property depends upon exclusion by law from interference, and a person is not excluded from using any combination of words merely because someone has used it before, even if it took labor and genius to make it. If a given person is to be prohibited from making the use of words that his neighbors are free to make some other ground must be found. One such ground is vaguely expressed in the phrase unfair trade. This means that the words are repeated by a competitor in business in such a way as to convey a misrepresentation that materially injures the person who first used them, by appropriating credit of some kind which the first user has earned. The ordinary case is a representation by device, appearance, or other indirection that the defendant's goods come from the plaintiff. But the only reason why it is actionable to make such a representation is that it tends to give the defendant an advantage in his competition with the plaintiff and that it is thought undesirable that an advantage should be gained in that way. Apart from that the defendant may use such unpatented devices and uncopyrighted combinations of words as he likes. The ordinary case, I say, is palming off the defendant's product as the plaintiff's, but the same evil may follow from the opposite falsehood—from saying, whether in words or by implication, that the plaintiff's product is the defendant's, and that, it seems to me, is what has happened here.

Fresh news is got only by enterprise and expense. To produce such news as it is produced by the defendant represents by implication that it has been acquired by the defendant's enterprise and at its expense. When it comes from one of the great news-collecting agencies like the Associated Press, the source generally is indicated, plainly importing that credit; and that such a representation is implied may be inferred with some confidence from the unwillingness of the defendant to give the credit and tell the truth. If the plaintiff produces the news at the same time that the defendant does, the defendant's presentation impliedly denies to the plaintiff the credit of collecting the facts and assumes that credit to the defendant. If the plaintiff is later in western cities it naturally will be supposed to have obtained its information from the defendant. The falsehood is a little more subtle, the injury a little more indirect, than in ordinary cases of unfair trade, but I think that the principle that condemns the one condemns the other. It is a question of how strong an infusion of fraud is necessary to turn a flavor into a poison. The dose seems to me strong enough here to need a remedy from the law. But as, in my view, the only ground of complaint that can be recognized without legislation is the implied misstatement, it can be corrected by stating the truth; and a suitable acknowledgment of the source is all that the plaintiff can require. I think that within the limits recognized by the decision of the Court the defendant should be enjoined from publishing news obtained from the Associated Press for hours after publication by the plaintiff unless it gives express credit to the Associated Press; the number of hours and the form of acknowledgment to be settled by the District Court.

Mr. Justice McKENNA concurs in this opinion.

Mr. Justice BRANDEIS dissenting.

There are published in the United States about 2,500 daily papers. More than 800 of them are supplied with domestic and foreign news of general interest by the Associated Press—a corporation without capital stock which does not sell news or earn or seek to earn profits, but serves merely as an instrumentality by means of which these papers supply themselves at joint expense with such news. Papers not members of the Associated Press depend for their news of general interest largely upon agencies organized for profit. Among these agencies is the International News Service which supplies news to about 400 subscribing papers. It has, like the Associated Press, bureaus and correspondents in this and foreign countries; and its annual expenditure in gathering and distributing news is about $ 2,000,000. Ever since its organization in 1909, it has included among the sources from which it gathers news, copies (purchased in the open market) of early editions of some papers published by members of the Associated Press and the bulletins publicly posted by them. These items, which constitute but a small part of the news transmitted to its subscribers, are generally verified by the International News Service before transmission; but frequently items are transmitted without verification; and occasionally even without being re-written. In no case is the fact disclosed that such item was suggested by or taken from a paper or bulletin published by an Associated Press member.

No question of statutory copyright is involved. The sole question for our consideration is this: Was the International News Service properly enjoined from using, or causing to be used gainfully, news of which it acquired knowledge by lawful means (namely, by reading publicly posted bulletins or papers purchased by it in the open market) merely because the news had been originally gathered by the Associated Press and continued to be of value to some of its members, or because it did not reveal the source from which it was acquired?

The "ticker" cases, the cases concerning literary and artistic compositions, and cases of unfair competition were relied upon in support of the injunction. But it is admitted that none of those cases affords a complete analogy with that before us. The question presented for decision is new; and it is important.

News is a report of recent occurrences. The business of the news agency is to gather systematically knowledge of such occurrences of interest and to distribute reports thereof. The Associated Press contended that knowledge so acquired is property, because it costs money and labor to produce and because it has value for which those who have it not are ready to pay; that it remains property and is entitled to protection as long as it has commercial value as news; and that to protect it effectively the defendant must be enjoined from making, or causing to be made, any gainful use of it while it retains such value. An essential element of individual property is the legal right to exclude others from enjoying it. If the property is private, the right of exclusion may be absolute; if the property is affected with a public interest, the right of exclusion is qualified. But the fact that a product of the mind has cost its producer money and labor, and has a value for which others are willing to pay, is not sufficient to ensure to it this legal attribute of property. The general rule of law is, that the noblest of human productions—knowledge, truths ascertained, conceptions, and ideas—become, after voluntary communication to others, free as the air to common use. Upon these incorporeal productions the attribute of property is continued after such communication only in certain classes of cases where public policy has seemed to demand it. These exceptions are confined to productions which, in some degree, involve creation, invention, or discovery. But by no means all such are endowed with this attribute of property. The creations which are recognized as property by the common law are literary, dramatic, musical, and other artistic creations; and these have also protection under the copyright statutes. The inventions and discoveries upon which this attribute of property is conferred only by statute, are the few comprised within the patent law. There are also many other cases in which courts interfere to prevent curtailment of plaintiff's enjoyment of incorporeal productions; and in which the right to relief is often called a property right, but is such only in a special sense. In those cases, the plaintiff has no absolute right to the protection of his production; he has merely the qualified right to be protected as against the defendant's acts, because of the special relation in which the latter stands or the wrongful method or means employed in acquiring the knowledge or the manner in which it is used. Protection of this character is afforded where the suit is based upon breach of contract or of trust or upon unfair competition.

The knowledge for which protection is sought in the case at bar is not of a kind upon which the law has heretofore conferred the attributes of property; nor is the manner of its acquisition or use nor the purpose to which it is applied, such as has heretofore been recognized as entitling a plaintiff to relief. . . .

Plaintiff further contended that defendant's practice constitutes unfair competition, because there is "appropriation without cost to itself of values created by" the plaintiff; and it is upon this ground that the decision of this court appears to be based. To appropriate and use for profit, knowledge and ideas produced by other men, without making compensation or even acknowledgment, may be inconsistent with a finer sense of propriety; but, with the exceptions indicated above, the law has heretofore sanctioned the practice. Thus it was held that one may ordinarily make and sell anything in any form, may copy with exactness that which another has produced, or may otherwise use his ideas without his consent and without the payment of compensation, and yet not inflict a legal injury; and that ordinarily one is at perfect liberty to find out, if he can by lawful means, trade secrets of another, however valuable, and then use the knowledge so acquired gainfully, although it cost the original owner much in effort and in money to collect or produce.

Such taking and gainful use of a product of another which, for reasons of public policy, the law has refused to endow with the attributes of property, does not become unlawful because the product happens to have been taken from a rival and is used in competition with him. The unfairness in competition which hitherto has been recognized by the law as a basis for relief, lay in the manner or means of conducting the business; and the manner or means held legally unfair, involves either fraud or force or the doing of acts otherwise prohibited by law. In the "passing off" cases (the typical and most common case of unfair competition), the wrong consists in fraudulently representing by word or act that defendant's goods are those of plaintiff. See *Hanover Milling Co. v. Metcalf*. In the other cases, the diversion of trade was effected through physical or moral coercion, or by inducing breaches of contract or of trust or by enticing away employees. In some others, called cases of simulated competition, relief was granted because defendant's purpose was unlawful; namely, not competition but deliberate and wanton destruction of plaintiff's business. . . .

That competition is not unfair in a legal sense, merely because the profits gained are unearned, even if made at the expense of a rival, is shown by many cases besides those referred to above. He who follows the pioneer into a new market, or who engages in the manufacture of an article newly introduced by another, seeks profits due largely to the labor and expense of the first adventurer; but the law sanctions, indeed encourages, the pursuit. He who makes a city known through his product, must submit to sharing the resultant trade with others who, perhaps for that reason, locate there later. *Canal Co. v. Clark*; *Elgin National Watch Co. v. Illinois Watch Co.* He who has made his name a guaranty of quality, protests in vain when another with the same name engages, perhaps for that reason, in the same lines of business; provided, precaution is taken to prevent the public from being deceived into the belief that what he is selling was made by his competitor. One bearing a name made famous by another is permitted to enjoy the unearned benefit which necessarily flows from such use, even though the use proves harmful to him who gave the name value.

The means by which the International News Service obtains news gathered by the Associated Press is also clearly unobjectionable. It is taken from papers bought in the open market or from bulletins publicly posted. No breach of contract such as the court considered to exist in *Hitchman Coal & Coke Co. v. Mitchell*; or of trust such as was present in *Morison v. Moat*; and neither fraud nor force, is involved. The manner of use is likewise unobjectionable. No reference is made by word or by act to the Associated Press, either in transmitting the news to subscribers or by them in publishing it in their papers. Neither the International News Service nor its subscribers is gaining or seeking to gain in its business a benefit from the reputation of the Associated Press. They are merely using its product without making compensation. See *Bamforth v. Douglass Post Card & Machine Co.*; *Tribune Co. of Chicago v. Associated Press*. That, they have a legal right to do; because the product is not property, and they do not stand in any relation to the Associated Press, either of contract or of trust, which otherwise precludes such use. The argument is not advanced by characterizing such taking and use a misappropriation.

It is also suggested, that the fact that defendant does not refer to the Associated Press as the source of the news may furnish a basis for the relief. But the defendant and its subscribers, unlike members of the Associated Press, were under no contractual obligation to disclose the source of the news; and there is no rule of law requiring acknowledgment to be made where uncopyrighted matter is reproduced. The International News Service is said to mislead its subscribers into believing that the news transmitted was originally gathered by it and that they in turn mislead their readers. There is, in fact, no representation by either of any kind. Sources of information are sometimes given because required by contract; sometimes because naming the source gives authority to an otherwise incredible statement; and sometimes the source is named because the agency does not wish to take the responsibility itself of giving currency to the news. But no representation can properly be implied from omission to mention the source of information except that the International News Service is transmitting news which it believes to be credible. . . .

The rule for which the plaintiff contends would effect an important extension of property rights and a corresponding curtailment of the free use of knowledge and of ideas; and the facts of this case admonish us of the danger involved in recognizing such a property right in news, without imposing upon news-gatherers corresponding obligations. A large majority of the newspapers and perhaps half the newspaper readers of the United States are dependent for their news of general interest upon agencies other than the Associated Press. The channel through which about 400 of these papers received, as the plaintiff alleges, "a large amount of news relating to the European war of the greatest importance and of intense interest to the newspaper reading public" was suddenly closed. The closing to the International News Service of these channels for foreign news (if they were closed) was due not to unwillingness on its part to pay the cost of collecting the news, but to the prohibitions imposed by foreign governments upon its securing news from their respective countries and from using cable or telegraph lines running therefrom. For aught that appears, this prohibition may have been wholly undeserved; and at all events the 400 papers and their readers may be assumed to have been innocent. For aught that appears, the International News Service may have sought then to secure temporarily by arrangement with the Associated Press the latter's foreign news service. For aught that appears, all of the 400 subscribers of the International News Service would gladly have then become members of the Associated Press, if they could have secured election thereto. It is possible, also, that a large part of the readers of these papers were so situated that they could not secure prompt access to papers served by the Associated Press. The prohibition of the foreign governments might as well have been extended to the channels through which news was supplied to the more than a thousand other daily papers in the United States not served by the Associated Press; and a large part of their readers may also be so located that they can not procure prompt access to papers served by the Associated Press.

A legislature, urged to enact a law by which one news agency or newspaper may prevent appropriation of the fruits of its labors by another, would consider such facts and possibilities and others which appropriate enquiry might disclose. Legislators might conclude that it was impossible to put an end to the obvious injustice involved in such appropriation of news, without opening the door to other evils, greater than that sought to be remedied. Such appears to have been the opinion of our Senate which reported unfavorably a bill to give news a few hours' protection; and which ratified, on February 15, 1911, the convention adopted at the Fourth International American Conference; and such was evidently the view also of the signatories to the International Copyright Union Of November 13, 1908; as both these conventions expressly exclude news from copyright protection.

Or legislators dealing with the subject might conclude, that the right to news values should be protected to the extent of permitting recovery of damages for any unauthorized use, but that protection by injunction should be denied, just as courts of equity ordinarily refuse (perhaps in the interest of free speech) to restrain actionable libels, and for other reasons decline to protect by injunction mere political rights; and as Congress has prohibited courts from enjoining the illegal assessment or collection of federal taxes. If a legislature concluded to recognize property in published news to the extent of permitting recovery at law, it might, with a view to making the remedy more certain and adequate, provide a fixed measure of damages, as in the case of copyright infringement. . . .

Courts are ill-equipped to make the investigations which should precede a determination of the limitations which should be set upon any property right in news or of the circumstances under which news gathered by a private agency should be deemed affected with a public interest. Courts would be powerless to prescribe the detailed regulations essential to full enjoyment of the rights conferred or to introduce the machinery required for enforcement of such regulations. Considerations such as these should lead us to decline to establish a new rule of law in the effort to redress a newly-disclosed wrong, although the propriety of some remedy appears to be clear.

Questions:

Examine the arguments made by Pitney, Holmes and Brandeis in *INS v. AP*.

1.) Look back at the three basic questions asked on pages 2–3 of this book. How would each judge answer them?

2.) Compare the legal tools proposed by Pitney and Holmes to solve the problems they see. What type of "property" right is being proposed by each? What are its limits? Why?

3.) What position would each judge take on the FANtasy football hypothetical laid out in Problem 1-2? Do they add anything to the arguments you already made?

4.) Is Pitney using the same arguments for property given in chapter 1 of *The Public Domain*? In the excerpt from Locke?

5.) Does *INS v. AP* support or undermine Barlow's thesis about law's inability to regulate information using the jurisprudential tools of property rights?

6.) Can we solve public goods problems without intellectual property rights? What would Brandeis say?

7.) Does it change your attitude towards the case if you are told that the British government had denied the use of the only transatlantic telegraph network to INS—owned by William Randolph Hearst (the man on whom *Citizen Kane* was based)—because the government objected to the INS's coverage of the war? Hearst and his newspapers were thought to take a pro-German line and to exaggerate the amount of war-related damage in the UK. As a result of the ban, only the Associated Press had the ability to do real time reporting; taking data from bulletin boards and published newspapers was the only way for INS papers to report the war. How, if at all, does this change the way you structure or analyze the questions posed in the case? How would you use these facts if you were the lawyer for INS?

8.) The next excerpt is *The New York Times* article on the argument that INS put forward in the Supreme Court. How does Mr. Untermyer present the issue? What is his answer to the questions on pages 2–3? What alternative framings of the dispute does he offer?

The New York Times

NEWS PIRATING CASE IN SUPREME COURT

Untermyer Argues for Dissolution of Associated Press Injunction Against Hearst.

MAKES MONOPOLY CHARGE

Admits, However, That International Has Sold News Sent Out by the Other Service.

WASHINGTON, May 2.—Arguments in proceedings brought in an effort to have set aside injunctions restraining the International News Service, or Hearst Service, from pirating news dispatches of The Associated Press began today in the Supreme Court. The opening argument was made by Samuel Untermyer, representing the Hearst Service, who will conclude tomorrow, after which Frederick W. Lehmann will present The Associated Press's side of the suit. Senator Johnson of California will close for the Hearst Service.

Mr. Untermyer attacked especially the contention of The Associated Press that news had property value, and charged that if the lower court injunctions were sustained The Associated Press would be allowed to become a "despotic monopoly."

Admitting that the International News Service had been guilty of selling news sent out by the other organization, the attorney insisted The Associated Press had been guilty of the same practice despite affidavits of employees of The Associated Press denying it.

The Associated Press also was attacked by Mr. Untermyer for bringing the present proceedings at a time when Great Britain and the allied Governments had denied the use of their cables to the International News Service for the transmission of news. He declared The Associated Press took advantage of this situation to institute the suit "because they thought the International News Service could be destroyed."

In explanation of the action of the Allied Governments, Mr. Untermyer declared it was due to news matter sent by the International News Service to its office in this country regarding the torpedoing of the British battleship Audacious and the naval battle of Jutland, and because headlines printed in one newspaper receiving the Hearst Service described London as being in flames.

Frequent questions were asked during the argument by members of the court regarding the property value of news. They wanted to know also why, although the lower courts restrained the International News Service from pirating Associated Press news through employees of newspapers taking the latter service, an appeal was taken to the Supreme Court only from the part of the injunctions enjoining the taking of news from bulletin boards and early editions of Associated Press newspapers.

Property Value of News

Mr. Untermyer summarized the questions involved as follows:

"Is there a right of property in news or knowledge of the news or in the quality of 'firstness' in the news that will survive its publication by the gatherer in any of the newspapers to which it has been delivered for the express purpose of publication and sale until the gatherer of the news and all of its customers have secured their reward; or does this news become public property as soon as it has been published by any of the papers to which it has been surrendered without restriction for that specific purpose? In other words, is there a sanctity of property right reserved to the news gatherer against the effects of publication as to matter that is admittedly uncopyrightable greater than that given by the statute to copyright matter?

"Assuming that the court would create a precedent in a case where it would be necessary to preserve a business against piracy in this case both parties and their respective members and customers have apparently from the time of their organization acted upon exactly opposite construction and understanding of the law. News displayed on bulletin boards and printed and sold in early editions of newspapers has been regarded as public property, which it is in law and in fact. Each of these parties has freely taken the other's news and they are bound by that practical construction of their rights and obligations. The fact that one of them claims that it verifies and rewrites the story it takes from the other, while the other does not, is purely a question of business policy that in no wise affects their legal rights as determined by their long continued acts.

"There can be no remedy in law or equity unless actual damage is shown. Courts are not established to try out moot or academic questions. The complainant says it is not organized for profit, and that it makes no money difference to it what is the financial outcome of its activities. That being so, if there are any remedies, they inhere in the members and not in the corporation, which is organized on the grotesque theory that it is not engaged in business.

"The attempt by this order to protect complainant's members in their local news in a suit to which they are not parties and in which the judgment could not, therefore, be binding or reciprocal is without precedent or reason. Conversely, if the defendant sued the complainant, could it secure an injunction that would run in favor of all the defendant's stockholders and customers?

Element of Competition

"There is no element of unfair competition involved. The defendant is not seeking to palm off complainant's news as its (defendant's) news, nor as complainant's news, but simply as news that has been made available to everyone. It has not secured it surreptitiously or as the result of a breach of contract, but publicly by paying for the paper containing it and in which it was authorized to be published. If defendant is right in its contention that it is public property, as the parties have always regarded it, there is nothing unfair in taking it. If, contrary to precedent and to the acts of the parties as evidencing their constructions of their rights—both parties—it is now held to be private property, its use would be enjoined on that ground, but in no event on the theory of what is known as unfair competition. There is no such element in this case.

"Both the parties are in the position with respect to news that has been published of the man with an unpatentable idea or trade secret that has cost him years of labor and vast sums of money to develop. Or of the architect who has created a beautiful structure, or the landscape gardener who has laid out a novel garden, or of any one of the many inventions in beauty, usefulness, and science, that are not patentable. So long as he keeps these things to himself he will be protected against their surreptitious taking. When he releases them they belong to the public.

"What the complainant is here trying to do is to release the news and at the same time hold on to it. That is impossible and in this case it is inequitable, for in the past it has been taken from the defendant, and now that events have temporarily changed, it seeks to escape from the consequences of its own action.

Calls Decision Dangerous.

"There is a manifest inconsistency in the attitude of the District Court, when it very properly declined to differentiate between 'tips' and 're-writes,' decided that the practice was universal in the newspaper trade and yet enjoined the defendant from continuing it on condition that the complainant would submit to a like injunction which the later was, of course, delighted to do at that particular juncture.

"This decision sets up a new and dangerous rule. The measure of a plaintiff's right is now made dependent, not on the extent to which the defendant has infringed a definite known rule of law, but upon an intangible unknown element that depends upon the extent of the activities of the plaintiff and those whom it happens at the moment to represent. If the news is taken from a paper of local circulation it may be immediately taken and used all over the United States except in that locality, for its commercial value will have passed away after the paper has been circulated in its own town. If, however, it happens to be a member of The Associated Press that same item of local news becomes ipso facto inviolate until every one of the 1,630 Associated Press newspapers in the United States and possibly until after The Associated Press agencies in foreign countries have utilized it. Is not this a reductio ad absurdum?"

James Boyle, Thomas Jefferson Writes a Letter
Please read The Public Domain *pp 17–41*

On August 13, 1813, Thomas Jefferson took up his pen to write to Isaac McPherson. It was a quiet week in Jefferson's correspondence. He wrote a letter to Madison about the appointment of a tax assessor, attempted to procure a government position for an acquaintance, produced a fascinating and lengthy series of comments on a new "Rudiments of English Grammar," discussed the orthography of nouns ending in "y," accepted the necessary delay in the publication of a study on the anatomy of mammoth bones, completed a brief biography of Governor Lewis, and, in general, confined himself narrowly in subject matter. But on the 13th of August, Jefferson's mind was on intellectual property, and most specifically, patents.

Jefferson's writing is, as usual, apparently effortless. Some find his penmanship a little hard to decipher. To me, used to plowing through the frenzied chicken tracks that law students produce during exams, it seems perfectly clear. If handwriting truly showed the architecture of the soul, then Jefferson's would conjure up Monticello or the University of Virginia. There are a few revisions and interlineations, a couple of words squeezed in with a caret at the bottom of the line, but for the most part the lines of handwriting simply roll on and on—"the fugitive fermentation of an individual brain," to quote a phrase from the letter, caught in vellum and ink, though that brain has been dust for more than a century and a half. . . .   *Read the rest*

Questions:

Jefferson is a deeply problematic figure. Polymath. Principal drafter of the Declaration of Independence, with its majestic words about equality and inalienable rights. (He included a draft clause disavowing slavery, which was rejected by others.) Yet he himself was a slaveholder! He had over 600 slaves, freeing only 2 during his life and 7 after his death. Knowing that, why pay any attention to his words? First, just as the Declaration of Independence continues to be important to American law, so too does Jefferson's vision of intellectual property, a vision that appears to have been central to the Constitutional framework for copyright and patent and one that continues to be referenced, explicitly and implicitly, by courts. Jefferson even played a major role in the drafting of the first patent act and served on the country's first patent examination board. Second, Jefferson's ideas about intellectual property deserve attention in their own right, the evil of his actions notwithstanding. They force us to articulate the differences between intellectual property and tangible property in ways that are central to the subject.

1.) What problems is Jefferson concerned with? Beyond the question of incentives what additional dangers did he and Macaulay see? Does Macaulay see intellectual property as a matter of necessary incentive, restraint on competition, or restriction of speech?

2.) What are the basic differences between the baseline assumptions of Diderot and Condorcet? What are the strongest arguments for and against the notion of a natural right to intellectual property?

3.) Boyle lays out a multi-part "Jefferson Warning" that he says is vital to making good intellectual property decisions. How would you respond to that formulation of good policy if you were General Counsel of the Recording Industry Association of America? Of Google? Of the National Academy of Sciences? Diderot?

CHAPTER TWO

Intellectual Property & the Constitution

[The Congress shall have power] "To promote the progress of science and useful arts, by securing for limited times to authors and inventors the exclusive right to their respective writings and discoveries;"

U.S. Constitution Art. I, § 8, cl. 8.

Introduction

In this chapter, we explore the constitutional sources of (and possible limitations) on Congress's powers to make intellectual property law. There are two reasons to want to do this. First, it will help us understand the reach of, and the limits on, Federal intellectual property law, and in particular the way those limits are shaped by interaction between three constitutional provisions, Art. I, § 8, cl. 8 quoted above,[‡] the Commerce Clause and the First Amendment. Second, and perhaps more important, understanding the animating constitutional provisions, their goals, and their inner tensions, will shine a light on the way that the courts *interpret* existing intellectual property law. There are three basic conceptual boxes in the Federal intellectual property system (together with a newly created Federal trade secrecy regime) and Congress, and the happenstance of technological development, keep depositing new material, new social practices and new technology into those conceptual boxes. The ideas expressed in the constitutional sources and limitations explored in this sector may shape the way that judges interpret the law in the process that follows.

Congress's power to legislate in any given field must be founded on one of the powers enumerated in Article I, section 8 of the Constitution. Its power to offer exclusive rights to authors and inventors (i.e. copyright and patent) derives from the Intellectual Property Clause which is reproduced at the top of this page.

At the outset, there are a few notable things about this grant of power. First, it is the only clause that comes with its own, built-in justification: "to promote the progress of science and useful arts." None of the other clauses list a rationale. For example, Congress also has the power:

- To borrow money on the credit of the United States;
- To regulate commerce with foreign nations, and among the several states, and with the Indian tribes;
- To establish a uniform rule of naturalization, and uniform laws on the subject of bankruptcies throughout the United States;
- To coin money, regulate the value thereof, and of foreign coin, and fix the standard of weights and measures;
- To provide for the punishment of counterfeiting the securities and current coin of the United States;
- To establish post offices and post roads.

Like some other clauses, the Intellectual Property Clause contains obvious modifiers: "by securing for limited Times." But as we will see, the courts have also found

---

‡ This clause is variously referred to as the Copyright Clause, Copyright and Patent Clause, and Intellectual Property Clause.

other, less immediately obvious, limitations in the clause. The *Trade-Mark Cases*, which follow this introduction, represent one example of such a limitation, the requirement of originality, though the constricted vision of Congress's Commerce Clause power is no longer good law. (Today, the Federal Trademark statute, the Lanham Act, is seen as well within Congress's power under the Commerce Clause. The same is true of Federal trade secrecy protection.) *Feist* reiterates that originality is constitutionally required for grants of copyright. The excerpted fragment of the *John Deere* case provides a robust assertion of the limits of Congressional power in the context of patent law. But important questions remain. If there are any strong limitations imposed by the Intellectual Property Clause, do they also limit the power of the Congress under the other clauses of the Constitution? For example, if under the Intellectual Property Clause, Congress is forbidden from creating permanent copyrights or rights over unoriginal collections of facts, may it do so under the Commerce Clause instead?

These questions are given particular saliency by two developments; first, the increased importance of intellectual property rights in an information age that runs from the Internet to the Human Genome project and second, a relatively uniform expansion of intellectual property rights over the last fifty years.

We will turn first to the question of the *sources* of Congressional power to make intellectual property law, the limits those sources impose and the interaction between different grants of power. After that, we will turn to the limitations imposed by the First Amendment. Before heading into the cases, though, we are going to think through the Intellectual Property Clause. The goal is to come up with a range of its possible meanings.

PROBLEM 2-1
CONSTITUTIONAL INTERPRETATION.

[The Congress shall have power] "To promote the progress of science and useful arts, by securing for limited times to authors and inventors the exclusive right to their respective writings and discoveries;" U.S. Constitution Art. I, § 8, cl. 8.

Find each word or phrase in this clause that could constitute a limitation on Congress's power. Explain *what* the limitation would be, *why* one might believe that such a limitation should be read into the clause and what kind of assumptions your possible reasoning makes about the *goal or function or meaning* of the clause. In addition, explain what implication each interpretation would have for a judge or other decision maker trying to interpret a piece of legislation made *under* the clause.

1.) Limitations on Congressional Power: Originality

The Trade-Mark Cases
U.S. v. Steffens; U.S. v. Wittemann; U.S. v. Johnson
100 U.S. 82 (1879)

Mr. Justice MILLER delivered the opinion of the court.

The three cases whose titles stand at the head of this opinion are criminal prosecutions for violations of what is known as the trade-mark legislation of Congress. The first two are indictments in the southern district of New York, and the last is an information in the southern district of Ohio. In all of them the judges of the circuit courts in which they are pending have certified to a difference of opinion on what is substantially the same question; namely, are the acts of Congress on the subject of trade-marks founded on any rightful authority in the Constitution of the United States?

. . . The right to adopt and use a symbol or a device to distinguish the goods or property made or sold by the person whose mark it is, to the exclusion of use by all other persons, has been long recognized by the common law and the chancery courts of England and of this country, and by the statutes of some of the States. It is a property right for the violation of which damages may be recovered in an action at law, and the continued violation of it will be enjoined by a court of equity, with compensation for past infringement. This exclusive right was not created by the act of Congress, and does not now depend upon it for its enforcement. The whole system of trade-mark property and the civil remedies for its protection existed long anterior to that act, and have remained in full force since its passage.

These propositions are so well understood as to require neither the citation of authorities nor an elaborate argument to prove them.

As the property in trade-marks and the right to their exclusive use rest on the laws of the States, and, like the great body of the rights of person and of property, depend on them for security and protection, the power of Congress to legislate on the subject, to establish the conditions on which these rights shall be enjoyed and exercised, the period of their duration, and the legal remedies for their enforcement, if such power exist at all, must be found in the Constitution of the United States, which is the source of all powers that Congress can lawfully exercise.

In the argument of these cases this seems to be conceded, and the advocates for the validity of the acts of Congress on this subject point to two clauses of the Constitution, in one or in both of which, as they assert, sufficient warrant may be found for this legislation.

The first of these is the eighth clause of sect. 8 of the first article. That section, manifestly intended to be an enumeration of the powers expressly granted to Congress, and closing with the declaration of a rule for the ascertainment of such powers as are necessary by way of implication to carry into efficient operation those expressly given, authorizes Congress, by the clause referred to, 'to promote the progress of science and useful arts, by securing for limited times, to authors and inventors, the exclusive right to their respective writings and discoveries.'

As the first and only attempt by Congress to regulate the right of trade-marks is to be found in the act of July 8, 1870, to which we have referred, entitled 'An Act to revise, consolidate, and amend the statutes relating to patents and copyrights,' terms which have long since become technical, as referring, the one to inventions and the other to the writings of authors, it is a reasonable inference that this part of the statute also was, in the opinion of Congress, an exercise of the power found in that clause of the Constitution. It may also be safely assumed that until a critical examination of the subject in the courts became necessary, it was mainly if not wholly to this clause that the advocates of the law looked for its support.

Any attempt, however, to identify the essential characteristics of a trade-mark with inventions and discoveries in the arts and sciences, or with the writings of authors, will show that the effort is surrounded with insurmountable difficulties.

The ordinary trade-mark has no necessary relation to invention or discovery. The trade-mark recognized by the common law is generally the growth of a considerable period of use, rather than a sudden invention. It is often the result of accident rather than design, and when under the act of Congress it is sought to establish it by registration, neither originality, invention, discovery, science, nor art is in any way essential to the right conferred by that act. If we should endeavor to classify it under the head of writings of authors, the objections are equally strong. In this, as in regard to inventions, originality is required. And while the word writings may be liberally construed, as it has been, to include original designs for engravings, prints, &c., it is only such as are original, and are founded in the creative powers of the mind. The writings which are to be protected are the fruits of intellectual labor, embodied in the form of books, prints, engravings, and the like. The trade-mark may be, and generally is, the adoption of something already in existence as the distinctive symbol of the party using it. At common law the exclusive right to it grows out of its use, and not its mere adoption. By the act of Congress this exclusive right attaches upon registration. But in neither case does it depend upon novelty, invention, discovery, or any work of the brain. It requires no fancy or imagination, no genius, no laborious thought. It is simply founded on priority of appropriation. We look in vain in the statute for any other qualification or condition. If the symbol, however plain, simple, old, or well-known, has been first appropriated by the claimant as his distinctive trade-mark, he may by registration secure the right to its exclusive use. While such legislation may be a judicious aid to the common law on the subject of trade-marks, and may be within the competency of legislatures whose general powers embrace that class of subjects, we are unable to see any such power in the constitutional provision concerning authors and inventors, and their writings and discoveries.

The other clause of the Constitution supposed to confer the requisite authority on Congress is . . . as follows: 'The Congress shall have power to regulate commerce with foreign nations, and among the several States, and with the Indian tribes.'

The argument is that the use of a trade-mark—that which alone gives it any value—is to identify a particular class or quality of goods as the manufacture, produce, or property of the person who puts them in the general market for sale; that the sale of the article so distinguished is commerce; that the trade-mark is, therefore, a useful and valuable aid or instrument of commerce, and its regulation by virtue of the clause belongs to Congress, and that the act in question is a lawful exercise of this power. . . .

The question, therefore, whether the trade-mark bears such a relation to commerce in general terms as to bring it within congressional control, when used or applied to the classes of commerce which fall within that control, is one which, in the present case, we propose to leave undecided. We adopt this course because when this court is called on in the course of the administration of the law to consider whether an act of Congress, or of any other department of the government, is within the constitutional authority of that department, a due respect for a co-ordinate branch of the government requires that we shall decide that it has transcended its powers only when that is so plain that we cannot avoid the duty.

In such cases it is manifestly the dictate of wisdom and judicial propriety to decide no more than is necessary to the case in hand. That such has been the uniform course of this court in regard to statutes passed by Congress will readily appear to any one who will consider the vast amount of argument presented to us assailing them as unconstitutional, and he will count, as he may do on his fingers, the instances in which this court has declared an act of Congress void for want of constitutional power.

Governed by this view of our duty, we proceed to remark that a glance at the commerce clause of the Constitution discloses at once what has been often the subject of comment in this court and out of it, that the power of regulation there conferred on Congress is limited to commerce with foreign nations, commerce among the States, and commerce with the Indian tribes. . . .

When, therefore, Congress undertakes to enact a law, which can only be valid as a regulation of commerce, it is reasonable to expect to find on the face of the law, or from its essential nature, that it is a regulation of commerce with foreign nations, or among the several States, or with the Indian tribes. If not so limited, it is in excess of the power of Congress. If its main purpose be to establish a regulation applicable to all trade, to commerce at all points, especially if it be apparent that it is designed to govern the commerce wholly between citizens of the same State, it is obviously the exercise of a power not confided to Congress.

We find no recognition of this principle in the chapter on trade-marks in the Revised Statutes. We would naturally look for this in the description of the class of persons who are entitled to register a trade-mark, or in reference to the goods to which it should be applied. If, for instance, the statute described persons engaged in a commerce between the different States, and related to the use of trade-marks in such commerce, it would be evident that Congress believed it was acting under the clause of the Constitution which authorizes it to regulate commerce among the States. So if, when the trade-mark has been registered, Congress had protected its use on goods sold by a citizen of one State to another, or by a citizen of a foreign State to a citizen of the United States, it would be seen that Congress was at least intending to exercise the power of regulation conferred by that clause of the Constitution. But no such idea is found or suggested in this statute. . . .

The questions in each of these cases being an inquiry whether these statutes can be upheld in whole or in part as valid and constitutional, must be answered in the negative.

Questions:

1.) The Court says "[i]f we should endeavor to classify it under the head of writings of authors, the objections are equally strong. In this, as in regard to inventions, originality is required." Where does this limitation appear in the Intellectual Property Clause? Is there a textual basis? A philosophical basis? Both?

2.) "In such cases it is manifestly the dictate of wisdom and judicial propriety to decide no more than is necessary to the case in hand. That such has been the uniform course of this court in regard to statutes passed by Congress will readily appear to any one who will consider the vast amount of argument presented to us assailing them as unconstitutional, and he will count, as he may do on his fingers, the instances in which this court has declared an act of Congress void for want of constitutional power." Yet this time the Court does declare the Act unconstitutional, despite the fact that the word "original" does not appear in the Intellectual Property Clause. Why? Does the discussion of the Commerce Clause, and its assumptions about Federal power, suggest an answer? Or is the originality requirement, in your view, well grounded in the purpose and language of the Intellectual Property Clause?

Feist v. Rural Telephone Service
499 U.S. 340 (1991)

The *Feist* opinion can be found in Chapter 11, starting at page 287. Please read it and then answer the following questions.

Questions:

1.) What would Justice Pitney, who wrote the majority in *INS v. AP*, say about this case?

2.) Is this merely a case about statutory interpretation? Or does it reinforce the *Trade-Mark Cases'* originality requirement?

3.) From an information economics point of view, telephone directories look like "public goods." They are non-excludable and non-rival. Yet this decision refuses to extend copyright to them. Is there an economic justification for such a result as well as a constitutional one?

4.) Think of innovation and culture as an input-output system. There are inputs (the raw material from which the innovation or the cultural product is produced) and outputs (the book, the invention, the movie, the software program.) Intellectual property schemes give control and limited monopolies over outputs, but this also risks raising the cost of the inputs for the next generation of innovation or culture. What "balance" does the *Feist* case set in terms of the inputs and outputs of copyright? Why leave unoriginal compilations of fact free?

5.) It is the day after the *Feist* decision and you are the lawyer for the winners. Might you still try and negotiate a license with the telephone company for their directory information, even if at a lower price? Why, when you could take it for free? Does this tell you anything about how excludable and non-rival the telephone directory truly is?

2.) Limitations on Congressional Power: Purpose and Novelty/Non-Obviousness

Graham v. John Deere Co.
383 U.S. 1 (1966)

Please read sections I–IV of the opinion, which can be found on page 744.

Questions:

1.) Give the most expansive possible reading of the holding of *Graham* in terms of the limitations set by the Copyright and Patent Clause on Congress's power. Now the most limited. Which is correct, in your view? Is there some middle position?

2.) Does this ruling apply only to Congress's patent legislation or does it apply equally to patent and copyright? Why?

3.) Does *Graham* also offer *interpretive* guidance to courts seeking to interpret intellectual property legislation? If so, how would you describe that guidance?

3.) Limitations on Congressional Power: Fixation & the Interaction Between Clauses

---

PROBLEM 2-2

CONSTITUTIONAL INTERPRETATION.

Read *Moghadam* and *Martignon* and answer the following questions:

1.) *Why* do we have a fixation requirement in copyright? Offer reasons that resonate with a.) the Copyright Clause's goal of encouraging creative activity that leads to actual access to the works for citizens and consumers, followed by an entry of the work into the public domain b.) the need to make copyright consistent with the First Amendment c.) the issue of "formal realizability"—defining the metes and bounds of the right so that one can tell what activities do and do not infringe.

2.) You are a plaintiff challenging the constitutionality of the anti-bootlegging statute discussed in *Moghadam* and *Martignon*—both the civil and criminal provisions. What specific challenges should you bring? How should the Court rule?

3.) More generally, does the Intellectual Property Clause ever constrain Congress's power under the Commerce clause? When and under what circumstances?

U.S. v. Moghadam
175 F.3d 1269 (11th Cir. 1999)

ANDERSON, Chief Judge.

In 1994, Congress passed a statute criminalizing the unauthorized recording, the transmission to the public, and the sale or distribution of or traffic in unauthorized recordings of live musical performances. *See* 18 U.S.C. § 2319A. Appellant Ali Moghadam was convicted of violating that law (herein sometimes referred to as the "anti-bootlegging statute") after he pleaded guilty to knowingly distributing, selling, and trafficking in bootleg (unauthorized) compact discs featuring live musical performances by recording artists including Tori Amos and the Beastie Boys. . . . In the district court, Moghadam moved to dismiss the indictment, arguing that the statute was unconstitutional because it did not fall within any of the federal legislative powers enumerated in Article I, § 8 of the Constitution. The government responded that it was constitutional under either the Copyright Clause or the Commerce Clause. . . . For the reasons that follow, and in the limited circumstances of this case, we reject Moghadam's constitutional challenge, and therefore affirm Moghadam's conviction.

I. Background on the Anti-Bootlegging Statute

A brief overview of the history of statutory protection for music and musical performances is in order. Musicians or performers may enjoy copyright or copyright-like protection in three things, which are important to keep distinct. . . . First, [there is the] musical composition. . . . [Second, i]n 1971, Congress extended copyright protection to sound recordings. This meant that persons who made unauthorized reproductions of records or tapes . . . could be prosecuted or face civil liability for copyright infringement. . . .

However . . . [n]o protection at the federal level extended directly to unrecorded live musical performances. Therefore, a bootlegger could surreptitiously record a live musical performance and engage in unauthorized distribution of the recording or copies thereof, without having violated copyright law. . . . [The anti-bootlegging statute was enacted as part of the URAA, a statute implementing the agreements reached as part of the TRIPS Uruguay Round. It forbade making, distributing or trafficking in such (unauthorized) recordings for commercial gain or private financial advantage.] The URAA also enacted a similar provision establishing civil liability for the same conduct (but omitting the commercial advantage or private financial gain requirement). . . . [W]hat little legislative history exists tends to suggest that Congress viewed the anti-bootlegging provisions as enacted pursuant to its Copyright Clause authority.

The rights created by the anti-bootlegging provisions in URAA are actually hybrid rights that in some ways resemble the protections of copyright law but in other ways are distinct from them. . . . Congress could have amended 17 U.S.C. § 102 to include live musical performances in the list of protectable subject matter, but it did not do so. Likewise, it is unclear whether longstanding concepts generally applicable to copyright law such as fair use, the work-for-hire doctrine, limited duration, and the statute of limitations, carry over to the anti-bootlegging provisions. Finally, in contrast to the six exclusive rights of a copyright owner spelled out in 17 U.S.C. § 106, it appears that the only exclusive right created by the anti-bootlegging statute is to record and/or re-communicate one's performance. For all of these reasons, the protections that the anti-bootlegging statutes confer on musicians are best described as "quasi-copyright" or *sui generis* protections.

II. Whether the Anti-Bootlegging Statute Can Be Sustained Under the Copyright Clause of the Constitution

Our analysis of the constitutionality of § 2319A begins with the Copyright Clause of the United States Constitution. By that Clause, Congress is empowered "to promote the Progress of Science and the useful Arts, by securing for limited Times to Authors and Inventors the exclusive Right to their respective Writings and Discoveries." U.S. Const. art. I, § 8, cl. 8. This positive grant of legislative authority includes several limitations. *See, e.g., Feist* (holding that the word "Writings" in the Copyright Clause allows Congress to extend protection only to works of authorship that are original). Of these limitations, Moghadam has relied in the instant case only on the concept of "fixation" which is said to be embedded in the term "Writings."

The concept of fixation suggests that works are not copyrightable unless reduced to some tangible form. . . . Of course, the term "Writings" has been interpreted so broadly as to include much more than writings in the literal sense, or the lay definition of the word. In fact, since a sound recording qualifies as a "Writing" in the constitutional sense "it is now clear that a writing may be perceptible either visually or aurally." But the fixation requirement seems to have persisted through this expansion. Thus, although in the modern era the term "Writings" allows Congress to extend copyright protection to a great many things, those things have always involved some fixed, tangible and durable form.

Moghadam argues that a live performance, by definition, has not been reduced to a tangible form or fixed as of the time of the performance. *See* Nimmer, *The End of Copyright* ("No respectable interpretation of the word 'writings' embraces an untaped performance of someone singing at Carnegie Hall.") Moghadam argues that, but for the bootlegger's decision to record, a live performance is fleeting and evanescent.

Because we affirm the conviction in the instant case on the basis of an alternative source of Congressional power, we decline to decide in this case whether the fixation concept of Copyright Clause can be expanded so as to encompass live performances that are merely capable of being reduced to tangible form, but have not been.[9] For purposes of this case, we assume *arguendo,* without deciding, that the above described problems with the fixation requirement would preclude the use of the Copyright Clause as a source of Congressional power for the anti-bootlegging statute.

III. Whether the Anti-Bootlegging Statute Can Be Sustained Under the Commerce Clause of the Constitution

The government contends, however, that the anti-bootlegging statute is permissible legislation under Congress's Commerce Clause power.[10] Congress has the legislative authority "to regulate Commerce with foreign Nations, and among the several States." U.S. Const. art. I, § 8, cl. 3. . . . Because Congress thought it was acting under the Copyright Clause, predictably there are no legislative findings in the record regarding the effect of bootlegging of live musical performances on interstate or foreign commerce. . . . However, the lack of such findings does not rule out the Commerce Clause as a possible source of legislative authority applicable to the statute under challenge. . . .

Section 2319A clearly prohibits conduct that has a substantial effect on both commerce between the several states and commerce with foreign nations. The link between bootleg compact discs and interstate commerce and commerce with foreign nations is self-evident. . . . Moreover, the type of conduct that Congress intended to regulate by passing the anti-bootlegging statute is by its very nature economic activity, which distinguishes the statute from the Gun-Free School Zones Act struck down in *Lopez,* which in criminalizing the possession of handguns within 1000 feet of a school, "had nothing to do with 'commerce' or any sort of economic enterprise, however broadly one might define those terms." We hold that the anti-bootlegging statute has a sufficient connection to interstate and foreign commerce to meet the *Lopez* test.

The more difficult question in this case is whether Congress can use its Commerce Clause power to avoid the limitations that might prevent it from passing the same legislation under the Copyright Clause. As noted above, we assume *arguendo* that the Copyright Clause could not sustain this legislation because live performances, being unfixed, are not encompassed by the term "Writings" which includes a fixation requirement. The government argues that the anti-bootlegging conviction in this case can be sustained under the Commerce Clause. We turn now to this issue.

In general, the various grants of legislative authority contained in the Constitution stand alone and must be independently analyzed. In other words, each of the powers of Congress is alternative to all of the other powers, and what cannot be done under one of them may very well be doable under another. Perhaps the most prominent example of this principle is *Heart of Atlanta Motel, Inc. v. United States* (1964). There, the Supreme Court considered the constitutionality of the public accommodation provisions of the Civil Rights Act of 1964. The earlier *Civil Rights Cases* (1883) had declared unconstitutional

---

[9] We note that the anti-bootlegging statute may be faced with another constitutional problem under the Copyright Clause. The Clause allows Congress to extend protection to authors only for "Limited Times." The protection afforded to live performances by § 2319A, however, contains no express time limitation and would arguably persist indefinitely. However, Moghadam has not preserved this argument, *see infra,* and we decline to address the argument in light of our disposition of this case.

[10] Congress's failure to cite the Commerce Clause as grounds for § 2319A does not eliminate the possibility that the Commerce Clause can sustain this legislation. "The constitutionality of action taken by Congress does not depend on recitals of the power which it undertakes to exercise," *Woods v. Cloyd W. Miller Co.* (1948), and "in exercising the power of judicial review," we look only at "the *actual* powers of the national government," *Timmer v. Michigan Dept. of Commerce* (1997).

similar provisions of the Civil Rights Act of 1875 because they regulated private conduct beyond the scope of the legislative authority granted by § 5 of the Fourteenth Amendment. Yet, the *Heart of Atlanta Motel* Court held, the Civil Rights Act of 1964 was predicated on the Commerce Clause and possessed sufficient connection to interstate commerce. The Court's reasoning illustrates that, as a general matter, the fact that legislation reaches beyond the limits of one grant of legislative power has no bearing on whether it can be sustained under another.

This general approach has been applied in a context involving the Copyright Clause and the Commerce Clause as alternative sources of Congressional power. *The Trade-Mark Cases* (1879) involved an 1876 Congressional enactment of a primitive sort of trademark protection, long before the modern-day Lanham Act. Act of Aug. 14, 1876, 19 Stat. 141 ("1876 Act"). . . . Apparently, just as was the case with the anti-bootlegging statute, Congress labored under the impression that it was acting pursuant to its Copyright Clause power. The *Trade-Mark Cases* ("Until a critical examination of the subject in the courts became necessary, it was mainly if not wholly to [the Copyright C]lause that the advocates of the law looked for its support."). Nevertheless, the Supreme Court held that the Copyright Clause could not sustain the 1876 Act because "the ordinary trade-mark has no necessary relation to invention or discovery," which were the hallmarks of protectable subject matter under the Copyright Clause. . . .

The Court next considered whether Congress could enact the 1876 Act under the Commerce Clause. . . . The Court appeared receptive to this argument. However, it must be remembered that the *Trade-Mark Cases* predated the New Deal-era expansion of the Commerce Clause. . . . Although the 1876 Act did not survive due to the restrictive view of the Commerce Clause prevailing at that time, the Supreme Court's analysis in the *Trade-Mark Cases* stands for the proposition that legislation which would not be permitted under the Copyright Clause *could* nonetheless be permitted under the Commerce Clause, provided that the independent requirements of the latter are met. . . .

On the other hand, it might be argued that some of the grants of legislative authority in Article I, § 8 contain significant limitations that can be said to represent the Framers' judgment that Congress should be affirmatively prohibited from passing certain types of legislation, no matter under which provision. The Supreme Court touched on such a situation in *Railway Labor Executives' Ass'n v. Gibbons* (1982). Congress had enacted a statute that purported to alter a pending bankruptcy case by requiring the debtor railroad company's bankruptcy estate to pay $75 million to the company's former employees. This statute directly clashed with the Bankruptcy Clause, U.S. Const. art. I, § 8, cl. 4, which provides that Congress is empowered to pass "uniform" bankruptcy laws, because the law targeted a particular situation and was anything but uniform. The Court quickly brushed off the possibility that the legislation could nevertheless be sustained under the Commerce Clause (which contains no uniformity requirement), stating that "if we were to hold that Congress had the power to enact nonuniform bankruptcy laws pursuant to the Commerce Clause, we would eradicate from the Constitution a limitation on the power of Congress to enact bankruptcy laws." . . . *Cf.* Paul J. Heald, *The Vices of Originality* (arguing that Congress would not be able to circumvent the *originality* requirement inherent in the term "Writings" in the Copyright Clause by passing a statute under the Commerce Clause which extended copyright-like protection to unoriginal works).

We note that there is some tension between the former line of cases (*Heart of Atlanta Motel*, the *Trade-Mark Cases* and *Authors League*) and the *Railway Labor Executives* case. The former cases suggest that in some circumstances the Commerce Clause can be used by Congress to accomplish something that the Copyright Clause might not allow. But the *Railway Labor Executives* case suggests that in some circumstances the Commerce Clause cannot be used to eradicate a limitation placed upon Congressional power in another grant of power. For purposes of the instant case, we resolve this tension in the following manner . . . [w]e undertake a circumscribed analysis, deciding only what is necessary to decide this case, and we reach a narrow conclusion. First . . . we hold the anti-bootlegging statute satisfies the "substantial effects" test of the post-*Lopez* Commerce Clause jurisprudence. Second, following the former line of cases (*Heart of Atlanta Hotel*, the *Trade-Mark Cases* and *Authors League*), we hold that in some circumstances the Commerce Clause indeed may be used to accomplish that which may not have been permissible under the Copyright Clause. We hold that the instant case is one such circumstance in which the Commerce Clause may be thus used. It is at this point that we must resolve the tension with *Railway Labor Executives*.

Resolving this tension, we take as a given that there are some circumstances, as illustrated by *Railway Labor Executives*, in which the Commerce Clause cannot be used by Congress to eradicate a limitation placed upon Congress in another grant of power.[12] For the reasons that follow, we hold that the instant case is not one such circumstance. We hold that the Copyright Clause does not envision that Congress is positively forbidden from extending copyright-like protection under other constitutional clauses, such as the Commerce Clause, to works of authorship that may not meet the fixation requirement inherent in the term "Writings." The grant itself is stated in positive terms, and does not imply any negative pregnant that suggests that the term "Writings" operates as a ceiling on Congress' ability to legislate pursuant to other grants. Extending quasi-copyright protection to unfixed live musical performances is in no way inconsistent with the Copyright Clause. . . . A live musical performance clearly satisfies the originality requirement. Extending quasi-copyright protection also furthers the purpose of the Copyright Clause to promote the progress of the useful arts by securing some exclusive rights to the creative author. Finally, with respect to the fixation requirement, upon which this opinion focuses, although a live musical performance may not have been fixed, or reduced to tangible form, as of the time the bootleg copy was made, it certainly was subject to having been thus fixed. . . . Common sense does not indicate that extending copyright-like protection to a live performance is fundamentally inconsistent with the Copyright Clause.

For the foregoing reasons, we conclude that extending copyright-like protection in the instant case is not fundamentally inconsistent with the fixation requirement of the Copyright Clause. By contrast, the nonuniform bankruptcy statute at issue in *Railway Labor Executives* was irreconcilably inconsistent with the uniformity requirement of the Bankruptcy Clause of the Constitution.[14]

We note that there is another limitation in the Copyright Clause that may be implicated by the anti-bootlegging statute: the "Limited Times" requirement that forbids Congress from conferring intellectual property rights of perpetual duration. On its face, the protection created by the anti-bootlegging statute is apparently perpetual and contains

---

[12] We assume *arguendo*, without deciding, that the Commerce Clause could not be used to avoid a limitation in the Copyright Clause if the particular use of the Commerce Clause (e.g., the anti-bootlegging statute) were fundamentally inconsistent with the particular limitation in the Copyright Clause (e.g., the fixation requirement).

[14] Our holding is limited to the fixation requirement, and should not be taken as authority that the other various limitations in the Copyright Clause can be avoided by reference to the Commerce Clause. *Compare* Nimmer, *The End of Copyright, supra,* at 1413 (decrying that Congress may "jettison *Feist*" by analogy to the URAA because "why is a telephone book any further afield than a performance at Carnegie Hall?"), *with* Gerdes, *supra,* at 1461 (proposing that Congress legislatively overrule *Feist* and extend copyright protection to unoriginal works by relying on the Commerce Clause).

no express time limit; therefore phonorecords of live musical performances would presumably never fall into the public domain. However, because Moghadam has not challenged the constitutionality of § 2319A on this basis,[15] we decline to raise the issue *sua sponte*. Thus, we do not decide in this case whether extending copyright-like protection under the anti-bootlegging statute might be fundamentally inconsistent with the "Limited Times" requirement of the Copyright Clause, and we do not decide in this case whether the Commerce Clause can provide the source of Congressional power to sustain the application of the anti-bootlegging statute in some other case in which such an argument is preserved. We reserve those issues for another day.

Summarizing our narrow holding in this case, we assume *arguendo,* without deciding, that the anti-bootlegging statute cannot satisfy the fixation requirement of the Copyright Clause; we hold that the statute satisfies the "substantial effects" test of the post-*Lopez* Commerce Clause jurisprudence; we hold that the Commerce Clause can provide the source of Congressional power in this case because the extension of copyright-like protection here is not fundamentally inconsistent with the fixation requirement of the Copyright Clause;[16] and thus under the circumstances of this case,[17] we reject Moghadam's constitutional challenge to his conviction.

IV. CONCLUSION

For the foregoing reasons, the judgment of the district court is AFFIRMED.

Questions:

1.) Bootlegging *Tori Amos*? Sorry, that wasn't a question.

2.) If Mr. Moghadam were reading this decision in his prison cell, what might he wish intensely that his lawyers had done differently?

3.) The court sees a danger in assuming that a limitation on Congress's power in one clause implies that Congress cannot "get around" that limitation under another clause. Yet it also sees a danger in assuming the reverse. Explain each danger, as the court describes it. What technique does the court use to avoid both dangers and to explain when such limitations should, and should not, be implied?

---

[15] Moghadam did not make this argument in the district court or in his brief on appeal. He fleetingly mentions the "Limited Times" requirement for the first time in his reply brief on appeal, and even then does not argue that extending copyright-like protection in this case pursuant to the Commerce Clause would be prohibited by an inconsistency with the "Limited Times" requirement of the Copyright Clause. The government has not had any opportunity to present a defense to such an argument, and it would be unfair to entertain the argument at this late date.

[16] Because we find no such inconsistency, we need not decide the consequences if there were inconsistency. *See* note 12, *supra.*

[17] As noted above, Moghadam has waived any constitutional challenge based on the "Limited Times" requirement of the Copyright Clause, and thus our holding in this case is further narrowed by the fact that we do not address potential arguments based on the "Limited Times" requirement.

U.S. v. Martignon
492 F.3d 140 (2d Cir. 2007)

[In *Martignon,* the plaintiff explicitly claimed that the URAA violated *both* the fixation and the limited times restrictions of the Copyright Clause. Thus, the court could not rely on the *Moghadam* court's carefully limited reasoning.]

The Supreme Court has indicated that Congress can sometimes enact legislation under one constitutional provision that it could not have enacted under another. *See, e.g., Heart of Atlanta.* However, this power is not unlimited. *See Gibbons.* Because the parties attach different import to these cases and to the *Trade-Mark Cases,* we examine them to determine where to draw the line between (1) a law which, while related to one constitutional provision and unauthorized by it, can be validly enacted under a different provision; and (2) legislative action that is prohibited under one provision and cannot be enacted under another even though it is seemingly within the purview of the second provision. . . .

We believe that the Supreme Court's cases allow the regulation of matters that could not be regulated under the Copyright Clause in a manner arguably inconsistent with that clause unless the statute at issue is a copyright law. We draw this lesson from *Heart of Atlanta* and from *Gibbons.* In *Heart of Atlanta,* the Court found authority for Congress to enact a statute that prohibited race discrimination in public accommodations affecting interstate commerce, even though the prohibition ran to discrimination not involving "state action," under the Commerce Clause although the Fourteenth Amendment did not allow Congress to enact a similar statute. The *Gibbons* Court found that RITA was actually a bankruptcy law, not that it was very close to a bankruptcy law or that it was bankruptcy-like. . . . We will judge the constitutionality of Section 2319A under the same standard that the *Gibbons* Court used; that is, in order to demonstrate unconstitutionality, Martignon must establish that Section 2319A is a copyright law and not just that it is copyright-like. . . .

Section 2319A does not create and bestow property rights upon authors or inventors, or allocate those rights among claimants to them. It is a criminal statute, falling in its codification (along with Section 2319B about bootlegged films) between the law criminalizing certain copyright infringement and the law criminalizing "trafficking in counterfeit goods or services." It is, perhaps, analogous to the law of criminal trespass. Rather than creating a right in the performer him- or herself, it creates a power in the government to protect the interest of performers from commercial predations. Section 2319A does not grant the performer the right to exclude others from the performance— only the government can do that. Neither may the performer transfer his or her interests under Section 2319A to another. . . . Section 2319A is not a law "secur[ing] . . . rights," nor is it a copyright law. Thus . . . Section 2319A is not subject to the limitations of Article I, Section 8, cl. 8. . . .

In sum, Section 2319A does not create, bestow, or allocate property rights in expression, it does not share the defining characteristics of other laws that are concededly "copyright laws," and it differs significantly from the Copyright Act that was passed pursuant to the Copyright Clause (and that is valid under it). We therefore conclude that it was not enacted under the Copyright Clause. We have no need to examine whether it violates limits of the Copyright Clause and proceed instead to an examination of its sustainability under the Commerce Clause.[7]

---

[7] We acknowledge that our analysis necessarily triggers concerns about the ability of Congress to criminalize other conduct that would be permitted under the Copyright Clause and the copyright laws of this country,

Commerce Clause Authority

. . . Section 2319A has substantial commercial and economic aspects. . . . Because Section 2319A is not a copyright law and its enactment was well within the scope of Congress's Commerce Clause authority, it is constitutionally permissible unless some other constitutional provision prevents its enforcement. . . .

Questions:

1.) How does the *Martignon* court solve the problem that the *Moghadam* court had? How do the two solutions differ? Which solution is best in your view? Which gives Congress the greatest freedom to make laws that do not fit within the Intellectual Property Clause, narrowly construed?

2.) According to this court, what are the key features of a 'copyright law'? Do you agree with the description? With the way it is applied in this case?

4.) Limitations on Congressional Power: Limited Times, Term Extension and the First Amendment

Eldred v. Ashcroft
537 U.S. 186 (2003)

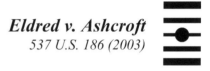

Justice GINSBURG delivered the opinion of the Court. Justices STEVENS and BREYER dissented and filed opinions.

This case concerns the authority the Constitution assigns to Congress to prescribe the duration of copyrights. The Copyright and Patent Clause of the Constitution, Art. I, § 8, cl. 8, provides as to copyrights: "Congress shall have Power . . . [t]o promote the Progress of Science . . . by securing [to Authors] for limited Times . . . the exclusive Right to their . . . Writings." In 1998, in the measure here under inspection, Congress enlarged the duration of copyrights by 20 years. As in the case of prior extensions, principally in 1831, 1909, and 1976, Congress provided for application of the enlarged terms to existing and future copyrights alike.

Petitioners are individuals and businesses whose products or services build on copyrighted works that have gone into the public domain. They seek a determination that the CTEA fails constitutional review under both the Copyright Clause's "limited Times" prescription and the First Amendment's free speech guarantee. Under the 1976 Copyright Act, copyright protection generally lasted from the work's creation until 50 years after the author's death. Under the CTEA, most copyrights now run from creation until 70 years after the author's death. 17 U.S.C. § 302(a). Petitioners do not challenge the "life-plus-70-years" timespan itself. "Whether 50 years is enough, or 70 years too much," they acknowledge, "is not a judgment meet for this Court."[1] Congress went awry, petitioners

---

for instance the reproduction and sale of a literary work that has long lost its copyright protection. Because such statutes are not before us, we cannot address them. We do note, however, that there could be other constitutional problems associated with such statutes, including possible violations of the Due Process Clause and the First Amendment.

[1] Justice Breyer's dissent is not similarly restrained. He makes no effort meaningfully to distinguish existing

maintain, not with respect to newly created works, but in enlarging the term for published works with existing copyrights. The "limited Tim[e]" in effect when a copyright is secured, petitioners urge, becomes the constitutional boundary, a clear line beyond the power of Congress to extend. As to the First Amendment, petitioners contend that the CTEA is a content-neutral regulation of speech that fails inspection under the heightened judicial scrutiny appropriate for such regulations.

In accord with the District Court and the Court of Appeals, we reject petitioners' challenges to the CTEA. In that 1998 legislation, as in all previous copyright term extensions, Congress placed existing and future copyrights in parity. In prescribing that alignment, we hold, Congress acted within its authority and did not transgress constitutional limitations.

I
A

We evaluate petitioners' challenge to the constitutionality of the CTEA against the backdrop of Congress' previous exercises of its authority under the Copyright Clause. The Nation's first copyright statute, enacted in 1790, provided a federal copyright term of 14 years from the date of publication, renewable for an additional 14 years if the author survived the first term. . . . The 1790 Act's renewable 14-year term applied to existing works (*i.e.,* works already published and works created but not yet published) and future works alike. Congress expanded the federal copyright term to 42 years in 1831 (28 years from publication, renewable for an additional 14 years), and to 56 years in 1909 (28 years from publication, renewable for an additional 28 years). Both times, Congress applied the new copyright term to existing and future works.

In 1976, Congress altered the method for computing federal copyright terms. For works created by identified natural persons, the 1976 Act provided that federal copyright protection would run from the work's creation, not—as in the 1790, 1831, and 1909 Acts—its publication; protection would last until 50 years after the author's death. § 302(a). In these respects, the 1976 Act aligned United States copyright terms with the then-dominant international standard adopted under the Berne Convention for the Protection of Literary and Artistic Works. For anonymous works, pseudonymous works, and works made for hire, the 1976 Act provided a term of 75 years from publication or 100 years from creation, whichever expired first. § 302(c). . . .

The measure at issue here, the CTEA, installed the fourth major duration extension of federal copyrights. Retaining the general structure of the 1976 Act, the CTEA enlarges the terms of all existing and future copyrights by 20 years. For works created by identified natural persons, the term now lasts from creation until 70 years after the author's death. 17 U.S.C. § 302(a). This standard harmonizes the baseline United States copyright term with the term adopted by the European Union in 1993. For anonymous works, pseudonymous works, and works made for hire, the term is 95 years from publication or 120 years from creation, whichever expires first. 17 U.S.C. § 302(c). . . .

II
A

We address first the determination of the courts below that Congress has authority under the Copyright Clause to extend the terms of existing copyrights. Text, history, and precedent, we conclude, confirm that the Copyright Clause empowers Congress to prescribe "limited Times" for copyright protection and to secure the same level and

---

copyrights from future grants. Under his reasoning, the CTEA's 20-year extension is globally unconstitutional.

duration of protection for all copyright holders, present and future.

The CTEA's baseline term of life plus 70 years, petitioners concede, qualifies as a "limited Tim[e]" as applied to future copyrights. Petitioners contend, however, that existing copyrights extended to endure for that same term are not "limited." Petitioners' argument essentially reads into the text of the Copyright Clause the command that a time prescription, once set, becomes forever "fixed" or "inalterable." The word "limited," however, does not convey a meaning so constricted. At the time of the Framing, that word meant what it means today: "confine[d] within certain bounds," "restrain[ed]," or "circumscribe[d]." Thus understood, a timespan appropriately "limited" as applied to future copyrights does not automatically cease to be "limited" when applied to existing copyrights. And as we observe, *infra,* there is no cause to suspect that a purpose to evade the "limited Times" prescription prompted Congress to adopt the CTEA.

To comprehend the scope of Congress' power under the Copyright Clause, "a page of history is worth a volume of logic." *New York Trust Co. v. Eisner* (1921) (Holmes, J.). History reveals an unbroken congressional practice of granting to authors of works with existing copyrights the benefit of term extensions so that all under copyright protection will be governed evenhandedly under the same regime. As earlier recounted, the First Congress accorded the protections of the Nation's first federal copyright statute to existing and future works alike. 1790 Act § 1. Since then, Congress has regularly applied duration extensions to both existing and future copyrights.

Because the Clause empowering Congress to confer copyrights also authorizes patents, congressional practice with respect to patents informs our inquiry. We count it significant that early Congresses extended the duration of numerous individual patents as well as copyrights. The courts saw no "limited Times" impediment to such extensions; renewed or extended terms were upheld in the early days, for example, by Chief Justice Marshall and Justice Story sitting as circuit justices. . . . (Congresses ". . . are not restrained from renewing a patent or prolonging" it.).[7] . . .

Satisfied that the CTEA complies with the "limited Times" prescription, we turn now to whether it is a rational exercise of the legislative authority conferred by the Copyright Clause. On that point, we defer substantially to Congress. *Sony,* 464 U.S. at 429 ("[I]t is Congress that has been assigned the task of defining the scope of the limited monopoly that should be granted to authors . . . in order to give the public appropriate access to their work product.").[10]

The CTEA reflects judgments of a kind Congress typically makes, judgments we cannot dismiss as outside the Legislature's domain. As respondent describes, a key factor in the CTEA's passage was a 1993 European Union directive instructing EU members to

---

[7] Justice Stevens would sweep away these decisions, asserting that *Graham v. John Deere Co. of Kansas City* (1966), "flatly contradicts" them. *Post,* at 798. Nothing but wishful thinking underpins that assertion. The controversy in *Graham* involved no patent extension. *Graham* addressed an invention's very eligibility for patent protection, and spent no words on Congress' power to enlarge a patent's duration.

[10] Justice Breyer would adopt a heightened, three-part test for the constitutionality of copyright enactments. *Post,* at 802. He would invalidate the CTEA as irrational in part because, in his view, harmonizing the United States and European Union baseline copyright terms "apparent[ly]" fails to achieve "significant" uniformity. *Post,* at 812. But see *infra,* at 782. The novelty of the "rational basis" approach he presents is plain. (Breyer, J., dissenting) ("Rational-basis review—with its presumptions favoring constitutionality—is 'a paradigm of *judicial* restraint.'" (quoting *FCC v. Beach Communications, Inc.* (1993))). Rather than subjecting Congress' legislative choices in the copyright area to heightened judicial scrutiny, we have stressed that "it is not our role to alter the delicate balance Congress has labored to achieve." Congress' exercise of its Copyright Clause authority must be rational, but Justice Breyer's stringent version of rationality is unknown to our literary property jurisprudence.

establish a copyright term of life plus 70 years. Consistent with the Berne Convention, the EU directed its members to deny this longer term to the works of any non-EU country whose laws did not secure the same extended term. By extending the baseline United States copyright term to life plus 70 years, Congress sought to ensure that American authors would receive the same copyright protection in Europe as their European counterparts.

In addition to international concerns, Congress passed the CTEA in light of demographic, economic, and technological changes,[14] and rationally credited projections that longer terms would encourage copyright holders to invest in the restoration and public distribution of their works.

In sum, we find that the CTEA is a rational enactment; we are not at liberty to second-guess congressional determinations and policy judgments of this order, however debatable or arguably unwise they may be. Accordingly, we cannot conclude that the CTEA—which continues the unbroken congressional practice of treating future and existing copyrights in parity for term extension purposes—is an impermissible exercise of Congress' power under the Copyright Clause.

B

1

Petitioners contend that even if the CTEA's 20-year term extension is literally a "limited Tim[e]," permitting Congress to extend existing copyrights allows it to evade the "limited Times" constraint by creating effectively perpetual copyrights through repeated extensions. We disagree.

As the Court of Appeals observed, a regime of perpetual copyrights "clearly is not the situation before us." Nothing before this Court warrants construction of the CTEA's 20-year term extension as a congressional attempt to evade or override the "limited Times" constraint. Critically, we again emphasize, petitioners fail to show how the CTEA crosses a constitutionally significant threshold with respect to "limited Times" that the 1831, 1909, and 1976 Acts did not. . . .

2

Petitioners dominantly advance a series of arguments all premised on the proposition that Congress may not extend an existing copyright absent new consideration from the author. They pursue this main theme under three headings. Petitioners contend that the CTEA's extension of existing copyrights (1) overlooks the requirement of "originality," (2) fails to "promote the Progress of Science," and (3) ignores copyright's *quid pro quo*.

Petitioners' "originality" argument draws on *Feist* (1991). In *Feist,* we observed that "[t]he *sine qua non* of copyright is originality," and held that copyright protection is unavailable to "a narrow category of works in which the creative spark is utterly lacking or so trivial as to be virtually nonexistent." Relying on *Feist,* petitioners urge that even if a work is sufficiently "original" to qualify for copyright protection in the first instance, any extension of the copyright's duration is impermissible because, once published, a work is no longer original. *Feist,* however, did not touch on the duration of copyright protection. . . . The decision did not construe the "limited Times" for which a work may be protected, and the originality requirement has no bearing on that prescription.

More forcibly, petitioners contend that the CTEA's extension of existing copyrights

---

[14] Members of Congress expressed the view that, as a result of increases in human longevity and in parents' average age when their children are born, the pre-CTEA term did not adequately secure "the right to profit from licensing one's work during one's lifetime and to take pride and comfort in knowing that one's children—and perhaps their children—might also benefit from one's posthumous popularity." . . .

does not "promote the Progress of Science" as contemplated by the preambular language of the Copyright Clause. Art. I, § 8, cl. 8. To sustain this objection, petitioners do not argue that the Clause's preamble is an independently enforceable limit on Congress' power. Rather, they maintain that the preambular language identifies the sole end to which Congress may legislate; accordingly, they conclude, the meaning of "limited Times" must be "determined in light of that specified end." The CTEA's extension of existing copyrights categorically fails to "promote the Progress of Science," petitioners argue, because it does not stimulate the creation of new works but merely adds value to works already created.

As petitioners point out, we have described the Copyright Clause as "both a grant of power and a limitation," *Graham v. John Deere Co. of Kansas City* (1966), and have said that "[t]he primary objective of copyright" is "[t]o promote the Progress of Science." *Feist*. The "constitutional command," we have recognized, is that Congress, to the extent it enacts copyright laws at all, create a "system" that "promote[s] the Progress of Science."

We have also stressed, however, that it is generally for Congress, not the courts, to decide how best to pursue the Copyright Clause's objectives. See *Stewart v. Abend* (1990) ("Th[e] evolution of the duration of copyright protection tellingly illustrates the difficulties Congress faces. . . . [I]t is not our role to alter the delicate balance Congress has labored to achieve.") The justifications we earlier set out for Congress' enactment of the CTEA provide a rational basis for the conclusion that the CTEA "promote[s] the Progress of Science." . . .

Closely related to petitioners' preambular argument, or a variant of it, is their assertion that the Copyright Clause "imbeds a *quid pro quo*." They contend, in this regard, that Congress may grant to an "Autho[r]" an "exclusive Right" for a "limited Tim[e]," but only in exchange for a "Writin[g]." Extending an existing copyright without demanding additional consideration, petitioners maintain, bestows an unpaid-for benefit on copyright holders and their heirs, in violation of the *quid pro quo* requirement. . . .

We note, furthermore, that patents and copyrights do not entail the same exchange, and that our references to a *quid pro quo* typically appear in the patent context. . . .

Further distinguishing the two kinds of intellectual property, copyright gives the holder no monopoly on any knowledge. A reader of an author's writing may make full use of any fact or idea she acquires from her reading. See § 102(b). The grant of a patent, on the other hand, does prevent full use by others of the inventor's knowledge. In light of these distinctions, one cannot extract from language in our patent decisions—language not trained on a grant's duration—genuine support for petitioners' bold view. Accordingly, we reject the proposition that a *quid pro quo* requirement stops Congress from expanding copyright's term in a manner that puts existing and future copyrights in parity. . . .

III

Petitioners separately argue that the CTEA is a content-neutral regulation of speech that fails heightened judicial review under the First Amendment. We reject petitioners' plea for imposition of uncommonly strict scrutiny on a copyright scheme that incorporates its own speech-protective purposes and safeguards. The Copyright Clause and First Amendment were adopted close in time. This proximity indicates that, in the Framers' view, copyright's limited monopolies are compatible with free speech principles. Indeed, copyright's purpose is to *promote* the creation and publication of free expression. As *Harper & Row* observed: "[T]he Framers intended copyright itself to be the engine of free expression. By establishing a marketable right to the use of one's expression, copyright supplies the economic incentive to create and disseminate ideas."

In addition to spurring the creation and publication of new expression, copyright law contains built-in First Amendment accommodations. First, it distinguishes between ideas and expression and makes only the latter eligible for copyright protection. As we said in *Harper & Row,* this "idea/expression dichotomy strike[s] a definitional balance between the First Amendment and the Copyright Act by permitting free communication of facts while still protecting an author's expression." Due to this distinction, every idea, theory, and fact in a copyrighted work becomes instantly available for public exploitation at the moment of publication. See *Feist.*

Second, the "fair use" defense allows the public to use not only facts and ideas contained in a copyrighted work, but also expression itself in certain circumstances. Codified at 17 U.S.C. § 107, the defense provides: "[T]he fair use of a copyrighted work, including such use by reproduction in copies . . ., for purposes such as criticism, comment, news reporting, teaching (including multiple copies for classroom use), scholarship, or research, is not an infringement of copyright." The fair use defense affords considerable "latitude for scholarship and comment," *Harper & Row*, and even for parody, see *Campbell v. Acuff-Rose Music, Inc.* (1994) (rap group's musical parody of Roy Orbison's "Oh, Pretty Woman" may be fair use).

Finally, the case petitioners principally rely upon for their First Amendment argument, *Turner Broadcasting System, Inc. v. FCC* (1994), bears little on copyright. The statute at issue in *Turner* required cable operators to carry and transmit broadcast stations through their proprietary cable systems. . . . The CTEA, in contrast, does not oblige anyone to reproduce another's speech against the carrier's will. Instead, it protects authors' original expression from unrestricted exploitation. Protection of that order does not raise the free speech concerns present when the government compels or burdens the communication of particular facts or ideas. The First Amendment securely protects the freedom to make—or decline to make—one's own speech; it bears less heavily when speakers assert the right to make other people's speeches. To the extent such assertions raise First Amendment concerns, copyright's built-in free speech safeguards are generally adequate to address them. We recognize that the D.C. Circuit spoke too broadly when it declared copyrights "categorically immune from challenges under the First Amendment." But when, as in this case, Congress has not altered the traditional contours of copyright protection, further First Amendment scrutiny is unnecessary.

IV

. . . Beneath the facade of their inventive constitutional interpretation, petitioners forcefully urge that Congress pursued very bad policy in prescribing the CTEA's long terms. The wisdom of Congress' action, however, is not within our province to second guess. Satisfied that the legislation before us remains inside the domain the Constitution assigns to the First Branch, we affirm the judgment of the Court of Appeals.
It is so ordered.

Justice STEVENS, dissenting.

Writing for a unanimous Court in 1964, Justice Black stated that it is obvious that a State could not "extend the life of a patent beyond its expiration date." *Sears, Roebuck & Co. v. Stiffel Co.* (1964). As I shall explain, the reasons why a State may not extend the life of a patent apply to Congress as well. If Congress may not expand the scope of a patent monopoly, it also may not extend the life of a copyright beyond its expiration date. Accordingly, insofar as the 1998 Sonny Bono Copyright Term Extension Act, 112 Stat. 2827, purported to extend the life of unexpired copyrights, it is invalid. Because the majority's contrary conclusion rests on the mistaken premise that this Court has virtually no role in reviewing congressional grants of monopoly privileges to authors, inventors, and their successors, I respectfully dissent.

I

The authority to issue copyrights stems from the same Clause in the Constitution that created the patent power. . . . It is well settled that the Clause is "both a grant of power and a limitation" and that Congress "may not overreach the restraints imposed by the stated constitutional purpose." *Graham* (1966). As we have made clear in the patent context, that purpose has two dimensions. Most obviously the grant of exclusive rights to their respective writings and discoveries is intended to encourage the creativity of "Authors and Inventors." But the requirement that those exclusive grants be for "limited Times" serves the ultimate purpose of promoting the "Progress of Science and useful Arts" by guaranteeing that those innovations will enter the public domain as soon as the period of exclusivity expires. . . .

Neither the purpose of encouraging new inventions nor the overriding interest in advancing progress by adding knowledge to the public domain is served by retroactively increasing the inventor's compensation for a completed invention and frustrating the legitimate expectations of members of the public who want to make use of it in a free market. Because those twin purposes provide the only avenue for congressional action under the Copyright/Patent Clause of the Constitution, any other action is manifestly unconstitutional.

II

We have recognized that these twin purposes of encouraging new works and adding to the public domain apply to copyrights as well as patents. Thus, with regard to copyrights on motion pictures, we have clearly identified the overriding interest in the "release to the public of the products of [the author's] creative genius." And, as with patents, we have emphasized that the overriding purpose of providing a reward for authors' creative activity is to motivate that activity and "to allow the public access to the products of their genius after the limited period of exclusive control has expired." *Ex post facto* extensions of copyrights result in a gratuitous transfer of wealth from the public to authors, publishers, and their successors in interest. Such retroactive extensions do not even arguably serve either of the purposes of the Copyright/Patent Clause. The reasons why such extensions of the patent monopoly are unconstitutional apply to copyrights as well. . . .

IV

. . . A more complete and comprehensive look at the history of congressional action under the Copyright/Patent Clause demonstrates that history, in this case, does not provide the "'volume of logic'" necessary to sustain the Sonny Bono Act's constitutionality. . . .

The first example relied upon by respondent, the extension of Oliver Evans' patent in 1808, ch. 13, 6 Stat. 70, demonstrates the pitfalls of relying on an incomplete historical analysis. . . . This legislation, passed January 21, 1808, restored a patent monopoly for an invention that had been in the public domain for over four years. As such, this Act unquestionably exceeded Congress' authority under the Copyright/Patent Clause: "The Congress in the exercise of the patent power may not overreach the restraints imposed by the stated constitutional purpose. . . . *Congress may not authorize the issuance of patents whose effects are to remove existent knowledge from the public domain, or to restrict free access to materials already available.*" *Graham* (emphasis added).

. . . Congress passed private bills either directly extending patents or allowing otherwise untimely applicants to apply for patent extensions for approximately 75 patents between 1790 and 1875. Of these 75 patents, at least 56 had already fallen into the public domain. The fact that this repeated practice was patently unconstitutional completely undermines the majority's reliance on this history as "significant."

Copyright legislation has a similar history. Respondent argues that that historical practice effectively establishes the constitutionality of retroactive extensions of unexpired copyrights. Of course, the practice buttresses the presumption of validity that attaches to every Act of Congress. But, as our decision in *INS v. Chadha* (1983) demonstrates, the fact that Congress has repeatedly acted on a mistaken interpretation of the Constitution does not qualify our duty to invalidate an unconstitutional practice when it is finally challenged in an appropriate case. . . . For, as this Court has long recognized, "[i]t is obviously correct that no one acquires a vested or protected right in violation of the Constitution by long use, even when that span of time covers our entire national existence." *Walz v. Tax Comm'n of City of New York* (1970). . . . The fact that the Court has not previously passed upon the constitutionality of retroactive copyright extensions does not insulate the present extension from constitutional challenge. . . .

VI

Finally, respondent relies on concerns of equity to justify the retroactive extension. If Congress concludes that a longer period of exclusivity is necessary in order to provide an adequate incentive to authors to produce new works, respondent seems to believe that simple fairness requires that the same lengthened period be provided to authors whose works have already been completed and copyrighted. This is a classic *non sequitur*. The reason for increasing the inducement to create something new simply does not apply to an already-created work. To the contrary, the equity argument actually provides strong support for petitioners. Members of the public were entitled to rely on a promised access to copyrighted or patented works at the expiration of the terms specified when the exclusive privileges were granted. . . .

One must indulge in two untenable assumptions to find support in the equitable argument offered by respondent—that the public interest in free access to copyrighted works is entirely worthless and that authors, as a class, should receive a windfall solely based on completed creative activity. [A]s our cases repeatedly and consistently emphasize, ultimate public access is the overriding purpose of the constitutional provision. *Ex post facto* extensions of existing copyrights, unsupported by any consideration of the public interest, frustrate the central purpose of the Clause.

VII

The express grant of a perpetual copyright would unquestionably violate the textual requirement that the authors' exclusive rights be only "for limited Times." Whether the extraordinary length of the grants authorized by the 1998 Act are invalid because they are the functional equivalent of perpetual copyrights is a question that need not be answered in this case because the question presented by the certiorari petition merely challenges Congress' power to extend retroactively the terms of existing copyrights. . . . It is important to note, however, that a categorical rule prohibiting retroactive extensions would effectively preclude perpetual copyrights. More important-ly, as the House of Lords recognized when it refused to amend the Statute of Anne in 1735, unless the Clause is construed to embody such a categorical rule, Congress may extend existing monopoly privileges *ad infinitum* under the majority's analysis.

By failing to protect the public interest in free access to the products of inventive and artistic genius—indeed, by virtually ignoring the central purpose of the Copyright/ Patent Clause—the Court has quitclaimed to Congress its principal responsibility in this area of the law. Fairly read, the Court has stated that Congress' actions under the Copyright/Patent Clause are, for all intents and purposes, judicially unreviewable. That result cannot be squared with the basic tenets of our constitutional structure. It is not hyperbole to recall the trenchant words of Chief Justice John Marshall: "It is emphatically the province and duty of the judicial department to say what the law is." *Marbury v. Madison* (1803). We should discharge that responsibility as we did in *Chadha*.

I respectfully dissent.

Justice BREYER, dissenting.

. . . The economic effect of this 20-year extension—the longest blanket extension since the Nation's founding—is to make the copyright term not limited, but virtually perpetual. Its primary legal effect is to grant the extended term not to authors, but to their heirs, estates, or corporate successors. And most importantly, its practical effect is not to promote, but to inhibit, the progress of "Science"—by which word the Framers meant learning or knowledge.

. . . Although the Copyright Clause grants broad legislative power to Congress, that grant has limits. And in my view this statute falls outside them.

I

The "monopoly privileges" that the Copyright Clause confers "are neither unlimited nor primarily designed to provide a special private benefit." This Court has made clear that the Clause's limitations are judicially enforceable.

The Copyright Clause and the First Amendment seek related objectives—the creation and dissemination of information. When working in tandem, these provisions mutually reinforce each other, the first serving as an "engine of free expression," the second assuring that government throws up no obstacle to its dissemination. At the same time, a particular statute that exceeds proper Copyright Clause bounds may set Clause and Amendment at cross-purposes, thereby depriving the public of the speech-related benefits that the Founders, through both, have promised.

Consequently, I would review plausible claims that a copyright statute seriously, and unjustifiably, restricts the dissemination of speech somewhat more carefully than reference to this Court's traditional Copyright Clause jurisprudence might suggest. . . . I would find that the statute lacks the constitutionally necessary rational support (1) if the significant benefits that it bestows are private, not public; (2) if it threatens seriously to undermine the expressive values that the Copyright Clause embodies; and (3) if it cannot find justification in any significant Clause-related objective. Where, after examination of the statute, it becomes difficult, if not impossible, even to dispute these characterizations, Congress' "choice is clearly wrong." *Helvering v. Davis* (1937).

II
A

Because we must examine the relevant statutory effects in light of the Copyright Clause's own purposes, we should begin by reviewing the basic objectives of that Clause. The Clause authorizes a "tax on readers for the purpose of giving a bounty to writers." (Lord Macaulay). Why? What constitutional purposes does the "bounty" serve?

The Constitution itself describes the basic Clause objective as one of "promot[ing] the Progress of Science," *i.e.,* knowledge and learning. The Clause exists not to "provide a special private benefit," but "to stimulate artistic creativity for the general public good." It does so by "motivat[ing] the creative activity of authors" through "the provision of a special reward." *Sony, supra,* at 429. The "reward" is a means, not an end. And that is why the copyright term is limited. It is limited so that its beneficiaries—the public—"will not be permanently deprived of the fruits of an artist's labors."

That is how the Court previously has described the Clause's objectives. And, in doing so, the Court simply has reiterated the views of the Founders.

Madison, like Jefferson and others in the founding generation, warned against the dangers of monopolies . . . (arguing against even copyright monopolies); (statement of Rep. Jackson in the First Congress, Feb. 1791) ("What was it drove our forefathers to this country? Was it not the ecclesiastical corporations and perpetual monopolies of England and Scotland?"). Madison noted that the Constitution had "limited them to two cases, the authors of Books, and of useful inventions." He thought that in those two cases monopoly is justified because it amounts to "compensation for" an actual community "benefit" and because the monopoly is "temporary"—the term originally being 14 years (once renewable). Madison concluded that "under that limitation a sufficient recompence and encouragement may be given." But he warned in general that monopolies must be "guarded with strictness against abuse." . . .

For present purposes, then, we should take the following as well established: that copyright statutes must serve public, not private, ends; that they must seek "to promote the Progress" of knowledge and learning; and that they must do so both by creating incentives for authors to produce and by removing the related restrictions on dissemination after expiration of a copyright's "limited Tim[e]"—a time that (like "a *limited* monarch") is "restrain[ed]" and "circumscribe[d]," "not [left] at large." . . .

B

This statute, like virtually every copyright statute, imposes upon the public certain expression-related costs in the form of (1) royalties that may be higher than necessary to evoke creation of the relevant work, and (2) a requirement that one seeking to reproduce a copyrighted work must obtain the copyright holder's permission. The first of these costs translates into higher prices that will potentially restrict a work's dissemination. The second means search costs that themselves may prevent reproduction even where the author has no objection. Although these costs are, in a sense, inevitable concomitants of copyright protection, there are special reasons for thinking them especially serious here.

First, the present statute primarily benefits the holders of existing copyrights, *i.e.,* copyrights on works already created. And a Congressional Research Service (CRS) study prepared for Congress indicates that the added royalty-related sum that the law will transfer to existing copyright holders is large. In conjunction with official figures on copyright renewals, the CRS Report indicates that only about 2% of copyrights between 55 and 75 years old retain commercial value—*i.e.,* still generate royalties after that time. But books, songs, and movies of that vintage still earn about $400 million per year in royalties. [O]ne might conservatively estimate that 20 extra years of copyright protection will mean the transfer of several billion extra royalty dollars to holders of existing copyrights—copyrights that, together, already will have earned many billions of dollars in royalty "reward."

The extra royalty payments will not come from thin air. Rather, they ultimately come from those who wish to read or see or hear those classic books or films or recordings that have survived. Further, the likely amounts of extra royalty payments are large enough to suggest that unnecessarily high prices will unnecessarily restrict distribution of classic works (or lead to disobedience of the law)—not just in theory but in practice. Cf. CRS Report 3 ("[N]ew, cheaper editions can be expected when works come out of copyright"); Brief for College Art Association et al. as *Amici Curiae* 24.

A second, equally important, cause for concern arises out of the fact that copyright extension imposes a "permissions" requirement—not only upon potential users of "classic" works that still retain commercial value, but also upon potential users of *any other work* still in copyright. Again using CRS estimates, one can estimate that, by 2018, the number of such works 75 years of age or older will be about 350,000. Because the Copyright Act of 1976 abolished the requirement that an owner must renew a copyright, such still-in-copyright works (of little or no commercial value) will eventually number in the millions.

The potential users of such works include not only movie buffs and aging jazz fans, but also historians, scholars, teachers, writers, artists, database operators, and researchers of all kinds—those who want to make the past accessible for their own use or for that of others. The permissions requirement can inhibit their ability to accomplish that task. Indeed, in an age where computer-accessible databases promise to facilitate research and learning, the permissions requirement can stand as a significant obstacle to realization of that technological hope.

The reason is that the permissions requirement can inhibit or prevent the use of old works (particularly those without commercial value): (1) because it may prove expensive to track down or to contract with the copyright holder, (2) because the holder may prove impossible to find, or (3) because the holder when found may deny permission either outright or through misinformed efforts to bargain. The CRS, for example, has found that the cost of seeking permission "can be prohibitive."

Thus, the American Association of Law Libraries points out that the clearance process associated with creating an electronic archive, Documenting the American South, "consumed approximately a dozen man-hours" *per work.* The College Art Association says that the costs of obtaining permission for use of single images, short excerpts, and other short works can become prohibitively high; it describes the abandonment of efforts to include, *e.g.,* campaign songs, film excerpts, and documents exposing "horrors of the chain gang" in historical works or archives; and it points to examples in which copyright holders in effect have used their control of copyright to try to control the content of historical or cultural works. . . . *Amici* for petitioners describe how electronic databases tend to avoid adding to their collections works whose copyright holders may prove difficult to contact.

. . . Similarly, the costs of obtaining permission, now perhaps ranging in the millions of dollars, will multiply as the number of holders of affected copyrights increases from several hundred thousand to several million. The costs to the users of nonprofit databases, now numbering in the low millions, will multiply as the use of those computer-assisted databases becomes more prevalent. And the qualitative costs to education, learning, and research will multiply as our children become ever more dependent for the content of their knowledge upon computer-accessible databases—thereby condemning that which is not so accessible, say, the cultural content of early 20th-century history, to a kind of intellectual purgatory from which it will not easily emerge. . . .

The majority also invokes the "fair use" exception, and it notes that copyright law itself is restricted to protection of a work's expression, not its substantive content. Neither the exception nor the restriction, however, would necessarily help those who wish to obtain from electronic databases material that is not there—say, teachers wishing their students to see albums of Depression Era photographs, to read the recorded words of those who actually lived under slavery, or to contrast, say, Gary Cooper's heroic portrayal of Sergeant York with filmed reality from the battlefield of Verdun. Such harm, and more will occur despite the 1998 Act's exemptions and despite the other "First Amendment safeguards" in which the majority places its trust.

I should add that the Motion Picture Association of America also finds my concerns overstated, at least with respect to films, because the extension will sometimes make it profitable to reissue old films, saving them from extinction. Other film preservationists note, however, that only a small minority of the many films, particularly silent films, from the 1920's and 1930's have been preserved. (Half of all pre-1950 feature films and more than 80% of all such pre-1929 films have already been lost); cf. Brief for Hal Roach Studios et al. as *Amici Curiae* 18 (Out of 1,200 Twenties Era silent films still under copyright, 63 are now available on digital video disc). They seek to preserve the remainder. And they tell us that copyright extension will impede preservation by forbidding the reproduction of films within their own or within other public collections. . . .

C

What copyright-related benefits might justify the statute's extension of copyright protection? First, no one could reasonably conclude that copyright's traditional economic rationale applies here. The extension will not act as an economic spur encouraging authors to create new works. . . . And any remaining monetary incentive is diminished dramatically by the fact that the relevant royalties will not arrive until 75 years or more into the future, when, not the author, but distant heirs, or shareholders in a successor corporation, will receive them. Using assumptions about the time value of money provided us by a group of economists (including five Nobel prize winners), it seems fair to say that, for example, a 1% likelihood of earning $100 annually for 20 years, starting *75 years into the future,* is worth less than seven cents today.

What potential Shakespeare, Wharton, or Hemingway would be moved by such a sum? What monetarily motivated Melville would not realize that he could do better for his grandchildren by putting a few dollars into an interest-bearing bank account? The Court itself finds no evidence to the contrary. It refers to testimony before Congress (1) that the copyright system's incentives encourage creation, and (2) (referring to Noah Webster) that income earned from one work can help support an artist who "'continue[s] to create.'"

[E]ven if this cited testimony were meant more specifically to tell Congress that somehow, somewhere, some potential author might be moved by the thought of great-grandchildren receiving copyright royalties a century hence, so might some potential author also be moved by the thought of royalties being paid for two centuries, five centuries, 1,000 years, "'til the End of Time." And from a rational economic perspective the time difference among these periods *makes no real difference.* The present extension will produce a copyright period of protection that, even under conservative assumptions, is worth more than *99.8%* of protection *in perpetuity* (more than *99.99%* for a songwriter like Irving Berlin and a song like Alexander's Ragtime Band). The lack of a practically meaningful distinction from an author's *ex ante* perspective between (a) the statute's extended terms and (b) an infinite term makes this latest extension difficult to square with the Constitution's insistence on "limited Times."

I am not certain why the Court considers it relevant in this respect that "[n]othing . . . warrants construction of the [1998 Act's] 20-year term extension as a congressional attempt to evade or override the 'limited Times' constraint." Of course Congress did not intend to act unconstitutionally. But it may have sought to test the Constitution's limits. After all, the statute was named after a Member of Congress, who, the legislative history records, "wanted the term of copyright protection to last forever." 144 Cong. Rec. H9952 (daily ed. Oct. 7, 1998) (stmt. of Rep. Mary Bono). See also (stmt. of Rep. Sonny Bono) (questioning why copyrights should ever expire); (stmt. of Rep. Berman) ("I guess we could . . . just make a permanent moratorium on the expiration of copyrights"); (stmt. of Rep. Hoke) ("Why 70 years? Why not forever? Why not 150 years?"); (stmt. of the

Register of Copyrights) (In Copyright Office proceedings, "[t]he Songwriters Guild suggested a perpetual term"); (statement of Quincy Jones) ("I'm particularly fascinated with Representative Hoke's statement. . . . [W]hy not forever?"); (stmt. of Quincy Jones) ("If we can start with 70, add 20, it would be a good start"). And the statute ended up creating a term so long that (were the vesting of 19th-century real property at issue) it would typically violate the traditional rule against perpetuities.

In any event, the incentive-related numbers are far too small for Congress to have concluded rationally, even with respect to new works, that the extension's economic-incentive effect could justify the serious expression-related harms earlier described. And, of course, in respect to works already created—the source of many of the harms previously described—*the statute creates no economic incentive at all.*

Second, the Court relies heavily for justification upon international uniformity of terms. . . . Despite appearances, the statute does *not* create a uniform American-European term with respect to the lion's share of the economically significant works that it affects—*all* works made "for hire" and *all* existing works created prior to 1978. With respect to those works the American statute produces an extended term of 95 years while comparable European rights in "for hire" works last for periods that vary from 50 years to 70 years to life plus 70 years. Neither does the statute create uniformity with respect to anonymous or pseudonymous works.

The statute does produce uniformity with respect to copyrights in new, post-1977 works attributed to natural persons. But these works constitute only a subset (likely a minority) of works that retain commercial value after 75 years. And the fact that uniformity comes so late, if at all, means that bringing American law into conformity with this particular aspect of European law will neither encourage creation nor benefit the long-dead author in any other important way.

In sum, the partial, future uniformity that the 1998 Act promises cannot reasonably be said to justify extension of the copyright term for new works. And concerns with uniformity cannot possibly justify the extension of the new term to older works, for the statute there creates no uniformity at all.

Third, several publishers and filmmakers argue that the statute provides incentives to *those who act as publishers* to republish and to redistribute older copyrighted works. This claim cannot justify this statute, however, because the rationale is inconsistent with the basic purpose of the Copyright Clause—as understood by the Framers and by this Court. The Clause assumes an initial grant of monopoly, designed primarily to encourage creation, followed by termination of the monopoly grant in order to promote dissemination of already-created works. It assumes that it is the *disappearance* of the monopoly grant, not its *perpetuation,* that will, on balance, promote the dissemination of works already in existence. This view of the Clause finds strong support in the writings of Madison, in the antimonopoly environment in which the Framers wrote the Clause, and in the history of the Clause's English antecedent, the Statute of Anne—a statute which sought to break up a publishers' monopoly by offering, as an alternative, an author's monopoly of limited duration.

This view finds virtually conclusive support in the Court's own precedents. See *Sony* (The Copyright Clause is "intended . . . to allow the public access . . . after the limited period of exclusive control").

This view also finds textual support in the Copyright Clause's word "limited." It finds added textual support in the word "Authors," which is difficult to reconcile with a rationale that rests entirely upon incentives given to publishers perhaps long after the death of the work's creator.

It finds empirical support in sources that underscore the wisdom of the Framers' judgment. And it draws logical support from the endlessly self-perpetuating nature of the publishers' claim and the difficulty of finding any kind of logical stopping place were this Court to accept such a uniquely publisher-related rationale. . . .

Given this support, it is difficult to accept the conflicting rationale that the publishers advance, namely, that extension, rather than limitation, of the grant will, by rewarding publishers with a form of monopoly, promote, rather than retard, the dissemination of works already in existence. Indeed, given these considerations, this rationale seems constitutionally perverse—unable, constitutionally speaking, to justify the blanket extension here at issue.

Fourth, the statute's legislative history suggests another possible justification. That history refers frequently to the financial assistance the statute will bring the entertainment industry, particularly through the promotion of exports. I recognize that Congress has sometimes found that suppression of competition will help Americans sell abroad—though it has simultaneously taken care to protect American buyers from higher domestic prices. In doing so, however, Congress has exercised its commerce, not its copyright, power. I can find nothing in the Copyright Clause that would authorize Congress to enhance the copyright grant's monopoly power, likely leading to higher prices both at home and abroad, *solely* in order to produce higher foreign earnings. That objective is not a *copyright* objective. Nor, standing alone, is it related to any other objective more closely tied to the Clause itself. Neither can higher corporate profits alone justify the grant's enhancement. The Clause seeks public, not private, benefits.

Finally, the Court mentions as possible justifications "demographic, economic, and technological changes"—by which the Court apparently means the facts that today people communicate with the help of modern technology, live longer, and have children at a later age. The first fact seems to argue not for, but instead against, extension. The second fact seems already corrected for by the 1976 Act's life-plus-50 term, which automatically grows with lifespans. And the third fact—that adults are having children later in life—is a makeweight at best, providing no explanation of why the 1976 Act's term of 50 years after an author's death—a longer term than was available to authors themselves for most of our Nation's history—is an insufficient potential bequest. The weakness of these final rationales simply underscores the conclusion that emerges from consideration of earlier attempts at justification: There is no legitimate, serious copyright-related justification for this statute.

III

The Court is concerned that our holding in this case not inhibit the broad decisionmaking leeway that the Copyright Clause grants Congress. It is concerned about the implications of today's decision for the Copyright Act of 1976—an Act that changed copyright's basic term from 56 years (assuming renewal) to life of the author plus 50 years. It is concerned about having to determine just how many years of copyright is too many—a determination that it fears would require it to find the "right" constitutional number, a task for which the Court is not well suited.

I share the Court's initial concern, about intrusion upon the decisionmaking authority of Congress. But I do not believe it intrudes upon that authority to find the statute unconstitutional on the basis of (1) a legal analysis of the Copyright Clause's objectives; (2) the total implausibility of any incentive effect; and (3) the statute's apparent failure to provide significant international uniformity. Nor does it intrude upon congressional authority to consider rationality in light of the expressive values underlying the Copyright Clause, related as it is to the First Amendment, and given the constitutional importance of correctly drawing the relevant Clause/Amendment boundary. We cannot avoid the need to examine the statute carefully by saying that "Congress has not altered the traditional contours of copyright protection," for the sentence points to the question, rather than the answer. Nor should we avoid that examination here. That degree of judicial vigilance—at the far outer boundaries of the Clause—is warranted if we are to avoid the monopolies and consequent restrictions of expression that the Clause, read consistently with the First Amendment, seeks to preclude. And that vigilance is all the more necessary in a new Century that will see intellectual property rights and the forms of expression that underlie them play an ever more important role in the Nation's economy and the lives of its citizens.

I do not share the Court's concern that my view of the 1998 Act could automatically doom the 1976 Act. . . . Regardless, the law provides means to protect those who have reasonably relied upon prior copyright statutes. See *Heckler v. Mathews* (1984). And, in any event, we are not here considering, and we need not consider, the constitutionality of other copyright statutes.

Neither do I share the Court's aversion to line-drawing in this case. Even if it is difficult to draw a single clear bright line, the Court could easily decide (as I would decide) that this particular statute simply goes too far. And such examples—of what goes too far— sometimes offer better constitutional guidance than more absolute-sounding rules. In any event, "this Court sits" in part to decide when a statute exceeds a constitutional boundary.

Finally, the Court complains that I have not "restrained" my argument or "train[ed] my] fire, as petitioners do, on Congress' choice to place existing and future copyrights in parity." . . . A desire for "parity" between *A* (old copyrights) and *B* (new copyrights) cannot justify extending *A* when there is no rational justification for extending *B*. At the very least, (if I put aside my rationality characterization) to ask *B* to support *A* here is like asking Tom Thumb to support Paul Bunyan's ox. Where the case for extending new copyrights is itself so weak, what "justice," what "policy," what "equity" can warrant the tolls and barriers that extension of existing copyrights imposes?

IV

This statute will cause serious expression-related harm. It will likely restrict traditional dissemination of copyrighted works. It will likely inhibit new forms of dissemination through the use of new technology. It threatens to interfere with efforts to preserve our Nation's historical and cultural heritage and efforts to use that heritage, say, to educate our Nation's children. It is easy to understand how the statute might benefit the private financial interests of corporations or heirs who own existing copyrights. But I cannot find any constitutionally legitimate, copyright-related way in which the statute will benefit the public. Indeed, in respect to existing works, the serious public harm and the virtually nonexistent public benefit could not be more clear.

I have set forth the analysis upon which I rest these judgments. This analysis leads inexorably to the conclusion that the statute cannot be understood rationally to advance a constitutionally legitimate interest. The statute falls outside the scope of legislative power that the Copyright Clause, read in light of the First Amendment, grants to Congress. I would hold the statute unconstitutional.

I respectfully dissent.

APPENDIX TO OPINION OF BREYER, J.
A

The text's estimates of the economic value of 1998 Act copyrights relative to the economic value of a perpetual copyright, as well as the incremental value of a 20-year extension of a 75-year term, rest upon the conservative future value and discount rate assumptions set forth in the brief of economist *amici.* Under these assumptions, if an author expects to live 30 years after writing a book, the copyright extension (by increasing the copyright term from "life of the author plus 50 years" to "life of the author plus 70 years") increases the author's expected income from that book—*i.e.,* the economic incentive to write—by no more than about 0.33%.

The text assumes that the extension creates a term of 95 years (the term corresponding to works made for hire and for all existing pre-1978 copyrights). Under the economists' conservative assumptions, the value of a 95-year copyright is slightly more than 99.8% of the value of a perpetual copyright. If a "life plus 70" term applies, and if an author lives 78 years after creation of a work (as with Irving Berlin and Alexander's Ragtime Band), the same assumptions yield a figure of 99.996%. . . .

Questions:

1.) Under *Eldred,* would a copyright term of 10,000 years, imposed both prospectively and retrospectively, be constitutional—if accompanied by Congressional findings that this was necessary to promote the progress of science?

2.) Reread pp 9–16 of *The Public Domain.* Justice Ginsburg believes that the internal limitations of the copyright system (such as fair use and the idea expression distinction) coupled with the expression-*promoting* effect of copyright, are together enough to make copyright law presumptively (though not categorically) immune from First Amendment scrutiny.

> [The CTEA] protects authors' original expression from unrestricted exploitation. Protection of that order does not raise the free speech concerns present when the government compels or burdens the communication of particular facts or ideas. The First Amendment securely protects the freedom to make—or decline to make—one's own speech; it bears less heavily when speakers assert the right to make other people's speeches. To the extent such assertions raise First Amendment concerns, copyright's built-in free speech safeguards are generally adequate to address them.

Are archivists and librarians trying to digitize orphan works asserting "the right to make other people's speeches"? Does retrospective term extension—as to those works— have an expression-promoting effect? Are the internal limitations of copyright enough to protect their activity?

3.) What is the strongest criticism that could be made of Justice Breyer's opinion? If his proposed standard of review should be used here, why not in Commerce Clause cases?

4.) Justice Ginsburg and Justice Breyer both seem to think that "copyright is different," that its rules present special constitutional issues, though they disagree strongly on what those differences are. If you had to sum up why Justice Ginsburg believes Congress deserves judicial deference and that copyright legislation should be presumptively free from First Amendment scrutiny, how would you do so? If you had to sum up why Justice Breyer thinks that this issue deserves heightened scrutiny, how would you do so? How do they frame the issue differently?

5.) Justice Breyer focuses on the lopsided ratio of harm to benefits imposed by term extension. His argument is summarized in the comic book page that follows these notes. What are the best arguments that the expressive costs and benefits of term extension are i.) irrelevant constitutionally? ii.) vitally important in both the First Amendment *and* Copyright Clause analysis?

Note: The Classics Protection and Access Act

The works whose copyright extension was upheld in *Eldred* began to enter the public domain in 2019; there has been no push to further expand their copyright terms. However, there has been a legislative development regarding the copyright term for a specific subset of works: pre-1972 sound recordings. In 2018, Congress passed the "Classics Protection and Access Act" ("Classics Act") as part of the Orrin G. Hatch–Bob Goodlatte Music Modernization Act ("MMA"). This law grants certain federal rights to pre-1972 sound recordings (previously, federal copyright law did not cover sound recordings fixed before February 15, 1972; instead they were covered, if at all, by a patchwork of state laws). These older recordings will enter the public domain gradually, beginning in 2022: recordings published before 1923 will enter the public domain in 2022, and recordings published between 1923–1946 will enter the public domain after the end of a 100-year term, from 2024–2029. Intriguingly, the Classics Act also contains a limited exception allowing the use of orphan works: it exempts noncommercial uses of pre-1972 sound recordings that are not being commercially exploited, so long as the user has conducted a good faith, reasonable search for the rights owner, and the rights owner has not objected within 90 days. (Note that the MMA contains other revisions that are beyond the scope of this chapter. For example, the "Music Licensing Modernization Act" provides a blanket licensing scheme for digital music services under 17 U.S.C. § 115.)

***

Golan v. Holder
565 U.S. 302 (2012)

GINSBURG, J., delivered the opinion of the Court. BREYER, J., filed a dissenting opinion, in which ALITO, J., joined.

Justice GINSBURG delivered the opinion of the Court.

The Berne Convention for the Protection of Literary and Artistic Works (Berne Convention or Berne), which took effect in 1886, is the principal accord governing international copyright relations. Latecomer to the international copyright regime launched by Berne, the United States joined the Convention in 1989. To perfect U.S. implementation of Berne, and as part of our response to the Uruguay Round of multilateral trade negotiations, Congress, in 1994, gave works enjoying copyright protection abroad the same full term of protection available to U.S. works. Congress did so in § 514 of the Uruguay Round Agreements Act (URAA), which grants copyright protection to preexisting works of Berne member countries, protected in their country of origin, but lacking protection in the United States for any of three reasons: The United States did not protect works from the country of origin at the time of publication; the United States did not protect sound recordings fixed before 1972; or the author had failed to comply with U.S. statutory formalities (formalities Congress no longer requires as prerequisites to copyright protection).

The URAA accords no protection to a foreign work after its full copyright term has expired, causing it to fall into the public domain, whether under the laws of the country of origin or of this country. Works encompassed by § 514 are granted the protection they would have enjoyed had the United States maintained copyright relations with the author's country or removed formalities incompatible with Berne. . . . To cushion the impact of their placement in protected status, Congress included in § 514 ameliorating accommodations for parties who had exploited affected works before the URAA was enacted.

Petitioners include orchestra conductors, musicians, publishers, and others who formerly enjoyed free access to works § 514 removed from the public domain. They maintain that the Constitution's Copyright and Patent Clause, Art. I, § 8, cl. 8, and First

Amendment both decree the invalidity of § 514. Under those prescriptions of our highest law, petitioners assert, a work that has entered the public domain, for whatever reason, must forever remain there.

In accord with the judgment of the Tenth Circuit, we conclude that § 514 does not transgress constitutional limitations on Congress' authority. Neither the Copyright and Patent Clause nor the First Amendment, we hold, makes the public domain, in any and all cases, a territory that works may never exit. . . .

II

We first address petitioners' argument that Congress lacked authority, under the Copyright Clause, to enact § 514. . . . Petitioners find in this grant of authority an impenetrable barrier to the extension of copyright protection to authors whose writings, for whatever reason, are in the public domain. We see no such barrier in the text of the Copyright Clause, historical practice, or our precedents. . . .

Carried to its logical conclusion, petitioners persist, the Government's position would allow Congress to institute a second "limited" term after the first expires, a third after that, and so on. Thus, as long as Congress legislated in installments, perpetual copyright terms would be achievable. As in *Eldred,* the hypothetical legislative misbehavior petitioners posit is far afield from the case before us. . . . Congress rationally could have concluded that adherence to Berne "promotes the diffusion of knowledge." A well-functioning international copyright system would likely encourage the dissemination of existing and future works. . . . The provision of incentives for the creation of new works is surely an essential means to advance the spread of knowledge and learning. We hold, however, that it is not the sole means Congress may use "[t]o promote the Progress of Science." . . .

III
A

We next explain why the First Amendment does not inhibit the restoration authorized by § 514. To do so, we first recapitulate the relevant part of our pathmarking decision in *Eldred.* . . .

Concerning the First Amendment, we recognized that some restriction on expression is the inherent and intended effect of every grant of copyright. Noting that the "Copyright Clause and the First Amendment were adopted close in time," we observed that the Framers regarded copyright protection not simply as a limit on the manner in which expressive works may be used. They also saw copyright as an "engine of free expression." . . .

We then described the "traditional contours" of copyright protection, *i.e.,* the "idea/expression dichotomy" and the "fair use" defense. Both are recognized in our jurisprudence as "built-in First Amendment accommodations." . . .

Given the "speech-protective purposes and safeguards" embraced by copyright law, we concluded in *Eldred* that there was no call for the heightened review petitioners sought in that case. We reach the same conclusion here. . . .

B

Petitioners attempt to distinguish their challenge from the one turned away in *Eldred.* First Amendment interests of a higher order are at stake here, petitioners say, because they— unlike their counterparts in *Eldred*—enjoyed "vested rights" in works that had already entered the public domain. The limited rights they retain under copyright law's "built-in safeguards" are, in their view, no substitute for the unlimited use they enjoyed before § 514's enactment. Nor, petitioners urge, does § 514's "unprecedented" foray into the public domain possess the historical pedigree that supported the term extension at issue in *Eldred*.

    ... To copyright lawyers, the "vested rights" formulation might sound exactly backwards: Rights typically vest at the *outset* of copyright protection, in an author or rightholder. Once the term of protection ends, the works do not revest in any rightholder. Instead, the works simply lapse into the public domain. Anyone has free access to the public domain, but no one, after the copyright term has expired, acquires ownership rights in the once-protected works. . . .

    Section 514, we add, does not impose a blanket prohibition on public access. Petitioners protest that fair use and the idea/expression dichotomy "are plainly inadequate to protect the speech and expression rights that § 514 took from petitioners, or . . . the public"—that is, "the unrestricted right to perform, copy, teach and distribute the *entire* work, for any reason." "Playing a few bars of a Shostakovich symphony," petitioners observe, "is no substitute for performing the entire work." But Congress has not put petitioners in this bind. The question here, as in *Eldred,* is whether would-be users must pay for their desired use of the author's expression, or else limit their exploitation to "fair use" of that work. Prokofiev's Peter and the Wolf could once be performed free of charge; after § 514 the right to perform it must be obtained in the marketplace. . . .

IV

    Congress determined that U.S. interests were best served by our full participation in the dominant system of international copyright protection. . . . The judgment § 514 expresses lies well within the ken of the political branches. It is our obligation, of course, to determine whether the action Congress took, wise or not, encounters any constitutional shoal. For the reasons stated, we are satisfied it does not. The judgment of the Court of Appeals for the Tenth Circuit is therefore
Affirmed.

Justice BREYER, with whom Justice ALITO joins, dissenting.

    In order "[t]o promote the Progress of Science" (by which term the Founders meant "learning" or "knowledge"), the Constitution's Copyright Clause grants Congress the power to "secur[e] for limited Times to Authors . . . the exclusive Right to their . . . Writings." Art. I, § 8, cl. 8. This "exclusive Right" allows its holder to charge a fee to those who wish to use a copyrighted work, and the ability to charge that fee encourages the production of new material. In this sense, a copyright is, in Macaulay's words, a "tax on readers for the purpose of giving a bounty to writers"—a bounty designed to encourage new production. As the Court said in *Eldred*, "'[t]he economic philosophy behind the [Copyright] [C]lause . . . is the conviction that encouragement of individual effort by personal gain is the best way to advance public welfare through the talents of authors and inventors.'"

    The statute before us, however, does not encourage anyone to produce a single new work. By definition, it bestows monetary rewards only on owners of old works—works that have already been created and already are in the American public domain. At the same time, the statute inhibits the dissemination of those works, foreign works published abroad after 1923, of which there are many millions, including films, works of art, innumerable photographs, and, of course, books—books that (in the absence of the statute) would assume their rightful places in computer-accessible databases, spreading knowledge throughout the world. In my view, the Copyright Clause does not authorize Congress to enact this statute. And I consequently dissent.

I

The possibility of eliciting new production is, and always has been, an essential precondition for American copyright protection. . . .

Yet, as the Founders recognized, monopoly is a two-edged sword. On the one hand, it can encourage production of new works. In the absence of copyright protection, anyone might freely copy the products of an author's creative labor, appropriating the benefits without incurring the nonrepeatable costs of creation, thereby deterring authors from exerting themselves in the first place. On the other hand, copyright tends to restrict the dissemination (and use) of works once produced either because the absence of competition translates directly into higher consumer prices or because the need to secure copying permission sometimes imposes administrative costs that make it difficult for potential users of a copyrighted work to find its owner and strike a bargain. . . .

. . . [T]ext, history, and precedent demonstrate that the Copyright Clause places great value on the power of copyright to elicit new production. Congress in particular cases may determine that copyright's ability to do so outweighs any concomitant high prices, administrative costs, and restrictions on dissemination. And when it does so, we must respect its judgment. But does the Clause empower Congress to enact a statute that withdraws works from the public domain, brings about higher prices and costs, and in doing so seriously restricts dissemination, particularly to those who need it for scholarly, educational, or cultural purposes—all *without providing any additional incentive* for the production of new material? That is the question before us. And, as I have said, I believe the answer is no. Congress in this statute has exceeded what are, under any plausible reading of the Copyright Clause, its permissible limits.

II
A

The provision before us takes works from the public domain, at least as of January 1, 1996. It then restricts the dissemination of those works in two ways.

First, "restored copyright" holders can now charge fees for works that consumers previously used for free. The price of a score of Shostakovich's Preludes and Fugues Op. 87, for example, has risen by a multiple of seven. . . . If a school orchestra or other nonprofit organization cannot afford the new charges, so be it. They will have to do without. . . .

Second, and at least as important, the statute creates administrative costs, such as the costs of determining whether a work is the subject of a "restored copyright," searching for a "restored copyright" holder, and negotiating a fee. Congress has tried to ease the administrative burden of contacting copyright holders and negotiating prices for those whom the statute calls "reliance part[ies]," namely those who previously had used such works when they were freely available in the public domain. But Congress has done nothing to ease the administrative burden of securing permission from copyright owners that is placed upon those who want to use a work that they did not previously use, and this is a particular problem when it comes to "orphan works"—older and more obscure works with minimal commercial value that have copyright owners who are difficult or impossible to track down. . . .

There are millions of such works. For example, according to European Union figures, there are 13 million orphan books in the European Union (13% of the total number of books in-copyright there), 225,000 orphan films in European film archives, and 17 million orphan photographs in United Kingdom museums. How is a university, a film collector, a musician, a database compiler, or a scholar now to obtain permission to use any such lesser known foreign work previously in the American public domain? Consider the questions that any such individual, group, or institution usually must answer: Is the work eligible for restoration under the statute? If so, who now holds the copyright—the author? an heir? a publisher? an association? a long-lost cousin? Whom must we contact? What is the address? Suppose no one answers? How do we conduct a negotiation?

It is consequently not surprising to learn that the Los Angeles Public Library has been unable to make its collection of Mexican folk music publicly available because of problems locating copyright owners, that a Jewish cultural organization has abandoned similar efforts to make available Jewish cultural music and other materials, or that film preservers, museums, universities, scholars, database compilers, and others report that the administrative costs associated with trying to locate foreign copyright owners have forced them to curtail their cultural, scholarly, or other work-preserving efforts. . . .

B

. . . Worst of all, "restored copyright" protection removes material from the public domain. In doing so, it reverses the payment expectations of those who used, or intended to use, works that they thought belonged to them. Were Congress to act similarly with respect to well-established property rights, the problem would be obvious. This statute analogously restricts, and thereby diminishes, Americans' preexisting freedom to use formerly public domain material in their expressive activities.

Thus, while the majority correctly observes that the dissemination-restricting harms of copyright normally present problems appropriate for legislation to resolve, the question is whether the Copyright Clause permits Congress seriously to exacerbate such a problem by taking works out of the public domain without a countervailing benefit. This question *is* appropriate for judicial resolution. Indeed, unlike *Eldred* where the Court had to decide a complicated line-drawing question—when is a copyright term too long?—here an easily administrable standard is available—a standard that would require works that have already fallen into the public domain to stay there.

The several, just mentioned features of the present statute are important, for they distinguish it from other copyright laws. By removing material from the public domain, the statute, in literal terms, "abridges" a preexisting freedom to speak. In practical terms, members of the public might well have decided what to say, as well as when and how to say it, in part by reviewing with a view to repeating, expression that they reasonably believed was, or would be, freely available. Given these speech implications, it is not surprising that Congress has long sought to protect public domain material when revising the copyright laws. And this Court has assumed the particular importance of public domain material in roughly analogous circumstances. See *Graham,* 383 U.S. at 6 ("Congress may not authorize the issuance of patents whose effects are to remove existent knowledge from the public domain"); *Kewanee Oil Co. v. Bicron Corp.* (1974) (trade secret protection is not incompatible with "policy that matter once in the public domain must remain in the public domain"); *Cox Broadcasting Corp. v. Cohn* (1975) (First Amendment prohibits sanctioning press for publishing material disclosed in public court documents); see also *Dastar Corp. v. Twentieth Century Fox Film Corp.* (2003) ("The right to copy . . . once a copyright has expired . . . passes to the public"). . . .

Taken together, these speech-related harms (*e.g.,* restricting use of previously available material; reversing payment expectations; rewarding rent-seekers at the public's expense) at least show the presence of a First Amendment interest. And that is enough. For present purposes, I need not decide whether the harms to that interest show a violation of the First Amendment. I need only point to the importance of interpreting the Constitution as a single document—a document that we should not read as setting the Copyright Clause and the First Amendment at cross-purposes. Nor need I advocate the application here of strict or specially heightened review. I need only find that the First Amendment interest is important enough to require courts to scrutinize with some care the reasons claimed to justify the Act in order to determine whether they constitute reasonable copyright-related justifications for the serious harms, including speech-related harms, which the Act seems likely to impose.

C

The majority makes several other arguments. First, it argues that the Clause does not require the "creation of at least one new work," but may instead "promote the Progress of Science" in other ways. And it specifically mentions the "dissemination of existing and future works" as determinative here. The industry experts to whom the majority refers argue that copyright protection of already existing works can help, say, music publishers or film distributers raise prices, produce extra profits and consequently lead them to publish or distribute works they might otherwise have ignored. . . . But this kind of argument, which can be made by distributers of all sorts of goods, ranging from kiwi fruit to Swedish furniture, has little if anything to do with the nonrepeatable costs of initial creation, which is the special concern of copyright protection.

Moreover, the argument proves too much. . . . It is the kind of argument that could justify a legislature's withdrawing from the public domain the works, say, of Hawthorne or of Swift or for that matter the King James Bible in order to encourage further publication of those works; and, it could even more easily justify similar action in the case of lesser known early works, perhaps those of the Venerable Bede. . . .

III

The fact that, by withdrawing material from the public domain, the statute inhibits an important preexisting flow of information is sufficient, when combined with the other features of the statute that I have discussed, to convince me that the Copyright Clause, interpreted in the light of the First Amendment, does not authorize Congress to enact this statute.

I respectfully dissent from the Court's contrary conclusion.

PROBLEM 2-3
TERM LIMITS.

Citing the importance to commerce of investments in innovation, whether artistic or commercial, and the uncertainty "in this modern technological age" about when investments in innovation will finally pay off, the Congress passes the "Defense of Innovation & Science, New Extension Years" Act (or DISNEY). DISNEY grants a supplementary right to holders of copyrights and patents. The supplementary right lasts for an additional 20 years. It applies both to existing copyrights and patents and those that expired during the last 20 years. The accompanying Legislative Report explicitly states that Congress is taking its authority, not from the Copyright Clause, but from the Commerce Clause.

Is DISNEY constitutional in whole or part? What type of constitutional analysis should the court perform in cases like this?

CHAPTER THREE
Intellectual Property &
the First Amendment

San Francisco Arts & Athletics v. U.S. Olympic Committee

483 U.S. 522 (1987)

Justice POWELL delivered the opinion of the Court.

In this case, we consider the scope and constitutionality of a provision of the Amateur Sports Act of 1978, 36 U.S.C. §§ 371–396, that authorizes the United States Olympic Committee to prohibit certain commercial and promotional uses of the word "Olympic."

Petitioner San Francisco Arts & Athletics, Inc. (SFAA), is a nonprofit California corporation. The SFAA originally sought to incorporate under the name "Golden Gate Olympic Association," but was told by the California Department of Corporations that the word "Olympic" could not appear in a corporate title. After its incorporation in 1981, the SFAA nevertheless began to promote the "Gay Olympic Games," using those words on its letterheads and mailings and in local newspapers. The games were to be a 9-day event to begin in August 1982, in San Francisco, California. The SFAA expected athletes from hundreds of cities in this country and from cities all over the world. . . . To cover the cost of the planned Games, the SFAA sold T-shirts, buttons, bumper stickers, and other merchandise bearing the title "Gay Olympic Games."[2]

Poster and flyer from the Gay Olympic Games

Section 110 of the Amateur Sports Act (Act), grants respondent United States Olympic Committee (USOC) the right to prohibit certain commercial and promotional uses of the word "Olympic" and various Olympic symbols.[4] In late December 1981, the

---

[2] The 1982 athletic event ultimately was held under the name "Gay Games I." A total of 1,300 men and women from 12 countries, 27 States, and 179 cities participated. . . .

[4] Section 110 of the Act, as set forth in 36 U.S.C. § 380, provides:

"Without the consent of the [USOC], any person who uses for the purpose of trade, to induce the sale of any goods or services, or to promote any theatrical exhibition, athletic performance, or competition—

"(1) the symbol of the International Olympic Committee, consisting of 5 interlocking rings;

"(2) the emblem of the [USOC], consisting of an escutcheon having a blue chief and vertically extending red and white bars on the base with 5 interlocking rings displayed on the chief;

"(3) any trademark, trade name, sign, symbol, or insignia falsely representing association with, or authorization by, the International Olympic Committee or the [USOC]; or

"(4) the words 'Olympic', 'Olympiad', 'Citius Altius Fortius', or any combination or simulation thereof tending to cause confusion, to cause mistake, to deceive, or to falsely suggest a connection

executive director of the USOC wrote to the SFAA, informing it of the existence of the Amateur Sports Act, and requesting that the SFAA immediately terminate use of the word "Olympic" in its description of the planned Games. The SFAA at first agreed to substitute the word "Athletic" for the word "Olympic," but, one month later, resumed use of the term. . . . In August, the USOC brought suit in the Federal District Court for the Northern District of California to enjoin the SFAA's use of the word "Olympic." The District Court granted a temporary restraining order and then a preliminary injunction. The Court of Appeals for the Ninth Circuit affirmed. After further proceedings, the District Court granted the USOC summary judgment and a permanent injunction. . . .

III

This Court has recognized that "[n]ational protection of trademarks is desirable . . . because trademarks foster competition and the maintenance of quality by securing to the producer the benefits of good reputation." . . .

The protection granted to the USOC's use of the Olympic words and symbols differs from the normal trademark protection in two respects: the USOC need not prove that a contested use is likely to cause confusion, and an unauthorized user of the word does not have available the normal statutory defenses. The SFAA argues, in effect, that the differences between the Lanham Act and § 110 are of constitutional dimension. First, the SFAA contends that the word "Olympic" is a generic[7] word that could not gain trademark protection under the Lanham Act. The SFAA argues that this prohibition is constitutionally required and thus that the First Amendment prohibits Congress from granting a trademark in the word "Olympic." Second, the SFAA argues that the First Amendment prohibits Congress from granting exclusive use of a word absent a requirement that the authorized user prove that an unauthorized use is likely to cause confusion. We address these contentions in turn.

A

This Court has recognized that words are not always fungible, and that the suppression of particular words "run[s] a substantial risk of suppressing ideas in the process." *Cohen v. California* (1971). The SFAA argues that this principle prohibits Congress from granting the USOC exclusive control of uses of the word "Olympic," a word that the SFAA views as generic.[8] Yet this recognition always has been balanced against the principle that when a word acquires value "as the result of organization and the expenditure of labor, skill, and money" by an entity, that entity constitutionally may obtain a limited property right in the word. *International News Service v. Associated Press* (1918).

---

with the [USOC] or any Olympic activity;

"shall be subject to suit in a civil action by the [USOC] for the remedies provided in the Act of July 5, 1946 (60 Stat. 427; popularly known as the Trademark Act of 1946 [Lanham Act]) [15 U.S.C. § 1051 et seq.].["] . . .

[7] A common descriptive name of a product or service is generic. Because a generic name by definition does not distinguish the identity of a particular product, it cannot be registered as a trademark under the Lanham Act. See §§ 2, 14(c), 15 U.S.C. §§ 1052, 1064(c). See also 1 J. McCarthy, Trademarks and Unfair Competition § 12:1, p. 520 (1984).

[8] This grant by statute of exclusive use of distinctive words and symbols by Congress is not unique. Violation of some of these statutes may result in criminal penalties. See, e.g., 18 U.S.C. § 705 (veterans' organizations); § 706 (American National Red Cross); § 707 (4-H Club); § 711 ("Smokey Bear"); § 711a ("Woodsy Owl"). See also *FTC v. A.P.W. Paper Co.* (1946) (reviewing application of Red Cross statute). Others, like the USOC statute, provide for civil enforcement. See, e.g., 36 U.S.C. § 18c (Daughters of the American Revolution); § 27 (Boy Scouts); § 36 (Girl Scouts); § 1086 (Little League Baseball); § 3305 (1982 ed., Supp. III) (American National Theater and Academy).

There is no need in this case to decide whether Congress ever could grant a private entity exclusive use of a generic word. Congress reasonably could conclude that the commercial and promotional value of the word "Olympic" was the product of the USOC's "own talents and energy, the end result of much time, effort, and expense." *Zacchini v. Scripps-Howard Broadcasting Co.* (1977). The USOC, together with respondent International Olympic Committee (IOC), have used the word "Olympic" at least since 1896, when the modern Olympic Games began. Baron Pierre de Coubertin of France, acting pursuant to a government commission, then proposed the revival of the ancient Olympic Games to promote international understanding. De Coubertin sought to identify the "spirit" of the ancient Olympic Games that had been corrupted by the influence of money and politics. De Coubertin thus formed the IOC, that has established elaborate rules and procedures for the conduct of the modern Olympics. In addition, these rules direct every national committee to protect the use of the Olympic flag, symbol, flame, and motto from unauthorized use. Under the IOC Charter, the USOC is the national Olympic committee for the United States with the sole authority to represent the United States at the Olympic Games. Pursuant to this authority, the USOC has used the Olympic words and symbols extensively in this country to fulfill its object under the Olympic Charter of "ensur[ing] the development and safeguarding of the Olympic Movement and sport."

The history of the origins and associations of the word "Olympic" demonstrates the meritlessness of the SFAA's contention that Congress simply plucked a generic word out of the English vocabulary and granted its exclusive use to the USOC. Congress reasonably could find that since 1896, the word "Olympic" has acquired what in trademark law is known as a secondary meaning—it "has become distinctive of [the USOC's] goods in commerce." The right to adopt and use such a word "to distinguish the goods or property [of] the person whose mark it is, to the exclusion of use by all other persons, has been long recognized." *Trade-Mark Cases.* Because Congress reasonably could conclude that the USOC has distinguished the word "Olympic" through its own efforts, Congress' decision to grant the USOC a limited property right in the word "Olympic" falls within the scope of trademark law protections, and thus certainly within constitutional bounds.

B

Congress also acted reasonably when it concluded that the USOC should not be required to prove that an unauthorized use of the word "Olympic" is likely to confuse the public. To the extent that § 110 applies to uses "for the purpose of trade [or] to induce the sale of any goods or services," 36 U.S.C. § 380(a), its application is to commercial speech. Commercial speech "receives a limited form of First Amendment protection." Section 110 also allows the USOC to prohibit the use of "Olympic" for promotion of theatrical and athletic events. Although many of these promotional uses will be commercial speech, some uses may go beyond the "strictly business" context. See *Friedman v. Rogers* (1979). In this case, the SFAA claims that its use of the word "Olympic" was intended to convey a political statement about the status of homosexuals in society.[13] Thus, the SFAA claims that in this case § 110 suppresses political speech.

---

[13] According to the SFAA's president, the Gay Olympic Games would have offered three "very important opportunities":

"1) To provide a healthy recreational alternative to a suppressed minority.

"2) To educate the public at large towards a more reasonable characterization of gay men and women.

"3) To attempt, through athletics, to bring about a positive and gradual assimilation of gay men and women, as well as gays and non-gays, and to diminish the ageist, sexist and racist divisiveness existing in all communities regardless of sexual orientation."

App. 93. His expectations

By prohibiting the use of one word for particular purposes, neither Congress nor the USOC has prohibited the SFAA from conveying its message. The SFAA held its athletic event in its planned format under the names "Gay Games I" and "Gay Games II" in 1982 and 1986, respectively. Nor is it clear that § 110 restricts purely expressive uses of the word "Olympic." Section 110 restricts only the manner in which the SFAA may convey its message. The restrictions on expressive speech properly are characterized as incidental to the primary congressional purpose of encouraging and rewarding the USOC's activities. The appropriate inquiry is thus whether the incidental restrictions on First Amendment freedoms are greater than necessary to further a substantial governmental interest. *United States v. O'Brien* (1968).

One reason for Congress to grant the USOC exclusive control of the word "Olympic," as with other trademarks, is to ensure that the USOC receives the benefit of its own efforts so that the USOC will have an incentive to continue to produce a "quality product," that, in turn, benefits the public. But in the special circumstance of the USOC, Congress has a broader public interest in promoting, through the activities of the USOC, the participation of amateur athletes from the United States in "the great four-yearly sport festival, the Olympic Games." . . .

The restrictions of § 110 are not broader than Congress reasonably could have determined to be necessary to further these interests. Section 110 primarily applies to all uses of the word "Olympic" to induce the sale of goods or services. Although the Lanham Act protects only against confusing uses, Congress' judgment respecting a certain word is not so limited. Congress reasonably could conclude that most commercial uses of the Olympic words and symbols are likely to be confusing. It also could determine that unauthorized uses, even if not confusing, nevertheless may harm the USOC by lessening the distinctiveness and thus the commercial value of the marks.

In this case, the SFAA sought to sell T-shirts, buttons, bumper stickers, and other items, all emblazoned with the title "Gay Olympic Games." The possibility for confusion as to sponsorship is obvious. Moreover, it is clear that the SFAA sought to exploit the "commercial magnetism" of the word given value by the USOC. There is no question that this unauthorized use could undercut the USOC's efforts to use, and sell the right to use, the word in the future, since much of the word's value comes from its limited use. Such an adverse effect on the USOC's activities is directly contrary to Congress' interest. Even though this protection may exceed the traditional rights of a trademark owner in certain circumstances, the application of the Act to this commercial speech is not broader than necessary to protect the legitimate congressional interest and therefore does not violate the First Amendment.

Section 110 also extends to promotional uses of the word "Olympic," even if the promotion is not to induce the sale of goods. Under § 110, the USOC may prohibit purely promotional uses of the word only when the promotion relates to an athletic or theatrical event. The USOC created the value of the word by using it in connection with an athletic event. Congress reasonably could find that use of the word by other entities to promote an athletic event would directly impinge on the USOC's legitimate right of exclusive use. The

---

"were that people of all persuasions would be drawn to the event because of its Olympic format and that its nature of 'serious fun' would create a climate of friendship and co-operation[;] false images and misconceptions about gay people would decline as a result of a participatory [sic] educational process, and benefit ALL communities."

Id., at 93–94. He thought "[t]he term 'Olympic' best describe[d] [the SFAA's] undertaking" because it embodied the concepts of "peace, friendship and positive social interaction." *Id.*, at 99.

SFAA's proposed use of the word is an excellent example. The "Gay Olympic Games" were to take place over a 9-day period and were to be held in different locations around the world. They were to include a torch relay, a parade with uniformed athletes of both sexes divided by city, an "Olympic anthem" and "Olympic Committee," and the award of gold, silver, and bronze medals, and were advertised under a logo of three overlapping rings. All of these features directly parallel the modern-day Olympics, not the Olympic Games that occurred in ancient Greece. The image the SFAA sought to invoke was exactly the image carefully cultivated by the USOC. The SFAA's expressive use of the word cannot be divorced from the value the USOC's efforts have given to it. The mere fact that the SFAA claims an expressive, as opposed to a purely commercial, purpose does not give it a First Amendment right to "appropriat[e] to itself the harvest of those who have sown." *International News Service v. Associated Press* (1918).[19] The USOC's right to prohibit use of the word "Olympic" in the promotion of athletic events is at the core of its legitimate property right.

IV

The SFAA argues that even if the exclusive use granted by § 110 does not violate the First Amendment, the USOC's enforcement of that right is discriminatory in violation of the Fifth Amendment.[21] The fundamental inquiry is whether the USOC is a governmental actor to whom the prohibitions of the Constitution apply.[22] The USOC is a "private corporatio[n] established under Federal law." 36 U.S.C. § 1101(46). In the Act, Congress granted the USOC a corporate charter, § 371, imposed certain requirements on the USOC, and provided for some USOC funding through exclusive use of the Olympic words and symbols, § 380, and through direct grants.

---

[19] The SFAA claims a superior right to the use of the word "Olympic" because it is a nonprofit corporation and its athletic event was not organized for the primary purpose of commercial gain. But when the question is the scope of a legitimate property right in a word, the SFAA's distinction is inapposite. As this Court has noted in the analogous context of "fair use" under the Copyright Act:

"The crux of the profit/nonprofit distinction is not whether the sole motive of the use is monetary gain but whether the user stands to profit from exploitation of the [protected] material without paying the customary price."

Harper & Row (1985). Here, the SFAA's proposed use of the word "Olympic" was a clear attempt to exploit the imagery and goodwill created by the USOC.

[21] The SFAA invokes the Fourteenth Amendment for its discriminatory enforcement claim. The Fourteenth Amendment applies to actions by a State. The claimed association in this case is between the USOC and the Federal Government. Therefore, the Fourteenth Amendment does not apply. The Fifth Amendment, however, does apply to the Federal Government and contains an equal protection component. *Bolling v. Sharpe* (1954). "This Court's approach to Fifth Amendment equal protection claims has . . . been precisely the same as to equal protection claims under the Fourteenth Amendment." *Weinberger v. Wiesenfeld* (1975). See *Buckley v. Valeo* (1976) (per curiam). The Petitioners raised the issue of discriminatory enforcement in their petition for certiorari, and both petitioners and respondents have briefed the issue fully. Accordingly, we address the claim as one under the Fifth Amendment.

[22] Because we find no governmental action, we need not address the merits of the SFAA's discriminatory enforcement claim. We note, however, that the SFAA's claim of discriminatory enforcement is far from compelling. As of 1982 when this suit began, the USOC had brought 22 oppositions to trademark applications and one petition to cancel. For example, the USOC successfully prohibited registration of the mark "Golden Age Olympics." The USOC also litigated numerous suits prior to bringing this action, prohibiting use of the Olympic words and symbols by such entities as the National Amateur Sports Foundation, a shoe company, the International Federation of Body Builders, and a bus company. Since 1982, the USOC has brought a number of additional suits against various companies and the March of Dimes Birth Defects Foundation. The USOC has authorized the use of the word "Olympic" to organizations that sponsor athletic competitions and events for handicapped persons ("Special Olympics") and for youth ("Junior Olympics" and "Explorer Olympics"). Both of these uses directly relate to a purpose of the USOC established by its charter. See 36 U.S.C. §§ 374(7), (13), reprinted supra, at 2981, n.17. The USOC has not consented to any other uses of the

Most fundamentally, this Court has held that a government "normally can be held responsible for a private decision only when it has exercised coercive power or has provided such significant encouragement, either overt or covert, that the choice must in law be deemed to be that of the [government]." The USOC's choice of how to enforce its exclusive right to use the word "Olympic" simply is not a governmental decision. There is no evidence that the Federal Government coerced or encouraged the USOC in the exercise of its right. At most, the Federal Government, by failing to supervise the USOC's use of its rights, can be said to exercise "[m]ere approval of or acquiescence in the initiatives" of the USOC. *Blum v. Yaretsky* (1982). This is not enough to make the USOC's actions those of the Government. Because the USOC is not a governmental actor, the SFAA's claim that the USOC has enforced its rights in a discriminatory manner must fail.

V

Accordingly, we affirm the judgment of the Court of Appeals for the Ninth Circuit. *It is so ordered.*

Justice O'CONNOR, with whom Justice BLACKMUN joins, concurring in part and dissenting in part.

I agree with the Court's construction of § 110 of the Amateur Sports Act, 92 Stat. 3048, 36 U.S.C. § 380, and with its holding that the statute is "within constitutional bounds." Therefore, I join Parts I through III of the Court's opinion. But largely for the reasons explained by Justice Brennan in Part I-B of his dissenting opinion, I believe the United States Olympic Committee and the United States are joint participants in the challenged activity and as such are subject to the equal protection provisions of the Fifth Amendment. Accordingly, I would reverse the Court of Appeals' finding of no Government action and remand the case for determination of petitioners' claim of discriminatory enforcement.

Justice BRENNAN, with whom Justice MARSHALL joins, dissenting.

The Court wholly fails to appreciate both the congressionally created interdependence between the United States Olympic Committee (USOC) and the United States, and the significant extent to which § 110 of the Amateur Sports Act of 1978, 36 U.S.C. § 380, infringes on noncommercial speech. I would find that the action of the USOC challenged here is Government action, and that § 110 is both substantially overbroad and discriminates on the basis of content. I therefore dissent.

I

For two independent reasons, the action challenged here constitutes Government action. First, the USOC performs important governmental functions and should therefore be considered a governmental actor. Second, there exists "a sufficiently close nexus between the [Government] and the challenged action" of the USOC that "the action of the latter may be fairly treated as that of the [Government] itself." *Jackson v. Metropolitan Edison Co.* (1974).

A

Examination of the powers and functions bestowed by the Government upon the

---

word in connection with athletic competitions or events.

The USOC necessarily has discretion as to when and against whom it files opposition to trademark applications, and when and against whom it institutes suits. The record before us strongly indicates that the USOC has acted strictly in accord with its charter and that there has been no actionable discrimination.

USOC makes clear that the USOC must be considered a Government actor. . . .

The Court has repeatedly held, however, that "when private individuals or groups *are endowed by the State* with powers or functions governmental in nature, they become agencies or instrumentalities of the State and subject to its constitutional limitations." *Evans v. Newton* (1966). See *Terry v. Adams* (1953) (private political association and its elections constitute state action); *Marsh v. Alabama* (1946) (privately owned "company town" is a state actor). Moreover, a finding of government action is particularly appropriate when the function performed is "traditionally the exclusive prerogative" of government. *Jackson v. Metropolitan Edison Co.* Patently, Congress has endowed the USOC with traditional governmental powers that enable it to perform a governmental function. . . .

C

A close examination of the USOC and the Government thus reveals a unique interdependence between the two. Although at one time amateur sports was a concern merely of private entities, and the Olympic Games an event of significance only to individuals with a particular interest in athletic competition, that era is passed. In the Amateur Sports Act of 1978, Congress placed the power and prestige of the United States Government behind a single, central sports organization. Congress delegated to the USOC functions that Government actors traditionally perform—the representation of the Nation abroad and the administration of all private organizations in a particular economic sector. The representation function is of particular significance here, in my view, because an organization that need not adhere to the Constitution cannot meaningfully represent this Nation. The Government is free, of course, to "privatize" some functions it would otherwise perform. But such privatization ought not automatically release those who perform Government functions from constitutional obligations. . . .

II

Section 110(a)(4) prohibits "any person" from using the word "Olympic" "[w]ith-out the consent of the [USOC] for the purpose of trade, to induce the sale of any goods or services, or to promote any theatrical exhibition, athletic performance, or competition." The Court construes this section to give the USOC authority over use of the word "Olympic" which far surpasses that provided by a standard trademark. The Court ignores the serious First Amendment problems created by its interpretation. It holds that § 110(a)(4) regulates primarily commercial speech, and that this section imposes only those incidental restrictions on expressive speech necessary to further a substantial governmental interest.

I disagree. The statute is overbroad on its face because it is susceptible of application to a substantial amount of noncommercial speech, and vests the USOC with unguided discretion to approve and disapprove others' noncommercial use of "Olympic." Moreover, by eliminating even noncommercial uses of a particular word, it unconstitutionally infringes on the SFAA's right to freedom of expression. The Act also restricts speech in a way that is not content neutral. The Court's justifications of these infringements on First Amendment rights are flimsy. The statute cannot be characterized as a mere regulation of the "manner" of speech, and does not serve any Government purpose that would not effectively be protected by giving the USOC a standard commercial trademark. Therefore, as construed by the Court, § 110(a)(4) cannot withstand the First Amendment challenge presented by petitioners.

A

The USOC has held a trademark in the word "Olympic" since 1896, and § 110(a)(3) of the Amateur Sports Act perpetuates the USOC's protection against infringement of its trademarks. To be more than statutory surplusage, then, § 110(a)(4) must provide something more than a normal trademark. Thus, the Court finds that § 110(a)(4) grants to the USOC a novel and expansive word-use authority. In my view, the Act, as interpreted by the Court, is substantially overbroad, violating the First Amendment because it prohibits "a substantial amount of constitutionally protected conduct." The Amateur Sports Act is substantially overbroad in two respects. First, it grants the USOC the remedies of a commercial trademark to regulate the use of the word "Olympic," but refuses to interpret the Act to incorporate the defenses to trademark infringement provided in the Lanham Act. These defenses are essential safeguards which prevent trademark power from infringing upon constitutionally protected speech. Second, the Court construes § 110(a)(4) to grant the USOC unconstitutional authority to prohibit use of "Olympic" in the "promotion of theatrical and athletic events," even if the promotional activities are *noncommercial* or expressive.

1

The first part of § 110 prohibits use of the word "Olympic" "for the purpose of trade" or "to induce the sale of any goods or services." There is an important difference between the word-use authority granted by this portion of § 110 and a Lanham Act trademark: the former primarily affects noncommercial speech, while the latter does not.

Charitable solicitation and political advocacy by organizations such as SFAA may in part consist of commercial speech regulated by trademark law, but the expressive element of such speech has been sheltered from unconstitutional harm by Lanham Act defenses. Without them, the Amateur Sports Act prohibits a substantial amount of noncommercial speech.

Trademark protection has been carefully confined to the realm of commercial speech by two important limitations in the Lanham Act. First, the danger of substantial regulation of noncommercial speech is diminished by denying enforcement of a trademark against uses of words that are not likely "to cause confusion, to cause mistake, or to deceive." See 15 U.S.C. § 1066. Confusion occurs when consumers make an incorrect mental association between the involved commercial products or their producers. In contrast, § 110(a)(4) regulates even nonconfusing uses of "Olympic." . . . Because § 110 does not incorporate the requirement that a defendant's use of the word be confusing to consumers, it regulates an extraordinary range of noncommercial speech.

The fair-use defense also prevents the award of a trademark from regulating a substantial amount of noncommercial speech. See 15 U.S.C. § 1115(b)(4). The Lanham Act allows "the use of the name, term, or device . . . which is descriptive of and used fairly and in good faith only to describe to users the goods or services of such party." . . . Congress' failure to incorporate this important defense in § 110(a)(4) confers an unprecedented right on the USOC. See *Park 'N Fly, Inc. v. Dollar Park and Fly, Inc.* (1985) (noting that fair-use doctrine assists in preventing the "unprecedented" creation of "an exclusive right to use language that is descriptive of a product").

In sum, while the USOC's trademark of "Olympic" allows the USOC to regulate use of the word in the "strictly business" context, the USOC's authority under § 110(a)(4) to regulate nonconfusing and good-faith descriptive uses of the word "Olympic" grants the USOC discretion to prohibit a substantial amount of noncommercial speech. Section 110(a)(4) is therefore substantially overbroad.

2

A key Lanham Act requirement that limits the impact of trademarks on noncommercial speech is the rule that a trademark violation occurs only when an offending trademark is applied to commercial goods and services. See 15 U.S.C. §§ 1066 and 1127. The Amateur Sports Act is not similarly qualified. Section 110(a)(4) "allows the USOC to prohibit the use of 'Olympic' for promotion of theatrical and athletic events," even if such uses "go beyond the 'strictly business' context." While the USOC has unquestioned authority to enforce its "Olympic" trademark against the SFAA, § 110(a)(4) gives it additional authority to regulate a substantial amount of noncommercial speech that serves to promote social and political ideas. The SFAA sponsors a number of nonprofit-making theatrical and athletic events, including concerts, film screenings, and plays. These public events are aimed at educating the public about society's alleged discrimination based on sexual orientation, age, sex, and nationality. In conjunction with these events, the SFAA distributes literature describing the meaning of the Gay Olympic Games. References to "Olympic" in this literature were deleted in response to the injunction, because of § 110's application to the promotion of athletic and theatrical events.

3

Thus, contrary to the belief of the Court, § 110 may prohibit a substantial amount of noncommercial speech, and is therefore unconstitutionally overbroad. *Schaumburg v. Citizens for a Better Environment* (1980).This overbreadth is particularly significant in light of the unfettered discretion the Act affords to the USOC to prohibit other entities from using the word "Olympic." Given the large number of such users,[32] this broad discretion creates the potential for significant suppression of protected speech. "[A] law subjecting the exercise of First Amendment freedoms to the prior restraint of a license, without narrow, objective, and definite standards to guide the licensing authority, is unconstitutional." This broad discretion, with its potential for abuse, also renders § 110 unconstitutionally overbroad on its face.

B

The Court concedes that "some" uses of "Olympic" prohibited under § 110 may involve expressive speech. But it contends that "[b]y prohibiting the use of one word for particular purposes, neither Congress nor the USOC has prohibited the SFAA from conveying its message. . . . Section 110 restricts only the manner in which the SFAA may convey its message." Section 110(a)(4) cannot be regarded as a mere time, place, and manner statute, however. By preventing the use of the word "Olympic," the statute violates the First Amendment by prohibiting dissemination of a message for which there is no adequate translation.

In *Cohen v. California* (1971), we rejected the very notion advanced today by the Court when considering the censorship of a single four-letter expletive:

> "[W]e cannot indulge the facile assumption that one can forbid particular words without also running a substantial risk of suppressing ideas in the process. Indeed, governments might soon seize upon the censorship of particular words as a convenient guise for banning the expression of unpopular views. We have been able . . . to discern little social benefit that might result from running the risk of opening the door to such grave results."

The Amateur Sports Act gives a single entity exclusive control over a wide range of uses of a word with a deep history in the English language and Western culture. Here, the SFAA

---

[32] In Los Angeles and Manhattan alone, there are over 200 enterprises and organizations listed in the telephone directories whose names start with the word "Olympic." 789 F.2d 1319, 1323 (CA9 1986) (Kozinski, J., dissenting).

intended, by use of the word "Olympic," to promote a realistic image of homosexual men and women that would help them move into the mainstream of their communities. As Judge Kozinski observed in dissent in the Court of Appeals, just as a jacket reading "I Strongly Resent the Draft" would not have conveyed Cohen's message, so a title such as "The Best and Most Accomplished Amateur Gay Athletes Competition" would not serve as an adequate translation of petitioners' message. Indeed, because individual words carry "a life and force of their own," translations never fully capture the sense of the original. The First Amendment protects more than the right to a mere translation. By prohibiting use of the word "Olympic," the USOC substantially infringes upon the SFAA's right to communicate ideas.

C

The Amateur Sports Act also violates the First Amendment because it restricts speech in a way that is not content neutral. A wide variety of groups apparently wish to express particular sociopolitical messages through the use of the word "Olympic," but the Amateur Sports Act singles out certain of the groups for favorable treatment. As the Court observes, Congress encouraged the USOC to allow the use of "Olympic" in athletic competitions held for youth ("Junior Olympics" and "Explorer Olympics") and handicapped persons ("Special Olympics"), 36 U.S.C. § 374(13), while leaving to the USOC's unfettered discretion the question whether other groups may use it. . . . Such a scheme is unacceptable under the First Amendment. . . .

D

Even if § 110(a)(4) may fairly be characterized as a statute that directly regulates only commercial speech, its incidental restrictions on First Amendment freedoms are greater than necessary to further a substantial Government interest. . . . At minimum, it is necessary to consider whether the USOC's interest in use of the word "Olympic" could not adequately be protected by rights coextensive with those in the Lanham Act, or by some other restriction on use of the word.

In the absence of § 110(a)(4), the USOC would have authority under the Lanham Act to enforce its "Olympic" trademark against commercial uses of the word that might cause consumer confusion and a loss of the mark's distinctiveness. There is no evidence in the record that this authority is insufficient to protect the USOC from economic harm. . . . The Court contends that § 110 may prohibit uses of "Olympic" because it protects an "image carefully cultivated by the USOC." Again, there is no proof in the record that the Lanham Act inadequately protects the USOC's commercial interest in its image or that the SFAA has harmed the USOC's image by its speech.[36]

Language, even in a commercial context, properly belongs to the public, unless the

---

[36] Nor is there any evidence that SFAA's expressive speech caused economic or reputational harm to the USOC's image. In *Spence v. Washington* (1974), a State asserted a similar interest in the integrity of America's flag as "'an unalloyed symbol of our country,'" and contended that there is a substantial Government interest in "preserving the flag as 'an important symbol of nationhood and unity.'" The Court considered whether a State could withdraw "a unique national symbol from the roster of materials that may be used as a background for communications." It reviewed a state law that limited the use of the American flag and forbade the public exhibition of a flag that was distorted or marked. The appellant was convicted for violating the statute by displaying the flag upside down in the window of his apartment with a peace symbol attached to it. Eight Members of the Court held that the statute was unconstitutional as applied to appellant's activity. "There was no risk that appellant's acts would mislead viewers into assuming that the Government endorsed his viewpoint," and "his message was direct, likely to be understood, and within the contours of the First Amendment." The Court concluded that since the state interest was not "significantly impaired," the conviction violated the First Amendment. Similarly, in this case, the SFAA's primary purpose was to convey a political message that is nonmisleading and direct. This message, like the symbolic speech in *Spence*, is protected by the First Amendment.

Government's asserted interest is substantial, and unless the limitation imposed is no more extensive than necessary to serve that interest. The Lanham Act is carefully crafted to prevent commercial monopolization of language that otherwise belongs in the public domain. The USOC demonstrates no need for additional protection. In my view, the SFAA therefore is entitled to use the word "Olympic" in a nonconfusing and nonmisleading manner in the noncommercial promotion of a theatrical or athletic event, absent proof of resultant harm to the USOC.

I dissent.

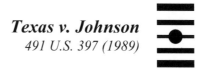

Texas v. Johnson
491 U.S. 397 (1989)

Justice BRENNAN delivered the opinion of the Court.

After publicly burning an American flag as a means of political protest, Gregory Lee Johnson was convicted of desecrating a flag in violation of Texas law. This case presents the question whether his conviction is consistent with the First Amendment. We hold that it is not.

I

While the Republican National Convention was taking place in Dallas in 1984, respondent Johnson participated in a political demonstration dubbed the "Republican War Chest Tour." As explained in literature distributed by the demonstrators and in speeches made by them, the purpose of this event was to protest the policies of the Reagan administration and of certain Dallas-based corporations. The demonstrators marched through the Dallas streets, chanting political slogans and stopping at several corporate locations to stage "die-ins" intended to dramatize the consequences of nuclear war. On several occasions they spray-painted the walls of buildings and overturned potted plants, but Johnson himself took no part in such activities. He did, however, accept an American flag handed to him by a fellow protestor who had taken it from a flagpole outside one of the targeted buildings.

The demonstration ended in front of Dallas City Hall, where Johnson unfurled the American flag, doused it with kerosene, and set it on fire. While the flag burned, the protestors chanted, "America, the red, white, and blue, we spit on you." After the demonstrators dispersed, a witness to the flag burning collected the flag's remains and buried them in his backyard. No one was physically injured or threatened with injury, though several witnesses testified that they had been seriously offended by the flag burning.

Of the approximately 100 demonstrators, Johnson alone was charged with a crime. The only criminal offense with which he was charged was the desecration of a venerated object in violation of Tex. Penal Code Ann. § 42.09(a)(3) (1989). After a trial, he was convicted, sentenced to one year in prison, and fined $2,000. The Court of Appeals for the Fifth District of Texas at Dallas affirmed Johnson's conviction, but the Texas Court of Criminal Appeals reversed, holding that the State could not, consistent with the First Amendment, punish Johnson for burning the flag in these circumstances.

The Court of Criminal Appeals began by recognizing that Johnson's conduct was symbolic speech protected by the First Amendment:

> Given the context of an organized demonstration, speeches, slogans, and
> the distribution of literature, anyone who observed appellant's act would

> have understood the message that appellant intended to convey. The act
> for which appellant was convicted was clearly "speech" contemplated
> by the First Amendment.

To justify Johnson's conviction for engaging in symbolic speech, the State asserted two interests: preserving the flag as a symbol of national unity and preventing breaches of the peace. The Court of Criminal Appeals held that neither interest supported his conviction.

Acknowledging that this Court had not yet decided whether the Government may criminally sanction flag desecration in order to preserve the flag's symbolic value, the Texas court nevertheless concluded that our decision in *West Virginia Board of Education v. Barnette* (1943), suggested that furthering this interest by curtailing speech was impermissible. "Recognizing that the right to differ is the centerpiece of our First Amendment freedoms," the court explained,

> a government cannot mandate by fiat a feeling of unity in its citizens.
> Therefore, that very same government cannot carve out a symbol of
> unity and prescribe a set of approved messages to be associated with that
> symbol when it cannot mandate the status or feeling the symbol purports
> to represent.

We never before have held that the Government may ensure that a symbol be used to express only one view of that symbol or its referents. Indeed, in *Schacht v. United States*, we invalidated a federal statute permitting an actor portraying a member of one of our armed forces to "'wear the uniform of that armed force if the portrayal does not tend to discredit that armed force.'" ([Q]uoting 10 U.S.C. § 772(f).) This proviso, we held,

> which leaves Americans free to praise the war in Vietnam but can send
> persons like Schacht to prison for opposing it, cannot survive in a
> country which has the First Amendment.

We perceive no basis on which to hold that the principle underlying our decision in *Schacht* does not apply to this case. To conclude that the government may permit designated symbols to be used to communicate only a limited set of messages would be to enter territory having no discernible or defensible boundaries. Could the government, on this theory, prohibit the burning of state flags? Of copies of the Presidential seal? Of the Constitution? In evaluating these choices under the First Amendment, how would we decide which symbols were sufficiently special to warrant this unique status? To do so, we would be forced to consult our own political preferences, and impose them on the citizenry, in the very way that the First Amendment forbids us to do. See *Carey v. Brown* (1980).

Chief Justice REHNQUIST, C.J., with whom Justice WHITE and Justice O'CONNOR join, dissenting.

. . . Only two Terms ago, in *San Francisco Arts & Athletics, Inc. v. United States Olympic Committee* (1987), the Court held that Congress could grant exclusive use of the word "Olympic" to the United States Olympic Committee. The Court thought that this "re-strictio[n] on expressive speech properly [was] characterized as incidental to the primary congressional purpose of encouraging and rewarding the USOC's activities." As the Court stated, "when a word [or symbol] acquires value "as the result of organization and the expenditure of labor, skill, and money" by an entity, that entity constitutionally may obtain a limited property right in the word [or symbol]." *Id.* at 532, quoting *International News Service v. Associated Press* (1918). Surely Congress or the States may recognize a similar interest in the flag.

H.R. 2723
102d Congress (1st Session)

To grant the United States a copyright to the Flag of the United States
and to impose criminal penalties for the destruction of a copyrighted Flag.

IN THE HOUSE OF REPRESENTATIVES
June 20, 1991

Mr. TORRICELLI introduced the following bill; which was referred to the Committee on the Judiciary

A BILL

To grant the United States a copyright to the Flag of the United States and to impose criminal penalties for the destruction of a copyrighted Flag.

Be it enacted by the Senate and House of Representatives of the United States of America in Congress assembled,

SECTION 1. United States Granted Copyright to the Flag of the United States.

The United States is hereby granted a copyright to the Flag of the United States.

SEC. 2. License To Manufacture, Sell, or Distribute the Flag of the United States.

The United States hereby grants a license to any person to manufacture in the United States the Flag of the United States, and to sell and distribute such Flag.

SEC. 3. Requirements of the Display of the Flag of the United States.

Any Flag of the United States may only be displayed in accordance with chapter 1 of title 4, United States Code, (relating to the Flag of the United States) and the joint resolution entitled 'Joint Resolution to codify and emphasize existing rules and customs pertaining to the display and use of the flag of the United States of America', approved June 22, 1942 (36 U.S.C. 174–178).

SEC. 4. Criminal Penalties for Burning or Mutilating the Flag of the United States.

(a) IN GENERAL—Whoever burns or otherwise mutilates a Flag of the United States shall be punished as follows:

(1) If the damage to such Flag exceeds $100, by a fine of not more than $10,000 or imprisonment for not more than 10 years, or both.

(2) If the damage to such Flag does not exceed $100, by a fine of not more than $1,000 or imprisonment for not more than one year, or both.

(b) EXCEPTION—Subsection (a) shall not apply with respect to whoever destroys a Flag of the United States in accordance with section 4 of the joint resolution referred to in section 3.

SEC. 5. Definitions.

As used in this Act—

(1) the term 'Flag of the United States' means a rectangular design which consists of 13 horizontal stripes, alternate red and white, with a union of 50 white stars in a blue field, and which the average person, upon seeing such design, may believe without deliberation to represent the Flag of the United States of America; and

(2) the term 'United States', when used in the geographical sense, means the 50

States, the District of Columbia, the Commonwealth of Puerto Rico, any possession of the United States, the Commonwealth of the Northern Mariana Islands, and the Trust Territory of the Pacific Islands.

Questions:

1.) Would Mr. Torricelli's bill to copyright the flag have been constitutional, if enacted? If not, why and on how many distinct constitutional grounds?

2.) One important question in any case involving intellectual property and the First Amendment is whether the defendant *needed* the material protected by property rights in order to exercise "the freedom of speech." Why does the Court believe that the SFAA does not need the word "Olympic"? Do you agree?

3.) Why does the majority focus on the effort and labor that the USOC has spent in giving Olympic a positive connotation? What is the relevance of that argument to an analysis of whether this statute violates the First Amendment?

4.) One part of the challenged law gives the USOC the right to decide who is allowed to use the logo or symbol and who not. Congress strongly urged, in a resolution, that the USOC allow the Special Olympics to keep using the name. Why did Congress itself not simply pick and choose which groups could use the term?

5.) *Texas v. Johnson* is often described as standing for the position that the Constitution does not tolerate the creation of "venerated objects," symbols about which only one attitude or method of expression is permitted. Is *SFAA v. USOC* consistent with this position?

PROBLEM 3-1
INTELLECTUAL PROPERTY AND THE FIRST AMENDMENT.

Citing the need to avoid "political confusion among voters," and to "reward the Democratic Party for their ingenuity and labor in giving the word 'Democrat' a uniquely positive connotation," the Congress grants to the Democratic National Committee ("DNC") a permanent right to the word "democrat" (upper or lower case). The "Democrat Protection Act"—or DPA—forbids any person, without the consent of the Democratic National Committee, to use the word 'democrat' or 'democratic' in any commercial (or non-profit fund-raising) activity. The right is protected by the remedies provided in the Act of July 5, 1946 (60 Stat. 427; popularly known as the Trademark Act of 1946 [Lanham Act]) [15 U.S.C. § 1051 et seq.] but expands their reach to include non-profit activities and eliminates the requirement that the DNC show the likelihood of confusion produced by the challenged use. The DNC has announced its intention of emphasizing the "New Democrat" shift to the center by denying usage of the word 'democrat' to both "left and right-wing extremists." Having been denied usage for their fund raising activities, the Democratic Socialists, Committee for a Well-Armed Democratic Citizenry, Gay Democrats PAC, and the "luncheon meat" SPAN, (whose proposed new slogan is "the Democrat of Luncheon Meats") all challenge the law.

Is the DPA constitutional? Are the actions of the DNC constitutional?

Dallas Cowboys Cheerleaders v. Pussycat Cinema
604 F.2d 200 (2d Cir. 1979)

Plaintiff in this trademark infringement action is Dallas Cowboys Cheerleaders, Inc., a wholly owned subsidiary of the Dallas Cowboys Football Club, Inc. Plaintiff employs thirty-six women who perform dance and cheerleading routines at Dallas Cowboys football games. The cheerleaders have appeared frequently on television programs and make commercial appearances at such public events as sporting goods shows and shopping center openings. In addition, plaintiff licenses others to manufacture and distribute posters, calendars, T-shirts, and the like depicting Dallas Cowboys Cheerleaders in their uniforms. These products have enjoyed nationwide commercial success, due largely to the national exposure the Dallas Cowboys Cheerleaders have received through the news and entertainment media. Moreover, plaintiff has expended large amounts of money to acquaint the public with its uniformed cheerleaders and earns substantial revenue from their commercial appearances.

At all the football games and public events where plaintiff's cheerleaders appear and on all commercial items depicting the cheerleaders, the women are clad in plaintiff's distinctive uniform. The familiar outfit consists of white vinyl boots, white shorts, a white belt decorated with blue stars, a blue bolero blouse, and a white vest decorated with three blue stars on each side of the front and a white fringe around the bottom. In this action plaintiff asserts that it has a trademark in its uniform and that defendants have infringed and diluted that trademark in advertising and exhibiting "Debbie Does Dallas."

Pussycat Cinema, Ltd., is a New York corporation which owns a movie theatre in New York City; Zaffarano is the corporation's sole stockholder. In November 1978 the Pussycat Cinema began to show "Debbie Does Dallas," a gross and revolting sex film whose plot, to the extent that there is one, involves a cheerleader at a fictional high school, Debbie, who has been selected to become a "Texas Cowgirl."[1] In order to raise enough money to send Debbie, and eventually the entire squad, to Dallas, the cheerleaders perform sexual services for a fee. The movie consists largely of a series of scenes graphically depicting the sexual escapades of the "actors." In the movie's final scene Debbie dons a uniform strikingly similar to that worn by the Dallas Cowboys Cheerleaders and for approximately twelve minutes of film footage engages in various sex acts while clad or partially clad in the uniform. Defendants advertised the movie with marquee posters depicting Debbie in the allegedly infringing uniform and containing such captions as "Starring Ex Dallas Cowgirl Cheerleader Bambi Woods" and "You'll do more than cheer for this X Dallas Cheerleader."[2] Similar advertisements appeared in the newspapers.

Plaintiff brought this action alleging trademark infringement under section 43(a) of the Lanham Act (15 U.S.C. s 1125(a)), unfair competition, and dilution of trademark in violation of section 368-d of the New York General Business Law. The district court, in its oral opinion of February 13, 1979, found that "plaintiff ha(d) succeeded in proving by overwhelming evidence the merits of each one of its contentions." Defendants challenge the validity of all three claims.

A preliminary issue raised by defendants is whether plaintiff has a valid trademark

---

[1] The official appellation of plaintiff's cheerleaders is "Dallas Cowboys Cheerleaders," but the district court found that plaintiff also has a trademark in the names "Dallas Cowgirls" and "Texas Cowgirls" which have been made popular by the media.

[2] Bambi Woods, the woman who played the role of Debbie, is not now and never has been a Dallas Cowboys Cheerleader.

in its cheerleader uniform.[3] Defendants argue that the uniform is a purely functional item necessary for the performance of cheerleading routines and that it therefore is not capable of becoming a trademark. We do not quarrel with defendants' assertion that a purely functional item may not become a trademark. However, we do not agree that all of characteristics of plaintiff's uniform serve only a functional purpose or that, because an item is in part incidentally functional, it is necessarily precluded from being designated as a trademark. Plaintiff does not claim a trademark in all clothing designed and fitted to allow free movement while performing cheerleading routines, but claims a trademark in the particular combination of colors and collocation of decorations that distinguish plaintiff's uniform from those of other squads.[4] It is well established that, if the design of an item is nonfunctional and has acquired secondary meaning,[5] the design may become a trademark even if the item itself is functional. Moreover, when a feature of the construction of the item is arbitrary, the feature may become a trademark even though it serves a useful purpose. Thus, the fact that an item serves or performs a function does not mean that it may not at the same time be capable of indicating sponsorship or origin, particularly where the decorative aspects of the item are nonfunctional. In the instant case the combination of the white boots, white shorts, blue blouse, and white star-studded vest and belt is an arbitrary design which makes the otherwise functional uniform trademarkable.

Having found that plaintiff has a trademark in its uniform, we must determine whether the depiction of the uniform in "Debbie Does Dallas" violates that trademark. The district court found that the uniform worn in the movie and shown on the marquee closely resembled plaintiff's uniform and that the public was likely to identify it as plaintiff's uniform. Our own comparison of the two uniforms convinces us that the district court was correct, and defendants do not seriously contend that the uniform shown in the movie is not almost identical with plaintiff's.

Defendants assert that the copyright doctrine of "fair use" should be held applicable to trademark infringement actions and that we should apply the doctrine to sanction their use of a replica of plaintiff's uniform. Fair use is "a 'privilege in others than the owner of a copyright to use the copyrighted material in a reasonable manner without his consent. . . .'" The fair use doctrine allows adjustments of conflicts between the first amendment and the copyright laws, and is designed primarily to balance "the exclusive rights of a copyright holder with the public's interest in dissemination of information affecting areas of universal concern, such as art, science and industry." It is unlikely that the fair use doctrine is applicable to trademark infringements; however, we need not reach that question. Although, as defendants assert, the doctrine of fair use permits limited copyright infringement for purposes of parody, defendants' use of plaintiff's uniform hardly qualifies as parody or any other form of fair use.

Nor does any other first amendment doctrine protect defendants' infringement of plaintiff's trademark. That defendants' movie may convey a barely discernible message

---

[3] At present plaintiff does not have a registered trademark or service mark in its uniform. However, plaintiff still may prevail if it establishes that it has a common law trademark or service mark. Whether plaintiff's uniform is considered as a trademark or a service mark, the standards for determining infringement are the same. *West &Co. v. Arica Institute, Inc.* (1977).

[4] Plaintiff's design imparts a western flavor appropriate for a Texas cheerleading squad. The design is in no way essential to the performance of cheerleading routines and to that extent is not a functional aspect of the uniform.

[5] Secondary meaning is "(t)he power of a name or other configuration to symbolize a particular business, product or company. . . ." *Ideal Toy Corp. v. Kenner Products Division of General Mills Fun Group, Inc.* (1977). There is no dispute in this case that plaintiff's uniform is universally recognized as the symbol of the Dallas Cowboys Cheerleaders.

does not entitle them to appropriate plaintiff's trademark in the process of conveying that message. Plaintiff's trademark is in the nature of a property right, and as such it need not "yield to the exercise of First Amendment rights under circumstances where adequate alternative avenues of communication exist." Because there are numerous ways in which defendants may comment on "sexuality in athletics" without infringing plaintiff's trademark, the district court did not encroach upon their first amendment rights in granting a preliminary injunction.

For similar reasons, the preliminary injunction did not constitute an unconstitutional "prior restraint". This is not a case of government censorship, but a private plaintiff's attempt to protect its property rights. The propriety of a preliminary injunction where such relief is sought is so clear that courts have often issued an injunction without even mentioning the first amendment. The prohibition of the Lanham Act is content neutral, *Cf. Schacht v. United States* (1970), and therefore does not arouse the fears that trigger the application of constitutional "prior restraint" principles.

Questions:

1.) What do you think of Pussycat Cinema's parody and First Amendment defense? Can you offer a better one?

2.) *Debbie Does Dallas* was enjoined because it violated a property right held by the Dallas Cowboys Football Club, namely an unregistered common trademark/trade dress right in the uniforms worn by its cheerleaders. You have read the reasoning of the court. Did that right exist before the case was brought? Does that fact raise any First Amendment issues?

L.L. Bean, Inc. v. Drake Publishers, Inc.
811 F.2d 26 (1st Cir. 1987)

BOWNES, Circuit Judge.

Imitation may be the highest form of flattery, but plaintiff-appellee L.L. Bean, Inc., was neither flattered nor amused when High Society magazine published a prurient parody of Bean's famous catalog. Defendant-appellant Drake Publishers, Inc., owns High Society, a monthly periodical featuring adult erotic entertainment. Its October 1984 issue contained a two-page article entitled "L.L. Beam's Back-To-School-Sex-Catalog." The article was labelled on the magazine's contents page as "humor" and "parody." The article displayed a facsimile of Bean's trademark and featured pictures of nude models in sexually explicit positions using "products" that were described in a crudely humorous fashion.

L.L. Bean sought a temporary restraining order to remove the October 1984 issue from circulation. The complaint alleged trademark infringement, unfair competition, trademark dilution, deceptive trade practices, interference with prospective business advantage and trade libel.... [Among other things, the district court granted] Bean summary judgment with respect to the trademark dilution claim raised under Maine law. Me. Rev. Stat. Ann. tit. 10, § 1530 (1981). It ruled that the article had tarnished Bean's trademark by undermining the goodwill and reputation associated with the mark. . . . The court also held that enjoining the publication of a parody to prevent trademark dilution did not offend the first amendment. An injunction issued prohibiting further publication or distribution of the "L.L. Beam Sex Catalog." [Drake appealed.]

I

. . . One need only open a magazine or turn on television to witness the pervasive influence of trademarks in advertising and commerce. Designer labels appear on goods ranging from handbags to chocolates to every possible form of clothing. Commercial advertising slogans, which can be registered as trademarks, have become part of national political campaigns. "Thus, trademarks have become a natural target of satirists who seek to comment on this integral part of the national culture." The ridicule conveyed by parody inevitably conflicts with one of the underlying purposes of the Maine anti-dilution statute, which is to protect against the tarnishment of the goodwill and reputation associated with a particular trademark. The court below invoked this purpose as the basis for its decision to issue an injunction. The issue before us is whether enjoining the publication of appellant's parody violates the first amendment guarantees of freedom of expression.

II

The district court disposed of the first amendment concerns raised in this matter by relying on the approach taken in *Dallas Cowboys Cheerleaders, Inc. v. Pussycat Cinema, Ltd.* (1979). In rejecting Drake's claim that the first amendment protects the unauthorized use of another's trademark in the process of conveying a message, the district court cited the following language from Dallas Cowboys Cheerleaders: "Plaintiffs trademark is in the nature of a property right . . . and as such it need not 'yield to the exercise of First Amendment rights under circumstances where adequate alternative avenues of communication exist.' *Lloyd Corp. v. Tanner* (1972)." We do not believe that the first amendment concerns raised here can be resolved as easily as was done in *Dallas Cowboys Cheerleaders*. Aside from our doubts about whether there are alternative means of parodying plaintiffs catalog, we do not think the court fully assessed the nature of a trademark owner's property rights.

The limits on the scope of a trademark owner's property rights was considered recently in *Lucasfilm Ltd. v. High Frontier* (1985). In that case, the owners of the trade-mark "Star Wars" alleged injury from public interest groups that used the term in commercial advertisements presenting their views on President Reagan's Strategic Defense Initiative. Judge Gesell stressed that the sweep of a trademark owner's rights extends only to injurious, unauthorized commercial uses of the mark by another. Trademark rights do not entitle the owner to quash an unauthorized use of the mark by another who is communicating ideas or expressing points of view.

III

The district court's opinion suggests that tarnishment may be found when a trade-mark is used without authorization in a context which diminishes the positive associations with the mark. Neither the strictures of the first amendment nor the history and theory of anti-dilution law permit a finding of tarnishment based solely on the presence of an unwholesome or negative context in which a trademark is used without authorization. Such a reading of the anti-dilution statute unhinges it from its origins in the marketplace. A trademark is tarnished when consumer capacity to associate it with the appropriate products or services has been diminished. The threat of tarnishment arises when the goodwill and reputation of a plaintiffs trademark is linked to products which are of shoddy quality or which conjure associations that clash with the associations generated by the owner's lawful use of the mark. . . .

[T]he dilution injury stems from an unauthorized effort to market incompatible products or services by trading on another's trademark. The Constitution is not offended when the anti-dilution statute is applied to prevent a defendant from using a trademark without permission in order to merchandise dissimilar products or services. Any residual effect on first amendment freedoms should be balanced against the need to fulfill the legitimate purpose of the anti-dilution statute. The law of trademark dilution has developed to combat an unauthorized and harmful appropriation of a trademark by another for the purpose of identifying, manufacturing, merchandising or promoting dissimilar products or services. The harm occurs when a trademark's identity and integrity—its capacity to command respect in the market—is undermined due to its inappropriate and unauthorized use by other market actors. When presented with such circumstances, courts have found that trademark owners have suffered harm despite the fact that redressing such harm entailed some residual impact on the rights of expression of commercial actors. See, e.g., *Chemical Corp. of America v. Anheuser-Busch, Inc.* (1962) (floor wax and insecticide maker's slogan, "Where there's life, there's bugs," harmed strength of defendant's slogan, "Where there's life, there's Bud."); *Original Appalachian Artworks, Inc. v. Topps Chewing Gum* (1986) (merchandiser of "Garbage Pail Kids" stickers and products injured owner of Cabbage Patch Kids mark); *General Electric Co. v. Alumpa Coal Co.* (1979) ("Genital Electric" monogram on underpants and T-shirts harmful to plaintiffs trademark).

While the cases cited above might appear at first glance to be factually analogous to the instant one, they are distinguishable for two reasons. First, they all involved unauthorized commercial uses of another's trademark. Second, none of those cases involved a defendant using a plaintiff's trademark as a vehicle for an editorial or artistic parody. In contrast to the cases cited, the instant defendant used plaintiffs mark solely for non-commercial purposes. Appellant's parody constitutes an editorial or artistic, rather than a commercial, use of plaintiffs mark. The article was labeled as "humor" and "parody" in the magazine's table of contents section; it took up two pages in a one-hundred-page issue; neither the article nor appellant's trademark was featured on the front or back cover of the magazine. Drake did not use Bean's mark to identify or promote goods or services to consumers; it never intended to market the "products" displayed in the parody.

We think the Constitution tolerates an incidental impact on rights of expression of commercial actors in order to prevent a defendant from unauthorizedly merchandising his products with another's trademark.[4] In such circumstances, application of the anti-dilution statute constitutes a legitimate regulation of commercial speech, which the Supreme Court has defined as "expression related solely to the economic interests of the speaker and its audience." *Central Hudson Gas & Elec. v. Public Serv. Comm'n* (1980). It offends the Constitution, however, to invoke the anti-dilution statute as a basis for enjoining the non-commercial use of a trademark by a defendant engaged in a protected form of expression.

Our reluctance to apply the anti-dilution statute to the instant case also stems from a recognition of the vital importance of parody. Although, as we have noted, parody is often offensive, it is nevertheless "deserving of substantial freedom—both as entertainment and as a form of social and literary criticism." *Berlin v. E.C. Publications, Inc.* (1964). It would be anomalous to diminish the protection afforded parody solely because

---

[4] We have no occasion to consider the constitutional limits which might be imposed on the application of anti-dilution statutes to unauthorized uses of trademarks on products whose principal purpose is to convey a message. *Mutual of Omaha Ins. Co. v. Novak* (1985) (plaintiff entitled to preliminary injunction against peace activist protesting nuclear weapons proliferation by marketing "Mutant of Omaha" T-shirts). Such a situation undoubtedly would require a balancing of the harm suffered by the trademark owner against the benefit derived by the parodist and the public from the unauthorized use of a trademark on a product designed to convey a message.

a parodist chooses a famous trade name, rather than a famous personality, author or creative work, as its object.[5]

The district court's injunction falls not only because it trammels upon a protected form of expression, but also because it depends upon an untoward judicial evaluation of the offensiveness or unwholesomeness of the appellant's materials. The Supreme Court has recognized the threat to free speech inherent in sanctioning such evaluations. *Cohen v. California* (1971).

Reversed and remanded.

LEVIN H. CAMPBELL, Chief Judge (dissenting). [Omitted.]

Question:

1.) Why does the court rule in favor of Drake but against Pussycat Cinema?

PROBLEM 3-2
CONSTITUTIONAL INTERPRETATION: REVIEW.

Review the materials in the previous two chapters. What are the most difficult lines to draw and rules to formulate in a constitutional theory that explains:

1.) The general contours of the Congressional power to create, extend and define intellectual property rights?

2.) The limits (if any) that the First Amendment puts on intellectual property rights and remedies? Before answering, consider this sentence from the Breyer-Alito dissent in *Golan*. "The fact that, by withdrawing material from the public domain, the statute inhibits an important preexisting flow of information is sufficient, when combined with the other features of the statute that I have discussed, to convince me that the Copyright Clause, interpreted in the light of the First Amendment, does not authorize Congress to enact this statute." How does Justice Breyer's understanding of the way the First Amendment should inflect the interpretation of the Copyright Clause differ from that of Justice Ginsburg?

---

[5] We recognize that the plaintiffs in *Pillsbury Co. v. Milky Way Productions, Inc.* (1981), obtained injunctive relief against Screw magazine, which had published pictures of facsimiles of Pillsbury's trade characters, "Poppin Fresh" and "Poppie Fresh," engaged in sexual intercourse and fellatio. The pictorial also featured plaintiff's trademark and the refrain of its jingle, "The Pillsbury Baking Song." While the district court granted relief under Georgia's anti-dilution statute, it did so only after specifically declining to consider whether defendants' presentation constituted a parody. The defendants in Pillsbury had tried to proffer parody as a defense to plaintiffs copyright infringement claim; they did not assert it as a defense to the dilution claim. Pillsbury, therefore, does not stand for the proposition that the publication of a parody properly may be enjoined under an anti-dilution statute, since the court never considered whether defendants had presented a parody, and defendants never asserted parody as a defense to the dilution claim.

CHAPTER FOUR

Trademark: Introduction

Modern developments in the law of unfair competition offer many examples of . . . circular reasoning. There was once a theory that the law of trade marks and trade names was an attempt to protect the consumer against the "passing off" of inferior goods under misleading labels. Increasingly the courts have departed from any such theory and have come to view this branch of law as a protection of property rights in divers economically valuable sale devices. In practice, injunctive relief is being extended today to realms where no actual danger of confusion to the consumer is present, and this extension has been vigorously supported and encouraged by leading writers in the field. . . . The current legal argument runs: One who by the ingenuity of his advertising or the quality of his product has induced consumer responsiveness to a particular name, symbol, form of packaging, etc., has thereby created a thing of value; a thing of value is property; the creator of property is entitled to protection against third parties who seek to deprive him of his property. This argument may be embellished, in particular cases, with animadversions upon the selfish motives of the infringing defendant, a summary of the plaintiff's evidence (naturally uncontradicted) as to the amount of money he has spent in advertising, and insinuations (seldom factually supported) as to the inferiority of the infringing defendant's product. The vicious circle inherent in this reasoning is plain. It purports to base legal protection upon economic value, when, as a matter of actual fact, the economic value of a sales device depends upon the extent to which it will be legally protected. If commercial exploitation of the word "Palmolive" is not restricted to a single firm, the word will be of no more economic value to any particular firm than a convenient size, shape, mode of packing, or manner of advertising, common in the trade. Not being of economic value to any particular firm, the word would be regarded by courts as "not property," and no injunction would be issued. In other words, the fact that courts did not protect the word would make the word valueless, and the fact that it was valueless would then be regarded as a reason for not protecting it.

Felix Cohen, *Transcendental Nonsense and the Functional Approach* (1935)

Felix Cohen's article comes from the time before the Lanham Act, which provided a Federal legislative source of authority in place of the common law reasoning he disdains here. It also antedates many developments and extensions in trademark law, including some with which he would probably have disagreed, to say nothing of the social and technological transformations that make the world of brand, logo and advertising very different from the one in which he lived. But his article still asks a valid question.

Why do we have trademark rights? Why do we have this "homestead law for the language," to use Cohens words? To return to Chapter 1, is this a Lockean story in which one mixes one's labor with a word or a logo, and therefore is entitled to a property right? Is it a Justice Pitney-style assumption that others should not benefit freely from positive externalities created by my actions, including my actions in creating a trademark? Both of those ideas clearly influenced the common law of trademarks and unfair competition, a body of law which partly shaped the contours of Federal protection. Both continue to operate in cases today. Think back to the Supreme Court's discussion in *SFAA v. USOC* of the *labor and ingenuity* that the USOC had expended creating the *valuable* brand "Olympic." The right at issue there was not technically a trademark. In fact, it was stronger. Yet, the Court tried to analogize the USOC's rights to those provided by trademark law, to show how Congress routinely handed out property rights in valuable words without offending the First Amendment. To make that analogy, it turned immediately to a discussion of labor invested and uncompensated benefit conferred. So those themes continue to resonate and have considerable force. We will encounter them in the cases in this book.

Yet today both scholars and courts largely offer a different set of justifications for trademark law, one that escapes—or at least tries to escape—from the circular reasoning Cohen mocked. That set of justifications is a utilitarian one and it focuses on informational efficiency—efficient communication between consumers and producers. In fact, there are two utilitarian justifications, one focused on preventing consumer confusion and one on encouraging producer investment in stable brands.

Let us start with the consumer. As you rush through the aisles of the grocery store, throwing things in your cart, how much time do you spend assessing the qualities of each good purchased? Certainly, you look at the date on the milk and the meat, perhaps double check whether there is MSG in an unfamiliar brand of Hoisin sauce, but most of the time your purchases are probably almost automatic. Detergent? The orange one in the square box with concentric red and yellow circles on the logo. Soap? Ivory. Toilet paper? The one with the puppies on it (because nothing says anal cleanliness like a dog. Or a bear.). If you are like most consumers, most of these purchases are reflexive, sometimes even pre-verbal. You have tried a number of soaps and whether or not you were convinced by Ivory's slogan "so pure it floats"—a *non sequitur* if there ever was one—you now just buy Ivory. But how do you know that the "Ivory soap" you buy will be the same as the "Ivory soap" you settled on? Absent the legal creation of this right over a name or logo, the product name is a "public good"—non-excludable and non rival. If anyone could call their soap "Ivory" or their detergent "Palmolive" would you have to scrutinize the label each time to make sure the ingredients were the same? From an economic point of view, that is very inefficient. In other words, the economic rationale for the Ivory trademark is not that Ivory has labored hard to build it up and advertise it. Nor is it that, without trademark protection, other soap companies could use the same name and "reap where they had not sown." Instead, we focus on the benefits to the consumer of stable nomenclature and thus the social gains produced by efficient information flow in the market.

Of course, trademarks do not in fact guarantee stable brand identity. They just guarantee that product-meddling will be solely in the hands of the trademark owner. If Coke wants to change its formula, or the Pears soap trademark has been bought by a company that wants to lower the quality of ingredients, my consumer expectations will be upset, nonetheless. But at least the trademark owner might be presumed to make rational calculations about when to do so.

So the first rationale for trademark is preventing consumer confusion and encouraging efficient consumer information flow. The second one is producer-focused. Trademarks provide an incentive to producers to invest in building up a stable brand meaning, which in turn will be useful to consumers. Notice: *stable* brand meaning, not *high quality* brand meaning. The trademark protects White Castle burgers no less than it protects Ruth's Chris Steak House, Econo Lodge no less than the Four Seasons, Pabst no less than Dogfish. Whatever slice of the market a producer chooses to go for, from *haute cuisine* or high fashion to cheap and nasty but dependable, trademark is there to help incentivize the investment in semantic stability. Again, without the mark, the name is a public good. Why should Apple or the Four Seasons seek to build a reputation for that kind of style or quality? Why should McDonald's try to convince me that the burgers will be exactly the same level of grey mediocrity from Maine to Monterey, never reaching Escoffier heights or *E. coli* lows? Anyone could slap Apple, Four Seasons or McDonald's on their product. By telling the *producer* that it will be able to exclude others from the name, goes the theory, we encourage investment in a stable brand that then becomes a useful and efficient communication to the *consumer*. The two arguments meet, a semantic handshake enabled by a legal right. Or so says the theory.

Of course, if we *really* wanted to promote semantic stability, we might force producers to internalize the costs of sub-par performance as well as the benefits of consistency. We do not. Do you have a positive image of Blackwater Security, the firm whose employees killed 17 Iraqi civilians in a single 2007 incident? Whatever your impressions, you are unlikely to find the company. It was renamed Xe Services in 2009. It is now called Academi. Remember ValuJet and their rather questionable safety record? Want to avoid them and fly AirTran instead? They were the same company (and later AirTran became part of Southwest Airlines). Because producers can always change their brand names or even their corporate names, they always have the option to declare semantic bankruptcy and start afresh. But we digress.

In each area of intellectual property law, we first try to understand the problem the right is supposed to solve, as a way of understanding the contours, the extent, the duration and the limitations and exceptions of the right. So the trademark is a legal right to exclude others from a name or logo or other distinguishing characteristic that would otherwise be a non-excludable and non-rival public good. The rationale we have discussed is that this minimizes consumer confusion, thus maximizing informational efficiency in the market, and provides an incentive for the creation of information-packed stable brands. If you were trying to further that purpose, what shape would you give the right? Please look again at the chart on page *xii* of the Introduction, comparing the three main forms of Federal intellectual property.

This chart omits a lot. It must in order to fit on one page. But it does give a sense of the varied designs of the three intellectual property rights we are discussing, each over a differed type of subject matter, each covering or applying to a different "thing"—a legally protected *res*—each procured through a different process, lasting for a different period of time, shaped by different limitations and exceptions and regulating or prohibiting different types of behavior in others.

Returning to the shape or design of the right suggested by trademark's rationale, one can see that the right is designed (or *should be* designed) to fulfill the functions of efficient consumer communication. First, note that trademarks do not convey ownership of a word—a mistake that non-lawyers (and some trademark owners) sometimes make. They convey the right to forbid a particular kind of *use*. Teachers of intellectual property love to use Bass Ale as an example, because the label itself says that it was the first registered trademark in the United Kingdom. In the US, Bass got a registered mark in 1912 for pale ale, with a first date of use of 1856. In 1990 it broadened that to cover beer, ale, stout, lager and porter.

Int. Cl.: 32

Prior U.S. Cl.: 48

United States Patent and Trademark Office

Reg. No. 1,598,860

Registered May 29, 1990

TRADEMARK
PRINCIPAL REGISTER

BASS PUBLIC LIMITED COMPANY (UNITED KINGDOM COMPANY)
HIGH STREET
BURTON-ON-TRENT, ENGLAND

FOR: BEER, ALE, STOUT, LAGER AND PORTER, IN CLASS 32 (U.S. CL. 48).

FIRST USE 0–0–1856; IN COMMERCE 11–30–1985.

OWNER OF U.S. REG. NOS. 88,266, 1,490,420 AND OTHERS.

NO CLAIM IS MADE TO THE EXCLUSIVE RIGHT TO USE "COS.", "PALE ALE", "ENG-LAND'S FIRST REGD. TRADEMARK", AND "I.P.A.", APART FROM THE MARK AS SHOWN.

THE LINING ON THE DRAWING IS A FEATURE OF THE MARK AND DOES NOT REPRESENT COLOR, AND THE STIPPLING APPEARING THEREIN IS FOR SHADING PURPOSES ONLY.

SER. NO. 73–719,218, FILED 3–28–1988.

CRAIG K. MORRIS, EXAMINING ATTORNEY

There are a few things worth noticing about this. First, look at the field that says "For:" This mark is for use selling beer, ale, stout, lager and porter. It does not interfere with Bass "for medical apparatus, namely, a system consisting of collectors and suctioning equipment to collect fluids from medical procedures." That is a registered mark. It does not interfere with Bass for electric lights and LED circuit boards. It does not interfere with all those businesses whose name contains a reference to bass the fish, or bass the instrument, or bass the sound range. G.H. Bass, the maker of Weejuns shoes, is not infringing Bass Ale's trademark. The mark does not stop you saying that you drank a lot of Bass last night, or posting a picture on your Facebook page with you holding a Bass, or praising or criticizing Bass Ale. What it does stop you from doing, is selling beer under the name Bass, or using any mark on your beer that is likely to cause confusion with the Bass ale trademark. It also stops you registering a trademark that would be likely to cause confusion. So when a Mr. Michael Massa applied for a trademark over "Bass Hole Ale: The Brew That Makes Your Stories True"[1] the holders of the Bass Ale trademark opposed

---

[1] The applicant stressed the fact that the "bass" referred to was the fish. "The mark consists of a representation of a fisherman in green waders with brown suspenders and a golden colored hat holding a bent fishing rod.

the registration of that mark. Mr. Massa eventually abandoned the application.

Of course, companies can leverage their popular trademarks into other fields. Bass holds a trademark for the use of its logos on mirrors, glassware and shopping bags, among other things. But the claim is always mark X for use Y, not for the ownership of a word outright.

The second thing to notice is the limitations and exceptions that further cabin the reach of the right. To pick one example: Generic terms can *never* have or keep trademark status, even if they were novel terms invented, and successfully registered as marks, by the owner. If people start to use "Shredded Wheat" to describe all cereals of that type, not just the ones from the National Biscuit Company (now Nabisco), or "Murphy beds" to describe all beds that fold down from the wall, not just the ones from the original manufacturer, then the trademark is canceled. We cannot take away from the public the ability to use the standard term for the goods. The owners of Kleenex, Xerox and Rollerblades spend a great deal of time policing usages of their mark to try and stop this from happening. Instead they promote an alternative term for the general category ("facial tissue," "photocopying" and "in-line skates") and admonish those who use the trademark to describe the type of good. No matter how hard they try, however, if the public starts to use that as the generic term, the trademark is canceled. The term has moved into the public domain.

(handwritten margin note: Generic terms NEVER TM)

To pick another example: nominative use—using the name of a competing product in order to identify it, in comparative advertising, say—is not a violation of the trademark. Notice how both of these exceptions allow us to test various theories of why we have the right. If trademarks were an incentive to come up with novel goods with novel names—in the same way that a patent does—then we would want to incentivize, not penalize, the person who came up with the good and the term used to describe it. Yet if the term suffers genericide—comes to describe the product *category* rather than the original product source—then the mark is subject to cancellation. Similarly, it may seem unfair that makers of competing hybrid cars can favorably compare theirs to the Prius. Surely they are "reaping where they have not sown," capturing a positive externality by using the familiar brand to help the consumer understand the new one? Yet if that facilitates communication to the consumer about what kind of a product this is, then trademark would be undermining its own rationale to forbid it. The rationales will help you understand the rules and predict how they might apply to new facts or new technologies. In the next section we will lead you through the basics of trademark law. In each case, think about the feature of the law being described and try and relate it back to trademark's central goal. Does it fit well or badly?

(handwritten margin note: Nominative use okay in TM)

Trademark Basics

A trademark is a word, phrase, logo, or any other indicator that identifies the source of a particular product. (Technically, a "trademark" distinguishes goods while a "service mark" distinguishes services; in this section, "trademark" will be used to refer to both trademarks and service marks.) The key here is "source indicative." Think of a triangle composed of the producer, the good and the consumer. The mark is the sign that tells the consumer where the good came from, that identifies its source. "Nike", "Just Do It", and

---

In the background a largemouth bass with a lure in his mouth is beginning to jump. The bass is surrounded by a field of bluish-green water. In the foreground the fisherman is standing against a stand of cattails with a lone dragonfly perched on a blade of cattail. The words BASS HOLE BEER appear in an arc across the top of the label in green with black edging. The words "The Brew That Makes Your Stories True" are in the foreground in black on a stretched blue oval banner." Application 77165782.

the checkmark Swoosh are trademarks owned by Nike, Inc. When you spend $180 on shoes that say Nike®, that trademark indicates that the shoes were made by Nike rather than another manufacturer, and has the quality or appeal associated with Nike products. "Apple", "iTunes", and the bitten apple logo are trademarks that indicate that your stylish hardware and proprietary software came from Apple, Inc.

Trademark protection can extend to product features beyond conventional words or logos, such as color, shape, or sound. (Some of these are referred to as "trade dress," a category we will discuss later.) Examples include the lacquered red soles on Louboutin shoes, the undulating tapered shape of the Coca-Cola bottle, or the roar of the MGM lion. Under no circumstances, however, can a *functional* feature of the product be trademarked. I might be the first person to make bright yellow life vests or stainless steel vacuum flasks, but I can never trademark those features—high visibility and stainless durability are obviously functional in those products. To give a trademark over them would convey a patent-like monopoly (and potentially, a perpetual one) rather than truly protecting a source indicator.

What are the sources of trademark law?

Trademark law has its roots in state unfair competition laws that prohibited competitors from "passing off" other producers' goods as their own. (In the quotation that began this chapter, Cohen argues that such reasoning could balloon too far.) The first federal trademark statutes date from 1870 and 1876 but, as you read in Chapter 2, they were struck down as being beyond Congress's power under both the Intellectual Property Clause and the Commerce Clause. In 1881 Congress passed another, much narrower statute, justified under its Commerce Clause power and limited only to marks used in interstate and international commerce, or in trade with the Indian tribes. These limitations were included specifically to make that Act comply with the ruling in *The Trade-Mark Cases*.

The current federal statute is the Lanham Act, originally enacted in 1946 and amended many times since. As we will see, the Lanham Act's reach is much broader than the narrow 1881 statute. This expansion reflects the Supreme Court's broadening vision of the meaning of "commerce" after the New Deal. Though the Lanham Act reaches broadly, it does not supplant state systems. Unlike the Federal copyright and patent systems, which "preempt" state regulation of their subject matter, the Federal trademark system coexists with a thriving set of state trademark regimes, which share many of its features, and which provide protection to businesses with no desire to spread nationally. However, for obvious reasons—geographic reach and economic significance among them—the Federal system is the central focus of large-scale legal attention.

We will examine 5 types of protection in the Federal trademark system. The statutory sections cited below are from the Lanham Act.

1.) **Registered Marks.** At the center is the system of registered Federal marks (and registered Federal trade dress, such as the Coke bottle design). These are the rights centered in § 1114 (or § 32) of the Lanham Act. Only the trademark holder can sue to enforce the mark.

2.) **Unregistered marks, unregistered trade dress and false designation of origin.** Beyond registered marks, the Federal system also provides a similar but weaker set of prohibitions against false or misleading designation of origin. Those rights, developing out of § 1125(a) (§ 43(a)) give protection—among other things—to unregistered marks and unregistered trade dress. While only the trademark owner can sue to enforce a registered mark, § 1125(a) says that suit can be brought "by any person who believes that he or she is or is likely to be damaged by such act." The Supreme Court held that the "damage" referred to here must be to a valid commercial interest of a competitor, partly because there are obvious constitutional problems in premising standing on a "belief" one has been harmed.

3.) **Dilution.** Marks that are "famous" to the national consuming public are also protected from "dilution" that blurs or tarnishes their strength. These rights find their home in § 1125(c) (§ 43(c)).

4.) **Cybersquatting.** The Lanham Act has been amended to deal with the intersection of domain names and trademark law. § 1125(d) explicitly covers "cybersquatting"—the "bad faith" registration of domain names in the hope of extracting rent from a trademark owner. It should be noted, however, that the other protections of the Act are also of relevance. For example, a domain name can also be a registered mark in its own right.

5.) **False or Misleading Statements of Fact.** The Lanham Act also prohibits false or misleading statements of fact ("My new diet will lose you 30 pounds in 3 weeks") even when there appears to be no "mark" of any kind involved. These provisions, too, are rooted in section § 1125(a). Judicial interpretation of the Lanham Act has effectively broadened it to become a Federal law of false advertising and unfair competition, a considerable expansion. Again, the more relaxed definition of standing applies, though the interest vindicated must be that of a competitor, not a consumer.

Registered Marks

The Lanham Act creates a national system for registering trademarks, and determining which marks enjoy priority over others. It also spells out causes of action for trademark infringement and dilution, as well as available remedies. The key here is *registering.* Many people believe that the little symbol ™ indicates a valid Federal trademark. It does not. At best, ™ and its equivalent for service marks, ˢᴹ, mean that the company wants to use the term as a common law mark, or that it hopes one day to register the mark but has not attempted to do so, and is attempting to build brand identity in the meantime. The sign of a Federal Mark is the "R" inside a circle: ®. The "R" stands for "registered." It shows that the mark has been examined by the PTO and registered on the Principal or Supplemental Register. (The Supplemental Register lists a variety of marks that have not yet received full Federal protection, such as descriptive terms that have not yet developed sufficient distinctiveness.)

To be sure, Federal registration is not a prerequisite for acquiring trademark rights. Absent registration, a trademark owner may gain common law rights by being the first to use the mark in commerce. However, these rights are limited to the geographical area where the mark is used. For example, a "Wiener King" restaurant would enjoy rights in Durham but could not prevent Wiener Kings in other cities from using the same mark. With federal registration, the default is flipped: trademark rights extend nationwide, with the exception of areas where an earlier (or as trademark lawyers say, "senior") user has already been using the mark. So Federal registration would give Wiener King rights from Durham to San Francisco, minus areas where a preexisting Wiener King has been using the mark.

In addition to nationwide rights, federal registration confers a number of other benefits. These include: a legal presumption of exclusive rights in the mark, constructive notice to the public of trademark ownership, the ability to prevent the Federal registration of confusingly similar marks, an array of remedies, and a basis for registering in foreign countries.

Why build the center of the Federal system around registration? After all, we do not require that writers, musicians or filmmakers register in order to acquire copyright. (Though they must register in order to sue for infringement.) It is important to remember that the Federal system of registered marks is supposed to complement and act as an adjunct to the state system. It is the functions those other systems cannot perform that the Federal registration system seeks to fulfill. On the Federal level, registration fulfills multiple functions centering around information costs.

- It lowers search costs, both for those with existing marks and those seeking to create new marks. If I am looking for a name for my new nationwide 'rapid oil change' franchise, I can learn quickly that "Jiffy Lube" is taken. I will not waste time or money developing a campaign around that name, or laboriously searching, state by state, to find available semantic real estate. In addition, the Supplemental Register will show me that someone else is working to develop a brand identity over a term like "Quik Oil," even if that mark has not yet developed sufficient distinctiveness to merit registration on the Principal Register.

- It allows businesses to plan to expand nationally, secure in the knowledge their mark will not have to change when they reach new territory. In the example given above, Wiener King does not invest in developing a local following, only to find that it cannot use that name elsewhere in the country and must invent a new one.

- We hope that the process of review and approval that is required to get onto the Federal Register sets a high enough bar so that businesses are deterred from claiming to have legal rights over generic, functional or misleading marks, which in turn would suppress competition or confuse consumers. (This hope is not always well-founded.)

- The Register lists both "Live" and "Dead" marks, the latter including those that have been abandoned, fallen out of use, or been successfully challenged. By listing "Dead" marks no less than "Live" ones the Register gives a map of both those semantic areas that are already taken and those that have once again become free. It is a map both of current property and of areas that have fallen back into the public domain. The requirement that registrations be continuously maintained and renewed provides a natural "pruning" function.

We will start with the center of the system—registered marks—and will go through the requirements for registration. It will turn out that many of the requirements for registering marks—such as use in commerce—are also requirements for unregistered marks, just as many of the tests for the *infringement* of registered marks are also tests for the infringement of unregistered marks. Thus, it is important to remember that while many cases in the next chapter focus on registered marks, their implications are much broader.

Notes: Use-based and Intent-To-Use Applications

The requirement that a trademark be used in commerce (discussed in detail in the next chapter) applies to both common law marks and federally registered marks. Use-based applications for federally registered marks must indicate the date of first use in commerce and include a specimen showing that the mark is actively being used on all of the goods and services listed in the application. For those seeking federal registration, the requirement of use in commerce before the mark could be registered led in practice to applicants trying through "token" or "pretextual" uses to establish that the mark had been used in commerce. Courts rejected some of these and allowed others.

Since 1988, however, the story has changed. Congress amended § 1051 of the Lanham Act to allow "intent to use" applications. (Foreign applicants have a third option—international agreements allow them to file based on an active registration or application in another country.) Parties who are not yet using a mark can file based on intent-to-use, meaning that (in the words of the PTO) "you have more than just an idea but are less than market ready (for example, having a business plan, creating samples products, or performing other initial business activities)." A successful use-based application results in registration. A successful intent-to-use application results in a "Notice of Allowance" that gives the applicant six months to verify in a "Statement of Use" that she has begun using the mark in commerce. If six months is not enough time, the applicant can file for a series of six-month extensions; the maximum extension period is three years from the Notice of Allowance. After the first six month period, "good cause" statements must be filed showing the reasons for requiring the extension.

Until the 1988 amendments to section 1051, domestic applicants were at a disadvantage *vis à vis* foreign applicants who could effectively jump in line ahead of domestic applicants because international agreements allowed them to file U.S. applications claiming earlier filing dates from countries with less stringent requirements. This gave the foreign applications "priority" as against the domestic applicants. Recognizing applications based on a *bona fide* intent-to-use helped to level the playing field.

"Priority" is an important concept in trademark law. A mark cannot be registered if it is confusingly similar to a mark that has priority because it is already registered or the subject of a prior application. (If a mark is confusingly similar to an unregistered mark, then it can still obtain a federal registration, but exclusive rights will not extend to the geographical area where the senior common law mark is being used.) As between two applications for confusingly similar marks, the filing date—the date that the PTO receives either the electronic or paper application—establishes priority. The second application is suspended until the first is either registered or abandoned. However, if the second applicant actually has stronger rights—for example, by using the mark for a much longer time—she can bring an opposition proceeding during the registration process and, if successful, prevent the mark from being registered.

After a trademark application is submitted, a PTO examiner determines whether it satisfies the eligibility requirements summarized above and publishes it in the "Official Gazette." There is then a 30-day period for anyone who feels they would be damaged by registration of the mark to oppose it. Opposition proceedings are held before the Trademark Trial and Appeal Board (TTAB). The TTAB also handles appeals from the PTO's denials of registration. Appeals from the TTAB can go to the Federal Circuit (for a direct appeal) or to a federal district court (for a de novo review).

After registration, trademark rights last for as long as a mark is in use, as long as the trademark owner submits the required recurring paperwork and fees. (Trademark maintenance documentation is first due between 5 and 6 years after registration, and then every 10 years after registration.) However, registered marks may be subject to cancellation proceedings. *See* 15 U.S.C. 1064. Among other reasons, a registration can be cancelled if the mark has become generic or functional, or if the registration was obtained contrary to certain provisions in section 1052 (discussed in Chapter 6).

Notes: International Trademark Protection

Though trademark law is territorial, both in terms of registration and enforcement, there are a number of international agreements that harmonize international trademark laws in order to facilitate more global protection. One of the main instruments is the Paris Convention for the Protection of Industrial Property or "Paris Convention" (1883). It currently has 175 signatories, including the United States. It provides for "national treatment," meaning that signatories must offer the same application process and post-registration rights to trademark owners from other contracting parties as they give to their nationals. In addition, signatories must refuse to grant national registrations to marks that are confusingly similar to well-known international marks. This keeps the door open for the global expansion of famous brands. Finally, an applicant can claim the filing date in one Paris Convention country as the priority date in all participating countries as long as the other filings occur within six months. (This is the provision that inspired the U.S. to allow intent-to-use applications.)

The Trade Related Aspects of Intellectual Property Agreement or "TRIPS Agreement" (1994) is another important international agreement that—like the Paris Convention—provides for national treatment and priority filing dates. In addition, it establishes minimum standards of protection, such as protection for geographic indications.

The Protocol Relating to the Madrid Agreement Concerning the International Registration of Marks or "Madrid Protocol" (1989) supplements the Madrid Agreement for the International Registration of Trademarks or "Madrid Agreement" (1891), and provides a mechanism for filing a single international application after securing a registration in a participating country. This saves trademark owners from filing different applications in every additional country where they seek protection. The Madrid Protocol only streamlines filing, not protection; each contracting party designated in the application can determine whether to grant protection. The U.S. did not join the Madrid Agreement until 2003 because, before the Madrid Protocol, our laws set a higher bar for trademark registration than many other countries, and the single international application disfavored U.S. trademark owners by giving foreign applicants a shortcut into the U.S. registration process.

PROBLEM 4-1

Look back at Chapter 1 and then review the contours of trademark protection as described in this chapter and in the chart on page *xii*. The goal is to see which features of trademark law mesh with the rationales and world-views described in Chapter 1.

1.) Would Cohen, quoted on the first page of this chapter, have agreed with the baseline for intellectual property set out by Brandeis, by Holmes or by Pitney? Why? Is there a tension between the "unfair competition" roots of trademark law and the theory that trademarks are intended to facilitate efficient producer-consumer information flow?

2.) This chapter argues that one particular rationale for trademark law best explains the loss of rights to a novel, invented term—Escalator, Thermos, Aspirin—through genericide. Do you agree? What other rules of trademark law are explained by the same rationale?

3.) Of the three intellectual property rights we will look at, only trademarks can (so long as continually used and renewed) last for an unlimited period of time. Why? If your answer is that the Constitution requires that copyright and patent be for limited times, why do we also find that rule in other countries not bound by the U.S. Constitution?

4.) Critics of "brand fetishism," such as Naomi Klein, author of *No Logo*, argue that we define ourselves in terms of brands (both those we accept and those we reject), that we obsess about the messages that come with these symbols and that, as a consequence, the public space for debate, self-definition and meaning is increasingly privatized. The social harms attributed to this process range from thefts or crimes of violence to acquire favored status-symbols such as branded jackets or shoes, to the claim that in turning over our visions of self to private logoed creations, we impoverish our culture and ourselves. One central thesis of this argument is that trademarks have long since left the rationale of efficient consumer information flow behind. The logo does not tell us something about the producer of the good. The logo *is* the good. The person who purchases a plain white cotton T-shirt with a large Nike swoosh is not buying the shirt. The shirt is merely the transport mechanism for the logo. Do you agree with any or all of this? What criticisms could be made of this idea? What implications does the brand fetishism critique have for trademark law and specifically for the protection of famous marks under anti-dilution law?

Note: A Trademark Law Flow Chart

On the next page you will find one of the tools we use in the book to make intellectual property law easier to understand. It is a humble one—a flow-chart. You can use it in two different ways.

First, please use it as a map of what you will be learning. The chart explains what we will be covering in each chapter and how the legal questions discussed will play a role in trademark analysis. Take the time to read it carefully and think through each stage. You will find that pays remarkable dividends. It is too easy to get buried in minutia, to forget why you are covering a particular question, or what role it plays in the larger analysis. Of course, one can hope for the 3am epiphany the morning of the test in which the structure of the whole edifice becomes clear, but we want you to have that big picture view from the beginning.

Second, you can use the chart to help you with the Problems. The casebook uses a series of practical doctrinal exercises to ensure you actually understand the material, and to give you the analytical skills you will need for real mastery. Problems will be focused on a particular issue you have just studied: "Can your client register this mark? What are the requirements for registration? What if the mark is scandalous? Or merely descriptive? Or another company has registered an identical mark to sell a completely different type of product?" The Problems are based on former exams, so they provide a useful method of review. When you are doing the Problems, the flow chart functions not just as a map but as a check-list: a structured set of questions designed to lead you through the analysis step-by-step.

The map is not the terrain. This is a single page covering hundreds of pages of material. There is much more to the analysis than it can cover. Also, this is the intro–ductory Intellectual Property course; there are many more specialized issues in trademark law that our coverage here necessarily skips over. Still, even with those limitations, we hope you will find it useful.

TRADEMARK FLOW CHART
(This is a (highly) simplified preview of what you will learn and a tool to use in the problems. Refer to it often.)

Does the plaintiff own a valid trademark? (Chapters 5 and 6)

Was the mark 1) USED IN COMMERCE 2) AS A MARK, and is it 3) DISTINCTIVE— does it identify the source of the product?

Trademarks can consist of words, logos, colors, packaging, design, and more. FUNCTIONAL product features and GENERIC terms are *never protectable*.

The "use in commerce" must be *bona fide* and sufficiently public to create an association between the mark and the product. The "use as a mark" must be as a source identifier, not merely a motto or mission statement. Some marks are considered "inherently distinctive," because they immediately signal a product's source. Others— including merely descriptive marks, colors, and product design—require "secondary meaning" before they qualify as distinctive.

Federal registration is not necessary for protection, but it does confer additional benefits.

→ **NO** →

YES

Did the defendant infringe that trademark? (Chapter 7)

Did the defendant make a USE IN COMMERCE of a similar mark in connection with goods or services, and did that use cause a LIKELIHOOD OF CONFUSION about source or sponsorship, such that consumers are likely to mistakenly associate the defendant's products with the plaintiff?

Courts use multifactor tests to determine whether there is a likelihood of consumer confusion. Key factors include the similarity of the plaintiff's and defendant's marks and the proximity of their products. Some courts expand the inquiry beyond confusion at the point of sale to encompass "initial interest" and "post-sale" confusion.

→ **NO** →

YES

Do any defenses apply? (Chapter 8)

Was the defendant's use a CLASSIC FAIR USE or a NOMINATIVE USE? Was it sufficiently PARODIC to preclude the likelihood of confusion?

Classic fair use applies when a defendant uses a term over which the plaintiff has a mark, fairly and in good faith, only to describe his own product, and *not at all to refer to the plaintiff's product*. ("Microcolor" permanent makeup.) Nominative use exists where the defendant uses the plaintiff's mark to *describe the plaintiff's product*, ("Want Prius values, but race car style? Buy a Tesla."), even if the defendant's ultimate goal is to describe his own product. Nominative uses are often for the purposes of comparison, criticism, or point of reference. They are subject to limitations based on the need and scope of use, and cannot suggest sponsorship or endorsement by the mark owner.

→ **YES** →

NO

NO TRADEMARK INFRINGEMENT

TRADEMARK INFRINGEMENT

Note about other causes of action: Chapter 7 also covers liability for *contributory infringement*— facilitating someone else's infringement. Chapter 9 covers *false advertising*—liability for false or misleading statements of fact in advertising (§ 1125(a)), *anti-dilution*—special protection for "famous" marks against dilution by "blurring" and "tarnishment" (§ 1125(c)), and *"cyberpiracy"*—remedies against the registration with "bad faith intent to profit" of domain names that are identical or confusingly similar to trademarks (§ 1125(d)).

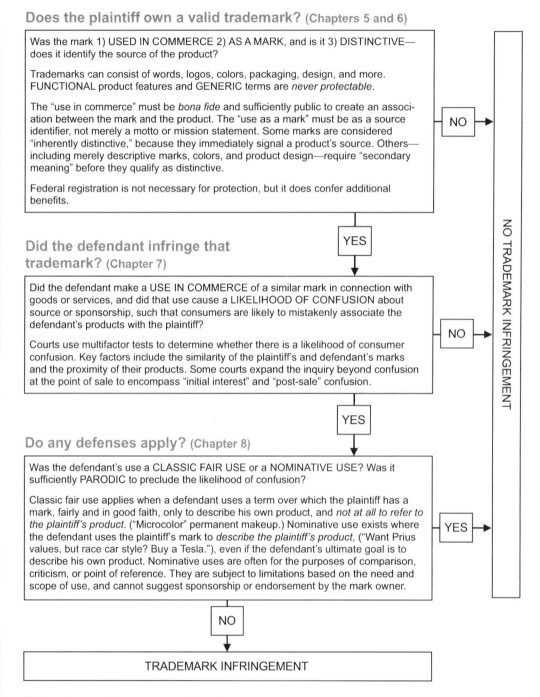

CHAPTER FIVE
Subject Matter: Requirements for Trademark Protection

1.) Use as a Mark in Commerce

For each intellectual property right that we look at in this course, the first, crucial, question is: what subject matter does it cover? Look back at the "subject matter" row in the chart in the Introduction. Notice how differently the subject matter of each right is defined, how each subject matter design tells you something about the goals that property regime was supposed to serve. Trademark subject matter is defined, in part, by the way the producer uses it and the consumer perceives it as a symbol. Copyrightable subject matter is defined, in part, in terms of qualities of the content produced – original expression, fixed in a tangible medium. Patentable subject matter is defined, in part, in terms of the relationship of the innovation to the field of technology as understood by its practitioners at the time.

How does trademark law define its subject matter? The easiest way to state the foundational requirements for both registered and unregistered trademarks is to say that we require "use as a mark in commerce." But this simple phrase conceals some complexities. What do we mean by *use in commerce*? What do we mean by use *as a mark*? It turns out that the latter phrase contains two requirements. The first focuses on the actions of the producer. The source company must actually be using the putative mark as a mark, something connected (physically where possible, but also cognitively) to a particular good or service. The key here is that the source company must be using the mark *as a mark*, as a source identifier, rather than just as a slogan, mission statement or favorite turn of phrase. The second focuses on the interaction between the consumer and the mark. It is the requirement of *distinctiveness*. Even if the producer is clearly trying to use the mark as a mark, is it capable of functioning as a mark? Can it distinguish this source for goods or services from others in the minds of consumers? Is it a source identifier or really a functional characteristic of the product? We will deal with these requirements in turn.

Use in Commerce

As always, it is good to start with some of the statutory definitions. Develop the habit of going to the definitions section of an intellectual property statute first when you seek to understand the field, not just after you think you see an ambiguity. You will not regret it.

§ 1127—Construction and definitions
In the construction of this chapter, unless the contrary is plainly apparent from the context: . . .

. . . The word "commerce" means all commerce which may lawfully be regulated by Congress. . . .

. . . The term "use in commerce" means the bona fide use of a mark in the ordinary course of trade, and not made merely to reserve a right in a mark. For purposes of this chapter, a mark shall be deemed to be in use in commerce—

(1) on goods when—

> (A) it is placed in any manner on the goods or their containers or the displays associated therewith or on the tags or labels affixed thereto, or if the nature of the goods makes such placement impracticable, then on documents associated with the goods or their sale, and
>
> (B) the goods are sold or transported in commerce, and
>
> (2) on services when it is used or displayed in the sale or advertising of services and the services are rendered in commerce, or the services are rendered in more than one State or in the United States and a foreign country and the person rendering the services is engaged in commerce in connection with the services.

Notice how the first definition of "commerce" above is very broad. If commerce is anything that Congress can regulate under the Commerce Clause then almost anything could be commerce. Even after *Lopez* and *Morrison,* the Federal government's ability to regulate actual economic activity is a sweeping one. Then notice how the second clause quoted, defining *use* in commerce, is narrower.

The following cases and materials will explore how broadly or narrowly the Federal system defines "use in commerce." One note before we begin. We are considering "use in commerce" as a requirement for trademark protection. But "use in commerce" also plays another role—as one of the requirements for *infringement*. We will come back to that requirement in the section of the casebook on infringement—to infringe, I must be using your mark in commerce. Should the definition of "use in commerce" required to get a mark be the same as that required to infringe it? We will return to that question later.

Use in Commerce: Free and Open Source Software

The following case deals with whether or not free distribution of an open source email program on the internet constituted use in commerce. The software was offered under the GNU "General Public License" or "GPL" which we will consider later in the course. The GPL gives users the rights freely to copy and to modify the program, but if they redistribute modified versions of the program, they must do so under the same license—preserving the open qualities of the program for future users. Could the developer of the open source software called Coolmail, distributed freely online, claim a trademark over it? Was this a use in commerce?

Planetary Motion, Inc. v. Techsplosion, Inc.
261 F.3d 1188 (11th Cir. 2001)

RESTANI, Judge.

. . .

Under the Lanham Act, the term "use in commerce" is defined in relevant part as follows:

> the bona fide use of a mark in the ordinary course of trade, and not made merely to reserve a right in a mark. . . . [A] mark shall be deemed to be in use in commerce . . . on goods when (A) it is placed in any manner on the goods or their containers or the displays associated therewith or on the tags or labels affixed thereto, or if the nature of the goods makes such

placement impracticable, then on documents associated with the goods
or their sale, and (B) the goods are sold or transported in commerce. . . .
15 U.S.C. § 1127.

The district court found that because the statute is written in the disjunctive (i.e.,
"sale or transport"), Darrah's wide distribution of the Coolmail software over the
Internet, even absent any sales thereof, was sufficient to establish ownership rights in the
"CoolMail" mark. Appellants contend that "transport in commerce" alone—here,
Darrah's free distribution of software over the Internet "with no existing business, no
intent to form a business, and no sale under the mark"—is insufficient to create trademark
rights. Appellants' argument lacks merit.

The parties do not make clear the two different contexts in which the phrase "use in
commerce" is used. The term "use in commerce" as used in the Lanham Act "denotes Congress's authority under the Commerce Clause rather than an intent to limit the [Lanham]
Act's application to profit making activity." Because Congress's authority under the Commerce Clause extends to activity that "substantially affects" interstate commerce, the
Lanham Act's definition of "commerce" is concomitantly broad in scope: "all commerce
which may lawfully be regulated by Congress." Nevertheless, the use of a mark in commerce also must be sufficient to establish ownership rights for a plaintiff to recover against
subsequent users under section 43(a). The court in *Mendes* set forth a two part test to determine whether a party has established "prior use" of a mark sufficient to establish ownership:

> [E]vidence showing, first, adoption, and, second, use in a way sufficiently
> public to identify or distinguish the marked goods in an appropriate
> segment of the public mind as those of the adopter of the mark, is
> competent to establish ownership, even without evidence of actual sales.

Under the "totality of circumstances" analysis, a party may establish "use in
commerce" even in the absence of sales. Similarly, not every transport of a good is
sufficient to establish ownership rights in a mark. To warrant protection, use of a mark
"need not have gained wide public recognition," but "[s]ecret, undisclosed internal
shipments are generally inadequate." In general, uses that are de minimis may not
establish trademark ownership rights.

We find that, under these principles, Darrah's activities under the "Coolmail" mark
constitute a "use in commerce" sufficiently public to create ownership rights in the mark.
First, the distribution was widespread, and there is evidence that members of the targeted
public actually associated the mark Coolmail with the Software to which it was affixed.
Darrah made the software available not merely to a discrete or select group (such as
friends and acquaintances, or at a trade show with limited attendance), but to numerous
end-users via the Internet. Third, the mark served to identify the source of the Software.
The "Coolmail" mark appeared in the subject field and in the text of the announcement
accompanying each release of the Software, thereby distinguishing the Software from
other programs that might perform similar functions available on the Internet or sold in
software compilations. The announcements also apparently indicated that Darrah was the
"Author/Maintainer of Coolmail" and included his e-mail address. The user manual also
indicated that the Software was named "Coolmail."

[S]oftware is commonly distributed without charge under a GNU General Public
License. The sufficiency of use should be determined according to the customary
practices of a particular industry. That the Software had been distributed pursuant to a
GNU General Public License does not defeat trademark ownership, nor does this in any
way compel a finding that Darrah abandoned his rights in trademark. Appellants
misconstrue the function of a GNU General Public License. Software distributed

pursuant to such a license is not necessarily ceded to the public domain and the licensor purports to retain ownership rights, which may or may not include rights to a mark.

Appellants also rely on *DeCosta v. Columbia Broad. Sys.* (1st Cir. 1975), to argue that Darrah is an eleemosynary individual and therefore unworthy of protection under unfair competition laws. The *DeCosta* court did not hold that the absence of a profit-oriented enterprise renders one an eleemosynary individual, nor did it hold that such individuals categorically are denied protection. Rather, the *DeCosta* court expressed "misgivings" of extending common law unfair competition protection, clearly available to eleemosynary organizations, to eleemosynary individuals. The court's reluctance to extend protection to eleemosynary individuals was based on an apparent difficulty in establishing a line of demarcation between those eleemosynary individuals engaged in commerce and those that are not. But as the sufficiency of use to establish trademark ownership is inherently fact-driven, the court need not have based its decision on such a consideration. Common law unfair competition protection extends to non-profit organizations because they nonetheless engage in competition with other organizations. *See Girls Clubs of Am., Inc. v. Boys Clubs of Am., Inc.* (2d Cir. 1988). Thus, an eleemosynary individual that uses a mark in connection with a good or service may nonetheless acquire ownership rights in the mark if there is sufficient evidence of competitive activity.

Here, Darrah's activities bear elements of competition, notwithstanding his lack of an immediate profit-motive. By developing and distributing software under a particular mark, and taking steps to avoid ceding the Software to the public domain, Darrah made efforts to retain ownership rights in his Software and to ensure that his Software would be distinguishable from other developers who may have distributed similar or related Software. Competitive activity need not be fueled solely by a desire for direct monetary gain. Darrah derived value from the distribution because he was able to improve his Software based on suggestions sent by end-users. Just as any other consumers, these end-users discriminate among and share information on available software. It is logical that as the Software improved, more end-users used his Software, thereby increasing Darrah's recognition in his profession and the likelihood that the Software would be improved even further.

In light of the foregoing, the use of the mark in connection with the Software constitutes significant and substantial public exposure of a mark sufficient to have created an association in the mind of public.

Questions:

1.) Many of the virtual "goods" you receive online—apps, email programs, downloaded browsers—are distributed without charge. Of that group, a subset is not even "advertising supported," they are simply distributed for the use of others. Some of them are also "free" in the larger GPL sense that users are permitted to modify and redistribute them. How does *Planetary Motion* apply the requirement of use in commerce to such activities? Do you agree?

2.) Much of the court's analysis focuses on whether a widespread association in the mind of the public is created. Why? Does this collapse the "use in commerce" requirement into the "use as a mark" requirement, the requirement of cognitive association between the good and the mark?

3.) What are the benefits of describing "use in commerce" so broadly? What are the potential harms? Does your listing of the potential harms depend on whether the same definition of "use in commerce" is used in both establishing and infringing a trademark?

4.) One of the arguments used against Darrah was that he was an individual engaged in eleemosynary (or charitable) activity, and therefore that his use was not a use in commerce. The court noted that charitable or non-profit *organizations* were routinely granted trademarks—presumably on the ground that this constituted "commerce" that Congress could regulate. But it also felt that non-profit individuals could still acquire marks if there were suitable evidence of competitive activity. Why should we care about "competitive activity" when it comes to granting charitable or non-profit organizations or individuals trademark rights? Because of Justice Pitney's vision of unfair competition—the danger that others will benefit from your labor in doing good, perhaps being able to raise funds for their charity because of goodwill you have generated? Because it means that trademarks are still fulfilling a function of efficiently communicating with the consumer—or in this case the donor? If I want to give to the Red Cross or Amnesty International or Occupy Wall St, does it help me that those organizations can get trademarks?

Use in commerce was only the first requirement for trademark protection (both for registration and for common law protection). The second is use *as a mark*, a concept that requires us to analyze both whether the mark is actually being used by the producer to identify itself as the source of a product, and whether it is distinctive enough to do so.

2.) Use as a Mark: Source Identification Function

a.) Actions of the Source

MicroStrategy Inc. v. Motorola, Inc.
245 F.3d 335 (4th Cir. 2001)

DIANA GRIBBON MOTZ, Circuit Judge.

. . . In June 2000, Motorola held a business summit of its marketing officers to determine how to market more effectively its services and products on a worldwide basis. The company decided to develop a new brand, which would cut across its various business interests, to establish a more cohesive corporate identity. In early July, Motorola contacted three advertising agencies, inviting each to compete in creating this new brand. The company met with all three agencies during the week of August 7, 2000. One agency, Ogilvy & Mather, suggested the use of "Intelligence Everywhere" as a trademark and global brand for Motorola products. Ogilvy & Mather also represented that its attorneys had conducted a trademark search for "Intelligence Everywhere," which revealed no conflicting use of the phrase as a trademark.

Motorola selected Ogilvy & Mather as its agency and began its normal procedures for clearing "Intelligence Everywhere" as a trademark. In-house trademark counsel for Motorola performed and commissioned various trademark searches for "Intelligence Everywhere" and turned up no conflicting trademark uses of the phrase. On October 5, 2000, in-house counsel informed Motorola management that no conflicting marks had been found and that the phrase was available for use as a mark in the United States and throughout the world. However, in-house counsel also informed Motorola management that a Canadian company, Cel Corporation, had registered the domain name "intelligenceeverywhere.com" and further investigation revealed that Cel might be using the name as a trademark on some products. A month later, Motorola obtained Cel's rights to "Intelligence Everywhere."

On October 19, 2000, Motorola filed an intent-to-use application with the United States Patent and Trademark Office for the registration of the trademark "Intelligence Everywhere," indicating its intent to use this mark on a vast array of its products and services. On December 10, 2000, Motorola registered the domain name "intelligenceeverywhere.com" with Network Solutions, Inc. in Herndon, Virginia.

On January 8, 2001, MicroStrategy, a producer of communication software, notified Motorola that MicroStrategy had been using "Intelligence Everywhere" as a trademark since "at least as early as 1998." MicroStrategy further stated that the mark had obtained common law protection, and that Motorola's intended use of the mark would constitute unlawful infringement. Motorola responded by expressing its belief that its use of the mark would not violate state or federal law and its intent to continue using the mark. MicroStrategy then submitted its own application to the United States Patent and Trademark Office seeking to register the trademark, "Intelligence Everywhere."

On February 13, 2001, MicroStrategy filed this action in the United States District Court for the Eastern District of Virginia, raising claims of trademark infringement, trademark dilution, and cybersquatting. On February 23, 2001, the district court heard oral argument and denied the motion for a preliminary injunction. MicroStrategy then moved this court for expedited consideration of that appeal. We granted the request and, after receiving briefs from the parties, heard oral argument on the matter on March 15, 2001. Immediately following argument, we issued a written order, which affirmed the district court's judgment denying the injunction. We explain here our reasons for that order. . . .[3]

. . . [W]e turn to the question of whether MicroStrategy has demonstrated substantial likelihood of success on the merits in its trademark infringement claim. For a plaintiff to prevail on a claim of trademark infringement, the plaintiff must first and most fundamentally prove that it has a valid and protectable mark. The district court held that MicroStrategy had failed to show a likelihood of success on this critical, initial burden. The court reasoned that although the record demonstrated that MicroStrategy had registered approximately 50 marks, it failed to register "Intelligence Everywhere" as a mark and, therefore, did not qualify for protection under 15 U.S.C. § 1114(1). With

---

[3] Although MicroStrategy makes only the general argument noted in text with respect to irreparable harm, Motorola has offered evidence detailing the particulars of the harm it would suffer if a preliminary injunction was granted. For example, Motorola has submitted affidavits explaining that it has previewed the "Intelligence Everywhere" mark to its "key customers," and has told those customers that the mark would be the basis of a "joint co-marketing and advertising campaign with Motorola," to be launched the week of March 19, 2001 to coincide with three international technology trade shows. An injunction would assertedly cause Motorola incalculable harm to its "reputation and good will within the industry" and "negatively impact key business ventures." Motorola has submitted evidence as to print and television advertisements, new packaging, and website redesign—all featuring the "Intelligence Everywhere" mark—that it has developed for the same mid-March campaign to accompany the three trade shows. The company has also outlined its financial investment in developing the "Intelligence Everywhere" mark, which as of February 20, 2001 totaled more than $24 million. Undoubtedly, Motorola incurred some of these expenses after it received notification of MicroStrategy's claim in January 2001, but not even MicroStrategy contends that Motorola had not spent substantial sums on its global campaign prior to any notice from MicroStrategy. Moreover, the record clearly demonstrates that, after conducting an extensive trademark search and carefully evaluating MicroStrategy's claims, Motorola believed that MicroStrategy had no valid claim to the "Intelligence Everywhere" mark. It seems entirely reasonable for Motorola, considering its significant sunk costs, to continue preparations for its campaign in face of what it viewed as a meritless claim. The dissent's contrary contention, that Motorola acted in bad faith, assumes that MicroStrategy's claim to the mark was not only valid, but clearly valid; to adopt this view is to have already adjudicated MicroStrategy's ownership of the mark in its favor. Not only is this an inappropriate starting place, but, as we explain above, an insupportable conclusion. . . .

respect to MicroStrategy's claim under the common law of Virginia, the court concluded that "a careful review" of the record did "not reveal" that MicroStrategy used the term "Intelligence Everywhere" to "identif[y] MicroStrategy as a source of goods or services."

Of course, as MicroStrategy points out, a mark need not be registered to garner federal trademark protection. Rather, "it is common ground that § 43(a) of the Lanham Act, 15 U.S.C. § 1125 protects qualifying unregistered trademarks." *Two Pesos, Inc. v. Taco Cabana, Inc.* (1992). But § 43(a) of the Lanham Act, like Virginia common law, does require that in order to obtain trademark protection "a designation must be proven to perform the job of identification: to identify one source and distinguish it from other sources. . . . Not every single word [or] phrase . . . that appears on a label or in an advertisement qualifies as a protectable mark." If a purported mark fails to identify its source, it is not protectable—under state or federal law. See also 15 U.S.C. § 1127 (1994) ("'trademark' includes any word, name, symbol, or device, or any combination thereof . . . used by a person . . . to identify and distinguish his or her goods"). As the Sixth Circuit recently put it, "a plaintiff must show that it has actually used the designation at issue as a trademark; thus the designation or phrase must be used to 'perform[]' the trademark function of identifying the source of the merchandise to the customers." *Rock and Roll Hall of Fame v. Gentile Prods.* (6th Cir. 1998).

After careful examination of the 252 pages of MicroStrategy documents that the company has submitted in support of its motion for preliminary injunction, we agree with the district court: MicroStrategy has failed to demonstrate that it has likely used "Intelligence Everywhere" to identify MicroStrategy as the source of its goods or services.

MicroStrategy has offered 24 documents dating from March 1999 through early 2001, in which it has used the term "Intelligence Everywhere." These include two annual reports, several press releases, brochures, sales presentations, a product manual, a business card, and newspaper articles. Although most of these documents contain several pages of densely printed material and some are quite lengthy, typically each refers only once to "Intelligence Everywhere," and that reference follows no particular design or sequence, i.e., sometimes it's on the cover, sometimes not, most often "Intelligence Everywhere" appears in the midst of text. Use of a trademark to identify goods and services and distinguish them from those of others "does not contemplate that the public will be required or expected to browse through a group of words, or scan an entire page in order to decide that a particular word, separated from its context, may or may not be intended, or may or may not serve to identify the product." Yet that is precisely the sort of examination one is forced to employ even to find the term "Intelligence Everywhere" in many of MicroStrategy's materials.

Moreover, MicroStrategy has not used any "constant pattern" or design to highlight "Intelligence Everywhere." A trademark need not be "particularly large in size or appear in any particular position on the goods, but it must be used in such a manner that its nature and function are readily apparent and recognizable without extended analysis or research and certainly without legal opinion." Unlike certain MicroStrategy trademarks, e.g., "Intelligent E-Business," MicroStrategy has not consistently placed "Intelligence Everywhere" on a particular part of the page, or in a particular type, or labeled it with "TM," or consistently used a distinctive font, color, typeset or any other method that makes "its nature and function readily apparent and recognizable without extended analysis." . . .

On its business card and elsewhere, MicroStrategy characterizes "Intelligence Everywhere" as the company "mission," "vision," "effort," "motto," or "dream." Although in the proper context, a mission statement, like a slogan, can serve as a trademark, a company mission statement or slogan is certainly not by definition a trademark. Rather, mission statements, like "[s]logans often appear in such a context that they do not identify and distinguish the source of goods or services. In such cases, they are neither protectable nor registrable as trademarks." So it is here. MicroStrategy has not demonstrated that it has used the mission statement to identify and distinguish the source of its products or services. If anything, the phrase has been used to advertise MicroStrategy's goods, without identifying the source of those goods. Unless used in a context whereby they take on a dual function, advertisements are not trademarks. . . .

For these reasons, MicroStrategy has at this juncture utterly failed to provide a basis for a court to find the probability of its trademark usage, let alone trademark infringement by Motorola. Rather, MicroStrategy has presented a record of limited, sporadic, and inconsistent use of the phrase "Intelligence Everywhere." Obviously, this does not constitute "a clear and strong case" of likelihood of success on the merits. Of course, MicroStrategy may yet prevail on its infringement claim at trial. But the company has not demonstrated that this is likely, let alone that the district court abused its discretion in refusing to grant the requested preliminary injunction. The judgment of the district court is therefore *AFFIRMED*.

NIEMEYER Circuit Judge, dissenting. . . .[3]

. . . [W]hile MicroStrategy has not consistently used the mark in all of its corporate documents, the record certainly does reflect that MicroStrategy has used the mark consistently as a trademark with respect to its "Broadcaster" software. On the cover of the software user's manual, which is distributed with the software, the mark is set out in prominent, highlighted text. Moreover, every MicroStrategy business card features the mark, set off with quotation marks, in initial capital letters, with the TM signal next to it. Either of these consistent uses alone could be enough to establish the adoption of "Intelligence Everywhere" as a mark, and together, they provide MicroStrategy with considerable evidence to present at trial on the first element of its infringement claim.

If it is able to establish this element, MicroStrategy is almost certain to prevail on the other elements of its infringement claim. Despite the district court's contrary conclusion, it cannot seriously be contended that MicroStrategy's use of "Intelligence Everywhere" is descriptive rather than suggestive. The phrase does not impart information about MicroStrategy or its products directly—the hallmark of a descriptive mark—but instead "requires some operation of the imagination to connect" the meaning of the phrase to MicroStrategy and its products, the very definition of a suggestive mark. A potential customer faced solely with the slogan would be unable to describe precisely what product or services were offered by MicroStrategy, unlike in the cases of marks held to be descriptive, e.g., "After Tan post-tanning lotion, 5 Minute glue, King Size men's clothing, and the Yellow Pages telephone directory."

Because the district court applied the controlling legal standards improperly and, in addition, considered irrelevant factors in determining the relative harms to the parties, I would reverse its ruling and remand for entry of a preliminary injunction pending trial. I would also direct the district court to conduct that trial expeditiously so as to minimize any harm that might be caused by further delay. For these reasons, I respectfully dissent.

---

[3] That the district judge and two members of this court have been impressed by the amount spent on a trademark by a potential infringer, a theoretically irrelevant factor, would seem to indicate that companies wishing to escape infringement liability will best be served by heeding the advice of Martin Luther, that if you sin, "sin boldly" (*pecca fortiter*). Letter from Luther to Melanchthon (1521), in *Epistolæ* (1556). The majority's suggestion, albeit ambiguous, that "bad faith" infringement can only be proved in a case where a claim to a mark is "not only valid, but clearly valid," is simply an inaccurate statement of what is required to recover profits, actual damages, and attorney fees under 15 U.S.C. § 1117(a).

Questions:

1.) Why does the majority mention that Motorola hired Ogilvy & Mather, which conducted a trademark search, and that it purchased the rights to "Intelligence Everywhere" and "intelligenceeverywhere.com" from the Cel Corporation? Is the court merely seeking to show that Motorola acted in good faith or is it implicitly referring back to one of the functions of the trademark system?

2.) Of what relevance are the amounts of money Motorola had spent on its upcoming ad campaign? Are you persuaded by the dissent's nicely snarky invocation of Martin Luther—claiming that the majority is effectively telling those who might use the marks of others, "if you sin, sin boldly"?

b.) Nature of the Mark: Distinctiveness and Functionality

Abercrombie & Fitch Co. v. Hunting World, Inc.
537 F.2d 4 (2d Cir. 1976)

FRIENDLY, Circuit Judge.

This action in the District Court for the Southern District of New York by Abercrombie & Fitch Company (A&F), owner of well-known stores at Madison Avenue and 45th Street in New York City and seven places in other states, against Hunting World, Incorporated (HW), operator of a competing store on East 53rd Street, is for infringement of some of A&F's registered trademarks using the word 'Safari'. It has had a long and, for A&F, an unhappy history. On this appeal from a judgment which not only dismissed the complaint but canceled all of A&F's 'Safari' registrations, including several that were not in suit, we relieve A&F of some of its unhappiness but not of all.

I.

The complaint, filed in January, 1970, after describing the general nature of A&F's business, reflecting its motto "The Greatest Sporting Goods Store in the World," alleged as follows: For many years A&F has used the mark 'Safari' on articles "exclusively offered and sold by it." Since 1936 it has used the mark on a variety of men's and women's outer garments. Its United States trademark registrations include:

Trademark	Number	Issued	Goods
Safari	358,781	7/26/38	Men's and Women's outer garments, including hats.
Safari Mills	125,531	5/20/19	Cotton Piece goods.
Safari	652,098	9/24/57	Men's and Women's outer garments, including shoes.
Safari	703,279	8/23/60	Woven cloth, sporting goods, apparel, etc.

A&F has spent large sums of money in advertising and promoting products identified with its mark 'Safari' and in policing its right in the mark, including the successful conduct of trademark infringement suits. HW, the complaint continued, has engaged in the retail marketing of sporting apparel including hats and shoes, some identified by use of 'Safari' alone or by expressions such as 'Minisafari' and 'Safariland'. Continuation of HW's acts would confuse and deceive the public and impair "the distinct and unique quality of the plaintiff's trademark." A&F sought an injunction against infringement and an accounting for damages and profits.

HW filed an answer and counterclaim. This alleged, inter alia, that "the word 'safari' is an ordinary, common, descriptive, geographic, and generic word" which "is commonly used and understood by the public to mean and refer to a journey or expedition, especially for hunting or exploring in East Africa, and to the hunters, guides, men, animals, and equipment forming such an expedition" and is not subject to exclusive appropriation as a trademark. HW sought cancellation of all of A&F's registrations using the word 'Safari' on the ground that A&F had fraudulently failed to disclose the true nature of the term to the Patent Office. . . .

II.

It will be useful at the outset to restate some basic principles of trademark law, which, although they should be familiar, tend to become lost in a welter of adjectives.

The cases, and in some instances the Lanham Act, identify four different categories of terms with respect to trademark protection. Arrayed in an ascending order which roughly reflects their eligibility to trademark status and the degree of protection accorded, these classes are (1) generic, (2) descriptive, (3) suggestive, and (4) arbitrary or fanciful. The lines of demarcation, however, are not always bright. Moreover, the difficulties are compounded because a term that is in one category for a particular product may be in quite a different one for another, because a term may shift from one category to another in light of differences in usage through time, because a term may have one meaning to one group of users and a different one to others, and because the same term may be put to different uses with respect to a single product. In various ways, all of these complications are involved in the instant case.

A generic term is one that refers, or has come to be understood as referring, to the genus of which the particular product is a species. At common law neither those terms which were generic nor those which were merely descriptive could become valid trademarks[.] . . . While, as we shall see, the Lanham Act makes an important exception with respect to those merely descriptive terms which have acquired secondary meaning, it offers no such exception for generic marks. The Act provides for the cancellation of a registered mark if at any time it "becomes the common descriptive name of an article or substance," § 14(c). This means that even proof of secondary meaning, by virtue of which some "merely descriptive" marks may be registered, cannot transform a generic term into a subject for trademark. [N]o matter how much money and effort the user of a generic term has poured into promoting the sale of its merchandise and what success it has achieved in securing public identification, it cannot deprive competing manufacturers of the product of the right to call an article by its name. We have recently had occasion to apply this doctrine of the impossibility of achieving trademark protection for a generic term. The pervasiveness of the principle is illustrated by a series of well known cases holding that when a suggestive or fanciful term has become generic as a result of a manufacturer's own advertising efforts, trademark protection will be denied save for those markets where the term still has not become generic and a secondary meaning has been shown to continue. A term may thus be generic in one market and descriptive or suggestive or fanciful in another.

The term which is descriptive but not generic stands on a better basis. Although § 1052 forbids the registration of a mark which, when applied to the goods of the applicant, is "merely descriptive," § 2(f) removes a considerable part of the sting by providing that "except as expressly excluded in paragraphs (a)–(d) of this section, nothing in this chapter shall prevent the registration of a mark used by the applicant which has become distinctive of the applicant's goods in commerce" and that the Commissioner may accept, as prima facie evidence that the mark has become distinctive, proof of substantially exclusive and continuous use of the mark applied to the applicant's goods for five years preceding the application. As indicated in the cases cited in the discussion of the unregistrability of generic terms, "common descriptive name" refers to generic terms applied to products and not to terms that are "merely descriptive." In the former case any claim to an exclusive right must be denied since this in effect would confer a monopoly not only of the mark but of the product by rendering a competitor unable effectively to name what it was endeavoring to sell. In the latter case the law strikes the balance, with respect to registration, between the hardships to a competitor in hampering the use of an appropriate word and those to the owner who, having invested money and energy to endow a word with the good will adhering to his enterprise, would be deprived of the fruits of his efforts.

The category of "suggestive" marks was spawned by the felt need to accord protection to marks that were neither exactly descriptive on the one hand nor truly fanciful on the other. Having created the category the courts have had great difficulty in defining it. Judge Learned Hand made the not very helpful statement:

> "It is quite impossible to get any rule out of the cases beyond this: That the validity of the mark ends where suggestion ends and description begins."

Another court has observed, somewhat more usefully, that:

> "A term is suggestive if it requires imagination, thought and perception to reach a conclusion as to the nature of goods. A term is descriptive if it forthwith conveys an immediate idea of the ingredients, qualities or characteristics of the goods."

Also useful is the approach taken by this court in *Aluminum Fabricating Co. of Pittsburgh v. Season-All Window Corp.*, that the reason for restricting the protection accorded descriptive terms, namely the undesirability of preventing an entrant from using a descriptive term for his product, is much less forceful when the trademark is a suggestive word since, as Judge Lumbard wrote:

> "The English language has a wealth of synonyms and related words with which to describe the qualities which manufacturers may wish to claim for their products and the ingenuity of the public relations profession supplies new words and slogans as they are needed."

If a term is suggestive, it is entitled to registration without proof of secondary meaning. Moreover, as held in the *Season-All* case, the decision of the Patent Office to register a mark without requiring proof of secondary meaning affords a rebuttable presumption that the mark is suggestive or arbitrary or fanciful rather than merely descriptive.

It need hardly be added that fanciful or arbitrary terms enjoy all the rights accorded to suggestive terms as marks—without the need of debating whether the term is "merely descriptive" and with ease of establishing infringement.

In the light of these principles we must proceed to a decision of this case.

III.

We turn first to an analysis of A&F's trademarks to determine the scope of protection to which they are entitled. We have reached the following conclusions: (1) applied to specific types of clothing 'safari' has become a generic term and 'minisafari' may be used for a smaller brim hat; (2) 'safari' has not, however, become a generic term for boots or shoes; it is either "suggestive" or "merely descriptive" and is a valid trademark even if "merely descriptive" since it has become incontestable under the Lanham Act; but (3) in light of the justified finding below that 'Camel Safari,' 'Hippo Safari' and 'Safari Chukka' were devoted by HW to a purely descriptive use on its boots, HW has a defense against a charge of infringement with respect to these on the basis of "fair use." We now discuss how we have reached these conclusions.

It is common ground that A&F could not apply 'Safari' as a trademark for an expedition into the African wilderness. This would be a clear example of the use of 'Safari' as a generic term. What is perhaps less obvious is that a word may have more than one generic use. The word 'Safari' has become part of a family of generic terms which, although deriving no doubt from the original use of the word and reminiscent of its milieu, have come to be understood not as having to do with hunting in Africa, but as terms within the language referring to contemporary American fashion apparel. These terms name the components of the safari outfit well-known to the clothing industry and its customers: the 'Safari hat,' a broad flat-brimmed hat with a single, large band; the 'Safari jacket,' a belted bush jacket with patch pockets and a buttoned shoulder loop; when the jacket is accompanied by pants, the combination is called the 'Safari suit.' Typically these items are khaki-colored.

This outfit, and its components, were doubtless what Judge Ryan had in mind when he found that "the word 'safari' in connection with wearing apparel is widely used by the general public and people in the trade." The record abundantly supports the conclusion that many stores have advertised these items despite A&F's attempts to police its mark. In contrast, a search of the voluminous exhibits fails to disclose a single example of the use of 'Safari,' by anyone other than A&F and HW, on merchandise for which A&F has registered 'Safari' except for the safari outfit and its components as described above.

What has been thus far established suffices to support the dismissal of the complaint with respect to many of the uses of 'Safari' by HW. Describing a publication as a "Safariland Newsletter" containing bulletins as to safari activity in Africa, was clearly a generic use which is nonenjoinable, see *CES Publishing Co. v. St. Regis Publications, Inc.* A&F also was not entitled to an injunction against HW's use of the word in advertising goods of the kind included in the safari outfit as described above. And if HW may advertise a hat of the kind worn on safaris as a safari hat, it may also advertise a similar hat with a smaller brim as a minisafari. Although the issue may be somewhat closer, the principle against giving trademark protection to a generic term also sustains the denial of an injunction against HW's use of 'Safariland' as a name of a portion of its store devoted at least in part to the sale of clothing as to which the term 'Safari' has become generic.

A&F stands on stronger ground with respect to HW's use of 'Camel Safari,' 'Hippo Safari' and Chukka 'Safari' as names for boots imported from Africa. As already indicated, there is no evidence that 'Safari' has become a generic term for boots. Since, as will appear, A&F's registration of 'Safari' for use on its shoes has become incontestable, it is immaterial (save for HW's contention of fraud which is later rejected) whether A&F's use of 'Safari' for boots was suggestive or "merely descriptive."

HW contends, however, that even if 'Safari' is a valid trademark for boots, it is entitled to the defense of "fair use" within § 33(b)(4) of the Lanham Act, 15 U.S.C. § 1115(b)(4). That section offers such a defense even as against marks that have become incontestable when the term charged to be an infringement is not used as a trademark "and is used fairly and in good faith only to describe to users the goods and services of such party, or their geographic origin."

Here, Lee Expeditions, Ltd., the parent company of HW, has been primarily engaged in arranging safaris to Africa since 1959; Robert Lee, the president of both companies, is the author of a book published in 1959 entitled "Safari Today—The Modern Safari

Handbook" and has, since 1961, booked persons on safaris as well as purchased safari clothing in Africa for resale in America. These facts suffice to establish, absent a contrary showing, that defendant's use of 'Safari' with respect to boots was made in the context of hunting and traveling expeditions and not as an attempt to garner A&F's good will. . . . When a plaintiff has chosen a mark with some descriptive qualities, he cannot altogether exclude some kinds of competing uses even when the mark is properly on the register. We do not have here a situation similar to those in *Venetianaire* and *Feathercombs, Inc.*, in both of which we rejected "fair use" defenses, wherein an assertedly descriptive use was found to have been in a trademark sense. It is significant that HW did not use 'Safari' alone on its shoes, as it would doubtless have done if confusion had been intended.

We thus hold that the district court was correct in dismissing the complaint.

IV.

We find much greater difficulty in the court's broad invalidation of A&F's trademark registrations. Section 37 of the Lanham Act, 15 U.S.C. § 1119, provides authority for the court to cancel those registrations of any party to an action involving a registered mark. The cases cited above establish that when a term becomes the generic name of the product to which it is applied, grounds for cancellation exist. . . . [C]ancellation may be decreed at any time if the registered mark has become "the common descriptive name of an article or substance." The whole of Registration No. 358,781 thus was properly canceled. With respect to Registration No. 703,279 only a part has become generic and cancellation on that ground should be correspondingly limited. . . .

. . . The generic term for A&F's 'safari cloth Bermuda shorts,' for example, is 'Bermuda shorts,' not 'safari'; indeed one would suppose this garment to be almost ideally unsuited for the forest or the jungle and there is no evidence that it has entered into the family for which 'Safari' has become a generic adjective. The same analysis holds for luggage, portable grills, and the rest of the suburban paraphernalia, from swimtrunks and raincoats to belts and scarves, included in these registrations.

So much of the judgment as dismissed the complaint is affirmed; so much of the judgment as directed cancellation of the registrations is affirmed in part and reversed in part, and the cause is remanded for the entry of a new judgment consistent with this opinion. No costs.

Zatarain's, Inc. v. Oak Grove Smokehouse, Inc.
698 F.2d 786 (5th Cir. 1983)

GOLDBERG, Circuit Judge.

This appeal of a trademark dispute presents us with a menu of edible delights sure to tempt connoisseurs of fish and fowl alike. At issue is the alleged infringement of two trademarks, "Fish-Fri" and "Chick-Fri," held by appellant Zatarain's, Inc. ("Zatarain's"). . . .

Throughout this litigation, Zatarain's has maintained that the term "Fish-Fri" is a suggestive mark automatically protected from infringing uses by virtue of its registration in 1962. Oak Grove and Visko's assert that "fish fry" is a generic term identifying a class of foodstuffs used to fry fish; alternatively, Oak Grove and Visko's argue that "fish fry" is merely descriptive of the characteristics of the product. The district court found that "Fish-Fri" was a descriptive term identifying a function of the product being sold. Having reviewed this finding under the appropriate "clearly erroneous" standard, we affirm.

We are mindful that "[t]he concept of descriptiveness must be construed rather broadly." Whenever a word or phrase conveys an immediate idea of the qualities, characteristics, effect, purpose, or ingredients of a product or service, it is classified as descriptive and cannot be claimed as an exclusive trademark. Courts and commentators have formulated a number of tests to be used in classifying a mark as descriptive.

A suitable starting place is the dictionary, for "[t]he dictionary definition of the word is an appropriate and relevant indication 'of the ordinary significance and meaning of words' to the public." Webster's Third New International Dictionary 858 (1966) lists the following definitions for the term "fish fry": "1. a picnic at which fish are caught, fried, and eaten; . . . 2. fried fish." Thus, the basic dictionary definitions of the term refer to the preparation and consumption of fried fish. This is at least preliminary evidence that the term "Fish-Fri" is descriptive of Zatarain's product in the sense that the words naturally direct attention to the purpose or function of the product.

The "imagination test" is a second standard used by the courts to identify descriptive terms. This test seeks to measure the relationship between the actual words of the mark and the product to which they are applied. If a term "requires imagination, thought and perception to reach a conclusion as to the nature of goods," it is considered a suggestive term. Alternatively, a term is descriptive if standing alone it conveys information as to the characteristics of the product. In this case, mere observation compels the conclusion that a product branded "Fish-Fri" is a prepackaged coating or batter mix applied to fish prior to cooking. The connection between this merchandise and its identifying terminology is so close and direct that even a consumer unfamiliar with the product would doubtless have an idea of its purpose or function. It simply does not require an exercise of the imagination to deduce that "Fish-Fri" is used to fry fish. Accordingly, the term "Fish-Fri" must be considered descriptive when examined under the "imagination test."

A third test used by courts and commentators to classify descriptive marks is "whether competitors would be likely to need the terms used in the trademark in describing their products." A descriptive term generally relates so closely and directly to a product or service that other merchants marketing similar goods would find the term useful in identifying their own goods. Common sense indicates that in this case merchants other than Zatarain's might find the term "fish fry" useful in describing their own particular batter mixes. While Zatarain's has argued strenuously that Visko's and Oak Grove could have chosen from dozens of other possible terms in naming their coating mix, we find this position to be without merit. As this court has held, the fact that a term is not the only or even the most common name for a product is not determinative, for there is no legal foundation that a product can be described in only one fashion. There are many edible fish in the sea, and as many ways to prepare them as there are varieties to be prepared. Even piscatorial gastronomes would agree, however, that frying is a form of preparation accepted virtually around the world, at restaurants starred and unstarred. The paucity of synonyms for the words "fish" and "fry" suggests that a merchant whose batter mix is specially spiced for frying fish is likely to find "fish fry" a useful term for describing his product.

A final barometer of the descriptiveness of a particular term examines the extent to which a term actually has been used by others marketing a similar service or product. This final test is closely related to the question whether competitors are likely to find a mark useful in describing their products. As noted above, a number of companies other than Zatarain's have chosen the word combination "fish fry" to identify their batter mixes. Arnaud's product, "Oyster Shrimp and Fish Fry," has been in competition with Zatarain's "Fish-Fri" for some ten to twenty years. When companies from A to Z, from

Arnaud to Zatarain's, select the same term to describe their similar products, the term in question is most likely a descriptive one.

The correct categorization of a given term is a factual issue; consequently, we review the district court's findings under the "clearly erroneous" standard of Fed.R.Civ.P. 52. The district court in this case found that Zatarain's trademark "Fish-Fri" was descriptive of the function of the product being sold. Having applied the four prevailing tests of descriptiveness to the term "Fish-Fri," we are convinced that the district court's judgment in this matter is not only not clearly erroneous, but clearly correct.

2. Secondary Meaning

Descriptive terms are not protectable by trademark absent a showing of secondary meaning in the minds of the consuming public. To prevail in its trademark infringement action, therefore, Zatarain's must prove that its mark "Fish-Fri" has acquired a secondary meaning and thus warrants trademark protection. The district court found that Zatarain's evidence established a secondary meaning for the term "Fish-Fri" in the New Orleans area. We affirm.

The existence of secondary meaning presents a question for the trier of fact, and a district court's finding on the issue will not be disturbed unless clearly erroneous. The burden of proof rests with the party seeking to establish legal protection for the mark— the plaintiff in an infringement suit. The evidentiary burden necessary to establish secondary meaning for a descriptive term is substantial.

In assessing a claim of secondary meaning, the major inquiry is the consumer's attitude toward the mark. The mark must denote to the consumer "a single thing coming from a single source," to support a finding of secondary meaning. Both direct and circumstantial evidence may be relevant and persuasive on the issue.

Factors such as amount and manner of advertising, volume of sales, and length and manner of use may serve as circumstantial evidence relevant to the issue of secondary meaning. While none of these factors alone will prove secondary meaning, in combination they may establish the necessary link in the minds of consumers between a product and its source. It must be remembered, however, that "the question is not the extent of the promotional efforts, but their effectiveness in altering the meaning of [the term] to the consuming public."

Since 1950, Zatarain's and its predecessor have continuously used the term "Fish-Fri" to identify this particular batter mix. Through the expenditure of over $400,000 for advertising during the period from 1976 through 1981, Zatarain's has promoted its name and its product to the buying public. Sales of twelve-ounce boxes of "Fish-Fri" increased from 37,265 cases in 1969 to 59,439 cases in 1979. From 1964 through 1979, Zatarain's sold a total of 916,385 cases of "Fish-Fri." The district court considered this circumstantial evidence of secondary meaning to weigh heavily in Zatarain's favor.

In addition to these circumstantial factors, Zatarain's introduced at trial two surveys conducted by its expert witness, Allen Rosenzweig. In one survey, telephone interviewers questioned 100 women in the New Orleans area who fry fish or other seafood three or more times per month. Of the women surveyed, twenty-three percent specified Zatarain's "Fish-Fri" as a product they "would buy at the grocery to use as a coating" or a "product on the market that is especially made for frying fish." In a similar survey conducted in person at a New Orleans area mall, twenty-eight of the 100 respondents answered "Zatarain's 'Fish-Fri'" to the same questions.

The authorities are in agreement that survey evidence is the most direct and persuasive way of establishing secondary meaning. The district court believed that the survey evidence produced by Zatarain's, when coupled with the circumstantial evidence of advertising and usage, tipped the scales in favor of a finding of secondary meaning. Were we considering the question of secondary meaning de novo, we might reach a different conclusion than did the district court, for the issue is close. Mindful, however, that there is evidence in the record to support the finding below, we cannot say that the district court's conclusion was clearly erroneous. Accordingly, the finding of secondary meaning in the New Orleans area for Zatarain's descriptive term "Fish-Fri" must be affirmed. . . .

• • • • • • • • • •

Note: The Spectrum of Distinctiveness

As *Abercrombie* explains, in order for a mark to be registrable, it must be distinctive. It lays out four categories of marks, from strongest to weakest. Only the first two are inherently distinctive.

1.) **Fanciful or arbitrary** marks are protectable. Fanciful marks are invented words such as Kodak or Pantene. (This category can also include obsolete or scientific terms that are unfamiliar to the ordinary consumer.) Arbitrary marks are existing words or names that have no relationship to the product, such as "Apple" for computers, or "Starbucks" for coffee. (Starbuck was the mate on the *Pequod*, the whaler in the novel Moby Dick.)

2.) **Suggestive** marks are also protectable. They suggest—but do not directly describe— a quality or characteristic of the underlying product. Connecting the mark with the product requires some cognitive or imaginative effort. Examples of suggestive marks provided by the PTO are "Quick N' Neat" for piecrust (do you agree?) and "Glance-A-Day" for calendars.

3.) **Descriptive** marks are not protectable unless they acquire distinctiveness, because granting exclusive rights over mere descriptions would impede the ability of others to describe similar items. Building upon the PTO's examples above, "Flaky Round Piecrust" for piecrust or "365-Day Calendar" for calendars would be merely descriptive. As you may gather from these examples, however, the line between suggestive and descriptive can be difficult to draw. *Zatarain's* usefully lays out some guidelines for doing so.

A descriptive mark can be eligible for protection if it acquires distinctiveness through "secondary meaning." This occurs when the consuming public connects the mark with the source of the product, rather than simply with the product itself. An example of a descriptive mark that has acquired secondary meaning is "Holiday Inn."

While merely descriptive marks are not eligible for registration on the main trademark register, which is called the "Principal Register," they can be registered on the "Supplemental Register" if they are used in commerce and capable of acquiring distinctiveness. Unlike the Principal Register, the Supplemental Register does not convey the presumption of validity, constructive notice of ownership, or right to enjoin others from using the mark. However, it does offer actual notice and the right to use the ® symbol, and prevent later registration of confusingly similar marks. The PTO's normal practice is to assume that marks gain secondary meaning after five years on the Supplemental Register, at which point they become eligible for the Principal Register.

4.) **Generic** terms for products are never registrable under the Lanham Act. The public retains the right to use these basic terms for goods and services. "Apple" for apples or "Hammer" for hammers would be generic. Over time, some arbitrary marks become so widely used to describe particular products that they become generic words (this is referred to as genericity or genericide)—examples include "Escalator" and "THERMOS."

5.) In June 2020, the Supreme Court decided *USPTO v. Booking.com*. Before this case, the PTO and courts had followed the general rule that the combination of a generic word and ".com" is still generic: "mattress.com" and "lawyers.com" were just as generic as "mattress" and "lawyers" when used in connection with mattresses and legal services. The Supreme Court rejected this *per se* rule, which had led the PTO to refuse registration for "booking.com" because it was generic for online hotel-reservation services. As a result, "booking.com" – a composite of two generic terms, "booking" and ".com" – could be descriptive, and protectable with acquired distinctiveness. The Court reasoned that an unyielding rule that disregards *consumer perception* is incompatible with the principles of trademark law. The protectability of "generic.com" turns on its meaning to consumers: "While we reject the rule proffered by the PTO that 'generic.com' terms are generic names, we do not embrace a rule automatically classifying such terms as nongeneric. Whether any given 'generic.com' term is generic, we hold, depends on whether consumers in fact perceive that term as the name of a class or, instead, as a term capable of distinguishing among members of the class." The Court distinguished "generic.com" from "generic company," and the rule that adding "company" to a generic term does not confer trademark eligibility. Adding ".com" to a generic term was different, the Court explained, because only one entity can occupy a particular Internet domain name at a time. Therefore, "generic.com" could "convey to consumers a source-identifying characteristic: an association with a particular website."

PROBLEM 5-1

1.) Go into your kitchen or bathroom and do a "trademark audit." List at least 10 products and classify them according to the four categories above. [Those who do not have at least 10 products in their home may be reported to the authorities for insufficient consumerism.]

2.) Find a product—in or out of your house—that a.) has the ® symbol indicating a registered mark and b.) seems descriptive. Go to the USPTO Trademark Search Page http://tmsearch.uspto.gov/ (The site is not that user-friendly, but repays with interest the time spent mastering it. Hint: click the TSDR button and the "Documents" tab to see the details.) Did the PTO agree with you? How was the mark registered?

3.) Are the following terms generic? Google? Rollerblades? (As in "I need to buy some new Rollerblades before I start practicing law in L.A.") "Scotch tape" (As in "Do you have any Scotch Tape? I need to wrap my Mother's Day present.") Kleenex? Purell? Is Uber generic for all ride share services?

• • • • • • • • • •

Note: Survey Evidence in Trademark Cases

Consumer perception is at the heart of trademark law. The cases you're currently reading focus on whether consumers will see a term or product feature as a distinctive "source-identifier." Subsequent chapters will ask the questions: Is there a likelihood of confusion? Will the defendant's mark blur the distinctiveness of a famous mark or tarnish its reputation? Did misleading advertisements materially affect purchasing decisions?

The answers to all of these lies in the mind of the relevant purchaser.

So how do we peer into the consumer's mind? One way is through surveys. You just saw an example in *Zatarain's*, where survey evidence was used to suggest that "Fish-Fri" had obtained secondary meaning in the New Orleans area. And you'll see a discussion of surveys in upcoming cases involving Levi's jeans, Starbucks, and Papa John's. Trademark litigants hire experts to design their surveys, and the methodology is contentious—parties employ different approaches that yield divergent results, and courts may disregard survey evidence on grounds of bias or other flaws, both because of the initial survey design and because of problems in the way the survey was conducted.

Compare the following methods for assessing whether "Teflon" is a generic term for non-stick coating. (These examples are based on the opposing surveys in *E. I. DuPont de Nemours & Co. v. Yoshida International, Inc.* (E.D.N.Y. 1975), the case holding that "Teflon" was not generic, and was infringed by "Eflon" for a nylon zipper. They have been simplified for purposes of comparison.) The first example uses the "Thermos" method from *American Thermos Products Co. v. Aladdin Industries, Inc.* (2d Cir. 1963) (holding that "thermos" in lower-case was generic for vacuum-insulated containers, but preserving trademark rights in capitalized "Thermos"). The second uses what became called the "Teflon" method after the *DuPont* court endorsed its approach.

#1   The "Thermos" survey method
- Respondents (in the actual case, the group conducting the survey believed the relevant group was "adult women") are asked: "Are you familiar with substances that manufacturers sometimes apply to the surfaces of certain products in order to prevent things from sticking to them?" 90% say yes.
- Those who answered "yes" are then asked: "What name or names are those substances called?" Over 80% say "Teflon." They are also asked: "What name or names would you use to describe those substances to a store clerk or friend?" Over 70% say "Teflon."

The defendant argues that this shows "Teflon" is generic.

#2   The "Teflon" survey method
- Respondents are first given this brief introduction to the difference between trademarks and generic terms: "By brand name, I mean a word like Chevrolet which is made by one company; by common name, I mean a word like automobile which is made by a number of different companies."
- Respondents are then asked whether a range of eight terms, including "Teflon," is a brand name or a common name, with the option of answering "don't know." Here are the results (the remainder in each category answered "don't know"). The plaintiff argues that the numbers below show "Teflon" is not generic.

NAME	BRAND/%	COMMON/%
STP	90	5
THERMOS	51	46
MARGARINE	9	91
TEFLON	68	31
JELLO	75	25
REFRIGERATOR	6	94
ASPIRIN	13	86
COKE	76	24

Both of these methods are accepted by courts, though the "Teflon" format is more widely accepted. *See McCarthy on Trademarks and Unfair Competition* § 12:16. (Of course, litigants will customize the general methodology to the facts at hand.) Which approach do you think is more persuasive in answering the key question in genericity cases: whether, in the mind of the consumer, the primary significance of the mark is the *producer*, or the underlying *product itself*? Look at the "Thermos" questions—if I walk into Bed, Bath and Beyond and ask for "Teflon" pans, does that tell you anything about whether I'm referring to DuPont's brand, or to non-stick coating generally? If you're representing the owner of an especially famous mark, what concerns might you have about a "Thermos" survey? As for the "Teflon" survey, the *DuPont* court opined that "the responses of the survey reveal that the public is quite good at sorting out brand names from common names." Do you agree?

Returning to one of the questions in Problem 5-1, the Ninth Circuit recently confirmed that "Google" is not generic for internet search engines. *Elliott v. Google* (9th Cir. 2017). In that case, Elliott (the challenger to the "Google" mark) used a "Thermos" survey, while Google conducted a "Teflon" survey. (Why? Do you agree with that tactical judgment by the lawyers?) The "Thermos" survey asked: "If you were going to ask a friend to search for something on the Internet, what word or phrase would you use to tell him/her what you want him/her to do?" Over half of the respondents answered by using "google" as a verb, and Elliott argued that this showed "Google" was generic, on the theory that verb use constitutes generic use. (Do you agree? The court did not, and further found that this approach failed to link the mark to the relevant good or service—"Google" for "internet search engines.") In Google's "Teflon" survey, the majority of respondents classified "Refrigerator," "Margarine," "Browser," and "Website" as common names, while the following percentages suggested strong brand recognition for "Google" and other familiar marks:

NAME	BRAND/%	COMMON/%
AMAZON	96.51	2.99
GOOGLE	93.77	5.25
YAHOO!	93.52	5.99
COKE	89.53	6.73

Do you find these results persuasive? In order to answer, would you need to know what percentage of consumers use only Google as a search engine, or would that be irrelevant? How would you design a survey to determine whether "Google" is generic? The goal of survey evidence is to replace the judge or jury's subjective hunches about trademarks with empirical evidence that goes to the source-identification function of the mark. Do you think that goal can ever be fully achieved?

• • • • • • • • • •

Abercrombie and *Zatarain's* focused on *verbal* marks. The cases that follow focus on the protectability of *non-verbal* marks such as color and trade dress (generally, product packaging or design), where *functionality* becomes an important consideration.

Qualitex Co. v. Jacobson Products Co., Inc.
514 U.S. 159 (1995)

Justice BREYER delivered the opinion of the Court.

The question in this case is whether the Lanham Trademark Act of 1946 permits the registration of a trademark that consists, purely and simply, of a color. We conclude that, sometimes, a color will meet ordinary legal trademark requirements. And, when it does so, no special legal rule prevents color alone from serving as a trademark.

I.

The case before us grows out of petitioner Qualitex Company's use (since the 1950's) of a special shade of green-gold color on the pads that it makes and sells to dry cleaning firms for use on dry cleaning presses. In 1989 respondent Jacobson Products (a Qualitex rival) began to sell its own press pads to dry cleaning firms; and it colored those pads a similar green-gold. In 1991 Qualitex registered the special green-gold color on press pads with the Patent and Trademark Office as a trademark. Qualitex subsequently added a trademark infringement count, 15 U.S.C. § 1114(1), to an unfair competition claim, § 1125(a), in a lawsuit it had already filed challenging Jacobson's use of the green-gold color.

Qualitex won the lawsuit in the District Court. But, the Court of Appeals for the Ninth Circuit set aside the judgment in Qualitex's favor on the trademark infringement claim because, in that Circuit's view, the Lanham Act does not permit Qualitex, or anyone else, to register "color alone" as a trademark.

The courts of appeals have differed as to whether or not the law recognizes the use of color alone as a trademark. Therefore, this Court granted certiorari. We now hold that there is no rule absolutely barring the use of color alone, and we reverse the judgment of the Ninth Circuit.

II.

The Lanham Act gives a seller or producer the exclusive right to "register" a trademark, 15 U.S.C. § 1052, and to prevent his or her competitors from using that trademark, § 1114(1). Both the language of the Act and the basic underlying principles of trademark law would seem to include color within the universe of things that can qualify as a trademark. The language of the Lanham Act describes that universe in the broadest of terms. It says that trademarks "includ[e] any word, name, symbol, or device, or any combination thereof." § 1127. Since human beings might use as a "symbol" or "device" almost anything at all that is capable of carrying meaning, this language, read literally, is not restrictive. The courts and the Patent and Trademark Office have authorized for use as a mark a particular shape (of a Coca-Cola bottle), a particular sound (of NBC's three chimes), and even a particular scent (of plumeria blossoms on sewing thread). If a shape, a sound, and a fragrance can act as symbols why, one might ask, can a color not do the same?

A color is also capable of satisfying the more important part of the statutory definition of a trademark, which requires that a person "us[e]" or "inten[d] to use" the mark

> "to identify and distinguish his or her goods, including a unique product,
> from those manufactured or sold by others and to indicate the source of
> the goods, even if that source is unknown." 15 U.S.C. § 1127.

True, a product's color is unlike "fanciful," "arbitrary," or "suggestive" words or designs, which almost *automatically* tell a customer that they refer to a brand. *Abercrombie & Fitch v. Hunting World* (Friendly, J.). The imaginary word "Suntost," or the words "Suntost Marmalade," on a jar of orange jam immediately would signal a brand or a product "source"; the jam's orange color does not do so. But, over time, customers may come to treat a particular color on a product or its packaging (say, a color that in context seems unusual, such as pink on a firm's insulating material or red on the head of a large industrial bolt) as signifying a brand. And, if so, that color would have come to identify and distinguish the goods—*i.e.* "to indicate" their "source"—much in the way that descriptive words on a product (say, "Trim" on nail clippers or "Car-Freshner" on deodorizer) can come to indicate a product's origin. In this circumstance, trademark law says that the word (*e.g.*, "Trim"), although not inherently distinctive, has developed "secondary meaning." Again, one might ask, if trademark law permits a descriptive word with secondary meaning to act as a mark, why would it not permit a color, under similar circumstances, to do the same?

We cannot find in the basic objectives of trademark law any obvious theoretical objection to the use of color alone as a trademark, where that color has attained "secondary meaning" and therefore identifies and distinguishes a particular brand (and thus indicates its "source"). In principle, trademark law, by preventing others from copying a source-identifying mark, "reduce[s] the customer's costs of shopping and making purchasing decisions" for it quickly and easily assures a potential customer that *this* item—the item with this mark—is made by the same producer as other similarly marked items that he or she liked (or disliked) in the past. At the same time, the law helps assure a producer that it (and not an imitating competitor) will reap the financial, reputation-related rewards associated with a desirable product. The law thereby "encourage[s] the production of quality products," and simultaneously discourages those who hope to sell inferior products by capitalizing on a consumer's inability quickly to evaluate the quality of an item offered for sale. It is the source-distinguishing ability of a mark—not its ontological status as color, shape, fragrance, word, or sign—that permits it to serve these basic purposes. See Landes & Posner, Trademark Law: An Economic Perspective, 30 J. Law & Econ. 265, 290 (1987). And, for that reason, it is difficult to find, in basic trademark objectives, a reason to disqualify absolutely the use of a color as a mark.

Neither can we find a principled objection to the use of color as a mark in the important "functionality" doctrine of trademark law. The functionality doctrine prevents trademark law, which seeks to promote competition by protecting a firm's reputation, from instead inhibiting legitimate competition by allowing a producer to control a useful product feature. It is the province of patent law, not trademark law, to encourage invention by granting inventors a monopoly over new product designs or functions for a limited time, 35 U.S.C. §§ 154, 173, after which competitors are free to use the innovation. If a product's functional features could be used as trademarks, however, a monopoly over such features could be obtained without regard to whether they qualify as patents and could be extended forever (because trademarks may be renewed in perpetuity). See *Inwood Laboratories, Inc.* (White, J., concurring in result) ("A functional characteristic is 'an important ingredient in the commercial success of the product,' and, after expiration of a patent, it is no more the property of the originator than the product itself"). Functionality doctrine therefore would require, to take an imaginary example, that even if customers have come to identify the special illumination-enhancing shape of a new patented light bulb with a particular manufacturer, the manufacturer may not use that shape as a trademark, for doing so, after the patent had expired, would impede competition—not by protecting the reputation of the original bulb maker, but by frustrating competitors' legitimate efforts to produce an equivalent illumination-enhancing bulb (trademark law cannot be used to extend monopoly over "pillow" shape of shredded wheat biscuit after the patent for that shape had expired). This Court consequently has explained that, "[i]n general terms, a product feature is functional," and cannot serve as a trademark, "if it is essential to the use or purpose of the article or if it affects the cost or quality of the article," that is, if exclusive use of the feature would put competitors at a significant non-reputation-related disadvantage. Although sometimes color plays an important role (unrelated to source identification) in making a product more desirable, sometimes it does not. And, this latter fact—the fact that sometimes color is not essential to a product's use or purpose and does not affect cost or quality—indicates that the doctrine of "functionality" does not create an absolute bar to the use of color alone as a mark.

It would seem, then, that color alone, at least sometimes, can meet the basic legal requirements for use as a trademark. It can act as a symbol that distinguishes a firm's goods and identifies their source, without serving any other significant function. See U.S. Dept. of Commerce, Patent and Trademark Office, Trademark Manual of Examining Procedure (approving trademark registration of color alone where it "has become distinctive of the applicant's goods in commerce," provided that "there is [no] competitive need for colors to remain available in the industry" and the color is not "functional"). Indeed, the District Court, in this case, entered findings (accepted by the Ninth Circuit) that show Qualitex's green-gold press pad color has met these requirements. The green-gold color acts as a symbol. Having developed secondary meaning (for customers identified the green-gold color as Qualitex's), it identifies the press pads' source. And, the green-gold color serves no other function. (Although it is important to use *some* color on press pads to avoid noticeable stains, the court found "no competitive need in the press pad industry for the green-gold color, since other colors are equally usable.") Accordingly, unless there is some special reason that convincingly militates against the use of color alone as a trademark, trademark law would protect Qualitex's use of the green-gold color on its press pads.

III.

Respondent Jacobson Products says that there are four special reasons why the law should forbid the use of color alone as a trademark. We shall explain, in turn, why we, ultimately, find them unpersuasive.

First, Jacobson says that, if the law permits the use of color as a trademark, it will produce uncertainty and unresolvable court disputes about what shades of a color a competitor may lawfully use. Because lighting (morning sun, twilight mist) will affect perceptions of protected color, competitors and courts will suffer from "shade confusion" as they try to decide whether use of a similar color on a similar product does, or does not, confuse customers and thereby infringe a trademark. Jacobson adds that the "shade confusion" problem is "more difficult" and "far different from" the "determination of the similarity of words or symbols."

We do not believe, however, that color, in this respect, is special. Courts traditionally decide quite difficult questions about whether two words or phrases or symbols are sufficiently similar, in context, to confuse buyers. They have had to compare, for example, such words as "Bonamine" and "Dramamine" (motion-sickness remedies); "Huggies" and "Dougies" (diapers); "Cheracol" and "Syrocol" (cough syrup); "Cyclone" and "Tornado" (wire fences); and "Mattres" and "1–800–Mattres" (mattress franchisor telephone numbers). Legal standards exist to guide courts in making such comparisons. We do not see why courts could not apply those standards to a color, replicating, if necessary, lighting conditions under which a colored product is normally sold. Indeed, courts already have done so in cases where a trademark consists of a color plus a design, *i.e.*, a colored symbol such as a gold stripe (around a sewer pipe), a yellow strand of wire rope, or a "brilliant yellow" band (on ampules).

Second, Jacobson argues, as have others, that colors are in limited supply. Jacobson claims that, if one of many competitors can appropriate a particular color for use as a trademark, and each competitor then tries to do the same, the supply of colors will soon be depleted. Put in its strongest form, this argument would concede that "[h]undreds of color pigments are manufactured and thousands of colors can be obtained by mixing." But, it would add that, in the context of a particular product, only some colors are usable. By the time one discards colors that, say, for reasons of customer appeal, are not usable, and adds the shades that competitors cannot use lest they risk infringing a similar, registered shade, then one is left with only a handful of possible colors. And, under these circumstances, to permit one, or a few, producers to use colors as trademarks will "deplete" the supply of usable colors to the point where a competitor's inability to find a suitable color will put that competitor at a significant disadvantage.

This argument is unpersuasive, however, largely because it relies on an occasional problem to justify a blanket prohibition. When a color serves as a mark, normally alternative colors will likely be available for similar use by others. See, e.g., *Owens-Corning* (pink insulation). Moreover, if that is not so—if a "color depletion" or "color scarcity" problem does arise—the trademark doctrine of "functionality" normally would seem available to prevent the anticompetitive consequences that Jacobson's argument posits, thereby minimizing that argument's practical force.

The functionality doctrine, as we have said, forbids the use of a product's feature as a trademark where doing so will put a competitor at a significant disadvantage because the feature is "essential to the use or purpose of the article" or "affects [its] cost or quality." *Inwood.* The functionality doctrine thus protects competitors against a disadvantage (unrelated to recognition or reputation) that trademark protection might otherwise impose, namely their inability reasonably to replicate important non-reputation-related product features.

For example, this Court has written that competitors might be free to copy the color of a medical pill where that color serves to identify the kind of medication (*e.g.*, a type of blood medicine) in addition to its source. ("[S]ome patients commingle medications in a container and rely on color to differentiate one from another"); see also J. Ginsburg, D. Goldberg, & A. Greenbaum, Trademark and Unfair Competition Law (noting that drug color cases "have more to do with public health policy" regarding generic drug substitution "than with trademark law"). And, the federal courts have demonstrated that they can apply this doctrine in a careful and reasoned manner, with sensitivity to the effect on competition. Although we need not comment on the merits of specific cases, we note that lower courts have permitted competitors to copy the green color of farm machinery (because customers wanted their farm equipment to match) and have barred the use of black as a trademark on outboard boat motors (because black has the special functional attributes of decreasing the apparent size of the motor and ensuring compatibility with many different boat colors). See *Deere & Co. v. Farmhand, Inc.*; *Brunswick Corp. v. British Seagull Ltd.*; see also *Nor-Am Chemical v. O.M. Scott & Sons Co.* (blue color of fertilizer held functional because it indicated the presence of nitrogen). The Restatement (Third) of Unfair Competition adds that, if a design's "aesthetic value" lies in its ability to "confe[r] a significant benefit that cannot practically be duplicated by the use of alternative designs," then the design is "functional." The "ultimate test of aesthetic functionality," it explains, "is whether the recognition of trademark rights would significantly hinder competition."

The upshot is that, where a color serves a significant nontrademark function—whether to distinguish a heart pill from a digestive medicine or to satisfy the "noble instinct for giving the right touch of beauty to common and necessary things," G. K. Chesterton, Simplicity and Tolstoy 61 (1912)—courts will examine whether its use as a mark would permit one competitor (or a group) to interfere with legitimate (nontrademark-related) competition through actual or potential exclusive use of an important product ingredient. That examination should not discourage firms from creating aesthetically pleasing mark designs, for it is open to their competitors to do the same. But, ordinarily, it should prevent the anticompetitive consequences of Jacobson's hypothetical "color depletion" argument, when, and if, the circumstances of a particular case threaten "color depletion."

Third, Jacobson points to many older cases—including Supreme Court cases—in support of its position. In 1878, this Court described the common-law definition of trademark rather broadly to "consist of a name, symbol, figure, letter, form, or device, if adopted and used by a manufacturer or merchant in order to designate the goods he manufactures or sells to distinguish the same from those manufactured or sold by another." Yet, in interpreting the Trademark Acts of 1881 and 1905, which retained that common-law definition, the Court questioned "[w]hether mere color can constitute a valid trade-mark," and suggested that the "product including the coloring matter is free to all who make it." Even though these statements amounted to dicta, lower courts interpreted them as forbidding protection for color alone.

These Supreme Court cases, however, interpreted trademark law as it existed *before* 1946, when Congress enacted the Lanham Act. The Lanham Act significantly changed and liberalized the common law to "dispense with mere technical prohibitions," S.Rep. No. 1333, 79th Cong., 2d Sess., 3 (1946), most notably, by permitting trademark registration of descriptive words (say, "U-Build-It" model airplanes) where they had acquired "secondary meaning." See *Abercrombie & Fitch Co.* (Friendly, J.). The Lanham Act extended protection to descriptive marks by making clear that (with certain explicit exceptions not relevant here)

> "nothing . . . shall prevent the registration of a mark used by the applicant which has become distinctive of the applicant's goods in commerce." 15 U.S.C. § 1052(f).

This language permits an ordinary word, normally used for a nontrademark purpose (e.g., description), to act as a trademark where it has gained "secondary meaning." Its logic would appear to apply to color as well. . . .

Fourth, Jacobson argues that there is no need to permit color alone to function as a trademark because a firm already may use color as part of a trademark, say, as a colored circle or colored letter or colored word, and may rely upon "trade dress" protection, under § 43(a) of the Lanham Act, if a competitor copies its color and thereby causes consumer confusion regarding the overall appearance of the competing products or their packaging, see 15 U.S.C. § 1125(a). The first part of this argument begs the question. One can understand why a firm might find it difficult to place a usable symbol or word on a product (say, a large industrial bolt that customers normally see from a distance); and, in such instances, a firm might want to use color, pure and simple, instead of color as part of a design. Neither is the second portion of the argument convincing. Trademark law helps the holder of a mark in many ways that "trade dress" protection does not. See 15 U.S.C. § 1124 (ability to prevent importation of confusingly similar goods); § 1072 (constructive notice of ownership); § 1065 (incontestable status); § 1057(b) (prima facie evidence of validity and ownership). Thus, one can easily find reasons why the law might provide trademark protection in addition to trade dress protection.

IV.

Having determined that a color may sometimes meet the basic legal requirements for use as a trademark and that respondent Jacobson's arguments do not justify a special legal rule preventing color alone from serving as a trademark (and, in light of the District Court's here undisputed findings that Qualitex's use of the green-gold color on its press pads meets the basic trademark requirements), we conclude that the Ninth Circuit erred in barring Qualitex's use of color as a trademark. For these reasons, the judgment of the Ninth Circuit is
Reversed.

Wal-Mart Stores, Inc. v. Samara Brothers, Inc.
529 U.S. 205 (2000)

Justice SCALIA delivered the opinion of the Court.

In this case, we decide under what circumstances a product's design is distinctive, and therefore protectible, in an action for infringement of unregistered trade dress under § 43(a) of the Trademark Act of 1946 (Lanham Act), 60 Stat. 441, as amended, 15 U.S.C. § 1125(a).

I

Respondent Samara Brothers, Inc., designs and manufactures children's clothing. Its primary product is a line of spring/summer one-piece seersucker outfits decorated with appliqués of hearts, flowers, fruits, and the like. A number of chain stores, including JCPenney, sell this line of clothing under contract with Samara.

Petitioner Wal-Mart Stores, Inc., is one of the nation's best known retailers, selling among other things children's clothing. In 1995, Wal-Mart contracted with one of its suppliers, Judy-Philippine, Inc., to manufacture a line of children's outfits for sale in the 1996 spring/summer season. Wal-Mart sent Judy-Philippine photographs of a number of garments from Samara's line, on which Judy-Philippine's garments were to be based; Judy-Philippine duly copied, with only minor modifications, 16 of Samara's garments, many of which contained copyrighted elements. In 1996, Wal-Mart briskly sold the so-called knockoffs, generating more than $1.15 million in gross profits. . . .

After sending cease-and-desist letters, Samara brought this action in the United States District Court

A Samara Brothers outfit purchased from JC Penney

for the Southern District of New York against Wal-Mart, Judy-Philippine, Kmart, Caldor, Hills, and Goody's for copyright infringement under federal law, consumer fraud and unfair competition under New York law, and—most relevant for our purposes—infringement of unregistered trade dress under § 43(a) of the Lanham Act, 15 U.S.C. § 1125(a). All of the defendants except Wal-Mart settled before trial.

After a weeklong trial, the jury found in favor of Samara on all of its claims. Wal-Mart then renewed a motion for judgment as a matter of law, claiming, inter alia, that there was insufficient evidence to support a conclusion that Samara's clothing designs could be legally protected as distinctive trade dress for purposes of § 43(a). The District Court denied the motion, and awarded Samara damages, interest, costs, and fees totaling almost $1.6 million, together with injunctive relief. The Second Circuit affirmed the denial of the motion for judgment as a matter of law, and we granted certiorari.

II

. . . In addition to protecting registered marks, the Lanham Act, in § 43(a), gives a producer a cause of action for the use by any person of "any word, term, name, symbol, or device, or any combination thereof . . . which . . . is likely to cause confusion . . . as to the origin, sponsorship, or approval of his or her goods. . . ." 15 U.S.C. § 1125(a). It is the latter provision that is at issue in this case.

The breadth of the definition of marks registrable under § 2, and of the confusion-producing elements recited as actionable by § 43(a), has been held to embrace not just word marks, such as "Nike," and symbol marks, such as Nike's "swoosh" symbol, but also "trade dress"—a category that originally included only the packaging, or "dressing," of a product, but in recent years has been expanded by many courts of appeals to encompass the design of a product. See, e.g., *Ashley Furniture Industries, Inc. v. Sangiacomo* (bedroom furniture); *Knitwaves, Inc. v. Lollytogs* (sweaters); *Stuart Hall Co., Inc. v. Ampad Corp.* (notebooks). These courts have assumed, often without discussion, that trade dress constitutes a "symbol" or "device" for purposes of the relevant sections, and we conclude likewise. "Since human beings might use as a 'symbol' or 'device' almost anything at all that is capable of carrying meaning, this language, read literally, is not restrictive." *Qualitex Co. v. Jacobson Products Co.* This reading of § 2 and § 43(a) is buttressed by a recently added subsection of § 43(a), § 43(a)(3), which refers specifically to "civil action[s] for trade dress infringement under this chapter for trade dress not registered on the principal register." 15 U.S.C. A. § 1125(a)(3).

The text of § 43(a) provides little guidance as to the circumstances under which unregistered trade dress may be protected. It does require that a producer show that the allegedly infringing feature is not "functional," see § 43(a)(3), and is likely to cause confusion with the product for which protection is sought, see § 43(a)(1)(A), 15 U.S.C. § 1125(a)(1)(A). Nothing in § 43(a) explicitly requires a producer to show that its trade dress is distinctive, but courts have universally imposed that requirement, since without distinctiveness the trade dress would not "cause confusion . . . as to the origin, sponsorship, or approval of [the] goods," as the section requires. Distinctiveness is, moreover, an explicit prerequisite for registration of trade dress under § 2, and "the general principles qualifying a mark for registration under § 2 of the Lanham Act are for the most part applicable in determining whether an unregistered mark is entitled to protection under § 43(a)." *Two Pesos, Inc. v. Taco Cabana, Inc.*

In evaluating the distinctiveness of a mark under § 2 (and therefore, by analogy, under § 43(a)), courts have held that a mark can be distinctive in one of two ways. First, a mark is inherently distinctive if "[its] intrinsic nature serves to identify a particular source." In the context of word marks, courts have applied the now-classic test originally formulated by Judge Friendly, in which word marks that are "arbitrary" ("Camel" cigarettes), "fanciful" ("Kodak" film), or "suggestive" ("Tide" laundry detergent) are held to be inherently distinctive. See *Abercrombie & Fitch Co. v. Hunting World, Inc.* Second, a mark has acquired distinctiveness, even if it is not inherently distinctive, if it has developed secondary meaning, which occurs when, "in the minds of the public, the primary significance of a [mark] is to identify the source of the product rather than the product itself." *Inwood Laboratories, Inc. v. Ives Laboratories, Inc.* (1982).*

The judicial differentiation between marks that are inherently distinctive and those that have developed secondary meaning has solid foundation in the statute itself. Section 2 requires that registration be granted to any trademark "by which the goods of the applicant may be distinguished from the goods of others"—subject to various limited exceptions. 15 U.S.C. § 1052. It also provides, again with limited exceptions, that "nothing in this chapter shall prevent the registration of a mark used by the applicant which has become distinctive of the applicant's goods in commerce"—that is, which is not inherently distinctive but has become so only through secondary meaning. § 2(f), 15 U.S.C. § 1052(f). Nothing in § 2, however, demands the conclusion that every category of mark necessarily includes some marks "by which the goods of the applicant may be distinguished from the goods of others" without secondary meaning—that in every category some marks are inherently distinctive.

Indeed, with respect to at least one category of mark—colors—we have held that no mark can ever be inherently distinctive. See *Qualitex*. In *Qualitex*, petitioner manufactured and sold green-gold dry-cleaning press pads. After respondent began selling pads of a similar color, petitioner brought suit under § 43(a), then added a claim under § 32 after obtaining registration for the color of its pads. We held that a color could be protected as a trademark, but only upon a showing of secondary meaning. Reasoning by analogy to the *Abercrombie & Fitch* test developed for word marks, we noted that a product's color is unlike a "fanciful," "arbitrary," or "suggestive" mark, since it does not "almost automatically tell a customer that [it] refer[s] to a brand," and does not "immediately . . . signal a brand or a product 'source.'" However, we noted that, "over time, customers may come to treat a particular color on a product or its packaging . . . as signifying a brand." Because a color, like a "descriptive" word mark, could eventually "come to indicate a product's origin," we concluded that it could be protected upon a showing of secondary meaning.

It seems to us that design, like color, is not inherently distinctive. The attribution of inherent distinctiveness to certain categories of word marks and product packaging derives from the fact that the very purpose of attaching a particular word to a product, or encasing it in a distinctive packaging, is most often to identify the source of the product. Although the words and packaging can serve subsidiary functions—a suggestive word mark (such as "Tide" for laundry detergent), for instance, may invoke positive connotations in the consumer's mind, and a garish form of packaging (such as Tide's squat, brightly decorated plastic bottles for its liquid laundry detergent) may attract an otherwise indifferent consumer's attention on a crowded store shelf—their predominant function remains source identification. Consumers are therefore predisposed to regard those symbols as indication of the producer, which is why such symbols "almost automatically tell a customer that they refer to a brand," and "immediately . . . signal a brand or a product 'source.'" And where it is not reasonable to assume consumer predisposition to take an affixed word or packaging as indication of source—where, for example, the affixed word is descriptive of the product ("Tasty" bread) or of a geographic

---

* The phrase "secondary meaning" originally arose in the context of word marks, where it served to distinguish the source-identifying meaning from the ordinary, or "primary," meaning of the word. "Secondary meaning" has since come to refer to the acquired, source-identifying meaning of a non-word mark as well. It is often a misnomer in that context, since non-word marks ordinarily have no "primary" meaning. Clarity might well be served by using the term "acquired meaning" in both the word-mark and the non-word-mark contexts—but in this opinion we follow what has become the conventional terminology.

origin ("Georgia" peaches)—inherent distinctiveness will not be found. That is why the statute generally excludes, from those word marks that can be registered as inherently distinctive, words that are "merely descriptive" of the goods. § 1052(e)(1), or "primarily geographically descriptive of them," § 1052(e). In the case of product design, as in the case of color, we think consumer predisposition to equate the feature with the source does not exist. Consumers are aware of the reality that, almost invariably, even the most unusual of product designs—such as a cocktail shaker shaped like a penguin—is intended not to identify the source, but to render the product itself more useful or more appealing.

The fact that product design almost invariably serves purposes other than source identification not only renders inherent distinctiveness problematic; it also renders application of an inherent-distinctiveness principle more harmful to other consumer interests. Consumers should not be deprived of the benefits of competition with regard to the utilitarian and esthetic purposes that product design ordinarily serves by a rule of law that facilitates plausible threats of suit against new entrants based upon alleged inherent distinctiveness. How easy it is to mount a plausible suit depends, of course, upon the clarity of the test for inherent distinctiveness, and where product design is concerned we have little confidence that a reasonably clear test can be devised. Respondent and the United States as amicus curiae urge us to adopt for product design relevant portions of the test formulated by the Court of Customs and Patent Appeals for product packaging in *Seabrook Foods v. Bar-Well Foods* (1977). That opinion, in determining the inherent distinctiveness of a product's packaging, considered, among other things, "whether it was a 'common' basic shape or design, whether it was unique or unusual in a particular field, [and] whether it was a mere refinement of a commonly-adopted and well-known form of ornamentation for a particular class of goods viewed by the public as a dress or ornamentation for the goods." Such a test would rarely provide the basis for summary disposition of an anticompetitive strike suit. Indeed, at oral argument, counsel for the United States quite understandably would not give a definitive answer as to whether the test was met in this very case, saying only that "[t]his is a very difficult case for that purpose."

It is true, of course, that the person seeking to exclude new entrants would have to establish the nonfunctionality of the design feature, see § 43(a)(3), 15 U.S.C. A. § 1125(a)(3)—a showing that may involve consideration of its esthetic appeal, see *Qualitex*. Competition is deterred, however, not merely by successful suit but by the plausible threat of successful suit, and given the unlikelihood of inherently source-identifying design, the game of allowing suit based upon alleged inherent distinctiveness seems to us not worth the candle. That is especially so since the producer can ordinarily obtain protection for a design that is inherently source identifying (if any such exists), but that does not yet have secondary meaning, by securing a design patent or a copyright for the design—as, indeed, respondent did for certain elements of the designs in this case. The availability of these other protections greatly reduces any harm to the producer that might ensue from our conclusion that a product design cannot be protected under § 43(a) without a showing of secondary meaning.

Respondent contends that our decision in *Two Pesos* forecloses a conclusion that product-design trade dress can never be inherently distinctive. In that case, we held that the trade dress of a chain of Mexican restaurants, which the plaintiff described as "a festive eating atmosphere having interior dining and patio areas decorated with artifacts, bright colors, paintings and murals," could be protected under § 43(a) without a showing of secondary meaning. *Two Pesos* unquestionably establishes the legal principle that trade dress can be inherently distinctive, but it does not establish that product-design trade dress can be. *Two Pesos* is inapposite to our holding here because the trade dress at issue, the décor of a restaurant, seems to us not to constitute product design. It was either product packaging—which, as we have discussed, normally is taken by the consumer to indicate origin—or else some tertium quid that is akin to product packaging and has no bearing on the present case.

Respondent replies that this manner of distinguishing *Two Pesos* will force courts to draw difficult lines between product-design and product-packaging trade dress. There will indeed be some hard cases at the margin: a classic glass Coca-Cola bottle, for instance, may constitute packaging for those consumers who drink the Coke and then discard the bottle, but may constitute the product itself for those consumers who are bottle collectors, or part of the product itself for those consumers who buy Coke in the classic glass bottle, rather than a can, because they think it more stylish to drink from the former. We believe, however, that the frequency and the difficulty of having to distinguish between product design and product packaging will be much less than the frequency and the difficulty of having to decide when a product design is inherently distinctive. To the extent there are close cases, we believe that courts should err on the side of caution and classify ambiguous trade dress as product design, thereby requiring secondary meaning. The very closeness will suggest the existence of relatively small utility in adopting an inherent-distinctiveness principle, and relatively great consumer benefit in requiring a demonstration of secondary meaning. . . .

We hold that, in an action for infringement of unregistered trade dress under § 43(a) of the Lanham Act, a product's design is distinctive, and therefore protectible, only upon a showing of secondary meaning. The judgment of the Second Circuit is reversed, and the case is remanded for further proceedings consistent with this opinion. *It is so ordered.*

Questions:

1.) Wal-Mart told its supplier to rip off this poor designer's offerings. They did. They profited. And the Supreme Court is fine with that? Why?

2.) The Supreme Court here sets up a different test for product *design* trade dress than for product packaging trade dress. The former is registrable only on proof of secondary meaning. Why?

3.) Why does the Supreme Court rule as it does in *Wal-Mart*? Is this not a classic example of free-riding on the part of the defendants, once Samara has come up with an appealing design? The Court says,

> In the case of product design, as in the case of color, we think consumer predisposition to equate the feature with the source does not exist. Consumers are aware of the reality that, almost invariably, even the most unusual of product designs—such as a cocktail shaker shaped like a penguin—is intended not to identify the source, but to render the product itself more useful or more appealing.

Do you agree? Is the court offering an empirical prediction? ("If surveyed, most consumers would agree that most designs are not source identifying but rather serve to make the product more appealing or useful.") Or is it offering a per se rule designed to facilitate imitation and competition—at least in the realms of color and design—in order to drive prices down, even if consumers do regard the designs as source identifying?

Jessica Litman, The Exclusive Right to Read
13 CARDOZO ARTS & ENT. L.J. 29 (1994)

Imagine for a moment that some upstart revolutionary proposed that we eliminate all intellectual property protection for fashion design. No longer could a designer secure federal copyright protection for the cut of a dress or the sleeve of a blouse. Unscrupulous mass-marketers could run off thousands of knock-off copies of any designer's evening ensemble, and flood the marketplace with cheap imitations of *haute couture*. In the short run, perhaps, clothing prices would come down as legitimate designers tried to meet the prices of their free-riding competitors. In the long run, though, as we know all too well, the diminution in the incentives for designing new fashions would take its toll. Designers would still wish to design, at least initially, but clothing manufacturers with no exclusive rights to rely on would be reluctant to make the investment involved in manufacturing those designs and distributing them to the public. The dynamic American fashion industry would wither, and its most talented designers would forsake clothing design for some more remunerative calling like litigation. And all of us would be forced either to wear last year's garments year in and year out, or to import our clothing from abroad.

    Or, perhaps, imagine that Congress suddenly repealed federal intellectual property protection for food creations. Recipes would become common property. Downscale restaurants could freely recreate the signature chocolate desserts of their upscale sisters. Uncle Ben's would market Minute Risotto (microwavable!); the Ladies' Home Journal would reprint recipes it had stolen from Gourmet Magazine. Great chefs would be unable to find book publishers willing to buy their cookbooks. Then, expensive gourmet restaurants would reduce their prices to meet the prices of the competition; soon they would either close or fire their chefs to cut costs; promising young cooks would either move to Europe or get a day job (perhaps the law) and cook only on weekends. Ultimately, we would all be stuck eating Uncle Ben's Minute Risotto (eleven yummy flavors!!) for every meal.

    But, I'm boring you, you tell me; you've heard all of this before. It's the same argument motion picture producers make about why we need to extend the duration of copyright protection another 20 years; the same argument software publishers make about what will happen if we permit other software publishers to decompile and reverse-engineer their software products; the same argument database proprietors make about the huge social cost of a failure to protect their rights in their data. Perhaps the most important reason why we have intellectual property protection is our conclusion that incentives are required to spur the creation and dissemination of a sufficient number and variety of intellectual creations like films, software, databases, fashions and food.

    Of course, we don't give copyright protection to fashions or food. We never have.

Questions:

1.) If this is true, what are we debating in this course? What does Litman's argument add to the discussions of intellectual property theory in the first chapter? To the Supreme Court's analysis in *Wal-Mart*?

2.) Litman is talking about copyright protection – there is very little for fashion. One can copyright the design on the fabric, but not the cut of the dress. In *Wal-Mart*, Justice Scalia emphasizes that *trademark* also offers little in the way of design protection. Certainly, a manufacturer can cover the object with its trademarked logo. That is one reason why bags, clothes and the like have become billboards for the Vuitton or Gucci symbol. The trademark is protected even if the design of the bag or scarf on which it rests is not. But so long as one does not copy the mark, one can imitate designs freely without interference from either copyright or trademark law. Why, then, have the horrors Litman describes not come about? What forms of "exclusion" continue to function in the worlds of fashion and food? Forms of emulation? Types of exclusivity for which intellectual property is not necessary (or is wielded in a different way)? Demand for "authenticity" in which the availability of knockoffs is actually a positive, not a negative thing? Credit economies with different methods for disciplining those who take and do not give back? Are there limiting principles to these types of mechanisms? When are they likely to work well or work badly?

For further reading on these subjects, see Christine Cox and Jennifer Jenkins, "Between the Seams, A Fertile Commons," in Ready To Share: Fashion and the Ownership of Creativity (Norman Lear Center 2005); Kal Raustiala & Christopher Sprigman, "The Piracy Paradox: Innovation and Intellectual Property in Fashion Design," 92 Virginia Law Review 8 (2006); Kal Raustiala & Christopher Sprigman, The Knockoff Economy: How Imitation Sparks Innovation (2012).

TrafFix Devices, Inc. v. Marketing Displays, Inc.
532 U.S. 23 (2001)

Justice KENNEDY delivered the opinion of the Court.

Temporary road signs with warnings like "Road Work Ahead" or "Left Shoulder Closed" must withstand strong gusts of wind. An inventor named Robert Sarkisian obtained two utility patents for a mechanism built upon two springs (the dual-spring design) to keep these and other outdoor signs upright despite adverse wind conditions. The holder of the now-expired Sarkisian patents, respondent Marketing Displays, Inc. (MDI), established a successful business in the manufacture and sale of sign stands incorporating the patented feature. MDI's stands for road signs were recognizable to buyers and users (it says) because the dual-spring design was visible near the base of the sign.

This litigation followed after the patents expired and a competitor, TrafFix Devices, Inc., sold sign stands with a visible spring mechanism that looked like MDI's. MDI and TrafFix products looked alike because they were. When TrafFix started in business, it sent an MDI product abroad to have it reverse

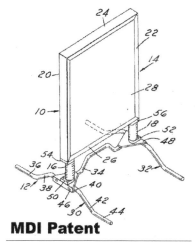

MDI Patent

Patent drawing from USPTO record

engineered, that is to say copied. Complicating matters, TrafFix marketed its sign stands under a name similar to MDI's. MDI used the name "WindMaster," while TrafFix, its new competitor, used "WindBuster."

MDI brought suit under the Trademark Act of 1946, as amended, 15 U.S.C. § 1051 et seq., against TrafFix for trademark infringement (based on the similar names), trade dress infringement (based on the copied dual-spring design) and unfair competition. TrafFix counterclaimed on antitrust theories. After the United States District Court for the

Eastern District of Michigan considered cross-motions for summary judgment, MDI prevailed on its trademark claim for the confusing similarity of names and was held not liable on the antitrust counterclaim; and those two rulings, affirmed by the Court of Appeals, are not before us.

I

We are concerned with the trade dress question. The District Court ruled against MDI on its trade dress claim. After determining that the one element of MDI's trade dress at issue was the dual-spring design, it held that "no reasonable trier of fact could determine that MDI has established secondary meaning" in its alleged trade dress. In other words, consumers did not associate the look of the dual-spring design with MDI. As a second, independent reason to grant summary judgment in favor of TrafFix, the District Court determined the dual-spring design was functional. On this rationale secondary meaning is irrelevant because there can be no trade dress protection in any event. In ruling on the functional aspect of the design, the District Court noted that Sixth Circuit precedent indicated that the burden was on MDI to prove that its trade dress was nonfunctional, and not on TrafFix to show that it was functional (a rule since adopted by Congress, see 15 U.S.C. § 1125(a)(3)), and then went on to consider MDI's arguments that the dual-spring design was subject to trade dress protection. Finding none of MDI's contentions persuasive, the District Court concluded MDI had not "proffered sufficient evidence which would enable a reasonable trier of fact to find that MDI's vertical dual-spring design is non-functional." Summary judgment was entered against MDI on its trade dress claims.

The Court of Appeals for the Sixth Circuit reversed the trade dress ruling. The Court of Appeals held the District Court had erred in ruling MDI failed to show a genuine issue of material fact regarding whether it had secondary meaning in its alleged trade dress, and had erred further in determining that MDI could not prevail in any event because the alleged trade dress was in fact a functional product configuration. The Court of Appeals suggested the District Court committed legal error by looking only to the dual-spring design when evaluating MDI's trade dress. Basic to its reasoning was the Court of Appeals' observation that it took "little imagination to conceive of a hidden dual-spring mechanism or a tri or quad-spring mechanism that might avoid infringing [MDI's] trade dress." The Court of Appeals explained that "[i]f TrafFix or another competitor chooses to use [MDI's] dual-spring design, then it will have to find some other way to set its sign apart to avoid infringing [MDI's] trade dress." It was not sufficient, according to the Court of Appeals, that allowing exclusive use of a particular feature such as the dual-spring design in the guise of trade dress would "hinde[r] competition somewhat." Rather, "[e]xclusive use of a feature must 'put competitors at a significant non-reputation-related disadvantage' before trade dress protection is denied on functionality grounds." ([Q]uoting *Qualitex Co. v. Jacobson Products Co.* (1995)). In its criticism of the District Court's ruling on the trade dress question, the Court of Appeals took note of a split among Courts of Appeals in various other Circuits on the issue whether the existence of an expired utility patent forecloses the possibility of the patentee's claiming trade dress protection in the product's design. To resolve the conflict, we granted certiorari.

II

It is well established that trade dress can be protected under federal law. The design or packaging of a product may acquire a distinctiveness which serves to identify the product with its manufacturer or source; and a design or package which acquires this secondary meaning, assuming other requisites are met, is a trade dress which may not be used in a manner likely to cause confusion as to the origin, sponsorship, or approval of the goods. In these respects protection for trade dress exists to promote competition. As we explained just last Term, see *Wal-Mart Stores v. Samara Brothers* (2000), various Courts of Appeals have allowed claims of trade dress infringement relying on the general provision of the Lanham Act which provides a cause of action to one who is injured when a person uses "any word, term name, symbol, or device, or any combination thereof . . . which is likely to cause confusion . . . as to the origin, sponsorship, or approval of his or her goods." 15 U.S.C. § 1125(a)(1)(A). Congress confirmed this statutory protection for trade dress by amending the Lanham Act to recognize the concept. Title 15 U.S.C. § 1125(a)(3) provides: "In a civil action for trade dress infringement under this chapter for trade dress not registered on the principal register, the person who asserts trade dress protection has the burden of proving that the matter sought to be protected is not functional." This burden of proof gives force to the well-established rule that trade dress protection may not be claimed for product features that are functional. And in *WalMart*, we were careful to caution against misuse or over-extension of trade dress. We noted that "product design almost invariably serves purposes other than source identification."

Trade dress protection must subsist with the recognition that in many instances there is no prohibition against copying goods and products. In general, unless an intellectual property right such as a patent or copyright protects an item, it will be subject to copying. As the Court has explained, copying is not always discouraged or disfavored by the laws which preserve our competitive economy. Allowing competitors to copy will have salutary effects in many instances. "Reverse engineering of chemical and mechanical articles in the public domain often leads to significant advances in technology."

The principal question in this case is the effect of an expired patent on a claim of trade dress infringement. A prior patent, we conclude, has vital significance in resolving the trade dress claim. A utility patent is strong evidence that the features therein claimed are functional. If trade dress protection is sought for those features the strong evidence of functionality based on the previous patent adds great weight to the statutory presumption that features are deemed functional until proved otherwise by the party seeking trade dress protection. Where the expired patent claimed the features in question, one who seeks to establish trade dress protection must carry the heavy burden of showing that the feature is not functional, for instance by showing that it is merely an ornamental, incidental, or arbitrary aspect of the device.

In the case before us, the central advance claimed in the expired utility patents (the Sarkisian patents) is the dual-spring design; and the dual-spring design is the essential feature of the trade dress MDI now seeks to establish and to protect. The rule we have explained bars the trade dress claim, for MDI did not, and cannot, carry the burden of overcoming the strong evidentiary inference of functionality based on the disclosure of the dual-spring design in the claims of the expired patents.

The dual springs shown in the Sarkisian patents were well apart (at either end of a frame for holding a rectangular sign when one full side is the base) while the dual springs at issue here are close together (in a frame designed to hold a sign by one of its corners). As the District Court recognized, this makes little difference. The point is that the springs are necessary to the operation of the device. The fact that the springs in this very different-looking device fall within the claims of the patents is illustrated by MDI's own position in earlier litigation. In the late 1970's, MDI engaged in a long-running intellectual property battle with a company known as Winn-Proof. Although the precise claims of the Sarkisian patents cover sign stands with springs "spaced apart," the Winn-Proof sign stands (with springs much like the sign stands at issue here) were found to infringe the patents by the United States District Court for the District of Oregon, and the Court of Appeals for the Ninth Circuit affirmed the judgment. . . . In light of this past ruling—a ruling procured at MDI's own insistence—it must be concluded the products here at issue would have been covered by the claims of the expired patents.

The rationale for the rule that the disclosure of a feature in the claims of a utility patent constitutes strong evidence of functionality is well illustrated in this case. The dual-spring design serves the important purpose of keeping the sign upright even in heavy wind conditions; and, as confirmed by the statements in the expired patents, it does so in a unique and useful manner. As the specification of one of the patents recites, prior art "devices, in practice, will topple under the force of a strong wind." The dual-spring design allows sign stands to resist toppling in strong winds. Using a dual-spring design rather than a single spring achieves important operational advantages. For example, the specifications of the patents note that the "use of a pair of springs . . . as opposed to the use of a single spring to support the frame structure prevents canting or twisting of the sign around a vertical axis," and that, if not prevented, twisting "may cause damage to the spring structure and may result in tipping of the device." In the course of patent prosecution, it was said that "[t]he use of a pair of spring connections as opposed to a single spring connection . . . forms an important part of this combination" because it "forc[es] the sign frame to tip along the longitudinal axis of the elongated ground-engaging members." The dual-spring design affects the cost of the device as well; it was acknowledged that the device "could use three springs but this would unnecessarily increase the cost of the device." These statements made in the patent applications and in the course of procuring the patents demonstrate the functionality of the design. MDI does not assert that any of these representations are mistaken or inaccurate, and this is further strong evidence of the functionality of the dual-spring design.

III

In finding for MDI on the trade dress issue the Court of Appeals gave insufficient recognition to the importance of the expired utility patents, and their evidentiary significance, in establishing the functionality of the device. The error likely was caused by its misinterpretation of trade dress principles in other respects. As we have noted, even if there has been no previous utility patent the party asserting trade dress has the burden to establish the nonfunctionality of alleged trade dress features. MDI could not meet this burden. Discussing trademarks, we have said "'[i]n general terms, a product feature is functional,' and cannot serve as a trademark, 'if it is essential to the use or purpose of the article or if it affects the cost or quality of the article.'" Expanding upon the meaning of this phrase, we have observed that a functional feature is one the "exclusive use of [which] would put competitors at a significant non-reputation-related disadvantage." The Court of Appeals in the instant case seemed to interpret this language to mean that a necessary test for functionality is "whether the particular product configuration is a competitive necessity." This was incorrect as a comprehensive definition. As explained in *Qualitex* and *Inwood*, a feature is also functional when it is essential to the use or purpose of the device or when it affects the cost or quality of the device. The *Qualitex* decision did not purport to displace this traditional rule. Instead, it quoted the rule as *Inwood* had set it forth. It is proper to inquire into a "significant non-reputation-related disadvantage" in cases of aesthetic functionality, the question involved in *Qualitex*. Where the design is functional under the *Inwood* formulation there is no need to proceed further to consider if there is a competitive necessity for the feature. In *Qualitex*, by contrast, aesthetic functionality was the central question, there having been no indication that the green-gold color of the laundry press pad had any bearing on the use or purpose of the product or its cost or quality.

The Court has allowed trade dress protection to certain product features that are inherently distinctive. *Two Pesos*. In *Two Pesos*, however, the Court at the outset made the explicit analytic assumption that the trade dress features in question (decorations and other features to evoke a Mexican theme in a restaurant) were not functional. The trade dress in those cases did not bar competitors from copying functional product design features. In the instant case, beyond serving the purpose of informing consumers that the sign stands are made by MDI (assuming it does so), the dual-spring design provides a unique and useful mechanism to resist the force of the wind. Functionality having been established, whether MDI's dual-spring design has acquired secondary meaning need not be considered.

There is no need, furthermore, to engage, as did the Court of Appeals, in speculation about other design possibilities, such as using three or four springs which might serve the same purpose. Here, the functionality of the spring design means that competitors need not explore whether other spring juxtapositions might be used. The dual-spring design is not an arbitrary flourish in the configuration of MDI's product; it is the reason the device works. Other designs need not be attempted.

Because the dual-spring design is functional, it is unnecessary for competitors to explore designs to hide the springs, say by using a box or framework to cover them, as suggested by the Court of Appeals. The dual-spring design assures the user the device will work. If buyers are assured the product serves its purpose by seeing the operative mechanism that in itself serves an important market need. It would be at cross-purposes to those objectives, and something of a paradox, were we to require the manufacturer to conceal the very item the user seeks.

In a case where a manufacturer seeks to protect arbitrary, incidental, or ornamental aspects of features of a product found in the patent claims, such as arbitrary curves in the legs or an ornamental pattern painted on the springs, a different result might obtain. There the manufacturer could perhaps prove that those aspects do not serve a purpose within the terms of the utility patent. The inquiry into whether such features, asserted to be trade dress, are functional by reason of their inclusion in the claims of an expired utility patent could be aided by going beyond the claims and examining the patent and its prosecution history to see if the feature in question is shown as a useful part of the invention. No such claim is made here, however. MDI in essence seeks protection for the dual-spring design alone. The asserted trade dress consists simply of the dual-spring design, four legs, a base, an upright, and a sign. MDI has pointed to nothing arbitrary about the components of its device or the way they are assembled. The Lanham Act does not exist to reward manufacturers for their innovation in creating a particular device; that is the purpose of the patent law and its period of exclusivity. The Lanham Act, furthermore, does not protect trade dress in a functional design simply because an investment has been made to encourage the public to associate a particular functional feature with a single manufacturer or seller. The Court of Appeals erred in viewing MDI as possessing the right to exclude competitors from using a design identical to MDI's and to require those competitors to adopt a different design simply to avoid copying it. MDI cannot gain the exclusive right to produce sign stands using the dual-spring design by asserting that consumers associate it with the look of the invention itself. Whether a utility patent has expired or there has been no utility patent at all, a product design which has a particular appearance may be functional because it is "essential to the use or purpose of the article" or "affects the cost or quality of the article."

TrafFix and some of its *amici* argue that the Patent Clause of the Constitution, Art. I, § 8, cl. 8, of its own force, prohibits the holder of an expired utility patent from claiming trade dress protection. We need not resolve this question. If, despite the rule that functional features may not be the subject of trade dress protection, a case arises in

which trade dress becomes the practical equivalent of an expired utility patent, that will be time enough to consider the matter. The judgment of the Court of Appeals is reversed, and the case is remanded for further proceedings consistent with this opinion.
It is so ordered.

Questions:

1.) As both *TrafFix* and *Qualitex* explain, functional aspects of a product can *never* be trademarked. How does *TrafFix* describe the test for functionality? How is that different than the Court of Appeals' definition of the concept? What philosophical differences do these positions reflect?

2.) What position does *TrafFix* take about the desirability of deliberate copying? What position does *Wal-Mart v. Samara* take on the same issue? Look back at the *INS* opinion. Who would be most likely to agree? Pitney, Holmes or Brandeis?

CHAPTER SIX

Grounds for Refusing Registration

Section 1052 of the Lanham Act contains a series of grounds for refusing federal registration of trademarks. We will take its subsections in turn.

1.) 1052(a)

> **No trademark by which the goods of the applicant may be distinguished from the goods of others shall be refused registration on the principal register on account of its nature unless it—**
>
> > **(a) Consists of or comprises ~~immoral~~, deceptive, ~~or scandalous~~ matter; or matter which may ~~disparage or~~ falsely suggest a connection with persons, living or dead, institutions, beliefs, or national symbols, ~~or bring them into contempt, or disrepute~~; or a geographical indication which, when used on or in connection with wines or spirits, identifies a place other than the origin of the goods and is first used on or in connection with wines or spirits by the applicant on or after one year after the date on which the WTO Agreement (as defined in section 3501 (9) of title 19) enters into force with respect to the United States.[1]**

Why the crossed-out text? In 2017, two landmark cases struck down longstanding provisions of section 1052(a) as violations of the First Amendment. You may recall the First Amendment cases from Chapters 2 and 3—there, the freedom of speech (whether it was the right to use 20 years of material set to enter the public domain, the word "Olympic," a cheerleader uniform, or a brand name) was in conflict with intellectual property rights. In the cases that follow, the framework is a little different. It is the parties *seeking* federally registered intellectual property rights who are bringing First Amendment claims, namely that the statutory prohibitions against registering their trademarks are unconstitutional restrictions of speech.

i.) Disparaging marks. In June 2017, the Supreme Court invalidated § 1052(a)'s prohibition on registering marks that "may disparage [persons, beliefs, etc.] or bring them into contempt, or disrepute," holding that it violates the First Amendment. The opinion in this case—*Matal v. Tam*—follows.

You may have read about the REDSKINS trademark litigation, on which this case bears. Before the *Tam* decision, the federal registrations of six trademarks containing the term REDSKINS had been cancelled because they were found disparaging to Native Americans in violation of § 1052(a). When those cancellations were appealed, the lower

---

[1] The last clause of § 1052(a) was inserted to comply with the TRIPS Agreement. It prohibits geographical indications on wines and spirits that identify a place other than their origin, even if the term is not misleading; "Champagne" cannot be used on sparkling wine unless it comes from Champagne, France. (Or unless the wine was grandfathered in by being used before the relevant date. Hence the excellent Chandon Brut sparkling wine from California may not use the term "champagne" but Cooks Champagne may.)

courts echoed the reasoning of earlier cases – holding that the refusal to register disparaging marks does not impermissibly restrict free speech, because the trademark holder is free to go on using the disparaging mark, just without the benefits of federal registration. *See Pro-Football, Inc. v. Blackhorse* (E.D. Va. 2015). Those cases are no longer good law. After the *Tam* decision, such marks *can* be registered, since the provision under which they were refused has been found unconstitutional. As you read the case below, remember that the question here is *constitutionality*. One might find some marks offensive but believe that the government does not get to deny them registration for that reason alone.

Matal v. Tam
137 S. Ct. 1744 (2017)

ALITO, J., announced the judgment of the Court. . . . GORSUCH, J., took no part in the consideration or decision of the case. [The Justices who joined on each portion are noted below.]

This case concerns a dance-rock band's application for federal trademark registration of the band's name, "The Slants." "Slants" is a derogatory term for persons of Asian descent, and members of the band are Asian-Americans. But the band members believe that by taking that slur as the name of their group, they will help to "reclaim" the term and drain its denigrating force.

The dance-rock band "The Slants"

The Patent and Trademark Office (PTO) denied the application based on a provision of federal law prohibiting the registration of trademarks that may "disparage . . . or bring . . . into contemp[t] or disrepute" any "persons, living or dead." 15 U.S.C. § 1052(a). We now hold that this provision violates the Free Speech Clause of the First Amendment. It offends a bedrock First Amendment principle: Speech may not be banned on the ground that it expresses ideas that offend.

I
[unanimous]
A

"The principle underlying trademark protection is that distinctive marks—words, names, symbols, and the like—can help distinguish a particular artisan's goods from those of others." . . . "[F]ederal law does not create trademarks." Trademarks and their precursors have ancient origins, and trademarks were protected at common law and in equity at the time of the founding of our country. For most of the 19th century, trademark protection was the province of the States. Eventually, Congress stepped in to provide a degree of national uniformity, passing the first federal legislation protecting trademarks in 1870. The foundation of current federal trademark law is the Lanham Act, enacted in 1946. . . . Under the Lanham Act, trademarks that are "used in commerce" may be placed on the "principal register," that is, they may be federally registered. . . . There are now more than two million marks that have active federal certificates of registration. . . .

B

Without federal registration, a valid trademark may still be used in commerce. And an unregistered trademark can be enforced against would-be infringers in several ways. Most important, even if a trademark is not federally registered, it may still be enforceable under § 43(a) of the Lanham Act, which creates a federal cause of action for trademark infringement.[1] Unregistered trademarks may also be entitled to protection under other federal statutes, such as the Anticybersquatting Consumer Protection Act, 15 U.S.C. § 1125(d). And an unregistered trademark can be enforced under state common law, or if it has been registered in a State, under that State's registration system.

Federal registration, however, "confers important legal rights and benefits on trademark owners who register their marks." Registration on the principal register (1) "serves as 'constructive notice of the registrant's claim of ownership' of the mark" (15 U.S.C. § 1072); (2) "is 'prima facie evidence of the validity of the registered mark and of the registration of the mark, of the owner's ownership of the mark, and of the owner's exclusive right to use the registered mark in commerce on or in connection with the goods or services specified in the certificate'" (§ 1057(b)); and (3) can make a mark "'incontestable'" once a mark has been registered for five years (§§ 1065, 1115(b)). Registration also enables the trademark holder "to stop the importation into the United States of articles bearing an infringing mark." See 15 U.S.C. § 1124.

C

The Lanham Act contains provisions that bar certain trademarks from the principal register. For example, a trademark cannot be registered if it is "merely descriptive or deceptively misdescriptive" of goods, § 1052(e)(1), or if it is so similar to an already registered trademark or trade name that it is "likely . . . to cause confusion, or to cause mistake, or to deceive," § 1052(d). At issue in this case is one such provision, which we will call "the

---

[1] In the opinion below, the Federal Circuit opined that although "Section 43(a) allows for a federal suit to protect an unregistered trademark," "it is not at all clear" that respondent could bring suit under § 43(a) because "there is no authority extending § 43(a) to marks denied under § 2(a)'s disparagement provision." When drawing this conclusion, the Federal Circuit relied in part on our statement in Two Pesos that "the general principles qualifying a mark for registration under § 2 of the Lanham Act are for the most part applicable in determining whether an unregistered mark is entitled to protection under § 43(a)." We need not decide today whether respondent could bring suit under § 43(a) if his application for federal registration had been lawfully denied under the disparagement clause.

disparagement clause." This provision prohibits the registration of a trademark "which may disparage . . . persons, living or dead, institutions, beliefs, or national symbols, or bring them into contempt, or disrepute." § 1052(a). . . . When deciding whether a trademark is disparaging, an examiner at the PTO generally applies a "two-part test." The examiner first considers "the likely meaning of the matter in question, taking into account not only dictionary definitions, but also the relationship of the matter to the other elements in the mark, the nature of the goods or services, and the manner in which the mark is used in the marketplace in connection with the goods or services." "If that meaning is found to refer to identifiable persons, institutions, beliefs or national symbols," the examiner moves to the second step, asking "whether that meaning may be disparaging to a substantial composite of the referenced group." If the examiner finds that a "substantial composite, although not necessarily a majority, of the referenced group would find the proposed mark . . . to be disparaging in the context of contemporary attitudes," a prima facie case of disparagement is made out, and the burden shifts to the applicant to prove that the trademark is not disparaging. What is more, the PTO has specified that "[t]he fact that an applicant may be a member of that group or has good intentions underlying its use of a term does not obviate the fact that a substantial composite of the referenced group would find the term objectionable."

D

Simon Tam is the lead singer of "The Slants." He chose this moniker in order to "reclaim" and "take ownership" of stereotypes about people of Asian ethnicity. The group "draws inspiration for its lyrics from childhood slurs and mocking nursery rhymes" and has given its albums names such as "The Yellow Album" and "Slanted Eyes, Slanted Hearts."

Tam sought federal registration of "THE SLANTS," on the principal register, but an examining attorney at the PTO rejected the request, applying the PTO's two-part framework and finding that "there is . . . a substantial composite of persons who find the term in the applied for mark offensive." The examining attorney relied in part on the fact that "numerous dictionaries define 'slants' or 'slant-eyes' as a derogatory or offensive term." The examining attorney also relied on a finding that "the band's name has been found offensive numerous times"—citing a performance that was canceled because of the band's moniker and the fact that "several bloggers and commenters to articles on the band have indicated that they find the term and the applied-for mark offensive."

Tam contested the denial of registration before the examining attorney and before the PTO's Trademark Trial and Appeal Board (TTAB) but to no avail. Eventually, he took the case to federal court, where the *en banc* Federal Circuit ultimately found the disparagement clause facially unconstitutional under the First Amendment's Free Speech Clause. The majority found that the clause engages in viewpoint-based discrimination, that the clause regulates the expressive component of trademarks and consequently cannot be treated as commercial speech, and that the clause is subject to and cannot satisfy strict scrutiny. The majority also rejected the Government's argument that registered trademarks constitute government speech, as well as the Government's contention that federal registration is a form of government subsidy. And the majority opined that even if the disparagement clause were analyzed under this Court's commercial speech cases, the clause would fail the "intermediate scrutiny" that those cases prescribe. . . .

The Government filed a petition for certiorari, which we granted in order to decide whether the disparagement clause "is facially invalid under the Free Speech Clause of the First Amendment." . . .

III

Because the disparagement clause applies to marks that disparage the members of a racial or ethnic group, we must decide whether the clause violates the Free Speech Clause of the First Amendment. And at the outset, we must consider three arguments that would either eliminate any First Amendment protection or result in highly permissive rational-basis review. Specifically, the Government contends (1) that trademarks are government speech, not private speech, (2) that trademarks are a form of government subsidy, and (3) that the constitutionality of the disparagement clause should be tested under a new "government-program" doctrine. We address each of these arguments below.

A
[unanimous]

The First Amendment prohibits Congress and other government entities and actors from "abridging the freedom of speech"; the First Amendment does not say that Congress and other government entities must abridge their own ability to speak freely. And our cases recognize that "[t]he Free Speech Clause . . . does not regulate government speech."

As we have said, "it is not easy to imagine how government could function" if it were subject to the restrictions that the First Amendment imposes on private speech. "'[T]he First Amendment forbids the government to regulate speech in ways that favor some viewpoints or ideas at the expense of others,'" but imposing a requirement of viewpoint-neutrality on government speech would be paralyzing. When a government entity embarks on a course of action, it necessarily takes a particular viewpoint and rejects others. . . .

But while the government-speech doctrine is important—indeed, essential—it is a doctrine that is susceptible to dangerous misuse. If private speech could be passed off as government speech by simply affixing a government seal of approval, government could silence or muffle the expression of disfavored viewpoints. For this reason, we must exercise great caution before extending our government-speech precedents.

At issue here is the content of trademarks that are registered by the PTO, an arm of the Federal Government. The Federal Government does not dream up these marks, and it does not edit marks submitted for registration. Except as required by the statute involved here, 15 U.S.C. § 1052(a), an examiner may not reject a mark based on the viewpoint that it appears to express. . . . In light of all this, it is far-fetched to suggest that the content of a registered mark is government speech. If the federal registration of a trademark makes the mark government speech, the Federal Government is babbling prodigiously and incoherently. It is saying many unseemly things. It is expressing contradictory views.[9] It is unashamedly endorsing a vast array of commercial products and services. And it is providing Delphic advice to the consuming public.

For example, if trademarks represent government speech, what does the Government have in mind when it advises Americans to "make.believe" (Sony), "Think different" (Apple), "Just do it" (Nike), or "Have it your way" (Burger King)? Was the Government warning about a coming disaster when it registered the mark "EndTime Ministries"?

The PTO has made it clear that registration does not constitute approval of a mark.

---

[9] Compare "Abolish Abortion," Registration No. 4,935,774 (Apr. 12, 2016), with "I Stand With Planned Parenthood," Registration No. 5,073,573 (Nov. 1, 2016); compare "Capitalism Is Not Moral, Not Fair, Not Freedom," Registration No. 4,696,419 (Mar. 3, 2015), with "Capitalism Ensuring Innovation," Registration No. 3,966,092 (May 24, 2011); compare "Global Warming Is Good," Registration No. 4,776,235 (July 21, 2015), with "A Solution to Global Warming," Registration No. 3,875,271 (Nov. 10, 2010).

And it is unlikely that more than a tiny fraction of the public has any idea what federal registration of a trademark means. . . .

This brings us to the case on which the Government relies most heavily, *Walker v. Texas Div., Sons of Confederate Veterans, Inc.* (2015), which likely marks the outer bounds of the government-speech doctrine. Holding that the messages on Texas specialty license plates are government speech, the *Walker* Court cited three factors distilled from *Pleasant Grove City v. Summum* (2009). First, license plates have long been used by the States to convey state messages. Second, license plates "are often closely identified in the public mind" with the State, since they are manufactured and owned by the State, generally designed by the State, and serve as a form of "government ID." Third, Texas "maintain[ed] direct control over the messages conveyed on its specialty plates." As explained above, none of these factors are present in this case.

In sum, the federal registration of trademarks is vastly different from . . . even the specialty license plates in *Walker*. Holding that the registration of a trademark converts the mark into government speech would constitute a huge and dangerous extension of the government-speech doctrine. For if the registration of trademarks constituted government speech, other systems of government registration could easily be characterized in the same way.

Perhaps the most worrisome implication of the Government's argument concerns the system of copyright registration. If federal registration makes a trademark government speech and thus eliminates all First Amendment protection, would the registration of the copyright for a book produce a similar transformation?

The Government attempts to distinguish copyright on the ground that it is "'the engine of free expression,'" but as this case illustrates, trademarks often have an expressive content. Companies spend huge amounts to create and publicize trademarks that convey a message. It is true that the necessary brevity of trademarks limits what they can say. But powerful messages can sometimes be conveyed in just a few words.

Trademarks are private, not government, speech.

B
[Alito, Roberts, Thomas, Breyer]

We next address the Government's argument that this case is governed by cases in which this Court has upheld the constitutionality of government programs that subsidized speech expressing a particular viewpoint. These cases implicate a notoriously tricky question of constitutional law. "[W]e have held that the Government 'may not deny a benefit to a person on a basis that infringes his constitutionally protected . . . freedom of speech even if he has no entitlement to that benefit.'" But at the same time, government is not required to subsidize activities that it does not wish to promote. Determining which of these principles applies in a particular case "is not always self-evident," but no difficult question is presented here.

Unlike the present case, the decisions on which the Government relies all involved cash subsidies or their equivalent. In *Rust v. Sullivan* (1991), a federal law provided funds to private parties for family planning services. . . . In other cases, we have regarded tax benefits as comparable to cash subsidies.

The federal registration of a trademark is nothing like the programs at issue in these cases. The PTO does not pay money to parties seeking registration of a mark. Quite the contrary is true: An applicant for registration must pay the PTO a filing fee of $225-$600. (Tam submitted a fee of $275 as part of his application to register THE SLANTS.) And to maintain federal registration, the holder of a mark must pay a fee of $300-$500 every

10 years. The Federal Circuit concluded that these fees have fully supported the registration system for the past 27 years.

The Government responds that registration provides valuable non-monetary benefits that "are directly traceable to the resources devoted by the federal government to examining, publishing, and issuing certificates of registration for those marks." But just about every government service requires the expenditure of government funds. . . .

Trademark registration is not the only government registration scheme. For example, the Federal Government registers copyrights and patents. State governments and their sub-divisions register the title to real property and security interests; they issue driver's licenses, motor vehicle registrations, and hunting, fishing, and boating licenses or permits. . . .

C
[Alito, Roberts, Thomas, Breyer]

Finally, the Government urges us to sustain the disparagement clause under a new doctrine that would apply to "government-program" cases. For the most part, this argument simply merges our government-speech cases and the previously discussed subsidy cases in an attempt to construct a broader doctrine that can be applied to the registration of trademarks. . . . Potentially more analogous are cases in which a unit of government creates a limited public forum for private speech. . . . However, even in such cases, what we have termed "viewpoint discrimination" is forbidden.

Our cases use the term "viewpoint" discrimination in a broad sense, and in that sense, the disparagement clause discriminates on the bases of "viewpoint." To be sure, the clause evenhandedly prohibits disparagement of all groups. It applies equally to marks that damn Democrats and Republicans, capitalists and socialists, and those arrayed on both sides of every possible issue. It denies registration to any mark that is offensive to a substantial percentage of the members of any group. But in the sense relevant here, that is viewpoint discrimination: Giving offense is a viewpoint.

We have said time and again that "the public expression of ideas may not be prohibited merely because the ideas are themselves offensive to some of their hearers." For this reason, the disparagement clause cannot be saved by analyzing it as a type of government program in which some content- and speaker-based restrictions are permitted.

IV
[Alito, Roberts, Thomas, Breyer]

Having concluded that the disparagement clause cannot be sustained under our government-speech or subsidy cases or under the Government's proposed "government program" doctrine, we must confront a dispute between the parties on the question whether trademarks are commercial speech and are thus subject to the relaxed scrutiny outlined in *Central Hudson Gas & Elec. Corp. v. Public Serv. Comm'n of N.Y.* (1980). The Government and *amici* supporting its position argue that all trademarks are commercial speech. They note that the central purposes of trademarks are commercial and that federal law regulates trademarks to promote fair and orderly interstate commerce. Tam and his *amici,* on the other hand, contend that many, if not all, trademarks have an expressive component. In other words, these trademarks do not simply identify the source of a product or service but go on to say something more, either about the product or service or some broader issue. The trademark in this case illustrates this point. The name "The Slants" not only identifies the band but expresses a view about social issues.

We need not resolve this debate between the parties because the disparagement clause cannot withstand even *Central Hudson* review. Under *Central Hudson,* a restriction of speech must serve "a substantial interest," and it must be "narrowly drawn." This means, among other things, that "[t]he regulatory technique may extend only as far as the interest it serves." The disparagement clause fails this requirement.

It is claimed that the disparagement clause serves two interests. The first is phrased in a variety of ways in the briefs. Echoing language in one of the opinions below, the Government asserts an interest in preventing "'underrepresented groups'" from being "'bombarded with demeaning messages in commercial advertising.'" An *amicus* supporting the Government refers to "encouraging racial tolerance and protecting the privacy and welfare of individuals." But no matter how the point is phrased, its unmistakable thrust is this: The Government has an interest in preventing speech expressing ideas that offend. And, as we have explained, that idea strikes at the heart of the First Amendment. Speech that demeans on the basis of race, ethnicity, gender, religion, age, disability, or any other similar ground is hateful; but the proudest boast of our free speech jurisprudence is that we protect the freedom to express "the thought that we hate."

The second interest asserted is protecting the orderly flow of commerce. Commerce, we are told, is disrupted by trademarks that "involv[e] disparagement of race, gender, ethnicity, national origin, religion, sexual orientation, and similar demographic classification." Such trademarks are analogized to discriminatory conduct, which has been recognized to have an adverse effect on commerce. A simple answer to this argument is that the disparagement clause is not "narrowly drawn" to drive out trademarks that support invidious discrimination. The clause reaches any trademark that disparages *any person, group, or institution.* It applies to trademarks like the following: "Down with racists," "Down with sexists," "Down with homophobes." It is not an anti-discrimination clause; it is a happy-talk clause. In this way, it goes much further than is necessary to serve the interest asserted.

The clause is far too broad in other ways as well. The clause protects every person living or dead as well as every institution. Is it conceivable that commerce would be disrupted by a trademark saying: "James Buchanan was a disastrous president" or "Slavery is an evil institution"?

There is also a deeper problem with the argument that commercial speech may be cleansed of any expression likely to cause offense. The commercial market is well stocked with merchandise that disparages prominent figures and groups, and the line between commercial and non-commercial speech is not always clear, as this case illustrates. If affixing the commercial label permits the suppression of any speech that may lead to political or social "volatility," free speech would be endangered.

* * *

For these reasons, we hold that the disparagement clause violates the Free Speech Clause of the First Amendment. The judgment of the Federal Circuit is affirmed.

It is so ordered.

[Justice KENNEDY, with whom JUSTICE GINSBURG, JUSTICE SOTOMAYOR, and JUSTICE KAGAN joined, concurred in the judgment and argued further that "the First Amendment's protections against viewpoint discrimination apply to the trademark here." They concluded, "the viewpoint discrimination rationale renders unnecessary any extended treatment of other questions raised by the parties."]

Justice THOMAS, concurring in part and concurring in the judgment.

. . . I also write separately because "I continue to believe that when the government seeks to restrict truthful speech in order to suppress the ideas it conveys, strict scrutiny is appropriate, whether or not the speech in question may be characterized as 'commercial.'" I nonetheless join Part IV of JUSTICE ALITO's opinion because it correctly concludes that the disparagement clause, 15 U.S.C. § 1052(a), is unconstitutional even under the less stringent test announced in *Central Hudson.*

Questions:

1.) What reasons does the court give for the claim that registered trademarks are private speech rather than government speech?

2.) Do you think that the disparagement clause constitutes viewpoint discrimination? Why? Why not?

3.) Do you foresee a flood of trademark applications seeking federal registration for "offensive" marks?

4.) Is this case consistent with *SFAA v. USOC*? Why? Why not?

ii.) Immoral or scandalous marks. Does the reasoning in *Matal v. Tam* also invalidate § 1052(a)'s bar on registering immoral or scandalous marks? The Supreme Court answered that question in the affirmative in 2019.

Iancu v. Brunetti
588 U.S. _____ (2019)

KAGAN, J., delivered the opinion of the Court, in which THOMAS, GINSBURG, ALITO, GORSUCH and KAVANAUGH, JJ., joined. ALITO, J., filed a concurring opinion. ROBERTS, C.J., and BREYER, J., filed opinions concurring in part and dissenting in part. SOTOMAYOR, J., filed an opinion concurring in part and dissenting in part, in which BREYER, J., joined.

Two Terms ago, in *Matal v. Tam*, this Court invalidated the Lanham Act's bar on the registration of "disparag[ing]" trademarks. 15 U.S.C. § 1052(a). Although split between two non-majority opinions, all Members of the Court agreed that the provision violated the First Amendment because it discriminated on the basis of viewpoint. Today we consider a First Amendment challenge to a neighboring provision of the Act, prohibiting the registration of "immoral[ ] or scandalous" trademarks. We hold that this provision infringes the First Amendment for the same reason: It too disfavors certain ideas.

I

Respondent Erik Brunetti is an artist and entrepreneur who founded a clothing line that uses the trademark FUCT. According to Brunetti, the mark (which functions as the clothing's brand name) is pronounced as four letters, one after the other: F-U-C-T. But you might read it differently and, if so, you would hardly be alone. That common perception caused difficulties for Brunetti when he tried to register his mark with the U.S. Patent and Trademark Office (PTO). . . .

II

. . . [In *Matal*,] [t]he Justices thus found common ground in a core postulate of free speech law: The government may not discriminate against speech based on the ideas or opinions it conveys. . . . So the key question becomes: Is the "immoral or scandalous" criterion in the Lanham Act viewpoint-neutral or viewpoint-based?

It is viewpoint-based. The meanings of "immoral" and "scandalous" are not mysterious, but resort to some dictionaries still helps to lay bare the problem. When is expressive material "immoral"? According to a standard definition, when it is "inconsistent with rectitude, purity, or good morals"; "wicked"; or "vicious." Webster's New International Dictionary 1246 (2d ed. 1949). Or again, when it is "opposed to or violating morality"; or "morally evil." Shorter Oxford English Dictionary 961 (3d ed. 1947). So the Lanham Act permits registration of marks that champion society's sense of rectitude and morality, but not marks that denigrate those concepts. And when is such material "scandalous"? Says a typical definition, when it "giv[es] offense to the conscience or moral feelings"; "excite[s] reprobation"; or "call[s] out condemnation." Webster's New International Dictionary, at 2229. Or again, when it is "shocking to the sense of truth, decency, or propriety"; "disgraceful"; "offensive"; or "disreputable." Funk & Wagnalls New Standard Dictionary 2186 (1944). So the Lanham Act allows registration of marks when their messages accord with, but not when their messages defy, society's sense of decency or propriety. Put the pair of overlapping terms together and the statute, on its face, distinguishes between two opposed sets of ideas: those aligned with conventional moral standards and those hostile to them; those inducing societal nods of approval and those provoking offense and condemnation. The statute favors the former, and disfavors the latter. "Love rules"? "Always be good"? Registration follows. "Hate rules"? "Always be cruel"? Not according to the Lanham Act's "immoral or scandalous" bar.

The facial viewpoint bias in the law results in viewpoint-discriminatory application. Recall that the PTO itself describes the "immoral or scandalous" criterion using much the same language as in the dictionary definitions recited above. The PTO, for example, asks whether the public would view the mark as "shocking to the sense of truth, decency, or propriety"; "calling out for condemnation"; "offensive"; or "disreputable." Using those guideposts, the PTO has refused to register marks communicating "immoral" or "scandalous" views about (among other things) drug use, religion, and terrorism. But all the while, it has approved registration of marks expressing more accepted views on the same topics. . . . [A]s the Court made clear in *Tam*, a law disfavoring "ideas that offend" discriminates based on viewpoint, in violation of the First Amendment. . . .

We accordingly affirm the judgment of the Court of Appeals.

It is so ordered.

· · · · · · · · · ·

iii.) Marks that falsely suggest a connection to persons. § 1052(a) still prohibits the registration of marks that "falsely suggest a connection with persons, living or dead, institutions, beliefs, or national symbols." Note that this is different from disparagement – falsely suggesting a connection need not be disparaging. It is also distinct from § 1052(c)'s prohibition on using names of particular living individuals, and § 1052(e)'s prohibition on marks that are "primarily merely a surname" (both discussed below). The provision barring false associations with "persons" emerged from the concepts of rights of publicity and privacy. It only precludes registration when, among other things, "the plaintiff's name or identity is of sufficient fame or reputation that when the defendant's mark is used on its goods or services, a connection with the plaintiff would be presumed." So, for example, BO BALL with a baseball/football design could not be registered because it falsely suggested a connection with the famous athlete Bo Jackson, but DA VINCI could be registered for jewelry and leather giftware because reasonable buyers would not assume a connection between Leonardo Da Vinci and the trademark owner's products.[2]

iv.) Deceptive marks. A deceptive mark can never be registered, unlike "deceptively misdescriptive" marks (see the discussion of § 1052(e) below), which can be registered upon acquiring secondary meaning. A mark is deceptive if its misrepresentation materially affects purchasing decisions. LOVEE LAMB for car seat covers made entirely of synthetic fibers and WHITE JASMINE for tea that contained no white tea were found to be deceptive because they were likely to affect the purchasing decisions of customers who wanted sheepskin seats, or the purported health benefits of white tea.[3]

2.) 1052(b)

> **Consists of or comprises the flag or coat of arms or other insignia of the United States, or of any State or municipality, or of any foreign nation, or any simulation thereof.**

Flags and other government insignia. Section 1052(b) denies registration to a mark that "consists of or comprises the flag or coat of arms or other insignia of the United States, or of any State or municipality, or of any foreign nation, or any simulation thereof." Government "insignia" is a narrow category, and only includes "specific designs formally adopted to serve as emblems of governmental authority," such as flags and official seals.[4] Other national symbols, such as the Statue of Liberty or the Capitol building, may be part of a registered mark, as long as the mark does not falsely suggest a connection with the government in violation of § 1052(a).[5] What is the policy behind keeping core "emblems of governmental authority" from serving as registered trademarks, but allowing the registration of other national symbols?

Government entities are also precluded from registering official insignia as trademarks.[6] Outside of this narrow prohibition, however, the government owns many marks. In the wake of recent wars, there has been an uptick in trademark registrations by the Marines and other armed forces, along with efforts to protect their brands. The Navy successfully objected to Disney's efforts to trademark the name SEAL TEAM 6. The Marines have objected to uses ranging from Marine-themed toilet paper called "Leatherneck Wipes" to a Star Trek fan site called "Starfleet Marine Corps Academy" that used the Marine Eagle (the website could keep the name but had to remove the eagle). They have also objected to uses by veterans—for example, a veteran who started a company called *Semper Fidelis* Garage Doors was required to remove the Marine emblem

---

[2] *See In re Sauer* (T.T.A.B. 1993), *aff'd* (Fed. Cir. 1994); *Lucien Piccard Watch Corp. v. Crescent Corp.* (S.D.N.Y. 1970).

[3] *See In re Budge Mfg. Co.* (Fed. Cir. 1988); *In re White Jasmine LLC* (T.T.A.B. 2013).

[4] *Trademark Manual of Examining Procedure* § 1204.

[5] *Liberty Mut. Ins. Co. v. Liberty Ins. Co. of Tex.* (E.D. Ark. 1960) (Liberty Mutual Insurance Company had a valid registration of a mark using the Statue of Liberty); *Heroes, Inc. v. Boomer Esiason Hero's Foundation, Inc.* (D.D.C. 1997) (charity had a valid registration for a mark that included an image of the Capitol building).

[6] *In re City of Houston* (T.T.A.B. 2012) (Houston could not register its city seal).

from his trademark. Who should have the exclusive right to use something like the Marine emblem as a source indicator? The government? Veterans? Disney? Entrepreneurs who successfully associate it with a product?

3.) 1052(c)

> **Consists of or comprises a name, portrait, or signature identifying a particular living individual except by his written consent, or the name, signature, or portrait of a deceased President of the United States during the life of his widow, if any, except by the written consent of the widow.**

Names and portraits of living individuals. Section 1052(c) bars the registration of a mark that "consists of or comprises a name, portrait, or signature identifying a particular living individual" or "deceased President of the United States during the life of his widow," unless there is written consent. (Does this language need to be amended if a woman becomes president?) This section only applies when "the person is so well known that the public would assume a connection or there will be an association of the name and the mark as used on the goods because the individual is publicly connected with the field in which the mark is being used."[7] For example, registration of the marks OBAMA PAJAMA, OBAMA BAHAMA PAJAMAS and BARACK'S JOCKS DRESS TO THE LEFT was rejected because they clearly identified President Obama.[8] By contrast, the authors of this casebook do not have § 1052(c) claims against BOYLES or JENNIFER HOME FURNITURE, both registered marks for furniture stores, because the public would not associate them with those trademarks.

4.) 1052(d)

> **Consists of or comprises a mark which so resembles a mark registered in the Patent and Trademark Office, or a mark or trade name previously used in the United States by another and not abandoned, as to be likely, when used on or in connection with the goods of the applicant, to cause confusion, or to cause mistake, or to deceive. . . .**

Confusingly similar to existing marks. Section 1052(d) provides that a mark cannot be registered if it is likely to cause confusion with another active mark, though concurrent registration may be allowed in limited circumstances based on good faith prior use. The test for likelihood of confusion at the registration stage is the same as that used for infringement, and is explored in detail in Chapter 7. If you practice trademark law after graduation, this question may account for a lot of your billable hours: whether marks proposed for registration are likely to cause confusion with existing marks. You will only be able to answer that question properly once we have covered likelihood of confusion in Chapter 7, but we think it is worth it to set the issue up now.

Applicants trying to federally register a mark may face refusal under § 1052(d) when i.) the examining attorney at the PTO has determined that their mark is likely to cause

---

[7] *Ross v. Analytical Technology Inc.* (TTAB 1999) (James W. Ross, Jr. was sufficiently well-known in the field to bar registration of ROSS for electrochemical analysis equipment).

[8] *In re Richard M. Hoefflin* (T.T.A.B. 2010).

confusion with a preexisting mark, or ii.) when the owner of such a mark has initiated an "opposition" proceeding claiming potential confusion. (Trademark owners vigilantly track trademark applications for this purpose. Duke University is particularly vigilant, if not overzealous, as it turns out; in fact, it has been named a leading trademark bully.)

Numerous factors are considered in determining whether registration is barred by § 1052(d) on confusion grounds, but as with infringement, two key factors are the similarity of the marks "in their entireties as to appearance, sound, connotation and commercial impression" and the "relatedness of the goods or services" connected to those marks. *Trademark Manual of Examining Procedure* § 1207.01. The PTO does not look at the products in isolation, or the marks in isolation. Rather, it asks the question, given the similarity or dissimilarity of the marks and the related or unrelated nature of the goods or services, is there a likelihood of confusion as to the source or the sponsorship of the applicant's product? With this in mind, do you think there was a likelihood of confusion in the following cases?

- The trademark owner of MR. CLEAN for "sudsing cleaner, cleanser and detergent" opposed the registration of MISTER STAIN for a stain removing compound
- The owner of the same MR. CLEAN mark opposed the registration of MASTER KLEEN for dry cleaning services

What about design marks, where the similarity of the marks is assessed primarily on the basis of appearance? Are the following confusingly similar?

 Registered mark for "moisturizing skin c   Applicant's mark for "distributorship services in the field of health and beauty aids"

 Ocean Spray's registered mark for various foods and drinks made with cranberries   Applicant's mark for "seafood"

5.) 1052(e)

> **Consists of a mark which**
> **(1) when used on or in connection with the goods of the applicant is merely descriptive or deceptively misdescriptive of them,**
> **(2) when used on or in connection with the goods of the applicant is primarily geographically descriptive of them, except as indications of regional origin may be registrable under section 1054 of this title,**
> **(3) when used on or in connection with the goods of the applicant is primarily geographically deceptively misdescriptive of them,**
> **(4) is primarily merely a surname, or**
> **(5) comprises any matter that, as a whole, is functional.**

Section 1052(e) precludes registration of a mark that is: functional; merely descriptive or "deceptively misdescriptive"; "primarily geographically descriptive" or "primarily geographically deceptively misdescriptive"; or "primarily merely a surname." However, marks within some of these categories can become registrable after they acquire distinctiveness (see § 1052(f) below).

i.) § 1052(e) "deceptively misdescriptive" v. § 1052(a) "deceptive." Marks that are *functional* or *merely descriptive*, and the reasons they are ineligible for protection, have already been discussed elsewhere in this chapter. But what about deceptively misdescriptive marks? Like merely descriptive marks, these marks describe their products in a way that falls short of being suggestive; however, the description is misleading. The mark TITANIUM for RVs might be "merely descriptive" if the vehicles are made of titanium, but is "deceptively misdescriptive" if the RVs do not contain titanium.[9] The test is "(i) whether the mark misdescribes the goods to which it applies; and (ii) whether consumers are likely to believe the misdescription."[10] If the misdescription is one that materially affects purchasing decisions— for example, if consumers purchased TITANIUM RVs *because* they thought they were made of titanium—then the mark goes beyond being deceptive misdescriptive and is flat out "deceptive" under § 1052(a). The distinction between "deceptive" under § 1052(a) and "deceptively misdescriptive" under § 1052(e) is important because deceptive marks are never registrable, while deceptively misdescriptive marks can be registered if they acquire distinctiveness (see § 1052(f) below).

ii.) Primarily geographically descriptive, or geographically deceptively misdescriptive. For a mark to be geographically descriptive, consumers must assume that the goods or services originated from the place designated in the mark. So, for example, CALIFORNIA PIZZA KITCHEN was found geographically descriptive. "[E]ven if applicant may have opened a branch of its restaurant outside of California, we believe customers encountering this out-of-state restaurant would believe that the services originated in California. It should be noted that restaurant services would include the restaurant concept, menu, recipes, etc., and even though a customer in Atlanta, Georgia would obviously recognize that the particular branch of the restaurant was physically located outside of California, he would be likely to assume that the restaurant services such as the concept, recipes and even possibly the food originated in the state of California. Thus, we believe that the primary significance of "CALIFORNIA" in applicant's mark would be its geographical significance."[11] Registration was thus refused. Similarly, CAROLINA APPAREL for a clothing store was found geographically descriptive. "Accordingly, although applicant acknowledges that its services are rendered in the state of North Carolina, the actual items of clothing may come from a variety of locations, applicant contends. It is applicant's position, therefore, that the asserted mark is not primarily geographically descriptive of its services." The Board was not convinced by this reasoning. "It is clear that the primary significance of the designation CAROLINA APPAREL, APPAREL being generic and disclaimed by applicant, is geographic. The addition of a generic term to a geographic term does not avoid the refusal of primary geographic descriptiveness. Inasmuch as the services admittedly do or will come from the place named in the mark, a public association of the services with the place named in the mark is presumed. . . . Accordingly, there is clearly an association of applicant's retail

---

[9] *See Glendale Intern. Corp. v. U.S. Patent & Trademark Office* (E.D. Va. 2005) (registration of TITANIUM for RVs that were not made of titanium was properly rejected).

[10] *Id.*

[11] *In re California Pizza Kitchen Inc* (T.T.A.B. 1988).

clothing store services with the place named in the mark."[12] Registration was refused. Do you agree with these conclusions? On the other hand, AMAZON for the online marketplace, SATURN for cars, and ATLANTIC for the magazine are not geographically descriptive because there is no goods/place association. While geographically descriptive marks are initially unregistrable, they can be registered if they acquire distinctiveness (see 1052(f) below).

Examples of "geographically deceptively misdescriptive" marks include HAVANA CLUB for cigars that were not from Cuba and NEAPOLITAN for sausages made in Florida instead of Naples.[13] However, a misleading mark might not be deemed geographically deceptively misdescriptive if it does not mislead a "substantial portion of the intended audience." MOSKOVSKAYA—Russian for "of or from Moscow"—on vodka that was not from Moscow was initially rejected for registration, but this decision was vacated and remanded because it was not clear that the mark would deceive a substantial portion of relevant consumers, as only 0.25% of the U.S. population speaks Russian.[14] Consider the following: the mark SWISS ARMY KNIFE is used on penknives that are made in China rather than Switzerland. Is the mark registrable? Why or why not?

Some geographical terms, such as SWISS cheese and PEKING duck, have become generic and cannot serve as trademarks at all. But if geographical terms cease being generic, and gain secondary meaning, they may become registrable. At one time, BUDWEISER was the generic term for beer brewed according to a method pioneered in the town of Budweis. However, it is now associated in the minds of consumers with Anheuser-Busch and registrable in the US (though not in the EU because of preexisting use of the mark by the Czech company Budvar).

iii.) Primarily merely a surname. On its face, this prohibition focuses on surnames rather than full names. So JOHN SMITH might be registrable, but SMITH would not, absent secondary meaning (see 1052(f) below). What is the general policy behind this provision? Why not allow a business owner to register SMITH for her products, without a showing of secondary meaning? Of course, many surnames have secondary meaning and are famous registered marks, such as FORD, DUPONT, or MCDONALD'S. What about J. SMITH— is this still "primarily merely a surname"? How about J.D. SMITH? SMITH ELECTRONICS? The touchstone for answering such questions is "the primary significance of the mark to the purchasing public."[15] So, for example, when surnames are combined with other terms (DELL COMPUTERS, DUKE UNIVERSITY), registrability would turn on whether or not the public perceives the mark as a whole as "primarily merely a surname." Similarly, when a mark consists of a surname that is a double entendre (BIRD, COOK, KING), courts will look at the predominant meaning in the minds of consumers encountering the mark (does BIRD refer to the surname or the feathered vertebrate?). When the name of a famous person is used as a mark, it is unlikely to be "primarily merely a surname" because the public will instead associate it with the well-known personality.[16]

---

[12] *In re Carolina Apparel* (T.T.A.B. 1998).

[13] *Corporacion Habanos, S.A. v. Anncas, Inc* (T.T.A.B. 2008); *In re Jack's Hi-Grade Foods, Inc* (T.T.A.B. 1985).

[14] *In re Spirits Intern., N.V* (Fed. Cir. 2009) (noting that if a larger percentage of vodka consumers speak Russian, or non-Russian speakers would understand MOSKOVSKAYA to suggest "from Moscow," then this might amount to a substantial portion).

[15] *Ex Parte Rivera Watch Corporation* (Comm'r Pat. & Trademarks 1955).

[16] *Michael S. Sachs, Inc.* (T.T.A.B. 2000) ("The mark M.C. ESCHER would no more be perceived as primarily merely a surname than the personal names P.T. Barnum, T.S. Eliot, O.J. Simpson, I.M. Pei and Y.A. Tittle.").

6.) 1052(f)

Except as expressly excluded in subsections (a), (b), (c), (d), (e)(3), and (e)(5) of this section, nothing in this chapter shall prevent the registration of a mark used by the applicant which has become distinctive of the applicant's goods in commerce. The Director may accept as prima facie evidence that the mark has become distinctive, as used on or in connection with the applicant's goods in commerce, proof of substantially exclusive and continuous use thereof as a mark by the applicant in commerce for the five years before the date on which the claim of distinctiveness is made. Nothing in this section shall prevent the registration of a mark which, when used on or in connection with the goods of the applicant, is primarily geographically deceptively misdescriptive of them, and which became distinctive of the applicant's goods in commerce before December 8, 1993.

Registration of otherwise problematic marks with secondary meaning. Section 2(f) provides that marks that are *merely descriptive, deceptively misdescriptive, primarily geographically descriptive*, or *primarily merely a surname* can be registered if they acquire secondary meaning. Proof of exclusive and continuous use in commerce for five years can constitute prima facie evidence of distinctiveness. As a result of international agreements, marks that are *primarily geographically deceptively misdescriptive* can be registered only if they acquired secondary meaning before December 8, 1993. The remaining categories of marks addressed in § 1052—those that are deceptive, functional, falsely suggest connections with people or institutions, use flags or government seals, identify living individuals, or are likely to cause confusion with another mark—are not registrable even if they acquire distinctiveness. Why do we allow the registration of some categories of marks if they acquire secondary meaning and not allow others? What distinctions do you see between the various categories?

Section 2(f) also specifies proceedings for opposing or canceling marks on the basis of dilution, which we will deal with later in this book. Only "famous" marks are protected against dilution. There are two types of dilution, blurring and tarnishment. "[D]ilution by blurring" is "association arising from the similarity between a mark or trade name and a famous mark that impairs the distinctiveness of the famous mark." "[D]ilution by tarnishment" is "association arising from the similarity between a mark or trade name and a famous mark that harms the reputation of the famous mark."[17] Note that this provision requires the owner of the mark to bring the action to refuse registration, not the PTO to refuse it on application.

A mark which would be likely to cause dilution by blurring or dilution by tarnishment under section 1125(c) of this title, may be refused registration only pursuant to a proceeding brought under section 1063 of this title. A registration for a mark which would be likely to cause dilution by blurring or dilution by tarnishment under section 1125(c) of this title, may be canceled pursuant to a proceeding brought under either section 1064 of this title or section 1092 of this title.

---

[17] § 1125(c).

PROBLEM 6-1

(We will be returning to this problem in future chapters, but you are asked here only about one aspect of it.)

Alan Turning is the brilliant computer scientist behind a new program known as Faceplant. Mr. Turning is a long-time vocal critic of Facebook, the social network site. He believes that its privacy practices are poor and less than transparent, that it imposes on its users a tightening spiral of narcissism and withdrawal from the "real" world, and that its network structure and architecture is overly controlling and anti-competitive. Mr. Turning is fond of pointing out that Facebook was able to supplant Myspace as the dominant social network because there was "open competition on the open web." Facebook, by contrast, has boasted that its goal is to be the portal through which users get *all* their content, e-commerce services and forms of communication. Mr. Turning believes that Facebook is trying to replace the "open" structure of the World Wide Web with its own carefully controlled gated community, from which competitors or rivals can be excluded. His saying, "Their goal is to be the *last* social network!" has become something of a rallying cry for Facebook's critics.

Mr. Turning's solution was to create a program called Faceplant that he claimed would restore "control of privacy to the user and control of competition to the free market." Mr. Turning's program simplifies the process of selecting and fine-tuning one's privacy preferences by automating the process of jumping through Facebook's cumbersome sets of menus. It also "nags" users if they stayed on Facebook for too long, sending messages such as "Enough with the profile tweaks!" "Only losers stalk their high school boyfriends!" and "It's Spring! Go for a walk outside!" Finally, the program "unlocks" Facebook's integration with other apps, so that users can use any app or play any game "inside" Facebook, not merely those approved by the Facebook app store. Mr. Turning made clear by both the name of his program and the logo he selected that his product was critical of Facebook. He claimed that the name "Faceplant" was designed to highlight two of his criticisms – that users become effectively unconscious because of Facebook's influence ("doing a faceplant" is a slang expression for falling rapidly asleep) and that they turn away from more imaginative engagement with forms of culture such as *books,* into vegetative recipients of manipulative advertising, mere "*plants.*"

Both Facebook's name and its original logo have been registered on the Principal Register since 2005. The logo is shown below.

Mr. Turning's logo for Faceplant is based on a modification of that image to send a very different message.

Mr. Turning has applied for a Federal trademark on both the name "Faceplant" and the logo above which changes Facebook's "like" symbol by rotating it 90 degrees and adding a raised middle finger. He is giving the app away for free, but he does make a considerable amount of money from advertisements seen by the millions of users flocking to his website, Faceplant.com.

Would Mr. Turning be able to register his proposed marks? Why? Would Facebook be able to oppose registration? On what grounds and how? Bonus question: If refused registration on the Principal Register, would Mr. Turning be able to seek any other kind of protection for the name "Faceplant" and the logo?

CHAPTER SEVEN

Trademark Infringement

We have stressed that one has to know the "reach" of an intellectual property right—how far it extends and what is needed to trigger it—in order to understand what that right means. Even more than with physical property rights, intellectual property rights are not absolute. In the cases that follow, we explore the conduct that is found to constitute infringement under both § 1114, protecting registered marks, and § 1125 protecting unregistered marks. As we go through these cases, measure the outlines of the property right revealed by the conduct required to infringe. How do they relate to the basic rationales of trademark law? We begin with the requirement of use in commerce, turn to the basic test for infringement, which is 'likelihood of confusion,' and conclude with the reach of *contributory* trademark infringement.

1.) Use in Commerce

Earlier, we discussed the requirement of use in commerce in order to get a trademark—registered or not. But use in commerce is also a requirement for *infringement*.

Rescuecom Corp. v. Google, Inc.
562 F.3d 123 (2d Cir. 2009)

LEVAL, Circuit Judge.

Appeal by Plaintiff Rescuecom Corp. from a judgment of the United States District Court for the Northern District of New York dismissing its action against Google, Inc., under Rule 12(b)(6) for failure to state a claim upon which relief may be granted. Rescuecom's Complaint alleges that Google is liable under §§ 32 and 43 of the Lanham Act, 15 U.S.C. §§ 1114 & 1125, for infringement, false designation of origin, and dilution of Rescuecom's eponymous trademark. The district court believed the dismissal of the action was compelled by our holding in *1-800 Contacts, Inc. v. WhenU.Com, Inc.*, because, according to the district court's understanding of that opinion, Rescuecom failed to allege that Google's use of its mark was a "use in commerce" within the meaning of § 45 of the Lanham Act, 15 U.S.C. § 1127. We believe this misunderstood the holding of *1-800*. While we express no view as to whether Rescuecom can prove a Lanham Act violation, an actionable claim is adequately alleged in its pleadings. Accordingly, we vacate the judgment dismissing the action and remand for further proceedings.

BACKGROUND

Rescuecom is a national computer service franchising company that offers on-site computer services and sales. Rescuecom conducts a substantial amount of business over the Internet and receives between 17,000 to 30,000 visitors to its website each month. It also advertises over the Internet, using many web-based services, including those offered by Google. Since 1998, "Rescuecom" has been a registered federal trademark, and there is no dispute as to its validity.

Google operates a popular Internet search engine, which users access by visiting www.google.com. Using Google's website, a person searching for the website of a particular entity in trade (or simply for information about it) can enter that entity's name or trademark into Google's search engine and launch a search. Google's proprietary system responds to such a search request in two ways. First, Google provides a list of links to websites, ordered in what Google deems to be of descending relevance to the user's search terms based on its proprietary algorithms. Google's search engine assists the public not only in obtaining information about a provider, but also in purchasing products and services. If a prospective purchaser, looking for goods or services of a particular provider, enters the provider's trademark as a search term on Google's website and clicks to activate a search, within seconds, the Google search engine will provide on the searcher's computer screen a link to the webpage maintained by that provider (as well as a host of other links to sites that Google's program determines to be relevant to the search term entered). By clicking on the link of the provider, the searcher will be directed to the provider's website, where the searcher can obtain information supplied by the provider about its products and services and can perhaps also make purchases from the provider by placing orders.

The second way Google responds to a search request is by showing context-based advertising. When a searcher uses Google's search engine by submitting a search term, Google may place advertisements on the user's screen. Google will do so if an advertiser, having determined that its ad is likely to be of interest to a searcher who enters the particular term, has purchased from Google the placement of its ad on the screen of the searcher who entered that search term. What Google places on the searcher's screen is more than simply an advertisement. It is also a link to the advertiser's website, so that in response to such an ad, if the searcher clicks on the link, he will open the advertiser's website, which offers not only additional information about the advertiser, but also perhaps the option to purchase the goods and services of the advertiser over the Internet. Google uses at least two programs to offer such context-based links: AdWords and Keyword Suggestion Tool.

AdWords is Google's program through which advertisers purchase terms (or keywords). When entered as a search term, the keyword triggers the appearance of the advertiser's ad and link. An advertiser's purchase of a particular term causes the advertiser's ad and link to be displayed on the user's screen whenever a searcher launches a Google search based on the purchased search term. Advertisers pay Google based on the number of times Internet users "click" on the advertisement, so as to link to the advertiser's website. For example, using Google's AdWords, Company Y, a company engaged in the business of furnace repair, can cause Google to display its advertisement and link whenever a user of Google launches a search based on the search term, "furnace repair." Company Y can also cause its ad and link to appear whenever a user searches for the term "Company X," a competitor of Company Y in the furnace repair business. Thus, whenever a searcher interested in purchasing furnace repair services from Company X launches a search of the term X (Company X's trademark), an ad and link would appear on the searcher's screen, inviting the searcher to the furnace repair services of X's competitor, Company Y. And if the searcher clicked on Company Y's link, Company Y's website would open on the searcher's screen, and the searcher might be able to order or purchase Company Y's furnace repair services.

In addition to AdWords, Google also employs Keyword Suggestion Tool, a program that recommends keywords to advertisers to be purchased. The program is designed to improve the effectiveness of advertising by helping advertisers identify keywords related to their area of commerce, resulting in the placement of their ads before users who are likely to be responsive to it. Thus, continuing the example given above, if Company Y employed Google's Keyword Suggestion Tool, the Tool might suggest to Company Y that it purchase not only the term "furnace repair" but also the term "X," its competitor's brand name and trademark, so that Y's ad would appear on the screen of a searcher who searched Company X's trademark, seeking Company X's website.

Once an advertiser buys a particular keyword, Google links the keyword to that advertiser's advertisement. The advertisements consist of a combination of content and a link to the advertiser's webpage. Google displays these advertisements on the search result page either in the right margin or in a horizontal band immediately above the column of relevance-based search results. These advertisements are generally associated with a label, which says "sponsored link." Rescuecom alleges, however, that a user might easily be misled to believe that the advertisements which appear on the screen are in fact part of the relevance-based search result and that the appearance of a competitor's ad and link in response to a searcher's search for Rescuecom is likely to cause trademark confusion as to affiliation, origin, sponsorship, or approval of service. This can occur, according to the Complaint, because Google fails to label the ads in a manner which would clearly identify them as purchased ads rather than search results. The Complaint alleges that when the sponsored links appear in a horizontal bar at the top of the search results, they may appear to the searcher to be the first, and therefore the most relevant, entries responding to the search, as opposed to paid advertisements.

Google's objective in its AdWords and Keyword Suggestion Tool programs is to sell keywords to advertisers. Rescuecom alleges that Google makes 97% of its revenue from selling advertisements through its AdWords program. Google therefore has an economic incentive to increase the number of advertisements and links that appear for every term entered into its search engine.

Many of Rescuecom's competitors advertise on the Internet. Through its Keyword Suggestion Tool, Google has recommended the Rescuecom trademark to Rescuecom's competitors as a search term to be purchased. Rescuecom's competitors, some responding to Google's recommendation, have purchased Rescuecom's trademark as a keyword in Google's AdWords program, so that whenever a user launches a search for the term "Rescuecom," seeking to be connected to Rescuecom's website, the competitors' advertisement and link will appear on the searcher's screen. This practice allegedly allows Rescuecom's competitors to deceive and divert users searching for Rescuecom's website. According to Rescuecom's allegations, when a Google user launches a search for the term "Rescuecom" because the searcher wishes to purchase Rescuecom's services, links to websites of its competitors will appear on the searcher's screen in a manner likely to cause the searcher to believe mistakenly that a competitor's advertisement (and website link) is sponsored by, endorsed by, approved by, or affiliated with Rescuecom.

The district court granted Google's 12(b)(6) motion and dismissed Rescuecom's claims. The court believed that our *1-800* decision compels the conclusion that Google's allegedly infringing activity does not involve use of Rescuecom's mark in commerce, which is an essential element of an action under the Lanham Act.

DISCUSSION
I. Google's Use of Rescuecom's Mark Was a "Use in Commerce"

The district court believed that this case was on all fours with *1-800*, and that its dismissal was required for the same reasons as given in *1-800*. We believe the cases are materially different. The allegations of Rescuecom's complaint adequately plead a use in commerce.

In *1-800*, the plaintiff alleged that the defendant infringed the plaintiff's trademark through its proprietary software, which the defendant freely distributed to computer users who would download and install the program on their computer. The program provided contextually relevant advertising to the user by generating pop-up advertisements to the user depending on the website or search term the user entered in his browser. For example, if a user typed "eye care" into his browser, the defendant's program would randomly display a pop-up advertisement of a company engaged in the field of eye care. Similarly, if the searcher launched a search for a particular company engaged in eye care, the defendant's program would display the pop-up ad of a company associated with eye care. The pop-up ad appeared in a separate browser window from the website the user accessed, and the defendant's brand was displayed in the window frame surrounding the ad, so that there was no confusion as to the nature of the pop-up as an advertisement, nor as to the fact that the defendant, not the trademark owner, was responsible for displaying the ad, in response to the particular term searched.

Sections 32 and 43 of the Act, which we also refer to by their codified designations, 15 U.S.C. §§ 1114 & 1125, inter alia, impose liability for unpermitted "use in commerce" of another's mark which is "likely to cause confusion, or to cause mistake, or to deceive," § 1114, "as to the affiliation . . . or as to the origin, sponsorship or approval of his or her goods [or] services . . . by another person." § 1125(a)(1)(A). The *1-800* opinion looked to the definition of the term "use in commerce" provided in § 45 of the Act, 15 U.S.C. § 1127. That definition provides in part that "a mark shall be deemed to be in use in commerce . . . (2) on services when it is used or displayed in the sale or advertising of services and the services are rendered in commerce." 15 U.S.C. § 1127. Our court found that the plaintiff failed to show that the defendant made a "use in commerce" of the plaintiff's mark, within that definition.

At the outset, we note two significant aspects of our holding in *1-800*, which distinguish it from the present case. A key element of our court's decision in *1-800* was that under the plaintiff's allegations, the defendant did not use, reproduce, or display the plaintiff's mark at all. The search term that was alleged to trigger the pop-up ad was the plaintiff's website address. *1-800* noted, notwithstanding the similarities between the website address and the mark, that the website address was not used or claimed by the plaintiff as a trademark. Thus, the transactions alleged to be infringing were not transactions involving use of the plaintiff's trademark. *1-800* suggested in dictum that is highly relevant to our case that had the defendant used the plaintiff's trademark as the trigger to pop-up an advertisement, such conduct might, depending on other elements, have been actionable.

Second, as an alternate basis for its decision, *1-800* explained why the defendant's program, which might randomly trigger pop-up advertisements upon a searcher's input of the plaintiff's website address, did not constitute a "use in commerce," as defined in § 1127. In explaining why the plaintiff's mark was not "used or displayed in the sale or advertising of services," *1-800* pointed out that, under the defendant's program, advertisers could not request or purchase keywords to trigger their ads. Even if an advertiser wanted to display its advertisement to a searcher using the plaintiff's trademark as a search term, the defendant's program did not offer this possibility. In fact, the defendant "did not disclose the proprietary contents of [its] directory to its advertising clients. . . ." In addition to not selling trademarks of others to its customers to trigger these ads, the defendant did not "otherwise manipulate which category-related advertisement will pop up in response to any particular terms on the internal directory." The display of a particular advertisement was controlled by the category associated with the website or keyword, rather than the website or keyword itself.

The present case contrasts starkly with those important aspects of the *1-800* decision. First, in contrast to *1-800*, where we emphasized that the defendant made no use whatsoever of the plaintiff's trademark, here what Google is recommending and selling to its advertisers is Rescuecom's trademark. Second, in contrast with the facts of *1-800* where the defendant did not "use or display," much less sell, trademarks as search terms to its advertisers, here Google displays, offers, and sells Rescuecom's mark to Google's advertising customers when selling its advertising services. In addition, Google encourages the purchase of Rescuecom's mark through its Keyword Suggestion Tool. Google's utilization of Rescuecom's mark fits literally within the terms specified by 15 U.S.C. § 1127. According to the Complaint, Google uses and sells Rescuecom's mark "in the sale . . . of [Google's advertising] services . . . rendered in commerce." § 1127.

Google, supported by *amici*, argues that *1-800* suggests that the inclusion of a trademark in an internal computer directory cannot constitute trademark use. Several district court decisions in this Circuit appear to have reached this conclusion. This over-reads the *1-800* decision. First, regardless of whether Google's use of Rescuecom's mark in its internal search algorithm could constitute an actionable trademark use, Google's recommendation and sale of Rescuecom's mark to its advertising customers are not internal uses. Furthermore, *1-800* did not imply that use of a trademark in a software program's internal directory precludes a finding of trademark use. Rather, influenced by the fact that the defendant was not using the plaintiff's trademark at all, much less using it as the basis of a commercial transaction, the court asserted that the particular use before it did not constitute a use in commerce. We did not imply in *1-800* that an alleged infringer's use of a trademark in an internal software program insulates the alleged infringer from a charge of infringement, no matter how likely the use is to cause confusion in the marketplace. If we were to adopt Google and its amici's argument, the operators of search engines would be free to use trademarks in ways designed to deceive and cause consumer confusion. This is surely neither within the intention nor the letter of the Lanham Act.

Google and its amici contend further that its use of the Rescuecom trademark is no different from that of a retail vendor who uses "product placement" to allow one vender to benefit from a competitors' name recognition. An example of product placement occurs when a store-brand generic product is placed next to a trademarked product to induce a customer who specifically sought out the trademarked product to consider the typically less expensive, generic brand as an alternative. Google's argument misses the point. From the fact that proper, non-deceptive product placement does not result in liability under the Lanham Act, it does not follow that the label "product placement" is a magic shield against liability, so that even a deceptive plan of product placement designed to confuse consumers would similarly escape liability. It is not by reason of absence of a use of a mark in commerce that benign product placement escapes liability; it escapes liability because it is a benign practice which does not cause a likelihood of consumer confusion. In contrast, if a retail seller were to be paid by an off-brand purveyor to arrange product display and delivery in such a way that customers seeking to purchase a famous brand would receive the off-brand, believing they had gotten the brand they were seeking, we see no reason to believe the practice would escape liability merely because it could claim the mantle of "product placement." The practices attributed to Google by the Complaint, which at this stage we must accept as true, are significantly different from benign product placement that does not violate the Act.

Unlike the practices discussed in *1-800*, the practices here attributed to Google by Rescuecom's complaint are that Google has made use in commerce of Rescuecom's mark. Needless to say, a defendant must do more than use another's mark in commerce to violate the Lanham Act. The gist of a Lanham Act violation is an unauthorized use, which "is likely to cause confusion, or to cause mistake, or to deceive as to the affiliation, . . . or as to the origin, sponsorship, or approval of . . . goods [or] services." We have no idea whether Rescuecom can prove that Google's use of Rescuecom's trademark in its AdWords program causes likelihood of confusion or mistake. Rescuecom has alleged that it does, in that would-be purchasers (or explorers) of its services who search for its website on Google are misleadingly directed to the ads and websites of its competitors in a manner which leads them to believe mistakenly that these ads or websites are sponsored by, or affiliated with Rescuecom. This is particularly so, Rescuecom alleges, when the advertiser's link appears in a horizontal band at the top of the list of search results in a manner which makes it appear to be the most relevant search result and not an advertisement. What Rescuecom alleges is that by the manner of Google's display of sponsored links of competing brands in response to a search for Rescuecom's brand name (which fails adequately to identify the sponsored link as an advertisement, rather than a relevant search result), Google creates a likelihood of consumer confusion as to trademarks. If the searcher sees a different brand name as the top entry in response to the search for "Rescuecom," the searcher is likely to believe mistakenly that the different name which appears is affiliated with the brand name sought in the search and will not suspect, because the fact is not adequately signaled by Google's presentation, that this is not the most relevant response to the search. Whether Google's actual practice is in fact benign or confusing is not for us to judge at this time.

We conclude that the district court was mistaken in believing that our precedent in *1-800* requires dismissal.

CONCLUSION

The judgment of the district court is vacated and the case is remanded for further proceedings.

Questions:

1.) *Rescuecom* is a case about "use in commerce" as a requirement of infringement. The earlier case we looked at, *Planetary Motion v. Techsplosion*, was about the "use in commerce" required to gain a mark in the first place, either through the federal registration process or as a common law mark. Are the two definitions of "use in commerce" the same? Are there good policy reasons to want them to be different? Would we want a higher bar to get a trademark, or to infringe it? Or should the line be exactly the same? The definition of use in commerce is in § 1127. Courts have disagreed as to whether this definition is relevant only to the question of ownership or also to infringement.

2.) Are you convinced by the court's distinction between using the company's domain name as opposed to its trademark as the basis for search? If I search for Ford.com am I not doing both?

3.) The court here is careful to distinguish what Google was doing here from the "internal" use of trademarks in the *1-800 Contacts, Inc. v. WhenU.Com* case, a case that was about cost-free, but advertising-supported, software. The argument is that this "internal" use is different than Google's commercial use of the trademarks—namely selling them as contextual prompts for searches. Do you agree?

People for the Ethical Treatment of Animals v. Michael T. Doughney
263 F.3d 359 (4th Cir. 2001)

People for the Ethical Treatment of Animals ("PETA") sued Michael Doughney ("Doughney") after he registered the domain name peta.org and created a website called "People Eating Tasty Animals." PETA alleged claims of service mark infringement under 15 U.S.C. § 1114 and Virginia common law, unfair competition under 15 U.S.C. § 1125(a) and Virginia common law, and service mark dilution and cybersquatting under 15 U.S.C. § 1123(c). [Sic. The court presumably meant § 1125(d).] Doughney appeals the district court's decision granting PETA's motion for summary judgment and PETA cross-appeals the district court's denial of its motion for attorney's fees and costs. Finding no error, we affirm.

I.

PETA is an animal rights organization with more than 600,000 members worldwide. PETA "is dedicated to promoting and heightening public awareness of animal protection issues and it opposes the exploitation of animals for food, clothing, entertainment and vivisection."

Doughney is a former internet executive who has registered many domain names since 1995. For example, Doughney registered domain names such as dubyadot.com, dubyadot.net, deathbush.com, RandallTerry.org (Not Randall Terry for Congress), bwtel.com (Baltimore-Washington Telephone Company), pmrc.org ("People's Manic Repressive Church"), and ex-cult.org (Ex-Cult Archive). At the time the district court issued its summary judgment ruling, Doughney owned 50–60 domain names.

Doughney registered the domain name peta.org in 1995 with Network Solutions, Inc. ("NSI"). When registering the domain name, Doughney represented to NSI that the registration did "not interfere with or infringe upon the rights of any third party," and that a "non-profit educational organization" called "People Eating Tasty Animals" was registering the domain name. Doughney made these representations to NSI despite knowing that no corporation, partnership, organization or entity of any kind existed or traded under that name. Moreover, Doughney was familiar with PETA and its beliefs and had been for at least 15 years before registering the domain name.

After registering the peta.org domain name, Doughney used it to create a website purportedly on behalf of "People Eating Tasty Animals." Doughney claims he created the website as a parody of PETA. A viewer accessing the website would see the title "People Eating Tasty Animals" in large, bold type. Under the title, the viewer would see a statement that the website was a "resource for those who enjoy eating meat, wearing fur and leather, hunting, and the fruits of scientific research." The website contained links to various meat, fur, leather, hunting, animal research, and other organizations, all of which held views generally antithetical to PETA's views. Another statement on the website asked the viewer whether he/she was

Doughney's website

"Feeling lost? Offended? Perhaps you should, like, exit immediately." The phrase "exit immediately" contained a hyperlink to PETA's official website.

Doughney's website appeared at "www.peta.org" for only six months in 1995–96. In 1996, PETA asked Doughney to voluntarily transfer the peta.org domain name to PETA because PETA owned the "PETA" mark ("the Mark"), which it registered in 1992. See U.S. Trademark Registration No. 1705,510. When Doughney refused to transfer the domain name to PETA, PETA complained to NSI, whose rules then required it to place the domain name on "hold" pending resolution of Doughney's dispute with PETA. Consequently, Doughney moved the website to www.mtd.com/tasty and added a disclaimer stating that "People Eating Tasty Animals is in no way connected with, or endorsed by, People for the Ethical Treatment of Animals."

In response to Doughney's domain name dispute with PETA, *The Chronicle of Philanthropy* quoted Doughney as stating that, "[i]f they [PETA] want one of my domains, they should make me an offer." Doughney does not dispute making this statement. Additionally, Doughney posted the following message on his website on May 12, 1996:

> "PeTa" has no legal grounds whatsoever to make even the slightest demands of me regarding this domain name registration. If they disagree, they can sue me. And if they don't, well, perhaps they can behave like the polite ladies and gentlemen that they evidently aren't and negotiate a settlement with me. Otherwise, "PeTa" can wait until the significance and value of a domain name drops to nearly nothing, which is inevitable as each new web search engine comes on-line, because that's how long it's going to take for this dispute to play out.

PETA sued Doughney in 1999, asserting claims for service mark infringement, unfair competition, dilution and cybersquatting. PETA did not seek damages, but sought only to enjoin Doughney's use of the "PETA" Mark and an order requiring Doughney to transfer the peta.org domain name to PETA.

Doughney responded to the suit by arguing that the website was a constitutionally-protected parody of PETA. Nonetheless, the district court granted PETA's motion for summary judgment on June 12, 2000. The district court rejected Doughney's parody defense, explaining that

> [o]nly after arriving at the "PETA.ORG" web site could the web site browser determine that this was not a web site owned, controlled or sponsored by PETA. Therefore, the two images: (1) the famous PETA name and (2) the "People Eating Tasty Animals" website was not a parody because [they were not] simultaneous. . . .

A. Trademark Infringement/Unfair Competition

A plaintiff alleging causes of action for trademark infringement and unfair competition must prove (1) that it possesses a mark; (2) that the defendant used the mark; (3) that the defendant's use of the mark occurred "in commerce"; (4) that the defendant used the mark "in connection with the sale, offering for sale, distribution, or advertising" of goods or services; and (5) that the defendant used the mark in a manner likely to confuse consumers. 15 U.S.C. §§ 1114, 1125(a).

There is no dispute here that PETA owns the "PETA" Mark, that Doughney used it, and that Doughney used the Mark "in commerce." Doughney disputes the district court's findings that he used the Mark in connection with goods or services and that he used it in a manner engendering a likelihood of confusion.

1.

To use PETA's Mark "in connection with" goods or services, Doughney need not have actually sold or advertised goods or services on the www.peta.org website. Rather, Doughney need only have prevented users from obtaining or using PETA's goods or services, or need only have connected the website to others' goods or services.

While sparse, existing caselaw on infringement and unfair competition in the Internet context clearly weighs in favor of this conclusion. For example, in *OBH, Inc. v. Spotlight Magazine, Inc.*, the plaintiffs owned the "The Buffalo News" registered trademark used by the newspaper of the same name. The defendants registered the domain name thebuffalonews.com and created a website parodying *The Buffalo News* and providing a public forum for criticism of the newspaper. The site contained hyperlinks to other local news sources and a site owned by the defendants that advertised Buffalo-area apartments for rent. The court held that the defendants used the mark "in connection with" goods or services because the defendants' website was "likely to prevent or hinder Internet users from accessing plaintiffs' services on plaintiffs' own web site":

> Prospective users of plaintiffs' services who mistakenly access defendants' web site may fail to continue to search for plaintiffs' web site due to confusion or frustration. Such users, who are presumably looking for the news services provided by the plaintiffs on their web site, may instead opt to select one of the several other news-related hyperlinks contained in defendants' web site. These news-related hyperlinks will directly link the user to other news-related web sites that are in direct competition with plaintiffs in providing news-related services over the Internet. Thus, defendants' action in appropriating plaintiff's mark has a connection to plaintiffs' distribution of its services.

Moreover, the court explained that defendants' use of the plaintiffs' mark was in connection with goods or services because it contained a link to the defendants' apartment-guide website.

Similarly, in *Planned Parenthood Federation of America, Inc. v. Bucci*, the plaintiff owned the "Planned Parenthood" mark, but the defendant registered the domain name plannedparenthood.com. Using the domain name, the defendant created a website containing information antithetical to the plaintiff's views. The court ruled that the defendant used the plaintiff's mark "in connection with" the distribution of services

> because it is likely to prevent some Internet users from reaching plaintiff's own Internet web site. Prospective users of plaintiff's services who mistakenly access defendant's web site may fail to continue to search for plaintiff's own home page, due to anger, frustration, or the belief that plaintiff's home page does not exist.

The same reasoning applies here. As the district court explained, Doughney's use of PETA's Mark in the domain name of his website

> is likely to prevent Internet users from reaching [PETA's] own Internet web site. The prospective users of [PETA's] services who mistakenly access Defendant's web site may fail to continue to search for [PETA's] own home page, due to anger, frustration, or the belief that [PETA's] home page does not exist.

Moreover, Doughney's web site provides links to more than 30 commercial operations offering goods and services. By providing links to these commercial operations, Doughney's use of PETA's Mark is "in connection with" the sale of goods or services.

Questions:

1.) Why does the court say "There is no dispute here that PETA owns the "PETA" Mark, that Doughney used it, and that Doughney used the Mark 'in commerce.' Doughney disputes the district court's findings that he used the Mark in connection with goods or services. . . ." If § 1127 is the benchmark, is "using the mark in connection with goods and services" not part of the *definition* of "use in commerce" in § 1127?

2.) The court says,

> To use PETA's Mark "in connection with" goods or services, Doughney need not have actually sold or advertised goods or services on the www.peta.org website. Rather, Doughney need only have prevented users from obtaining or using PETA's goods or services. . . .

It goes on to list several possible ways that this might have happened, including one known technically as initial interest confusion. Although Doughney's disclaimer reveals to the web searcher once they arrive at his domain that this is not the PETA they have been looking for (bonus for identifying the classical reference), PETA is harmed nevertheless. The searcher may give up, frustrated, or they may become genuinely interested in the material offered on the People Eating Tasty Animals site. Either one, the court suggests, is enough to provide the link to goods or services.

a.) If we read the PETA opinion broadly it could be seen as defining "use in commerce" to include having a negative, displacing or substitute effect on the commercial activities of others. If so, what activities are swept into trademark's domain? A noisy protest outside a Walmart that includes signs with Walmart's logo on them? A website criticizing Apple's labor practices in China, and urging a consumer boycott, that superimposes the Apple logo over pictures of sweatshops? How might the court seek to cabin or curtail such overreach?

b.) The court here uses a concept called "initial interest confusion"—the person who initially searches for one brand but, finding another because of a momentary confusion, once informed of her error decides to purchase the new brand instead, or gives up the search. Initial interest confusion is a controversial topic in trademark law and some courts have rejected it. "[T]he kind of confusion that is more likely to result [here] namely, that consumers will realize they are at the wrong site and go to an Internet search engine to find the right one—is not substantial enough to be legally significant. '[A]n initial confusion on the part of web browsers . . . is not cognizable under trademark law.'" *Hasbro, Inc. v. Clue Computing, Inc.* (D. Mass. 1999) (*aff'd.* 1st Cir. 2000). The Ninth Circuit has been more equivocal.

Here the important point to note is that the *PETA* court is using initial interest confusion (normally, as the name suggests, part of the analysis of whether there is *confusion*) as part of the analysis of whether the mark was *used in commerce* in connection with goods and services. Under the *PETA* approach negative initial interest confusion caused by the use of the mark, such as in a protest website, would appear to be enough to satisfy the use in commerce test. This aspect of the opinion (itself a contestable interpretation of the *PETA* decision) has been widely criticized by scholars and rejected by some courts. For example, the Ninth Circuit, which has sometimes accepted the idea of initial interest confusion as one form of actionable infringement, has declined to consider such effects *also* to constitute "commercial" activity. Ironically, it did so by quoting the 4th Circuit, the court that produced the *PETA* decision.

> Nissan Motor argues that disparaging remarks or links to websites with disparaging remarks at nissan.com is commercial because the comments

have an effect on its own commerce. . . . However, we have never adopted an "effect on commerce" test to determine whether speech is commercial and decline to do so here. We are persuaded by the Fourth Circuit's reasoning in a similar case involving negative material about Skippy Peanut Butter posted on skippy.com, a website hosted by the owner of the trademark SKIPPY for a cartoon comic strip. CPC, which makes Skippy Peanut Butter, successfully sought an injunction that ordered removal of the material. The court of appeals reversed. *CPC Int'l, Inc. v. Skippy Inc.* (4th Cir. 2000). Recognizing that criticism was vexing to CPC, the court emphasized how important it is that "trademarks not be 'transformed from rights against unfair competition to rights to control language.'" Id. at 462 (quoting Mark A. Lemley, "The Modern Lanham Act and the Death of Common Sense," 108 Yale L.J. 1687, 1710–11 (1999)). It held that speech critical of CPC was informational, not commercial speech. Likewise here, links to negative commentary about Nissan Motor, and about this litigation, reflect a point of view that we believe is protected. *Nissan Motor Co. v. Nissan Computer Corp.* (9th Cir. 2004).

2.) Likelihood of Confusion

"Likelihood of confusion" is a, perhaps *the,* fundamental test in trademark law. It is the standard for determining trademark infringement of both **registered marks under § 1114** and **unregistered marks under § 1125(a)**, and **for determining whether § 1052(d) bars federal registration of a mark** (as you read in Chapter 6). (**It is also used for assessing infringement of state marks.**) The basic question is whether, because of the similarity of the defendant's and plaintiff's marks, the consumer is likely to mistakenly associate the defendant's goods or services with the plaintiff.

Each federal circuit has developed a multifactor test to "help grapple with the 'vexing' problem of resolving the likelihood of confusion issue" (quoting *Lois Sportswear v. Levi Strauss*, below). These tests are named after seminal cases, so the Ninth Circuit uses the *Sleekcraft* test, the Fourth Circuit the *Pizzeria Uno* test, the Eighth Circuit the *SquirtCo* test, etc.; in *Lois Sportswear*, you'll see an application of the Second Circuit's *Polaroid* test. While the formulation and terminology of these tests vary from circuit to circuit, the key factors are similar. All of the circuits look at some variant of the following: **the similarity of the plaintiff's and defendant's marks**, **the proximity of their goods or services**, **the strength of the plaintiff's mark**, and **evidence of actual confusion.** Twelve circuits explicitly consider the **defendant's intent**, and ten circuits consider **consumer sophistication**. Before turning to *Lois Sportswear*'s treatment of these factors, here is a summary of some case law and considerations.

Similarity of the marks. Remember from Chapter 4 that trademark rights cover mark X for product Y, not the word or symbol itself. Therefore, this factor is linked to the next one (proximity of the products), and the degree of similarity necessary to prove infringement varies inversely with the proximity of the goods or services. "Delta" for faucets does not infringe "Delta" for airlines, but "Deltoid Airlines" might. For closely related products, a lesser degree of resemblance between the marks may suffice; for linked but dissimilar products, something closer to exact identity may be required, while for completely distinct categories of goods or services even identity is irrelevant.

Similarity is not confined to the appearance of a mark. Marks are compared in terms of **sight**, **sound**, **meaning**, and **overall "commercial impression."** Of course, establishing the commercial impression that a trademark ultimately conjures in the mind of the consumer is not an exact science. Do you think the following marks are confusingly similar? Why or why not?

- "Bonamine" and "Dramamine," both for motion sickness drugs
- "Blue Lightning" and "Blue Thunder," both for automotive audio components
- "Beauty Sleep" and "BeautyRest," both for mattresses
- "RestMaster" and "Sleepmaster," both for mattresses

These are all based on actual cases; likelihood of confusion was found in the first three examples, but not in the fourth. And remember the § 1052(d) hypotheticals from Chapter 6? "Mister Stain" was found confusingly similar to "Mr. Clean," but "Master Kleen" for dry cleaning services was not. And registration of the silhouette mark for health and beauty aids was refused on confusion grounds, while registration of the wave mark for seafood was not.

Proximity of the goods or services. The focus here is on whether the plaintiff's and defendant's products are sufficiently related in the mind of the consumer to support a finding of likelihood of confusion; the products in question need not be in direct competition. As mentioned above, this factor is connected to the similarity of the marks: the more similar the marks, the less related the goods or services need to be to suggest potential confusion. The multifactor tests in some circuits include related inquiries into how the products are marketed, channels of trade, their comparative quality, and whether the plaintiff will "bridge the gap" into the defendant's market.

Not surprisingly, analysis of this factor is highly dependent on context and evidence. For example, while food or beverage products are frequently found to be related to restaurant services, there is no *per se* rule connecting these categories; the evidence must show "something more" to support a finding of likelihood of confusion. This requirement was met with the following marks: COLOMBIANO COFFEE HOUSE for "providing food and drink" and COLOMBIAN for "coffee" (coffee houses emphasize coffee beverages); OPUS ONE for "restaurant services" and OPUS ONE for "wine" (the "Opus One" restaurant actually served "Opus One" wine); and AMAZON (with a parrot design) for "chili sauce and pepper sauce" and AMAZON for "restaurant services" (restaurants commonly market their own sauces). *See Trademark Manual of Examining Procedure* § 1207.01(a)(ii)(A). But the evidence pointed the other way with BLUE MOON (with an associated moon design) for "beer" and BLUE MOON (with a different moon design) for "restaurant services." In *In re Coors Brewing Co.* (Fed. Cir. 2003), the Federal Circuit acknowledged that the BLUE MOON marks were similar, but found that even though some restaurants make their own beer and some breweries are also restaurants, the "degree of overlap between the sources of restaurant services and the sources of beer is *de minimis*." Despite the existing BLUE MOON restaurant, Coors successfully registered BLUE MOON as a mark for beer, by presenting evidence that there were around 815,000 restaurants in the US and only 1,450 breweries (this number has doubtless increased since then), and the court reasoned that even if all of these breweries were also restaurants, this would only account for a minuscule percentage of overall restaurants (fewer than one in 500).

Strength of the plaintiff's mark. Stronger marks enjoy broader protection against trademark infringement, with strength being defined both in terms of inherent distinctiveness (recall the spectrum of distinctiveness in Chapter 5—fanciful, arbitrary, and suggestive marks are inherently distinctive) and acquired distinctiveness (the amount of fame or consumer recognition a mark has achieved). The theory is that the more distinctive or widely recognized the mark, the more likely it is to come to mind when purchasers encounter a similar mark. Do you agree? Are stronger marks more susceptible to confusion? Or does their strength mean consumers will more easily distinguish them from similar marks?

Actual confusion. Because the question is *likelihood* of confusion, evidence of actual confusion is not necessary to establish trademark infringement. However, such evidence—if convincing, and not beset by methodological defects or bias—can be persuasive proof of likelihood of confusion.

Survey evidence (discussed briefly in Chapter 5) can be used to show actual confusion (or lack thereof). Two prominent approaches are the "Eveready" format and the "Squirt" format (from *Union Carbide Corp. v. Ever-Ready, Inc.* (7th Cir. 1976) and *Squirt Co. v. Seven-Up Co.* (8th Cir. 1980)). An "Eveready" survey shows respondents the defendant's product and asks: "Who do you think puts out [the defendant's product] shown here?" "What makes you think so?" "Please name any other products put out by the same concern which puts out the [defendant's product] shown here." Responses referring to the plaintiff or its products suggest consumer confusion. A "Squirt" survey shows respondents *both* defendant's and plaintiff's products and asks: "Do you think [defendant's and plaintiff's products] are put out by the same company or by different companies?" "What makes you think that?" This format has been criticized for "priming" the participants to find confusion where none exists, and for fabricating marketplace conditions. (In practice, courts may limit the admissibility of "Squirt" surveys to cases in which the products in question also appear side-by-side in the real world.) Which approach do you think is preferable for plaintiffs whose mark is not well-known? For plaintiffs whose mark is famous and readily called to mind?

Note that while surveys can be important in likelihood of confusion cases, they are also too expensive for many litigants. As a result, survey evidence features prominently in high-profile litigation, but studies suggest a more limited role in trademark cases as a whole. *See* Barton Beebe, *An Empirical Study of the Multifactor Tests for Trademark Infringement*, 94 Calif. L. Rev. 1581 (2006).

Defendant's intent. If the focus is on the confusion of the *consumer*, why is the defendant's intent relevant? If I'm not confused about the source of a product, no amount of bad faith on the part of its producer will change that. Accordingly, courts have acknowledged that this factor is "more pertinent to issues other than likelihood of confusion, such as harm to plaintiff's reputation and choice of remedy." *Virgin Enterprises Ltd. v. Nawab* (2d Cir. 2003).

Are some of these factors more important than others in practice? An empirical study by Professor Barton Beebe suggests that the similarity of the marks tends to be the most important factor, and that in order to show a likelihood of confusion, a plaintiff must prevail on it (out of 192 opinions studied by Professor Beebe, the 65 opinions finding that the marks were not similar all ultimately found no likelihood of confusion). *See* Barton Beebe, *An Empirical Study of the Multifactor Tests for Trademark Infringement*, 94 CALIF. L. REV. 1581 (2006). Interestingly, the study suggests that the second most important factor is the defendant's intent, notwithstanding the observation above that it's more pertinent to peripheral issues (of 67 opinions finding bad faith, 65 also decided confusion was likely, and the 2 opinions deciding otherwise also found that the marks weren't similar). After these two factors, the more important factors appeared to be (in order of decreasing importance) the proximity of the products, evidence of actual confusion, and the strength of the plaintiff's mark.

Modern trademark law has expanded the scope of likelihood of confusion beyond "source" confusion (I mistakenly buy "Duke" ketchup because I think it's made by the producers of delicious "Duke's" mayonnaise, only to discover it's a lower quality condiment). Trademark infringement also encompasses "sponsorship or affiliation" confusion (I buy "Duke" ketchup because I'm a Duke fan and assume there must have been some licensing deal with Duke University, not because I think Duke University made the ketchup or have any corresponding expectations about its quality). Should Duke University be able to claim trademark infringement? Section 1125(a) explicitly refers not only to confusion as to "origin," but also as to "affiliation, connection, or association" and "sponsorship or approval." But some courts have stretched this kind of penumbral confusion to extremes. In one example, the owner of the familiar "Dairy Queen" trademark for frozen dairy treats was able to enjoin New Line Productions from using the title "Dairy Queens" for a mockumentary about beauty contests in the rural Minnesota (part of "dairy country"). *American Dairy Queen v. New Line Productions* (D. Minn. 1998) (noting that consumers might think New Line had received Dairy Queen's "endorsement or permission.") For a criticism of this trend, *see* Mark A. Lemley & Mark McKenna, *Irrelevant Confusion*, 62 STAN. L. REV. 413 (2010).

Other expansive readings of "likelihood of confusion" extend it beyond the point of sale. You've just encountered "initial interest confusion" in *Rescuecom* and *PETA*. The *Lois Sportswear* case below deals with "post-sale confusion" on the other side of the purchasing decision.

Lois Sportswear, U.S.A., Inc. v. Levi Strauss & Co.
799 F.2d 867 (2d Cir. 1986)

TIMBERS, Circuit Judge.

Appellee is a world famous clothing manufacturer. One of its most popular products is a line of casual pants known as Levi Jeans. Appellee began manufacturing its denim jeans in the 1850s. Each pair of jeans contains numerous identifying features. One such feature is a distinct back pocket stitching pattern. This pattern consists of two intersecting arcs which roughly bisect both pockets of appellee's jeans. Appellee has an incontestable federal trademark in this stitching pattern. See 15 U.S.C. § 1065 (1982). Appellee has used this pattern on all its jeans continuously since 1873. In many ways the back pocket stitching pattern has become the embodiment of Levi Jeans in the minds of jeans buyers. The record is replete with undisputed examples of the intimate association between the stitching pattern and appellee's products in the buying public's mind. Not only has appellee spent considerable sums on promoting the stitching pattern, but various competitors have run nationwide advertisement campaigns touting the advantages of their jeans' back pockets over appellee's. In addition, one of the largest chains of jeans retailers, the Gap Stores, has run numerous advertisements featuring pictures of appellee's back pocket stitching pattern as the entire visual portion of the ad. The record also contains numerous examples of the public's phenomenal reaction to the stitching pattern and the jeans it epitomizes. These examples range from national magazine cover stories to high school yearbook dedications.

Appellant Lois Sportswear, U.S.A., Inc. ("Lois") imports into the United States jeans manufactured in Spain by Textiles Y Confecciones Europeas, S.A. ("Textiles"). The instant litigation was commenced because appellants' jeans bear a back pocket stitching pattern substantially similar to appellee's trademark stitching pattern. On appeal appellants do not challenge the district court's conclusion that the two stitching patterns are substantially similar. Nor could they; the two patterns are virtually identical when viewed from any appreciable distance. In fact, the results from a survey based on showing consumers videotapes of the back pockets of various jeans, including appellants', indicate that 44% of those interviewed mistook appellants' jeans for appellee's jeans. Appellants instead rely on their use of various labels, some permanent and some temporary, to distinguish their jeans and defeat appellee's trademark infringement and unfair competition claims.

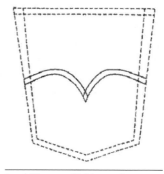

Levi Strauss stitching pattern. Image from the USPTO trademark record.

On July 12, 1985 the court held a hearing on the motions at which depositions, exhibits and memoranda were received. Most of the evidence sought to show that appellee's back pocket stitching pattern had achieved a strong secondary meaning, i.e., that jeans consumers associated the pattern with appellee's products. This evidence is undisputed for the most part. The remainder of the evidence is focused on the respective quality of the two products at issue and the likelihood that consumers somehow would confuse the source of appellants' jeans.

The evidence is undisputed that appellants and appellee manufacture and sell a similar product. While stratifying the jeans market with various styles and grades seems to be the current rage, there can be no dispute that the parties before us compete to sell their jeans to the public. The record does indicate that appellants have attempted to target their "designer" jeans at a decidedly upscale market segment. There also was evidence, however, that appellants' jeans were selling at deep discount in cut-rate clothing outlets. Moreover, there was substantial evidence which indicated that appellee's jeans, although originally marketed as work pants, had achieved a certain elan among the fashion conscious. The evidence suggests that appellee's jeans have achieved fad popularity in all sectors of the jeans market. Finally, appellee produced affidavits stating that it was planning to enter the designer jeans market.

In short, the uncontested facts show that appellants' jeans exhibit a back pocket stitching pattern substantially similar to appellee's incontestable registered trademark back pocket stitching pattern. The record also makes plain that the stitching pattern is closely associated with appellee's jeans, and that appellants' use of the stitching pattern on arguably competing jeans at least presents the possibility that consumers will be confused as to the source of appellants' jeans or the relationship between appellants and appellee. With these facts in mind, we turn to the relevant law of trademark infringement and unfair competition in our Court.

II.

Appellants' arguments, for the most part, focus only on the likelihood that consumers will buy appellants' jeans thinking they are appellee's jeans due to the similar stitching patterns. Appellants point to their labeling as conclusive proof that no such confusion is likely. We agree with the district court, however, that the two principal areas of confusion raised by appellants' use of appellee's stitching pattern are: (1) the likelihood that jeans consumers will be confused as to the relationship between appellants and appellee; and (2) the likelihood that consumers will be confused as to the source of appellants' jeans when the jeans are observed in the post-sale context. We hold that the Lanham Act, 15 U.S.C. §§ 1051–1127 (1982), as interpreted by our Court, was meant to prevent such likely confusion.

As a threshold matter, in the past we have found it useful to decide how much protection a particular trademark is to be given by first determining what type of trademark is at issue. In *Abercrombie & Fitch Co. v. Hunting World, Inc.*, Judge Friendly set forth what has become the governing law of trademark classification: "Arrayed in an ascending order which roughly reflects their eligibility to trademark status and the degree of protection accorded, these classes are (1) generic, (2) descriptive, (3) suggestive, and (4) arbitrary or fanciful."

Superimposed on this framework is the rule that registered trademarks are presumed to be distinctive and should be afforded the utmost protection.

It is clear under this framework that appellee's back pocket stitching pattern deserves the highest degree of protection. First, the mark is registered and incontestable. This, of course, entitles the mark to significant protection. Second, the mark, being a fanciful pattern of interconnected arcs, is within Judge Friendly's fourth category and is entitled to the most protection the Lanham Act can provide. In deciding the likelihood of confusion issues, therefore, appellee's mark is entitled to a liberal application of the law.

Turning to the principal issues under the Lanham Act, in either a claim of trademark infringement under § 32 or a claim of unfair competition under § 43, a prima facie case is made out by showing the use of one's trademark by another in a way that is likely to confuse consumers as to the source of the product. See *Mushroom Makers, Inc. v. R.G. Barry Corp.* (2d Cir. 1978) ("The ultimate inquiry in most actions for false designation of origin, as with actions for trademark infringement, is whether there exists a 'likelihood that an appreciable number of ordinarily prudent purchasers [will] be misled, or indeed simply confused, as to the source of the goods in question.'").

In deciding the issue of likelihood of confusion in the instant case, the district court relied on the multifactor balancing test set forth by Judge Friendly in *Polaroid Corp. v. Polarad Electronics Corp.* (2d Cir. 1961). At the outset, it must be remembered just what the *Polaroid* factors are designed to test. The factors are designed to help grapple with the "vexing" problem of resolving the likelihood of confusion issue. Therefore, each factor must be evaluated in the context of how it bears on the ultimate question of likelihood of confusion as to the source of the product. It also must be emphasized that the ultimate conclusion as to whether a likelihood of confusion exists is not to be determined in accordance with some rigid formula. The *Polaroid* factors serve as a useful guide through a difficult quagmire. Appellants place great reliance on their labeling as a means of preventing any confusion. While such labeling may prevent appellants' use of appellee's stitching pattern from confusing consumers at the point of sale into believing that appellee manufactured and marketed appellants' jeans, the labeling does nothing to alleviate other forms of likely confusion that are equally actionable.

First, a distinct possibility raised by appellants' use of appellee's immediately identifiable stitching pattern is that consumers will be confused into believing that appellee either somehow is associated with appellants or has consented to appellants' use of its trademark. In *Dallas Cowboys Cheerleaders, Inc. v. Pussycat Cinema, Ltd.* (2d Cir. 1979), we held that "[t]he public's belief that the mark's owner sponsored or otherwise approved of the use of the trademark satisfies the confusion requirement." Likewise, in *Grotrian, Helfferich, Schulz, Th. Steinweg Nachf. v. Steinway & Sons* (2d Cir. 1975), we held that "[t]he harm to [the trademark owner], rather, is the likelihood that a consumer, hearing the [similar sounding] name and thinking it had some connection with [the trademark owner] would consider [the product] on that basis. The [similar sounding] name therefore would attract potential customers based on the reputation built up by [the trademark owner] in this country for many years." In *Steinway*, we held that the Lanham Act was designed to prevent a competitor from such a bootstrapping of a trademark owner's goodwill by the use of a substantially similar mark. Therefore, the *Polaroid* factors must be applied in the instant case with an eye to how they bear on the likelihood that appellants' use of appellee's trademark stitching pattern will confuse consumers into thinking that appellee is somehow associated with appellants or has consented to their use of the stitching pattern regardless of labeling.

Second, it is equally clear that post-sale confusion as to source is actionable under the Lanham Act. In the instant case, this post-sale confusion would involve consumers seeing appellant's jeans outside of the retail store, perhaps being worn by a passer-by. The confusion the Act seeks to prevent in this context is that a consumer seeing the familiar stitching pattern will associate the jeans with appellee and that association will influence his buying decisions. Clearly, in this post-sale context appellants' labels, most of which having been long since discarded, will be of no help. The Ninth Circuit case of *Levi Strauss & Co. v. Blue Bell, Inc.* (9th Cir. 1980), is very persuasive on this point. In *Blue Bell*, the court upheld an injunction preventing the manufacturer of Wrangler jeans from using a back pocket name tag similar to the one used on Levi's jeans. The court held that Wrangler's extensive labeling, including its own name on the very tag at issue, was not sufficient to avoid confusion as to source in the post-sale context. The court held that "Wrangler's use of its projecting label is likely to cause confusion among prospective purchasers who carry even an imperfect recollection of Strauss's mark and who observe Wrangler's projecting label after the point of sale." Precisely the same considerations apply in the instant case. The *Polaroid* factors therefore must be applied with an eye toward post-sale confusion also.

The first factor—the strength of the mark—weighs heavily in appellee's favor. We have defined the strength of a mark as "its tendency to identify the goods sold under the mark as emanating from a particular source." As discussed above, appellee's back pocket stitching pattern is a fanciful registered trademark with a very strong secondary meaning. Virtually all jeans consumers associate the stitching pattern with appellee's products. We agree with the district court that the evidence indicates as a matter of law that appellee's stitching pattern is a very strong mark. This factor is crucial to the likelihood of confusion analysis since appellee's intimate association with the trademark makes it much more likely that consumers will assume wrongly that appellee is somehow associated with appellants' jeans or has authorized the use of its mark, or, in the post-sale context, that appellee has manufactured the jeans.

The second factor—the degree of similarity of the marks—also weighs in favor of appellee. As the district court correctly observed, the two stitching patterns are "essentially identical." Both patterns consist of two intersecting arcs placed in the exact same position on the back pockets of the jeans. The only difference—the fact that appellants' arcs extend 3/4 inch further down the pocket at their intersection—is imperceptible at any significant distance. In light of the fact that the stitching pattern is in no way dictated by function and an infinite number of patterns are possible, the similarity of the two patterns is striking. When this striking similarity is factored into the likelihood of confusion analysis, its great importance becomes clear. In view of the trademark's strength, this nearly identical reproduction of the stitching pattern no doubt is likely to cause consumers to believe that appellee somehow is associated with appellants or at least has consented to the use of its trademark. In the post-sale context, this striking similarity no doubt will cause consumers to transfer the goodwill they feel for appellee to appellants, at least initially. This misuse of goodwill is at the heart of unfair competition. Appellants' reliance on the effect of their labeling with respect to this factor underscores their misguided focus on only the most obvious form of consumer confusion. Appellants' labeling in no way dispels the likelihood that consumers will conclude that appellants' jeans are somehow connected to appellee by virtue of the nearly identical stitching patterns.

The third factor—the proximity of the products—also weighs in favor of appellee. Both products are jeans. Although appellants argue that their jeans are designer jeans and are sold to a different market segment than appellee's jeans, there is significant evidence in the record of an overlap of market segments. Moreover, even if the two jeans are in different segments of the jeans market, such a finding would not switch this factor to appellants' side of the scale. We are trying to determine if it is likely that consumers mistakenly will assume either that appellants' jeans somehow are associated with appellee or are made by appellee. The fact that appellants' jeans arguably are in a different market segment makes this type of confusion more likely. Certainly a consumer observing appellee's striking stitching pattern on appellants' designer jeans might assume that appellee had chosen to enter that market segment using a subsidiary corporation, or that appellee had allowed appellants' designers to use appellee's trademark as a means of reaping some profits from the designer jeans fad without a full commitment to that market segment. Likewise, in the post-sale context a consumer seeing appellants' jeans on a passer-by might think that the jeans were appellee's long-awaited entry into the designer jeans market segment. Motivated by this mistaken notion—appellee's goodwill—the consumer might then buy appellants' jeans even after discovering his error. After all, the way the jeans look is a primary consideration to most designer jeans buyers.

The fourth factor—bridging the gap—is closely related to the proximity of the products and does not aid appellants' case. Under this factor, if the owner of a trademark can show that it intends to enter the market of the alleged infringer, that showing helps to establish a future likelihood of confusion as to source. We have held that the trademark laws are designed in part to protect "the senior user's interest in being able to enter a related field at some future time." In the instant case, the district court rejected as irrelevant appellee's affidavits which stated that appellee was planning to enter the designer jeans market, since the affidavits did not assert that appellee's designer jeans entry would utilize the stitching pattern. We do not believe, however, that the form appellee's entry into the market segment might take is especially relevant to the likelihood of confusion issue. Appellee's entry into the market, regardless of the form it might take, would increase the chances of consumer confusion as to the source of appellants' jeans because of likely consumer expectations that appellee's designer jeans would bear its famous stitching pattern. If one knew only that appellee had entered the designer jeans market and then saw appellants' jeans in a post-sale context, it is very likely that one could confuse them for appellee's entry. See *McGregor-Doniger* ("Because consumer confusion is the key, the assumptions of the typical consumer, whether or not they match reality, must be taken into account."). Also, appellee has an interest in preserving its trademark should it ever wish to produce designer jeans with the stitching pattern. The Lanham Act is meant to protect this interest. *Scarves by Vera, Inc.* (scarf designer has right to prevent use of her tradename on cosmetics even without proof that she presently intends to enter cosmetic market).

The fifth factor—actual confusion—while not helping appellee, does not really hurt its case. Appellee's only evidence of actual confusion was a consumer survey which the district court discounted due to methodological defects in simulating the post-sale environment. Of course, it is black letter law that actual confusion need not be shown to prevail under the Lanham Act, since actual confusion is very difficult to prove and the Act requires only a likelihood of confusion as to source. While the complete absence of actual confusion evidence after a significant period of competition may weigh in a defendant's favor, such an inference is unjustified in the instant case in view of the survey evidence, even with its methodological defects. While these defects go to the weight of the survey, it is still somewhat probative of actual confusion in the post-sale context. In any event, the record indicates that sales of appellants' jeans have been minimal in the United States thus far and there has been little chance for actual confusion as yet. It would be unfair to penalize appellee for acting to protect its trademark rights before serious damage has occurred.

The sixth factor—the junior user's good faith in adopting the mark—weighs in favor of appellants. The evidence before the district court, when viewed in a light favorable to appellants, indicates that appellants happened on the stitching pattern serendipitously. It must be remembered, however, that intentional copying is not a requirement under the Lanham Act. Also, intent is largely irrelevant in determining if consumers likely will be confused as to source. The history of advertising suggests that consumer reactions usually are unrelated to manufacturer intentions.

The seventh factor—the quality of the respective goods—does add some weight to appellants' position. Appellee has conceded that appellants' jeans are not of an inferior quality, arguably reducing appellee's interest in protecting its reputation from debasement. It must be noted, however, that under the circumstances of this case the good quality of appellants' product actually may increase the likelihood of confusion as to source. Particularly in the post-sale context, consumers easily could assume that quality jeans bearing what is perceived as appellee's trademark stitching pattern to be a Levi's product. The fact that appellants have produced a quality copy suggests that the possibility of their profiting from appellee's goodwill is still likely.

The eighth and final factor—the sophistication of relevant buyers—does not, under the circumstances of this case, favor appellants. The district court found, and the parties do not dispute, that the typical buyer of "designer" jeans is sophisticated with respect to jeans buying. Appellants argue that this sophistication prevents these consumers from becoming confused by nearly identical back pocket stitching patterns. On the contrary, we believe that it is a sophisticated jeans consumer who is most likely to assume that the presence of appellee's trademark stitching pattern on appellants' jeans indicates some sort of association between the two manufacturers. Presumably it is these sophisticated jeans buyers who pay the most attention to back pocket stitching patterns and their "meanings". Likewise, in the post-sale context, the sophisticated buyer is more likely to be affected by the sight of appellee's stitching pattern on appellants' jeans and, consequently, to transfer goodwill. Finally, to the extent the sophisticated buyer is attracted to appellee's jeans because of the exclusiveness of its stitching pattern, appellee's sales will be affected adversely by these buyers' ultimate realization that the pattern is no longer exclusive.

Our review of the district court's application of the *Polaroid* factors convinces us that the court correctly concluded that consumers are likely to mistakenly associate appellants' jeans with appellee or will confuse the source of appellants' jeans when the jeans are observed in the post-sale context. This result is eminently reasonable in view of the undisputed evidence of the use by one jeans manufacturer of the trademark back pocket stitching pattern of another jeans manufacturer, coupled with the fact that the trademark stitching pattern is instantly associated with its owner and is important to consumers. There is simply too great a risk that appellants will profit from appellee's hard-earned goodwill to permit the use.

We affirm the eminently sound decision of Judge Sweet based on the well established law of this Circuit.

MINER, Circuit Judge, dissenting. [Omitted.]

Questions:

1.) The court emphasizes that the mark not only protects the goods in question, but the owner's right to expand the mark to other areas and product lines. The market in question here—designer jeans—is a close one to the original product, but the court also favorably quotes another case in which a scarf designer had the "right to prevent use of her tradename on cosmetics even without proof that she presently intends to enter cosmetic market." Do you agree with the court's conclusion that "The Lanham Act is meant to protect this interest"? How does this idea of "room to expand the brand," of an entitlement to grow beyond the current product category, fit with the rationales of trademark law? If this is true, why can Bass beer not enjoin Bass shoes and Bass electronics, and Delta Airlines enjoin Delta faucets? Is there a distinguishing factor that separates these cases?

2.) After deciding most of the factors against Lois, the court finds, strangely, both that Levi's is a hugely famous brand and its stitching pattern iconic, and that "appellants [Lois] happened on the stitching pattern serendipitously." (?) It goes on to say "It must be remembered, however, that intentional copying is not a requirement under the Lanham Act" and concludes "[t]here is simply too great a risk that appellants will profit from appellee's hard-earned goodwill to permit the use." How is this different from the kind of "reaping where one has not sown" that Justice Pitney condemned in *INS v. AP*? Does it matter, should it matter, if I am serendipitously, not deliberately, benefiting from a positive externality created by another? Why does the Lanham Act nevertheless not require intentional copying?

3.) Look back at the Cohen quote at the beginning of Chapter 4. He said,

> In practice, injunctive relief is being extended today to realms where no actual danger of confusion to the consumer is present, and this extension has been vigorously supported and encouraged by leading writers in the field. . . . The current legal argument runs: One who by the ingenuity of his advertising or the quality of his product has induced consumer responsiveness to a particular name, symbol, form of packaging, etc., has thereby created a thing of value; a thing of value is property; the creator of property is entitled to protection against third parties who seek to deprive him of his property.

Does Cohen accurately describe the reasoning of this case or is the court, in fact, concerned about consumer confusion, efficient producer-consumer communication, and the protection of investment in stable brand names?

4.) As mentioned earlier, the court finds that the Lanham Act does not merely protect against confusion at the point of sale—I think I am buying Dove soap but actually it is *Dave's* soap in similar packaging. It also protects against *post* point of sale confusion, where labels and disclaimers are of no use. Thus it prevents Lois jeans, bought knowingly by a savvy consumer, from being mistaken on the street for Levi's by a *non*-purchaser. Do you agree? Does this stretch the rationale of trademark law?

5.) When considering the seventh factor, the quality of the goods, the court acknowledges that Lois jeans are of high quality, but goes on to say that "the good quality of appellants' product actually may increase the likelihood of confusion as to source." If Lois jeans had been markedly inferior to Levi's would this have helped them? What if they were of identical quality? Under the court's reasoning, is there *any* level of quality under which Lois would not lose this factor?

6.) To summarize the points made in the preceding questions, no matter the formal factors a court must look at in order to determine likelihood of confusion, the results will still differ depending on the underlying vision of the scope of the trademark right.

One vision of the scope of a trademark confines it tightly to the semantic interaction between *this* good or service, *this* mark, *this* consumer and *this* manufacturer. Dove for soap does not infringe Dove for chocolate. The rationale for the right is to maintain stable meaning of the symbols that producers use and consumers rely on. The key *market* is the one the trademark owner is already in, with perhaps a small room for expansion to closely related markets (Levi designer jeans not Levi Jeep interiors). The key *person* whose confusion is relevant is the purchaser (and thus labels that explicitly disclaim connection to another producer are very strong evidence that consumers will not be likely to be confused). The key *moment* is the moment of sale. Confusion before the moment of sale (as with the person who clicks on a Google advertisement served up by her search for "Coach bags," only to be shown Kate Spade bags that she ends up preferring to Coach) is irrelevant. Confusion *after* the moment of sale (as when the Chrysler 300 is seen on the street and mistaken for a Bentley, when the driver knows very well it is not) is irrelevant. Wherever the narrow reach of the right does not extend, competition—including competition built on deliberately copying non-trademarked features of another product—is to be welcomed.

The second, broader, vision of the scope of a trademark right views it partly as a device to avoid (current) consumer confusion and diminution of the utility of trademark symbols. In that, it agrees with the narrower view. But it goes beyond that to see the trademark right as rooted in broader themes of unfair competition law, protecting acquired goodwill which can be leveraged into new markets whenever the producer wants, and preventing other producers from "reaping where they have not sown" even if the *consumer* is not at all confused. The right is no longer confined tightly to the semantic interaction between this consumer, this mark, this good and this producer. It is extended to cover possible *future* markets. It is as if, by having the mark, I have planted a semantic claim stake on the empty range next door. The relevant *moment* is expanded both before and after the point of sale, to cover initial interest confusion and post point of sale confusion. If the consumer was interested initially in my mark, I deserve to get that consumer, even if they come to prefer the goods of my rival. The person whose likelihood of confusion is relevant is not merely the actual consumer, but the bystander and possible future purchaser. This vision of the right protects a larger swath of time, reaches a larger swath of markets and protects against (as a legal realist, Cohen would say 'judicially creates') "harms" that the first vision simply does not reach.

Federal courts offer decisions that resonate with both of these two visions. For example, the courts that find initial interest confusion actionable are obviously closer to the broader idea of trademark rights, while those rejecting it are closer to the narrower view. In *Walmart* the court seemed happy to sacrifice acquired goodwill in a product design, because of the greater interest in encouraging competition. The general rule that trademarks are specific to the actual good or service with which the mark is connected expresses the narrow view. An expansive vision of "room to expand beyond the brand," or the interest of famous marks being protected against non-confusing dilution, reflects the broader.

The *Lois* court makes many points that seem to resonate with the second, broader vision of trademark. Does it need to in order to find likelihood of confusion? After all, these are two types of jeans that look almost identical. Would the first, narrower, vision of trademark not easily find that eventuality likely to produce confusion?

3.) Contributory Infringement

The Lois jeans case gives us the standard for straightforward, primary, trademark infringement as well as the infringement of the rights § 1125(a) gives to unregistered marks and trade dress. But what about secondary infringement? What about an entity that *facilitates* or *encourages* or *controls and profits from* the trademark infringement of others but does not itself infringe?

In the online world, secondary liability for violation of intellectual property rights—particularly copyright and trademark rights—is vital. Increasingly, rights holders want to curtail the activities of intermediaries—internet service providers, online marketplaces, search engines, social networks and file lockers. These services can be used legally but can also be used by customers to violate intellectual property rights. Why not go directly after the individuals who are violating the rights? First, the primary infringers are hard (and expensive) to find and to control once found. They do not have deep pockets. Second, from the point of the right-holder, the intermediaries are profiting from the portion of their activities that facilitates infringement. Why should they not internalize the costs, the "negative externalities" as economists would put it, that their activities are helping to create? Would this not appropriately incentivize them to cut down on infringement, like the polluting factory forced to internalize the costs of its own pollution? Finally, are the intermediaries not morally culpable? Are they not aware of high levels of illegal activity? Do they not turn a deliberate blind eye to it?

The opposing position sees the attempt to impose secondary liability—liability for contributing to infringement—as fraught with extraordinary difficulty. Google copies the entire web every day. That is what a search engine does. Must it therefore be liable when it copies infringing pages along with non-infringing ones? These intermediaries—viewed by rights owners as facilitators of piracy—are also a central part of the architecture of the internet, the entities whose activities facilitate all the expressive, commercial and communicative possibilities the internet involves, the revolution in "disintermediation" it has brought about. Finally, some critics view attempts to expand secondary liability as an attempt by incumbent industries to immunize themselves against the disruption to their business models wrought by the internet. We will be dealing with secondary liability both in trademark and, later in the course, in copyright. As you look at the legal regime the judges and legislators carve out, ask yourself how they are balancing these two competing views.

Tiffany Inc. v. eBay Inc.
600 F.3d 93 (2d Cir. 2010)

SACK, Circuit Judge.

eBay, Inc. ("eBay"), through its eponymous online marketplace, has revolutionized the online sale of goods, especially used goods. It has facilitated the buying and selling by hundreds of millions of people and entities, to their benefit and eBay's profit. But that marketplace is sometimes employed by users as a means to perpetrate fraud by selling counterfeit goods.

Plaintiffs Tiffany (NJ) Inc. and Tiffany and Company (together, "Tiffany") have created and cultivated a brand of jewelry bespeaking high-end quality and style. Based on Tiffany's concern that some use eBay's website to sell counterfeit Tiffany merchandise, Tiffany has instituted this action against eBay, asserting various causes of action—sounding in trademark infringement, trademark dilution and false advertising—arising from eBay's advertising and listing practices.

Background

[The court summarized the findings of fact in the district court. Internal citations omitted. Eds.]

eBay is the proprietor of www.ebay.com, an Internet-based marketplace that allows those who register with it to purchase goods from and sell goods to one another. It "connect[s] buyers and sellers and [] enable[s] transactions, which are carried out directly between eBay members." In its auction and listing services, it "provides the venue for the sale [of goods] and support for the transaction[s], [but] it does not itself sell the items" listed for sale on the site, nor does it ever take physical possession of them. Thus, "eBay generally does not know whether or when an item is delivered to the buyer."

eBay has been enormously successful. More than six million new listings are posted on its site daily. At any given time it contains some 100 million listings.

eBay generates revenue by charging sellers to use its listing services. For any listing, it charges an "insertion fee" based on the auction's starting price for the goods being sold and ranges from $0.20 to $4.80. For any completed sale, it charges a "final value fee" that ranges from 5.25% to 10% of the final sale price of the item. Sellers have the option of purchasing, at additional cost, features "to differentiate their listings, such as a border or bold-faced type."

eBay also generates revenue through a company named PayPal, which it owns and which allows users to process their purchases. PayPal deducts, as a fee for each transaction that it processes, 1.9% to 2.9% of the transaction amount, plus $0.30. This gives eBay an added incentive to increase both the volume and the price of the goods sold on its website.

Tiffany is a world-famous purveyor of, among other things, branded jewelry. Since 2000, all new Tiffany jewelry sold in the United States has been available exclusively through Tiffany's retail stores, catalogs, and website, and through its Corporate Sales Department. It does not use liquidators, sell overstock merchandise, or put its goods on sale at discounted prices. It does not—nor can it, for that matter—control the "legitimate secondary market in authentic Tiffany silvery jewelry," i.e., the market for second-hand Tiffany wares. The record developed at trial "offere[d] little basis from which to discern the actual availability of authentic Tiffany silver jewelry in the secondary market."

Sometime before 2004, Tiffany became aware that counterfeit Tiffany merchandise was being sold on eBay's site. . . . Tiffany conducted two surveys known as "Buying Programs," one in 2004 and another in 2005, in an attempt to assess the extent of this practice. Under those programs, Tiffany bought various items on eBay and then inspected and evaluated them to determine how many were counterfeit. Tiffany found that 73.1% of the purported Tiffany goods purchased in the 2004 Buying Program and 75.5% of those purchased in the 2005 Buying Program were counterfeit. The district court concluded, however, that the Buying Programs were "methodologically flawed and of questionable value," and "provide[d] limited evidence as to the total percentage of counterfeit goods available on eBay at any given time." The court nonetheless decided that during the period in which the Buying Programs were in effect, a "significant portion of the 'Tiffany' sterling silver jewelry listed on the eBay website . . . was counterfeit," and that eBay knew "that some portion of the Tiffany goods sold on its website might be counterfeit." The court found, however, that "a substantial number of authentic Tiffany goods are [also] sold on eBay."

Reducing or eliminating the sale of all second-hand Tiffany goods, including genuine Tiffany pieces, through eBay's website would benefit Tiffany in at least one sense: It would diminish the competition in the market for genuine Tiffany merchandise. ([The District Court noted] that "there is at least some basis in the record for eBay's assertion that one of Tiffany's goals in pursuing this litigation is to shut down the legitimate secondary market in authentic Tiffany goods.") The immediate effect would be loss of revenue to eBay, even though there might be a countervailing gain by eBay resulting from increased consumer confidence about the bona fides of other goods sold through its website.

Anti-Counterfeiting Measures

Because eBay facilitates many sales of Tiffany goods, genuine and otherwise, and obtains revenue on every transaction, it generates substantial revenues from the sale of purported Tiffany goods, some of which are counterfeit. "eBay's Jewelry & Watches category manager estimated that, between April 2000 and June 2004, eBay earned $4.1 million in revenue from completed listings with 'Tiffany' in the listing title in the Jewelry & Watches category." Although eBay was generating revenue from all sales of goods on its site, including counterfeit goods, the district court found eBay to have "an interest in eliminating counterfeit Tiffany merchandise from eBay . . . to preserve the reputation of its website as a safe place to do business." The buyer of fake Tiffany goods might, if and when the forgery was detected, fault eBay. Indeed, the district court found that "buyers . . . complain[ed] to eBay" about the sale of counterfeit Tiffany goods. "[D]uring the last six weeks of 2004, 125 consumers complained to eBay about purchasing 'Tiffany' items through the eBay website that they believed to be counterfeit."

Because eBay "never saw or inspected the merchandise in the listings," its ability to determine whether a particular listing was for counterfeit goods was limited. Even had it been able to inspect the goods, moreover, in many instances it likely would not have had the expertise to determine whether they were counterfeit. ("[I]n many instances, determining whether an item is counterfeit will require a physical inspection of the item, and some degree of expertise on the part of the examiner.").

Notwithstanding these limitations, eBay spent "as much as $20 million each year on tools to promote trust and safety on its website." For example, eBay and PayPal set up "buyer protection programs," under which, in certain circumstances, the buyer would be reimbursed for the cost of items purchased on eBay that were discovered not to be genuine. eBay also established a "Trust and Safety" department, with some 4,000 employees "devoted to trust and safety" issues, including over 200 who "focus exclusively on combating infringement" and 70 who "work exclusively with law enforcement."

By May 2002, eBay had implemented a "fraud engine," "which is principally dedicated to ferreting out illegal listings, including counterfeit listings." eBay had theretofore employed manual searches for keywords in listings in an effort to "identify blatant instances of potentially infringing . . . activity." "The fraud engine uses rules and complex models that automatically search for activity that violates eBay policies." In addition to identifying items actually advertised as counterfeit, the engine also incorporates various filters designed to screen out less-obvious instances of counterfeiting using "data elements designed to evaluate listings based on, for example, the seller's Internet protocol address, any issues associated with the seller's account on eBay, and the feedback the seller has received from other eBay users." In addition to general filters, the fraud engine incorporates "Tiffany-specific filters," including "approximately 90 different keywords" designed to help distinguish between genuine and counterfeit Tiffany goods. During the period in dispute, eBay also "periodically conducted [manual] reviews of listings in an effort to remove those that might be selling counterfeit goods, including Tiffany goods."

For nearly a decade, including the period at issue, eBay has also maintained and administered the "Verified Rights Owner ('VeRO') Program"—a "'notice-and-takedown' system" allowing owners of intellectual property rights, including Tiffany, to "report to eBay any listing offering potentially infringing items, so that eBay could remove such reported listings." Any such rights-holder with a "good-faith belief that [a particular listed] item infringed on a copyright or a trademark" could report the item to eBay, using a "Notice of Claimed Infringement form or NOCI form." During the period under consideration, eBay's practice was to remove reported listings within twenty-four hours of receiving a NOCI, but eBay in fact deleted seventy to eighty percent of them within twelve hours of notification.

On receipt of a NOCI, if the auction or sale had not ended, eBay would, in addition to removing the listing, cancel the bids and inform the seller of the reason for the cancellation. If bidding had ended, eBay would retroactively cancel the transaction. In the event of a cancelled auction, eBay would refund the fees it had been paid in connection with the auction.

In some circumstances, eBay would reimburse the buyer for the cost of a purchased item, provided the buyer presented evidence that the purchased item was counterfeit. During the relevant time period, the district court found, eBay "never refused to remove a reported Tiffany listing, acted in good faith in responding to Tiffany's NOCIs, and always provided Tiffany with the seller's contact information."

In addition, eBay has allowed rights owners such as Tiffany to create an "About Me" webpage on eBay's website "to inform eBay users about their products, intellectual property rights, and legal positions." eBay does not exercise control over the content of those pages in a manner material to the issues before us.

Tiffany, not eBay, maintains the Tiffany "About Me" page. With the headline "**BUYER BEWARE**," the page begins: "**Most of the purported TIFFANY & CO. silver jewelry and packaging available on eBay is counterfeit.**" It also says, *inter alia:*

> The only way you can be certain that you are purchasing a genuine TIFFANY & CO. product is to purchase it from a Tiffany & Co. retail store, via our website (www.tiffany.com) or through a Tiffany & Co. catalogue. Tiffany & Co. stores do not authenticate merchandise. A good jeweler or appraiser may be able to do this for you.

In 2003 or early 2004, eBay began to use "special warning messages when a seller attempted to list a Tiffany item." These messages "instructed the seller to make sure that the item was authentic Tiffany merchandise and informed the seller that eBay 'does not tolerate the listing of replica, counterfeit, or otherwise unauthorized items' and that violation of this policy 'could result in suspension of [the seller's] account.'" The messages also provided a link to Tiffany's "About Me" page with its "buyer beware" disclaimer. If the seller "continued to list an item despite the warning, the listing was flagged for review."

In addition to cancelling particular suspicious transactions, eBay has also suspended from its website "'hundreds of thousands of sellers every year,' tens of thousands of whom were suspected [of] having engaged in infringing conduct." eBay primarily employed a "'three strikes rule'" for suspensions, but would suspend sellers after the first violation if it was clear that "the seller 'listed a number of infringing items,' and '[selling counterfeit merchandise] appears to be the only thing they've come to eBay to do.'" But if "a seller listed a potentially infringing item but appeared overall to be a legitimate seller, the 'infringing items [were] taken down, and the seller [would] be sent a warning on the first offense and given the educational information, [and] told that . . . if they do this again, they will be suspended from eBay.'"

By late 2006, eBay had implemented additional anti-fraud measures: delaying the ability of buyers to view listings of certain brand names, including Tiffany's, for 6 to 12 hours so as to give rights-holders such as Tiffany more time to review those listings; developing the ability to assess the number of items listed in a given listing; and restricting one-day and three-day auctions and cross-border trading for some brand-name items.

The district court concluded that "eBay consistently took steps to improve its technology and develop anti-fraud measures as such measures became technologically feasible and reasonably available."

eBay's Advertising

At the same time that eBay was attempting to reduce the sale of counterfeit items on its website, it actively sought to promote sales of premium and branded jewelry, including Tiffany merchandise, on its site. Among other things, eBay "advised its sellers to take advantage of the demand for Tiffany merchandise as part of a broader effort to grow the Jewelry & Watches category." And prior to 2003, eBay advertised the availability of Tiffany merchandise on its site. eBay's advertisements trumpeted "Mother's Day Gifts!," a "Fall FASHION BRAND BLOWOUT," "GREAT BRANDS, GREAT PRICES," or "Top Valentine's Deals," among other promotions. It encouraged the viewer to "GET THE FINER THINGS." These advertisements provided the reader with hyperlinks, at least one of each of which was related to Tiffany merchandise—"Tiffany," "Tiffany & Co. under $150," "Tiffany & Co," "Tiffany Rings," or "Tiffany & Co. under $50."

eBay also purchased sponsored-link advertisements on various search engines to promote the availability of Tiffany items on its website. In one such case, in the form of a printout of the results list from a search on Yahoo! for "tiffany," the second sponsored link read "Tiffany on eBay. Find tiffany items at low prices. With over 5 million items for sale every day, you'll find all kinds of unique [unreadable] Marketplace. www.ebay.com." Tiffany complained to eBay of the practice in 2003, and eBay told Tiffany that it had ceased buying sponsored links. The district court found, however, that eBay continued to do so indirectly through a third party.

Procedural History

By amended complaint dated July 15, 2004, Tiffany initiated this action. It alleged, *inter alia*, that eBay's conduct—i.e., facilitating and advertising the sale of "Tiffany" goods that turned out to be counterfeit—constituted direct and contributory trademark infringement, trademark dilution, and false advertising. On July 14, 2008, following a bench trial, the district court, in a thorough and thoughtful opinion, set forth its findings of fact and conclusions of law, deciding in favor of eBay on all claims. Tiffany appeals from the district court's judgment for eBay.

DISCUSSION

I. Direct Trademark Infringement

Tiffany alleges that eBay infringed its trademark in violation of section 32 of the Lanham Act. The district court described this as a claim of "direct trademark infringement," and we adopt that terminology. Under section 32, "the owner of a mark registered with the Patent and Trademark Office can bring a civil action against a person alleged to have used the mark without the owner's consent." We analyze such a claim "under a familiar two-prong test. The test looks first to whether the plaintiff's mark is entitled to protection, and second to whether the defendant's use of the mark is likely to cause consumers confusion as to the origin or sponsorship of the defendant's goods." *Savin Corp. v. Savin Group* (2d Cir. 2004).

In the district court, Tiffany argued that eBay had directly infringed its mark by using it on eBay's website and by purchasing sponsored links containing the mark on Google and Yahoo! Tiffany also argued that eBay and the sellers of the counterfeit goods using its site were jointly and severally liable. The district court rejected these arguments on the ground that eBay's use of Tiffany's mark was protected by the doctrine of nominative fair use.

The doctrine of nominative fair use allows "[a] defendant [to] use a plaintiff's trademark to identify the plaintiff's goods so long as there is no likelihood of confusion about the source of [the] defendant's product or the mark-holder's sponsorship or affiliation." The doctrine apparently originated in the Court of Appeals for the Ninth Circuit. See *New Kids on the Block v. News Am. Publ'g, Inc.* (9th Cir. 1992). To fall within the protection, according to that court: "First, the product or service in question must be one not readily identifiable without use of the trademark; second, only so much of the mark or marks may be used as is reasonably necessary to identify the product or service; and third, the user must do nothing that would, in conjunction with the mark, suggest sponsorship or endorsement by the trademark holder."

The Court of Appeals for the Third Circuit has endorsed these principles. We have referred to the doctrine, albeit without adopting or rejecting it. Other circuits have done similarly.

We need not address the viability of the doctrine to resolve Tiffany's claim, however. We have recognized that a defendant may lawfully use a plaintiff's trademark where doing so is necessary to describe the plaintiff's product and does not imply a false affiliation or endorsement by the plaintiff of the defendant. "While a trademark conveys an exclusive right to the use of a mark in commerce in the area reserved, that right generally does not prevent one who trades a branded product from accurately describing it by its brand name, so long as the trader does not create confusion by implying an affiliation with the owner of the product." ("As a general rule, trademark law does not reach the sale of genuine goods bearing a true mark even though the sale is not authorized by the mark owner.")

We agree with the district court that eBay's use of Tiffany's mark on its website and in sponsored links was lawful. eBay used the mark to describe accurately the genuine Tiffany goods offered for sale on its website. And none of eBay's uses of the mark suggested that Tiffany affiliated itself with eBay or endorsed the sale of its products through eBay's website.

In addition, the "About Me" page that Tiffany has maintained on eBay's website since 2004 states that "[m]ost of the purported 'TIFFANY & CO.' silver jewelry and packaging available on eBay is counterfeit." The page further explained that Tiffany itself sells its products only through its own stores, catalogues, and website.

Tiffany argues, however, that even if eBay had the right to use its mark with respect to the resale of genuine Tiffany merchandise, eBay infringed the mark because it knew or had reason to know that there was "a substantial problem with the sale of counterfeit [Tiffany] silver jewelry" on the eBay website. As we discuss below, eBay's knowledge *vel non* that counterfeit Tiffany wares were offered through its website is relevant to the issue of whether eBay contributed to the direct infringement of Tiffany's mark by the counterfeiting vendors themselves, or whether eBay bears liability for false advertising. But it is not a basis for a claim of direct trademark infringement against eBay, especially inasmuch as it is undisputed that eBay promptly removed all listings that Tiffany challenged as counterfeit and took affirmative steps to identify and remove illegitimate Tiffany goods. To impose liability because eBay cannot guarantee the genuineness of all of the purported Tiffany products offered on its website would unduly inhibit the lawful resale of genuine Tiffany goods.

We conclude that eBay's use of Tiffany's mark in the described manner did not constitute direct trademark infringement.

II. Contributory Trademark Infringement

The more difficult issue is whether eBay is liable for contributory trademark infringement—i.e., for culpably facilitating the infringing conduct of the counterfeiting vendors. Acknowledging the paucity of case law to guide us, we conclude that the district court correctly granted judgment on this issue in favor of eBay.

A. Principles

Contributory trademark infringement is a judicially created doctrine that derives from the common law of torts. The Supreme Court most recently dealt with the subject in *Inwood Laboratories, Inc. v. Ives Laboratories, Inc.* (1982). There, the plaintiff, Ives, asserted that several drug manufacturers had induced pharmacists to mislabel a drug the defendants produced to pass it off as Ives'. According to the Court, "if a manufacturer or distributor intentionally induces another to infringe a trademark, or if it continues to supply its product to one whom it knows or has reason to know is engaging in trademark infringement, the manufacturer or distributor is contributorially responsible for any harm done as a result of the deceit." The Court ultimately decided to remand the case to the Court of Appeals after concluding it had improperly rejected factual findings of the district court favoring the defendant manufacturers.

Inwood's test for contributory trademark infringement applies on its face to manufacturers and distributors of goods. Courts have, however, extended the test to providers of services. The Seventh Circuit applied *Inwood* to a lawsuit against the owner of a swap meet, or "flea market," whose vendors were alleged to have sold infringing Hard Rock Café T-shirts. The court "treated trademark infringement as a species of tort" and analogized the swap meet owner to a landlord or licensor, on whom the common law "imposes the same duty . . . [as *Inwood*] impose[s] on manufacturers and distributors."

Speaking more generally, the Ninth Circuit concluded that *Inwood*'s test for contributory trademark infringement applies to a service provider if he or she exercises sufficient control over the infringing conduct. *Lockheed Martin Corp. v. Network Solutions, Inc.* (9th Cir. 1999) ("Direct control and monitoring of the instrumentality used by a third party to infringe the plaintiff's mark permits the expansion of Inwood Lab.'s 'supplies a product' requirement for contributory infringement."). . . .

The limited case law leaves the law of contributory trademark infringement ill-defined. Although we are not the first court to consider the application of *Inwood* to the Internet, we are apparently the first to consider its application to an online marketplace.

B. Discussion
1. Does *Inwood* Apply?

. . . On appeal, eBay no longer maintains that it is not subject to *Inwood*. We therefore assume without deciding that *Inwood*'s test for contributory trademark infringement governs.

2. Is eBay Liable Under *Inwood*?

The question that remains, then, is whether eBay is liable under the *Inwood* test on the basis of the services it provided to those who used its website to sell counterfeit Tiffany products. As noted, when applying *Inwood* to service providers, there are two ways in which a defendant may become contributorially liable for the infringing conduct of another: first, if the service provider "intentionally induces another to infringe a trademark," and second, if the service provider "continues to supply its [service] to one whom it knows or has reason to know is engaging in trademark infringement." *Inwood*. Tiffany does not argue that eBay induced the sale of counterfeit Tiffany goods on its website—the circumstances addressed by the first part of the *Inwood* test. It argues instead, under the second part of the *Inwood* test, that eBay continued to supply its services to the sellers of counterfeit Tiffany goods while knowing or having reason to know that such sellers were infringing Tiffany's mark.

The district court rejected this argument. First, it concluded that to the extent the NOCIs that Tiffany submitted gave eBay reason to know that particular listings were for counterfeit goods, eBay did not continue to carry those listings once it learned that they were specious. The court found that eBay's practice was promptly to remove the challenged listing from its website, warn sellers and buyers, cancel fees it earned from that listing, and direct buyers not to consummate the sale of the disputed item. The court therefore declined to hold eBay contributorially liable for the infringing conduct of those sellers. On appeal, Tiffany does not appear to challenge this conclusion. In any event, we agree with the district court that no liability arises with respect to those terminated listings.

Tiffany disagrees vigorously, however, with the district court's further determination that eBay lacked sufficient knowledge of trademark infringement by sellers behind other, non-terminated listings to provide a basis for *Inwood* liability. Tiffany argued in the district court that eBay knew, or at least had reason to know, that counterfeit Tiffany goods were being sold ubiquitously on its website. As evidence, it pointed to, inter alia, the demand letters it sent to eBay in 2003 and 2004, the results of its Buying Programs that it shared with eBay, the thousands of NOCIs it filed with eBay alleging its good faith belief that certain listings were counterfeit, and the various complaints eBay received from buyers claiming that they had purchased one or more counterfeit Tiffany items through eBay's website. Tiffany argued that taken together, this evidence established eBay's knowledge of the widespread sale of counterfeit Tiffany products on its website. Tiffany urged that eBay be held contributorially liable on the basis that despite that knowledge, it continued to make its services available to infringing sellers.

The district court rejected this argument. It acknowledged that "[t]he evidence produced at trial demonstrated that eBay had *generalized* notice that some portion of the Tiffany goods sold on its website might be counterfeit." The court characterized the issue before it as "whether eBay's generalized knowledge of trademark infringement on its website was sufficient to meet the 'knowledge or reason to know' prong of the *Inwood* test." eBay had argued that "such generalized knowledge is insufficient, and that the law demands more specific knowledge of individual instances of infringement and infringing sellers before imposing a burden upon eBay to remedy the problem."

The district court concluded that "while eBay clearly possessed general knowledge as to counterfeiting on its website, such generalized knowledge is insufficient under the *Inwood* test to impose upon eBay an affirmative duty to remedy the problem." The court reasoned that *Inwood*'s language explicitly imposes contributory liability on a defendant who "continues to supply its product [—in eBay's case, its service—] to one whom it knows or has reason to know is engaging in trademark infringement." The court also noted that plaintiffs "bear a high burden in establishing 'knowledge' of contributory infringement," and that courts have been reluctant to extend contributory trademark liability to defendants where there is some uncertainty as to the extent or the nature of the infringement. In *Inwood*, Justice White emphasized in his concurring opinion that a defendant is not "require[d] . . . to refuse to sell to dealers who merely might pass off its goods."

Accordingly, the district court concluded that for Tiffany to establish eBay's contributory liability, Tiffany would have to show that eBay "knew or had reason to know of specific instances of actual infringement" beyond those that it addressed upon learning of them. Tiffany failed to make such a showing.

On appeal, Tiffany argues that the distinction drawn by the district court between eBay's general knowledge of the sale of counterfeit Tiffany goods through its website, and its specific knowledge as to which particular sellers were making such sales, is a "false" one not required by the law. Tiffany posits that the only relevant question is "whether all of the knowledge, when taken together, puts [eBay] on notice that there is a substantial problem of trademark infringement. If so and if it fails to act, [eBay] is liable for contributory trademark infringement."

We agree with the district court. For contributory trademark infringement liability to lie, a service provider must have more than a general knowledge or reason to know that its service is being used to sell counterfeit goods. Some contemporary knowledge of which particular listings are infringing or will infringe in the future is necessary.

We are not persuaded by Tiffany's proposed interpretation of *Inwood*. Tiffany understands the "lesson of *Inwood*" to be that an action for contributory trademark infringement lies where "the evidence [of infringing activity]—direct or circumstantial, taken as a whole—. . . provide[s] a basis for finding that the defendant knew or should have known that its product or service was being used to further illegal counterfeiting activity." We think that Tiffany reads *Inwood* too broadly. Although the *Inwood* Court articulated a "knows or has reason to know" prong in setting out its contributory liability test, the Court explicitly declined to apply that prong to the facts then before it. The Court applied only the inducement prong of the test. See *Inwood*.

We therefore do not think that *Inwood* establishes the contours of the "knows or has reason to know" prong. Insofar as it speaks to the issue, though, the particular phrasing that the Court used—that a defendant will be liable if it "continues to supply its product to one whom it knows or has reason to know is engaging in trademark infringement," supports the district court's interpretation of *Inwood*, not Tiffany's.

We find helpful the Supreme Court's discussion of *Inwood* in a subsequent copyright case, *Sony Corp. of America v. Universal City Studios, Inc.* (1984). There, defendant Sony manufactured and sold home video tape recorders. Plaintiffs Universal Studios and Walt Disney Productions held copyrights on various television programs that individual television-viewers had taped using the defendant's recorders. The plaintiffs contended that this use of the recorders constituted copyright infringement for which the defendants should be held contributorially liable. In ruling for the defendants, the Court discussed *Inwood* and the differences between contributory liability in trademark versus copyright law.

> If *Inwood*'s narrow standard for contributory trademark infringement
> governed here, [the plaintiffs'] claim of contributory infringement would
> merit little discussion. Sony certainly does not 'intentionally induce[]' its
> customers to make infringing uses of [the plaintiffs'] copyrights, nor does

it supply its products to *identified individuals known by it* to be engaging
in continuing infringement of [the plaintiffs'] copyrights.

Thus, the Court suggested, had the *Inwood* standard applied in *Sony*, the fact that Sony might have known that some portion of the purchasers of its product used it to violate the copyrights of others would not have provided a sufficient basis for contributory liability. *Inwood*'s "narrow standard" would have required knowledge by Sony of "identified individuals" engaging in infringing conduct. Tiffany's reading of *Inwood* is therefore contrary to the interpretation of that case set forth in *Sony*.

Although the Supreme Court's observations in *Sony*, a copyright case, about the "knows or has reason to know" prong of the contributory trademark infringement test set forth in *Inwood* were dicta, they constitute the only discussion of that prong by the Supreme Court of which we are aware. We think them to be persuasive authority here.

Applying *Sony*'s interpretation of *Inwood*, we agree with the district court that "Tiffany's general allegations of counterfeiting failed to provide eBay with the knowledge required under *Inwood*." Tiffany's demand letters and Buying Programs did not identify particular sellers who Tiffany thought were then offering or would offer counterfeit goods. And although the NOCIs and buyer complaints gave eBay reason to know that certain sellers had been selling counterfeits, those sellers' listings were removed and repeat offenders were suspended from the eBay site. Thus Tiffany failed to demonstrate that eBay was supplying its service to individuals who it knew or had reason to know were selling counterfeit Tiffany goods.

Accordingly, we affirm the judgment of the district court insofar as it holds that eBay is not contributorially liable for trademark infringement.

3. Willful Blindness.

Tiffany and its amici express their concern that if eBay is not held liable except when specific counterfeit listings are brought to its attention, eBay will have no incentive to root out such listings from its website. They argue that this will effectively require Tiffany and similarly situated retailers to police eBay's website—and many others like it—"24 hours a day, and 365 days a year." They urge that this is a burden that most mark holders cannot afford to bear.

First, and most obviously, we are interpreting the law and applying it to the facts of this case. We could not, even if we thought it wise, revise the existing law in order to better serve one party's interests at the expense of the other's.

But we are also disposed to think, and the record suggests, that private market forces give eBay and those operating similar businesses a strong incentive to minimize the counterfeit goods sold on their websites. eBay received many complaints from users claiming to have been duped into buying counterfeit Tiffany products sold on eBay. The risk of alienating these users gives eBay a reason to identify and remove counterfeit listings. Indeed, it has spent millions of dollars in that effort.

Moreover, we agree with the district court that if eBay had reason to suspect that counterfeit Tiffany goods were being sold through its website, and intentionally shielded itself from discovering the offending listings or the identity of the sellers behind them, eBay might very well have been charged with knowledge of those sales sufficient to satisfy *Inwood*'s "knows or has reason to know" prong. A service provider is not, we think, permitted willful blindness. When it has reason to suspect that users of its service are infringing a protected mark, it may not shield itself from learning of the particular infringing transactions by looking the other way. See, e.g., *Hard Rock Café* ("To be willfully blind, a person must suspect wrongdoing and deliberately fail to investigate.");

Fonovisa (applying *Hard Rock Café*'s reasoning to conclude that "a swap meet can not disregard its vendors' blatant trademark infringements with impunity"). In the words of the Seventh Circuit, "willful blindness is equivalent to actual knowledge for purposes of the Lanham Act." *Hard Rock Café*.

eBay appears to concede that it knew as a general matter that counterfeit Tiffany products were listed and sold through its website. Without more, however, this knowledge is insufficient to trigger liability under *Inwood*. The district court found, after careful consideration, that eBay was not willfully blind to the counterfeit sales. That finding is not clearly erroneous. eBay did not ignore the information it was given about counterfeit sales on its website.

III. Trademark Dilution

A. Principles

Federal law allows the owner of a "famous mark" to enjoin a person from using "a mark or trade name in commerce that is likely to cause dilution by blurring or dilution by tarnishment of the famous mark." 15 U.S.C. § 1125(c)(1).

"Dilution by blurring" is an "association arising from the similarity between a mark or trade name and a famous mark that impairs the distinctiveness of the famous mark." § 1125(c)(2)(B). It can occur "regardless of the presence or absence of actual or likely confusion, of competition, or of actual economic injury." § 1125(c)(1). "Some classic examples of blurring include 'hypothetical anomalies as Dupont shoes, Buick aspirin tablets, Schlitz varnish, Kodak pianos, Bulova gowns, and so forth.'" *Starbucks Corp. v. Wolfe's Borough Coffee, Inc.* (2d Cir. 2009) (quoting *Mead Data Cent., Inc. v. Toyota Motor Sales, U.S.A., Inc.* (2d Cir. 1989)). It is not a question of confusion; few consumers would likely confuse the source of a Kodak camera with the source of a "Kodak" piano. Dilution by blurring refers instead to "'the whittling away of [the] established trademark's selling power and value through its unauthorized use by others.'" (Quoting *Mead Data Cent.*)

Federal law identifies a non-exhaustive list of six factors that courts "may consider" when determining whether a mark is likely to cause dilution by blurring. These are: (1) "[t]he degree of similarity between the mark or trade name and the famous mark"; (2) "[t]he degree of inherent or acquired distinctiveness of the famous mark"; (3) "[t]he extent to which the owner of the famous mark is engaging in substantially exclusive use of the mark"; (4) "[t]he degree of recognition of the famous mark"; (5) "[w]hether the user of the mark or trade name intended to create an association with the famous mark"; and (6) "[a]ny actual association between the mark or trade name and the famous mark." 15 U.S.C. § 1125(c)(2)(B)(i–vi).

In contrast to dilution by blurring, "dilution by tarnishment" is an "association arising from the similarity between a mark or trade name and a famous mark that harms the reputation of the famous mark." 15 U.S.C. § 1125(c)(2)(C). This "generally arises when the plaintiff's trademark is linked to products of shoddy quality, or is portrayed in an unwholesome or unsavory context likely to evoke unflattering thoughts about the owner's product." *Deere & Co. v. MTD Prods., Inc.* (2d Cir. 1994).

B. Discussion

The district court rejected Tiffany's dilution by blurring claim on the ground that "eBay never used the TIFFANY Marks in an effort to create an association with its own product, but instead, used the marks directly to advertise and identify the availability of authentic Tiffany merchandise on the eBay website." The court concluded that "just as the dilution by blurring claim fails because eBay has never used the [Tiffany] Marks to refer to eBay's own product, the dilution by tarnishment claim also fails." We agree. There is no second mark or product at issue here to blur with or to tarnish "Tiffany." Tiffany argues that counterfeiting dilutes the value of its product. Perhaps. But insofar as eBay did not itself sell the goods at issue, it did not itself engage in dilution.

IV. False Advertising

[The court remanded to the District Court on the issue of whether eBay's advertising implied to a reasonable consumer that the Tiffany products on eBay were genuine. Eds.]

CONCLUSION

For the foregoing reasons, we affirm the judgment of the district court with respect to the claims of trademark infringement and dilution. . . . [W]e return the cause to the district court for further proceedings with respect to Tiffany's false advertising claim.

PROBLEM 7-1

You have recently been appointed as General Counsel for Google, which is facing a number of legal problems. Early this year, Google began a new service called Google Store. Google Store is designed to compete with eBay, Craigslist, uBid and other consumer-to-consumer and small business-to-consumer online shopping sites. These sites allow sellers who have goods or services to sell to "list" them online. The sites provide convenient advertising and payment options, in return for a percentage of the sale. "Google Store will allow us to leverage our core-competency in search and the synergies of our global reach to provide the world's greatest integrated search and shopping Web 2.0 experience!" announced Sergey Brin, one of Google's founders.

The exciting thing about Google Store is the way it is integrated into the Google search process. The standard Google search page has a number of hyperlinks along the top—Web, Images, Maps, Shopping and Video being the most prominent. If a user clicks on "Images," for example, her existing search is confined only to pictorial search results. "Shopping" will yield only products for sale and so on. In order to understand the way listings are generated on the Shopping page, it is necessary to explain two of Google's programs—Google AdWords Featured Listings (AdWords) and Google Store (Store).

AdWords allows advertisers to "purchase" certain words or phrases. When those words or phrases are used by someone searching Google, the advertiser's chosen advertisement is featured on top of the search result, inside a yellow highlighted box. (An example of a Google Shopping search is reproduced on the next page.) Google chooses to include as AdWords available for purchase both simple descriptive terms ("designer bags," "discount travel") and trademarked phrases or words. The trademark owner is free to "purchase" its own name as an AdWord, as Louis Vuitton and Prada have apparently done in the featured page. In addition, some of the advertisements are from vendors who wish to resell the item in question. For example, vendors who claim to be selling second-hand Louis Vuitton or Prada bags could "purchase" the words 'Louis Vuitton' or 'Dior bags' and would then have their advertisements appear in the highlighted box when someone searched for that word or phrase. Some may buy the trademarked word for reasons entirely unrelated to its trademark status, as the person who purchased "Hermes" in order to sell a "weird old Greek God Belly Fat Diet" has apparently done. Finally, competitors to the trademark owner can purchase the trade-marked AdWord on the theory that someone searching for, say, Louis Vuitton, might

Figure One: (This was created for Problem 7-1. It is not a real screenshot.)

Google   louis vuitton handbags authentic   🎤   🔍

Web   Images   Maps   **Shopping**   More ⌄

Clear all filters   Handbags › Louis Vuitton

YOU SEARCHED "LOUIS VUITTON." FOR COMPARISON PURPOSES, GOOGLE'S "CLUSTERSEARCH" AUTOMATICALLY LISTS OTHER DESIGNERS AND MERCHANTS WITH RELATED OFFERINGS
(All listings sole responsibility of posters.)

Ads related to "Louis Vuitton" 🛈
Louis Vuitton. Sole Authorized Seller. Louisvuitton.com
Genine Louise Vuittion Bags at Insanly Low Prices. Подделка.ru
Try "Lou Vutton!" It's like Louis Vuitton, but for men! Falsificación.es
5 x Better than Louis Vuitton! Coach bags. Coach.com
Pre-owned Louis Vuitton! $15-$35! Visit Google Store
         More listings tagged "Louis Vuitton" at Google Store . . .

Ads related to "Chanel" 🛈
Channel Desiner Bags On Sale! Super Cheep. Sketchy.ru
KoKo Chanel Bags at KnocKdown prices. Contrefaçon.com
Get Genuine Coach Bags Direct from Manufacturer! Coach.com
Make a Chanel Bag to order! Logo extra. Visit Google Store
         More listings tagged "Chanel" at Google Store . . .

Ads related to "Hermes" 🛈
Greek Gods' weird old belly fat diet! MessengerOfGreekGods.com
Buy 2nd hand HERMÈS from sellers **upgrading** to Coach? Coach.com
HERMÈS ON SALE! Direct from Paris, TX.
CheeseEatingSurrenderMonkey.com
Hermes, Schmermes! Look at these prices! Visit Google Store
         More listings tagged "Hermes" at Google Store . . .

Ads related to "Christian Dior" 🛈
Christian Single Dating but with Dior Elegance. ChicChristiandate.com
Get Genuine Coach Bags Direct from Manufacturer! Coach.com
Christian Dior Bags #1 Reseller. Insane prices! Visit Google Store
Make a genuine Dior Bag to order! Logo extra. Visit Google Store
         More listings tagged "Christian Dior" at Google Store . . .

Ads related to "Prada" 🛈
Prada. Original. Incomparable. Prada.com
The Devil Wore Prada. You can too! Heavenly prices. Sketchy.ru
Get Genuine Coach Bags Direct from Manufacturer! Coach.com
Make a genuine Prada Bag to order! Logo extra. Visit Google Store
Strut your 2nd hand Prada style for under $20! Visit Google Store
         More listings tagged "Prada" at Google Store . . .

Ads related to "Gucci" 🛈
Too Poochy for Gucci? Biggirlsknockoffs.com
Get Genuine Coach Bags Direct from Manufacturer! Coach.com
Make your genuine Gucci Bag to order! Logo extra. Visit Google Store
Pre-owned Gucci designer chic under $25! Visit Google Store
         More listings tagged "Gucci" at Google Store . . .

All logos owned by their respective trademark holders, used here for search-convenience only and not as a signal of endorsement. Google does not inspect listings in search results or Google Store for authenticity. Buyer beware!

be interested in the wider category of designer bags. As you can see, Coach has done this with several of the designer bags featured on the page.

Above the yellow highlighted advertisements is a header that says "Ads related to X." Next to it appears an information icon: If that icon is clicked, the following message appears: "Google is not responsible for these listings and does not warrant their accuracy. If you believe this advertisement makes inappropriate use of your intellectual property, please go to our "Abuse" page." As you can see, there are additional warnings at the top and bottom of the page that express in different language the point that Google does not screen or endorse the listings.

Please examine the layout of the search page included as an illustration on the previous page. The user initially searched for Louis Vuitton handbags and so that is the first result shown. In addition, Google's famous search technology has revealed "clusters" of trademarked names. Those who search for "Prius" are statistically likely also be interested in and to click upon ads related to other hybrid or electric vehicles, but not those for Jaguar or Lamborghini. Those who search for Prada are statistically likely to be interested in other high-end designers, but not in Payless Shoe Source or Walmart. Having uncovered this pattern of interest, Google's "Clustersearch" algorithm facilitates it by automatically constructing a page that features "related" brands to those for which the consumer is actually searching. The program has been extremely successful with a high rate of "click through," demonstrating, as far as Google engineers are concerned, that they are giving their users the goods and services for which they really wanted to search.

At the top of the page, Google inserts the following description. "YOU SEARCHED FOR '[Trademark Name].' FOR COMPARISON PURPOSES GOOGLE'S "CLUSTERSEARCH" AUTOMATICALLY LISTS OTHER DESIGNERS AND MERCHANTS WITH RELATED OFFERINGS. (All listings sole responsibility of posters.)" The latter limitation is included because Google cannot know exactly what the vendor is selling—only that it was willing to signal its interest by purchasing the AdWord or, in the case of Google Store, "tagging" its advertisement with the word in question. (When sellers list goods for sale in Google Store, the procedure is slightly different than for AdWords. For no additional fee they can "tag" their post with any keyword they choose—Google does not suggest the tags. Goods tagged with famous brand names will automatically be featured in Google searches for those brand names.)

As you can see, Google offers a useful visual cue to each cluster of advertisements by featuring the logo for the brand in question on the left hand side of the page. Google's research has shown that as many as 20% of consumers visually recognize the logo even when they do not know the actual name of the brand. For example, the Louis Vuitton interlocking LV pattern shown in Figure One is recognized as a trademark for "a fancy designer" by many clueless males buying bags as gifts, though they could not name or spell the actual designer involved. A disclaimer at the bottom of the page states, "All logos owned by their respective trademark holders, used here for search-convenience only and not as a signal of endorsement."

Google Store adds to the existing features on Google Shopping search pages, a service equivalent to Craigslist or eBay. For a percentage of any sale, Store lists advertisements of individual sellers, provides a reputational "ranking" system that offers feedback on reliability, and facilitates payment. The Store listings are displayed immediately below the highlighted listings. Your predecessor as General Counsel pondered the design of the system at length and decided that Google could not and should not attempt to screen or vet listings in order to judge the truth of the advertising or the authenticity of the product. Indeed, its entire policy is purposefully "hands off." "It is just like search!" he said, "We can't examine every webpage on the Internet for copyright infringement and we can't comb through 100 million listings to figure out who is selling shoddy or counterfeit goods!" Indeed, he says that attempting to screen listings would appear to offer a guarantee of authenticity that Google could not back up.

Instead of vetting individual listings, Google offers a "takedown" system through its "Abuse" page for those who believe their intellectual property has been misused. For example, if a copyright or trademark owner complains about an individual listing—either in the "featured listings" or in the Google Store—on grounds that it infringes their rights, Google will remove it. Thousands of such takedown requests are received and processed every day, though trademark owners complain that it is "like trying to empty the ocean with a teacup." Though it does process all these requests, Google refuses to block the use of the trademarked term preemptively by anyone but the owner of the mark. Your predecessor was very clear on this point. "The ability to buy competitors' trademarks as AdWords is a feature, not a bug!"

In addition, Google will not comply with takedown requests on advertisements that are not claiming to sell the complainant's actual trademarked goods. For example, when Coach bags are listed in the Louis Vuitton advertisements, because Coach has purchased "Louis Vuitton" as an AdWord, Google refused to remove the advertisement even when Vuitton complained. "They aren't selling Vuitton, they are selling Coach! It says that right in the ad," said your pugnacious predecessor. Only if a reseller claims to be selling exactly the trademarked goods in question, referred to by a letter for letter identical trademark name, will Google take the word of the trademark owner that the goods are counterfeit and thus remove the listing. You have noticed that new "resale" postings immediately crop up after every takedown and you assume some of them must be genuine; indeed, Google receives some complaints from sellers who claim that their legitimate second-hand sale has been blocked by an overly zealous rights-holder.

As part of your welcome to the job, your bosses have asked you to take a look at the problem above because they think "there might be a couple of Lanham Act issues."

1.) Is AdWords using the marks of others in commerce? Is Clustersearch? Why?

2.) Does Google violate registered trademarks by creating a likelihood of consumer confusion through the AdWords program? Through Clustersearch? Why or why not? What are Google's best defenses?

3.) Is Google Store guilty of contributory trademark infringement?

CHAPTER EIGHT

Defenses to Trademark Infringement: Fair & Nominative Use

We have already seen many of the internal limitations of trademark law. Its rights are constrained from their creation—ownership not of the word, or the image, but rather the word or image used in relationship to a particular good or service. They are constrained by the requirements of *use in commerce*, not only before the rights are obtained, but as a continuing requirement for the right to exist. They are constrained by the requirement of *use as a mark*—both that the signals must be deliberately sent by the producer *as trademarks*—not mottos or mission statements—and in the *distinctiveness*, acquired or inherent, perceived by the consumer. They are constrained by the limitations that trademarks can never be over *functional* features of the product; *TrafFix* provides one obvious example, but so does the discussion in *Qualitex* of all the occasions on which color cannot be owned, such as green for farm equipment, given that fashion-conscious farmers may want their tractors to match. They are constrained by the limitation of *genericide*, or "genericity." Even if the producer created an entirely new name—fanciful and arbitrary—that mark will be lost if it becomes the generic term for the goods or services involved. Finally, they are constrained by the reach—however indeterminate—of the requirements of the First Amendment, to allow speech and commentary about the mark, and of the requirements of efficient competitive consumer communication in the marketplace.

In this chapter, we focus on two particular defenses, fair use and nominative use, which reflect these limitations but also illustrate their operation in action, particularly in the context of new business models and new technologies such as the internet.

The first defense, "descriptive" or "classic" fair use, is laid out in the Lanham Act in § 1115(b), which describes limitations on the § 1065 "incontestability" of a mark that has been registered on the Principal Register for five years. ("Incontestable" could more accurately be described as "contestable for fewer reasons.") But fair use has been judicially developed to be a more general limitation on trademarks, even if they are not registered or incontestable. From the language below, courts have extracted the following three-part test for descriptive fair use: the mark must be used (1) other than as a mark (i.e. not to identify the product's source), (2) in a descriptive sense (though the mark does not have to *literally* describe the defendant's product, it can instead describe an aspirational effect—both "Come on Strong" for menswear or "Seal it with a Kiss" for lipstick were found to be descriptive), and (3) in good faith.

> **1115(b) To the extent that the right to use the registered mark has become incontestable the registration shall be conclusive evidence of the registrant's exclusive right to use the registered mark in commerce . . . subject to the following defenses. . . .**
>
> **4.) That the use of the name, term, or device charged to be an infringement is a use, <u>otherwise than as a mark</u>, of the party's individual name in his own business, or of the individual name of anyone in privity with such party, or of a term or device which is <u>descriptive of and used fairly and in good faith only to describe the goods or services</u> of such party, or their geographic origin. . . .**

KP Permanent Make-Up, Inc. v. Lasting Impression I, Inc., et al.
543 U.S. 111 (2004)

Justice SOUTER delivered the opinion of the Court.

The question here is whether a party raising the statutory affirmative defense of fair use to a claim of trademark infringement, 15 U.S.C. § 1115(b)(4), has a burden to negate any likelihood that the practice complained of will confuse consumers about the origin of the goods or services affected. We hold it does not.

I

Each party to this case sells permanent makeup, a mixture of pigment and liquid for injection under the skin to camouflage injuries and modify nature's dispensations, and each has used some version of the term "micro color" (as one word or two, singular or plural) in marketing and selling its product. Petitioner KP Permanent Make-Up, Inc., claims to have used the single-word version since 1990 or 1991 on advertising flyers and since 1991 on pigment bottles. Respondents Lasting Impression I, Inc., and its licensee, MCN International, Inc. (Lasting, for simplicity), deny that KP began using the term that early, but we accept KP's allegation as true for present purposes; the District and Appeals Courts took it to be so, and the disputed facts do not matter to our resolution of the issue. In 1992, Lasting applied to the United States Patent and Trademark Office (PTO) under 15 U.S.C. § 1051 for registration of a trademark consisting of the words "Micro Colors" in white letters separated by a green bar within a black square. The PTO registered the mark to Lasting in 1993, and in 1999 the registration became incontestable. § 1065.

It was also in 1999 that KP produced a 10-page advertising brochure using "microcolor" in a large, stylized typeface, provoking Lasting to demand that KP stop using the term. Instead, KP sued Lasting in the Central District of California, seeking, on more than one ground, a declaratory judgment that its language infringed no such exclusive right as Lasting claimed. Lasting counterclaimed, alleging, among other things, that KP had infringed Lasting's "Micro Colors" trademark.

KP sought summary judgment on the infringement counterclaim, based on the statutory affirmative defense of fair use, 15 U.S.C. § 1115(b)(4). After finding that Lasting had conceded that KP used the term only to describe its goods and not as a mark, the District Court held that KP was acting fairly and in good faith because undisputed facts showed that KP had employed the term "microcolor" continuously from a time before Lasting adopted the two-word, plural variant as a mark. Without enquiring whether the practice was likely to cause confusion, the court concluded that KP had made out its affirmative defense under § 1115(b)(4).

On appeal, the Court of Appeals for the Ninth Circuit thought it was error for the District Court to have addressed the fair use defense without delving into the matter of possible confusion on the part of consumers about the origin of KP's goods. The reviewing court took the view that no use could be recognized as fair where any consumer confusion was probable, and although the court did not pointedly address the burden of proof, it appears to have placed it on KP to show absence of consumer confusion. We now vacate the judgment of the Court of Appeals.

II
A

The Trademark Act of 1946, known for its principal proponent as the Lanham Act,

60 Stat. 427, as amended, 15 U.S.C. § 1051 et seq., provides the user of a trade or service mark with the opportunity to register it with the PTO, §§ 1051, 1053. If the registrant then satisfies further conditions including continuous use for five consecutive years, "the right . . . to use such registered mark in commerce" to designate the origin of the goods specified in the registration "shall be incontestable" outside certain listed exceptions. § 1065.

The holder of a registered mark (incontestable or not) has a civil action against anyone employing an imitation of it in commerce when "such use is likely to cause confusion, or to cause mistake, or to deceive." § 1114(1)(a). Although an incontestable registration is "conclusive evidence . . . of the registrant's exclusive right to use the . . . mark in commerce," § 1115(b), the plaintiff's success is still subject to "proof of infringement as defined in section 1114." And that, as just noted, requires a showing that the defendant's actual practice is likely to produce confusion in the minds of consumers about the origin of the goods or services in question. This plaintiff's burden has to be kept in mind when reading the relevant portion of the further provision for an affirmative defense of fair use, available to a party whose

> "use of the name, term, or device charged to be an infringement is a use, otherwise than as a mark, . . . of a term or device which is descriptive of and used fairly and in good faith only to describe the goods or services of such party, or their geographic origin. . . ." § 1115(b)(4).

Two points are evident. Section 1115(b) places a burden of proving likelihood of confusion (that is, infringement) on the party charging infringement even when relying on an incontestable registration. And Congress said nothing about likelihood of confusion in setting out the elements of the fair use defense in § 1115(b)(4).

Starting from these textual fixed points, it takes a long stretch to claim that a defense of fair use entails any burden to negate confusion. It is just not plausible that Congress would have used the descriptive phrase "likely to cause confusion, or to cause mistake, or to deceive" in § 1114 to describe the requirement that a markholder show likelihood of consumer confusion, but would have relied on the phrase "used fairly" in § 1115(b)(4) in a fit of terse drafting meant to place a defendant under a burden to negate confusion. . . .

Finally, a look at the typical course of litigation in an infringement action points up the incoherence of placing a burden to show nonconfusion on a defendant. If a plaintiff succeeds in making out a prima facie case of trademark infringement, including the element of likelihood of consumer confusion, the defendant may offer rebutting evidence to undercut the force of the plaintiff's evidence on this (or any) element, or raise an affirmative defense to bar relief even if the prima facie case is sound, or do both. But it would make no sense to give the defendant a defense of showing affirmatively that the plaintiff cannot succeed in proving some element (like confusion); all the defendant needs to do is to leave the factfinder unpersuaded that the plaintiff has carried its own burden on that point. A defendant has no need of a court's true belief when agnosticism will do. Put another way, it is only when a plaintiff has shown likely confusion by a preponderance of the evidence that a defendant could have any need of an affirmative defense, but under Lasting's theory the defense would be foreclosed in such a case. "[I]t defies logic to argue that a defense may not be asserted in the only situation where it even becomes relevant." *Shakespeare Co. v. Silstar Corp.* Nor would it make sense to provide an affirmative defense of no confusion plus good faith, when merely rebutting the plaintiff's case on confusion would entitle the defendant to judgment, good faith or not. . . .

Since the burden of proving likelihood of confusion rests with the plaintiff, and the fair use defendant has no free-standing need to show confusion unlikely, it follows (contrary to the Court of Appeals's view) that some possibility of consumer confusion must be compatible with fair use, and so it is. The common law's tolerance of a certain degree of confusion on the part of consumers followed from the very fact that in cases like this one an originally descriptive term was selected to be used as a mark, not to mention the undesirability of allowing anyone to obtain a complete monopoly on use of a descriptive term simply by grabbing it first. The Lanham Act adopts a similar leniency, there being no indication that the statute was meant to deprive commercial speakers of the ordinary utility of descriptive words. "If any confusion results, that is a risk the plaintiff accepted when it decided to identify its product with a mark that uses a well known descriptive phrase." *Cosmetically Sealed Industries, Inc. v. Chesebrough-Pond's USA Co.* See also *Park 'N Fly, Inc. v. Dollar Park & Fly, Inc.* (1985) (noting safeguards in Lanham Act to prevent commercial monopolization of language); *Car-Freshner Corp. v. S.C. Johnson & Son, Inc.* (2d Cir. 1995) (noting importance of "protect[ing] the right of society at large to use words or images in their primary descriptive sense"). This right to describe is the reason that descriptive terms qualify for registration as trademarks only after taking on secondary meaning as "distinctive of the applicant's goods," 15 U.S.C. § 1052(f), with the registrant getting an exclusive right not in the original, descriptive sense, but only in the secondary one associated with the markholder's goods. . . .

III

In sum, a plaintiff claiming infringement of an incontestable mark must show likelihood of consumer confusion as part of the prima facie case, 15 U.S.C. § 1115(b), while the defendant has no independent burden to negate the likelihood of any confusion in raising the affirmative defense that a term is used descriptively, not as a mark, fairly, and in good faith, § 1115(b)(4).

Because we read the Court of Appeals as requiring KP to shoulder a burden on the issue of confusion, we vacate the judgment and remand the case for further proceedings consistent with this opinion. It is so ordered.

Questions:

1.) The Ninth Circuit thought that the fair use defense was subject to the limitation that the defendant must show that the use is not likely to confuse the consuming public. It would seem they have a strong argument on their side. Is the purpose of trademark law not to avoid the likelihood of consumer confusion? Why does the Supreme Court disagree?

2.) In intellectual property, as elsewhere in the law, burdens of proof are all important, and the way they are set up can tell us much about the goals of the statutory scheme. Explain what the Court means when it says:

> Put another way, it is only when a plaintiff has shown likely confusion by a preponderance of the evidence that a defendant could have any need of an affirmative defense, but under Lasting's theory the defense would be foreclosed in such a case.

3.) You may recall that the *Abercrombie* case from Chapter 5 ultimately concluded that, even though Abercrombie had a valid trademark in "safari" for boots, Hunting World's use of "Camel Safari" "Hippo Safari" and "Safari Chukka" for boots from Africa was a descriptive fair use "to apprise the public of the type of product by referring to its origin and use." Another oft-cited example is Ocean Spray's use of "sweet-tart" to describe the taste of its cranberry juice—because this was a fair use, it did not infringe the "Sweetarts" mark for candy. *Sunmark v. Ocean Spray Cranberries* (7th Cir. 1995).

New Kids on the Block v. New America Pub., Inc.

971 F.2d 302 (9th Cir. 1992)

KOZINSKI, Circuit Judge.

The individual plaintiffs perform professionally as The New Kids on the Block, reputedly one of today's hottest musical acts. This case requires us to weigh their rights in that name against the rights of others to use it in identifying the New Kids as the subjects of public opinion polls.

Background

No longer are entertainers limited to their craft in marketing themselves to the public. This is the age of the multi-media publicity blitzkrieg: Trading on their popularity, many entertainers hawk posters, T-shirts, badges, coffee mugs and the like—handsomely supplementing their incomes while boosting their public images. The New Kids are no exception; the record in this case indicates there are more than 500 products or services bearing the New Kids trademark. Among these are services taking advantage of a recent development in telecommunications: 900 area code numbers, where the caller is charged a fee, a portion of which is paid to the call recipient. Fans can call various New Kids 900 numbers to listen to the New Kids talk about themselves, to listen to other fans talk about the New Kids, or to leave messages for the New Kids and other fans.

The defendants, two newspapers of national circulation, conducted separate polls of their readers seeking an answer to a pressing question: Which one of the New Kids is the most popular? USA Today's announcement contained a picture of the New Kids and asked, "Who's the best on the block?" The announcement listed a 900 number for voting, noted that "any USA Today profits from this phone line will go to charity," and closed with the following:

> New Kids on the Block are pop's hottest group. Which of the five is your fave? Or are they a turn off? . . . Each call costs 50 cents. Results in Friday's Life section.

The *USA Today* poll and winner

The Star's announcement, under a picture of the New Kids, went to the heart of the matter: "Now which kid is the sexiest?" The announcement, which appeared in the middle of a page containing a story on a New Kids concert, also stated:

> Which of the New Kids on the Block would you most like to move next door? STAR wants to know which cool New Kid is the hottest with our readers.

Readers were directed to a 900 number to register their votes; each call cost 95 cents per minute.

Fearing that the two newspapers were undermining their hegemony over their fans, the New Kids filed a shotgun complaint in federal court raising no fewer than ten claims: (1) common law trademark infringement; (2) Lanham Act false advertising; (3) Lanham Act false designation of origin; (4) Lanham Act unfair competition; (5) state trade name infringement; (6) state false advertising; (7) state unfair competition; (8) commercial misappropriation; (9) common-law misappropriation; and (10) intentional interference with prospective economic advantage. The two papers raised the First Amendment as a defense, on the theory that the polls were part and parcel of their "news-gathering activities." The district court granted summary judgment for defendants.

Discussion

. . . [W]e consider first whether the New Kids have stated viable claims on their various causes of action.

I

A. Since at least the middle ages, trademarks have served primarily to identify the source of goods and services, "to facilitate the tracing of 'false' or defective wares and the punishment of the offending craftsman." F. Schechter, The Historical Foundations of the Law Relating to Trademarks 47 (1925). . . . Throughout the development of trademark law, the purpose of trademarks remained constant and limited: Identification of the manufacturer or sponsor of a good or the provider of a service. And the wrong protected against was traditionally equally limited: Preventing producers from free-riding on their rivals' marks. . . . The core protection of the Lanham Act remains faithful to this conception. . . .

A trademark is a limited property right in a particular word, phrase or symbol. And although English is a language rich in imagery, we need not belabor the point that some words, phrases or symbols better convey their intended meanings than others. See *San Francisco Arts & Athletics, Inc. v. U.S.O.C.* (1987) (Brennan, J., dissenting) ("[A] jacket reading 'I Strongly Resent the Draft' would not have conveyed Cohen's message."). Indeed, the primary cost of recognizing property rights in trademarks is the removal of words from (or perhaps non-entrance into) our language. Thus, the holder of a trademark will be denied protection if it is (or becomes) generic, i.e., if it does not relate exclusively to the trademark owner's product. See, e.g., *Kellogg Co. v. National Biscuit Co.* (1938) ("shredded wheat"); *Eastern Air Lines, Inc. v. New York Air Lines, Inc.* (S.D.N.Y. 1983) ("air-shuttle" to describe hourly plane service). This requirement allays fears that producers will deplete the stock of useful words by asserting exclusive rights in them. When a trademark comes to describe a class of goods rather than an individual product, the courts will hold as a matter of law that use of that mark does not imply sponsorship or endorsement of the product by the original holder.

A related problem arises when a trademark also describes a person, a place or an attribute of a product. If the trademark holder were allowed exclusive rights in such use, the language would be depleted in much the same way as if generic words were protectable. Thus trademark law recognizes a defense where the mark is used only "to describe the goods or services of [a] party, or their geographic origin." 15 U.S.C. § 1115(b)(4). "The 'fair-use' defense, in essence, forbids a trademark registrant to appropriate a descriptive term for his exclusive use and so prevent others from accurately describing a characteristic of their goods." *Soweco, Inc. v. Shell Oil Co.* (5th Cir. 1980). Once again, the courts will hold as a matter of law that the original producer does not sponsor or endorse another product that uses his mark in a descriptive manner. See, e.g., *Schmid Laboratories v. Youngs Drug Products Corp.* (D.N.J. 1979) ("ribbed" condoms).

With many well-known trademarks, such as Jell-O, Scotch tape and Kleenex, there are equally informative non-trademark words describing the products (gelatin, cellophane tape and facial tissue). But sometimes there is no descriptive substitute, and a problem closely related to genericity and descriptiveness is presented when many goods and services are effectively identifiable only by their trademarks. For example, one might refer to "the two-time world champions" or "the professional basketball team from Chicago," but it's far simpler (and more likely to be understood) to refer to the Chicago Bulls. In such cases, use of the trademark does not imply sponsorship or endorsement of the product because the mark is used only to describe the thing, rather than to identify its source.

Indeed, it is often virtually impossible to refer to a particular product for purposes of comparison, criticism, point of reference or any other such purpose without using the mark. For example, reference to a large automobile manufacturer based in Michigan would not differentiate among the Big Three; reference to a large Japanese manufacturer of home electronics would narrow the field to a dozen or more companies. Much useful social and commercial discourse would be all but impossible if speakers were under threat of an infringement lawsuit every time they made reference to a person, company or product by using its trademark.

A good example of this is *Volkswagenwerk Aktiengesellschaft v. Church* (9th Cir. 1969), where we held that Volkswagen could not prevent an automobile repair shop from using its mark. We recognized that in "advertising [the repair of Volkswagens, it] would be difficult, if not impossible, for [Church] to avoid altogether the use of the word 'Volkswagen' or its abbreviation 'VW,' which are the normal terms which, to the public at large, signify appellant's cars." Church did not suggest to customers that he was part of the Volkswagen organization or that his repair shop was sponsored or authorized by VW; he merely used the words "Volkswagen" and "VW" to convey information about the types of cars he repaired. Therefore, his use of the Volkswagen trademark was not an infringing use.

The First Circuit confronted a similar problem when the holder of the trademark "Boston Marathon" tried to stop a television station from using the name:

> T]he words "Boston Marathon" ... do more than call attention to Channel 5's program; they also describe the event that Channel 5 will broadcast. Common sense suggests (consistent with the record here) that a viewer who sees those words flash upon the screen will believe simply that Channel 5 will show, or is showing, or has shown, the marathon, not that Channel 5 has some special approval from the [trademark holder] to do so. In technical trademark jargon, the use of words for descriptive purposes is called a "fair use," and the law usually permits it even if the words themselves also constitute a trademark.

WCVB-TV v. Boston Athletic Ass'n (1st Cir. 1991). Similarly, competitors may use a rival's trademark in advertising and other channels of communication if the use is not false or misleading. See, e.g., *Smith v. Chanel, Inc.* (9th Cir. 1968) (maker of imitation perfume may use original's trademark in promoting product).

Cases like these are best understood as involving a non-trademark use of a mark—a use to which the infringement laws simply do not apply, just as videotaping television shows for private home use does not implicate the copyright holder's exclusive right to reproduction. See *Sony Corp. v. Universal City Studios, Inc.* (1984). Indeed, we may generalize a class of cases where the use of the trademark does not attempt to capitalize on consumer confusion or to appropriate the cachet of one product for a different one.

Such nominative use of a mark—where the only word reasonably available to describe a particular thing is pressed into service—lies outside the strictures of trademark law: Because it does not implicate the source-identification function that is the purpose of trademark, it does not constitute unfair competition; such use is fair because it does not imply sponsorship or endorsement by the trademark holder.

To be sure, this is not the classic fair use case where the defendant has used the plaintiff's mark to describe the defendant's own product. Here, the New Kids trademark is used to refer to the New Kids themselves. We therefore do not purport to alter the test applicable in the paradigmatic fair use case. If the defendant's use of the plaintiff's trademark refers to something other than the plaintiff's product, the traditional fair use inquiry will continue to govern. But, where the defendant uses a trademark to describe the plaintiff's product, rather than its own, we hold that a commercial user is entitled to a nominative fair use defense provided he meets the following three requirements: First, the product or service in question must be one not readily identifiable without use of the trademark; second, only so much of the mark or marks may be used as is reasonably necessary to identify the product or service; and third, the user must do nothing that would, in conjunction with the mark, suggest sponsorship or endorsement by the trademark holder. . . .

The New Kids argue that, even if the newspapers are entitled to a nominative fair use defense for the announcements, they are not entitled to it for the polls themselves, which were money-making enterprises separate and apart from the newspapers' reporting businesses. According to plaintiffs, defendants could have minimized the intrusion into their rights by using an 800 number or asking readers to call in on normal telephone lines which would not have resulted in a profit to the newspapers based on the conduct of the polls themselves.

The New Kids see this as a crucial difference, distinguishing this case from *Volkswagenwerk*, *WCBV-TV* and other nominative use cases. The New Kids' argument in support of this distinction is not entirely implausible: They point out that their fans, like everyone else, have limited resources. Thus a dollar spent calling the newspapers' 900 lines to express loyalty to the New Kids may well be a dollar not spent on New Kids products and services, including the New Kids' own 900 numbers. In short, plaintiffs argue that a nominative fair use defense is inapplicable where the use in question competes directly with that of the trademark holder.

We reject this argument. While the New Kids have a limited property right in their name, that right does not entitle them to control their fans' use of their own money. Where, as here, the use does not imply sponsorship or endorsement, the fact that it is carried on for profit and in competition with the trademark holder's business is beside the point. Voting for their favorite New Kid may be, as plaintiffs point out, a way for fans to articulate their loyalty to the group, and this may diminish the resources available for products and services they sponsor. But the trademark laws do not give the New Kids the right to channel their fans' enthusiasm (and dollars) only into items licensed or authorized by them. See *International Order of Job's Daughters v. Lindeburg & Co.* (9th Cir. 1990) (no infringement where unauthorized jewelry maker produced rings and pins bearing fraternal organization's trademark). The New Kids could not use the trademark laws to prevent the publication of an unauthorized group biography or to censor all parodies or satires which use their name. We fail to see a material difference between these examples and the use here.

Summary judgment was proper as to the first seven causes of action because they all hinge on a theory of implied endorsement; there was none here as the uses in question were purely nominative.

Questions:

1.) Is anything more reflective of life's ephemeral nature, its transitory enthusiasms, its fleeting follies than . . . yesterday's embarrassing boy band? (Not for credit.)

2.) What is the key difference between the situations in *K.P. Makeup* and *New Kids*? Is this the same defense? Reflective of the same policies?

3.) The band argues, probably correctly, that in the 1-900 number polls they set up, the newspapers are deliberately exploiting the consumer goodwill and strength of name recognition of the band. They are reaping where they have not sown, intentionally profiting from a positive externality (consumer goodwill and brand recognition) created by another. Under the broader vision of trademark discussed in the last chapter, this is exactly what trademark is designed to prevent. Yet Judge Kozinski resolutely says such uses are allowed. Why? What analogies does he use—actions we clearly wish to allow—to show the undesirability of a more expansive conception of the reach of trademark law?

4.) How does the following passage from the case fit with the views put forward by Pitney in *INS*? With the *Lois* jeans court's vision of "room to expand the brand"?

> While the New Kids have a limited property right in their name, that right does not entitle them to control their fans' use of their own money. Where, as here, the use does not imply sponsorship or endorsement, the fact that it is carried on for profit and in competition with the trademark holder's business is beside the point. Voting for their favorite New Kid may be, as plaintiffs point out, a way for fans to articulate their loyalty to the group, and this may diminish the resources available for products and services they sponsor. But the trademark laws do not give the New Kids the right to channel their fans' enthusiasm (and dollars) only into items licensed or authorized by them.

What distinctions might Kozinski offer to explain the difference between those situations and this one?

Mattel Inc. v. Walking Mountain Productions
353 F.3d 792 (9th Cir. 2003)

PREGERSON, Circuit Judge.

In the action before us, Plaintiff Mattel Corporation asks us to prohibit Defendant artist Thomas Forsythe from producing and selling photographs containing Mattel's "Barbie" doll. Most of Forsythe's photos portray a nude Barbie in danger of being attacked by vintage household appliances. Mattel argues that his photos infringe on their copyrights, trademarks, and trade dress. We have jurisdiction pursuant to 28 U.S.C. § 1291 and affirm the district court's grant of summary judgment to Forsythe.

BACKGROUND

Thomas Forsythe, aka "Walking Mountain Productions," is a self-taught photographer who resides in Kanab, Utah. He produces photographs with social and political overtones. In 1997, Forsythe developed a series of 78 photographs entitled

"Food Chain Barbie," in which he depicted Barbie in various absurd and often sexualized positions. Forsythe uses the word "Barbie" in some of the titles of his works. While his works vary, Forsythe generally depicts one or more nude Barbie dolls juxtaposed with vintage kitchen appliances. For example, "Malted Barbie" features a nude Barbie placed on a vintage Hamilton Beach malt machine. "Fondue a la Barbie" depicts Barbie heads in a fondue pot. "Barbie Enchiladas" depicts four Barbie dolls wrapped in tortillas and covered with salsa in a casserole dish in a lit oven.

In his declaration in support of his motion for summary judgment, Forsythe describes the message behind his photographic series as an attempt to "critique[] the objectification of women associated with [Barbie], and [][to] lambast[] the conventional beauty myth and the societal acceptance of women as objects because this is what Barbie embodies." He explains that he chose to parody Barbie in his photographs because he believes that "Barbie is the most enduring of those products that feed on the insecurities of our beauty and perfection-obsessed consumer culture." Forsythe claims that, throughout his series of photographs, he attempts to communicate, through artistic expression, his serious message with an element of humor. . . .

Tom Forsythe, Food Chain Barbie (1999). Image from the Univ. of Iowa Interventionist Collage exhibit.

On August 22, 2001, the Los Angeles federal district court granted Forsythe's motion for summary judgment. . . . The court found that Forsythe's use of Mattel's trademark and trade dress caused no likelihood of confusion as to Mattel's sponsorship of Forsythe's works. The court dismissed Mattel's trademark dilution claim because it found that Forsythe's use had been "noncommercial." . . .

Mattel appeals the Los Angeles federal district court's grant of summary judgment in favor of Forsythe on the trademark, copyright, and state law claims. Mattel also appeals the Los Angeles federal district court's dismissal of its false advertising claim. . . .

We now address whether the district court erred in granting summary judgment in favor of Forsythe on Mattel's claims of trademark and trade dress infringement and dilution. . . .

A. Trademark

As we recently recognized in *MCA*, . . . when marks "transcend their identifying purpose" and "enter public discourse and become an integral part of our vocabulary," they "assume[] a role outside the bounds of trademark law." Where a mark assumes such cultural significance, First Amendment protections come into play. In these situations, "the trademark owner does not have the right to control public discourse whenever the public imbues his mark with a meaning beyond its source-identifying function." See also *New Kids on the Block v. News Am. Publ'g Inc.* (9th Cir. 1992).

As we determined in *MCA*, Mattel's "Barbie" mark has taken on such a role in our culture. In *MCA*, Mattel brought an identical claim against MCA Records, producers of a song entitled "Barbie Girl" that contained lyrics that parodied and mocked Barbie. Recognizing that First Amendment concerns in free expression are particularly present in the realm of artistic works, we rejected Mattel's claim. In doing so, we adopted the Second Circuit's First Amendment balancing test for applying the Lanham Act to titles of artistic works as set forth in *Rogers v. Grimaldi* (2d Cir. 1989). The *Rogers* balancing test requires courts to construe the Lanham Act "to apply to artistic works only where the public interest in avoiding consumer confusion outweighs the public interest in free expression." *Rogers*. Accordingly, the *Rogers* test prohibits application of the Lanham Act to titles of artistic works unless the title "has no artistic relevance to the underlying work whatsoever or, if it has some artistic relevance, unless the title explicitly misleads as to the source or the content of the work."

Application of the *Rogers* test here leads to the same result as it did in *MCA*. Forsythe's use of the Barbie mark is clearly relevant to his work. . . . Accordingly, the public interest in free and artistic expression greatly outweighs its interest in potential consumer confusion about Mattel's sponsorship of Forsythe's works.

B. Trade dress

Mattel also claims that Forsythe misappropriated its trade dress in Barbie's appearance, in violation of the Lanham Act, 15 U.S.C. § 1125. Mattel claims that it possesses a trade dress in the Superstar Barbie head and the doll's overall appearance. The district court concluded that there was no likelihood that the public would be misled into believing that Mattel endorsed Forsythe's photographs despite Forsythe's use of the Barbie figure.

Arguably, the Barbie trade dress also plays a role in our culture similar to the role played by the Barbie trademark—namely, symbolization of an unattainable ideal of femininity for some women. Forsythe's use of the Barbie trade dress, therefore, presumably would present First Amendment concerns similar to those that made us reluctant to apply the Lanham Act as a bar to the artistic uses of Mattel's Barbie trademark in both *MCA* and this case. But we need not decide how the *MCA/Rogers* First Amendment balancing might apply to Forsythe's use of the Barbie trade dress because we find, on a narrower ground, that it qualifies as nominative fair use. In the trademark context, we recently held that a defendant's use is classic fair use where "a defendant has used the plaintiff's mark *only* to describe his own product, *and not at all to describe the plaintiff's product.*" *Cairns* (emphasis in original). In contrast, a defendant's use of a plaintiff's mark is nominative where he or she "used the plaintiff's mark to describe the plaintiff's product, *even if the defendant's ultimate goal is to describe his own product.*" *Cairns* (emphasis in original). The goal of a nominative use is generally for the "purposes of comparison, criticism [or] point of reference." *New Kids on the Block.* These two mutually exclusive forms of fair use are equally applicable here in the trade dress context.

Applying these fair use standards to the trade dress context, we hold that a defendant's use is classic fair use where the defendant has used the plaintiff's dress to describe or identify the defendant's own product and not at all to describe or identify the plaintiff's product. Likewise, a defendant's use is nominative where he or she used the plaintiff's dress to describe or identify the plaintiff's product, even if the defendant's ultimate goal is to describe or identify his or her own product.

Forsythe's use of the Barbie trade dress is nominative. Forsythe used Mattel's Barbie figure and head in his works to conjure up associations of Mattel, while at the same time to identify his own work, which is a criticism and parody of Barbie. See *Cairns.* Where use of the trade dress or mark is grounded in the defendant's desire to refer to the plaintiff's product as a point of reference for defendant's own work, a use is nominative.

Fair use may be either nominative or classic. We recognize a fair use defense in claims brought under § 1125 where the use of the trademark "does not imply sponsorship or endorsement of the product because the mark is used only to describe the thing, rather than to identify its source." *New Kids on the Block.* Thus, we recently reiterated that, in the trademark context, nominative use becomes nominative fair use when a defendant proves three elements:

> First, the plaintiff's product or service in question must be one not readily identifiable without use of the trademark; second, only so much of the mark or marks may be used as is reasonably necessary to identify the plaintiff's product or service; and third, the user must do nothing that would, in conjunction with the mark, suggest sponsorship or endorsement by the trademark holder. . . .

We hold that Forsythe's use of Mattel's Barbie qualifies as nominative fair use. All three elements weigh in favor of Forsythe. Barbie would not be readily identifiable in a photographic work without use of the Barbie likeness and figure. Forsythe used only so much as was necessary to make his parodic use of Barbie readily identifiable, and it is highly unlikely that any reasonable consumer would have believed that Mattel sponsored or was affiliated with his work. The district court's grant of summary judgment to Forsythe on Mattel's trade dress infringement claim was, therefore, proper.

C. Dilution

Mattel also appeals the district court's grant of summary judgment on its trademark and dress dilution claims. The district court found that Forsythe was entitled to summary judgment because his use of the Barbie mark and trade dress was parody and thus "his expression is a non-commercial use."

Dilution may occur where use of a trademark "whittle[s] away . . . the value of a trademark" by "blurring their uniqueness and singularity" or by "tarnishing them with negative associations." *MCA.* However, "[t]arnishment caused merely by an editorial or artistic parody which satirizes plaintiff's product or its image is not actionable under an anti-dilution statute because of the free speech protections of the First Amendment. . . ." 4 McCarthy, § 24:105. A dilution action only applies to purely commercial speech. Parody is a form of noncommercial expression if it does more than propose a commercial transaction. Under *MCA*, Forsythe's artistic and parodic work is considered noncommercial speech and, therefore, not subject to a trademark dilution claim.

We reject Mattel's Lanham Act claims and affirm the district court's grant of summary judgment in favor of Forsythe. Mattel cannot use "trademark laws to . . . censor all parodies or satires which use [its] name" or dress. *New Kids on the Block.*

Question:

1.) The *Mattel* court says, helpfully for the purposes of this chapter,

> In the trademark context, we recently held that a defendant's use is classic fair use where "a defendant has used the plaintiff's mark *only* to describe his own product, *and not at all to describe the plaintiff's product.*" *Cairns* (emphasis in original). In contrast, a defendant's use of a plaintiff's mark is nominative where he or she "used the plaintiff's mark to describe the plaintiff's product, *even if the defendant's ultimate goal is to describe his own product.*" *Cairns* (emphasis in original). The goal of a nominative use is generally for the "purposes of comparison, criticism [or] point of reference." *New Kids on the Block.* These two mutually exclusive forms of fair use are equally applicable here in the trade dress context.

Give examples, not from our reading, of both fair and nominative use. Are they really mutually exclusive? How would you classify this imaginary advertisement for Tesla electric cars? "Tesla: the style of a Ferrari for someone with Prius values." Does it qualify for either defense? Does it violate 1125(a)?

Playboy Enterprises, Inc. v. Welles
279 F.3d 796 (9th Cir. 2002)

T.G. NELSON, Circuit Judge.

Playboy Enterprises, Inc. (PEI), appeals the district court's grant of summary judgment as to its claims of trademark infringement, unfair competition, and breach of contract against Terri Welles. . . .

I.
Background

Terri Welles was on the cover of Playboy in 1981 and was chosen to be the Playboy Playmate of the Year for 1981. Her use of the title "Playboy Playmate of  the Year 1981," and her use of other trademarked terms on her website are at issue in this suit. During the relevant time period, Welles' website offered information about and free photos of Welles, advertised photos for sale, advertised memberships in her photo club, and promoted her services as a spokesperson. A biographical section described Welles' selection as Playmate of the Year in 1981 and her years modeling for PEI. After the lawsuit began, Welles included discussions of the suit and criticism of PEI on her website and included a note disclaiming any association with PEI.

PEI complains of four different uses of its trademarked terms on Welles' website: (1) the terms "Playboy" and "Playmate" in the metatags of the website; (2) the phrase "Playmate of the Year 1981" on the masthead of the website; (3) the phrases "Playboy Playmate of the Year 1981" and "Playmate of the Year 1981" on various banner ads, which may be transferred to other websites; and (4) the repeated use of the abbreviation "PMOY '81" as the watermark on the pages of the website. PEI claimed that these uses of its marks constituted trademark infringement, dilution, false designation of origin, and unfair competition. The district court granted defendants' motion for summary judgment. PEI appeals the grant of summary judgment on its infringement and dilution claims. We affirm in part and reverse in part.

Discussion

A. Trademark Infringement

Except for the use of PEI's protected terms in the wallpaper of Welles' website, we conclude that Welles' uses of PEI's trademarks are permissible, nominative uses. They imply no current sponsorship or endorsement by PEI. Instead, they serve to identify Welles as a past PEI "Playmate of the Year."

We articulated the test for a permissible, nominative use in *New Kids On The Block v. New America Publishing, Inc.* . . . Unlike a traditional fair use scenario, the defendant newspaper was using the trademarked term to describe not its own product, but the plaintiff's. Thus, the factors used to evaluate fair use were inapplicable. The use was nonetheless permissible, we concluded, based on its nominative nature.

We adopted the following test for nominative use:

> First, the product or service in question must be one not readily identifiable without use of the trademark; second, only so much of the mark or marks may be used as is reasonably necessary to identify the product or service; and third, the user must do nothing that would, in conjunction with the mark, suggest sponsorship or endorsement by the trademark holder.

We noted in *New Kids* that a nominative use may also be a commercial one.

In cases in which the defendant raises a nominative use defense, the above three-factor test should be applied instead of the test for likelihood of confusion set forth in *Sleekcraft*. The three-factor test better evaluates the likelihood of confusion in nominative use cases. When a defendant uses a trademark nominally, the trademark will be identical to the plaintiff's mark, at least in terms of the words in question. Thus, application of the *Sleekcraft* test, which focuses on the similarity of the mark used by the plaintiff and the defendant, would lead to the incorrect conclusion that virtually all nominative uses are confusing. The three-factor test—with its requirements that the defendant use marks only when no descriptive substitute exists, use no more of the mark than necessary, and do nothing to suggest sponsorship or endorsement by the mark holder—better addresses concerns regarding the likelihood of confusion in nominative use cases.

1. Headlines and banner advertisements.

To satisfy the first part of the test for nominative use, "the product or service in question must be one not readily identifiable without use of the trademark[.]" This situation arises "when a trademark also describes a person, a place or an attribute of a product" and there is no descriptive substitute for the trademark. In such a circumstance, allowing the trademark holder exclusive rights would allow the language to "be depleted in much the same way as if generic words were protectable." In *New Kids*, we gave the example of the trademarked term, "Chicago Bulls." We explained that "one might refer to the 'two-time world champions' or 'the professional basketball team from Chicago,' but it's far simpler (and more likely to be understood) to refer to the Chicago Bulls." Moreover, such a use of the trademark would "not imply sponsorship or endorsement of the product because the mark is used only to describe the thing, rather than to identify its source." Thus, we concluded, such uses must be excepted from trademark infringement law.

The district court properly identified Welles' situation as one which must also be excepted. No descriptive substitute exists for PEI's trademarks in this context. The court explained:

> [T]here is no other way that Ms. Welles can identify or describe herself and her services without venturing into absurd descriptive phrases. To describe herself as the "nude model selected by Mr. Hefner's magazine as its number-one prototypical woman for the year 1981" would be impractical as well as ineffectual in identifying Terri Welles to the public.

We agree. . . .

The second part of the nominative use test requires that "only so much of the mark or marks may be used as is reasonably necessary to identify the product or service." Welles' banner advertisements and headlines satisfy this element because they use only the trademarked words, not the font or symbols associated with the trademarks.

The third element requires that the user do "nothing that would, in conjunction with the mark, suggest sponsorship or endorsement by the trademark holder." Welles does nothing in conjunction with her use of the marks to suggest sponsorship or endorsement by PEI. The marks are clearly used to describe the title she received from PEI in 1981, a title that helps describe who she is. In addition to doing nothing in conjunction with her use of the marks to suggest sponsorship or endorsement by PEI, Welles affirmatively disavows any sponsorship or endorsement. Her site contains a clear statement disclaiming any connection to PEI. Moreover, the text of the site describes her ongoing legal battles with the company.

For the foregoing reasons, we conclude that Welles' use of PEI's marks in her headlines and banner advertisements is a nominative use excepted from the law of trademark infringement.

2. Metatags.

Welles includes the terms "playboy" and "playmate" in her metatags. Metatags describe the contents of a website using keywords. Some search engines search metatags to identify websites relevant to a search. Thus, when an internet searcher enters "playboy" or "playmate" into a search engine that uses metatags, the results will include Welles' site. Because Welles' metatags do not repeat the terms extensively, her site will not be at the top of the list of search results. Applying the three-factor test for nominative use, we conclude that the use of the trademarked terms in Welles' metatags is nominative. As we discussed above with regard to the headlines and banner advertisements, Welles has no practical way of describing herself without using trademarked terms. In the context of metatags, we conclude that she has no practical way of identifying the content of her website without referring to PEI's trademarks. A large portion of Welles' website discusses her association with Playboy over the years. Thus, the trademarked terms accurately describe the contents of Welles' website, in addition to describing Welles. Forcing Welles and others to use absurd turns of phrase in their metatags, such as those necessary to identify Welles, would be particularly damaging in the internet search context. Searchers would have a much more difficult time locating relevant websites if they could do so only by correctly guessing the long phrases necessary to substitute for trademarks. We can hardly expect someone searching for Welles' site to imagine the same phrase proposed by the district court to describe Welles without referring to Playboy—"the nude model selected by Mr. Hefner's organization. . . ." Yet if someone could not remember her name, that is what they would have to do. Similarly, someone searching for critiques of Playboy on the internet would have a difficult time if internet sites could not list the object of their critique in their metatags.

There is simply no descriptive substitute for the trademarks used in Welles' metatags. Precluding their use would have the unwanted effect of hindering the free flow of information on the internet, something which is certainly not a goal of trademark law. Accordingly, the use of trademarked terms in the metatags meets the first part of the test for nominative use. We conclude that the metatags satisfy the second and third elements of the test as well. The metatags use only so much of the marks as reasonably necessary and nothing is done in conjunction with them to suggest sponsorship or endorsement by the trademark holder. We note that our decision might differ if the metatags listed the trademarked term so repeatedly that Welles' site would regularly appear above PEI's in searches for one of the trademarked terms.

3. Wallpaper/watermark.

The background, or wallpaper, of Welles' site consists of the repeated abbreviation "PMOY '81," which stands for "Playmate of the Year 1981." Welles' name or likeness does not appear before or after "PMOY '81." The pattern created by the repeated abbreviation appears as the background of the various pages of the website. Accepting, for the purposes of this appeal, that the abbreviation "PMOY" is indeed entitled to protection, we conclude that the repeated, stylized use of this abbreviation fails the nominative use test. The repeated depiction of "PMOY '81" is not necessary to describe Welles. "Playboy Playmate of the Year 1981" is quite adequate. Moreover, the term does not even appear to describe Welles—her name or likeness do not appear before or after each "PMOY '81." Because the use of the abbreviation fails the first prong of the nominative use test, we need not apply the next two prongs of the test.

Because the defense of nominative use fails here, and we have already determined that the doctrine of fair use does not apply, we remand to the district court. The court must determine whether trademark law protects the abbreviation "PMOY," as used in the wallpaper.

· · · · · · · · · ·

Notes: Background on Search Technology

We start with trademark's assumption that a mark is a word that points from a particular type of good to the source of that good. But we *think* of the mark doing that to the consumer's eyeball, the consumer's brain, in the context of a storefront, a supermarket shelf or a billboard. Along comes the internet, or more accurately in this case, the world wide web. (If you do not know the difference, you should probably Google "history of the internet," and "history of the world wide web." It will be fun. Honest.) And on the search engine, the experienced reality is very different.

If you are walking through the aisles of the grocery store and I have a large picture on my cereal box that looks like a single Cheerio, but no use of that brand's name or logos, then you—as a loyal Cheerio eater—may be interested by the similarly shaped product, but you are not likely to be confused. If I have a sign by my mouthwash that says "compare to Listerine" then I am using Listerine's trademark to show consumers that this is a product I claim to be comparable—a nominative use of the kind discussed in this chapter. But what if the metatags on my website say "Listerine" many times, attracting Listerine-seeking visitors, who later stay on the site, intrigued, even after realizing their initial mistake. What if the search engine displays other mouthwash ads whenever someone searches for Listerine? We have to make a choice. Is this just (benign) product comparison? In that situation, the brand name is used to convey useful information to a consumer making a choice—like "compare to Listerine," or "considering a Prius? Try our even more advanced electric car." Or is this like posting a Pizza Hut billboard at the exit to the freeway, which leads hungry drivers to a restaurant that turns out to be Domino's, which they would not have chosen but where they may eat anyway, just because it was convenient?

Law is context-dependent and technology is a context.

That goes not just for the way trademark needs to adapt to search engines, but *within* the world of search engines, because we need to understand what the search engine is actually doing.

When *Welles* was decided search engines prioritized their search results (among other things) according to word-frequency and metatag description. If a site had the words "online shoe store" 1000 times in one point white font on a white background in its "wallpaper" and if it put in the html metatags for the site <meta name="keywords" "shoe sale," "designer shoes" "cute shoes" "designer shoe sale" "really cute shoes"> that site would be more highly ranked in a search for shoe stores online.

To see what metatags are, pick an old, unfashionable website and click "view source," or something comparable, in your browser's command menu. Here is an imaginary one for a Duke basketball fan site.

```
<!DOCTYPE HTML PUBLIC "-//W3C//DTD HTML 4.0 Transitional//EN">
<html>
  <head>
  <title>Duke basketball fan site.</title>
  <meta name="keywords" content="Duke basketball, ACC
    basketball, Duke fan, etc">
 <meta name="description" content="The Number One Site for
    Duke Basketball Fans!!">
  </head>
  <body>
  Welcome to the Duke Basketball Fanatics page. (Not affiliated
  with Duke University)
  </body>
</html>
```

The metatags are, as their name suggests, meta. They are not the page. They are talking *about* the page. The <title> tag tells your browser what the title of the page is. (Look at the name that appears in the tab at the top of your browser screen.) The <keywords> metatag tells search engines what the creator of the site thinks are the search keywords that someone looking for a page like this might choose to search. The <description> metatag provides the page creator's own description of the page.

Insiders will know that this description is about as current a representation of the way web pages are set up and search engines operate, as a diagram of a 1968 VW Beetle would be for contemporary car design. There are still metatags, they are important and search engines do look at them. But, precisely because search results were so easily "gamed" with strategies like Ms. Welles', search engineers had to find a better way. They settled instead on what some have called the water-hole strategy. If you want to know where the water is, do not look at a map, look at the tracks the animals leave on the ground. The animals know where the water is. On the web, the users know where the best pages are and they link to them. Rather than searching words and metatags, search engines—led by Google's Page Rank algorithm (hint Sergey Brin and Larry *Page*)—looked for patterns of linkage. If James Boyle's site http://thepublicdomain.org has lots of links *from* people who seem knowledgeable about copyright, he gets a higher page rank. If he then links to another page about copyright, then that page in turn is seen as more relevant to a copyright search. It is a lay version of peer review. In the world of search engines that use such techniques, while word frequency and metatags will still influence a result, they will have less impact relative to other factors, perhaps changing the balance of interests. On the other hand, "link bombing" which attempts to game search engine algorithms by creating hundreds of spurious links to the owner's site, might assume a greater importance.

Question:

1.) Look at the discussion above about how to apply trademark law to search engines. Does one's answer to that question depend on an analysis of the technology, or a choice between the broad and narrow vision of trademark law discussed in the last chapter? Both? What normative questions about the ultimate justification for trademark and its temporal reach both before and after the moment of purchase would be relevant?

PROBLEM 8-1

1) Look back at Problem 7-1, and in particular at Figure One on page 194 and the paragraph at the bottom of page 206 that describes Google's use of the company logos. **May Google use these logos to facilitate search in the way shown in Figure One? Why or why not?**

2) Now, doing your own research, **find two examples in the real world of uses in commerce that you think qualify as *descriptive fair uses* of others' trademarks, and two examples of uses in commerce that you think are *nominative uses* of others' trademarks. In each instance, explain why you think those uses meet the criteria for the relevant defense.**

CHAPTER NINE

False Advertising, Dilution & 'Cyberpiracy'

We have seen how the Lanham Act reaches beyond registered marks to also protect unregistered marks and trade dress. But it also provides other legal rights. We will deal with three in this chapter—the § 1125(a) prohibition of false advertising and false or misleading statements of fact, the § 1125(c) "anti dilution" provisions that offer special protection to famous marks, and the § 1125(d) prohibition of "cyberpiracy" or "cyber-squatting" that gives trademark owners, under certain circumstances, the right to prevent "bad faith" registering of domain names.

1.) False Advertising: False or Misleading Statements of Fact

Section 1125(a) not only prohibits false or misleading designations of origin—the provision that allows Federal enforcement of unregistered marks and trade dress—it also prohibits false or misleading statements of *fact*. The cause of action for false advertising is in 1125(a)(1)(B).

> **1125(a) Civil action**
> **(1) Any person who, on or in connection with any goods or services, or any container for goods, uses in commerce any word, term, name, symbol, or device, or any combination thereof, or any false designation of origin, false or misleading description of fact, or false or misleading representation of fact, which—**
>> **(A) is likely to cause confusion, or to cause mistake, or to deceive as to the affiliation, connection, or association of such person with another person, or as to the origin, sponsorship, or approval of his or her goods, services, or commercial activities by another person, or**
>> **(B) in commercial advertising or promotion, misrepresents the nature, characteristics, qualities, or geographic origin of his or her or another person's goods, services, or commercial activities,**
> **shall be liable in a civil action by any person who believes that he or she is or is likely to be damaged by such act. . . .**

Read the language of the statute closely. Do we need such a broad regulation of commercial speech in the Federal trademark statute? What goals does it serve?

Unlike the § 1114 trademark infringement provisions, which can only be invoked by the owner of the mark, § 1125(a)'s standing criteria are very broad: "shall be liable in a civil action by any person who *believes* that he or she is or is likely to be damaged by such act." In practice, courts have narrowed this standing considerably, requiring the presence of an actual economic or commercial interest. In *Lexmark Int'l, Inc. v. Static Control Components, Inc.* (2014), the Supreme Court confirmed that, consistent with the Lanham Act's stated goal of "protect[ing] persons engaged in [commerce within the control of Congress] against unfair competition," in order to bring a § 1125(a) false advertising claim, "a plaintiff must allege an injury to a commercial interest in reputation or sales. A consumer who is hoodwinked into purchasing a disappointing product may well have an injury-in-fact cognizable under Article III, but he cannot invoke the protection of the Lanham Act." (This chapter focuses only on the cause of action for false advertising in § 1125. Note that consumers can bring complaints for false advertising under other schemes, including through the Federal Trade Commission or state laws.)

Pizza Hut, Inc. v. Papa John's Intern., Inc.
227 F.3d 489 (5th Cir. 2000)

E. GRADY JOLLY, Circuit Judge:

This appeal presents a false advertising claim under section 43(a) of the Lanham Act, resulting in a jury verdict for the plaintiff, Pizza Hut. At the center of this appeal is Papa John's four word slogan "Better Ingredients. Better Pizza." . . .

I
A

Pizza Hut is a wholly owned subsidiary of Tricon Global Restaurants. With over 7000 restaurants (both company and franchisee-owned), Pizza Hut is the largest pizza chain in the United States. In 1984, John Schnatter founded Papa John's Pizza in the back of his father's tavern. Papa John's has grown to over 2050 locations, making it the third largest pizza chain in the United States.

In May 1995, Papa John's adopted a new slogan: "Better Ingredients. Better Pizza." In 1996, Papa John's filed for a federal trademark registration for this slogan with the United States Patent & Trademark Office ("PTO"). Its application for registration was ultimately granted by the PTO. Since 1995, Papa John's has invested over $300 million building customer goodwill in its trademark "Better Ingredients. Better Pizza." The slogan has appeared on millions of signs, shirts, menus, pizza boxes, napkins and other items, and has regularly appeared as the "tag line" at the end of Papa John's radio and television ads, or with the company logo in printed advertising.

On May 1, 1997, Pizza Hut launched its "Totally New Pizza" campaign. This campaign was the culmination of "Operation Lightning Bolt," a nine-month, $50 million project in which Pizza Hut declared "war" on poor quality pizza. From the deck of a World War II aircraft carrier, Pizza Hut's president, David Novak, declared "war" on "skimpy, low quality pizza." National ads aired during this campaign touted the "better taste" of Pizza Hut's pizza, and "dared" anyone to find a "better pizza."

In early May 1997, Papa John's launched its first national ad campaign. The campaign was directed towards Pizza Hut, and its "Totally New Pizza" campaign. In a pair of TV ads featuring Pizza Hut's co-founder Frank Carney, Carney touted the superiority of Papa John's pizza over Pizza Hut's pizza. Although Carney had left the pizza business in the 1980's, he returned as a franchisee of Papa John's because he liked the taste of Papa John's pizza better than any other pizza on the market. The ad campaign was remarkably successful. During May 1997, Papa John's sales increased 11.7 percent over May 1996 sales, while Pizza Hut's sales were down 8 percent.

On the heels of the success of the Carney ads, in February 1998, Papa John's launched a second series of ads touting the results of a taste test in which consumers were asked to compare Papa John's and Pizza Hut's pizzas. In the ads, Papa John's boasted that it "won big time" in taste tests. The ads were a response to Pizza Hut's "dare" to find a "better pizza."

The taste test showed that consumers preferred Papa John's traditional crust pizzas over Pizza Hut's comparable pizzas by a 16-point margin (58% to 42%). Additionally, consumers preferred Papa John's thin crust pizzas by a fourteen-point margin (57% to 43%).

Following the taste test ads, Papa John's ran a series of ads comparing specific ingredients used in its pizzas with those used by its "competitors." During the course of these ads, Papa John's touted the superiority of its sauce and its dough. During the sauce campaign, Papa John's asserted that its sauce was made from "fresh, vine-ripened tomatoes," which were canned through a process called "fresh pack," while its competitors—including Pizza Hut—make their sauce from remanufactured tomato paste. During the dough campaign, Papa John's stated that it used "clear filtered water" to make its pizza dough, while the "biggest chain" uses "whatever comes out of the tap." Additionally, Papa John's asserted that it gives its yeast "several days to work its magic," while "some folks" use "frozen dough or dough made the same day." At or near the close of each of these ads, Papa John's punctuated its ingredient comparisons with the slogan "Better Ingredients. Better Pizza."

Pizza Hut does not appear to contest the truthfulness of the underlying factual assertions made by Papa John's in the course of these ads. Pizza Hut argues, however, that its own independent taste tests and other "scientific evidence" establishes that filtered water makes no difference in pizza dough, that there is no "taste" difference between Papa John's "fresh-pack" sauce and Pizza Hut's "remanufactured" sauce, and that fresh dough is not superior to frozen dough. In response to Pizza Hut's "scientific evidence," Papa John's asserts that "each of these 'claims' involves a matter of common sense choice (fresh versus frozen, canned vegetables and fruit versus remanufactured paste, and filtered versus unfiltered water) about which individual consumers can and do form preferences every day without 'scientific' or 'expert' assistance."

In November 1997, Pizza Hut filed a complaint regarding Papa John's "Better Ingredients. Better Pizza." advertising campaign with the National Advertising Division of the Better Business Bureau, an industry self-regulatory body. This complaint, however, did not produce satisfactory results for Pizza Hut.

B

. . . The district court, without objection, submitted the liability issue to the jury through special interrogatories. The special issues submitted to the jury related to (1) the slogan and (2) over Papa John's objection, certain classes of groups of advertisements referred to as "sauce claims," "dough claims," "taste test claims," and "ingredients claims."

On November 17, 1999, the jury returned its responses to the special issues finding that Papa John's slogan, and its "sauce claims" and "dough claims" were false or misleading and deceptive or likely to deceive consumers.[2] . . .

On January 3, 2000, the trial court, based upon the jury's verdict and the evidence presented by the parties in support of injunctive relief and on the issue of damages, entered a Final Judgment and issued a Memorandum Opinion and Order. The court concluded that the "Better Ingredients. Better Pizza." slogan was "consistent with the legal definition of non-actionable puffery" from its introduction in 1995 until May 1997. However, the slogan "became tainted . . . in light of the entirety of Papa John's post-May 1997 advertising." Based on this conclusion, the magistrate judge permanently enjoined Papa

---

[2] . . . Although the jury was specifically asked whether the advertisements were likely to deceive consumers, the interrogatories failed to ask whether the deception created by these advertisements was material to the consumers to which the ads were directed—that is, whether consumers actually relied on the misrepresentations in making purchasing decisions.

John's from "using any slogan in the future that constitutes a recognizable variation of the phrase 'Better Ingredients. Better Pizza.' or which uses the adjective 'Better' to modify the terms 'ingredients' and/or 'pizza'." Additionally, the court enjoined Papa John's from identifying Frank Carney as a co-founder of Pizza Hut, "unless such advertising includes a voice-over, printed statement or a superimposed message which states that Frank Carney has not been affiliated with Pizza Hut since 1980," and enjoined the dissemination of any advertising that was produced or disseminated prior to the date of this judgment and that explicitly or implicitly states or suggested that "Papa John's component is superior to the same component of Pizza Hut's pizzas." Finally, the court enjoined Papa John's from "explicitly or implicitly claim[ing] that a component of Papa John's pizza is superior to the same component of Pizza Hut's unless the superiority claim is supported by either (1) scientifically demonstrated attributes of superiority or (2) taste test surveys." Additionally, the injunction required that if the claim is supported by taste test surveys, the advertising shall include a printed statement, voice-over or "super," whichever is appropriate, stating the localities where the tests were conducted, the inclusive dates on which the surveys were performed, and the specific pizza products that were tested. . . .

II

We review the district court's denial of a motion for judgment as a matter of law de novo applying the same standards as the district court. . . . Thus, for purposes of this appeal, we will review the evidence, in the most favorable light to Pizza Hut, to determine if, as a matter of law, it is sufficient to support a claim of false advertising under section 43(a) of the Lanham Act.

III
A

Section 43(a) of the Lanham Act, codified at 15 U.S.C. § 1125, provides in relevant part:

> Any person who . . . in commercial advertising or promotion, misrepresents the nature, characteristics, quality, or geographic origin of his or another person's goods, services, or commercial activities, shall be liable in a civil action by any person who believes that he or she is likely to be damaged by such act.

15 U.S.C. § 1125(a)(1)(B). We have interpreted this section of the Lanham Act as providing "protection against a 'myriad of deceptive commercial practices,' including false advertising or promotion."

A prima facie case of false advertising under section 43(a) requires the plaintiff to establish:

> (1) A false or misleading statement of fact about a product;
> (2) Such statement either deceived, or had the capacity to deceive a substantial segment of potential consumers;
> (3) The deception is material, in that it is likely to influence the consumer's purchasing decision;
> (4) The product is in interstate commerce; and
> (5) The plaintiff has been or is likely to be injured as a result of the statement at issue.

The failure to prove the existence of any element of the prima facie case is fatal to the plaintiff's claim.

B

The law governing false advertising claims under section 43(a) of the Lanham Act is well settled. In order to obtain monetary damages or equitable relief in the form of an injunction, "a plaintiff must demonstrate that the commercial advertisement or promotion is either literally false, or that [if the advertisement is not literally false,] it is likely to mislead and confuse consumers." If the statement is shown to be misleading, the plaintiff must also introduce evidence of the statement's impact on consumers, referred to as materiality.

(1)
(a)

Essential to any claim under section 43(a) of the Lanham Act is a determination of whether the challenged statement is one of fact—actionable under section 43(a)—or one of general opinion—not actionable under section 43(a). Bald assertions of superiority or general statements of opinion cannot form the basis of Lanham Act liability. Rather the statements at issue must be a "specific and measurable claim, capable of being proved false or of being reasonably interpreted as a statement of objective fact." As noted by our court in *Presidio:* "[A] statement of fact is one that (1) admits of being adjudged true or false in a way that (2) admits of empirical verification."

(b)

One form of non-actionable statements of general opinion under section 43(a) of the Lanham Act has been referred to as "puffery." Puffery has been discussed at some length by other circuits. The Third Circuit has described "puffing" as "advertising that is not deceptive for no one would rely on its exaggerated claims." Similarly, the Ninth Circuit has defined "puffing" as "exaggerated advertising, blustering and boasting upon which no reasonable buyer would rely and is not actionable under 43(a)."

These definitions of puffery are consistent with the definitions provided by the leading commentaries in trademark law. A leading authority on unfair competition has defined "puffery" as an "exaggerated advertising, blustering, and boasting upon which no reasonable buyer would rely," or "a general claim of superiority over a comparative product that is so vague, it would be understood as a mere expression of opinion." McCarthy on Trademark and Unfair Competition. Similarly, Prosser and Keeton on Torts defines "puffing" as "a seller's privilege to lie his head off, so long as he says nothing specific, on the theory that no reasonable man would believe him, or that no reasonable man would be influenced by such talk."

Drawing guidance from the writings of our sister circuits and the leading commentators, we think that non-actionable "puffery" comes in at least two possible forms: (1) an exaggerated, blustering, and boasting statement upon which no reasonable buyer would be justified in relying; or (2) a general claim of superiority over comparable products that is so vague that it can be understood as nothing more than a mere expression of opinion.

(2)
(a)

With respect to materiality, when the statements of fact at issue are shown to be literally false, the plaintiff need not introduce evidence on the issue of the impact the statements had on consumers. In such a circumstance, the court will assume that the statements actually misled consumers. On the other hand, if the statements at issue are either ambiguous or true but misleading, the plaintiff must present evidence of actual deception. The plaintiff may not rely on the judge or the jury to determine, "based solely upon his or her own intuitive reaction, whether the advertisement is deceptive." Instead, proof of actual deception requires proof that "consumers were actually deceived by the defendant's ambiguous or true-but-misleading statements." [Such proof often includes testimony from consumers, surveys, and consumer reaction tests.]. . . .

IV

We turn now to consider the case before us. Reduced to its essence, the question is whether the evidence, viewed in the most favorable light to Pizza Hut, established that Papa John's slogan "Better Ingredients. Better Pizza." is misleading and violative of section 43(a) of the Lanham Act. In making this determination, we will first consider the slogan "Better Ingredients. Better Pizza." standing alone to determine if it is a statement of fact capable of deceiving a substantial segment of the consuming public to which it was directed. Second, we will determine whether the evidence supports the district court's conclusion that after May 1997, the slogan was tainted, and therefore actionable, as a result of its use in a series of ads comparing specific ingredients used by Papa John's with the ingredients used by its "competitors."

A

The jury concluded that the slogan itself was a "false or misleading" statement of fact, and the district court enjoined its further use. Papa John's argues, however, that this statement "quite simply is not a statement of fact, [but] rather, a statement of belief or opinion, and an argumentative one at that." Papa John's asserts that because "a statement of fact is either true or false, it is susceptible to being proved or disproved. A statement of opinion or belief, on the other hand, conveys the speaker's state of mind, and even though it may be used to attempt to persuade the listener, it is a subjective communication that may be accepted or rejected, but not proven true or false." Papa John's contends that its slogan "Better Ingredients. Better Pizza." falls into the latter category, and because the phrases "better ingredients" and "better pizza" are not subject to quantifiable measures, the slogan is non-actionable puffery.

We will therefore consider whether the slogan standing alone constitutes a statement of fact under the Lanham Act. Bisecting the slogan "Better Ingredients. Better Pizza.," it is clear that the assertion by Papa John's that it makes a "Better Pizza." is a general statement of opinion regarding the superiority of its product over all others. This simple statement, "Better Pizza.," epitomizes the exaggerated advertising, blustering, and boasting by a manufacturer upon which no consumer would reasonably rely. *See, e.g., In re Boston Beer Co.* (Fed.Cir. 1999) (stating that the phrase "The Best Beer in America" was "trade puffery" and that such a general claim of superiority "should be freely available to all competitors in any given field to refer to their products or services"). Consequently, it appears indisputable that Papa John's assertion "Better Pizza." is non-actionable puffery.[8]

Moving next to consider separately the phrase "Better Ingredients.," the same conclusion holds true. Like "Better Pizza.," it is typical puffery. The word "better," when used in this context is unquantifiable. What makes one food ingredient "better" than another comparable ingredient, without further description, is wholly a matter of individual taste or preference not subject to scientific quantification. Indeed, it is difficult to think of any product, or any component of any product, to which the term "better," without more, is quantifiable. As our court stated in *Presidio:*

The law recognizes that a vendor is allowed some latitude in claiming

---

[8] It should be noted that Pizza Hut uses the slogan "The Best Pizza Under One Roof." Similarly, other nationwide pizza chains employ slogans touting their pizza as the "best": (1) Domino's Pizza uses the slogan "Nobody Delivers Better."; (2) Danato's uses the slogan "Best Pizza on the Block."; (3) Mr. Gatti's uses the slogan "Best Pizza in Town: Honest!"; and (4) Pizza Inn uses the slogans "Best Pizza Ever." and "The Best Tasting Pizza."

merits of his wares by way of an opinion rather than an absolute guarantee, so long as he hews to the line of rectitude in matters of fact. Opinions are not only the lifestyle of democracy, they are the brag in advertising that has made for the wide dissemination of products that otherwise would never have reached the households of our citizens. If we were to accept the thesis set forth by the appellees, [that all statements by advertisers were statements of fact actionable under the Lanham Act,] the advertising industry would have to be liquidated in short order.

Thus, it is equally clear that Papa John's assertion that it uses "Better Ingredients." is one of opinion not actionable under the Lanham Act.

Finally, turning to the combination of the two non-actionable phrases as the slogan "Better Ingredients. Better Pizza.," we fail to see how the mere joining of these two statements of opinion could create an actionable statement of fact. Each half of the slogan amounts to little more than an exaggerated opinion of superiority that no consumer would be justified in relying upon. It has not been explained convincingly to us how the combination of the two phrases, without more, changes the essential nature of each phrase so as to make it actionable. We assume that "Better Ingredients." modifies "Better Pizza." and consequently gives some expanded meaning to the phrase "Better Pizza," i.e., our pizza is better because our ingredients are better. Nevertheless, the phrase fails to give "Better Pizza." any more quantifiable meaning. Stated differently, the adjective that continues to describe "pizza" is "better," a term that remains unquantifiable, especially when applied to the sense of taste. Consequently, the slogan as a whole is a statement of non-actionable opinion. Thus, there is no legally sufficient basis to support the jury's finding that the slogan standing alone is a "false or misleading" statement of fact.

B

We next will consider whether the use of the slogan "Better Ingredients. Better Pizza." in connection with a series of comparative ads found by the jury to be misleading—specifically, ads comparing Papa John's sauce and dough with the sauce and dough of its competitors—"tainted" the statement of opinion and made it misleading under section 43(a) of the Lanham Act. Before reaching the ultimate question of whether the slogan is actionable under the Lanham Act, we will first examine the sufficiency of the evidence supporting the jury's conclusion that the comparison ads were misleading. . . .

(2)

We are obligated to accept the findings of the jury unless the facts point so overwhelmingly in favor of one party that no reasonable person could arrive at a different conclusion. In examining the record evidence, we must view it the way that is most favorable to upholding the verdict. Viewed in this light, it is clear that there is sufficient evidence to support the jury's conclusion that the sauce and dough ads were misleading statements of fact actionable under the Lanham Act.

Turning first to the sauce ads, the evidence establishes that despite the differences in the methods used to produce their competing sauces: (1) the primary ingredient in both Pizza Hut and Papa John's sauce is vine-ripened tomatoes; (2) at the point that the competing sauces are placed on the pizza, just prior to putting the pies into the oven for cooking, the consistency and water content of the sauces are essentially identical; and (3) as noted by the district court, at no time "prior to the close of the liability phase of trial was any credible evidence presented [by Papa John's] to demonstrate the existence of demonstrable differences" in the competing sauces. Consequently, the district court was correct in concluding that: "Without any scientific support or properly conducted taste preference test, by the written and/or oral negative connotations conveyed that pizza made from tomato paste concentrate is inferior to the 'fresh pack' method used by Papa John's, its sauce advertisements conveyed an impression which is misleading. . . ." Turning our focus to the dough ads, while the evidence clearly established that Papa John's and Pizza Hut employ different methods in making their pizza dough, again, the evidence established that there is no quantifiable difference between pizza dough produced through the "cold or slow-fermentation method" (used by Papa John's), or the "frozen dough method" (used by Pizza Hut). Further, although there is some evidence indicating that the texture of the dough used by Papa John's and Pizza Hut is slightly different, this difference is not related to the manufacturing process used to produce the dough. Instead, it is due to a difference in the wheat used to make the dough. Finally, with respect to the differences in the pizza dough resulting from the use of filtered water as opposed to tap water, the evidence was sufficient for the jury to conclude that there is no quantifiable difference between dough produced with tap water, as opposed to dough produced with filtered water.

We should note again that Pizza Hut does not contest the truthfulness of the underlying factual assertions made by Papa John's in the course of the sauce and dough ads. Pizza Hut concedes that it uses "remanufactured" tomato sauce to make its pizza sauce, while Papa John's uses "fresh-pack." Further, in regard to the dough, Pizza Hut concedes the truth of the assertion that it uses tap water in making its pizza dough, which is often frozen, while Papa John's uses filtered water to make its dough, which is fresh—never frozen. Consequently, because Pizza Hut does not contest the factual basis of Papa John's factual assertions, such assertions cannot be found to be factually false, but only impliedly false or misleading.

Thus, we conclude by saying that although the ads were true about the ingredients Papa John's used, it is clear that there was sufficient evidence in the record to support the jury's conclusion that Papa John's sauce and dough ads were misleading—but not false—in their suggestion that Papa John's ingredients were superior.

(3)

Thus, having concluded that the record supports a finding that the sauce and dough ads are misleading statements of fact, we must now determine whether the district court was correct in concluding that the use of the slogan "Better Ingredients. Better Pizza." in conjunction with these misleading ads gave quantifiable meaning to the slogan making a general statement of opinion misleading within the meaning of the Lanham Act.

In support of the district court's conclusion that the slogan was transformed, Pizza Hut argues that "in construing any advertising statement, the statement must be considered in the overall context in which it appears." Building on the foundation of this basic legal principle, Pizza Hut argues that "[t]he context in which Papa John's slogan must be viewed is the 2½ year campaign during which its advertising served as 'chapters' to demonstrate the truth of the 'Better Ingredients. Better Pizza.' book." Pizza Hut argues, that because Papa John's gave consumers specific facts supporting its assertion that its sauce and dough are "better"—specific facts that the evidence, when viewed in the light most favorable to the verdict, are irrelevant in making a better pizza—Papa John's statement of opinion that it made a "Better Pizza" became misleading. In essence, Pizza Hut argues, that by using the slogan "Better Ingredients. Better Pizza." in combination with the ads comparing Papa John's sauce and dough with the sauce and dough of its competitions, Papa John's gave quantifiable meaning to the word "Better" rendering it actionable under section 43(a) of the Lanham Act.

We agree that the message communicated by the slogan "Better Ingredients. Better Pizza." is expanded and given additional meaning when it is used as the tag line in the misleading sauce and dough ads. The slogan, when used in combination with the comparison ads, gives consumers two fact-specific reasons why Papa John's ingredients are "better." Consequently, a reasonable consumer would understand the slogan, *when considered in the context of the comparison ads,* as conveying the following message: Papa John's uses "better ingredients," which produces a "better pizza" because Papa John's uses "fresh-pack" tomatoes, fresh dough, and filtered water. In short, Papa John's has given definition to the word "better." Thus, when the slogan is used in this context, it is no longer mere opinion, but rather takes on the characteristics of a statement of fact. When used in the context of the sauce and dough ads, the slogan is misleading for the same reasons we have earlier discussed in connection with the sauce and dough ads.

(4)

Concluding that when the slogan was used as the tag line in the sauce and dough ads it became misleading, we must now determine whether reasonable consumers would have a tendency to rely on this misleading statement of fact in making their purchasing decisions. We conclude that Pizza Hut has failed to adduce evidence establishing that the misleading statement of fact conveyed by the ads and the slogan was material to the consumers to which the slogan was directed. Consequently, because such evidence of materiality is necessary to establish liability under the Lanham Act, the district court erred in denying Papa John's motion for judgment as a matter of law.

As previously discussed, none of the underlying facts supporting Papa John's claims of ingredient superiority made in connection with the slogan were literally false. Consequently, in order to satisfy its prima facie case, Pizza Hut was required to submit evidence establishing that the impliedly false or misleading statements were material to, that is, they had a tendency to influence the purchasing decisions of, the consumers to which they were directed.[12] We conclude that the evidence proffered by Pizza Hut fails to make an adequate showing.

In its appellate brief and during the course of oral argument, Pizza Hut directs our attention to three items of evidence in the record that it asserts establishes materiality to consumers. First, Pizza Hut points to the results of a survey conducted by an "independent expert" (Dr. Dupont) regarding the use of the slogan "Better Ingredients. Better Pizza." as written on Papa John's pizza box (the box survey). The results of the box survey, however, were excluded by the district court.[14] Consequently, these survey results provide no basis for the jury's finding.

Second, Pizza Hut points to two additional surveys conducted by Dr. Dupont that attempted to measure consumer perception of Papa John's "taste test" ads. This survey evidence, however, fails to address Pizza Hut's claim of materiality with respect to the slogan. Moreover, the jury rejected Pizza Hut's claims of deception with regard to Papa John's "taste test" ads—the very ads at issue in these surveys.

Finally, Pizza Hut attempts to rely on Papa John's own tracking studies and on the alleged subjective intent of Papa John's executives "to create a perception that Papa John's in fact uses better ingredients" to demonstrate materiality. Although Papa John's 1998 Awareness, Usage & Attitude Tracking Study showed that 48% of the respondents believe that "Papa John's has better ingredients than other national pizza chains," the study failed

---

[12] Since Pizza Hut sought only equitable relief and no monetary damages, it was required to offer evidence sufficient to establish that the claims made by Papa John's had the "*tendency to deceive consumers,*" rather than evidence indicating that the claims made by Papa John's *actually deceived consumers.*

[14] Pizza Hut has not sought review on appeal of the district court's ruling that the results of the box survey were inadmissible.

to indicate whether the conclusions resulted from the advertisements at issue, or from personal eating experiences, or from a combination of both. Consequently, the results of this study are not reliable or probative to test whether the slogan was material. Further, Pizza Hut provides no precedent, and we are aware of none, that stands for the proposition that the subjective intent of the defendant's corporate executives to convey a particular message is evidence of the fact that consumers in fact relied on the message to make their purchases. Thus, this evidence does not address the ultimate issue of materiality.

In short, Pizza Hut has failed to offer probative evidence on whether the misleading facts conveyed by Papa John's through its slogan were material to consumers: that is to say, there is no evidence demonstrating that the slogan had the tendency to deceive consumers so as to affect their purchasing decisions. Thus, the district court erred in denying Papa John's motion for judgment as a matter of law.

V

In sum, we hold that the slogan "Better Ingredients. Better Pizza." standing alone is not an objectifiable statement of fact upon which consumers would be justified in relying. Thus, it does not constitute a false or misleading statement of fact actionable under section 43(a) of the Lanham Act.

Additionally, while the slogan, when appearing in the context of some of the post-May 1997 comparative advertising—specifically, the sauce and dough campaigns—was given objectifiable meaning and thus became misleading and actionable, Pizza Hut has failed to adduce sufficient evidence establishing that the misleading facts conveyed by the slogan were material to the consumers to which it was directed. Thus, Pizza Hut failed to produce evidence of a Lanham Act violation, and the district court erred in denying Papa John's motion for judgment as a matter of law.

Therefore, the judgment of the district court denying Papa John's motion for judgment as a matter of law is REVERSED; the final judgment of the district court is VACATED; and the case is REMANDED for entry of judgment for Papa John's.

Questions:

1.) A timely question: What is a fact? Also, what is puffery and why is it non-actionable?

2.) On what elements of the false advertising claim does Pizza Hut prevail? On what does Papa John's prevail? Were you surprised by the outcome of the case? If you were Pizza Hut's lawyer, with the benefit of hindsight, what would you do differently?

3.) Why is the evidentiary standard different for statements that are *literally false* and those that are ambiguous or true, but *misleading*?

2.) Dilution

Section 1125(c) of the Lanham Act gives a special right to "famous" marks, one that reaches considerably further than conventional trademark infringement.

> **1125(c) Dilution by blurring; dilution by tarnishment**
> **(1) Injunctive relief**
> **Subject to the principles of equity, the owner of a famous mark that**
> **is distinctive, inherently or through acquired distinctiveness, shall**

be entitled to an injunction against another person who, at any time after the owner's mark has become famous, commences use of a mark or trade name in commerce that is likely to cause dilution by blurring or dilution by tarnishment of the famous mark, regardless of the presence or absence of actual or likely confusion, of competition, or of actual economic injury.

(2) **Definitions**

(A) For purposes of paragraph (1), a mark is famous if it is widely recognized by the general consuming public of the United States as a designation of source of the goods or services of the mark's owner. In determining whether a mark possesses the requisite degree of recognition, the court may consider all relevant factors, including the following:

(i) The duration, extent, and geographic reach of advertising and publicity of the mark, whether advertised or publicized by the owner or third parties.

(ii) The amount, volume, and geographic extent of sales of goods or services offered under the mark.

(iii) The extent of actual recognition of the mark.

(iv) Whether the mark was registered under the Act of March 3, 1881, or the Act of February 20, 1905, or on the principal register.

(B) For purposes of paragraph (1), "dilution by blurring" is association arising from the similarity between a mark or trade name and a famous mark that impairs the distinctiveness of the famous mark. In determining whether a mark or trade name is likely to cause dilution by blurring, the court may consider all relevant factors, including the following:

(i) The degree of similarity between the mark or trade name and the famous mark.

(ii) The degree of inherent or acquired distinctiveness of the famous mark.

(iii) The extent to which the owner of the famous mark is engaging in substantially exclusive use of the mark.

(iv) The degree of recognition of the famous mark.

(v) Whether the user of the mark or trade name intended to create an association with the famous mark.

(vi) Any actual association between the mark or trade name and the famous mark.

(C) For purposes of paragraph (1), "dilution by tarnishment" is association arising from the similarity between a mark or trade name and a famous mark that harms the reputation of the famous mark.

(3) **Exclusions**

The following shall not be actionable as dilution by blurring or dilution by tarnishment under this subsection:

(A) Any fair use, including a nominative or descriptive fair use, or facilitation of such fair use, of a famous mark by another person other than as a designation of source for the person's own goods or services, including use in connection with—

(i) advertising or promotion that permits consumers to

> compare goods or services; or
> **(ii) identifying and parodying, criticizing, or commenting upon the famous mark owner or the goods or services of the famous mark owner.**
> **(B) All forms of news reporting and news commentary.**
> **(C) Any noncommercial use of a mark. . . .**

Note that, once a mark has shown itself to be famous, it does not have to clear many of the hurdles that the owner of a conventional mark does in a classic § 1114 infringement suit. Dilution by blurring or tarnishment can be found "regardless of the presence or absence of actual or likely confusion, of competition, or of actual economic injury." This language was inserted by the Trademark Dilution Revision Act (TDRA) of 2006 to undo the Supreme Court's decision in *Moseley, DBA Victor's Little Secret v. V Secret Catalogue, Inc.* (2003), which had required more proof on harm for a dilution claim. Why would Congress want to do this?

But while the TDRA lowered the standards required to prove blurring or tarnishment, it raised the standards required to prove that the mark was "famous." The result was to leave an extremely strong right, with a low standard to prove injury, but to confine the possession of that right to a few megabrands. Is there a good normative or economic reason to choose that legal design? A political science explanation based on lobbying power? Both?

a.) The Requirement that the Mark be Famous

Coach Services, Inc. v. Triumph Learning LLC
668 F.3d 1356 (Fed. Cir. 2012)

O'MALLEY, Circuit Judge.

Coach Services, Inc. ("CSI") appeals from the final decision of the Trademark Trial and Appeal Board ("the Board") dismissing its opposition to Triumph Learning, LLC's

("Triumph") use-based applications to register the mark COACH for educational materials used to prepare students for standardized tests. The Board found that: (1) there was no likelihood of confusion between the parties' COACH marks; (2) CSI failed to prove likelihood of dilution. . . .

The Board found that CSI could not succeed on its dilution claims because it failed to show that its COACH mark was famous for dilution purposes. For the reasons explained below, we agree. Because we find that CSI failed to prove fame for dilution, we need not address the other statutory factors courts can consider to determine whether a mark is likely to cause dilution by blurring.

1. Fame for Dilution

A threshold question in a federal dilution claim is whether the mark at issue is "famous." Under the TDRA, a mark is famous if it "is widely recognized by the general consuming public of the United States as a designation of source of the goods or services of the mark's owner." 15 U.S.C. § 1125(c)(2)(A). By using the "general consuming public" as the benchmark, the TDRA eliminated the possibility of "niche fame," which some courts had recognized under the previous version of the statute. The TDRA lists four non-exclusive factors for courts to consider when determining whether a mark is famous:

> (i) The duration, extent, and geographic reach of advertising and publicity of the mark, whether advertised or publicized by the owner or third parties.
>
> (ii) The amount, volume, and geographic extent of sales of goods or services offered under the mark.
>
> (iii) The extent of actual recognition of the mark.
>
> (iv) Whether the mark was registered under the Act of March 3, 1881, or the Act of February 20, 1905, or on the principal register.

15 U.S.C. § 1125(c)(2)(A). Whether a mark is famous under the TDRA is a factual question reviewed for substantial evidence.

Fame for likelihood of confusion and fame for dilution are distinct concepts, and dilution fame requires a more stringent showing. While fame for dilution "is an either/or proposition"—it either exists or does not—fame for likelihood of confusion is a matter of degree along a continuum. *Palm Bay*. Accordingly, a mark can acquire "sufficient public recognition and renown to be famous for purposes of likelihood of confusion without meeting the more stringent requirement for dilution fame." *7-Eleven*.

It is well-established that dilution fame is difficult to prove. *Everest Capital, Ltd. v. Everest Funds Mgmt. LLC* (8th Cir. 2005) ("The judicial consensus is that 'famous' is a rigorous standard."); see also 4 McCarthy, § 24:104 at 24–286, 24–293 (noting that fame for dilution is "a difficult and demanding requirement" and that, although "all 'trademarks' are 'distinctive'—very few are 'famous'"). This is particularly true where, as here, the mark is a common English word that has different meanings in different contexts. Importantly, the owner of the allegedly famous mark must show that its mark became famous "prior to the filing date of the trademark application or registration against which it intends to file an opposition or cancellation proceeding." *Toro*.

As noted, fame for dilution requires widespread recognition by the general public. 15 U.S.C. § 1125(c)(2)(A). To establish the requisite level of fame, the "mark's owner must demonstrate that the common or proper noun uses of the term and third-party uses of the mark are now eclipsed by the owner's use of the mark." *Toro*. An opposer must show that, when the general public encounters the mark "in almost any context, it associates the term, at least initially, with the mark's owner." In other words, a famous mark is one that has become a "household name." With this framework in mind, we turn to CSI's evidence of fame.

2. CSI Failed to Introduce Sufficient Evidence of Fame for Dilution

The Board found that CSI's evidence of fame was insufficient to support a dilution claim. On appeal, CSI argues that the same evidence establishing fame for likelihood of confusion also establishes fame for dilution purposes. Specifically, CSI argues that the Board disregarded: (1) sales and advertising figures for years 2000–2008; (2) its sixteen federal trademark registrations; (3) unsolicited media attention; (4) joint marketing efforts; (5) two Second Circuit decisions finding the Coach hangtag, which features the COACH mark, to be famous; and (6) CSI's internal brand awareness survey showing awareness among 18–24 year old consumers. We address each category of evidence in turn. For the reasons set forth below, we find substantial evidence supporting the Board's decision that CSI failed to show the requisite level of fame for dilution.

Turning first to CSI's evidence of sales and advertising expenditures, CSI argues that the Board erred when it ignored the annual reports that were attached to a Notice of Reliance.

As previously discussed, however, the Board correctly held that these reports were unauthenticated and thus inadmissible. The only sales and advertising figures in the record via Ms. Sadler's testimony were for one year—2008—which, notably, is after Triumph filed its use-based applications in December 2004. We agree with the Board that this limited evidence of sales and advertising is insufficient to show fame. Even if the Board had considered the annual reports, moreover, such evidence, standing alone, would be insufficient. See *Toro* ("Merely providing evidence that a mark is a top-selling brand is insufficient to show this general fame without evidence of how many persons are purchasers.").

With respect to CSI's registrations, the Board found that the mere existence of federally registered trademarks is insufficient to show that the mark is famous for purposes of dilution because ownership of a registration is not proof of fame. On appeal, CSI argues that the Board erred in this determination because one of the statutory factors a court can consider in the fame analysis is whether the mark is registered on the principal register. See 15 U.S.C. § 1125(c)(2)(A)(iv). As Triumph points out, however, "[o]ne cannot logically infer fame from the fact that a mark is one of the millions on the Federal Register." 4 McCarthy, § 24:106 at 24–310. While ownership of a trademark registration is relevant to the fame inquiry, and—to the extent the Board decision implies otherwise—the Board erred on this point, proof of registration is not conclusive evidence of fame.

With respect to media attention, the Board found that CSI's evidence fell short of showing "widespread recognition of opposer's mark [by] the general population." Specifically, the Board found that: "the vast majority of unsolicited media recognition for opposer's COACH mark comprises a reference to one of opposer's products as one of many different fashion buys or trends, and the news articles noting opposer's renown are too few to support a finding that opposer's mark has been transformed into a household name." On appeal, CSI argues that the Board ignored hundreds of unsolicited articles mentioning the COACH mark over the years. CSI points to several examples, including the following:

- "In fact, Coach's growth . . . has been phenomenal. When Sara Lee acquired the firm in 1985, its volume was about $18 million. In Sara Lee's latest fiscal year, which ended last June 30, Coach's sales exceeded $500 million. The name also resonates with consumers. The brand ranked eighth among the top 10 in accessories firms in the latest Fairchild 100 consumer survey of fashion labels, in 1995." (*Women's Wear Daily*, May 5, 1997).
- "Coach, one of the top makers of status handbags in the United States. . . ." (*The New York Times*, Jan. 27, 1999).
- "Coach's creative director has helped transform the 60-year old company into a must-have American icon." (*Women's Wear Daily*, June 2001).
- "Will Coach Become Too Popular? . . . Coach, the maker and retailer of stylish handbags, just had a blowout season. . . . Clearly Coach has recorded some of the best growth numbers of any retailer or accessories maker in recent years." (*Business Week*, Jan. 24, 2007).

Looking at the media attention in the record, there is certainly evidence that CSI's COACH mark has achieved a substantial degree of recognition. That said, many of the articles submitted are dated after Triumph filed its registration applications and thus do not show that CSI's mark was famous prior to the filing date. See *Toro* ("an owner of an allegedly famous mark must establish that its mark had become famous prior to the filing date of the trademark application" which it opposes). And, there is substantial evidence supporting the Board's determination that many of the references are limited to mentioning one of CSI's COACH products among other brands. Accordingly, even though there is some evidence of media attention, substantial evidence supports the Board's conclusion that the media evidence submitted fails to show widespread recognition.

With respect to joint marketing efforts, CSI argued that other popular brands, including LEXUS and CANON, have used the COACH mark in connection with their products. The Board found that CSI "failed to provide any testimony regarding the success of the joint marketing efforts and the effect of those efforts in promoting opposer's mark." Board Decision, 96 U.S.P.Q.2d at 1611, n.37. We agree. Without evidence as to the success of these efforts or the terms of any contracts involved, they have little value here.

Next, the Board found that CSI's 2008 brand awareness study was "of dubious probative value" because it did not offer a witness with first-hand knowledge of the study to explain how it was conducted. The Board further noted that, although the study showed a high level of brand awareness among women ages 13–24, it provided no evidence of brand awareness among women generally, or among men. See *Top Tobacco* (noting that the TDRA eliminated the possibility of "niche fame" as a basis for finding a mark famous). And, the survey was conducted in 2007, several years after Triumph filed its applications. Given these circumstances, we find no error in the Board's decision to give this survey limited weight.

CSI also argues that the Board failed to adequately consider two Second Circuit decisions finding that the hangtag attached to its various handbags, which features the COACH mark, is distinctive. See *Coach Leatherware Co., Inc. v. AnnTaylor, Inc.* (2d Cir. 1991) (finding that Coach's lozenge-shaped leather tags embossed with the name "Coach Leatherware," which are attached to Coach's handbags by beaded brass chains, "have become distinctive and valuable through Coach's promotional efforts and by virtue of its upscale reputation"); see also *Coach, Inc. v. We Care Trading Co., Inc.* (2d Cir. 2002) (affirming the jury's dilution verdict on grounds that "the jury's determination that the hang tag was famous and distinctive was not unreasonable" and "the substantial similarity of the two marks here coupled with the use of Coach's very distinctive hang tag shape amply justified the jury's verdict"). Although the Board did not specifically address these cases, we agree with Triumph that they are unrelated and irrelevant, particularly because: (1) the 1991 case did not involve a dilution claim; and (2) both cases focus on the hangtag feature on CSI's handbags, not on the alleged fame of the COACH mark generally.

Based on the foregoing, we agree with the Board that CSI failed to provide sufficient evidence of fame for dilution purposes. Absent a showing of fame, CSI's dilution claim fails, and we need not address the remaining statutory factors for dilution by blurring.

Before moving on, we pause to emphasize the fact-specific nature of our holding today. While the burden to show fame in the dilution context is high—and higher than that for likelihood of confusion purposes—it is not insurmountable. We do not hold that CSI could never establish the requisite level of fame for dilution purposes. We hold only that, on the record presented to it, the Board had substantial support for its conclusion that CSI's evidentiary showing was just too weak to do so here.

Questions:

1.) Why protect famous marks from dilution or tarnishment in the first place? Why should we not have Rolex beer or Prada hemorrhoid cream, so long as no consumer thinks that this is the "long awaited entry" (to quote *Lois*) of those companies into this new market? (A potential confusion against which § 1114 and § 1125(a) already guard.) Does this represent an expansion of trademark's ambit? On what theory?

2.) Why does the court set such a seemingly high bar in this case for proof that a mark is famous? Does the particular controversy in this case—a luggage maker trying to stop a company using "Coach" for educational products—explain the heightened proof the court requires? Look at the passage where the court says "This is particularly true where, as here, the mark is a common English word that has different meanings in different contexts." Does this mean there is no general standard for "fame" but rather one that is relative? Or is the court simply delineating the amount of fame needed in such a situation, so that the average person hearing "Coach" would think "handbag" rather than "K" or "basketball" or any other relevant connotation?

3.) What other marks should count as famous? How about Viagra, Visa, "Just Do It," Newport cigarettes or the University of Texas's longhorn logo? [Of this group, the longhorn was the only one found *not* to be famous. Do you agree?]

---

b.) The Requirement of "Commercial Speech"; Dilution by Tarnishment

Smith v. Wal-Mart Stores, Inc.
537 F. Supp. 2d 1302 (N.D. Ga. 2008)

TIMOTHY C. BATTEN, Sr., District Judge.

This action arises from the contention of Defendant Wal-Mart Stores, Inc. that its registered trademarks "WALMART"; "WAL-MART"; and "WAL★MART"; its registered word mark "ALWAYS LOW PRICES. ALWAYS"; and its "well-known smiley face mark" were infringed by Plaintiff Charles Smith's anti-Wal-Mart merchandise. Smith petitions the Court to declare his activities legal so that he may resume them without fear of incurring liability for damages; Wal-Mart counterclaims for an award of ownership of Smith's Wal-Mart-related domain names, an injunction precluding Smith from making commercial use of any designation beginning with the prefix "WAL," and an award of nominal damages. . . .

I. Background

Wal-Mart Stores, Inc., which had approximately $283 billion in gross domestic revenue in fiscal year 2008, sells retail goods and services through a large chain of nearly 6500 physical stores and its Internet site, www.wal-mart.com. The company also owns and operates additional domain names, including www.walmartstores.com and www.walmartfacts.com, that link to the www.wal-mart.com website.

The company owns and has continuously used the well-known WAL-MART trademark and service mark in the United States for retail department store services since 1962 and has longstanding registered trademark rights in the marks. WAL-MART and WALMART are used alone or in conjunction with Wal-Mart's blue five-pointed star. Wal-Mart also owns a trademark registration in the word mark "ALWAYS LOW PRICES. ALWAYS." . . .

Smith is an avid and vocal critic of Wal-Mart. He believes that Wal-Mart has a destructive effect on communities, treats workers badly, and has a damaging influence on the United States as a whole—an influence so detrimental to the United States and its communities that Smith likens it to that of the Nazi regime. With the goals of stimulating discussions about Wal-Mart and getting others of like mind to join him in expressing strongly negative views about Wal-Mart, Smith created various designs and slogans that incorporated the word "Walocaust," a word Smith invented by combining the first three letters of Wal-Mart's name with the last six letters of the word "holocaust."

Smith created four basic Walocaust designs. One design depicted a blue stylized bird modeled to resemble a Nazi eagle grasping a yellow smiley face in the same manner that a Nazi eagle is typically depicted grasping a swastika. Above the bird image, the word "WAL★ OCAUST" was printed in a blue font comparable to that  commonly used by Wal-Mart. Two designs were text only: one design read, "I ♥ WAL ★OCAUST They have FAMILY VALUES and their ALCOHOL, TOBACCO and FIREARMS are 20% OFF"; and another design read, "WAL★OCAUST Come for the LOW prices[,] stay for the KNIFE fights." The fourth was a graphical design that depicted the word WAL★OCAUST on a Wal-Mart-like storefront that also included the Nazi eagle image, a poster advertising family values and discounted alcohol, tobacco and firearms, and other images commenting negatively on Wal-Mart.

Smith does not claim any exclusive right to his Wal-Mart-related creations; in fact, he says that he would like to see the general public use the terms freely. He hoped that the word "Walocaust" would become such a commonly used term to describe Wal-Mart that it might eventually appear in the dictionary.

In late July 2005, to help draw attention to his Walocaust concept and his views about Wal-Mart in general, Smith arranged for some of his designs to be printed on t-shirts and other items like mugs, underwear, camisoles, teddy bears, bumper stickers and bibs that could be purchased through www.CafePress.com. He also placed text on his CafePress account home page that included harsh statements about Wal-Mart, such as "Walocaust: The World is Our Labor Camp. Walmart Sucks" and "Say hello to the Walocaust, say hello to low prices, say hello to child labor, say hello to unpaid overtime, say hello to 60 hour work weeks, say hello to low pay, say hello to poverty[.] Say hello to the Walocaust, say goodbye to health insurance, say goodbye to weekends, say goodbye to vacation, say goodbye to retirement, say goodbye to living indoors[.] The Walocaust: coming soon to your occupation. A real web site is coming soon. Contact: Walocaust@yahoo.com[.]"

Although CafePress offered the option to open a "basic shop" at no charge, which would have allowed Smith to sell his items at cost, Smith instead chose to pay $6.95 per month for a "premium account," which offered several automated functions that allowed him to set up a website without knowing HTML code. This enabled Smith to display on his CafePress website his products, his other designs, and content more fully expressing his views about Wal-Mart. It also enabled him to have his www.walocaust.com domain name bring viewers to the home page of his CafePress account. In hopes that profit from his CafePress site would cover the costs of his premium fees and domain name, Smith retained CafePress's default "medium" mark-up setting, which set his items' sale price at approximately thirty percent above cost.

On December 28, 2005, and again on February 1, 2006, Wal-Mart wrote to Smith and to CafePress, asserting that Smith's Walocaust CafePress webpage was violating Wal-Mart's trademark rights, and demanding that they cease selling all products imprinted with his various anti-Wal-Mart designs. Wal-Mart also objected to Smith's registration and use of the domain name www.walocaust.com, demanding that Smith cease using the domain name and transfer ownership of it to Wal-Mart.

In response, CafePress removed all of Smith's Wal-Mart-related merchandise from his online store so that only non-Wal-Mart-related merchandise remained available at www.cafepress.com/walocaust.

On March 6, 2006, Smith filed this action, seeking a declaratory judgment of his right to sell his Walocaust merchandise and demanding costs and attorneys' fees.

After learning that some courts of appeals had approved disclaimers as a technique for minimizing possible trademark confusion, Smith added one to the top of his Walocaust webpage, stating that the site is unaffiliated with Wal-Mart and containing, the URL for Wal-Mart's official website to help redirect any visitors who may have intended to visit www.wal-mart.com but instead accessed the Walocaust site by mistake. He also updated the site to denounce Wal-Mart's role in forcing this litigation and filing counterclaims, and he posted a link to an entity called "Public Citizen" through which visitors have donated $1040.01 in support of his legal activities.

On or about March 8, 2006, after filing his declaratory judgment complaint, Smith also registered the domain names www.wal-qaeda.com and www.walqaeda.com. "Wal-Qaeda" was another portmanteau word Smith coined, this time combining the name "Wal-Mart" with "Al-Qaeda." Smith intended the word "Wal-Qaeda" as a comment on what he considered to be Wal-Mart's terrorist-like attack on his free speech through threats of litigation.

On a new site that was accessible via both www.wal-qaeda.com and www.walqaeda.com, Smith displayed various graphics incorporating his new word. He also posted other anti-Wal-Mart slogans such as "FREEDOM-HATER-MART STOP Stomping on our free speech!" and "Freedom-Haters ALWAYS," intended to call to mind Wal-Mart's trademark "ALWAYS LOW PRICES. ALWAYS."

Once he became certain that CafePress was open to carrying his new Wal-Qaeda concepts, he created a new Wal-Qaeda CafePress webpage where he again offered various items commenting on Wal-Mart. . . . The site offered two text-only designs that depicted the word "WAL-QAEDA" in a blue block letter font similar to Wal-Mart's: one with the legend "SUPPORT OUR TROOPS[.] BOYCOTT WAL-QADA" and another reading, "WAL-QADA[.] Freedom Haters ALWAYS." The site also offered products imprinted with five other graphical concepts. One of those concepts was a revision of the Walocaust storefront design, altered to replace "WAL★OCAUST" with "WAL-QAEDA[.] THE DIME STORE FROM HELL"; to replace the Nazi eagle with "FREEDOM HATERS ALWAYS" and "2 days without a k[n]ife fight"; and to make other small changes. Another concept depicted an American flag in the shape of a United States map with the word "DECEASED" stamped over it. Above the flag was printed "WAL-QAEDA[.] THE DIME STORE FROM HELL," and under the flag appeared the phrase "CAUSE OF DEATH: A Dime Store." In the third concept, the slogan "ATTENTION WAL★QAEDA[.] THESE COLORS DON'T RUN" was imprinted over a modified American flag, and in the last two concepts, Hillary Clinton was named the "WAL-QAEDA Employee of the Year 1986–1992," and Chairman Mao Zedong was awarded the "WAL-QAEDA Human Resource Achievement Award."

Although he hoped to help finance this lawsuit with the proceeds, Smith did not actively market his designs. He did, however, post his new Wal-Qaeda home page, his Wal-Qaeda CafePress account and a link to the Wal-Qaeda home page from his Walocaust website at a time when he knew that reporters were working on stories about this litigation. As a result, news about his new Wal-Qaeda designs was reported in the press and on blogs, and almost all of the sales of Smith's Wal-Qaeda items occurred within a month of the first publicity that followed upon the press and bloggers discovering those designs. The revenues from Smith's CafePress Walocaust and Wal-Qaeda account sales have been less than his costs for the domain names and CafePress account fees.

On April 28, 2006, Wal-Mart filed its answer and counterclaim, asserting various federal trademark claims and related state law claims against Smith for both the Walocaust and the Wal-Qaeda products. Wal-Mart contends that Smith has engaged in (1) trademark infringement in violation of 15 U.S.C. § 1114(1) and common law; (2) unfair competition in violation of 15 U.S.C. § 1125(a); (3) trademark dilution by tarnishment in violation of 15 U.S.C. § 1125(c); and (4) cybersquatting in violation of 15 U.S.C. § 1125(d).

II. Analysis

Wal-Mart contends that Smith is a merchant who misappropriated its trademarks and business reputation in pursuit of illegal profit and who disingenuously seeks to cloak those activities under the First Amendment. Smith alleges that Wal-Mart is attempting to misuse trademark laws to censor his criticism of the company. According to Smith, at stake in this case is a person's right to publicly criticize the world's largest retailer—or any other business. . . .

C. Trademark Infringement, Unfair Competition, Cybersquatting and Deceptive Trade Practices Claims

To prove that Smith committed trademark infringement or cybersquatting, or subjected Wal-Mart to unfair competition or deceptive trade practices, Wal-Mart must also show that Smith's use of its trademarks is likely to cause an appreciable number of potential buyers to be confused about the source, affiliation or sponsorship of Smith's products. See 15 U.S.C. § 1125(d)(1)(A) (subjecting to a cybersquatting claim only domain names that are "identical or confusingly similar" to a senior mark).

In making this inquiry, courts consider a variety of factors, including the strength of the allegedly infringed mark, whether the designs that incorporate the registered mark are similar, whether the products sold by the parties are similar, whether the retail outlets and purchasers are similar, whether the parties use the same advertising media, whether the defendant intended to usurp the registered trademark, and whether any consumers were actually confused. The Court must balance the factors according to its own judgment based on the facts in the case before it. . . .

Because Smith's arguments with regard to the *Safeway* factors depend heavily on whether his designs are successful parodies, the Court must first consider whether the contested designs are in fact parodies of Wal-Mart's registered marks. See *Dr. Seuss Enters. v. Penguin Books USA, Inc.* (9th Cir. 1997) (noting that the claim that a secondary use is a parody is not a separate defense to a charge of trademark infringement but is instead is considered within the likelihood of confusion analysis). For the purposes of trademark analysis, "a parody is defined as a simple form of entertainment conveyed by juxtaposing the irreverent representation of the trademark with the idealized image created by the mark's owner." *Louis Vuitton Malletier v. Haute Diggity Dog, LLC* (4th Cir. 2007). To be considered successful, the alleged parody must both call to mind and differentiate itself from the original, and it must "communicate some articulable element of satire, ridicule, joking or amusement."

When applying these criteria to the facts of the case, it is clear that Smith's concepts are parodies of the registered Wal-Mart marks. Smith successfully calls Wal-Mart to mind by using either "WAL" or "MART" as part of the concept; by mimicking its fonts and storefront design; by mentioning Bentonville, the location of Wal-Mart's headquarters; or by including various other icons typically associated with Wal-Mart. As Wal-Mart fervently contends, it is obvious that Smith's concepts use Wal-Mart imagery to evoke the company in the mind of his viewers.

It is equally obvious that Smith's concepts are not the "idealized image" of the registered Wal-Mart marks. "Walocaust," "Wal-Qaeda" and "Freedom-Hater-Mart" are not "Wal-Mart." The imagery on Smith's t-shirts includes portraits of Mao Zedong, a United States map with the word "DECEASED" stamped over it, and the slogan "FREEDOM HATERS ALWAYS."

Finally, the juxtaposition of the similar and dissimilar—the satirical representation and the idealized image of Wal-Mart—conveys a scathing parody. In the "smiley eagle" Walocaust concept, the reference to the Holocaust and the image of the Nazi eagle clutching a smiley face at once portrays and contradicts the benign image that Wal-Mart portrays to the community. In the "SUPPORT OUR TROOPS" Wal-Qaeda concept, Smith transforms all-American "Wal-Mart" into the terrorist group "Wal-Qaeda" and satirically urges the viewer to support Wal-Qaeda's troops, apparently commenting both on what Smith considers to be Wal-Mart's ruthless business tactics and its detrimental impact on the United States. Other concepts juxtapose Wal-Mart's reputation for low prices with a reference to poor store security and the company's family values imagery with the fact that it offers for sale inexpensive alcohol, tobacco and firearms—products known better for destroying families.

The Court thus concludes that Smith's concepts adequately evoke Wal-Mart while maintaining their differentiation, and they convey Smith's satirical commentary; thus, they are successful parodies. See *Louis Vuitton*.

The finding that Smith's concepts are parodies does not preclude the likelihood of confusion analysis, however; it merely influences the way the likelihood of confusion factors are applied. "[A]n effective parody will actually diminish the likelihood of confusion, while an ineffective parody does not." Because even a parody may constitute trademark infringement if that parody is confusing, the Court will next consider the likelihood of confusion factors. . . .

Evaluating the overall balance of the seven likelihood of confusion factors, the Court finds that Wal-Mart has failed to demonstrate a likelihood that its trademarks "WALMART," "WAL-MART," and "WAL★MART" and its word mark "ALWAYS LOW PRICES. ALWAYS." would be confused with Smith's "WALOCAUST," "WAL-QAEDA," "FREEDOM HATER MART," or "BENTON★VILLEBULLIES ALWAYS" concepts. In so finding, the Court concludes that factors three (similarity of the marks), five (similarity of sales methods) and six (similarity of advertising methods), weigh in Smith's favor, with particular emphasis on how different the appearance and usage of the marks were and how vastly the parties' advertising methods differed. The Court concludes that factors one (actual confusion), two (strength of the mark), four (similarity of product) and seven (Smith's intent) favor neither party.

In sum, the Court is convinced that no fair-minded jury could find that a reasonable consumer is likely to be confused by the challenged marks. As a result, the Court GRANTS summary judgment to Smith on Wal-Mart's claims of trademark infringement, unfair business competition, cybersquatting and deceptive trade practices.

D. Trademark Dilution by Tarnishment

Wal-Mart contends that Smith's Walocaust and Wal-Qaeda concepts, by associating Wal-Mart with "the perpetrators of such atrocities as the Holocaust and the attacks of September 11, 2001, unquestionably tarnish the Wal-Mart marks." Dilution by tarnishment recognizes an injury when a "trademark is . . . portrayed in an unwholesome or unsavory context likely to evoke unflattering thoughts about the owner's product." *Deere & Co. v.*

MTD Prods., Inc. (2d Cir. 1994).

"However, tarnishment caused merely by an editorial or artistic parody which satirizes [the complainant's] product or its image is not actionable under an anti-dilution statute because of the free speech protections of the First Amendment." *Mattel, Inc. v. Walking Mountain Prods.* (9th Cir. 2003). "Parody is a form of noncommercial expression if it does more than propose a commercial transaction." *Bolger v. Youngs Drug Prods. Corp.* (1983).

A claim of dilution applies only to purely commercial speech. *Mattel.* See also *Bolger* (finding that materials do not become "commercial speech" simply because the author had economic motivation to create them). "The question whether an economic motive existed is more than a question whether there was an economic incentive for the speaker to make the speech; the *Bolger* test also requires that the speaker acted substantially out of economic motivation." *Procter & Gamble Co. v. Amway Corp.* (5th Cir. 2001) "Thus, for example, speech that is principally based on religious or political convictions, but which may also benefit the speaker economically, would fall short of the requirement that the speech was economically motivated" and therefore would be considered noncommercial.

At least one court of appeals has specifically addressed whether a social advocate selling t-shirts that carried the group's social message was engaging in noncommercial speech, despite the fact that the group sold the t-shirts to the public for profit. See *Ayres v. City of Chicago* (7th Cir. 1997). In *Ayres*, the court distinguished limitations on "the sale of goods that are not themselves forms of protected speech," noting that precedent allows more restriction on sales of nonexpressive goods than it does on goods that are forms of protected speech. The court likened t-shirts carrying messages of social advocacy to "the sandwich boards that union pickets sometimes wear." As such, the t-shirts were "a medium of expression prima facie protected by the free-speech clause of the First Amendment, and they do not lose their protection by being sold rather than given away."

The Court is convinced that a reasonable juror could only find that Smith primarily intended to express himself with his Walocaust and Wal-Qaeda concepts and that commercial success was a secondary motive at most. Smith has strongly adverse opinions about Wal-Mart; he believes that it has a destructive effect on communities, treats workers badly and has a damaging influence on the United States as a whole. He invented the term "Walocaust" to encapsulate his feelings about Wal-Mart, and he created his Walocaust designs with the intent of calling attention to his beliefs and his cause. He never expected to have any exclusive rights to the word. He created the term "Wal-Qaeda" and designs incorporating it with similar expressive intent. The Court has found those designs to be successful parodies.

Thus, Smith's parodic work is considered noncommercial speech and therefore not subject to Wal-Mart's trademark dilution claims, despite the fact that Smith sold the designs to the public on t-shirts and other novelty merchandise. Consequently, Smith's motion for summary judgment on Wal-Mart's trademark dilution claims is hereby GRANTED.

III. Conclusion

Smith's motion for summary judgment is hereby GRANTED, and Wal-Mart's motion for summary judgment is DENIED. The Court hereby issues a declaratory judgment that Smith's activities have not violated any of Wal-Mart's trademark rights. Smith may maintain his domain names and websites. He may also resume offering for sale via his Walocaust and Wal-Qaeda CafePress webstores his parodic WALOCAUST, WAL-QAEDA, FREEDOM

HATER MART, and BENTON★VILLEBULLIES ALWAYS concepts printed on novelty merchandise; on any webpage or other channel offering such merchandise for sale, Smith must continue to include prominent disclaimers of affiliation with Wal-Mart.

Questions:

1.) Commercial/Noncommercial Use v. Use in Commerce: We have said repeatedly that the "commercial/non commercial" line is one way that courts and legislatures seek to trim the ambit of intellectual property rights, to fine tune them so that they are neither under nor over inclusive. So far, we have looked at two definitions of "use in commerce"—one in the context of the use required to *obtain* a mark and one in the context of the use required to *infringe* a mark. How is the definition of commercial speech here in the context of dilution different? Why is it different? [Hint: what would be the ambit of the 'non commercial' defense to dilution if we took a broad definition of commercial, such as "anything Congress can regulate under the commerce clause?"]

2.) Smith was selling, for profit, T shirts that used portions of Walmart's logos. Why is this not commercial? List the reasons the court gives, starting with those you think most important.

3.) The court draws a distinction between "speech goods", those that carry a message though they are distributed for profit, and those that offer no such message. Is this distinction of relevance in the *PETA* case? Should it have been?

c.) Dilution by Blurring

Starbucks Corp. v. Wolfe's Borough Coffee, Inc.
736 F.3d 198 (2d Cir. 2013)

[This is the culmination of a long-running attempt by Starbucks to enjoin Wolfe's Borough Coffee, doing business as Black Bear Micro Roastery, from using "Mister Charbucks," "Mr. Charbucks," and "Charbucks Blend." The litigation was extended in part by the intervening passage of the TDRA.]

LOHIER, Circuit Judge:

. . . [T]he District Court concluded that Starbucks failed to prove that the Charbucks Marks are likely to dilute Starbucks' famous "Starbucks" marks (the "Starbucks Marks") and denied Starbucks' request for an injunction. . . . For the following reasons, we conclude that the District Court did not err in its factual findings, and, balancing the statutory factors de novo, we agree with the District Court that Starbucks failed to prove a likelihood of dilution. We therefore affirm. . . .

[At the bench trial] Starbucks introduced the testimony of Warren J. Mitofsky, a scientist in the field of consumer research and polling. Mitofsky explained the results of a telephone survey he had conducted of six hundred participants, designed to be representative of the United States population. The survey found that when asked, "What is the first thing that comes to your mind when you hear the name 'Charbucks,' spelled

C-H-A-R-B-U-C-K-S?," 30.5 percent of participants answered "Starbucks," while 9 percent answered "coffee."[5] When the participants were asked, "Can you name any company or store that you think might offer a product called 'Charbucks'?," 3.1 percent responded "Starbucks," and another 1.3 percent responded "coffee house."[6] Mitofsky concluded that "[t]he number one association of the name 'Charbucks' in the minds of consumers is with the brand 'Starbucks.'" . . .

In Starbucks IV [the Second Circuit's previous decision in this case] [w]e held that "the District Court did not clearly err in finding that the Charbucks Marks were minimally similar to the Starbucks Marks," because the context of the Charbucks Marks (on Black Bear's packaging, on its website, and in the phrases "Charbucks Blend" and "Mister Charbucks") differentiated them from the famous marks. We concluded, however, that "the District Court erred to the extent it required 'substantial' similarity between the marks," and we suggested that the District Court had overemphasized the similarity factor. In particular, we stated that the inclusion of "the degree of similarity" as only one of six factors in the revised statute indicates that even a low degree of similarity would not categorically bar a dilution-by-blurring claim.

Turning to the fifth and sixth factors—intent to associate and actual association—we held that the District Court had erred by requiring "bad faith" to find that the intent to associate factor favored Starbucks. Noting the survey results, which demonstrated some degree of association between "Charbucks" and "Starbucks," we also held that the District Court erred by relying on evidence supporting the absence of "actual confusion" to conclude that the actual association factor did not weigh in Starbucks' favor "to any significant degree." The absence of actual or likely confusion, we reasoned, does not bear directly on whether dilution is likely. . . .

DISCUSSION
C. Factual Findings: The Statutory Factors

On appeal, Starbucks challenges two of the District Court's findings: (1) that there is only a minimal degree of similarity between the Starbucks Marks and the Charbucks Marks; and (2) that Starbucks demonstrated only a weak association between the marks. The District Court did not clearly err with regard to either finding.

1. Degree of Similarity

In Starbucks IV we held that "[w]ith respect to the first factor—the degree of similarity between the marks—the District Court did not clearly err in finding that the Charbucks Marks were minimally similar to the Starbucks Marks." We highlighted the difference between the Starbucks Marks and Charbucks Marks when the latter are placed in the context of Black Bear's packaging and the word "Charbucks" is incorporated into the phrases "Charbucks Blend" and "Mister Charbucks." . . .

2. Actual Association

Starbucks next contends that the District Court's finding that actual association "weighs no more than minimally" in Starbucks' favor was error for two reasons. First, Starbucks argues, Black Bear's admitted intent to create an association—the fifth statutory factor—raises a "presumption of association," or at least is strong evidence of

---

[5] Other common responses included "barbeque" or "charcoal" (7.9 percent); "restaurant" or "grill" (7.5 percent); "meat," "steak," or "hamburger" (4.6 percent); and "money" (3.9 percent).

[6] More popular responses to this second question included: "grocery store" (18.3 percent); "discount store" (16.9 percent); "restaurant" (7.0 percent); "department store" (4.8 percent); and "hardware store" or "home improvement store" (3.7 percent).

actual association—the sixth statutory factor. Second, it argues that the District Court improperly discounted the Mitofsky survey evidence, which, in Starbucks' view, proves a high degree of actual association. We reject both arguments.

a. *Intent to Create an Association*

As an initial matter, an intent to create an association is a separate factor under the TDRA and does not constitute *per se* evidence that the actual association factor weighs in favor of the owner of the famous mark. In support of its argument to the contrary, Starbucks quotes McCarthy's treatise, which states, "If the junior [user] intended to create an association, the law may assume that it succeeded." Starbucks similarly relies on *Federal Express Corp. v. Federal Espresso, Inc.* (2d Cir. 2000), a dilution case in which we stated that the trier of fact "may well find that the marks are of sufficient similarity so that, in the mind of the consumer, the junior mark will conjure an association with the senior, especially in light of the testimony of [Federal Espresso's founder] that she chose the name Federal Espresso, in part, precisely because it would call to mind Federal Express."

Both *Federal Espresso* and McCarthy's treatise acknowledge the importance of the intent factor in determining likelihood of dilution. This makes sense, as district courts must evaluate whether a junior mark is "likely to cause" "association arising from the similarity" between the marks "that impairs the distinctiveness of the famous mark," 15 U.S.C. §§ 1125(c)(1), (c)(2)(B), and the intent to associate may bear directly on the likelihood that the junior mark will cause such an association.

That said, "we interpret statutes to give effect, if possible, to every clause and word and to avoid statutory interpretations that render provisions superfluous." Adopting Starbucks' presumption argument would effectively merge the intent to associate and the actual association factors, by making the former determinative of the latter, rather than treating them as distinct but related considerations. We therefore conclude that the District Court did not clearly err in finding that Clark's [Black Bear's founder] testimony concerning the origin of the Charbucks Marks was not an "admission" of actual association and that his intentions were not definitive proof of an actual association between the marks.

b. *Mitofsky Survey*

Nor did the District Court err when it discounted the Mitofsky survey evidence because the survey measured only how respondents reacted to the isolated word "Charbucks," rather than to the Charbucks Marks in context, and because the share of respondents who indicated an association between the marks was "relatively small." We arrive at this conclusion for two reasons.

First, it coheres with our decision in *Starbucks IV,* in which we discerned no clear error in the District Court's consideration of context—including the addition of "Mister" or "Blend" to "Charbucks" and Black Bear's packaging—in assessing the marks' similarity, as consumers are likely to experience the product only in the context of those full phrases and Black Bear's packaging or website. In our analysis of Starbucks' infringement claim, we similarly determined that the District Court did not clearly err when it found (1) that the survey failed to demonstrate significant actual confusion, "[p]articularly in light of the fact that the survey was administered by telephone and did not present the term 'Charbucks' in the context in which Black Bear used it," and (2) that the survey should have examined the effects of "a hypothetical coffee named either 'Mister Charbucks' or 'Charbucks Blend'" on the respondents' impressions of Starbucks coffee as a measure of dilution by tarnishment.

Second, our conclusion also comports with our prior precedents and other cases unrelated to Starbucks. In *Playtex Products, Inc. v. Georgia-Pacific Corp.* (2d Cir.2004), a case interpreting the pre-revision FTDA, we held that the results of a consumer survey showing an association between the marks "Moist-Ones" and "Wet Ones" were inadmissible as evidence of actual dilution because the defendant's product was "presented and packaged" as "*Quilted Northern* Moist-Ones." District courts within our Circuit have applied the same reasoning in evaluating surveys in the infringement context. *See, e.g., WE Media, Inc. v. Gen. Elec. Co.* (S.D.N.Y. 2002) ("Germane survey evidence should make some effort to compare the impressions the marks have on potential customers under marketplace conditions."). . . . As in *Playtex,* the District Court was within its rights to conclude that the Mitofsky survey had limited probative value because the defendant's marks were not presented to survey respondents as they are actually "presented and packaged" in commerce.

Citing our decision in *Nabisco,* Starbucks nevertheless argues that consumers are likely to hear and view the term "Charbucks" outside the context of Black Bear's packaging and without the full phrases "Mister Charbucks" and "Charbucks Blend." But Starbucks presented no record evidence that "Charbucks" is ever read or heard in isolation, and in the absence of such evidence, we are not persuaded by the argument. To the contrary, as we noted in *Starbucks IV,* "it is unlikely that 'Charbucks' will appear to consumers outside the context of its normal use," and "it was not clearly erroneous for the District Court to find that the 'Mister' prefix or 'Blend' suffix lessened the similarity between the [marks]."

Starbucks also challenges the District Court's finding that the association between "Charbucks" and Starbucks was "relatively small." It contends that the Mitofsky survey in fact provided evidence of substantial actual association. We disagree.

It is true that in response to Mitofsky's question most probative of actual association—"What is the FIRST THING that comes to your mind when you hear the name 'Charbucks,' spelled C-H-A-R-B-U-C-K-S?"—30.5 percent of respondents said "Starbucks," and 9 percent said "coffee." Both of these responses suggest an association between "Charbucks" and the Starbucks Marks. In *Jada Toys,* for example, the Ninth Circuit held that a survey demonstrated actual association because it showed that 28 percent of respondents thought Jada's product was made by Mattel when asked who they thought produced the item. Here, however, the equivalent question in Mitofsky's survey was: "Can you name any company or store that you think might offer a product called 'Charbucks'?" In response to that question concerning source on the Mitofsky survey, however, only 3.1 percent of respondents answered "Starbucks" and 1.3 percent answered "coffee house." These percentages are far below that for the equivalent question in Jada Toys and fail to demonstrate anything more than minimal actual association.[15]

Ultimately, on this factor, we consider only whether the District Court clearly erred when it found that the Mitofsky survey tilts the "actual association" factor "no more than minimally in [Starbucks'] favor." Had the Mitofsky survey presented the Charbucks Marks as they appear in commerce, we might well conclude that the District Court erred. But the word "Charbucks" was presented outside of its marketplace context, and Starbucks, which bears the burden of proof, failed to show that this flaw did not materially impact the survey results. We therefore conclude that the record supports the District Court's decision to discount the survey and consider the actual association factor as weighing only minimally in Starbucks' favor.

---

[15] Although some other respondents gave answers consistent with an association with Starbucks—18.3 percent answered "grocery store," 16.9 percent answered "discount store," 7 percent answered "restaurant," and 4.8 percent answered "department store"—these responses are also consistent with other views of what "Charbucks" could be, including meat or a charcoal grilling product, as 38.5 percent of respondents suggested.

D. *Balancing*

We next balance the factors enumerated in § 1125(c)(2)(B), along with any other factors that bear on a likelihood of dilution, *de novo.* In balancing these factors, we are again mindful that the test is not an inflexible one, and that the ultimate question is whether the Charbucks Marks are likely to cause an association arising from their similarity to the Starbucks Marks, which impairs the Starbucks Marks' tendency to identify the source of Starbucks products in a unique way.

We have already affirmed the District Court's finding of minimal similarity between the Charbucks Marks and the Starbucks Marks. That finding weighs heavily in Black Bear's favor. Certainly, a plaintiff may show a likelihood of dilution notwithstanding only minimal similarity. But here, minimal similarity strongly suggests a relatively low likelihood of an association diluting the senior mark. The statute itself emphasizes the similarity of marks. *See* § 1125(c)(2)(B) (defining "dilution by blurring" as "association arising from the *similarity* between a mark or a trade name and a famous mark that impairs the distinctiveness of the famous mark" (emphasis added)). Indeed, in *Starbucks IV,* we stated that "'similarity' is an integral element in the definition of 'blurring'" under the TDRA and suggested that, without *any* similarity, there could be no dilution by blurring.

The next three factors—the degrees of distinctiveness, exclusive use, and recognition—are features of the senior mark itself that do not depend on the use of the junior mark. "[T]he *degree* of distinctiveness of the senior mark has a considerable bearing on the question whether a junior use will have a diluting effect. . . . [T]he more distinctiveness the mark possesses, the greater the interest to be protected." There is no question that "Starbucks"—an arbitrary mark as applied to coffee—is highly distinctive. Moreover, because, as the District Court found, the Starbucks Marks are in substantially exclusive use, "the mark's distinctiveness is more likely to be impaired by the junior use." Lastly, as 79 percent of Mitofsky survey respondents were familiar with Starbucks, it is undisputed that Starbucks constitutes a widely recognized mark, and that this factor favors Starbucks.

Although the three factors of distinctiveness, recognition, and exclusivity favor Starbucks and bear to some degree on our assessment of the likelihood of dilution by blurring, the more important factors in the context of this case are the similarity of the marks and actual association. We agree with the District Court that the distinctiveness, recognition, and exclusive use of the Starbucks Marks do not overcome the weak evidence of actual association between the Charbucks and Starbucks marks. To the contrary, viewed in light of Starbucks' fame, both globally and among the Mitofsky survey participants more particularly, the fact that more survey participants did not think of "Starbucks" upon hearing "Charbucks" reinforces the District Court's finding that the marks are only minimally similar, and therefore unlikely to prompt an association that impairs the Starbucks Marks. Likewise, although the distinctiveness and exclusive use of the Starbucks Marks help Starbucks prove *susceptibility* to dilution by association arising from similarity between the Charbucks and Starbucks marks, they do not demonstrate that such an association is likely to arise, as Starbucks needed to show to obtain an injunction. Accordingly, these factors weigh only weakly in Starbucks' favor.

In this case, we attribute a moderate amount of significance to the fifth factor, intent to create an association. Clark's testimony indicated that Black Bear was capitalizing on an historic connection between the word "Charbucks" and "Starbucks," which arose out of the so-called "coffee-wars" in Boston, Massachusetts, and that he "meant to evoke an image of dark-roasted coffee of the type offered by Starbucks." "[W]here, as here, the allegedly diluting mark was created with an intent to associate with the famous mark," we agree with the District Court that this factor favors a finding of a likelihood of dilution.

The final, disputed factor, actual association, is highly relevant to likelihood of association. In the analogous context of determining the "likelihood of confusion" for trademark infringement claims, we have noted that "[t]here can be no more positive or substantial proof of the likelihood of confusion than proof of actual confusion," even though a showing of actual confusion is not necessary to prevail on such a claim. The same principle obtains with respect to proof of actual association in dilution claims. And as noted, the Mitofsky survey demonstrated weak actual association, at best.

Weighing the factors above *de novo,* we agree with the District Court that Starbucks did not demonstrate a likelihood of dilution by blurring. Ultimately what tips the balance in this case is that Starbucks bore the burden of showing that it was entitled to injunctive relief on this record. Because Starbucks' principal evidence of association, the Mitofsky survey, was fundamentally flawed, and because there was minimal similarity between the marks at issue, we agree with the District Court that Starbucks failed to show that Black Bear's use of its Charbucks Marks in commerce is likely to dilute the Starbucks Marks.

CONCLUSION

We have considered all of Starbucks' contentions on this appeal and have concluded that they are without merit. For the foregoing reasons, we AFFIRM the judgment of the District Court.

Questions:

1.) Really? "Charbucks" on coffee doesn't dilute the "Starbucks" mark? What would Starbucks need to show to bring a successful dilution claim against "Charbucks"?

2.) Do you agree with the court's interpretation of the six statutory factors for "dilution by blurring"? What factors are the most relevant for determining whether a challenged mark "impairs the distinctiveness" of a famous mark?

PROBLEM 9-1
DILUTION OF (BY) ALCOHOL?

John Wayne, the legendary actor, was also known by the nickname "The Duke.' John Wayne Enterprises—owned by his heirs—has sought to register "Duke" for a variety of goods and services over the years: including restaurants, celebrity licensing services and gaming machines. Now they want to register it for alcoholic beverages, and in particular, bourbon. Duke University—the venerable educational institution—strongly objects to the registration of "Duke" for alcohol, alleging that it will cause confusion but also that it will dilute Duke's "famous" mark.

What sections of the Lanham Act can Duke rely on in attempting to block registration? [Be

Image from the producers of Duke bourbon at http://www.dukespirits.com/

specific.] **Will any of those challenges succeed? If the mark is registered and John Wayne Enterprises attempts to market the bourbon, will Duke succeed in an anti-dilution action? Is the mark famous? Is there a likelihood of dilution? By blurring or by tarnishment?**

[Those who are interested in a real-life empirical study of whether a university can be a trademark bully may read Boyle & Jenkins, *Mark of the Devil: The University as Brand Bully*. Unfortunately, the university is Duke, and the answer is "yes, a university can be a brand bully."]

3.) "Cybersquatting" and "Cyberpiracy"

1125(d) Cyberpiracy prevention

(1)(A) A person shall be liable in a civil action by the owner of a mark, including a personal name which is protected as a mark under this section, if, without regard to the goods or services of the parties, that person—

(i) has a bad faith intent to profit from that mark, including a personal name which is protected as a mark under this section; and

(ii) registers, traffics in, or uses a domain name that—

(I) in the case of a mark that is distinctive at the time of registration of the domain name, is identical or confusingly similar to that mark;

(II) in the case of a famous mark that is famous at the time of registration of the domain name, is identical or confusingly similar to or dilutive of that mark; or

(III) is a trademark, word, or name protected by reason of section 706 of title 18 or section 220506 of title 36.

(B)(i) In determining whether a person has a bad faith intent described under subparagraph (A), a court may consider factors such as, but not limited to—

(I) the trademark or other intellectual property rights of the person, if any, in the domain name;

(II) the extent to which the domain name consists of the legal name of the person or a name that is otherwise commonly used to identify that person;

(III) the person's prior use, if any, of the domain name in connection with the bona fide offering of any goods or services;

(IV) the person's bona fide noncommercial or fair use of the mark in a site accessible under the domain name;

(V) the person's intent to divert consumers from the mark owner's online location to a site accessible under the domain name that could harm the goodwill represented by the mark, either for commercial gain or with the intent to tarnish or disparage the mark, by creating a likelihood of confusion as to the source, sponsorship, affiliation, or endorsement of the site;

(VI) the person's offer to transfer, sell, or otherwise assign the

domain name to the mark owner or any third party for financial gain without having used, or having an intent to use, the domain name in the bona fide offering of any goods or services, or the person's prior conduct indicating a pattern of such conduct;

(VII) the person's provision of material and misleading false contact information when applying for the registration of the domain name, the person's intentional failure to maintain accurate contact information, or the person's prior conduct indicating a pattern of such conduct;

(VIII) the person's registration or acquisition of multiple domain names which the person knows are identical or confusingly similar to marks of others that are distinctive at the time of registration of such domain names, or dilutive of famous marks of others that are famous at the time of registration of such domain names, without regard to the goods or services of the parties; and

(IX) the extent to which the mark incorporated in the person's domain name registration is or is not distinctive and famous within the meaning of subsection (c).

(ii) Bad faith intent described under subparagraph (A) shall not be found in any case in which the court determines that the person believed and had reasonable grounds to believe that the use of the domain name was a fair use or otherwise lawful.

(C) In any civil action involving the registration, trafficking, or use of a domain name under this paragraph, a court may order the forfeiture or cancellation of the domain name or the transfer of the domain name to the owner of the mark.

(D) A person shall be liable for using a domain name under subparagraph (A) only if that person is the domain name registrant or that registrant's authorized licensee.

(E) As used in this paragraph, the term "traffics in" refers to transactions that include, but are not limited to, sales, purchases, loans, pledges, licenses, exchanges of currency, and any other transfer for consideration or receipt in exchange for consideration.

Notes

Section 1125(d), the so-called cyberpiracy or cybersquatting provision, is part of a continuing attempt by the courts and Congress to delineate the relationship between trademark law on the one hand and internet domain names on the other. What is the internet's Domain Name System?

The Domain Name System (DNS) is a hierarchical distributed naming system for computers, services, or any resource connected to the Internet or a private network. It associates various [types of] information with domain names assigned to each of the participating entities. Most prominently, it translates easily memorized domain names to the numerical IP addresses needed for the purpose of locating computer services and devices worldwide. The Domain Name System is an essential component of the functionality of the Internet. An often-used analogy to explain the Domain Name System is that it serves as the phone book for the Internet by translating human-friendly computer hostnames into IP addresses. For example, the domain name www.example.com translates to the addresses 93.184.216.119 (IPv4) and 2606:2800:220:6d:26bf:1447: 1097:aa7 (IPv6). Unlike a phone book, the DNS can be quickly updated, allowing a service's location on the network to change without affecting the end users, who continue to use the same host name. Users take advantage of this when they use meaningful Uniform Resource Locators (URLs), and e-mail addresses without having to know how the computer actually locates the services.[1]

Domain names are organized in subdomains of this DNS system. You are probably familiar with the suffixes indicating the top level domain names (TLD) such as .com, .org, .edu and so on. You may also know the country code top level domain names such as .uk and .fr. What happens when this domain name system meets trademark law? This is another of the central themes in this book—technological happenstance produces conflicts with a set of legal premises, conflicts that the law has to work out.

At the beginning of the trademark section we discussed the fact that trademark law does not convey ownership of a word. Bass for ale does not infringe Bass for electronics or circuit boards, nor is it infringed by bass fishing companies or those who want to teach you to play a bass guitar like Jaco Pastorius. (Not that anyone could.) The word bass is not "rivalrous" and trademark law does not seek to make it rivalrous, unless 1.) its use would cause a likelihood of confusion or 2.) in the case of famous marks, there would be blurring or tarnishment. But there is only one bass.com—the most desirable top level domain name. Who is to own it and what does trademark law say about that? (It is owned by Anheuser-Busch, as it turns out.) True, there are other top level domains and their suffixes offer some ability to segregate different types of activities just as non digital reality allows many uses of the word to coexist. For example, .org was originally reserved for non-profits, though it is now unrestricted. (Bass.org is devoted to a now defunct mailing list discussing playing the electronic bass.) .edu signifies educational activities, so you expect duke.edu to be different from duke.com (which at present carries an "under construction" message and points to sites selling Duke merchandise, among other things). .xxx is reserved for porn sites. .gov is reserved for government sites, so Whitehouse.gov will get you the White House web site, while Whitehouse.com will get you advertisements for Ukrainian dating sites (to use the most salubrious example there). And finally, the country level domain names such as .uk and .fr mean that a little of the *geographic* boundedness that trademark relied on (no one in Portugal knows Delta faucets, but they all know Delta coffee) can be restored. It should be noted, though, that there is no requirement that companies only use country level domain names pointing to their nation, and that many entities use the country domain names for reasons other than nationality. .tv is popular for television related sites, though it really signifies Tuvalu.

Despite the multiple uses made possible by the varied TLDs and CCTLDs (country-code top level domains) there is clearly a shortage of desirable domains for those businesses or activities that both use the same word. A body of law that presumes that a word is "rivalrous" only within the bounds of a type of commercial activity (because that is all the trademark covers) meets a technology where the use of the word is rival in a different way. One immediate problem (though hardly the only one) is that of "cybersquatting" or "cyberpiracy." While the term is actually a broad one, as you can

---

[1] "Domain Name System" http://en.wikipedia.org/wiki/Domain_Name_System (as posted in July 2014).

see from 1125(d), the core prohibition against cyberpiracy is aimed at a practice that was most prominent in the early days of the web. The cybersquatter is the person who buys up a domain name that a trademark owner might want and has not yet purchased. Often, he or she does not use the domain in commerce. (Doing *that* might have triggered conventional trademark liability, depending on what goods and services were being offered and whether they were similar to the trademark owner's products.) Instead, he or she leaves the site with an "under construction" sign and offers it to the trademark owner at a price, generally a hefty price. 1125(d) was designed to deal with this problem.[2] But what is the nature of the "problem"?

PROBLEM 9-2

John Wayne, Daddy Warbucks and Joe Dotcom all have interesting business opportunities—at different moments in history. Wayne reads the speeches of the politicians and believes that a transcontinental railroad must be coming soon. He pores over maps and realizes that there are certain geographical choke points, valleys through which the tracks must pass. Quietly, he starts buying up the land. He can do so for pennies, because it is unattractive and not very fertile. He has no intention of farming himself, he just waits for the railroad to come to town at which point he will confidently name a very high price. The cost of bypassing the valley would be even greater.

Years later, Warbucks is also keeping a close eye on the news. He believes that a new World War is about to break out. Knowing that aviation gasoline and various metals will be in high demand, he manages to corner a nice chunk of the market on them, buying "options" to purchase at a set price. He believes the prices will skyrocket and he will be able to flip his options to eager, even desperate, buyers. He has no intention of flying planes or smelting metal himself. He just wants to "bring the information to market" and make a lot of money doing so. He is proud of his "all-American" ingenuity in figuring out where the market is going.

Joe Dotcom is an early user of the internet. He believes this will be the future of commerce and speech and he thinks that incumbent industries will be slow to realize this.

---

[2] § 1125(d) is largely mirrored by an agreement called the UDRP (or Uniform Domain Name Dispute Resolution Policy) imposed by the Internet Corporation on Assigned Names and Numbers (ICANN). ICANN effectively runs the decentralized registrar system by which new websites are registered. Anyone registering a domain name with an ICANN sanctioned registrar must follow that agreement, which sets up an arbitration system to resolve domain name disputes. (The UDRP is included in the statutory supplement.)

> All registrars must follow the Uniform Domain-Name Dispute-Resolution Policy (often referred to as the "UDRP"). Under the policy, most types of trademark-based domain-name disputes must be resolved by agreement, court action, or arbitration before a registrar will cancel, suspend, or transfer a domain name. Disputes alleged to arise from abusive registrations of domain names (for example, cybersquatting) may be addressed by expedited administrative proceedings that the holder of trademark rights initiates by filing a complaint with an approved dispute-resolution service provider. To invoke the policy, a trademark owner should either (a) file a complaint in a court of proper jurisdiction against the domain-name holder (or where appropriate an in-rem action concerning the domain name) or (b) in cases of abusive registration submit a complaint to an approved dispute-resolution service provider.

https://www.icann.org/resources/pages/help/dndr/udrp-en (last visited July 20, 2018). While trademark law provides the broad outlines of the rules, on a day-to-day basis, disputes are more likely to be settled in the cheaper and quicker arbitration system outlined in the UDRP. Yet the UDRP arbitrators will often consult the same principles that you are reading about in these trademark cases.

He goes on a spending spree, buying up Ford.com, Pfizer.com, Cocacola.com and many others. He has no intention of using the domains, he is simply "safeguarding them" he says. When the companies awake to the power of the internet, he will be ready with an offer to sell the domain. In the case of companies competing for the same domain, such as bass.com, he will propose a simple auction. For the others, he will propose that they ask themselves how much it is worth to have the correct domain name. He is sure they can agree on a price. And if they cannot, he is asked? Then the domain will not be transferred, the way it normally goes in a market if a willing buyer and a willing seller cannot agree to a price. "It is not as though anyone will be confused by the big 'under construction' notices that are currently the only thing on those pages," he tells you.

Are Warbucks and Wayne breaking the law? If not, why is Dotcom? What is he doing that is different from what they are doing? (This is not a rhetorical question; please list the differences.) How do the words cyber*piracy* and cyber*squatting* morally frame the issue? What are the arguments that it is socially better (more efficient, more just) for him to be forbidden from this kind of activity and for the trademark owners to be given the legal right to compel transfer of the domains at no cost to them? Are you convinced?

Lamparello v. Falwell
420 F.3d 309 (4th Cir. 2005)

MOTZ, Circuit Judge.

Christopher Lamparello appeals the district court's order enjoining him from maintaining a gripe website critical of Reverend Jerry Falwell. For the reasons stated below, we reverse.

I.

Reverend Falwell is "a nationally known minister who has been active as a commentator on politics and public affairs." *Hustler Magazine v. Falwell* (1988). He holds the common law trademarks "Jerry Falwell" and "Falwell," and the registered trademark "Listen America with Jerry Falwell." Jerry Falwell Ministries can be found online at "www.falwell.com," a website which receives 9,000 hits (or visits) per day.

Lamparello registered the domain name "www.fallwell.com" on February 11, 1999, after hearing Reverend Falwell give an interview "in which he expressed opinions about gay people and homosexuality that [Lamparello] considered . . . offensive." Lamparello created a website at that domain name to respond to what he believed were "untruths about gay people." Lamparello's website included headlines such as "Bible verses that Dr. Falwell chooses to ignore" and "Jerry Falwell has been bearing false witness (Exodus 20:16) against his gay and lesbian neighbors for a long time." The site also contained indepth criticism of Reverend Falwell's views. For example, the website stated:

> Dr. Falwell says that he is on the side of truth. He says that he will preach that homosexuality is a sin until the day he dies. But we believe that if the reverend were to take another thoughtful look at the scriptures, he would discover that they have been twisted around to support an anti-gay political agenda . . . at the expense of the gospel.

Although the interior pages of Lamparello's website did not contain a disclaimer, the homepage prominently stated, "This website is NOT affiliated with Jerry Falwell or his ministry"; advised, "If you would like to visit Rev. Falwell's website, you may click here"; and provided a hyperlink to Reverend Falwell's website.

At one point, Lamparello's website included a link to the Amazon.com webpage for a book that offered interpretations of the Bible that Lamparello favored, but the parties agree that Lamparello has never sold goods or services on his website. The parties also agree that "Lamparello's domain name and web site at www.fallwell.com," which received only 200 hits per day, "had no measurable impact on the quantity of visits to [Reverend Falwell's] web site at www.falwell.com."

Lamparello's website for www.fallwell.com

Nonetheless, Reverend Falwell sent Lamparello letters in October 2001 and June 2003 demanding that he cease and desist from using www.fallwell.com or any variation of Reverend Falwell's name as a domain name. Ultimately, Lamparello filed this action against Reverend Falwell and his ministries (collectively referred to hereinafter as "Reverend Falwell"), seeking a declaratory judgment of noninfringement. Reverend Falwell counter-claimed, alleging trademark infringement under 15 U.S.C. § 1114 (2000), false designation of origin under 15 U.S.C. § 1125(a), unfair competition under 15 U.S.C. § 1126 and the common law of Virginia, and cybersquatting under 15 U.S.C. § 1125(d).

The district court granted summary judgment to Reverend Falwell, enjoined Lamparello from using Reverend Falwell's mark at www.fallwell.com, and required Lamparello to transfer the domain name to Reverend Falwell. However, the court denied Reverend Falwell's request for statutory damages or attorney fees, reasoning that the "primary motive" of Lamparello's website was "to put forth opinions on issues that were contrary to those of [Reverend Falwell]" and "not to take away monies or to profit."

Lamparello appeals the district court's order; Reverend Falwell cross-appeals the denial of statutory damages and attorney fees.

II.

We first consider Reverend Falwell's claims of trademark infringement and false designation of origin. . . .

Trademark law serves the important functions of protecting product identification, providing consumer information, and encouraging the production of quality goods and services. See *Qualitex Co. v. Jacobson Prods. Co.* (1995). But protections "'against unfair competition'" cannot be transformed into "'rights to control language.'" *CPC Int'l, Inc. v. Skippy Inc.* (4th Cir. 2000) (quoting Mark A. Lemley, The Modern Lanham Act and the Death of Common Sense, 108 Yale L.J. 1687, 1710–11 (1999)). "Such a transformation" would raise serious First Amendment concerns because it would limit the ability to discuss the products or criticize the conduct of companies that may be of widespread public concern and importance. Much useful social and commercial discourse would be all but impossible if speakers were under threat of an infringement lawsuit every time they made reference to a person, company or product by using its trademark.

  Lamparello and his *amici* argue at length that application of the Lanham Act must be restricted to "commercial speech" to assure that trademark law does not become a tool for unconstitutional censorship. The Sixth Circuit has endorsed this view, see *Taubman Co. v. Webfeats* (6th Cir. 2003), and the Ninth Circuit recently has done so as well, see *Bosley Med. Inst., Inc. v. Kremer* (9th Cir. 2005).

  In its two most significant recent amendments to the Lanham Act, the Federal Trademark Dilution Act of 1995 ("FTDA") and the Anticybersquatting Consumer Protection Act of 1999 ("ACPA"), Congress left little doubt that it did not intend for trademark laws to impinge [on] the First Amendment rights of critics and commentators. The dilution statute applies to only a "commercial use in commerce of a mark," 15 U.S.C. § 1125(c)(1), and explicitly states that the "[n]oncommercial use of a mark" is not actionable. § 1125(c)(4). Congress explained that this language was added to "adequately address[] legitimate First Amendment concerns," and "incorporate[d] the concept of 'commercial' speech from the 'commercial speech' doctrine." Similarly, Congress directed that in determining whether an individual has engaged in cybersquatting, the courts may consider whether the person's use of the mark is a "bona fide noncommercial or fair use." 15 U.S.C. § 1125(d)(1)(B)(i)(IV). The legislature believed this provision necessary to "protect[ ] the rights of Internet users and the interests of all Americans in free speech and protected uses of trademarked names for such things as parody, comment, criticism, comparative advertising, news reporting, etc."

  In contrast, the trademark infringement and false designation of origin provisions of the Lanham Act (Sections 32 and 43(a), respectively) do not employ the term "noncommercial." They do state, however, that they pertain only to the use of a mark "in connection with the sale, offering for sale, distribution, or advertising of any goods or services," 15 U.S.C. § 1114(1)(a), or "in connection with any goods or services," § 1125(a)(1). But courts have been reluctant to define those terms narrowly. Rather, as the Second Circuit has explained, "[t]he term 'services' has been interpreted broadly" and so "[t]he Lanham Act has . . . been applied to defendants furnishing a wide variety of non-commercial public and civic benefits." *United We Stand Am., Inc. v. United We Stand, Am. N.Y., Inc.* (2d Cir. 1997). Similarly, in *PETA* we noted that a website need not actually sell goods or services for the use of a mark in that site's domain name to constitute a use "'in connection with' goods or services." *PETA*; see also *Taubman Co.* (concluding that website with two links to websites of for-profit entities violated the Lanham Act).

  Thus, even if we accepted Lamparello's contention that Sections 32 and 43(a) of the Lanham Act apply only to commercial speech, we would still face the difficult question of what constitutes such speech under those provisions. In the case at hand, we need not resolve that question or determine whether Sections 32 and 43(a) apply exclusively to commercial speech because Reverend Falwell's claims of trademark infringement and false designation fail for a more obvious reason. The hallmark of such claims is a likelihood of confusion—and there is no likelihood of confusion here.

B. 1.

  "[T]he use of a competitor's mark that does not cause confusion as to source is per-missible." *Dorr-Oliver, Inc. v. Fluid-Quip, Inc.* (7th Cir. 1996). Accordingly, Lamparello can only be liable for infringement and false designation if his use of Reverend Falwell's mark would be likely to cause confusion as to the source of the website found at www.fallwell.com. This likelihood-of-confusion test "generally strikes a comfortable balance" between the First Amendment and the rights of markholders.

We have identified seven factors helpful in determining whether a likelihood of confusion exists as to the source of a work, but "not all these factors are always relevant or equally emphasized in each case." *Pizzeria Uno Corp. v. Temple* (4th Cir. 1984) The factors are: "(a) the strength or distinctiveness of the mark; (b) the similarity of the two marks; (c) the similarity of the goods/services the marks identify; (d) the similarity of the facilities the two parties use in their businesses; (e) the similarity of the advertising used by the two parties; (f) the defendant's intent; (g) actual confusion."

Reverend Falwell's mark is distinctive, and the domain name of Lamparello's website, www.fallwell.com, closely resembles it. But, although Lamparello and Reverend Falwell employ similar marks online, Lamparello's website looks nothing like Reverend Falwell's; indeed, Lamparello has made no attempt to imitate Reverend Falwell's website. Moreover, Reverend Falwell does not even argue that Lamparello's website constitutes advertising or a facility for business, let alone a facility or advertising similar to that of Reverend Falwell. Furthermore, Lamparello clearly created his website intending only to provide a forum to criticize ideas, not to steal customers.

Most importantly, Reverend Falwell and Lamparello do not offer similar goods or services. Rather they offer opposing ideas and commentary. Reverend Falwell's mark identifies his spiritual and political views; the website at www.fallwell.com criticizes those very views. After even a quick glance at the content of the website at www.fallwell.com, no one seeking Reverend Falwell's guidance would be misled by the domain name—www.fallwell.com—into believing Reverend Falwell authorized the content of that website. No one would believe that Reverend Falwell sponsored a site criticizing himself, his positions, and his interpretations of the Bible.[3]

Finally, the fact that people contacted Reverend Falwell's ministry to report that they found the content at www.fallwell.com antithetical to Reverend Falwell's views does not illustrate, as Reverend Falwell claims, that the website engendered actual confusion. To the contrary, the anecdotal evidence Reverend Falwell submitted shows that those searching for Reverend Falwell's site and arriving instead at Lamparello's site quickly realized that Reverend Falwell was not the source of the content therein.

For all of these reasons, it is clear that the undisputed record evidences no likelihood of confusion. In fact, Reverend Falwell even conceded at oral argument that those viewing the content of Lamparello's website probably were unlikely to confuse Reverend Falwell with the source of that material.

2.

Nevertheless, Reverend Falwell argues that he is entitled to prevail under the "initial interest confusion" doctrine. This relatively new and sporadically applied doctrine holds that "the Lanham Act forbids a competitor from luring potential customers away from a producer by initially passing off its goods as those of the producer's, even if confusion as to the source of the goods is dispelled by the time any sales are consummated." *Dorr-Oliver*. According to Reverend Falwell, this doctrine requires us to compare his mark with Lamparello's website domain name, www.fallwell.com, without considering the content of Lamparello's website. Reverend Falwell argues that some

---

[3] If Lamparello had neither criticized Reverend Falwell by name nor expressly rejected Reverend Falwell's teachings, but instead simply had quoted Bible passages and offered interpretations of them subtly different from those of Reverend Falwell, this would be a different case. For, while a gripe site, or a website dedicated to criticism of the markholder, will seldom create a likelihood of confusion, a website purporting to be the official site of the markholder and, for example, articulating positions that could plausibly have come from the markholder may well create a likelihood of confusion.

people who misspell his name may go to www.fallwell.com assuming it is his site, thus giving Lamparello an unearned audience—albeit one that quickly disappears when it realizes it has not reached Reverend Falwell's site. This argument fails for two reasons.

First, we have never adopted the initial interest confusion theory; rather, we have followed a very different mode of analysis, requiring courts to determine whether a likelihood of confusion exists by "examin[ing] the allegedly infringing use *in the context in which it is seen by the ordinary consumer.*" *Anheuser-Busch, Inc. v. L & L Wings, Inc.* (4th Cir. 1992).

Contrary to Reverend Falwell's arguments, we did not abandon this approach in *PETA*. Our inquiry in *PETA* was limited to whether Doughney's use of the domain name "www.peta.org" constituted a successful enough parody of People for the Ethical Treatment of Animals that no one was likely to believe www.peta.org was sponsored or endorsed by that organization. For a parody to be successful, it "must convey two simultaneous—and contradictory—messages: that it is the original, but also that it is not the original and is instead a parody." *PETA*. Doughney argued that his domain name conveyed the first message (that it was PETA's website) and that the content of his website conveyed the requisite second message (that it was not PETA's site). Although "[t]he website's content ma[de] it clear that it [wa]s not related to PETA," we concluded that the website's content could not convey the requisite second message because the site's content "[wa]s not conveyed simultaneously with the first message, [i.e., the domain name itself,] as required to be considered a parody." Accordingly, we found the "district court properly rejected Doughney's parody defense."

PETA simply outlines the parameters of the parody defense; it does not adopt the initial interest confusion theory or otherwise diminish the necessity of examining context when determining whether a likelihood of confusion exists. Indeed, in *PETA* itself, rather than embracing a new approach, we reiterated that "[t]o determine whether a likelihood of confusion exists, a court should not consider how closely a fragment of a given use duplicates the trademark, but must instead consider whether the use in its entirety creates a likelihood of confusion." When dealing with domain names, this means a court must evaluate an allegedly infringing domain name in conjunction with the content of the website identified by the domain name.[4]

Moreover, even if we did endorse the initial interest confusion theory, that theory would not assist Reverend Falwell here because it provides no basis for liability in circumstances such as these. The few appellate courts that have followed the Ninth Circuit and imposed liability under this theory for using marks on the Internet have done so only in cases involving a factor utterly absent here—one business's use of another's mark for its own financial gain.

Profiting financially from initial interest confusion is thus a key element for imposition of liability under this theory.[5] When an alleged infringer does not compete with the markholder for sales, "some initial confusion will not likely facilitate free riding

---

[4] Contrary to Reverend Falwell's suggestions, this rule does not change depending on how similar the domain name or title is to the mark. Hence, Reverend Falwell's assertion that he objects only to Lamparello using the domain name www.fallwell.com and has no objection to Lamparello posting his criticisms at "www .falwelliswrong.com," or a similar domain name, does not entitle him to a different evaluation rule. Rather it has long been established that even when alleged infringers use the very marks at issue in titles, courts look to the underlying content to determine whether the titles create a likelihood of confusion as to source.

[5] Offline uses of marks found to cause actionable initial interest confusion also have involved financial gain. See *Elvis Presley Enters., Inc. v. Capece* (5th Cir. 1998); *Mobil Oil Corp. v. Pegasus Petroleum Corp.* (2d Cir. 1987). And even those courts recognizing the initial interest confusion theory of liability but finding no actionable initial confusion involved one business's use of another's mark for profit.

on the goodwill of another mark, or otherwise harm the user claiming infringement. Where confusion has little or no meaningful effect in the marketplace, it is of little or no consequence in our analysis." *Checkpoint Sys.* For this reason, even the Ninth Circuit has stated that a firm is not liable for using another's mark in its domain name if it "could not financially capitalize on [a] misdirected consumer [looking for the markholder's site] even if it so desired." *Interstellar Starship Servs., Ltd. v. Epix, Inc.* (9th Cir. 2002).

This critical element—use of another firm's mark to capture the markholder's customers and profits—simply does not exist when the alleged infringer establishes a gripe site that criticizes the markholder. See Hannibal Travis, *The Battle For Mindshare: The Emerging Consensus that the First Amendment Protects Corporate Criticism and Parody on the Internet*, 10 Va. J.L. & Tech. 3, 85 (Winter 2005) ("The premise of the 'initial interest' confusion cases is that by using the plaintiff's trademark to divert its customers, the defendant is engaging in the old 'bait and switch.' But because . . . Internet users who find [gripe sites] are not sold anything, the mark may be the 'bait,' but there is simply no 'switch.'").[6] Applying the initial interest confusion theory to gripe sites like Lamparello's would enable the markholder to insulate himself from criticism—or at least to minimize access to it. We have already condemned such uses of the Lanham Act, stating that a markholder cannot "'shield itself from criticism by forbidding the use of its name in commentaries critical of its conduct.'" *CPC Int'l* (quoting *L.L. Bean, Inc. v. Drake Publishers, Inc.* (1st Cir. 1987)). "[J]ust because speech is critical of a corporation and its business practices is not a sufficient reason to enjoin the speech."

In sum, even if we were to accept the initial interest confusion theory, that theory would not apply in the case at hand. Rather, to determine whether a likelihood of confusion exists as to the source of a gripe site like that at issue in this case, a court must look not only to the allegedly infringing domain name, but also to the underlying content of the website. When we do so here, it is clear, as explained above, that no likelihood of confusion exists. Therefore, the district court erred in granting Reverend Falwell summary judgment on his infringement, false designation, and unfair competition claims.

III.

We evaluate Reverend Falwell's cybersquatting claim separately because the elements of a cybersquatting violation differ from those of traditional Lanham Act violations. To prevail on a cybersquatting claim, Reverend Falwell must show that Lamparello: (1) "had a bad faith intent to profit from using the [www.fallwell.com] domain name," and (2) the domain name www.fallwell.com "is identical or confusingly similar to, or dilutive of, the distinctive and famous [Falwell] mark." *PETA* (citing 15 U.S.C. § 1125(d)(1)(A)).

"The paradigmatic harm that the ACPA was enacted to eradicate" is "the practice of

---

[6] Although the appellate courts that have adopted the initial interest confusion theory have only applied it to profit-seeking uses of another's mark, the district courts have not so limited the application of the theory. Without expressly referring to this theory, two frequently-discussed district court cases have held that using another's domain name to post content antithetical to the markholder constitutes infringement. See *Planned Parenthood Fed'n of Am., Inc. v. Bucci*, No. 97 Civ. 0629, 1997 WL 133313 (S.D.N.Y. 1997), *aff'd*, 152 F.3d 920 (2d Cir. 1998) (table) (finding use of domain name "www.plannedparenthood.com" to provide links to passages of anti-abortion book constituted infringement); *Jews for Jesus v. Brodsky* (D.N.J. 1998), *aff'd* (3d Cir. 1998) (table) (finding use of "www.jewsforjesus.org" to criticize religious group constituted infringement). We think both cases were wrongly decided to the extent that in determining whether the domain names were confusing, the courts did not consider whether the websites' content would dispel any confusion. In expanding the initial interest confusion theory of liability, these cases cut it off from its moorings to the detriment of the First Amendment.

cybersquatters registering several hundred domain names in an effort to sell them to the legitimate owners of the mark." *Lucas Nursery & Landscaping, Inc. v. Grosse* (6th Cir. 2004). The Act was also intended to stop the registration of multiple marks with the hope of selling them to the highest bidder, "distinctive marks to defraud consumers" or "to engage in counterfeiting activities," and "well-known marks to prey on consumer confusion by misusing the domain name to divert customers from the mark owner's site to the cybersquatter's own site, many of which are pornography sites that derive advertising revenue based on the number of visits, or 'hits,' the site receives." The Act was not intended to prevent "noncommercial uses of a mark, such as for comment, criticism, parody, news reporting, etc.," and thus they "are beyond the scope" of the ACPA.

To distinguish abusive domain name registrations from legitimate ones, the ACPA directs courts to consider nine nonexhaustive factors. . . . [These statutory factors are listed at the beginning of this section on page 242.]

These factors attempt "to balance the property interests of trademark owners with the legitimate interests of Internet users and others who seek to make lawful uses of others' marks, including for purposes such as comparative advertising, comment, criticism, parody, news reporting, fair use, etc." H.R.Rep. No. 106-412. "The first four [factors] suggest circumstances that may tend to indicate an absence of bad-faith intent to profit from the goodwill of a mark, and the others suggest circumstances that may tend to indicate that such bad-faith intent exists." However, "[t]here is no simple formula for evaluating and weighing these factors. For example, courts do not simply count up which party has more factors in its favor after the evidence is in." *Harrods Ltd. v. Sixty Internet Domain Names* (4th Cir. 2002). In fact, because use of these listed factors is permissive, "[w]e need not . . . march through" them all in every case. *Virtual Works, Inc. v. Volkswagen of Am., Inc.* (4th Cir. 2001). "The factors are given to courts as a guide, not as a substitute for careful thinking about whether the conduct at issue is motivated by a bad faith intent to profit." *Lucas Nursery & Landscaping*.

After close examination of the undisputed facts involved in this case, we can only conclude that Reverend Falwell cannot demonstrate that Lamparello "had a bad faith intent to profit from using the [www.fallwell.com] domain name." Lamparello clearly employed www.fallwell.com simply to criticize Reverend Falwell's views. Factor IV of the ACPA, 15 U.S.C. § 1125(d)(1)(B)(i)(IV), counsels against finding a bad faith intent to profit in such circumstances because "use of a domain name for purposes of . . . comment, [and] criticism," constitutes a "bona fide noncommercial or fair use" under the statute, 15 U.S.C. § 1125(d)(1)(B)(i)(IV).[7] That Lamparello provided a link to an Amazon.com webpage selling a book he favored does not diminish the communicative function of his website. The use of a domain name to engage in criticism or commentary "even where done for profit" does not alone evidence a bad faith intent to profit, and Lamparello did not even stand to gain financially from sales of the book at Amazon.com. Thus factor IV weighs heavily in favor of finding Lamparello lacked a bad faith intent to profit from the

---

[7] We note that factor IV does not protect a *faux* noncommercial site, that is, a noncommercial site created by the registrant for the sole purpose of avoiding liability under the FTDA, which exempts noncommercial uses of marks, see 15 U.S.C. § 1125(c)(4)(B), or under the ACPA. As explained by the Senate Report discussing the ACPA, an individual cannot avoid liability for registering and attempting to sell a hundred domain names incorporating famous marks by posting noncommercial content at those domain names. See S.Rep. No. 106-140, 1999 WL 594571, at *14 (citing *Panavision Int'l v. Toeppen* (9th Cir. 1998)). But Lamparello's sole purpose for registering www.fallwell.com was to criticize Reverend Falwell, and this noncommercial use was not a ruse to avoid liability. Therefore, factor IV indicates that Lamparello did not have a bad faith intent to profit.

use of the domain name.

Equally important, Lamparello has not engaged in the type of conduct described in the statutory factors as typifying the bad faith intent to profit essential to a successful cybersquatting claim. First, we have already held, *supra* Part II.B, that Lamparello's domain name does not create a likelihood of confusion as to source or affiliation. Accordingly, Lamparello has not engaged in the type of conduct—"creating a likelihood of confusion as to the source, sponsorship, affiliation, or endorsement of the site," 15 U.S.C. § 1125(d)(1)(B)(i)(V)—described as an indicator of a bad faith intent to profit in factor V of the statute.

Factors VI and VIII also counsel against finding a bad faith intent to profit here. Lamparello has made no attempt—or even indicated a willingness—"to transfer, sell, or otherwise assign the domain name to [Reverend Falwell] or any third party for financial gain." 15 U.S.C. § 1125(d)(1)(B)(i)(VI). Similarly, Lamparello has not registered "multiple domain names," 15 U.S.C. § 1125(d)(1)(B)(i)(VIII); rather, the record indicates he has registered only one. Thus, Lamparello's conduct is not of the suspect variety described in factors VI and VIII of the Act.

Notably, the case at hand differs markedly from those in which the courts have found a bad faith intent to profit from domain names used for websites engaged in political commentary or parody. For example, in *PETA* we found the registrant of www.peta.org engaged in cybersquatting because www.peta.org was one of fifty to sixty domain names Doughney had registered, *PETA*, and because Doughney had evidenced a clear intent to sell www.peta.org to PETA, stating that PETA should try to "'settle' with him and 'make him an offer.'" Similarly, in *Coca-Cola Co. v. Purdy* (8th Cir. 2004), the Eighth Circuit found an anti-abortion activist who had registered domain names incorporating famous marks such as "Washington Post" liable for cybersquatting because he had registered almost seventy domain names, had offered to stop using the *Washington Post* mark if the newspaper published an opinion piece by him on its editorial page, and posted content that created a likelihood of confusion as to whether the famous markholders sponsored the anti-abortion sites and "ha[d] taken positions on hotly contested issues." In contrast, Lamparello did not register multiple domain names, he did not offer to transfer them for valuable consideration, and he did not create a likelihood of confusion.

Instead, Lamparello, like the plaintiffs in two cases recently decided by the Fifth and Sixth Circuits, created a gripe site. Both courts expressly refused to find that gripe sites located at domain names nearly identical to the marks at issue violated the ACPA. In *TMI, Inc. v. Maxwell* (5th Cir. 2004), Joseph Maxwell, a customer of homebuilder TMI, registered the domain name "www.trendmakerhome.com," which differed by only one letter from TMI's mark, TrendMaker Homes, and its domain name, "www .trendmakerhomes.com." Maxwell used the site to complain about his experience with TMI and to list the name of a contractor whose work pleased him. After his registration expired, Maxwell registered "www.trendmakerhome.info." TMI then sued, alleging cybersquatting. The Fifth Circuit reversed the district court's finding that Maxwell violated the ACPA, reasoning that his site was noncommercial and designed only "to inform potential customers about a negative experience with the company."

Similarly, in *Lucas Nursery & Landscaping*, a customer of Lucas Nursery registered the domain name "www.lucasnursery.com" and posted her dissatisfaction with the company's landscaping services. Because the registrant, Grosse, like Lamparello, registered a single domain name, the Sixth Circuit concluded that her conduct did not constitute that which Congress intended to proscribe—i.e., the registration of multiple domain names. *Lucas Nursery & Landscaping*. Noting that Grosse's gripe site did not create any confusion as to sponsorship and that she had never attempted to sell the domain name to the markholder, the court found that Grosse's conduct was not actionable under the ACPA. The court explained: "One of the ACPA's main objectives is the protection of consumers from slick internet peddlers who trade on the names and reputations of established brands. The practice of informing fellow consumers of one's experience with a particular service provider is surely not inconsistent with this ideal."

Like Maxwell and Grosse before him, Lamparello has not evidenced a bad faith intent to profit under the ACPA. To the contrary, he has used www.fallwell.com to engage in the type of "comment[] [and] criticism" that Congress specifically stated militates against a finding of bad faith intent to profit. And he has neither registered multiple domain names nor attempted to transfer www.fallwell.com for valuable consideration. We agree with the Fifth and Sixth Circuits that, given these circumstances, the use of a mark in a domain name for a gripe site criticizing the markholder does not constitute cybersquatting.

IV.

For the foregoing reasons, Lamparello, rather than Reverend Falwell, is entitled to summary judgment on all counts. Accordingly, the judgment of the district court is reversed and the case is remanded for entry of judgment for Lamparello.
REVERSED AND REMANDED.

PROBLEM 9-3

Lamparello is from the 4th Circuit, the same Circuit that decided *PETA* (excerpted in Chapter 7). **Are the two cases consistent?** In your answer you should first offer the strongest reasons that they are not—listing arguments, decisions on points of law, legal definitions, or jurisprudential approaches towards trademark that you think make the two decisions inconsistent, not just as a matter of law, but as a matter of trademark philosophy. Then you should make the strongest counter arguments. In particular, you should list the distinguishing features between the two cases that actually show that the decisions—though one favors plaintiff and one defendant—are consistent. **Which side of the debate do you think is stronger, and why? To the extent you do think the cases represent diverging views, with which do you agree, and why?**

Note: A Trademark Check List

The next page provides you with a check list to review the material we have covered in trademark. Use it and the flow chart as bookends in your review.

TRADEMARK CHECKLIST

(Highly simplified. Use this to review our coverage of trademark
law and to test your understanding of the doctrine.)

Does the plaintiff own a valid trademark/trade dress?

- Is there a "use in commerce"? *Planetary Motion*
- Is it used "as a mark"? *Microstrategy*
- Is it distinctive? *Abercrombie* (spectrum of distinctiveness)*; Zatarains* (descriptive or suggestive)
- Does it fall into a category that requires acquired distinctiveness (e.g. merely descriptive, *Zatarains,* color, *Qualitex*, design as opposed to packaging, *Wal-Mart*)? If so, does it have acquired distinctiveness? § 1052(f)
- Is it functional; utilitarian or aesthetic? Functional product features are never protectable. *TrafFix*
- Does it fall into another category that is never protectable (generic, deceptive, etc.)?
- For federal registration of marks, is registration barred by any of the provisions in § 1052 (deceptive marks, names, geographic terms, etc.)? *See* Chapter 6; note the provisions of § 1052 invalidated by *Matal* and *Brunetti*. For unregistered marks, § 1125(a), many if not all of § 1052's limitations also apply.

Was there confusion-based infringement?

- Did the defendant use a similar mark in commerce in connection with goods or services? *Rescuecom, PETA* (note: the reasoning in *PETA* has been disavowed or limited by subsequent courts)
- Was there a likelihood of confusion as to source or sponsorship? *Lois,* § 1114, § 1125. (note: some courts consider initial interest confusion and post-sale confusion) *Lois*; Chapter 7 summary
- Did the defendant engage in *direct* infringement (infringed through their own actions) or *contributory* infringement (facilitated someone *else*'s infringement)? *Tiffany*

Do any defenses apply?

- Was the defendant's use a *classic* fair use (aka "descriptive fair use")? *KP Permanent Make-Up*, § 1115(b)(4)
- Was the defendant's use a *nominative* use? *New Kids on the Block, Mattel, Playboy*
- Did the defendant use the trademark in the title of an artistic work? *Mattel* (applying *Rogers*)
- Was it a successful parody? (Effective parodies diminish likelihood of confusion) *Smith*

Was there false advertising under § 1125(a)?

- Was there a false or misleading statement of fact? *Pizza Hut*
- If it was true but misleading, was there materiality? *Pizza Hut*

Was there dilution under § 1125(c)?

- Was the plaintiff's mark "famous"? *Coach*
- Was there dilution by blurring? *Starbucks*
- Was there dilution by tarnishment? *Smith*
- Do any exceptions apply? *Smith,* § 1125(c)(3)(c)

Was there cyberpiracy under § 1125(d)?

- Was there a domain name registration with a "bad faith intent to profit"? *Lamparello*

CHAPTER TEN
Introduction to Copyright: Theory & History

Imagine that you have to craft a scheme of intellectual property from scratch. Your subject matter is books. And later music and film. But initially books. What do you do? What material should the right cover? What material should the right leave free? What exceptions and limitations should there be? Again we have a resource that—once we get to a certain technological level—is non-rivalrous and non-excludable. True, the *degree* of rivalrousness and excludability will change over time. It is harder to typeset an illicit edition of *Bleak House* on a Victorian printing press than to download an epub of *Fifty Shades of Grey* from a "warez" site. But you wish to encourage authors (and publishers) to produce these wonderful objects, and yet make sure they can be read by your fellow citizens and even built upon by future authors. How do you do so?

Copyright starts with a remarkable and dramatic choice. It does not cover ideas or unoriginal compilations of fact. When I publish my book, the ideas and facts within it go immediately into the public domain—no need to wait for my lifetime plus another seventy years to get them. Copyright covers only the *original expression*.

© covers expression, not ideas or facts

When I report on a momentous assassination of a politician, reveal the assassin's name and offer the prediction that this may lead to the death of a peace process, copyright gives me no rights over the facts of the death, or the assassin's name or the idea that this may set off national and regional conflict with tragic consequences for those who had hoped peace was within their grasp. My copyright covers only the way in which those ideas and facts are expressed.

In the readings that follow, you will find first that neither this idea/expression dichotomy, nor the drawing of a limited legal right around its contours, seemed obvious or normal when first introduced. Yet you will also find that it was subsequently woven into an edifice of remarkable rhetorical force and power.

Copyright and the Invention of Authorship

Excerpt from
James Boyle, Shamans, Software and Spleens: Law and the Construction of the Information Society
(Harvard University Press, 1997)[1]

In personal or real property, . . . one can point to a pair of sneakers or a house, say "I own that," and have some sense of confidence that the statement means something. As the *LeRoy Fibre* case [you probably read the *Leroy Fibre* case as a 1L—the Supreme Court held that "the rights of one man in the use of his property cannot be limited by the wrongs of another"] shows, of course, it is not at all clear that such confidence is justified, but at least

---
[1] Footnotes omitted.

property presents itself as an apparently coherent feature of social reality, and this is a fact of considerable ideological and political significance. In intellectual property, the response to the claim "I own that" might be "what do you mean?"

As Martha Woodmansee discovered, this point was made with startling clarity in the debates over copyright in Germany in the eighteenth century. Encouraged by an enormous reading public, several apocryphal tales of writers who were household names, yet still living in poverty, and a new, more romantic vision of authorship, writers began to demand greater economic returns from their labors. One obvious strategy was to lobby for some kind of legal right in the text—the right that we would call copyright. To many participants in the debate, the idea was ludicrous. Christian Sigmund Krause, writing in 1783, expressed the point pungently.

> "But the ideas, the content! that which actually constitutes a book! which only the author can sell or communicate!"—Once expressed, it is impossible for it to remain the author's property . . . It is precisely for the purpose of *using* the ideas that most people buy books—pepper dealers, fishwives, and the like and literary pirates excepted . . . Over and over again it comes back to the same question: I can read the contents of a book, learn, abridge, expand, teach, and translate it, write about it, laugh over it, find fault with it, deride it, use it poorly or well—in short, do with it whatever I will. But the one thing I should be prohibited from doing is copying or reprinting it? . . . A published book is a secret divulged. With what justification would a preacher forbid the printing of his homilies, since he cannot prevent any of his listeners from transcribing his sermons? Would it not be just as ludicrous for a professor to demand that his students refrain from using some new proposition he had taught them as for him to demand the same of book dealers with regard to a new book? *No, no it is too obvious that the concept of intellectual property is useless. My property must be exclusively mine; I must be able to dispose of it and retrieve it unconditionally.* Let someone explain to me how that is possible in the present case. Just let someone try taking back the ideas he has originated once they have been communicated so that they are, as before, nowhere to be found. All the money in the world could not make that possible.

Along with this problem go two other, more fundamental ones. The first is the recurrent question of how we can give property rights in intellectual products and yet still have the inventiveness and free flow of information which liberal social theory demands. I shall return to this question in a moment. The second problem is the more fundamental one. On what grounds should we give the author this kind of unprecedented property right at all, even if the conceptual problems could be overcome? We do not think it is necessary to give car workers residual property rights in the cars that they produce—wage labor is thought to work perfectly well. Surely, an author is merely taking public goods—language, ideas, culture, humor, genre—and converting them to his or her own use? Where is the moral or utilitarian justification for the existence of this property right in the first place? The most obvious answer is that authors are special, but why? And since when?

Even the most cursory historical study reveals that our notion of "authorship" is a concept of relatively recent provenance. Medieval church writers actively disapproved of the elements of originality and creativeness which we think of as an essential component of authorship: "They valued extant old books more highly than any recent elucubrations and they put the work of the scribe and copyist above that of the authors. The real task of the scholar was not the vain excogitation of novelties but a discovery of great old books, their multiplication and the placing of copies where they would be accessible to future generations of readers."

Martha Woodmansee quotes a wonderful definition of "Book" from a mid-eighteenth-century dictionary that merely lists the writer as one mouth among many—"the scholar, . . . the paper-maker, the type-founder and setter, the proof-reader, the publisher and book-binder, sometimes even the gilder and brass worker"—all of whom are "fed by this branch of manufacture." Other studies show that authors seen as craftsmen—an appellation which Shakespeare might not have rejected—or at their most exalted, as the crossroads where learned tradition met external divine inspiration. But since the tradition was mere craft and the glory of the divine inspiration should be offered to God rather than to the vessel he had chosen, where was the justification for preferential treatment in the creation of property rights? As authors ceased to think of themselves as either craftsmen, gentlemen, or amanuenses for the Divine spirit, a recognizably different, more romantic vision of authorship began to emerge. At first, it was found mainly in self-serving tracts, but little by little it spread through the culture so that by the middle of the eighteenth century it had come to be seen as a "universal truth about art."

Woodmansee explains how the decline of the craft-inspiration model of writing and the elevation of the romantic author both presented and seemed to solve the question of property rights in intellectual products: "Eighteenth-century theorists departed from this compound model of writing in two significant ways. They minimized the element of craftsmanship (in some instances they simply discarded it) in favor of the element of inspiration, and they internalized the source of that inspiration. That is, inspiration came to be regarded as emanating not from outside or above, but from within the writer himself. 'Inspiration' came to be explicated in terms of original genius with the consequence that the inspired work was made peculiarly and distinctively the product—and the property—of the writer."

In this vision, the author was not the journeyman who learned a craft and then hoped to be well paid for it. The romantic author was defined not by the mastery of a prior set of rules, but instead by the transformation of genre, the revision of form. Originality became the watchword of artistry and the warrant for property rights. To see how complete a revision this is, one need only examine Shakespeare's wholesale lifting of plot, scene, and language from other writers, both ancient and contemporary. To an Elizabethan playwright, the phrase "imitation is the sincerest form of flattery" might have seemed entirely without irony. "Not only were Englishmen from 1500 to 1625 without any feeling analogous to the modern attitude toward plagiarism; they even lacked the *word* until the very end of that period." To the theorists and polemicists of romantic authorship, however, the reproduction of orthodoxy would have been proof they were not the unique and transcendent spirits they imagined themselves to be.

It is the *originality* of the author, the novelty which he or she adds to the raw materials provided by culture and the common pool, which "justifies" the property right and at the same time offers a strategy for resolving the basic conceptual problem pointed out by Krause—what concept of property would allow the author to retain some property rights in the work but not others? In the German debates, the best answer was provided by the great idealist Fichte. In a manner that is now familiar to lawyers trained in legal realism and Hohfeldian analysis, but that must have seemed remarkable at the time, Fichte disaggregated the concept of property in books. The buyer gets the physical thing and the ideas contained in it. Precisely because the originality of his spirit was converted into an originality of form, the author retains the right to the form in which those ideas were expressed: "Each writer must give his own thoughts a certain form, and he can give them no other form than his own because he has no other. But neither can he be willing to hand over this form in making his thoughts public, for no one can appropriate his thoughts without thereby altering their form. This latter thus remains forever his exclusive property."

A similar theme is struck in American copyright law. In the famous case of *Bleistein v. Donaldson Lithographing Company*, concerning the copyrightability of a circus poster, Oliver Wendell Holmes was still determined to claim that the work could become the subject of an intellectual property right because it was the original creation of a unique individual spirit. Holmes's opinion shows us both the advantages and the disadvantages of a rhetoric which bases property rights on "originality." As a hook on which to hang a property right, "originality" seems to have at least a promise of formal realizability. It connects nicely to the romantic vision of authorship which I described earlier and to which I will return. It also seems to limit a potentially expansive principle, the principle that those who create may be entitled to retain some legally protected interest in the objects they make—even after those objects have been conveyed through the marketplace. But while the idea that an original spirit conveys its uniqueness to worked matter seems intuitively plausible when applied to Shakespeare or Dante, it has less obvious relevance to a more humdrum act of creation by a less credibly romantic creator—a commercial artist in a shopping mall, say. The tension between the rhetoric of Wordsworth and the reality of suburban corporate capitalism is one that continues to bedevil intellectual property discourse today. In *Bleistein*, this particular original spirit had only managed to rough out a picture of energetic-looking individuals performing unlikely acts on bicycles, but to Holmes the principle was the same. "The copy is the personal reaction of an individual upon nature. Personality always contains something unique. It expresses its singularity even in handwriting, and a very modest grade of art has in it something irreducible, which is one man's alone. That something he may copyright."

This quality of "uniqueness," recognized first in great spirits, then in creative spirits, and finally in advertising executives, expresses itself in originality of form, of expression. Earlier I quoted a passage from Jessica Litman which bears repeating here: "Why is it that copyright does not protect ideas? Some writers have echoed the justification for failing to protect facts by suggesting that ideas have their origin in the public domain. Others have implied that 'mere ideas' may not be worthy of the status of private property. Some authors have suggested that ideas are not protected because of the strictures imposed on copyright by the first amendment. The task of distinguishing ideas from expression in order to explain why private ownership is inappropriate for one but desirable for the other, however, remains elusive."

I would say that we find the answer to this question in the romantic vision of authorship, of the genius whose style forever expresses a single unique persona. The rise of this powerful (and historically contingent) stereotype provided the necessary raw material to fashion some convincing mediation of the tension between the imagery of "public" and "private" in information production.

To sum up, then, if our starting place is the romantic idea of authorship, then the idea/expression division which has so fascinated and puzzled copyright scholars apparently manages, at a stroke, to do four things:

- First, it provides a conceptual basis for partial, limited property rights, without completely collapsing the notion of property into the idea of a temporary, limited, utilitarian state grant, revocable at will. The property right still seems to be based on something real—on a distinction which sounds formally realizable, even if, on closer analysis, it turns out to be impossible to maintain.

- Second, this division provides a moral and philosophical justification for fencing in the commons, giving the author property in something built from the resources of the public domain—language, culture, genre, scientific community, or what have you. If one makes originality of spirit the assumed feature of authorship and the touchstone for property rights, one can see the author as creating something entirely new—not recombining the resources of the commons. Thus we reassure ourselves both that the grant to the author is justifiable and that it will not have the effect of diminishing the commons for future creators. After all, if a work of authorship is original—by definition—we believe that it only adds to our cultural supply. With originality first defended and then routinely assumed, intellectual property no longer looks like a zero sum game. There is always "enough and as good" left over—by definition. The distinguished intellectual property scholar Paul Goldstein captures both the power and the inevitable limitations of this view very well. "Copyright, in a word, is about authorship. Copyright is about sustaining the conditions of creativity that enable an individual to craft out of thin air an *Appalachian Spring*, a *The Sun Also Rises*, a *Citizen Kane*." But of course, even these—remarkable and "original"—works are not crafted out of thin air. As Northrop Frye put it in 1957, when Michel Foucault's work on authorship was only a gleam in the eye of the episteme, "Poetry can only be made out of other poems; novels out of other novels. All of this was much clearer before the assimilation of literature to private enterprise."

- Third, the idea/expression division circumscribes the ambit of a labor theory of property. At times, it seems that the argument is almost like Locke's labor theory; one gains property by mixing one's labor with an object. But where Locke's theory, if applied to a modern economy, might have a disturbingly socialist ring to it, Fichte's theory bases the property right on the originality of every spirit as expressed through words. Every author gets the right—the writer of the roman à clef as well as Goethe—but because of the concentration on originality of expression, the residual property right is only for the workers of the word and the image, not the workers of the world. Even after that right is extended by analogy to sculpture and painting, software and music, it will still have an attractively circumscribed domain.

- Fourth, the idea/expression division resolves (or at least conceals) the tension between public and private. In the double life which Marx described, information is both the life blood of the noble disinterested citizens of the public world and a commodity in the private sphere to which we must attach property rights if we wish our self-interested producers to continue to produce. By disaggregating the book into "idea" and "expression," we can give the idea (and the facts on which it is based) to the public world and the expression to the writer, thus apparently mediating the contradiction between public good and private need (or greed).

Thus the combination of the romantic vision of authorship and the distinction between idea and expression appeared to provide a conceptual basis and a moral justification for intellectual property, to do so in a way which did not threaten to spread dangerous notions of entitlement to other kinds of workers, and to mediate the tension between the halves of the liberal world view. Small wonder that it was a success.

Questions:

1.) Reread the indented quote from Krause. What does he assume that the property right in a book would have to cover? And what does he assume about the "reach" of the right? How absolute or total does he assume that property right would have to be in order to be coherent? Why does he say such a right would be impossible?

2.) What does he mean when he says "It is precisely for the purpose of using the ideas that most people buy books—*pepper dealers, fishwives, and the like and literary pirates excepted*"?

3.) Boyle sets up a checklist of functions that any theory of copyright has to fulfill: The two most important are to explain how the author gets to own something she drew in part from the public domain, and to explain how this particular property right balances property with freedom of expression (think of the framings we discussed in Chapter 1). How does the idea of a limited property right drawn around the idea-expression dichotomy fulfill those tasks?

4.) Do current artists and critics believe that the mark of an artist, the measurement of her worth, is above all her originality? Does the public? Compare our view of soap operas, formula action movies and high culture novels or movies. Would Shakespeare have agreed with our implicit aesthetic criteria?

Three Views of Copyright (and the *droits d'auteur*)

One approach to the background theory of copyright is to give you excerpts from the writings of philosophers or property theorists. We would be the last people to deprecate such an approach: one of us has just engaged in it. But we have taken a different tack here. In the excerpts that follow we have tried to give you a snapshot of *the actual political debates over copyright*. This was a battle of ideas, make no mistake about that. But it was a battle of ideas that had to be changed into the coin of the day, that had to be cashed out in language that legislators and citizens could understand and appreciate. We have taken a series of snippets drawn from writers with very different views—Macaulay (whom you have already encountered), Victor Hugo, and Samuel Clemens (Mark Twain.) The topics they are discussing will be familiar to you—free expression, term extension, access to culture—but we want you to focus more on their premises. What is copyright *for*? How should it be judged? What balance—if any—should it strike between authors, readers and future creators? How does its split between idea and expression play in that discussion? When is access to the idea not sufficient, so that one needs access to the actual expression?

Thomas Babington Macaulay,
First Speech to the House of Commons on Copyright
February 5, 1841

It is painful to me to take a course which may possibly be misunderstood or misrepresented as unfriendly to the interests of literature and literary men. It is painful to me, I will add, to oppose my honorable and learned friend on a question which he has taken up from the purest motives, and which he regards with a parental interest. These feelings have hitherto kept me silent when the law of copyright has been under discussion. But as I am, on full consideration, satisfied that the measure before us will, if adopted, inflict grievous injury on the public, without conferring any compensating advantage on men of letters, I think it my duty to avow that opinion and to defend it.

The first thing to be done, Sir, is to settle on what principles the question is to be argued. Are we free to legislate for the public good, or are we not? Is this a question of expediency, or is it a question of right? Many of those who have written and petitioned against the existing state of things treat the question as one of right. The law of nature, according to them, gives to every man a sacred and indefeasible property in his own ideas, in the fruits of his own reason and imagination. The legislature has indeed the power to take away this property, just as it has the power to pass an act of attainder for cutting off an innocent man's head without a trial. But, as such an act of attainder would be legal murder, so would an act invading the right of an author to his copy be, according to these gentlemen, legal robbery.

Now, Sir, if this be so, let justice be done, cost what it may. I am not prepared, like my honorable and learned friend, to agree to a compromise between right and expediency, and to commit an injustice for the public convenience. But I must say, that his theory soars far beyond the reach of my faculties. It is not necessary to go, on the present occasion, into a metaphysical inquiry about the origin of the right of property; and certainly nothing but the strongest necessity would lead me to discuss a subject so likely to be distasteful to the House. I agree, I own, with Paley in thinking that property is the creature of the law, and that the law which creates property can be defended only on this ground, that it is a law beneficial to mankind. But it is unnecessary to debate that point. For, even if I believed in a natural right of property, independent of utility and anterior to legislation, I should still deny that this right could survive the original proprietor. . . . Surely, Sir, even those who hold that there is a natural right of property must admit that rules prescribing the manner in which the effects of deceased persons shall be distributed are purely arbitrary, and originate altogether in the will of the legislature. If so, Sir, there is no controversy between my honorable and learned friend and myself as to the principles on which this question is to be argued. For the existing law gives an author copyright during his natural life; nor do I propose to invade that privilege, which I should, on the contrary, be prepared to defend strenuously against any assailant. The only point in issue between us is, how long after an author's death the state shall recognize a copyright in his representatives and assigns; and it can, I think, hardly be disputed by any rational man that this is a point which the legislature is free to determine in the way which may appear to be most conducive to the general good.

We may now, therefore, I think, descend from these high regions, where we are in danger of being lost in the clouds, to firm ground and clear light. Let us look at this question like legislators, and after fairly balancing conveniences and inconveniences, pronounce between the existing law of copyright, and the law now proposed to us. The question of copyright, Sir, like most questions of civil prudence, is neither black nor white, but gray. The system of copyright has great advantages and great disadvantages; and it is our business to ascertain what these are, and then to make an arrangement under which the advantages may be as far as possible secured, and the disadvantages as far as possible excluded. The charge which I bring against my honorable and learned friend's bill is this, that it leaves the advantages nearly what they are at present, and increases the disadvantages at least fourfold.

The advantages arising from a system of copyright are obvious. It is desirable that we should have a supply of good books; we cannot have such a supply unless men of letters are liberally remunerated: and the least objectionable way of remunerating them is by means of copyright. You cannot depend for literary instruction and amusement on the leisure of men occupied in the pursuits of active life. Such men may occasionally produce compositions of great merit. But you must not look to such men for works which require deep meditation and long research. Works of that kind you can expect only from persons who make literature the business of their lives. Of these persons few will be found among the rich and the noble. The rich and the noble are not impelled to intellectual exertion by necessity. They may be impelled to intellectual exertion by the desire of distinguishing themselves, or by the desire of benefiting the community. But it is generally within these walls that they seek to signalize themselves and to serve their fellow-creatures. Both their ambition and their public spirit, in a country like this, naturally take a political turn. It is then on men whose profession is literature, and whose private means are not ample, that you must rely for a supply of valuable books. Such men must be remunerated for their literary labor. And there are only two ways in which they can be remunerated. One of those ways is patronage; the other is copyright.

There have been times in which men of letters looked, not to the public, but to the government, or to a few great men, for the reward of their exertions. It was thus in the time of Mæcenas and Pollio at Rome, of the Medici at Florence, of Louis the Fourteenth in France, of Lord Halifax and Lord Oxford in this country. Now, Sir, I well know that there are cases in which it is fit and graceful, nay, in which it is a sacred duty to reward the merits or to relieve the distresses of men of genius by the exercise of this species of liberality. But these cases are exceptions. I can conceive no system more fatal to the integrity and independence of literary men than one under which they should be taught to look for their daily bread to the favor of ministers and nobles. I can conceive no system more certain to turn those minds which are formed by nature to be the blessings and ornaments of our species into public scandals and pests.

We have, then, only one resource left. We must betake ourselves to copyright, be the inconveniences of copyright what they may. Those inconveniences, in truth, are neither few nor small. Copyright is monopoly, and produces all the effects which the general voice of mankind attributes to monopoly. My honorable and learned friend talks very contemptuously of those who are led away by the theory that monopoly makes things dear. That monopoly makes things dear is certainly a theory, as all the great truths which have been established by the experience of all ages and nations, and which are taken for granted in all reasonings, may be said to be theories. It is a theory in the same sense in which it is a theory that day and night follow each other, that lead is heavier than water, that bread nourishes, that arsenic poisons, that alcohol intoxicates.

If, as my honorable and learned friend seems to think, the whole world is in the wrong on this point, if the real effect of monopoly is to make articles good and cheap, why does he stop short in his career of change? Why does he limit the operation of so salutary a principle to sixty years? Why does he consent to anything short of a perpetuity? He told us that in consenting to anything short of a perpetuity he was making a compromise between extreme right and expediency. But if his opinion about monopoly be correct, extreme right and expediency would coincide. Or rather, why should we not restore the monopoly of the East India trade to the East India Company? Why should we not revive all those old monopolies which, in Elizabeth's reign, galled our fathers so severely that, maddened by intolerable wrong, they opposed to their sovereign a resistance before which her haughty spirit quailed for the first and for the last time? Was it the cheapness and excellence of commodities that then so violently stirred the indignation of the English people? I believe, Sir, that I may safely take it for granted that the effect of monopoly generally is to make articles scarce, to make them dear, and to make them bad. And I may with equal safety challenge my honorable friend to find out any distinction between copyright and other privileges of the same kind; any reason why a monopoly of books should produce an effect directly the reverse of that which was produced by the East India Company's monopoly of tea, or by Lord Essex's monopoly of sweet wines. Thus, then, stands the case. It is good that authors should be remunerated; and the least exceptionable way of remunerating them is by a monopoly. Yet monopoly is an evil. For the sake of the good we must submit to the evil; but the evil ought not to last a day longer than is necessary for the purpose of securing the good.

Now, I will not affirm that the existing law is perfect, that it exactly hits the point at which the monopoly ought to cease; but this I confidently say, that the existing law is very much nearer that point than the law proposed by my honorable and learned friend. For consider this; the evil effects of the monopoly are proportioned to the length of its duration. But the good effects for the sake of which we bear with the evil effects are by no means proportioned to the length of its duration. A monopoly of sixty years produces twice as much evil as a monopoly of thirty years, and thrice as much evil as a monopoly of twenty years. But it is by no means the fact that a posthumous monopoly of sixty years gives to an author thrice as much pleasure and thrice as strong a motive as a posthumous monopoly of twenty years. On the contrary, the difference is so small as to be hardly perceptible. We all know how faintly we are affected by the prospect of very distant advantages, even when they are advantages which we may reasonably hope that we shall ourselves enjoy. But an advantage that is to be enjoyed more than half a century after we are dead, by somebody, we know not by whom, perhaps by somebody unborn, by somebody utterly unconnected with us, is really no motive at all to action. It is very probable that in the course of some generations land in the unexplored and unmapped heart of the Australasian continent will be very valuable. But there is none of us who would lay down five pounds for a whole province in the heart of the Australasian continent. We know, that neither we, nor anybody for whom we care, will ever receive a farthing of rent from such a province. And a man is very little moved by the thought that in the year 2000 or 2100, somebody who claims through him will employ more shepherds than Prince Esterhazy, and will have the finest house and gallery of pictures at Victoria or Sydney. Now, this is the sort of boon which my honorable and learned friend holds out to authors. Considered as a boon to them, it is a mere nullity; but considered as an impost on the public, it is no nullity, but a very serious and pernicious reality.

The principle of copyright is this. It is a tax on readers for the purpose of giving a bounty to writers. The tax is an exceedingly bad one; it is a tax on one of the most innocent and most salutary of human pleasures; and never let us forget, that a tax on innocent pleasures is a premium on vicious pleasures. I admit, however, the necessity of giving a bounty to genius and learning. In order to give such a bounty, I willingly submit even to this severe and burdensome tax. Nay, I am ready to increase the tax, if it can be shown that by so doing I should proportionally increase the bounty. My complaint is, that my honorable and learned friend doubles, triples, quadruples, the tax, and makes scarcely any perceptible addition to the bounty. Why, Sir, what is the additional amount of taxation which would have been levied on the public for Dr. Johnson's works alone, if my honorable and learned friend's bill had been the law of the land? I have not data sufficient to form an opinion. But I am confident that the taxation on his dictionary alone would have amounted to many thousands of pounds. In reckoning the whole additional sum which the holders of his copyrights would have taken out of the pockets of the public during the last half century at twenty thousand pounds, I feel satisfied that I very greatly underrate it. Now, I again say that I think it but fair that we should pay twenty thousand pounds in consideration of twenty thousand pounds' worth of pleasure and encouragement received by Dr. Johnson. But I think it very hard that we should pay twenty thousand pounds for what he would not have valued at five shillings. . . .

But this is not all. I think it right, Sir, to call the attention of the House to an evil, which is perhaps more to be apprehended when an author's copyright remains in the hands of his family, than when it is transferred to booksellers. I seriously fear that, if such a measure as this should be adopted, many valuable works will be either totally suppressed or grievously mutilated. I can prove that this danger is not chimerical; and I am quite certain that, if the danger be real, the safeguards which my honorable and learned friend has devised are altogether nugatory. That the danger is not chimerical may easily be shown. Most of us, I am sure, have known persons who, very erroneously as I think, but from the best motives, would not choose to reprint Fielding's novels or Gibbon's "History of the Decline and Fall of the Roman Empire." Some gentlemen may perhaps be of opinion that it would be as well if "Tom Jones" and Gibbon's "History" were never reprinted. I will not, then, dwell on these or similar cases. I will take cases respecting which it is not likely that there will be any difference of opinion here; cases, too, in which the danger of which I now speak is not matter of supposition, but matter of fact.

Take Richardson's novels. Whatever I may, on the present occasion, think of my honorable and learned friend's judgment as a legislator, I must always respect his judgment as a critic. He will, I am sure, say that Richardson's novels are among the most valuable, among the most original, works in our language. No writings have done more to raise the fame of English genius in foreign countries. No writings are more deeply pathetic. No writings, those of Shakespeare excepted, show more profound knowledge of the human heart. . . . Sir, it is my firm belief, that if the law had been what my honorable and learned friend proposes to make it, they would have been suppressed.

I remember Richardson's grandson well; he was a clergyman in the city of London; he was a most upright and excellent man; but he had conceived a strong prejudice against works of fiction. He thought all novel-reading not only frivolous but sinful. He said,— this I state on the authority of one of his clerical brethren who is now a bishop,—he said that he had never thought it right to read one of his grandfather's books. Suppose, Sir, that the law had been what my honorable and learned friend would make it. Suppose that the copyright of Richardson's novels had descended, as might well have been the case, to this gentleman. I firmly believe that he would have thought it sinful to give them a wide circulation. I firmly believe that he would not for a hundred thousand pounds have deliberately done what he thought sinful. He would not have reprinted them.

And what protection does my honorable and learned friend give to the public in such a case? Why, Sir, what he proposes is this: if a book is not reprinted during five years, any person who wishes to reprint it may give notice in the London Gazette: the advertisement must be repeated three times: a year must elapse; and then, if the proprietor of the copyright does not put forth a new edition, he loses his exclusive privilege. Now, what protection is this to the public? What is a new edition? Does the law define the number of copies that make an edition? Does it limit the price of a copy? Are twelve copies on large paper, charged at thirty guineas each, an edition? It has been usual, when monopolies have been granted, to prescribe numbers and to limit prices. But I do not find that my honorable and learned friend proposes to do so in the present case. And, without some such provision, the security which he offers is manifestly illusory. It is my conviction that, under such a system as that which he recommends to us, a copy of "Clarissa" would have been as rare as an Aldus or a Caxton.

I will give another instance. One of the most instructive, interesting, and delightful books in our language is Boswell's "Life of Johnson." Now it is well known that Boswell's eldest son considered this book, considered the whole relation of Boswell to Johnson, as a blot in the escutcheon of the family. He thought, not perhaps altogether without reason, that his father had exhibited himself in a ludicrous and degrading light. And thus he became so sore and irritable that at last he could not bear to hear the "Life of Johnson" mentioned. Suppose that the law had been what my honorable and learned friend wishes to make it. Suppose that the copyright of Boswells "Life of Johnson" had belonged, as it well might, during sixty years, to Boswell's eldest son. What would have been the consequence? An unadulterated copy of the finest biographical work in the world would have been as scarce as the first edition of Camden's "Britannia."

. . . Sir, of the kindness with which the House has listened to me, that I will not detain you longer. I will only say this, that if the measure before us should pass, and should produce one tenth part of the evil which it is calculated to produce, and which I fully expect it to produce, there will soon be a remedy, though of a very objectionable kind. Just as the absurd Acts which prohibited the sale of game were virtually repealed by the poacher, just as many absurd revenue Acts have been virtually repealed by the smuggler, so will this law be virtually repealed by piratical booksellers.

At present the holder of copyright has the public feeling on his side. Those who invade copyright are regarded as knaves who take the bread out of the mouths of deserving men. Everybody is well pleased to see them restrained by the law, and compelled to refund their ill-gotten gains. No tradesman of good repute will have anything to do with such disgraceful transactions. Pass this law: and that feeling is at an end. Men very different from the present race of piratical booksellers will soon infringe this intolerable monopoly. Great masses of capital will be constantly employed in the violation of the law. Every art will be employed to evade legal pursuit; and the whole nation will be in the plot. On which side indeed should the public sympathy be when the question is whether some book as popular as "Robinson Crusoe" or the "Pilgrim's Progress" shall be in every cottage, or whether it shall be confined to the libraries of the rich for the advantage of the great-grandson of a bookseller who, a hundred years before, drove a hard bargain for the copyright with the author when in great distress? Remember too that, when once it ceases to be considered as wrong and discreditable to invade literary property, no person can say where the invasion will stop. The public seldom makes nice distinctions. The wholesome copyright which now exists will share in the disgrace and danger of the new copyright which you are about to create. And you will find that, in attempting to impose unreasonable restraints on the reprinting of the works of the dead, you have, to a great extent, annulled those restraints which now prevent men from pillaging and defrauding the living.

Questions:

1.) How does Macaulay link possible private censorship and *inherited* interests in copyright? Why do these same concerns not arise with the author's original private right to control reproduction?

2.) Is copyright a matter of right or a matter of utility for Macaulay?

3.) Why does he think copyright superior to patronage as a method of encouraging literary production? What would he think of crowdsourcing sites such as Kickstarter?

4.) What would he think of our current copyright system?

5.) The Bill he was discussing dealt with the possibility that publishers might "sit on their rights" and that works would become commercially unavailable, subverting copyright's goal of access. What mechanism did the Bill have to avoid that danger? Would it be a good idea for us to have such a mechanism today?

6.) Ever read Richardson's novels? Hmm.

Victor Hugo, Speech to the Congress of Literary, Industrial and Artistic Property
Paris, 1878[2]

Literary property is of *general* utility.

All the old monarchical laws denied and still deny literary property. For what purpose? For the purpose of *control*. The writer-owner is a free writer. To take his property, is to take away his independence. One wishes that it were not so. [That is the danger in] the remarkable fallacy, which would be childish if it were not so perfidious, "thought belongs to everyone, so it cannot be property, so literary property does not exist." What a strange confusion! First, to confuse the ability to think, which is general, with the thought, which is individual; my thought is *me*. Then, to confuse thought, an abstract thing, with the book, a material thing. The thought of the writer, as thought, evades the grasping hand. It flies from soul to soul; it has this gift and this force—*virum volitare per ora*—that it is everywhere on the lips of men. But the book is distinct from thought; as a book, it is "seizable," so much so that it is sometimes "seized." [illicitly copied, but also impounded, censored.] (Laughter.)

The book, a product of printing, belongs to industry and is the foundation, in all its forms, of a large commercial enterprise. It is bought and sold; it is a form of property, a value created, uncompensated, riches added by the writer to the national wealth. Indeed all must agree, this is the most *compelling* form of property.

Despotic governments violate this property right; they confiscate the book, hoping thus to confiscate the writer. Hence the system of royal pensions. [Pensions for writers, in the place of author's rights.] Take away everything and give back a pittance! This is the attempt to dispossess and to subjugate the writer. One steals, and *then* one buys back a fragment of what one has stolen. It is a wasted effort, however. The writer always escapes. We became poor, he remains free. (Applause.) Who could buy these great minds, Rabelais, Molière, Pascal? But the attempt is nonetheless made, and the result is dismal. Monarchic patronage drains the vital forces of the nation. Historians give Kings the title the "father of the nation" and "fathers of letters"; . . . the result? These two sinister facts: the people without bread, Corneille [the great French author] without shoes. (Long applause).

Gentlemen, let us return to the basic principle: respect for property. Create a system of literary property, but at the same time, create the public domain! Let us go further. Let us expand the idea. The law could give to all publishers the right to publish any book after the death of the author, the only requirement would be to pay the direct heirs a very low fee, which in no case would exceed five or ten percent of the net profit. This simple system, which combines the unquestionable property of the writer with the equally incontestable right of the public domain was suggested by the 1836 commission [on the rights of authors]; and you can find this solution, with all its details, in the minutes of the board, then published by the Ministry of the Interior.

The principle is twofold, do not forget. The book, as a book, is owned by the author, but as a thought, it is owned, it *belongs*—the word is not too extreme—to the human

---

[2] This is our own translation and it is a free one—one that tries to convey the impact that Hugo's powerful, soaring rhetoric would have had to a contemporary French audience, rather than translating literally, word for word. French has its own rhythms and stylistic flourishes; a mixture of passion and formality that can seem odd to the English ear—we have tried to give a sense of those, and probably failed. All the emphases in the text are ours. His are not recorded.

race. All intelligences, all minds, are eligible, all own it. If one of these two rights, the right of the writer and the right of the human mind, were to be sacrificed, it would certainly be the right of the writer, because the public interest is our only concern, and that must take precedence in anything that comes before us. [Numerous sounds of approval.] But, as I just said, this sacrifice is not necessary.

· · · · · · · · · ·

Notes

Hugo was a fabulous—inspiring, passionate—proponent of the rights of authors, and the connection of those rights to free expression and free ideas. He went beyond giving speeches to play a serious role in setting up the current international copyright system. He is held out today as the ultimate proponent of the *droits d'auteur*—the person who said (and he did) that the author's right was the most sacred form of property: unlike other property rights it impoverished no one, because it was over something that was entirely new. (Think of Locke and his point that all property took from the common store. Not so with copyright, said Hugo.) But Hugo was a more subtle thinker than that, as this passage shows.

Questions:

1.) Could Hugo and Macaulay come to agreement?

2.) Hugo calls on the delegates to the Conference (who were to offer suggestions on a new Copyright Bill) to create, or found, a system of literary property but at the same time to create the public domain. How?

3.) Does Hugo think that the public's interest in access is satisfied by the free availability of ideas alone, or does he also want the public to have access to the expression?

4.) In *Golan* Justice Ginsburg said:

> As petitioners put it in this Court, Congress impermissibly revoked their right to exploit foreign works that "belonged to them" once the works were in the public domain. To copyright lawyers, the "vested rights" formulation might sound exactly backwards: Rights typically vest at the *outset* of copyright protection, in an author or rightholder. See, *e.g.,* 17 U.S.C. § 201(a) ("Copyright in a work protected . . . vests initially in the author. . . ."). Once the term of protection ends, the works do not revest in any rightholder. Instead, the works simply lapse into the public domain. See, *e.g.*, Berne, Art. 18(1), 828 U.N.T.S., at 251 ("This Convention shall apply to all works which . . . have not yet fallen into the public domain. . . ."). Anyone has free access to the public domain, but no one, after the copyright term has expired, acquires ownership rights in the once-protected works.

Would Hugo agree?

Samuel L. Clemens [Mark Twain], Statement before the Committee of Patents of the Senate and House to discuss amending the Copyright Act

June 1906

Mr. Clemens. I have read the bill. At least I have read such portions of it as I could understand; and indeed I think no one but a practiced legislator can read the bill and thoroughly understand it, and I am not a practiced legislator. I have had no practice at all in unraveling confused propositions or bills. Not that this is more confused than any other bill. I suppose they are all confused. It is natural that they should be, in a legal paper of that kind, as I understand it. Nobody can understand a legal paper, merely on account of the language that is in it. It is on account of the language that is in it that no one can understand it except an expert.

Necessarily I am interested particularly and especially in the part of the bill which concerns my trade. I like that bill, and I like that extension from the present limit of copyright life of forty-two years to the author's life and fifty years after. I think that will satisfy any reasonable author, because it will take care of his children. Let the grandchildren take care of themselves. "Sufficient unto the day." That would satisfy me very well. That would take care of my daughters, and after that I am not particular. I shall then long have been out of this struggle and independent of it. Indeed, I like the whole bill. It is not objectionable to me. Like all the trades and occupations of the United States, ours is represented and protected in that bill. I like it. I want them to be represented and protected and encouraged. They are all worthy, all important, and if we can take them under our wing by copyright, I would like to see it done. I should like to have you encourage oyster culture and anything else. I have no illiberal feeling toward the bill. I like it. I think it is just. I think it is righteous, and I hope it will pass without reduction or amendment of any kind.

I understand, I am aware, that copyright must have a term, must have a limit, because that is required by the Constitution of the United States, which sets aside the earlier constitution, which we call the Decalogue. The Decalogue says that you shall not take away from any man his property. I do not like to use the harsher term, "Thou shalt not steal."

But the laws of England and America do take away property from the owner. They select out the people who create the literature of the land. Always talk handsomely about the literature of the land. Always say what a fine, a great monumental thing a great literature is. In the midst of their enthusiasm they turn around and do what they can to crush it, discourage it, and put it out of existence. I know that we must have that limit. But forty-two years is too much of a limit. I do not know why there should be a limit at all. I am quite unable to guess why there should be a limit to the possession of the product of a man's labor. There is no limit to real estate. As Doctor Hale has just suggested, you might just as well, after you had discovered a coal mine and worked it twenty-eight years, have the Government step in and take it away—under what pretext?

The excuse for a limited copyright in the United States is that an author who has produced a book and has had the benefit of it for that term has had the profit of it long enough, and therefore the Government takes the property, which does not belong to it, and generously gives it to the eighty-eight millions. That is the idea. If it did that, that would be one thing. But it does not do anything of the kind. It merely takes the author's property, merely takes from his children the bread and profit of that book, and gives the publisher double profit. The publisher, and some of his confederates who are in the conspiracy, rear families in affluence, and they continue the enjoyment of these ill-gotten gains generation after generation. They live forever, the publishers do.

As I say, this limit is quite satisfactory to me—for the author's life, and fifty years after. In a few weeks, or months, or years I shall be out of it. I hope to get a monument. I hope I shall not be entirely forgotten. I shall subscribe to the monument myself. But I shall not be caring what happens if there is fifty years' life of my copyright. My copyrights produce to me annually a good deal more money than I have any use for. But those children of mine have use for that. I can take care of myself as long as I live. I know half a dozen trades, and I can invent a half a dozen more. I can get along. But I like the fifty years' extension, because that benefits my two daughters, who are not as competent to earn a living as I am, because I have carefully raised them as young ladies, who don't know anything and can't do anything. So I hope Congress will extend to them that charity which they have failed to get from me.

Why, if a man who is mad—not mad, but merely strenuous—about race suicide should come to me and try to get me to use my large political or ecclesiastical influence for the passage of a bill by this Congress limiting families to 22 children by one mother, I should try to calm him down. I should reason with him. I should say to him, "That is the very parallel to the copyright limitation by statute. Leave it alone. Leave it alone and it will take care of itself." There is only one couple in the United States that can reach that limit. Now, if they reach that limit let them go on. Make the limit a thousand years. Let them have all the liberty they want. You are not going to hurt anybody in that way. Don't cripple that family and restrict it to 22 children. In doing so you are merely offering this opportunity for activity to one family per year in a nation of eighty millions. It is not worth the while at all.

The very same with copyright. One author per year produces a book which can outlive the forty-two year limit, and that is all. This nation can not produce two authors per year who can create a book that will outlast forty-two years. The thing is demonstrably impossible. It can not be done. To limit copyright is to take the bread out of the mouths of the children of that one author per year, decade, century in and century out. That is all you get out of limiting copyright.

I made an estimate once when I was to be called before the copyright committee of the House of Lords, as to the output of books, and by my estimate we had issued and published in this country since the Declaration of Independence 220,000 books. What was the use of protecting those books by copyright? They are all gone. They had all perished before they were 10 years old. There is only about one book in a thousand that can outlive forty-two years of copyright. Therefore why put a limit at all? You might just as well limit a family to 22. It will take care of itself. If you try to recall to your minds the number of men in the nineteenth century who wrote books in America which books lived forty-two years you will begin with Fennimore Cooper, follow that with Washington Irving, Harriet Beecher Stowe, and Edgar A. Poe, and you will not go far until you begin to find that the list is limited.

You come to Whittier and Holmes and Emerson, and you find Howells and Thomas Bailey Aldrich, and then the list gets pretty thin and you question if you can find 20 persons in the United States in a whole century who have produced books that could outlive or did outlive the forty-two year limit. You can take all the authors in the United States whose books have outlived the forty-two year limit and you can seat them on one bench there. Allow three children to each of them, and you certainly can put the result down at 100 persons. Add two or three more benches. You have plenty of room left. That is the limit of the insignificant number whose bread and butter are to be taken away. For what purpose? For what profit to anybody? Nobody can tell what that profit is. It is only those books that will outlast the forty-two-year limit that have any value after ten or fifteen years. The rest are all dead. Then you turn those few books into the hands of the pirate—into the hands of the legitimate publisher—and they go on, and they get the profit that properly should have gone to wife and children. I do not think that is quite right. I told you what the idea was in this country for a limited copyright.

The English idea of copyright, as I found, was different, when I was before the committee of the House of Lords, composed of seven members I should say. The spokesman was a very able man, Lord Thring, a man of great reputation, but he didn't know anything about copyright and publishing. Naturally he didn't, because he hadn't been brought up to this trade. It is only people who have had intimate personal experience with the triumphs and griefs of an occupation who know how to treat it and get what is justly due.

Now that gentleman had no purpose or desire in the world to rob anybody or anything, but this was the proposition—fifty years' extension—and he asked me what I thought the limit of copyright ought to be.

"Well," I said, "perpetuity." I thought it ought to last forever.

Well, he didn't like that idea very much. I could see some resentment in his manner, and he went on to say that the idea of a perpetual copyright was illogical, and so forth, and so on. And here was his reason—for the reason that it has long ago been decided that ideas are not property, that there can be no such thing as property in ideas. . . . That there could be no such thing as property in an intangible idea. He said, "What is a book? A book is just built from base to roof with ideas, and there can be no property in them." I said I wished he could mention any kind of property existing on this planet, property that had a pecuniary value, which was not derived from an idea or ideas.

"Well," he said, "landed estate—real estate."

"Why," I said, "Take an assumed case, of a dozen Englishmen traveling through the South—Africa—they camp out; eleven of them see nothing at all; they are mentally blind. But there is one in the party who knows what that harbor means, what this lay of the land means; to "him it means that some day—you can not tell when—a railway will come through here, and there on that harbor a great city will spring up. That is his idea. And he has another idea, which is to get a trade, and so, perhaps, he sacrifices his last bottle of Scotch whisky and gives a horse blanket to the principal chief of that region and buys a piece of land the size of Pennsylvania. There is the value of an idea applied to real estate. That day will come, as it was to come when the Cape-to-Cairo Railway should pierce Africa and cities should be built, though there was some smart person who bought the land from the chief and received his everlasting gratitude, just as was the case with William Penn, who bought for $40 worth of stuff the area of Pennsylvania. He did a righteous thing. We have to be enthusiastic over it, because that was a thing that never happened before probably. There was the application of an idea to real estate. Every improvement that is put upon real estate is the result of an idea in somebody's head. A skyscraper is another idea. The railway was another idea. The telephone and all those things are merely symbols which represent ideas. The washtub was the result of an idea. The thing hadn't existed before. There is no property on this earth that does not derive pecuniary value from ideas and association of ideas applied and applied and applied again and again and again, as in the case of the steam engine. You have several hundred people contributing their ideas to the improvement and the final perfection of that great thing, whatever it is—telephone, telegraph, and all."

So if I could have convinced that gentleman that a book which does consist solely of ideas, from the base to the summit, then that would have been the best argument in the world that it is property, like any other property, and should not be put under the ban of any restriction, but that it should be the property of that man and his heirs forever and ever, just as a butcher shop would be, or—I don't care—anything, I don't care what it is. It all has the same basis. The law should recognize the right of perpetuity in this and every other kind of property. But for this property I do not ask that at all. Fifty years from now I shall not be here. I am sorry, but I shall not be here. Still, I should like to see it.

Of course we have to move by slow stages. When a great event happens in this world, like that of 1714, [sic] under Queen Anne, it stops everything, but still, all the world imagines there was an element of justice in that act. They do not know why they imagine it, but it is because somebody else has said so. And that process must continue until our day, and keep constantly progressing on and on. First twenty-eight years was added, and then a renewal for fourteen years; and then you encountered Lord Macaulay, who made a speech on copyright when it was going to achieve a life of sixty years which reduced it to forty years—a speech that was read all over the world by everybody who does not know that Lord Macaulay did not know what he was talking about. So he inflicted this disaster upon his successors in the authorship of books. It has to undergo regular and slow development—evolution.

Here is this bill, one instance of it. Make the limit the author's life and fifty years after, and, as I say, fifty years from now they will see that that has not convulsed the world at all. It has not destroyed any San Francisco. No earthquakes concealed in it anywhere. It has changed nobody. It has merely fed some starving author's children. Mrs. Stowe's [Harriet Beacher Stowe, author of *Uncle Tom's Cabin*] two daughters were close neighbors of mine, and—well, they had their living very much limited. . . .

I say again, as I said in the beginning, I have no enmities, no animosities toward this bill. This bill is plenty righteous enough for me. I like to see all these industries and arts propagated and encouraged by this bill. This bill will do that, and I do hope that it will pass and have no deleterious effect. I do seem to have an extraordinary interest in a whole lot of arts and things. The bill is full of those that I have nothing to do with. But that is in line with my generous, liberal nature. I can't help it. I feel toward those same people the same sort of charity of the man who arrived at home at 2 o'clock in the morning from the club. He was feeling perfect satisfaction with life—was happy, was comfortable. There was his house weaving and weaving and weaving around. So he watched his chance, and by and by when the steps got in his neighborhood he made a jump and he climbed up on the portico. The house went on weaving. He watched his door, and when it came around his way he climbed through it. He got to the stairs, went up on all fours. The house was so unsteady he could hardly make his way, but at last he got up and put his foot down on the top step, but his toe hitched on that step, and of course he crumpled all down and rolled all the way down the stairs and fetched up at the bottom with his arm around the newel post, and he said, "God pity a poor sailor out at sea on a night like this."

The committee adjourned until 10 o'clock a.m. tomorrow.

• • • • • • • • • •

Notes

Samuel Clemens gives a robust argument for perpetual copyright—for the idea that the book is the author's, not by utilitarian privilege but by *right*—and he neatly flips today's assumptions about term extension on their heads. But he is also hilariously cynical, perhaps mindful of the fact that the legislators to whom his words are addressed might be familiar with his prior pronouncements about both them and the law they were considering. "It could probably be shown by facts and figures that there is no distinctly native American criminal class except Congress." "Whenever a copyright law is to be made or altered, then the idiots assemble." "Only one thing is impossible for God: to find any sense in any copyright law on the planet." He is particularly pointed in attacking the compromises with which any copyright bill is loaded—the special provisions that gave American printers special rights to print the books (and thus the unions a strong barrier against foreign competition), that gave libraries certain privileges, indeed that allowed the expiration of copyright at all. All these compromises, from his point of view, are simply takings from authors for the benefit of activities that have little or nothing to do with their art. He even waxes a little absurdist about it. "Like all the trades and occupations of the United States, ours [that of the actual author] is represented and protected in that bill. I like it. I want them to be represented and protected and encouraged. They are all worthy, all important, and if we can take them under our wing by copyright, I would like to see it done. I should like to have you encourage oyster culture and anything else. . . . I do seem to have an extraordinary interest in a whole lot of arts and things. The bill is full of those that I have nothing to do with. But that is in line with my generous, liberal nature." The committee members, eager to shower other celebrities such as John Philip Sousa with questions, offered none after his remarks. Clemens was an old lion—he speaks of his own awareness of mortality in his remarks, and he in fact had only four more years to live— but he still had teeth and a savaging by him might have ended up on the front page of *The New York Times*. And so after his remarks . . . the committee quietly adjourned.

Questions:

1.) Clemens has obviously read Macaulay. On what do they disagree?

2.) He argues that taking away his copyright is as unjust as the government taking away his mine after a certain period of time, saying he had already reaped enough benefit from it. Do you agree? What differences do you see? How would Jefferson and Macaulay respond? Would Hugo agree?

3.) Clemens argues that there would be no real negative effects of term extension because he notes (correctly) that very, very few works retain any commercial value after 42 years. Thus the public loses little, because there are very few works still available for it to buy for which it will now pay higher prices. He was arguing in this testimony for a "life plus fifty" system, which did not in fact get enacted until 1976. We now have a "life plus seventy" system. Is he right that there have been no negative consequences?

Excerpt from
Jennifer Jenkins, In Ambiguous Battle: The Promise (and Pathos) of Public Domain Day, 2014
12 DUKE L. & TECH. REV. 1 (December 31, 2013)

INTRODUCTION: WHAT STREAMS FEED THE PUBLIC DOMAIN?

In Europe, January 1st, 2014 will be the day when the works of Fats Waller, Nikola Tesla, Sergei Rachmaninoff, Elinor Glyn, and hundreds of other authors emerge into the public domain. In Canada, where the copyright term is shorter, a wealth of material—including works from W.E.B. Du Bois, Robert Frost, Aldous Huxley, C.S. Lewis, and Sylvia Plath—will join the realm of free culture.

What is entering the public domain in the United States on January 1? Not a single published work. Why? In 1998, Congress added twenty years to the copyright term. But this term extension was not only granted to future works; it was retroactively applied to existing works. For works created after 1977, the term was extended to life plus 70 years for natural authors, and to 95 years after publication for works of corporate authorship. For works published between 1923 and 1977 that were still in copyright, the terms were extended to 95 years from publication, keeping them out of the public domain for an additional 20 years. The public domain was frozen in time, and artifacts from 1923 won't enter it until 2019.

The Supreme Court rejected a challenge to this retroactive term extension in 2003. Deferring substantially to Congress, the Court held that the law did not violate the constitutional requirement that copyrights last for "limited Times." In addition, the Court declined to apply heightened First Amendment scrutiny, rejecting the petitioners' argument that term extension unconstitutionally restricted the public's ability to make speech- related uses of older works. Then, in 2012, the Court went a step further, and ruled that Congress may constitutionally *remove* works from the public domain, even though citizens—including orchestra conductors, educators, librarians, and film archivists—were already legally using them. According to the majority opinion, while copyright owners had legally protected rights during the copyright term, the public had no First Amendment rights to use material in the public domain: "Anyone has free access to the public domain, but no one, after the copyright term has expired, acquires ownership rights in the once-protected works." The dissenting Justices' disagreement was forceful: "By removing material from the public domain, the statute, in literal terms, 'abridges' a preexisting freedom to speak."

This impoverishment of the public domain stands in stark contrast to the original purpose and history of our copyright laws. As Justice Story explained, the Constitutional purpose of copyright is to "promote the progress of science and the useful arts, and admit the people at large, after a short interval, to the full possession and enjoyment of all writings and inventions without restraint." Accordingly, the original copyright term lasted for 14 years, with the option to renew for another 14 years. Until 1978, the maximum copyright term was 56 years: 28 years from the date of publication, renewable for another 28 years.

Under that relatively recent term, works published in 1957 would enter the public domain on January 1, 2014. These include books ranging from Jack Kerouac's *On The Road* to Ayn Rand's *Atlas Shrugged* to Dr. Seuss's *The Cat in the Hat.* (A variety of constituencies would have cause for celebration.) Joining those books would be the classic films *The Bridge on the River Kwai, Funny Face,* and *A Farewell to Arms,* as well as the first episodes of *Leave It to Beaver.* Under current law, they will remain under copyright until 2053. And famous creations like these are only the beginning. Most works from 1957 are out of circulation—a Congressional Research Service study suggested that only 2 percent of works between 55 and 75 years old continue to retain commercial value.

Those who wish to use such works legally face a series of potential roadblocks. Finding the rights holders of commercially unavailable works can be especially difficult, as the relevant documentation is often lost or buried. These challenges are compounded by the abandonment of "formalities," which coincided with the term extension. Until 1978, the law required copyright owners either to affix a simple notice to their works showing their name and the year of publication, or to register unpublished works with the Copyright Office, in order to receive copyright protection. To maintain copyright, they needed to renew claims with the Copyright Office after an initial term. These requirements produced an evidentiary trail that, in practice, provided the public with basic information about copyright ownership and status—a predicate to efficiently obtaining permission or a license. Without this information, the initial "search costs" can themselves be insurmountable—those who wish to negotiate terms of use cannot find the rights holders in the first place—giving rise to "orphan works." Productive uses are foregone, and forgotten works remain off limits. This legal gridlock entrenches the dividing line between copyright and the public domain, but its costs fall on both sides of that line; in the absence of information *neither* works under copyright, nor those in the public domain, will be efficiently used.

The removal of the renewal requirement further diminished the public domain, by creating copyrights that persisted over works that had exhausted their commercial potential. With renewal, if works were still valuable at the end of their first term, that would provide the incentive to renew; but if not, then the work could pass into the public domain, where it might prove valuable to others. A 1961 study showed that 85 percent of all copyrights were not renewed, and some 93 percent of copyrights in books were not renewed. All of those works went immediately into the public domain. Under current law, however, for the majority of older works, no one is reaping the benefits from continued protection, yet they remain presumptively copyrighted.

The general elimination of formalities had an additional effect. It meant that for the first time the realm of "informal culture"—diaries, home movies, personal photographs—entered the realm of copyright, whether the creators wished it or not. These amateur works, invaluable in detailing our cultural history, are even more likely to be "orphan works" and thus, barring assertions of fair use, effectively off limits to those who would digitize them or use them to chronicle our past. Because these works, too, were subject to the twenty-year term extension, a large swath of informal history became practically unavailable.

These costs in terms of speech and accessibility are high, but what about the countervailing benefits? Copyright's central economic rationale is that exclusive rights spur creativity. However, the incentive effect from prospective term extension is negligible, and from *retrospective* term extension, nonexistent. The 1998 law lengthened the term from life plus 50 to life plus 70 years for natural authors, and from 75 years to 95 years after publication for corporate "works made for hire." Could this extra 20 years of protection, decades in the future, provide additional incentives to authors? The economic evidence suggests that the answer is *no*. Only a minuscule percentage of works retain commercial value by this time. For the term extension to stimulate new creation, authors would have to be incentivized by the remote possibility that their heirs or successors-in-interest would continue to receive revenue beyond the previous terms of life plus 50 years or 75 years after publication. A team of eminent economists estimated that "a 1% likelihood of earning $100 annually for 20 years, starting *75 years into the future*, is worth less than seven cents today"—hardly a compelling economic incentive. And, of course, lengthening the term for works that have already been produced provides no new incentives at all.

Incentives aside, another purported benefit of term extension was that the additional twenty years would encourage rights holders to restore and redistribute their older works. Empirical studies show otherwise: it is not rights holders who wish to digitize and redistribute their older catalogues. It is non-owners who are waiting to do so. When books fall out of copyright, they are more likely to be in print, and available in more editions and formats. Preservationists, not copyright holders, are digitizing deteriorating films and sound recordings, and term extension is inhibiting their efforts. Therefore, keeping older works under copyright frequently frustrates, rather than promotes, their maintenance and dissemination. In the end, while reasonable minds can disagree about the constitutionality of retrospective term extension, it is difficult to argue that the benefits outweigh the costs. The available evidence strongly suggests otherwise.

So, one answer to "What will enter the public domain in 2014?" is simple, and distressing: "Nothing."

Copyright's History

If a page of history is worth a chapter of theory, you are in luck. We now turn to the actual history of copyright and in particular, to the way that copyright has expanded over the years. US copyright law has its roots in England's first copyright law: the Statute of Anne, enacted in 1710. The Statute of Anne marked a significant departure from previous laws in England that had granted an effective monopoly to the Stationers' Company—a printers' guild—by giving its members exclusive privileges to print and distribute books. These privileges were perpetual, as long as a book remained in print. Not only did this system enable a monopoly, it also gave the government a powerful censorship tool, as rights were conferred in exchange for the guild's refusal to print materials that were considered seditious or heretical. The Statute of Anne changed the law by vesting printing rights in authors, rather than printers (although authors often had to transfer their rights to printers in order to make a living). The term of protection was no longer perpetual—it lasted 14 years for new books, plus another 14 years if the author was still living at the end of the first term; books already in print received a single 21 year term. And the new law expressly stated a utilitarian purpose: it was an "Act for the Encouragement of Learning."

The first US Copyright law was passed in 1790, pursuant to the power granted to Congress under the Intellectual Property Clause to "promote the progress . . . by securing for limited times to authors . . . the exclusive rights to their . . . writings." Like the English law, the US law was "an act for the encouragement of learning"; and the initial term of protection was 14 years, with the option to renew for another 14 years if the author was still alive. The scope of copyright was limited: it only covered the "printing, reprinting, publishing and vending" of "maps, charts, and books."

Over the next decades, copyright grew to cover additional subject matter such as music (1831), photographs (1865), and paintings, drawings, and other works of fine art (1870). While musical compositions became eligible for copyright protection in 1831, it wasn't until 1897 that music copyright holders gained the exclusive right to publicly perform their compositions for profit. Until then, they could prevent others from printing and vending their compositions, but not from performing them.

The next major copyright act was enacted in 1909. Under this new law, the copyright term was extended to 28 years from publication, with the option to renew for another 28 years. Copyright holders also gained additional exclusive rights, most notably the right to make an array of derivative works including translations, dramatizations, and adaptations. (An 1870 law had given authors more limited rights to control translations and dramatizations, but those rights were part of an opt-in system.) Before derivative work rights were reserved to authors, you needed permission to print or "vend"—we would now say "distribute"—a copyrighted work, but it was perfectly legal to translate, adapt, or otherwise build upon those works, because the policy behind copyright favored such follow-on creativity.

Perhaps the most striking difference between the 1909 Act and current copyright law (see below) was that copyright protection was conditioned upon "formalities": namely, 1) *publication* of a work with 2) a copyright *notice*—e.g. Copyright 2014, John Smith. To maintain copyright after the first 28-year term, authors had to *renew* their rights. Works published without proper notice went into the public domain, as did works whose subsisting copyrights were not renewed. At the time, *unpublished* works were generally subject to state common law copyright rather than the federal scheme. (Note that "publication" under the 1909 Act had a specific legal meaning that can make the determination of whether or not a work was published less than obvious.)

While 1909 may seem somewhat distant, the 1909 Act is still relevant in many circumstances because some of its key provisions govern works that were created up until 1978. For example, its formalities requirements may affect the copyright status of certain pre-1978 works. Successive extensions of the copyright term (see below) mean that only works published almost a century ago are conclusively in the public domain. Works published before 1978 go into the public domain on January 1st the year after a 95-year copyright term—so works published in 1930 go into the public domain on 1/1/2026 (1930+95+1). However, because of the 1909 Act's notice and renewal requirements, works from before 1978 published without notice, as well as works from before 1964 that were published with notice but whose copyrights were not renewed, are also in the public domain. Before you make plans to use these works, however, note that tracking down publication, notice, and renewal information for older works can be prohibitively difficult.

The 1976 Copyright Act

The basic framework of today's copyright law is provided by the 1976 Copyright Act, which has been amended many times. It took effect on January 1, 1978, and has been amended numerous times. Unlike the 1909 Act, the 1976 Act covers both published and unpublished works, and preempts state common law. 17 U.S.C. § 301. Its provisions will be the subject of the bulk of the readings in this book. Here is a brief summary of its key features; you will be learning more about them in the coming weeks.

In terms of subject matter, current copyright law has expanded over time to include motion pictures, choreographic works, architectural works, computer programs, and more. Within those categories, copyright protection only subsists in "original" works that are "fixed in any tangible medium of expression." 17 U.S.C. § 102(a). "Original" does not mean novel, it merely means that the work was independently created, and not copied from other works. (If we both write exactly the same love song without copying one another, we are both entitled to a copyright.) In addition, copyright only covers creative "expression," and never extends to "any idea, procedure, process, system, method of operation, concept, principle, or discovery." 17 U.S.C. § 102(b). Some subject matter, such as sound recordings, semiconductor chips, and boat hulls, are subject to their own special rules under the Copyright Act.

In terms of rights, copyright holders now enjoy the exclusive rights of 1) reproduction, 2) making derivative works, 3) distribution, 4) public performance, 5) and public display. 17 U.S.C. § 106. Outside of the scope of these rights, the copyright owner is not entitled to control other uses of her work, such as private performance. In addition, the exclusive rights themselves are subject to limitations and exceptions, such as fair use and first sale. 17 U.S.C. §§ 107, 109. When an exclusive right is infringed, however, innocent intent is not a defense, because copyright is a strict liability system. (Innocent infringement can limit remedies, for example by reducing the damage award.)

While copyrights initially vest in the "author," this does not necessarily mean that they are owned by the individual who created the work. In the case of "works made for hire," the corporation or employer is considered the author. When multiple parties contribute to a work, the copyright can be owned by "joint authors." Copyrights are transferrable, and are often transferred numerous times during the course of their (now very long) lifespan. The complex rules about copyright ownership and transfer are in 17 U.S.C. §§ 201–05 of the Copyright Act.

Regarding duration, the 1976 Copyright Act initially expanded the copyright term from a possible total of 56 years under the 1909 Act (28 years plus the optional 28-year renewal term) to a single term of life plus 50 years for natural authors, and 75 years after publication for corporate works. In 1998, the term was further expanded to life of the author plus 70 years, and 95 years from publication for works of corporate authorship. This 20-year term extension did not just apply to new works, but also retrospectively to works already in existence, meaning that no published works entered the public domain until 2019. The rules governing copyright duration can be found at 17 U.S.C. §§ 302–04.

Current copyright law has also eliminated the "formalities" required by the 1909 Act. Copyright now automatically attaches to an eligible work the moment it is fixed in a tangible medium of expression. There is no need to include a copyright notice or renew the copyright after a specified period of time. There is also no need to register the work with the Copyright Office. That said, registration does become necessary if a copyright holder wants to bring an action for infringement. 17 U.S.C. § 411(a). (If the Copyright Office refuses registration, a plaintiff can still sue as long as she notifies the Register of Copyrights, who then has the option of intervening on the issue of registrability.) Registration also confers a number of benefits in the event of a lawsuit: registration within 3 months of publication (or within 1 month of learning about the infringement, if that is earlier) is a prerequisite for statutory damages and attorneys' fees, and registration within five years of publication provides prima facie evidence of copyright validity. 17 U.S.C. §§ 412, 410(c).

One reason that the US removed formalities was to comply with the Berne Convention for the Protection of Literary and Artistic Works, a major international copyright treaty. The US began relaxing formalities with passage of the 1976 Act, and then eliminated them on March 1, 1989 when it officially joined the Berne Convention, which requires that rights "shall not be subject to any formality." (Like many international IP treaties, the Berne Convention provides for both minimum standards and "national treatment," meaning that signatories must grant nationals from other participating countries the same rights as they give to their own nationals. Whether the US is currently in compliance with all aspects of the Berne Convention is the subject of continuing debate, and something you may explore in courses on international intellectual property.) Aside from adhering with Berne, another reason that the US removed formalities involved practical and policy concerns. Authors who were unfamiliar or unable to comply with formalities might unwittingly forfeit protection; automatic copyright ensured that this would not happen.

In 1998, Congress amended the Copyright Act by passing the Digital Millennium

Copyright Act ("DMCA"). Among its key features are new legal protections for "technological measures" that control access to copyrighted works, and safe harbors for providers of a variety of online services, including internet access, hosting, and linking. The DMCA will be explored in more detail in subsequent chapters.

In 2020, Congress passed the "Copyright Alternative in Small-Claims Enforcement Act of 2019" ("CASE Act"), as part of a COVID-19 relief bill. (No, copyright enforcement has nothing to do with COVID relief; this was an irrelevant provision inserted into the omnibus bill.) The CASE Act establishes an administrative tribunal called the Copyright Claims Board ("CCB") within the US Copyright Office that will decide copyright claims of $30,000 or less. Determinations are rendered by three attorneys serving as Copyright Claims Officers, two having "substantial experience" with copyright claims, and one with alternative dispute resolution expertise. A defendant wishing to proceed in court rather than the CCB can opt out within 60 days after notification of the claim. If the defendant fails to opt out and receives an adverse determination, there are limited grounds for appeal: the decision can be challenged on the basis of fraud, corruption, misrepresentation, or misconduct, but not substantive error. Proponents of the CASE Act argue that it will help rightsholders keep up with the frequency of infringement online by giving them a cheaper, more efficient enforcement mechanism for small claims. Opponents argue that, in practice, the process will be used by large copyright holders and "copyright trolls" to extract payments from less savvy defendants who may not know how to opt out or successfully defend against a claim. (Copyright trolls were defined by a judge as those who bring copyright claims "as a profit-making scheme rather than as a deterrent.") Copyright is complex, and these streamlined proceedings may be ill-suited to handle nuanced issues like "fair use" (covered in Chapter 13), making it difficult for respondents to avail themselves of such defenses.

Copyright Expansions and Policy

Take a moment to review the copyright history briefly sketched above, and consider the way that copyright has expanded over time in response to technological and market developments. The original copyright act from 1790 only governed the printing, publishing, and vending of books, maps, and charts. In 1850, even though musical compositions had recently been added to this list, your school orchestra could freely perform any composition because public performances were not reserved to the copyright holder. Nor were any derivative works rights—as a follow-on creator, you could translate books into other languages, or adapt them for theater, or build upon them in your own work.

The term of protection has lengthened markedly in recent years. Until 1978, it lasted for a possible total of 56 years—28 years from the date of publication, plus the option to renew for another 28 years—with the majority of works entering the public domain after the first 28-year term (studies put the rate of non-renewal for all works at 85%, and for books alone at 93%). Now the term is 70 years after the death of the author, and 95 years after publication for corporate works. Because this span outlasts the economic viability of most works, only a small percentage of copyrighted works benefits from this longer term; a Congressional study suggested that only 2 percent of works between 55 and 75 years old continue to retain commercial value. As time goes on, an increasing amount of material is out of print, but still in copyright. Many libraries, creators, and others are prevented from using this material because the expanded term, along with the elimination of formalities, has made it especially difficult to find the rights holders. The result is a growing corpus of "orphan works"—those whose authors cannot be identified or located, keeping them off limits to users who are seeking permission. As the Copyright Office has explained: "For good faith users, orphan works are a frustration, a liability risk, and a major cause of gridlock in the digital marketplace. . . . This outcome is difficult if not impossible to reconcile with the objectives of the copyright system and may unduly restrict access to millions of works that might otherwise be available to the public." This is the flip-side of the argument Samuel Clemens made in 1906. He assumed that there would be no loss to the public, because—while the term was extended—the demand for the book would not be. Thus no one would lose. Do you agree after reading the excerpt from Jenkins' article? Of course in 1906, the idea of scanning and digitizing the world's cultural heritage would have seemed like a fever-dream.

To address the orphan works problem, there is currently a push toward reform. In addition, the Register of Copyrights has suggested that, toward the end of the term, continued copyright should be conditioned upon registration with the Copyright Office, so that older works are not unnecessarily kept from the public, while successful works can still register and maintain protection.

As you have read elsewhere in these materials, the primary purpose of US copyright law is to benefit the public. (Hugo, interestingly, accepts this formulation. Clemens does so only with great irony.) It does so by granting limited exclusive rights to authors, in order to provide an economic incentive to create and distribute creative material. But the ultimate goal is to ensure that the public will benefit from the diffusion of knowledge and culture. In the words of the Supreme Court, "The immediate effect of our copyright law is to secure a fair return for an 'author's' creative labor. But the ultimate aim is, by this incentive, to stimulate artistic creativity for the general public good." *Twentieth Century Music Corp. v. Aiken* (1975). Copyright law is, at its core, "[a]n act for the encouragement of learning." Its ability to achieve this objective depends upon a continually recalibrated balance between that which is subject to private control, and that which is free for the public to use and build upon.

As you read through the upcoming materials, consider the following questions. Is copyright in its current form fulfilling its purpose? How have its scope, duration, and impact changed? How about countervailing limitations and exceptions? How do the challenges posed by new technologies inflect your analysis?

Copyright Office

As part of your introduction to copyright, please spend some time exploring the Copyright Office website at http://www.copyright.gov. You can find out how to register copyright, search the Copyright Office's records, and read their explanatory Circulars and Brochures. In general, registering a copyright is more straightforward (and much cheaper) than registering a trademark. If you are a creator, consider registering your work *via* the Copyright Office website as an introductory exercise.

Note: A Copyright Flow Chart

On the next page you will find a copyright flow chart which parallels the trademark law flow chart you may already have encountered. The chart explains what we will be covering in each chapter and how the legal questions discussed will play a role in a copyright analysis. Second, you can refer to the chart to help you with the Problems in this section. Use it to remind yourself of the structure of the analysis and to make sure you are not missing an issue.

COPYRIGHT FLOW CHART
(This is a (highly) simplified preview of what you will learn and a tool to use in the problems. Refer to it often.)

Does the plaintiff own a valid copyright? (Chapter 11)

Is the copied material ORIGINAL, CREATIVE EXPRESSION?

For copyright purposes, "original" doesn't mean novel, it means that the plaintiff "independently created" the material—in other words, that she didn't copy it from other works—AND that it possessed a "modicum of creativity."

"Expression" is protected, but facts and "ideas" are not; nor is expression that "merges" with the idea.

NO →

YES

Did the defendant infringe that copyright? (Chapter 12)

Is there sufficient evidence of ACCESS?

"Access" means that the defendant had a reasonable opportunity to copy the plaintiff's work. It is typically shown through 1) widespread dissemination of the plaintiff's work or 2) a chain of events linking the plaintiff and defendant. In some cases, STRIKING SIMILARITY can allow for a presumption of access.

NO →

Is there direct evidence of copying?

NO →

YES

YES

NO COPYRIGHT INFRINGEMENT

Is there SUBSTANTIAL SIMILARITY between the plaintiff's and defendant's works? Only similarities to copyright-protected elements of plaintiff's work are relevant. Copying material such as ideas, facts, and *scènes à faire* (elements that have become standard or indispensable for a topic or genre) is not infringement.

There is no bright line rule about the necessary degree of similarity. Substantiality can be either quantitative (a large amount of plaintiff's work was copied) or qualitative (an important part of plaintiff's work was copied). In either case, the similarity must be to portions protected by copyright. Trivial or *de minimis* copying falls beneath the threshold of substantial similarity.

(In practice, if the defendant has engaged in wholesale, direct copying, a full analysis of access and similarity will obviously be unnecessary.)

NO →

YES

Was the copying FAIR USE? (Chapter 13) ——————— **YES** →

NO

COPYRIGHT INFRINGEMENT

CHAPTER ELEVEN

Copyrightable Subject Matter

What does copyright cover?

Images from Aoki, Boyle, and Jenkins, *Theft! A History of Music* (available for free online at https://law.duke.edu/musiccomic/).

Copyrightable Subject Matter

As with trademark, the first question to ask with copyright is "what subject matter does it cover?" By that we do not merely mean "what media forms does copyright cover?" Before we even get to the question of when copyright came to cover music, recordings, or photographs, there is a deeper premise we have to understand. As the last chapter made clear, copyright starts with a remarkable and dramatic choice, the choice that Krause was unable to understand, but that Hugo and Fichte stressed. It does not cover ideas or unoriginal compilations of fact. When I publish my book, the ideas and facts within it go immediately into the public domain—no need to wait for my lifetime plus another seventy years to get them. Copyright covers only the *original expression*. This point comes with a corollary. There is no original expression in the design of a water filter or a mousetrap. There may be *genius*, in the sense of making a technological leap that is way beyond the current state of the art, but we do not look at the lightbulb and say "Ah, the filament— that's just so Edison! That's just the way that he, and only he, would express the idea *'glow, sucker, glow!'*" Focusing only on expression, copyright never covers purely functional or useful articles, never covers discoveries or inventions. If they are to be covered by rights at all, those are in the domain of patent.

This chapter will go through the criteria for copyrightable subject matter, many of which, as we saw in Chapter 3, have a constitutional dimension. As you consider them, compare them to the limitations on trademark subject matter. Notice how the subject matter limitations trace both the functional goals that the right is to fulfill and the need to limit the ambit of the right in order to allow for the requirements of speech, debate and competition. But notice also how those reasons do not explain *all* of the subject matter delineations— and in some cases may be flatly contradictory to them.

We will look at:

- the requirement of originality, meeting the *Feist* case again,
- the idea/expression (and idea/fact) distinction,
- the linked idea of "merger" where the expression merges with the idea and therefore cannot be owned,
- the "useful articles" doctrine—which limits the reach of copyright on designs that are both functional and expressive,
- the exclusion of "methods of operation" from copyright, and
- the requirement of fixation in material form.

But it is easy to get lost in the picky details of each subsection. As you will see, many of these cases could be classified as dealing with multiple subject matter limitations. When I refuse to extend copyright to the way an accounting method is implemented, is that the idea/expression distinction, a method of operation or something else altogether? The important question is the basic one, "Why do we have this limitation on copyright's subject matter? How does including or excluding this material further the constitutional and statutory scheme?"

In addition, this section leads into another of the central and recurrent themes of the book: the interaction between intellectual property and technology. This entire chapter, but in particular the last two sections—on methods of operation and on fixation—begin a unit dealing with copyright and software. The software unit is layered on top of the doctrinal material of the course. We will be learning the rules about copyrightable subject matter, infringement and substantial similarity, fair use, the interaction between copyright and licenses—all subjects that transcend the technology. But at the same time many of those subjects have a particular twist or valence when they are inside the world of computing.

Thus we will simultaneously be studying the way the courts took the ancient niches of copyright and trimmed and stretched them to fit the new threats and opportunities of software. (As you read the later sections of this chapter, compare what you see to the way courts adapted trademark law to fit the world of domain names and search engines.)

§ 102 Subject matter of copyright: In general

(a) Copyright protection subsists, in accordance with this title, in original works of authorship fixed in any tangible medium of expression, now known or later developed, from which they can be perceived, reproduced, or otherwise communicated, either directly or with the aid of a machine or device. Works of authorship include the following categories:

> **(1) literary works;**
>
> **(2) musical works, including any accompanying words;**
>
> **(3) dramatic works, including any accompanying music;**
>
> **(4) pantomimes and choreographic works;**
>
> **(5) pictorial, graphic, and sculptural works;**
>
> **(6) motion pictures and other audiovisual works;**
>
> **(7) sound recordings; and**
>
> **(8) architectural works.**

(b) In no case does copyright protection for an original work of authorship extend to any idea, procedure, process, system, method of operation, concept, principle, or discovery, regardless of the form in which it is described, explained, illustrated, or embodied in such work.

1.) Originality: Independent Creation and a Modicum of Creativity

Feist v. Rural Telephone Service
499 U.S. 340 (1991)

Justice O'CONNOR delivered the opinion of the Court.

This case requires us to clarify the extent of copyright protection available to telephone directory white pages.

I

Rural Telephone Service Company, Inc., is a certified public utility that provides telephone service to several communities in northwest Kansas. It is subject to a state regulation that requires all telephone companies operating in Kansas to issue annually an updated telephone directory. Accordingly, as a condition of its monopoly franchise, Rural publishes a typical telephone directory, consisting of white pages and yellow pages. The white pages list in alphabetical order the names of Rural's subscribers, together with their towns and telephone numbers. The yellow pages list Rural's business subscribers alphabetically by category and feature classified advertisements of various sizes. Rural distributes its directory free of charge to its subscribers, but earns revenue by selling yellow pages advertisements.

Feist Publications, Inc., is a publishing company that specializes in area-wide telephone directories. Unlike a typical directory, which covers only a particular calling area, Feist's area-wide directories cover a much larger geographical range, reducing the need to call directory assistance or consult multiple directories. The Feist directory that is the subject of this litigation covers 11 different telephone service areas in 15 counties and contains 46,878 white pages listings—compared to Rural's approximately 7,700 listings. Like Rural's directory, Feist's is distributed free of charge and includes both white pages and yellow pages. Feist and Rural compete vigorously for yellow pages advertising.

Feist area-wide telephone directory

As the sole provider of telephone service in its service area, Rural obtains subscriber information quite easily. Persons desiring telephone service must apply to Rural and provide their names and addresses; Rural then assigns them a telephone number. Feist is not a telephone company, let alone one with monopoly status, and therefore lacks independent access to any subscriber information. To obtain white pages listings for its area-wide directory, Feist approached each of the 11 telephone companies operating in northwest Kansas and offered to pay for the right to use its white pages listings.

Of the 11 telephone companies, only Rural refused to license its listings to Feist. Rural's refusal created a problem for Feist, as omitting these listings would have left a gaping hole in its area-wide directory, rendering it less attractive to potential yellow pages advertisers. In a decision subsequent to that which we review here, the District Court determined that this was precisely the reason Rural refused to license its listings. The refusal was motivated by an unlawful purpose "to extend its monopoly in telephone service to a monopoly in yellow pages advertising."

Unable to license Rural's white pages listings, Feist used them without Rural's consent. Feist began by removing several thousand listings that fell outside the geographic range of its area-wide directory, then hired personnel to investigate the 4,935 that remained. These employees verified the data reported by Rural and sought to obtain additional information. As a result, a typical Feist listing includes the individual's street address; most of Rural's listings do not. Notwithstanding these additions, however, 1,309 of the 46,878 listings in Feist's 1983 directory were identical to listings in Rural's 1982–1983 white pages. Four of these were fictitious listings that Rural had inserted into its directory to detect copying.

II

A

This case concerns the interaction of two well-established propositions. The first is that facts are not copyrightable; the other, that compilations of facts generally are. Each of these propositions possesses an impeccable pedigree. That there can be no valid copyright in facts is universally understood. The most fundamental axiom of copyright law is that "[n]o author may copyright his ideas or the facts he narrates." *Harper & Row* (1985). Rural wisely concedes this point, noting in its brief that "[f]acts and discoveries, of course, are not themselves subject to copyright protection." At the same time, however, it is beyond dispute that compilations of facts are within the subject matter of copyright. . . .

There is an undeniable tension between these two propositions. Many compilations consist of nothing but raw data—*i.e.,* wholly factual information not accompanied by any original written expression. On what basis may one claim a copyright in such a work? Common sense tells us that 100 uncopyrightable facts do not magically change their status when gathered together in one place. Yet copyright law seems to contemplate that compilations that consist exclusively of facts are potentially within its scope.

The key to resolving the tension lies in understanding why facts are not copy-rightable. The *sine qua non* of copyright is originality. To qualify for copyright protection, a work must be original to the author. See *Harper & Row*. Original, as the term is used in copyright, means only that the work was independently created by the author (as opposed to copied from other works), and that it possesses at least some minimal degree of creativity. To be sure, the requisite level of creativity is extremely low; even a slight amount will suffice. The vast majority of works make the grade quite easily, as they possess some creative spark, "no matter how crude, humble or obvious" it might be. Originality does not signify novelty; a work may be original even though it closely resembles other works so long as the similarity is fortuitous, not the result of copying. To illustrate, assume that two poets, each ignorant of the other, compose identical poems. Neither work is novel, yet both are original and, hence, copyrightable.

Originality is a constitutional requirement. The source of Congress' power to enact copyright laws is Article I, § 8, cl. 8, of the Constitution, which authorizes Congress to "secur[e] for limited Times to Authors . . . the exclusive Right to their respective Writings." In two decisions from the late 19th century—*The Trade-Mark Cases* (1879); and *Burrow-Giles Lithographic Co. v. Sarony* (1884)—this Court defined the crucial terms "authors" and "writings." In so doing, the Court made it unmistakably clear that these terms presuppose a degree of originality.

In *The Trade-Mark Cases*, the Court addressed the constitutional scope of "writings." For a particular work to be classified "under the head of writings of authors," the Court determined, "originality is required." The Court explained that originality requires independent creation plus a modicum of creativity: "[W]hile the word *writings* may be liberally construed, as it has been, to include original designs for engraving, prints, &c., it is only such as are *original*, and are founded in the creative powers of the mind. The writings which are to be protected are *the fruits of intellectual labor*, embodied in the form of books, prints, engravings, and the like."

In *Burrow-Giles*, the Court distilled the same requirement from the Constitution's use of the word "authors." The Court defined "author," in a constitutional sense, to mean "he to whom anything owes its origin; originator; maker." As in *The Trade-Mark Cases*, the Court emphasized the creative component of originality. It described copyright as being limited to "original intellectual conceptions of the author," and stressed the importance of requiring an author who accuses another of infringement to prove "the existence of those facts of originality, of intellectual production, of thought, and conception."

The originality requirement articulated in *The Trade-Mark Cases* and *Burrow-Giles* remains the touchstone of copyright protection today. See *Goldstein v. California* (1973). It is the very "premise of copyright law." *Miller v. Universal City Studios, Inc.* (1981). Leading scholars agree on this point. As one pair of commentators succinctly puts it: "The originality requirement is *constitutionally mandated* for all works." Patterson & Joyce 763 (1989).

It is this bedrock principle of copyright that mandates the law's seemingly disparate treatment of facts and factual compilations. "No one may claim originality as to facts." Nimmer § 2.11[A]. This is because facts do not owe their origin to an act of authorship. The distinction is one between creation and discovery: The first person to find and report a particular fact has not created the fact; he or she has merely discovered its existence. To borrow from *Burrow-Giles*, one who discovers a fact is not its "maker" or "originator." "The discoverer merely finds and records." Nimmer § 2.03[E]. Census-takers, for example, do not "create" the population figures that emerge from their efforts; in a sense, they copy these figures from the world around them. Census data therefore do not trigger copyright because these data are not "original" in the constitutional sense. The same is true of all facts—scientific, historical, biographical, and news of the day. "They may not be copyrighted and are part of the public domain available to every person." *Miller*.

Factual compilations, on the other hand, may possess the requisite originality. The compilation author typically chooses which facts to include, in what order to place them, and how to arrange the collected data so that they may be used effectively by readers. These choices as to selection and arrangement, so long as they are made independently by the compiler and entail a minimal degree of creativity, are sufficiently original that Congress may protect such compilations through the copyright laws. Thus, even a directory that contains absolutely no protectible written expression, only facts, meets the constitutional minimum for copyright protection if it features an original selection or arrangement. See *Harper & Row*.

This protection is subject to an important limitation. The mere fact that a work is copyrighted does not mean that every element of the work may be protected. Originality remains the *sine qua non* of copyright; accordingly, copyright protection may extend only to those components of a work that are original to the author. Thus, if the compilation author clothes facts with an original collocation of words, he or she may be able to claim a copyright in this written expression. Others may copy the underlying facts from the publication, but not the precise words used to present them. In *Harper & Row*, for example, we explained that President Ford could not prevent others from copying bare historical facts from his autobiography, but that he could prevent others from copying his "subjective descriptions and portraits of public figures." Where the compilation author adds no written expression but rather lets the facts speak for themselves, the expressive element is more elusive. The only conceivable expression is the manner in which the compiler has selected and arranged the facts. Thus, if the selection and arrangement are original, these elements of the work are eligible for copyright protection. No matter how original the format, however, the facts themselves do not become original through association.

This inevitably means that the copyright in a factual compilation is thin. Notwithstanding a valid copyright, a subsequent compiler remains free to use the facts contained in another's publication to aid in preparing a competing work, so long as the competing work does not feature the same selection and arrangement. As one commentator explains it: "[N]o matter how much original authorship the work displays, the facts and ideas it exposes are free for the taking. . . . [T]he very same facts and ideas may be divorced from the context imposed by the author, and restated or reshuffled by second comers, even if the author was the first to discover the facts or to propose the ideas." Ginsburg, Creation and Commercial Value: Copyright Protection of Works of Information (1990).

It may seem unfair that much of the fruit of the compiler's labor may be used by others without compensation. As Justice Brennan has correctly observed, however, this is not "some unforeseen byproduct of a statutory scheme." *Harper & Row*. It is, rather, "the essence of copyright" and a constitutional requirement. The primary objective of copyright is not to reward the labor of authors, but "[t]o promote the Progress of Science and useful Arts." Art. I, § 8, cl. 8. To this end, copyright assures authors the right to their original expression, but encourages others to build freely upon the ideas and information conveyed by a work. This principle, known as the idea-expression or fact-expression dichotomy, applies to all works of authorship. As applied to a factual compilation, assuming the absence of original written expression, only the compiler's selection and arrangement may be protected; the raw facts may be copied at will. This result is neither unfair nor unfortunate. It is the means by which copyright advances the progress of science and art.

This Court has long recognized that the fact-expression dichotomy limits severely the scope of protection in fact-based works. More than a century ago, the Court observed: "The very object of publishing a book on science or the useful arts is to communicate to the world the useful knowledge which it contains. But this object would be frustrated if the knowledge could not be used without incurring the guilt of piracy of the book." *Baker v. Selden* (1880). We reiterated this point in *Harper & Row*:

"[N]o author may copyright facts or ideas. The copyright is limited to those aspects of the work—termed 'expression'—that display the stamp of the author's originality.

"[C]opyright does not prevent subsequent users from copying from a prior author's work those constituent elements that are not original—for example . . . facts, or materials in the public domain—as long as such use does not unfairly appropriate the author's original contributions."

This, then, resolves the doctrinal tension: Copyright treats facts and factual compilations in a wholly consistent manner. Facts, whether alone or as part of a compilation, are not original and therefore may not be copyrighted. A factual compilation is eligible for copyright if it features an original selection or arrangement of facts, but the copyright is limited to the particular selection or arrangement. In no event may copyright extend to the facts themselves.

III

There is no doubt that Feist took from the white pages of Rural's directory a substantial amount of factual information. At a minimum, Feist copied the names, towns, and telephone numbers of 1,309 of Rural's subscribers. Not all copying, however, is copyright infringement. To establish infringement, two elements must be proven: (1) ownership of a valid copyright, and (2) copying of constituent elements of the work that are original. See *Harper & Row*. The first element is not at issue here; Feist appears to concede that Rural's directory, considered as a whole, is subject to a valid copyright because it contains some foreword text, as well as original material in its yellow pages advertisements.

The question is whether Rural has proved the second element. In other words, did Feist, by taking 1,309 names, towns, and telephone numbers from Rural's white pages, copy anything that was "original" to Rural? Certainly, the raw data does not satisfy the originality requirement. Rural may have been the first to discover and report the names, towns, and telephone numbers of its subscribers, but this data does not "'ow[e] its origin'" to Rural. *Burrow-Giles*. Rather, these bits of information are uncopyrightable facts; they existed before Rural reported them and would have continued to exist if Rural had never published a telephone directory. The originality requirement "rule[s] out protecting . . . names, addresses, and telephone numbers of which the plaintiff by no stretch of the imagination could be called the author." Patterson & Joyce 776.

The question that remains is whether Rural selected, coordinated, or arranged these uncopyrightable facts in an original way. As mentioned, originality is not a stringent standard; it does not require that facts be presented in an innovative or surprising way. It is equally true, however, that the selection and arrangement of facts cannot be so mechanical or routine as to require no creativity whatsoever. The standard of originality is low, but it does exist. As this Court has explained, the Constitution mandates some minimal degree of creativity, see *The Trade-Mark Cases*, and an author who claims infringement must prove "the existence of . . . intellectual production, of thought, and conception." *Burrow-Giles*.

The selection, coordination, and arrangement of Rural's white pages do not satisfy the minimum constitutional standards for copyright protection. As mentioned at the outset, Rural's white pages are entirely typical. Persons desiring telephone service in Rural's service area fill out an application and Rural issues them a telephone number. In preparing its white pages, Rural simply takes the data provided by its subscribers and lists it alphabetically by surname. The end product is a garden-variety white pages directory, devoid of even the slightest trace of creativity.

Rural's selection of listings could not be more obvious: It publishes the most basic information—name, town, and telephone number—about each person who applies to it for telephone service. This is "selection" of a sort, but it lacks the modicum of creativity necessary to transform mere selection into copyrightable expression. Rural expended sufficient effort to make the white pages directory useful, but insufficient creativity to make it original.

We note in passing that the selection featured in Rural's white pages may also fail the originality requirement for another reason. Feist points out that Rural did not truly "select" to publish the names and telephone numbers of its subscribers; rather, it was required to do so by the Kansas Corporation Commission as part of its monopoly franchise. Accordingly, one could plausibly conclude that this selection was dictated by state law, not by Rural.

Nor can Rural claim originality in its coordination and arrangement of facts. The white pages do nothing more than list Rural's subscribers in alphabetical order. This arrangement may, technically speaking, owe its origin to Rural; no one disputes that Rural undertook the task of alphabetizing the names itself. But there is nothing remotely creative about arranging names alphabetically in a white pages directory. It is an age-old practice, firmly rooted in tradition and so commonplace that it has come to be expected as a matter of course. It is not only unoriginal, it is practically inevitable. This time-honored tradition does not possess the minimal creative spark required by the Copyright Act and the Constitution.

We conclude that the names, towns, and telephone numbers copied by Feist were not original to Rural and therefore were not protected by the copyright in Rural's combined white and yellow pages directory. As a constitutional matter, copyright protects only those constituent elements of a work that possess more than a *de minimis* quantum of creativity. Rural's white pages, limited to basic subscriber information and arranged alphabetically, fall short of the mark. As a statutory matter, 17 U.S.C. § 101 does not afford protection from copying to a collection of facts that are selected, coordinated, and arranged in a way that utterly lacks originality. Given that some works must fail, we cannot imagine a more likely candidate. Indeed, were we to hold that Rural's white pages pass muster, it is hard to believe that any collection of facts could fail.

Because Rural's white pages lack the requisite originality, Feist's use of the listings cannot constitute infringement. This decision should not be construed as demeaning Rural's efforts in compiling its directory, but rather as making clear that copyright rewards originality, not effort. As this Court noted more than a century ago, "'great praise may be due to the plaintiffs for their industry and enterprise in publishing this paper, yet the law does not contemplate their being rewarded in this way.'" *Baker v. Selden.* The judgment of the Court of Appeals is
Reversed.

Questions:

1.) What balance does *Feist* strike between efficient information flow and property rights? Between property in *innovation* and property in *information*?

2.) Let us return to a question we asked in Chapter 2 about the constitutional limitations on intellectual property. In *The Trade-Mark Cases* the Court said: "If we should endeavor to classify [a trademark] under the head of writings of authors, the objections are equally strong. In this, as in regard to inventions, originality is required." Where does this limitation appear in the Intellectual Property Clause? Is there a textual basis? A philosophical basis? Both? Revisiting this question in the light of the *Feist* case, what is your answer?

The next two cases, which provide additional fodder for Problem 11-1, take the statutory and constitutional originality limitation and add to it an additional statutory subject matter wrinkle. Under § 105 of the Copyright Act, "Copyright protection under this title is not available for any work of the United States Government, but the United States Government is not precluded from receiving and holding copyrights transferred to it by assignment, bequest, or otherwise." This is a hugely important and consequential component of U.S. information policy. Unoriginal compilations of fact are not covered by copyright and even expressive works are not covered by copyright if they are works of the Federal government. From the free availability of weather and navigational data, to the public domain status of government reports, NASA photographs and the *CIA World Factbook*, the combination of the originality requirement and § 105 operates to shape our information environment in profound ways. (For example, whatever other laws Edward Snowden or Bradley/Chelsea Manning may or may not have broken, they did *not* violate copyright, and neither did those who reproduced the documents they leaked.) But this combination also shapes the availability of Federal legal materials, as the next two cases will show.

Matthew Bender & Co., Inc. v. West Publishing Co.
158 F.3d 674 (2d Cir. 1998)

JACOBS, Circuit Judge.

West Publishing Co. and West Publishing Corp. (collectively "West") publish compilations of reports of judicial opinions ("case reports"). Each case report consists of the text of the judicial opinion with enhancements that for the purposes of this case can be put in two categories: (i) independently composed features, such as a syllabus (which digests and heralds the opinion's general holdings), headnotes (which summarize the specific points of law recited in each opinion), and key numbers (which categorize points of law into different legal topics and subtopics), and (ii) additions of certain factual information to the text of the opinions, including parallel or alternative citations to cases, attorney information, and data on subsequent procedural history. HyperLaw, Inc. publishes compact disc-read only memory ("CD-ROM") compilations of Supreme Court and United States Court of Appeals decisions, and intervened as a plaintiff to seek a judgment declaring that the individual West case reports that are left after redaction of the first category of alterations (i.e., the independently composed features), do not contain copyrightable material. . . .

It is true that neither novelty nor invention is a requisite for copyright protection, but minimal creativity is required. Aside from its syllabi, headnotes and key numbers—none of which HyperLaw proposes to copy—West makes four different types of changes to judicial opinions that it claimed at trial are copyrightable: (i) rearrangement of information specifying the parties, court, and date of decision; (ii) addition of certain information concerning counsel; (iii) annotation to reflect subsequent procedural developments such as amendments and denials of rehearing; and (iv) editing of parallel and alternate citations to cases cited in the opinions in order to redact ephemeral and obscure citations and to add standard permanent citations (including West reporters). All of West's alterations to judicial opinions involve the addition and arrangement of facts, or the rearrangement of data already included in the opinions, and therefore any creativity in these elements of West's case reports lies in West's selection and arrangement of this information. In light of accepted legal conventions and other external constraining factors, West's choices on selection and arrangement can reasonably be viewed as obvious, typical, and lacking even minimal creativity. Therefore, we cannot conclude that the district court clearly erred in finding that those elements that HyperLaw seeks to copy from West's case reports are not copyrightable, and affirm. . . .

The principal trial witness was Donna Bergsgaard, the manager of West's manuscript department. She specified four kinds of alterations made by West to the opinions that it publishes in the Supreme Court Reporter and Federal Reporter and that HyperLaw intends to copy: (i) the arrangement of prefatory information, such as parties, court, and date of decision; (ii) the selection and arrangement of the attorney information; (iii) the arrangement of information relating to subsequent procedural developments; and (iv) the selection of parallel and alternative citations. [T]he district court ruled that West's revisions to judicial opinions were merely trivial variations from the public domain works, and that West's case reports were therefore not copyrightable as derivative works. In reaching this conclusion, the district court reviewed each type of alteration and found that "West does not have a protectible interest in any of the portions of the opinions that HyperLaw copies or intends to copy" because West's alterations lack even minimal creativity.

DISCUSSION
II

Works of the federal government are not subject to copyright protection; the text of judicial decisions may therefore be copied at will. 17 U.S.C. § 105. Federal judicial opinions may, however, form part of a compilation. The Copyright Act defines "compilation" as "a work formed by the collection and assembling of preexisting materials or of data that are selected, coordinated, or arranged in such a way that the resulting work as a whole constitutes an original work of authorship." 17 U.S.C. § 101. West has filed a certificate of copyright registration for every paperbacked advance sheet and bound permanent volume of the Supreme Court Reporter and Federal Reporter, and each certificate characterizes the copyrighted work as a "compilation." Under *Feist Publications, Inc. v. Rural Telephone Serv. Co.* (1991), an infringement claim for a compilation has two elements: "(1) ownership of a valid copyright, and (2) copying of constituent elements of the work that are original."

But HyperLaw has not signaled its intent to copy the text of every case included in particular volumes of West case reporters or the case reporters' selection and arrangement of cases; HyperLaw's intent is to copy particular, though numerous, individual case reports. HyperLaw seeks a declaratory judgment that these case reports—after removal of the syllabus, headnotes, and key numbers—contain no copyrightable material.

A.

HyperLaw contends that each case report should be analyzed as a derivative work, which is defined under the Copyright Act as, inter alia, "[a] work consisting of editorial revisions, annotations, elaborations, or other modifications which, as a whole, represent an original work of authorship." 17 U.S.C. § 101. The district court adopted this view and analyzed the individual case report as a derivative work, but found it wanting in the requisite originality. West contends that each case report is a compilation, i.e., a collection of facts that have been distinctively selected and arranged. No one claims that a case report is anything other than a derivative work or a compilation.

The House Report on the 1976 Copyright Act distinguishes between a derivative work and a compilation:

> Between them the terms . . . comprehend every copyrightable work that employs preexisting material or data of any kind. There is necessarily some overlapping between the two, but they basically represent different concepts. A "compilation" results from a process of selecting, bringing together, organizing, and arranging previously existing material of all kinds, regardless of whether the individual items in the material have been or ever could have been subject to copyright. A "derivative work," on the other hand, requires a process of recasting, transforming, or adapting "one or more preexisting works"; the "preexisting work" must come within the general subject matter of copyright set forth in section 102, regardless of whether it is or was ever copyrighted. . . .

We need not categorize West's case reports as either derivative works or compilations in order to decide this case. Copyright protection is unavailable for both derivative works and compilations alike unless, when analyzed as a whole, they display sufficient originality so as to amount to an "original work of authorship." . . . As West and HyperLaw seemingly agree, the question presented is whether West's alterations to the case reports, when considered collectively, demonstrate sufficient originality and creativity to be copyrightable. . . .

Our decision in this case does not mean that an editor seeking to create the most accurate edition of another work never exercises creativity.[13] As West argues, our decisions establish a low threshold of creativity, even in works involving selection from among facts. But those cases involved the exercise of judgments more evaluative and creative than West exercises in the four elements of the case reports that HyperLaw intends to copy. For instance, in *Kregos* thousands of different permutations of pitching statistics were available for inclusion in the publisher's pitching chart. See *Kregos*; see also *Eckes v. Card Prices Update* (2d Cir. 1984) (baseball card guide which selected 5,000 "premium" baseball cards from among 18,000 eligible baseball cards was copyrightable). In *Key Publications*, we found sufficient creativity because the author of the yellow pages "excluded from the directory those businesses she did not think would remain open for very long." In *CCC Information Services*, we found sufficient creativity in the selection of optional car features and number of years' models to be included in a used-car price compilation. . . . In each of these cases, the compiler selected from among numerous choices, exercising subjective judgments relating to taste and value that were not obvious and that were not dictated by industry convention. . . .

---

[13] It is true that some types of editing require little creativity. See, e.g., *Grove Press, Inc. v. Collectors Publication, Inc.* (C.D. Cal. 1967) ("Plaintiff made approximately forty thousand changes from the Verlag copy in producing its edition. These changes consisted almost entirely of elimination and addition of punctuation, changes of spelling of certain words, elimination and addition of quotation marks, and correction of typographical errors. These changes required no skill beyond that of a [1967] high school English student and displayed no originality. These changes are found to be trivial."). In addition, convention and external forces may, as here, limit the practical choices available so as to eliminate any creativity. On the other hand, preparing an edition from multiple prior editions, or creating an accurate version of the missing parts of an ancient document by using conjecture to determine the probable content of the document may take a high amount of creativity. See, e.g., Abraham Rabinovich, Scholar: Reconstruction of Dead Sea Scroll Pirated, Wash. Times: Nat'l Wkly. Edition, Apr. 12, 1998, at 26 (discussing scholar's copyright infringement claim in Israeli Supreme Court relating to his reconstruction of the missing parts of a "Dead Sea Scroll" through the use of "educated guesswork" based on knowledge of the sect that authored work).

CONCLUSION

The district court did not clearly err in concluding that the elements of West's case reports that HyperLaw seeks to copy are not copyrightable. The judgment of the district court is affirmed.

SWEET, District Judge.

The key issue in this appeal is whether West's Supreme Court Reporter and Federal Reporter case reports in the context of its overall reporter citation system meet the constitutional and statutory requirement of creative originality. Because the majority imposes a standard that demands significantly more than the "modicum" of originality required by *Feist Publications, Inc. v. Rural Telephone Service Company, Inc.*, and far more than the "non-trivial" variation required by this Court for derivative-work and compilation copyright protection, I respectfully dissent. . . .

Contrary to the majority's holding, however, I find that West's selection and arrangement of factual annotations to public domain judicial opinions, considered as a whole, is copyrightable.

Originality alone—whether the "author make[s] the selection or arrangement independently (i.e. without copying that selection or arrangement from another work)"—is not sufficient. *Feist.* The work must also "display some minimal level of creativity." Creativity for copyright purposes is not a philosophical question: the "creative spark" need only pass "the narrowest and most obvious limits." The "modicum of creativity" requires simply that the author prove "the existence of . . . intellectual production, of thought, and conception." *Feist.* Thus, while the majority is correct that it is "not a goal of copyright law" to encourage the creation of compilations which lack "sufficient creativity," it is well-established that the required level of creativity is "extremely low." *Feist.* . . .

The fact that federal judges publish written opinions differently than West is sufficient reason to conclude that West's version requires some "thought" and is sufficiently "creative" to satisfy the modicum necessary for copyrightability. . . .

For the reasons stated, I conclude the summary judgment granted in favor of HyperLaw should be reversed.

Matthew Bender & Co., Inc. v. West Publishing Co.
158 F.3d 693 (2d Cir. 1998)

JACOBS, Circuit Judge.

Defendants-appellants West Publishing Co. and West Publishing Corp. (collectively "West") create and publish printed compilations of federal and state judicial opinions. Plaintiff-appellee Matthew Bender & Company, Inc. and intervenor-plaintiff-appellee HyperLaw, Inc. (collectively "plaintiffs") manufacture and market compilations of judicial opinions stored on compact disc-read only memory ("CD-ROM") discs, in which opinions they embed (or intend to embed) citations that show the page location of the particular text in West's printed version of the opinions (so-called "star pagination").[1] Bender and HyperLaw seek judgment declaring that star pagination will not infringe West's copyrights in its compilations of judicial opinions.

---

[1] This cross-reference method is called "star pagination" because an asterisk and citation or page number are inserted in the text of the judicial opinion to indicate when a page break occurs in a different version of the case.

West's primary contention on appeal is that star pagination to West's case reporters allows a user of plaintiffs' CD-ROM discs (by inputting a series of commands) to "perceive" West's copyright-protected arrangement of cases, and that plaintiffs' products (when star pagination is added) are unlawful copies of West's arrangement. We reject West's argument for two reasons:

A. Even if plaintiffs' CD-ROM discs (when equipped with star pagination) amounted to unlawful copies of West's arrangement of cases under the Copyright Act, (i) West has conceded that specification of the initial page of a West case reporter in plaintiffs' products ("parallel citation") is permissible under the fair use doctrine, (ii) West's arrangement may be perceived through parallel citation and thus the plaintiffs may lawfully create a copy of West's arrangement of cases, (iii) the incremental benefit of star pagination is that it allows the reader to perceive West's page breaks within each opinion, which are not protected by its copyright, and (iv) therefore star pagination does not create a "copy" of any protected elements of West's compilations or infringe West's copyrights.

B. In any event, under a proper reading of the Copyright Act, the insertion of star pagination does not amount to infringement of West's arrangement of cases. . . .

[The court rejected an earlier decision from the 8th Circuit, called *West Publishing Co.* which had found for West.] At bottom, *West Publishing Co.* rests upon the now defunct "sweat of the brow" doctrine. That court found that LEXIS had infringed West's copyright simply because it supplanted much of the need for West's case reporters through wholesale appropriation of West's page numbers. In reaching this conclusion, the court (i) noted that LEXIS's appropriation would deprive West of a large part of what it "[had] spent so much labor and industry in compiling," [and cited] classic "sweat of the brow" cases that were overruled in *Feist*. Thus, the Eighth Circuit in *West Publishing Co.* erroneously protected West's industrious collection rather than its original creation. Because *Feist* undermines the reasoning of *West Publishing Co.*, see *United States v. Thomson Corp.* (D.D.C. 1996), we decline to follow it.

CONCLUSION

We hold that Bender and HyperLaw will not infringe West's copyright by inserting star pagination to West's case reporters in their CD-ROM disc version of judicial opinions. The judgement of the district court is affirmed.

SWEET, District Judge.

I respectfully dissent.

This appeal from the grant of summary judgment in favor of the appellee Bender presents challenging issues, the extent of copyright protection for compilations under the § 501(a) and § 106(1) and (3) of Title 17, U.S.C., what constitutes copying in the electronic age, and the propriety of summary judgment in determining issues of fair use. Because the majority reaches conclusions on the first two issues, with which I disagree, and consequently failed to address the third issue, I feel required to dissent, emboldened by the holdings of the three other courts which have considered the issue, *West Pub. Co. v. Mead Data Central, Inc.* (D. Minn. 1985), [*aff'd*, 799 F.2d 1219 (8th Cir. 1986), *cert. denied*, 479 U.S. 1070 (1987)]; *Oasis Pub. Co. v. West Pub. Co.* (D. Minn. 1996), and reached conclusions contrary to those stated by the majority. By concluding that page numbers in the context of the West citation system are facts rather than an expression of originality the majority permits the appellee Bender and the intervenor HyperLaw to appropriate the practical and commercial value of the West compilation.

The West page numbers which are inserted by appellee Bender in the text of each of its CD-ROM disks by star pagination result from the totality of the West compilation process which includes its concededly original and copyrightable work, i.e. attorney description, headnotes, method of citation and emending of parallel or alternate citations. These result in a compilation work with page numbers assigned mechanically. The West page numbers and the corresponding Bender and HyperLaw star pagination are the keys which open the door to the entire West citation system which as the majority noted is an accepted, and in some instances, a required element for the citation of authorities.

In my view West's case arrangements, an essential part of which is page citations, are original works of authorship entitled to copyright protection. Comprehensive documentation of West's selection and arrangement of judicial opinions infringes the copyright in that work.

This reasoning is consistent with *Feist*. As discussed above, the majority notes that the compiler's copyright is "thin." *Feist*. Therefore, "a subsequent compiler remains free to use the facts contained in another's publication to aid in preparing a competing work, *so long as the competing work does not feature the same selection and arrangement*." In this case, allowing plaintiffs to use the page numbers contained in West's publication enables them to feature West's same selection and arrangement.[2] Indeed, were it not for the ability to reproduce West's arrangement, its pagination would be of limited (if any) use. . . .

Some of the most seminal developments in copyright law have been driven by technological change. There was a time when people questioned whether photographs or advertisements were copyrightable. Here again it is necessary to reconcile technology with pre-electronic principles of law. Clearly, plaintiffs' CD-ROM disks are not "copies" in the traditional sense. Yet, plaintiffs provide the ability for a user to push a button or two and obtain West's exact selection and arrangement. This technological capacity presents a new question. The majority's answer threatens to eviscerate copyright protection for compilations. . . .

For these reasons I believe the grant of summary judgment granting the declaratory judgment requested by Bender was error, and I therefore dissent from the majority's affirmance of that judgment.

Questions:

1.) Does any user actually *want* West's selection and arrangement, or just the page numbers that that selection and arrangement results in, because those are the authoritative way to cite the case? Does that matter?

2.) Judge Sweet claims a user could "push a button or two and obtain West's exact selection and arrangement." But a user could also push "a button or two" and arrange the cases by alphabetical ordering of case name, of defendant's name(s), of judge's name, of day of the week, of the type of law being decided, or any of a hundred more possible methods. If *many* forms of ordering, selection or arrangement can be cybernetically imposed, by software, on a mass of material dumped, unordered, on a hard drive or DVD, does Judge Sweet's answer not bring up an opposite problem? *All* compilations could

---

[2] It is immaterial that plaintiffs' products may display other arrangements as well as West's. The capability of a CD-ROM to display more than one arrangement does not make the encoding of an original selection and arrangement such as West's any less of an infringement.

It is also irrelevant that plaintiffs' products may contain material beyond West's selection and arrangement. Infringement is determined by how much of the copyright owner's work was taken, not by what else the copier's work contains. See e.g., *Warner Bros., Inc. v. American Broadcasting Cos., Inc.* (2d Cir. 1983).

potentially be "immanent within," implicitly present within, the database. Does that therefore mean that any system for flexibly arranging data inherently violates compilation copyrights on *all* of the arrangements it *could* be used to emulate?

Note

The *West* cases involved Federal legal materials, which are clearly in the public domain under § 105's exclusion for "any work of the United States Government." But what about the laws of states and municipalities—can they be copyrighted? In *Veeck v. Southern Building Code Congress International* (5th Cir. 2002), an *en banc* panel held that once a privately authored building code was enacted into local laws, it could no longer be copyrighted. Citing to two early Supreme Court cases "holding that 'the law' is not copyrightable," the court stated: "as *law*, the model codes enter the public domain and are not subject to the copyright holder's exclusive prerogatives" (emphasis in original). *See Wheaton v. Peters* (1834); *Banks v. Manchester* (1888). Alternatively, the court held that the building codes were either uncopyrightable "facts," or uncopyrightable under the merger doctrine as "the unique, unalterable expression of the 'idea' that constitutes local law."

More recently, in *Georgia v. Public.Resource.Org (PRO)* (2020), the Supreme Court held that the Official Code of Georgia Annotated ("OCGA") was not copyrightable. In doing so, it revisited *Wheaton* and *Banks*, which had developed what the Court dubbed the "government edicts doctrine." "Officials empowered to speak with the force of law cannot be the authors of—and therefore cannot copyright—the works they create in the course of their official duties." The Court explained: "The animating principle behind this rule is that no one can own the law. 'Every citizen is presumed to know the law,' and 'it needs no argument to show . . . that all should have free access' to its contents." Those earlier cases had dealt with works by judges, including opinions and non-binding materials such as syllabi and headnotes. In this case, the work was the annotations to the state code, actually written by an outside contractor, but *deemed* to be "authored" by the legislature by the Court in this case. Thus the annotations were not copyrightable, even though the annotations did not carry the force of law.

After *PRO*, it is clear that state and local laws *produced* by the government are in the public domain. But what about privately authored codes and standards, such as the model building code in *Veeck*, that are subsequently adopted into law? If you want to "bring your house up to code" in Durham and a private trade association has written a code, which the state enacts as the law of North Carolina, does this code enter the public domain when it gains the force of law as *Veeck* would imply? If the focus is merger (there is only one correct way of stating the ideas and facts of the law), or even due process (citizens are presumed to know the law) and the question of who initially *wrote* the code would be irrelevant. *PRO* on the other hand focused on the question of government "authorship," though it then proceeded to define that authorship very broadly, perhaps for the reasons *Veeck* put forward.

True, the *PRO* Court also stated more categorically that "no one can own the law," indicating that government authorship does not mark the outer bounds of its holding. At the time of writing this book, organizations such as the International Code Council continue to bring lawsuits asserting copyright over model codes that are both "*the law*," and were privately drafted. Are these codes in the public domain, so that anyone can make them available to those who need them? Under *Veeck*, of course, those codes are not copyrightable. Both its reading of Supreme Court precedent and of copyright's idea-fact/expression dichotomy and merger doctrine make this clear. We believe this answer is correct, but *PRO*'s curious mixture of formalism on the surface and constitutional and policy concerns beneath, makes it hard to know.

James Boyle, A Natural Experiment
Financial Times, *Nov. 22, 2004*

Imagine a process of reviewing prescription drugs which goes like this: representatives from the drug company come to the regulators and argue that their drug works well and should be approved. They have no evidence of this beyond a few anecdotes about people who want to take it and perhaps some very simple models of how the drug might affect the human body. The drug is approved. No trials, no empirical evidence of any kind, no follow-up. Or imagine a process of making environmental regulations in which there were no data, and no attempts to gather data, about the effects of the particular pollutants being studied. Even the harshest critics of drug regulation or environmental regulation would admit we generally do better than this. But this is often the way we make intellectual property policy.

So how do we decide the ground-rules of the information age? Representatives of interested industries come to regulators and ask for another heaping slice of monopoly rent in the form of an intellectual property right. They have doom-laden predictions, they have anecdotes, carefully selected to pluck the heartstrings of legislators, they have celebrities who testify—often incoherently, but with palpable charisma—and they have very, very simple economic models. The basic economic model here is "If you give me a larger right, I will have a larger incentive to innovate. Thus the bigger the rights, the more innovation we will get. Right?" Well, not exactly. Even without data, the models are obviously flawed—copyrighting the alphabet will not produce more books, patenting $E=mc^2$ will not yield more scientific innovation. Intellectual property creates barriers to, as well as incentives towards, innovation. Clearly the "more is better" argument has limits. Extensions of rights can help or hurt, but without economic evidence beforehand and review afterwards, we will never know. In the absence of evidence on either side, the presumption should obviously be against creating a *new* legalised monopoly, but still the empirical emptiness of the debates is frustrating.

This makes the occasion where there actually is some evidence a time for celebration. What we really need is a test case where one country adopts the proposed new intellectual property right and another does not, and we can assess how they are both doing after a number of years.

There is such a case. It is the "database right." Europe adopted a Database Directive in 1996 which both gave a high level of copyright protection to databases, and conferred a new "sui generis" database right even on unoriginal compilations of facts. In the United States, by contrast, in a 1991 case called *Feist*, the Supreme Court made it clear that unoriginal compilations of facts are not copyrightable. (The case is not as revolutionary as it is claimed to be. Most of the appeals courts in the United States had long held this to be the case. In fact, a tenet of the US intellectual property system is that neither facts nor ideas can be owned.) Since 1991 the U.S. Congress has managed to resist frenzied attempts by a few database companies to create a special database right over facts. Interestingly, apart from academics, scientists and civil libertarians, many database companies, and even those well-known communist property-haters, the U.S. Chamber of Commerce, oppose the creation of such a right. They believe that database providers can adequately protect themselves with contracts, technical means such as passwords, can rely on providing tied services and so on. Moreover, they argue that strong database protection may make it harder to generate databases in the first place; the facts you need may be locked up. The pressure to create a new right continues, however, aided by the cries that US must "harmonise" with Europe. So here we have our natural experiment. Presumably the government economists are hard at work both in the US and the EU, seeing if the right actually worked? Umm. . . . No.

Despite the fact that the European Commission has a legal obligation to review the Database Directive for its effects on competition (they are three years late in issuing their report) no attention appears to be being paid to the actual evidence of whether the Directive helps or hurts in the EU, or whether the database industry in the US has collapsed or flourished. That is a shame, because the evidence is there, and it is fairly shocking.

Intellectual property rights are a form of state-created monopoly and "the general tendency of monopolies," as Macaulay pointed out, is to "make things dear, to make them scarce, and to make them bad." Monopolies are an evil, but they must sometimes be accepted when they are necessary to the production of some good, some particular social goal. In this case, the "evil" is obviously going to be an increase in price of databases, and the legal ability to exclude competitors from their use—that, after all is the point of granting the new right. The "good" is that we are supposed to get lots of new databases, databases that we would not have had but for the existence of the database right.

If the database right were working, we would expect positive answers to three crucial questions. First, has the European database industry's rate of growth increased since 1996, while the US database industry has languished? (The drop off in the US database industry ought to be particularly severe after 1991 if the proponents of database protection are correct; they argued the *Feist* case was a change in current law and a great surprise to the industry.)

Second, are the principal beneficiaries of the database right in Europe producing databases they would not have produced otherwise? Obviously if a society is handing over a database right for a database that would have been created anyway, it is overpaying—needlessly increasing prices for consumers and burdens for competitors. This goes to the design of the right—has it been crafted too broadly, so that it is not being targeted to those areas where it is needed to encourage innovation?

Third, and this one is harder to judge, is the right promoting innovation and competition rather than stifling it? For example, if the existence of the right allowed a one-time surge of newcomers to the market who then used their rights to discourage new entrants, or if we promoted some increase in databases but made scientific aggregation of large amounts of data harder overall, then the database right might actually be stifling the innovation it is designed to foment.

Those are the three questions that any review of the Database Directive must answer. But we have preliminary answers to those three questions and they are either strongly negative or extremely doubtful.

Are database rights necessary for a thriving database industry? The answer is a clear "no." In the United States, the database industry has grown more than 25-fold since 1979 and—contrary to those who paint the *Feist* case as a revolution—for that entire period, in most of the United States, it was clear that unoriginal databases were not covered by copyright. The figures are even more interesting in the legal database market. The two major proponents of database protection in the United States are Reed Elsevier, the owner of Lexis, and Thomson Publishing, the owner of Westlaw. Fascinatingly, both companies made their key acquisitions in the US legal database market after the *Feist* decision, at which point no one could have thought unoriginal databases were copyrightable. This seems to be some evidence that they believe they could make money even without a database right. How? In the old-fashioned way: competing on features, accuracy, tied services, making users pay for entry to the database and so on.

If those companies believed there were profits to be made, they were right. Jason Gelman, one of our students, points out in a recent paper that Thomson's Legal Regulatory division had a profit margin of over 26% for the first quarter of 2004. Reed Elsevier's 2003 profit margin for LexisNexis was 22.8%. Both profit margins were significantly higher than the company average and both are earned primarily in the $6 billion US legal database market, a market which is thriving without strong intellectual property protection over databases. (First rule of thumb for regulators: when someone with a profit margin over 20% asks you for additional monopoly protection, pause before agreeing.)

What about Europe? There is some good news for the proponents of database protection. As Hugenholtz, Maurer, and Onsrud point out in a nice article in Science Magazine, there was a sharp, one-time spike in numbers of companies entering the European database market immediately following the implementation of the Directive in member states. Yet their work, and "Across Two Worlds," a fascinating study by Maurer, suggests that the rate of entry then falls back to levels similar to those before the Directive. Maurer's analysis shows that the attrition rate is also very high in some European markets in the period following the passage of the Directive—even with the new right, many companies drop out.

At the end of the day, the British database industry—the strongest performer in Europe—adds about 200 databases in the three years immediately after the implementation of the Directive. In France there is little net change in the number of databases and the number of providers falls sharply. In Germany, the industry added nearly 300 databases immediately following the Directive—a remarkable surge—about 200 of which rapidly disappeared. During the same period the US industry adds about 900 databases. Bottom line? Europe's industry did get a one-time boost, and some of those firms have stayed in the market; that is a benefit, though a costly one. But database growth rates have gone back to pre-Directive levels, while the anti-competitive costs of database protection are now a permanent fixture of the European landscape. The US, by contrast, gets a nice steady growth rate in databases without paying the monopoly cost. (Second rule of thumb for regulators: Do no harm! Do not create rights without strong evidence that the incentive effect is worth the anti-competitive cost.)

Now the second question. Is the Database Directive encouraging the production of databases we would not have got otherwise? Here the evidence is clear and disturbing. Again, Hugenholtz et al, point out that the majority of cases brought under the Directive have been about databases that would have been created anyway—telephone numbers, television schedules, concert times. A review of more recent cases reveals the same pattern. These databases are inevitably generated by the operation of the business in question and cannot be independently compiled by a competitor. The database right simply serves to limit competition in the provision of the information. Last week, the European Court of Justice implicitly underscored this point in a series of cases concerning football scores, horse-racing results and so on. Rejecting a stunningly protectionist and one-sided opinion from its Advocate General, the court ruled that the mere running of a business which generates data does not count as "substantial investment" enough to trigger the database right. It would be nice to think that this is the beginning of some scepticism about the reach of the Directive, scepticism that might even penetrate the Commission's review of the Directive's anti-competitive effects. Yet the Court provides little discussion for the economic reasons behind its interpretation; the analysis is merely semantic and definitional, a sharp contrast to its competition decisions.

So what kinds of databases are being generated by this bold new right? The answer is somewhere between bathos and pathos. Here are some of the wonderful "databases" that people found it worthwhile litigating over: A website, consisting of a collection of 259 hyper-links to "parenting resources," a collection of poems, an assortment of advertisements, headings referring to local news, charts of popular music. The sad list goes on and on. The European Commission might ask itself whether these are really the kind of "databases" which we need a legal monopoly to encourage, and that we want to tie up judicial resources protecting. The point that many more such factual resources can be found online in the United States without such protection, also seems worthy of note. At very least, the evidence indicates that the right is drawn much too broadly and triggered too easily in ways that are profoundly anti-competitive.

Finally, is the database right encouraging scientific innovation or hurting it? Here the evidence is merely suggestive. Scientists have claimed that the European database right, together with the perverse failure of European governments to take advantage of the limited scientific research exceptions allowed by the Directive, have made it much harder to aggregate data, to replicate studies, and to judge published articles. In fact, academic scientific bodies have been among the strongest critics of database protection. But negative evidence, by its nature, is hard to produce; "show me the science that did not get done!" Certainly, both US science and commerce have benefited extraordinarily from the openness of US data policy. This is an issue I will deal with in a later column.

I was not always opposed to intellectual property rights over data. Indeed, in a book written before the enactment of the Database Directive, I said that there was a respectable economic argument that such protection might be warranted and that we needed research on the issue. Unfortunately, Europe got the right without the research. The facts are now in. If the European Database Directive were a drug, the government would be pulling it from the market until its efficacy and harmfulness could be reassessed. At the very least, the Commission needs a detailed empirical review of the Directive's effects, and needs to adjust the Directive's definitions and to fine-tune its limitations. But there is a second lesson. There is more discussion of the empirical economic effects of the Database Directive in this 2000 word column than there is in the 600 page review of the effects of the Directive that the European Commission paid a private company to conduct. That is a scandal. And it is a scandal that is altogether typical of the way we make intellectual property policy.

PROBLEM 11-1

You represent the West Corporation which has asked for your advice after its two losses in the *HyperLaw* cases. West has asked you to advise them on the relative merits of three different solutions to the problem presented to the company by these cases.

1.) Amendment of the copyright act to specify that page numbers in a law report are copyrightable.

2.) a.) Amendment of the copyright act to specify that any purposeful arrangement in sequence is sufficiently original to warrant copyright protection over the resulting sequence *and* that b.) "any reproduction of uncopyrightable textual material, accompanied by textual, numerical or technological references that allow a user to identify precisely the place of any given bit of text in an authoritative sequence produced by another, shall constitute a violation of the exclusive rights held by the creator of that authoritative sequence."

3.) [And it is on this alternative that we will concentrate our time.] The passage of a statute, justified under the Congress' Commerce Clause power, which prohibits (*inter alia*) the following: (*cf.* HR Bill 3261: Database and Collections of Information Misappropriation Act (Introduced in House)).

Sec. 3. Prohibition Against Misappropriation Of Databases.

(a) LIABILITY—Any person who makes available in commerce to others a quantitatively substantial part of the information in a database generated, gathered, or maintained by another person, knowing that such making available in commerce is without the authorization of that person (including a successor in interest) or that person's licensee, when acting within the scope of its license, shall be liable for the remedies set forth in section 7 if—

> (1) the database was generated, gathered, or maintained through a substantial expenditure of financial resources or time;
> (2) the unauthorized making available in commerce occurs in a time sensitive manner and inflicts injury on the database or a product or service offering access to multiple databases; and
> (3) the ability of other parties to free ride on the efforts of the plaintiff would so reduce the incentive to produce the product or service that its existence or quality would be substantially threatened.

(b) INJURY—For purposes of subsection (a), the term 'inflicts an injury' means serving as a functional equivalent in the same market as the database in a manner that causes the displacement, or the disruption of the sources, of sales, licenses, advertising, or other revenue.

(c) TIME SENSITIVE—In determining whether an unauthorized making available in commerce occurs in a time sensitive manner, the court shall consider the temporal value of the information in the database, within the context of the industry sector involved.

Which of these alternatives do you think is best for your client to pursue? Why? What are the particular obstacles to the third alternative? Statutory drafting is a kind of advocacy—aiming to reassure possible opponents, while still providing the protection desired. Why was this section drafted the way it was? In particular, how far would this new intellectual property right reach? Is this the same definition of time-sensitivity as is implied in the *INS v. AP* case? Is Section 3 constitutional? Does it outlaw the FANtasy football games discussed in Chapter 1?

2.) The Idea-Expression Distinction

Baker v. Selden
101 U.S. 99 (1880)

Mr. Justice BRADLEY delivered the opinion of the court.

Charles Selden, the testator of the complainant in this case, in the year 1859 took the requisite steps for obtaining the copyright of a book, entitled "Selden's Condensed Ledger, or Book-keeping Simplified," the object of which was to exhibit and explain a peculiar system of book-keeping. In 1860 and 1861, he took the copyright of several other books, containing additions to and improvements upon the said system. The bill of complaint was filed against the defendant, Baker, for an alleged infringement of these copyrights. The latter, in his answer, denied that Selden was the author or designer of the books, and denied the infringement charged, and contends on the argument that the matter alleged to be infringed is not a lawful subject of copyright. . . .

Image from *Selden's Condensed Ledger and Condensed Memorandum Book* (1861).

The book or series of books of which the complainant claims the copyright consists of an introductory essay explaining the system of book-keeping referred to, to which are annexed certain forms or blanks, consisting of ruled lines, and headings, illustrating the system and showing how it is to be used and carried out in practice. This system effects the same results as book-keeping by double entry; but, by a peculiar arrangement of columns and headings, presents the entire operation, of a day, a week, or a month, on a single page, or on two pages facing each other, in an account-book. The defendant uses a similar plan so far as results are concerned; but makes a different arrangement of the columns, and uses different headings. If the complainant's testator had the exclusive right to the use of the system explained in his book, it would be difficult to contend that the defendant does not infringe it, notwithstanding the difference in his form of arrangement; but if it be assumed that the system is open to public use, it seems to be equally difficult to contend that the books made and sold by the defendant are a violation of the copyright of the complainant's book considered merely as a book explanatory of the system. Where the truths of a science or the methods of an art are the common property of the whole world, any author has the right to express the one, or explain and use the other, in his own way. As an author, Selden explained the system in a particular way. It may be conceded that Baker makes and uses account-books arranged on substantially the same system; but the proof fails to show that he has violated the copyright of Selden's book, regarding the latter merely as an explanatory work; or that he has infringed Selden's right in any way, unless the latter became entitled to an exclusive right in the system.

The evidence of the complainant is principally directed to the object of showing that Baker uses the same system as that which is explained and illustrated in Selden's books. It becomes important, therefore, to determine whether, in obtaining the copyright of his books, he secured the exclusive right to the use of the system or method of book-keeping which the said books are intended to illustrate and explain. It is contended that he has secured such exclusive right, because no one can use the system without using substantially the same ruled lines and headings which he has appended to his books in illustration of it. In other words, it is contended that the ruled lines and headings, given to illustrate the system, are a part of the book, and, as such, are secured by the copyright; and that no one can make or use similar ruled lines and headings, or ruled lines and headings made and arranged on substantially the same system, without violating the copyright. And this is really the question to be decided in this case. Stated in another form, the question is, whether the exclusive property in a system of book-keeping can be claimed, under the law of copyright, by means of a book in which that system is explained? The complainant's bill, and the case made under it, are based on the hypothesis that it can be. . . .

There is no doubt that a work on the subject of book-keeping, though only explanatory of well-known systems, may be the subject of a copyright; but, then, it is claimed only as a book. Such a book may be explanatory either of old systems, or of an entirely new system; and, considered as a book, as the work of an author, conveying information on the subject of book-keeping, and containing detailed explanations of the art, it may be a very valuable acquisition to the practical knowledge of the community. But there is a clear distinction between the book, as such, and the art which it is intended to illustrate. The mere statement of the proposition is so evident, that it requires hardly any argument to support it. The same distinction may be predicated of every other art as well as that of book-keeping. A treatise on the composition and use of medicines, be they old or new; on the construction and use of ploughs, or watches, or churns; or on the mixture and application of colors for painting or dyeing; or on the mode of drawing lines to produce the effect of perspective,—would be the subject of copyright; but no one would contend that the copyright of the treatise would give the exclusive right to the art or manufacture described therein. The copyright of the book, if not pirated from other works, would be valid without regard to the novelty, or want of novelty, of its subject-matter. The novelty of the art or thing described or explained has nothing to do with the validity of the copyright. To give to the author of the book an exclusive property in the art described therein, when no examination of its novelty has ever been officially made, would be a surprise and a fraud upon the public. That is the province of letters-patent, not of copyright. The claim to an invention or discovery of an art or manufacture must be subjected to the examination of the Patent Office before an exclusive right therein can be obtained; and it can only be secured by a patent from the government.

The difference between the two things, letters-patent and copyright, may be illustrated by reference to the subjects just enumerated. Take the case of medicines. Certain mixtures are found to be of great value in the healing art. If the discoverer writes and publishes a book on the subject (as regular physicians generally do), he gains no exclusive right to the manufacture and sale of the medicine; he gives that to the public. If he desires to acquire such exclusive right, he must obtain a patent for the mixture as a new art, manufacture, or composition of matter. He may copyright his book, if he pleases; but that only secures to him the exclusive right of printing and publishing his book. So of all other inventions or discoveries.

The copyright of a book on perspective, no matter how many drawings and illustrations it may contain, gives no exclusive right to the modes of drawing described, though they may never have been known or used before. By publishing the book, without getting a patent for the art, the latter is given to the public. The fact that the art described in the book by illustrations of lines and figures which are reproduced in practice in the application of the art, makes no difference. Those illustrations are the mere language employed by the author to convey his ideas more clearly. Had he used words of description instead of diagrams (which merely stand in the place of words), there could not be the slightest doubt that others, applying the art to practical use, might lawfully draw the lines and diagrams which were in the author's mind, and which he thus described by words in his book.

The copyright of a work on mathematical science cannot give to the author an exclusive right to the methods of operation which he propounds, or to the diagrams which he employs to explain them, so as to prevent an engineer from using them whenever occasion requires. The very object of publishing a book on science or the useful arts is to communicate to the world the useful knowledge which it contains. But this object would be frustrated if the knowledge could not be used without incurring the guilt of piracy of the book. And where the art it teaches cannot be used without employing the methods and diagrams used to illustrate the book, or such as are similar to them, such methods and diagrams are to be considered as necessary incidents to the art, and given therewith to the public; not given for the purpose of publication in other works explanatory of the art, but for the purpose of practical application.

Of course, these observations are not intended to apply to ornamental designs, or pictorial illustrations addressed to the taste. Of these it may be said, that their form is their essence, and their object, the production of pleasure in their contemplation. This is their final end. They are as much the product of genius and the result of composition, as are the lines of the poet or the historian's periods. On the other hand, the teachings of science and the rules and methods of useful art have their final end in application and use; and this application and use are what the public derive from the publication of a book which teaches them. But as embodied and taught in a literary composition or book, their essence consists only in their statement. This alone is what is secured by the copyright. The use by another of the same methods of statement, whether in words or illustrations, in a book published for teaching the art, would undoubtedly be an infringement of the copyright.

Recurring to the case before us, we observe that Charles Selden, by his books, explained and described a peculiar system of book-keeping, and illustrated his method by means of ruled lines and blank columns, with proper headings on a page, or on successive pages. Now, whilst no one has a right to print or publish his book, or any material part thereof, as a book intended to convey instruction in the art, any person may practise and use the art itself which he has described and illustrated therein. The use of the art is a totally different thing from a publication of the book explaining it. The copyright of a book on book-keeping cannot secure the exclusive right to make, sell, and use account-books prepared upon the plan set forth in such book. Whether the art might or might not have been patented, is a question which is not before us. It was not patented, and is open and free to the use of the public. And, of course, in using the art, the ruled lines and headings of accounts must necessarily be used as incident to it.

The plausibility of the claim put forward by the complainant in this case arises from a confusion of ideas produced by the peculiar nature of the art described in the books which have been made the subject of copyright. In describing the art, the illustrations and diagrams employed happen to correspond more closely than usual with the actual work performed by the operator who uses the art. Those illustrations and diagrams consist of ruled lines and headings of accounts; and it is similar ruled lines and headings of accounts which, in the application of the art, the book-keeper makes with his pen, or the stationer with his press;

whilst in most other cases the diagrams and illustrations can only be represented in concrete forms of wood, metal, stone, or some other physical embodiment. But the principle is the same in all. The description of the art in a book, though entitled to the benefit of copyright, lays no foundation for an exclusive claim to the art itself. The object of the one is explanation; the object of the other is use. The former may be secured by copyright. The latter can only be secured, if it can be secured at all, by letters-patent. . . .

The conclusion to which we have come is, that blank account-books are not the subject of copyright; and that the mere copyright of Selden's book did not confer upon him the exclusive right to make and use account-books, ruled and arranged as designated by him and described and illustrated in said book.

The decree of the Circuit Court must be reversed, and the cause remanded with instructions to dismiss the complainant's bill; and it is
So ordered.

Questions:

1.) Some courts derived from *Baker v. Selden* what they called "the blank form doctrine": one could not get a copyright in a book that consisted merely of headings and ruled lines and blank space under those headings. Does this understate or overstate the importance of the actual rule enunciated in *Baker*?

2.) Is this a case about copyright not applying to ideas? To inventions? To functional articles? To schemes in which expressive choice is impossible? To schemes where expressive choice *is* possible (one could choose different schemes for classifying how to "book" expenses and income) but once those are chosen, and become "industry standard"—as in Generally Accepted Accounting Principles—it would hold up progress to have the standard subject to a copyright? All of the above?

3.) Merger of Idea and Expression

Herbert Rosenthal Jewelry Corp. v. Kalpakian
446 F.2d 738 (9th Cir. 1971)

BROWNING, Circuit Judge.

Plaintiff and defendants are engaged in the design, manufacture, and sale of fine jewelry.

Plaintiff charged defendants with infringing plaintiff's copyright registration of a pin in the shape of a bee formed of gold encrusted with jewels. A consent decree was entered, reciting that the parties had agreed to a settlement of the action and entry of the decree. It provided that plaintiff's copyright of the jeweled bee was "good and valid in law," that defendants had manufactured a jeweled bee "alleged to be similar," and that defendants were enjoined from infringing plaintiff's copyright and from manufacturing or selling copies of plaintiff's jeweled bee pin.

Later plaintiff filed a motion for an order holding defendants in contempt of the consent decree. The district court, after an evidentiary hearing, found that while defendants had manufactured and sold a line of jeweled bee pins, they designed their pins themselves

Handwritten margin note:
© protects expression, not ideas → description of book-keeping © (expression), visual not © (idea) but potentially patentable

after a study of bees in nature and in published works and did not copy plaintiff's copyrighted bee. The court further found that defendants' jeweled bees were "not substantially similar" to plaintiff's bees, except that both "do look like bees." The court concluded that defendants had neither infringed plaintiff's copyright nor violated the consent decree. . . . We affirm. . . .

II

Plaintiff contends that its copyright registration of a jeweled bee entitles it to protection from the manufacture and sale by others of any object that to the ordinary observer is substantially similar in appearance. The breadth of this claim is evident. For example, while a photograph of the copyrighted bee pin attached to the complaint depicts a bee with nineteen small white jewels on its back, plaintiff argues that its copyright is infringed by defendants'

Plaintiff's jeweled bee design alongside four of defendants' jeweled bees

entire line of a score or more jeweled bees in three sizes decorated with from nine to thirty jewels of various sizes, kinds, and colors.

Although plaintiff's counsel asserted that the originality of plaintiff's bee pin lay in a particular arrangement of jewels on the top of the pin, the elements of this arrangement were never identified. Defendants' witnesses testified that the "arrangement" was simply a function of the size and form of the bee pin and the size of the jewels used. Plaintiff's counsel, repeatedly pressed by the district judge, was unable to suggest how jewels might be placed on the back of a pin in the shape of a bee without infringing plaintiff's copyright. He eventually conceded, "not being a jeweler, I can't conceive of how he might rearrange the design so it is dissimilar."

If plaintiff's understanding of its rights were correct, its copyright would effectively prevent others from engaging in the business of manufacturing and selling jeweled bees. We think plaintiff confuses the balance Congress struck between protection and competition under the Patent Act and the Copyright Act.

The owner of a patent is granted the exclusive right to exploit for a period of seventeen years (a maximum of fourteen years for design patents) the conception that is the subject matter of the patent. 35 U.S.C. §§ 154, 173. The grant of this monopoly, however, is carefully circumscribed by substantive and procedural protections. To be patentable the subject matter must be new and useful, and represent a nonobvious advance—one requiring "more ingenuity and skill than that possessed by an ordinary mechanic acquainted with the business"; an advance that would not be obvious to a hypothetical person skilled in the art and charged with knowledge of all relevant developments publicly known to that point in time. *Graham v. John Deere Co.* (1966). A patent is granted only after an independent administrative inquiry and determination that these substantive standards have been met. This determination is subject to both administrative and court review.

Copyright registration, on the other hand, confers no right at all to the conception reflected in the registered subject matter. "Unlike a patent, a copyright gives no exclusive right to the art disclosed; protection is given only to the expression of the idea—not the idea itself." *Mazer v. Stein* (1954). Accordingly, the prerequisites for copyright registration are minimal. The work offered for registration need only be the product of the registrant. So long as it is not a plagiarized copy of another's effort, there is no requirement that the work differ substantially from prior works or that it contribute anything of value. "The copyright protects originality rather than novelty or invention." ... Because the registrant's protection is limited and the social cost therefore small, the life of the copyright is long and, under current proposals, potentially even longer—now twenty-eight years plus a renewal period of twenty-eight more, 17 U.S.C. § 24, and, under Copyright Revision Bill § 543, 91st Congress, 1st Session, the life of the author plus fifty years.

Obviously a copyright must not be treated as equivalent to a patent lest long continuing private monopolies be conferred over areas of gainful activity without first satisfying the substantive and procedural prerequisites to the grant of such privileges.

Because copyright bars only copying, perhaps this case could be disposed of on the district court's finding that defendants did not copy plaintiff's bee pin. ... Any inference of copying based upon similar appearance lost much of its strength because both pins were lifelike representations of a natural creature. Moreover, there were differences between defendants' and plaintiff's bees—notably in the veining of the wings.

Although this evidence would support a finding that defendants' bees were their own work rather than copied from plaintiff's, this resolution of the problem is not entirely satisfactory, particularly in view of the principle that copying need not be conscious, but "may be the result of subconscious memory derived from hearing, seeing or reading the copyrighted work at some time in the past." Howell's Copyright Law 129 (4th ed. 1962). It seems unrealistic to suppose that defendants could have closed their minds to plaintiff's highly successful jeweled bee pin as they designed their own.

What is basically at stake is the extent of the copyright owner's monopoly—from how large an area of activity did Congress intend to allow the copyright owner to exclude others? We think the production of jeweled bee pins is a larger private preserve than Congress intended to be set aside in the public market without a patent. A jeweled bee pin is therefore an "idea" that defendants were free to copy. Plaintiff seems to agree, for it disavows any claim that defendants cannot manufacture and sell jeweled bee pins and concedes that only plaintiff's particular design or "expression" of the jeweled bee pin "idea" is protected under its copyright. The difficulty, as we have noted, is that on this record the "idea" and its "expression" appear to be indistinguishable. There is no greater similarity between the pins of plaintiff and defendants than is inevitable from the use of jewel-encrusted bee forms in both.

When the "idea" and its "expression" are thus inseparable, copying the "expression" will not be barred, since protecting the "expression" in such circumstances would confer a monopoly of the "idea" upon the copyright owner free of the conditions and limitations imposed by the patent law.
Affirmed.

Questions:

1.) "The court further found that defendants' jeweled bees were 'not substantially similar' to plaintiff's bees, except that both 'do look like bees.'" Is the court being funny, or is this the *point* of the merger doctrine? Both?

2.) To establish copyright infringement, a plaintiff must prove "(1) ownership of a valid copyright, and (2) copying of constituent elements of the work that are original." *Feist Publications, Inc. v. Rural Tel. Serv. Co.* (1991). As a procedural matter, when should merger be considered? As negating the cause of action in the first place since this is not copyrightable subject matter? Or as excusing infringement by denying that it was really "copying"? What difference does it make?

Morrissey v. Procter & Gamble Co.
379 F.2d 675 (1st Cir. 1967)

ALDRICH, Chief Judge.

This is an appeal from a summary judgment for the defendant. The plaintiff, Morrissey, is the copyright owner of a set of rules for a sales promotional contest of the "sweepstakes" type involving the social security numbers of the participants. Plaintiff alleges that the defendant, Procter & Gamble Company, infringed, by copying, almost precisely, Rule 1. In its motion for summary judgment, based upon affidavits and depositions, defendant denies that plaintiff's Rule 1 is copyrightable material, and denies access. The district court held for the defendant on both grounds.

Taking the second ground first, the defendant offered affidavits or depositions of all of its allegedly pertinent employees, all of whom denied having seen plaintiff's rules. Although the plaintiff, by deposition, flatly testified that prior to the time the defendant conducted its contest he had mailed to the defendant his copyrighted rules with an offer to sell, the court ruled that the defendant had "proved" nonaccess, and stated that it was "satisfied that no material issue as to access * * * lurks * * * [in the record.]"

The court did not explain whether it considered defendant's showing to have constituted proof overcoming the presumption of receipt arising from plaintiff's testimony of mailing, or whether it felt there was an unsatisfied burden on the plaintiff to show that the particularly responsible employees of the defendant had received his communication. Either view would have been error. A notice to the defendant at its principal office, as this one assertedly was, is proper notice. There is at least an inference that the letter reached its proper destination. . . . The presumption arising from mailing remained in the case.[1] . . .

The second aspect of the case raises a more difficult question. Before discussing it we recite plaintiff's Rule 1, and defendant's Rule 1, the italicizing in the latter being ours to note the defendant's variations or changes.

> "1. Entrants should print name, address and social security number on a boxtop, or a plain paper. Entries must be accompanied by * * * boxtop or by plain paper on which the name * * * is copied from any source. Official rules are explained on * * * packages or leaflets obtained from dealer. If you do not have a social security number you may use the name and number of any member of your immediate family living with you. Only the person named on the entry will be deemed an entrant and may qualify for prize.
>
> "Use the correct social security number belonging to the person named on entry * * * wrong number will be disqualified."

(Plaintiff's Rule)

> "1. Entrants should print name, address and Social Security number on a Tide boxtop, or on [a] plain paper. Entries must be accompanied by Tide boxtop (any size) or by plain paper on which the name 'Tide' is copied from any source. Official rules are *available* on Tide Sweepstakes packages, or on leaflets at Tide dealers, *or you can send a*

---

[1] The court did not discuss, nor need we, the additional fact that the almost exact following of plaintiff's wording and format in an area in which there is at least some room for maneuverability, might be found of itself to contradict defendant's denial of access. *Cf. Arnstein v. Porter.*

stamped, self-addressed envelope to: Tide 'Shopping Fling' Sweep-stakes, P.O. Box 4459, Chicago 77, Illinois.

"If you do not have a Social Security number, you may use the name and number of any member of your immediate family living with you. Only the person named on the entry will be deemed an entrant and may qualify for a prize.

"Use the correct Social Security number, belonging to the person named on the entry wrong numbers will be disqualified."

(Defendant's Rule)

The district court, following an earlier decision, *Gaye v. Gillis* (D. Mass. 1958), took the position that since the substance of the contest was not copyrightable, which is unquestionably correct, *Baker v. Selden* (1879); and the substance was relatively simple, it must follow that plaintiff's rule sprung directly from the substance and "contains no original creative authorship." This does not follow. Copyright attaches to form of expression, and defendant's own proof, introduced to deluge the court on the issue of access, itself established that there was more than one way of expressing even this simple substance. Nor, in view of the almost precise similarity of the two rules, could defendant successfully invoke the principle of a stringent standard for showing infringement which some courts apply when the subject matter involved admits of little variation in form of expression.

Nonetheless, we must hold for the defendant. When the uncopyrightable subject matter is very narrow, so that "the topic necessarily requires," if not only one form of expression, at best only a limited number, to permit copyrighting would mean that a party or parties, by copyrighting a mere handful of forms, could exhaust all possibilities of future use of the substance. In such circumstances it does not seem accurate to say that any particular form of expression comes from the subject matter. However, it is necessary to say that the subject matter would be appropriated by permitting the copyrighting of its expression. We cannot recognize copyright as a game of chess in which the public can be checkmated. *Cf. Baker v. Selden.*

Upon examination the matters embraced in Rule 1 are so straightforward and simple that we find this limiting principle to be applicable. Furthermore, its operation need not await an attempt to copyright all possible forms. It cannot be only the last form of expression which is to be condemned, as completing defendant's exclusion from the substance. Rather, in these circumstances, we hold that copyright does not extend to the subject matter at all, and plaintiff cannot complain even if his particular expression was deliberately adopted.

Affirmed.

Questions:

1.) Is the court saying that the defendant did not copy the rule? That it might well have copied the rule but that it does not matter? Is copying in the case of merger a.) a *prima facie* wrong excusable because of a dearth of alternatives, b.) not a violation of a legally protected interest in the first place and thus neutral as a matter of law and policy or c.) a positive good?

2.) The court first says that there *are* other ways in which the rule could have been stated and then says "We cannot recognize copyright as a game of chess in which the public can be checkmated." What does this mean?

Kregos v. Associated Press
937 F.2d 700 (2d Cir. 1991); cert. denied,
510 U.S. 1112 (1994)

NEWMAN, Circuit Judge.

The primary issue on this appeal is whether the creator of a baseball pitching form is entitled to a copyright. The appeal requires us to consider the extent to which the copyright law protects a compiler of information. George L. Kregos appeals from the April 30, 1990, judgment of the District Court for the Southern District of New York (Gerard L. Goettel, Judge) dismissing on motion for summary judgment his copyright and trademark claims against the Associated Press ("AP") and Sports Features Syndicate, Inc. ("Sports Features"). We affirm dismissal of the trademark claims, but conclude that Kregos is entitled to a trial on his copyright claim, though the available relief may be extremely limited.

Facts

The facts are fully set forth in Judge Goettel's thorough opinion. The reader's attention is particularly called to the appendices to that opinion, which set forth Kregos' pitching form and the allegedly infringing forms. Kregos distributes to newspapers a pitching form, discussed in detail below, that displays information concerning the past performances of the opposing pitchers scheduled to start each day's baseball games. The form at issue in this case, first distributed in 1983, is a redesign of an earlier form developed by Kregos in the 1970's. Kregos registered his form with the Copyright Office and obtained a copyright. Though the form, as distributed to subscribing newspapers, includes statistics, the controversy in this case concerns only Kregos' rights to the form without each day's data, in other words, his rights to the particular selection of categories of statistics appearing on his form.

In 1984, AP began publishing a pitching form provided by Sports Features. The AP's 1984 form was virtually identical to Kregos' 1983 form. AP and Sports Features changed their form in 1986 in certain respects, which are discussed in part I(D) below. Kregos' 1983 form lists four items of information about each day's games-the teams, the starting pitchers, the game time, and the betting odds, and then lists nine items of information about each pitcher's past performance, grouped into three categories. Since there can be no claim of a protectable interest in the categories of information concerning each day's game, we confine our attention to the categories of information concerning the pitchers' past performances. For convenience, we will identify each performance item by a number from 1 to 9 and use that number whenever referring to the same item in someone else's form.

The first category in Kregos' 1983 form, performance during the entire season, comprises two items—won/lost record (1) and earned run average (2). The second category, performance during the entire season against the opposing team at the site of the game, comprises three items—won/lost record (3), innings pitched (4), and earned run average (5). The third category, performance in the last three starts, comprises four items—won/lost record (6), innings pitched (7), earned run average (8), and men on base average (9). This last item is the average total of hits and walks given up by a pitcher per nine innings of pitching.

It is undisputed that prior to Kregos' 1983 form, no form had listed the same nine items collected in his form. Kregos pulled his categories of data from a "universe of available data." It is also undisputed that some but not all of the nine items of information had previously appeared in other forms. In the earlier forms, however, the few items common to Kregos' form were grouped with items different from those in Kregos' form.

The District Court granted summary judgment for the defendants on both Kregos' copyright and trademark claims. On the copyright side of the case, the Court ruled that Kregos lacked a copyrightable interest in his pitching form on three grounds. First, the Court concluded that Kregos' pitching form was insufficiently original in its selection of statistics to warrant a copyright as a compilation. Second, the Court concluded that, in view of the limited space available for displaying pitching forms in newspapers, the possible variations in selections of pitching statistics were so limited that the idea of a pitching form had merged into its expression. Third, the Court ruled that Kregos' pitching form was not entitled to a copyright because of the so-called "blank form" doctrine.

Discussion
I. Copyright Claim
A. Copyright for a Compilation of Facts

The basic principles concerning copyright protection for compilations of facts are clear and have recently been authoritatively restated in the Supreme Court's decision rejecting copyright protection for telephone book white pages. *Feist Publications, Inc. v. Rural Telephone Service Co., Inc.* (1991) ("*Feist*"). Thus, as to compilations of facts, independent creation as to selection and arrangement will not assure copyright protection; the requirement of minimal creativity becomes an important ingredient of the test for copyright entitlement.

Prior to *Feist*, we had applied these principles to require some minimal level of creativity in two fairly recent cases that illustrate compilations of facts one of which is and one of which is not entitled to a copyright, *Eckes v. Card Prices Update* (2d Cir. 1984), and *Financial Information, Inc. v. Moody's Investors Service* (2d Cir. 1986) ("*FFI*"), *cert. denied*, 484 U.S. 820 (1987). In *Eckes* we upheld a District Court's finding, made after trial, that a selection of 5,000 out of 18,000 baseball cards to be considered "premium" was entitled to a copyright. *Eckes.* In *FFI* we upheld a District Court's finding, also made after trial, that the listing of five items of information concerning municipal bond calls lacked sufficient selection to warrant a copyright; in almost all instances, the five items for the various bond issues had all appeared in "tombstone" ads, and only "minor additional research" was needed to complete the listings. *FFI.*

Kregos' pitching form presents a compilation of facts that falls between the extremes illustrated by *Eckes* and *FFI*. Kregos has selected nine items of information concerning a pitcher's performance. "The universe of available data" available only from inspection of box scores of prior games is considerably greater than nine, though perhaps not as great as the quantity of 18,000 cards in *Eckes*. For example, Kregos could have selected past performances from any number of recent starts, instead of using the three most recent starts. And he could have chosen to include strikeouts, walks, balks, or hit batters. In short, there are at least scores of available statistics about pitching performance available to be calculated from the underlying data and therefore thousands of combinations of data that a selector can choose to include in a pitching form.[2]

It cannot be said as a matter of law that in selecting the nine items for his pitching form out of the universe of available data, Kregos has failed to display enough selectivity to satisfy the requirement of originality. Whether in selecting his combination of nine items he has displayed the requisite degree of creativity is a somewhat closer question. Plainly, he has done better than the compiler in *FFI* who "selected" only the five facts

---

[2] If the universe of available data included even 20 items and a selector was limited to 9 items, there would be 167,960 combinations of items available.

about bond calls already grouped together in nearly all tombstone ads. Judge Goettel was persuaded to rule against Kregos, at least in part, because "most of the statistics . . . had been established in previously existing forms." But that observation is largely irrelevant to the issue of whether Kregos' selection of statistics displays sufficient creativity to warrant a copyright. Nearly all copyrighted compilations of facts convey facts that have been published elsewhere. Each of the cards selected for the "premium" category in *Eckes* had previously been published. To hold a valid copyright, a compiler of facts need not be a discoverer of facts. Indeed, any discovered fact, or, in Kregos' case, any newly devised statistic, would not, in and of itself, be eligible for copyright protection. It's the originality shown what the finder does with the fact that allows for copyrightability.

[T]he record discloses no prior pitching form with more than three of the pitching performance statistics that are included in Kregos' selection of nine statistics. Neither a prior identical form to his nor one which varies in only a trivial degree exists. The validity of his copyright in a compilation of facts cannot be rejected as a matter of law for lack of the requisite originality and creativity.

B. Idea/Expression Merger

The fundamental copyright principle that only the expression of an idea and not the idea itself is protectable, see *Mazer v. Stein* (1954), has produced a corollary maxim that even expression is not protected in those instances where there is only one or so few ways of expressing an idea that protection of the expression would effectively accord protection to the idea itself. Our Circuit has considered this so-called "merger" doctrine in determining whether actionable infringement has occurred, rather than whether a copyright is valid, see *Durham Industries, Inc. v. Tomy Corp.* (2d Cir. 1980), an approach the Nimmer treatise regards as the "better view." See 3 NIMMER ON COPYRIGHT § 13.03[B][3] (1990). Assessing merger in the context of alleged infringement will normally provide a more detailed and realistic basis for evaluating the claim that protection of expression would inevitably accord protection to an idea.

In this case, Judge Goettel understood Kregos' idea to be "to publish an outcome predictive pitching form." In dissent, Judge Sweet contends that Kregos' idea is that the nine statistics he has selected are the most significant ones to consider when attempting to predict the outcome of a baseball game. Unquestionably, if that is the idea for purposes of merger analysis, then merger of that idea and its expression has occurred-by definition.

Though there is room for fair debate as to the identification of the pertinent idea whenever merger analysis is applied to a compilation of facts, we think the "idea" in this case is the one as formulated by Judge Goettel. Kregos has not devised a system that he seeks to withdraw from the public domain by virtue of copyright. He does not present his selection of nine statistics as a method of predicting the outcome of baseball games. His idea is that of "an outcome predictive pitching form" in the general sense that it selects the facts that he thinks newspaper readers should consider in making their own predictions of outcomes. He does not purport to weigh the nine statistics, much less provide a method for comparing the aggregate value of one pitcher's statistics against that of the opposing pitcher in order to predict an outcome or even its probability of occurring. He has not devised a system, as had the deviser of a bookkeeping system in *Baker v. Selden* (1879). He has compiled facts, or at least categories of facts, and selected those facts from a vast pool of information.

Though formulating the idea as "an outcome predictive pitching form," Judge Goettel applied the merger doctrine, concluding that the idea of selecting outcome predictive statistics to rate pitching performance was capable of expression in only a very limited number of ways.

As the various pitching forms in the record indicate, the past performances of baseball pitchers can be measured by a variety of statistics. Kregos' selection of categories includes three statistics for the pitcher's current season performance against the day's opponent at the site of the day's game; other charts select "at site" performance against the opponent during the prior season, and some select performance against the opponent over the pitcher's career, both home and away. Some charts include average men on base per nine innings; others do not. The data for most recent starts could include whatever number of games the compiler thought pertinent. These variations alone (and there are others) abundantly indicate that there are a sufficient number of ways of expressing the idea of rating pitchers' performances; this variety of expression precludes a ruling that the idea has merged into its expression.

In reaching this conclusion, we confess to some unease because of the risk that protection of selections of data, or, as in this case, categories of data, have the potential for according protection to ideas. Our concern may be illustrated by an example of a doctor who publishes a list of symptoms that he believes provides a helpful diagnosis of a disease. There might be many combinations of symptoms that others could select for the same purpose, but a substantial question would nonetheless arise as to whether that doctor could obtain a copyright in his list, based on the originality of his selection. If the idea that the doctor is deemed to be expressing is the general idea that the disease in question can be identified by observable symptoms, then the idea might not merge into the doctor's particular expression of that idea by his selection of symptoms. That general idea might remain capable of many other expressions. But it is arguable that the doctor has conceived a more precise idea—namely, the idea that his selection of symptoms is a useful identifier of the disease. That more limited idea can be expressed only by his selection of symptoms, and therefore might be said to have merged into his expression.

As long as selections of facts involve matters of taste and personal opinion, there is no serious risk that withholding the merger doctrine will extend protection to an idea. That was surely the case with the selection of premium baseball cards in *Eckes* where the compiler selected 5,000 premium baseball cards from over 18,000 cards. It is also true of a selection of prominent families for inclusion in a social directory. See *Social Register Ass'n v. Murphy* (C.C.R.I. 1904). However, where a selection of data is the first step in an analysis that yields a precise result or even a better-than-average probability of some result, protecting the "expression" of the selection would clearly risk protecting the idea of the analysis.

Kregos' pitching form is part way along the continuum spanning matters of pure taste to matters of predictive analysis. He is doing more than simply saying that he holds the opinion that his nine performance characteristics are the most pertinent. He implies that his selections have some utility in predicting outcomes. On the other hand, he has not gone so far as to provide a system for weighing the combined value of the nine characteristics for each of two opposing pitchers and determining a probability as to which is more likely to win. Like the compilers of horse racing statistics, Kregos has been content to select categories of data that he obviously believes have some predictive power, but has left its interpretation to all sports page readers as to the likely outcomes from the sets of data he has selected. His "idea," for purposes of the merger doctrine, remains the general idea that statistics can be used to assess pitching performance rather than the precise idea that his selection yields a determinable probability of outcome. Since there are various ways of expressing that general idea, the merger doctrine need not be applied to assure that the idea will remain in the public domain.

C. "Blank Form" Doctrine

The District Court also ruled that Kregos could not obtain a valid copyright in his pitching form because of the so-called "blank form" doctrine. The doctrine derives from the Supreme Court's decision in *Baker v. Selden*. The Court there denied copyright protection to blank forms contained in a book explaining a system of double-entry bookkeeping. The forms displayed an arrangement of columns and headings that permitted entries for a day, a week, or a month to be recorded on one page or two facing pages. The Court made clear that the author could not obtain copyright protection for an "art" that "might or might not have been patented" and reasoned that since the "art" was available to the public, "the ruled lines and headings of accounts must necessarily be used as incident to it." Then, in a concluding statement that is susceptible to overreading, the Court said that "blank account-books are not the subject of copyright." Similarly, a check book account register, a baby book for growth information and measurements for cooking or otherwise probably will not be copyrightable. Simply stated, it depends upon the pool of information from which the selection is taken.

Though there are some statements suggesting broadly that no blank forms are copyrightable, many courts have recognized that there can be protectable elements of forms that include considerable blank space.[3]

The regulations of the Copyright Office are careful to preclude copyright registration to:

> Blank forms, such as . . . account books, diaries, bank checks, scorecards, address books, report forms, order forms and the like, which are designed
> for recording information *and do not in themselves convey information.*

37 C.F.R. § 202.l(c)(1990)(emphasis added).

Of course, a form that conveys no information and serves only to provide blank space for recording information contains no expression or selection of information that could possibly warrant copyright protection. At the same time, it should be equally obvious that a writing that does contain a *selection* of categories of information worth recording, sufficiently original and creative to deserve a copyright as a compilation of facts, cannot lose that protection simply because the work also contains blank space for recording the information. When the Copyright Office denies a copyright to scorecards or diaries that "do not in themselves convey information," it must be contemplating works with headings so obvious that their selection cannot be said to satisfy even minimal creativity (a baseball scorecard with columns headed "innings" and lines headed "players"; a travel diary with headings for "cities" "hotels," and "restaurants"). Such a work conveys no information, not just because it contains blanks, but because its selection of headings is totally uninformative. On the other hand, if a scorecard or diary contained a group of headings whose selection (or possibly arrangement) displayed cognizable creativity, the author's choice of those headings would convey to users the information that this group of categories was something out of the ordinary. See 1 NIMMER ON COPYRIGHT § 2.18[C][1] at 2-201 (1990) ("Thus books intended to record the events of baby's first year, or a record of a European trip, or anyone of a number of other subjects, *may* evince considerable originality in suggestions of specific items of information which are to be recorded, and in the arrangement of such items.") (emphasis added).

The Ninth Circuit has rejected this approach. With deference, we suggest that this

---

[3] We are concerned with protectable elements in the selection (and perhaps arrangement) of the categories of information to be recorded on the forms. There is widespread agreement that a work containing a blank form may be copyrightable because of the protectable elements of the textual matter accompanying the form.

critique of cases recognizing a copyright in the selection of categories of information for forms is not well taken. All forms may convey that the information called for is important (or at least worth recording), but the form-maker does not necessarily display even minimal creativity by selecting categories of "important" information. [C]ourts are obliged to determine as to forms, as with all compilations of information, whether the author's selection of categories of data to be recorded displays at least minimal creativity. However, all forms need not be denied protection simply because many of them fail to display sufficient creativity.

In the pending case, once it is determined that Kregos' selection of categories of statistics displays sufficient creativity to preclude a ruling as a matter of law that it is not a copyrightable compilation of information, that same conclusion precludes rejecting his copyright as a "blank form."

D. Extent of Protection

Our ruling that Kregos' copyright claim survives defendants' motion for summary judgment does not, of course, mean that he will necessarily obtain much of a victory. If Kregos prevails at trial on the factual issues of originality and creativity, he will be entitled to protection only against infringement of the protectable features of his form. Only the selection of statistics might be entitled to protection. We agree entirely with Judge Goettel that nothing in Kregos' arrangement of the selected statistics displays the requisite creativity. As to the arrangement, Kregos' form is surely a "garden-variety" pitching form. The statistics are organized into the "obvious" arrangement of columns, and the form follows the pattern of most other forms: the statistics are organized into three groups, first the statistics about each pitcher's performance for the season, then the statistics about the pitcher's performance against the day's opponent, and finally the statistics concerning the pitcher's recent starts.

Even as to the selection of statistics, if Kregos establishes entitlement to protection, he will prevail only against other forms that can be said to copy his selection. That would appear to be true of the AP's 1984 form, which, as Judge Goettel noted, is "identical in virtually every sense to plaintiff's form." Whether it is also true of the AP's current form, revised in 1986, is far less certain. That form contains six of Kregos' nine items (1, 2, 6, 7, 8, 9). It also includes four items that Kregos does not have. Three of these items concern performance against the day's opposing team-won-lost record, innings pitched, and earned run average; though these three statistics appear on Kregos' form, the AP's 1986 form shows data for the current season both home and away, whereas Kregos' form shows data for the pitcher's current season at the site of that day's game. The fourth item on the AP's 1986 form and not on Kregos' form shows the team's record in games started by that day's pitcher during the season.

The reason for doubting that the AP's 1986 form infringes Kregos' form arises from the same consideration that supports Kregos' claim to a copyright. Kregos can obtain a copyright by displaying the requisite creativity in his selection of statistics. But if someone else displays the requisite creativity by making a selection that differs in more than a trivial degree, Kregos cannot complain. Kregos contends that the AP's 1986 form makes insignificant changes from its 1984 form. But Kregos cannot have it both ways. If his decision to select, in the category of performance against the opposing team, statistics for the pitcher's current season at the site of today's game displays, in combination with his other selections, enough creativity to merit copyright protection, then a competitor's decision to select in that same category performance statistics for the pitcher's season performance both home and away may well insulate the competitor from a claim of infringement. Thus, though issues remain to be explored before any determination can be made, it may well be that Kregos will have a valid claim only as to the AP's 1984 form.

[In part II of the opinion, the court affirmed the district court's grant of summary judgment for the defendants on the trademark claims because the plaintiff did not demonstrate secondary meaning in his form.]

APPENDIX 1

(Kregos' 1983 Pitching Form)

THE HARTFORD COURANT: Sunday, May 6, 1984

SCOREBOARD

Today's Games

Team	Probable Pitcher (H)	Time	Odds	1984 W/L	1984 ERA	vs.team at site W/L	vs.team at site IP	vs.team at site ERA	Last 3 starts W/L	Last 3 starts IP	Last 3 starts ERA	MBA
AMERICAN LEAGUE												
DET	Wilcox (R)		Even–6	3–0	3.34	0–2	10	9.00	2–0	22	2.05	11.05
CLEV	Blyleven (R)	1:35	*	3–2	3.14	0–0	6	3.00	1–1	22	3.68	12.68
K.C.	Gura (L)		*	4–0	2.55	0–2	9⅔	9.31	2–0	21⅓	1.89	9.28
TORN	Alexander (R)	1:35	5½–6½	1–1	3.82	*	*	*	1–1	21⅔	2.91	9.97
CHIC	Bannister (L)		Even–6	2–2	5.12	0–1	8	2.25	1–1	19⅔	5.03	15.10
BOST	Hurst (L)	2:05	*	3–3	2.02	1–1	13⅓	4.73	2–1	18	1.50	15.00
OAK	Warren (R)		Even–6	3–3	3.82	*	*	*	2–1	18	5.00	15.50
MINN	Hodge (L)	2:15	*	0–0	7.20	*	*	*	0–0	5	7.20	23.40
N.Y.	Fontenot (L)		*	0–4	4.88	1–0	7	5.14	0–2	16⅓	2.76	13.22
MIL	Cocanower (R)	2:30	5½–6½	0–4	3.00	*	*	*	0–3	23⅔	1.90	12.55
BALT	Boddicker (R)		5–7	1–3	3.19	1–0	8	4.50	1–1	23	1.57	10.17
TEX	Darwin (R)	3:05	*	3–0	2.40	1–0	6⅔	0.00	2–0	25	1.08	7.54
CAL	John (L)		5½–6½	2–2	2.04	*	*	*	1–1	21⅓	2.11	11.39
SEAT	Young (L)	4:35	*	2–2	6.52	1–0	11⅔	0.77	0–1	11⅔	8.49	20.83
NATIONAL LEAGUE												
ATL	McMurtry (R)		*	2–3	3.58	1–0	7	3.86	1–1	20⅓	3.10	13.28
MONT	Lea (R)	1:05	6–7	4–1	2.61	0–1	7	6.43	2–0	20	2.70	13.05
ATL	Camp (R)		*	2–0	2.31	0–1	4	4.50	2–0	11⅔	2.31	10.03
MONT	Palmer (R)		6–7	2–0	2.29	*	*	*	1–0	14⅔	2.45	5.52
L.A.	Pena (R)		*	4–1	1.41	0–0	7⅔	2.35	3–0	24⅔	1.11	7.40
PITT	McWilliams (L)	1:35	Pick 'em	0–3	3.24	0–0	8	2.25	0–2	17	3.18	12.18
L.A.	Valenzuela (L)		5½–6½	3–2	2.93	0–0	7⅓	3.68	3–0	27	0.67	6.33
PITT	Tudor (L)		*	1–1	2.91	*	*	*	0–1	19⅓	4.19	14.43
CINN	Russell (R)		*	1–3	3.14	*	*	*	0–2	22	1.23	11.45
PHIL	Carlton (L)	1:35	7½–8½	1–1	2.60	1–0	8	4.50	0–1	21	2.14	11.57
HOUS	Ryan (R)		*	1–2	3.65	2–0	15⅔	2.30	0–1	16	5.06	12.94
METS	Gooden (R)	1:35	Pick 'em	2–1	2.63	*	*	*	1–0	19	0.47	9.95
S.F.	Laskey (R)		*	0–3	2.20	*	*	*	0–2	19⅔	2.29	10.98
STL	Andujar (R)	2:15	6½–7½	4–2	3.09	0–1	15⅔	2.87	2–1	25	3.24	10.08
S.D.	Show (R)		*	4–1	1.89	2–0	14	1.93	2–1	17⅓	1.56	10.90
CUBS	Ruthven (R)	2:20	Even–6	2–2	5.35	*	*	*	0–2	17⅓	7.79	12.98

Bottom team is home team. Favored team is designated by odds beside pitcher's name. All pitching data reflects the pitcher's past performance as a "starter." 1984—Pitcher's 1984 record as "starter." Vs Team at site—Pitcher's past performance vs. today's opponent at the site of today's game. Last 3 Starts—Reflects how pitcher is currently going. Details his performance over his last three starts. W/L—Won/lost record as a "starter". IP—Innings pitched. ERA—Earned run average. MBA—Men on base average. (Average number of men allowed to reach base via hits and walks per nine innings pitched.) The odds are estimated lines. Time is Eastern Daylight Time

APPENDIX 2

(AP's 1984 Pitching Form)

FRIDAY'S PITCHERS

Away Home	Probable Pitcher	Time	Line	1983 W-L	1983 ERA	vs. opp. at site W-L	vs. opp. at site IP	vs. opp. at site ERA	last 3 starts W-L	last 3 starts IP	last 3 starts ERA	AHWG
American												
DET	Matt Wilcox (R)		EV–6	11–10	.397	0–0	90	0.00	0–0	00.0	0.00	0.0
at CHI	Rich Dotson (R)	1:30		22–7	3.22	1–0	60	2.25	0–0	00.0	0.00	0.0
NY	John Montefusco (R)		5.5–6.5	14–4	3.31	0–0	00	00	000	00.0	0.00	0.0
at TEX	Frank Tanana (L)	7:35		7–9	3.05	0–1	71	6.14	0–0	00.0	0.00	0.0
CLE	Bert Blyleven (R)			7–10	3.91	0–0	00	00	00.0	0.00	0.00	0.0
at KC	Mark Gubicza (R)	7:35	PK	0–0	0–0	0.0	00	00.0	0.00	0.00	0.00	0.0
BALT	Mike Boddiker (R)		5.5–6.5	16–8	2.77	1–0	70	0.0	0–0	00.0	0.00	0.0
at MINN	Mike Smithson (R)	7:35		10–11	3.91	0–0	00	0–0	00.0	0.00	0.00	0.0
TOR	Doyle Alexander (R)		5.5–6.5	7–8	4.41	1–0	111	1.59	0–0	00	0.00	0.0
at CAL	Steve Brown (R)	9:30		3–4	4.50	1–1	32	7.36	0.0	00.0	0.00	0.0
BOST	Dennis Boyd (R)			4–8	3.34	0–0	00	0–0	00.0	00.0	0.00	0.0
at OAK	Larry Sorensen (R)	9:35	EV–6	12–11	4.24	0–0	00	0–0	0.00	00.0	0.00	0.0
MILW	Moose Haas (R)		7.5–8.5	13–3	3.27	0–0	70	129	0–0	00.0	0.00	0.0
at SEA	Matt Young (L)	9:35		11–15	3.27	0–0	00	0–0	00.0	0.00	0.00	0.0
National												
PHIL	Charles Hudson (R)		EV–6	8–8	3.35	0–0	52	9.53	0–0	00.0	0.00	0.0
at CINN	Joe Price (L)	6:35		10–6	3.38	1–0	81	1.08	0–0	0.00	00.0	0.0
MONT	Bryn Smith (R)			6–11	.349	0–0	12	5.40	0–0	00.0	0.00	0.0
at ATL	Ken Dayley (L)	6:40	6–7	5–8	4.30	0–1	61	2.84	0–0	00.0	0.00	0.0
NY	Walt Terrell (R)			8–8	3.50	1–0	60	1.50	0–0	00.0	0.00	0.0
at HOU	Tony Scott (R)	7:35	7.5–8.5	10–8	3.72	1–1	161	2.20	0–0	00.0	0.00	0.0
CHI	Scott Sanderson (R)			6–7	.445	0–0	10	27.00	0–0	00.0	0.00	0.0
at SD	Tim Lollar (L)	9:05	6.5–7.5	7–12	4.58	1–1	131	3.38	0–0	00.0	0.00	0.0
PITT	John Tudor (L)			13–12	4.05	0–3	00	0–0	00.0	0.00	0.00	0.0
at LA	Bob Welch (R)	9:35	6.5–7.5	15–12	2.65	0–0	70	2.57	0–0	00.0	0.00	0.0
ST L	Joaquin Andujar (R)			7–16	4.00	0–1	80	5.63	0–0	00.0	0.00	0.0
at SF	Bill Laskey (R)	10:05	EV–6	13–10	4.19	1–0	90	1.00	0–0	00.0	0.00	0.0

Legend W–L Won–Lost IP Innings pitched ERA Earned run average AHWG Average hits and walks per nine innings

APPENDIX 3
(AP's 1986 Pitching Form)

	PITCHERS	LINE	1987 W–L	ERA	TEAM REC	1987 W–L	VS IP	OPP ERA	LAST 3 STARTS W–L	IP	ERA†	AHWG
Minnesota	Niekro (R)	2:35p	7–12	5.00	6–11	1–1	10.0	3.60	1–1	17.2	4.58	13.2
Kansas City	Gubicza (R)	6–7	12–18	4.10	14–20	0–1	6.0	7.50	1–2	23.0	2.35	12.1
Seattle	Langston (L)	3:05p	18–13	3.86	20–14	2–0	18.0	1.00	1–2	21.0	3.00	15.4
Texas	Hough (R)	5½–6½	18–12	3.78	22–17	1–0	12.0	4.50	1–1	25.0	2.88	9.7
Cleveland	Farrell (R)	3:10p	4–1	3.21	3–5	No Record			0–1	21.0	4.71	14.1
California	Witt (R)	6–7	16–13	3.85	18–17	No Record			1–1	23.0	3.91	11.3

KEY=

TEAM REC—Team's record in games started by today's pitcher.
AHWG—Average hits and walks allowed per 9 innings.
VS OPP—Pitcher's record versus this opponent, 1987 statistics.
Copyright 1987 Sports Features Syndicate, Inc. and Computer Sports World.
AP–NY–01–25–89 1635 EST <

SWEET, District Judge, concurring in part and dissenting in part.

While I concur in the majority's conclusion that Kregos has displayed sufficient creativity to satisfy the *Feist Publications* standard for copyrightability, I would affirm the district court's grant of summary judgment because I conclude that Kregos' idea here has merged into his expression.

1. Kregos' Idea

I respectfully disagree with the majority's statement that Kregos' idea was the abstract "general idea that statistics can be used to assess pitching performance," because I do not believe that the majority has set forth convincing grounds for its determination as to the idea at issue here.

In my opinion, Kregos' form constitutes an explanation of his preferred system of handicapping baseball games, and he seeks to use his copyright here to prevent others from practicing that system.

The majority characterizes Kregos' work as dealing with "matters of taste and opinion," and therefore compares it to the list of baseball card prices in *Eckes v. Card Prices Update* (2d Cir. 1984) or to a listing of socially prominent families rather than to the hypothetical doctor's diagnostic chart. In my view, both the pitching form and the diagnostic chart are expressions intended to assist in predicting particular outcomes, with the data intended to be used as a basis for that prediction. In contrast, neither the card price list nor the social register is associated with any defined event or result, and the information reported-the card prices, the names of the families-is itself the primary feature or attraction.

Finally, in light of the majority's agreement with the district court that Kregos' arrangement of the statistics was not itself creative or original, and therefore that his particular ordering is not protected, it is difficult to grasp exactly what "expression" the majority intends to protect, if not the fundamental expression that these nine items are valuable in predicting games. This difficulty becomes apparent as the majority speculates about the extent of protection to be given to Kregos' form.

2. The Application of the Merger Doctrine

As a secondary matter, I disagree with the majority's characterization of how the merger doctrine is applied in this Circuit.

I believe the proper approach requires the court first to decide whether the copyrighted work satisfies the primary requirement of creativity, then to determine whether there is merger before extending copyright protection. This is based on the wording of § 102(b) of the Copyright Act, which provides

> In no case does copyright protection for an original work of authorship
> extend to any idea, procedure, process, system, method of operation,

concept, principle, or discovery, regardless of the form in which it is described, explained, illustrated, or embodied in such work.

I interpret this language as indicating that protection cannot be given to a work which is inseparable from its underlying idea.

The Nimmer treatise supports the majority's approach, suggesting that merger must be considered in the context of determining whether infringement has occurred rather than in deciding the issue of copyrightability. Under this approach, a court which finds that merger exists should hold that the two works in question are not "substantially similar," even where they are in fact identical, a result which I view as a not useful variety of doublespeak.

Nimmer notwithstanding, the majority of cases have rejected this approach and instead followed the method in which merger becomes an issue only when the two works in question—the copyrighted one and the alleged infringement—appear on the surface to be similar, and under which merger is used as a reason for denying all copyright protection to the plaintiff and thereby excusing the defendant's use of a similar or even identical expression.

The difference in applying these two approaches is not insignificant. Nimmer's method lends itself much more readily to the erroneous conclusion that merger is only available where the defendant has independently created an expression which happens coincidentally to be similar to the plaintiffs work. Merger is then viewed as a means of explaining the unintentional similarity between the two works-thus Nimmer's characterization of it as a means of negating substantial similarity. In other words, if a defendant has actually copied the plaintiffs work, it is unlikely to be allowed to rely on merger to avoid liability. This approach owes little if anything to the strictures of § 102(b), and instead depends on the fundamental principle of copyright law that independent creation is never infringement.

The more common approach, in which merger is considered as part of the determination of copyrightability, absolves even a defendant who has directly copied the plaintiffs work if the idea of that work is merged into the expression. I believe this approach accords more fully with both the language and the purpose of § 102(b), and serves to focus consideration on the proper definition of the idea at the outset of the inquiry.

Questions:

1.) What idea does the court say the form is expressing? What idea does Judge Sweet say the form is expressing? Which convinces you?

2.) Is the holding of this case that the more accurate a prediction system, the less copyrightable? Why or why not?

3.) Reconcile Judge Sweet's dissent here and in the *West* cases.

PROBLEM 11-2

[With thanks to David Nimmer, Rochelle Dreyfuss and Roberta Kwall.*]

Indiana Jones finds the Dead Sea Scrolls in a cave, sealed inside amphorae. The scrolls have badly deteriorated so that what remains is a jumble of fragments, some legible and some not. Dr. Jones painstakingly tries to reconstruct the scrolls. He uses many types of evidence. For example, because he knows what size the scrolls were and roughly what their margins were, if there is a gap in the reconstructed scroll, he can deduce how big the word is, and come up with all the Hebrew words (or Aramaic or Greek if the scroll is in that language) that might fit. Jones is an expert in early Jewish sects, so he knows what type of wording is most likely. Then he can look at contemporary religious texts, at word frequency distributions, and predict which word fits the gap. If that makes sense linguistically and in the context of the religious text he is looking at, he can have greater certainty that the two fragments on either side are indeed from that particular scroll. Jones' unparalleled linguistic, religious and archeological knowledge give him many clues like this—his colleagues describe his ability to synthesize all of these sources of information as nothing short of genius. At the end of 2 years of work, he claims to have the definitive "historical reconstruction" of the scroll.

May Jones claim copyright in the reconstructed text? Argue both sides. In each case, explain the analogies you would make, the doctrines you would invoke and the particular precedents to which you would appeal.

4.) Useful Articles

As defined by the Copyright Act, a "useful article" is "an article having an intrinsic utilitarian function that is not merely to portray the appearance of the article or to convey information." Such useful articles, along with "any article that is normally a part of a useful article," cannot be copyrighted; they are protectable, if at all, only by patent law. However, the *"design of a useful article" can* be copyrighted as a "pictorial, graphic, or sculptural work" if "such design incorporates pictorial, graphic, or sculptural features that *can be identified separately from, and are capable of existing independently of, the utilitarian aspects of the article*," 17 U.S.C. § 101, a standard known as "separability." But how does one determine whether a useful article's design features are sufficiently separable from its utilitarian aspects, particularly when (unlike a hood ornament on a car, for example) they cannot physically be detached from the underlying article? This is the "metaphysical quandary"[4] of conceptual separability.

Sometimes form and function merge—as with a sculptural work that also serves as a bicycle rack, or a mannequin, or a belt buckle.[5] Are these copyrightable "works of applied art" or uncopyrightable "industrial designs"? Sometimes design elements serve functional purposes—as with the sequins and beads on the bodice of a prom dress that "cover the body

---

* David Nimmer, *Copyright in the Dead Sea Scrolls*, 38 HOUSTON L. REV. 1; Rochelle Dreyfuss and Roberta Kwall, *Intellectual Property* 224 (2d edition 2004).

[4] Quoting *Universal Furniture Int'l, Inc. v. Collezione Europa USA, Inc.* (4th Cir. 2010).

[5] *See Brandir Int'l, Inc. v. Cascade Pac. Lumber Co.* (2d Cir. 1987) (bicycle rack not copyrightable); *Carol Barnhart, Inc. v. Economy Cover Corp.* (2d Cir. 1985) (mannequin torso not copyrightable); *Kieselstein-Cord v. Accessories by Pearl, Inc.* (2d Cir. 1980) (belt buckle copyrightable).

in a particularly attractive way for that special occasion" or the chevrons, stripes, and color blocks on a cheerleader uniform that appear to identify the wearer as a cheerleader (and apparently make the wearer appear both "slimmer" and "curvier").[6] Can these aesthetic features "exist independently" of their utilitarian function? How do we know—do we look at the perception of an ordinary observer? The motivations of the designer? At whether they are primarily ornamental or functional? Or whether, taking away any functionality, they're still marketable as art? At stake is a dividing line between copyright and patent law. Draw it too far one way, and copyright confers 95 years (or life plus 70 years) of exclusivity over utilitarian subject matter without ensuring that patent eligibility thresholds are satisfied. Draw it too far the other way, and copyright excludes legitimate works of art from its purview.

Not surprisingly, courts have "struggled mightily to formulate a test" for conceptual separability.[7] In 2017, in the case involving cheerleader uniforms, the Supreme Court sought to "resolve widespread disagreement over the proper test for implementing § 101's separate identification and independent-existence requirements." The appellate decision in that case had listed *nine* different approaches to analyzing conceptual separability from courts, scholars, and the Copyright Office, and arguably added a tenth one. The Supreme Court's majority opinion largely ignored those prior formulations, and provided its own standard. In theory, therefore, we now have a definitive test.

This Supreme Court decision is below. But first, consider the analysis in an earlier case, *Brandir Int'l, Inc. v. Cascade Pacific Lumber Co.* (2d Cir. 1987). There, the Second Circuit addressed the question of whether a bicycle rack called the "RIBBON Rack" was copyrightable. The sculptor had originally come up with a minimalist sine wave sculpture made of metal. One of his friends, an avid cyclist, opined that it would make a great bike rack. Rather than beating the friend with his own bike in a fit of artistic pique, the sculptor saw a business opportunity and modified the ribbon rack to make it more suitable for such a task. But was it copyrightable as a sculpture?

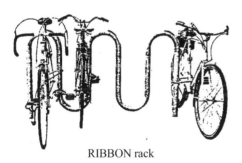

RIBBON rack

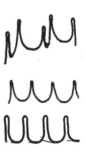

Previous sculptures that led to the RIBBON rack

The court in *Brandir* summarized several possible approaches to "conceptual separability . . . including whether the primary use is as a utilitarian article as opposed to an artistic work, whether the aesthetic aspects of the work can be said to be 'primary,' and whether the article is marketable as art, none of which is very satisfactory." But the court finally adopted an approach drawn from a law review article by Professor Robert

---

[6] *Jovani Fashion, Inc. v. Cinderella Divine, Inc.* (S.D.N.Y. 2011) (prom dress design not copyrightable, affirmed by the Second Circuit); *Star Athletica v. Varsity Brands, Inc.* (2017) (cheerleader uniform designs copyrightable). Please note that the Supreme Court in *Star Athletica* did not find that identifying the wearer as a cheerleader was the purpose of these design features. The claims about enhancing the wearer's appearance are from the oral argument in that case.

[7] *Varsity Brands, Inc. v. Star Athletica* (6th Cir. 2015).

Denicola (*Applied Art and Industrial Design: A Suggested Approach to Copyright in Useful Articles*, 1983). Professor Denicola had proposed a test that focused on the motivations of the artist, rather than the mind of the beholder, concluding that "copyrightability 'ultimately should depend on the extent to which the work reflects artistic expression uninhibited by functional considerations.'" Writing for the majority, Judge Oakes summarized Denicola's test as follows: "if design elements reflect a merger of aesthetic and functional considerations, the artistic aspects of a work cannot be said to be conceptually separable from the utilitarian elements. Conversely, where design elements can be identified as reflecting the designer's artistic judgment exercised independently of functional influences, conceptual separability exists."

Applying this standard, the majority held that the RIBBON Rack was not copyrightable. While the rack originated as a series of wire sculptures (see above), the final form at issue in the case had "adapted the original aesthetic elements to accommodate and further a utilitarian purpose"—among other things, the regular undulations allowed multiple types of bicycles and mopeds to park both under and over the curves. The majority concluded:

> Using the test we have adopted, it is not enough that . . . the rack may stimulate in the mind of the reasonable observer a concept separate from the bicycle rack concept. While the RIBBON Rack may be worthy of admiration for its aesthetic qualities alone, it remains nonetheless the product of industrial design. Form and function are inextricably intertwined in the rack, its ultimate design being as much the result of utilitarian pressures as aesthetic choices. . . . Thus there remains no artistic element of the RIBBON Rack that can be identified as separate and "capable of existing independently, of, the utilitarian aspects of the article."

Judge Winter filed a dissenting opinion, explaining "The grounds of my disagreement are that: (1) my colleagues' adaptation of Professor Denicola's test diminishes the statutory concept of 'conceptual separability' to the vanishing point; and (2) their focus on the process or sequence followed by the particular designer makes copyright protection depend upon largely fortuitous circumstances concerning the creation of the design in issue." Judge Winter proposed a standard focusing on how the final work is perceived: "the relevant question is whether the design of a useful article, however intertwined with the article's utilitarian aspects, causes an ordinary reasonable observer to perceive an aesthetic concept not related to the article's use. The answer to this question is clear in the instant case because any reasonable observer would easily view the Ribbon Rack as an ornamental sculpture."

Take a look at the RIBBON rack above. How would you vote? Copyrightable or not?

Star Athletica v. Varsity Brands, Inc.
137 S. Ct. 1002 (2017)

Justice THOMAS delivered the opinion of the Court.

Congress has provided copyright protection for original works of art, but not for industrial designs. The line between art and industrial design, however, is often difficult to draw. This is particularly true when an industrial design incorporates artistic elements. Congress has afforded limited protection for these artistic elements by providing that "pictorial, graphic, or sculptural features" of the "design of a useful article" are eligible for copyright protection as artistic works if those features "can be identified separately from, and are capable of existing independently of, the utilitarian aspects of the article." 17 U.S.C. § 101. We granted certiorari to resolve widespread disagreement over the proper test for implementing § 101's separate-identification and independent-existence requirements. We hold that a feature incorporated into the design of a useful article is eligible for copyright protection only if the feature (1) can be perceived as a two- or three-dimensional work of art separate from the useful article and (2) would qualify as a protectable pictorial, graphic, or sculptural work—either on its own or fixed in some other tangible medium of expression—if it were imagined separately from the useful article into which it is incorporated. Because that test is satisfied in this case, we affirm.

I

Respondents Varsity Brands, Inc., Varsity Spirit Corporation, and Varsity Spirit Fashions & Supplies, Inc., design, make, and sell cheerleading uniforms. Respondents have obtained or acquired more than 200 U.S. copyright registrations for two-dimensional designs appearing on the surface of their uniforms and other garments. These designs are primarily "combinations, positionings, and arrangements of elements" that include "chevrons . . .,

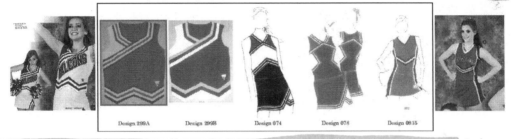

lines, curves, stripes, angles, diagonals, inverted [chevrons], coloring, and shapes." At issue in this case are Designs 299A, 299B, 074, 078, and 0815. [Above are images of these designs from Varsity's submissions to the Copyright Office, alongside images of two of the designs worn as uniforms.]

Petitioner Star Athletica, L.L.C., also markets and sells cheerleading uniforms. Respondents sued petitioner for infringing their copyrights in the five designs. . . .

II
B

We must now decide when a feature incorporated into a useful article "can be identified separately from" and is "capable of existing independently of" "the utilitarian aspects" of the article. This is not a free-ranging search for the best copyright policy, but rather "depends solely on statutory interpretation." "The controlling principle in this case is the basic and unexceptional rule that courts must give effect to the clear meaning of statutes as written." . . .

1

The statute provides that a "pictorial, graphic, or sculptural featur[e]" incorporated into the "design of a useful article" is eligible for copyright protection if it (1) "can be identified separately from," and (2) is "capable of existing independently of, the utilitarian aspects of the article." § 101. The first requirement—separate identification—is not onerous. The decisionmaker need only be able to look at the useful article and spot some two- or three-dimensional element that appears to have pictorial, graphic, or sculptural qualities.

The independent-existence requirement is ordinarily more difficult to satisfy. The decisionmaker must determine that the separately identified feature has the capacity to exist apart from the utilitarian aspects of the article. . . . In other words, the feature must be able to exist as its own pictorial, graphic, or sculptural work as defined in § 101 once it is imagined apart from the useful article. If the feature is not capable of existing as a pictorial, graphic, or sculptural work once separated from the useful article, then it was not a pictorial, graphic, or sculptural feature of that article, but rather one of its utilitarian aspects.

Of course, to qualify as a pictorial, graphic, or sculptural work on its own, the feature cannot itself be a useful article or "[a]n article that is normally a part of a useful article" (which is itself considered a useful article). § 101. Nor could someone claim a copyright in a useful article merely by creating a replica of that article in some other medium—for example, a cardboard model of a car. Although the replica could itself be copyrightable, it would not give rise to any rights in the useful article that inspired it. . . .

3

This interpretation is . . . consistent with the history of the Copyright Act. In *Mazer v. Stein* (1954), a case decided under the 1909 Copyright Act, the respondents copyrighted a statuette depicting a dancer. The statuette was intended for use as a lamp base, "with electric wiring, sockets and lamp shades attached." Copies of the statuette were sold both as lamp bases and separately as statuettes. . . . [T]he Court held that the respondents owned a copyright in the statuette even though it was intended for use as a lamp base. . . . Congress

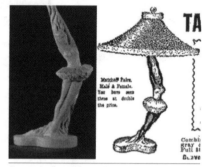

Statuette/lamp base from *Mazer v. Stein*.

essentially lifted the language governing protection for the design of a useful article directly from the post-*Mazer* regulations and placed it into § 101 of the 1976 Act. Consistent with *Mazer*, the approach we outline today interprets §§ 101 and 113 in a way that would afford copyright protection to the statuette in *Mazer* regardless of whether it was first created as a standalone sculptural work or as the base of the lamp.

C

In sum, a feature of the design of a useful article is eligible for copyright if, when identified and imagined apart from the useful article, it would qualify as a pictorial, graphic, or sculptural work either on its own or when fixed in some other tangible medium.

Applying this test to the surface decorations on the cheerleading uniforms is straightforward. First, one can identify the decorations as features having pictorial, graphic, or sculptural qualities. Second, if the arrangement of colors, shapes, stripes, and chevrons on the surface of the cheerleading uniforms were separated from the uniform and applied in another medium—for example, on a painter's canvas—they would qualify as "two-dimensional . . . works of . . . art," § 101. And imaginatively removing the surface decorations from the uniforms and applying them in another medium would not replicate the uniform itself. Indeed, respondents have applied the designs in this case to other media of expression—different types of clothing—without replicating the uniform. The decorations are therefore separable from the uniforms and eligible for copyright protection.[1] . . .

. . . To be clear, the only feature of the cheerleading uniform eligible for a copyright in this case is the two-dimensional work of art fixed in the tangible medium of the uniform

---

[1] We do not today hold that the surface decorations are copyrightable. We express no opinion on whether these works are sufficiently original to qualify for copyright protection, or on whether any other prerequisite of a valid copyright has been satisfied.

fabric. Even if respondents ultimately succeed in establishing a valid copyright in the surface decorations at issue here, respondents have no right to prohibit any person from manufacturing a cheerleading uniform of identical shape, cut, and dimensions to the ones on which the decorations in this case appear. They may prohibit only the reproduction of the surface designs in any tangible medium of expression—a uniform or otherwise.[2]

D

Petitioner and the Government raise several objections to the approach we announce today. None is meritorious.

1

Petitioner first argues that our reading of the statute is missing an important step. It contends that a feature may exist independently only if it can stand alone as a copyrightable work *and* if the useful article from which it was extracted would remain equally useful. . . . The designs here are not protected, it argues, because they are necessary to two of the uniforms' "inherent, essential, or natural functions"—identifying the wearer as a cheerleader and enhancing the wearer's physical appearance. Because the uniforms would not be equally useful without the designs, petitioner contends that the designs are inseparable from the "utilitarian aspects" of the uniform. . . . The debate over the relative utility of a plain white cheerleading uniform is unnecessary. The focus of the separability inquiry is on the extracted feature and not on any aspects of the useful article that remain after the imaginary extraction. The statute does not require the decisionmaker to imagine a fully functioning useful article without the artistic feature. Instead, it requires that the separated feature qualify as a nonuseful pictorial, graphic, or sculptural work on its own. . . . Were we to accept petitioner's argument that the only protectable features are those that play absolutely no role in an article's function, we would effectively abrogate the rule of *Mazer* and read "applied art" out of the statute.

Because we reject the view that a useful article must remain after the artistic feature has been imaginatively separated from the article, we necessarily abandon the distinction between "physical" and "conceptual" separability, which some courts and commentators have adopted based on the Copyright Act's legislative history. According to this view, a feature is *physically* separable from the underlying useful article if it can "be physically separated from the article by ordinary means while leaving the utilitarian aspects of the article completely intact." *Conceptual* separability applies if the feature physically could not be removed from the useful article by ordinary means.

The statutory text indicates that separability is a conceptual undertaking. Because separability does not require the underlying useful article to remain, the physical-conceptual distinction is unnecessary.

2

Petitioner next argues that we should incorporate two "objective" components into our test to provide guidance to the lower courts: (1) "whether the design elements can be identified as reflecting the designer's artistic judgment exercised independently of functional influence" and (2) whether "there is [a] substantial likelihood that the pictorial,

---

[2] The dissent suggests that our test would lead to the copyrighting of shovels. But a shovel, like a cheerleading uniform, even if displayed in an art gallery, is "an article having an intrinsic utilitarian function that is not merely to portray the appearance of the article or to convey information." 17 U.S.C. § 101. It therefore cannot be copyrighted. A drawing of a shovel could, of course, be copyrighted. And, if the shovel included any artistic features that could be perceived as art apart from the shovel, and which would qualify as protectable pictorial, graphic, or sculptural works on their own or in another medium, they too could be copyrighted. But a shovel as a shovel cannot.

graphic, or sculptural feature would still be marketable to some significant segment of the community without its utilitarian function."

We reject this argument because neither consideration is grounded in the text of the statute. The first would require the decisionmaker to consider evidence of the creator's design methods, purposes, and reasons. The statute's text makes clear, however, that our inquiry is limited to how the article and feature are perceived, not how or why they were designed. The same is true of marketability. Nothing in the statute suggests that copyrightability depends on market surveys. Moreover, asking whether some segment of the market would be interested in a given work threatens to prize popular art over other forms, or to substitute judicial aesthetic preferences for the policy choices embodied in the Copyright Act.

3

Finally, petitioner argues that allowing the surface decorations to qualify as a "work of authorship" is inconsistent with Congress' intent to entirely exclude industrial design from copyright. Petitioner notes that Congress refused to pass a provision that would have provided limited copyright protection for industrial designs, including clothing, when it enacted the 1976 Act, and that it has enacted laws protecting designs for specific useful articles—semiconductor chips and boat hulls—while declining to enact other industrial design statutes. . . . It therefore urges us to approach this question with a presumption against copyrightability.

We do not share petitioner's concern. As an initial matter, "[c]ongressional inaction lacks persuasive significance" in most circumstances. Moreover, we have long held that design patent and copyright are not mutually exclusive. Congress has provided for limited copyright protection for certain features of industrial design, and approaching the statute with presumptive hostility toward protection for industrial design would undermine Congress' choice. In any event, as explained above, our test does not render the shape, cut, and physical dimensions of the cheerleading uniforms eligible for copyright protection. . . .

Justice BREYER, with whom Justice KENNEDY joins, dissenting.

I agree with much in the Court's opinion. But I do not agree that the designs that Varsity Brands, Inc., submitted to the Copyright Office are eligible for copyright protection. Even applying the majority's test, the designs cannot "be perceived as . . . two- or three-dimensional work[s] of art separate from the useful article."

Look at the designs that Varsity submitted to the Copyright Office. You will see only pictures of cheerleader uniforms. And cheerleader uniforms are useful articles. A picture of the relevant design features, whether separately "perceived" on paper or in the imagination, is a picture of, and thereby "replicate[s]," the underlying useful article of which they are a part. Hence the design features that Varsity seeks to protect are not "capable of existing independently o[f] the utilitarian aspects of the article." 17 U.S.C. § 101.

I

The relevant statutory provision says that the "design of a useful article" is copyrightable "only if, and only to the extent that, such design incorporates pictorial, graphic, or sculptural features that can be identified separately from, and are capable of existing independently of, the utilitarian aspects of the article." But what, we must ask, do the words "identified separately" mean? Just when is a design separate from the "utilitarian aspect of the [useful] article?" The most direct, helpful aspect of the Court's opinion answers this question by stating:

    Nor could someone claim a copyright in a useful article merely by creating a replica of that article in some other medium—for example, a cardboard model of a car. Although the replica could itself be copyrightable, it would not give rise to any rights in the useful article that inspired it.

Exactly so. These words help explain the Court's statement that a copyrightable work of art must be "perceived as a two- or three-dimensional work of art separate from the useful article." . . .

Consider, for example, the explanation that the House Report for the Copyright Act of 1976 provides. It says:

Unless the shape of an automobile, airplane, ladies' dress, food processor, television set, or any other industrial product contains some element that, physically or conceptually, can be identified as separable from the utilitarian aspects of that article, the design would not be copyrighted. . . .

These words suggest two exercises, one physical, one mental. Can the design features (the picture, the graphic, the sculpture) be physically removed from the article (and considered separately), all the while leaving the fully functioning utilitarian object in place? If not, can one nonetheless conceive of the design features separately without replicating a picture of the utilitarian object? If the answer to either of these questions is "yes," then the design is eligible for copyright protection. Otherwise, it is not. The abstract nature of these questions makes them sound difficult to apply. But with the Court's words in mind, the difficulty tends to disappear.

An example will help. Imagine a lamp with a circular marble base, a vertical 10-inch tall brass rod (containing wires) inserted off center on the base, a light bulb fixture emerging from the top of the brass rod, and a lampshade sitting on top. In front of the brass rod a porcelain Siamese cat sits on the base facing outward. Obviously, the Siamese cat is *physically separate* from the lamp, as it could be easily removed while leaving both cat and lamp intact. And, assuming it otherwise qualifies, the designed cat is eligible for copyright protection.

Now suppose there is no long brass rod; instead the cat sits in the middle of the base and the wires run up through the cat to the bulbs. The cat is not physically separate from the lamp, as the reality of the lamp's construction is such that an effort to physically separate the cat and lamp will destroy both cat and lamp. The two are integrated into a single functional object, like the similar configuration of the ballet dancer statuettes that formed the lamp bases at issue in *Mazer v. Stein* (1954). But we can easily imagine the cat on its own. . . . In doing so, we do not create a mental picture of a lamp (or, in the Court's words, a "replica" of the lamp), which is a useful article. We simply perceive the cat separately, as a small cat figurine that could be a copyrightable design work standing alone that does not replicate the lamp. Hence the cat is *conceptually separate* from the utilitarian article that is the lamp.

Case law, particularly case law that Congress and the Copyright Office have considered, reflects the same approach. Congress cited examples of copyrightable design works, including "a carving on the back of a chair" and "a floral relief design on silver flatware." Copyright Office guidance on copyrightable designs in useful articles include "an engraving on a vase," "[a]rtwork printed on a t-shirt," "[a] colorful pattern decorating the surface of a shopping bag," "[a] drawing on the surface of wallpaper," and "[a] floral relief decorating the handle of a spoon." Courts have found copyrightable matter in a plaster ballet dancer statuette encasing the lamp's electric cords and forming its base, as well as carvings engraved onto furniture, and designs on laminated floor tiles.

By way of contrast, Van Gogh's painting of a pair of old shoes, though beautifully executed and copyrightable as a painting, would not qualify for a shoe design copyright. Courts have similarly denied copyright protection to objects that begin as three-dimensional designs, such as measuring spoons shaped like heart-tipped arrows, candleholders shaped like sailboats, and wire spokes on a wheel cover. None of these designs could qualify for copyright protection that would prevent others from selling spoons, candleholders, or wheel covers with the same design. Why not? Because in each case the design is not separable from the utilitarian aspects of the object to which it relates. The designs cannot be physically separated because they themselves make up the shape of the spoon, candleholders, or wheel covers of which they are a part. And spoons, candleholders, and wheel covers are useful objects, as are the old shoes depicted in Van Gogh's painting. More importantly, one cannot easily imagine or otherwise conceptualize the design of the spoons or the candleholders or the shoes without that picture, or image, or replica being a picture of spoons, or candleholders, or wheel covers, or shoes. The designs necessarily bring along the underlying utilitarian object. Hence each design is not conceptually separable from the physical useful object.

The upshot is that one could copyright the floral design on a soupspoon but one could not copyright the shape of the spoon itself, no matter how beautiful, artistic, or esthetically pleasing that shape might be: A picture of the shape of the spoon is also a picture of a spoon; the picture of a floral design is not.

To repeat: A separable design feature must be "capable of existing independently" of the useful article as a separate artistic work that is not itself the useful article. If the claimed feature could be extracted without replicating the useful article of which it is a part, and the result would be a copyrightable artistic work standing alone, then there is a separable design. But if extracting the claimed features would necessarily bring along the underlying useful article, the design is not separable from the useful article. . . . The law has long recognized that drawings or photographs of real world objects are copyrightable as drawings or photographs, but the copyright does not give protection against others making the underlying useful objects. That is why a copyright on Van Gogh's painting would prevent others from reproducing that painting, but it would not prevent others from reproducing and selling the comfortable old shoes that the painting depicts. Indeed, the purpose of § 113(b) was to ensure that "'copyright in a pictorial, graphic, or sculptural work, portraying a useful article as such, does not extend to the manufacture of the useful article itself.'"

II

To ask this kind of simple question—does the design picture the useful article?—will not provide an answer in every case, for there will be cases where it is difficult to say whether a picture of the design is, or is not, also a picture of the useful article. But the question will avoid courts focusing primarily upon what I believe is an unhelpful feature of the inquiry, namely, whether the design can be imagined as a "two- or three-dimensional work of art." That is because virtually any industrial design can be thought of separately as a "work of art" . . . Indeed, great industrial design may well include design that is inseparable from the useful article—where, as Frank Lloyd Wright put it, "form and function are one." Where they are one, the designer may be able to obtain 15 years of protection through a design patent. But, if they are one, Congress did not intend a century or more of copyright protection.

III

The conceptual approach that I have described reflects Congress' answer to a problem that is primarily practical and economic. Years ago Lord Macaulay drew attention to the problem when he described copyright in books as a "tax on readers for the purpose of giving a bounty to writers." He called attention to the main benefit of copyright protection, which is to provide an incentive to produce copyrightable works and thereby "promote the Progress of Science and useful Arts." But Macaulay also made clear that copyright protection imposes costs. Those costs include the higher prices that can accompany the grant of a copyright monopoly. They also can include (for those wishing to display, sell, or perform a design, film, work of art, or piece of music, for example) the costs of discovering whether there are previous copyrights, of contacting copyright holders, and of securing permission to copy. Sometimes, as Thomas Jefferson wrote to James Madison, costs can outweigh "the benefit even of limited monopolies." And that is particularly true in light of the fact that Congress has extended the "limited Times" of protection, U.S. Const. Art. I, § 8, cl. 8, from the "14 years" of Jefferson's day to potentially more than a century today.

The Constitution grants Congress primary responsibility for assessing comparative costs and benefits and drawing copyright's statutory lines. Courts must respect those lines and not grant copyright protection where Congress has decided not to do so. And it is clear that Congress has not extended broad copyright protection to the fashion design industry. Congress has left "statutory . . . protection . . . largely unavailable for dress designs." 1 Nimmer § 2A.08[H][3][a].

Congress' decision not to grant full copyright protection to the fashion industry has not left the industry without protection. Patent design protection is available. A maker of clothing can obtain trademark protection under the Lanham Act for signature features of the clothing. And a designer who creates an original textile design can receive copyright protection for that pattern as placed, for example, on a bolt of cloth, or anything made with that cloth.

The fashion industry has thrived against this backdrop, and designers have contributed immeasurably to artistic and personal self-expression through clothing. But a decision by this Court to grant protection to the design of a garment would grant the designer protection that Congress refused to provide. It would risk increased prices and unforeseeable disruption in the clothing industry, which in the United States alone encompasses nearly $370 billion in annual spending and 1.8 million jobs. That is why I believe it important to emphasize those parts of the Court's opinion that limit the scope of its interpretation. That language, as I have said, makes clear that one may not "claim a copyright in a useful article merely by creating a replica of that article in some other medium," which "would not give rise to any rights in the useful article that inspired it."

IV

If we ask the "separateness" question correctly, the answer here is not difficult to find. The majority's opinion, in its appendix, depicts the cheerleader dress designs that Varsity submitted to the Copyright Office. Can the design features in Varsity's pictures exist separately from the utilitarian aspects of a dress? Can we extract those features as copyrightable design works standing alone, without bringing along, via picture or design, the dresses of which they constitute a part?

Consider designs 074, 078, and 0815. They certainly look like cheerleader uniforms. That is to say, they look like pictures of cheerleader uniforms, just like Van Gogh's old shoes look like shoes. I do not see how one could see them otherwise. Designs 299A and 299B present slightly closer questions. They omit some of the dresslike context that the other designs possess. But the necklines, the sleeves, and the cut of the skirt suggest that they too are pictures of dresses. Looking at all five of Varsity's pictures, I do not see how one could conceptualize the design features in a way that does not picture, not just artistic designs, but dresses as well.

Were I to accept the majority's invitation to "imaginatively remov[e]" the chevrons and stripes as they are arranged on the neckline, waistline, sleeves, and skirt of each uniform, and apply them on a "painter's canvas," that painting would be of a cheerleader's dress. The esthetic elements on which Varsity seeks protection exist only as part of the uniform design—there is nothing to separate out but for dress-shaped lines that replicate the cut and style of the uniforms. Hence, each design is not physically separate, nor is it conceptually separate, from the useful article it depicts, namely, a cheerleader's dress. They cannot be copyrighted.

Varsity, of course, could have sought a design patent for its designs. Or, it could have sought a copyright on a textile design, even one with a similar theme of chevrons and lines.

But that is not the nature of Varsity's copyright claim. It has instead claimed ownership of the particular "'treatment and arrangement'" of the chevrons and lines of the design as they appear at the neckline, waist, skirt, sleeves, and overall cut of each uniform. The majority imagines that Varsity submitted something different—that is, only the surface decorations of chevrons and stripes, as in a textile design. As the majority sees it, Varsity's copyright claim would be the same had it submitted a plain rectangular space depicting chevrons and stripes, like swaths from a bolt of fabric. But considered on their own, the simple stripes are plainly unoriginal. Varsity, then, seeks to do indirectly what it cannot do directly: bring along the design and cut of the dresses by seeking to protect surface decorations whose "treatment and arrangement" are coextensive with that design and cut. As Varsity would have it, it would prevent its competitors from making useful three-dimensional cheerleader uniforms by submitting plainly unoriginal chevrons and stripes as cut and arranged on a useful article. But with that cut and arrangement, the resulting pictures on which Varsity seeks protection do not simply depict designs. They depict clothing. They depict the useful articles of which the designs are inextricable parts. And Varsity cannot obtain copyright protection that would give them the power to prevent others from making those useful uniforms, any more than Van Gogh can copyright comfortable old shoes by painting their likeness.

I fear that, in looking past the three-dimensional design inherent in Varsity's claim by treating it as if it were no more than a design for a bolt of cloth, the majority has lost sight of its own important limiting principle. One may not "claim a copyright in a useful article merely by creating a replica of that article in some other medium," such as in a picture. That is to say, one cannot obtain a copyright that would give its holder "any rights in the useful article that inspired it."

With respect, I dissent.

Questions:

1.) *Star Athletica* holds that

A feature incorporated into the design of a useful article is eligible for copyright protection only if the feature (1) can be perceived as a two- or

> three-dimensional work of art separate from the useful article and (2) would qualify as a protectable pictorial, graphic, or sculptural work— either on its own or fixed in some other tangible medium of expression— if it were *imagined* separately from the useful article into which it is incorporated. . . . [T]he statute does not require the imagined *remainder* to be a fully functioning useful article at all, much less an equally useful one.

If one can copyright a feature of a useful article *that makes that article useful*, has the useful articles doctrine been silently abolished? Surely that is not what the majority intended, but is that the result? For the majority, is any design feature now potentially copyrightable[8], as long as it is not a complete replica of the useful article? What about other industrial designs—is Breyer correct that, if the majority opinion is broadly construed, one might copyright a shovel, *imagining* the curve of the blade and the ledge for one's foot floating free? The luminous stripes on a safety vest or straps on a life vest? A banana costume?

2.) The appellate decision in *Star Athletica* had listed *nine* different approaches to analyzing conceptual separability from courts, scholars, and the Copyright Office, and arguably added a tenth one to the list. The Supreme Court's majority opinion sought to resolve this long-standing and intractable problem. The answer, Justice Thomas explained, was simple. The Court should read the statute. "This is not a free-ranging search for the best copyright policy, but rather "depends solely on statutory interpretation. . . . We thus begin and end our inquiry with the text." One can imagine the many, many judges and scholars who had wrestled with this issue over the years striking their collective foreheads. *"The text of the statute! Why didn't we think of that?!"* Textualism is very much in vogue now in the Supreme Court—or at least it is often invoked. Are you convinced that Justice Thomas's opinion simply offers the plain meaning of § 101's separability requirement? Even if the provision were self-explicating, is textualism— without focus on the goals of the system—the best approach? Consistent with Art 1 § 8 cl. 8—the Copyright Clause?

3.) *Star Athletica* has been widely criticized as an incoherent decision laying down a test with no obvious limiting principles. What effect has the decision had in the lower courts?

We are glad you asked. Do the two banana costumes on the right infringe a copyright in the costume on the left? In 2019, the Third Circuit had the occasion to address the age-old question of banana costume copyright-ability in the case of *Silvertop Associates v. Kangaroo Manu-facturing* (3d Cir. 2019). The re-

sult was a predictable prat-fall. Does this "design incorporate[] pictorial, graphic, or sculptural features that *can be identified separately from, and are capable of existing independently of, the utilitarian aspects of the article*" as § 101 requires? The answer of

---

[8] Note that the court explicitly says it is not ruling on "originality," so this requirement would still need to be satisfied. However, in her concurrence Justice Ginsburg notes "In view of the dissent's assertion that Varsity's designs are 'plainly unoriginal,' however, I note this Court's recognition that 'the requisite level of creativity [for copyrightability] is extremely low; even a slight amount will suffice.'"

course, should be an easy "no." One cannot separate the graphic and sculptural features of a banana costume designed to look like a banana from its utilitarian function (looking like a banana) since those graphic and sculptural features consist in . . . looking like a banana. The utilitarian functions are the same as the pictorial and graphic ones. Not only can they not be separated, there is in fact *nothing to separate.* Map, meet terrain.

Or that would have been the conclusion before *Star Athletica.* After extensively quoting the case, the 3rd Circuit goes on to explain the application of its ruling thus:

> To begin with, Rasta's banana costume is a "useful article." The artistic features of the costume, in combination, prove both separable and capable of independent existence as a copyrightable work: a sculpture. Those sculptural features include the banana's combination of colors, lines, shape, and length. They do not include the cutout holes for the wearer's arms, legs, and face; the holes' dimensions; or the holes' locations on the costume, because those features are utilitarian. Although more difficult to imagine separately from the costume's "non-appearance related utility" (*i.e.,* wearability) than many works, one can still imagine the banana apart from the costume as an original sculpture. That sculpted banana, once split from the costume, is not intrinsically utilitarian and does not merely replicate the costume, so it may be copyrighted.

Notice the tortured logic by which the court narrows the utility of the costume by insisting that it be the "non-appearance related" attribute of "wearability," as if the purchaser were simply searching through the contents of his closet looking for the appropriate thing to wear. "I am thinking something warm and loose, so maybe a sweatshirt and jeans, or—I don't know—a banana?" But of course, it is precisely the utility of a costume that *it looks like the thing it portrays.* Otherwise, it is not a *costume.*

The court's discussion of the merger doctrine merely continues the judicial theatre of the absurd. Surely the idea of a banana merges with its expression, a costume portrayal of a banana, and thus threatens to allow someone to monopolize the very idea of a banana costume? In the following remarkable passage, the court explains that it would not.

> Here too, copyrighting the banana costume's non-utilitarian features in combination would not threaten such monopolization. Kangaroo points to no specific feature that *necessarily* results from the costume's subject matter (a banana). *Although a banana costume is likely to be yellow, it could be any shade of yellow—or green or brown for that matter. Although a banana costume is likely to be curved, it need not be—*let alone in any particular manner. And although a banana costume is likely to have ends that resemble a natural banana's, those tips need not look like Rasta's black tips (in color, shape, or size). [Emphasis added]

So, while the court admits that a banana costume is *likely* to be yellow and curved, it says it could also be brown and straight. On Halloween, when your child goes out in her brown, straight, banana costume and her friends ask "why are you dressed up as a *stick*!?" she will be able to respond with a simple, terse explanation. "*Star Athletica,*" she will say.

Mockery is irresistible yet perhaps unworthy. Is this not what inevitably happens when a distinguished Appeals Court struggles to apply an incoherent test laid down by the Supreme Court? The silliness comes from the top, but proliferates rapidly.

4.) Is *Silvertop* consistent with *Kalpakian,* the bee pin case?

5.) Would the Ribbon Rack now be copyrightable?

6.) In the trademark context, in *Wal-Mart*, the Court held that product design (in that case, the design of children's seersucker outfits) can never be inherently distinctive, drawing a "bright line" that favored competition:

> Consumers should not be deprived of the benefits of competition with regard to the utilitarian and esthetic purposes that product design ordinarily serves by a rule of law that facilitates plausible threats of suit against new entrants based upon alleged inherent distinctiveness. How easy it is to mount a plausible suit depends, of course, upon the clarity of the test. . . . Competition is deterred, however, not merely by successful suit but by the plausible threat of successful suit, and given the unlikelihood of inherently source-identifying design, the game of allowing suit based upon alleged inherent distinctiveness seems to us not worth the candle.

Why is the same not true of *copyright* in product design? Where does *Star Athletica* draw the "bright line"? In *TrafFix*, the Court explained that "copying is not always discouraged or disfavored by the laws which preserve our competitive economy. Allowing competitors to copy will have salutary effects in many instances." Is that the approach the court adopts here?

7.) Congress has repeatedly declined to extend copyright to fashion designs, expressing concern that this "would create a new monopoly which has not been justified by a showing that its benefits will outweigh the disadvantage of removing such designs from free public use." Breyer echoes this with his concern that the majority's opinion, if interpreted broadly, could "risk increased prices and unforeseeable disruption in the clothing industry, which in the United States alone encompasses nearly $370 billion in annual spending and 1.8 million jobs." During oral argument in *Star Athletica*, Justice Sotomayor said: "You're killing knock-offs with copyright. You haven't been able to do it with trademark law. You haven't been able to do it with patent designs. We are now going to use copyright law to kill the knockoff industry. I don't know that that's bad. I'm just saying." After the decision came out, many news reports hailed it as a victory for the fashion industry. True?

8.) You encountered cheerleader uniforms in *Dallas Cowboys* and may have wondered, "what *is* the function of a cheerleader uniform"? In the Sixth Circuit decision in *Star Athletica*, much turned on this question. The majority held that the uniform's function was to "cover the body, permit free movement, and wick moisture," and not to "identify the wearer as a cheerleader." The dissent disagreed: "That broad definition could be used to describe all athletic gear. But the particular athletic uniforms before us serve to identify the wearer as a cheerleader. Without stripes, braids, and chevrons, we are left with a blank white pleated skirt and crop top. As the district court recognized, the reasonable observer would not associate this blank outfit with cheerleading. This may be appropriate attire for a match at the All England Lawn Tennis Club, but not for a member of a cheerleading squad." Do you agree?

5.) Methods of Operation: Introduction to Computer Software

Lotus Development Corp. v. Borland Intern'l, Inc.

49 F.3d 807 (1st Cir. 1995)

STAHL, Circuit Judge.

This appeal requires us to decide whether a computer menu command hierarchy is copyrightable subject matter. In particular, we must decide whether, as the district court held, plaintiff-appellee Lotus Development Corporation's copyright in Lotus 1-2-3, a computer spreadsheet program, was infringed by defendant-appellant Borland International, Inc., when Borland copied the Lotus 1-2-3 menu command hierarchy into its Quattro and Quattro Pro computer spreadsheet programs.

I.
Background

Lotus 1-2-3 is a spreadsheet program that enables users to perform accounting functions electronically on a computer. Users manipulate and control the program via a series of menu commands, such as "Copy," "Print," and "Quit." Users choose commands either by highlighting them on the screen or by typing their first letter. In all, Lotus 1-2-3 has 469 commands arranged into more than 50 menus and submenus.

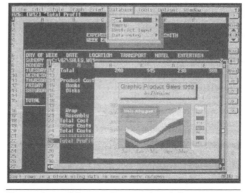

Image information available at http://en .wikipedia.org/wiki/File:Lotus-123-3.0-dos.png.

Screenshot of Quattro Pro reprinted from *Personal Computing*, issue 4/1990, at http://www.aresluna.org/attached/computer history/articles/spreadsheets/quattroprounify andconquer/.

Lotus 1-2-3, like many computer programs, allows users to write what are called "macros." By writing a macro, a user can designate a series of command choices with a single macro keystroke. Then, to execute that series of commands in multiple parts of the spreadsheet, rather than typing the whole series each time, the user only needs to type the single pre-programmed macro keystroke, causing the program to recall and perform the designated series of commands automatically. Thus, Lotus 1-2-3 macros shorten the time needed to set up and operate the program.

The district court found, and Borland does not now contest, that Borland included in its Quattro and Quattro Pro version 1.0 programs "a virtually identical copy of the entire 1-2-3 menu tree." *Borland III.* In so doing, Borland did not copy any of Lotus's underlying computer code; it copied only the words and structure of Lotus's menu command hierarchy. Borland included the Lotus menu command hierarchy in its programs to make them compatible with Lotus 1-2-3 so that spreadsheet users who were already familiar with Lotus 1-2-3 would be able to switch to the Borland programs without having to learn new commands or rewrite their Lotus macros.

In its Quattro and Quattro Pro version 1.0 programs, Borland achieved compatibility with Lotus 1-2-3 by offering its users an alternate user interface, the "Lotus Emulation Interface." By activating the Emulation Interface, Borland users would see the Lotus menu commands on their screens and could interact with Quattro or Quattro Pro as if using Lotus 1-2-3, albeit with a slightly different looking screen and with many Borland options not available on Lotus 1-2-3. In effect, Borland allowed users to choose how they wanted to communicate with Borland's spreadsheet programs: either by using menu commands designed by Borland, or by using the commands and command structure used in Lotus 1-2-3 augmented by Borland-added commands.

Lotus filed this action against Borland in the District of Massachusetts on July 2, 1990, four days after a district court held that the Lotus 1-2-3 "menu structure, taken as a whole—including the choice of command terms [and] the structure and order of those terms," was protected expression covered by Lotus's copyrights.

Lotus and Borland filed cross motions for summary judgment; the district court denied both motions on March 20, 1992, concluding that "neither party's motion is supported by the record." *Borland I.* The district court invited the parties to file renewed summary judgment motions that would "focus their arguments more precisely" in light of rulings it had made in conjunction with its denial of their summary judgment motions. Both parties filed renewed motions for summary judgment on April 24, 1992. In its motion, Borland contended that the Lotus 1-2-3 menus were not copyrightable as a matter of law and that no reasonable trier of fact could find that the similarity between its products and Lotus 1-2-3 was sufficient to sustain a determination of infringement. Lotus contended in its motion that Borland had copied Lotus 1-2-3's entire user interface and had thereby infringed Lotus's copyrights.

On July 31, 1992, the district court denied Borland's motion and granted Lotus's motion in part. The district court ruled that the Lotus menu command hierarchy was copyrightable expression because

> [a] very satisfactory spreadsheet menu tree can be constructed using
> different commands and a different command structure from those of
> Lotus 1-2-3. In fact, Borland has constructed just such an alternate tree
> for use in Quattro Pro's native mode. Even if one holds the arrangement
> of menu commands constant, it is possible to generate literally millions
> of satisfactory menu trees by varying the menu commands employed.

Borland II. The district court demonstrated this by offering alternate command words for the ten commands that appear in Lotus's main menu. For example, the district court stated that "[t]he 'Quit' command could be named 'Exit' without any other modifications," and that "[t]he 'Copy' command could be called 'Clone,' 'Ditto,' 'Duplicate,' 'Imitate,' 'Mimic,' 'Replicate,' and 'Reproduce,' among others." Because so many variations were possible, the district court concluded that the Lotus developers' choice and arrangement of command terms, reflected in the Lotus menu command hierarchy, constituted copyrightable expression.

In granting partial summary judgment to Lotus, the district court held that Borland had infringed Lotus's copyright in Lotus 1-2-3:

[A]s a matter of law, Borland's Quattro products infringe the Lotus 1-2-3 copyright because of (1) the extent of copying of the "menu commands" and "menu structure" that is not genuinely disputed in this case, (2) the extent to which the copied elements of the "menu commands" and "menu structure" contain expressive aspects separable from the functions of the "menu commands" and "menu structure," and (3) the scope of those copied expressive aspects as an integral part of Lotus 1-2-3.

Borland II. The court nevertheless concluded that while the Quattro and Quattro Pro programs infringed Lotus's copyright, Borland had not copied the entire Lotus 1-2-3 user interface, as Lotus had contended. Accordingly, the court concluded that a jury trial was necessary to determine the scope of Borland's infringement, including whether Borland copied the long prompts[2] of Lotus 1-2-3, whether the long prompts contained expressive elements, and to what extent, if any, functional constraints limited the number of possible ways that the Lotus menu command hierarchy could have been arranged at the time of its creation. See *Borland III.* Additionally, the district court granted Lotus summary judgment on Borland's affirmative defense of waiver, but not on its affirmative defenses of laches and estoppel. *Borland II.*

Immediately following the district court's summary judgment decision, Borland removed the Lotus Emulation Interface from its products. Thereafter, Borland's spreadsheet programs no longer displayed the Lotus 1-2-3 menus to Borland users, and as a result Borland users could no longer communicate with Borland's programs as if they were using a more sophisticated version of Lotus 1-2-3. Nonetheless, Borland's programs continued to be partially compatible with Lotus 1-2-3, for Borland retained what it called the "Key Reader" in its Quattro Pro programs. Once turned on, the Key Reader allowed Borland's programs to understand and perform some Lotus 1-2-3 macros.[3] With the Key Reader on, the Borland programs used Quattro Pro menus for display, interaction, and macro execution, except when they encountered a slash ("/") key in a macro (the starting key for any Lotus 1-2-3 macro), in which case they interpreted the macro as having been written for Lotus 1-2-3. Accordingly, people who wrote or purchased macros to shorten the time needed to perform an operation in Lotus 1-2-3 could still use those macros in Borland's programs. The district court permitted Lotus to file a supplemental complaint alleging that the Key Reader infringed its copyright.

In its Phase I-trial decision, the district court found that "each of the Borland emulation interfaces contains a virtually identical copy of the 1-2-3 menu tree and that the 1-2-3 menu tree is capable of a wide variety of expression."

In its Phase II-trial decision, the district court found that Borland's Key Reader file

---

[2] Lotus 1-2-3 utilizes a two-line menu; the top line lists the commands from which the user may choose, and the bottom line displays what Lotus calls its "long prompts." The long prompts explain, as a sort of "help text," what the highlighted menu command will do if entered. For example, the long prompt for the "Worksheet" command displays the submenu that the "Worksheet" command calls up; it reads "Global, Insert, Delete, Column, Erase, Titles, Window, Status, Page." The long prompt for the "Copy" command explains what function the "Copy" command will perform: "Copy a cell or range of cells." The long prompt for the "Quit" command reads, "End 1-2-3 session (Have you saved your work?)."

Prior to trial, the parties agreed to exclude the copying of the long prompts from the case; Lotus agreed not to contend that Borland had copied the long prompts, Borland agreed not to argue that it had not copied the long prompts, and both sides agreed not to argue that the issue of whether Borland had copied the long prompts was material to any other issue in the case. See *Borland III.*

[3] Because Borland's programs could no longer display the Lotus menu command hierarchy to users, the Key Reader did not allow debugging or modification of macros, nor did it permit the execution of most interactive macros.

included "a virtually identical copy of the Lotus menu tree structure, but represented in a different form and with first letters of menu command names in place of the full menu command names." In other words, Borland's programs no longer included the Lotus command terms, but only their first letters. The district court held that "the Lotus menu structure, organization, and first letters of the command names . . . constitute part of the protectable expression found in [Lotus 1-2-3]." Accordingly, the district court held that with its Key Reader, Borland had infringed Lotus's copyright. The district court then entered a permanent injunction against Borland, from which Borland appeals.

This appeal concerns only Borland's copying of the Lotus menu command hierarchy into its Quattro programs and Borland's affirmative defenses to such copying. Lotus has not cross-appealed; in other words, Lotus does not contend on appeal that the district court erred in finding that Borland had not copied other elements of Lotus 1-2-3, such as its screen displays.

II.
Discussion

On appeal, Borland does not dispute that it factually copied the words and arrangement of the Lotus menu command hierarchy. Rather, Borland argues that it "lawfully copied the unprotectable menus of Lotus 1-2-3." Borland contends that the Lotus menu command hierarchy is not copyrightable because it is a system, method of operation, process, or procedure foreclosed from protection by 17 U.S.C. § 102(b). Borland also raises a number of affirmative defenses.

A. Copyright Infringement Generally

To establish copyright infringement, a plaintiff must prove "(1) ownership of a valid copyright, and (2) copying of constituent elements of the work that are original." *Feist Publications, Inc. v. Rural Tel. Serv. Co.* (1991). To show ownership of a valid copyright and therefore satisfy *Feist*'s first prong, a plaintiff must prove that the work as a whole is original and that the plaintiff complied with applicable statutory formalities. See *Engineering Dynamics, Inc. v. Structural Software, Inc.* (5th Cir. 1994). "In judicial proceedings, a certificate of copyright registration constitutes prima facie evidence of copyrightability and shifts the burden to the defendant to demonstrate why the copyright is not valid." *Bibbero Sys., Inc. v. Colwell Sys., Inc.* (9th Cir. 1990); see also 17 U.S.C. § 410(c); *Folio Impressions, Inc. v. Byer California* (2d Cir. 1991) (presumption of validity may be rebutted).

To show actionable copying and therefore satisfy *Feist*'s second prong, a plaintiff must first prove that the alleged infringer copied plaintiff's copyrighted work as a factual matter; to do this, he or she may either present direct evidence of factual copying or, if that is unavailable, evidence that the alleged infringer had access to the copyrighted work and that the offending and copyrighted works are so similar that the court may infer that there was factual copying (i.e., probative similarity). *Engineering Dynamics*; see also *Concrete Mach.* The plaintiff must then prove that the copying of copyrighted material was so extensive that it rendered the offending and copyrighted works substantially similar.

In this appeal, we are faced only with whether the Lotus menu command hierarchy is copyrightable subject matter in the first instance, for Borland concedes that Lotus has a valid copyright in Lotus 1-2-3 as a whole[5] and admits to factually copying the Lotus

---

[5] Computer programs receive copyright protection as "literary works." See 17 U.S.C. § 102(a)(1) (granting protection to "literary works") and 17 U.S.C. § 101 (defining "literary works" as "works . . . expressed in words, numbers, or other verbal or numerical symbols or indicia, regardless of the nature of the material

menu command hierarchy. As a result, this appeal is in a very different posture from most copyright-infringement cases, for copyright infringement generally turns on whether the defendant has copied protected expression as a factual matter. Because of this different posture, most copyright-infringement cases provide only limited help to us in deciding this appeal. This is true even with respect to those copyright-infringement cases that deal with computers and computer software.

B. Matter of First Impression

Whether a computer menu command hierarchy constitutes copyrightable subject matter is a matter of first impression in this court. While some other courts appear to have touched on it briefly in dicta, see, e.g., *Autoskill, Inc. v. National Educ. Support Sys., Inc.*, [*cert. denied*, 510 U.S. 916] (1993), we know of no cases that deal with the copyrightability of a menu command hierarchy standing on its own (i.e., without other elements of the user interface, such as screen displays, in issue). Thus we are navigating in uncharted waters.

Borland vigorously argues, however, that the Supreme Court charted our course more than 100 years ago when it decided *Baker v. Selden* (1879). In *Baker v. Selden*, the Court held that Selden's copyright over the textbook in which he explained his new way to do accounting did not grant him a monopoly on the use of his accounting system.[6]

Borland argues:

> "The facts of *Baker v. Selden*, and even the arguments advanced by the parties in that case, are identical to those in this case. The only difference is that the "user interface" of Selden's system was implemented by pen and paper rather than by computer."

To demonstrate that *Baker v. Selden* and this appeal both involve accounting systems, Borland even supplied this court with a video that, with special effects, shows Selden's paper forms "melting" into a computer screen and transforming into Lotus 1-2-3.

We do not think that *Baker v. Selden* is nearly as analogous to this appeal as Borland claims. Of course, Lotus 1-2-3 is a computer spreadsheet, and as such its grid of horizontal rows and vertical columns certainly resembles an accounting ledger or any other paper spreadsheet. Those grids, however, are not at issue in this appeal for, unlike Selden, Lotus does not claim to have a monopoly over its accounting system. Rather, this appeal involves Lotus's monopoly over the commands it uses to operate the computer. Accordingly, this appeal is not, as Borland contends, "identical" to *Baker v. Selden*.

C. *Altai*

Before we analyze whether the Lotus menu command hierarchy is a system, method of operation, process, or procedure, we first consider the applicability of the test the Second Circuit set forth in *Computer Assoc. Int'l, Inc. v. Altai, Inc.* (2d Cir. 1992). The Second Circuit designed its *Altai* test to deal with the fact that computer programs, copyrighted as "literary works," can be infringed by what is known as "nonliteral" copying, which is copying that is paraphrased or loosely paraphrased rather than word for word. . . .

The *Altai* test involves three steps: abstraction, filtration, and comparison. The abstraction step requires courts to "dissect the allegedly copied program's structure and

---

objects, such as books, periodicals, phonorecords, film, tapes, *disks*, or cards, in which they are embodied" (emphasis added)); see also H.R.Rep. No. 1476, 94th Cong., 2d Sess. 54 (1976), reprinted in 1976 U.S.C.C.A.N. 5659, 5667 ("The term 'literary works' . . . includes computer data bases, and computer programs to the extent that they incorporate authorship in the programmer's expression of original ideas, as distinguished from the ideas themselves.").

[6] Selden's system of double-entry bookkeeping is the now almost-universal T-accounts system.

isolate each level of abstraction contained within it." *Altai*. This step enables courts to identify the appropriate framework within which to separate protectable expression from unprotected ideas. Second, courts apply a "filtration" step in which they examine "the structural components at each level of abstraction to determine whether their particular inclusion at that level was 'idea' or was dictated by considerations of efficiency, so as to be necessarily incidental to that idea; required by factors external to the program itself; or taken from the public domain." Finally, courts compare the protected elements of the infringed work (i.e., those that survived the filtration screening) to the corresponding elements of the allegedly infringing work to determine whether there was sufficient copying of protected material to constitute infringement.

In the instant appeal, we are not confronted with alleged nonliteral copying of computer code. Rather, we are faced with Borland's deliberate, literal copying of the Lotus menu command hierarchy. Thus, we must determine not whether nonliteral copying occurred in some amorphous sense, but rather whether the literal copying of the Lotus menu command hierarchy constitutes copyright infringement.

While the *Altai* test may provide a useful framework for assessing the alleged nonliteral copying of computer code, we find it to be of little help in assessing whether the literal copying of a menu command hierarchy constitutes copyright infringement. In fact, we think that the *Altai* test in this context may actually be misleading because, in instructing courts to abstract the various levels, it seems to encourage them to find a base level that includes copyrightable subject matter that, if literally copied, would make the copier liable for copyright infringement. While that base (or literal) level would not be at issue in a nonliteral-copying case like *Altai*, it is precisely what is at issue in this appeal. We think that abstracting menu command hierarchies down to their individual word and menu levels and then filtering idea from expression at that stage, as both the *Altai* and the district court tests require, obscures the more fundamental question of whether a menu command hierarchy can be copyrighted at all. The initial inquiry should not be whether individual components of a menu command hierarchy are expressive, but rather whether the menu command hierarchy as a whole can be copyrighted.

D. The Lotus Menu Command Hierarchy: A "Method of Operation"

Borland argues that the Lotus menu command hierarchy is uncopyrightable because it is a system, method of operation, process, or procedure foreclosed from copyright protection by 17 U.S.C. § 102(b). Section 102(b) states: "In no case does copyright protection for an original work of authorship extend to any idea, procedure, process, system, method of operation, concept, principle, or discovery, regardless of the form in which it is described, explained, illustrated, or embodied in such work." Because we conclude that the Lotus menu command hierarchy is a method of operation, we do not consider whether it could also be a system, process, or procedure.

We think that "method of operation," as that term is used in § 102(b), refers to the means by which a person operates something, whether it be a car, a food processor, or a computer. Thus a text describing how to operate something would not extend copyright protection to the method of operation itself; other people would be free to employ that method and to describe it in their own words. Similarly, if a new method of operation is used rather than described, other people would still be free to employ or describe that method.

We hold that the Lotus menu command hierarchy is an uncopyrightable "method of operation." The Lotus menu command hierarchy provides the means by which users control and operate Lotus 1-2-3. If users wish to copy material, for example, they use the "Copy" command. If users wish to print material, they use the "Print" command. Users must use the command terms to tell the computer what to do. Without the menu command hierarchy, users would not be able to access and control, or indeed make use of, Lotus 1-2-3's functional capabilities.

The Lotus menu command hierarchy does not merely explain and present Lotus 1-2-3's functional capabilities to the user; it also serves as the method by which the program is operated and controlled. The Lotus menu command hierarchy is different from the Lotus long prompts, for the long prompts are not necessary to the operation of the program; users could operate Lotus 1-2-3 even if there were no long prompts.[9] The Lotus menu command hierarchy is also different from the Lotus screen displays, for users need not "use" any expressive aspects of the screen displays in order to operate Lotus 1-2-3; because the way the screens look has little bearing on how users control the program, the screen displays are not part of Lotus 1-2-3's "method of operation."[10] The Lotus menu command hierarchy is also different from the underlying computer code, because while code is necessary for the program to work, its precise formulation is not. In other words, to offer the same capabilities as Lotus 1-2-3, Borland did not have to copy Lotus's underlying code (and indeed it did not); to allow users to operate its programs in substantially the same way, however, Borland had to copy the Lotus menu command hierarchy. Thus the Lotus 1-2-3 code is not a uncopyrightable "method of operation."

The district court held that the Lotus menu command hierarchy, with its specific choice and arrangement of command terms, constituted an "expression" of the "idea" of operating a computer program with commands arranged hierarchically into menus and submenus. *Borland II*. Under the district court's reasoning, Lotus's decision to employ hierarchically arranged command terms to operate its program could not foreclose its competitors from also employing hierarchically arranged command terms to operate their programs, but it did foreclose them from employing the specific command terms and arrangement that Lotus had used. In effect, the district court limited Lotus 1-2-3's "method of operation" to an abstraction.

Accepting the district court's finding that the Lotus developers made some expressive choices in choosing and arranging the Lotus command terms, we nonetheless hold that that expression is not copyrightable because it is part of Lotus 1-2-3's "method of operation." We do not think that "methods of operation" are limited to abstractions; rather, they are the means by which a user operates something. If specific words are essential to operating something, then they are part of a "method of operation" and, as such, are unprotectable. This is so whether they must be highlighted, typed in, or even spoken, as computer programs no doubt will soon be controlled by spoken words.

The fact that Lotus developers could have designed the Lotus menu command hierarchy differently is immaterial to the question of whether it is a "method of operation." In other words, our initial inquiry is not whether the Lotus menu command hierarchy incorporates any expression. Rather, our initial inquiry is whether the Lotus menu command hierarchy is a "method of operation." Concluding, as we do, that users operate Lotus 1-2-3 by using the Lotus menu command hierarchy, and that the entire Lotus menu command

---

[9] As the Lotus long prompts are not before us on appeal, we take no position on their copyrightability, although we do note that a strong argument could be made that the brief explanations they provide "merge" with the underlying idea of explaining such functions. See *Morrissey v. Procter & Gamble Co.*, (1st Cir. 1967) (when the possible ways to express an idea are limited, the expression "merges" with the idea and is therefore uncopyrightable; when merger occurs, identical copying is permitted).

[10] As they are not before us on appeal, we take no position on whether the Lotus 1-2-3 screen displays constitute original expression capable of being copyrighted.

hierarchy is essential to operating Lotus 1-2-3, we do not inquire further whether that method of operation could have been designed differently. The "expressive" choices of what to name the command terms and how to arrange them do not magically change the uncopyrightable menu command hierarchy into copyrightable subject matter.

Our holding that "methods of operation" are not limited to mere abstractions is bolstered by *Baker v. Selden*. In *Baker*, the Supreme Court explained that

> the teachings of science and the rules and methods of useful art have their final end in application and use; and this application and use are what the public derive from the publication of a book which teaches them. . . . The description of the art in a book, though entitled to the benefit of copyright, lays no foundation for an exclusive claim to the art itself. The object of the one is explanation; the object of the other is use. The former may be secured by copyright. The latter can only be secured, if it can be secured at all, by letters-patent.

Lotus wrote its menu command hierarchy so that people could learn it and use it. Accordingly, it falls squarely within the prohibition on copyright protection established in *Baker v. Selden* and codified by Congress in § 102(b).

In many ways, the Lotus menu command hierarchy is like the buttons used to control, say, a video cassette recorder ("VCR"). A VCR is a machine that enables one to watch and record video tapes. Users operate VCRs by pressing a series of buttons that are typically labelled "Record, Play, Reverse, Fast Forward, Pause, Stop/Eject." That the buttons are arranged and labeled does not make them a "literary work," nor does it make them an "expression" of the abstract "method of operating" a VCR via a set of labeled buttons. Instead, the buttons are themselves the "method of operating" the VCR.

When a Lotus 1-2-3 user chooses a command, either by highlighting it on the screen or by typing its first letter, he or she effectively pushes a button. Highlighting the "Print" command on the screen, or typing the letter "P," is analogous to pressing a VCR button labeled "Play."

Just as one could not operate a buttonless VCR, it would be impossible to operate Lotus 1-2-3 without employing its menu command hierarchy. Thus the Lotus command terms are not equivalent to the labels on the VCR's buttons, but are instead equivalent to the buttons themselves. Unlike the labels on a VCR's buttons, which merely make operating a VCR easier by indicating the buttons' functions, the Lotus menu commands are essential to operating Lotus 1-2-3. Without the menu commands, there would be no way to "push" the Lotus buttons, as one could push unlabeled VCR buttons. While Lotus could probably have designed a user interface for which the command terms were mere labels, it did not do so here. Lotus 1-2-3 depends for its operation on use of the precise command terms that make up the Lotus menu command hierarchy.

One might argue that the buttons for operating a VCR are not analogous to the commands for operating a computer program because VCRs are not copyrightable, whereas computer programs are. . . . Computer programs, unlike VCRs, are copyrightable as "literary works." 17 U.S.C. § 102(a). Accordingly, one might argue, the "buttons" used to operate a computer program are not like the buttons used to operate a VCR, for they are not subject to a useful-article exception. The response, of course, is that the arrangement of buttons on a VCR would not be copyrightable even without a useful-article exception, because the buttons are an uncopyrightable "method of operation." Similarly, the "buttons" of a computer program are also an uncopyrightable "method of operation."

That the Lotus menu command hierarchy is a "method of operation" becomes clearer when one considers program compatibility. Under Lotus's theory, if a user uses several different programs, he or she must learn how to perform the same operation in a different way for each program used. For example, if the user wanted the computer to print material, then the user would have to learn not just one method of operating the computer such that it prints, but many different methods. We find this absurd. The fact that there may be many different ways to operate a computer program, or even many different ways to operate a computer program using a set of hierarchically arranged command terms, does not make the actual method of operation chosen copyrightable; it still functions as a method for operating the computer and as such is uncopyrightable.

Consider also that users employ the Lotus menu command hierarchy in writing macros. Under the district court's holding, if the user wrote a macro to shorten the time needed to perform a certain operation in Lotus 1-2-3, the user would be unable to use that macro to shorten the time needed to perform that same operation in another program. Rather, the user would have to rewrite his or her macro using that other program's menu command hierarchy. This is despite the fact that the macro is clearly the user's own work product. We think that forcing the user to cause the computer to perform the same operation in a different way ignores Congress's direction in § 102(b) that "methods of operation" are not copyrightable. That programs can offer users the ability to write macros in many different ways does not change the fact that, once written, the macro allows the user to perform an operation automatically. As the Lotus menu command hierarchy serves as the basis for Lotus 1-2-3 macros, the Lotus menu command hierarchy is a "method of operation."

In holding that expression that is part of a "method of operation" cannot be copyrighted, we do not understand ourselves to go against the Supreme Court's holding in *Feist*. In *Feist*, the Court explained:

> The primary objective of copyright is not to reward the labor of authors, but to promote the Progress of Science and useful Arts. To this end, copyright assures authors the right to their original expression, but encourages others to build freely upon the ideas and information conveyed by a work.

Feist. We do not think that the Court's statement that "copyright assures authors the right to their original expression" indicates that all expression is necessarily copyrightable; while original expression is necessary for copyright protection, we do not think that it is alone sufficient. Courts must still inquire whether original expression falls within one of the categories foreclosed from copyright protection by § 102(b), such as being a "method of operation."

We also note that in most contexts, there is no need to "build" upon other people's expression, for the ideas conveyed by that expression can be conveyed by someone else without copying the first author's expression.[13] In the context of methods of operation, however, "building" requires the use of the precise method of operation already employed; otherwise, "building" would require dismantling, too. Original developers are not the only people entitled to build on the methods of operation they create; anyone can. Thus, Borland may build on the method of operation that Lotus designed and may use the Lotus menu command hierarchy in doing so. . . .

III.
Conclusion

Because we hold that the Lotus menu command hierarchy is uncopyrightable

---

[13] When there are a limited number of ways to express an idea, however, the expression "merges" with the idea and becomes uncopyrightable. *Morrissey*, 379 F.2d at 678–79.

subject matter, we further hold that Borland did not infringe Lotus's copyright by copying it. Accordingly, we need not consider any of Borland's affirmative defenses. The judgment of the district court is
Reversed.

BOUDIN, Circuit Judge, concurring.

The importance of this case, and a slightly different emphasis in my view of the underlying problem, prompt me to add a few words to the majority's tightly focused discussion.

I.

Most of the law of copyright and the "tools" of analysis have developed in the context of literary works such as novels, plays, and films. In this milieu, the principal problem—simply stated, if difficult to resolve—is to stimulate creative expression without unduly limiting access by others to the broader themes and concepts deployed by the author. The middle of the spectrum presents close cases; but a "mistake" in providing too much protection involves a small cost: subsequent authors treating the same themes must take a few more steps away from the original expression.

The problem presented by computer programs is fundamentally different in one respect. The computer program is a means for causing something to happen; it has a mechanical utility, an instrumental role, in accomplishing the world's work. Granting protection, in other words, can have some of the consequences of patent protection in limiting other people's ability to perform a task in the most efficient manner. Utility does not bar copyright (dictionaries may be copyrighted), but it alters the calculus.

Of course, the argument for protection is undiminished, perhaps even enhanced, by utility: if we want more of an intellectual product, a temporary monopoly for the creator provides incentives for others to create other, different items in this class. But the "cost" side of the equation may be different where one places a very high value on public access to a useful innovation that may be the most efficient means of performing a given task. Thus, the argument for extending protection may be the same; but the stakes on the other side are much higher.

It is no accident that patent protection has preconditions that copyright protection does not—notably, the requirements of novelty and non-obviousness—and that patents are granted for a shorter period than copyrights. This problem of utility has sometimes manifested itself in copyright cases, such as *Baker v. Selden* (1879), and been dealt with through various formulations that limit copyright or create limited rights to copy. But the case law and doctrine addressed to utility in copyright have been brief detours in the general march of copyright law.

Requests for the protection of computer menus present the concern with fencing off access to the commons in an acute form. A new menu may be a creative work, but over time its importance may come to reside more in the investment that has been made by users in learning the menu and in building their own mini-programs—macros—in reliance upon the menu. Better typewriter keyboard layouts may exist, but the familiar QWERTY keyboard dominates the market because that is what everyone has learned to use. See P. David, CLIO and the Economics of QWERTY, 75 Am. Econ. Rev. 332 (1985). The QWERTY keyboard is nothing other than a menu of letters.

Thus, to assume that computer programs are just one more new means of expression, like a filmed play, may be quite wrong. The "form"—the written source code or the menu structure depicted on the screen—look hauntingly like the familiar stuff of copyright; but the "substance" probably has more to do with problems presented in patent law or, as already noted, in those rare cases where copyright law has confronted industrially useful expressions. Applying copyright law to computer programs is like assembling a jigsaw puzzle whose pieces do not quite fit.

All of this would make no difference if Congress had squarely confronted the issue, and given explicit directions as to what should be done. The Copyright Act of 1976 took a different course. While Congress said that computer programs might be subject to copyright protection, it said this in very general terms; and, especially in § 102(b), Congress adopted a string of exclusions that if taken literally might easily seem to exclude most computer programs from protection. The only detailed prescriptions for computers involve narrow issues (like back-up copies) of no relevance here.

Of course, one could still read the statute as a congressional command that the familiar doctrines of copyright law be taken and applied to computer programs, in cookie cutter fashion, as if the programs were novels or play scripts. Some of the cases involving computer programs embody this approach. It seems to be mistaken on two different grounds: the tradition of copyright law, and the likely intent of Congress.

The broad-brush conception of copyright protection, the time limits, and the formalities have long been prescribed by statute. But the heart of copyright doctrine— what may be protected and with what limitations and exceptions—has been developed by the courts through experience with individual cases. B. Kaplan, An Unhurried View of Copyright 40 (1967). Occasionally Congress addresses a problem in detail. For the most part the interstitial development of copyright through the courts is our tradition.

Nothing in the language or legislative history of the 1976 Act, or at least nothing brought to our attention, suggests that Congress meant the courts to abandon this case-by-case approach. Indeed, by setting up § 102(b) as a counterpoint theme, Congress has arguably recognized the tension and left it for the courts to resolve through the development of case law. And case law development is adaptive: it allows new problems to be solved with help of earlier doctrine, but it does not preclude new doctrines to meet new situations.

II.

In this case, the raw facts are mostly, if not entirely, undisputed. Although the inferences to be drawn may be more debatable, it is very hard to see that Borland has shown any interest in the Lotus menu except as a fall-back option for those users already committed to it by prior experience or in order to run their own macros using 1-2-3 commands. At least for the amateur, accessing the Lotus menu in the Borland Quattro or Quattro Pro program takes some effort.

Put differently, it is unlikely that users who value the Lotus menu for its own sake—independent of any investment they have made themselves in learning Lotus' commands or creating macros dependent upon them—would choose the Borland program in order to secure access to the Lotus menu. Borland's success is due primarily to other features. Its rationale for deploying the Lotus menu bears the ring of truth.

Now, any use of the Lotus menu by Borland is a commercial use and deprives Lotus of a portion of its "reward," in the sense that an infringement claim if allowed would increase Lotus' profits. But this is circular reasoning: broadly speaking, every limitation on copyright or privileged use diminishes the reward of the original creator. Yet not every writing is copyrightable or every use an infringement. The provision of reward is one concern of copyright law, but it is not the only one. If it were, copyrights would be perpetual and there would be no exceptions.

The present case is an unattractive one for copyright protection of the menu. The menu commands (e.g., "print," "quit") are largely for standard procedures that Lotus did not invent and are common words that Lotus cannot monopolize. What is left is the particular combination and sub-grouping of commands in a pattern devised by Lotus. This arrangement may have a more appealing logic and ease of use than some other configurations; but there is a certain arbitrariness to many of the choices.

If Lotus is granted a monopoly on this pattern, users who have learned the command structure of Lotus 1-2-3 or devised their own macros are locked into Lotus, just as a typist who has learned the QWERTY keyboard would be the captive of anyone who had a monopoly on the production of such a keyboard. Apparently, for a period Lotus 1-2-3 has had such sway in the market that it has represented the de facto standard for electronic spreadsheet commands. So long as Lotus is the superior spreadsheet—either in quality or in price—there may be nothing wrong with this advantage.

But if a better spreadsheet comes along, it is hard to see why customers who have learned the Lotus menu and devised macros for it should remain captives of Lotus because of an investment in learning made by the users and not by Lotus. Lotus has already reaped a substantial reward for being first; assuming that the Borland program is now better, good reasons exist for freeing it to attract old Lotus customers: to enable the old customers to take advantage of a new advance, and to reward Borland in turn for making a better product. If Borland has not made a better product, then customers will remain with Lotus anyway.

Thus, for me the question is not whether Borland should prevail but on what basis. Various avenues might be traveled, but the main choices are between holding that the menu is not protectable by copyright and devising a new doctrine that Borland's use is privileged. No solution is perfect and no intermediate appellate court can make the final choice.

To call the menu a "method of operation" is, in the common use of those words, a defensible position. After all, the purpose of the menu is not to be admired as a work of literary or pictorial art. It is to transmit directions from the user to the computer, i.e., to operate the computer. The menu is also a "method" in the dictionary sense because it is a "planned way of doing something," an "order or system," and (aptly here) an "orderly or systematic arrangement, sequence or the like." Random House Webster's College Dictionary 853 (1991).

A different approach would be to say that Borland's use is privileged because, in the context already described, it is not seeking to appropriate the advances made by Lotus' menu; rather, having provided an arguably more attractive menu of its own, Borland is merely trying to give former Lotus users an option to exploit their own prior investment in learning or in macros. The difference is that such a privileged use approach would not automatically protect Borland if it had simply copied the Lotus menu (using different codes), contributed nothing of its own, and resold Lotus under the Borland label.

The closest analogue in conventional copyright is the fair use doctrine. E.g., *Harper & Row, Publishers, Inc. v. Nation Enters.* (1985). Although invoked by Borland, it has largely been brushed aside in this case because the Supreme Court has said that it is "presumptively" unavailable where the use is a "commercial" one. [*Harper & Row*]. But see *Campbell v. Acuff-Rose Music, Inc.* (1994). In my view, this is something less than a definitive answer; "presumptively" does not mean "always" and, in any event, the doctrine of fair use was created by the courts and can be adapted to new purposes.

But a privileged use doctrine would certainly involve problems of its own. It might more closely tailor the limits on copyright protection to the reasons for limiting that protection; but it would entail a host of administrative problems that would cause cost and delay, and would also reduce the ability of the industry to predict outcomes. Indeed, to the extent that Lotus' menu is an important standard in the industry, it might be argued that any use ought to be deemed privileged.

In sum, the majority's result persuades me and its formulation is as good, if not better, than any other that occurs to me now as within the reach of courts. Some solutions (e.g., a very short copyright period for menus) are not options at all for courts but might be for Congress. In all events, the choices are important ones of policy, not linguistics, and they should be made with the underlying considerations in view.

Lotus Development Corp. v. Borland Intern'l, Inc.
516 U.S. 233 (1996)

On writ of *certiorari* from the United States Court of Appeals for the First Circuit.

PER CURIAM.

The judgment of the United States Court of Appeals for the First Circuit is affirmed by an equally divided Court.

(Justice STEVENS took no part in the consideration or decision of this case.)

Note

Lotus is included in the book not merely because it was a pathbreaking case on copyrightable subject matter, affirmed by an equally divided Supreme Court, but because of three additional factors.

- First, *Lotus* is a nice example of the courts taking a series of doctrines developed in other contexts and applying them to a new technology.
- Second, the majority and concurrence demonstrate two different judicial methodologies for that process of technological and statutory "translation." The majority looks at the existing limitations within the statutory structure, rejects a straightforward application of *Baker v. Selden* (do you agree?) and fits the menu prompts and command hierarchy into the language of "methods of operation"—explicitly declared to be non-copyrightable under § 102. Judge Boudin concurs but says "[t]he importance of this case, and a slightly different emphasis in my view of the underlying problem, prompt me to add a few words to the majority's tightly focused discussion." (What does "tightly focused" mean here in judicial language?) He rejects the idea that copyright doctrine should be applied literally to the new technology. "Of course, one could still read the statute as a congressional command that the familiar doctrines of copyright law be taken and applied to computer programs, in cookie cutter fashion, as if the programs were novels or play scripts. Some of the cases involving computer programs embody this approach. It seems to be mistaken on two different grounds: the tradition of copyright law, and the likely intent of Congress." He concludes "the choices are important ones of policy, not linguistics, and they should be made with the underlying considerations in view." This question of judicial method—how should judges apply intellectual property law?—is a central theme of the course.
- Finally, *Lotus* is an excellent introduction to the particular features of "network goods" or network effects, and the implication these have for intellectual

property. If you read *Fifty Shades of Grey* it does not affect my decision on whether to read Thomas Pynchon or Neil Stephenson. But if you (and everyone else) uses Microsoft Word, I may need to use that program even if I believe Open Office to be better.

Questions:

1.) Compare Boudin's approach with the majority's. Which is more appropriate? More faithful to the judicial role? In your answer which of the following factors are relevant:

- A belief that Congress's copyright and patent powers contain an explicit purposive and utilitarian goal—promoting the progress?
- A belief that utilitarian reasoning in judicial decisions is inherently suspect— that belief being derived either from the separation of powers or the nature of the judicial role or both?
- The Jeffersonian tradition described in the earlier excerpt from *The Public Domain*?
- Absence of specific guidance from Congress about how courts should integrate new technologies into copyright and patent?
- The idea that a judge's role is merely that of an umpire who "calls strikes"?
- A belief that literal rather than purposive interpretation is somehow less political?
- A belief that both literal and purposive interpretation are laden with value judgments?

2.) Would your answers be different if the field of law was antitrust? Why? Why not?

3.) At the very beginning of his concurrence, Boudin makes a vitally important point about "error costs" in the context of protecting goods such as software, comparing that to the error costs of protecting more traditional copyrightable subject matter. What is it?

4.) How does the following quotation resonate with the arguments used by Pitney, Holmes or Brandeis in *INS v. AP*? With Jefferson? With Diderot or Condorcet? With the quote from Felix Cohen that begins Chapter 4 on trademark? Why does Boudin say this argument is *circular*?

> Now, any use of the Lotus menu by Borland is a commercial use and deprives Lotus of a portion of its "reward," in the sense that an infringement claim if allowed would increase Lotus' profits. But this is circular reasoning: broadly speaking, every limitation on copyright or privileged use diminishes the reward of the original creator. Yet not every writing is copyrightable or every use an infringement. The provision of reward is one concern of copyright law, but it is not the only one. If it were, copyrights would be perpetual and there would be no exceptions.

Note: The *Oracle v. Google* Case

For 25 years, the decision in *Lotus v. Borland* was assumed to lay out the law of copyrightable subject matter as applied to computer software methods of operation— menu hierarchies, interfaces and so on. That premise was challenged in *Oracle v. Google,* a closely watched case that culminated in a Supreme Court decision in 2021.

Oracle concerned the copyrightability of "APIs"—Application Programming Interfaces. The last word there is the key. The API governs the way one program works with another. Without knowledge of the API, or the ability to reverse engineer it, the "interoperability" of programs will be limited. (Imagine trying to play a piano without knowing which key corresponded to which note.)

When writing the Android operating system, Google copied the declaring code and structure, sequence, and organization ("SSO")[9] of 37 API packages from Oracle's Java software, in order to enable Java developers to write applications for Android. (The relevant technology is described in more detail in Chapter 13.) In 2012, the Northern District of California held that the declaring code and SSO were not subject to copyright protection: the declaring code was uncopyrightable because idea and expression had merged, and the SSO, like the menu command hierarchy in *Lotus*, was a "method of operation" under § 102(b). The district court's decision was animated in part by concerns about the consequences that Oracle's copyright claim might have on *interoperability*: "To accept Oracle's claim would be to allow anyone to copyright one version of code to carry out a system of commands and thereby bar all others from writing their own different versions to carry out all or part of the same commands. No holding has ever endorsed such a sweeping proposition."

In 2014, the Federal Circuit reversed. (The case was in the Federal Circuit because of earlier patent claims; for the copyright claims, the court declared itself to be bound by Ninth Circuit law.) For the Federal Circuit, the presence of expressive choices in the APIs precluded them from being uncopyrightable methods of operation. Otherwise, all computer programs (which are methods of operating computers) could become uncopyrightable as a result. Compare the court's reasoning to the *Lotus* opinion you have just read.

> The problem with the district court's approach is that computer programs are by definition functional—they are all designed to accomplish some task. . . . If we were to accept the district court's suggestion that a computer program is uncopyrightable simply because it "carr[ies] out pre-assigned functions," no computer program is protectable. That result contradicts Congress's express intent to provide copyright protection to computer programs, as well as binding Ninth Circuit case law finding computer programs copyrightable, despite their utilitarian or functional purpose. Though the trial court did add the caveat that it "does not hold that the structure, sequence and organization of all computer programs may be stolen," it is hard to see how its method of operation analysis could lead to any other conclusion. [W]e conclude that a set of commands to instruct a computer to carry out desired operations may contain expression that is eligible for copyright protection. We agree with Oracle that, under Ninth Circuit law, an original work—even one that serves a function—is entitled to copyright protection as long as the author had multiple ways to express the underlying idea.

---

[9] "Structure, sequence and organization" is a term introduced in *Whelan Associates v. Jaslow Dental Laboratory* (3d Cir. 1986) for the purpose of separating the copyrightable and uncopyrightable portions of software. That decision was widely criticized by scholars for extending copyright to merely functional components of the program—in that case, the task of managing a dentist's office. The term had largely fallen out of use in the Ninth Circuit since the late 1980's but it was used by both the District Court (which believed it to be uncopyrightable) and the Federal Circuit (which believed it was copyrightable). Regardless of the terminology, the central question here is whether interfaces are uncopyrightable methods of operation, or copyrightable expressive choices—the term used should not obscure that fact.

After this decision, the case proceeded to trial where, in 2016, the jury found that Google's use of Oracle's APIs was "fair use." Then in 2018, the Federal Circuit reversed—taking the unusual step of overturning a jury verdict on fair use. Finally in 2021 the Supreme Court decided the case, but not on subject matter grounds.

> Given the rapidly changing technological, economic, and business-related circumstances, we believe we should not answer more than is necessary to resolve the parties' dispute. We shall assume, but purely for argument's sake, that the entire Sun Java API falls within the definition of that which can be copyrighted. We shall ask instead whether Google's use of part of that API was a "fair use." Unlike the Federal Circuit, we conclude that it was.

You will read that decision in Chapter 13. Strikingly, the majority opinion, written by Justice Breyer, returns again and again to the arguments made in *Lotus* and in particular to the concerns raised by Judge Boudin in his concurrence. Yet it enunciates those concerns through the lens of fair use, not the "in or out" bright line question of copyrightable subject matter.

Notice how all of these decisions have to navigate not one, but two slippery slopes in dealing with software's mixture of expressive and functional aspects. Make the decision too broad one way and no software is protected by copyright. Make it too broad the other way and copyright monopolies of enormous length are added to a technology rich in network effects and lock-in. What is the best policy argument in favor of the *Lotus* approach? The Federal Circuit's approach? Which is more consistent with the language of § 102(b) of the Copyright Act? "In *no case* does copyright protection for an original work of authorship extend to any . . . method of operation, *regardless of the form in which it is . . . embodied*"?

This leaves us with an unresolved question. Is *Lotus* still good law? The authors believe it is the correct decision, both textually and on policy grounds. As you will see in Chapter 13, its *logic* was enthusiastically embraced in the Supreme Court's decision, even if the legal ground was different—fair use not subject matter. Or, in assuming for the sake of argument that APIs *can* be copyrightable, is the Court implicitly endorsing the Federal Circuit's view? Will *Oracle* make it easier to raise copyright suits over software, because the issue can rarely be resolved at the summary judgment level? Or is the Supreme Court, in signaling emphatic approval of Judge Boudin's logic, actually directing the lower courts to focus intently on interoperability and network effects, regardless of the legal pigeon-hole in which they are raised?

PROBLEM 11-3

Lotus v. Borland uses copyright's subject matter limitations—in this case, over "methods of operation"—to exclude menu commands and interfaces from copyrightable subject matter. Judge Boudin's concurrence muses on the desirability of a more dynamic and flexible privilege-based approach—a kind of super fair use—focusing on a pragmatic inquiry into whether the particular case featured the negative consequences of network effects or lock in. In the end though, he joins the majority's "tightly focused" decision on methods of operation. When the Federal Circuit decided *Oracle v. Google*, it rejected *Lotus*, finding that Application Programming Interfaces—which as their name suggests, seem to be methods of operation—*were* copyrightable subject matter under § 102. To hold otherwise, the CAFC declared, would be to cast into doubt the copyrightability of all computer programs which, at base, are obviously methods of operating a computer. When SCOTUS decided the *Oracle* case it declined to reach the question of whether APIs were copyrightable subject matter, instead deciding the case on fair use grounds. It overturned the CAFC's decision on that front and found fair use on Google's part. You will read that opinion in Chapter 13. You thus have three approaches: 1.) Interfaces and APIs are methods of operation and thus not copyrightable subject matter under § 102. (*Lotus*). 2.) Interfaces and APIs can be copyrightable subject matter. (The CAFC approach in *Oracle*.) 3.) We will not decide on subject matter grounds but will rule in particular cases on whether the use of the particular code or interface is fair use. (SCOTUS *Oracle*.) Which is the best approach? Why?

6.) Fixation (Copyright Meets Software, continued)

We saw in the *Moghadam* and *Martignon* cases featured in Chapter 2 that fixation was not merely a statutory requirement but a constitutional one where copyright was concerned. At the same time, we were left uncertain about whether that constitutional requirement could easily be circumvented using Congress' commerce clause power. In the case that follows, we consider a very different fixation-related question, the attempt to define the statutory meaning of fixation. More specifically, the Ninth Circuit has to define "fixation" in the context of computer memory, and in particular the volatile "Random Access Memory" that holds a temporary copy of the program being executed. Should the constitutional and statutory inquiries into fixation have anything to do with each other? Do they? (It should be noted that while this chapter discusses subject matter requirements for copyright, *MAI* deals with fixation in terms of finding copyright *infringement*. We include the case here because of its importance to our discussion of software and because, in each instance, we are defining the limits and extent of the copyright monopoly.)

MAI Systems Corp. v. Peak Computer, Inc.
991 F.2d 511 (9th Cir. 1993)

BRUNETTI, Circuit Judge.

Peak Computer, Inc. and two of its employees appeal the district court's order issuing a preliminary injunction pending trial as well as the district court's order issuing a permanent injunction following the grant of partial summary judgment.

I. FACTS

MAI Systems Corp., until recently, manufactured computers and designed software to run those computers. The company continues to service its computers and the software necessary to operate the computers. MAI software includes operating system software, which is necessary to run any other program on the computer.

Peak Computer, Inc. is a company organized in 1990 that maintains computer systems for its clients. Peak maintains MAI computers for more than one hundred clients in Southern California. This accounts for between fifty and seventy percent of Peak's business.

Peak's service of MAI computers includes routine maintenance and emergency repairs. Malfunctions often are related to the failure of circuit boards inside the computers, and it may be necessary for a Peak technician to operate the computer and its operating system software in order to service the machine.

In August, 1991, Eric Francis left his job as customer service manager at MAI and joined Peak. Three other MAI employees joined Peak a short time later. Some businesses that had been using MAI to service their computers switched to Peak after learning of Francis's move.

II. PROCEDURAL HISTORY

. . . The district court granted partial summary judgment for MAI and entered a permanent injunction on the issues of copyright infringement and misappropriation of trade secrets on February 2, 1993 which provides:

A. Defendants [and certain others] are hereby permanently enjoined as follows:

1. Peak [and certain others] are permanently enjoined from copying, disseminating, selling, publishing, distributing, loaning, or otherwise infringing MAI's copyrighted works, or any derivatives thereof, including those works for which registrations have issued, and works for which registrations may issue in the future. The "copying" enjoined herein specifically includes the acts of loading, or causing to be loaded, directly or indirectly, any MAI software from any magnetic storage or read only memory device into the electronic random access memory of the central processing unit of a computer system. As used herein, "computer system" means an MAI central processing unit in combination with either a video display, printer, disk drives, and/or keyboard.

2. (a) Peak and Francis [and certain others] are permanently enjoined from misappropriating, using in any manner in their business, including advertising connected therewith, and/or disclosing to others MAI's trade secrets. . . .

(b) In particular, the persons identified in subparagraph (a) herein are permanently enjoined from soliciting any MAI computer maintenance customer and from maintaining any contract with any former MAI computer maintenance customer where knowledge of any such customers was obtained by Francis during his employment with MAI. . . .

IV. COPYRIGHT INFRINGEMENT

The district court granted summary judgment in favor of MAI on its claims of copyright infringement and issued a permanent injunction against Peak on these claims. The alleged copyright violations include: (1) Peak's running of MAI software licenced to Peak customers; (2) Peak's use of unlicensed software at its headquarters; and, (3) Peak's loaning of MAI computers and software to its customers. Each of these alleged violations must be considered separately.

A. Peak's running of MAI software licensed to Peak customers

To prevail on a claim of copyright infringement, a plaintiff must prove ownership of a copyright and a "'copying' of protectable expression" beyond the scope of a license. *S.O.S., Inc. v. Payday, Inc.* (9th Cir. 1989).

MAI software licenses allow MAI customers to use the software for their own internal information processing.[3] This allowed use necessarily includes the loading of the software into the computer's random access memory ("RAM") by a MAI customer. However, MAI software licenses do not allow for the use or copying of MAI software by third parties such as Peak. Therefore, any "copying" done by Peak is "beyond the scope" of the license.

It is not disputed that MAI owns the copyright to the software at issue here, however, Peak vigorously disputes the district court's conclusion that a "copying" occurred under the Copyright Act.

The Copyright Act defines "copies" as:

material objects, other than phonorecords, in which a work is fixed by any method now known or later developed, and from which the work can be perceived, reproduced, or otherwise communicated, either directly or with the aid of a machine or device.

17 U.S.C. § 101.

The Copyright Act then explains:

A work is "fixed" in a tangible medium of expression when its embodiment in a copy or phonorecord, by or under the authority of the author, is sufficiently permanent or stable to permit it to be perceived, reproduced, or otherwise communicated for a period of more than transitory duration.

17 U.S.C. § 101.

The district court's grant of summary judgment on MAI's claims of copyright infringement reflects its conclusion that a "copying" for purposes of copyright law occurs when a computer program is transferred from a permanent storage device to a computer's RAM. This conclusion is consistent with its finding, in granting the preliminary injunction, that: "the loading of copyrighted computer software from a storage medium (hard disk, floppy disk, or read only memory) into the memory of a central processing unit ("CPU") causes a copy to be made. In the absence of ownership of the copyright or express permission by license, such acts constitute copyright infringement." We find that this conclusion is supported by the record and by the law.

Peak concedes that in maintaining its customer's computers, it uses MAI operating software "to the extent that the repair and maintenance process necessarily involves

---

[3] A representative MAI software license provides in part:

4. Software License.
(a) License. . . . Customer may use the Software (one version with maximum of two copies permitted—a working and a backup copy) . . . solely to fulfill Customer's own internal information processing needs on the particular items of Equipment . . . for which the Software is configured and furnished by [MAI]. . . . The term "Software" includes, without limitation, all basic operating system software. . . .
(b) Customer Prohibited Acts. . . . Any possession or use of the Software . . . not expressly authorized under this License or any act which might jeopardize [MAI]'s rights or interests in the Software . . . is prohibited, including without limitation, examination, disclosure, copying, modification, reconfiguration, augmentation, adaptation, emulation, visual display or reduction to visually perceptible form or tampering. . . .
(c) Customer Obligations. Customer acknowledges that the Software is [MAI]'s valuable and exclusive property, trade secret and copyrighted material. Accordingly, Customer shall . . . (i) use the Software . . . strictly as prescribed under this License, (ii) keep the Software . . . confidential and not make [it] available to others. . . .
A representative diagnostic license agreement provides in part:
6. Access/Non-Disclosure.
Licensee shall not give access nor shall it disclose the Diagnostics (in any form) . . . to any person . . . without the written permission of [MAI]. Licensee may authorize not more than three (3) of its bona fide employees to utilize the Diagnostics . . . if, and only if, they agree to be bound by the terms hereof.

turning on the computer to make sure it is functional and thereby running the operating system." It is also uncontroverted that when the computer is turned on the operating system is loaded into the computer's RAM. As part of diagnosing a computer problem at the customer site, the Peak technician runs the computer's operating system software, allowing the technician to view the systems error log, which is part of the operating system, thereby enabling the technician to diagnose the problem.[4]

Peak argues that this loading of copyrighted software does not constitute a copyright violation because the "copy" created in RAM is not "fixed." However, by showing that Peak loads the software into the RAM and is then able to view the system error log and diagnose the problem with the computer, MAI has adequately shown that the representation created in the RAM is "sufficiently permanent or stable to permit it to be perceived, reproduced, or otherwise communicated for a period of more than transitory duration."

After reviewing the record, we find no specific facts (and Peak points to none) which indicate that the copy created in the RAM is not fixed. While Peak argues this issue in its pleadings, mere argument does not establish a genuine issue of material fact to defeat summary judgment. A party opposing a properly supported motion for summary judgment may not rest upon the mere allegations or denials in pleadings, but "must set forth specific facts showing that there is a genuine issue for trial." Fed.R.Civ.Proc. 56(e); *Anderson v. Liberty Lobby, Inc.* (1986); *Harper v. Wallingford* (9th Cir. 1989).

The law also supports the conclusion that Peak's loading of copyrighted software into RAM creates a "copy" of that software in violation of the Copyright Act. In *Apple Computer, Inc. v. Formula Int'l, Inc.* (C.D. Cal. 1984), the district court held that the copying of copy-righted software onto silicon chips and subsequent sale of those chips is not protected by § 117 of the Copyright Act. Section 117 allows "the 'owner'[5] of a copy of a computer pro-gram to make or authorize the making of another copy" without infringing copyright law, if it "is an essential step in the utilization of the computer program" or if the new copy is "for archival purposes only." 17 U.S.C. § 117 (Supp. 1988).[6] One of the grounds for finding that § 117 did not apply was the court's conclusion that the permanent copying of the software onto the silicon chips was not an "essential step" in the utilization of the software because the software could be used through RAM without making a permanent copy. The court stated:

> RAM can be simply defined as a computer component in which data and computer programs can be temporarily recorded. Thus, the purchaser of [software] desiring to utilize all of the programs on the diskette could arrange to copy [the software] into RAM. This would only be a temporary fixation. It is a property of RAM that when the computer is turned off, the

---

[4] MAI also alleges that Peak runs its diagnostic software in servicing MAI computers. Since Peak's running of the operating software constitutes copyright violation, it is not necessary for us to directly reach the issue of whether Peak also runs MAI's diagnostic software. However, we must note that Peak's field service manager, Charles Weiner, admits that MAI diagnostic software is built into the MAI MPx system and, further, that if Peak loads the MAI diagnostic software from whatever source into the computer's RAM, that such loading will produce the same copyright violation as loading the operating software.

[5] Since MAI licensed its software, the Peak customers do not qualify as "owners" of the software and are not eligible for protection under § 117.

[6] The current § 117 was enacted by Congress in 1980, as part of the Computer Software Copyright Act. This Act adopted the recommendations contained in the Final Report of the National Commission on New Technological Uses of Copyrighted Works ("CONTU") (1978). The CONTU was established by Congress in 1974 to perform research and make recommendations concerning copyright protection for computer programs. The new § 117 reflects the CONTU's conclusion that: "Because the placement of a work into a computer is the preparation of a copy, the law should provide that persons in rightful possession of copies of programs be able to use them freely without fear of exposure to copyright liability." Final Report at 13.

copy of the program recorded in RAM is lost.

Apple Computer at 622.

While we recognize that this language is not dispositive, it supports the view that the copy made in RAM is "fixed" and qualifies as a copy under the Copyright Act.

We have found no case which specifically holds that the copying of software into RAM creates a "copy" under the Copyright Act. However, it is generally accepted that the loading of software into a computer constitutes the creation of a copy under the Copyright Act. See e.g. *Vault Corp. v. Quaid Software Ltd.* (5th Cir. 1988) ("the act of loading a program from a medium of storage into a computer's memory creates a copy of the program"); 2 NIMMER ON COPYRIGHT, § 8.08 at 8-105 (1983) ("Inputting a computer program entails the preparation of a copy."); Final Report of the National Commission on the New Technological Uses of Copyrighted Works, at 13 (1978) ("the placement of a work into a computer is the preparation of a copy"). We recognize that these authorities are somewhat troubling since they do not specify that a copy is created regardless of whether the software is loaded into the RAM, the hard disk or the read only memory ("ROM"). However, since we find that the copy created in the RAM can be "perceived, reproduced, or otherwise communicated," we hold that the loading of software into the RAM creates a copy under the Copyright Act. 17 U.S.C. § 101. We affirm the district court's grant of summary judgment as well as the permanent injunction as it relates to this issue. . . .

Questions:

1.) Should the question of whether a RAM copy of a computer program is sufficiently "fixed" to constitute infringement depend on some linguistic analysis? A technical analysis? One that considers the effect of the decision on the degree of control that the owner of the software copyright could exercise in the aftermarket—for example, by controlling maintenance and repair? What would Judge Boudin say about the approach that the *MAI* court adopts?

2.) We have talked about implicit moral framing in intellectual property questions. What facts does the court give early in its decision that suggested which way it was going to rule? How would you describe the implicit narrative presented?

3.) You are the lawyer responsible for the appeal of this case. The judges are not technically savvy. Your job is to come up with analogies to the world of copyright that *they* are familiar with that either confirm or deny the court's conclusion. In particular, you should focus on their implicit definition of what it means to be fixed. ("To say that this is fixed is like saying ___ is fixed. To say that this is not fixed is like saying ___ does not count as fixation.") You should also focus in your analogical quest on the *consequences* of their ruling. ("This is like saying that ___ [traditional copyright holder] can forbid ___. To say they cannot prohibit this activity would be like saying a ___ [traditional copyright holder] is unable to prevent someone from ___.")

4.) How does this decision relate to the goals of the fixation requirement in the Constitution?

5.) Read § 117 of the Copyright Act. This section was amended after the *MAI* decision specifically to address the legality of computer repair. Does this solve the potential problem created by *MAI*?

6.) How much software do you own? Search the web for the licenses covering some piece of software on your computer, such as iTunes, or Microsoft Word (assuming that you did not carefully read those terms when you clicked "I accept"). What does the license say? Why is *MAI* relevant to this question?

Religious Technology Center v. Netcom
907 F. Supp. 1361 (N.D. Cal. 1995)

WHYTE, District Judge.

This case concerns an issue of first impression regarding intellectual property rights in cyberspace. Specifically, this order addresses whether the operator of a computer bulletin board service ("BBS"), and the large Internet access provider that allows that BBS to reach the Internet, should be liable for copyright infringement committed by a subscriber of the BBS.

Plaintiffs Religious Technology Center ("RTC") and Bridge Publications, Inc. ("BPI") hold copyrights in the unpublished and published works of L. Ron Hubbard, the late founder of the Church of Scientology ("the Church"). Defendant Dennis Erlich ("Erlich")[3] is a former minister of Scientology turned vocal critic of the Church, whose pulpit is now the Usenet newsgroup[4] alt.religion.scientology ("a.r.s."), an on-line forum for discussion and criticism of Scientology. Plaintiffs maintain that Erlich infringed their copyrights when he posted portions of their works on a.r.s. Erlich gained his access to the Internet through defendant Thomas Klemesrud's ("Klemesrud's") BBS "support.com." Klemesrud is the operator of the BBS, which is run out of his home and has approximately 500 paying users. Klemesrud's BBS is not directly linked to the Internet, but gains its connection through the facilities of defendant Netcom On-Line Communications, Inc. ("Netcom"), one of the largest providers of Internet access in the United States.

After failing to convince Erlich to stop his postings, plaintiffs contacted defendants Klemesrud and Netcom. Klemesrud responded to plaintiffs' demands that Erlich be kept off his system by asking plaintiffs to prove that they owned the copyrights to the works posted by Erlich. However, plaintiffs refused Klemesrud's request as unreasonable. Netcom similarly refused plaintiffs' request that Erlich not be allowed to gain access to the Internet through its system. Netcom contended that it would be impossible to prescreen Erlich's postings and that to kick Erlich off the Internet meant kicking off the hundreds of

---

[3] Issues of Erlich's liability were addressed in this court's order of September 22, 1995. That order concludes in part that a preliminary injunction against Erlich is warranted because plaintiffs have shown a likelihood of success on their copyright infringement claims against him. Plaintiffs likely own valid copyrights in Hubbard's published and unpublished works and Erlich's near-verbatim copying of substantial portions of plaintiffs' works was not likely a fair use.

[4] The Usenet has been described as a worldwide community of electronic BBSs that is closely associated with the Internet and with the Internet community. The messages in Usenet are organized into thousands of topical groups, or "Newsgroups". . . . As a Usenet user, you read and contribute ("post") to your local Usenet site. Each Usenet site distributes its users' postings to other Usenet sites based on various implicit and explicit configuration settings, and in turn receives postings from other sites. Usenet traffic typically consists of as much as 30 to 50 Mbytes of messages per day. Usenet is read and contributed to on a daily basis by a total population of millions of people. . . . There is no specific network that is the Usenet. Usenet traffic flows over a wide range of networks, including the Internet and dial-up phone links.

users of Klemesrud's BBS. Consequently, plaintiffs named Klemesrud and Netcom in their suit against Erlich, although only on the copyright infringement claims. . . . For the reasons set forth below, the court grants in part and denies in part Netcom's motion for summary judgment and Klemesrud's motion for judgment on the pleadings and denies plaintiffs' motion for a preliminary injunction. . . .

B. Copyright Infringement

To establish a claim of copyright infringement, a plaintiff must demonstrate (1) ownership of a valid copyright and (2) "copying"[7] of protectable expression by the defendant. Infringement occurs when a defendant violates one of the exclusive rights of the copyright holder. 17 U.S.C. § 501(a). These rights include the right to reproduce the copyrighted work, the right to prepare derivative works, the right to distribute copies to the public, and the right to publicly display the work. 17 U.S.C. §§ 106(1)–(3) & (5). The court has already determined that plaintiffs have established that they own the copyrights to all of the Exhibit A and B works, except item 4 of Exhibit A. The court also found plaintiffs likely to succeed on their claim that defendant Erlich copied the Exhibit A and B works and was not entitled to a fair use defense. Plaintiffs argue that, although Netcom was not itself the source of any of the infringing materials on its system, it nonetheless should be liable for infringement, either directly, contributorily, or vicariously. Netcom disputes these theories of infringement and further argues that it is entitled to its own fair use defense.

1. Direct Infringement

Infringement consists of the unauthorized exercise of one of the exclusive rights of the copyright holder delineated in section 106. 17 U.S.C. § 501. Direct infringement does not require intent or any particular state of mind,[10] although willfulness is relevant to the award of statutory damages. 17 U.S.C. § 504(c).

Many of the facts pertaining to this motion are undisputed. The court will address the relevant facts to determine whether a theory of direct infringement can be supported based on Netcom's alleged reproduction of plaintiffs' works. . . . The court will additionally examine whether Netcom is liable for infringing plaintiffs' exclusive rights to publicly distribute and display their works.

a. Undisputed Facts

The parties do not dispute the basic processes that occur when Erlich posts his allegedly infringing messages to a.r.s. Erlich connects to Klemesrud's BBS using a telephone and a modem. Erlich then transmits his messages to Klemesrud's computer, where they are automatically briefly stored. According to a prearranged pattern established by Netcom's software, Erlich's initial act of posting a message to the Usenet results in the automatic copying of Erlich's message from Klemesrud's computer onto Netcom's computer and onto

---

[7] In this context, "copying" is "shorthand for the infringing of any of the copyright owner's five exclusive rights." *S.O.S., Inc. v. Payday, Inc.* (9th Cir. 1989).

[10] The strict liability for copyright infringement is in contrast to another area of liability affecting online service providers: defamation. Recent decisions have held that where a BBS exercised little control over the content of the material on its service, it was more like a "distributor" than a "republisher" and was thus only liable for defamation on its system where it knew or should have known of the defamatory statements. *Cubby, Inc. v. CompuServe, Inc.* (S.D.N.Y. 1991). By contrast, a New York state court judge found that Prodigy was a publisher because it held itself out to be controlling the content of its services and because it used software to automatically prescreen messages that were offensive or in bad taste. *Stratton Oakmont, Inc. v. Prodigy Services Co.* [The latter case was one prompt for § 230 of the CDA. Eds.]

other computers on the Usenet. In order to ease transmission and for the convenience of Usenet users, Usenet servers maintain postings from newsgroups for a short period of time—eleven days for Netcom's system and three days for Klemesrud's system. Once on Netcom's computers, messages are available to Netcom's customers and Usenet neighbors, who may then download the messages to their own computers. Netcom's local server makes available its postings to a group of Usenet servers, which do the same for other servers until all Usenet sites worldwide have obtained access to the postings, which takes a matter of hours.

Unlike some other large on-line service providers, such as CompuServe, America Online, and Prodigy, Netcom does not create or control the content of the information available to its subscribers. It also does not monitor messages as they are posted. It has, however, suspended the accounts of subscribers who violated its terms and conditions, such as where they had commercial software in their posted files. Netcom admits that, although not currently configured to do this, it may be possible to reprogram its system to screen postings containing particular words or coming from particular individuals. Netcom, however, took no action after it was told by plaintiffs that Erlich had posted messages through Netcom's system that violated plaintiffs' copyrights, instead claiming that it could not shut out Erlich without shutting out all of the users of Klemesrud's BBS.

b. Creation of Fixed Copies

The Ninth Circuit addressed the question of what constitutes infringement in the context of storage of digital information in a computer's random access memory ("RAM"). *MAI Systems Corp. v. Peak Computer, Inc.* (9th Cir. 1993). In *MAI*, the Ninth Circuit upheld a finding of copyright infringement where a repair person, who was not authorized to use the computer owner's licensed operating system software, turned on the computer, thus loading the operating system into RAM for long enough to check an "error log." Copyright protection subsists in original works of authorship "*fixed* in any tangible medium of expression, now known or later developed, from which they can be perceived, reproduced, or otherwise communicated, either directly or with the aid of a machine or device." 17 U.S.C. § 102 (emphasis added). A work is "fixed" when its "embodiment in a copy . . . is sufficiently permanent or stable to permit it to be perceived, reproduced, or otherwise communicated for a period of more than transitory duration." [17 U.S.C.] § 101. *MAI* established that the loading of data from a storage device into RAM constitutes copying because that data stays in RAM long enough for it to be perceived.

In the present case, there is no question after *MAI* that "copies" were created, as Erlich's act of sending a message to a.r.s. caused reproductions of portions of plaintiffs' works on both Klemesrud's and Netcom's storage devices. Even though the messages remained on their systems for at most eleven days, they were sufficiently "fixed" to constitute recognizable copies under the Copyright Act.

c. Is Netcom Directly Liable for Making the Copies?

Accepting that copies were made, Netcom argues that Erlich, and not Netcom, is directly liable for the copying. *MAI* did not address the question raised in this case: whether possessors of computers are liable for incidental copies automatically made on their computers using their software as part of a process initiated by a third party. Netcom correctly distinguishes *MAI* on the ground that Netcom did not take any affirmative action that directly resulted in copying plaintiffs' works other than by installing and maintaining a system whereby software automatically forwards messages received from subscribers onto the Usenet, and temporarily stores copies on its system. Netcom's actions, to the extent that they created a copy of plaintiffs' works, were necessary to having a working system for transmitting Usenet postings to and from the Internet.

Unlike the defendants in *MAI*, neither Netcom nor Klemesrud initiated the copying. The defendants in *MAI* turned on their customers' computers thereby creating temporary copies of the operating system, whereas Netcom's and Klemesrud's systems can operate without any human intervention. Thus, unlike *MAI*, the mere fact that Netcom's system incidentally makes temporary copies of plaintiffs' works does not mean Netcom has caused the copying.[11] The court believes that Netcom's act of designing or implementing a system that automatically and uniformly creates temporary copies of all data sent through it is not unlike that of the owner of a copying machine who lets the public make copies with it.[12] Although some of the people using the machine may directly infringe copyrights, courts analyze the machine owner's liability under the rubric of contributory infringement, not direct infringement. Elkin-Koren [argued that] "contributory in-fringement is more appropriate for dealing with BBS liability, first, because it focuses attention on the BBS-users relationship and the way imposing liability on BBS operators may shape this relationship, and second because it better addresses the complexity of the relationship between BBS operators and subscribers"). Plaintiffs' theory would create many separate acts of infringement and, carried to its natural extreme, would lead to unreasonable liability.

It is not difficult to conclude that Erlich infringes by copying a protected work onto his computer and by posting a message to a newsgroup. However, plaintiffs' theory further implicates a Usenet server that carries Erlich's message to other servers regardless of whether that server acts without any human intervention beyond the initial setting up of the system. It would also result in liability for every single Usenet server in the worldwide

---

[11] One commentator addressed the difficulty in translating copyright concepts, including the public/private dichotomy, to the digitized environment. See Niva Elkin-Koren, Copyright Law and Social Dialogue on the Information Superhighway: The Case Against Copyright Liability of Bulletin Board Operators, 13 CARDOZO ARTS & ENT. L.J. 345, 390 (1995). This commentator noted that one way to characterize a BBS operation is that it "provides subscribers with access and services. As such, BBS operators do not create copies, and do not transfer them in any way. Users post the copies on the BBS, which other users can then read or download."

[12] Netcom compares itself to a common carrier that merely acts as a passive conduit for information. In a sense, a Usenet server that forwards all messages acts like a common carrier, passively retransmitting every message that gets sent through it. Netcom would seem no more liable than the phone company for carrying an infringing facsimile transmission or storing an infringing audio recording on its voice mail. As Netcom's counsel argued, holding such a server liable would be like holding the owner of the highway, or at least the operator of a toll booth, liable for the criminal activities that occur on its roads. Since other similar carriers of information are not liable for infringement, there is some basis for exempting Internet access providers from liability for infringement by their users. The IITF Report concluded that "[i]f an entity provided only the wires and conduits—such as the telephone company, it would have a good argument for an exemption if it was truly in the same position as a common carrier and could not control who or what was on its system." IITF Report at 122. Here, perhaps, the analogy is not completely appropriate as Netcom does more than just "provide the wire and conduits." Further, Internet providers are not natural monopolies that are bound to carry all the traffic that one wishes to pass through them, as with the usual common carrier. Section 111 of the Copyright Act codifies the exemption for passive carriers who are otherwise liable for a secondary transmission. However, the carrier must not have any direct or indirect control over the content or selection of the primary transmission In any event, common carriers are granted statutory exemptions for liability that might otherwise exist. Here, Netcom does not fall under this statutory exemption, and thus faces the usual strict liability scheme that exists for copyright. Whether a new exemption should be carved out for online service providers is to be resolved by Congress, not the courts. Compare Comment, "Online Service Providers and Copyright Law: The Need for Change," 1 SYRACUSE J. LEGIS. & POL'Y 197, 202 (1995) (citing recommendations of online service providers for amending the Copyright Act to create liability only where a "provider has 'actual knowledge that a work that is being or has been transmitted onto, or stored on, its system is infringing,' and has the 'ability and authority' to stop the transmission, and has, after a reasonable amount of time, allowed the infringing activity to continue") with IITF Report at 122 (recommending that Congress not exempt service providers from strict liability for direct infringements).

link of computers transmitting Erlich's message to every other computer. These parties, who are liable under plaintiffs' theory, do no more than operate or implement a system that is essential if Usenet messages are to be widely distributed. There is no need to construe the Act to make all of these parties infringers. Although copyright is a strict liability statute, there should still be some element of volition or causation which is lacking where a defendant's system is merely used to create a copy by a third party.

Plaintiffs point out that the infringing copies resided for eleven days on Netcom's computer and were sent out from it onto the "Information Superhighway." However, under plaintiffs' theory, any storage of a copy that occurs in the process of sending a message to the Usenet is an infringement. While it is possible that less "damage" would have been done if Netcom had heeded plaintiffs' warnings and acted to prevent Erlich's message from being forwarded,[13] this is not relevant to its direct liability for copying. The same argument is true of Klemesrud and any Usenet server. Whether a defendant makes a direct copy that constitutes infringement cannot depend on whether it received a warning to delete the message. This distinction may be relevant to contributory infringement, however, where knowledge is an element. [Contributory infringement will be dealt with in later chapters, Eds.]

The court will now consider two district court opinions that have addressed the liability of BBS operators for infringing files uploaded by subscribers. . . .

. . . g. Conclusion

The court is not persuaded by plaintiffs' argument that Netcom is directly liable for the copies that are made and stored on its computer. Where the infringing subscriber is clearly directly liable for the same act, it does not make sense to adopt a rule that could lead to the liability of countless parties whose role in the infringement is nothing more than setting up and operating a system that is necessary for the functioning of the Internet. Such a result is unnecessary as there is already a party directly liable for causing the copies to be made. Plaintiffs occasionally claim that they only seek to hold liable a party that refuses to delete infringing files after they have been warned. However, such liability cannot be based on a theory of direct infringement, where knowledge is irrelevant. The court does not find workable a theory of infringement that would hold the entire Internet liable for activities that cannot reasonably be deterred. Billions of bits of data flow through the Internet and are necessarily stored on servers throughout the network and it is thus practically impossible to screen out infringing bits from noninfringing bits. Because the court cannot see any meaningful distinction (without regard to knowledge) between what Netcom did and what every other Usenet server does, the court finds that Netcom cannot be held liable for direct infringement. Cf. IITF Report at 69 (noting uncertainty regarding whether BBS operator should be directly liable for reproduction or distribution of files uploaded by a subscriber).[19]

---

[13] The court notes, however, that stopping the distribution of information once it is on the Internet is not easy. The decentralized network was designed so that if one link in the chain be closed off, the information will be dynamically rerouted through another link. This was meant to allow the system to be used for communication after a catastrophic event that shuts down part of it.

[19] Despite that uncertainty, the IITF Report recommends a strict liability paradigm for BBS operators. See IITF Report at 122–24. It recommends that Congress not exempt on-line service providers from strict liability because this would prematurely deprive the system of an incentive to get providers to reduce the damage to copyright holders by reducing the chances that users will infringe by educating them, requiring indemnification, purchasing insurance, and, where efficient, developing technological solutions to screening out infringement. Denying strict liability in many cases would leave copyright owners without an adequate remedy since direct infringers may act anonymously or pseudonymously or may not have the resources to pay a judgment.

2. Contributory Infringement

Netcom is not free from liability just because it did not directly infringe plaintiffs' works; it may still be liable as a contributory infringer. . . . [Issues of contributory and vicarious infringement will be taken up in later chapters, however this case will be an important reference. Eds.]

4. First Amendment Argument

Netcom argues that plaintiffs' theory of liability contravenes the First Amendment, as it would chill the use of the Internet because every access provider or user would be subject to liability when a user posts an infringing work to a Usenet newsgroup. While the court agrees that an overbroad *injunction* might implicate the First Amendment, imposing *liability* for infringement where it is otherwise appropriate does not necessarily raise a First Amendment issue. The copyright concepts of the idea/expression dichotomy and the fair use defense balance the important First Amendment rights with the constitutional authority for "promot[ing] the progress of science and useful arts," U.S. Const. art. I, § 8, cl. 8. Netcom argues that liability here would force Usenet servers to perform the impossible—screening all the information that comes through their systems. However, the court is not convinced that Usenet servers are directly liable for causing a copy to be made, and absent evidence of knowledge and participation or control and direct profit, they will not be contributorily or vicariously liable. If Usenet servers were responsible for screening all messages coming through their systems, this could have a serious chilling effect on what some say may turn out to be the best public forum for free speech yet devised. Finally, Netcom admits that its First Amendment argument is merely a consideration in the fair use argument, which the court will now address. . . .

C. Conclusion

The court finds that plaintiffs have raised a genuine issue of fact regarding whether Netcom should have known that Erlich was infringing their copyrights after receiving a letter from plaintiffs, whether Netcom substantially participated in the infringement, and whether Netcom has a valid fair use defense. Accordingly, Netcom is not entitled to summary judgment on plaintiffs' claim of contributory copyright infringement. However, plaintiffs' claims of direct and vicarious infringement fail. . . .

IV. ORDER

The court denies Netcom's motion for summary judgment and Klemesrud's motion for judgment on the pleadings, as a triable issue of fact exists on the claim of contributory infringement. The court also gives plaintiffs 30 days leave in which to amend to state a claim for vicarious liability against defendant Klemesrud, if they can do so in good faith. Plaintiffs' application for a preliminary injunction against defendants Netcom and Klemesrud is denied.

Questions:

1.) "Netcom correctly distinguishes *MAI* on the ground that Netcom did not take any affirmative action that directly resulted in copying plaintiffs' works other than by installing and maintaining a system whereby software automatically forwards messages received from subscribers onto the Usenet, and temporarily stores copies on its system." This is a distinction. Did the technician who turned on a computer in order to service it take such an affirmative action? What vision of strict liability does *Netcom* espouse?

2.) Is *Netcom* a.) ingenious, b.) a mangling of precedent, c.) correct, or all three?

3.) What would Judge Boudin think? Should those thoughts be left to Congress? Or is that what the common law does, and has always done?

4.) Why does the court mention the reach of defamation law in the context of the First Amendment?

5.) *Netcom*—though a District Court case ingeniously distinguishing binding precedent in its own Circuit—anticipates some of the broad outlines of the compact that now governs the Internet. We will see in later chapters that limitations of liability are fundamental to that compact. Judge Whyte's decision, with its focus on "actual knowledge" and merely "installing and maintaining a system," suggests the lines that were ultimately drawn. Is there any suggestion in the opinion that he was focused on those ultimate issues and aware of the stakes? Where precisely?

James Boyle, The Internet Threat
Please read <u>The Public Domain</u> *pp 54–63*

The conventional wisdom is that governments respond slowly to technological change. In the case of the Internet, nothing could be further from the truth. In 1994 and 1995, "dot-com" was still a mystical term for many. Most stories about the Internet dealt with sexual predation rather than possibilities of extreme wealth. Internet commerce itself was barely an idea, and some of the most exciting sites on the Web had pictures of coffeepots in university departments far away. ("See," one would proudly say to a technological neophyte friend when introducing him to the wonders of the Net, "the pot is empty and we can see that live from here! This changes everything!") It was an innocent time. Yet the U.S. government was already turning the wheels of intellectual property policy to respond to the threat (and promise) of the Internet. More precisely, they were trying to shape the future of the cumbersomely named "National Information Infrastructure," the official name for the "information superhighway" that it was presumed would replace the "immature" technology of the Net. The government was wrong about that, and about a lot else.

The blueprint for new intellectual property policy online came from the Patent and Trademark Office. That office promulgated first a Green Paper and then, after further hearings, a White Paper, on "Intellectual Property and the National Information Infrastructure." As policy and legal documents these are in one sense long out of date. Some of their legal arguments were successfully challenged. Some of their most important proposals were rejected, while many others have become law. But as a starting point from which to trace the frame of mind that has come to dominate intellectual property policy online, they are hard to equal. These documents contained proposals that nowadays would be seen as fairly controversial. Internet service providers were said to be "strictly liable" for copyright violations committed by their subscribers; that is to say, they were legally responsible whether or not they knew about the violation or were at fault in any way. Loading a document into your browser's transient cache memory while reading it was said to be making a "copy." There was more: the beginnings of what later became the Digital Millennium Copyright Act, making it illegal to cut through the digital fences which content providers put around their products. The attitude toward fair use was particularly revealing. At one point in the White Paper it was hinted that fair use might be a relic of the inconveniences of the analog age, to be discarded now that we could have automated fractional payments for even the most insignificant use. (It was noted, however, that some disagreed with this conclusion.) At another point, fair use was described as a "tax" on rights holders and a "subsidy" to those who benefited from it, such as educational institutions. The White Paper also suggested that while any potential loss to rights holders caused by the new technology needed to be countered with new rights and new protections, any potential gain to them through the new technology was simply theirs. Potential gain did not offset the need to compensate for potential loss.

So what views of intellectual property were we carrying forward into the Internet age? Intellectual property is just like other property. Rights are presumptively absolute. Any limitations on them, such as fair use, are taxes on property owners, subsidies to the society at large. It sounds like a perfect time to administer the Jefferson Warning I sketched out in Chapter 2. After all, Jefferson was specifically warning against each of these errors two hundred years ago. To find them in a student paper would be disappointing—irritating, even. But this document was the blueprint for the intellectual property regime of cyberspace.

But do these mistakes matter? How important is it that we get the rules of intellectual property right? To me, a number of my colleagues, some librarians, a few software gurus, the White Paper was more than just a bit of bad policy in a technical field—like a poorly drafted statute about the witnessing of wills, say. When you set up the property rules in some new space, you determine much about the history that follows. Property rules have a huge effect on power relationships and bargaining positions. Think of rules setting out water rights or the right to drive cattle over homesteaders' land in the American West. But they also are part of a larger way of seeing the world; think of the early-twentieth-century rules treating unions as "conspiracies in restraint of trade" or the Supreme Court decisions that dispossessed the American Indians on the theory that they did not comprehend the concept of property and thus did not "own" the land being taken from them. We were at a comparable point in the history of cyberspace. What was being set up here was a vision of economy and culture, a frame of mind about how the world of cultural exchange operates, and eventually a blueprint for our systems of communication. At this stage, the range of possibilities is extremely wide. A lot of different choices could be made, but subsequent changes would be harder and harder as people and companies built their activities around the rules that had been laid down. This was, in short, a tipping point where it was particularly important that we make the right decisions. . . .   *Read the rest*

Question:

1.) Boyle argues that the proposals that would have imposed strict liability on all internet intermediaries—in part based on the logic of *MAI*, that even transient copies count as copies, and copyright is a strict liability system—would have destroyed the internet as we know it. ISPs, search engines, social media sites, cyberlockers—all would be liable for any unauthorized copy on their systems, regardless of knowledge or volition. But would this not have been the appropriate solution? After all, we impose strict liability on manufacturers and sellers of products and hold them liable even where the defect that causes harm could not have been detected or prevented. The theory is that they should internalize the loss and that this will cause them to take appropriate safety precautions for those harms that can be prevented and to pay for those harms that cannot. Why not here? Would this not have saved the copyright industries from all the harm they have suffered from rampant downloading?

Notes

In the 2008 case *Cartoon Network v. CSC Holdings*[10] (often referred to as the "*Cablevision*" case—Cablevision was one of the defendants), the Second Circuit limited one aspect of *MAI*'s holding regarding fixation. As a reminder, the Copyright Act defines fixation as follows:

> A work is "fixed" in a tangible medium of expression when its embodiment in a copy or phonorecord, by or under the authority of the author, is sufficiently permanent or stable to permit it to be perceived, reproduced, or otherwise communicated for a period of more than transitory duration.

The *Cartoon Network* court read this definition as follows: "We believe that this language plainly imposes two distinct but related requirements: the work must be embodied in a medium, i.e., placed in a medium such that it can be perceived, reproduced, etc., from that medium (the 'embodiment requirement') and it must remain thus embodied 'for a period of more than transitory duration' (the 'duration requirement')." It distinguished *MAI* by finding that it only applied the first requirement: "We do not read *MAI Systems* as holding that, as a matter of law, loading a program into a form of RAM *always* results in copying. Such a holding would read the 'transitory duration' language out of the definition, and we do not believe our sister circuit would dismiss this statutory language without even discussing it." Accordingly, it held that "buffering" the data that comprised a movie or TV show for no more than 1.2 seconds did not create a fixed "copy" and was therefore not a "reproduction" and not infringing. ("Buffering" temporarily stores data while it is being transferred—you have seen it in action when the progress bar at the bottom of your video inches ahead of what you're watching.) In addition to amending *MAI*, *Cartoon Network* also adopted *Netcom*'s volitional copying requirement, finding that "volitional conduct is an important element of direct liability." This allowed it to hold that a DVR system was not subject to direct liability even when it made "fixed" copies in the course of streaming video, because it was the *customer* ordering the video, and not the system, that engaged in volitional conduct.

---

[10] 536 F.3d 121 (2d Cir. 2008).

CHAPTER TWELVE
Copyright's "Reach": Infringement

Introduction

Once one knows what subject matter copyright *covers*, the next and linked question is "what conduct *infringes* copyright?" Obviously, to answer this question fully we would have to consider the limitations and exceptions to copyright and we have not yet covered those. Our question is different. How far does the right reach? Answering that question will bring in the material covered in the last chapter—since, by definition, the copyright will only cover the copyrightable aspects of a work; expression but not idea, for example. But it will also bring up separate questions: What are the exclusive rights that copyright provides and what does it take to infringe them? Where does idea stop and expression begin? Does a paraphrase infringe? What counts as "too little to count as copying"? Should the same rules apply to infringing a novel and a computer program? How does one go through the actual process of separating copyrightable wheat from un-copyrightable chaff?

PROBLEM 12-1

These problems are designed to test your intuitions about copyright infringement before reading the cases that lay out the doctrinal framework. After finishing the chapter, reassess your answers.

a.) James visits a bookstore that sells both new and used books. One of its most expensive offerings is a prime condition, unopened, edition of Madonna's *Sex*, a 1992 book that, famously, has pictures of Madonna eating pizza naked, hitch hiking naked and so on and, less famously, has an exploration of sexuality, power dynamics and S&M. James is a shallow guy and just wants to look at the nudie photos. But he is also cheap and does not want to pay the requisite price. The book is held closed by a sealed paper band so that readers cannot see the images inside. The paper band clearly announces that it can only be broken by a purchaser, that breaking the band without paying, since the contents are copyrighted, constitutes copyright infringement. James waits until the shopkeeper is not looking and breaks the band. He peeks inside, and—his curiosity satisfied and his mind teeming with prurient imagery—replaces the broken band and takes his leave without buying anything. **Has James infringed copyright? Is the answer different if James is one of the original "Google Glassholes"?** (Early adopters of the Google Glass device, which looks like a pair of spectacles and permits real time recording.)

b.) Jennifer has long been fascinated by the kind of business strategy and self-improvement books sold in airport bookstores. She studies the people who buy *The Seven Habits of Highly Effective People*, *Lean In* and *What Color is Your Parachute?* Then she watches them as they flip through their purchases in the waiting area and on the plane. She notes that while people buy these books in large numbers, they rarely *read* them. She concludes that even these short offerings are too lengthy for the average traveler and comes up with a brilliant business idea. She decides to write 10 page *précis* versions of each book. While she does not use the same words as the originals, she meticulously lays out all of the concepts, arguments and conclusions they contain. Jennifer's versions contain no criticism or commentary on the original, merely a condensed summary of their points. She thinks this will allow busy business travelers to pretend to have read the books without going through the time and expense of doing so. Her service is wildly popular and she sells it to the SkyMall catalog whose slightly greasy, *E. coli* encrusted pages now contain "Jennifer's 'Fake It To Make It' Bookshelf," summarizing business bestsellers. She is sued by the copyright owners. **Has Jennifer violated copyright?**

c.) Irritated by all the law suits, Jennifer searches for an alternative business idea. She notes that the only books more popular than self-help and business improvement titles are diet books. She decides to write her own. Called *The Last Diet Book,* it consists of two sentences printed in 48 point type. "Eat less. Exercise more." The remaining 200 pages of the book are blank. The book is a huge success. James sees it and decides to publish his own book. It is called *The Last Diet Book, Abridged Edition.* It has the same two sentences, but only 100 blank pages following them, to cut down on costs. Meanwhile Anthony starts up a blog called "Eat Less. Exercise More." The blog makes fun of diet crazes. Anthony concludes each posting with the tag line "Eat Less. Exercise More." **Has James or Anthony violated copyright? (Bonus question: Has James violated trademark law? Has Anthony?)**

d.) Sergey is a computer programmer who discovers an apparently universal truth. In every serious relationship, friendship or work partnership, one person will be a time-realist and one a time-fantasist. One party will accurately predict when it is necessary to leave in order to get to the airport on time, or when one needs to start the paper in order to finish it in a timely manner. The other person in the relationship will have an expansive, optimistic sense of duration in which it is always possible to clean the kitchen, do the taxes and learn Russian before packing for the flight that departs in one and a half hours. Sergey writes an app called "Leave now!" that, once you have put in your schedule and answered a number of questions, will tell you when you need to leave, start writing or what have you. The app is wildly popular. Intrigued, Larry—who was once a programmer but now installs cable for Time Warner—decides to write his own app that exactly what "Leave Now" does. He carefully studies the functions Sergey provided—such as integrating data on traffic and airport delays into its answers—and offers each of those functions in his competing app, "It's Later Than You Think." **Has Larry infringed Sergey's copyright?**

e.) Imagine that Shakespeare's works have been taken out of the public domain. (Shakespeare's works were never actually under copyright so it is not technically a *restoration*.) Congress has conveyed the new copyright over Shakespeare's works to the Folger Shakespeare Library in Washington DC for its tireless work to promote the Bard and because the Folger "will be a good conservator of his literary heritage." James has long been a fan of *Hamlet*. He writes a novel featuring a gloomy and indecisive Scandinavian prince who has strangely intense feelings for his mother, a correspondingly poor relationship with his uncle/stepfather, and a *really* flaky girl-friend who talks about flowers a lot. The prince is called Hamnet (the name of Shakespeare's son, who died young). **Could the Folger Library sue James for copyright infringement? [Bonus assignment: Find the lines in the *Golan* majority opinion that indicate it would be unconstitutional to withdraw Shakespeare's works from the public domain and give copyright in them to the Folger Library.]**

A Limited List of Exclusive Rights

Exclusive Rights

17 U.S. Code § 106—Exclusive rights in copyrighted works
Subject to sections 107 through 122, the owner of copyright under this title has the exclusive rights to do and to authorize any of the following:

(1) to reproduce the copyrighted work in copies or phonorecords;

(2) to prepare derivative works based upon the copyrighted work;

(3) to distribute copies or phonorecords of the copyrighted work to the public by sale or other transfer of ownership, or by rental, lease, or lending;

(4) in the case of literary, musical, dramatic, and choreographic works, pantomimes, and motion pictures and other audiovisual works, to perform the copyrighted work publicly;

(5) in the case of literary, musical, dramatic, and choreographic works, pantomimes, and pictorial, graphic, or sculptural works, including the individual images of a motion picture or other audiovisual work, to display the copyrighted work publicly; and

(6) in the case of sound recordings, to perform the copyrighted work publicly by means of a digital audio transmission.

Remember the naïve young thing who arrived in law school, dewy-eyed and thinking that property was pretty simple? One either owned something or one did not. Perhaps that was never you, but in any case exposure to the first year curriculum would soon have changed that misimpression. In place of the binary, "property or not" conception, one learns that property is a "bundle of rights" of varying shape and design. Does one have the right to exclude, to demand compensation but not to exclude, to alienate, to use for a defined period but not to alienate? What is true of real and personal property is doubly so for copyright. Just as trademark was not "absolute ownership of the *word*" so copyright is not "absolute ownership of the *work*."

§ 106 defines the exclusive rights owned by a copyright holder. (§ 1201, which we will cover later, adds a special set of rights over digital copyrighted works protected by technical measures that control one's ability to access or to reproduce the work.) Read through the rights enumerated. Notice how much is *not* covered. Reading is not copyright infringement. Selling one's used copy of the book is not copyright infringement. Privately performing a dramatic or musical work is not copyright infringement.

As we learned in the last chapter, by definition, copyright can only cover copyrightable subject matter. This is the first, vital, restriction of copyright's ambit. Even within that subject matter copyright's reach is restricted to certain actions—"§ 106 significant acts"—copying, distributing, publicly performing and so on. This is the second limit on copyright's reach. But even when one has engaged in one of the actions covered by a § 106 exclusive right, the question is has one actually done enough to *violate* the right. In this chapter we will focus largely on two of the rights of § 106—the reproduction and derivative works rights. We will ask, when does copying constitute infringement? (The questions of whether something is a public performance, public display, or distribution are no less vexed. We just do not have space for them here, though in the next chapter you will be reading a fascinating case about whether "in-line linking" and "framing" by an image search engine implicate the public display right.)

It may be helpful to remember this: the discussion of copyrightable *subject matter* also suffuses the discussion of copyright *infringement*. This is not a situation in which some areas are completely public and not subject to property rights (a Hawaiian beach, a white pages telephone directory) while others (your farm, a song) are completely private and completely owned. This is more like a situation in which even the farm that is clearly private property has public rights of way running through it, rights of overflight running over it. Property and commons exist in a tight braid, not as two separate plots on a map.

Feist tells us that "To establish infringement, two elements must be proven: (1) ownership of a valid copyright, and (2) copying of constituent elements of the work that are original." There must be copying. It must be enough copying. And it must be copying of material subject to the copyright—the ideas and facts in a work are not. But how do those abstractions work themselves out in concrete cases?

1.) The Idea/Expression Distinction in Infringement Analysis

Nichols v. Universal Pictures Corp. et al.
45 F.2d 119 (2d Cir. 1930)

L. HAND, Circuit Judge.

The plaintiff is the author of a play, "Abie's Irish Rose," which it may be assumed was properly copyrighted under section five, subdivision (d), of the Copyright Act, 17 USCA § 5(d). The defendant produced publicly a motion picture play, "The Cohens and The Kellys," which the plaintiff alleges was taken from it. As we think the defendant's play too unlike the plaintiff's to be an infringement, we may assume, *arguendo*, that in some details the defendant used the plaintiff's play, as will subsequently appear, though we do not so decide. It therefore becomes necessary to give an outline of the two plays.

Abie's Irish Rose image information available at http://en.wikipedia.org/wiki/File:Abiesirish.jpg. *The Cohens and the Kellys* image information available at https://en.wikipedia.org/wiki/The_Cohens_and_Kellys #/media/File:Cohens_and_Kellys_poster.jpg.

"Abie's Irish Rose" presents a Jewish family living in prosperous circumstances in New York. The father, a widower, is in business as a merchant, in which his son and only child helps him. The boy has philandered with young women, who to his father's great disgust have always been Gentiles, for he is obsessed with a passion that his daughter-in-law shall be an orthodox Jewess. When the play opens the son, who has been courting a young Irish Catholic girl, has already married her secretly before a Protestant minister, and is concerned to soften the blow for his father, by securing a favorable impression of his bride, while concealing her faith and race. To accomplish this he introduces her to his father at his home as a Jewess, and lets it appear that he is interested in her, though he conceals the marriage. The girl somewhat reluctantly falls in with the plan; the father takes the bait, becomes infatuated with the girl, concludes that they must marry, and assumes that of course they will, if he so decides. He calls in a rabbi, and prepares for the wedding according to the Jewish rite.

Meanwhile the girl's father, also a widower, who lives in California, and is as intense in his own religious antagonism as the Jew, has been called to New York, supposing that his daughter is to marry an Irishman and a Catholic. Accompanied by a priest, he arrives at the house at the moment when the marriage is being celebrated, but too late to prevent it, and the two fathers, each infuriated by the proposed union of his child to a heretic, fall into unseemly and grotesque antics. The priest and the rabbi become friendly, exchange trite sentiments about religion, and agree that the match is good. Apparently out of abundant caution, the priest celebrates the marriage for a third time, while the girl's father is inveigled away. The second act closes with each father, still outraged, seeking to find some way by which the union, thus trebly insured, may be dissolved.

The last act takes place about a year later, the young couple having meanwhile been abjured by each father, and left to their own resources. They have had twins, a boy and a girl, but their fathers know no more than that a child has been born. At Christmas each, led by his craving to see his grandchild, goes separately to the young folks' home, where they encounter each other, each laden with gifts, one for a boy, the other for a girl. After some slapstick comedy, depending upon the insistence of each that he is right about the sex of the grandchild, they become reconciled when they learn the truth, and that each child is to bear the given name of a grandparent. The curtain falls as the fathers are exchanging amenities, and the Jew giving evidence of an abatement in the strictness of his orthodoxy.

"The Cohens and The Kellys" presents two families, Jewish and Irish, living side by side in the poorer quarters of New York in a state of perpetual enmity. The wives in both cases are still living, and share in the mutual animosity, as do two small sons, and even the respective dogs. The Jews have a daughter, the Irish a son; the Jewish father is in the clothing business; the Irishman is a policeman. The children are in love with each other, and secretly marry, apparently after the play opens. The Jew, being in great financial straits, learns from a lawyer that he has fallen heir to a large fortune from a great-aunt, and moves into a great house, fitted luxuriously. Here he and his family live in vulgar ostentation, and here the Irish boy seeks out his Jewish bride, and is chased away by the angry father. The Jew then abuses the Irishman over the telephone, and both become hysterically excited. The extremity of his feelings makes the Jew sick, so that he must go to Florida for a rest, just before which the daughter discloses her marriage to her mother.

On his return the Jew finds that his daughter has borne a child; at first he suspects the lawyer, but eventually learns the truth and is overcome with anger at such a low alliance. Meanwhile, the Irish family who have been forbidden to see the grandchild, go to the Jew's house, and after a violent scene between the two fathers in which the Jew disowns his daughter, who decides to go back with her husband, the Irishman takes her back with her baby to his own poor lodgings. The lawyer, who had hoped to marry the Jew's daughter, seeing his plan foiled, tells the Jew that his fortune really belongs to the Irishman, who was also related to the dead woman, but offers to conceal his knowledge, if the Jew will share the loot. This the Jew repudiates, and, leaving the astonished lawyer, walks through the rain to his enemy's house to surrender the property. He arrives in great dejection, tells the truth, and abjectly turns to leave. A reconciliation ensues, the Irishman agreeing to share with him equally. The Jew shows some interest in his grandchild, though this is at most a minor motive in the reconciliation, and the curtain falls while the two are in their cups, the Jew insisting that in the firm name for the business, which they are to carry on jointly, his name shall stand first.

It is of course essential to any protection of literary property, whether at common-law or under the statute, that the right cannot be limited literally to the text, else a plagiarist would escape by immaterial variations. That has never been the law, but, as soon as literal appropriation ceases to be the test, the whole matter is necessarily at large, so that, as was recently well said by a distinguished judge, the decisions cannot help much in a new case. When plays are concerned, the plagiarist may excise a separate scene; or he may appropriate part of the dialogue. Then the question is whether the part so taken is "substantial," and therefore not a "fair use" of the copyrighted work; it is the same question as arises in the case of any other copyrighted work. But when the plagiarist does not take out a block in situ, but an abstract of the whole, decision is more troublesome. Upon any work, and especially upon a play, a great number of patterns of increasing generality will fit equally well, as more and more of the incident is left out. The last may perhaps be no more than the most general statement of what the play is about, and at times might consist only of its title; but there is a point in this series of abstractions where they are no longer protected, since otherwise the playwright could prevent the use of his "ideas," to which, apart from their expression, his property is never extended. Nobody has ever been able to fix that boundary, and nobody ever can. In some cases the question has been treated as though it were analogous to lifting a portion out of the copyrighted work; but the analogy is not a good one, because, though the skeleton is a part of the body, it pervades and supports the whole. In such cases we are rather concerned with the line between expression and what is expressed. As respects plays, the controversy chiefly centers upon the characters and sequence of incident, these being the substance.

We did not in *Dymow v. Bolton* hold that a plagiarist was never liable for stealing a plot; that would have been flatly against our rulings in *Dam v. Kirk La Shelle Co.*, and *Stodart v. Mutual Film Co.*, neither of which we meant to overrule. We found the plot of the second play was too different to infringe, because the most detailed pattern, common to both, eliminated so much from each that its content went into the public domain; and for this reason we said, "this mere subsection of a plot was not susceptible of copyright." But we do not doubt that two plays may correspond in plot closely enough for infringement. How far that correspondence must go is another matter. Nor need we hold that the same may not be true as to the characters, quite independently of the "plot" proper, though, as far as we know, such a case has never arisen. If Twelfth Night were copyrighted, it is quite possible that a second comer might so closely imitate Sir Toby Belch or Malvolio as to infringe, but it would not be enough that for one of his characters he cast a riotous knight who kept wassail to the discomfort of the household, or a vain and foppish steward who became amorous of his mistress. These would be no more than Shakespeare's "ideas" in the play, as little capable of monopoly as Einstein's Doctrine of Relativity, or Darwin's theory of the Origin of Species. It follows that the less developed the characters, the less they can be copyrighted; that is the penalty an author must bear for marking them too indistinctly.

In the two plays at bar we think both as to incident and character, the defendant took no more—assuming that it took anything at all—than the law allowed. The stories are quite different. One is of a religious zealot who insists upon his child's marrying no one outside his faith; opposed by another who is in this respect just like him, and is his foil. Their difference in race is merely an obbligato to the main theme, religion. They sink their differences through grandparental pride and affection. In the other, zealotry is wholly absent; religion does not even appear. It is true that the parents are hostile to each other in part because they differ in race; but the marriage of their son to a Jew does not apparently offend the Irish family at all, and it exacerbates the existing animosity of the Jew, principally because he has become rich, when he learns it. They are reconciled through the honesty of the Jew and the generosity of the Irishman; the grandchild has nothing whatever to do with it. The only matter common to the two is a quarrel between a Jewish and an Irish father, the marriage of their children, the birth of grandchildren and a reconciliation.

If the defendant took so much from the plaintiff, it may well have been because her amazing success seemed to prove that this was a subject of enduring popularity. Even so, granting that the plaintiff's play was wholly original, and assuming that novelty is not essential to a copyright, there is no monopoly in such a background. Though the plaintiff discovered the vein, she could not keep it to herself; so defined, the theme was too generalized an abstraction from what she wrote. It was only a part of her "ideas."

Nor does she fare better as to her characters. It is indeed scarcely credible that she should not have been aware of those stock figures, the low comedy Jew and Irishman. The defendant has not taken from her more than their prototypes have contained for many decades. If so, obviously so to generalize her copyright, would allow her to cover what was not original with her. But we need not hold this as matter of fact, much as we might be justified. Even though we take it that she devised her figures out of her brain *de novo*, still the defendant was within its rights.

There are but four characters common to both plays, the lovers and the fathers. The lovers are so faintly indicated as to be no more than stage properties. They are loving and fertile; that is really all that can be said of them, and anyone else is quite within his rights if he puts loving and fertile lovers in a play of his own, wherever he gets the cue. The plaintiff's Jew is quite unlike the defendant's. His obsession is his religion, on which depends such racial animosity as he has. He is affectionate, warm and patriarchal. None of these fit the defendant's Jew, who shows affection for his daughter only once, and who has none but the most superficial interest in his grandchild. He is tricky, ostentatious and vulgar, only by misfortune redeemed into honesty. Both are grotesque, extravagant and quarrelsome; both are fond of display; but these common qualities make up only a small part of their simple pictures, no more than any one might lift if he chose. The Irish fathers are even more unlike; the plaintiff's a mere symbol for religious fanaticism and patriarchal pride, scarcely a character at all. Neither quality appears in the defendant's, for while he goes to get his grandchild, it is rather out of a truculent determination not to be forbidden, than from pride in his progeny. For the rest he is only a grotesque hobbledehoy, used for low comedy of the most conventional sort, which any one might borrow, if he chanced not to know the exemplar.

. . . We assume that the plaintiff's play is altogether original, even to an extent that in fact it is hard to believe. We assume further that, so far as it has been anticipated by earlier plays of which she knew nothing, that fact is immaterial. Still, as we have already said, her copyright did not cover everything that might be drawn from her play; its content went to some extent into the public domain. We have to decide how much, and while we are as aware as any one that the line, wherever it is drawn, will seem arbitrary, that is no excuse for not drawing it; it is a question such as courts must answer in nearly all cases. Whatever may be the difficulties a priori, we have no question on which side of the line this case falls. A comedy based upon conflicts between Irish and Jews, into which the marriage of their children enters, is no more susceptible of copyright than the outline of Romeo and Juliet.

The plaintiff has prepared an elaborate analysis of the two plays, showing a "quadrangle" of the common characters, in which each is represented by the emotions which he discovers. She presents the resulting parallelism as proof of infringement, but the adjectives employed are so general as to be quite useless. Take for example the attribute of "love" ascribed to both Jews. The plaintiff has depicted her father as deeply attached to his son, who is his hope and joy; not so, the defendant, whose father's conduct is throughout not actuated by any affection for his daughter, and who is merely once overcome for the moment by her distress when he has violently dismissed her lover. "Anger" covers emotions aroused by quite different occasions in each case; so do "anxiety," "despondency" and "disgust." It is unnecessary to go through the catalogue for emotions are too much colored by their causes to be a test when used so broadly. This is not the proper approach to a solution; it must be more ingenuous, more like that of a spectator, who would rely upon the complex of his impressions of each character.

We cannot approve the length of the record, which was due chiefly to the use of expert witnesses. Argument is argument whether in the box or at the bar, and its proper place is the last. The testimony of an expert upon such issues, especially his cross-examination, greatly extends the trial and contributes nothing which cannot be better heard after the evidence is all submitted. It ought not to be allowed at all; and while its admission is not a ground for reversal, it cumbers the case and tends to confusion, for the more the court is led into the intricacies of dramatic craftsmanship, the less likely it is to stand upon the firmer, if more naïve, ground of its considered impressions upon its own perusal. We hope that in this class of cases such evidence may in the future be entirely excluded, and the case confined to the actual issues; that is, whether the copyrighted work was original, and whether the defendant copied it, so far as the supposed infringement is identical. Decree affirmed.

Questions:

1.) Think back to the speech of Victor Hugo in Chapter 10. Copyright depends on the ability of law to police the boundary between protectable expression and unprotectable idea. *Nichols* is the leading case on that point. It contains the line "[n]obody has ever been able to fix that boundary, and nobody ever can." Can a property regime survive with boundaries as vague as this? Could we have property in real estate if Blackacre's dimensions were outlined on a surrealist map that changed depending on who viewed it? Property in money if a $10 bill might stand for a range of monetary values from $9.50 to $11? What is Learned Hand's response to this problem?

2.) "If the defendant took so much from the plaintiff, it may well have been because her amazing success seemed to prove that this was a subject of enduring popularity. Even so, granting that the plaintiff's play was wholly original, and assuming that novelty is not essential to a copyright, there is no monopoly in such a background." How is it that it can be legal to copy aspects of a copyrighted work, for profit, in the hope of reaping some of the success the original enjoyed? How does your answer relate to the notion of "promote the progress"? To Larry and Sergey's punctuality apps?

2.) Copyright Meets Computer Software: The Infringement Edition

James Boyle, A Machine that Contains All Other Machines
Please read The Public Domain *pp 161–168*

Imagine a person staring at an infinite roll of paper tape. On the paper are symbols in some alphabet or number system. The reader carries out simple, operable instructions on the basis of that data. "Add together the next two digits you are presented with and write down the answer. If the answer is odd, go to step 2. If the answer is even, go to step 3." Now replace the person with a mechanical head that can "read" the instructions, carry out the desired operations, and write the answer down. The British mathematician Alan Turing imagined something like this—a little more complicated, perhaps, but fairly similar. What is it? We have the reading head, the set of instructions, the data on which the instructions are to be performed, the record of the result, and some kind of "state table" that tells the machine where it is in the process. These are the component parts of Turing machines— or as we know them better, computers. More accurately, Turing machines are a method of simulating the operation of computers, a metaphor that enables us to imitate their logical processes. In the words of Wikipedia, "despite their simplicity—[they] can be adapted to simulate the logic of any computer that could possibly be constructed." And to give lawyers fits. But that is getting ahead of ourselves.

In Greek mythology, Procrustes had a bed to which he fitted its prospective occupants, whether they liked it or not. The tall were trimmed down. The short stretched on the rack. Intellectual property lawyers have many similarities to Procrustes. The technologies that are brought before them are made to fit the conceptual boxes the law provides, boxes with names such as "copyright" and "patent." Occasionally, new conceptual boxes are made, but—for very good reasons—most of the time we stick with the boxes we have. As with Procrustes, things do not always fit and the process can be distressing for its subjects.

It is important to realize that the process of trimming and stretching can be done well or badly. If it is done really badly, the technology is stunted, deformed, even destroyed. If it is done well, the law aids the development of the technology in exactly the happy way described in Chapter 1. What did our Procrustean legal system do with computers and computer science?   *Read the rest*

· · · · · · · · · ·

Notes

The next case is long. (Apologies). Why? First, it has some nice, plain English explanations of computer programming—seen through the lens of copyright. You need to understand how computer programming works, at least at the highest, most abstract level. (You began this journey by reading *Lotus* and *Oracle* in the previous chapter; it continues here.) So that part of the decision has been left only mildly edited—it is not "Physics for Poets" but it might be "Coding for Law Student, Humanities Majors." We hope you find it of interest. Resist the inexorable tendency to have your IQ plummet toward zero whenever someone says "parameter," "function call" or "API—(application programming interface)." This is a description of a system of *code*, normally expressed in *a highly technical language most people do not fully understand* (thus needing smart people to decipher it) *that runs a lot of important things.* Guess what you hope to do for a living? Not so different, is it?

The second reason the decision is long is that it is a classic case—maybe *the* classic case together with *Lotus v. Borland* and *Sega v. Accolade*—demonstrating a court wrestling with the incorporation of a new technology into copyright. One could look at the decision as frankly policy-oriented in its concerns about how copyright will affect innovation and competition—and its close tailoring of the doctrine in order to achieve that result. On the other hand, you could see this as a classic example of the common law method. Note how the court uses existing traditional copyright doctrines—the idea-expression distinction, merger, *scènes à faire*—as it deals with this new technology.

Finally, *Computer Associates*, together with other cases you have yet to read, ended up shaping the law of software copyright on the most fundamental level. Ask yourself the following, is it really true now that a copyright over a book or a piece of music is *the same* as a software copyright? Do we really have a different law of copyright for software? Or is it simply that the subject matter's own peculiarities demand different answers to the same questions?

Computer Associates v. Altai, Inc.
982 F.2d 693 (2d Cir. 1992)

WALKER, Circuit Judge.

In recent years, the growth of computer science has spawned a number of challenging legal questions, particularly in the field of copyright law. As scientific knowledge advances, courts endeavor to keep pace, and sometimes—as in the area of computer technology—they are required to venture into less than familiar waters. This is not a new development, though. "From its beginning, the law of copyright has developed in response to significant changes in technology." *Sony Corp. v. Universal City Studios, Inc.* (1984).

Article I, section 8 of the Constitution authorizes Congress "[t]o promote the Progress of Science and useful Arts, by securing for limited Times to Authors and Inventors the exclusive Right to their respective Writings and Discoveries." The Supreme Court has stated that "[t]he economic philosophy behind the clause . . . is the conviction that encouragement of individual effort by personal gain is the best way to advance public welfare. . . ." *Mazer v. Stein* (1954). The author's benefit, however, is clearly a "secondary" consideration. "[T]he ultimate aim is, by this incentive, to stimulate artistic creativity for the general public good." *Twentieth Century Music Corp. v. Aiken* (1975).

Thus, the copyright law seeks to establish a delicate equilibrium. On the one hand, it affords protection to authors as an incentive to create, and, on the other, it must appropriately limit the extent of that protection so as to avoid the effects of monopolistic stagnation. In applying the federal act to new types of cases, courts must always keep this symmetry in mind.

Among other things, this case deals with the challenging question of whether and to what extent the "non-literal" aspects of a computer program, that is, those aspects that are not reduced to written code, are protected by copyright. While a few other courts have already grappled with this issue, this case is one of first impression in this circuit. As we shall discuss, we find the results reached by other courts to be less than satisfactory. Drawing upon long-standing doctrines of copyright law, we take an approach that we think better addresses the practical difficulties embedded in these types of cases. In so doing, we have kept in mind the necessary balance between creative incentive and industrial competition.

BACKGROUND
I. COMPUTER PROGRAM DESIGN

Certain elementary facts concerning the nature of computer programs are vital to the following discussion. The Copyright Act defines a computer program as "a set of statements or instructions to be used directly or indirectly in a computer in order to bring about a certain result." 17 U.S.C. § 101. In writing these directions, the programmer works "from the general to the specific." *Whelan Assocs., Inc. v. Jaslow Dental Lab., Inc.* (3d Cir. 1986).

The first step in this procedure is to identify a program's ultimate function or purpose. An example of such an ultimate purpose might be the creation and maintenance of a business ledger. Once this goal has been achieved, a programmer breaks down or "decomposes" the program's ultimate function into "simpler constituent problems or 'subtasks,'" which are also known as subroutines or modules. In the context of a business ledger program, a module or subroutine might be responsible for the task of updating a list of outstanding accounts receivable. Sometimes, depending upon the complexity of its task, a subroutine may be broken down further into sub-subroutines.

Having sufficiently decomposed the program's ultimate function into its component elements, a programmer will then arrange the subroutines or modules into what are known as organizational or flow charts. Flow charts map the interactions between modules that achieve the program's end goal.

In order to accomplish these intra-program interactions, a programmer must carefully design each module's parameter list. A parameter list, according to the expert appointed and fully credited by the district court, Dr. Randall Davis, is "the information sent to and received from a subroutine." The term "parameter list" refers to the form in which information is passed between modules (e.g. for accounts receivable, the designated time frame and particular customer identifying number) and the information's actual content (e.g. 8/91–7/92; customer No. 3). With respect to form, interacting modules must share similar parameter lists so that they are capable of exchanging information.

"The functions of the modules in a program together with each module's relationships to other modules constitute the 'structure' of the program." Additionally, the term structure may include the category of modules referred to as "macros." A macro is a single instruction that initiates a sequence of operations or module interactions within the program. Very often the user will accompany a macro with an instruction from the parameter list to refine the instruction (e.g. current total of accounts receivable (macro), but limited to those for 8/91 to 7/92 from customer No. 3 (parameters)).

In fashioning the structure, a programmer will normally attempt to maximize the program's speed, efficiency, as well as simplicity for user operation, while taking into consideration certain externalities such as the memory constraints of the computer upon which the program will be run. . . .

Once each necessary module has been identified, designed, and its relationship to the other modules has been laid out conceptually, the resulting program structure must be embodied in a written language that the computer can read. This process is called "coding," and requires two steps. First, the programmer must transpose the program's structural blue-print into a source code. This step has been described as "comparable to the novelist fleshing out the broad outline of his plot by crafting from words and sentences the paragraphs that convey the ideas." The source code may be written in any one of several computer languages, such as COBAL, FORTRAN, BASIC, EDL, etc., depending upon the type of computer for which the program is intended. Once the source code has been completed, the second step is to translate or "compile" it into object code. Object code is the binary language comprised of zeros and ones through which the computer directly receives its instructions. After the coding is finished, the programmer will run the program on the computer in order to find and correct any logical and syntactical errors. This is known as "debugging" and, once done, the program is complete.

II. FACTS

CA is a Delaware corporation, with its principal place of business in Garden City, New York. Altai is a Texas corporation, doing business primarily in Arlington, Texas. Both companies are in the computer software industry—designing, developing and marketing various types of computer programs.

The subject of this litigation originates with one of CA's marketed programs entitled CA-SCHEDULER. CA-SCHEDULER is a job scheduling program designed for IBM mainframe computers. Its primary functions are straightforward: to create a schedule specifying when the computer should run various tasks, and then to control the computer as it executes the schedule. CA-SCHEDULER contains a sub-program entitled ADAPTER, also developed by CA. ADAPTER is not an independently marketed product of CA; it is a wholly integrated component of CA-SCHEDULER and has no capacity for independent use.

Nevertheless, ADAPTER plays an extremely important role. It is an "operating system compatibility component," which means, roughly speaking, it serves as a translator. An "operating system" is itself a program that manages the resources of the computer, allocating those resources to other programs as needed. The IBM System 370 family of computers, for which CA-SCHEDULER was created, is, depending upon the computer's size, designed to contain one of three operating systems: DOS/VSE, MVS, or CMS. As the district court noted, the general rule is that "a program written for one operating system, e.g., DOS/VSE, will not, without modification, run under another operating system such as MVS." ADAPTER's function is to translate the language of a given program into the particular language that the computer's own operating system can understand. . . .

A program like ADAPTER, which allows a computer user to change or use multiple operating systems while maintaining the same software, is highly desirable. It saves the user the costs, both in time and money, that otherwise would be expended in purchasing new programs, modifying existing systems to run them, and gaining familiarity with their operation. The benefits run both ways. The increased compatibility afforded by an ADAPTER-like component, and its resulting popularity among consumers, makes whatever software in which it is incorporated significantly more marketable.

Starting in 1982, Altai began marketing its own job scheduling program entitled ZEKE. The original version of ZEKE was designed for use in conjunction with a VSE operating system. By late 1983, in response to customer demand, Altai decided to rewrite ZEKE so that it could be run in conjunction with an MVS operating system.

At that time, James P. Williams ("Williams"), then an employee of Altai and now its President, approached Claude F. Arney, III ("Arney"), a computer programmer who worked for CA. Williams and Arney were longstanding friends, and had in fact been co-workers at CA for some time before Williams left CA to work for Altai's predecessor. Williams wanted to recruit Arney to assist Altai in designing an MVS version of ZEKE.

At the time he first spoke with Arney, Williams was aware of both the CA-SCHEDULER and ADAPTER programs. However, Williams was not involved in their development and had never seen the codes of either program. When he asked Arney to come work for Altai, Williams did not know that ADAPTER was a component of CA-SCHEDULER.

Arney, on the other hand, was intimately familiar with various aspects of ADAPTER. While working for CA, he helped improve the VSE version of ADAPTER, and was permitted to take home a copy of ADAPTER'S source code. This apparently developed into an irresistible habit, for when Arney left CA to work for Altai in January, 1984, he took with him copies of the source code for both the VSE and MVS versions of ADAPTER. He did this in knowing violation of the CA employee agreements that he had signed.

Once at Altai, Arney and Williams discussed design possibilities for adapting ZEKE to run on MVS operating systems. Williams, who had created the VSE version of ZEKE, thought that approximately 30% of his original program would have to be modified in order to accommodate MVS. Arney persuaded Williams that the best way to make the needed modifications was to introduce a "common system interface" component into ZEKE. He did not tell Williams that his idea stemmed from his familiarity with ADAPTER. They decided to name this new component-program OSCAR.

Arney went to work creating OSCAR at Altai's offices using the ADAPTER source code. The district court accepted Williams' testimony that no one at Altai, with the exception of Arney, affirmatively knew that Arney had the ADAPTER code, or that he was using it to create OSCAR/VSE. However, during this time period, Williams' office was adjacent to Arney's. Williams testified that he and Arney "conversed quite frequently" while Arney was "investigating the source code of ZEKE" and that Arney was in his office "a number of times daily, asking questions." In three months, Arney successfully completed the OSCAR/VSE project. In an additional month he developed an OSCAR/MVS version. When the dust finally settled, Arney had copied approximately 30% of OSCAR's code from CA's ADAPTER program.

The first generation of OSCAR programs was known as OSCAR 3.4. From 1985 to August 1988, Altai used OSCAR 3.4 in its ZEKE product, as well as in programs entitled ZACK and ZEBB. In late July 1988, CA first learned that Altai may have appropriated parts of ADAPTER. After confirming its suspicions, CA secured copyrights on its 2.1 and 7.0 versions of CA-SCHEDULER. CA then brought this copyright and trade secret misappropriation action against Altai.

Apparently, it was upon receipt of the summons and complaint that Altai first learned that Arney had copied much of the OSCAR code from ADAPTER. After Arney confirmed to Williams that CA's accusations of copying were true, Williams immediately set out to survey the damage. Without ever looking at the ADAPTER code himself, Williams learned from Arney exactly which sections of code Arney had taken from ADAPTER.

Upon advice of counsel, Williams initiated OSCAR's rewrite. The project's goal was to save as much of OSCAR 3.4 as legitimately could be used, and to excise those portions which had been copied from ADAPTER. Arney was entirely excluded from the process, and his copy of the ADAPTER code was locked away. Williams put eight other programmers on the project, none of whom had been involved in any way in the development of OSCAR 3.4. Williams provided the programmers with a description of the ZEKE operating system services so that they could rewrite the appropriate code. The rewrite project took about six months to complete and was finished in mid-November 1989. The resulting program was entitled OSCAR 3.5.

From that point on, Altai shipped only OSCAR 3.5 to its new customers. Altai also shipped OSCAR 3.5 as a "free upgrade" to all customers that had previously purchased OSCAR 3.4. While Altai and Williams acted responsibly to correct Arney's literal copying of the ADAPTER program, copyright infringement had occurred. . . .

I. COPYRIGHT INFRINGEMENT

In any suit for copyright infringement, the plaintiff must establish its ownership of a valid copyright, and that the defendant copied the copyrighted work. The plaintiff may prove defendant's copying either by direct evidence or, as is most often the case, by showing that (1) the defendant had access to the plaintiff's copyrighted work and (2) that defendant's work is substantially similar to the plaintiff's copyrightable material. For the purpose of analysis, the district court assumed that Altai had access to the ADAPTER code when creating OSCAR 3.5. Thus, in determining whether Altai had unlawfully copied protected aspects of CA's ADAPTER, the district court narrowed its focus of inquiry to ascertaining whether Altai's OSCAR 3.5 was substantially similar to ADAPTER. Because we approve Judge Pratt's conclusions regarding substantial similarity, our analysis will proceed along the same assumption.

As a general matter, and to varying degrees, copyright protection extends beyond a literary work's strictly textual form to its non-literal components. As we have said, "[i]t is of course essential to any protection of literary property . . . that the right cannot be limited literally to the text, else a plagiarist would escape by immaterial variations." *Nichols v. Universal Pictures Co.* (2d Cir. 1930) Thus, where "the fundamental essence or structure of one work is duplicated in another," 3 Nimmer, § 13.03[A][1], courts have found copyright infringement. See, e.g., *Horgan v. Macmillan* (2d Cir. 1986) (recognizing that a book of photographs might infringe ballet choreography); *Twentieth Century-Fox Film Corp. v. MCA, Inc.* (9th Cir. 1983) (motion picture and television series); *Sid & Marty Krofft Television Prods., Inc. v. McDonald's Corp.* (9th Cir. 1977) (television commercial and television series); *Sheldon v. Metro-Goldwyn Pictures Corp.* (2d Cir.), *cert. denied*, 298 U.S. 669 (1936) (play and motion picture); *accord Stewart v. Abend* (1990) (recognizing that motion picture may infringe copyright in book by using its "unique setting, characters, plot, and sequence of events"). This black letter proposition is the springboard for our discussion.

A. Copyright Protection for the Non-literal Elements of Computer Programs

It is now well settled that the literal elements of computer programs, i.e., their source and object codes, are the subject of copyright protection. Here, as noted earlier, Altai admits having copied approximately 30% of the OSCAR 3.4 program from CA's ADAPTER source code, and does not challenge the district court's related finding of infringement.

In this case, the hotly contested issues surround OSCAR 3.5. As recounted above, OSCAR 3.5 is the product of Altai's carefully orchestrated rewrite of OSCAR 3.4. After the purge, none of the ADAPTER source code remained in the 3.5 version; thus, Altai made sure that the literal elements of its revamped OSCAR program were no longer substantially similar to the literal elements of CA's ADAPTER.

According to CA, the district court erroneously concluded that Altai's OSCAR 3.5 was not substantially similar to its own ADAPTER program. CA argues that this occurred because the district court "committed legal error in analyzing [its] claims of copyright infringement by failing to find that copyright protects expression contained in the non-literal elements of computer software." We disagree.

CA argues that, despite Altai's rewrite of the OSCAR code, the resulting program remained substantially similar to the structure of its ADAPTER program. As discussed above, a program's structure includes its non-literal components such as general flow charts as well as the more specific organization of inter-modular relationships, parameter lists, and macros. In addition to these aspects, CA contends that OSCAR 3.5 is also substantially similar to ADAPTER with respect to the list of services that both ADAPTER and OSCAR obtain from their respective operating systems. We must decide whether and to what extent these elements of computer programs are protected by copyright law. . . .

The Copyright Act affords protection to "original works of authorship fixed in any tangible medium of expression. . . ." 17 U.S.C. § 102(a). This broad category of protected "works" includes "literary works," which are defined by the Act as

> works, other than audiovisual works, expressed in words, numbers, or other verbal or numerical symbols or indicia, regardless of the nature of the material objects, such as books, periodicals, manuscripts, phonorecords, film tapes, disks, or cards, in which they are embodied.

17 U.S.C. § 101. While computer programs are not specifically listed as part of the above statutory definition, the legislative history leaves no doubt that Congress intended them to be considered literary works.

The syllogism that follows from the foregoing premises is a powerful one: if the non-literal structures of literary works are protected by copyright; and if computer programs are literary works, as we are told by the legislature; then the non-literal structures of computer programs are protected by copyright. See *Whelan* ("By analogy to other literary works, it would thus appear that the copyrights of computer programs can be infringed even absent copying of the literal elements of the program."). We have no reservation in joining the company of those courts that have already ascribed [sic] to this logic. However, that conclusion does not end our analysis. We must determine the scope of copyright protection that extends to a computer program's non-literal structure.

As a caveat, we note that our decision here does not control infringement actions regarding categorically distinct works, such as certain types of screen displays. These items represent products of computer programs, rather than the programs themselves, and fall under the copyright rubric of audiovisual works. If a computer audiovisual display is copyrighted separately as an audiovisual work, apart from the literary work that generates it (i.e., the program), the display may be protectable regardless of the underlying program's copyright status. Of course, the copyright protection that these displays enjoy extends only so far as their expression is protectable. See *Data East USA, Inc. v. Epyx, Inc.* (9th Cir. 1988). In this case, however, we are concerned not with a program's display, but the program itself, and then with only its non-literal components. In considering the copyrightability of these components, we must refer to venerable doctrines of copyright law.

1) Idea vs. Expression Dichotomy

It is a fundamental principle of copyright law that a copyright does not protect an idea, but only the expression of the idea. This axiom of common law has been incorporated into the governing statute. Section 102(b) of the Act provides:

> In no case does copyright protection for an original work of authorship extend to any idea, procedure, process, system, method of operation, concept, principle, or discovery, regardless of the form in which it is described, explained, illustrated, or embodied in such work.

17 U.S.C. § 102(b). *See also House Report* ("Copyright does not preclude others from using ideas or information revealed by the author's work.").

Congress made no special exception for computer programs. To the contrary, the legislative history explicitly states that copyright protects computer programs only "to the extent that they incorporate authorship in programmer's expression of original ideas, as distinguished from the ideas themselves."

Similarly, the National Commission on New Technological Uses of Copyrighted Works ("CONTU") established by Congress to survey the issues generated by the interrelationship of advancing technology and copyright law, see Pub. L. No. 93-573, § 201, 88 Stat. 1873 (1974), recommended, inter alia, that the 1976 Copyright Act "be amended . . . to make it explicit that computer programs, to the extent that they embody the author's original creation, are proper subject matter for copyright." To that end, Congress adopted CONTU's suggestions and amended the Copyright Act by adding, among other things, a provision to 17 U.S.C. § 101 which defined the term "computer program." CONTU also "concluded that the idea-expression distinction should be used to determine which aspects of computer programs are copyrightable."

Drawing the line between idea and expression is a tricky business. Judge Learned Hand noted that "[n]obody has ever been able to fix that boundary, and nobody ever can." *Nichols*. Thirty years later his convictions remained firm. "Obviously, no principle can be stated as to when an imitator has gone beyond copying the 'idea,' and has borrowed its 'expression,'" Judge Hand concluded. "Decisions must therefore inevitably be ad hoc." *Peter Pan Fabrics, Inc. v. Martin Weiner Corp.* (2d Cir. 1960).

The essentially utilitarian nature of a computer program further complicates the task of distilling its idea from its expression. In order to describe both computational processes and abstract ideas, its content "combines creative and technical expression." The variations of expression found in purely creative compositions, as opposed to those contained in utilitarian works, are not directed towards practical application. For example, a narration of Humpty Dumpty's demise, which would clearly be a creative composition, does not serve the same ends as, say, a recipe for scrambled eggs—which is a more process-oriented text. Thus, compared to aesthetic works, computer programs hover even more closely to the elusive boundary line described in § 102(b).

The doctrinal starting point in analyses of utilitarian works, is the seminal case of *Baker v. Selden* (1879). In Baker, the Supreme Court faced the question of "whether the exclusive property in a system of bookkeeping can be claimed, under the law of copyright, by means of a book in which that system is explained?" . . .

The Supreme Court found nothing copyrightable in Selden's bookkeeping system, and rejected his infringement claim regarding the ledger sheets. The Court held that:

> The fact that the art described in the book by illustrations of lines and figures which are reproduced in practice in the application of the art, makes no difference. Those illustrations are the mere language employed by the author to convey his ideas more clearly. Had he used words of description instead of diagrams (which merely stand in the place of words), there could not be the slightest doubt that others, applying the art to practical use, might lawfully draw the lines and diagrams which were in the author's mind, and which he thus described by words in his book.
>
> The copyright of a work on mathematical science cannot give to the author an exclusive right to the methods of operation which he propounds, or to the diagrams which he employs to explain them, so as to prevent an engineer from using them whenever occasion requires.

To the extent that an accounting text and a computer program are both "a set of statements or instructions . . . to bring about a certain result," 17 U.S.C. § 101, they are roughly analogous. In the former case, the processes are ultimately conducted by human agency; in the latter, by electronic means. In either case, as already stated, the processes themselves are not protectable. But the holding in *Baker* goes farther. The Court concluded that those aspects of a work, which "must necessarily be used as incident to" the idea, system or process that the work describes, are also not copyrightable. Selden's ledger sheets, therefore, enjoyed no copyright protection because they were "necessary incidents to" the system of accounting that he described. From this reasoning, we conclude that those elements of a computer program that are necessarily incidental to its function are similarly unprotectable.

While *Baker v. Selden* provides a sound analytical foundation, it offers scant guidance on how to separate idea or process from expression, and moreover, on how to further distinguish protectable expression from that expression which "must necessarily be used as incident to" the work's underlying concept. In the context of computer programs, the Third Circuit's noted decision in *Whelan* has, thus far, been the most thoughtful attempt to accomplish these ends.

The court in *Whelan* faced substantially the same problem as is presented by this case. There, the defendant was accused of making off with the non-literal structure of the plaintiff's copyrighted dental lab management program, and employing it to create its own competitive version. In assessing whether there had been an infringement, the court had to determine which aspects of the programs involved were ideas, and which were expression. In separating the two, the court settled upon the following conceptual approach:

> The line between idea and expression may be drawn with reference to the end sought to be achieved by the work in question. In other words, the purpose or function of a utilitarian work would be the work's idea, and everything that is not necessary to that purpose or function would be part of the expression of the idea. . . . Where there are various means of achieving the desired purpose, then the particular means chosen is not necessary to the purpose; hence, there is expression, not idea.

[*Whelan*]. The "idea" of the program at issue in *Whelan* was identified by the court as simply "the efficient management of a dental laboratory."

So far, in the courts, the *Whelan* rule has received a mixed reception. . . .

Whelan has fared even more poorly in the academic community, where its standard for distinguishing idea from expression has been widely criticized for being conceptually overbroad.

The leading commentator in the field has stated that "[t]he crucial flaw in [*Whelan*'s] reasoning is that it assumes that only one 'idea,' in copyright law terms, underlies any computer program, and that once a separable idea can be identified, everything else must be expression." 3 Nimmer § 13.03(F). This criticism focuses not upon the program's ultimate purpose but upon the reality of its structural design. As we have already noted, a computer program's ultimate function or purpose is the composite result of interacting subroutines. Since each subroutine is itself a program, and thus, may be said to have its own "idea," *Whelan*'s general formulation that a program's overall purpose equates with the program's idea is descriptively inadequate.

Accordingly, we think that Judge Pratt wisely declined to follow *Whelan*. . . . Rightly, the district court found *Whelan*'s rationale suspect because it is so closely tied to what can now be seen—with the passage of time—as the opinion's somewhat outdated appreciation of computer science.

2) Substantial Similarity Test for Computer Program Structure: Abstraction-Filtration-Comparison

We think that *Whelan*'s approach to separating idea from expression in computer programs relies too heavily on metaphysical distinctions and does not place enough emphasis on practical considerations. As the cases that we shall discuss demonstrate, a satisfactory answer to this problem cannot be reached by resorting, a priori, to philosophical first principals [*sic*].

As discussed herein, we think that district courts would be well-advised to undertake a three-step procedure, based on the abstractions test utilized by the district court, in order to determine whether the non-literal elements of two or more computer programs are substantially similar. This approach breaks no new ground; rather, it draws on such familiar copyright doctrines as merger, *scènes à faire*, and public domain. In taking this approach, however, we are cognizant that computer technology is a dynamic field which can quickly outpace judicial decisionmaking. Thus, in cases where the technology in question does not allow for a literal application of the procedure we outline below, our opinion should not be read to foreclose the district courts of our circuit from utilizing a modified version.

In ascertaining substantial similarity under this approach, a court would first break down the allegedly infringed program into its constituent structural parts. Then, by examining each of these parts for such things as incorporated ideas, expression that is necessarily incidental to those ideas, and elements that are taken from the public domain, a court would then be able to sift out all non-protectable material. Left with a kernel, or possible kernels, of creative expression after following this process of elimination, the court's last step would be to compare this material with the structure of an allegedly infringing program. The result of this comparison will determine whether the protectable elements of the programs at issue are substantially similar so as to warrant a finding of infringement. It will be helpful to elaborate a bit further.

Step One: Abstraction

As the district court appreciated, the theoretic framework for analyzing substantial similarity expounded by Learned Hand in the *Nichols* case is helpful in the present context. In *Nichols*, we enunciated what has now become known as the "abstractions" test for separating idea from expression:

> Upon any work . . . a great number of patterns of increasing generality will fit equally well, as more and more of the incident is left out. The last may perhaps be no more than the most general statement of what the [work] is about, and at times might consist only of its title; but there is a point in this series of abstractions where they are no longer protected, since otherwise the [author] could prevent the use of his "ideas," to which, apart from their expression, his property is never extended. *Nichols*.

While the abstractions test was originally applied in relation to literary works such as novels and plays, it is adaptable to computer programs. In contrast to the *Whelan* approach, the abstractions test "implicitly recognizes that any given work may consist of a mixture of numerous ideas and expressions." 3 Nimmer § 13.03[F].

As applied to computer programs, the abstractions test will comprise the first step in the examination for substantial similarity. Initially, in a manner that resembles reverse engineering on a theoretical plane, a court should dissect the allegedly copied program's structure and isolate each level of abstraction contained within it. This process begins with the code and ends with an articulation of the program's ultimate function. Along the way, it is necessary essentially to retrace and map each of the designer's steps—in the opposite order in which they were taken during the program's creation.

Step Two: Filtration

Once the program's abstraction levels have been discovered, the substantial similarity inquiry moves from the conceptual to the concrete. Professor Nimmer suggests, and we endorse, a "successive filtering method" for separating protectable expression from non-protectable material. See generally 3 Nimmer § 13.03[F]. This process entails examining the structural components at each level of abstraction to determine whether their particular inclusion at that level was "idea" or was dictated by considerations of efficiency, so as to be necessarily incidental to that idea; required by factors external to the program itself; or taken from the public domain and hence is nonprotectable expression. See also Kretschmer (arguing that program features dictated by market externalities or efficiency concerns are unprotectable). The structure of any given program may reflect some, all, or none of these considerations. Each case requires its own fact specific investigation.

Strictly speaking, this filtration serves "the purpose of defining the scope of plaintiff's copyright." *Brown Bag Software v. Symantec Corp.* (9th Cir.) (endorsing "analytic dissection" of computer programs in order to isolate protectable expression). By applying well developed doctrines of copyright law, it may ultimately leave behind a "core of protectable material." 3 Nimmer § 13.03[F][5]. Further explication of this second step may be helpful.

(a) Elements Dictated by Efficiency

The portion of *Baker v. Selden*, discussed earlier, which denies copyright protection to expression necessarily incidental to the idea being expressed, appears to be the cornerstone for what has developed into the doctrine of merger. See *Morrissey v. Proctor & Gamble Co.* (1st Cir. 1967) (relying on *Baker* for the proposition that expression embodying the rules of a sweepstakes contest was inseparable from the idea of the contest itself, and therefore were not protectable by copyright); see also *Digital Communications*. The doctrine's underlying principle is that "[w]hen there is essentially only one way to express an idea, the idea and its expression are inseparable and copyright is no bar to copying that expression." *Concrete Machinery Co. v. Classic Lawn Ornaments, Inc.* (1st Cir. 1988). Under these circumstances, the expression is said to have "merged" with the idea itself. In order not to confer a monopoly of the idea upon the copyright owner, such expression should not be protected. See *Herbert Rosenthal Jewelry Corp. v. Kalpakian* (9th Cir. 1971).

CONTU recognized the applicability of the merger doctrine to computer programs. In its report to Congress it stated that:

> [C]opyrighted language may be copied without infringing when there is but a limited number of ways to express a given idea. . . . In the computer context, this means that when specific instructions, even though previously copyrighted, are the only and essential means of accomplishing a given task, their later use by another will not amount to infringement.

CONTU Report.

Furthermore, when one considers the fact that programmers generally strive to create programs "that meet the user's needs in the most efficient manner," Menell, the applicability of the merger doctrine to computer programs becomes compelling. In the context of computer program design, the concept of efficiency is akin to deriving the most concise logical proof or formulating the most succinct mathematical computation. Thus, the more efficient a set of modules are, the more closely they approximate the idea or process embodied in that particular aspect of the program's structure.

While, hypothetically, there might be a myriad of ways in which a programmer may effectuate certain functions within a program,—i.e., express the idea embodied in a given subroutine—efficiency concerns may so narrow the practical range of choice as to make only one or two forms of expression workable options. . . . It follows that in order to determine whether the merger doctrine precludes copyright protection to an aspect of a program's structure that is so oriented, a court must inquire "whether the use of this particular set of modules is necessary efficiently to implement that part of the program's process" being implemented. If the answer is yes, then the expression represented by the programmer's choice of a specific module or group of modules has merged with their underlying idea and is unprotected.

Another justification for linking structural economy with the application of the merger doctrine stems from a program's essentially utilitarian nature and the competitive forces that exist in the software marketplace. See Kretschmer. Working in tandem, these factors give rise to a problem of proof which merger helps to eliminate.

Efficiency is an industry-wide goal. Since, as we have already noted, there may be only a limited number of efficient implementations for any given program task, it is quite possible that multiple programmers, working independently, will design the identical method employed in the allegedly infringed work. Of course, if this is the case, there is no copyright infringement.

Under these circumstances, the fact that two programs contain the same efficient structure may as likely lead to an inference of independent creation as it does to one of copying. Thus, since evidence of similarly efficient structure is not particularly probative of copying, it should be disregarded in the overall substantial similarity analysis. See 3 Nimmer § 13.03[F][2].

[The court summarized other cases that dealt with the issue.] We agree with the approach taken in these decisions, and conclude that application of the merger doctrine in this setting is an effective way to eliminate non-protectable expression contained in computer programs.

(b) Elements Dictated By External Factors

We have stated that where "it is virtually impossible to write about a particular historical era or fictional theme without employing certain 'stock' or standard literary devices," such expression is not copyrightable. *Hoehling v. Universal City Studios, Inc.* (2d Cir. 1980). For example, the *Hoehling* case was an infringement suit stemming from several works on the Hindenburg disaster. There we concluded that similarities in representations of German beer halls, scenes depicting German greetings such as "Heil Hitler," or the singing of certain German songs would not lead to a finding of infringement because they were "'indispensable, or at least standard, in the treatment of'" life in Nazi Germany. This is known as the *scènes à faire* doctrine, and like "merger," it has its analogous application to computer programs.

Professor Nimmer points out that "in many instances it is virtually impossible to write a program to perform particular functions in a specific computing environment without employing standard techniques." 3 Nimmer § 13.03[F][3]. This is a result of the fact that a programmer's freedom of design choice is often circumscribed by extrinsic considerations such as

(1) the mechanical specifications of the computer on which a particular program is intended to run;

(2) compatibility requirements of other programs with which a program is designed to operate in conjunction;

(3) computer manufacturers' design standards;

(4) demands of the industry being serviced; and

(5) widely accepted programming practices within the computer industry.

Courts have already considered some of these factors in denying copyright protection to various elements of computer programs. In the *Plains Cotton* case, the Fifth Circuit refused to reverse the district court's denial of a preliminary injunction against an alleged program infringer because, in part, "many of the similarities between the . . . programs [were] dictated by the externalities of the cotton market."

In *Manufacturers Technologies*, the district court noted that the program's method of screen navigation "is influenced by the type of hardware that the software is designed to be used on." Because, in part, "the functioning of the hardware package impact[ed] and constrain[ed] the type of navigational tools used in plaintiff's screen displays," the court denied copyright protection to that aspect of the program. *[C]f. Data East USA* (reversing a district court's finding of audiovisual work infringement because, inter alia, "the use of the Commodore computer for a karate game intended for home consumption is subject to various constraints inherent in the use of that computer"). Finally, the district court in *Q-Co Industries* rested its holding on what, perhaps, most closely approximates a traditional *scènes à faire* rationale. There, the court denied copyright protection to four program modules employed in a teleprompter program. This decision was ultimately based upon the court's finding that "the same modules would be an inherent part of any prompting program."

Building upon this existing case law, we conclude that a court must also examine the structural content of an allegedly infringed program for elements that might have been dictated by external factors.

(c) Elements taken From the Public Domain

Closely related to the non-protectability of *scènes à faire*, is material found in the public domain. Such material is free for the taking and cannot be appropriated by a single author even though it is included in a copyrighted work. We see no reason to make an exception to this rule for elements of a computer program that have entered the public domain by virtue of freely accessible program exchanges and the like. See 3 Nimmer § 13.03[F][4]; see also *Brown Bag Software* (affirming the district court's finding that "'[p]laintiffs may not claim copyright protection of an . . . expression that is, if not standard, then commonplace in the computer software industry.'"). Thus, a court must also filter out this material from the allegedly infringed program before it makes the final inquiry in its substantial similarity analysis.

Step Three: Comparison

The third and final step of the test for substantial similarity that we believe appropriate for non-literal program components entails a comparison. Once a court has sifted out all elements of the allegedly infringed program which are "ideas" or are dictated by efficiency or external factors, or taken from the public domain, there may remain a core of protectable expression. In terms of a work's copyright value, this is the golden nugget. See *Brown Bag Software*. At this point, the court's substantial similarity inquiry focuses on whether the defendant copied any aspect of this protected expression, as well as an assessment of the copied portion's relative importance with respect to the plaintiff's overall program. See 3 Nimmer § 13.03[F][5]; *Data East USA* ("To determine whether similarities result from unprotectable expression, analytic dissection of similarities may be performed. If . . . all similarities in expression arise from use of common ideas, then no substantial similarity can be found.").

3) Policy Considerations

We are satisfied that the three step approach we have just outlined not only comports with, but advances the constitutional policies underlying the Copyright Act. Since any method that tries to distinguish idea from expression ultimately impacts on the scope of copyright protection afforded to a particular type of work, "the line [it draws] must be a pragmatic one, which also keeps in consideration 'the preservation of the balance between competition and protection. . . .'" *Apple Computer*.

CA and some amici argue against the type of approach that we have set forth on the grounds that it will be a disincentive for future computer program research and development. At bottom, they claim that if programmers are not guaranteed broad copyright protection for their work, they will not invest the extensive time, energy and funds required to design and improve program structures. While they have a point, their argument cannot carry the day. The interest of the copyright law is not in simply conferring a monopoly on industrious persons, but in advancing the public welfare through rewarding artistic creativity, in a manner that permits the free use and development of non-protectable ideas and processes.

In this respect, our conclusion is informed by Justice Stewart's concise discussion of the principles that correctly govern the adaptation of the copyright law to new circumstances. In *Twentieth Century Music Corp. v. Aiken*, he wrote:

> The limited scope of the copyright holder's statutory monopoly, like the limited copyright duration required by the Constitution, reflects a balance of competing claims upon the public interest: Creative work is to be encouraged and rewarded, but private motivation must ultimately serve the cause of promoting broad public availability of literature, music, and the other arts. The immediate effect of our copyright law is to secure a fair return for an "author's" creative labor. But the ultimate aim is, by this incentive, to stimulate artistic creativity for the general public good. . . .
>
> When technological change has rendered its literal terms ambiguous, the Copyright Act must be construed in light of this basic purpose.

Recently, the Supreme Court has emphatically reiterated that "[t]he primary objective of copyright is not to reward the labor of authors. . . ." *Feist Publications, Inc. v. Rural Tel. Serv. Co.* (1991). . . .

Feist teaches that substantial effort alone cannot confer copyright status on an otherwise uncopyrightable work. As we have discussed, despite the fact that significant labor and expense often goes into computer program flow-charting and debugging, that process does not always result in inherently protectable expression. Thus, *Feist* implicitly undercuts the *Whelan* rationale, "which allow[ed] copyright protection beyond the literal computer code . . . [in order to] provide the proper incentive for programmers by protecting their most valuable efforts. . . ." *Whelan*. We note that *Whelan* was decided prior to *Feist* when the "sweat of the brow" doctrine still had vitality.

Furthermore, we are unpersuaded that the test we approve today will lead to the dire consequences for the computer program industry that plaintiff and some amici predict. To the contrary, serious students of the industry have been highly critical of the sweeping scope of copyright protection engendered by the *Whelan* rule, in that it "enables first comers to 'lock up' basic programming techniques as implemented in programs to perform particular tasks." Menell; see also Spivack (*Whelan* "results in an inhibition of creation by virtue of the copyright owner's quasi-monopoly power").

To be frank, the exact contours of copyright protection for non-literal program structure are not completely clear. We trust that as future cases are decided, those limits will become better defined. Indeed, it may well be that the Copyright Act serves as a relatively weak barrier against public access to the theoretical interstices behind a program's source and object codes. This results from the hybrid nature of a computer program, which, while it is literary expression, is also a highly functional, utilitarian component in the larger process of computing.

Generally, we think that copyright registration—with its indiscriminating availability—is not ideally suited to deal with the highly dynamic technology of computer science. Thus far, many of the decisions in this area reflect the courts' attempt to fit the proverbial square peg in a round hole. The district court and at least one commentator have suggested that patent registration, with its exacting up-front novelty and non-obviousness requirements, might be the more appropriate rubric of protection for intellectual property of this kind. . . .

In the meantime, Congress has made clear that computer programs are literary works entitled to copyright protection. Of course, we shall abide by these instructions, but in so doing we must not impair the overall integrity of copyright law. While incentive based arguments in favor of broad copyright protection are perhaps attractive from a pure policy perspective, see *Lotus Dev. Corp.*, ultimately, they have a corrosive effect on certain fundamental tenets of copyright doctrine. If the test we have outlined results in narrowing the scope of protection, as we expect it will, that result flows from applying, in accordance with Congressional intent, long-standing principles of copyright law to computer programs. Of course, our decision is also informed by our concern that these fundamental principles remain undistorted.

B. The District Court Decision

At the outset, we must address CA's claim that the district court erred by relying too heavily on the court appointed expert's "personal opinions on the factual and legal issues before the court."

1) Use of Expert Evidence in Determining Substantial Similarity Between Computer Programs

Pursuant to Fed.R.Evid. 706, and with the consent of both Altai and CA, Judge Pratt appointed and relied upon Dr. Randall Davis of the Massachusetts Institute of Technology as the court's own expert witness on the issue of substantial similarity. Dr. Davis submitted a comprehensive written report that analyzed the various aspects of the computer programs at issue and evaluated the parties' expert evidence. At trial, Dr. Davis was extensively cross-examined by both CA and Altai.

The well-established general rule in this circuit has been to limit the use of expert opinion in determining whether works at issue are substantially similar. As a threshold matter, expert testimony may be used to assist the fact finder in ascertaining whether the defendant had copied any part of the plaintiff's work. See *Arnstein v. Porter* (2d Cir. 1946). To this end, "the two works are to be compared in their entirety . . . [and] in making such comparison resort may properly be made to expert analysis. . . ." 3 Nimmer § 13.03[E][2].

However, once some amount of copying has been established, it remains solely for the trier of fact to determine whether the copying was "illicit," that is to say, whether the "defendant took from plaintiff's works so much of what is pleasing to [lay observers] who comprise the audience for whom such [works are] composed, that defendant wrongfully appropriated something which belongs to the plaintiff." *Arnstein*. Since the test for illicit copying is based upon the response of ordinary lay observers, expert testimony is thus "irrelevant" and not permitted. We have subsequently described this method of inquiry as "merely an alternative way of formulating the issue of substantial similarity." *Ideal Toy Corp. v. Fab-Lu Ltd. (Inc.)* (2d Cir. 1966).

Historically, *Arnstein*'s ordinary observer standard had its roots in "an attempt to apply the 'reasonable person' doctrine as found in other areas of the law to copyright." 3 Nimmer § 13.03[E][2]. That approach may well have served its purpose when the material under scrutiny was limited to art forms readily comprehensible and generally familiar to the average lay person. However, in considering the extension of the rule to the present case, we are reminded of Holmes' admonition that, "[t]he life of the law has not been logic: it has been experience." O.W. Holmes, Jr., THE COMMON LAW 1 (1881).

Thus, in deciding the limits to which expert opinion may be employed in ascertaining the substantial similarity of computer programs, we cannot disregard the highly complicated and technical subject matter at the heart of these claims. Rather, we recognize the reality that computer programs are likely to be somewhat impenetrable by lay observers—whether they be judges or juries—and, thus, seem to fall outside the category of works contemplated by those who engineered the *Arnstein* test. *Cf. Dawson v. Hinshaw Music Inc.* (4th Cir.) ("departure from the lay characterization is warranted only where the intended audience possesses 'specialized expertise'").

In making its finding on substantial similarity with respect to computer programs, we believe that the trier of fact need not be limited by the strictures of its own lay perspective. Rather, we leave it to the discretion of the district court to decide to what extent, if any, expert opinion, regarding the highly technical nature of computer programs, is warranted in a given case. In so holding, we do not intend to disturb the traditional role of lay observers in judging substantial similarity in copyright cases that involve the aesthetic arts, such as music, visual works or literature. In this case, Dr. Davis' opinion was instrumental in dismantling the intricacies of computer science so that the court could formulate and apply an appropriate rule of law. While Dr. Davis' report and testimony undoubtedly shed valuable light on the subject matter of the litigation, Judge Pratt remained, in the final analysis, the trier of fact. The district court's use of the expert's assistance, in the context of this case, was entirely appropriate.

2) Evidentiary Analysis

The district court had to determine whether Altai's OSCAR 3.5 program was substantially similar to CA's ADAPTER. We note that Judge Pratt's method of analysis effectively served as a road map for our own, with one exception—Judge Pratt filtered out the non-copyrightable aspects of OSCAR 3.5 rather than those found in ADAPTER, the allegedly infringed program. We think that our approach—i.e., filtering out the unprotected aspects of an allegedly infringed program and then comparing the end product to the structure of the suspect program—is preferable, and therefore believe that district courts should proceed in this manner in future cases.

We opt for this strategy because, in some cases, the defendant's program structure might contain protectable expression and/or other elements that are not found in the plaintiff's program. Since it is extraneous to the allegedly copied work, this material would have no bearing on any potential substantial similarity between the two programs. Thus, its filtration would be wasteful and unnecessarily time consuming. Furthermore, by focusing the analysis on the infringing rather than on the infringed material, a court may mistakenly place too little emphasis on a quantitatively small misappropriation which is, in reality, a qualitatively vital aspect of the plaintiff's protectable expression.

The fact that the district court's analysis proceeded in the reverse order, however, had no material impact on the outcome of this case. Since Judge Pratt determined that OSCAR effectively contained no protectable expression whatsoever, the most serious charge that can be levelled against him is that he was overly thorough in his examination.

The district court took the first step in the analysis set forth in this opinion when it separated the program by levels of abstraction. The district court stated:

> As applied to computer software programs, this abstractions test would progress in order of "increasing generality" from object code, to source code, to parameter lists, to services required, to general outline. In discussing the particular similarities, therefore, we shall focus on these levels.

While the facts of a different case might require that a district court draw a more particularized blueprint of a program's overall structure, this description is a workable one for the case at hand.

Moving to the district court's evaluation of OSCAR 3.5's structural components, we agree with Judge Pratt's systematic exclusion of non-protectable expression. With respect to code, the district court observed that after the rewrite of OSCAR 3.4 to OSCAR 3.5, "there remained virtually no lines of code that were identical to ADAPTER." Accordingly, the court found that the code "present[ed] no similarity at all."

Next, Judge Pratt addressed the issue of similarity between the two programs' parameter lists and macros. He concluded that, viewing the conflicting evidence most favorably to CA, it demonstrated that "only a few of the lists and macros were similar to protected elements in ADAPTER; the others were either in the public domain or dictated by the functional demands of the program." As discussed above, functional elements and elements taken from the public domain do not qualify for copyright protection. With respect to the few remaining parameter lists and macros, the district court could reasonably conclude that they did not warrant a finding of infringement given their relative contribution to the overall program. In any event, the district court reasonably found that, for lack of persuasive evidence, CA failed to meet its burden of proof on whether the macros and parameter lists at issue were substantially similar.

The district court also found that the overlap exhibited between the list of services required for both ADAPTER and OSCAR 3.5 was "determined by the demands of the operating system and of the applications program to which it [was] to be linked through ADAPTER or OSCAR. . . ." In other words, this aspect of the program's structure was dictated by the nature of other programs with which it was designed to interact and, thus, is not protected by copyright.

Finally, in his infringement analysis, Judge Pratt accorded no weight to the similarities between the two programs' organizational charts, "because [the charts were] so simple and obvious to anyone exposed to the operation of the program[s]." CA argues that the district court's action in this regard "is not consistent with copyright law"—that "obvious" expression is protected, and that the district court erroneously failed to realize this. However, to say that elements of a work are "obvious," in the manner in which the district court used the word, is to say that they "follow naturally from the work's theme rather than from the author's creativity." 3 Nimmer § 13.03[F][3]. This is but one formulation of the *scènes à faire* doctrine, which we have already endorsed as a means of weeding out unprotectable expression. . . .

CONCLUSION

In adopting the above three step analysis for substantial similarity between the non-literal elements of computer programs, we seek to insure [sic] two things: (1) that programmers may receive appropriate copyright protection for innovative utilitarian works containing expression; and (2) that non-protectable technical expression remains in the public domain for others to use freely as building blocks in their own work. At first blush, it may seem counter-intuitive that someone who has benefitted to some degree from illicitly obtained material can emerge from an infringement suit relatively unscathed. However, so long as the appropriated material consists of non-protectable expression, "[t]his result is neither unfair nor unfortunate. It is the means by which copyright advances the progress of science and art." *Feist.*

Furthermore, we underscore that so long as trade secret law is employed in a manner that does not encroach upon the exclusive domain of the Copyright Act, it is an appropriate means by which to secure compensation for software espionage.

Accordingly, we affirm the judgment of the district court in part; vacate in part; and remand for further proceedings. The parties shall bear their own costs of appeal, including the petition for rehearing.

Note: Scènes à Faire

As you saw in the flow chart after chapter 10, copying "scènes à faire" is not infringement. "Scènes à faire" is French for "scenes that must be done," and refers to elements that have become standard for treating a particular topic or creating within a style or genre. Courts do not always use the term "scènes à faire" to describe this material; they sometimes describe it as too "common," "trite," "stereotypical," "clichéd," "stock," or "hackneyed" to be protectable. Whatever the terminology, anyone can use this material without infringing copyright, even if it would otherwise qualify as original, creative expression.

In *Computer Associates* the court excluded "scènes à faire" in computer programming from copyright protection. What are some examples of scènes à faire in other art forms? The image gives an example of scènes à faire in a copyright case about country music lyrics. In movies, courts have explained that "parties, alcohol, co-eds, and wild behavior are natural elements in a story about a college fraternity," "elements such as drunks, prostitutes, vermin and derelict cars would appear in any realistic work about the work of policemen in the South Bronx," and "[g]etting drunk, spending a 'one-nighter' with someone you just met, waking up disoriented the next morning at the individual's house or apartment, and putting on the clothes worn the night before are also plot devices that are necessary to a walk of shame." As you can tell from these examples, as our culture (and the Bronx real estate market, for that matter) changes, scènes à faire may also evolve. Bonus question: what are scènes à faire for your favorite type of movie, or style of music? Seriously. Try to list them.

"HAVING CHOSEN THE FAMILIAR THEME OF A BROKEN-HEARTED LOVER SEEKING SOLACE IN COUNTRY MUSIC, THE CHOICE OF A BARROOM WITH A JUKEBOX AS THE SETTING IN WHICH TO UNFOLD THIS IDEA SIMPLY CANNOT BE ATTRIBUTED TO ANY UNIQUE CREATIVITY ON THE PART OF THE SONGWRITER."

Black v. Gosdin, 740 F. Supp. 1288 (M.D. Tenn. 1990)

SCÈNES À FAIRE

Questions:

1.) Having read the case, what is your answer—do we have a separate law of copyright for software?

2.) How would you describe the extent of copyright protection for software after this decision? Copying Windows 7, bit for bit, is illegal. What about writing a competing operating system that borrows all of Windows 7's ideas about how to present and open programs, retrieve information and so on, but does not copy the code. Is that infringing?

3.) Look back at problem 12-1 d.). Has Larry infringed Sergey's copyright?

3.) Copyright in Characters

Anderson v. Stallone
11 U.S.P.Q.2d 1161 (C.D. Cal. 1989)

WILLIAM D. KELLER, District Judge.

Factual Background

The movies Rocky I, II, and III were extremely successful motion pictures. Sylvester Stallone wrote each script and played the role of Rocky Balboa, the dominant character in each of the movies. In May of 1982, while on a promotional tour for the movie Rocky III, Stallone informed members of the press of his ideas for Rocky IV. Although Stallone's description of his ideas would vary slightly in each of the press conferences, he would generally describe his ideas as follows:

> I'd do it [Rocky IV] if Rocky himself could step out a bit. Maybe tackle world problems. So what would happen, say, if Russia allowed her boxers to enter the professional ranks? Say Rocky is the United States' representative and the White House wants him to fight with the Russians before the Olympics. It's in Russia with everything against him. It's a giant stadium in Moscow and everything is Russian Red. It's a fight of astounding proportions with 50 monitors sent to 50 countries. It's the World Cup—a war between 2 countries.

In June of 1982, after viewing the movie Rocky III, Timothy Anderson wrote a thirty-one page treatment entitled "Rocky IV" that he hoped would be used by Stallone and MGM as a sequel to Rocky III. The treatment incorporated the characters created by Stallone in his prior movies and cited Stallone as a co-author. In October of 1982, Mr. Anderson met with Art Linkletter, who was a member of MGM's board of directors. Mr. Linkletter set up a meeting on October 11, 1982, between Mr. Anderson and Mr. Fields, who was president of MGM at the time. Mr. Linkletter was also present at this October 11, 1982 meeting. During the meeting, the parties discussed the possibility that plaintiff's treatment would be used by defendants as the script for Rocky IV. At the suggestion of Mr. Fields, the plaintiff, who is a lawyer and was accompanied by a lawyer at the meeting, signed a release that purported to relieve MGM from liability stemming from use of the treatment. Plaintiff alleges that Mr. Fields told him and his attorney that "if they [MGM & Stallone] use his stuff [Anderson's treatment] it will be big money, big bucks for Tim."

On April 22, 1984, Anderson's attorney wrote MGM requesting compensation for the alleged use of his treatment in the forthcoming Rocky IV movie. On July 12, 1984, Stallone described his plans for the Rocky IV script on the Today Show before a national television audience. Anderson, in his deposition, states that his parents and friends called him to tell him that Stallone was telling "his story" on television. In a diary entry of July 12, 1984, Anderson noted that Stallone "explained my story" on national television.

Stallone completed his Rocky IV script in October of 1984. Rocky IV was released in November of 1985. The complaint in this action was filed on January 29, 1987.

1. Visually Depicted Characters Can Be Granted Copyright Protection

The precise legal standard this Court should apply in determining when a character may be afforded copyright protection is fraught with uncertainty. The Second Circuit has followed Judge Learned Hand's opinion in *Nichols v. Universal Pictures*, Judge Hand set forth a test, simple in theory but elusive in application, to determine when a character should be granted copyright protection. Essentially, under this test, copyright protection is granted to a character if it is developed with enough specificity so as to constitute protectable expression.

This circuit originally created a more rigorous test for granting copyright protection to characters. In *Warner Bros. Pictures, Inc. v. Columbia Broadcasting System, Inc.*, (hereinafter the "Sam Spade" opinion) this circuit held that the literary character Sam Spade was not copyrightable, opining that a character could not be granted copyright protection unless it "constituted the story being told." The Sam Spade case has not been explicitly overruled by this circuit and its requirement that a character "constitute the story being told" appears to greatly circumscribe the protection of characters in this circuit.

Subsequent decisions in the Ninth Circuit cast doubt on the reasoning and implicitly limit the holding of the Sam Spade case. In *Walt Disney Productions v. Air Pirates*, this circuit held that several Disney comic characters were protected by copyright. In doing so the Court of Appeals reasoned that because "comic book characters . . . are distinguishable from literary characters, the Warner Bros language does not preclude protection of Disney's characters." *Air Pirates* can be interpreted as either attempting to harmonize granting copyright protection to graphic characters with the "story being told" test enunciated in the Sam Spade case or narrowing the "story being told" test to characters in literary works. If *Air Pirates* is construed as holding that the graphic characters in question constituted the story being told, it does little to alter the Sam Spade opinion. However, it is equally as plausible to interpret *Air Pirates* as applying a less stringent test for protectability of graphic characters.

Professor Nimmer has adopted the latter reading as he interprets *Air Pirates* as limiting the story being told requirement to word portraits. Further, Professor Nimmer finds that the reasoning of the Sam Spade case is undermined by the *Air Pirates* opinion, even as it relates to word portraits. This is true because the use of a less stringent test for protection of characters in the graphic medium casts doubt on the vitality of the more stringent story being told test for graphic characters. As a practical matter, a graphically depicted character is much more likely than a literary character to be fleshed out in sufficient detail so as to warrant copyright protection. But this fact does not warrant the creation of separate analytical paradigms for protection of characters in the two mediums.

This circuit's most recent decision on the issue of copyrightability of characters, *Olson v. National Broadcasting Corp.* (9th Cir. 1988) does little to clarify the uncertainties in this circuit as to how the *Air Pirates* decision effects the continued viability of the *Sam Spade* test. In *Olson*, the Court of Appeals cited with approval the Sam Spade "story being told test" and declined to characterize this language as dicta. The Court then cited *Air Pirates* along with Second Circuit precedent and "recognize[d] that cases subsequent to *Warner Bros* [Sam Spade] have allowed copyright protection for characters who are especially distinctive." *Olson* also stated definitively that "copyright protection may be afforded to characters visually depicted in a television series or in a movie." But later in the opinion, the court in *Olson* distanced itself from the character delineation test that these cases employed, referring to it as "the more lenient standards adopted elsewhere."

In an implicit acknowledgment of the unsettled state of the law, in considering the characters at issue in *Olson*, the circuit court evaluates the characters in the suit under both tests.

2. The Rocky Characters Are Entitled To Copyright Protection as a Matter of Law

Olson's evaluation of literary characters is clearly distinguishable from the visually depicted characters of the first three Rocky movies for which the defendant seeks protection here. Thus, the more restrictive "story being told test" is inapplicable to the facts of this case. However, out of an abundance of caution this Court will determine the protectability of the Rocky characters under both tests. As shown below, the Rocky characters are protected from bodily appropriation under either standard.

The Rocky characters are one of the most highly delineated group of characters in modern American cinema. The physical and emotional characteristics of Rocky Balboa and the other characters were set forth in tremendous detail in the three Rocky movies before Anderson appropriated the characters for his treatment. The interrelationships and development of Rocky, Adrian, Apollo Creed, Clubber Lang, and Paulie are central to all three movies. Rocky Balboa is such a highly delineated character that his name is the title of all four of the Rocky movies and his character has become identified with specific character traits ranging from his speaking mannerisms to his physical characteristics. This Court has no difficulty ruling as a matter of law that the Rocky characters are delineated so extensively that they are protected from bodily appropriation when taken as a group and transposed into a sequel by another author. Plaintiff has not and cannot put before this Court any evidence to rebut the defendants' showing that Rocky characters are so highly delineated that they warrant copyright protection.

Plaintiff's unsupported assertions that Rocky is merely a stock character, made in the face of voluminous evidence that the Rocky characters are copyrightable, do not bar this Court from granting summary judgment on this issue. If any group of movie characters is protected by copyright, surely the Rocky characters are protected from bodily appropriation into a sequel which merely builds on the relationships and characteristics which these characters developed in the first three Rocky movies. No reasonable jury could find otherwise.

This Court need not and does not reach the issue of whether any single character alone, apart from Rocky, is delineated with enough specificity so as to garner copyright protection. Nor does the Court reach the issue of whether these characters are protected from less than bodily appropriation. See 1 M. Nimmer, § 2.12 (copyrightability of characters is "more properly framed as relating to the degree of substantial similarity required to constitute infringement rather than in terms of copyrightability per se").

This Court also finds that the Rocky characters were so highly developed and central to the three movies made before Anderson's treatment that they "constituted the story being told." All three Rocky movies focused on the development and relationships of the various characters. The movies did not revolve around intricate plots or story lines. Instead, the focus of these movies was the development of the Rocky characters. The same evidence which supports the finding of delineation above is so extensive that it also warrants a finding that the Rocky characters—Rocky, Adrian, Apollo Creed, Clubber Lang, and Paulie—"constituted the story being told" in the first three Rocky movies.

3. Anderson's Work is An Unauthorized Derivative Work

Under 17 U.S.C. section 106(2), the holder of a copyright has the exclusive right to prepare derivative works based upon his copyrighted work. In this circuit a work is derivative "only if it would be considered an infringing work if the material which it had derived from a prior work had been taken without the consent of the copyright proprietor of the prior work." *Litchfield v. Spielberg* (9th Cir. 1984).This Court must now examine whether Anderson's treatment is an unauthorized derivative work under this standard.

Usually a court would be required to undertake the extensive comparisons under the *Krofft* substantial similarity test to determine whether Anderson's work is a derivative work. However, in this case, Anderson has bodily appropriated the Rocky characters in his treatment. This Court need not determine whether the characters in Anderson's treatment are substantially similar to Stallone's characters, as it is uncontroverted that the characters were lifted lock, stock, and barrel from the prior Rocky movies. Anderson retained the names, relationships and built on the experiences of these characters from the three prior Rocky movies. 1 M. Nimmer, § 2.12 (copying names of characters is highly probative evidence of infringement). His characters are not merely substantially similar to Stallone's, they are Stallone's characters. As Professor Nimmer stated, "Where there is literal similarity. . . . [i]t is not necessary to determine the level of abstraction at which similarity ceases to consist of an 'expression of ideas' since literal similarity by definition is always a similarity as to the expression of ideas." 3 M. Nimmer, § 13.03[3]. Anderson's bodily appropriation of these characters infringes upon the protected expression in the Rocky characters and renders his work an unauthorized derivative work. By bodily appropriating the significant elements of protected expression in the Rocky characters, Anderson has copied protected expression and his treatment infringes on Stallone's copyrighted work.

4. Since Anderson's Work Is an Unauthorized Derivative Work, No Part of the Treatment Can Be Granted Copyright Protection

Stallone owns the copyrights for the first three Rocky movies. Under 17 U.S.C. section 106(2), he has the exclusive right to prepare derivative works based on these copyrighted works. This Court has determined that Anderson's treatment is an unauthorized derivative work. Thus, Anderson has infringed upon Stallone's copyright.

Nevertheless, plaintiff contends that his infringing work is entitled to copyright protection and he can sue Stallone for infringing upon his treatment. Plaintiff relies upon 17 U.S.C. section 103(a) as support for his position that he is entitled to copyright protection for the non-infringing portions of his treatment. 17 U.S.C section 103(a) reads:

> The subject matter of copyright as specified by section 102 includes compilations and derivative works, but protection for a work employing preexisting material in which copyright subsists does not extend to any part of the work in which the material has been used unlawfully.

Plaintiff has not argued that section 103(a), on its face, requires that an infringer be granted copyright protection for the non-infringing portions of his work. He has not and cannot provide this Court with a single case that has held that an infringer of a copyright is entitled to sue a third party for infringing the original portions of his work. Nor can he provide a single case that stands for the extraordinary proposition he proposes here, namely, allowing a plaintiff to sue the party whose work he has infringed upon for infringement of his infringing derivative work. . . .

The Court finds that Rocky IV is not substantially similar to Anderson's work. Nor is any portion of Anderson's work entitled to copyright protection under 17 U.S.C. sections 103(a) & 106(2). The Court GRANTS defendants summary judgment on Anderson's claim that they infringed Anderson's copyright.

Questions:

1.) If the characters are under copyright, and Anderson's "treatment" is thus an unauthorized derivative work, not eligible for copyright protection, what does it matter that

Stallone had publicly offered ideas similar to the ones Anderson put in the screenplay prior to seeing it? Why does the court mention it? To pose the counterfactual, suppose Stallone had never thought about *any* of these plot twists, had access to a screenplay of Anderson's and taken *all* of it—down to the exact language of the script—does Anderson still lose on the copyright claim?

2.) Should we have copyright over characters? Why? Why not? Think of the blockbuster movies featuring comic book characters. Are these an argument for copyright protection of characters or against it?

3.) Has James infringed copyright with his Hamnet character described in problem 12-1 e.)?

4.) In *DC Comics v. Towle* (9th Cir. 2015), the Ninth Circuit held that the Batmobile is a copyrightable character. It set out the following three-part test for the copyright eligibility of characters:

- the character must generally have physical as well as conceptual qualities
- the character must be sufficiently delineated to be recognizable as the same character whenever it appears
- the character must be especially distinctive and contain some unique elements of expression

The court explained: "Even when a character lacks sentient attributes and does not speak (like a car), it can be a protectable character if it meets this standard." So, under this standard, is Hogwarts a copyrightable character? What might infringe it? In *DC Comics*, the court's holding meant that the defendant—Mark Towle, the owner of Gotham Garage—infringed the Batmobile copyright when he built *actual cars* that were replicas of Batmobiles. Here is one of Towle's replicas.

4.) A Two-Part Test for Copyright Infringement

We have discussed the line courts must draw between idea and expression, the process by which unprotectable elements are filtered from computer software and the reach of copyright over characters. We now turn to the way (actually, the *ways*) that courts assess claims of illicit copying. Portions of this discussion should be familiar from *Computer Associates v. Altai*, but there they were in the specialized context of software.

In the 1946 case *Arnstein v. Porter*, the Second Circuit laid out a seminal two-pronged test for copyright infringement. This was one of many lawsuits brought by songwriter Ira Arnstein, who was convinced that more successful songwriters were stealing his music and made sometimes outlandish allegations of copying. In this case, he claimed that several songs by Cole Porter infringed his works, even though there were few significant similarities. While Arnstein lost his other lawsuits at the summary judgment stage, here the court denied Porter's summary judgment motion and set an unusually high bar for winning these motions. Later cases tempered *Arnstein's* summary judgment standard, and the current requirement is that there is "no genuine issue of material fact." But its bifurcated test endures, and it is excerpted below.

Arnstein v. Porter
154 F.2d 464 (2d Cir. 1946)

FRANK, Circuit Judge.

. . . [I]t is important to avoid confusing two separate elements essential to a plaintiff's case in such a suit: (a) that defendant copied from plaintiff's copyrighted work and (b) that the copying (assuming it to be proved) went so far as to constitute improper appropriation.

As to the first—copying—the evidence may consist (a) of defendant's admission that he copied or (b) of circumstantial evidence—usually evidence of access—from which the trier of the facts may reasonably infer copying. Of course, if there are no similarities, no amount of evidence of access will suffice to prove copying. If there is evidence of access and similarities exist, then the trier of the facts must determine whether the similarities are sufficient to prove copying. On this issue, analysis ('dissection') is relevant, and the testimony of experts may be received to aid the trier of the facts. If evidence of access is absent, the similarities must be so striking as to preclude the possibility that plaintiff and defendant independently arrived at the same result.

If copying is established, then only does there arise the second issue, that of illicit copying (unlawful appropriation). On that issue (as noted more in detail below) the test is the response of the ordinary lay hearer; accordingly, on that issue, 'dissection' and expert testimony are irrelevant.

In some cases, the similarities between the plaintiff's and defendant's work are so extensive and striking as, without more, both to justify an inference of copying and to prove improper appropriation. But such double-purpose evidence is not required; that is, if copying is otherwise shown, proof of improper appropriation need not consist of similarities which, standing alone, would support an inference of copying. . . .

Assuming that adequate proof is made of copying, that is not enough; for there can be 'permissible copying,' copying which is not illicit. Whether (if he copied) defendant unlawfully appropriated presents, too, an issue of fact. The proper criterion on that issue is not an analytic or other comparison of the respective musical compositions as they appear on paper or in the judgment of trained musicians. The plaintiff's legally protected interest is not, as such, his reputation as a musician but his interest in the potential financial returns from his compositions which derive from the lay public's approbation of his efforts. The question, therefore, is whether defendant took from plaintiff's works so much of what is pleasing to the ears of lay listeners, who comprise the audience for whom such popular music is composed, that defendant wrongfully appropriated something which belongs to the plaintiff. . . .

• • • • • • • • •

Notes

(handwritten margin note: 2-part test for © infringement! ☆)

> "[There are] two separate elements essential to a plaintiff's case in such a suit:
>
> > "a) that defendant copied from plaintiff's copyrighted work and
> > b) that the copying (assuming it to be proved) went too far as to constitute improper appropriation."

This two-part test from *Arnstein* has served as a basic template for copyright infringement tests in many other Circuits. The general contours of each prong are as follows.

(handwritten margin note: ☆) First, there is the question of whether the defendant copied from the plaintiff's work *at all*, as opposed to independently creating her own work. This is a factual rather than legal question. It is easily resolved if the defendant admits to copying; in cases of digital music sampling, for example, there is no debate over whether the defendant copied, just whether she took enough for that copying to be unlawful. Often there is no such admission, however, and courts turn to analyzing whether circumstantial evidence of similarities between the works, often called "probative similarity," and evidence of "access" are together enough to suggest copying.

Probative Similarity: At this stage, similarities are being assessed to answer the initial question of whether there was copying, not the legal question of whether there was infringement. Thus courts look at the question of similarity broadly, even including similarities in unprotected material such as ideas. (Courts look at all the similarities because they may show that I did copy from you as a factual matter, even if they do not show that I infringed as a legal matter.) Do you agree with this technique? Obviously, it poses the danger that juries will later conflate both protectable and unprotectable similarities when judging infringement.

Access: A full exploration of access is beyond the scope of this chapter, but, generally, there must be a "reasonable possibility" that the defendant had access to the plaintiff's work, either through a chain of events (my producer met you at a bar where you gave her a demo of a song that you now claim I copied), or widespread dissemination of the plaintiff's work (your song was played so often that I must have heard it). As we saw in *Computer Associates*, programmers try to devise "clean room" programming techniques, in which coders are kept away from the code to be emulated functionally, precisely to preclude access. However, few of us create in hermetically sealed environments, and courts will sometimes presume access even in the absence of any evidence if similarities between the works are so "striking" as to make independent creation implausible. These evidentiary questions are complex. As *Arnstein* suggests, analytical dissection and expert testimony about the nature of those similarities (and thus the likelihood that they are accidental) are appropriate to resolve them.

In this chapter, we have focused on the second question: whether the copying "went so far as to constitute improper appropriation"—that is, copyright infringement. *Arnstein* provides two general guidelines with regard to this inquiry:

- unlawful appropriation should be determined by the "lay listener" or observer, and
- analytical dissection and expert testimony are "irrelevant."

What is the court's reasoning here? Why leave this determination to the lay juror, without the aid (or distraction) of dissection and expert testimony? Should expert testimony be permitted to assist the jury with certain discrete determinations, such as distinguishing between protectable and unprotectable material? More broadly, do you agree with *Arnstein* that "improper appropriation" should turn on whether the defendant has unduly impinged on the plaintiff's market interest "in the potential financial returns from his compositions which derive from the lay public's approbation of his efforts"?

The Ninth Circuit has adopted and reformulated *Arnstein v. Porter*'s two-part test. After establishing factual copying, it separates the unlawful appropriation inquiry into two prongs: an "extrinsic" inquiry—an objective comparison of the protectable elements of the two works, with the assistance of expert testimony, and an "intrinsic" inquiry—a subjective comparison of the works by the jury from the point of view of the ordinary reasonable person. *See Skidmore v. Zeppelin* (9th Cir. 2020) (summarizing the current test in light of conflicting precedent; finding that Led Zeppelin's song "Stairway to Heaven" did not infringe the copyright in the song "Taurus").

The following case engages with the "ordinary observer" test as introduced in *Arnstein* and developed in other Circuits, and suggests a limited modification.

Dawson v. Hinshaw Music
905 F.2d 731 (4th Cir. 1990)

[In this case, the plaintiff claimed that the defendant had infringed his musical arrangement of the spiritual "Ezekiel Saw De Wheel." The court held that applying the ordinary lay observer test was inappropriate, and adopted an "intended audience" test. Here, the intended audience for the spiritual arrangements could be "choral directors who possess specialized expertise relevant to their selection of one arrangement instead of another."]

MURNAGHAN, Circuit Judge.

Arnstein v. Porter provides the source of modern theory regarding the ordinary observer test. *Arnstein* involved the alleged infringement of a popular musical composition. Writing for the panel, Judge Jerome Frank first explained that "the plaintiff's legally protected interest is not, as such, his reputation as a musician but his interest in the potential financial returns from his compositions which derive from the lay public's approbation." This initial observation gave force to the recognized purpose of the copyright laws of providing creators with a financial incentive to create for the ultimate benefit of the public.

Consistent with its economic incentive view of copyright law, the *Arnstein* court concluded that "the question, therefore, is whether defendant took from plaintiff's works so much of what is pleasing to the ears of lay listeners, *who comprise the audience for whom such popular music is composed,* that defendant wrongfully appropriated something which belongs to plaintiff." (emphasis added). Thus, under *Arnstein,* a court should look to the reaction of "lay listeners," because they comprise the audience of the plaintiff's work. The lay listener's reaction is relevant because it gauges the effect of the defendant's work on the plaintiff's market.

Although *Arnstein* established a sound foundation for the appeal to audience reaction, its reference to "lay listeners" may have fostered the development of a rule that has come to be stated too broadly. Under the facts before it, with a popular composition at issue, the *Arnstein* court appropriately perceived "lay listeners" and the works' "audience" to be the same. However, under *Arnstein*'s sound logic, the lay listeners are relevant only because they comprise the relevant audience. Although *Arnstein* does not address the question directly, we read the case's logic to require that where the intended audience is significantly more specialized than the pool of lay listeners, the reaction of the intended audience would be the relevant inquiry. In light of the copyright law's purpose of protecting a creator's market, we think it sensible to embrace *Arnstein*'s command that the ultimate comparison of the works at issue be oriented towards the works' intended audience.

Our reading of *Arnstein* brings our analysis into line with *Sid & Marty Krofft Television v. McDonald's Corp.* (9th Cir. 1977), another landmark case involving questions of substantial similarity. *Krofft* announced that the test for determining substantial similarity in the expression of ideas of two works "shall be labeled an intrinsic one-depending on the response of the ordinary reasonable person." When applying its intrinsic test, the *Krofft* court noted the particular audience to which the works in question were directed. The court wrote:

> The present case demands an even more intrinsic determination because both plaintiff's and defendants' works are directed to an audience of children. This raises the particular factual issue of the impact of the respective works upon the minds and imaginations of young people.

Thus, the *Krofft* court believed that the perspective of the specific audience for which the products were intended (children) was the relevant perspective for the ordinary observer test.

We suspect that courts have been slow to recognize explicitly the need for refining the ordinary observer test in such a way that it would adopt the perspective of the intended audience because, in most fact scenarios, the general lay public fairly represents the works' intended audience. As a result, "a considerable degree of ambiguity exists in this area; courts have not always made it apparent whether they were using a member of a specific audience, or simply an average lay observer as their spectator." Fortunately, the advent of computer programming infringement actions has forced courts to recognize that sometimes the non-interested or uninformed lay observer simply lacks the necessary expertise to determine similarities or differences between products. In *Whelan Associates v. Jaslow Dental Laboratory* (3d Cir. 1986), the Third Circuit concluded that the ordinary observer arm of the substantial similarity test was not appropriate for the complex computer program copyright case before it. Writing for a unanimous panel, Judge Becker reasoned that the complexity of computer programs, combined with the general public's unfamiliarity with such programs, rendered the ordinary observer test senseless. He further reasoned that where the finder of fact is the same for both the extrinsic and intrinsic tests, it seems silly to ask the finder of fact to "forget" the expert testimony when considering similarity of expression. Judge Becker relied also on Federal Rule of Evidence 702, which permits expert testimony where it will be useful to a trier of fact.

We believe the *Whelan* analysis further supports our view. As *Whelan* reveals, only a reckless indifference to common sense would lead a court to embrace a doctrine that requires a copyright case to turn on the opinion of someone who is ignorant of the relevant differences and similarities between two works. Instead, the judgment should be informed by people who are familiar with the media at issue. . . .

Under the foregoing logic, we state the law to be as follows. When conducting the second prong of the substantial similarity inquiry, a district court must consider the nature of the intended audience of the plaintiff's work. If, as will most often be the case, the lay public fairly represents the intended audience, the court should apply the lay observer formulation of the ordinary observer test. However, if the intended audience is more narrow in that it possesses specialized expertise, relevant to the purchasing decision, that lay people would lack, the court's inquiry should focus on whether a member of the intended audience would find the two works to be substantially similar. Such an inquiry may include, and no doubt in many cases will require, admission of testimony from members of the intended audience or, possibly, from those who possess expertise with reference to the tastes and perceptions of the intended audience. . . .

. . . [I]n any given case, a court should be hesitant to find that the lay public does not fairly represent a work's intended audience. In our opinion, departure from the lay characterization is warranted only where the intended audience possesses "specialized expertise." We thereby pay heed to the need for hesitancy when departing from the indiscriminately selected lay public in applying the test. To warrant departure from the lay characterization of the ordinary observer test, "specialized expertise" must go beyond mere differences in taste and instead must rise to the level of the possession of knowledge that the lay public lacks.

Questions:

1.) Why does the court believe that the audience for the work is also the relevant audience to determine substantial similarity? Because they would have the relevant levels of expertise? Or because they are the relevant purchasers? Imagine a contemporary jazz composer who writes a song riffing on the styles of prior jazz greats, from Bird to Coltrane, in a way that knowledgeable jazz audiences would have realized was merely a tip of the hat to his predecessors, common among sophisticated jazz musicians. Then imagine a few themes of his work are included in a massively popular hip hop song, which also—and independently—refers back to the same greats in jazz history. To the ear of someone unfamiliar with jazz the two sound strikingly similar. To the ear of an *aficionado*, the similarities are revealed to be independent references to the same cultural store. The jazz composer sues the hip hop artist. Which is the relevant audience?

2.) Though many observers have agreed that *Arnstein*'s test may sweep in too much in assessing infringement, the "intended audience" test has not commanded much support from courts. Should that change?

3.) Apply the *Arnstein* test to Jennifer's summaries of airport self-help and business books. What result?

4.) Apply what you have read so far to the diet books in Problem 12-1 c.). Do you think that James' abridged diet book or Anthony's blog infringe Jennifer's copyright?

Note: Substantial Similarity

Whether determined by the lay juror or intended audience, the basic test for illicit copying is whether there is substantial similarity between protectable elements in the plaintiff's and defendant's works. Assessing substantial similarity requires numerous exercises in line-drawing, and to quote Judge Hand in Nichols, "the line, wherever it is drawn, will seem arbitrary." What elements are protected by copyright, and what elements are unprotectable facts, ideas, scènes à faire, unoriginal material, or instances of merger? At what point does copying become "substantial" and therefore unlawful? The legal standards vary from Circuit to Circuit, and have changed over time. They also vary medium to medium: assessing similarities becomes very different depending on whether one is considering music (melody, harmony, rhythm, instrumentation, etc.), or novels (plot, dialogue, setting, sequence, characters, etc.), or computer programs (as you saw in Computer Associates).

Consider the difference between the following tests for substantial similarity:

- The jury is asked to decide whether the "total concept and feel" of the original and allegedly infringing works is substantially similar.
- The jury is asked to focus exclusively on substantial similarities between *protected* materials.

How might these tests be over- or under-inclusive? (In practice, tests have evolved and overlapped over time, and courts have tried to fine-tune them so that they converge on a reasonable, fact-specific analysis of whether there has been appropriation sufficient to amount to infringement.)

Questions:

Apply the tests for substantial similarity to the following fact patterns. How do these come out under a "total concept and feel" test? How about a targeted comparison of only the protected material?

1.) Hallmark creates a romantic greeting card showing an original arrangement of a cute puppy with a bouquet of flowers and balloons under a rainbow with the superimposed text "i wuv you." American Greetings creates a card with an almost identical arrangement of its own cute puppy with flowers and balloons, and a generic rainbow that also reads "i wuv you."

2.) DJ JJ samples the catchy four-note hook from your song and includes it in the introduction to her song, which is otherwise entirely different from your work.

3.) A fan develops a South Park trivia game that contains multiple-choice questions about the key characters and events in all of the episodes to date, duplicating fragmentary details from the series in an entirely different (text-only) format.

4.) Revisit James's novel about Hamnet. Under which test is he most likely to win?

Subconscious Copying: One final wrinkle. Because copyright is a strict liability system, infringement may result even when one *subconsciously* copies another's work. In the words of Learned Hand: "Everything registers somewhere in our memories, and no one can tell what may evoke it. . . . The author's copyright is an absolute right to prevent others from copying his original collocation of words or notes, and does not depend upon the infringer's good faith. Once it appears that another has in fact used the copyright as the source of his production, he has invaded the author's rights. It is no excuse that in so doing his memory has played him a trick." *Fred Fisher, Inc. v. Dillingham* (S.D.N.Y. 1924); *see also Bright Tunes Music v. Harrisongs Music* (S.D.N.Y. 1976), *aff'd, ABKCO Music, Inc. v. Harrisongs Music, Ltd.* (2d Cir. 1983). Do you agree? What are the dangers of holding creators liable for subconscious copying? How about the dangers of limiting infringement to instances of intentional copying? How does this doctrine fit with the idea that independent creation—us both coming up with the same sonnet independently—is not copyright infringement?

5.) *"De minimis"* Copying

When is copying not copying? When it is *de minimis*. It is hornbook law that trivial or "*de minimis*" copying does not constitute actionable copyright infringement. This is a copyright specific embodiment of the general common law principle that "*de minimis non curat lex*"—the law does not concern itself with trifles. (Any first year law student could tell you that the law *frequently* concerns itself with trifles, but the principle is a general one.)

Before we begin: Please note that it's *de minimis*, not de minimUS, a common misspelling.

Many people assume that there is an accepted quantitative threshold for *de minimis* copying, and that—depending on the medium—any use of fewer than 10 seconds, 2 sentences, 6 notes, or the like is non-infringing. As you will see below, there is no bright-line rule, and the inquiry is much more complex and fact-specific.

Newton v. Diamond
388 F.3d 1189 (9th Cir. 2004)

SCHROEDER, Chief Judge.

[This case involved an intricate performance by an avant-garde flutist, and included much debate about what musical elements within that performance should be considered part of the *musical composition*, as opposed to the *sound recording* of that composition, because compositions and sound recordings are covered by two different copyrights. The copyright claim in this case only involved the composition because the defendants had properly licensed the sound recording. Therefore, the scope of the composition copyright mattered—the less the composition included, the more likely its copying would be *de minimis*. This extraneous discussion is not included in the excerpt below, which focuses on the application of the *de minimis* doctrine. Eds.]

. . .

Background and Procedural History

The plaintiff and appellant in this case, James W. Newton, is an accomplished avant-garde jazz flutist and composer. In 1978, he composed the song "Choir." . . .

The defendants and appellees include the members of the rap and hip-hop group Beastie Boys, and their business associates. In 1992, Beastie Boys obtained a license from ECM Records to use portions of the sound recording of "Choir" in various renditions of their song "Pass the Mic" in exchange for a one-time fee of $1000. Beastie Boys did not obtain a license from Newton to use the underlying composition.

The portion of the composition at issue consists of three notes, C–D flat–C, sung over a background C note played on the flute. . . . Beastie Boys digitally sampled the opening six seconds of Newton's sound recording of "Choir." . . .

Whether Defendants' Use was De Minimis

. . .

For an unauthorized use of a copyrighted work to be actionable, the use must be significant enough to constitute infringement. This means that even where the fact of copying is conceded, no legal consequences will follow from that fact unless the copying is substantial. The principle that trivial copying does not constitute actionable infringement has long been a part of copyright law. Indeed, as Judge Learned Hand observed over 80 years ago: "Even where there is some copying, that fact is not conclusive of infringement. Some copying is permitted. In addition to copying, it must be shown that this has been done to an unfair extent." This principle reflects the legal maxim, *de minimis non curat lex* (often rendered as, "the law does not concern itself with trifles").

A leading case on *de minimis* infringement in our circuit is *Fisher v. Dees*, where we observed that a use is *de minimis* only if the average audience would not recognize the appropriation. ("[A] taking is considered *de minimis* only if it is so meager and fragmentary that the average audience would not recognize the appropriation."). This observation reflects the relationship between the *de minimis* maxim and the general test for substantial similarity, which also looks to the response of the average audience, or ordinary observer, to determine whether a use is infringing. To say that a use is *de minimis* because no audience would recognize the appropriation is thus to say that the use is not sufficiently significant. . . .

The high degree of similarity between the works here (i.e., "Pass the Mic" and

"Choir"), but the limited scope of the copying, place Newton's claim for infringement into the class of cases that allege what Nimmer refers to as "fragmented literal similarity." Fragmented literal similarity exists where the defendant copies a portion of the plaintiff's work exactly or nearly exactly, without appropriating the work's overall essence or structure. Because the degree of similarity is high in such cases, the dispositive question is whether the copying goes to trivial or substantial elements. Substantiality is measured by considering the qualitative and quantitative significance of the copied portion in relation to the plaintiff's work as a whole. This focus on the sample's relation to the plaintiff's work as a whole embodies the fundamental question in any infringement action, as expressed more than 150 years ago by Justice Story: whether "so much is taken[] that the value of the original is sensibly diminished, or the labors of the original author are substantially to an injurious extent appropriated by another." Courts also focus on the relationship to the plaintiff's work because a contrary rule that measured the significance of the copied segment in the defendant's work would allow an unscrupulous defendant to copy large or qualitatively significant portions of another's work and escape liability by burying them beneath non-infringing material in the defendant's own work, even where the average audience might recognize the appropriation. Thus, as the district court properly concluded, the fact that Beastie Boys "looped" the sample throughout "Pass the Mic" is irrelevant in weighing the sample's qualitative and quantitative significance.

On the undisputed facts of this record, no reasonable juror could find the sampled portion of the composition to be a quantitatively or qualitatively significant portion of the composition as a whole. Quantitatively, the three-note sequence appears only once in Newton's composition. It is difficult to measure the precise relationship between this segment and the composition as a whole, because the score calls for between 180 and 270 seconds of improvisation. When played, however, the segment lasts six seconds and is roughly two percent of the four-and-a-half-minute "Choir" sound recording licensed by Beastie Boys. Qualitatively, this section of the composition is no more significant than any other section. Indeed, with the exception of two notes, the entirety of the scored portions of "Choir" consist of notes separated by whole and half-steps from their neighbors and is played with the same technique of singing and playing the flute simultaneously; the remainder of the composition calls for sections of improvisation that range between 90 and 180 seconds in length. . . .

Conclusion

. . . We hold that Beastie Boys' use of a brief segment of that composition, consisting of three notes separated by a half-step over a background C note, is not sufficient to sustain a claim for infringement of Newton's copyright in the composition "Choir". We affirm the district court's grant of summary judgment on the ground that Beastie Boys' use of the composition was de minimis and therefore not actionable.

GRABER, Circuit Judge, dissenting.
. . . [O]n the record before us, a finder of fact reasonably could find that Beastie Boys' use of the sampled material was not *de minimis*. Therefore, summary judgment is inappropriate.
. . . Even passages with relatively few notes may be qualitatively significant. The opening melody of Beethoven's Fifth Symphony is relatively simple and features only four notes, but it certainly is compositionally distinctive and recognizable. . . .
Because Newton has presented evidence establishing that reasonable ears differ over

the qualitative significance of the composition of the sampled material, summary judgment is inappropriate in this case. Newton should be allowed to present his claims of infringement to a factfinder. I therefore dissent from the majority's conclusion to the contrary.

• • • • • • • • • •

Notes:

We would like to be able to give you a succinct description of the *de minimis* doctrine but we cannot. Consider three possibilities.

1.) There is a certain level of copying—in either amount taken or impact produced on the market—that is just too little for the law to worry about. Yes, there is copying in the factual sense, identifiable copying, but the law will not concern itself with such a trifle—for reasons of judicial economy, or the preservation of a sphere of individual liberty, or protection of a certain degree of cultural reference, or all three.

2.) A related but separate point: The test for infringement is "substantial similarity." If I have taken only a little, then the works are not substantially similar, because most of yours went un-copied and most of mine is not taken from yours. But this now requires us to enter into the similarity analysis. We move away from the prospect of a bright line *de minimis* rule that stops the analysis before it even gets started. And the substantial similarity inquiry implicitly focuses us on the amount question (both as a quantitative and qualitative matter), not the market impact question—perhaps appropriately so, because impact can be considered under fair use.

3.) *De minimis* is conflated into some of the 4 factors in the fair use analysis, making it effectively a subdivision of fair use. This could be true *either* because very little was copied or because that copying had no real impact on the plaintiff.

Which of these represents the *de minimis* doctrine as the law currently stands? Elements of all three versions can be found.

The *Newton* case situates the *de minimis* analysis within the context of substantial similarity: "To say that a use is *de minimis* . . . is thus to say that the works are not substantially similar." But what about instances where there *is* substantial similarity, but the copying is nevertheless too insignificant or inconsequential to merit adjudication? What if I copy your photograph for my law school collage, but never show it to anyone? Should the principle that "the law does not concern itself with trifles" have a more general application to copyright claims, as it does in other areas of law? Consider this quote from Judge Pierre Leval in *Davis v. Gap, Inc.* (2d Cir. 2001):

> "The *de minimis* doctrine is rarely discussed in copyright opinions because suits are rarely brought over trivial instances of copying. Nonetheless, it is an important aspect of the law of copyright. Trivial copying is a significant part of modern life. Most honest citizens in the modern world frequently engage, without hesitation, in trivial copying that, but for the *de minimis* doctrine, would technically constitute a violation of law. We do not hesitate to make a photocopy of a letter from a friend to show to another friend, or of a favorite cartoon to post on the refrigerator. Parents in Central Park photograph their children perched on Jose de Creeft's Alice in Wonderland sculpture. We record television programs aired while we are out, so as to watch them at a more convenient hour. Waiters at a restaurant sing "Happy Birthday" at a patron's table. When we do such things, it is not that we are breaking the

law but unlikely to be sued given the high cost of litigation. Because of the *de minimis* doctrine, in trivial instances of copying, we are in fact not breaking the law. If a copyright owner were to sue the makers of trivial copies, judgment would be for the defendants. The case would be dismissed because trivial copying is not an infringement."

Notice that Judge Leval (whose own articles on fair use have been very influential) conflates multiple types of copying here, some of them clearly—as in the case of home taping—covered not by *de minimis* but fair use. Do Judge Leval's assertions about mundane copying—the cartoon on the fridge—still hold in the internet age, where trivial copying is both a more "significant part of modern life," and more detectable and preventable by copyright holders? Do they hold even more strongly? Think back to *MAI v. Peak*. Should that RAM copy have been deemed the type of "trivial" copying that Judge Leval is discussing?

In *Davis v. Gap*, the court did not ultimately find the *de minimis* doctrine applicable. There, The Gap had run an advertising campaign in which one of the models wore the plaintiff's "nonfunctional" eyeware jewelry. The court found that The Gap's use of the copyrighted eyeware was too noticeable to qualify for *de minimis* protection. Another famous case rejecting a *de minimis* argument was *Ringgold v. Black Entertainment TV* (2d Cir. 1997). There, a poster of a copyrighted artwork appeared in the background of a TV show in nine scenes ranging from 1.86 to 4.16 seconds and totaling 26.75 seconds. The court ruled that the use was not *de minimis*. Sound? What would you have to think, to think this a good result? What is the vision of copyright's role or reach?

As mentioned above, some courts have further confused the meaning of *de minimis* in the copyright context by applying it to yet another inquiry: fair use. Judge Leval's quote above suggests the same tendency. They tend to use the term "*de minimis*" when discussing either of two fair use factors that you will encounter in the upcoming readings: the "amount and substantiality" of the defendant's use and the degree of "market harm" to the plaintiff.

Bottom line, there may be coherence to the doctrine, but if there is . . . it is *de minimis*.

CHAPTER THIRTEEN

Limitations on Exclusive Rights: Fair Use

§ 107. Limitations on exclusive rights: Fair use

Notwithstanding the provisions of sections 106 and 106A, the fair use of a copyrighted work, including such use by reproduction in copies or phonorecords or by any other means specified by that section, for purposes such as criticism, comment, news reporting, teaching (including multiple copies for classroom use), scholarship, or research, is not an infringement of copyright. In determining whether the use made of a work in any particular case is a fair use the factors to be considered shall include—

> **(1) the purpose and character of the use, including whether such use is of a commercial nature or is for nonprofit education-al purposes;**
> **(2) the nature of the copyrighted work;**
> **(3) the amount and substantiality of the portion used in relation to the copyrighted work as a whole; and**
> **(4) the effect of the use upon the potential market for or value of the copyrighted work.**

The fact that a work is unpublished shall not itself bar a finding of fair use if such finding is made upon consideration of all the above factors.

Section 107 of the Copyright Act contains its most famous limitation—fair use—though not its most *important* limitation, which is clearly the idea-expression distinction. The idea/expression and fact/expression dichotomy says that while you cannot have the expression, the facts and ideas in any work are yours. But what if you *need* the expression? Or if you *should have* the expression in order to promote the progress, the foundational goal of copyright? That is where fair use comes in. We have said many times—in *SFAA v. USOC,* for example—that the most common defense of intellectual property against First Amendment claims is "you don't need the protected material! Paraphrase!" Fair use is for when the paraphrase will not work. (To use Justice Brennan's non intellectual property example, a T shirt saying 'I strongly resent the draft' would not be the same.) And fair use also covers those cases where the right to prevent copying should have no role in the first place.

But fair use is something else as well—it has become the duct tape of copyright, the thing courts turn to when something systemic needs to be fixed right now.

Congress (and the happenstance of technological development) continue to drop new technologies and forms of media into the bed marked "copyright," with scant guidance to judges about how they are to deal with the resulting chaos. We are not referring only to software. There is the reality of a global web that is spidered, *copied*, every day by search engines, and must be if it is to be navigable. We now live constantly with devices on which reading is also necessarily copying. We work and play with systems in which making a compatible widget—the generic razor blade of the digital era—requires decompiling copyrighted code. In each case, activities—reading, indexing, making compatible generic goods—that in an analog world did not implicate copyright at all, are suddenly within its sway. One way to deal with that process is the kind of Procrustean trimming and stretching we saw in *Lotus* or *Computer Associates*. Feel free to add the descriptions "inappropriately interventionist and policy driven," "responsibly focused on substance not form, with an eye to the constitutional goals of the system" or "working within the classic common law methods in a process of judicial evolution" to your account of what the judges did in those cases. We would go with the second two descriptions, but a reasonable case can be made for the first.

Yet sometimes redefining the subject matter criteria or the test for infringement is not enough. That is when fair use is called upon.

We do not mean to say that fair use is only important to deal with the *technological* transformations of copyright, though that will be one important theme of this chapter. Fair use also deals with the *speech* side of copyright—the places where "paraphrasing around" is not enough. It is the conjunction of these two themes from the class that causes us to concentrate so heavily on fair use—this is the place where these arguments are brought together, weighed and decided.

And so in this chapter we will read about whether you have a legal privilege (a right?) to videotape or DVR copyrighted TV shows for time-shifting purposes, and to decompile video games to make interoperable games. We will discuss the scanning of millions of books under copyright, without permission, in order to create the 'digital index of Alexandria' according to the defendants, or engage 'in the greatest act of illicit copying the world has ever known,' according to the plaintiffs. But we will also read about parodic rap versions of songs that the Supreme Court (wrongly) seems to think are about prostitution, and why Margaret Mitchell's estate thought they had the power to tell an African-American novelist that it would be breaking the law to retell *Gone With the Wind* from the slaves' perspective. We will even talk about reproducing sections of copyrighted books for educational purposes in coursepacks. We will meet again two of the "framings" we discussed in Chapter 1. As you might guess, one will be 'incentives for investment in creativity' versus 'promotion of competition and avoidance of monopoly in technological development.' But the other will be the classic 'speech versus property' divide. The readings and arguments from both Chapters 1 and 2 will be very relevant. It will turn out that cases developed within one of those frames can inform the other. Cases about Google image search draw on cases about rap parodies, and cases about appropriationist art draw on cases about technological transformation.

PROBLEM 13-1

Section 107 is short. We want you to bring out your best legislative parsing skills.

1.) Look at the clauses one by one. **What is the *textual* structure of § 107? For example, is it open-ended or closed? Does the first clause determine the analysis of the subsequent clauses, or is it mere legislative throat clearing? What roles do the examples play? The 4 factors? The examples and the factors in combination?**

2.) "The factors to be considered shall include. . . ." **Are they positive or negative? How can you tell? How is the judge to consider them?**

3.) Look at this clause—"whether such use is of a commercial nature or is for nonprofit educational purposes. . . ." Parse it. **Is there a difference between a use being commercial and a use "of a commercial nature"? Is *The New York Times*'**

report featuring unauthorized reproduction of Abu Ghraib prisoner-abuse pictures "commercial" because *The Times* is a for profit company? Is a professor at (for profit) Phoenix University who wants to copy an article for his class engaged in activities of a commercial nature? Or a (nonprofit) educational purpose? Something in between? And what does the Venn diagram of commercial and nonprofit educational purposes look like? Are the only nonprofit activities those that are also educational?

4.) Section 107 focuses on the nature of "the fair use." **What does that mean? What counts as a use for the purposes of the section? If I tell the copy shop to copy something for class, whose "use" should we look at? Mine or theirs? How can you tell?**

The first case we will read is a famous one: *Sony v. Universal*, which established the legality of home taping. *Sony* actually contains two very important contributions to copyright's interaction with technology, and the fair use portion is probably the less important of the two. It is in the discussion of the requirements of "contributory infringement" that *Sony* has had its biggest impact. Some casebooks separate the two portions of the case; but we think they make more sense when read together.

1.) Fair Use, Technology and Contributory Infringement

Sony Corp. of America v. Universal City Studios, Inc.
464 U.S. 417 (1984)

Justice STEVENS delivered the opinion of the Court.

Petitioners manufacture and sell home video tape recorders. Respondents own the copyrights on some of the television programs that are broadcast on the public airwaves. Some members of the general public use video tape recorders sold by petitioners to record some of these broadcasts, as well as a large number of other broadcasts. The question presented is whether the sale of petitioners' copying equipment to the general public violates any of the rights conferred upon respondents by the Copyright Act.

Respondents commenced this copyright infringement action against petitioners in the United States District Court for the Central District of California in 1976. Respondents alleged that some individuals had used Betamax video tape recorders (VTR's) to record some of respondents' copyrighted works which had been exhibited on commercially sponsored television and contended that these individuals had thereby infringed respondents' copyrights. Respondents further maintained that petitioners were liable for the copyright infringement allegedly committed by Betamax consumers because of petitioners' marketing of the Betamax VTR's.

Image from the Rush Forum discussion of video cassettes, available at http://www.therushforum.com/index.php?/topic/ 49589-the-early-days-of-video-cassettes/.

Respondents sought no relief against any Betamax consumer. Instead, they sought money damages and an equitable accounting of profits from petitioners, as well as an injunction against the manufacture and marketing of Betamax VTR's.

After a lengthy trial, the District Court denied respondents all the relief they sought and entered judgment for petitioners. The United States Court of Appeals for the Ninth Circuit reversed the District Court's judgment on respondent's copyright claim, holding petitioners liable for contributory infringement and ordering the District Court to fashion appropriate relief. We granted *certiorari*; since we had not completed our study of the case last Term, we ordered reargument. We now reverse.

An explanation of our rejection of respondents' unprecedented attempt to impose copyright liability upon the distributors of copying equipment requires a quite detailed recitation of the findings of the District Court. In summary, those findings reveal that the average member of the public uses a VTR principally to record a program he cannot view as it is being televised and then to watch it once at a later time. This practice, known as "time-shifting," enlarges the television viewing audience. For that reason, a significant amount of television programming may be used in this manner without objection from the owners of the copyrights on the programs. For the same reason, even the two respondents in this case, who do assert objections to time-shifting in this litigation, were unable to prove that the practice has impaired the commercial value of their copyrights or has created any likelihood of future harm. Given these findings, there is no basis in the Copyright Act upon which respondents can hold petitioners liable for distributing VTR's to the general public. The Court of Appeals' holding that respondents are entitled to enjoin the distribution of VTR's, to collect royalties on the sale of such equipment, or to obtain other relief, if affirmed, would enlarge the scope of respondents' statutory monopolies to encompass control over an article of commerce that is not the subject of copyright protection. Such an expansion of the copyright privilege is beyond the limits of the grants authorized by Congress.

I

The two respondents in this action, Universal Studios, Inc. and Walt Disney Productions, produce and hold the copyrights on a substantial number of motion pictures and other audiovisual works. In the current marketplace, they can exploit their rights in these works in a number of ways: by authorizing theatrical exhibitions, by licensing limited showings on cable and network television, by selling syndication rights for repeated airings on local television stations, and by marketing programs on prerecorded videotapes or videodiscs. Some works are suitable for exploitation through all of these avenues, while the market for other works is more limited. . . .

The respondents and Sony both conducted surveys of the way the Betamax machine was used by several hundred owners during a sample period in 1978. Although there were some differences in the surveys, they both showed that the primary use of the machine for most owners was "time-shifting,"—the practice of recording a program to view it once at a later time, and thereafter erasing it. Time-shifting enables viewers to see programs they otherwise would miss because they are not at home, are occupied with other tasks, or are viewing a program on another station at the time of a broadcast that they desire to watch. Both surveys also showed, however, that a substantial number of interviewees had accumulated libraries of tapes. Sony's survey indicated that over 80% of the interviewees watched at least as much regular television as they had before owning a Betamax. Respondents offered no evidence of decreased television viewing by Betamax owners.

Sony introduced considerable evidence describing television programs that could be copied without objection from any copyright holder, with special emphasis on sports, religious, and educational programming. For example, their survey indicated that 7.3% of all Betamax use is to record sports events, and representatives of professional baseball, football, basketball, and hockey testified that they had no objection to the recording of their televised events for home use.

Respondents offered opinion evidence concerning the future impact of the unrestricted sale of VTR's on the commercial value of their copyrights. The District Court found, however, that they had failed to prove any likelihood of future harm from the use of VTR's for time-shifting. . . .

The District Court concluded that noncommercial home use recording of material broadcast over the public airwaves was a fair use of copyrighted works and did not constitute copyright infringement. . . .

The Court of Appeals reversed the District Court's judgment on respondents' copyright claim. It did not set aside any of the District Court's findings of fact. Rather, it concluded as a matter of law that the home use of a VTR was not a fair use because it was not a "productive use." It therefore held that it was unnecessary for plaintiffs to prove any harm to the potential market for the copyrighted works, but then observed that it seemed clear that the cumulative effect of mass reproduction made possible by VTR's would tend to diminish the potential market for respondents' works. . . .

II

Article I, Sec. 8 of the Constitution provides that: "The Congress shall have Power . . . to Promote the Progress of Science and useful Arts, by securing for limited Times to Authors and Inventors the exclusive Right to their respective Writings and Discoveries."

The monopoly privileges that Congress may authorize are neither unlimited nor primarily designed to provide a special private benefit. Rather, the limited grant is a means by which an important public purpose may be achieved. It is intended to motivate the creative activity of authors and inventors by the provision of a special reward, and to allow the public access to the products of their genius after the limited period of exclusive control has expired.

> "The copyright law, like the patent statute, makes reward to the owner a secondary consideration. In *Fox Film Corp. v. Doyal*, Chief Justice Hughes spoke as follows respecting the copyright monopoly granted by Congress, 'The sole interest of the United States and the primary object in conferring the monopoly lie in the general benefits derived by the public from the labors of authors.' It is said that reward to the author or artist serves to induce release to the public of the products of his creative genius." *United States v. Paramount Pictures* (1948).

As the text of the Constitution makes plain, it is Congress that has been assigned the task of defining the scope of the limited monopoly that should be granted to authors or to inventors in order to give the public appropriate access to their work product. Because this task involves a difficult balance between the interests of authors and inventors in the control and exploitation of their writings and discoveries on the one hand, and society's competing interest in the free flow of ideas, information, and commerce on the other hand, our patent and copyright statutes have been amended repeatedly.

From its beginning, the law of copyright has developed in response to significant changes in technology.[11] Indeed, it was the invention of a new form of copying equipment—the printing press—that gave rise to the original need for copyright protection.[12] Repeatedly, as new developments have occurred in this country, it has been the Congress that has fashioned the new rules that new technology made necessary. Thus, long before the enactment of the Copyright Act of 1909, it was settled that the protection given to copyrights is wholly statutory. The remedies for infringement "are only those prescribed by Congress."

The judiciary's reluctance to expand the protections afforded by the copyright without explicit legislative guidance is a recurring theme. Sound policy, as well as history, supports our consistent deference to Congress when major technological innovations alter the market for copyrighted materials. Congress has the constitutional authority and the institutional ability to accommodate fully the varied permutations of competing interests that are inevitably implicated by such new technology.

In a case like this, in which Congress has not plainly marked our course, we must be circumspect in construing the scope of rights created by a legislative enactment which never contemplated such a calculus of interests. In doing so, we are guided by Justice Stewart's exposition of the correct approach to ambiguities in the law of copyright:

"The limited scope of the copyright holder's statutory monopoly, like the limited copyright duration required by the Constitution, reflects a balance of competing claims upon the public interest: Creative work is to be encouraged and rewarded, but private motivation must ultimately serve the cause of promoting broad public availability of literature, music, and the other arts. The immediate effect of our copyright law is to secure a fair return for an 'author's' creative labor. But the ultimate aim is, by this incentive, to stimulate artistic creativity for the general public good. 'The sole interest of the United States and the primary object in conferring the monopoly,' this Court has said, 'lie in the general benefits derived by the public from the labors of authors.' *Fox Film Corp. v. Doyal* (1932). When technological change has rendered its literal terms ambiguous, the Copyright Act must be construed in light of this basic purpose." *Twentieth Century Music Corp. v. Aiken* (1975).

Copyright protection "subsists . . . in original works of authorship fixed in any tangible medium of expression." This protection has never accorded the copyright owner complete control over all possible uses of his work.[13] Rather, the Copyright Act grants

---

[11] Thus, for example, the development and marketing of player pianos and perforated roles of music, preceded the enactment of the Copyright Act of 1909; innovations in copying techniques gave rise to the statutory exemption for library copying embodied in § 108 of the 1976 revision of the Copyright law; the development of the technology that made it possible to retransmit television programs by cable or by microwave systems, prompted the enactment of the complex provisions set forth in 17 U.S.C. § 111(d)(2)(B) and § 111(d)(5) after years of detailed congressional study. . . .

[12] "Copyright protection became necessary with the invention of the printing press and had its early beginnings in the British censorship laws. The fortunes of the law of copyright have always been closely connected with freedom of expression, on the one hand, and with technological improvements in means of dissemination, on the other. Successive ages have drawn different balances among the interest of the writer in the control and exploitation of his intellectual property, the related interest of the publisher, and the competing interest of society in the untrammeled dissemination of ideas." Foreword to B. Kaplan, An Unhurried View of Copyright vii–viii (1967).

[13] . . . While the law has never recognized an author's right to absolute control of his work, the natural tendency of legal rights to express themselves in absolute terms to the exclusion of all else is particularly pronounced in the history of the constitutionally sanctioned monopolies of the copyright and the patent.

the copyright holder "exclusive" rights to use and to authorize the use of his work in five qualified ways, including reproduction of the copyrighted work in copies. All reproductions of the work, however, are not within the exclusive domain of the copyright owner; some are in the public domain. Any individual may reproduce a copyrighted work for a "fair use;" the copyright owner does not possess the exclusive right to such a use.

The two respondents in this case do not seek relief against the Betamax users who have allegedly infringed their copyrights. Moreover, this is not a class action on behalf of all copyright owners who license their works for television broadcast, and respondents have no right to invoke whatever rights other copyright holders may have to bring infringement actions based on Betamax copying of their works. As was made clear by their own evidence, the copying of the respondents' programs represents a small portion of the total use of VTR's. It is, however, the taping of respondents' own copyrighted programs that provides them with standing to charge Sony with contributory infringement. To prevail, they have the burden of proving that users of the Betamax have infringed their copyrights and that Sony should be held responsible for that infringement.

III

The Copyright Act does not expressly render anyone liable for infringement committed by another. In contrast, the Patent Act expressly brands anyone who "actively induces infringement of a patent" as an infringer, and further imposes liability on certain individuals labeled "contributory" infringers. The absence of such express language in the copyright statute does not preclude the imposition of liability for copyright infringements on certain parties who have not themselves engaged in the infringing activity.[17] For vicarious liability is imposed in virtually all areas of the law, and the concept of contributory infringement is merely a species of the broader problem of identifying the circumstances in which it is just to hold one individual accountable for the actions of another.

Such circumstances were plainly present in *Kalem Co. v. Harper Brothers* (1911), the copyright decision of this Court on which respondents place their principal reliance. In *Kalem,* the Court held that the producer of an unauthorized film dramatization of the copyrighted book *Ben Hur* was liable for his sale of the motion picture to jobbers, who in turn arranged for the commercial exhibition of the film. Justice Holmes, writing for the Court, explained:

> "The defendant not only expected but invoked by advertisement the use of its films for dramatic reproduction of the story. That was the most conspicuous purpose for which they could be used, and the one for which especially they were made. If the defendant did not contribute to the infringement it is impossible to do so except by taking part in the final act. It is liable on principles recognized in every part of the law."

---

[17] As the District Court correctly observed, however, "the lines between direct infringement, contributory infringement, and vicarious liability are not clearly drawn. . . ." The lack of clarity in this area may, in part, be attributable to the fact that an infringer is not merely one who uses a work without authorization by the copyright owner, but also one who authorizes the use of a copyrighted work without actual authority from the copyright owner.

We note the parties' statements that the questions of petitioners' liability under the "doctrines" of "direct infringement" and "vicarious liability" are not nominally before this Court. We also observe, however, that reasoned analysis of respondents' unprecedented contributory infringement claim necessarily entails consideration of arguments and case law which may also be forwarded under the other labels, and indeed the parties to a large extent rely upon such arguments and authority in support of their respective positions on the issue of contributory infringement.

The use for which the item sold in *Kalem* had been "especially" made was, of course, to display the performance that had already been recorded upon it. The producer had personally appropriated the copyright owner's protected work and, as the owner of the tangible medium of expression upon which the protected work was recorded, authorized that use by his sale of the film to jobbers. But that use of the film was not his to authorize: the copyright owner possessed the exclusive right to authorize public performances of his work. Further, the producer personally advertised the unauthorized public performances, dispelling any possible doubt as to the use of the film which he had authorized.

Respondents argue that *Kalem* stands for the proposition that supplying the "means" to accomplish an infringing activity and encouraging that activity through advertisement are sufficient to establish liability for copyright infringement. This argument rests on a gross generalization that cannot withstand scrutiny. The producer in *Kalem* did not merely provide the "means" to accomplish an infringing activity; the producer supplied the work itself, albeit in a new medium of expression. Petitioners in the instant case do not supply Betamax consumers with respondents' works; respondents do. Petitioners supply a piece of equipment that is generally capable of copying the entire range of programs that may be televised: those that are uncopyrighted, those that are copyrighted but may be copied without objection from the copyright holder, and those that the copyright holder would prefer not to have copied. The Betamax can be used to make authorized or unauthorized uses of copyrighted works, but the range of its potential use is much broader than the particular infringing use of the film *Ben Hur* involved in *Kalem*. *Kalem* does not support respondents' novel theory of liability.

Justice Holmes stated that the producer had "contributed" to the infringement of the copyright, and the label "contributory infringement" has been applied in a number of lower court copyright cases involving an ongoing relationship between the direct infringer and the contributory infringer at the time the infringing conduct occurred. In such cases, as in other situations in which the imposition of vicarious liability is manifestly just, the "contributory" infringer was in a position to control the use of copyrighted works by others and had authorized the use without permission from the copyright owner.[18] This case, however, plainly does not fall in that category. The only contact between Sony and the users of the Betamax that is disclosed by this record occurred at the moment of sale. The District Court expressly found that "no employee of Sony, Sonam or DDBI had either direct involvement with the allegedly infringing activity or direct contact with purchasers of Betamax who recorded copyrighted works off-the-air." And it further found that "there was no evidence that any of the copies made by Griffiths or the other individual witnesses in this suit were influenced or encouraged by [Sony's] advertisements."

If vicarious liability is to be imposed on petitioners in this case, it must rest on the fact that they have sold equipment with constructive knowledge of the fact that their customers may use that equipment to make unauthorized copies of copyrighted material. There is no precedent in the law of copyright for the imposition of vicarious liability on such a theory. The closest analogy is provided by the patent law cases to which it is

---

[18] The so-called "dance hall cases," *Famous Music Corp. v. Bay State Harness Horse Racing and Breeding Ass'n* (1st Cir. 1977) (racetrack retained infringer to supply music to paying customers); *KECA MUSIC, Inc. v. Dingus McGee's Co.* (W.D. Mo. 1977) (cocktail lounge hired musicians to supply music to paying customers); *Dreamland Ball Room v. Shapiro, Bernstein & Co.* (7th Cir. 1929) (dance hall hired orchestra to supply music to paying customers) are often contrasted with the so-called landlord-tenant cases, in which landlords who leased premises to a direct infringer for a fixed rental and did not participate directly in any infringing activity were found not to be liable for contributory infringement. . . .

appropriate to refer because of the historic kinship between patent law and copyright law.[19]

In the Patent Code both the concept of infringement and the concept of contributory infringement are expressly defined by statute. The prohibition against contributory infringement is confined to the knowing sale of a component especially made for use in connection with a particular patent. There is no suggestion in the statute that one patentee may object to the sale of a product that might be used in connection with other patents. Moreover, the Act expressly provides that the sale of a "staple article or commodity of commerce suitable for substantial noninfringing use" is not contributory infringement. 35 U.S.C. § 271(c).

When a charge of contributory infringement is predicated entirely on the sale of an article of commerce that is used by the purchaser to infringe a patent, the public interest in access to that article of commerce is necessarily implicated. A finding of contributory infringement does not, of course, remove the article from the market altogether; it does, however, give the patentee effective control over the sale of that item. Indeed, a finding of contributory infringement is normally the functional equivalent of holding that the disputed article is within the monopoly granted to the patentee.[21]

For that reason, in contributory infringement cases arising under the patent laws the Court has always recognized the critical importance of not allowing the patentee to extend his monopoly beyond the limits of his specific grant. These cases deny the patentee any right to control the distribution of unpatented articles unless they are "unsuited for any commercial noninfringing use." *Dawson Chemical Co. v. Rohm & Hass Co.* (1980). . . .

We recognize there are substantial differences between the patent and copyright laws. But in both areas the contributory infringement doctrine is grounded on the recognition that adequate protection of a monopoly may require the courts to look beyond actual duplication of a device or publication to the products or activities that make such duplication possible. The staple article of commerce doctrine must strike a balance between a copyright holder's legitimate demand for effective—not merely symbolic—protection of the statutory monopoly, and the rights of others freely to engage in substantially unrelated areas of commerce. Accordingly, the sale of copying equipment,

---

[19] The two areas of the law, naturally, are not identical twins, and we exercise the caution which we have expressed in the past in applying doctrine formulated in one area to the other.

We have consistently rejected the proposition that a similar kinship exists between copyright law and trademark law, and in the process of doing so have recognized the basic similarities between copyrights and patents. Given the fundamental differences between copyright law and trademark law, in this copyright case we do not look to the standard for contributory infringement set forth in *Inwood Laboratories, Inc. v. Ives Laboratories, Inc.* (1982), which was crafted for application in trademark cases. There we observed that a manufacturer or distributor could be held liable to the owner of a trademark if it intentionally induced a merchant down the chain of distribution to pass off its product as that of the trademark owner's or if it continued to supply a product which could readily be passed off to a particular merchant whom it knew was mislabeling the product with the trademark owner's mark. If *Inwood*'s narrow standard for contributory trademark infringement governed here, respondents' claim of contributory infringement would merit little discussion. Sony certainly does not "intentionally induc[e]" its customers to make infringing uses of respondents' copyrights, nor does it supply its products to identified individuals known by it to be engaging in continuing infringement of respondents' copyrights.

[21] It seems extraordinary to suggest that the Copyright Act confers upon all copyright owners collectively, much less the two respondents in this case, the exclusive right to distribute VTR's simply because they may be used to infringe copyrights. That, however, is the logical implication of their claim. The request for an injunction below indicates that respondents seek, in effect, to declare VTR's contraband. Their suggestion in this Court that a continuing royalty pursuant to a judicially created compulsory license would be an acceptable remedy merely indicates that respondents, for their part, would be willing to license their claimed monopoly interest in VTR's to petitioners in return for a royalty.

like the sale of other articles of commerce, does not constitute contributory infringement if the product is widely used for legitimate, unobjectionable purposes. Indeed, it need merely be capable of substantial noninfringing uses.

IV

The question is thus whether the Betamax is capable of commercially significant noninfringing uses. In order to resolve that question, we need not explore *all* the different potential uses of the machine and determine whether or not they would constitute infringement. Rather, we need only consider whether on the basis of the facts as found by the district court a significant number of them would be non-infringing. Moreover, in order to resolve this case we need not give precise content to the question of how much use is commercially significant. For one potential use of the Betamax plainly satisfies this standard, however it is understood: private, noncommercial time-shifting in the home. It does so both (A) because respondents have no right to prevent other copyright holders from authorizing it for their programs, and (B) because the District Court's factual findings reveal that even the unauthorized home time-shifting of respondents' programs is legitimate fair use.

A. Authorized Time Shifting

Each of the respondents owns a large inventory of valuable copyrights, but in the total spectrum of television programming their combined market share is small. The exact percentage is not specified, but it is well below 10%. If they were to prevail, the outcome of this litigation would have a significant impact on both the producers and the viewers of the remaining 90% of the programming in the Nation. No doubt, many other producers share respondents' concern about the possible consequences of unrestricted copying. Nevertheless the findings of the District Court make it clear that time-shifting may enlarge the total viewing audience and that many producers are willing to allow private time-shifting to continue, at least for an experimental time period.

The District Court found:

> "Even if it were deemed that home-use recording of copyrighted material constituted infringement, the Betamax could still legally be used to record noncopyrighted material or material whose owners consented to the copying. An injunction would deprive the public of the ability to use the Betamax for this noninfringing off-the-air recording.

> "Defendants introduced considerable testimony at trial about the potential for such copying of sports, religious, educational and other programming. This included testimony from representatives of the Offices of the Commissioners of the National Football, Basketball, Baseball and Hockey Leagues and Associations, the Executive Director of National Religious Broadcasters and various educational communications agencies. Plaintiffs attack the weight of the testimony offered and also contend that an injunction is warranted because infringing uses outweigh noninfringing uses."

> "Whatever the future percentage of legal versus illegal home-use recording might be, an injunction which seeks to deprive the public of the very tool or article of commerce capable of some noninfringing use would be an extremely harsh remedy, as well as one unprecedented in copyright law."

Although the District Court made these statements in the context of considering the propriety of injunctive relief, the statements constitute a finding that the evidence concerning "sports, religious, educational, and other programming" was sufficient to establish a significant quantity of broadcasting whose copying is now authorized, and a significant potential for future authorized copying. That finding is amply supported by the record. In addition to the religious and sports officials identified explicitly by the District Court, two items in the record deserve specific mention.

First is the testimony of John Kenaston, the station manager of Channel 58, an educational station in Los Angeles affiliated with the Public Broadcasting Service. He explained and authenticated the station's published guide to its programs. For each program, the guide tells whether unlimited home taping is authorized, home taping is authorized subject to certain restrictions (such as erasure within seven days), or home taping is not authorized at all. The Spring 1978 edition of the guide described 107 programs. Sixty-two of those programs or 58% authorize some home taping. Twenty-one of them or almost 20% authorize unrestricted home taping.

Second is the testimony of Fred Rogers, president of the corporation that produces and owns the copyright on *Mr. Rogers' Neighborhood*. The program is carried by more public television stations than any other program. Its audience numbers over 3,000,000 families a day. He testified that he had absolutely no objection to home taping for noncommercial use and expressed the opinion that it is a real service to families to be able to record children's programs and to show them at appropriate times.[27]

If there are millions of owners of VTR's who make copies of televised sports events, religious broadcasts, and educational programs such as *Mister Rogers' Neighborhood*, and if the proprietors of those programs welcome the practice, the business of supplying the equipment that makes such copying feasible should not be stifled simply because the equipment is used by some individuals to make unauthorized reproductions of respondents' works. The respondents do not represent a class composed of all copyright holders. Yet a finding of contributory infringement would inevitably frustrate the interests of broadcasters in reaching the portion of their audience that is available only through time-shifting.

Of course, the fact that other copyright holders may welcome the practice of time-shifting does not mean that respondents should be deemed to have granted a license to copy their programs. Third party conduct would be wholly irrelevant in an action for direct infringement of respondents' copyrights. But in an action for *contributory* infringement against the seller of copying equipment, the copyright holder may not prevail unless the relief that he seeks affects only his programs, or unless he speaks for virtually all copyright holders with an interest in the outcome. In this case, the record makes it perfectly clear that there are many important producers of national and local television programs who find nothing objectionable about the enlargement in the size of the television audience that results from the practice of time-shifting for private home

---

[27] "Some public stations, as well as commercial stations, program the 'Neighborhood' at hours when some children cannot use it. I think that it's a real service to families to be able to record such programs and show them at appropriate times. I have always felt that with the advent of all of this new technology that allows people to tape the 'Neighborhood' off-the-air, and I'm speaking for the 'Neighborhood' because that's what I produce, that they then become much more active in the programming of their family's television life. Very frankly, I am opposed to people being programmed by others. My whole approach in broadcasting has always been 'You are an important person just the way you are. You can make healthy decisions.' Maybe I'm going on too long, but I just feel that anything that allows a person to be more active in the control of his or her life, in a healthy way, is important."

use.[28] The seller of the equipment that expands those producers' audiences cannot be a contributory infringer if, as is true in this case, it has had no direct involvement with any infringing activity.

B. Unauthorized Time-Shifting

Even unauthorized uses of a copyrighted work are not necessarily infringing. An unlicensed use of the copyright is not an infringement unless it conflicts with one of the specific exclusive rights conferred by the copyright statute. Moreover, the definition of exclusive rights in § 106 of the present Act is prefaced by the words "subject to sections 107 through 118." Those sections describe a variety of uses of copyrighted material that "are not infringements of copyright notwithstanding the provisions of § 106." The most pertinent in this case is § 107, the legislative endorsement of the doctrine of "fair use."

That section identifies various factors that enable a Court to apply an "equitable rule of reason" analysis to particular claims of infringement. Although not conclusive, the first factor requires that "the commercial or nonprofit character of an activity" be weighed in any fair use decision. If the Betamax were used to make copies for a commercial or profit-making purpose, such use would presumptively be unfair. The contrary presumption is appropriate here, however, because the District Court's findings plainly establish that time-shifting for private home use must be characterized as a noncommercial, nonprofit activity. Moreover, when one considers the nature of a televised copyrighted audiovisual work, see 17 U.S.C. § 107(2), and that timeshifting merely enables a viewer to see such a work which he had been invited to witness in its entirety free of charge, the fact that the entire work is reproduced, § 107(3), does not have its ordinary effect of militating against a finding of fair use.[33]

---

[28] . . . In the context of television programming, some producers evidently believe that permitting home viewers to make copies of their works off the air actually enhances the value of their copyrights. Irrespective of their reasons for authorizing the practice, they do so, and in significant enough numbers to create a substantial market for a non-infringing use of the Sony VTR's. No one could dispute the legitimacy of that market if the producers had authorized home taping of their programs in exchange for a license fee paid directly by the home user. The legitimacy of that market is not compromised simply because these producers have authorized home taping of their programs without demanding a fee from the home user. The copyright law does not require a copyright owner to charge a fee for the use of his works, and as this record clearly demonstrates, the owner of a copyright may well have economic or noneconomic reasons for permitting certain kinds of copying to occur without receiving direct compensation from the copier. It is not the role of the courts to tell copyright holders the best way for them to exploit their copyrights: even if respondents' competitors were ill-advised in authorizing home videotaping, that would not change the fact that they have created a substantial market for a paradigmatic non-infringing use of petitioners' product.

[33] It has been suggested that "consumptive uses of copyrights by home VTR users are commercial even if the consumer does not sell the homemade tape because the consumer will not buy tapes separately sold by the copyrightholder." Home Recording of Copyrighted Works: Hearing before Subcommittee on Courts, Civil Liberties and the Administration of Justice of the House Committee on the Judiciary, 97th Congress, 2d Session, pt. 2, p. 1250 (1982) (memorandum of Prof. Laurence H. Tribe). Furthermore, "[t]he error in excusing such theft as noncommercial," we are told, "can be seen by simple analogy: jewel theft is not converted into a noncommercial veniality if stolen jewels are simply worn rather than sold." The premise and the analogy are indeed simple, but they add nothing to the argument. The use to which stolen jewelry is put is quite irrelevant in determining whether depriving its true owner of his present possessory interest in it is venial; because of the nature of the item and the true owner's interests in physical possession of it, the law finds the taking objectionable even if the thief does not use the item at all. Theft of a particular item of personal property of course may have commercial significance, for the thief deprives the owner of his right to sell that particular item to any individual. Timeshifting does not even remotely entail comparable consequences to the copyright owner. Moreover, the timeshifter no more steals the program by watching it once than does the live viewer, and the live viewer is no more likely to buy pre-recorded videotapes than is the

This is not, however, the end of the inquiry because Congress has also directed us to consider "the effect of the use upon the potential market for or value of the copyrighted work." § 107(4). The purpose of copyright is to create incentives for creative effort. Even copying for noncommercial purposes may impair the copyright holder's ability to obtain the rewards that Congress intended him to have. But a use that has no demonstrable effect upon the potential market for, or the value of, the copyrighted work need not be prohibited in order to protect the author's incentive to create. The prohibition of such noncommercial uses would merely inhibit access to ideas without any countervailing benefit.

Thus, although every commercial use of copyrighted material is presumptively an unfair exploitation of the monopoly privilege that belongs to the owner of the copyright, noncommercial uses are a different matter. A challenge to a noncommercial use of a copyrighted work requires proof either that the particular use is harmful, or that if it should become widespread, it would adversely affect the potential market for the copyrighted work. Actual present harm need not be shown; such a requirement would leave the copyright holder with no defense against predictable damage. Nor is it necessary to show with certainty that future harm will result. What is necessary is a showing by a preponderance of the evidence that *some* meaningful likelihood of future harm exists. If the intended use is for commercial gain, that likelihood may be presumed. But if it is for a noncommercial purpose, the likelihood must be demonstrated.

In this case, respondents failed to carry their burden with regard to home time-shifting. . . .

The District Court's conclusions are buttressed by the fact that to the extent time-shifting expands public access to freely broadcast television programs, it yields societal benefits. Earlier this year, in *Community Television of Southern California v. Gottfried*, we acknowledged the public interest in making television broadcasting more available. Concededly, that interest is not unlimited. But it supports an interpretation of the concept of "fair use" that requires the copyright holder to demonstrate some likelihood of harm before he may condemn a private act of time-shifting as a violation of federal law.

When these factors are all weighed in the "equitable rule of reason" balance, we must conclude that this record amply supports the District Court's conclusion that home time-shifting is fair use. In light of the findings of the District Court regarding the state of the empirical data, it is clear that the Court of Appeals erred in holding that the statute as presently written bars such conduct.[40]

---

timeshifter. Indeed, no live viewer would buy a pre-recorded videotape if he did not have access to a VTR.

[40] The Court of Appeals chose not to engage in any "equitable rule of reason" analysis in this case. Instead, it assumed that the category of "fair use" is rigidly circumscribed by a requirement that every such use must be "productive." It therefore concluded that copying a television program merely to enable the viewer to receive information or entertainment that he would otherwise miss because of a personal scheduling conflict could never be fair use. That understanding of "fair use" was erroneous.

Congress has plainly instructed us that fair use analysis calls for a sensitive balancing of interests. The distinction between "productive" and "unproductive" uses may be helpful in calibrating the balance, but it cannot be wholly determinative. Although copying to promote a scholarly endeavor certainly has a stronger claim to fair use than copying to avoid interrupting a poker game, the question is not simply two-dimensional. For one thing, it is not true that all copyrights are fungible. Some copyrights govern material with broad potential secondary markets. Such material may well have a broader claim to protection because of the greater potential for commercial harm. Copying a news broadcast may have a stronger claim to fair use than copying a motion picture. And, of course, not all uses are fungible. Copying for commercial gain has a much weaker claim to fair use than copying for personal enrichment. But the notion of social "productivity" cannot be a complete answer to this analysis. A teacher who copies to prepare lecture notes is clearly productive. But so is a teacher who copies for the sake of broadening his personal understanding of his specialty. Or a

In summary, the record and findings of the District Court lead us to two conclusions. First, Sony demonstrated a significant likelihood that substantial numbers of copyright holders who license their works for broadcast on free television would not object to having their broadcasts time-shifted by private viewers. And second, respondents failed to demonstrate that time-shifting would cause any likelihood of nonminimal harm to the potential market for, or the value of, their copyrighted works. The Betamax is, therefore, capable of substantial noninfringing uses. Sony's sale of such equipment to the general public does not constitute contributory infringement of respondent's copyrights.

V

> "The direction of Art. I is that Congress shall have the power to promote the progress of science and the useful arts. When, as here, the Constitution is permissive, the sign of how far Congress has chosen to go can come only from Congress." *Deepsouth Packing Co. v. Laitram Corp.* (1972).

One may search the Copyright Act in vain for any sign that the elected representatives of the millions of people who watch television every day have made it unlawful to copy a program for later viewing at home, or have enacted a flat prohibition against the sale of machines that make such copying possible.

It may well be that Congress will take a fresh look at this new technology, just as it so often has examined other innovations in the past. But it is not our job to apply laws that have not yet been written. Applying the copyright statute, as it now reads, to the facts as they have been developed in this case, the judgment of the Court of Appeals must be reversed.

It is so ordered.

Justice BLACKMUN, with whom Justice MARSHALL, Justice POWELL, and Justice REHNQUIST join, dissenting.

... IV
A

... The purpose of copyright protection, in the words of the Constitution, is to "promote the Progress of Science and useful Arts." Copyright is based on the belief that by granting authors the exclusive rights to reproduce their works, they are given an incentive to create, and that "encouragement of individual effort by personal gain is the best way to advance public welfare through the talents of authors and inventors in 'Science and the useful Arts.'" *Mazer v. Stein* (1954). The monopoly created by copyright thus rewards the individual author in order to benefit the public.

---

legislator who copies for the sake of broadening her understanding of what her constituents are watching; or a constituent who copies a news program to help make a decision on how to vote.

 Making a copy of a copyrighted work for the convenience of a blind person is expressly identified by the House Committee Report as an example of fair use, with no suggestion that anything more than a purpose to entertain or to inform need motivate the copying. In a hospital setting, using a VTR to enable a patient to see programs he would otherwise miss has no productive purpose other than contributing to the psychological well-being of the patient. Virtually any time-shifting that increases viewer access to television programming may result in a comparable benefit. The statutory language does not identify any dichotomy between productive and nonproductive time-shifting, but does require consideration of the economic consequences of copying.

There are situations, nevertheless, in which strict enforcement of this monopoly would inhibit the very "Progress of Science and useful Arts" that copyright is intended to promote. An obvious example is the researcher or scholar whose own work depends on the ability to refer to and to quote the work of prior scholars. Obviously, no author could create a new work if he were first required to repeat the research of every author who had gone before him. The scholar, like the ordinary user, of course could be left to bargain with each copyright owner for permission to quote from or refer to prior works. But there is a crucial difference between the scholar and the ordinary user. When the ordinary user decides that the owner's price is too high, and forgoes use of the work, only the individual is the loser. When the scholar forgoes the use of a prior work, not only does his own work suffer, but the public is deprived of his contribution to knowledge. The scholar's work, in other words, produces external benefits from which everyone profits. In such a case, the fair use doctrine acts as a form of subsidy—albeit at the first author's expense—to permit the second author to make limited use of the first author's work for the public good.

A similar subsidy may be appropriate in a range of areas other than pure scholarship. The situations in which fair use is most commonly recognized are listed in § 107 itself; fair use may be found when a work is used "for purposes such as criticism, comment, news reporting, teaching, . . . scholarship, or research." The House and Senate Reports expand on this list somewhat, and other examples may be found in the case law. Each of these uses, however, reflects a common theme: each is a productive use, resulting in some added benefit to the public beyond that produced by the first author's work. The fair use doctrine, in other words, permits works to be used for "socially laudable purposes." See *Copyright Office, Briefing Papers on Current Issues*, reprinted in 1975 House Hearings 2051, 2055. I am aware of no case in which the reproduction of a copyrighted work for the sole benefit of the user has been held to be fair use.

I do not suggest, of course, that every productive use is a fair use. A finding of fair use still must depend on the facts of the individual case, and on whether, under the circumstances, it is reasonable to expect the user to bargain with the copyright owner for use of the work. The fair use doctrine must strike a balance between the dual risks created by the copyright system: on the one hand, that depriving authors of their monopoly will reduce their incentive to create, and, on the other, that granting authors a complete monopoly will reduce the creative ability of others. The inquiry is necessarily a flexible one, and the endless variety of situations that may arise precludes the formulation of exact rules. But when a user reproduces an entire work and uses it for its original purpose, with no added benefit to the public, the doctrine of fair use usually does not apply. There is then no need whatsoever to provide the ordinary user with a fair use subsidy at the author's expense.

The making of a videotape recording for home viewing is an ordinary rather than a productive use of the Studios' copyrighted works. The District Court found that "Betamax owners use the copy for the same purpose as the original. They add nothing of their own." Although applying the fair use doctrine to home VTR recording, as Sony argues, may increase public access to material broadcast free over the public airwaves, I think Sony's argument misconceives the nature of copyright. Copyright gives the author a right to limit or even to cut off access to his work. A VTR recording creates no public benefit sufficient to justify limiting this right. Nor is this right extinguished by the copyright owner's choice to make the work available over the airwaves. Section 106 of the 1976 Act grants the copyright owner the exclusive right to control the performance and the reproduction of his work, and the fact that he has licensed a single television performance is really irrelevant to the existence of his right to control its reproduction. Although a television broadcast may be free to the viewer, this fact is equally irrelevant; a book borrowed from the public library may not be copied any more freely than a book that is purchased.

It may be tempting, as, in my view, the Court today is tempted, to stretch the doctrine of fair use so as to permit unfettered use of this new technology in order to increase access to television programming. But such an extension risks eroding the very basis of copyright law, by depriving authors of control over their works and consequently of their incentive to create. Even in the context of highly productive educational uses, Congress has avoided this temptation; in passing the 1976 Act, Congress made it clear that off-the-air videotaping was to be permitted only in very limited situations. And, the Senate Report adds, "[t]he committee does not intend to suggest . . . that off-the-air recording for convenience would under any circumstances, be considered 'fair use.'" I cannot disregard these admonitions. . . .

Questions:

1.) *Sony* is the first and perhaps the most important modern decision on secondary copyright liability. What requirements does it lay down for the imposition of such liability on a manufacturer of a device? Under that rule, was the fair use part of the holding necessary? Even if the court had held that home taping was *not* fair use, would *Sony* have been found liable?

2.) Why do you think that internet copyright debates have focused extensively on contributory or secondary types of infringement, rather than on the illicit copying by the direct infringer?

3.) Justice Blackmun thinks that the Court is stretching fair use to "increase access to television programming." Do you think that is the majority's main goal? What are they concerned about?

4.) The dissenting Justices stress a particular vision of fair use—one built around "productive use." In this vision, the second comer uses the original copyrighted expression to create something new—a critical book review, for example, or a scholarly discussion. Precisely because of the productive nature of the second use, we know that the constitutional purpose of "promoting the progress" is being furthered. Authors are standing on the shoulders of other authors—not merely passively receiving their works, but actively building something out of them. Viewed through this lens, the activity of a bunch of couch potatoes eating Doritos while watching reruns of *The Dukes of Hazzard* does not seem particularly compelling as a fair use. Through the eyes of the majority, though, the activity that is going on here looks very different. There is productivity and innovation involved, activities that should not be stifled by the copyright holder. Who is doing the innovating? Is the innovation involved in "the fair use" analyzed under § 107 or is it that copyright's reach needs to be trimmed lest it pull in and exert control over other activities? Do you agree with the majority or dissent?

5.) What rules does *Sony* lay down about the burden of proof on the market harm portion of the fair use analysis?

James Boyle, The Public Domain
Please read <u>The Public Domain</u> *pp. 63–71*

There is a fairly solid tradition in intellectual property policy of what I call "20/20 downside" vision. All of the threats posed by any new technology—the player piano, the jukebox, the photocopier, the VCR, the Internet—are seen with extraordinary clarity. The opportunities, however, particularly those which involve changing a business model or restructuring a market, are dismissed as phantoms. The downside dominates the field, the upside is invisible. The story of video recorders is the best-known example. When video recorders—another technology promising cheaper copying—first appeared, the reaction of movie studios was one of horror. Their business plans relied upon showing movies in theaters and then licensing them to television stations. VCRs and Betamaxes fit nowhere in this plan; they were seen merely as copyright violation devices. Hollywood tried to have them taxed to pay for the losses that would be caused. Their assumption? Cheaper copying demands stronger rights.

Having lost that battle, the movie studios tried to have the manufacturers of the recording devices found liable for contributory copyright infringement; liable, in other words, for assisting the copyright violations that could be carried out by the owners of Sony Betamaxes. This, of course, was exactly the same legal claim that would be made in the Napster case. In the *Sony* case, however, the movie companies lost. The Supreme Court said that recording of TV programs to "time-shift" them to a more convenient hour was a fair use. The movie studios' claims were rejected.

Freed from the threat of liability, the price of video recorders continued to fall. They flooded consumers' houses at a speed unparalleled until the arrival of the World Wide Web. All these boxes sitting by TVs now cried out for content, content that was provided by an emerging video rental market. Until the triumph of DVDs, the videocassette rental market made up more than 50 percent of the movie industry's revenues. Were losses caused by video recorders? To be sure. Some people who might have gone to see a movie in a theater because the TV schedule was inconvenient could instead record the show and watch it later. Videos could even be shared with friends and families—tattered copies of Disney movies recorded from some cable show could be passed on to siblings whose kids have reached the appropriate age. VCRs were also used for copying that was clearly illicit—large-scale duplication and sale of movies by someone other than the rights holder. A cheaper copying technology definitely caused losses. But it also provided substantial gains, gains that far outweighed the losses. Ironically, had the movie companies "won" in the *Sony* case, they might now be worse off.

The *Sony* story provides us with some useful lessons—first, this 20/20 downside vision is a poor guide to copyright policy. Under its sway, some companies will invariably equate greater control with profit and cheaper copying with loss. They will conclude, sometimes rightly, that their very existence is threatened, and, sometimes wrongly, that the threat is to innovation and culture itself rather than to their particular way of delivering it. They will turn to the legislature and the courts for guarantees that they can go on doing business in the old familiar ways. Normally, the marketplace is supposed to provide correctives to this kind of myopia. Upstart companies, not bound by the habits of the last generation, are supposed to move nimbly to harvest the benefits from the new technology and to out-compete the lumbering dinosaurs. In certain situations, though, competition will not work:

• if the dinosaurs are a cartel strong enough to squelch competition;

- if they have enlisted the state to make the threatening technology illegal, describing it as a predatory encroachment on the "rights" of the old guard rather than aggressive competition;
- if ingrained prejudices are simply so strong that the potential business benefits take years to become apparent; or
- if the market has "locked in" on a dominant standard—a technology or an operating system, say—to which new market entrants do not have legal access.

In those situations, markets cannot be counted on to self-correct. Unfortunately, and this is a key point, intellectual property policy frequently deals with controversies in which all of these conditions hold true. . . .   *Read the rest*

2.) Unpublished works, "Scoops" and Political Speech

Harper & Row v. Nation Enterprises
471 U.S. 539 (1985)

Justice O'CONNOR delivered the opinion of the Court.

In March 1979, an undisclosed source provided The Nation Magazine with the unpublished manuscript of "A Time to Heal: The Autobiography of Gerald R. Ford." Working directly from the purloined manuscript, an editor of The Nation produced a short piece entitled "The Ford Memoirs—Behind the Nixon Pardon." The piece was timed to "scoop" an article scheduled shortly to appear in Time Magazine. Time had agreed to purchase the exclusive right to print prepublication excerpts from the copyright holders, Harper & Row Publishers, Inc. (hereinafter Harper & Row), and Reader's Digest Association, Inc. (hereinafter Reader's Digest). As a result of The Nation article, Time canceled its agreement. Petitioners brought a successful copyright action against The Nation. On appeal, the Second Circuit reversed the lower court's finding of infringement, holding that The Nation's act was sanctioned as a "fair use" of the copyrighted material. We granted certiorari, 467 U. S. 1214 (1984), and we now reverse.

I

In February 1977, shortly after leaving the White House, former President Gerald R. Ford contracted with petitioners Harper & Row and Reader's Digest, to publish his as yet unwritten memoirs. The memoirs were to contain "significant hitherto unpublished material" concerning the Watergate crisis, Mr. Ford's pardon of former President Nixon and "Mr. Ford's reflections on this period of history, and the morality and personalities involved." In addition to the right to publish the Ford memoirs in book form, the agreement gave petitioners the exclusive right to license prepublication excerpts, known in the trade as "first serial rights." Two years later, as the memoirs were nearing completion, petitioners negotiated a prepublication licensing agreement with Time, a weekly news magazine. Time agreed to pay $25,000, $12,500 in advance and an additional $12,500 at publication, in exchange for the right to excerpt 7,500 words from Mr. Ford's account of the Nixon pardon. The issue featuring the excerpts was timed to appear approximately one week before shipment of the full length book version to bookstores. Exclusivity was an important consideration; Harper & Row instituted procedures designed to maintain the confidentiality of the manuscript, and Time retained the right to renegotiate the second payment should the material appear in print prior to its release of the excerpts.

The Nation.

THE FORD MEMOIRS
BEHIND THE NIXON PARDON

In his memoirs, *A Time to Heal*, which Harper & Row will publish in late May or early June, former President Gerald R. Ford says that the idea of giving a blanket pardon to Richard M. Nixon was raised before Nixon resigned from the Presidency by Gen. Alexander Haig, who was then the White House chief of staff.

Ford also writes that, but for a misunderstanding, he might have selected Ronald Reagan as his 1976 running mate, that Washington lawyer Edward Bennett Williams, a Democrat, was his choice for head of the Central Intelligence Agency, that Nixon was the one who first proposed Nelson Rockefeller for Vice President, and that he regretted his "cowardice" in allowing Rockefeller to remove himself from Vice Presidential contention. Ford also describes his often prickly relations with Henry Kissinger.

The Nation obtained the 655-page typescript before publication. Advance excerpts from the book will appear in *Time* in mid-April and in *The Reader's Digest* thereafter. Although the initial print order has not been decided, the figure is tentatively set at 50,000; it could change, depending upon the public reaction to the serialization.

Ford's account of the Nixon pardon contains significant new detail on the negotiations and considerations that surrounded it. According to Ford's version, the subject was first broached to him by General Haig on August 1, 1974, a week before Nixon resigned. General Haig revealed that the newly transcribed White House tapes were the equivalent of the "smoking gun" and that Ford should prepare himself to become President.

Ford was deeply hurt by Haig's revela-

(Continued on Page 363)

Excerpt from "The Ford Memoirs: Behind the Nixon Pardon," The Nation (April 7, 1979).

Two to three weeks before the Time article's scheduled release, an unidentified person secretly brought a copy of the Ford manuscript to Victor Navasky, editor of The Nation, a political commentary magazine. Mr. Navasky knew that his possession of the manuscript was not authorized and that the manuscript must be returned quickly to his "source" to avoid discovery. He hastily put together what he believed was "a real hot news story" composed of quotes, paraphrases, and facts drawn exclusively from the manuscript. Mr. Navasky attempted no independent commentary, research or criticism, in part because of the need for speed if he was to "make news" by "publish[ing] in advance of publication of the Ford book." The 2,250-word article, reprinted in the Appendix to this opinion, appeared on April 3, 1979. As a result of The Nation's article, Time canceled its piece and refused to pay the remaining $12,500.

. . . The District Court rejected respondents' argument that The Nation's piece was a "fair use" sanctioned by § 107 of the Act. . . . The court awarded actual damages of $12,500.

A divided panel of the Court of Appeals for the Second Circuit reversed. . . . The Court of Appeals was especially influenced by the "politically significant" nature of the subject matter and its conviction that it is not "the purpose of the Copyright Act to impede that harvest of knowledge so necessary to a democratic state" or "chill the activities of the press by forbidding a circumscribed use of copyrighted words."

II

. . . The Nation has admitted to lifting verbatim quotes of the author's original language totaling between 300 and 400 words and constituting some 13% of The Nation article. In using generous verbatim excerpts of Mr. Ford's unpublished manuscript to lend authenticity to its account of the forthcoming memoirs, The Nation effectively arrogated to itself the right of first publication, an important marketable subsidiary right. For the reasons set forth below, we find that this use of the copyrighted manuscript, even stripped to the verbatim quotes conceded by The Nation to be copyrightable expression, was not a fair use within the meaning of the Copyright Act.

III
A

. . . Perhaps because the fair use doctrine was predicated on the author's implied consent to "reasonable and customary" use when he released his work for public consumption, fair use traditionally was not recognized as a defense to charges of copying from an author's as yet unpublished works. Under common-law copyright, "the property of the author . . . in his intellectual creation [was] absolute until he voluntarily part[ed] with the same." *American Tobacco Co. v. Werckmeister* (1907). This absolute rule, however, was tempered in practice by the equitable nature of the fair use doctrine. In a given case, factors such as implied consent through de facto publication on performance or dissemination of a work may tip the balance of equities in favor of prepublication use. But it has never been seriously disputed that "the fact that the plaintiff's work is unpublished . . . is a factor tending to negate the defense of fair use." Publication of an author's expression before he has authorized its dissemination seriously infringes the author's right to decide when and whether it will be made public, a factor not present in fair use of published works. Respondents contend, however, that Congress, in including first publication among the rights enumerated in § 106, which are expressly subject to fair use under § 107, intended that fair use would apply *in pari materia* to published and unpublished works. The Copyright Act does not support this proposition. . . .

Though the right of first publication, like the other rights enumerated in § 106, is expressly made subject to the fair use provision of § 107, fair use analysis must always be tailored to the individual case. The nature of the interest at stake is highly relevant to whether a given use is fair. From the beginning, those entrusted with the task of revision recognized the "overbalancing reasons to preserve the common law protection of undisseminated works until the author or his successor chooses to disclose them." *Copyright Law Revision,* Report of the Register of Copyrights on the General Revision of the U. S. Copyright Law, 87th Cong., 1st Sess., 41 (Comm. Print 1961). The right of first publication implicates a threshold decision by the author whether and in what form to release his work. First publication is inherently different from other § 106 rights in that only one person can be the first publisher; as the contract with Time illustrates, the commercial value of the right lies primarily in exclusivity. Because the potential damage to the author from judicially enforced "sharing" of the first publication right with unauthorized users of his manuscript is substantial, the balance of equities in evaluating such a claim of fair use inevitably shifts. . . .

. . . We conclude that the unpublished nature of a work is "[a] key, though not necessarily determinative, factor" tending to negate a defense of fair use.

We also find unpersuasive respondents' argument that fair use may be made of a soon-to-be-published manuscript on the ground that the author has demonstrated he has no interest in nonpublication. This argument assumes that the unpublished nature of copyrighted material is only relevant to letters or other confidential writings not intended for dissemination. It is true that common-law copyright was often enlisted in the service of personal privacy. In its commercial guise, however, an author's right to choose when he will publish is no less deserving of protection. The period encompassing the work's initiation, its preparation, and its grooming for public dissemination is a crucial one for any literary endeavor. . . . The obvious benefit to author and public alike of assuring authors the leisure to develop their ideas free from fear of expropriation outweighs any short-term "news value" to be gained from premature publication of the author's expression. The author's control of first public distribution implicates not only his personal interest in creative control but his property interest in exploitation of prepublication rights, which are valuable in themselves and serve as a valuable adjunct to publicity and marketing. Under ordinary circumstances, the author's right to control the first public appearance of his undisseminated expression will outweigh a claim of fair use.

B

Respondents, however, contend that First Amendment values require a different rule under the circumstances of this case. The thrust of the decision below is that "[t]he scope of [fair use] is undoubtedly wider when the information conveyed relates to matters of high public concern." Respondents advance the substantial public import of the subject matter of the Ford memoirs as grounds for excusing a use that would ordinarily not pass muster as a fair use—the piracy of verbatim quotations for the purpose of "scooping" the authorized first serialization. Respondents explain their copying of Mr. Ford's expression as essential to reporting the news story it claims the book itself represents. In respondents' view, not only the facts contained in Mr. Ford's memoirs, but "the precise manner in which [he] expressed himself [were] as newsworthy as what he had to say." Respondents argue that the public's interest in learning this news as fast as possible outweighs the right of the author to control its first publication.

The Second Circuit noted, correctly, that copyright's idea/expression dichotomy "strike[s] a definitional balance between the First Amendment and the Copyright Act by permitting free communication of facts while still protecting an author's expression." No author may copyright his ideas or the facts he narrates. 17 U. S. C. § 102(b). As this Court long ago observed: "[T]he news element—the information respecting current events contained in the literary production—is not the creation of the writer, but is a report of matters that ordinarily are publici juris; it is the history of the day." *International News Service v. Associated Press* (1918). But copyright assures those who write and publish factual narratives such as "A Time to Heal" that they may at least enjoy the right to market the original expression contained therein as just compensation for their investment.

Respondents' theory, however, would expand fair use to effectively destroy any expectation of copyright protection in the work of a public figure. Absent such protection, there would be little incentive to create or profit in financing such memoirs, and the public would be denied an important source of significant historical information. . . .

Nor do respondents assert any actual necessity for circumventing the copyright scheme with respect to the types of works and users at issue here. Where an author and publisher have invested extensive resources in creating an original work and are poised to release it to the public, no legitimate aim is served by pre-empting the right of first publication. The fact that the words the author has chosen to clothe his narrative may of themselves be "newsworthy" is not an independent justification for unauthorized copying of the author's expression prior to publication. . . .

In our haste to disseminate news, it should not be forgotten that the Framers intended copyright itself to be the engine of free expression. By establishing a marketable right to the use of one's expression, copyright supplies the economic incentive to create and disseminate ideas. . . .

It is fundamentally at odds with the scheme of copyright to accord lesser rights in those works that are of greatest importance to the public. Such a notion ignores the major premise of copyright and injures author and public alike. "[T]o propose that fair use be imposed whenever the 'social value [of dissemination] . . . outweighs any detriment to the artist,' would be to propose depriving copyright owners of their right in the property precisely when they encounter those users who could afford to pay for it."

Moreover, freedom of thought and expression "includes both the right to speak freely and the right to refrain from speaking at all." *Wooley v. Maynard* (1977). Courts and commentators have recognized that copyright, and the right of first publication in particular, serve this countervailing First Amendment value.

In view of the First Amendment protections already embodied in the Copyright Act's distinction between copyrightable expression and uncopyrightable facts and ideas, and the latitude for scholarship and comment traditionally afforded by fair use, we see no warrant for expanding the doctrine of fair use to create what amounts to a public figure exception to copyright. . . .

IV

. . . *Purpose of the Use.* The Second Circuit correctly identified news reporting as the general purpose of The Nation's use. News reporting is one of the examples enumerated in § 107 to "give some idea of the sort of activities the courts might regard as fair use under the circumstances." Senate Report. This listing was not intended to be exhaustive, or to single out any particular use as presumptively a "fair" use. The drafters resisted pressures from special interest groups to create presumptive categories of fair use, but structured the provision as an affirmative defense requiring a case-by-case analysis. The fact that an article arguably is "news" and therefore a productive use is simply one factor in a fair use analysis.

We agree with the Second Circuit that the trial court erred in fixing on whether the information contained in the memoirs was actually new to the public. As Judge Meskill wisely noted, "[c]ourts should be chary of deciding what is and what is not news." The Nation has every right to seek to be the first to publish information. But The Nation went beyond simply reporting uncopyrightable information and actively sought to exploit the headline value of its infringement, making a "news event" out of its unauthorized first publication of a noted figure's copyrighted expression.

The fact that a publication was commercial as opposed to nonprofit is a separate factor that tends to weigh against a finding of fair use. "[E]very commercial use of copyrighted material is presumptively an unfair exploitation of the monopoly privilege that belongs to the owner of the copyright." *Sony Corp. of America v. Universal City Studios, Inc.* In arguing that the purpose of news reporting is not purely commercial, The Nation misses the point entirely. The crux of the profit/nonprofit distinction is not whether the sole motive of the use is monetary gain but whether the user stands to profit from exploitation of the copyrighted material without paying the customary price.

In evaluating character and purpose we cannot ignore The Nation's stated purpose of scooping the forthcoming hard-cover and Time abstracts. The Nation's use had not merely the incidental effect but the intended purpose of supplanting the copyright holder's commercially valuable right of first publication. Also relevant to the "character" of the use is "the propriety of the defendant's conduct." The trial court found that The Nation knowingly exploited a purloined manuscript. Unlike the typical claim of fair use, The Nation cannot offer up even the fiction of consent as justification. Like its competitor news-weekly, it was free to bid for the right of abstracting excerpts from "A Time to Heal." . . .

Nature of the Copyrighted Work. Second, the Act directs attention to the nature of the copyrighted work. "A Time to Heal" may be characterized as an unpublished historical narrative or autobiography. The law generally recognizes a greater need to disseminate factual works than works of fiction or fantasy. . . .

Some of the briefer quotes from the memoirs are arguably necessary adequately to convey the facts; for example, Mr. Ford's characterization of the White House tapes as the "smoking gun" is perhaps so integral to the idea expressed as to be inseparable from it. But The Nation did not stop at isolated phrases and instead excerpted subjective descriptions and portraits of public figures whose power lies in the author's individualized expression. Such use, focusing on the most expressive elements of the work, exceeds that necessary to disseminate the facts.

The fact that a work is unpublished is a critical element of its "nature." Our prior discussion establishes that the scope of fair use is narrower with respect to unpublished works. While even substantial quotations might qualify as fair use in a review of a published work or a news account of a speech that had been delivered to the public or disseminated to the press, the author's right to control the first public appearance of his expression weighs against such use of the work before its release. The right of first publication encompasses not only the choice whether to publish at all, but also the choices of when, where, and in what form first to publish a work.

In the case of Mr. Ford's manuscript, the copyright holders' interest in confidentiality is irrefutable; the copyright holders had entered into a contractual undertaking to "keep the manuscript confidential" and required that all those to whom the manuscript was shown also "sign an agreement to keep the manuscript confidential." While the copyright holders' contract with Time required Time to submit its proposed article seven days before publication, The Nation's clandestine publication afforded no such opportunity for creative or quality control. It was hastily patched together and contained "a number of inaccuracies." A use that so clearly infringes the copyright holder's interests in confidentiality and creative control is difficult to characterize as "fair."

Amount and Substantiality of the Portion Used. Next, the Act directs us to examine the amount and substantiality of the portion used in relation to the copyrighted work as a whole. In absolute terms, the words actually quoted were an insubstantial portion of "A Time to Heal." The District Court, however, found that "[T]he Nation took what was essentially the heart of the book." We believe the Court of Appeals erred in overruling the District Judge's evaluation of the qualitative nature of the taking. A Time editor described the chapters on the pardon as "the most interesting and moving parts of the entire manuscript." The portions actually quoted were selected by Mr. Navasky as among the most powerful passages in those chapters. He testified that he used verbatim excerpts because simply reciting the information could not adequately convey the "absolute certainty with which [Ford] expressed himself," or show that "this comes from President Ford," or carry the "definitive quality" of the original. In short, he quoted these passages precisely because they qualitatively embodied Ford's distinctive expression.

As the statutory language indicates, a taking may not be excused merely because it is insubstantial with respect to the infringing work. As Judge Learned Hand cogently remarked, "no plagiarist can excuse the wrong by showing how much of his work he did not pirate." *Sheldon v. Metro-Goldwyn Pictures Corp.* (2d Cir.). Conversely, the fact that a substantial portion of the infringing work was copied verbatim is evidence of the qualitative value of the copied material, both to the originator and to the plagiarist who seeks to profit from marketing someone else's copyrighted expression.

Stripped to the verbatim quotes, the direct takings from the unpublished manuscript constitute at least 13% of the infringing article. The Nation article is structured around the quoted excerpts which serve as its dramatic focal points. In view of the expressive value of the excerpts and their key role in the infringing work, we cannot agree with the Second Circuit that the "magazine took a meager, indeed an infinitesimal amount of Ford's original language."

Effect on the Market. Finally, the Act focuses on "the effect of the use upon the potential market for or value of the copyrighted work." This last factor is undoubtedly the single most important element of fair use.[9] "Fair use, when properly applied, is limited to copying by others which does not materially impair the marketability of the work which is copied." . . . Rarely will a case of copyright infringement present such clear-cut evidence of actual damage. Petitioners assured Time that there would be no other authorized publication of any portion of the unpublished manuscript prior to April 23, 1979. Any publication of material from chapters 1 and 3 would permit Time to renegotiate its final payment. Time cited The Nation's article, which contained verbatim quotes from the unpublished manuscript, as a reason for its nonperformance. . . . [O]nce a copyright holder establishes with reasonable probability the existence of a causal connection between the infringement and a loss of revenue, the burden properly shifts to

---

[9] Economists who have addressed the issue believe the fair use exception should come into play only in those situations in which the market fails or the price the copyright holder would ask is near zero. As the facts here demonstrate, there is a fully functioning market that encourages the creation and dissemination of memoirs of public figures. In the economists' view, permitting "fair use" to displace normal copyright channels disrupts the copyright market without a commensurate public benefit.

the infringer to show that this damage would have occurred had there been no taking of copyrighted expression. Petitioners established a prima facie case of actual damage that respondents failed to rebut. . . .

More important, to negate fair use one need only show that if the challenged use "should become widespread, it would adversely affect the *potential* market for the copyrighted work." *Sony Corp. of America v. Universal City Studios, Inc.* This inquiry must take account not only of harm to the original but also of harm to the market for derivative works. "If the defendant's work adversely affects the value of any of the rights in the copyrighted work (in this case the adaptation [and serialization] right) the use is not fair." 3 Nimmer § 13.05[B]. . . .

V

The Court of Appeals erred in concluding that The Nation's use of the copyrighted material was excused by the public's interest in the subject matter. . . . In sum, the traditional doctrine of fair use, as embodied in the Copyright Act, does not sanction the use made by The Nation of these copyrighted materials. Any copyright infringer may claim to benefit the public by increasing public access to the copyrighted work. But Congress has not designed, and we see no warrant for judicially imposing, a "compulsory license" permitting unfettered access to the unpublished copyrighted expression of public figures.

The Nation conceded that its verbatim copying of some 300 words of direct quotation from the Ford manuscript would constitute an infringement unless excused as a fair use. Because we find that The Nation's use of these verbatim excerpts from the unpublished manuscript was not a fair use, the judgment of the Court of Appeals is reversed, and the case is remanded for further proceedings consistent with this opinion.

It is so ordered.

Justice BRENNAN, with whom Justice WHITE and Justice MARSHALL join, dissenting. [Omitted.]

Questions:

1.) What "rules" can you extract from *Harper & Row*? (By rules, we mean something akin to *Sony*'s rulings on the effect of commercial and noncommercial use on the burden of proof on market harm—nuggets of relatively firm doctrine that instruct lower courts exactly how to apply the four factors.) Give both an expansive and a restricted version of its holding.

2.) Under what circumstances would the *Harper & Row* Court allow use of the actual expression of a copyrighted work in a way that was extremely likely to harm some of the markets for that work? Can you think of circumstances where such uses should be found as fair?

3.) What is the right of first publication? List *all* of the reasons that the *Harper & Row* Court gives for treating this right of the copyright holder in a different way from the other rights implicated by § 106.

4.) The majority describes *The Nation*'s goal as being merely to "scoop" *Time* in breaking the story—to get to market first with the same story. If you were representing *The Nation*, how would you describe its goals? Are there any details from the case you can use to support your account?

3.) Transformative Use, Parody, Commentary and Burdens of Proof Revisited

Campbell v. Acuff-Rose
510 U.S. 569 (1994)

Justice SOUTER delivered the opinion of the Court.

  We are called upon to decide whether 2 Live Crew's commercial parody of Roy Orbison's song, "Oh, Pretty Woman," may be a fair use within the meaning of the Copyright Act of 1976, 17 U.S.C. § 107. Although the District Court granted summary judgment for 2 Live Crew, the Court of Appeals reversed, holding the defense of fair use barred by the song's commercial character and excessive borrowing. Because we hold that a parody's commercial character is only one element to be weighed in a fair use enquiry, and that insufficient consideration was given to the nature of parody in weighing the degree of copying, we reverse and remand.

I

  In 1964, Roy Orbison and William Dees wrote a rock ballad called "Oh, Pretty Woman" and assigned their rights in it to respondent Acuff-Rose Music, Inc. Acuff-Rose registered the song for copyright protection.

  Petitioners Luther R. Campbell, Christopher Wongwon, Mark Ross, and David Hobbs are collectively known as 2 Live Crew, a popular rap music group.[1] In 1989, Campbell wrote a song entitled "Pretty Woman," which he later described in an affidavit

---

[1] Rap has been defined as a "style of black American popular music consisting of improvised rhymes performed to a rhythmic accompaniment." The Norton/Grove Concise Encyclopedia of Music 613 (1988). 2 Live Crew plays "[b]ass music," a regional, hip-hop style of rap from the Liberty City area of Miami, Florida.

as intended, "through comical lyrics, to satirize the original work. . . ." On July 5, 1989, 2 Live Crew's manager informed Acuff-Rose that 2 Live Crew had written a parody of "Oh, Pretty Woman," that they would afford all credit for ownership and authorship of the original song to Acuff-Rose, Dees, and Orbison, and that they were willing to pay a fee for the use they wished to make of it. Enclosed with the letter were a copy of the lyrics and a recording of 2 Live Crew's song. Acuff-Rose's agent refused permission, stating that "I am aware of the success enjoyed by 'The 2 Live Crews', but I must inform you that we cannot permit the use of a parody of 'Oh, Pretty Woman.'" Nonetheless, in June or July 1989, 2 Live Crew released records, cassette tapes, and compact discs of "Pretty Woman" in a collection of songs entitled "As Clean As They Wanna Be." The albums and compact discs identify the authors of "Pretty Woman" as Orbison and Dees and its publisher as Acuff-Rose. . . .

II

It is uncontested here that 2 Live Crew's song would be an infringement of Acuff-Rose's rights in "Oh, Pretty Woman," under the Copyright Act of 1976, 17 U.S.C. § 106, but for a finding of fair use through parody. From the infancy of copyright protection, some opportunity for fair use of copyrighted materials has been thought necessary to fulfill copyright's very purpose, "[t]o promote the Progress of Science and useful Arts. . . ." U.S. Const., Art. I, § 8, cl. 8. For as Justice Story explained, "[i]n truth, in literature, in science and in art, there are, and can be, few, if any, things, which in an abstract sense, are strictly new and original throughout. Every book in literature, science and art, borrows, and must necessarily borrow, and use much which was well known and used before." Similarly, Lord Ellenborough expressed the inherent tension in the need simultaneously to protect copyrighted material and to allow others to build upon it when he wrote, "while I shall think myself bound to secure every man in the enjoyment of his copy-right, one must not put manacles upon science." In copyright cases brought under the Statute of Anne of 1710, English courts held that in some instances "fair abridgements" would not infringe an author's rights, and although the First Congress enacted our initial copyright statute without any explicit reference to "fair use," as it later came to be known, the doctrine was recognized by the American courts nonetheless. . . .

. . . The fair use doctrine thus "permits [and requires] courts to avoid rigid application of the copyright statute when, on occasion, it would stifle the very creativity which that law is designed to foster."

The task is not to be simplified with bright-line rules, for the statute, like the doctrine it recognizes, calls for case-by-case analysis. The text employs the terms "including" and "such as" in the preamble paragraph to indicate the "illustrative and not limitative" function of the examples given, which thus provide only general guidance about the sorts of copying that courts and Congress most commonly had found to be fair uses. Nor may the four statutory factors be treated in isolation, one from another. All are to be explored, and the results weighed together, in light of the purposes of copyright.

A

The first factor in a fair use enquiry is "the purpose and character of the use, including whether such use is of a commercial nature or is for nonprofit educational purposes." § 107(1). This factor draws on Justice Story's formulation, "the nature and objects of the selections made." The enquiry here may be guided by the examples given in the preamble to § 107, looking to whether the use is for criticism, or comment, or news reporting, and the like, see § 107. The central purpose of this investigation is to see, in Justice Story's words, whether the new work merely "supersede[s] the objects" of the original creation, or instead adds something new, with a further purpose or different character, altering the first with new expression, meaning, or message; it asks, in other words, whether and to what extent the new work is "transformative." Although such transformative use is not absolutely necessary for a finding of fair use, the goal of copyright, to promote science and the arts, is generally furthered by the creation of transformative works. Such works thus lie at the heart of the fair use doctrine's guarantee of breathing space within the confines of copyright, and the more transformative the new work, the less will be the significance of other factors, like commercialism, that may weigh against a finding of fair use.

This Court has only once before even considered whether parody may be fair use, and that time issued no opinion because of the Court's equal division. Suffice it to say now that parody has an obvious claim to transformative value, as Acuff-Rose itself does not deny. Like less ostensibly humorous forms of criticism, it can provide social benefit, by shedding light on an earlier work, and, in the process, creating a new one. We thus line up with the courts that have held that parody, like other comment or criticism, may claim fair use under § 107.

The germ of parody lies in the definition of the Greek *parodeia*, quoted in Judge Nelson's Court of Appeals dissent, as "a song sung alongside another." Modern dictionaries accordingly describe a parody as a "literary or artistic work that imitates the characteristic style of an author or a work for comic effect or ridicule," or as a "composition in prose or verse in which the characteristic turns of thought and phrase in an author or class of authors are imitated in such a way as to make them appear ridiculous." For the purposes of copyright law, the nub of the definitions, and the heart of any parodist's claim to quote from existing material, is the use of some elements of a prior author's composition to create a new one that, at least in part, comments on that author's works. If, on the contrary, the commentary has no critical bearing on the substance or style of the original composition, which the alleged infringer merely uses to get attention or to avoid the drudgery in working up something fresh, the claim to fairness in borrowing from another's work diminishes accordingly (if it does not vanish), and other factors, like the extent of its commerciality, loom larger.[14] Parody needs to mimic an original to make its point, and so has some claim to use the creation of its victim's (or collective victims') imagination, whereas satire can stand on its own two feet and so requires justification for the very act of borrowing.[15]

The fact that parody can claim legitimacy for some appropriation does not, of course, tell either parodist or judge much about where to draw the line. Like a book review quoting the copyrighted material criticized, parody may or may not be fair use, and petitioners' suggestion that any parodic use is presumptively fair has no more

---

[14] A parody that more loosely targets an original than the parody presented here may still be sufficiently aimed at an original work to come within our analysis of parody. If a parody whose wide dissemination in the market runs the risk of serving as a substitute for the original or licensed derivatives, it is more incumbent on one claiming fair use to establish the extent of transformation and the parody's critical relationship to the original. By contrast, when there is little or no risk of market substitution, whether because of the large extent of transformation of the earlier work, the new work's minimal distribution in the market, the small extent to which it borrows from an original, or other factors, taking parodic aim at an original is a less critical factor in the analysis, and looser forms of parody may be found to be fair use, as may satire with lesser justification for the borrowing than would otherwise be required.

[15] Satire has been defined as a work "in which prevalent follies or vices are assailed with ridicule," or are "attacked through irony, derision, or wit".

justification in law or fact than the equally hopeful claim that any use for news reporting should be presumed fair. The Act has no hint of an evidentiary preference for parodists over their victims, and no workable presumption for parody could take account of the fact that parody often shades into satire when society is lampooned through its creative artifacts, or that a work may contain both parodic and nonparodic elements. Accordingly, parody, like any other use, has to work its way through the relevant factors, and be judged case by case, in light of the ends of the copyright law.

Here, the District Court held, and the Court of Appeals assumed, that 2 Live Crew's "Pretty Woman" contains parody, commenting on and criticizing the original work, whatever it may have to say about society at large. As the District Court remarked, the words of 2 Live Crew's song copy the original's first line, but then "quickly degenerat[e] into a play on words, substituting predictable lyrics with shocking ones . . . [that] derisively demonstrat[e] how bland and banal the Orbison song seems to them." Judge Nelson, dissenting below, came to the same conclusion, that the 2 Live Crew song "was clearly intended to ridicule the white-bread original" and "reminds us that sexual congress with nameless streetwalkers is not necessarily the stuff of romance and is not necessarily without its consequences. The singers (there are several) have the same thing on their minds as did the lonely man with the nasal voice, but here there is no hint of wine and roses." Although the majority below had difficulty discerning any criticism of the original in 2 Live Crew's song, it assumed for purposes of its opinion that there was some.

We have less difficulty in finding that critical element in 2 Live Crew's song than the Court of Appeals did, although having found it we will not take the further step of evaluating its quality. The threshold question when fair use is raised in defense of parody is whether a parodic character may reasonably be perceived. Whether, going beyond that, parody is in good taste or bad does not and should not matter to fair use. As Justice Holmes explained, "[i]t would be a dangerous undertaking for persons trained only to the law to constitute themselves final judges of the worth of [a work], outside of the narrowest and most obvious limits. At the one extreme some works of genius would be sure to miss appreciation. Their very novelty would make them repulsive until the public had learned the new language in which their author spoke."

While we might not assign a high rank to the parodic element here, we think it fair to say that 2 Live Crew's song reasonably could be perceived as commenting on the original or criticizing it, to some degree. 2 Live Crew juxtaposes the romantic musings of a man whose fantasy comes true, with degrading taunts, a bawdy demand for sex, and a sigh of relief from paternal responsibility. The later words can be taken as a comment on the naiveté of the original of an earlier day, as a rejection of its sentiment that ignores the ugliness of street life and the debasement that it signifies. It is this joinder of reference and ridicule that marks off the author's choice of parody from the other types of comment and criticism that traditionally have had a claim to fair use protection as transformative works.

The Court of Appeals, however, immediately cut short the enquiry into 2 Live Crew's fair use claim by confining its treatment of the first factor essentially to one relevant fact, the commercial nature of the use. The court then inflated the significance of this fact by applying a presumption ostensibly culled from Sony, that "every commercial use of copyrighted material is presumptively . . . unfair. . . ." In giving virtually dispositive weight to the commercial nature of the parody, the Court of Appeals erred.

The language of the statute makes clear that the commercial or nonprofit educational purpose of a work is only one element of the first factor enquiry into its purpose and character. Section 107(1) uses the term "including" to begin the dependent clause referring to commercial use, and the main clause speaks of a broader investigation into "purpose and character." As we explained in *Harper & Row*, Congress resisted attempts to narrow the ambit of this traditional enquiry by adopting categories of presumptively fair use, and it urged courts to preserve the breadth of their traditionally ample view of the universe of relevant evidence. Accordingly, the mere fact that a use is educational and not for profit does not insulate it from a finding of infringement, any more than the commercial character of a use bars a finding of fairness. If, indeed, commerciality carried presumptive force against a finding of fairness, the presumption would swallow nearly all of the illustrative uses listed in the preamble paragraph of § 107, including news reporting, comment, criticism, teaching, scholarship, and research, since these activities "are generally conducted for profit in this country." Congress could not have intended such a rule, which certainly is not inferable from the common-law cases, arising as they did from the world of letters in which Samuel Johnson could pronounce that "[n]o man but a blockhead ever wrote, except for money."

Sony itself called for no hard evidentiary presumption. There, we emphasized the need for a "sensitive balancing of interests," noted that Congress had "eschewed a rigid, bright-line approach to fair use," and stated that the commercial or nonprofit educational character of a work is "not conclusive," but rather a fact to be "weighed along with other[s] in fair use decisions." The Court of Appeals's elevation of one sentence from *Sony* to a *per se* rule thus runs as much counter to *Sony* itself as to the long common-law tradition of fair use adjudication. Rather, as we explained in *Harper & Row*, *Sony* stands for the proposition that the "fact that a publication was commercial as opposed to nonprofit is a separate factor that tends to weigh against a finding of fair use." But that is all, and the fact that even the force of that tendency will vary with the context is a further reason against elevating commerciality to hard presumptive significance. The use, for example, of a copyrighted work to advertise a product, even in a parody, will be entitled to less indulgence under the first factor of the fair use enquiry than the sale of a parody for its own sake, let alone one performed a single time by students in school.[18]

B

The second statutory factor, "the nature of the copyrighted work," § 107(2), draws on Justice Story's expression, the "value of the materials used." This factor calls for recognition that some works are closer to the core of intended copyright protection than others, with the consequence that fair use is more difficult to establish when the former works are copied. We agree with both the District Court and the Court of Appeals that the Orbison original's creative expression for public dissemination falls within the core of the copyright's protective purposes. This fact, however, is not much help in this case, or ever likely to help much in separating the fair use sheep from the infringing goats in a parody case, since parodies almost invariably copy publicly known, expressive works.

C

The third factor asks whether "the amount and substantiality of the portion used in relation to the copyrighted work as a whole," § 107(3) are reasonable in relation to the

---

[18] . . . [W]e reject Acuff-Rose's argument that 2 Live Crew's request for permission to use the original should be weighed against a finding of fair use. Even if good faith were central to fair use, 2 Live Crew's actions do not necessarily suggest that they believed their version was not fair use; the offer may simply have been made in a good-faith effort to avoid this litigation. If the use is otherwise fair, then no permission need be sought or granted. Thus, being denied permission to use a work does not weigh against a finding of fair use.

purpose of the copying. Here, attention turns to the persuasiveness of a parodist's justification for the particular copying done, and the enquiry will harken back to the first of the statutory factors, for, as in prior cases, we recognize that the extent of permissible copying varies with the purpose and character of the use. The facts bearing on this factor will also tend to address the fourth, by revealing the degree to which the parody may serve as a market substitute for the original or potentially licensed derivatives.

The District Court considered the song's parodic purpose in finding that 2 Live Crew had not helped themselves overmuch. The Court of Appeals disagreed, stating that "[w]hile it may not be inappropriate to find that no more was taken than necessary, the copying was qualitatively substantial. . . . We conclude that taking the heart of the original and making it the heart of a new work was to purloin a substantial portion of the essence of the original."

The Court of Appeals is of course correct that this factor calls for thought not only about the quantity of the materials used, but about their quality and importance, too. In *Harper & Row*, for example, the Nation had taken only some 300 words out of President Ford's memoirs, but we signaled the significance of the quotations in finding them to amount to "the heart of the book," the part most likely to be newsworthy and important in licensing serialization. We also agree with the Court of Appeals that whether "a substantial portion of the infringing work was copied verbatim" from the copyrighted work is a relevant question, for it may reveal a dearth of transformative character or purpose under the first factor, or a greater likelihood of market harm under the fourth; a work composed primarily of an original, particularly its heart, with little added or changed, is more likely to be a merely superseding use, fulfilling demand for the original.

Where we part company with the court below is in applying these guides to parody, and in particular to parody in the song before us. Parody presents a difficult case. Parody's humor, or in any event its comment, necessarily springs from recognizable allusion to its object through distorted imitation. Its art lies in the tension between a known original and its parodic twin. When parody takes aim at a particular original work, the parody must be able to "conjure up" at least enough of that original to make the object of its critical wit recognizable. What makes for this recognition is quotation of the original's most distinctive or memorable features, which the parodist can be sure the audience will know. Once enough has been taken to assure identification, how much more is reasonable will depend, say, on the extent to which the song's overriding purpose and character is to parody the original or, in contrast, the likelihood that the parody may serve as a market substitute for the original. But using some characteristic features cannot be avoided.

We think the Court of Appeals was insufficiently appreciative of parody's need for the recognizable sight or sound when it ruled 2 Live Crew's use unreasonable as a matter of law. It is true, of course, that 2 Live Crew copied the characteristic opening bass riff (or musical phrase) of the original, and true that the words of the first line copy the Orbison lyrics. But if quotation of the opening riff and the first line may be said to go to the "heart" of the original, the heart is also what most readily conjures up the song for parody, and it is the heart at which parody takes aim. Copying does not become excessive in relation to parodic purpose merely because the portion taken was the original's heart. If 2 Live Crew had copied a significantly less memorable part of the original, it is difficult to see how its parodic character would have come through.

This is not, of course, to say that anyone who calls himself a parodist can skim the cream and get away scot free. In parody, as in news reporting, context is everything, and the question of fairness asks what else the parodist did besides go to the heart of the original. It is significant that 2 Live Crew not only copied the first line of the original, but thereafter departed markedly from the Orbison lyrics for its own ends. 2 Live Crew not only copied the bass riff and repeated it,[19] but also produced otherwise distinctive sounds, interposing "scraper" noise, overlaying the music with solos in different keys, and altering the drum beat. This is not a case, then, where "a substantial portion" of the parody itself is composed of a "verbatim" copying of the original. It is not, that is, a case where the parody is so insubstantial, as compared to the copying, that the third factor must be resolved as a matter of law against the parodists.

Suffice it to say here that, as to the lyrics, we think the Court of Appeals correctly suggested that "no more was taken than necessary," but just for that reason, we fail to see how the copying can be excessive in relation to its parodic purpose, even if the portion taken is the original's "heart." As to the music, we express no opinion whether repetition of the bass riff is excessive copying, and we remand to permit evaluation of the amount taken, in light of the song's parodic purpose and character, its transformative elements, and considerations of the potential for market substitution sketched more fully below.

D

The fourth fair use factor is "the effect of the use upon the potential market for or value of the copyrighted work." § 107(4). It requires courts to consider not only the extent of market harm caused by the particular actions of the alleged infringer, but also "whether unrestricted and widespread conduct of the sort engaged in by the defendant . . . would result in a substantially adverse impact on the potential market" for the original. The enquiry "must take account not only of harm to the original but also of harm to the market for derivative works."

Since fair use is an affirmative defense, its proponent would have difficulty carrying the burden of demonstrating fair use without favorable evidence about relevant markets.[21] In moving for summary judgment, 2 Live Crew left themselves at just such a disadvantage when they failed to address the effect on the market for rap derivatives, and confined themselves to uncontroverted submissions that there was no likely effect on the market for the original. They did not, however, thereby subject themselves to the evidentiary presumption applied by the Court of Appeals. In assessing the likelihood of significant market harm, the Court of Appeals quoted from language in *Sony* that "'[i]f the intended use is for commercial gain, that likelihood may be presumed. But if it is for a noncommercial purpose, the likelihood must be demonstrated.'" The court reasoned that because "the use of the copyrighted work is wholly commercial, . . . we presume that a likelihood of future harm to Acuff-Rose exists." In so doing, the court resolved the fourth factor against 2 Live Crew, just as it had the first, by applying a presumption about the effect of commercial use, a presumption which as applied here we hold to be error.

No "presumption" or inference of market harm that might find support in *Sony* is applicable to a case involving something beyond mere duplication for commercial

---

[19] This may serve to heighten the comic effect of the parody, as one witness stated, or serve to dazzle with the original's music, as Acuff-Rose now contends.

[21] Even favorable evidence, without more, is no guarantee of fairness. Judge Leval gives the example of the film producer's appropriation of a composer's previously unknown song that turns the song into a commercial success; the boon to the song does not make the film's simple copying fair. This factor, no less than the other three, may be addressed only through a "sensitive balancing of interests." Market harm is a matter of degree, and the importance of this factor will vary, not only with the amount of harm, but also with the relative strength of the showing on the other factors.

purposes. *Sony*'s discussion of a presumption contrasts a context of verbatim copying of the original in its entirety for commercial purposes, with the noncommercial context of *Sony* itself (home copying of television programming). In the former circumstances, what *Sony* said simply makes common sense: when a commercial use amounts to mere duplication of the entirety of an original, it clearly "supersede[s] the objects," of the original and serves as a market replacement for it, making it likely that cognizable market harm to the original will occur. But when, on the contrary, the second use is transformative, market substitution is at least less certain, and market harm may not be so readily inferred. Indeed, as to parody pure and simple, it is more likely that the new work will not affect the market for the original in a way cognizable under this factor, that is, by acting as a substitute for it ("supersed[ing] [its] objects"). This is so because the parody and the original usually serve different market functions.

We do not, of course, suggest that a parody may not harm the market at all, but when a lethal parody, like a scathing theater review, kills demand for the original, it does not produce a harm cognizable under the Copyright Act. Because "parody may quite legitimately aim at garroting the original, destroying it commercially as well as artistically," the role of the courts is to distinguish between "[b]iting criticism [that merely] suppresses demand [and] copyright infringement[, which] usurps it." *Fisher v. Dees.*

This distinction between potentially remediable displacement and unremediable disparagement is reflected in the rule that there is no protectible derivative market for criticism. The market for potential derivative uses includes only those that creators of original works would in general develop or license others to develop. Yet the unlikelihood that creators of imaginative works will license critical reviews or lampoons of their own productions removes such uses from the very notion of a potential licensing market. "People ask . . . for criticism, but they only want praise." S. Maugham, Of Human Bondage 241 (Penguin ed. 1992). Thus, to the extent that the opinion below may be read to have considered harm to the market for parodies of "Oh, Pretty Woman," the court erred.[22]

In explaining why the law recognizes no derivative market for critical works, including parody, we have, of course, been speaking of the later work as if it had nothing but a critical aspect (i.e., "parody pure and simple"). But the later work may have a more complex character, with effects not only in the arena of criticism but also in protectible markets for derivative works, too. In that sort of case, the law looks beyond the criticism to the other elements of the work, as it does here. 2 Live Crew's song comprises not only parody but also rap music, and the derivative market for rap music is a proper focus of enquiry. Evidence of substantial harm to it would weigh against a finding of fair use, because the licensing of derivatives is an important economic incentive to the creation of originals. Of course, the only harm to derivatives that need concern us, as discussed above, is the harm of market substitution. The fact that a parody may impair the market for derivative uses by the very effectiveness of its critical commentary is no more relevant under copyright than the like threat to the original market.[24]

Although 2 Live Crew submitted uncontroverted affidavits on the question of market harm to the original, neither they, nor Acuff-Rose, introduced evidence or

---

[22] We express no opinion as to the derivative markets for works using elements of an original as vehicles for satire or amusement, making no comment on the original or criticism of it.

[24] In some cases it may be difficult to determine whence the harm flows. In such cases, the other fair use factors may provide some indicia of the likely source of the harm. A work whose overriding purpose and character is parodic and whose borrowing is slight in relation to its parody will be far less likely to cause cognizable harm than a work with little parodic content and much copying.

affidavits addressing the likely effect of 2 Live Crew's parodic rap song on the market for a nonparody, rap version of "Oh, Pretty Woman." And while Acuff-Rose would have us find evidence of a rap market in the very facts that 2 Live Crew recorded a rap parody of "Oh, Pretty Woman" and another rap group sought a license to record a rap derivative, there was no evidence that a potential rap market was harmed in any way by 2 Live Crew's parody, rap version. The fact that 2 Live Crew's parody sold as part of a collection of rap songs says very little about the parody's effect on a market for a rap version of the original, either of the music alone or of the music with its lyrics. The District Court essentially passed on this issue, observing that Acuff-Rose is free to record "whatever version of the original it desires," the Court of Appeals went the other way by erroneous presumption. Contrary to each treatment, it is impossible to deal with the fourth factor except by recognizing that a silent record on an important factor bearing on fair use disentitled the proponent of the defense, 2 Live Crew, to summary judgment. The evidentiary hole will doubtless be plugged on remand.

III

It was error for the Court of Appeals to conclude that the commercial nature of 2 Live Crew's parody of "Oh, Pretty Woman" rendered it presumptively unfair. No such evidentiary presumption is available to address either the first factor, the character and purpose of the use, or the fourth, market harm, in determining whether a transformative use, such as parody, is a fair one. The court also erred in holding that 2 Live Crew had necessarily copied excessively from the Orbison original, considering the parodic purpose of the use. We therefore reverse the judgment of the Court of Appeals and remand the case for further proceedings consistent with this opinion.
It is so ordered.

Justice KENNEDY, concurring.
    . . . The fair use factors thus reinforce the importance of keeping the definition of parody within proper limits. More than arguable parodic content should be required to deem a would-be parody a fair use. Fair use is an affirmative defense, so doubts about whether a given use is fair should not be resolved in favor of the self-proclaimed parodist. We should not make it easy for musicians to exploit existing works and then later claim that their rendition was a valuable commentary on the original. Almost any revamped modern version of a familiar composition can be construed as a "comment on the naiveté of the original," because of the difference in style and because it will be amusing to hear how the old tune sounds in the new genre. Just the thought of a rap version of Beethoven's Fifth Symphony or "Achy Breaky Heart" is bound to make people smile. If we allow any weak transformation to qualify as parody, however, we weaken the protection of copyright. And underprotection of copyright disserves the goals of copyright just as much as overprotection, by reducing the financial incentive to create.
    The Court decides it is "fair to say that 2 Live Crew's song reasonably could be perceived as commenting on the original or criticizing it, to some degree." While I am not so assured that 2 Live Crew's song is a legitimate parody, the Court's treatment of the remaining factors leaves room for the District Court to determine on remand that the song is not a fair use. As future courts apply our fair use analysis, they must take care to ensure that not just any commercial takeoff is rationalized *post hoc* as a parody.
    With these observations, I join the opinion of the Court.

APPENDIX A TO OPINION OF THE COURT

"Oh, Pretty Woman" by Roy Orbison and William Dees

Pretty Woman, walking down the street,
Pretty Woman, the kind I like to meet,
Pretty Woman, I don't believe you, you're not the truth,
No one could look as good as you Mercy
Pretty Woman, won't you pardon me,
Pretty Woman, I couldn't help but see,
Pretty Woman, that you look lovely as can be Are you lonely just like me?
Pretty Woman, stop a while,
Pretty Woman, talk a while,
Pretty Woman give your smile to me
Pretty Woman, yeah, yeah, yeah
Pretty Woman, look my way,
Pretty Woman, say you'll stay with me
'Cause I need you, I'll treat you right
Come to me baby, Be mine tonight
Pretty Woman, don't walk on by,
Pretty Woman, don't make me cry,
Pretty Woman, don't walk away,
Hey, O. K.
If that's the way it must be, O. K.
I guess I'll go on home, it's late
There'll be tomorrow night, but wait!
What do I see
Is she walking back to me?
Yeah, she's walking back to me!
Oh, Pretty Woman.

APPENDIX B TO OPINION OF THE COURT

"Pretty Woman" as Recorded by 2 Live Crew

Pretty woman walkin' down the street
Pretty woman girl you look so sweet
Pretty woman you bring me down to that knee
Pretty woman you make me wanna beg please
Oh, pretty woman
Big hairy woman you need to shave that stuff
Big hairy woman you know I bet it's tough
Big hairy woman all that hair it ain't legit
'Cause you look like 'Cousin It'
Big hairy woman
Bald headed woman girl your hair won't grow
Bald headed woman you got a teeny weeny afro
Bald headed woman you know your hair could look nice
Bald headed woman first you got to roll it with rice
Bald headed woman here, let me get this hunk of biz for ya

Ya know what I'm saying you look better than rice a roni
Oh bald headed woman
Big hairy woman come on in
And don't forget your bald headed friend
Hey pretty woman let the boys Jump in
Two timin' woman girl you know you ain't right
Two timin' woman you's out with my boy last night
Two timin' woman that takes a load off my mind
Two timin' woman now I know the baby ain't mine
Oh, two timin' woman
Oh pretty woman

Questions:

1.) Why did the Court think that, with commercial transformative works, market substitution was less certain or easily inferred? They are different from the original and thus not market-substitutes? The transformation indicates that it is more likely that the use is "fair" and not motivated by mere lazy and inequitable free-riding? Because we do not *care* as much about the economic loss to the original author if he or she is standing in the way of a potentially transformative subsequent work that might promote the progress? All three? Point to specific passages in the case to support your answer.

2.) Read (and listen) to both songs at issue in this case. Do you think the second is a parody? Why or why not? Does this depend on what 2 Live Crew had in mind? On what the audience perceives? On whether it is funny? On something else?

3.) Reconcile these two passages

> Although 2 Live Crew submitted uncontroverted affidavits on the question of market harm to the original, neither they, nor Acuff-Rose, introduced evidence or affidavits addressing the likely effect of 2 Live Crew's parodic rap song on the market for a *nonparody*, rap version of "Oh, Pretty Woman." [Emphasis added.]

and

> We do not, of course, suggest that a parody may not harm the market at all, but when a lethal parody, like a scathing theater review, kills demand for the original, it does not produce a harm cognizable under the Copyright Act. Because "parody may quite legitimately aim at garroting the original, destroying it commercially as well as artistically," the role of the courts is to distinguish between "[b]iting criticism [that merely] suppresses demand [and] copyright infringement[, which] usurps it."

4.) Does the ruling in *Acuff-Rose* apply to all transformative works or only to parody? Parody and satire? Does a parodist have a claim to take a greater amount from the original and if so, why?

Note: Burdens of Proof (and Persuasion)

Acuff-Rose changes (or "clarifies") two things about the law of fair use. First, beyond "mere duplication for commercial purposes" it is wrong to say that all commercial uses are presumptively unfair. (Rolling back the expansive language in

Sony.) Second, the fourth factor is important but not definitive or binary. As *Acuff-Rose* puts it, "this factor, no less than the other three, may be addressed only through a 'sensitive balancing of interests.' Market harm is a matter of degree, and the importance of this factor will vary, not only with the amount of harm, but also with the relative strength of the showing on the other factors." (Rolling back *Harper & Row.*) Yet where does it leave the law regarding burdens of proof on market harm? We know *Sony* said that with commercial works, market harm should be presumed, whereas with non-commercial works, market harm must be demonstrated by the plaintiff. We know that *Acuff-Rose* first denied that *Sony* called for any hard and fast presumption (?) and then said that if commercial uses are *transformative* "market substitution is at least less certain, and market harm may not be so readily inferred." Thus *Sony*'s presumption would not apply. That much is clear, but where does it leave us?

One possibility is that we should read *Acuff-Rose* as simply lumping commercial transformative uses into the same category as non-commercial uses in the *Sony* framework. If that were true, then transformative uses *and* non-commercial uses would effectively switch the burden of proof to the plaintiff on factor four. Because fair use is an affirmative defense, the defendant would have the burden of proof of showing that the work was in fact non-commercial or transformative, at which point the burden would switch to the plaintiff on market harm under factor four. This reading seems plausible to us, *particularly in the injunctive context,* but most subsequent Circuit Court cases have not adopted it. (Though District Courts sometimes adopt this interpretation.)

The more common approach in Circuit Courts is to hold that the burden of proof on *all* of the factors lies always with the defendant, because fair use is an affirmative defense. Courts also cite to *Acuff-Rose*'s critique of rigid "presumptions." However, three broad trends emerge. First, with the exception of "mere duplication for commercial use," courts have rejected the presumption that commercial uses are *ipso facto* unfair. Second, they have also rejected the proposition that if the use is transformative, the plaintiff bears the burden of showing market harm. Nimmer, for example, suggests the burden is still on the defendant on factor 4, even though, for transformative uses, "market substitution is at least less certain, and market harm may not be so readily inferred" (quoting *Acuff-Rose*). Finally, regardless of where the burden of proof lies as a matter of law, the finding that a use is transformative has a remarkable effect on *outcomes*. For example, Neil Netanel's excellent empirical study, *Making Sense of Fair Use,* found:

> In the period of 2006 to 2010—and this is essentially consistent with early cases in the post-*Campbell* period—84.21% of opinions that found that the use was unequivocally transformative and that opined on the issue of market harm found that there was no actual or potential harm to the plaintiff's market; only 1.3% found actual market harm.

Bottom line, although as a formal matter courts put the burden of proof on the absence of market harm on the defendant even in cases involving transformative use, they also tend overwhelmingly to *rule* for the defendant if a use is found to be transformative.

SunTrust Bank v. Houghton Mifflin Co.
268 F.3d 1257 (11th Cir. 2001)

BIRCH, Circuit Judge.

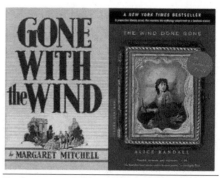

In this opinion, we decide whether publication of *The Wind Done Gone* ("*TWDG*"), a fictional work admittedly based on Margaret Mitchell's *Gone With the Wind* ("*GWTW*"), should be enjoined from publication based on alleged copyright violations. The district court granted a preliminary injunction against publication of *TWDG* because it found that Plaintiff-Appellee SunTrust Bank ("SunTrust") met the four-part test governing preliminary injunctions. We VACATE the injunction and REMAND for consideration of the remaining claims.

Book covers of *Gone With the Wind* and *The Wind Done Gone*

I. BACKGROUND

A. Procedural History

SunTrust is the trustee of the Mitchell Trust, which holds the copyright in *GWTW*. Since its publication in 1936, *GWTW* has become one of the best-selling books in the world, second in sales only to the Bible. The Mitchell Trust has actively managed the copyright, authorizing derivative works and a variety of commercial items. It has entered into a contract authorizing, under specified conditions, a second sequel to *GWTW* to be published by St. Martin's Press. The Mitchell Trust maintains the copyright in all of the derivative works as well.

Alice Randall, the author of *TWDG,* persuasively claims that her novel is a critique of *GWTW*'s depiction of slavery and the Civil-War-era American South. To this end, she appropriated the characters, plot and major scenes from *GWTW* into the first half of *TWDG*. According to SunTrust, *TWDG* "(1) explicitly refers to [*GWTW*] in its foreword; (2) copies core characters, character traits, and relationships from [*GWTW*]; (3) copies and summarizes famous scenes and other elements of the plot from [*GWTW*]; and (4) copies verbatim dialogues and descriptions from [*GWTW*]." Defendant-Appellant Houghton Mifflin, the publisher of *TWDG,* does not contest the first three allegations,[2] but nonetheless argues that there is no substantial similarity between the two works or, in the alternative, that the doctrine of fair use protects *TWDG* because it is primarily a parody of *GWTW*. . . .

II. DISCUSSION

Our primary focus at this stage of the case is on the appropriateness of the injunctive relief granted by the district court. In our analysis, we must evaluate the merits of SunTrust's copyright infringement claim, including Houghton Mifflin's affirmative defense of fair use. As we assess the fair-use defense, we examine to what extent a critic may use a work to communicate her criticism of the work without infringing the copyright in that work. . . .

. . . [T]he narrower question in this case is to what extent a critic may use the protected elements of an original work of authorship to communicate her criticism

---

[2] Houghton Mifflin denies that there are passages from *GWTW* copied verbatim in *TWDG*.

without infringing the copyright in that work. As will be discussed below, this becomes essentially an analysis of the fair use factors. . . .

Before considering a claimed fair-use defense based on parody, however, the Supreme Court has required that we ensure that "a parodic character may reasonably be perceived" in the allegedly infringing work. *Campbell v. Acuff-Rose Music, Inc.* (1994). The Supreme Court's definition of parody in *Campbell*, however, is somewhat vague. On the one hand, the Court suggests that the aim of parody is "comic effect or ridicule," but it then proceeds to discuss parody more expansively in terms of its "commentary" on the original. In light of the admonition in *Campbell* that courts should not judge the quality of the work or the success of the attempted humor in discerning its parodic character, we choose to take the broader view. For purposes of our fair-use analysis, we will treat a work as a parody if its aim is to comment upon or criticize a prior work by appropriating elements of the original in creating a new artistic, as opposed to scholarly or journalistic, work. Under this definition, the parodic character of *TWDG* is clear. *TWDG* is not a general commentary upon the Civil-War-era American South, but a specific criticism of and rejoinder to the depiction of slavery and the relationships between blacks and whites in *GWTW*. The fact that Randall chose to convey her criticisms of *GWTW* through a work of fiction, which she contends is a more powerful vehicle for her message than a scholarly article, does not, in and of itself, deprive *TWDG* of fair-use protection. We therefore proceed to an analysis of the four fair-use factors.

i. Purpose and Character of the Work

The first factor in the fair-use analysis, the purpose and character of the allegedly infringing work, has several facets. The first is whether *TWDG* serves a commercial purpose or nonprofit educational purpose. Despite whatever educational function *TWDG* may be able to lay claim to, it is undoubtedly a commercial product.[24] As the Supreme Court has stated, "[t]he crux of the profit/nonprofit distinction is not whether the sole motive of the use is monetary gain but whether the user stands to profit from exploitation of the copyrighted material without paying the customary price." *Harper & Row Publishing, Inc. v. Nation Enters.* (1985). The fact that *TWDG* was published for profit is the first factor weighing against a finding of fair use. However, *TWDG*'s for-profit status is strongly overshadowed and outweighed in view of its highly transformative use of *GWTW*'s copyrighted elements. . . .

The second factor in the "purpose and character" analysis relevant to this case is to what extent *TWDG*'s use of copyrighted elements of *GWTW* can be said to be "transformative." The inquiry is "whether the new work merely supersedes the objects of the original creation, or instead adds something new, with a further purpose or different character, altering the first with new expression, meaning, or message." *Campbell*. The issue of transformation is a double-edged sword in this case. On the one hand, the story of Cynara and her perception of the events in *TWDG* certainly adds new "expression, meaning, [and] message" to *GWTW*. From another perspective, however, *TWDG*'s success as a pure work of fiction depends heavily on copyrighted elements appropriated from *GWTW* to carry its own plot forward.

However, as noted above, *TWDG* is more than an abstract, pure fictional work. It is principally and purposefully a critical statement that seeks to rebut and destroy the perspective, judgments, and mythology of *GWTW*. Randall's literary goal is to explode the romantic, idealized portrait of the antebellum South during and after the Civil War. . . .

---

[24] Randall did not choose to publish her work of fiction on the internet free to all the world to read; rather, she chose a method of publication designed to generate economic profit.

In light of this, we find it difficult to conclude that Randall simply tried to "avoid the drudgery in working up something fresh." *Campbell*. It is hard to imagine how Randall could have specifically criticized *GWTW* without depending heavily upon copyrighted elements of that book. A parody is a work that seeks to comment upon or criticize another work by appropriating elements of the original. "Parody needs to mimic an original to make its point, and so has some claim to use the creation of its victim's (or collective victims') imagination." *Campbell*. Thus, Randall has fully employed those conscripted elements from *GWTW* to make war against it. . . .

While "transformative use is not absolutely necessary for a finding of fair use, . . . the more transformative the new work, the less will be the significance of other factors." In the case of *TWDG*, consideration of this factor certainly militates in favor of a finding of fair use, and, informs our analysis of the other factors, particularly the fourth, as discussed below.

ii. Nature of the Copyrighted Work

. . . *GWTW* is undoubtedly entitled to the greatest degree of protection as an original work of fiction. This factor is given little weight in parody cases, however. . . .

iii. Amount and Substantiality of the Portion Used

. . . *GWTW* is one of the most famous, popular, and enduring American novels ever written. Given the fame of the work and its primary characters, SunTrust argues that very little reference is required to conjure up *GWTW*. As we have already indicated in our discussion of substantial similarity, *TWDG* appropriates a substantial portion of the protected elements of *GWTW*. Houghton Mifflin argues that *TWDG* takes nothing from *GWTW* that does not serve a parodic purpose, the crux of the argument being that a large number of characters had to be taken from *GWTW* because each represents a different ideal or stereotype that requires commentary, and that the work as a whole could not be adequately commented upon without revisiting substantial portions of the plot, including its most famous scenes. Houghton Mifflin's argument is similar to that made by the defendants in *Harper & Row*, who argued for "expanding the doctrine of fair use to create what amounts to a public figure exception to copyright." To the extent Houghton Mifflin argues for extra latitude in copying from *GWTW* because of its fame, the Supreme Court has squarely foreclosed any such privilege. . . . Notably, however, the Court did not go so far as to grant well-known works a special, higher copyright status either.

There are numerous instances in which *TWDG* appropriates elements of *GWTW* and then transforms them for the purpose of commentary. . . .

On the other hand, however, we are told that not all of *TWDG*'s takings from *GWTW* are clearly justified as commentary. We have already determined that *TWDG* is a parody, but not every parody is a fair use. SunTrust contends that *TWDG*, at least at the margins, takes more of the protected elements of *GWTW* than was necessary to serve a parodic function. . . .

. . . [W]e are presented with conflicting and opposing arguments relative to the amount taken and whether it was too much or a necessary amount. . . .

. . . Based upon this record at this juncture, we cannot determine in any conclusive way whether "'the quantity and value of the materials used' are reasonable in relation to the purpose of the copying." *Campbell*.

iv. Effect on the Market Value of the Original

The final fair-use factor requires us to consider the effect that the publication of *TWDG* will have on the market for or value of SunTrust's copyright in *GWTW*, including the potential harm it may cause to the market for derivative works based on *GWTW*. *Campbell*. . . .

As for the potential market, SunTrust proffered evidence in the district court of the value of its copyright in *GWTW*. Several derivative works of *GWTW* have been authorized. . . .

. . . SunTrust focuses on the value of *GWTW* and its derivatives, but fails to address and offers little evidence or argument to demonstrate that *TWDG* would supplant demand for SunTrust's licensed derivatives. . . .

In contrast, the evidence proffered in support of the fair use defense specifically and correctly focused on market substitution and demonstrates why Randall's book is unlikely to displace sales of *GWTW*. Thus, we conclude, based on the current record, that SunTrust's evidence falls far short of establishing that *TWDG* or others like it will act as market substitutes for *GWTW* or will significantly harm its derivatives. Accordingly, the fourth fair use factor weighs in favor of *TWDG*. . . .

We reject the district court's conclusion that SunTrust has established its likelihood of success on the merits. To the contrary, based upon our analysis of the fair use factors we find, at this juncture, *TWDG* is entitled to a fair-use defense. . . .

. . . Accordingly, we vacate the district court's injunction. . . .

MARCUS, Circuit Judge, specially concurring.

I concur in Judge Birch's thoughtful and thorough opinion but write separately to emphasize that, on this limited record, SunTrust has fallen well short of establishing a likelihood of success on its copyright infringement claim. I stress three points. First, the district court erred by finding that the critical or parodic element of *The Wind Done Gone* is anything but clear-cut. Far from amounting to "unabated piracy," *The Wind Done Gone* is unequivocally parody, as both Judge Birch and the Supreme Court in *Campbell v. Acuff-Rose Music, Inc.*, define that term. Indeed, the book is critical by constitution, its main aim being to shatter *Gone With the Wind*'s window on life in the antebellum and Civil War South. Second, in service of this parodic design, Randall radically reshapes what she borrows from Mitchell. I would thus go even further than Judge Birch in underscoring the transformative nature of Randall's book; the "purpose and nature" prong of the fair use analysis is not a close call, in my view. Third, the preliminary record, if anything, suggests that *The Wind Done Gone* will not act as a substitute for Mitchell's original. What little evidence we have before us indicates that these two books aim at different readerships; to the extent that there is any overlap between these respective markets, further factfinding may well reveal that these two books will act as complements rather than substitutes. . . .

The Wind Done Gone's critical nature is clearer than that of other works courts have found to be protected parodies. This case does not involve a pop song that simply "comment[s] on the naiveté of the original of an earlier day." *Campbell*. . . .

. . . The two books' shared subject matter simply helps demonstrate how *The Wind Done Gone*'s critical character is more pronounced than many protected parodies. Our analysis might have been different had we faced a conflict between two literary worldviews of less perfect polarity, for example, or two works that differed over a matter of less sharp controversy. As Judge Birch explains in detail, though, *The Wind Done Gone*'s plain object is to make war on *Gone with the Wind*'s specific outlook—on a topic that itself tends to elicit no small comment and criticism. . . .

. . . Had Randall chosen to write *The Wind Done Gone* from the point of view of one of Mitchell's original characters, for example, and done no more than put a new gloss on the familiar tale without criticizing or commenting on its fundamental theme and spirit, Houghton Mifflin's case would have been much tougher.[3] . . .

The district court recognized that "the two works . . . present polar viewpoints," yet concluded that *The Wind Done Gone* recreates "the same fictional world, described in the same way and inhabited by the same people, who are doing the same things." Of course, both works are set in the antebellum South, but *The Wind Done Gone* creates an alter universe described in a wholly different style, and inhabited by shrewd slaves who manipulate incompetent masters and free blacks who thrive independent of the white plantation system. Like a political, thematic, and stylistic negative, *The Wind Done Gone* inverts *Gone With the Wind*'s portrait of race relations of the place and era.

Given this stark contrast, I would go further than Judge Birch in stressing the transformative nature of Randall's book. . . .

Questions:

1.) What does this case add to the definition and explanation of the relative roles of "parody," "satire," "commentary" and "transformation" in fair use?

2.) You are the lawyer for the Mitchell Estate, appealing to the Supreme Court. You need to convince the Justices that this decision puts us on a disastrous path. You realize that pitching your case with the soundbite "contemporary African American novelists should be forbidden from parodying the iconic novel romanticizing the slaveholding South" might not be a winning strategy. Thus you have to show convincingly how this case opens the door to a set of activities that the Justices would view as obviously undesirable. Rehearse your parade of horribles. Grease your slippery slope. Open your floodgates of litigation. Be prepared to show your work (and your mixed metaphors) in class.

3.) Note the court's acknowledgment of the commercial nature of Randall's work. "Randall did not choose to publish her work of fiction on the internet free to all the world to read; rather, she chose a method of publication designed to generate economic profit." In the past, anyone who wished to reach a wide audience—which one might do for distinctly "noncommercial reasons"—might have had to resort to a commercial publishing platform. Does the availability of the internet as a method of free distribution change this calculus, making the person who chooses a commercial publisher seem more focused on profit?

4.) In a portion of the *SunTrust* opinion that was not included above, Judge Birch says in a footnote: "I believe that fair use should be considered an affirmative *right* under the 1976 Act, rather than merely an affirmative defense, as it is defined in the Act as a use that is not a violation of copyright. However, fair use is commonly referred to as an affirmative defense, and, as we are bound by Supreme Court precedent, we will apply it as such. Nevertheless, the fact that the fair use right must be procedurally asserted as an affirmative

---

[3] It is hazardous to speculate too much about the legality of various hypothetical parodies, given the many forms literary parody may take, and the levels of sophistication it may reach. The irony and self-awareness common in contemporary literature, in particular, may one day pose difficulties for the fair use doctrine. It is not hard to imagine a copyrighted story that parodies itself by design, or an author who makes a career out of parodying his own work in each subsequent one. (Vladimir Nabokov, among others, hinted at the potential for such practices. *See, e.g.,* Vladimir Nabokov, *Pale Fire* (1962) (a novel consisting of a poem and substantial prose commentary on that poem).) Suppose that this hypothetical author in turn becomes the target of parody by another. Could the second author's work be said to usurp demand for the original author's self-parody? Here, we face a much simpler problem: *Gone With the Wind* lacks any apparent self-directed irony, and Randall's attack on it is just as straight-forward.

defense does not detract from its constitutional significance as a guarantor to access and use for First Amendment purposes" (emphasis in original). What difference does it make if fair use is considered an affirmative right rather than merely a defense to copyright infringement? Judge Birch says that fair use is "defined in the [Copyright] Act as a use that is not a violation of copyright." Look at the language in sections 106 and 107. § 106 begins "*Subject to sections 107* through 122, the owner of copyright under this title has the exclusive rights to do and to authorize any of the following. . . ." § 107 is titled "Limitations on exclusive rights: Fair use" and begins "Notwithstanding the provisions of section[] 106 . . . the fair use of a copyrighted work . . . is not an infringement of copyright." Does any of this language support Judge Birch's conclusion? Do you agree with him?

PROBLEM 13-2

You represent *The New York Times*. One of its reporters has just found a diary apparently belonging to Special Prosecutor Jonathan Edwards. Edwards is well-known because his recent investigations actually led to the impeachment, but not the conviction, of the President on charges of perjury and obstruction of justice. The prosecution was highly controversial and—in an unusual step—Edwards also released the full text of "the Edwards Report" online, complete with all of the embarrassing details of the President's relationship with a White House intern. Critics claimed he was trying to win a battle in the courts of public opinion that he would not win in Congress. Defenders praised him as operating in the noble tradition of whistle blowers who exposed presidential scandals such as Watergate.

In the diary, Edwards, in his famous and characteristically Biblical writing style, describes in apocalyptic and profanity-laden terms his envy of the President's hair, wife and status, and his distaste for the President's morals, and repeats many times his belief that "extremity in the pursuit of scoundrels is no vice." The tone is very different from the bland and regretful official prose of the Edwards Report. *The New York Times* reporter has planned an article, accompanied by a two page special pull-out, reproducing several thousand words of the diary verbatim in small print (in the style of the Unabomber manifesto) just to, as he says, "give the readers a true sense of his tone that they just cannot get any other way. It is the only way to show the reader the truth while freeing us from the claim that *The Times* is being selective or biased in what it excerpted!" He wants your opinion on this course of action. Alternatively, the reporter has planned an article which intersperses the wording of the Edwards Report sent to Congress with the profane fulminations of Edwards' diary—to ludicrous effect, it has to be said. Edwards' lawyers will move for an injunction to prevent publication. The reporter wants your advice on both courses of action.

What are your answers regarding the construction of the article, and possible fair use claims? How would your answers be different if the excerpts came from a purloined copy of Edwards' much-anticipated forthcoming autobiography, *"Bill"* of Attainder? In either case, would an injunction against publication have to meet certain First Amendment standards to avoid being a prior restraint of speech?

4.) Fair Use Meets Technology

Sega Enterprises Ltd. v. Accolade, Inc.
977 F.2d 1510 (9th Cir. 1992)

REINHARDT, Circuit Judge.

This case presents several difficult questions of first impression involving our copyright and trademark laws. We are asked to determine, first, whether the Copyright Act permits persons who are neither copyright holders nor licensees to disassemble a copyrighted computer program in order to gain an understanding of the unprotected functional elements of the program. In light of the public policies underlying the Act, we conclude that, when the person seeking the understanding has a legitimate reason for doing so and when no other means of access to the unprotected elements exists, such disassembly is as a matter of law a fair use of the copyrighted work. Second, we must decide the legal consequences under the Lanham Trademark Act of a computer manufacturer's use of a security system that affords access to its computers to software cartridges that include an initialization code which triggers a screen display of the computer manufacturer's trademark. The computer manufacturer also manufactures software cartridges; those cartridges all contain the initialization code. The question is whether the computer manufacturer may enjoin competing cartridge manufacturers from gaining access to its computers through the use of the code on the ground that such use will result in the display of a "false" trademark. Again, our holding is based on the public policies underlying the statute. We hold that when there is no other method of access to the computer that is known or readily available to rival cartridge manufacturers, the use of the initialization code by a rival does not violate the Act even though that use triggers a misleading trademark display. Accordingly, we reverse the district court's grant of a preliminary injunction in favor of plaintiff-appellee Sega Enterprises, Ltd. on its claims of copyright and trademark infringement. We decline, however, to order that an injunction *pendente lite* issue precluding Sega from continuing to use its security system, even though such use may result in a certain amount of false labeling. We prefer to leave the decision on that question to the district court initially.

I. Background

Plaintiff-appellee Sega Enterprises, Ltd. ("Sega"), a Japanese corporation, and its subsidiary, Sega of America, develop and market video entertainment systems, including the "Genesis" console (distributed in Asia under the name "Mega-Drive") and video game cartridges. Defendant-appellant Accolade, Inc., is an independent developer, manufacturer, and marketer of computer entertainment software, including game cartridges that are compatible with the Genesis console, as well as game cartridges that are compatible with other computer systems.

Sega licenses its copyrighted computer code and its "SEGA" trademark to a number of independent developers of computer game software. Those licensees develop and sell Genesis-compatible video games in competition with Sega. Accolade is not and never has been a licensee of Sega. Prior to rendering its own games compatible with the Genesis console, Accolade explored the possibility of entering into a licensing agreement with Sega, but abandoned the effort because the agreement would have required that Sega be the exclusive manufacturer of all games produced by Accolade.

Accolade used a two-step process to render its video games compatible with the Genesis console. First, it "reverse engineered" Sega's video game programs in order to discover the requirements for compatibility with the Genesis console. As part of the reverse engineering process, Accolade transformed the machine-readable object code contained in commercially available copies of Sega's game cartridges into human-readable source code using a process called "disassembly" or "decompilation".[2] Accolade purchased a Genesis console and three Sega game cartridges, wired a decompiler into the console circuitry, and generated printouts of the resulting source code. Accolade engineers studied and annotated the printouts in order to identify areas of commonality among the three game programs. They then loaded the disassembled code back into a computer, and experimented to discover the interface specifications for the Genesis console by modifying the programs and studying the results. At the end of the reverse engineering process, Accolade created a development manual that incorporated the information it had discovered about the requirements for a Genesis-compatible game. According to the Accolade employees who created the manual, the manual contained only functional descriptions of the interface requirements and did not include any of Sega's code.

III. Copyright Issues

Accolade raises four arguments in support of its position that disassembly of the object code in a copyrighted computer program does not constitute copyright infringement. First, it maintains that intermediate copying does not infringe the exclusive rights granted to copyright owners in section 106 of the Copyright Act unless the end product of the copying is substantially similar to the copyrighted work. Second, it argues that disassembly of object code in order to gain an understanding of the ideas and functional concepts embodied in the code is lawful under section 102(b) of the Act, which exempts ideas and functional concepts from copyright protection. Third, it suggests that disassembly is authorized by section 117 of the Act, which entitles the lawful owner of a copy of a computer program to load the program into a computer. Finally, Accolade contends that disassembly of object code in order to gain an understanding of the ideas and functional concepts embodied in the code is a fair use that is privileged by section 107 of the Act.

Neither the language of the Act nor the law of this circuit supports Accolade's first three arguments. Accolade's fourth argument, however, has merit. Although the question is fairly debatable, we conclude based on the policies underlying the Copyright Act that disassembly of copyrighted object code is, as a matter of law, a fair use of the copyrighted work if such disassembly provides the only means of access to those elements of the code that are not protected by copyright and the copier has a legitimate reason for seeking such access. Accordingly, we hold that Sega has failed to demonstrate a likelihood of success on the merits of its copyright claim. Because on the record before us the hardships do not

---

[2] Computer programs are written in specialized alphanumeric languages, or "source code". In order to operate a computer, source code must be translated into computer readable form, or "object code". Object code uses only two symbols, 0 and 1, in combinations which represent the alphanumeric characters of the source code. A program written in source code is translated into object code using a computer program called an "assembler" or "compiler", and then imprinted onto a silicon chip for commercial distribution. Devices called "disassemblers" or "decompilers" can reverse this process by "reading" the electronic signals for "0" and "1" that are produced while the program is being run, storing the resulting object code in computer memory, and translating the object code into source code. Both assembly and disassembly devices are commercially available, and both types of devices are widely used within the software industry.

tip sharply (or at all) in Sega's favor, the preliminary injunction issued in its favor must be dissolved, at least with respect to that claim.

A. Intermediate Copying

We have previously held that the Copyright Act does not distinguish between unauthorized copies of a copyrighted work on the basis of what stage of the alleged infringer's work the unauthorized copies represent. *Walker v. University Books* (9th Cir. 1979) ("[T]he fact that an allegedly infringing copy of a protected work may itself be only an inchoate representation of some final product to be marketed commercially does not in itself negate the possibility of infringement."). Our holding in *Walker* was based on the plain language of the Act. Section 106 grants to the copyright owner the exclusive rights "to reproduce the work in copies", "to prepare derivative works based upon the copyrighted work", and to authorize the preparation of copies and derivative works. 17 U.S.C. § 106(1)–(2). Section 501 provides that "[a]nyone who violates any of the exclusive rights of the copyright owner as provided by sections 106 through 118 . . . is an infringer of the copyright." § 501(a). On its face, that language unambiguously encompasses and proscribes "intermediate copying".

In order to constitute a "copy" for purposes of the Act, the allegedly infringing work must be fixed in some tangible form, "from which the work can be perceived, reproduced, or otherwise communicated, either directly or with the aid of a machine or device." 17 U.S.C. § 101. The computer file generated by the disassembly program, the printouts of the disassembled code, and the computer files containing Accolade's modifications of the code that were generated during the reverse engineering process all satisfy that requirement. The intermediate copying done by Accolade therefore falls squarely within the category of acts that are prohibited by the statute. . . .

. . . [T]he question whether intermediate copying of computer object code infringes the exclusive rights granted to the copyright owner in section 106 of the Copyright Act is a question of first impression. In light of the unambiguous language of the Act, we decline to depart from the rule set forth in *Walker* for copyrighted works generally. Accordingly, we hold that intermediate copying of computer object code may infringe the exclusive rights granted to the copyright owner in section 106 of the Copyright Act regardless of whether the end product of the copying also infringes those rights. If intermediate copying is permissible under the Act, authority for such copying must be found in one of the statutory provisions to which the rights granted in section 106 are subject.

B. The Idea/Expression Distinction

Accolade next contends that disassembly of computer object code does not violate the Copyright Act because it is necessary in order to gain access to the ideas and functional concepts embodied in the code, which are not protected by copyright. 17 U.S.C. § 102(b). Because humans cannot comprehend object code, it reasons, disassembly of a commercially available computer program into human-readable form should not be considered an infringement of the owner's copyright. Insofar as Accolade suggests that disassembly of object code is lawful *per se,* it seeks to overturn settled law.

Accolade's argument regarding access to ideas is, in essence, an argument that object code is not eligible for the full range of copyright protection. Although some scholarly authority supports that view, we have previously rejected it based on the language and legislative history of the Copyright Act. . . .

. . . Nor does the Act require that a work be directly accessible to humans in order to be eligible for copyright protection. Rather, it extends protection to all original works "which . . . can be perceived, reproduced, or otherwise communicated, either directly or with the aid of a machine or device." 17 U.S.C. § 102(a). The statutory language, read together with the CONTU report [the report from the National Commission on New Technological Uses of Copyrighted Works (CONTU) that led to the Copyright Act's extension of copyright protection to computer programs], leads inexorably to the conclusion that the copyright in a computer program extends to the object code version of the program.

Nor does a refusal to recognize a *per se* right to disassemble object code lead to an absurd result. The ideas and functional concepts underlying many types of computer programs, including word processing programs, spreadsheets, and video game displays, are readily discernible without the need for disassembly, because the operation of such programs is visible on the computer screen. The need to disassemble object code arises, if at all, only in connection with operations systems, system interface procedures, and other programs that are not visible to the user when operating—and then only when no alternative means of gaining an understanding of those ideas and functional concepts exists. In our view, consideration of the unique nature of computer object code thus is more appropriate as part of the case-by-case, equitable "fair use" analysis authorized by section 107 of the Act. Accordingly, we reject Accolade's second argument. . . .

D. Fair Use

Accolade contends, finally, that its disassembly of copyrighted object code as a necessary step in its examination of the unprotected ideas and functional concepts embodied in the code is a fair use that is privileged by section 107 of the Act. Because, in the case before us, disassembly is the only means of gaining access to those unprotected aspects of the program, and because Accolade has a legitimate interest in gaining such access (in order to determine how to make its cartridges compatible with the Genesis console), we agree with Accolade. Where there is good reason for studying or examining the unprotected aspects of a copyrighted computer program, disassembly for purposes of such study or examination constitutes a fair use. . . .

Section 107 lists the factors to be considered in determining whether a particular use is a fair one. . . . The statutory factors are not exclusive. Rather, the doctrine of fair use is in essence "an equitable rule of reason." *Harper & Row, Publishers, Inc. v. Nation Enterprises* (1985). Fair use is a mixed question of law and fact. "Where the district court has found facts sufficient to evaluate each of the statutory factors," an appellate court may resolve the fair use question as a matter of law.

In determining that Accolade's disassembly of Sega's object code did not constitute a fair use, the district court treated the first and fourth statutory factors as dispositive, and ignored the second factor entirely. Given the nature and characteristics of Accolade's direct use of the copied works, the ultimate use to which Accolade put the functional information it obtained, and the nature of the market for home video entertainment systems, we conclude that neither the first nor the fourth factor weighs in Sega's favor. In fact, we conclude that both factors support Accolade's fair use defense, as does the second factor, a factor which is important to the resolution of cases such as the one before us.

(a) With respect to the first statutory factor, we observe initially that the fact that copying is for a commercial purpose weighs against a finding of fair use. *Harper & Row*. However, the presumption of unfairness that arises in such cases can be rebutted by the characteristics of a particular commercial use. Further "[t]he commercial nature of a use is a matter of degree, not an absolute. . . ." *Maxtone-Graham v. Burtchaell* (2d Cir. 1986).

Sega argues that because Accolade copied its object code in order to produce a competing product, the *Harper & Row* presumption applies and precludes a finding of fair use. That analysis is far too simple and ignores a number of important considerations. We must consider other aspects of "the purpose and character of the use" as well. As we have noted, the use at issue was an intermediate one only and thus any commercial "exploitation" was indirect or derivative.

The declarations of Accolade's employees indicate, and the district court found, that Accolade copied Sega's software solely in order to discover the functional requirements for compatibility with the Genesis console—aspects of Sega's programs that are not protected by copyright. 17 U.S.C. § 102(b). With respect to the video game programs contained in Accolade's game cartridges, there is no evidence in the record that Accolade sought to avoid performing its own creative work. Indeed, most of the games that Accolade released for use with the Genesis console were originally developed for other hardware systems. Moreover, with respect to the interface procedures for the Genesis console, Accolade did not seek to avoid paying a customarily charged fee for use of those procedures, nor did it simply copy Sega's code; rather, it wrote its own procedures based on what it had learned through disassembly. Taken together, these facts indicate that although Accolade's ultimate purpose was the release of Genesis-compatible games for sale, its direct purpose in copying Sega's code, and thus its direct use of the copyrighted material, was simply to study the functional requirements for Genesis compatibility so that it could modify existing games and make them usable with the Genesis console. Moreover, as we discuss below, no other method of studying those requirements was available to Accolade. On these facts, we conclude that Accolade copied Sega's code for a legitimate, essentially non-exploitative purpose, and that the commercial aspect of its use can best be described as of minimal significance.

We further note that we are free to consider the public benefit resulting from a particular use notwithstanding the fact that the alleged infringer may gain commercially. Public benefit need not be direct or tangible, but may arise because the challenged use serves a public interest. In the case before us, Accolade's identification of the functional requirements for Genesis compatibility has led to an increase in the number of independently designed video game programs offered for use with the Genesis console. It is precisely this growth in creative expression, based on the dissemination of other creative works and the unprotected ideas contained in those works, that the Copyright Act was intended to promote. The fact that Genesis-compatible video games are not scholarly works, but works offered for sale on the market, does not alter our judgment in this regard. We conclude that given the purpose and character of Accolade's use of Sega's video game programs, the presumption of unfairness has been overcome and the first statutory factor weighs in favor of Accolade.

(b) As applied, the fourth statutory factor, effect on the potential market for the copyrighted work, bears a close relationship to the "purpose and character" inquiry in that it, too, accommodates the distinction between the copying of works in order to make independent creative expression possible and the simple exploitation of another's creative efforts. We must, of course, inquire whether, "if [the challenged use] should become widespread, it would adversely affect the potential market for the copyrighted work," *Sony Corp. v. Universal City Studios* (1984), by diminishing potential sales, interfering with marketability, or usurping the market. If the copying resulted in the latter effect, all other considerations might be irrelevant. The *Harper & Row* Court found a use that effectively usurped the market for the copyrighted work by supplanting that work to be dispositive.

However, the same consequences do not and could not attach to a use which simply enables the copier to enter the market for works of the same type as the copied work.

Image of box for Accolade's "Ishido" game from http://gamesdbase.com /game/sega-genesis/ishido-the-way-of-stones.aspx.

Unlike the defendant in *Harper & Row*, which printed excerpts from President Ford's memoirs verbatim with the stated purpose of "scooping" a *Time* magazine review of the book, Accolade did not attempt to "scoop" Sega's release of any particular game or games, but sought only to become a legitimate competitor in the field of Genesis-compatible video games. Within that market, it is the characteristics of the game program as experienced by the user that determine the program's commercial success. As we have noted, there is nothing in the record that suggests that Accolade copied any of those elements.

By facilitating the entry of a new competitor, the first lawful one that is not a Sega licensee, Accolade's disassembly of Sega's software undoubtedly "affected" the market for Genesis-compatible games in an indirect fashion. We note, however, that while no consumer except the most avid devotee of President Ford's regime might be expected to buy more than one version of the President's memoirs, video game users typically purchase more than one game. There is no basis for assuming that Accolade's "Ishido" has significantly affected the market for Sega's "Altered Beast," since a consumer might easily purchase both; nor does it seem unlikely that a consumer particularly interested in sports might purchase both Accolade's "Mike Ditka Power Football" and Sega's "Joe Montana Football," particularly if the games are, as Accolade contends, not substantially similar. In any event, an attempt to monopolize the market by making it impossible for others to compete runs counter to the statutory purpose of promoting creative expression and cannot constitute a strong equitable basis for resisting the invocation of the fair use doctrine. Thus, we conclude that the fourth statutory factor weighs in Accolade's, not Sega's, favor, notwithstanding the minor economic loss Sega may suffer.

(c) The second statutory factor, the nature of the copyrighted work, reflects the fact that not all copyrighted works are entitled to the same level of protection. The protection established by the Copyright Act for original works of authorship does not extend to the ideas underlying a work or to the functional or factual aspects of the work. 17 U.S.C. § 102(b). To the extent that a work is functional or factual, it may be copied, *Baker v. Selden* (1879), as may those expressive elements of the work that "must necessarily be used as incident to" expression of the underlying ideas, functional concepts, or facts. Works of fiction receive greater protection than works that have strong factual elements, such as historical or biographical works, or works that have strong functional elements, such as accounting textbooks, *Baker*. Works that are merely compilations of fact are copyrightable, but the copyright in such a work is "thin."

Computer programs pose unique problems for the application of the "idea/ expression distinction" that determines the extent of copyright protection. To the extent that there are many possible ways of accomplishing a given task or fulfilling a particular market demand, the programmer's choice of program structure and design may be highly creative and idiosyncratic. However, computer programs are, in essence, utilitarian articles—articles that accomplish tasks. As such, they contain many logical, structural, and visual display elements that are dictated by the function to be performed, by considerations of efficiency, or by external factors such as compatibility requirements and industry demands. *Computer Assoc. Int'l, Inc. v. Altai, Inc.* (2d Cir. 1992) ("*CAI*"). In some circumstances, even the exact set of commands used by the programmer is deemed functional rather than creative for purposes of copyright. "[W]hen specific instructions, even though previously copyrighted, are the only and essential means of accomplishing a given task, their later use by another will not amount to infringement." *CONTU Report.*[7]

Because of the hybrid nature of computer programs, there is no settled standard for identifying what is protected expression and what is unprotected idea in a case involving the alleged infringement of a copyright in computer software. We are in wholehearted agreement with the Second Circuit's recent observation that "[t]hus far, many of the decisions in this area reflect the courts' attempt to fit the proverbial square peg in a round hole." *CAI*. In 1986, the Third Circuit attempted to resolve the dilemma by suggesting that the idea or function of a computer program is the idea of the program as a whole, and "everything that is not necessary to that purpose or function [is] part of the expression of that idea." *Whelan Assoc., Inc. v. Jaslow Dental Laboratory, Inc.* (3d Cir. 1986) (emphasis omitted). The *Whelan* rule, however, has been widely—and soundly—criticized as simplistic and overbroad. *See CAI* (citing cases, treatises, and articles). In reality, "a computer program's ultimate function or purpose is the composite result of interacting subroutines. Since each subroutine is itself a program, and thus, may be said to have its own 'idea,' *Whelan*'s general formulation . . . is descriptively inadequate." For example, the computer program at issue in the case before us, a video game program, contains at least two such subroutines—the subroutine that allows the user to interact with the video game and the subroutine that allows the game cartridge to interact with the console. Under a test that breaks down a computer program into its component subroutines and sub-subroutines and then identifies the idea or core functional element of each, such as the test recently adopted by the Second Circuit in *CAI*, many aspects of the program are not protected by copyright. In our view, in light of the essentially utilitarian nature of computer programs, the Second Circuit's approach is an appropriate one.

Sega argues that even if many elements of its video game programs are properly characterized as functional and therefore not protected by copyright, Accolade copied protected expression. Sega is correct. The record makes clear that disassembly is wholesale copying. Because computer programs are also unique among copyrighted works in the form in which they are distributed for public use, however, Sega's observation does not bring us much closer to a resolution of the dispute.

The unprotected aspects of most functional works are readily accessible to the human eye. The systems described in accounting textbooks or the basic structural concepts embodied in architectural plans, to give two examples, can be easily copied

---

[7] We therefore reject Sega's belated suggestion that Accolade's incorporation of the code which "unlocks" the Genesis III console is not a fair use. Our decision on this point is entirely consistent with *Atari v. Nintendo* (Fed. Cir. 1992). Although *Nintendo* extended copyright protection to Nintendo's 10NES security system, that system consisted of an *original program* which generates an arbitrary data stream "key" which unlocks the NES console. Creativity and originality went into the design of that program. Moreover, the federal circuit concluded that there is a "multitude of different ways to generate a data stream which unlocks the NES console." The circumstances are clearly different here. Sega's key appears to be functional. It consists merely of 20 bytes of initialization code plus the letters S-E-G-A. There is no showing that there is a multitude of different ways to unlock the Genesis III console. Finally, we note that Sega's security code is of such de minimis length that it is probably unprotected under the words and short phrases doctrine.

without also copying any of the protected, expressive aspects of the original works. Computer programs, however, are typically distributed for public use in object code form, embedded in a silicon chip or on a floppy disk. For that reason, humans often cannot gain access to the unprotected ideas and functional concepts contained in object code without disassembling that code—i.e., making copies.[8]

Sega argues that the record does not establish that disassembly of its object code is the only available method for gaining access to the interface specifications for the Genesis console, and the district court agreed. An independent examination of the record reveals that Sega misstates its contents, and demonstrates that the district court committed clear error in this respect.

First, the record clearly establishes that humans cannot *read* object code. Sega makes much of Mike Lorenzen's statement that a reverse engineer can work directly from the zeroes and ones of object code but "[i]t's not as fun." In full, Lorenzen's statements establish only that the use of an *electronic* decompiler is not absolutely necessary. Trained programmers can disassemble object code by hand. Because even a trained programmer cannot possibly remember the millions of zeroes and ones that make up a program, however, he must make a written or computerized copy of the disassembled code in order to keep track of his work. The relevant fact for purposes of Sega's copyright infringement claim and Accolade's fair use defense is that *translation* of a program from object code into source code cannot be accomplished without making copies of the code.

Second, the record provides no support for a conclusion that a viable alternative to disassembly exists. . . .

In summary, the record clearly establishes that disassembly of the object code in Sega's video game cartridges was necessary in order to understand the functional requirements for Genesis compatibility. The interface procedures for the Genesis console are distributed for public use only in object code form, and are not visible to the user during operation of the video game program. Because object code cannot be read by humans, it must be disassembled, either by hand or by machine. Disassembly of object code necessarily entails copying. Those facts dictate our analysis of the second statutory fair use factor. If disassembly of copyrighted object code is *per se* an unfair use, the owner of the copyright gains a *de facto* monopoly over the functional aspects of his work—aspects that were expressly denied copyright protection by Congress. In order to enjoy a lawful monopoly over the idea or functional principle underlying a work, the creator of the work must satisfy the more stringent standards imposed by the patent laws. *Bonito Boats, Inc. v. Thunder Craft Boats, Inc.* (1989). Sega does not hold a patent on the Genesis console.

Because Sega's video game programs contain unprotected aspects that cannot be examined without copying, we afford them a lower degree of protection than more traditional literary works. . . .

(d) As to the third statutory factor, Accolade disassembled entire programs written by Sega. Accordingly, the third factor weighs against Accolade. The fact that an entire work was copied does not, however, preclude a finding a fair use. *Sony Corp.* In fact, where the ultimate (as opposed to direct) use is as limited as it was here, the factor is of very little weight.

---

[8] We do not intend to suggest that disassembly is always the only available means of access to those aspects of a computer program that are unprotected by copyright. As we noted in Part III(B), *supra,* in many cases the operation of a program is directly reflected on the screen display and therefore visible to the human eye. In those cases, it is likely that a reverse engineer would not need to examine the code in order to understand what the program does.

(e) In summary, careful analysis of the purpose and characteristics of Accolade's use of Sega's video game programs, the nature of the computer programs involved, and the nature of the market for video game cartridges yields the conclusion that the first, second, and fourth statutory fair use factors weigh in favor of Accolade, while only the third weighs in favor of Sega, and even then only slightly. Accordingly, Accolade clearly has by far the better case on the fair use issue.

We are not unaware of the fact that to those used to considering copyright issues in more traditional contexts, our result may seem incongruous at first blush. To oversimplify, the record establishes that Accolade, a commercial competitor of Sega, engaged in wholesale copying of Sega's copyrighted code as a preliminary step in the development of a competing product. However, the key to this case is that we are dealing with computer software, a relatively unexplored area in the world of copyright law. We must avoid the temptation of trying to force "the proverbial square peg in[to] a round hole."

In determining whether a challenged use of copyrighted material is fair, a court must keep in mind the public policy underlying the Copyright Act. "'The immediate effect of our copyright law is to secure a fair return for an "author's" creative labor. But the ultimate aim is, by this incentive, to stimulate artistic creativity for the general public good.'" *Sony Corp.* When technological change has rendered an aspect or application of the Copyright Act ambiguous, "'the Copyright Act must be construed in light of this basic purpose.'" As discussed above, the fact that computer programs are distributed for public use in object code form often precludes public access to the ideas and functional concepts contained in those programs, and thus confers on the copyright owner a *de facto* monopoly over those ideas and functional concepts. That result defeats the fundamental purpose of the Copyright Act—to encourage the production of original works by protecting the expressive elements of those works while leaving the ideas, facts, and functional concepts in the public domain for others to build on.

Sega argues that the considerable time, effort, and money that went into development of the Genesis and Genesis-compatible video games militate against a finding of fair use. Borrowing from antitrust principles, Sega attempts to label Accolade a "free rider" on its product development efforts. In *Feist Publications*, however, the Court unequivocally rejected the "sweat of the brow" rationale for copyright protection. Under the Copyright Act, if a work is largely functional, it receives only weak protection. "This result is neither unfair nor unfortunate. It is the means by which copyright advances the progress of science and art." *Feist* ("In truth, '[i]t is just such wasted effort that the proscription against the copyright of ideas and facts . . . [is] designed to prevent.'"). Here, while the work may not be largely functional, it incorporates functional elements which do not merit protection. The equitable considerations involved weigh on the side of public access. Accordingly, we reject Sega's argument.

(f) We conclude that where disassembly is the only way to gain access to the ideas and functional elements embodied in a copyrighted computer program and where there is a legitimate reason for seeking such access, disassembly is a fair use of the copyrighted work, as a matter of law. Our conclusion does not, of course, insulate Accolade from a claim of copyright infringement with respect to its finished products. Sega has reserved the right to raise such a claim, and it may do so on remand. . . .

Questions:

1.) *Sega* part of our case-study in copyright over software. The plaintiff in *Sega* might (and did) say something like this: "Fair use asks us to look at the nature of the activity, the nature of the work, the amount of copying and the effect on the market for the original work. This is a blatantly *commercial* copying of the *entirety* of a *copyrighted work* that may well have a *severe negative impact on the market*. Every factor clearly favors us or, at best, is neutral." Why did the defendant win?

2.) What is the relevant market in a fair use analysis? Should we focus on Sega's market or the market for the copyrighted work at issue? Are they the same?

3.) As in *Lotus* (but also in *Oracle*) the "stakes" here are interoperability and lock-in. The court says "where disassembly is the only way to gain access to the ideas and functional elements embodied in a copyrighted computer program and where there is a legitimate reason for seeking such access, disassembly is a fair use of the copyrighted work, as a matter of law." The court says we should not focus on the form of what is happening (copying!) but on the substance (reaching unprotectable elements!). Do you agree? In terms of its goals, how would you compare this ruling to other doctrines such as nominative use or genericide in trademark, or merger in copyright law, that override or limit the intellectual property right at issue in order to protect competition or prevent copyright holders from leveraging their rights over protectable material into control over unprotectable material?

4.) This case involves a complementary market—a platform (the game console) and an ecosystem of programs (the game cartridges). Similar markets can be found in phones and the apps that run on them, or particular MP3 players and the proprietary music stores that offer content for that player. Does this kind of market have any special significance for the fair use analysis? What is the best argument for keeping this ecosystem closed? Open? How should copyright law be involved in those arguments?

PROBLEM 13-3

You are the chief counsel for a prominent member of the Senate Judiciary Committee. She is deeply interested in the effect that copyright law has on technology. She has asked you to consider the cumulative effect of three cases: *Lotus v. Borland, Computer Associates v. Altai*, and *Sega v. Accolade*. First, she wants you to describe exactly what the courts did in each case—which doctrines of copyright law were involved. Second, she wants to know what policies or goals the courts were pursuing. Third, as someone who is expected to vote on the confirmation of Federal judges, she wants to know whether you think the judges in these cases showed fidelity to the judicial role. Finally, she wants to know whether the decision in *Sega* should be overturned, left as it is, or statutorily codified in section 107. **What are your answers to these questions?**

Perfect 10 v. Google
508 F.3d 1146 (9th Cir. 2007)

IKUTA, Circuit Judge.

    In this appeal, we consider a copyright owner's efforts to stop an Internet search engine from facilitating access to infringing images. Perfect 10, Inc. sued Google Inc., for infringing Perfect 10's copyrighted photographs of nude models, among other claims. . . . The district court preliminarily enjoined Google from creating and publicly displaying thumbnail versions of Perfect 10's images, but did not enjoin Google from linking to third-party websites that display infringing full-size versions of Perfect 10's images. . . .

I
Background

. . . Google operates a search engine, a software program that automatically accesses thousands of websites (collections of webpages) and indexes them within a database stored on Google's computers. When a Google user accesses the Google website and types in a search query, Google's software searches its database for websites responsive to that search query. Google then sends relevant information from its index of websites to the user's computer. Google's search engines can provide results in the form of text, images, or videos.

The Google search engine that provides responses in the form of images is called "Google Image Search." In response to a search query, Google Image Search identifies text in its database responsive to the query and then communicates to users the images associated with the relevant text. Google's software cannot recognize and index the images themselves. Google Image Search provides search results as a webpage of small images called "thumbnails," which are stored in Google's servers. The thumbnail images are reduced, lower-resolution versions of full-sized images stored on third-party computers.

When a user clicks on a thumbnail image, the user's browser program interprets HTML instructions on Google's webpage. These HTML instructions direct the user's browser to cause a rectangular area (a "window") to appear on the user's computer screen. The window has two separate areas of information. The browser fills the top section of the screen with information from the Google webpage, including the thumbnail image and text. The HTML instructions also give the user's browser the address of the website publisher's computer that stores the full-size version of the thumbnail. By following the HTML in-structions to access the third-party webpage, the user's browser connects to the website publisher's computer, downloads the full-size image, and makes the image appear at the bottom of the window on the user's screen. Google does not store the images that fill this lower part of the window and does not communicate the images to the user; Google simply provides HTML instructions directing a user's browser to access a third-party website. However, the top part of the window (containing the information from the Google web-page) appears to frame and comment on the bottom part of the window. Thus, the user's window appears to be filled with a single integrated presentation of the full-size image, but it is actually an image from a third-party website framed by information from Google's website. The process by which the webpage directs a user's browser to incorporate content from different computers into a single window is referred to as "in-line linking." The term "framing" refers to the process by which information from one computer appears to frame and annotate the in-line linked content from another computer. . . .

In addition to its search engine operations, Google generates revenue through a business program called "AdSense." Under this program, the owner of a website can register with Google to become an AdSense "partner." The website owner then places HTML instructions on its webpages that signal Google's server to place advertising on the webpages that is relevant to the webpages' content. Google's computer program selects the advertising automatically by means of an algorithm. AdSense participants agree to share the revenues that flow from such advertising with Google. . . .

Perfect 10 markets and sells copyrighted images of nude models. Among other enterprises, it operates a subscription website on the Internet. Subscribers pay a monthly fee to view Perfect 10 images in a "members' area" of the site. Subscribers must use a password to log into the members' area. Google does not include these password-protected images from the members' area in Google's index or database. Perfect 10 has also licensed Fonestarz Media Limited to sell and distribute Perfect 10's reduced-size copyrighted images for download and use on cell phones.

Some website publishers republish Perfect 10's images on the Internet without authorization. Once this occurs, Google's search engine may automatically index the webpages containing these images and provide thumbnail versions of images in response to user inquiries. When a user clicks on the thumbnail image returned by Google's search engine, the user's browser accesses the third-party webpage and in-line links to the full-sized infringing image stored on the website publisher's computer. This image appears, in its original context, on the lower portion of the window on the user's computer screen framed by information from Google's webpage. . . .

Because Perfect 10 has the burden of showing a likelihood of success on the merits, the district court held that Perfect 10 also had the burden of demonstrating a likelihood of overcoming Google's fair use defense under 17 U.S.C. § 107. *Perfect 10.* This ruling was erroneous. At trial, the defendant in an infringement action bears the burden of proving fair use. *See Campbell v. Acuff-Rose Music, Inc.* (1994). Because "the burdens at the preliminary injunction stage track the burdens at trial," once the moving party has carried its burden of showing a likelihood of success on the merits, the burden shifts to the nonmoving party to show a likelihood that its affirmative defense will succeed. Accordingly, once Perfect 10 has shown a likelihood of success on the merits, the burden shifts to Google to show a likelihood that its affirmative defenses will succeed.[1]

III
Direct Infringement

A. Display Right

. . . We have not previously addressed the question when a computer displays a copyrighted work for purposes of section 106(5). Section 106(5) states that a copyright owner has the exclusive right "to display the copyrighted work publicly." The Copyright Act explains that "display" means "to show a copy of it, either directly or by means of a film, slide, television image, or any other device or process. . . ." 17 U.S.C. § 101. Section 101 defines "copies" as "material objects, other than phonorecords, in which a work is fixed by any method now known or later developed, and from which the work can be perceived, reproduced, or otherwise communicated, either directly or with the aid of a machine or device." Finally, the Copyright Act provides that "[a] work is 'fixed' in a tangible medium of expression when its embodiment in a copy or phonorecord, by or under the authority of the author, is sufficiently permanent or stable to permit it to be perceived, reproduced, or otherwise communicated for a period of more than transitory duration."

We must now apply these definitions to the facts of this case. A photographic image is a work that is "'fixed' in a tangible medium of expression," for purposes of the Copyright Act, when embodied (i.e., stored) in a computer's server (or hard disk, or other

---

[1] [Editor's note. When the 9th Circuit first issued this opinion in May of 2007, it upheld the district court's ruling that the plaintiff bears the burden at the preliminary injunction stage of demonstrating the likelihood of overcoming the defendant's defense of fair use. In December, without comment, it withdrew that opinion and reissued it with the changed paragraph you find here.]

storage device). The image stored in the computer is the "copy" of the work for purposes of copyright law. The computer owner shows a copy "by means of a . . . device or process" when the owner uses the computer to fill the computer screen with the photographic image stored on that computer, or by communicating the stored image electronically to another person's computer. 17 U.S.C. § 101. In sum, based on the plain language of the statute, a person displays a photographic image by using a computer to fill a computer screen with a copy of the photographic image fixed in the computer's memory. There is no dispute that Google's computers store thumbnail versions of Perfect 10's copyrighted images and communicate copies of those thumbnails to Google's users. Therefore, Perfect 10 has made a prima facie case that Google's communication of its stored thumbnail images directly infringes Perfect 10's display right.

Google does not, however, display a copy of full-size infringing photographic images for purposes of the Copyright Act when Google frames in-line linked images that appear on a user's computer screen. Because Google's computers do not store the photographic images, Google does not have a copy of the images for purposes of the Copyright Act. In other words, Google does not have any "material objects . . . in which a work is fixed . . . and from which the work can be perceived, reproduced, or otherwise communicated" and thus cannot communicate a copy. 17 U.S.C. § 101.

Instead of communicating a copy of the image, Google provides HTML instructions that direct a user's browser to a website publisher's computer that stores the full-size photographic image. Providing these HTML instructions is not equivalent to showing a copy. First, the HTML instructions are lines of text, not a photographic image. Second, HTML instructions do not themselves cause infringing images to appear on the user's computer screen. The HTML merely gives the address of the image to the user's browser. The browser then interacts with the computer that stores the infringing image. It is this interaction that causes an infringing image to appear on the user's computer screen. Google may facilitate the user's access to infringing images. However, such assistance raises only contributory liability issues, and does not constitute direct infringement of the copyright owner's display rights. . . .

C. Fair Use Defense

. . . Google contends that its use of thumbnails is a fair use of the images and therefore does not constitute an infringement of Perfect 10's copyright. *See* 17 U.S.C. § 107.

The fair use defense permits the use of copyrighted works without the copyright owner's consent under certain situations. The defense encourages and allows the development of new ideas that build on earlier ones, thus providing a necessary counterbalance to the copyright law's goal of protecting creators' work product. "From the infancy of copyright protection, some opportunity for fair use of copyrighted materials has been thought necessary to fulfill copyright's very purpose. . . ." *Campbell v. Acuff-Rose* (1994). . . .

In applying the fair use analysis in this case, we are guided by *Kelly v. Arriba Soft Corp.*, which considered substantially the same use of copyrighted photographic images as is at issue here. In *Kelly*, a photographer brought a direct infringement claim against Arriba, the operator of an Internet search engine. The search engine provided thumbnail versions of the photographer's images in response to search queries. We held that Arriba's use of thumbnail images was a fair use primarily based on the transformative nature of a search engine and its benefit to the public. We also concluded that Arriba's use of the thumbnail images did not harm the photographer's market for his image.

In this case, the district court determined that Google's use of thumbnails was not a fair use and distinguished *Kelly*. We consider these distinctions in the context of the four-factor fair use analysis.

Purpose and character of the use. The first factor, 17 U.S.C. § 107(1), requires a court to consider "the purpose and character of the use, including whether such use is of a commercial nature or is for nonprofit educational purposes." The central purpose of this inquiry is to determine whether and to what extent the new work is "transformative." *Campbell*. A work is "transformative" when the new work does not "merely supersede the objects of the original creation" but rather "adds something new, with a further purpose or different character, altering the first with new expression, meaning, or message." Conversely, if the new work "supersede[s] the use of the original," the use is likely not a fair use. *Harper & Row Publishers, Inc. v. Nation Enters.* (1985).

As noted in *Campbell*, a "transformative work" is one that alters the original work "with new expression, meaning, or message." *Campbell*. "A use is considered transformative only where a defendant changes a plaintiff's copyrighted work or uses the plaintiff's copyrighted work in a different context such that the plaintiff's work is transformed into a new creation." *Wall Data Inc. v. L.A. County Sheriff's Dep't* (9th Cir. 2006).

Google's use of thumbnails is highly transformative. In *Kelly*, we concluded that Arriba's use of thumbnails was transformative because "Arriba's use of the images serve[d] a different function than Kelly's use—improving access to information on the [I]nternet versus artistic expression." *Kelly*. Although an image may have been created originally to serve an entertainment, aesthetic, or informative function, a search engine transforms the image into a pointer directing a user to a source of information. Just as a "parody has an obvious claim to transformative value" because "it can provide social benefit, by shedding light on an earlier work, and, in the process, creating a new one," *Campbell*, a search engine provides social benefit by incorporating an original work into a new work, namely, an electronic reference tool. Indeed, a search engine may be more transformative than a parody because a search engine provides an entirely new use for the original work, while a parody typically has the same entertainment purpose as the original work. In other words, a search engine puts images "in a different context" so that they are "transformed into a new creation." *Wall Data*.

The fact that Google incorporates the entire Perfect 10 image into the search engine results does not diminish the transformative nature of Google's use. As the district court correctly noted, we determined in *Kelly* that even making an exact copy of a work may be transformative so long as the copy serves a different function than the original work. For example, the First Circuit has held that the republication of photos taken for a modeling portfolio in a newspaper was transformative because the photos served to inform, as well as entertain. *See Nunez v. Caribbean Int'l News Corp.* (1st Cir. 2000). In contrast, duplicating a church's religious book for use by a different church was not transformative. *See Worldwide Church of God v. Phila. Church of God, Inc.* (9th Cir. 2000). Nor was a broadcaster's simple retransmission of a radio broadcast over telephone lines transformative, where the original radio shows were given no "new expression, meaning, or message." *Infinity Broad. Corp. v. Kirkwood* (2d Cir. 1998). Here, Google uses Perfect 10's images in a new context to serve a different purpose.

The district court nevertheless determined that Google's use of thumbnail images was less transformative than Arriba's use of thumbnails in *Kelly* because Google's use of thumbnails superseded Perfect 10's right to sell its reduced-size images for use on cell phones. The district court stated that "mobile users can download and save the thumbnails displayed by Google Image Search onto their phones," and concluded "to the extent that users may choose to download free images to their phone rather than purchase [Perfect 10's] reduced-size images, Google's use supersedes [Perfect 10's]."

Additionally, the district court determined that the commercial nature of Google's use weighed against its transformative nature. Although *Kelly* held that the commercial use of the photographer's images by Arriba's search engine was less exploitative than typical commercial use, and thus weighed only slightly against a finding of fair use, the district court here distinguished *Kelly* on the ground that some website owners in the AdSense program had infringing Perfect 10 images on their websites. The district court held that because Google's thumbnails "lead users to sites that directly benefit Google's bottom line," the AdSense program increased the commercial nature of Google's use of Perfect 10's images.

In conducting our case-specific analysis of fair use in light of the purposes of copyright, we must weigh Google's superseding and commercial uses of thumbnail images against Google's significant transformative use, as well as the extent to which Google's search engine promotes the purposes of copyright and serves the interests of the public. Although the district court acknowledged the "truism that search engines such as Google Image Search provide great value to the public," the district court did not expressly consider whether this value outweighed the significance of Google's superseding use or the commercial nature of Google's use. The Supreme Court, however, has directed us to be mindful of the extent to which a use promotes the purposes of copyright and serves the interests of the public.

We note that the superseding use in this case is not significant at present: the district court did not find that any downloads for mobile phone use had taken place. Moreover, while Google's use of thumbnails to direct users to AdSense partners containing infringing content adds a commercial dimension that did not exist in *Kelly*, the district court did not determine that this commercial element was significant. The district court stated that Google's AdSense programs as a whole contributed "$630 million, or 46% of total revenues" to Google's bottom line, but noted that this figure did not "break down the much smaller amount attributable to websites that contain infringing content."

We conclude that the significantly transformative nature of Google's search engine, particularly in light of its public benefit, outweighs Google's superseding and commercial uses of the thumbnails in this case. In reaching this conclusion, we note the importance of analyzing fair use flexibly in light of new circumstances. *Sony* ("'[Section 107] endorses the purpose and general scope of the judicial doctrine of fair use, but there is no disposition to freeze the doctrine in the statute, especially during a period of rapid technological change.'" (quoting H.R.Rep. No. 94-1476, p. 65–66 (1976)). We are also mindful of the Supreme Court's direction that "the more transformative the new work, the less will be the significance of other factors, like commercialism, that may weigh against a finding of fair use." *Campbell.*

Accordingly, we disagree with the district court's conclusion that because Google's use of the thumbnails could supersede Perfect 10's cell phone download use and because the use was more commercial than Arriba's, this fair use factor weighed "slightly" in favor of Perfect 10. Instead, we conclude that the transformative nature of Google's use is more significant than any incidental superseding use or the minor commercial aspects of Google's search engine and website. Therefore, this factor weighs heavily in favor of Google.

The nature of the copyrighted work. With respect to the second factor, "the nature of the copyrighted work," 17 U.S.C. § 107(2), our decision in *Kelly* is directly on point. There we held that the photographer's images were "creative in nature" and thus "closer to the core of intended copyright protection than are more fact-based works." *Kelly*. However, because the photos appeared on the Internet before Arriba used thumbnail versions in its search engine results, this factor weighed only slightly in favor of the photographer.

Here, the district court found that Perfect 10's images were creative but also previously published. The right of first publication is "the author's right to control the first public appearance of his expression." *Harper & Row*. Because this right encompasses "the choices of when, where, and in what form first to publish a work," an author exercises and exhausts this one-time right by publishing the work in any medium. Once Perfect 10 has exploited this commercially valuable right of first publication by putting its images on the Internet for paid subscribers, Perfect 10 is no longer entitled to the enhanced protection available for an unpublished work. Accordingly the district court did not err in holding that this factor weighed only slightly in favor of Perfect 10.

The amount and substantiality of the portion used. "The third factor asks whether the amount and substantiality of the portion used in relation to the copyrighted work as a whole . . . are reasonable in relation to the purpose of the copying." *Campbell*. In *Kelly*, we held Arriba's use of the entire photographic image was reasonable in light of the purpose of a search engine. *Kelly*. Specifically, we noted, "[i]t was necessary for Arriba to copy the entire image to allow users to recognize the image and decide whether to pursue more information about the image or the originating [website]. If Arriba only copied part of the image, it would be more difficult to identify it, thereby reducing the usefulness of the visual search engine." Accordingly, we concluded that this factor did not weigh in favor of either party. Because the same analysis applies to Google's use of Perfect 10's image, the district court did not err in finding that this factor favored neither party.

Effect of use on the market. The fourth factor is "the effect of the use upon the potential market for or value of the copyrighted work." 17 U.S.C. § 107(4). In *Kelly*, we concluded that Arriba's use of the thumbnail images did not harm the market for the photographer's full-size images. We reasoned that because thumbnails were not a substitute for the full-sized images, they did not harm the photographer's ability to sell or license his full-sized images. The district court here followed *Kelly*'s reasoning, holding that Google's use of thumbnails did not hurt Perfect 10's market for full-size images. We agree.

Perfect 10 argues that the district court erred because the likelihood of market harm may be presumed if the intended use of an image is for commercial gain. However, this presumption does not arise when a work is transformative because "market substitution is at least less certain, and market harm may not be so readily inferred." *Campbell*. As previously discussed, Google's use of thumbnails for search engine purposes is highly transformative, and so market harm cannot be presumed.

Perfect 10 also has a market for reduced-size images, an issue not considered in *Kelly*. The district court held that "Google's use of thumbnails likely does harm the potential market for the downloading of [Perfect 10's] reduced-size images onto cell phones." The district court reasoned that persons who can obtain Perfect 10 images free of charge from Google are less likely to pay for a download, and the availability of Google's thumbnail images would harm Perfect 10's market for cell phone downloads. As we discussed above, the district court did not make a finding that Google users have downloaded thumbnail images for cell phone use. This potential harm to Perfect 10's market remains hypothetical. We conclude that this factor favors neither party.

Having undertaken a case-specific analysis of all four factors, we now weigh these factors together "in light of the purposes of copyright." *Campbell*. In this case, Google has put Perfect 10's thumbnail images (along with millions of other thumbnail images) to a use fundamentally different than the use intended by Perfect 10. In doing so, Google has provided a significant benefit to the public. Weighing this significant transformative use against the unproven use of Google's thumbnails for cell phone downloads, and considering the other fair use factors, all in light of the purpose of copyright, we conclude that Google's use of Perfect 10's thumbnails is a fair use. Because the district court here "found facts sufficient to evaluate each of the statutory factors . . . [we] need not remand for further factfinding." *Harper & Row.* We conclude that Google is likely to succeed in proving its fair use defense and, accordingly, we vacate the preliminary injunction regarding Google's use of thumbnail images.

· · · · · · · · · ·

As you have seen, Google is involved in many intellectual property cases and, in particular, many cases involving fair use. It has sometimes been said that "Google pays Silicon Valley's legal bills." What does this phrase mean, and is the phenomenon a good or bad thing? Reflect on this question as you read the case below.

Authors Guild, Inc. v. Google Inc.
954 F. Supp. 2d 282 (S.D.N.Y. 2013)

[Editors' Note: This case involves legal challenges to the "Google Books" program, which Google offers in order to facilitate search of printed books. Google Books, in turn, includes material that Google has acquired from two sources. 1.) its "Partner Program"— under which Google has permission from copyright holders to have access to a digital version of their books—and 2.) the "Library Project." The Library Project was the focus of this case. Google had scanned physical books from libraries with which it had agreements. Where the book was in the public domain, no copyright issue arose. Users could search, see, and download, the full text of these books. In the case of books that were still under copyright, Google made the decision not to seek the permission of the copyright holders in advance of the scan. (They argued that seeking permission would, by definition, exclude from Google Books the orphan works that make up a substantial portion of library holdings.) Instead, Google allowed copyright holders to "opt out," by requesting that the work be removed. If the book was still under copyright—or seemed likely to be under copyright in that it had been published since 1923—Google would only show three "snippets" in response to a search query. As part of the deals made with the libraries that provided their collections to scan, Google also allowed the libraries to download a copy of each of the books scanned from their collections. Before the resumption of the case you are about to read, Google had attempted to negotiate with rightsholders a lengthy and elaborate Settlement—called "The Google Books Settlement." The details are complex, but basically the Settlement would have split revenues between all of the parties, and even made available "orphan works," escrowing the income earned. The settlement was eventually rejected by Judge Chin (who was then on the District Court) in part because the settlement would have bound parties not before the court. The lawsuit on fair use resumed. This is Judge Chin's decision.]

CHIN, Circuit Judge.

Since 2004, when it announced agreements with several major research libraries to digitally copy books in their collections, defendant Google Inc. ("Google") has scanned more than twenty million books. It has delivered digital copies to participating libraries, created an electronic database of books, and made text available for online searching through the use of "snippets." Many of the books scanned by Google, however, were under copyright, and Google did not obtain permission from the copyright holders for these usages of their copyrighted works. As a consequence, in 2005, plaintiffs brought this class action charging Google with copyright infringement. . . .

. . . Both in-print and out-of-print books are included, although the great majority are out-of-print. . . .

For books in "snippet view" . . . Google divides each page into eighths—each of which is a "snippet," a verbatim excerpt. Each search generates three snippets, but by performing multiple searches using different search terms, a single user may view far more than three snippets, as different searches can return different snippets. . . .

Google takes security measures to prevent users from viewing a complete copy of a snippet-view book. For example, a user cannot cause the system to return different sets of snippets for the same search query; the position of each snippet is fixed within the page and does not "slide" around the search term; only the first responsive snippet available on any given page will be returned in response to a query; one of the snippets on each page is "black-listed," meaning it will not be shown; and at least one out of ten entire pages in each book is black-listed. An "attacker" who tries to obtain an entire book by using a physical copy of the book to string together words appearing in successive passages would be able to obtain at best a patchwork of snippets that would be missing at least one snippet from every page and 10% of all pages. In addition, works with text organized in short "chunks," such as dictionaries, cookbooks, and books of haiku, are excluded from snippet view. . . .

DISCUSSION

. . . Google has digitally reproduced millions of copyrighted books, including the individual plaintiffs' books, maintaining copies for itself on its servers and backup tapes. See 17 U.S.C. § 106(1) (prohibiting unauthorized reproduction). Google has made digital copies available for its Library Project partners to download. See 17 U.S.C. § 106(3) (prohibiting unauthorized distribution). Google has displayed snippets from the books to the public. See 17 U.S.C. § 106(5) (prohibiting unauthorized display). Google has done all of this, with respect to in-copyright books in the Library Project, without license or permission from the copyright owners. The sole issue now before the Court is whether Google's use of the copyrighted works is "fair use" under the copyright laws. For the reasons set forth below, I conclude that it is. . . .

A key consideration is whether, as part of the inquiry into the first factor, the use of the copyrighted work is "transformative," that is, whether the new work merely "supersedes" or "supplants" the original creation, or whether it:

> instead adds something new, with a further purpose or different
> character, altering the first with new expression, meaning, or message;
> it asks, in other words, whether and to what extent the new work is
> "transformative." . . .

1. Purpose and Character of Use

The first factor is "the purpose and character of the use, including whether such use is of a commercial nature or is for nonprofit educational purposes." 17 U.S.C. § 107(1).

Google's use of the copyrighted works is highly transformative. Google Books digitizes books and transforms expressive text into a comprehensive word index that helps readers, scholars, researchers, and others find books. Google Books has become an important tool for libraries and librarians and cite-checkers as it helps to identify and find books. The use of book text to facilitate search through the display of snippets is transformative. . . . Google Books thus uses words for a different purpose—it uses snippets of text to act as pointers directing users to a broad selection of books.

Similarly, Google Books is also transformative in the sense that it has transformed book text into data for purposes of substantive research, including data mining and text mining in new areas, thereby opening up new fields of research. Words in books are being used in a way they have not been used before. Google Books has created something new in the use of book text—the frequency of words and trends in their usage provide substantive information.

Google Books does not supersede or supplant books because it is not a tool to be used to read books. Instead, it "adds value to the original" and allows for "the creation of new information, new aesthetics, new insights and understandings." Hence, the use is transformative.

It is true, of course, as plaintiffs argue, that Google is a for-profit entity and Google Books is largely a commercial enterprise. The fact that a use is commercial "tends to weigh against a finding of fair use." On the other hand, fair use has been found even where a defendant benefitted commercially from the unlicensed use of copyrighted works. Here, Google does not sell the scans it has made of books for Google Books; it does not sell the snippets that it displays; and it does not run ads on the About the Book pages that contain snippets. It does not engage in the direct commercialization of copyrighted works. Google does, of course, benefit commercially in the sense that users are drawn to the Google websites by the ability to search Google Books. While this is a consideration to be acknowledged in weighing all the factors, even assuming Google's principal motivation is profit, the fact is that Google Books serves several important educational purposes.

Accordingly, I conclude that the first factor strongly favors a finding of fair use.

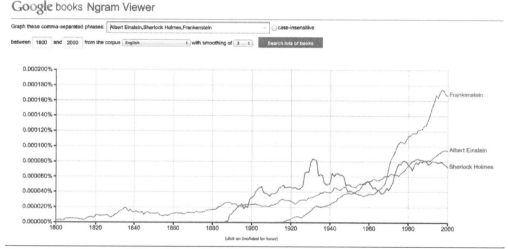

Google Books' Ngram project enables text-mining to track usage over time; image from https://books.google.com/ngrams/.

2. Nature of Copyrighted Works

The second factor is "the nature of the copyrighted work." Here, the works are books—all types of published books, fiction and non-fiction, in-print and out-of-print. While works of fiction are entitled to greater copyright protection, here the vast majority of the books in Google Books are non-fiction. Further, the books at issue are published and available to the public. These considerations favor a finding of fair use.

3. Amount and Substantiality of Portion Used

The third factor is "the amount and substantiality of the portion used in relation to the copyrighted work as a whole." Google scans the full text of books—the entire books—and it copies verbatim expression. On the other hand, courts have held that copying the entirety of a work may still be fair use. Here, as one of the keys to Google Books is its offering of full-text search of books, full-work reproduction is critical to the functioning of Google Books. Significantly, Google limits the amount of text it displays in response to a search.

On balance, I conclude that the third factor weighs slightly against a finding of fair use.

4. Effect of Use Upon Potential Market or Value

The fourth factor is "the effect of the use upon the potential market for or value of the copyrighted work." Here, plaintiffs argue that Google Books will negatively impact the market for books and that Google's scans will serve as a "market replacement" for books. It also argues that users could put in multiple searches, varying slightly the search terms, to access an entire book.

Neither suggestion makes sense. Google does not sell its scans, and the scans do not replace the books. While partner libraries have the ability to download a scan of a book from their collections, they owned the books already—they provided the original book to Google to scan. Nor is it likely that someone would take the time and energy to input countless searches to try and get enough snippets to comprise an entire book. Not only is that not possible as certain pages and snippets are blacklisted, the individual would have to have a copy of the book in his possession already to be able to piece the different snippets together in coherent fashion.

To the contrary, a reasonable factfinder could only find that Google Books enhances the sales of books to the benefit of copyright holders. An important factor in the success of an individual title is whether it is discovered—whether potential readers learn of its existence. Google Books provides a way for authors' works to become noticed, much like traditional in-store book displays. Indeed, both librarians and their patrons use Google Books to identify books to purchase. Many authors have noted that online browsing in general and Google Books in particular helps readers find their work, thus increasing their audiences. Further, Google provides convenient links to booksellers to make it easy for a reader to order a book. In this day and age of on-line shopping, there can be no doubt but that Google Books improves books sales.

Hence, I conclude that the fourth factor weighs strongly in favor of a finding of fair use.

5. Overall Assessment

Finally, the various non-exclusive statutory factors are to be weighed together, along with any other relevant considerations, in light of the purposes of the copyright laws.

In my view, Google Books provides significant public benefits. It advances the progress of the arts and sciences, while maintaining respectful consideration for the rights of authors and other creative individuals, and without adversely impacting the rights of copyright holders. It has become an invaluable research tool that permits students, teachers, librarians, and others to more efficiently identify and locate books. It has given scholars the ability, for the first time, to conduct full-text searches of tens of millions of books. It preserves books, in particular out-of-print and old books that have been forgotten in the bowels of libraries, and it gives them new life. It facilitates access to books for print-disabled and remote or underserved populations. It generates new audiences and creates new sources of income for authors and publishers. Indeed, all society benefits.

• • • • • • • • • •

Note:

In October 2015, the Second Circuit affirmed Judge Chin's decision. *Authors Guild v. Google* (2d Cir. 2015). The opinion was written by Judge Leval, the author of "Toward a Fair Use Standard," 103 Harv. L. Rev. 1105 (1990), the article that influenced the Supreme Court's "transformative" use analysis in *Campbell v. Acuff-Rose*. Judge Leval made clear that "while authors are undoubtedly important intended beneficiaries of copyright, the ultimate, primary intended beneficiary is the public," and that transformative uses further "copyright's overall objective of contributing to public knowledge." On the first fair use factor, the Second Circuit—like Judge Chin—found that Google Books served the "highly transformative" purposes of helping people identify and find books, and perform text and data mining through the Ngrams tool. Google's profit motive was secondary and did not defeat fair use, as "[m]any of the most universally accepted forms of fair use . . . are all normally done commercially for profit." On the question of how one distinguishes between "transformations" that fall within the copyright holder's derivative works right, and those that are protected by fair use, the court explained: "The statutory definition suggests that derivative works [such as translations and adaptations] generally involve transformations in the nature of *changes of form.* By contrast, copying from an original for the purpose of criticism or commentary on the original or provision of information about it, tends most clearly to satisfy *Campbell*'s notion of the 'transformative' purpose." [Is this a satisfying explanation? Is a translation not "transformative"? A parodic rap video of a nursery rhyme not a "change of form"?] As in many other cases, the court gave little weight to the second factor, the nature of the copyrighted work. [Why?] With regard to the third factor, the court found that Google legitimately copied entire books because "not only is the copying of the totality of the original reasonably appropriate to Google's transformative purpose, it is literally necessary to achieve that purpose." Moreover, "[w]hat matters in such cases is not so much 'the amount and substantiality of the portion used' *in making a copy,* but rather the amount and substantiality of *what is thereby made accessible* to a public for which it may serve as a competing substitute. . . ." Turning to the fourth factor, the court found that Google Books did not provide a market substitute for the original books, in part because of snippet view's built-in limitations: "Snippet view, at best and after a large commitment of manpower, produces discontinuous, tiny fragments. . . . This does not threaten the rights holders with any significant harm. . . ." In addition, the court explained that Google was free to convey the unprotected *facts* contained within books, even if this resulted in lost sales (as when a student does not purchase a book because she finds the factual information she seeks in a snippet). In addressing *potential* markets, the court returned to the scope of the derivative works right: "Nothing in the statutory definition of a derivative work, or of the logic that underlies it, suggests that the author of an original work enjoys an exclusive derivative right to supply information about that work of the sort communicated by Google's search functions." Therefore, Google did not harm protectable derivative markets. The licensing scheme contemplated by the proposed settlement agreement was irrelevant because it would have allowed "far more extensive" access to expressive content. In April 2016, the Supreme Court denied certiorari in this case.

· · · · · · · · · ·

In Chapter 11, you were introduced to the dispute between Oracle and Google over the copyrightability of APIs—Application Programming Interfaces. As we explained in that chapter, the "interoperability" aspect of those APIs is key. An API governs the way one program works with another. Without knowledge of the API, or the ability to reverse engineer it, the interoperability of programs will be limited. Imagine trying to play a piano without knowing which key corresponded to which note. Below is the Supreme Court's resolution of this case. This long-awaited decision on software copyright came some 25 years after the Court split 4–4 on granting *certiorari* in *Lotus v. Borland* in 1996.

Google v. Oracle
593 U.S. ____ (2021)

Justice BREYER delivered the opinion of the Court, in which Chief Justice ROBERTS, Justices SOTOMAYOR, KAGAN, GORSUCH, and KAVANAUGH, joined.

Oracle America, Inc., is the current owner of a copyright in Java SE, a computer program that uses the popular Java computer programming language. Google, without permission, has copied a portion of that program, a portion that enables a programmer to call up prewritten software that, together with the computer's hardware, will carry out a large number of specific tasks. The lower courts have considered (1) whether Java SE's owner could copyright the portion that Google copied, and (2) if so, whether Google's copying nonetheless constituted a "fair use" of that material, thereby freeing Google from copyright liability. The Federal Circuit held in Oracle's favor (*i.e.*, that the portion is copyrightable and Google's copying did not constitute a "fair use"). In reviewing that decision, we assume, for argument's sake, that the material was copyrightable. But we hold that the copying here at issue nonetheless constituted a fair use. Hence, Google's copying did not violate the copyright law.

I

In 2005, Google acquired Android, Inc., a startup firm that hoped to become involved in smartphone software. Google sought, through Android, to develop a software platform for mobile devices like smartphones. A platform provides the necessary infrastructure for computer programmers to develop new programs and applications. One might think of a software platform as a kind of factory floor where computer programmers (analogous to autoworkers, designers, or manufacturers) might come, use sets of tools found there, and create new applications for use in, say, smartphones.

Google envisioned an Android platform that was free and open, such that software developers could use the tools found there free of charge. Its idea was that more and more developers using its Android platform would develop ever more Android-based applications, all of which would make Google's Android-based smartphones more attractive to ultimate consumers. Consumers would then buy and use ever more of those phones. That vision required attracting a sizeable number of skilled programmers.

At that time, many software developers understood and wrote programs using the Java programming language, a language invented by Sun Microsystems (Oracle's predecessor). About six million programmers had spent considerable time learning, and then using, the Java language. . . .

The Android platform offered programmers the ability to program for that environment. To build the platform, Google wrote millions of lines of new code. Because Google wanted millions of programmers, familiar with Java, to be able easily to work with its new Android platform, it also copied roughly 11,500 lines of code from the Java SE program. The copied lines of code are part of a tool called an Application Programming Interface, or API.

What is an API? The Federal Circuit described an API as a tool that "allow[s] programmers to use . . . prewritten code to build certain functions into their own programs, rather than write their own code to perform those functions from scratch."

Consider in more detail just what an API does. A computer can perform thousands, perhaps millions, of different tasks that a programmer may wish to use. An API divides and organizes the world of computing tasks in a particular way. Programmers can then use the API to select the particular task that they need for their programs. In Sun's API (which we refer to as the Sun Java API), each individual task is known as a "method." The API groups somewhat similar methods into larger "classes," and groups somewhat similar classes into larger "packages." This method-class-package organizational structure is referred to as the Sun Java API's "structure, sequence, and organization," or SSO.

For each task, there is computer code, known as "implementing code," that in effect tells the computer how to execute the particular task you have asked it to perform (such as telling you, of two numbers, which is the higher). The implementing code (which Google independently wrote) is not at issue here. For a single task, the implementing code may be hundreds of lines long. It would be difficult, perhaps impossible, for a programmer to create complex software programs without drawing on prewritten task-implementing programs to execute discrete tasks.

But how do you as the programmer tell the computer which of the implementing code programs it should choose, *i.e.*, which task it should carry out? You do so by entering into your own program a command that corresponds to the specific task and calls it up. Those commands, known as "method calls," help you carry out the task by choosing those programs written in implementing code that will do the trick, *i.e.*, that will instruct the computer so that your program will find the higher of two numbers. If a particular computer might perform, say, a million different tasks, different method calls will tell the computer which of those tasks to choose. Those familiar with the Java language already know countless method calls that allow them to invoke countless tasks.

And how does the method call (which a programmer types) actually locate and invoke the particular implementing code that it needs to instruct the computer how to carry out a particular task? It does so through another type of code, which the parties have labeled "declaring code." Declaring code is part of the API. For each task, the specific command entered by the programmer matches up with specific declaring code inside the API. That declaring code provides both the name for each task and the location of each task within the API's overall organizational system (*i.e.,* the placement of a method within a particular class and the placement of a class within a particular package). In this sense, the declaring code and the method call form a link, allowing the programmer to draw upon the thousands of prewritten tasks, written in implementing code. Without that declaring code, the method calls entered by the programmer would not call up the implementing code.

The declaring code therefore performs at least two important functions in the Sun Java API. The first, more obvious, function is that the declaring code enables a set of shortcuts for programmers. By connecting complex implementing code with method calls, it allows a programmer to pick out from the API's task library a particular task without having to learn anything more than a simple command. For example, a programmer building a new application for personal banking may wish to use various tasks to, say, calculate a user's balance or authenticate a password. To do so, she need only learn the method calls associated with those tasks. In this way, the declaring code's shortcut function is similar to a gas pedal in a car that tells the car to move faster or the QWERTY keyboard on a typewriter that calls up a certain letter when you press a particular key. As those analogies demonstrate, one can think of the declaring code as part of an *interface* between human beings and a machine.

The second, less obvious, function is to reflect the way in which Java's creators have divided the potential world of different tasks into an actual world, *i.e.*, precisely which set of potentially millions of different tasks we want to have our Java-based computer systems perform and how we want those tasks arranged and grouped. In this sense, the declaring code performs an organizational function.

Consider a comprehensive, albeit farfetched, analogy that illustrates how the API is actually used by a programmer. Imagine that you can, via certain keystrokes, instruct a robot to move to a particular file cabinet, to open a certain drawer, and to pick out a specific recipe. With the proper recipe in hand, the robot then moves to your kitchen and gives it to a cook to prepare the dish. This example mirrors the API's task-related organizational system. Through your simple command, the robot locates the right recipe and hands it off to the cook. In the same way, typing in a method call prompts the API to locate the correct implementing code and hand it off to your computer. And importantly, to select the dish that you want for your meal, you do not need to know the recipe's contents, just as a programmer using an API does not need to learn the implementing code. In both situations, learning the simple command is enough.

Now let us consider the example that the District Court used to explain the precise technology here. A programmer wishes, as part of her program, to determine which of two integers is the larger. To do so in the Java language, she will first write **java.lang**. Those words (which we have put in bold type) refer to the "package" (or by analogy to the file cabinet). She will then write **Math**. That word refers to the "class" (or by analogy to the drawer). She will then write **max**. That word refers to the "method" (or by analogy to the recipe). She will then make two parentheses ( ). And, in between the parentheses she will put two integers, say 4 and 6, that she wishes to compare. The whole expression—the method call—will look like this: "**java.lang.Math.max(4, 6)**." The use of this expression will, by means of the API, call up a task-implementing program that will determine the higher number.

In writing this program, the programmer will use the very symbols we have placed in bold in the precise order we have placed them. But the symbols by themselves do nothing. She must also use software that connects the symbols to the equivalent of file cabinets, drawers, and files. The API is that software. It includes both the declaring code that links each part of the method call to the particular task-implementing program, and the implementing code that actually carries it out.

Google did not copy the implementing code from the Sun Java API. It wrote its own task-implementing programs, such as those that would determine which of two integers is the greater or carry out any other desired (normally far more complex) task. This implementing code constitutes the vast majority of both the Sun Java API and the API that Google created for Android. For most of the packages in its new API, Google also wrote its own declaring code. For 37 packages, however, Google copied the declaring code from the Sun Java API. As just explained, that means that, for those 37 packages, Google necessarily copied both the names given to particular tasks and the grouping of those tasks into classes and packages.

In doing so, Google copied that portion of the Sun Java API that allowed programmers expert in the Java programming language to use the "task calling" system that they had already learned. As Google saw it, the 37 packages at issue included those tasks that were likely to prove most useful to programmers working on applications for mobile devices. In fact, "three of these packages were . . . fundamental to being able to use the Java language at all." By using the same declaring code for those packages, programmers using the Android platform can rely on the method calls that they are already familiar with to call up particular tasks (*e.g.*, determining which of two integers is the greater); but Google's own implementing programs carry out those tasks. Without that copying, programmers would need to learn an entirely new system to call up the same tasks.

We add that the Android platform has been successful. Within five years of its release in 2007, Android-based devices claimed a large share of the United States market. As of 2015, Android sales produced more than $42 billion in revenue.

In 2010 Oracle Corporation bought Sun. Soon thereafter Oracle brought this lawsuit in the United States District Court for the Northern District of California. . . .

III A

Copyright and patents, the Constitution says, are to "promote the Progress of Science and useful Arts, by securing for limited Times to Authors and Inventors the exclusive Right to their respective Writings and Discoveries." Art. I, § 8, cl. 8. Copyright statutes and case law have made clear that copyright has practical objectives. It grants an author an exclusive right to produce his work (sometimes for a hundred years or more), not as a special reward, but in order to encourage the production of works that others might reproduce more cheaply. At the same time, copyright has negative features. Protection can raise prices to consumers. It can impose special costs, such as the cost of contacting owners to obtain reproduction permission. And the exclusive rights it awards can sometimes stand in the way of others exercising their own creative powers.

We have described the "fair use" doctrine, originating in the courts, as an "equitable rule of reason" that "permits courts to avoid rigid application of the copyright statute when, on occasion, it would stifle the very creativity which that law is designed to foster." The statutory provision that embodies the doctrine indicates, rather than dictates, how courts should apply it. [W]e have understood the provision to set forth general principles, the application of which requires judicial balancing, depending upon relevant circumstances, including "significant changes in technology." *Sony v. Universal* (1984); see also *Twentieth Century Music Corp. v. Aiken* (1975) ("When technological change has rendered its literal terms ambiguous, the Copyright Act must be construed in light of its basic purpose").

B

. . . Given the rapidly changing technological, economic, and business-related circumstances, we believe we should not answer more than is necessary to resolve the parties' dispute. We shall assume, but purely for argument's sake, that the entire Sun Java API falls within the definition of that which can be copyrighted. We shall ask instead whether Google's use of part of that API was a "fair use." Unlike the Federal Circuit, we conclude that it was.

. . . V

At the outset, Google argues that "fair use" is a question for a jury to decide; here the jury decided the question in Google's favor; and we should limit our review to determining whether "substantial evidence" justified the jury's decision. The Federal Circuit disagreed. It thought that the "fair use" question was a mixed question of fact and law; that reviewing courts should appropriately defer to the jury's findings of underlying facts; but that the ultimate question whether those facts showed a "fair use" is a legal question for judges to decide *de novo*.

We agree with the Federal Circuit's answer to this question. We have said, "[f]air use is a mixed question of law and fact." *Harper & Row*. We have explained that a reviewing court should try to break such a question into its separate factual and legal parts, reviewing each according to the appropriate legal standard. But when a question can be reduced no further, we have added that "the standard of review for a mixed question all depends—on whether answering it entails primarily legal or factual work." *U. S. Bank v. Village at Lakeridge* (2018).

In this case, the ultimate "fair use" question primarily involves legal work. "Fair use" was originally a concept fashioned by judges. Our cases still provide legal interpretations of the fair use provision. And those interpretations provide general guidance for future cases. See, *e.g., Campbell* (describing kinds of market harms that are not the concern of copyright); *Harper & Row* ("scope of fair use is narrower with respect to unpublished works"); *Sony* (wholesale copying aimed at creating a market substitute is presumptively unfair). This type of work is legal work.

Applying a legal "fair use" conclusion may, of course, involve determination of subsidiary factual questions, such as "whether there was harm to the actual or potential markets for the copyrighted work" or "how much of the copyrighted work was copied." In this case the Federal Circuit carefully applied the fact/law principles we set forth in *U. S. Bank*, leaving factual determinations to the jury and reviewing the ultimate question, a legal question, *de novo.* . . .

VI

We turn now to the basic legal question before us: Was Google's copying of the Sun Java API, specifically its use of the declaring code and organizational structure for 37 packages of that API, a "fair use." In answering this question, we shall consider the four factors set forth in the fair use statute as we find them applicable to the kind of computer programs before us. . . . For expository purposes, we begin with the second.

A. "The Nature of the Copyrighted Work"

The Sun Java API is a "user interface." It provides a way through which users (here the programmers) can "manipulate and control" task-performing computer programs "via a series of menu commands." *Lotus.* The API reflects Sun's division of possible tasks that a computer might perform into a set of actual tasks that certain kinds of computers actually will perform. Sun decided, for example, that its API would call up a task that compares one integer with another to see which is the larger. . . . No one claims that the decisions about what counts as a task are themselves copyrightable.

As discussed above, we can think of the technology as having three essential parts. First, the API includes "implementing code," which actually instructs the computer on the steps to follow to carry out each task. Google wrote its own programs (implementing programs) that would perform each one of the tasks that its API calls up.

Second, the Sun Java API associates a particular command, called a "method call," with the calling up of each task. The symbols **java.lang.**, for example, are part of the command that will call up the program (whether written by Sun or, as here, by Google) that instructs the computer to carry out the "larger number" operation. Oracle does not here argue that the use of these commands by programmers itself violates its copyrights.

Third, the Sun Java API contains computer code that will associate the writing of a method call with particular "places" in the computer that contain the needed implementing code. This is the declaring code. The declaring code both labels the particular tasks in the API and organizes those tasks, or "methods," into "packages" and "classes." We have referred to this organization, by way of rough analogy, as file cabinets, drawers, and files. Oracle does claim that Google's use of the Sun Java API's declaring code violates its copyrights.

The declaring code at issue here resembles other copyrighted works in that it is part of a computer program. Congress has specified that computer programs are subjects of copyright. It differs, however, from many other kinds of copyrightable computer code. It is inextricably bound together with a general system, the division of computing tasks, that no one claims is a proper subject of copyright. It is inextricably bound up with the idea of organizing tasks into what we have called cabinets, drawers, and files, an idea that is also not copyrightable. It is inextricably bound up with the use of specific commands known to programmers, known here as method calls (such as **java.lang.Math.max**, etc.), that Oracle does not here contest. And it is inextricably bound up with implementing code, which is copyrightable but was not copied.

Moreover, the copied declaring code and the uncopied implementing programs call for, and reflect, different kinds of capabilities. A single implementation may walk a computer through dozens of different steps. To write implementing programs, witnesses told the jury, requires balancing such considerations as how quickly a computer can execute a task or the likely size of the computer's memory. One witness described that creativity as "magic" practiced by an API developer when he or she worries "about things like power management" for devices that "run on a battery." This is the very creativity that was needed to develop the Android software for use not in laptops or desktops but in the very different context of smartphones.

The declaring code (inseparable from the programmer's method calls) embodies a different kind of creativity. Sun Java's creators, for example, tried to find declaring code names that would prove intuitively easy to remember. They wanted to attract programmers who would learn the system, help to develop it further, and prove reluctant to use another. Sun's business strategy originally emphasized the importance of using the API to attract programmers. It sought to make the API "open" and "then . . . compete on implementations." The testimony at trial was replete with examples of witnesses drawing this critical line between the user-centered declaratory code and the innovative implementing code.

These features mean that, as part of a user interface, the declaring code differs to some degree from the mine run of computer programs. Like other computer programs, it is functional in nature. But unlike many other programs, its use is inherently bound together with uncopyrightable ideas (general task division and organization) and new creative expression (Android's implementing code). Unlike many other programs, its value in significant part derives from the value that those who do not hold copyrights, namely, computer programmers, invest of their own time and effort to learn the API's system. And unlike many other programs, its value lies in its efforts to encourage programmers to learn and to use that system so that they will use (and continue to use) Sun-related implementing programs that Google did not copy.

Although copyrights protect many different kinds of writing, we have emphasized the need to "recogni[ze] that some works are closer to the core of [copyright] than others." In our view, for the reasons just described, the declaring code is, if copyrightable at all, further than are most computer programs (such as the implementing code) from the core of copyright. That fact diminishes the fear, expressed by both the dissent and the Federal Circuit, that application of "fair use" here would seriously undermine the general copyright protection that Congress provided for computer programs. And it means that this factor, "the nature of the copyrighted work," points in the direction of fair use.

B. "The Purpose and Character of the Use"

In the context of fair use, we have considered whether the copier's use "adds something new, with a further purpose or different character, altering" the copyrighted work "with new expression, meaning or message." Commentators have put the matter more broadly, asking whether the copier's use "fulfill[s] the objective of copyright law to stimulate creativity for public illumination." In answering this question, we have used the word "transformative" to describe a copying use that adds something new and important. An "'artistic painting'" might, for example, fall within the scope of fair use even though it precisely replicates a copyrighted "'advertising logo to make a comment about consumerism.'" Or, as we held in *Campbell*, a parody can be transformative because it comments on the original or criticizes it, for "[p]arody needs to mimic an original to make its point."

Google copied portions of the Sun Java API precisely, and it did so in part for the same reason that Sun created those portions, namely, to enable programmers to call up implementing programs that would accomplish particular tasks. But since virtually any unauthorized use of a copyrighted computer program (say, for teaching or research) would do the same, to stop here would severely limit the scope of fair use in the functional context of computer programs. Rather, in determining whether a use is "transformative," we must go further and examine the copying's more specifically described "purpose[s]" and "character."

Here Google's use of the Sun Java API seeks to create new products. It seeks to expand the use and usefulness of Android-based smartphones. Its new product offers programmers a highly creative and innovative tool for a smartphone environment. To the extent that Google used parts of the Sun Java API to create a new platform that could be readily used by programmers, its use was consistent with that creative "progress" that is the basic constitutional objective of copyright itself.

The jury heard that Google limited its use of the Sun Java API to tasks and specific programming demands related to Android. It copied the API (which Sun created for use in desktop and laptop computers) only insofar as needed to include tasks that would be useful in smartphone programs. And it did so only insofar as needed to allow program-mers to call upon those tasks without discarding a portion of a familiar programming language and learning a new one. To repeat, Google, through Android, provided a new collection of tasks operating in a distinct and different computing environment. Those tasks were carried out through the use of new implementing code (that Google wrote) designed to operate within that new environment. Some of the *amici* refer to what Google did as "reimplementation," defined as the "building of a system . . . that repurposes the same words and syntaxes" of an existing system—in this case so that programmers who had learned an existing system could put their basic skills to use in a new one.

The record here demonstrates the numerous ways in which reimplementing an interface can further the development of computer programs. The jury heard that shared interfaces are necessary for different programs to speak to each other. ("We have to agree on the APIs so that the application I write to show a movie runs on your device.") It heard that the reimplementation of interfaces is necessary if programmers are to be able to use their acquired skills. ("If the API labels change, then either the software wouldn't continue to work anymore or the developer . . . would have to learn a whole new language to be able to use these API labels.") It heard that the reuse of APIs is common in the industry. It heard that Sun itself had used pre-existing interfaces in creating Java. And it heard that Sun executives thought that widespread use of the Java programming language, including use on a smartphone platform, would benefit the company. *Amici* supporting Google have summarized these same points—points that witnesses explained to the jury. These and related facts convince us that the "purpose and character" of Google's copying was transformative—to the point where this factor too weighs in favor of fair use.

There are two other considerations that are often taken up under the first factor: commerciality and good faith. The text of § 107 includes various noncommercial uses, such as teaching and scholarship, as paradigmatic examples of privileged copying. There is no doubt that a finding that copying was not commercial in nature tips the scales in favor of fair use. But the inverse is not necessarily true, as many common fair uses are indisputably commercial. For instance, the text of § 107 includes examples like "news reporting," which is often done for commercial profit. So even though Google's use was a commercial endeavor—a fact no party disputed—that is not dispositive of the first factor, particularly in light of the inherently transformative role that the reimplementation played in the new Android system.

As for bad faith, our decision in *Campbell* expressed some skepticism about whether bad faith has any role in a fair use analysis. We find this skepticism justifiable, as "[c]opyright is not a privilege reserved for the well-behaved." We have no occasion here to say whether good faith is as a general matter a helpful inquiry. We simply note that given the strength of the other factors pointing toward fair use and the jury finding in Google's favor on hotly contested evidence, that fact-bound consideration is not determinative in this context.

C. "The Amount and Substantiality of the Portion Used"

If one considers the declaring code in isolation, the quantitative amount of what Google copied was large. Google copied the declaring code for 37 packages of the Sun Java API, totaling approximately 11,500 lines of code. Those lines of code amount to virtually all the declaring code needed to call up hundreds of different tasks. On the other hand, if one considers the entire set of software material in the Sun Java API, the quantitative amount copied was small. The total set of Sun Java API computer code, including implementing code, amounted to 2.86 million lines, of which the copied 11,500 lines were only 0.4 percent.

The question here is whether those 11,500 lines of code should be viewed in isolation or as one part of the considerably greater whole. We have said that even a small amount of copying may fall outside of the scope of fair use where the excerpt copied consists of the "'heart'" of the original work's creative expression. *Harper & Row*. On the other hand, copying a larger amount of material can fall within the scope of fair use where the material copied captures little of the material's creative expression or is central to a copier's valid purpose. See, *e.g.*, *Campbell*. If a defendant had copied one sentence in a novel, that copying may well be insubstantial. But if that single sentence set forth one of the world's shortest short stories—"When he awoke, the dinosaur was still there."—the question looks much different, as the copied material constitutes a small part of the novel but the entire short story.

Several features of Google's copying suggest that the better way to look at the numbers is to take into account the several million lines that Google did not copy. For one thing, the Sun Java API is inseparably bound to those task-implementing lines. Its purpose is to call them up. For another, Google copied those lines not because of their creativity, their beauty, or even (in a sense) because of their purpose. It copied them because programmers had already learned to work with the Sun Java API's system, and it would have been difficult, perhaps prohibitively so, to attract programmers to build its Android smartphone system without them. Further, Google's basic purpose was to create a different task-related system for a different computing environment (smartphones) and to create a platform—the Android platform—that would help achieve and popularize that objective. The "substantiality" factor will generally weigh in favor of fair use where, as here, the amount of copying was tethered to a valid, and transformative, purpose.

We do not agree with the Federal Circuit's conclusion that Google could have achieved its Java-compatibility objective by copying only the 170 lines of code that are "necessary to write in the Java language." In our view, that conclusion views Google's legitimate objectives too narrowly. Google's basic objective was not simply to make the Java programming language usable on its Android systems. It was to permit programmers to make use of their knowledge and experience using the Sun Java API when they wrote new programs for smartphones with the Android platform. In principle, Google might have created its own, different system of declaring code. But the jury could have found that its doing so would not have achieved that basic objective. In a sense, the declaring code was the key that it needed to unlock the programmers' creative energies. And it needed those energies to create and to improve its own innovative Android systems.

We consequently believe that this "substantiality" factor weighs in favor of fair use.

D. Market Effects

The fourth statutory factor focuses upon the "effect" of the copying in the "market for or value of the copyrighted work." 17 U. S. C. § 107(4). Consideration of this factor, at least where computer programs are at issue, can prove more complex than at first it may seem. It can require a court to consider the amount of money that the copyright owner might lose. Those losses normally conflict with copyright's basic objective: providing authors with exclusive rights that will spur creative expression.

But a potential loss of revenue is not the whole story. We here must consider not just the amount but also the source of the loss. As we pointed out in *Campbell*, a "lethal parody, like a scathing theatre review," may "kil[l] demand for the original." Yet this kind of harm, even if directly translated into foregone dollars, is not "cognizable under the Copyright Act."

Further, we must take into account the public benefits the copying will likely produce. Are those benefits, for example, related to copyright's concern for the creative production of new expression? Are they comparatively important, or unimportant, when compared with dollar amounts likely lost (taking into account as well the nature of the source of the loss)?

We do not say that these questions are always relevant to the application of fair use, not even in the world of computer programs. Nor do we say that these questions are the only questions a court might ask. But we do find them relevant here in helping to determine the likely market effects of Google's reimplementation.

As to the likely amount of loss, the jury could have found that Android did not harm the actual or potential markets for Java SE. And it could have found that Sun itself (now Oracle) would not have been able to enter those markets successfully whether Google did, or did not, copy a part of its API. First, evidence at trial demonstrated that, regardless of Android's smartphone technology, Sun was poorly positioned to succeed in the mobile phone market. The jury heard ample evidence that Java SE's primary market was laptops and desktops. Given the evidence showing that Sun was beset by business challenges in developing a mobile phone product, the jury was entitled to agree with that assessment.

Second, the jury was repeatedly told that devices using Google's Android platform were different in kind from those that licensed Sun's technology. For instance, witnesses explained that the broader industry distinguished between smartphones and simpler "feature phones." As to the specific devices that used Sun-created software, the jury heard that one of these phones lacked a touchscreen, while another did not have a QWERTY keyboard. For other mobile devices, the evidence showed that simpler products, like the Kindle, used Java software, while more advanced technology, like the Kindle Fire, were built on the Android operating system. This record evidence demonstrates that, rather than just "repurposing [Sun's] code from larger computers to smaller computers," Google's Android platform was part of a distinct (and more advanced) market than Java software.

Looking to these important differences, Google's economic expert told the jury that Android was not a market substitute for Java's software. As he explained, "the two products are on very different devices," and the Android platform, which offers "an entire mobile operating stack," is a "very different typ[e] of produc[t]" than Java SE, which is "just an applications programming framework."

Finally, the jury also heard evidence that Sun foresaw a benefit from the broader use of the Java programming language in a new platform like Android, as it would further expand the network of Java-trained programmers. In other words, the jury could have understood Android and Java SE as operating in two distinct markets. And because there are two markets at issue, programmers learning the Java language to work in one market (smartphones) are then able to bring those talents to the other market (laptops).

Sun presented evidence to the contrary. Indeed, the Federal Circuit held that the "market effects" factor militated against fair use in part because Sun had tried to enter the Android market. But those licensing negotiations concerned much more than 37 packages of declaring code, covering topics like "the implementation of [Java's] code" and "branding and cooperation" between the firms. See also Nimmer on Copyright (cautioning against the "danger of circularity posed" by considering unrealized licensing opportunities because "it is a given in every fair use case that plaintiff suffers a loss of a *potential* market if that potential is defined as the theoretical market for licensing the very use at bar").

On the other hand, Google's copying helped Google make a vast amount of money from its Android platform. And enforcement of the Sun Java API copyright might give Oracle a significant share of these funds. It is important, however, to consider why and how Oracle might have become entitled to this money. When a new interface, like an API or a spreadsheet program, first comes on the market, it may attract new users because of its expressive qualities, such as a better visual screen or because of its superior functionality. As time passes, however, it may be valuable for a different reason, namely, because users, including programmers, are just used to it. They have already learned how to work with it. See *Lotus* (Boudin, J., concurring).

The record here is filled with evidence that this factor accounts for Google's desire to use the Sun Java API. This source of Android's profitability has much to do with third parties' (say, programmers') investment in Sun Java programs. It has correspondingly less to do with Sun's investment in creating the Sun Java API. We have no reason to believe that the Copyright Act seeks to protect third parties' investment in learning how to operate a created work.

Finally, given programmers' investment in learning the Sun Java API, to allow enforcement of Oracle's copyright here would risk harm to the public. Given the costs and difficulties of producing alternative APIs with similar appeal to programmers, allowing enforcement here would make of the Sun Java API's declaring code a lock limiting the future creativity of new programs. Oracle alone would hold the key. The result could well prove highly profitable to Oracle (or other firms holding a copyright in computer interfaces). But those profits could well flow from creative improvements, new applications, and new uses developed by users who have learned to work with that interface. To that extent, the lock would interfere with, not further, copyright's basic creativity objectives. See also *Sega* ("An attempt to monopolize the market by making it impossible for others to compete runs counter to the statutory purpose of promoting creative expression").

The uncertain nature of Sun's ability to compete in Android's market place, the sources of its lost revenue, and the risk of creativity-related harms to the public, when taken together, convince that this fourth factor—market effects—also weighs in favor of fair use.

* * *

The fact that computer programs are primarily functional makes it difficult to apply traditional copyright concepts in that technological world. See *Lotus* (Boudin, J., concurring). In doing so here, we have not changed the nature of those concepts. We do not overturn or modify our earlier cases involving fair use—cases, for example, that involve "knockoff" products, journalistic writings, and parodies. Rather, we here recognize that application of a copyright doctrine such as fair use has long proved a cooperative effort of Legislatures and courts, and that Congress, in our view, intended that it so continue. As such, we have looked to the principles set forth in the fair use statute, § 107, and set forth in our earlier cases, and applied them to this different kind of copyrighted work.

We reach the conclusion that in this case, where Google reimplemented a user interface, taking only what was needed to allow users to put their accrued talents to work in a new and transformative program, Google's copying of the Sun Java API was a fair use of that material as a matter of law. The Federal Circuit's contrary judgment is reversed, and the case is remanded for further proceedings in conformity with this opinion.

It is so ordered.

Justice THOMAS, with whom Justice ALITO joins, dissenting. [Omitted.]

• • • • • • • • • •

Questions:

1.) This case gives a "fair use legal shield" or safe harbor to *some* software companies seeking to make their new programs interoperable with existing programs or existing programming languages. Is it stronger or weaker than the safe harbor provided by *Lotus v. Borland* on subject matter grounds? Both stronger and weaker?

2.) Which aspects of Judge Boudin's concurrence does Justice Breyer echo in this opinion? Why does Justice Breyer think that Oracle is not entitled to complete control over the positive externality created by its program and programming language?

3.) This case completes our case-study on fair use and technology—from video games to search engines, to the indexing of millions of books, to software. What themes do you see? What conception of the judicial role? What grade would you give the courts in their attempt to adapt the law to new technologies?

Note: Transformative Use, Appropriation Art and Mashups

As you have seen, "transformative use" became central in a surprising variety of cases. From its original role in *Acuff-Rose* and *SunTrust* where it protected parodic transformation, it came to be used by courts dealing with the interaction between copyright and technology—in the search engine cases and in the Google Books case, where the "transformation" is of a different kind, and most recently in *Google v. Oracle*, involving APIs in software.

Appropriation art. Returning to artistic reuses, the breadth of the transformative use concept reached what the Second Circuit called a "high-water mark" in the 2013 case of *Cariou v. Prince* (2d Cir. 2013). The plaintiff, Patrick Cariou, had published a book of photographs taken while living among Rastafarians in Jamaica called "Yes Rasta." Richard Prince—a famous appropriation artist—incorporated Cariou's photographs (sometimes in their entirety, sometimes using headshots or other cutouts) into thirty artworks at issue in the case. The district court had ruled for Cariou, finding that Prince's work was not transformative as a whole because "Prince did not intend to comment on Cariou, on Cariou's Photos, or on aspects of popular culture closely associated with Cariou." The Second Circuit disagreed on two grounds, espousing an especially broad interpretation of transformative use. First, it held that "[t]he law imposes no requirement that a work comment on the original or its author in order to be considered transformative, and a secondary work may constitute a fair use even if it serves some purpose other than those (criticism,

Prince's "Graduation" shown to the right of Cariou's original photograph. "Graduation" was one of the five works remanded to the district court for a determination of whether it was sufficiently transformative; Images from the Appendix of *Cariou v. Prince.*

comment, news reporting, teaching, scholarship, and research) identified in the preamble to the statute." It was sufficient that a work "alter the original with 'new expression, meaning, or message.'" Second, the court applied an objective test for assessing whether a work was transformative, focusing on how the work may "reasonably be perceived" rather than on the defendant's subjective intent. Accordingly, Prince's deposition testimony that he was not "trying to create anything with a new meaning or a new message" and did not "have any . . . interest in [Mr. Cariou's] original intent" was beside the point. Applying these standards, the court concluded that twenty-five of Prince's artworks were transformative as a matter of law because they "manifest[ed] an entirely different aesthetic from Cariou's photographs," but remanded to the district court regarding the five remaining artworks because it was not sufficiently clear whether they offered a "new expression, meaning, or message."

In 2021, the Second Circuit retreated from this expansive view of transformative use in *The Andy Warhol Foundation for the Arts v. Lynn Goldsmith* (2d Cir. 2021). This case dealt with Andy Warhol's "Prince Series," based on Lynn Goldsmith's photograph of the musical artist Prince. (Yes, both of these Second Circuit cases involved people named Prince.) Here are some of the works in question.

Goldsmith's photograph   Three of the sixteen works in Warhol's "Prince Series"

The district court had concluded that the Prince Series "can reasonably be perceived to have transformed Prince from a vulnerable, uncomfortable person to an iconic, larger-than-life figure." The Second Circuit disagreed, holding that the Prince Series did not qualify as fair use as a matter of law. The court rejected the notion that "any secondary work that adds a new aesthetic or new expression to its source material is necessarily transformative," but stopped short of overturning *Cariou*. Instead, it said this: "that decision has not been immune from criticism. While we remain bound by *Cariou,* and have no occasion or desire to question its correctness on its own facts, our review of the decision below persuades us that some clarification is in order."

Whereas *Cariou* drew criticism for widening the scope of transformative use beyond its legal moorings, the *Warhol* "clarification" has been criticized for swinging the pendulum too far in the opposite direction. Notably, the court attempted to draw a distinction between "derivative" and "transformative" works, placing the Prince Series closer to the "derivative" category. In doing so, it stated that "there exists an entire class of secondary works that add 'new expression, meaning, or message' to their source material but are nonetheless specifically *excluded* from the scope of fair use: derivative works" (emphasis in original). However, as you have already learned, this is backwards. The derivative works right does not circumscribe fair use; instead, the Copyright Act explicitly says that fair use is a limitation on the derivative works right. Section 106—which includes the derivative works right—begins with the qualification "*Subject to* section[] 107. . . .." Section 107 is then titled "*Limitations* on exclusive rights: Fair use" and states: "Notwithstanding the provisions of sections 106 . . . the fair use of a copyrighted work . . . is not an infringement of copyright." Plainly, the derivative works right is subject to the fair use limitation. Some derivative works will be fair uses, and others will not. On this point, the court appears simply to have misconstrued the law.

Turning to the works at hand, *Warhol* articulated a higher transformative use threshold for works of visual art that "share the same overarching purpose." It reviewed "conflicting guidance" from precedents involving visual art, and stated that "the bare assertion of a 'higher or different artistic use' is insufficient to render a work transformative. Rather, the secondary work itself *must reasonably be perceived as embodying an entirely distinct artistic purpose, one that conveys a "new meaning or message" entirely separate from its source material*." The court warned that judges "should not assume the role of art critic and seek to ascertain the intent behind or meaning of the works at issue" because "judges are typically unsuited to make aesthetic judgments." It then arguably proceeded to do just that in characterizing "the overarching purpose and function" of the two works and finding that "the cumulative effect" of Warhol's alterations in providing a "different impression of its subject" was insufficient to count as transformative.

Moving onto the other statutory factors, the court found that they also weighed against fair use. Under factor 2, the Goldsmith photograph was both unpublished and creative. For factor 3, rather than sifting out uncopyrightable material, the court decided that the copyrightable expression in Goldsmith's photograph included "the cumulative manifestation" of her artistic choices, so that "while Goldsmith has no monopoly on Prince's face, the law grants her a broad monopoly on its image as it appears in her photographs of him." This allowed the court to "readily conclude that the Prince Series borrows significantly from the Goldsmith Photograph, both quantitatively and qualitatively." This seems like another clear error. Goldsmith's copyright over the photograph covers only its *copyrightable subject matter*—the expressive choices in lighting, composition, framing and so on. The question should be whether Warhol copied (or copied but transformed) *those protectable elements*.

Finally, under factor 4, the court said that while Goldsmith might have an initial burden of "identifying" relevant markets, the Warhol Foundation had the burden of proving that its use did not cause market harm. (Remember, the court had held that Warhol's work was *not* transformative.) It held that "although the primary market for the Goldsmith Photograph and the Prince Series may differ, the Prince Series works pose cognizable harm to Goldsmith's market to license the Goldsmith Photograph to publications for editorial purposes and to other artists to create derivative works based on the Goldsmith Photograph and similar works."

We offer this summary of *Cariou* and *Warhol* because they are notable recent cases in a Circuit that is very important to copyright, not because we think they are correct. Both cases are significantly flawed. *Cariou* is a caricature of transformative use run wild, with judges legislating aesthetics from the bench as a matter of law. We would predict that *Warhol*, at least, will be overturned, possibly quite soon. Its apparent attempt to exempt derivative works from fair use is simply wrong as a matter of basic statutory interpretation, as well as being inconsistent with Supreme Court precedent. Since fair use reflects First Amendment concerns, it also raises troubling constitutional issues.

Mash-ups. When do mash-ups qualify for fair use? In *Dr. Seuss Enterprises v. ComicMix* (9th Cir. 2020), the Ninth Circuit held that the mash-up *Oh, the Place You'll Boldly Go! ("Boldly")*—which combined elements from works by Dr. Seuss including *Oh, the*

Places You'll Go! ("Go!") with elements from the Star Trek franchise—was not protected by fair use, reversing the district court's decision to the contrary. Here are some images from the books in question.

The district court had found the mash-up "highly transformative," explaining that "Defendants did not copy verbatim text from *Go!* in writing *Boldly*, nor did they replicate entire illustrations from *Go!* Although Defendants certainly borrowed from *Go!*—at times liberally—the elements borrowed were always adapted or transformed." The Ninth Circuit disagreed, concluding that *Boldly* was not transformative because it "merely repackaged" *Go!* rather than altering it: "While *Boldly* may have altered Star Trek by sending Captain Kirk and his crew to a strange new world, that world, the world of *Go!*, remains intact. *Go!* was merely repackaged into a new format, carrying the story of the Enterprise crew's journey through a strange star in a story shell already intricately illustrated by Dr. Seuss." Even though ComicMix claimed that *Boldly* had "extensive new content," the court said that "the addition of new expression to an existing work is not a get-out-of-jail-free card that renders the use of the original transformative." The court also found that *Boldly* was not a parody of *Go!* because "the juxtapositions of *Go!* and Star Trek elements do not 'hold [Seussian] style' up to ridicule. From the project's inception, ComicMix wanted *Boldly* to be a Star Trek primer that 'evoke[s]' rather than 'ridicule[s]' *Go!*. . . . We also reject as 'completely unconvincing' ComicMix's 'post-hoc characterization of the work' as criticizing the theme of banal narcissism in *Go!*."

The finding of non-transformative use under the first factor affected the analysis of the fourth factor. The district court, after finding that *Boldly* was transformative, had shifted the burden to Seuss on market harm, and concluded that "the harm to Plaintiff's market remains speculative." By contrast, the Ninth Circuit placed the burden firmly on the Defendants: "ComicMix's non-transformative and commercial use of Dr. Seuss's works likely leads to 'cognizable market harm to the original.' Not much about the fair use doctrine lends itself to absolute statements, but the Supreme Court and our circuit have unequivocally placed the burden of proof on the proponent of the affirmative defense of fair use." ComicMix's "scant evidence" was inadequate to carry this burden. Focusing on "Seuss's strong brand," the court found that *Boldly* harmed Seuss's extensive derivative works market, which included authorized *Go!* derivatives such as the books *Oh, The Things You Can Do That Are Good For You!*; *Oh, the Places I'll Go! By ME, Myself*; *Oh, Baby, the Places You'll Go!*; and *Oh, the Places I've Been! A Journal*. The court posited that "the unrestricted and widespread conduct of the sort ComicMix is engaged in could result in anyone being able to produce, without Seuss's permission, *Oh the Places Yoda'll Go!*, *Oh the Places You'll Pokemon Go!*, *Oh the Places You'll Yada Yada Yada!*, and countless other mash-ups." This "could 'create incentives to pirate intellectual property' and disincentivize the creation of illustrated books."

5.) A Fair Use Case-Study: Multiple Copies for Classroom Use

Princeton University Press v. Michigan Document Services, Inc.
99 F.3d 1381 (6th Cir. 1996 en banc)

DAVID A. NELSON, Circuit Judge.

This is a copyright infringement case. The corporate defendant, Michigan Document Services, Inc., is a commercial copyshop that reproduced substantial segments of copyrighted works of scholarship, bound the copies into "coursepacks," and sold the coursepacks to students for use in fulfilling reading assignments given by professors at the University of Michigan. The copyshop acted without permission from the copyright holders, and the main question presented is whether the "fair use" doctrine codified at 17 U.S.C. § 107 obviated the need to obtain such permission.

Answering this question "no," and finding the infringement willful, the district court entered a summary judgment order in which the copyright holders were granted equitable relief and were awarded damages that may have been enhanced for willfulness. *Princeton Univ. Press v. Michigan Document Servs., Inc.* (E.D. Mich. 1994). A three-judge panel of this court reversed the judgment on appeal, but a majority of the active judges of the court subsequently voted to rehear the case *en banc*. The appeal has now been argued before the full court.

We agree with the district court that the defendants' commercial exploitation of the copyrighted materials did not constitute fair use, and we shall affirm that branch of the district court's judgment. We believe that the district court erred in its finding of willfulness, however, and we shall vacate the damages award because of its possible linkage to that finding. . . .

Ann Arbor, the home of the University of Michigan, is also home to several copyshops. Among them is defendant Michigan Document Services (MDS), a corporation owned by defendant James Smith. We are told that MDS differs from most, if not all, of its competitors in at least one important way: it does not request permission from, nor does it pay agreed royalties to, copyright owners.

Mr. Smith has been something of a crusader against the system under which his competitors have been paying agreed royalties, or "permission fees" as they are known in the trade. The story begins in March of 1991, when Judge Constance Baker Motley, of the United States District Court for the Southern District of New York, decided the first reported case involving the copyright implications of educational coursepacks. See *Basic Books, Inc. v. Kinko's Graphics Corp.* (S.D.N.Y. 1991), holding that a Kinko's copyshop had violated the copyright statute by creating and selling coursepacks without permission from the publishing houses that held the copyrights. After *Kinko's,* we are told, many copyshops that had not previously requested permission from copyright holders began to obtain such permission. Mr. Smith chose not to do so. He consulted an attorney, and the attorney apparently advised him that while it was "risky" not to obtain permission, there were flaws in the *Kinko's* decision. Mr. Smith also undertook his own study of the fair use doctrine, reading what he could find on this subject in a law library. He ultimately concluded that the *Kinko's* case had been wrongly decided, and he publicized this conclusion through speeches, writings, and advertisements. His advertisements stressed that professors whose students purchased his coursepacks would not have to worry about delays attendant upon obtaining permission from publishers.

Not surprisingly, Mr. Smith attracted the attention of the publishing industry. Three publishers—Princeton University Press, MacMillan, Inc., and St. Martin's Press, Inc.—eventually brought the present suit against Mr. Smith and his corporation.

Each of the plaintiff publishers maintains a department that processes requests for permission to reproduce portions of copyrighted works. (In addition, copyshops may request such permission through the Copyright Clearance Center, a national clearinghouse.) Macmillan and St. Martin's, both of which are for-profit companies, claim that they generally respond within two weeks to requests for permission to make copies for classroom use. Princeton, a non-profit organization, claims to respond within two to four weeks. Mr. Smith has not put these claims to the test, and he has not paid permission fees. . . .

II

The fair use doctrine, which creates an exception to the copyright monopoly, "permits [and requires] courts to avoid rigid application of the copyright statute when, on occasion, it would stifle the very creativity which that law is designed to foster." *Campbell v. Acuff-Rose Music, Inc.* (1994). Initially developed by the courts, the doctrine was codified at 17 U.S.C. § 107 in 1976. Congress used the following formulation in Section 107:

> "[T]he fair use of a copyrighted work, including such use by reproduc-
> tion in copies . . . for purposes such as criticism, comment, news
> reporting, teaching (including multiple copies for classroom use). . . ."

This language does not provide blanket immunity for "multiple copies for classroom use." Rather, "whether a use referred to in the first sentence of Section 107 is a fair use in a particular case . . . depend[s] upon the application of the determinative factors." *Campbell*.[1]

The four statutory factors may not have been created equal. In determining whether a use is "fair," the Supreme Court has said that the most important factor is the fourth, the one contained in 17 U.S.C. § 107(4). See *Harper & Row Publishers, Inc. v. Nation Enters.* (But see *American Geophysical Union v. Texaco Inc.* (2d Cir. 1994), suggesting that the Supreme Court may now have abandoned the idea that the fourth factor is of paramount importance.) We take it that this factor, "the effect of the use upon the potential market for or value of the copyrighted work," is at least *primus inter pares,* figuratively speaking, and we shall turn to it first.

---

[1] Judge Merritt's dissent rejects this proposition and asserts, in effect, that under the plain language of the copyright statute the making of multiple copies for classroom use constitutes fair use *ipso facto.* Judge Merritt's reading of the statute would be unassailable if Congress had said that "the use of a copyrighted work for purposes such as teaching (including multiple copies for classroom use) is not an infringement of copyright." But that is not what Congress said. It said, rather, that "the fair use of a copyrighted work, *including such use* [*i.e.* including "fair use"] . . . for purposes such as . . . teaching (including multiple copies for classroom use) . . . is not an infringement of copyright."

When read in its entirety, as Judge Ryan's dissent correctly recognizes, the quoted sentence says that *fair use* of a copyrighted work for purposes such as teaching (including multiple copies for classroom use) is not an infringement. And the statutory factors set forth in the next sentence must be considered in determining whether the making of multiple copies for classroom use is a fair use in "any particular case," just as the statutory factors must be considered in determining whether any other use referred to in the first sentence is a fair use in a particular case. To hold otherwise would be to subvert the intent manifested in the words of the statute and confirmed in the pertinent legislative history.

The burden of proof as to market effect rests with the copyright holder if the challenged use is of a "noncommercial" nature. The alleged infringer has the burden, on the other hand, if the challenged use is "commercial" in nature. *Sony Corp. v. Universal City Studios, Inc.* (1984). In the case at bar the defendants argue that the burden of proof rests with the publishers because the use being challenged is "noncommercial." We disagree.

It is true that the use to which the materials are put by the students who purchase the coursepacks is noncommercial in nature. But the use of the materials by the students is not the use that the publishers are challenging. What the publishers are challenging is the duplication of copyrighted materials for sale by a for-profit corporation that has decided to maximize its profits—and give itself a competitive edge over other copyshops—by declining to pay the royalties requested by the holders of the copyrights.[2]

The defendants' use of excerpts from the books at issue here was no less commercial in character than was *The Nation* magazine's use of copyrighted material in *Harper & Row*, where publication of a short article containing excerpts from the still unpublished manuscript of a book by President Ford was held to be an unfair use. Like the students who purchased unauthorized coursepacks, the purchasers of *The Nation* did not put the contents of the magazine to commercial use—but that did not stop the Supreme Court from characterizing the defendant's use of the excerpts as "a publication [that] was commercial as opposed to nonprofit. . . ." *Harper & Row.* And like the use that is being challenged in the case now before us, the use challenged in *Harper & Row* was "presumptively an unfair exploitation of the monopoly privilege that belongs to the owner of the copyright." [Q]uoting *Sony*.[3]

The strength of the *Sony* presumption may vary according to the context in which it arises, and the presumption disappears entirely where the challenged use is one that transforms the original work into a new artistic creation. See *Campbell.* Perhaps the presumption is weaker in the present case than it would be in other contexts. There *is* a presumption of unfairness here, nonetheless, and we are not persuaded that the defendants have rebutted it.

If we are wrong about the existence of the presumption—if the challenged use is not commercial, in other words, and if the plaintiff publishers have the burden of proving an adverse effect upon either the potential market for the copyrighted work or the potential value of the work—we believe that the publishers have carried the burden of proving a diminution in potential market value.

---

[2] Two of the dissents suggest that a copyshop merely stands in the shoes of its customers and makes no "use" of copyrighted materials that differs materially from the use to which the copies are put by the ultimate consumer. But subject to the fair use exception, 17 U.S.C. § 106 gives the copyright owner the "exclusive" right "to reproduce the copyrighted work in copies. . . ." And if the fairness of making copies depends on what the ultimate consumer does with the copies, it is hard to see how the manufacture of pirated editions of any copyrighted work of scholarship could ever be an unfair use. As discussed *infra*, the dissenters' suggestion—which proposes no limiting principle—runs counter to the legislative history of the Copyright Act and has properly been rejected by the courts.

[3] Judge Ryan's dissent maintains that there cannot be an "exploitation" of a copyrighted work unless the exploiter assesses the work's market potential, makes a selection based on content, and realizes a profit from the substance of the work. But the dictionary defines "exploit" in terms that include "to take advantage of, utilize," see *Webster's Third New International Dictionary (Unabridged),* and nothing in *Harper & Row* suggests that the Supreme Court intended a narrower or more idiosyncratic meaning.

The dissent also points out that it was magazine employees, not outsiders, who obtained the unpublished manuscript of the Ford book and selected the portions that were included in the offending article. But nothing turns on the "in house" character of such activities. If a college professor had obtained the manuscript, selected the excerpts and peddled the article on a freelance basis, can anyone doubt that it would have been a violation of the copyright for *The Nation* to publish the professor's article?

One test for determining market harm—a test endorsed by the Supreme Court in *Sony*, *Harper & Row*, and *Campbell*—is evocative of Kant's categorical imperative. "[T]o negate fair use," the Supreme Court has said, "one need only show that *if the challenged use 'should become widespread, it would adversely affect the potential market* for the copyrighted work.'" *Harper & Row*, quoting *Sony*. Under this test, we believe, it is reasonably clear that the plaintiff publishers have succeeded in negating fair use.

As noted above, most of the copyshops that compete with MDS in the sale of coursepacks pay permission fees for the privilege of duplicating and selling excerpts from copyrighted works. The three plaintiffs together have been collecting permission fees at a rate approaching $500,000 a year. If copyshops across the nation were to start doing what the defendants have been doing here, this revenue stream would shrivel and the potential value of the copyrighted works of scholarship published by the plaintiffs would be diminished accordingly.

The defendants contend that it is circular to assume that a copyright holder is entitled to permission fees and then to measure market loss by reference to the lost fees. They argue that market harm can only be measured by lost sales of books, not permission fees. But the circularity argument proves too much. Imagine that the defendants set up a printing press and made exact reproductions—asserting that such reproductions constituted "fair use"—of a book to which they did not hold the copyright. Under the defendants' logic it would be circular for the copyright holder to argue market harm because of lost copyright revenues, since this would assume that the copyright holder had a right to such revenues.

A "circularity" argument indistinguishable from that made by the defendants here was rejected by the Second Circuit in *American Geophysical*, where the photocopying of scientific articles for use by Texaco researchers was held to be an unfair use. It is true, the Second Circuit acknowledged, that "a copyright holder can *always* assert some degree of adverse [e]ffect on its potential licensing revenues as a consequence of [the defendant's use] . . . simply because the copyright holder has not been paid a fee to permit that particular use." But such an assertion will not carry much weight if the defendant has "filled a market niche that the [copyright owner] simply had no interest in occupying." Where, on the other hand, the copyright holder clearly does have an interest in exploiting a licensing market—and especially where the copyright holder has actually succeeded in doing so—"it is appropriate that potential licensing revenues for photocopying be considered in a fair use analysis." *American Geophysical*. Only "traditional, reasonable, or likely to be developed markets" are to be considered in this connection, and even the availability of an existing system for collecting licensing fees will not be conclusive.[4] But Congress has implicitly suggested that licensing fees should be recognized in appropriate cases as part of the potential market for or value of the copyrighted work, and it was primarily because of lost licensing revenue that the Second Circuit agreed with the finding of the district court in *American Geophysical* that "the publishers have demonstrated a substantial harm to the value of their copyrights through [Texaco's] copying."

The approach followed by Judges Newman and Leval in the *American Geophysical*

---

[4] Although not conclusive, the existence of an established license fee system is highly relevant:

"[I]t is sensible that a particular unauthorized use should be considered 'more fair' when there is no ready market or means to pay for the use, while such an unauthorized use should be considered 'less fair' when there is a ready market or means to pay for the use. The vice of circular reasoning arises only if the availability of payment is conclusive against fair use."

litigation is fully consistent with the Supreme Court case law. In *Harper & Row*, where there is no indication in the opinion that the challenged use caused any diminution in sales of President Ford's memoirs, the Court found harm to the market for the licensing of excerpts. The Court's reasoning—which was obviously premised on the assumption that the copyright holder was entitled to licensing fees for use of its copyrighted materials—is no more circular than that employed here. And in *Campbell*, where the Court was unwilling to conclude that the plaintiff had lost licensing revenues under the fourth statutory factor, the Court reasoned that a market for critical parody was not one "that creators of original works would in general develop or license others to develop." *Campbell*.

The potential uses of the copyrighted works at issue in the case before us clearly include the selling of permission to reproduce portions of the works for inclusion in coursepacks—and the likelihood that publishers actually will license such reproduction is a demonstrated fact. A licensing market already exists here, as it did not in a case on which the plaintiffs rely, *Williams & Wilkins Co. v. United States* (1973). Thus there is no circularity in saying, as we do say, that the potential for destruction of this market by widespread circumvention of the plaintiffs' permission fee system is enough, under the *Harper & Row* test, "to negate fair use."

Our final point with regard to the fourth statutory factor concerns the affidavits of the three professors who assigned one or more of the copyrighted works to be read by their students. The defendants make much of the proposition that these professors only assigned excerpts when they would not have required their students to purchase the entire work. But what seems significant to us is that none of these affidavits shows that the professor executing the affidavit would have refrained from assigning the copyrighted work if the position taken by the copyright holder had been sustained beforehand.

It is true that Professor Victor Lieberman, who assigned the excerpt from the Olson and Roberts book on America and Vietnam, raises questions about the workability of the permission systems of "many publishers." In 1991, Professor Lieberman avers, a Kinko's copyshop to which he had given materials for inclusion in a coursepack experienced serious delays in obtaining permissions from unnamed publishers. Professor Lieberman does not say that timely permission could not have been obtained from the publisher of the Olson and Roberts book, however, and he does not say that he would have refrained from assigning the work if the copyshop had been required to pay a permission fee for it.

It is also true that the publisher of one of the copyrighted works in question here (*Public Opinion*, by Walter Lippmann) would have turned down a request for permission to copy the 45-page excerpt included in a coursepack prepared to the specifications of Professor Donald Kinder. The excerpt was so large that the publisher would have preferred that students buy the book itself, and the work was available in an inexpensive paperback edition. But Professor Kinder does not say that he would have refrained from assigning the excerpt from the Lippmann book if it could not have been included in the coursepack. Neither does he say that he would have refrained from assigning any of the other works mentioned in his affidavit had he known that the defendants would be required to pay permission fees for them.

The third professor, Michael Dawson, assigned a 95-page excerpt from the book on black politics by Nancy Weiss. Professor Dawson does not say that a license was not available from the publisher of the Weiss book, and he does not say that the license fee would have deterred him from assigning the book.

III

In the context of nontransformative uses, at least, and except insofar as they touch on the fourth factor, the other statutory factors seem considerably less important. We shall deal with them relatively briefly.

A

As to "the purpose and character of the use, including whether such use is of a commercial nature or is for nonprofit educational purposes," 17 U.S.C. § 107(1), we have already explained our reasons for concluding that the challenged use is of a commercial nature.

The defendants argue that the copying at issue here would be considered "nonprofit educational" if done by the students or professors themselves. The defendants also note that they can profitably produce multiple copies for less than it would cost the professors or the students to make the same number of copies. Most of the copyshops with which the defendants compete have been paying permission fees, however, and we assume that these shops too can perform the copying on a more cost-effective basis than the professors or students can. This strikes us as a more significant datum than the ability of a black market copyshop to beat the do-it-yourself cost.

As to the proposition that it would be fair use for the students or professors to make their own copies, the issue is by no means free from doubt. We need not decide this question, however, for the fact is that the copying complained of here was performed on a profit-making basis by a commercial enterprise. And "[t]he courts have . . . properly rejected attempts by for-profit users to stand in the shoes of their customers making nonprofit or noncommercial uses." Patry, *Fair Use in Copyright Law*. As the House Judiciary Committee stated in its report on the 1976 legislation,

> "[I]t would not be possible for a non-profit institution, by means of contractual arrangements with a commercial copying enterprise, to authorize the enterprise to carry out copying and distribution functions that would be exempt if conducted by the non-profit institution itself."

It should be noted, finally, that the degree to which the challenged use has transformed the original copyrighted works—another element in the first statutory factor—is virtually indiscernible. If you make verbatim copies of 95 pages of a 316-page book, you have not transformed the 95 pages very much—even if you juxtapose them to excerpts from other works and package everything conveniently. This kind of mechanical "transformation" bears little resemblance to the creative metamorphosis accomplished by the parodists in the *Campbell* case. . . .

V

We take as our text for the concluding part of this discussion of fair use Justice Stewart's well-known exposition of the correct approach to "ambiguities" in the copyright law:

> "The immediate effect of our copyright law is to secure a fair return for an 'author's' creative labor. But the ultimate aim is, by this incentive, to stimulate artistic creativity for the general public good. 'The sole interest of the United States and the primary object in conferring the monopoly,' this Court has said, 'lie in the general benefits derived by the public from the labors of authors.' . . . When technological change has rendered its literal terms ambiguous, the Copyright Act must be construed in light of

this basic purpose." *Twentieth Century Music Corp. v. Aiken* (1975).

The defendants attach considerable weight to the assertions of numerous academic authors that they do not write primarily for money and that they want their published writings to be freely copyable. The defendants suggest that unlicensed copying will "stimulate artistic creativity for the general public good."

This suggestion would be more persuasive if the record did not demonstrate that licensing income is significant to the publishers. It is the publishers who hold the copyrights, of course—and the publishers obviously need economic incentives to publish scholarly works, even if the scholars do not need direct economic incentives to write such works.

The writings of most academic authors, it seems fair to say, lack the general appeal of works by a Walter Lippmann, for example. (Lippmann is the only non-academic author whose writings are involved in this case.) One suspects that the profitability of at least some of the other books at issue here is marginal. If publishers cannot look forward to receiving permission fees, why should they continue publishing marginally profitable books at all? And how will artistic creativity be stimulated if the diminution of economic incentives for publishers to publish academic works means that fewer academic works will be published?

The fact that a liberal photocopying policy may be favored by many academics who are not themselves in the publishing business has little relevance in this connection. As Judge Leval observed in *American Geophysical*,

> "It is not surprising that authors favor liberal photocopying; generally such authors have a far greater interest in the wide dissemination of their work than in royalties—all the more so when they have assigned their royalties to the publisher. But the authors have not risked their capital to achieve dissemination. The publishers have. Once an author has assigned her copyright, her approval or disapproval of photocopying is of no further relevance."

In the case at bar the district court was not persuaded that the creation of new works of scholarship would be stimulated by depriving publishers of the revenue stream derived from the sale of permissions. Neither are we. On the contrary, it seems to us, the destruction of this revenue stream can only have a deleterious effect upon the incentive to publish academic writings.

VI

The district court's conclusion that the infringement was willful is somewhat more problematic, in our view. The Copyright Act allows the collection of statutory damages of between $500 and $20,000 for each work infringed. 17 U.S.C. § 504(c)(1). Where the copyright holder establishes that the infringement is willful, the court may increase the award to not more than $100,000. 17 U.S.C. § 504(c)(2). If the court finds that the infringement was innocent, on the other hand, the court may reduce the damages to not less than $200. Here the district court awarded $5,000 per work infringed, characterizing the amount of the award as "a strong admonition from this court."

Willfulness, under this statutory scheme, has a rather specialized meaning. As Professor Nimmer explains,

> "In other contexts ['willfulness'] might simply mean an intent to copy, without necessarily an intent to infringe. It seems clear that as here used, 'willfully' means with knowledge that the defendant's conduct constitutes copyright infringement. Otherwise, there would be no point in providing specially for the reduction of minimum awards in the case

of innocent infringement, because any infringement that was nonwillful would necessarily be innocent. This seems to mean, then, that one who has been notified that his conduct constitutes copyright infringement, but who reasonably and in good faith believes the contrary, is not 'willful' for these purposes."

The plaintiffs do not contest the good faith of Mr. Smith's belief that his conduct constituted fair use; only the reasonableness of that belief is challenged. "Reasonableness," in the present context, is essentially a question of law. The facts of the instant case are not in dispute, and the issue is whether the copyright law supported the plaintiffs' position so clearly that the defendants must be deemed as a matter of law to have exhibited a reckless disregard of the plaintiffs' property rights. We review this issue *de novo*.

Fair use is one of the most unsettled areas of the law. The doctrine has been said to be "so flexible as virtually to defy definition." *Time Inc. v. Bernard Geis Assoc.* (S.D.N.Y. 1968). The potential for reasonable disagreement here is illustrated by the forcefully argued dissents and the now-vacated panel opinion. In the circumstances of this case, we cannot say that the defendants' belief that their copying constituted fair use was so unreasonable as to bespeak willfulness. Accordingly, we shall remand the case for reconsideration of the statutory damages to be awarded. . . .

VIII

The grant of summary judgment on the fair use issue is AFFIRMED. The award of damages is VACATED, and the case is REMANDED for reconsideration of damages and for entry of a separate judgment not inconsistent with this opinion.

BOYCE F. MARTIN, Jr., Chief Judge, dissenting.

This case presents for me one of the more obvious examples of how laudable societal objectives, recognized by both the Constitution and statute, have been thwarted by a decided lack of judicial prudence. Copyright protection as embodied in the Copyright Act of 1976 is intended as a public service to both the creator and the consumer of published works. Although the Act grants to individuals limited control over their original works, it was drafted to stimulate the production of those original works for the benefit of the whole nation. The fair use doctrine, which requires unlimited public access to published works in educational settings, is one of the essential checks on the otherwise exclusive property rights given to copyright holders under the Copyright Act.

Ironically, the majority's rigid statutory construction of the Copyright Act grants publishers the kind of power that Article I, Section 8 of the Constitution is designed to guard against. The Copyright Clause grants Congress the power to create copyright interests that are *limited* in scope. Consequently, the Copyright Act adopted the fair use doctrine to protect society's vested interest in the sharing of ideas and information against pursuits of illegitimate or excessive private proprietary claims. While it may seem unjust that publishers must share, in certain situations, their work-product with others, free of charge, that is not some "unforeseen byproduct of a statutory scheme;" rather, it is the "essence of copyright" and a "constitutional requirement." *Feist Publications, Inc. v. Rural Tel. Serv. Co.* (1991).

Michigan Document Services provided a service to the University of Michigan that promoted scholarship and higher education. Michigan Document Services was paid for its services; however, that fact does not obviate a fair use claim under these facts. Requiring Michigan Document Services to pay permission fees in this instance is inconsistent with the primary mission of the Copyright Act. The individual rights granted by the Act are subservient to the Act's primary objective, which is the promotion of creativity generally. We must therefore consider the fair use provision of Section 107 of the Act in light of the sum total of public benefits intended by copyright law. In this instance, there is no adverse economic impact on Princeton University Press that can outweigh the benefits provided by Michigan Document Services. Indeed, to presume adverse economic impact, as has the majority, is to presume that the $50,000 in fees currently earned by plaintiff is mandated by the Act in every instance—something I hesitate to presume.

That the majority lends significance to the identity of the person operating the photocopier is a profound indication that its approach is misguided. Given the focus of the Copyright Act, the only practical difference between this case and that of a student making his or her own copies is that commercial photocopying is faster and more cost-effective. Censuring incidental private sector profit reflects little of the essence of copyright law. Would the majority require permission fees of the Professor's teaching assistant who at times must copy, at the Professor's behest, copyrighted materials for dissemination to a class, merely because such assistant is paid an hourly wage by the Professor for this work?

The majority's strict reading of the fair use doctrine promises to hinder scholastic progress nationwide. By charging permission fees on this kind of job, publishers will pass on expenses to colleges and universities that will, of course, pass such fees on to students. Students may also be harmed if added expenses and delays cause professors to opt against creating such specialized anthologies for their courses. Even if professors attempt to reproduce the benefits of such a customized education, the added textbook cost to students is likely to be prohibitive.

The Copyright Act does not suggest such a result. Rather, the fair use doctrine contemplates the creation and free flow of information; the unhindered flow of such information through, among other things, education in turn spawns the creation and free flow of new information.

In limiting the right to copy published works in the Copyright Act, Congress created an exception for cases like the one before us. When I was in school, you bought your books and you went to the library for supplemental information. To record this supplemental information, in order to learn and benefit from it, you wrote it out long-hand or typed out what you needed—not easy, but effective. Today, with the help of free enterprise and technology, this fundamental means of obtaining information for study has been made easier. Students may now routinely acquire inexpensive copies of the information they need without all of the hassle. The trend of an instructor giving information to a copying service to make a single set of copies for each student for a small fee is just a modern approach to the classic process of education. To otherwise enforce this statute is nonsensical. I therefore dissent.

MERRITT, Circuit Judge, dissenting.

The copying done in this case is permissible under the plain language of the copyright statute that allows "multiple copies for classroom use:" "[T]he fair use of a copyrighted work . . . for purposes such as . . . teaching (*including multiple copies for classroom use*), . . . is not an infringement of copyright." 17 U.S.C. § 107 (emphasis added). Also, the injunction the Court has upheld exceeds the protections provided by the Copyright Act of 1976 regardless of whether the use was a fair use and is so grossly overbroad that it violates the First Amendment.

I

This is a case of first impression with broad consequences. Neither the Supreme Court nor any other court of appeals has interpreted the exception allowing "multiple copies for classroom use" found in § 107 of the copyright statute. There is no legal precedent and no legal history that supports our Court's reading of this phrase in a way that outlaws the widespread practice of copying for classroom use by teachers and students.

For academic institutions, the practical consequences of the Court's decision in this case are highly unsatisfactory, to say the least. Anyone who makes multiple copies for classroom use for a fee is guilty of copyright infringement unless the portion copied is just a few paragraphs long. Chapters from a book or articles from a journal are verboten. No longer may Kinko's and other corner copyshops, or school bookstores, libraries and student-run booths and kiosks copy anything for a fee except a small passage. I do not see why we should so construe plain statutory language that on its face permits "multiple copies for classroom use." The custom of making copies for classroom use for a fee began during my college and law school days forty years ago and is now well-established. I see no justification for overturning this long-established practice.

I disagree with the Court's method of analyzing and explaining the statutory language of § 107 providing a fair use exception.[1] Except for "teaching," the statute is cast in general, abstract language that allows fair use for "criticism," "comment," "news reporting" and "research." The scope or extent of copying allowed for these uses is left undefined. Not so for "teaching." This purpose, and this purpose alone, is immediately followed by a definition. The definition allows "multiple copies for classroom use" of copyrighted material. The four factors to be considered, *e.g.,* market effect and the portion of the work used, are of limited assistance when the teaching use at issue fits squarely within the specific language of the statute, *i.e.,* "multiple copies for classroom use." In the present case that is all we have—"multiple copies for classroom use."

There is nothing in the statute that distinguishes between copies made for students by a third person who charges a fee for their labor and copies made by students themselves who pay a fee only for use of the copy machine. Our political economy generally encourages the division and specialization of labor. There is no reason why in this instance the law should discourage high schools, colleges, students and professors from hiring the labor of others to make their copies any more than there is a reason to discourage lawyers from hiring paralegals to make copies for clients and courts. The Court's distinction in this case based on the division of labor—who does the copying—is short sighted and unsound economically.

Our Court cites no authority for the proposition that the intervention of the copyshop changes the outcome of the case. The Court errs by focusing on the "use" of the materials made by the copyshop in making the copies rather than upon the real user of the materials—the students. Neither the District Court nor our Court provides a rationale as to why the copyshops cannot "stand in the shoes" of their customers in

---

[1] Both the majority opinion and Judge Ryan's dissent approach the determination of whether the use at issue here is infringing solely by use of the four statutory factors set out in § 107. Neither the plain language of the statute nor the case law requires that determination to be made solely on the narrow grounds of those four factors. Because the plain language of the statute is clear concerning "multiple copies for classroom use" and because determinations of infringement are to be made on a case-by-case basis taking into consideration the reasonableness of the copying from an equitable perspective, I do not believe that the four factors are controlling. The specific plain language should be given much more weight in this case than the four abstract considerations of little relevance to copying for classroom use.

making copies for noncommercial, educational purposes where the copying would be fair use if undertaken by the professor or the student personally. . . .

Turning to the effect of the use upon the potential market for or value of the copyrighted work, plaintiffs here have failed to demonstrate that the photocopying done by defendant has caused even marginal economic harm to their publishing business. As the Court concedes, the publishers would prefer that students purchase the publications containing the excerpts instead of receiving photocopies of excerpts from the publications. What the publishers would "prefer" is not part of the analysis to determine the effect on the potential market. We are to examine what the facts tell us about the market effect. The facts demonstrate that it is only wishful thinking on the part of the publishers that the professors who assigned the works in question would have directed their students to purchase the entire work if the excerpted portions were unavailable for copying. The excerpts copied were a small percentage of the total work, and, as the professors testified, it seems more likely that they would have omitted the work altogether instead of requiring the students to purchase the entire work.

The use complained of by plaintiffs here has been widespread for many years and the publishers have not been able to demonstrate any significant harm to the market for the original works during that time. The publishing industry tried to persuade Congress in 1976 to ban the type of copying done by defendant here. Congress declined to do so and the publishing industry has been trying ever since to work around the language of the statute to expand its rights.

It is also wrong to measure the amount of economic harm to the publishers by loss of a presumed license fee—a criterion that assumes that the publishers have the right to collect such fees in all cases where the user copies any portion of published works. The majority opinion approves of this approach by affirming the issuance of an injunction prohibiting defendant from copying any portion of plaintiffs' works. It does so without requiring a case-by-case determination of infringement as mandated by the Supreme Court.

The publishers have no right to such a license fee. Simply because the publishers have managed to make licensing fees a significant source of income from copyshops and other users of their works does not make the income from the licensing a factor on which we must rely in our analysis. If the publishers have no right to the fee in many of the instances in which they are collecting it, we should not validate that practice by now using the income derived from it to justify further imposition of fees. Our job is simply to determine whether the use here falls within the § 107 exception for "multiple copies for classroom use." If it does, the publisher cannot look to us to force the copyshop to pay a fee for the copying.

The Court states that defendant has declined to pay "agreed royalties" to the holders of the copyrights. Agreed to by whom? Defendant has not "agreed" to pay the publishers anything. It is fair to label a royalty as "agreed to" only when the publisher has appropriately negotiated a fee with the copyshop for use of the copy in question.

III

The injunction upheld by the Court, as it stands now, extends the rights of the copyright owners far beyond the limits prescribed by Congress.[2] It prohibits defendant

---

[2] Although the majority has modified its original draft of the opinion to order a remand directing the district court (1) to set out the injunction in a separate order as required by Federal Rule of Civil Procedure 65 and (2) to set forth "more precisely" the scope of the injunction, the remand instruction gives virtually no

from copying any excerpts from plaintiffs' materials, both those now in existence and any that may be published by plaintiffs in the future, regardless of whether the entire work is appropriately protected by copyright or whether the copying is for classroom use or is otherwise a fair use. The injunction prohibits defendant from copying from copyrighted works of the plaintiffs, without regard to length, content or purpose of the copying and without any recognition that the doctrine of fair use exists. The injunction avoids the necessity of determining whether the copying is an infringement or a fair use—any copying and dissemination is forbidden. The injunction also protects future publications of plaintiffs—works that have not yet even been created—without any knowledge as to the level of copyright protection the works would normally be afforded.

The gross overbreadth of the injunction appears to violate the First Amendment. The purpose of the First Amendment is to facilitate the widest possible dissemination of information. "From a first amendment viewpoint, the effect of an injunction is to restrain the infringing expression altogether—an effect which goes beyond what is necessary to secure the copyright property." Goldstein, Copyright and the First Amendment, 70 Colum. L. Rev. 983, 1030 (1970); 3 Nimmer § 14.06[B] (where public harm would result from the injunction, courts should award damages in lieu of injunction).

In sum, the injunction imposed here—an injunction that provides blanket copyright protection for all the works of a given publisher without regard to the limitations on copyright protection—is overbroad. The injunction is inappropriate because it prohibits the public from using defendant's copyshop for noninfringing copying of plaintiffs' works.

RYAN, Circuit Judge, dissenting.

It is clear from the application of the four fair use factors of 17 U.S.C. § 107 that MDS's copying of the publishers' copyrighted works in this case is fair use and, thus, no infringement of the publishers' rights. Indeed, it is a use which is merely an aspect of the professors' and students' classroom use, and, only in the narrowest and most technical sense, a use of a separate genre under section 107. And, so, I must dissent from the majority's contrary view and, in expressing my understanding of the matter, I shall identify three important subissues on which I think my colleagues' analysis has led them to mistakenly conclude that MDS's activity is not a fair use of the publishers' materials.

In my judgment, my colleagues have erred in

1. focusing on the loss of permission fees in evaluating "market effect" under section 107(4);

2. finding that the evidence supports the conclusion that permission fees provide an important incentive to authors to create new works or to publishers to publish new works; and

3. using legislative history, specifically the "Classroom Guidelines," to decide the issue of classroom use.

I.

The professors select the materials to be copied and deliver them to MDS with an estimate of the number of students expected in the course. The professors then assign the material to students enrolled in a particular class and inform them that they may purchase the required materials in coursepack form at MDS if they wish to do so. In the alternative,

---

guidance to the district court about curing the overbreadth of the injunction.

students are free to make copies of the excerpted material at the library themselves, to copy the material from other students, or to purchase the whole of the original work in which the assigned text appears. These coursepacks are sold only to students for use in a particular course; they are not sold to the general public. Any copies that are not purchased are simply discarded. The coursepacks are priced on a per-page basis, regardless of the contents of the page. The fee for a page reproducing copyrighted materials is the same as the fee for a blank page. The professors receive no commissions or other economic benefit from delivering coursepack materials to MDS. Each of the requesting professors signed a declaration stating that he does not request copies of excerpts where he would otherwise have assigned the entire work to his students.

III.
A.

At the very outset, it is critical to understand, as I have earlier stated, that MDS's "use" of this copyrighted material is of the same essential character as "use" by a student who chooses to personally make a photocopy of the designated excerpts. There are two differences: 1) the student will further "use" the material in the classroom; and 2) MDS does the copying for the student for a profit.

The question that must ultimately be answered is whether that which is a fair use for a student—copying—is not a fair use if done for the student by another, and for a profit. Plainly, the Copyright Act explicitly anticipates that use of a work by "reproduction in copies . . . for purposes such as . . . teaching (including multiple copies for classroom use)," will sometimes be a fair use even though teaching is commonly conducted for profit. 17 U.S.C. § 107. Thus, MDS's copying of materials, which indisputably are for "teaching (including multiple copies for classroom use)," must be tested for fair use under the four "factors to be considered" in section 107. *Id.*

The first factor that courts must evaluate in a fair use determination is "the purpose and character of the use, including whether such use is of a commercial nature or is for nonprofit educational purposes." 17 U.S.C. § 107(1). There are two parts to section 107's first factor: (1) the degree to which the challenged use has transformed the original, and (2) the profit or nonprofit character of the use. Both a non-transformative use determination and a "commercial" use determination weigh against a finding of fair use, though by no means conclusively.

The "purpose and character of the use" is examined to determine whether the questioned use would tend to advance or to thwart the goals of copyright law. The inquiry into the *transformative* aspect of the use assesses the likely benefit to society from the use—the more the original work has been transformed, the more likely it is that a distinct and valuable new product has been created. The inquiry into the profit or nonprofit aspect of the use assesses both the likely benefit to society and the likelihood that the use will threaten the creators' incentives.

The second prong of the first fair use factor asks whether the purpose of the *use* is commercial or nonprofit and educational. The point here "is not whether the sole motive of the use is monetary gain but whether the user stands to profit from exploitation of the copyrighted material without paying the customary price." In my judgment, a party profits from "exploiting copyrighted material" when it assesses the marketable potential of copyrighted material, selects material based on its content in order to reproduce those portions that will attract customers, and therefore profits from the *substance* of the copyrighted work.

As a preliminary matter, we must first decide whose *use* of the coursepacks must be evaluated. The majority accepts the publishers' position that the only relevant "use" under the first factor is MDS's sale of the coursepacks to students, not the use of the purchased coursepacks by the professors and students. Having limited its inquiry to MDS's mechanical reproduction of the excerpts and for-profit charge for the technology and labor required to reproduce the relevant pages, the majority easily finds that the copyshop's "use" of the copyrighted works is "commercial." I do not find support for this abbreviated analysis in either the statutory text or the case law.

Certainly nothing in the language of the statute supports the majority's decision to analyze the copyshop's production of multiple copies of the excerpts as a "use" completely independent from the classroom use of those copies. MDS, considered apart from the professors and students, does not "use" the "copyrighted work" in the sense primarily addressed in section 107; it uses a "master copy" of the excerpted material delivered to it by the professor, copy paper, ink, photocopying machines, mechanical binders, and related production materials to make the number of copies the professor has ordered. MDS could not care less whether Professor X asks it to copy selections from Walter Lippmann's *Public Opinion* or the 1996 University of Michigan Varsity Football roster. Either material is copied at a few cents a page, and MDS does not "use" the information from either—at least, not in the sense plainly contemplated by Congress in any of the language of section 107.

If the words used in section 107 are to be given their primary and generally accepted meaning, particularly in the context of the balance of the Copyright Act, it is obvious that the use that is to be evaluated for fairness in this case is the use to which the protected *substantive* text is put, not the mechanical process of copying it. Congress specifically identified "*teaching* (including *multiple copies* for classroom use)," § 107 (emphasis added), as an illustration of a possible fair use. Consequently, the act of copying (implicit in "multiple copies") is *within* the illustrative use of "teaching." MDS is not in the business of making copies of protected work in order to fill up warehouses or please the logging industry; it makes the copies *only* for classroom use. Neither the language of section 107 nor simple common sense warrant examining the production of multiple copies in a vacuum and ignoring their educational use on the facts of this case.

I would approach the "commercial purpose" determination under section 107's first factor in a different way than the majority does. A use is "commercial" within the meaning of section 107 if the user seeks to profit from "exploiting" the copyrighted material. *Profiting* from exploiting copyrighted material requires more than profit obtained from a mechanical service. Profiting from *exploiting* copyrighted material involves an active role in assessing the value of, selecting, and marketing copied material based on its substance. In *Harper & Row,* the defendant magazine assessed the value of President Ford's original work, selected the portions it believed to be the most "powerful," advertised, sold, and profited from the sale of the unauthorized copies, based on their substance. *Harper & Row* would be of some relevance to the market value component of this case only if MDS were selecting excerpts by assessing their commercial value to the public, assembling coursepacks for its own purposes, and marketing the coursepacks to professors or to the public without paying for the copyrighted materials. But that is not what MDS does or did. MDS's *profit* is attributable entirely to its provision of a mechanical service—running materials of value to others and selected by others through its photocopying machines and binding them. Because MDS made no attempt to assess the value of what it copied and did not select the materials for its copying services, it did not "exploit the copyrighted material without paying the customary price," as that was done in the *Harper & Row* case.

Certainly it is true that MDS "uses" the copyright work in the sense that it copies the copyrighted material that is handed to it by the professors. But it does not "use" the material independent of the university professors' and students' use; it is a participant in their use and its profits are derived only from photoreproduction services the students pay it to perform. The business of producing and selling coursepacks is more properly viewed as the commercial exploitation of professional copying technologies and of the inability of academic parties to reproduce printed materials efficiently, not the exploitation of copyrighted, creative materials. The copyshop is a printer, engaging *solely* in the business of reproducing images on paper at the direction of others. Because MDS does not control the length or substance of the excerpts that it copies, its profit motive does not provide information about the tendency of its activity to impinge upon the rightful territory of authors and does not interfere with the incentives orchestrated by the Copyright Act. The for-profit nature of MDS's service does not weigh against a finding of fair use because MDS, the for-profit actor, does not represent an institutional threat to authors and publishers' rightful profits.

The for-profit or nonprofit educational users whose purposes are linked to the authors' and publishers' incentives and therefore must be analyzed under this factor are the professors and students. The professors and students clearly do *use* Lippmann's work. The professors use Lippmann's ideas in meeting their professional obligation to teach their students, and the students use Lippmann's ideas in their effort to master the concepts of the course to which Lippmann's ideas pertain. The professors and students' classroom use of the excerpts of copyrighted material appears to be nonprofit. Although the professors and students are, in some sense, engaged in a for-profit endeavor—the professors teach for money and the students attend classes to obtain a commercially valuable degree—the purpose and character of the professors and students' use is not, on the facts of record in this case, "of a commercial nature." If "commerciality" meant only that the user employed the material while engaged in activity for profit, this one characteristic "would swallow nearly all of the illustrative uses listed in the preamble paragraph of § 107, including news reporting, comment, criticism, teaching, scholarship, and research, since these activities 'are generally conducted for profit in this country.'"

An assessment of the distinction between for-profit activity and exploitation is critical because the Supreme Court has commanded that we examine "'the nature and *objects* of the *selections* made'" in view of "the examples given in the preamble to § 107" and the purposes of copyright protection—that is, to promote science and the arts. Additionally, in determining whether MDS's use is commercial, it is important to bear in mind the practical effect of such a finding, not just in the analysis conducted under the first factor but in the impact that a finding of "commercial" or "educational" has in the analysis conducted under the fourth factor, which considers "the effect of the use upon the potential market for or value of the copyrighted work. . . ." 17 U.S.C. § 107(4). A conclusion that a use is "commercial" weighs against a finding of fair use and, in fact, creates a "presumption" of market harm in the fourth fair use factor. I conclude that the use of coursepacks in this case is not "commercial" within the meaning of section 107(1)'s "purpose and character of the use" language alone, but I am even more convinced that it is not "commercial" in view of section 107(4)'s "market harm" language: "the effect of the use upon the potential market for or value of the copyrighted work. . . ." § 107(4).

The Supreme Court has explained the presumption of market harm as follows:

The purpose of copyright is to create incentives for creative effort. Even copying for noncommercial purposes may impair the copyright holder's ability to obtain the rewards that Congress intended him to have. But a use that has no demonstrable effect upon the potential market for, or the value of, the copyrighted work need not be prohibited in order to protect the author's incentive to create. The prohibition of such noncommercial uses would merely inhibit access to ideas without any countervailing benefit.[ ] Thus, although every commercial use of copyrighted material is presumptively an unfair exploitation of the monopoly privilege that belongs to the owner of the copyright, noncommercial uses are a different matter. A challenge to a noncommercial use of a copyrighted work requires proof either that the particular use is harmful, or that if it should become widespread, it would adversely affect the potential market for the copyrighted work. (*Sony*)

To repeat, the content of the coursepacks was not controlled by MDS but by the professors; and "the nature and objects of the selections made" by the professors were plainly nonprofit and educational. The professors selected excerpts, not out of any motive for financial gain, but solely in order to enrich the educational experiences of their students. MDS made *no* selections; its motives for the activity that is challenged by the plaintiffs are not relevant.

It is consistent with the copyright scheme to find the use of these coursepacks to be noncommercial, to presume that they do not inflict market harm, and to require the publishers to prove that MDS's use is harmful to the value of the copyrighted works. Presuming that MDS's copying is not harmful to the value of the copyrighted works is appropriate because the identity and content of the excerpts is controlled entirely by persons whose motives are purely educational.

With regard to the professor-directed creation of coursepacks, it is not appropriate to presume that the practice of excerpting some materials harms the authors' rightful market and secures a benefit only to the excerpters. The more reasonable presumption is that society benefits from the additional circulation of ideas in the educational setting when those who direct the practice have no personal financial interests that would drive them to copy beyond the parameters of purely educational, and fair, use. The professors have no financial reason to copy mere excerpts when the entire works should be assigned, and their selections should not be presumed to harm the market for the original works and lessen the incentives for authors to write or publishers to publish new works. Rather, such harm must be demonstrated. Society benefits when professors provide diverse materials that are not central to the course but that may enrich or broaden the base of knowledge of the students. Society is not benefitted by establishing a presumption that *discourages* professors from exposing their students to anything but complete original works even when most of the work is irrelevant to the pedagogical purposes, and students are not benefitted or authors/publishers *justly* compensated if students are required to purchase entire works in order to read the 5% or 30% of the work that is relevant to the course.

And so, in my view, the majority's market harm analysis is fatally flawed: If market harm is presumed when excerpts are selected by professors and market harm is proven when fees are not paid, we have ceded benefits entirely to copyright holders when we are actually required to engage in "a sensitive balancing of interests," *Sony*, between "the interests of authors . . . in the control and exploitation of their writings . . . on the one hand, and society's competing interest in the free flow of ideas, information, and commerce on the other hand." The majority apparently does not really accept the firmly established principle that copyright monopoly privileges "are neither unlimited nor primarily designed to provide a special private benefit[; rather, the privileges exist to achieve] an important public purpose ... to motivate the creative activity of authors [*and*] to give the public appropriate access to their work product." ...

I have concluded that analysis under the first factor establishes the character of the use of coursepacks as noncommercial, and that, therefore, a proper analysis under the fourth factor begins with a rebuttable presumption that the plaintiffs have suffered no market harm and thus have the burden of proof on market effect. But, even in the absence of a presumption against market effect, the fourth factor, correctly construed, weighs in favor of a finding of fair use on the record before us.

For plaintiffs to prevail, there must be at least a meaningful likelihood that future harm to a potential market for the copyrighted works will occur. In *Sony*, the Court held:

> A challenge to a noncommercial use of a copyrighted work requires proof either that the particular use is harmful, or that if it should become widespread, it would adversely affect the potential market for the copyrighted work. ... What is necessary is a showing by a preponderance of the evidence that *some* meaningful likelihood of future harm exists.

Sony. Works or uses that creators of original works would "in general develop or license others to develop" make up the market for potential derivative uses. *Campbell*. The plaintiffs certainly have not demonstrated that the coursepacks affected the market for the original copyrighted works. Neither have they presented any evidence of likely harm to their potential market for derivative works, such as *published* anthologies. Remarkably, they have limited their showing of "market effect" to the loss of *permission fees* that they would like to receive from copyshops like MDS. But that is not a "market harm" within the meaning of section 107(4). To prove entitlement to permission fees, the publishers must show market harm and the market harm they claim is the loss of permission fees. MDS's coursepacks would inflict "market harm" if they damaged the *value* of the original work or the *value* of derivative products such as coursepacks the publishers might wish to market.

The original panel opinion, now vacated, stated:

> [E]vidence of lost permission fees does not bear on market effect. The right to permission fees is precisely what is at issue here. It is circular to argue that a use is unfair, and a fee therefore required, on the basis that the publisher is otherwise deprived of a fee.

The majority now claims that this charge of circular reasoning "proves too much." The majority asks the reader to

> [i]magine that the defendants set up a printing press and made exact reproductions—asserting that such reproductions constituted "fair use"—of a book to which they did not hold the copyright. Under the defendants' logic it would be circular for the copyright holder to argue market harm because of lost copyright revenues, since this would assume that the copyright holder had a right to such revenues.

The majority's logic would *always* yield a conclusion that the market had been harmed because *any* fees that a copyright holder could extract from a user if the use were found to be unfair would be "lost" if the use were instead found to be "fair use." The majority acknowledges that "a copyright owner will normally be able to complain that an asserted fair use may cause some loss of revenues in potential licensing fees" but resolves this problem by restricting its consideration of the loss of permission fees to the case of derivative markets that are "'traditional, reasonable, or likely to be developed markets.'" Under this approach, the majority would find that the copyright holders' monopoly over potential uses of the copyrighted works at issue in *Princeton* includes "the selling of permission to reproduce portions of the works for inclusion in coursepacks—and the likelihood that publishers actually will license such reproduction is a demonstrated fact."

The majority cites *Harper & Row* and *Campbell* as support for its reasoning that the mere loss of licensing fees—to which the copyright holder may or may not be entitled—is proof of market harm. The majority notes that in *Harper & Row*, the plaintiff did not challenge a use (the unauthorized article's direct quotes) based on its impact on sales of the entire work (the not-yet-published memoirs) but based on its harm to the market for the licensing of excerpts. There is a subtle but important distinction to be made between the facts in *Harper & Row* and the facts in this case. In *Harper & Row* there was proof that the copyright holder conceived of a potential derivative work (the planned *Time Magazine* articles) and took meaningful steps to aid in the creation of that derivative work and to capture profits from that creation. The *value* of the planned derivative work was harmed by the defendants' unauthorized use of the original work; the copyright holder lost its contract with *Time Magazine*—and concomitant fees—for the exclusive right to print prepublication excerpts of President Ford's memoirs when *The Nation Magazine* illicitly obtained a copy of the unpublished manuscript and produced a short article quoting from the heart of the manuscript. Thus, in *Harper & Row*, the *value* of the original work *in a derivative market that was targeted by the copyright holder* was harmed by the unauthorized use of the work. There is no similar evidence of injury to the value of a work in this case.

First, there is no evidence that the publishers, here, planned to create any products for a derivative market; no evidence, for instance, that the copyright holders sought to publish or license a competing compilation of excerpts to attract the interest, for instance, of the students in Professor Dawson's interdisciplinary course "Black Americans and the Political System." Second, even if there was evidence that the publishers had contemplated such a product, there is no evidence that the publishers' derivative compilation would be devalued by defendant's production of coursepacks; that is, there is no evidence that such a compilation would earn less because of the existence of coursepacks. In *Campbell*, for instance, the Court declined to find market harm based solely on undisputed evidence that the unauthorized user created a profitable product—rap-parody—from the original; the Court noted that the rap-parody version was not shown to affect the market for an authorized, non-parodic rap version of the original. It might at first appear that the publishers are, by definition, able to design and market a collection of excerpts and that the existence of other, unauthorized, collections will necessarily replace some of the authorized copies and thereby leach profits that the publishers could otherwise capture. However, neither the facts on this record nor any case law support such a leap in logic.

The fact is that the plaintiffs are not able to create a market for the product that MDS produces. To the extent that MDS serves a market at all, it is one created by the individual professors who have determined which excerpts from which writers they wish to comprise the required reading for a particular course. If the publishers decided to create an anthology of excerpts from its copyrighted works on, for example, "The Black Experience," it would not fill the market niche created by Professor X who is interested in very different materials. Indeed, the publishers do not claim to have lost an account for customized materials with a specific professor because of a copyshop coursepack; nor do they claim to be prepared to enter this highly-customized market. The argument that the publishers seek to enter the derivative market of customized materials by licensing MDS and other copyshops, who create such compilations, and that MDS's publication of unauthorized compilations interferes with their ability to obtain licensing fees from other copyshops simply returns the publishers to their original circular argument that they are entitled to permission fees, in part, because they are losing permission fees. . . .

The majority opinion stresses the fact that Congress "initiated and supervised negotiations among interested groups—groups that included authors, publishers, and educators—over specific legislative language [and that m]ost of the language that emerged was enacted into law or was made a part of the committee reports." However, what were not "enacted into law," but only made a part of the conference committee reports, are the Classroom Guidelines upon which the majority so heavily relies to decide how the language enacted into law applies. Indisputably, the Classroom Guidelines assure educators that nonprofit copying for educational purposes of "not more than 1,000 words" is fair use when "[t]he inspiration and decision to use the work and the moment of its use for maximum teaching effectiveness are so close in time that it would be unreasonable to expect a timely reply to a request for permission." The Classroom Guidelines "prohibit[ ] . . . [c]opying . . . used to create . . . anthologies, compilations or collective works." But, as the majority opinion acknowledges, that language did not survive congressional debate and was not enacted into law.

Despite the well-settled rule that legislative history is irrelevant and inappropriate to consider except to clarify an ambiguity in the text of a statute, the majority relies upon the legislative history without identifying any ambiguity in the statute, but only because "[t]he statutory factors are not models of clarity, . . . the fair use issue has long been a particularly troublesome one . . ., [and other] courts have often turned to the legislative history when considering fair use questions." I wish to emphasize in the strongest terms that it is entirely inappropriate to rely on the Copyright Act's legislative history at all.

As Justice Scalia has observed, "The greatest defect of legislative history is its illegitimacy. We are governed by laws, not by the intentions of legislators." The Classroom Guidelines do not become more authoritative by their adoption into a Committee Report. "[I]t is the statute, and not the Committee Report, which is the authoritative expression of the law." We may not permit the statutory text enacted by both Houses of Congress and signed by the President "to be expanded or contracted by the statements of individual legislators or committees during the course of the enactment process." That the Classroom Guidelines are not law should be reason enough for this court to refrain from using them to find infringement, but this is not the only reason to reject out of hand arguments based on legislative history. The members of Congress who voted for the statutory language of section 107 could have had any variety of understandings about the application of the fair use factors; all we know for certain is that the full House, the full Senate, and the President, pursuant to the procedures prescribed by the Constitution, enacted into law the text of section 107, and did not enact the standards of the Classroom Guidelines. Committee Reports do not reliably further consistent judicial construction. I subscribe wholeheartedly to Judge Harold Leventhal's observation that "the use of legislative history [is] the equivalent of entering a crowded cocktail party and looking over the heads of the guests for one's friends." "We use [Committee Reports] when it is convenient, and ignore them when it is not." . . .

The case for copyright infringement is very weak indeed if the court must rely on the unenacted theater of Committee Reports to find infringement. The fact that Congress saw fit, very likely in the interests of political expediency, to pay unusual deference to the "agreement" of interested parties about what *they* would like the law to be, even to the point of declaring (but not in the statute) that the parties' agreement was part of the committee's "understanding" of fair use, does not affect the rule of construction that binds this court.

In sum, even if the four statutory factors of section 107 are not "models of clarity" and their application to the facts of this case is "troublesome"—a challenge of the kind federal appellate judges are paid to face every day—the four factors are not ambiguous. Therefore, we may not properly resort to legislative history. I am satisfied to rely exclusively upon the evidence and lack of evidence on the record before us and the plain language of the Copyright Act and its construction in the case law; and they lead me to conclude that MDS's compilation into coursepacks of excerpts selected by professors is a "fair use" of the copyrighted materials.

· · · · · · · · · ·

Notes

We include this case because the opinions offer a master-class in fair use. In particular, they should teach you to avoid the sloppiness that lawyers often display in referring vaguely to "the use" or "the market" without actually connecting those phrases to either § 106 or § 107 and then explaining why their interpretation is correct. But we also include so many of the opinions because they are a lovely case-study in all of the *dimensions* of the fair use doctrine.

- What—or whose—is the relevant "use"? (And what are the criteria by which I would know?)
- What is the relevant market? How should we think about the copyright holder's rights over potential licensing markets?
- How does one interpret the clause "including multiple copies for classroom use"?
- How are the clauses of § 107 related to each other?
- Copyright is supposed "to promote the progress." How does one imagine that happening in the context of a case such as this?

Judges Nelson, Martin, Merritt and Ryan provide very different (and well-reasoned) answers to each of these questions. They differ on jurisprudential method: plain language, expanded context or purposive reading? They differ on the appropriateness of turning beyond the statute to glean Congressional intent from CONFU. They differ on the granularity of the rights copyright holders can claim over expanded licensing markets—markets beyond the original work—and the circularity of attempting to do so. They differ on the significance of coursepacks and monographs to education. Which of their arguments convinced you?

PROBLEM 13-4

You represent 15-501 Copies, a commercial copy shop, and the faculty of the Duke Law School. (For this purpose, you may ignore any potential conflicts of interest involved.) Both are being sued for copyright infringement by the Harvard Law

Review. The law school faculty has a single institutional subscription to the Harvard Law Review. When the most recent issue arrives, it is sent to 15-501, where the table of contents for each issue is copied and circulated to the faculty. Faculty members mark off on the table of contents any article they are interested in seeing. 15-501 receives these orders and then sends the individually labeled photocopies to the Duke Law School mail room, from whence they are distributed directly to the professors' offices. The Duke faculty has a large appetite for law review articles and this convenient procedure merely whets it; while no-one asks for copies of the entire review, individual articles will often be copied for twenty or thirty professors. Typically, professors pile these photocopies up in large, unstable piles in their offices. Eventually, they go through a batch, discarding most, annotating some and writing indignant rebuttals to others, rebuttals that may be published themselves, thus completing the cycle.

Like most law journals, the Harvard Law Review is believed by its critics to have all of the central features of a vanity press—that is to say, a press that does not pay its authors, takes their copyrights, makes editorial changes to the work submitted (in this case, adding useful footnotes that substantiate disputed points, such as the correlation of poverty with the absence of wealth), and finally charges the authors for copies of their own work—known as "reprints"—which the authors then give away for free, apparently believing that they will be read. The Law Review claims copyright over both the individual articles and to each issue as a whole. Despite the fact that its editorial labor and authorial content are effectively "free," Harvard Law Review currently runs at a loss, like most law reviews, and is partially subsidized by its host institution, a university near Boston. It makes some money by charging very high fees for institutional subscriptions and much lower, but still expensive, fees for individual subscriptions. It also makes a fairly substantial amount of money from "permission fees" paid by those who wish to include an article or a fragment of an article in a casebook or reader. Finally, it receives a considerable amount of money annually from Eastlaw, an online research service, for providing Eastlaw with a complete, fully searchable database of its articles.

The Duke faculty have free subscriptions to Eastlaw and could, if they wished, print any article directly from the database—though without the law review's attractive textual features, such as footnotes at the bottom of the page. Harvard Law Review does not currently have any service to license individual copies of individual articles though such a scheme might be technically possible—perhaps by direct download of a facsimile version from the Web. The editor in chief claims that she may "look into it," depending on the outcome of this litigation.

The proprietor of 15-501 is very upset; he had assumed that "anything done by a bunch of lawyers to their own books must be legal." He asks you if he will be liable for copyright infringement. The Duke faculty is also upset and have turned to you for legal advice; they claim that this kind of copying happens all the time behind the veil of ignorance, that it is protected by the First, Second and perhaps the Ninth Amendments, that the Warren Court, the Pre-Socratic philosophers and the Jacksonian Democrats would never have objected, that it is a Pareto superior allocation of entitlements and, in the alternative, (and you may concentrate your analysis here) that it is a fair use under section 107 of the Copyright Act. You may presume that you are in a Circuit that is not bound by the decision in *Princeton*

but is carefully attentive to all the arguments made there.

In your answer try hard to use the traditional common law skills of marshalling and distinguishing cases. On what aspects of this question would you focus to make this case seem less defensible than the copying in *Princeton*? More defensible? Be very clear about the following questions.

a.) What is the relevant "use" for the analysis? Explain what both the plaintiff and the defendant would say and the reasons why they would claim that their definition of use is the correct one.

b.) What is the relevant work?

c.) The relevant market for the work? Is it static or dynamic? Can a copyright holder claim all markets he might one day enter as relevant to the calculation? If not, how is the ambit of possible future markets to be limited?

Finally, hypotheticals (such as exam questions) often tweak the facts of an existing case to present a conflict more clearly or to come closer to some dividing line. Which of the "tweaks" to the facts in *Princeton* in this hypothetical is most favorable to the plaintiff? The defendant?

Conclusion

You are now experts in fair use—or at least considerably more expert than you were when you began the chapter. Fair use is a heated topic around the world. The United States is unusual in having such a flexible and open-ended limitation on copyright. A number of jurisdictions, including the UK, Ireland and Australia, have considered whether they should introduce some version of fair use into their copyright laws, as part of attempts to 'revamp copyright for the digital age.' The concerns addressed are often technological; the founders of Google are reported to have told the British Prime Minister that they could not have created the company without the protection of fair use. But they are also speech-related, and sometimes this involves speech that is enabled by a particular technology, such as an unauthorized YouTube remix. We would like you to answer some of those questions for yourself.

- What do you think of the current state of the law of fair use?
- Is its open ended, flexible and adaptable framework a strength or a weakness?
- Does it provide adequate protection to copyright holders?
- Adequate guidance to potential fair users?
- Adequate space for technological innovation? Focus here on the line from *Sony* through *Sega* to *Perfect 10, Google Books* and *Oracle.*

We will begin the next chapter with a case-study that raises many of these issues, and that links back to the place we began this chapter: *Sony* and its connection of fair use to contributory infringement. Finally, for those of you needing a light hearted review of the fair use doctrine, you can try the free online comic book, *Bound By Law.*[‡]

[‡] Keith Aoki, James Boyle, Jennifer Jenkins, *Tales from the Public Domain: Bound By Law?* https://law.duke.edu/cspd/comics/zoomcomic.html.

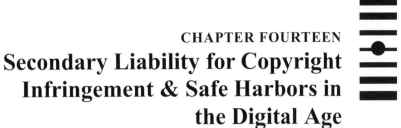

CHAPTER FOURTEEN
Secondary Liability for Copyright Infringement & Safe Harbors in the Digital Age

Introduction

Generally, in the common law, "secondary liability" is imposed on someone who does not commit the legal wrong directly, but is found responsible for encouraging, facilitating or profiting from it. As you will see, the Copyright Act has no provisions imposing secondary liability. (Compare to e.g. § 271 of the Patent Act.) As a result, the secondary liability provisions of copyright law are entirely judge-developed, without even an open-ended statutory basis like that given to fair use jurisprudence under § 107.

Until recently, there were two principal forms of secondary liability: contributory infringement and vicarious liability. (It should be noted here that the *Sony v. Universal* case does not clearly delineate whether and when it is talking about contributory infringement, vicarious liability or both.)

- Contributory infringement may be found if someone, with knowledge of the infringing activity, induces, causes or materially contributes to the infringing conduct of another.
- Vicarious liability—an outgrowth of *respondeat superior*—may be imposed on someone who has the right and ability to supervise the infringing activity and also has a direct financial interest in the activity.

In both cases, there needs to be underlying *direct* infringement. In other words, someone needs directly to violate the exclusive rights provided by § 106, before contributory or vicarious liability can be imposed on any third party.

Sony Corp. of America v. Universal City Studios, Inc.
464 U.S. 417 (1984)

Re-read sections I, II and III of the *Sony* opinion from Chapter 13, page 415.

PROBLEM 14-1
THE *NAPSTER* CASE.

This problem is designed to be used as either a free-standing hypothetical or as part of a video argument exercise. In the latter incarnation, a video we have edited, showing the *Napster* oral argument in the Ninth Circuit, is played in class. The video is available at http://youtu.be/5ftJ1pFLGQk. Students are placed in role as the lawyers in the case. The video is repeatedly paused throughout its length and the class as a whole is required to brainstorm about how to open their arguments, respond to

---

particular judges' questions and so on. Then the video is allowed to run and the class can compare its answers to those of the lawyers and the court—for good or ill.

Using the material we have read so far, particularly focusing on the *Sony* case, and the explanation of contributory and vicarious infringement above, please read the facts below and explain how you would argue that Napster is, or is not, infringing copyright law. For the purposes of this exercise, students do not need to read the *Napster* opinion. Indeed the exercise works much better (and is more enjoyable for all concerned) when they do not do so.

> [Excerpted statement of the facts] Napster facilitates the transmission of MP3 files between and among its users. Through a process commonly called "peer-to-peer" file sharing, Napster allows its users to: (1) make MP3 music files stored on individual computer hard drives available for copying by other Napster users; (2) search for MP3 music files stored on other users' computers; and (3) transfer exact copies of the contents of other users' MP3 files from one computer to another via the Internet. These functions are made possible by Napster's MusicShare software, available free of charge from Napster's Internet site, and Napster's network servers and server-side software. Napster provides technical support for the indexing and searching of MP3 files, as well as for its other functions, including a "chat room," where users can meet to discuss music, and a directory where participating artists can provide information about their music.
>
> **A. Accessing the System:** In order to copy MP3 files through the Napster system, a user must first access Napster's Internet site and download the MusicShare software to his individual computer. Once the software is installed, the user can access the Napster system. A first-time user is required to register with the Napster system by creating a "user name" and password.
>
> **B. Listing Available Files:** If a registered user wants to list available files stored in his computer's hard drive on Napster for others to access, he must first create a "user library" directory on his computer's hard drive. The user then saves his MP3 files in the library directory, using self-designated file names. He next must log into the Napster system using his user name and password. His MusicShare software then searches his user library and verifies that the available files are properly formatted. If in the correct MP3 format, the names of the MP3 files will be uploaded from the user's computer to the Napster servers. The content of the MP3 files remains stored in the user's computer. . . . Once uploaded to the Napster servers, the user's MP3 file names are stored in a server-side "library" under the user's name and become part of a "collective directory" of files available for transfer during the time the user is logged onto the Napster system. The collective directory is fluid; it tracks users who are connected in real time, displaying only file names that are immediately accessible.
>
> **C. Searching for Available Files:** Napster allows a user to locate other users' MP3 files in two ways: through Napster's search function and through its "hotlist" function.
>
> Software located on the Napster servers maintains a "search index" of Napster's collective directory. To search the files available from Napster users

currently connected to the network servers, the individual user accesses a form in the MusicShare software stored in his computer and enters either the name of a song or an artist as the object of the search. The form is then transmitted to a Napster server and automatically compared to the MP3 file names listed in the server's search index. Napster's server compiles a list of all MP3 file names pulled from the search index which include the same search terms entered on the search form and transmits the list to the searching user. The Napster server does not search the contents of any MP3 file; rather, the search is limited to "a text search of the file names indexed in a particular cluster. . . .

D. Transferring Copies of an MP3 file: To transfer a copy of the contents of a requested MP3 file, the Napster server software obtains the Internet address of the requesting user and the Internet address of the "host user" (the user with the available files). See generally *Brookfield Communications, Inc. v. West Coast Entm't Corp.* (9th Cir. 1999) (describing, in detail, the structure of the Internet). The Napster servers then communicate the host user's Internet address to the requesting user. The requesting user's computer uses this information to establish a connection with the host user and downloads a copy of the contents of the MP3 file from one computer to the other over the Internet, "peer-to-peer."

[T]he district court concluded that Napster harms the market in "at least" two ways: it reduces audio CD sales among college students and it 'raises barriers to plaintiffs' entry into the market for the digital downloading of music. . . ."[†]

What would you need to prove in order to find liability? What would be the defenses? How would you frame your argument? What would be your opening 60 seconds if you were the lawyer arguing either for the plaintiff or the defendant? [These are the crucial moments when you have a chance to frame the issue before the judges interrupt. If you are lucky.] Which, if any, of the frames discussed in Chapter 1 could each side use? On what precedents would you rely? What policy arguments would you stress? What "escape hatches" would you offer to a court contemplating the possibility that Napster might not be liable? What vision of doom would you conjure up were the court not to find Napster liable?

1.) The Stakes of Contributory Infringement

As *Tiffany v. eBay* showed in the trademark context, contributory infringement assumes particular importance in the world of the internet. Or perhaps, more broadly, in the world of devices and networks which give powers to individuals that were formerly held—to any significant extent—exclusively by large commercial intermediaries. The internet allows any individual to set up a global storefront. Your laptop or tablet or phone can implicate many of the rights in § 106 of the Copyright Act—a dramatic technologically enabled change to the legal significance of your actions. You can copy, distribute, and modify existing works—indeed on a daily basis, you would be hard put not to. At the same time, these devices and networks also allow an unprecedented flowering of creativity, innovation and disruptive business models. From Amazon and eBay to blogs, Wikipedia,

---

[†] *A & M Records v. Napster* (9th Cir. 2001).

open source software and the world of social media, the devices and networks of the digital era demonstrate a broad decentralization of creative tools and a "disintermediation" of previous business models and forms of social organization. ("Disintermediation" is an ugly, but useful, word meaning that it is possible to cut out the middle man—to go directly from musician or artist or technologist to the public or to the market.)

In this world, secondary liability will be crucial. For rights-holders, secondary liability will hold out the promise of being able to restrain the actions of swarms of anonymous infringers. If you can shut down the platform, the network or the technology—or bring it under your control financially or technologically—then you can strike at the root of infringement, rather than having to deal with a million individual instances. (Compare the arguments made by the trademark owner in a case such as *Tiffany* to the arguments made by copyright holders in the situation of a peer-to-peer network such as Napster.)

For technologists, many of whom will also be rights holders, the stakes are equally high. It is easy convincingly to portray *any* digital product or service in such a way as a.) to highlight its potential for massive infringement, b.) to point out that the developers of the technology or service "must have known of" this potential for infringement and c.) to show that the developers of the technology are profiting from demand that is *in part* fuelled by the potential for infringing uses. What would the demand be for an iPod that could only be filled with legally purchased music (for example by requiring DRM authentication that the music had been licitly purchased)? Do you think that Dropbox (or any cyberlocker) is popular among some users because it can be used to illicitly share copyrighted material? YouTube?

As you read the cases that follow try to be attentive both to the concerns of copyright holders and those of the technology developers. From the point of view of the copyright holder, consider the sheer scale and magnitude of the infringement. Surely this demands immediate and extensive intervention—particularly given the fact that the technology developers know that their products will be used to infringe and actually profit from it? From the perspective of the technology developer, do not assess the effect of the rules on technologies *ex post*—whether you think you could persuade a Federal District Court judge *today* that her existing iPod is illegal. Rather, consider the rule *ex ante*. Imagine yourself the lawyer in charge of vetting product development at a technology company *before* these products have been brought to market, widely used and accepted. The engineer comes and lays out the product or the service. "This will put 20,000 songs in your pocket!" "This search engine will allow users to search for and go directly to any content anywhere on the internet!" "This cyberlocker will allow anyone to exchange files of any size with anyone else in the world!"

Can you come up with a rule that protects the copyright holders without causing you—as a properly cautious lawyer vetting product development—to forbid *ex ante* the development of the iPod, Google, Dropbox and YouTube in the forms that we currently know? Or do you think that the correct answer would have been to impose secondary liability and veto all the technologies that could not internalize the costs of infringement? This chapter is about the attempt to answer these questions.

2.) Contributory and Vicarious Infringement

A & M Records, Inc. v. Napster, Inc.
239 F.3d 1004 (9th Cir. 2001)

BEEZER, Circuit Judge.

[In order to hold Napster liable for contributory or vicarious infringement, it is necessary for a court to find that there has been underlying direct infringement by Napster *users*.]

. . . Plaintiffs claim Napster users are engaged in the wholesale reproduction and distribution of copyrighted works, all constituting direct infringement. The district court agreed. . . .

A. Infringement

. . . [P]laintiffs have shown that Napster users infringe at least two of the copyright holders' exclusive rights: the rights of reproduction, § 106(1); and distribution, § 106(3). Napster users who upload file names to the search index for others to copy violate plaintiffs' distribution rights. Napster users who download files containing copyrighted music violate plaintiffs' reproduction rights.

Screenshot of the Napster system interface

Napster asserts an affirmative defense to the charge that its users directly infringe plaintiffs' copyrighted musical compositions and sound recordings.

B. Fair Use

Napster contends that its users do not directly infringe plaintiffs' copyrights because the users are engaged in fair use of the material. Napster identifies three specific alleged fair uses: sampling, where users make temporary copies of a work before purchasing; space-shifting, where users access a sound recording through the Napster system that they already own in audio CD format; and permissive distribution of recordings by both new and established artists. . . . The district court concluded that Napster users are not fair users. We agree. We first address the court's overall fair use analysis.

1. Purpose and Character of the Use

This factor focuses on whether the new work merely replaces the object of the original creation or instead adds a further purpose or different character. In other words, this factor asks "whether and to what extent the new work is 'transformative.'" *See Campbell v. Acuff-Rose Music, Inc.* (1994).

The district court first concluded that downloading MP3 files does not transform the copyrighted work. This conclusion is supportable. Courts have been reluctant to find fair use when an original work is merely retransmitted in a different medium.

This "purpose and character" element also requires the district court to determine whether the allegedly infringing use is commercial or noncommercial. A commercial use weighs against a finding of fair use but is not conclusive on the issue. The district court determined that Napster users engage in commercial use of the copyrighted materials largely because (1) "a host user sending a file cannot be said to engage in a personal use when distributing that file to an anonymous requester" and (2) "Napster users get for free something they would ordinarily have to buy." The district court's findings are not clearly erroneous.

Direct economic benefit is not required to demonstrate a commercial use. Rather, repeated and exploitative copying of copyrighted works, even if the copies are not offered for sale, may constitute a commercial use. In the record before us, commercial use is demonstrated by a showing that repeated and exploitative unauthorized copies of copyrighted works were made to save the expense of purchasing authorized copies. . . .

2. The Nature of the Use

Works that are creative in nature are "closer to the core of intended copyright protection" than are more fact-based works. The district court determined that plaintiffs' "copyrighted musical compositions and sound recordings are creative in nature . . . which cuts against a finding of fair use under the second factor." We find no error in the district court's conclusion.

3. The Portion Used

"While 'wholesale copying does not preclude fair use per se,' copying an entire work 'militates against a finding of fair use.'" The district court determined that Napster users engage in "wholesale copying" of copyrighted work because file transfer necessarily "involves copying the entirety of the copyrighted work." We agree. We note, however, that under certain circumstances, a court will conclude that a use is fair even when the protected work is copied in its entirety. *See, e.g., Sony Corp. v. Universal City Studios, Inc.*

4. Effect of Use on Market

"Fair use, when properly applied, is limited to copying by others which does not materially impair the marketability of the work which is copied." *Harper & Row Publishers, Inc. v. Nation Enters.* (1985). "[T]he importance of this [fourth] factor will vary, not only with the amount of harm, but also with the relative strength of the showing on the other factors." *Campbell*. The proof required to demonstrate present or future market harm varies with the purpose and character of the use:

> A challenge to a noncommercial use of a copyrighted work requires proof either that the particular use is harmful, or that if it should become widespread, it would adversely affect the potential market for the copyrighted work. . . . *If the intended use is for commercial gain, that likelihood [of market harm] may be presumed. But if it is for a noncommercial purpose, the likelihood must be demonstrated. Sony.*

Addressing this factor, the district court concluded that Napster harms the market in "at least" two ways: it reduces audio CD sales among college students and it "raises barriers to plaintiffs' entry into the market for the digital downloading of music." . . . Defendant has failed to show any basis for disturbing the district court's findings. . . .

Judge Patel did not abuse her discretion in reaching the above fair use conclusions, nor were the findings of fact with respect to fair use considerations clearly erroneous. We next address Napster's identified uses of sampling and space-shifting.

5. Identified Uses

Napster maintains that its identified uses of sampling and space-shifting were wrongly excluded as fair uses by the district court. . . . We find no error in the district court's factual findings or abuse of discretion in the court's conclusion that plaintiffs will likely prevail in establishing that sampling does not constitute a fair use.

b. Space-Shifting

Napster also maintains that space-shifting is a fair use. Space-shifting occurs when a Napster user downloads MP3 music files in order to listen to music he already owns on audio CD. Napster asserts that we have already held that space-shifting of musical compositions and sound recordings is a fair use. *See Recording Indus. Ass'n of Am. v. Diamond Multimedia Sys., Inc.* (9th Cir. 1999) ("Rio [a portable MP3 player] merely makes copies in order to render portable, or 'space-shift,' those files that already reside on a user's hard drive. . . . Such copying is a paradigmatic noncommercial personal use."). *See also generally Sony* (holding that "time-shifting," where a video tape recorder owner records a television show for later viewing, is a fair use).

We conclude that the district court did not err when it refused to apply the "shifting" analyses of *Sony* and *Diamond*. Both *Diamond* and *Sony* are inapposite because the methods of shifting in these cases did not also simultaneously involve distribution of the copyrighted material to the general public; the time or space-shifting of copyrighted material exposed the material only to the original user. In *Diamond*, for example, the copyrighted music was transferred from the user's computer hard drive to the user's portable MP3 player. So too *Sony*, where "the majority of VCR purchasers . . . did not distribute taped television broadcasts, but merely enjoyed them at home." Conversely, it is obvious that once a user lists a copy of music he already owns on the Napster system in order to access the music from another location, the song becomes "available to millions of other individuals," not just the original CD owner.

c. Other Uses

Permissive reproduction by either independent or established artists is the final fair use claim made by Napster. The district court noted that plaintiffs did not seek to enjoin this and any other noninfringing use of the Napster system, including: chat rooms, message boards and Napster's New Artist Program. Plaintiffs do not challenge these uses on appeal.

We find no error in the district court's determination that plaintiffs will likely succeed in establishing that Napster users do not have a fair use defense. Accordingly, we next address whether Napster is secondarily liable for the direct infringement under two doctrines of copyright law: contributory copyright infringement and vicarious copyright infringement.

IV

We first address plaintiffs' claim that Napster is liable for contributory copyright infringement. Traditionally, "one who, with knowledge of the infringing activity, induces, causes or materially contributes to the infringing conduct of another, may be held liable as a 'contributory' infringer." *Gershwin Publ'g Corp. v. Columbia Artists Mgmt., Inc.* (2d Cir. 1971).

The district court determined that plaintiffs in all likelihood would establish Napster's liability as a contributory infringer. The district court did not err; Napster, by its conduct, knowingly encourages and assists the infringement of plaintiffs' copyrights.

A. Knowledge

Contributory liability requires that the secondary infringer "know or have reason to know" of direct infringement. The district court found that Napster had both actual and constructive knowledge that its users exchanged copyrighted music. The district court also concluded that the law does not require knowledge of "specific acts of infringement" and rejected Napster's contention that because the company cannot distinguish infringing from noninfringing files, it does not "know" of the direct infringement.

It is apparent from the record that Napster has knowledge, both actual and constructive, of direct infringement. Napster claims that it is nevertheless protected from contributory liability by the teaching of *Sony Corp. v. Universal City Studios, Inc.* (1984).

We disagree. We observe that Napster's actual, specific knowledge of direct infringement renders *Sony*'s holding of limited assistance to Napster. We are compelled to make a clear distinction between the architecture of the Napster system and Napster's conduct in relation to the operational capacity of the system.

The *Sony* Court refused to hold the manufacturer and retailers of video tape recorders liable for contributory infringement despite evidence that such machines could be and were used to infringe plaintiffs' copyrighted television shows. *Sony* stated that if liability "is to be imposed on petitioners in this case, it must rest on the fact that *they have sold equipment with constructive knowledge of the fact that their customers may use that equipment to make unauthorized copies* of copyrighted material." The *Sony* Court declined to impute the requisite level of knowledge where the defendants made and sold equipment capable of both infringing and "substantial noninfringing uses."

We are bound to follow *Sony*, and will not impute the requisite level of knowledge to Napster merely because peer-to-peer file sharing technology may be used to infringe plaintiffs' copyrights. *See* [*Sony*] (rejecting argument that merely supplying the "'means' to accomplish an infringing activity" leads to imposition of liability). We depart from the reasoning of the district court that Napster failed to demonstrate that its system is capable of commercially significant noninfringing uses. The district court improperly confined the use analysis to current uses, ignoring the system's capabilities. *See generally Sony* (framing inquiry as whether the video tape recorder is "*capable* of commercially significant noninfringing uses"). Consequently, the district court placed undue weight on the proportion of current infringing use as compared to current and future noninfringing use. Nonetheless, whether we might arrive at a different result is not the issue here. The instant appeal occurs at an early point in the proceedings and "the fully developed factual record may be materially different from that initially before the district court. . . ." Regardless of the number of Napster's infringing versus noninfringing uses, the evidentiary record here supported the district court's finding that plaintiffs would likely prevail in establishing that Napster knew or had reason to know of its users' infringement of plaintiffs' copyrights. . . .

We agree that if a computer system operator learns of specific infringing material available on his system and fails to purge such material from the system, the operator knows of and contributes to direct infringement. Conversely, absent any specific information which identifies infringing activity, a computer system operator cannot be liable for contributory infringement merely because the structure of the system allows for the exchange of copyrighted material. To enjoin simply because a computer network allows for infringing use would, in our opinion, violate *Sony* and potentially restrict activity unrelated to infringing use.

We nevertheless conclude that sufficient knowledge exists to impose contributory liability when linked to demonstrated infringing use of the Napster system. The record supports the district court's finding that Napster has *actual* knowledge that *specific* infringing material is available using its system, that it could block access to the system by suppliers of the infringing material, and that it failed to remove the material.

B. Material Contribution

Under the facts as found by the district court, Napster materially contributes to the infringing activity. Relying on *Fonovisa, Inc. v. Cherry Auction, Inc.* (9th Cir. 1996), the district court concluded that "[w]ithout the support services defendant provides, Napster users could not find and download the music they want with the ease of which defendant boasts." We agree that Napster provides "the site and facilities" for direct infringement. The district court correctly applied the reasoning in *Fonovisa*, and properly found that

Napster materially contributes to direct infringement.

We affirm the district court's conclusion that plaintiffs have demonstrated a likelihood of success on the merits of the contributory copyright infringement claim. We will address the scope of the injunction in part VIII of this opinion.

V

We turn to the question whether Napster engages in vicarious copyright infringement. Vicarious copyright liability is an "outgrowth" of respondeat superior. *Fonovisa.* In the context of copyright law, vicarious liability extends beyond an employer/employee relationship to cases in which a defendant "has the right and ability to supervise the infringing activity and also has a direct financial interest in such activities."

Before moving into this discussion, we note that *Sony*'s "staple article of commerce" analysis has no application to Napster's potential liability for vicarious copyright infringement. *See generally* 3 NIMMER ON COPYRIGHT §§ 12.04[A][2] & [A][2][b] (2000) (confining *Sony* to contributory infringement analysis: "Contributory infringement itself is of two types—personal conduct that forms part of or furthers the infringement and contribution of machinery or goods that provide the means to infringe.") The issues of *Sony*'s liability under the "doctrines of 'direct infringement' and 'vicarious liability'" were not before the Supreme Court, although the Court recognized that the "lines between direct infringement, contributory infringement, and vicarious liability are not clearly drawn." Consequently, when the *Sony* Court used the term "vicarious liability," it did so broadly and outside of a technical analysis of the doctrine of vicarious copyright infringement. ("[V]icarious liability is imposed in virtually all areas of the law, and the concept of contributory infringement is merely a species of the broader problem of identifying the circumstances in which it is just to hold one individual accountable for the actions of another.")

A. Financial Benefit

The district court determined that plaintiffs had demonstrated they would likely succeed in establishing that Napster has a direct financial interest in the infringing activity. We agree. Financial benefit exists where the availability of infringing material "acts as a 'draw' for customers." *Fonovisa.* Ample evidence supports the district court's finding that Napster's future revenue is directly dependent upon "increases in userbase." More users register with the Napster system as the "quality and quantity of available music increases." We conclude that the district court did not err in determining that Napster financially benefits from the availability of protected works on its system.

B. Supervision

The district court determined that Napster has the right and ability to supervise its users' conduct. We agree in part.

The ability to block infringers' access to a particular environment for any reason whatsoever is evidence of the right and ability to supervise. Here, plaintiffs have demonstrated that Napster retains the right to control access to its system. Napster has an express reservation of rights policy, stating on its website that it expressly reserves the "right to refuse service and terminate accounts in [its] discretion, including, but not limited to, if Napster believes that user conduct violates applicable law . . . or for any reason in Napster's sole discretion, with or without cause."

To escape imposition of vicarious liability, the reserved right to police must be exercised to its fullest extent. Turning a blind eye to detectable acts of infringement for the sake of profit gives rise to liability.

The district court correctly determined that Napster had the right and ability to police its system and failed to exercise that right to prevent the exchange of copyrighted material. The district court, however, failed to recognize that the boundaries of the premises that Napster "controls and patrols" are limited. Put differently, Napster's reserved "right and ability" to police is cabined by the system's current architecture. As shown by the record, the Napster system does not "read" the content of indexed files, other than to check that they are in the proper MP3 format.

Napster, however, has the ability to locate infringing material listed on its search indices, and the right to terminate users' access to the system. The file name indices, therefore, are within the "premises" that Napster has the ability to police. We recognize that the files are user-named and may not match copyrighted material exactly (for example, the artist or song could be spelled wrong). For Napster to function effectively, however, file names must reasonably or roughly correspond to the material contained in the files, otherwise no user could ever locate any desired music. As a practical matter, Napster, its users and the record company plaintiffs have equal access to infringing material by employing Napster's "search function."

Our review of the record requires us to accept the district court's conclusion that plaintiffs have demonstrated a likelihood of success on the merits of the vicarious copyright infringement claim. Napster's failure to police the system's "premises," combined with a showing that Napster financially benefits from the continuing availability of infringing files on its system, leads to the imposition of vicarious liability. We address the scope of the injunction in part VIII of this opinion. . . .

VIII

The district court correctly recognized that a preliminary injunction against Napster's participation in copyright infringement is not only warranted but required. We believe, however, that the scope of the injunction needs modification in light of our opinion. Specifically, we reiterate that contributory liability may potentially be imposed only to the extent that Napster: (1) receives reasonable knowledge of specific infringing files with copyrighted musical compositions and sound recordings; (2) knows or should know that such files are available on the Napster system; and (3) fails to act to prevent viral distribution of the works. The mere existence of the Napster system, absent actual notice and Napster's demonstrated failure to remove the offending material, is insufficient to impose contributory liability.

Conversely, Napster may be vicariously liable when it fails to affirmatively use its ability to patrol its system and preclude access to potentially infringing files listed in its search index. Napster has both the ability to use its search function to identify infringing musical recordings and the right to bar participation of users who engage in the transmission of infringing files.

The preliminary injunction which we stayed is overbroad because it places on Napster the entire burden of ensuring that no "copying, downloading, uploading, transmitting, or distributing" of plaintiffs' works occur on the system. As stated, we place the burden on plaintiffs to provide notice to Napster of copyrighted works and files containing such works available on the Napster system before Napster has the duty to disable access to the offending content. Napster, however, also bears the burden of policing the system within the limits of the system. Here, we recognize that this is not an exact science in that the files are user named. In crafting the injunction on remand, the district court should recognize that Napster's system does not currently appear to allow Napster access to users' MP3 files.

Based on our decision to remand, Napster's additional arguments on appeal going to the scope of the injunction need not be addressed. We, however, briefly address Napster's First Amendment argument so that it is not reasserted on remand. Napster contends that the present injunction violates the First Amendment because it is broader than necessary. The company asserts two distinct free speech rights: (1) its right to publish a "directory" (here, the search index) and (2) its users' right to exchange information. We note that First Amendment concerns in copyright are allayed by the presence of the fair use doctrine. There was a preliminary determination here that Napster users are not fair users. Uses of copyrighted material that are not fair uses are rightfully enjoined. . . .

Questions:

1.) You had a chance to do Problem 14-1 and perhaps to see the video of the argument. How closely did the court decision mirror either your proposed framing of the issues or the way you thought the decision was going to come out? To what extent did the court attempt to *respond* to some of those proposed framings?

2.) "Get[ting] for free something they would ordinarily have to buy. . . ." The court finds that "commercial use is demonstrated by a showing that repeated and exploitative unauthorized copies of copyrighted works were made to save the expense of purchasing authorized copies." Do you agree with this definition of "commercial use"? *Harper & Row* offered a similar definition. Why does the court adopt it here? In *Harper*, after all, one commercial publisher was portrayed as scooping another commercial publisher. Here we have legions of private individuals "sharing" files for free. What is it about the disaggregated mass of millions of individuals that causes the court to label their collective, albeit uncompensated, efforts "commercial"?

3.) What would happen if the court held that this was *not* commercial? What would the record companies have to prove?

4.) Is the court correct in its characterization of the *Sony* opinion? Was *Sony* only a case about what knowledge could be attributed to the defendants, merely because of the capabilities of their technology, in the absence of more concrete information?

5.) *Napster* suggests that "*Sony*'s 'staple article of commerce' analysis has no application to Napster's potential liability for *vicarious* copyright infringement." Do you agree? Did the *Sony* court confine itself to contributory infringement, when it said that liability could not be imposed if the product was capable of substantial non-infringing uses? Which answer makes sense from the point of view of copyright policy?

6.) What burdens does the court impose on Napster to filter, block and monitor content on its system?

7.) Section 2, above, discusses the "stakes" of secondary liability. Does the line the court draws here manage to thread the needle between the concerns of the copyright holders and the technologists? Why? Why not?

3.) Inducement Liability

We said at the beginning of this chapter that contributory infringement and vicarious liability were, until recently, the only two forms of secondary liability for copyright infringement. But then came *MGM v. Grokster*.

MGM Studios Inc. v. Grokster, Ltd.
545 U.S. 913 (2005)

Justice SOUTER delivered the opinion of the Court.

The question is under what circumstances the distributor of a product capable of both lawful and unlawful use is liable for acts of copyright infringement by third parties using the product. We hold that one who distributes a device with the object of promoting its use to infringe copyright, as shown by clear expression or other affirmative steps taken to foster infringement, is liable for the resulting acts of infringement by third parties.

Respondents, Grokster, Ltd., and StreamCast Networks, Inc., defendants in the trial court, distribute free software products that allow computer users to share electronic files through peer-to-peer networks, so called because users' computers communicate directly with each other, not through central servers. The advantage of peer-to-peer networks over information networks of other types shows up in their substantial and growing popularity. Because they need no central computer server to mediate the exchange of information or files among users, the high-bandwidth communications capacity for a server may be dispensed with, and the need for costly server storage space is eliminated. Since copies of a file (particularly a popular one) are available on many users' computers, file requests and retrievals may be faster than on other types of networks, and since file exchanges do not travel through a server, communications can take place between any computers that remain connected to the network without risk that a glitch in the server will disable the network in its entirety. Given these benefits in security, cost, and efficiency, peer-to-peer networks are employed to store and distribute electronic files by universities, government agencies, corporations, and libraries, among others.

Other users of peer-to-peer networks include individual recipients of Grokster's and StreamCast's software, and although the networks that they enjoy through using the software can be used to share any type of digital file, they have prominently employed those networks in sharing copyrighted music and video files without authorization. A group of copyright holders (MGM for short, but including motion picture studios, recording companies, songwriters, and music publishers) sued Grokster and StreamCast for their users' copyright infringements, alleging that they knowingly and intentionally distributed their software to enable users to reproduce and distribute the copyrighted works in violation of the Copyright Act. MGM sought damages and an injunction.

Grokster's eponymous software employs what is known as FastTrack technology, a protocol developed by others and licensed to Grokster. StreamCast distributes a very similar product except that its software, called Morpheus, relies on what is known as Gnutella technology. A user who downloads and installs either software possesses the protocol to send requests for files directly to the computers of others using software compatible with FastTrack or Gnutella. On the FastTrack network opened by the Grokster software, the user's request goes to a computer given an indexing capacity by the software and designated a supernode, or to some other computer with comparable power and capacity to collect temporary indexes of the files available on the computers of users connected to it. The supernode (or indexing computer) searches its own index and may communicate the search request to other supernodes. If the file is found, the supernode discloses its location to the computer requesting it, and the requesting user can download the file directly from the computer located. The copied file is placed in a designated sharing folder on the requesting user's computer, where it is available for other users to download in turn, along with any other file in that folder.

In the Gnutella network made available by Morpheus, the process is mostly the same, except that in some versions of the Gnutella protocol there are no supernodes. In these versions, peer computers using the protocol communicate directly with each other. When a user enters a search request into the Morpheus software, it sends the request to computers connected with it, which in turn pass the request along to other connected peers. The search results are communicated to the requesting computer, and the user can download desired files directly from peers' computers. As this description indicates, Grokster and StreamCast use no servers to intercept the content of the search requests or to mediate the file transfers conducted by users of the software, there being no central point through which the substance of the communications passes in either direction.

Although Grokster and StreamCast do not therefore know when particular files are copied, a few searches using their software would show what is available on the networks the software reaches. MGM commissioned a statistician to conduct a systematic search, and his study showed that nearly 90% of the files available for download on the FastTrack system were copyrighted works. Grokster and StreamCast dispute this figure, raising methodological problems and arguing that free copying even of copyrighted works may be authorized by the rightholders. They also argue that potential noninfringing uses of their software are significant in kind, even if infrequent in practice. Some musical performers, for example, have gained new audiences by distributing their copyrighted works for free across peer-to-peer networks, and some distributors of unprotected content have used peer-to-peer networks to disseminate files, Shakespeare being an example. Indeed, StreamCast has given Morpheus users the opportunity to download the briefs in this very case, though their popularity has not been quantified.

As for quantification, the parties' anecdotal and statistical evidence entered thus far to show the content available on the FastTrack and Gnutella networks does not say much about which files are actually downloaded by users, and no one can say how often the software is used to obtain copies of unprotected material. But MGM's evidence gives reason to think that the vast majority of users' downloads are acts of infringement, and because well over 100 million copies of the software in question are known to have been downloaded, and billions of files are shared across the FastTrack and Gnutella networks each month, the probable scope of copyright infringement is staggering.

Grokster and StreamCast concede the infringement in most downloads, and it is uncontested that they are aware that users employ their software primarily to download copyrighted files, even if the decentralized FastTrack and Gnutella networks fail to reveal which files are being copied, and when. From time to time, moreover, the companies have learned about their users' infringement directly, as from users who have sent e-mail to each company with questions about playing copyrighted movies they had downloaded, to whom the companies have responded with guidance. And MGM notified the companies of 8 million copyrighted files that could be obtained using their software.

Grokster and StreamCast are not, however, merely passive recipients of information about infringing use. The record is replete with evidence that from the moment Grokster and StreamCast began to distribute their free software, each one clearly voiced the objective that recipients use it to download copyrighted works, and each took active steps to encourage infringement.

After the notorious file-sharing service, Napster, was sued by copyright holders for facilitation of copyright infringement, StreamCast gave away a software program of a kind known as OpenNap, designed as compatible with the Napster program and open to Napster users for downloading files from other Napster and OpenNap users' computers. Evidence indicates that "[i]t was always [StreamCast's] intent to use [its OpenNap network] to be able to capture email addresses of [its] initial target market so that [it] could promote [its] StreamCast Morpheus interface to them," indeed, the OpenNap program was engineered "'to leverage Napster's 50 million user base.'"

. . . Internal company documents indicate that StreamCast hoped to attract large numbers of former Napster users if that company was shut down by court order or otherwise, and that StreamCast planned to be the next Napster. A kit developed by StreamCast to be delivered to advertisers, for example, contained press articles about StreamCast's potential to capture former Napster users, and it introduced itself to some potential advertisers as a company "which is similar to what Napster was." It broadcast banner advertisements to users of other Napster-compatible software, urging them to adopt its OpenNap. An internal e-mail from a company executive stated: "'We have put this network in place so that when Napster pulls the plug on their free service . . . or if the Court orders them shut down prior to that . . . we will be positioned to capture the flood of their 32 million users that will be actively looking for an alternative.'"

Thus, StreamCast developed promotional materials to market its service as the best Napster alternative. One proposed advertisement read: "Napster Inc. has announced that it will soon begin charging you a fee. That's if the courts don't order it shut down first. What will you do to get around it?" Another proposed ad touted StreamCast's software as the "# 1 alternative to Napster" and asked "[w]hen the lights went off at Napster . . . where did the users go?" StreamCast even planned to flaunt the illegal uses of its software; when it launched the OpenNap network, the chief technology officer of the company averred that "[t]he goal is to get in trouble with the law and get sued. It's the best way to get in the new[s]."

The evidence that Grokster sought to capture the market of former Napster users is sparser but revealing, for Grokster launched its own OpenNap system called Swaptor and inserted digital codes into its Web site so that computer users using Web search engines to look for "Napster" or "[f]ree filesharing" would be directed to the Grokster Web site, where they could download the Grokster software. And Grokster's name is an apparent derivative of Napster.

StreamCast's executives monitored the number of songs by certain commercial artists available on their networks, and an internal communication indicates they aimed to have a larger number of copyrighted songs available on their networks than other file-sharing networks. The point, of course, would be to attract users of a mind to infringe, just as it would be with their promotional materials developed showing copyrighted songs as examples of the kinds of files available through Morpheus. Morpheus in fact allowed users to search specifically for "Top 40" songs, which were inevitably copyrighted.

In addition to this evidence of express promotion, marketing, and intent to promote further, the business models employed by Grokster and StreamCast confirm that their principal object was use of their software to download copyrighted works. Grokster and StreamCast receive no revenue from users, who obtain the software itself for nothing. Instead, both companies generate income by selling advertising space, and they stream the advertising to Grokster and Morpheus users while they are employing the programs. As the number of users of each program increases, advertising opportunities become worth more. While there is doubtless some demand for free Shakespeare, the evidence shows that substantive volume is a function of free access to copyrighted work. Users seeking Top 40 songs, for example, or the latest release by Modest Mouse, are certain to be far more numerous than those seeking a free Decameron, and Grokster and StreamCast translated that demand into dollars.

Finally, there is no evidence that either company made an effort to filter copyrighted material from users' downloads or otherwise impede the sharing of copyrighted files. Although Grokster appears to have sent e-mails warning users about infringing content when it received threatening notice from the copyright holders, it never blocked anyone from continuing to use its software to share copyrighted files. StreamCast not only rejected another company's offer of help to monitor infringement, but blocked the Internet Protocol addresses of entities it believed were trying to engage in such monitoring on its networks.

B

. . . The District Court limited its consideration to the asserted liability of Grokster and StreamCast for distributing the current versions of their software, leaving aside whether either was liable "for damages arising from past versions of their software, or from other past activities." The District Court held that those who used the Grokster and Morpheus software to download copyrighted media files directly infringed MGM's copyrights, a conclusion not contested on appeal, but the court nonetheless granted summary judgment in favor of Grokster and StreamCast as to any liability arising from distribution of the then current versions of their software. Distributing that software gave rise to no liability in the court's view, because its use did not provide the distributors with actual knowledge of specific acts of infringement.

The Court of Appeals affirmed. In the court's analysis, a defendant was liable as a contributory infringer when it had knowledge of direct infringement and materially contributed to the infringement. But the court read *Sony Corp. of America v. Universal City Studios, Inc.* (1984), as holding that distribution of a commercial product capable of substantial noninfringing uses could not give rise to contributory liability for infringement unless the distributor had actual knowledge of specific instances of infringement and failed to act on that knowledge. The fact that the software was capable of substantial noninfringing uses in the Ninth Circuit's view meant that Grokster and StreamCast were not liable, because they had no such actual knowledge, owing to the decentralized architecture of their software. The court also held that Grokster and StreamCast did not materially contribute to their users' infringement because it was the users themselves who searched for, retrieved, and stored the infringing files, with no involvement by the defendants beyond providing the software in the first place.

The Ninth Circuit also considered whether Grokster and StreamCast could be liable under a theory of vicarious infringement. The court held against liability because the defendants did not monitor or control the use of the software, had no agreed-upon right or current ability to supervise its use, and had no independent duty to police infringement. We granted *certiorari*.

II
A

MGM and many of the amici fault the Court of Appeals's holding for upsetting a sound balance between the respective values of supporting creative pursuits through copyright protection and promoting innovation in new communication technologies by limiting the incidence of liability for copyright infringement. The more artistic protection is favored, the more technological innovation may be discouraged; the administration of copyright law is an exercise in managing the trade-off.

The tension between the two values is the subject of this case, with its claim that digital distribution of copyrighted material threatens copyright holders as never before, because every copy is identical to the original, copying is easy, and many people (especially the young) use file-sharing software to download copyrighted works. This very breadth of the software's use may well draw the public directly into the debate over copyright policy, and the indications are that the ease of copying songs or movies using software like Grokster's and Napster's is fostering disdain for copyright protection. As the case has been presented to us, these fears are said to be offset by the different concern that imposing liability, not only on infringers but on distributors of software based on its potential for unlawful use, could limit further development of beneficial technologies.[8]

The argument for imposing indirect liability in this case is, however, a powerful one, given the number of infringing downloads that occur every day using StreamCast's and Grokster's software. When a widely shared service or product is used to commit infringement, it may be impossible to enforce rights in the protected work effectively against all direct infringers, the only practical alternative being to go against the distributor of the copying device for secondary liability on a theory of contributory or vicarious infringement.

One infringes contributorily by intentionally inducing or encouraging direct infringement, and infringes vicariously by profiting from direct infringement while declining to exercise a right to stop or limit it.[9] Although "[t]he Copyright Act does not expressly render anyone liable for infringement committed by another," *Sony Corp. v. Universal City Studios*, these doctrines of secondary liability emerged from common law principles and are well established in the law.

B

Despite the currency of these principles of secondary liability, this Court has dealt with secondary copyright infringement in only one recent case, and because MGM has tailored its principal claim to our opinion there, a look at our earlier holding is in order. In *Sony Corp. v. Universal City Studios*, this Court addressed a claim that secondary liability for infringement can arise from the very distribution of a commercial product. There, the product, novel at the time, was what we know today as the videocassette recorder or VCR. Copyright holders sued *Sony* as the manufacturer, claiming it was contributorily liable for infringement that occurred when VCR owners taped copyrighted programs because it supplied the means used to infringe, and it had constructive knowledge that infringement would occur. At the trial on the merits, the evidence showed that the principal use of the VCR was for "'time-shifting,'" or taping a program for later

---

[8] The mutual exclusivity of these values should not be overstated, however. On the one hand technological innovators, including those writing file-sharing computer programs, may wish for effective copyright protections for their work. On the other hand the widespread distribution of creative works through improved technologies may enable the synthesis of new works or generate audiences for emerging artists.

[9] We stated in *Sony Corp. of America v. Universal City Studios, Inc.* (1984), that "'the lines between direct infringement, contributory infringement and vicarious liability are not clearly drawn. . . .' [R]easoned analysis of [the *Sony* plaintiffs' contributory infringement claim] necessarily entails consideration of arguments and case law which may also be forwarded under the other labels, and indeed the parties . . . rely upon such arguments and authority in support of their respective positions on the issue of contributory infringement." In the present case MGM has argued a vicarious liability theory, which allows imposition of liability when the defendant profits directly from the infringement and has a right and ability to supervise the direct infringer, even if the defendant initially lacks knowledge of the infringement. Because we resolve the case based on an inducement theory, there is no need to analyze separately MGM's vicarious liability theory.

viewing at a more convenient time, which the Court found to be a fair, not an infringing, use. There was no evidence that *Sony* had expressed an object of bringing about taping in violation of copyright or had taken active steps to increase its profits from unlawful taping. Although *Sony*'s advertisements urged consumers to buy the VCR to "'record favorite shows'" or "'build a library'" of recorded programs, *Sony* (Blackmun, J., dissenting), neither of these uses was necessarily infringing.

On those facts, with no evidence of stated or indicated intent to promote infringing uses, the only conceivable basis for imposing liability was on a theory of contributory infringement arising from its sale of VCRs to consumers with knowledge that some would use them to infringe. But because the VCR was "capable of commercially significant noninfringing uses," we held the manufacturer could not be faulted solely on the basis of its distribution. . . .

In sum, where an article is "good for nothing else" but infringement there is no legitimate public interest in its unlicensed availability, and there is no injustice in presuming or imputing an intent to infringe. Conversely, the doctrine absolves the equivocal conduct of selling an item with substantial lawful as well as unlawful uses, and limits liability to instances of more acute fault than the mere understanding that some of one's products will be misused. It leaves breathing room for innovation and a vigorous commerce.

The parties and many of the *amici* in this case think the key to resolving it is the *Sony* rule and, in particular, what it means for a product to be "capable of commercially significant noninfringing uses." MGM advances the argument that granting summary judgment to Grokster and StreamCast as to their current activities gave too much weight to the value of innovative technology, and too little to the copyrights infringed by users of their software, given that 90% of works available on one of the networks was shown to be copyrighted. Assuming the remaining 10% to be its noninfringing use, MGM says this should not qualify as "substantial," and the Court should quantify *Sony* to the extent of holding that a product used "principally" for infringement does not qualify. As mentioned before, Grokster and StreamCast reply by citing evidence that their software can be used to reproduce public domain works, and they point to copyright holders who actually encourage copying. Even if infringement is the principal practice with their software today, they argue, the noninfringing uses are significant and will grow.

We agree with MGM that the Court of Appeals misapplied *Sony*, which it read as limiting secondary liability quite beyond the circumstances to which the case applied. *Sony* barred secondary liability based on presuming or imputing intent to cause infringement solely from the design or distribution of a product capable of substantial lawful use, which the distributor knows is in fact used for infringement. The Ninth Circuit has read *Sony*'s limitation to mean that whenever a product is capable of substantial lawful use, the producer can never be held contributorily liable for third parties' infringing use of it; it read the rule as being this broad, even when an actual purpose to cause infringing use is shown by evidence independent of design and distribution of the product, unless the distributors had "specific knowledge of infringement at a time at which they contributed to the infringement, and failed to act upon that information." Because the Circuit found the StreamCast and Grokster software capable of substantial lawful use, it concluded on the basis of its reading of *Sony* that neither company could be held liable, since there was no showing that their software, being without any central server, afforded them knowledge of specific unlawful uses.

This view of *Sony*, however, was error, converting the case from one about liability resting on imputed intent to one about liability on any theory. Because *Sony* did not displace other theories of secondary liability, and because we find below that it was error to grant summary judgment to the companies on MGM's inducement claim, we do not revisit *Sony* further, as MGM requests, to add a more quantified description of the point of balance between protection and commerce when liability rests solely on distribution with knowledge that unlawful use will occur. It is enough to note that the Ninth Circuit's judgment rested on an erroneous understanding of *Sony* and to leave further consideration of the *Sony* rule for a day when that may be required.

C

Sony's rule limits imputing culpable intent as a matter of law from the characteristics or uses of a distributed product. But nothing in *Sony* requires courts to ignore evidence of intent if there is such evidence, and the case was never meant to foreclose rules of fault-based liability derived from the common law. ("If vicarious liability is to be imposed on *Sony* in this case, it must rest on the fact that it has sold equipment with constructive knowledge" of the potential for infringement). Thus, where evidence goes beyond a product's characteristics or the knowledge that it may be put to infringing uses, and shows statements or actions directed to promoting infringement, *Sony*'s staple-article rule will not preclude liability.

The classic case of direct evidence of unlawful purpose occurs when one induces commission of infringement by another, or "entic[es] or persuad[es] another" to infringe, Black's Law Dictionary 790 (8th ed. 2004), as by advertising. Thus at common law a copyright or patent defendant who "not only expected but invoked [infringing use] by advertisement" was liable for infringement "on principles recognized in every part of the law." *Kalem Co. v. Harper Brothers* (copyright infringement).

The rule on inducement of infringement as developed in the early cases is no different today.[11] Evidence of "active steps . . . taken to encourage direct infringement," such as advertising an infringing use or instructing how to engage in an infringing use, show an affirmative intent that the product be used to infringe, and a showing that infringement was encouraged overcomes the law's reluctance to find liability when a defendant merely sells a commercial product suitable for some lawful use, see, e.g., *Water Technologies Corp. v. Calco, Ltd.* (Fed. Cir. 1988) (liability for inducement where one "actively and knowingly aid[s] and abet[s] another's direct infringement" (emphasis omitted)); *Fromberg, Inc. v. Thornhill* (5th Cir. 1963) (demonstrations by sales staff of infringing uses supported liability for inducement); *Haworth Inc. v. Herman Miller Inc.* (W.D. Mich. 1994) (evidence that defendant "demonstrate[d] and recommend[ed] infringing configurations" of its product could support inducement liability); *Sims v. Mack Trucks, Inc.* (E.D. Pa. 1978) (finding inducement where the use "depicted by the defendant in its promotional film and brochures infringes the . . . patent"), overruled on other grounds, 608 F.2d 87 (3d Cir. 1979).

For the same reasons that *Sony* took the staple-article doctrine of patent law as a model for its copyright safe-harbor rule, the inducement rule, too, is a sensible one for copyright. We adopt it here, holding that one who distributes a device with the object of promoting its use to infringe copyright, as shown by clear expression or other affirmative steps taken to foster infringement, is liable for the resulting acts of infringement by third parties. We are, of course, mindful of the need to keep from trenching on regular commerce or discouraging the development of technologies with lawful and unlawful potential. Accordingly, just as *Sony* did not find intentional inducement despite the knowledge of the VCR manufacturer that its device could be used to infringe, mere

---

[11] Inducement has been codified in patent law.

knowledge of infringing potential or of actual infringing uses would not be enough here to subject a distributor to liability. Nor would ordinary acts incident to product distribution, such as offering customers technical support or product updates, support liability in themselves. The inducement rule, instead, premises liability on purposeful, culpable expression and conduct, and thus does nothing to compromise legitimate commerce or discourage innovation having a lawful promise.

III
A

The only apparent question about treating MGM's evidence as sufficient to withstand summary judgment under the theory of inducement goes to the need on MGM's part to adduce evidence that StreamCast and Grokster communicated an inducing message to their software users. The classic instance of inducement is by advertisement or solicitation that broadcasts a message designed to stimulate others to commit violations. MGM claims that such a message is shown here. It is undisputed that StreamCast beamed onto the computer screens of users of Napster-compatible programs ads urging the adoption of its OpenNap program, which was designed, as its name implied, to invite the custom of patrons of Napster, then under attack in the courts for facilitating massive infringement. Those who accepted StreamCast's OpenNap program were offered software to perform the same services, which a factfinder could conclude would readily have been understood in the Napster market as the ability to download copyrighted music files. Grokster distributed an electronic newsletter containing links to articles promoting its software's ability to access popular copyrighted music. And anyone whose Napster or free file-sharing searches turned up a link to Grokster would have understood Grokster to be offering the same file-sharing ability as Napster, and to the same people who probably used Napster for infringing downloads; that would also have been the understanding of anyone offered Grokster's suggestively named Swaptor software, its version of OpenNap. And both companies communicated a clear message by responding affirmatively to requests for help in locating and playing copyrighted materials.

In StreamCast's case, of course, the evidence just described was supplemented by other unequivocal indications of unlawful purpose in the internal communications and advertising designs aimed at Napster users ("When the lights went off at Napster . . . where did the users go?"). Whether the messages were communicated is not to the point on this record. The function of the message in the theory of inducement is to prove by a defendant's own statements that his unlawful purpose disqualifies him from claiming protection (and incidentally to point to actual violators likely to be found among those who hear or read the message). Proving that a message was sent out, then, is the preeminent but not exclusive way of showing that active steps were taken with the purpose of bringing about infringing acts, and of showing that infringing acts took place by using the device distributed. Here, the summary judgment record is replete with other evidence that Grokster and StreamCast, unlike the manufacturer and distributor in *Sony*, acted with a purpose to cause copyright violations by use of software suitable for illegal use.

Three features of this evidence of intent are particularly notable. First, each company showed itself to be aiming to satisfy a known source of demand for copyright infringement, the market comprising former Napster users. StreamCast's internal documents made constant reference to Napster, it initially distributed its Morpheus software through an OpenNap program compatible with Napster, it advertised its OpenNap program to Napster users, and its Morpheus software functions as Napster did except that it could be used to distribute more kinds of files, including copyrighted movies and software programs. Grokster's name is apparently derived from Napster, it too initially offered an OpenNap program, its software's function is likewise comparable to Napster's, and it attempted to divert queries for Napster onto its own Web site. Grokster and StreamCast's efforts to supply services to former Napster users, deprived of a mechanism to copy and distribute what were overwhelmingly infringing files, indicate a principal, if not exclusive, intent on the part of each to bring about infringement.

Second, this evidence of unlawful objective is given added significance by MGM's showing that neither company attempted to develop filtering tools or other mechanisms to diminish the infringing activity using their software. While the Ninth Circuit treated the defendants' failure to develop such tools as irrelevant because they lacked an independent duty to monitor their users' activity, we think this evidence underscores Grokster's and StreamCast's intentional facilitation of their users' infringement.[12]

Third, there is a further complement to the direct evidence of unlawful objective. It is useful to recall that StreamCast and Grokster make money by selling advertising space, by directing ads to the screens of computers employing their software. As the record shows, the more the software is used, the more ads are sent out and the greater the advertising revenue becomes. Since the extent of the software's use determines the gain to the distributors, the commercial sense of their enterprise turns on high-volume use, which the record shows is infringing. This evidence alone would not justify an inference of unlawful intent, but viewed in the context of the entire record its import is clear.

The unlawful objective is unmistakable.

B

In addition to intent to bring about infringement and distribution of a device suitable for infringing use, the inducement theory of course requires evidence of actual infringement by recipients of the device, the software in this case. As the account of the facts indicates, there is evidence of infringement on a gigantic scale, and there is no serious issue of the adequacy of MGM's showing on this point in order to survive the companies' summary judgment requests. Although an exact calculation of infringing use, as a basis for a claim of damages, is subject to dispute, there is no question that the summary judgment evidence is at least adequate to entitle MGM to go forward with claims for damages and equitable relief.

* * *

In sum, this case is significantly different from *Sony* and reliance on that case to rule in favor of StreamCast and Grokster was error. *Sony* dealt with a claim of liability based solely on distributing a product with alternative lawful and unlawful uses, with knowledge that some users would follow the unlawful course. The case struck a balance between the interests of protection and innovation by holding that the product's capability of substantial lawful employment should bar the imputation of fault and consequent secondary liability for the unlawful acts of others.

MGM's evidence in this case most obviously addresses a different basis of liability for distributing a product open to alternative uses. Here, evidence of the distributors' words and deeds going beyond distribution as such shows a purpose to cause and profit from third-party acts of copyright infringement. If liability for inducing infringement is ultimately found, it will not be on the basis of presuming or imputing fault, but from inferring a patently

---

[12] Of course, in the absence of other evidence of intent, a court would be unable to find contributory infringement liability merely based on a failure to take affirmative steps to prevent infringement, if the device otherwise was capable of substantial noninfringing uses. Such a holding would tread too close to the *Sony* safe harbor.

illegal objective from statements and actions showing what that objective was.

There is substantial evidence in MGM's favor on all elements of inducement, and summary judgment in favor of Grokster and StreamCast was error. On remand, reconsideration of MGM's motion for summary judgment will be in order. The judgment of the Court of Appeals is vacated, and the case is remanded for further proceedings consistent with this opinion.

It is so ordered.

Justice GINSBURG, with whom THE CHIEF JUSTICE and Justice KENNEDY join, concurring.

I concur in the Court's decision . . . and write separately to clarify why I conclude that the Court of Appeals misperceived, and hence misapplied, our holding in *Sony Corp. of America v. Universal City Studios, Inc.* (1984). There is here at least a "genuine issue as to [a] material fact," Fed. Rule Civ. Proc. 56(c), on the liability of Grokster or StreamCast, not only for actively inducing copyright infringement, but also or alternatively, based on the distribution of their software products, for contributory copyright infringement. On neither score was summary judgment for Grokster and StreamCast warranted. . . .

This case differs markedly from *Sony*. Here, there has been no finding of any fair use and little beyond anecdotal evidence of noninfringing uses. In finding the Grokster and StreamCast software products capable of substantial noninfringing uses, the District Court and the Court of Appeals appear to have relied largely on declarations submitted by the defendants. These declarations include assertions (some of them hearsay) that a number of copyright owners authorize distribution of their works on the Internet and that some public domain material is available through peer-to-peer networks including those accessed through Grokster's and StreamCast's software. . . .[3]

Even if the absolute number of noninfringing files copied using the Grokster and StreamCast software is large, it does not follow that the products are therefore put to substantial noninfringing uses and are thus immune from liability. The number of noninfringing copies may be reflective of, and dwarfed by, the huge total volume of files shared. In sum, when the record in this case was developed, there was evidence that Grokster's and StreamCast's products were, and had been for some time, overwhelmingly used to infringe, and that this infringement was the overwhelming source of revenue from the products. Fairly appraised, the evidence was insufficient to demonstrate, beyond genuine debate, a reasonable prospect that substantial or commercially significant noninfringing uses were likely to develop over time. On this record, the District Court should not have ruled dispositively on the contributory

---

[3] Justice Breyer finds support for summary judgment in this motley collection of declarations and in a survey conducted by an expert retained by MGM. That survey identified 75% of the files available through Grokster as copyrighted works owned or controlled by the plaintiffs, and 15% of the files as works likely copyrighted. As to the remaining 10% of the files, "there was not enough information to form reasonable conclusions either as to what those files even consisted of, and/or whether they were infringing or non-infringing." Even assuming, as Justice Breyer does, that the *Sony* Court would have absolved *Sony* of contributory liability solely on the basis of the use of the Betamax for authorized time-shifting, summary judgment is not inevitably appropriate here. *Sony* stressed that the plaintiffs there owned "well below 10%" of copyrighted television programming, [*Sony*], and found, based on trial testimony from representatives of the four major sports leagues and other individuals authorized to consent to home recording of their copyrighted broadcasts, that a similar percentage of program copying was authorized. Here, the plaintiffs allegedly control copyrights for 70% or 75% of the material exchanged through the Grokster and StreamCast software, and the District Court does not appear to have relied on comparable testimony about authorized copying from copyright holders.

infringement charge by granting summary judgment to Grokster and StreamCast.

If, on remand, the case is not resolved on summary judgment in favor of MGM based on Grokster and StreamCast actively inducing infringement, the Court of Appeals, I would emphasize, should reconsider, on a fuller record, its interpretation of *Sony*'s product distribution holding.

Justice BREYER, with whom Justices STEVENS and O'CONNOR join, concurring.

I agree with the Court that the distributor of a dual-use technology may be liable for the infringing activities of third parties where he or she actively seeks to advance the infringement. I further agree that, in light of our holding today, we need not now "revisit" *Sony*. Other Members of the Court, however, take up the *Sony* question: whether Grokster's product is "capable of 'substantial' or 'commercially significant' noninfringing uses." And they answer that question by stating that the Court of Appeals was wrong when it granted summary judgment on the issue in Grokster's favor. I write to explain why I disagree with them on this matter. . . .

The Court's opinion in *Sony* and the record evidence (as described and analyzed in the many briefs before us) together convince me that the Court of Appeals' conclusion has adequate legal support. . . .

When measured against *Sony*'s underlying evidence and analysis, the evidence now before us shows that Grokster passes *Sony*'s test—that is, whether the company's product is capable of substantial or commercially significant noninfringing uses. For one thing, petitioners' (hereinafter MGM) own expert declared that 75% of current files available on Grokster are infringing and 15% are "likely infringing." That leaves some number of files near 10% that apparently are noninfringing, a figure very similar to the 9% or so of authorized time-shifting uses of the VCR that the Court faced in *Sony*. . . .

Importantly, *Sony* also used the word "capable," asking whether the product is "capable of" substantial noninfringing uses. Its language and analysis suggest that a figure like 10%, if fixed for all time, might well prove insufficient, but that such a figure serves as an adequate foundation where there is a reasonable prospect of expanded legitimate uses over time. [*Sony*] (noting a "significant potential for future authorized copying"). And its language also indicates the appropriateness of looking to potential future uses of the product to determine its "capability."

Here the record reveals a significant future market for noninfringing uses of Grokster-type peer-to-peer software. Such software permits the exchange of any sort of digital file—whether that file does, or does not, contain copyrighted material. As more and more uncopyrighted information is stored in swappable form, it seems a likely inference that lawful peer-to-peer sharing will become increasingly prevalent.

And that is just what is happening. Such legitimate noninfringing uses are coming to include the swapping of: research information (the initial purpose of many peer-to-peer networks); public domain films (e.g., those owned by the Prelinger Archive); historical recordings and digital educational materials (e.g., those stored on the Internet Archive); digital photos (OurPictures, for example, is starting a P2P photo-swapping service); "shareware" and "freeware" (e.g., Linux and certain Windows software); secure licensed music and movie files (Intent MediaWorks, for example, protects licensed content sent across P2P networks); news broadcasts past and present (the BBC Creative Archive lets users "rip, mix and share the BBC"); user-created audio and video files (including "podcasts" that may be distributed through P2P software); *and all manner of free "open content" works collected by Creative Commons* (one can search for Creative Commons material on StreamCast). I can find nothing in the record that suggests that this course of events will not continue to flow naturally as a consequence of the character of the software taken together with the foreseeable development of the Internet and of information technology. . . .

As I have said, *Sony* itself sought to "strike a balance between a copyright holder's legitimate demand for effective—not merely symbolic—protection of the statutory monopoly, and the rights of others freely to engage in substantially unrelated areas of commerce." Thus, to determine whether modification, or a strict interpretation, of *Sony* is needed, I would ask whether MGM has shown that *Sony* incorrectly balanced copyright and new-technology interests. In particular: (1) Has *Sony* (as I interpret it) worked to protect new technology? (2) If so, would modification or strict interpretation significantly weaken that protection? (3) If so, would new or necessary copyright-related benefits outweigh any such weakening?

A

The first question is the easiest to answer. *Sony*'s rule, as I interpret it, has provided entrepreneurs with needed assurance that they will be shielded from copyright liability as they bring valuable new technologies to market.

Sony's rule is clear. That clarity allows those who develop new products that are capable of substantial noninfringing uses to know, ex ante, that distribution of their product will not yield massive monetary liability. At the same time, it helps deter them from distributing products that have no other real function than—or that are specifically intended for—copyright infringement, deterrence that the Court's holding today reinforces (by adding a weapon to the copyright holder's legal arsenal).

Sony's rule is strongly technology protecting. The rule deliberately makes it difficult for courts to find secondary liability where new technology is at issue. It establishes that the law will not impose copyright liability upon the distributors of dual-use technologies (who do not themselves engage in unauthorized copying) unless the product in question will be used almost exclusively to infringe copyrights (or unless they actively induce infringements as we today describe). *Sony* thereby recognizes that the copyright laws are not intended to discourage or to control the emergence of new technologies, including (perhaps especially) those that help disseminate information and ideas more broadly or more efficiently. Thus *Sony*'s rule shelters VCRs, typewriters, tape recorders, photocopiers, computers, cassette players, compact disc burners, digital video recorders, MP3 players, Internet search engines, and peer-to-peer software. But *Sony*'s rule does not shelter descramblers, even if one could theoretically use a descrambler in a noninfringing way.

Sony's rule is forward looking. It does not confine its scope to a static snapshot of a product's current uses (thereby threatening technologies that have undeveloped future markets). Rather, as the VCR example makes clear, a product's market can evolve dramatically over time. And *Sony*—by referring to a capacity for substantial noninfringing uses—recognizes that fact. *Sony*'s word "capable" refers to a plausible, not simply a theoretical, likelihood that such uses will come to pass, and that fact anchors *Sony* in practical reality.

Sony's rule is mindful of the limitations facing judges where matters of technology are concerned. Judges have no specialized technical ability to answer questions about present or future technological feasibility or commercial viability where technology professionals, engineers, and venture capitalists themselves may radically disagree and where answers may differ depending upon whether one focuses upon the time of product development or the time of distribution.

Given the nature of the *Sony* rule, it is not surprising that in the last 20 years, there have been relatively few contributory infringement suits—based on a product distribution theory—brought against technology providers (a small handful of federal appellate court cases and perhaps fewer than two dozen District Court cases in the last 20 years). I have found nothing in the briefs or the record that shows that *Sony* has failed to achieve its innovation-protecting objective. . . .

The second, more difficult, question is whether a modified *Sony* rule (or a strict interpretation) would significantly weaken the law's ability to protect new technology. Justice Ginsburg's approach would require defendants to produce considerably more concrete evidence—more than was presented here—to earn *Sony*'s shelter. That heavier evidentiary demand, and especially the more dramatic (case-by-case balancing) modifications that MGM and the Government seek, would, I believe, undercut the protection that *Sony* now offers. . . .

The third question—whether a positive copyright impact would outweigh any technology-related loss—I find the most difficult of the three. I do not doubt that a more intrusive *Sony* test would generally provide greater revenue security for copyright holders. But it is harder to conclude that the gains on the copyright swings would exceed the losses on the technology roundabouts.

For one thing, the law disfavors equating the two different kinds of gain and loss; rather, it leans in favor of protecting technology. As *Sony* itself makes clear, the producer of a technology which permits unlawful copying does not himself engage in unlawful copying—a fact that makes the attachment of copyright liability to the creation, production, or distribution of the technology an exceptional thing. Moreover, *Sony* has been the law for some time. And that fact imposes a serious burden upon copyright holders like MGM to show a need for change in the current rules of the game, including a more strict interpretation of the test.

In any event, the evidence now available does not, in my view, make out a sufficiently strong case for change. . . . Will an unmodified *Sony* lead to a significant diminution in the amount or quality of creative work produced? Since copyright's basic objective is creation and its revenue objectives but a means to that end, this is the underlying copyright question. See *Twentieth Century Music Corp. v. Aiken* (1975) ("Creative work is to be encouraged and rewarded, but private motivation must ultimately serve the cause of promoting broad public availability of literature, music, and the other arts"). And its answer is far from clear.

Unauthorized copying likely diminishes industry revenue, though it is not clear by how much. . . . The extent to which related production has actually and resultingly declined remains uncertain, though there is good reason to believe that the decline, if any, is not substantial. See, e. g., M. Madden, Pew Internet & American Life Project, Artists, Musicians, and the Internet (nearly 70% of musicians believe that file sharing is a minor threat or no threat at all to creative industries); Benkler, *Sharing Nicely: On Shareable Goods and the Emergence of Sharing as a Modality of Economic Production*, 114 Yale L. J. 273, 351–352 (2004) ("Much of the actual flow of revenue to artists—from performances and other sources—is stable even assuming a complete displacement of the CD market by peer-to-peer distribution. . . . [I]t would be silly to think that music, a cultural form without which no human society has existed, will cease to be in our world [because of illegal file swapping]"). . . .

. . . As *Sony* recognized, the legislative option remains available. Courts are less well suited than Congress to the task of "accommodat[ing] fully the varied permutations of competing interests that are inevitably implicated by such new technology."

For these reasons, I disagree with Justice Ginsburg, but I agree with the Court and join its opinion.

Questions:

1.) A host of issues present themselves. We think one of the most important questions in intellectual property law (and perhaps law in general) is what role judges should play in elaborating its doctrines in the context of new technologies and new social realities. We discussed that extensively in the preceding two chapters, focusing in particular on software and on fair use. How should judges interpret the law and apply it, when the statutory text is either vague or absent, or the technological context clearly different from the ones to which the law initially applied? Your question is this: is it appropriate for Federal judges to fashion—with no statutory basis whatsoever—a law of secondary infringement? Whether your answer was affirmative or negative, did you have the *same* answer in the fair use and software cases? If not, why not?

2.) Having fashioned such a law—built around contributory infringement and vicarious liability—why does it make sense to add a new form of liability built around inducement? Describe Justice Souter's motivation for doing so. Justice Ginsburg's? Justice Breyer's?

3.) State the test that *Grokster* lays down for inducement liability.

PROBLEM 14-2

You are an associate product development lawyer for Apple. The *Grokster* decision has been taken back in time and has just landed on your desk. Five minutes later, the first iPod is laid in front of you. At the time, assume the principal competing digital music player (from *Sony*) only plays DRM-protected music and will not play MP3 files. Assume a deliberate engineering decision has been made that the iPod will play unprotected MP3 files. Assume the iPod can also hold dramatically more songs than any available competing player. The iPod will be marketed in conjunction with three advertising campaigns. "Rip, Mix and Burn!" "10,000 songs in your pocket!" and a dystopian, *1984*-like image of shackled slaves, listening to a droning Big Brother, suddenly revolting when exposed to Apple's new technology. "The revolution is here," says the ad, "free your head. Free the music!" The advertisements have been made and circulated internally at Apple, but not yet aired. One of the attractive features of iTunes is that it will automatically retrieve album art for any digital music found on your computer or iPod. To do this, iTunes relies on "digital signatures" of the tracks on your iPod or computer. This service does not restrict itself to the DRM-protected AARC files sold from the iTunes store, it also works for any album "ripped" from a CD into MP3 form (which would be a fair use, were the original CD owned by the person doing the ripping). By the same token, it works for any illicitly downloaded MP3.

You must tell your boss whether the iPod might violate the rules laid down in the new *Grokster* decision, or the more traditional rules of contributory and vicarious infringement. How do you advise? What factors inform your analysis? Would you advise any changes to the product, accompanying service or advertising?

4.) Safe Harbors: Section 512, Direct Infringement and Secondary Liability

Let us leave secondary infringement for a moment and turn back to *direct* infringement. Having read *MAI*, which suggests that even transitory copies count as copies for the purpose of § 106, and learned that copyright is a strict liability system, which does not require bad intent, or even negligence, for liability, you may be wondering why the entire internet is not illegal—or constantly subject to copyright suits for *direct* infringement. After all, Google's "spiders" copy the entire web every day in order to index it. Much of the material Google copies was itself illicitly copied—though Google does not "know" this when its spiders make copies. And those copies then sit on Google's titanic hard drives far longer than is needed to count as fixed; they are much more stable than a RAM copy. Google does this "on purpose"—there is much more intentionality about the copying than there was in the *Netcom* case. Hundreds of hours of video are uploaded to YouTube every *minute*: even though its digital fingerprinting and detection software is now very good, and even though some unauthorized uploads would be sufficiently transformative to count as fair use, that still leaves an enormous quantity of illicitly reproduced material. Facebook has millions of users posting content, some of which is illicitly copied (even if the users and Facebook sometimes do not know that). Dropbox and every other cyberlocker can be used to store both licit and infringing material. Gmail has billions of emails with infringing attachments passing through its systems, and sitting in its hard drives, every year. Time Warner Cable, Comcast and AT&T provide internet service to millions, and infringing material flows over those connections, and over the law school network you may be on right now. The networks temporarily "cache" material to speed up transmission. Some of the cached material is illicitly copied.

Why does this activity not make all of these intermediaries *directly* liable? (We will come to their potential indirect or secondary liability in a moment.) In each of these cases, the intermediary is *making* copies, on its own system, of infringing material. Is the whole internet somehow protected by *Netcom*, a single District Court decision that took a "creative" interpretation towards the law of its own circuit? (Revisit the *Netcom* decision from Chapter 11 to understand why we say that.)

The answer to this question is that, initially, it was the US government's official position that all these entities *should be*—indeed already were—strictly liable without any change in existing law, simply because of the combination of a broad conception of fixation and the fact that copyright was a strict liability system. As of 1995, the USPTO was saying that strict liability for internet intermediaries was a feature, not a bug. This is the way copyright infringement would be policed, just as products liability imposes strict liability on product sellers and then lets them decide how to keep their level of liability down.

Why did this not come to pass? The Digital Millennium Copyright Act—or more accurately, that part of it with the mellifluous name of the Online Copyright Infringement Liability Limitation Act (OCILLA)—provided a set of safe harbors which immunized many types of intermediaries, under certain conditions, from copyright liability. The key safe harbors are in § 512. It is no exaggeration to say that, without them, the internet as you know it would not exist. There would be a network, of course, but it would be wildly different from the one you know.

Look in the WIPO Copyright Treaty from the statutory supplement. You will see no requirement that there be § 512 limitations. In fact, while the EU E-Commerce Directive contains similar limitations, what is remarkable is that none of these are *required*. Rights are mandatory. Exceptions and limitations are optional. What would Jefferson say?

Section 512's structure is relatively simple. A series of types of online services are laid out. A set of requirements for the safe harbor is outlined for each type of service. But the safe harbor also contains *limitations*—patterns of behavior that will forfeit the safe harbor. The section is too long to reproduce in its entirety—please read it in the statutory supplement before reading the rest of this chapter. For illustration's sake, here is the beginning of section § 512(c). Ask yourself which specific services would benefit from it.

(c) Information Residing on Systems or Networks at Direction of Users.—

(1) In general.—A service provider shall not be liable for monetary relief, or, except as provided in subsection (j), for injunctive or other equitable relief, for infringement of copyright by reason of the storage at the direction of a user of material that resides on a system or network controlled or operated by or for the service provider, if the service provider—

(A)(i) does not have actual knowledge that the material or an activity using the material on the system or network is infringing;

(ii) in the absence of such actual knowledge, is not aware of facts or circumstances from which infringing activity is apparent; or

(iii) upon obtaining such knowledge or awareness, acts expeditiously to remove, or disable access to, the material;

(B) does not receive a financial benefit directly attributable to the infringing activity, in a case in which the service provider has the right and ability to control such activity; and

(C) upon notification of claimed infringement as described in paragraph (3), responds expeditiously to remove, or disable access to, the material that is claimed to be infringing or to be the subject of infringing activity.

The rest of the section goes on to detail the requirements of the "notice and takedown" procedure.

Notice subsection (B), which takes away the safe harbor if the service "receive[s] a financial benefit directly attributable to the infringing activity, in a case in which the service provider has the right and ability to control such activity." What does that sound like? It should be extremely reminiscent of the discussion we have just had of vicarious liability. So how are we to think of 512? Is it a limitation only on liability for *direct* copyright infringement? Is it a limitation on both direct and secondary copyright liability, but one that does not apply if the provider is vicariously liable? Or is it something else altogether?

To answer these questions we will start with the Copyright Office's excellent summary of § 512. The summary is from December 1998, shortly after the passage of the DMCA. Several high profile cases have been decided since then, including the 2012 *Viacom v. YouTube* case, which follows the summary. *Viacom* analyzes the applicability of the § 512(c) safe harbor we have just read, and addresses the questions we posed. As the internet has developed, this provision has become increasingly important because it potentially limits the copyright liability of video sharing, social networking, and cloud computing services for material stored on their systems by users. YouTube, Facebook, Instagram, and Dropbox rely on § 512(c). Therefore, the court's interpretation of its requirements has far-reaching consequences.

Title II: Online Copyright Infringement Liability Limitation
U.S. Copyright Office Summary

Title II of the DMCA adds a new section 512 to the Copyright Act to create four new limitations on liability for copyright infringement by online service providers. The limitations are based on the following four categories of conduct by a service provider:

1. Transitory communications;
2. System caching;
3. Storage of information on systems or networks at direction of users; and
4. Information location tools.

New section 512 also includes special rules concerning the application of these limitations to nonprofit educational institutions.

Each limitation entails a complete bar on monetary damages, and restricts the availability of injunctive relief in various respects. (Section 512(j)). Each limitation relates to a separate and distinct function, and a determination of whether a service provider qualifies for one of the limitations does not bear upon a determination of whether the provider qualifies for any of the other three. (Section 512(n)).

The failure of a service provider to qualify for any of the limitations in section 512 does not necessarily make it liable for copyright infringement. The copyright owner must still demonstrate that the provider has infringed, and the provider may still avail itself of any of the defenses, such as fair use, that are available to copyright defendants generally. (Section 512(l)).

In addition to limiting the liability of service providers, Title II establishes a procedure by which a copyright owner can obtain a subpoena from a federal court ordering a service provider to disclose the identity of a subscriber who is allegedly engaging in infringing activities. (Section 512(h)).

Section 512 also contains a provision to ensure that service providers are not placed in the position of choosing between limitations on liability on the one hand and preserving the privacy of their subscribers, on the other. Subsection (m) explicitly states that nothing in section 512 requires a service provider to monitor its service or access material in violation of law (such as the Electronic Communications Privacy Act) in order to be eligible for any of the liability limitations.

Eligibility for Limitations Generally

A party seeking the benefit of the limitations on liability in Title II must qualify as a "service provider." For purposes of the first limitation, relating to transitory communications, "service provider" is defined in section 512(k)(1)(A) as "an entity offering the transmission, routing, or providing of connections for digital online communications, between or among points specified by a user, of material of the user's choosing, without modification to the content of the material as sent or received." For purposes of the other three limitations, "service provider" is more broadly defined in section 512(k)(l)(B) as "a provider of online services or network access, or the operator of facilities therefore."

In addition, to be eligible for any of the limitations, a service provider must meet two overall conditions: (1) it must adopt and reasonably implement a policy of terminating in appropriate circumstances the accounts of subscribers who are repeat infringers; and (2) it must accommodate and not interfere with "standard technical measures." (Section 512(i)). "Standard technical measures" are defined as measures that copyright owners use to identify or protect copyrighted works, that have been developed pursuant to a broad consensus of copyright owners and service providers in an open, fair and voluntary multi-industry process, are available to anyone on reasonable nondiscriminatory terms, and do not impose substantial costs or burdens on service providers.

Limitation for Transitory Communications

In general terms, section 512(a) limits the liability of service providers in circumstances where the provider merely acts as a data conduit, transmitting digital information from one point on a network to another at someone else's request. This limitation covers acts of transmission, routing, or providing connections for the information, as well as the intermediate and transient copies that are made automatically in the operation of a network.

In order to qualify for this limitation, the service provider's activities must meet the following conditions:

- The transmission must be initiated by a person other than the provider.
- The transmission, routing, provision of connections, or copying must be carried out by an automatic technical process without selection of material by the service provider.
- The service provider must not determine the recipients of the material.
- Any intermediate copies must not ordinarily be accessible to anyone other than anticipated recipients, and must not be retained for longer than reasonably necessary.
- The material must be transmitted with no modification to its content.

Limitation for System Caching

Section 512(b) limits the liability of service providers for the practice of retaining copies, for a limited time, of material that has been made available online by a person other than the provider, and then transmitted to a subscriber at his or her direction. The service provider retains the material so that subsequent requests for the same material can be fulfilled by transmitting the retained copy, rather than retrieving the material from the original source on the network.

The benefit of this practice is that it reduces the service provider's bandwidth requirements and reduces the waiting time on subsequent requests for the same information. On the other hand, it can result in the delivery of outdated information to subscribers and can deprive website operators of accurate "hit" information—information about the number of requests for particular material on a website—from which advertising revenue is frequently calculated. For this reason, the person making the material available online may establish rules about updating it, and may utilize technological means to track the number of "hits."

The limitation applies to acts of intermediate and temporary storage, when carried out through an automatic technical process for the purpose of making the material available to subscribers who subsequently request it. It is subject to the following conditions:

- The content of the retained material must not be modified.
- The provider must comply with rules about "refreshing" material—replacing retained copies of material with material from the original location—when specified in accordance with a generally accepted industry standard data communication protocol.
- The provider must not interfere with technology that returns "hit" information to

the person who posted the material, where such technology meets certain requirements.

- The provider must limit users' access to the material in accordance with conditions on access (e.g., password protection) imposed by the person who posted the material.
- Any material that was posted without the copyright owner's authorization must be removed or blocked promptly once the service provider has been notified that it has been removed, blocked, or ordered to be removed or blocked, at the originating site.

Limitation for Information Residing on Systems or Networks at the Direction of Users

Section 512(c) limits the liability of service providers for infringing material on websites (or other information repositories) hosted on their systems. It applies to storage at the direction of a user. In order to be eligible for the limitation, the following conditions must be met:

- The provider must not have the requisite level of knowledge of the infringing activity, as described below.
- If the provider has the right and ability to control the infringing activity, it must not receive a financial benefit directly attributable to the infringing activity.
- Upon receiving proper notification of claimed infringement, the provider must expeditiously take down or block access to the material.

In addition, a service provider must have filed with the Copyright Office a designation of an agent to receive notifications of claimed infringement. The Office provides a suggested form for the purpose of designating an agent (https://www .copyright.gov/dmca-directory/) and maintains a list of agents on the Copyright Office website (https:/dmca.copyright.gov/osp/).

Under the knowledge standard, a service provider is eligible for the limitation on liability only if it does not have actual knowledge of the infringement, is not aware of facts or circumstances from which infringing activity is apparent, or upon gaining such knowl- edge or awareness, responds expeditiously to take the material down or block access to it.

The statute also establishes procedures for proper notification, and rules as to its effect. (Section 512(c)(3)). Under the notice and takedown procedure, a copyright owner submits a notification under penalty of perjury, including a list of specified elements, to the service provider's designated agent. Failure to comply substantially with the statutory requirements means that the notification will not be considered in determining the requisite level of knowledge by the service provider. If, upon receiving a proper notification, the service provider promptly removes or blocks access to the material identified in the notification, the provider is exempt from monetary liability. In addition, the provider is protected from any liability to any person for claims based on its having taken down the material. (Section 512(g)(1)).

In order to protect against the possibility of erroneous or fraudulent notifications, certain safeguards are built into section 512. Subsection (g)(1) gives the subscriber the opportunity to respond to the notice and takedown by filing a counter notification. In order to qualify for the protection against liability for taking down material, the service provider must promptly notify the subscriber that it has removed or disabled access to the material. If the subscriber serves a counter notification complying with statutory requirements, including a statement under penalty of perjury that the material was removed or disabled through mistake or misidentification, then unless the copyright owner files an action seeking a court order against the subscriber, the service provider must put the material back up within 10–14 business days after receiving the counter notification.

Penalties are provided for knowing material misrepresentations in either a notice or a counter notice. Any person who knowingly materially misrepresents that material is infringing, or that it was removed or blocked through mistake or misidentification, is liable for any resulting damages (including costs and attorneys' fees) incurred by the alleged infringer, the copyright owner or its licensee, or the service provider. (Section 512(f)).

Limitation for Information Location Tools

Section 512(d) relates to hyperlinks, online directories, search engines and the like. It limits liability for the acts of referring or linking users to a site that contains infringing material by using such information location tools, if the following conditions are met:

- The provider must not have the requisite level of knowledge that the material is infringing. The knowledge standard is the same as under the limitation for information residing on systems or networks.
- If the provider has the right and ability to control the infringing activity, the provider must not receive a financial benefit directly attributable to the activity.
- Upon receiving a notification of claimed infringement, the provider must expeditiously take down or block access to the material.

These are essentially the same conditions that apply under the previous limitation, with some differences in the notification requirements. The provisions establishing safeguards against the possibility of erroneous or fraudulent notifications, as discussed above, as well as those protecting the provider against claims based on having taken down the material apply to this limitation. (Sections 512(f)–(g)).

PROBLEM 14-3

a.) **List one service that you use that seems to fit into each of the safe harbors provided by § 512(a), (b), (c), and (d) (i.e., list one service per safe harbor). In each case describe what the service has to do in order to qualify for the safe harbor. Put differently, what specific types of behavior could cause it to *lose* the safe harbor? Finally, explain why the requirements for each type of service are different.**

b.) [As always, facts have been changed—or invented—for the purposes of this assignment.] Each year, James, a Duke law professor, assigns *The Grey Album* by DJ Danger Mouse as part of his Intellectual Property class. *The Grey Album* is a mashup of the Beatles' *The White Album* and an *a capella* version of Jay Z's *The Black Album*. James includes the audio and video of *The Grey Album* in his discussion of fair use under § 107. He uses it as a practice example and asks the students whether it is a fair use. (Responses vary.)

The Grey Album is controversial. The owners of the rights to the original works that Danger Mouse sampled have repeatedly claimed that it is a blatant copyright infringement. Through legal action, they were able to stop *The Grey Album* from being released commercially which, ironically, made it an online sensation. (*See* "Streisand Effect, The".) Finding they were unable to quell demand for the album, they have aimed at restricting supply. They have sent numerous DMCA takedown notices, as described in § 512(c), to sites such as YouTube. Even when counter-notices were sent by Danger Mouse, YouTube and other sites claimed that they were required to take the material down in order to keep their safe harbor. (True?) Thus, there are very few online sources for *The Grey Album*, or for the extremely amusing mashup videos that have been made using its soundtrack. Because of the dearth of online access, James declares that he has to make the music and videos available—"for educational purposes." All Duke professors have their own pages on the Duke network—"a foundational part of academic freedom," the Provost explains. James uploaded the audio and video to the Duke network and featured it prominently on his page, which is available not just to his students but to everyone on the internet. James's page presents the Danger Mouse audio and video in the middle of a dense commentary by him on fair use. Ego-bruisingly, most of those who come to the page just view or download the video and audio, and seem unmoved by the § 107 analysis. Not content with this, James created a "Grey Album Search Engine" which scans the web for other copies of Danger Mouse's classic work and supplies current and live hyperlinks to any searcher. Duke (and James) have been served with many takedown notices because of this behavior. Duke's beloved OIT department removes the material on James's page each time it receives a notice to the designated DMCA compliance agent, but James simply re-posts the files, and the links, again the next day. He claims that the copyright owners know this is a fair use and that Duke's administration "needs to make the crucial evolutionary leap from invertebrate to vertebrate."

Can James claim the DMCA safe harbor if he is sued personally for copyright infringement? Can Duke if it is sued for copyright infringement? [Hint: remember § 512(e).] Does failing to get the safe harbor mean that either James, or Duke, is liable?

Viacom International, Inc. v. YouTube, Inc.
676 F.3d 19 (2d Cir. 2012)

JOSÉ A. CABRANES, Circuit Judge.

This appeal requires us to clarify the contours of the "safe harbor" provision of the Digital Millennium Copyright Act (DMCA) that limits the liability of online service providers for copyright infringement that occurs "by reason of the storage at the direction of a user of material that resides on a system or network controlled or operated by or for the service provider." 17 U.S.C. § 512(c). . . .

The plaintiffs alleged direct and secondary copyright infringement based on the public performance, display, and reproduction of approximately 79,000 audiovisual "clips" that appeared on the YouTube website between 2005 and 2008. They demanded, inter alia, statutory damages pursuant to 17 U.S.C. § 504(c) or, in the alternative, actual damages from the alleged infringement, as well as declaratory and injunctive relief.

In a June 23, 2010 Opinion and Order (the "June 23 Opinion"), the District Court held that the defendants were entitled to DMCA safe harbor protection primarily because they had insufficient notice of the particular infringements in suit. In construing the statutory safe harbor, the District Court concluded that the "actual knowledge" or "aware[ness] of facts or circumstances" that would disqualify an online service provider from safe harbor protection under § 512(c)(1)(A) refer to "knowledge of specific and identifiable infringements." The District Court further held that item-specific knowledge of infringing activity is required for a service provider to have the "right and ability to control" infringing activity under § 512(c)(1)(B). . . .

These related cases present a series of significant questions of statutory construction. We conclude that the District Court correctly held that the § 512(c) safe harbor requires knowledge or awareness of specific infringing activity, but we vacate the order granting summary judgment because a reasonable jury could find that YouTube had actual knowledge or awareness of specific infringing activity on its website. We further hold that the District Court erred by interpreting the "right and ability to control" provision to require "item-specific" knowledge. . . .

BACKGROUND

A. The DMCA Safe Harbors

"The DMCA was enacted in 1998 to implement the World Intellectual Property Organization Copyright Treaty," *Universal City Studios, Inc. v. Corley* (2d Cir. 2001), and to update domestic copyright law for the digital age. Title II of the DMCA, separately titled the "Online Copyright Infringement Liability Limitation Act" (OCILLA), was designed to "clarif[y] the liability faced by service providers who transmit potentially infringing material over their networks." S.Rep. No. 105-190 at 2 (1998). But "[r]ather than embarking upon a wholesale clarification" of various copyright doctrines, Congress elected "to leave current law in its evolving state and, instead, to create a series of 'safe harbors[]' for certain common activities of service providers." To that end, OCILLA established a series of four "safe harbors" that allow qualifying service providers to limit their liability for claims of copyright infringement based on (a) "transitory digital network communications," (b) "system caching," (c) "information residing on systems or networks at [the] direction of users," and (d) "information location tools." 17 U.S.C. § 512(a)–(d).

To qualify for protection under any of the safe harbors, a party must meet a set of threshold criteria. First, the party must in fact be a "service provider," defined, in pertinent part, as "a provider of online services or network access, or the operator of facilities therefor." 17 U.S.C. § 512(k)(1)(B). A party that qualifies as a service provider must also satisfy certain "conditions of eligibility," including the adoption and reasonable implementation of a "repeat infringer" policy that "provides for the termination in appropriate circumstances of subscribers and account holders of the service provider's system or network." § 512(i)(1)(A). In addition, a qualifying service provider must accommodate "standard technical measures" that are "used by copyright owners to identify or protect copyrighted works." § 512(i)(1)(B), (i)(2).

Beyond the threshold criteria, a service provider must satisfy the requirements of a particular safe harbor. In this case, the safe harbor at issue is § 512(c), which covers infringement claims that arise "by reason of the storage at the direction of a user of material that resides on a system or network controlled or operated by or for the service provider." § 512(c)(1). The § 512(c) safe harbor will apply only if the service provider:

> (A)(i) does not have actual knowledge that the material or an activity using the material on the system or network is infringing;
>
>> (ii) in the absence of such actual knowledge, is not aware of facts or circumstances from which infringing activity is apparent; or
>>
>> (iii) upon obtaining such knowledge or awareness, acts expeditiously to remove, or disable access to, the material;
>
> (B) does not receive a financial benefit directly attributable to the infringing activity, in a case in which the service provider has the right

and ability to control such activity; and

(C) upon notification of claimed infringement as described in paragraph (3), responds expeditiously to remove, or disable access to, the material that is claimed to be infringing or to be the subject of infringing activity.

§ 512(c)(1)(A)–(C). Section 512(c) also sets forth a detailed notification scheme that requires service providers to "designate[] an agent to receive notifications of claimed infringement," § 512(c)(2), and specifies the components of a proper notification, commonly known as a "takedown notice," to that agent, see § 512(c)(3). Thus, actual knowledge of infringing material, awareness of facts or circumstances that make infringing activity apparent, or receipt of a takedown notice will each trigger an obligation to expeditiously remove the infringing material.

With the statutory context in mind, we now turn to the facts of this case.

B. Factual Background

YouTube was founded in February 2005 by Chad Hurley ("Hurley"), Steve Chen ("Chen"), and Jawed Karim ("Karim"), three former employees of the internet company PayPal. When YouTube announced the "official launch" of the website in December 2005, a press release described YouTube as a "consumer media company" that "allows people to watch, upload, and share personal video clips at www.YouTube.com." Under the slogan "Broadcast yourself," YouTube achieved rapid prominence and profitability, eclipsing competitors such as Google Video and Yahoo Video by wide margins. In November 2006, Google acquired YouTube in a stock-for-stock transaction valued at $1.65 billion. By March 2010, at the time of summary judgment briefing in this litigation, site traffic on YouTube had soared to more than 1 billion daily video views, with more than 24 hours of new video uploaded to the site every minute.

The basic function of the YouTube website permits users to "upload" and view video clips free of charge. Before uploading a video to YouTube, a user must register and create an account with the website. The registration process requires the user to accept YouTube's Terms of Use agreement, which provides, inter alia, that the user "will not submit material that is copyrighted . . . unless [he is] the owner of such rights or ha[s] permission from their rightful owner to post the material and to grant YouTube all of the license rights granted herein." When the registration process is complete, the user can sign in to his account, select a video to upload from the user's personal computer, mobile phone, or other device, and instruct the YouTube system to upload the video by clicking on a virtual upload "button."

Uploading a video to the YouTube website triggers a series of automated software functions. During the upload process, YouTube makes one or more exact copies of the video in its original file format. YouTube also makes one or more additional copies of the video in "Flash" format, a process known as "transcoding." The transcoding process ensures that YouTube videos are available for viewing by most users at their request. The YouTube system allows users to gain access to video content by "streaming" the video to the user's computer in response to a playback request. YouTube uses a computer algorithm to identify clips that are "related" to a video the user watches and display links to the "related" clips. . . .

DISCUSSION

A. Actual and "Red Flag" Knowledge: § 512(c)(1)(A)

The first and most important question on appeal is whether the DMCA safe harbor at issue requires "actual knowledge" or "aware[ness]" of facts or circumstances indicating "specific and identifiable infringements." We consider first the scope of the statutory provision and then its application to the record in this case.

1. The Specificity Requirement

"As in all statutory construction cases, we begin with the language of the statute," *Barnhart v. Sigmon Coal Co.* (2002). Under § 512(c)(1)(A), safe harbor protection is available only if the service provider:

> (i) does not have actual knowledge that the material or an activity using the material on the system or network is infringing;
>
> (ii) in the absence of such actual knowledge, is not aware of facts or circumstances from which infringing activity is apparent; or
>
> (iii) upon obtaining such knowledge or awareness, acts expeditiously to remove, or disable access to, the material. . . .

17 U.S.C. § 512(c)(1)(A). As previously noted, the District Court held that the statutory phrases "actual knowledge that the material . . . is infringing" and "facts or circumstances from which infringing activity is apparent" refer to "knowledge of specific and identifiable infringements." For the reasons that follow, we substantially affirm that holding.

Although the parties marshal a battery of other arguments on appeal, it is the text of the statute that compels our conclusion. In particular, we are persuaded that the basic operation of § 512(c) requires knowledge or awareness of specific infringing activity. Under § 512(c)(1)(A), knowledge or awareness alone does not disqualify the service provider; rather, the provider that gains knowledge or awareness of infringing activity retains safe-harbor protection if it "acts expeditiously to remove, or disable access to, the material." 17 U.S.C. § 512(c)(1)(A)(iii). Thus, the nature of the removal obligation itself contemplates knowledge or awareness of specific infringing material, because expeditious removal is possible only if the service provider knows with particularity which items to remove. Indeed, to require expeditious removal in the absence of specific knowledge or awareness would be to mandate an amorphous obligation to "take commercially reasonable steps" in response to a generalized awareness of infringement. Such a view cannot be reconciled with the language of the statute, which requires "expeditious[]" action to remove or disable "*the material*" at issue. 17 U.S.C. § 512(c)(1)(A)(iii) (emphasis added).

On appeal, the plaintiffs dispute this conclusion by drawing our attention to § 512(c)(1)(A)(ii), the so-called "red flag" knowledge provision. See § 512(c)(1)(A)(ii) (limiting liability where, "in the absence of such actual knowledge, [the service provider] is not aware of facts or circumstances from which infringing activity is apparent"). In their view, the use of the phrase "facts or circumstances" demonstrates that Congress did not intend to limit the red flag provision to a particular type of knowledge. The plaintiffs contend that requiring awareness of specific infringements in order to establish "aware[ness] of facts or circumstances from which infringing activity is apparent," 17 U.S.C. § 512(c)(1)(A)(ii), renders the red flag provision superfluous, because that provision would be satisfied only when the "actual knowledge" provision is also satisfied. For that reason, the plaintiffs urge the Court to hold that the red flag provision "requires less specificity" than the actual knowledge provision.

This argument misconstrues the relationship between "actual" knowledge and "red flag" knowledge. It is true that "we are required to 'disfavor interpretations of statutes that render language superfluous.'" *Conn. ex rel. Blumenthal v. U.S. Dep't of the Interior* (2d Cir. 2000). But contrary to the plaintiffs' assertions, construing § 512(c)(1)(A) to require actual knowledge or awareness of specific instances of infringement does not render the red flag provision superfluous. The phrase "actual knowledge," which appears in

§ 512(c)(1)(A)(i), is frequently used to denote subjective belief. By contrast, courts often invoke the language of "facts or circumstances," which appears in § 512(c)(1)(A)(ii), in discussing an objective reasonableness standard.

The difference between actual and red flag knowledge is thus not between specific and generalized knowledge, but instead between a subjective and an objective standard. In other words, the actual knowledge provision turns on whether the provider actually or "subjectively" knew of specific infringement, while the red flag provision turns on whether the provider was subjectively aware of facts that would have made the specific infringement "objectively" obvious to a reasonable person. The red flag provision, because it incorporates an objective standard, is not swallowed up by the actual knowledge provision under our construction of the § 512(c) safe harbor. Both provisions do independent work, and both apply only to specific instances of infringement.

The limited body of case law interpreting the knowledge provisions of the § 512(c) safe harbor comports with our view of the specificity requirement. Most recently, a panel of the Ninth Circuit addressed the scope of § 512(c) in *UMG Recordings, Inc. v. Shelter Capital Partners LLC* (9th Cir. 2011), a copyright infringement case against Veoh Networks, a video-hosting service similar to YouTube. As in this case, various music publishers brought suit against the service provider, claiming direct and secondary copyright infringement based on the presence of unauthorized content on the website, and the website operator sought refuge in the § 512(c) safe harbor. The Court of Appeals affirmed the district court's determination on summary judgment that the website operator was entitled to safe harbor protection. With respect to the actual knowledge provision, the panel declined to "adopt[] a broad conception of the knowledge requirement," holding instead that the safe harbor "[r]equir[es] specific knowledge of particular infringing activity." The Court of Appeals "reach[ed] the same conclusion" with respect to the red flag provision, noting that "[w]e do not place the burden of determining whether [materials] are actually illegal on a service provider."

Although *Shelter Capital* contains the most explicit discussion of the § 512(c) knowledge provisions, other cases are generally in accord. While we decline to adopt the reasoning of those decisions in toto, we note that no court has embraced the contrary proposition—urged by the plaintiffs—that the red flag provision "requires less specificity" than the actual knowledge provision.

Based on the text of § 512(c)(1)(A), as well as the limited case law on point, we affirm the District Court's holding that actual knowledge or awareness of facts or circumstances that indicate specific and identifiable instances of infringement will disqualify a service provider from the safe harbor.

2. The Grant of Summary Judgment

The corollary question on appeal is whether, under the foregoing construction of § 512(c)(1)(A), the District Court erred in granting summary judgment to YouTube on the record presented. For the reasons that follow, we hold that although the District Court correctly interpreted § 512(c)(1)(A), summary judgment for the defendants was premature.

i. Specific Knowledge or Awareness

The plaintiffs argue that, even under the District Court's construction of the safe harbor, the record raises material issues of fact regarding YouTube's actual knowledge or "red flag" awareness of specific instances of infringement. To that end, the plaintiffs draw our attention to various estimates regarding the percentage of infringing content on the YouTube website. For example, Viacom cites evidence that YouTube employees conducted website surveys and estimated that 75–80% of all YouTube streams contained copyrighted material. The class plaintiffs similarly claim that Credit Suisse, acting as financial advisor to Google, estimated that more than 60% of YouTube's content was "premium" copyrighted content—and that only 10% of the premium content was authorized. These approximations suggest that the defendants were conscious that significant quantities of material on the YouTube website were infringing. But such estimates are insufficient, standing alone, to create a triable issue of fact as to whether YouTube actually knew, or was aware of facts or circumstances that would indicate, the existence of particular instances of infringement.

Beyond the survey results, the plaintiffs rely upon internal YouTube communications that do refer to particular clips or groups of clips. The class plaintiffs argue that YouTube was aware of specific infringing material because, inter alia, YouTube attempted to search for specific Premier League videos on the site in order to gauge their "value based on video usage." In particular, the class plaintiffs cite a February 7, 2007 e-mail from Patrick Walker, director of video partnerships for Google and YouTube, requesting that his colleagues calculate the number of daily searches for the terms "soccer," "football," and "Premier League" in preparation for a bid on the global rights to Premier League content. On another occasion, Walker requested that any "clearly infringing, official broadcast footage" from a list of top Premier League clubs—including Liverpool Football Club, Chelsea Football Club, Manchester United Football Club, and Arsenal Football Club—be taken down in advance of a meeting with the heads of "several major sports teams and leagues." YouTube ultimately decided not to make a bid for the Premier League rights—but the infringing content allegedly remained on the website.

The record in the Viacom action includes additional examples. For instance, YouTube founder Jawed Karim prepared a report in March 2006 which stated that, "[a]s of today[,] episodes and clips of the following well-known shows can still be found [on YouTube]: Family Guy, South Park, MTV Cribs, Daily Show, Reno 911, [and] Dave Chapelle [sic]." Karim further opined that, "although YouTube is not legally required to monitor content . . . and complies with DMCA takedown requests, we would benefit from preemptively removing content that is blatantly illegal and likely to attract criticism." He also noted that "a more thorough analysis" of the issue would be required. At least some of the TV shows to which Karim referred are owned by Viacom. A reasonable juror could conclude from the March 2006 report that Karim knew of the presence of Viacom-owned material on YouTube, since he presumably located specific clips of the shows in question before he could announce that YouTube hosted the content "[a]s of today." A reasonable juror could also conclude that Karim believed the clips he located to be infringing (since he refers to them as "blatantly illegal"), and that YouTube did not remove the content from the website until conducting "a more thorough analysis," thus exposing the company to liability in the interim.

Furthermore, in a July 4, 2005 e-mail exchange, YouTube founder Chad Hurley sent an e-mail to his co-founders with the subject line "budlight commercials," and stated, "we need to reject these too." Steve Chen responded, "can we please leave these in a bit longer? another week or two can't hurt." Karim also replied, indicating that he "added back in all 28 bud videos." Similarly, in an August 9, 2005 e-mail exchange, Hurley urged his colleagues "to start being diligent about rejecting copyrighted / inappropriate content," noting that "there is a cnn clip of the shuttle clip on the site today, if the boys from Turner would come to the site, they might be pissed?" Again, Chen resisted:

> but we should just keep that stuff on the site. i really don't see what will
> happen. what? someone from cnn sees it? he happens to be someone
> with power? he happens to want to take it down right away. he gets in
> touch with cnn legal. 2 weeks later, we get a cease & desist letter. we

take the video down.

And again, Karim agreed, indicating that "the CNN space shuttle clip, I like. we can remove it once we're bigger and better known, but for now that clip is fine."

Upon a review of the record, we are persuaded that the plaintiffs may have raised a material issue of fact regarding YouTube's knowledge or awareness of specific instances of infringement. The foregoing Premier League e-mails request the identification and removal of "clearly infringing, official broadcast footage." The March 2006 report indicates Karim's awareness of specific clips that he perceived to be "blatantly illegal." Similarly, the Bud Light and space shuttle e-mails refer to particular clips in the context of correspondence about whether to remove infringing material from the website. On these facts, a reasonable juror could conclude that YouTube had actual knowledge of specific infringing activity, or was at least aware of facts or circumstances from which specific infringing activity was apparent. See § 512(c)(1)(A)(i)–(ii). Accordingly, we hold that summary judgment to YouTube on all clips-in-suit, especially in the absence of any detailed examination of the extensive record on summary judgment, was premature. . . .

ii. "Willful Blindness"

The plaintiffs further argue that the District Court erred in granting summary judgment to the defendants despite evidence that YouTube was "willfully blind" to specific infringing activity. On this issue of first impression, we consider the application of the common law willful blindness doctrine in the DMCA context.

"The principle that willful blindness is tantamount to knowledge is hardly novel." *Tiffany (NJ) Inc. v. eBay, Inc.* (2d Cir. 2010). A person is "willfully blind" or engages in "conscious avoidance" amounting to knowledge where the person "'was aware of a high probability of the fact in dispute and consciously avoided confirming that fact.'" *United States v. Aina-Marshall* (2d Cir. 2003). Writing in the trademark infringement context, we have held that "[a] service provider is not . . . permitted willful blindness. When it has reason to suspect that users of its service are infringing a protected mark, it may not shield itself from learning of the particular infringing transactions by looking the other way." *Tiffany*.

The DMCA does not mention willful blindness. As a general matter, we interpret a statute to abrogate a common law principle only if the statute "speak[s] directly to the question addressed by the common law." *Matar v. Dichter* (2d Cir. 2009). The relevant question, therefore, is whether the DMCA "speak[s] directly" to the principle of willful blindness. The DMCA provision most relevant to the abrogation inquiry is § 512(m), which provides that safe harbor protection shall not be conditioned on "a service provider monitoring its service or affirmatively seeking facts indicating infringing activity, except to the extent consistent with a standard technical measure complying with the provisions of subsection (i)." 17 U.S.C. § 512(m)(1). Section 512(m) is explicit: DMCA safe harbor protection cannot be conditioned on affirmative monitoring by a service provider. For that reason, § 512(m) is incompatible with a broad common law duty to monitor or otherwise seek out infringing activity based on general awareness that infringement may be occurring. That fact does not, however, dispose of the abrogation inquiry; as previously noted, willful blindness cannot be defined as an affirmative duty to monitor. Because the statute does not "speak[] directly" to the willful blindness doctrine, § 512(m) limits—but does not abrogate—the doctrine. Accordingly, we hold that the willful blindness doctrine may be applied, in appropriate circumstances, to demonstrate knowledge or awareness of specific instances of infringement under the DMCA.

The District Court cited § 512(m) for the proposition that safe harbor protection does not require affirmative monitoring, but did not expressly address the principle of willful blindness or its relationship to the DMCA safe harbors. As a result, whether the defendants made a "deliberate effort to avoid guilty knowledge," *In re Aimster*, remains a fact question for the District Court to consider in the first instance on remand.

B. Control and Benefit: § 512(c)(1)(B)

Apart from the foregoing knowledge provisions, the § 512(c) safe harbor provides that an eligible service provider must "not receive a financial benefit directly attributable to the infringing activity, in a case in which the service provider has the right and ability to control such activity." 17 U.S.C. § 512(c)(1)(B). The District Court addressed this issue in a single paragraph, quoting from § 512(c)(1)(B), the so-called "control and benefit" provision, and concluding that "[t]he 'right and ability to control' the activity requires knowledge of it, which must be item-specific." For the reasons that follow, we hold that the District Court erred by importing a specific knowledge requirement into the control and benefit provision, and we therefore remand for further fact-finding on the issue of control.

1. "Right and Ability to Control" Infringing Activity

On appeal, the parties advocate two competing constructions of the "right and ability to control" infringing activity. 17 U.S.C. § 512(c)(1)(B). Because each is fatally flawed, we reject both proposed constructions in favor of a fact-based inquiry to be conducted in the first instance by the District Court.

The first construction, pressed by the defendants, is the one adopted by the District Court, which held that "the provider must know of the particular case before he can control it." The Ninth Circuit recently agreed, holding that "until [the service provider] becomes aware of specific unauthorized material, it cannot exercise its 'power or authority' over the specific infringing item. In practical terms, it does not have the kind of ability to control infringing activity the statute contemplates." *UMG Recordings, Inc. v. Shelter Capital Partners LLC* (9th Cir. 2011). The trouble with this construction is that importing a specific knowledge requirement into § 512(c)(1)(B) renders the control provision duplicative of § 512(c)(1)(A). Any service provider that has item-specific knowledge of infringing activity and thereby obtains financial benefit would already be excluded from the safe harbor under § 512(c)(1)(A) for having specific knowledge of infringing material and failing to effect expeditious removal. No additional service provider would be excluded by § 512(c)(1)(B) that was not already excluded by § 512(c)(1)(A). Because statutory interpretations that render language superfluous are disfavored, we reject the District Court's interpretation of the control provision.

The second construction, urged by the plaintiffs, is that the control provision codifies the common law doctrine of vicarious copyright liability. The common law imposes liability for vicarious copyright infringement "[w]hen the right and ability to supervise coalesce with an obvious and direct financial interest in the exploitation of copyrighted materials—even in the absence of actual knowledge that the copyright mono[poly] is being impaired." *Shapiro, Bernstein & Co. v. H.L. Green Co.* (2d Cir. 1963). To support their codification argument, the plaintiffs rely on a House Report relating to a preliminary version of the DMCA: "The 'right and ability to control' language . . . codifies the second element of vicarious liability. . . . Subparagraph (B) is intended to preserve existing case law that examines all relevant aspects of the relationship between the primary and secondary infringer." H.R.Rep. No. 105-551(I), at 26 (1998). In response, YouTube notes that the codification reference was omitted from the committee reports describing the final legislation, and that Congress ultimately abandoned any attempt to "embark[] upon a wholesale clarification" of vicarious liability, electing instead "to create a series of 'safe harbors' for certain common activities of service providers." S.Rep. No. 105-190, at 19.

Happily, the future of digital copyright law does not turn on the confused legislative history of the control provision. The general rule with respect to common law codification is that when "Congress uses terms that have accumulated settled meaning under the common law, a court must infer, unless the statute otherwise dictates, that Congress means to incorporate the established meaning of those terms." *Neder v. United States* (1999). Under the common law vicarious liability standard, "'[t]he ability to block infringers' access to a particular environment for any reason whatsoever is evidence of the right and ability to supervise.'" *Arista Records LLC v. Usenet.com, Inc.* (S.D.N.Y. 2009). To adopt that principle in the DMCA context, however, would render the statute internally inconsistent. Section 512(c) actually presumes that service providers have the ability to "block . . . access" to infringing material. Indeed, a service provider who has knowledge or awareness of infringing material or who receives a takedown notice from a copyright holder is required to "remove, or disable access to, the material" in order to claim the benefit of the safe harbor. 17 U.S.C. § 512(c)(1)(A)(iii) & (C). But in taking such action, the service provider would—in the plaintiffs' analysis—be admitting the "right and ability to control" the infringing material. Thus, the prerequisite to safe harbor protection under § 512(c)(1)(A)(iii) & (C) would at the same time be a disqualifier under § 512(c)(1)(B).

Moreover, if Congress had intended § 512(c)(1)(B) to be coextensive with vicarious liability, "the statute could have accomplished that result in a more direct manner." *Shelter Capital*.

It is conceivable that Congress . . . intended that [service providers] which receive a financial benefit directly attributable to the infringing activity would not, under any circumstances, be able to qualify for the subsection (c) safe harbor. But if that was indeed their intention, it would have been far simpler and much more straightforward to simply say as much.

In any event, the foregoing tension—elsewhere described as a "predicament" and a "catch22"—is sufficient to establish that the control provision "dictates" a departure from the common law vicarious liability standard. Accordingly, we conclude that the "right and ability to control" infringing activity under § 512(c)(1)(B) "requires something more than the ability to remove or block access to materials posted on a service provider's website." *MP3tunes, LLC*. The remaining—and more difficult—question is how to define the "something more" that is required.

To date, only one court has found that a service provider had the right and ability to control infringing activity under § 512(c)(1)(B). In *Perfect 10, Inc. v. Cybernet Ventures, Inc.* (C.D. Cal. 2002), the court found control where the service provider instituted a monitoring program by which user websites received "detailed instructions regard[ing] issues of layout, appearance, and content." The service provider also forbade certain types of content and refused access to users who failed to comply with its instructions. Similarly, inducement of copyright infringement under *Metro-Goldwyn-Mayer Studios Inc. v. Grokster, Ltd.* (2005), which "premises liability on purposeful, culpable expression and conduct," might also rise to the level of control under § 512(c)(1)(B). Both of these examples involve a service provider exerting substantial influence on the activities of users, without necessarily—or even frequently—acquiring knowledge of specific infringing activity.

In light of our holding that § 512(c)(1)(B) does not include a specific knowledge requirement, we think it prudent to remand to the District Court to consider in the first instance whether the plaintiffs have adduced sufficient evidence to allow a reasonable jury to conclude that YouTube had the right and ability to control the infringing activity and received a financial benefit directly attributable to that activity. . . .

Questions:

1.) Explain succinctly why the court finds that § 512(c)'s limits are not the same as those imposed by vicarious liability.

2.) Is § 512(c) a limit against direct infringement? Secondary infringement? Both?

3.) Copyright holders in the entertainment industries were outraged by the YouTube ruling. Imagine you are acting for the RIAA and MPAA. What is your principal critique?

4.) Explain what "red flag knowledge" means. Use examples.

5.) YouTube itself has now implemented a fascinating, and apparently effective, system called Content ID, which allows rights-holders to register digital fingerprints of the works they own with YouTube. If such a work is subsequently uploaded to YouTube by someone else, Content ID allows the rights-holder to block, track or monetize the work. Blocking the work keeps it off YouTube. Tracking the work gives the rights-holders a wealth of valuable demographic data from YouTube's files—people who watch Justin Bieber also love Katy Perry. Serves them right. (In the academic literature, this is referred to as "mutually assured desecration.") Those who listen to Tori Amos are likely to have ineffectual constitutional advocates, and so on. Rights holders who choose to "monetize" the videos will get a share of any advertisements played alongside the video. All of this is done through code (software recognition of uploaded video) and contract (agreements with rightsholders). What does all this have to say about the future of copyright law? To the fair use provisions in particular? To the law of secondary liability? To the meaning of § 512?

CHAPTER FIFTEEN

Anti-Circumvention:
A New Statutory Scheme

§ 1201. Circumvention of copyright protection systems

(a) Violations Regarding Circumvention of Technological Measures

(1)(A) No person shall circumvent a technological measure that effectively controls access to a work protected under this title. The prohibition contained in the preceding sentence shall take effect at the end of the 2-year period beginning on the date of the enactment of this chapter. . . .

(2) No person shall manufacture, import, offer to the public, provide, or otherwise traffic in any technology, product, service, device, component, or part thereof, that—

(A) is primarily designed or produced for the purpose of circumventing a technological measure that effectively controls access to a work protected under this title;

(B) has only limited commercially significant purpose or use other than to circumvent a technological measure that effectively controls access to a work protected under this title; or

(C) is marketed by that person or another acting in concert with that person with that person's knowledge for use in circumventing a technological measure that effectively controls access to a work protected under this title.

(3) As used in this subsection—

(A) to "circumvent a technological measure" means to descramble a scrambled work, to decrypt an encrypted work, or otherwise to avoid, bypass, remove, deactivate, or impair a technological measure, without the authority of the copyright owner; and

(B) a technological measure "effectively controls access to a work" if the measure, in the ordinary course of its operation, requires the application of information, or a process or a treatment, with the authority of the copyright owner, to gain access to the work.

(b) Additional Violations

(1) No person shall manufacture, import, offer to the public, provide, or otherwise traffic in any technology, product, service, device, component, or part thereof, that—

(A) is primarily designed or produced for the purpose of circumventing protection afforded by a technological measure that effectively protects a right of a copyright owner under this title in a work or a portion thereof;

(B) has only limited commercially significant purpose or use other than to circumvent protection afforded by a technological measure that effectively protects a right of a copyright owner under this title in a work or a portion thereof; or

(C) is marketed by that person or another acting in concert with that person with that person's knowledge for use in circumventing protection afforded by a technological measure that effectively protects a right of a copyright owner under this title in a work or a portion thereof.

(2) As used in this subsection—

(A) to "circumvent protection afforded by a technological measure" means avoiding, bypassing, removing, deactivating, or otherwise impairing a technological measure; and

(B) a technological measure "effectively protects a right of a copyright owner under this title" if the measure, in the ordinary course of its operation, prevents, restricts, or otherwise limits the exercise of a right of a copyright owner under this title.

(c) Other Rights, Etc., Not Affected.—

(1) Nothing in this section shall affect rights, remedies, limitations, or defenses to copyright infringement, including fair use, under this title. . . .

Introduction

The Digital Millennium Copyright Act ("DMCA") was passed in 1998 with the purported mission of "updating copyright law for the digital age." In the last chapter, you read about one of its key provisions—the safe harbors for service providers in section 512. As explained by the legislative history, these *limited* liability in order to "ensure[] that the efficiency of the Internet will continue to improve and that the variety and quality of services on the Internet will continue to expand." This chapter explores the countervailing provision of the DMCA that *expanded* potential liability. Quoting again from the legislative history: "Due to the ease with which digital works can be copied and distributed worldwide virtually instantaneously, copyright owners will hesitate to make their works readily available on the Internet without reasonable assurance that they will be protected against massive piracy. [This legislation] provides this protection. . . ."

Specifically, Section 1201 of the DMCA added legal protection for "technological measures" employed by copyright owners either to prevent unauthorized access to their works ("access controls"), or to prevent copying, distribution, or other uses of their works that might infringe their exclusive rights ("rights controls"). You have probably encountered such technological measures—often referred to as "digital rights management" or "DRM." They might prevent you from "ripping" streaming audio or video, modding video games, installing software on unauthorized devices, or printing and sharing eBooks beyond certain limitations. Which of these do you think are access controls, and which are rights controls?

Section 1201 can be difficult to parse; to assist you with understanding its structure, its basic provisions are summarized in the chart on the following page.

Section 1201(a)(1)(A) (top left) prohibits users from circumventing technological measures that control access to copyrighted works. This focus on access was something new; before the DMCA, copyright law regulated *uses* that were reserved to rights holders by § 106, but did not regulate *access* to their works.

§ 1201(a)(1)(A)—user prohibition	§ 1201(a)(2)—trafficking ban
Makes it illegal for a person to "circumvent a technological measure" that "effectively controls access" to a copyrighted work	Prohibits *trafficking* in tools that enable circumvention of *access* controls
[Old-school copyright infringement: Person infringes the copyright owner's § 106 rights of reproduction, distribution, making derivative works, public performance or display]	§ 1201(b)(1)—additional violations Prohibits *trafficking* in tools that enable circumvention of technological measures that protect the copyright owner's § 106 *rights*

Section 1201 also added, in the right hand column, two provisions that go beyond the user, and prohibit anyone from "trafficking" in tools that defeat either access controls (§ 1201(a)(2)) or rights controls (§ 1201(b)(1)). For example, if the digital rights management (DRM) over your eBook prevents you from copying the book you just bought, a program that deactivates the DRM and allows you to store the book in an unprotected format would implicate § 1201(b)(1). Why? Because that DRM controlled *reproduction*, or copying, not access. By comparison, an "unlock" code that lets you watch a French Region 2 DVD on your American Region 1 DVD player would trigger § 1201(a)(2) because it gets around a measure that prevents *access* to the French film. (For those who haven't encountered "region coding," this is a technological measure used to geographically segment the movie market, so that customers in a given region can only watch movies officially released there.) These distinctions are not always clear-cut however; many technological measures both control access and protect § 106 rights. The tools that circumvent them could therefore violate both §§ 1201(a)(2) and (b)(1).

Moving into more contested territory: inevitably, many access controls will block both illegal and *legal* uses of a copyrighted work. DVD encryption might prevent you from making an illicit copy, but might also prevent you from excerpting a short clip for your class presentation within the bounds of "fair use." Can you be held liable for violating the DMCA if you decrypt the DVD in order to make a noninfringing use? What if someone else "traffics" in a tool—say, a decryption program—that allows you to make the noninfringing use; can that tool be enjoined? The cases in this chapter grapple with such questions, both in terms of statutory interpretation, and adherence with the Constitution. Does the language and structure of § 1201 flatly ban the circumvention of access controls, even when circumvention is necessary to engage in fair use? If so, can the DMCA be constitutional, when (as you read in *Eldred* and *Golan*) fair use is one of the two "traditional contours" that saves copyright law from running afoul of the First Amendment? Of course, the dangers might run the other way if a court were to allow certain circumvention tools in order to enable noninfringing uses: a decryption program that allows fair use could also be used to infringe copyright. Do we salvage user rights (such as fair use) at the expense of allowing some infringement? Or do we impose a blanket prohibition on circumvention at the expense of impinging on user rights?

As you have seen in previous chapters, inserting computer code into the mix introduces additional complexities. First, in terms of potential *claims*, the fact that many everyday products contain copyrightable code leads to some interesting fact patterns. If I make a garage door opener that contains copyrighted code, and you develop a generic hand-held transmitter that—in order to open the garage door—has to bypass a technological control to access that code, have you violated the DMCA? Would you expect the DMCA to have anything to do with garage door openers? (This is a real case, and it's in your readings.)

By enjoining the distribution of certain types of computer code, does § 1201 run into First Amendment issues? Let's say the defendant's allegedly infringing *tool*, a DVD decryption program, enables circumvention. If the DMCA enjoins the distribution of that decryption program under its anti-trafficking rules, is it unconstitutionally suppressing speech? Is computer code "speech"? How would you frame the issue so that it was, or was not? (This case is also in the readings. Also, a heads' up to gamers: the final case in this chapter is about World of Warcraft.)

The exceptions in DMCA § 1201 are beyond the scope of this chapter, but a few things are worth mentioning here. Sections 1201(a)(1)(B)–(E) spell out an administrative rulemaking proceeding that takes place every three years and is supposed to enumerate certain "classes of works" for which circumvention (just the act of circumvention, not the tools enabling it) is allowed in order to make certain "noninfringing uses." In practice, these rulemakings have only yielded a handful of narrow exceptions. (They have never granted many of the exceptions you might expect, such as allowing owners of lawfully purchased DVDs to circumvent in order to make backup copies or watch them on DVD players from other regions.) Moreover, any exceptions expire after 3 years unless proponents make a new evidentiary showing that they're still warranted. For example, the exception for "jailbreaking" smartphones in order to install third party applications has been renewed several times. However, circumventing to "*unlock*" mobile phones in order to connect to a different wireless network was allowed in 2009 but then curtailed in 2012. In 2014, Congress stepped in to overrule that 2012 determination by passing the "Unlocking Consumer Choice and Wireless Competition Act," a new law that allows mobile phone unlocking on a permanent basis. (Yes, the 2014 Congress could not agree on much, but there was bipartisan support for reversing the DMCA rulemaking.) Sections 1201(d) through (j) of the DMCA provide other limited exceptions for libraries, archives, and educational institutions; law enforcement; reverse engineering; encryption research; protecting minors; disabling cookies; and security testing. They vary in scope, and some are extremely circumscribed (read the text of § 1201(d) for an example of this).

James Boyle, The Public Domain
Please read The Public Domain *pp. 83–89*

Imagine that a bustling group of colonists has just moved into a new area, a huge, unexplored plain. (Again, assume the native inhabitants have conveniently disappeared.) Some of the colonists want to farm just as they always did in the old country. "Good fences make good neighbors" is their motto. Others, inspired by the wide-open spaces around them, declare that this new land needs new ways. They want to let their cattle roam as they will; their slogan is "Protect the open range." In practice, the eventual result is a mixture of the two regimes. Fields under cultivation can be walled off but there is a right of passage through the farmers' lands for all who want it, so long as no damage is done. This means travelers do not need to make costly and inefficient detours around each farm. In the long run, these "public roads" actually increase the value of the private property through which they pass. They also let the ranchers move their cattle around from one area of pasture to another. The ranchers become strong proponents of "public, open highways" (though some people muse darkly that they do very well out of that rule). Still, most people want open highways; the system seems to work pretty well, in fact. . . .

Read the rest

1.) Anti-Circumvention, Fair Use, and the First Amendment

Universal City Studios, Inc. v. Corley
273 F.3d 429 (2d Cir. 2001)

JON O. NEWMAN, Circuit Judge.

When the Framers of the First Amendment prohibited Congress from making any law "abridging the freedom of speech," they were not thinking about computers, computer programs, or the Internet. But neither were they thinking about radio, television, or movies. Just as the inventions at the beginning and middle of the 20th century presented new First Amendment issues, so does the cyber revolution at the end of that century. This appeal raises significant First Amendment issues concerning one aspect of computer technology—encryption to protect materials in digital form from unauthorized access. The appeal challenges the constitutionality of the Digital Millennium Copyright Act ("DMCA"), 17 U.S.C. § 1201 *et seq.* and the validity of an injunction entered to enforce the DMCA.

Defendant-Appellant Eric C. Corley and his company, 2600 Enterprises, Inc., appeal from the amended final judgment of the United States District Court for the Southern District of New York enjoining them from various actions concerning a decryption program known as "DeCSS." The injunction primarily bars the Appellants from posting DeCSS on their web site and from knowingly linking their web site to any other web site on which DeCSS is posted. We affirm.

Introduction

This appeal concerns the anti-trafficking provisions of the DMCA, which Congress enacted in 1998 to strengthen copyright protection in the digital age. Fearful that the ease with which pirates could copy and distribute a copyrightable work in digital form was overwhelming the capacity of conventional copyright enforcement to find and enjoin unlawfully copied material, Congress sought to combat copyright piracy in its earlier stages, before the work was even copied. The DMCA therefore backed with legal sanctions the efforts of copyright owners to protect their works from piracy behind digital walls such as encryption codes or password protections. In so doing, Congress targeted not only those pirates who would *circumvent* these digital walls (the "anti-circumvention provisions," contained in 17 U.S.C. § 1201(a)(1)), but also anyone who would *traffic* in a technology primarily designed to circumvent a digital wall (the "anti-trafficking provisions," contained in 17 U.S.C. §§ 1201(a)(2), (b)(1)).

Corley publishes a print magazine and maintains an affiliated web site geared towards "hackers," a digital-era term often applied to those interested in techniques for circumventing protections of computers and computer data from unauthorized access. The so-called hacker community includes serious computer-science scholars conducting research on protection techniques, computer buffs intrigued by the challenge of trying to circumvent access-limiting devices or perhaps hoping to promote security by exposing flaws in protection techniques, mischief-makers interested in disrupting computer operations, and thieves, including copyright infringers who want to acquire copyrighted material (for personal use or resale) without paying for it.

In November 1999, Corley posted a copy of the decryption computer program

"DeCSS" on his web site, http://www.2600.com.[2] DeCSS is designed to circumvent "CSS," the encryption technology that motion picture studios place on DVDs to prevent the unauthorized viewing and copying of motion pictures. Corley also posted on his web site links to other web sites where DeCSS could be found.

Plaintiffs-Appellees are eight motion picture studios that brought an action . . . seeking injunctive relief against Corley under the DMCA. . . . [T]he District Court entered a permanent injunction barring Corley from posting DeCSS on his web site or from knowingly linking via a hyperlink to any other web site containing DeCSS. The District Court rejected Corley's constitutional attacks on the statute and the injunction.

Corley renews his constitutional challenges on appeal. Specifically, he argues primarily that: (1) the DMCA oversteps limits in the Copyright Clause on the duration of copyright protection; (2) the DMCA as applied to his dissemination of DeCSS violates the First Amendment because computer code is "speech" entitled to full First Amendment protection and the DMCA fails to survive the exacting scrutiny accorded statutes that regulate "speech"; and (3) the DMCA violates the First Amendment and the Copyright Clause by unduly obstructing the "fair use" of copyrighted materials. Corley also argues that the statute is susceptible to, and should therefore be given, a narrow interpretation that avoids alleged constitutional objections.

Background

For decades, motion picture studios have made movies available for viewing at home in what is called "analog" format. Movies in this format are placed on videotapes, which can be played on a video cassette recorder ("VCR"). In the early 1990s, the studios began to consider the possibility of distributing movies in digital form as well. Movies in digital form are placed on disks, known as DVDs, which can be played on a DVD player (either a stand-alone device or a component of a computer). DVDs offer advantages over analog tapes, such as improved visual and audio quality, larger data capacity, and greater durability. However, the improved quality of a movie in a digital format brings with it the risk that a virtually perfect copy, *i.e.,* one that will not lose perceptible quality in the copying process, can be readily made at the click of a computer control and instantly distributed to countless recipients throughout the world over the Internet. This case arises out of the movie industry's efforts to respond to this risk by invoking the anti-trafficking provisions of the DMCA.

I. CSS

The movie studios were reluctant to release movies in digital form until they were confident they had in place adequate safeguards against piracy of their copyrighted movies. The studios took several steps to minimize the piracy threat. First, they settled on the DVD as the standard digital medium for home distribution of movies. The studios then sought an encryption scheme to protect movies on DVDs. They enlisted the help of members of the consumer electronics and computer industries, who in mid-1996 developed the Content Scramble System ("CSS"). CSS is an encryption scheme that employs an algorithm configured by a set of "keys" to encrypt a DVD's contents. The algorithm is a type of mathematical formula for transforming the contents of the movie file into gibberish; the "keys" are in actuality strings of 0's and 1's that serve as values for the mathematical

---

[2] "2600" has special significance to the hacker community. It is the hertz frequency of a signal that some hackers formerly used to explore the entire telephone system from "operator mode," which was triggered by the transmission of a 2600 hertz tone across a telephone line, or to place telephone calls without incurring long-distance toll charges. One such user reportedly discovered that the sound of a toy whistle from a box of Cap'n Crunch cereal matched the telephone company's 2600 hertz tone perfectly.

formula. Decryption in the case of CSS requires a set of "player keys" contained in compliant DVD players, as well as an understanding of the CSS encryption algorithm. Without the player keys and the algorithm, a DVD player cannot access the contents of a DVD. With the player keys and the algorithm, a DVD player can display the movie on a television or a computer screen, but does not give a viewer the ability to use the copy function of the computer to copy the movie or to manipulate the digital content of the DVD.

The studios developed a licensing scheme for distributing the technology to manufacturers of DVD players. Player keys and other information necessary to the CSS scheme were given to manufacturers of DVD players for an administrative fee. In exchange for the licenses, manufacturers were obliged to keep the player keys confidential. Manufacturers were also required in the licensing agreement to prevent the transmission of "CSS data" (a term undefined in the licensing agreement) from a DVD drive to any "internal recording device," including, presumably, a computer hard drive.

With encryption technology and licensing agreements in hand, the studios began releasing movies on DVDs in 1997, and DVDs quickly gained in popularity, becoming a significant source of studio revenue. In 1998, the studios secured added protection against DVD piracy when Congress passed the DMCA, which prohibits the development or use of technology designed to circumvent a technological protection measure, such as CSS. The pertinent provisions of the DMCA are examined in greater detail below.

II. DeCSS

In September 1999, Jon Johansen, a Norwegian teenager, collaborating with two unidentified individuals he met on the Internet, reverse-engineered a licensed DVD player designed to operate on the Microsoft operating system, and culled from it the player keys and other information necessary to decrypt CSS. The record suggests that Johansen was trying to develop a DVD player operable on Linux, an alternative operating system that did not support any licensed DVD players at that time. In order to accomplish this task, Johansen wrote a decryption program executable on Microsoft's operating system. That program was called, appropriately enough, "DeCSS."

If a user runs the DeCSS program . . . with a DVD in the computer's disk drive, DeCSS will decrypt the DVD's CSS protection, allowing the user to copy the DVD's files and place the copy on the user's hard drive. The result is a very large computer file that can be played on a non-CSS-compliant player and copied, manipulated, and transferred just like any other computer file. DeCSS comes complete with a fairly user-friendly interface that helps the user select from among the DVD's files and assign the decrypted file a location on the user's hard drive. The quality of the resulting decrypted movie is "virtually identical" to that of the encrypted movie on the DVD. And the file produced by DeCSS, while large, can be compressed to a manageable size by a compression software called "DivX," available at no cost on the Internet. This compressed file can be copied onto a DVD, or transferred over the Internet (with some patience).

Johansen posted the executable object code, but not the source code, for DeCSS on his web site. . . . Within months of its appearance in executable form on Johansen's web site, DeCSS was widely available on the Internet, in both object code and various forms of source code.

In November 1999, Corley wrote and placed on his web site, 2600.com, an article about the DeCSS phenomenon. His web site is an auxiliary to the print magazine, *2600: The Hacker Quarterly*, which Corley has been publishing since 1984. As the name suggests, the magazine is designed for "hackers," as is the web site. While the magazine and the web site cover some issues of general interest to computer users—such as threats to online privacy—the focus of the publications is on the vulnerability of computer security systems, and more specifically, how to exploit that vulnerability in order to circumvent the security systems. Representative articles explain how to steal an Internet domain name and how to break into the computer systems at Federal Express.

Corley's article about DeCSS detailed how CSS was cracked, and described the movie industry's efforts to shut down web sites posting DeCSS. It also explained that DeCSS could be used to copy DVDs. At the end of the article, the Defendants posted copies of the object and source code of DeCSS. In Corley's words, he added the code to the story because "in a journalistic world, . . . [y]ou have to show your evidence . . . and particularly in the magazine that I work for, people want to see specifically what it is that we are referring to," including "what evidence . . . we have" that there is in fact technology that circumvents CSS. Writing about DeCSS without including the DeCSS code would have been, to Corley, "analogous to printing a story about a picture and not printing the picture." Corley also added to the article links that he explained would take the reader to other web sites where DeCSS could be found.

2600.com was only one of hundreds of web sites that began posting DeCSS near the end of 1999. The movie industry tried to stem the tide by sending cease-and-desist letters to many of these sites. These efforts met with only partial success; a number of sites refused to remove DeCSS. In January 2000, the studios filed this lawsuit.

III. The DMCA

The DMCA was enacted in 1998 to implement the World Intellectual Property Organization Copyright Treaty ("WIPO Treaty"), which requires contracting parties to "provide adequate legal protection and effective legal remedies against the circumvention of effective technological measures that are used by authors in connection with the exercise of their rights under this Treaty or the Berne Convention and that restrict acts, in respect of their works, which are not authorized by the authors concerned or permitted by law." Even before the treaty, Congress had been devoting attention to the problems faced by copyright enforcement in the digital age. Hearings on the topic have spanned several years. This legislative effort resulted in the DMCA.

The Act contains three provisions targeted at the circumvention of technological protections. The first is subsection 1201(a)(1)(A), the anti-circumvention provision. This provision prohibits a person from "circumvent[ing] a technological measure that effectively controls access to a work protected under [Title 17, governing copyright]." The Librarian of Congress is required to promulgate regulations every three years exempting from this subsection individuals who would otherwise be "adversely affected" in "their ability to make noninfringing uses." 17 U.S.C. §§ 1201(a)(1)(B)–(E).

The second and third provisions are subsections 1201(a)(2) and 1201(b)(1), the "anti-trafficking provisions." Subsection 1201(a)(2), the provision at issue in this case, provides:

> No person shall manufacture, import, offer to the public, provide, or otherwise traffic in any technology, product, service, device, component, or part thereof, that—
>
>> (A) is primarily designed or produced for the purpose of circumventing a technological measure that effectively controls access to a work protected under this title;
>>
>> (B) has only limited commercially significant purpose or use other than to circumvent a technological measure that effectively controls access to a work protected under this title; or
>>
>> (C) is marketed by that person or another acting in concert with that

person with that person's knowledge for use in circumventing a technological measure that effectively controls access to a work protected under this title.

To "circumvent a technological measure" is defined, in pertinent part, as "to descramble a scrambled work . . . or otherwise to . . . bypass . . . a technological measure, without the authority of the copyright owner." § 1201(a)(3)(A).

Subsection 1201(b)(1) is similar to subsection 1201(a)(2), except that subsection 1201(a)(2) covers those who traffic in technology that can circumvent "a technological measure *that effectively controls access* to a work protected under" Title 17, whereas subsection 1201(b)(1) covers those who traffic in technology that can circumvent "protection afforded by a technological measure *that effectively protects a right of a copyright owner* under" Title 17. §§ 1201(a)(2), (b)(1) (emphases added). In other words, although both subsections prohibit trafficking in a circumvention technology, the focus of subsection 1201(a)(2) is circumvention of technologies designed to *prevent access* to a work, and the focus of subsection 1201(b)(1) is circumvention of technologies designed to *permit access* to a work but *prevent copying* of the work or some other act that infringes a copyright. Subsection 1201(a)(1) differs from both of these anti-trafficking subsections in that it targets the use of a circumvention technology, not the trafficking in such a technology.

The DMCA contains exceptions for schools and libraries that want to use circumvention technologies to determine whether to purchase a copyrighted product, 17 U.S.C. § 1201(d); individuals using circumvention technology "for the sole purpose" of trying to achieve "interoperability" of computer programs through reverse-engineering, § 1201(f); encryption research aimed at identifying flaws in encryption technology, if the research is conducted to advance the state of knowledge in the field, § 1201(g); and several other exceptions not relevant here.

The DMCA creates civil remedies, § 1203, and criminal sanctions, § 1204. It specifically authorizes a court to "grant temporary and permanent injunctions on such terms as it deems reasonable to prevent or restrain a violation." § 1203(b)(1).

IV. Procedural History

. . . After a trial on the merits, the [District] Court issued a comprehensive opinion, and granted a permanent injunction.

The Court explained that the Defendants' posting of DeCSS on their web site clearly falls within section 1201(a)(2)(A) of the DMCA, rejecting as spurious their claim that CSS is not a technological measure that "effectively controls access to a work" because it was so easily penetrated by Johansen, and as irrelevant their contention that DeCSS was designed to create a Linux-platform DVD player. The Court also held that the Defendants cannot avail themselves of any of the DMCA's exceptions, and that the alleged importance of DeCSS to certain fair uses of encrypted copyrighted material was immaterial to their statutory liability. The Court went on to hold that when the Defendants "proclaimed on their own site that DeCSS could be had by clicking on the hyperlinks" on their site, they were trafficking in DeCSS, and therefore liable for their linking as well as their posting.

Turning to the Defendants' numerous constitutional arguments, the Court first held that computer code like DeCSS is "speech" that is "protected" (in the sense of "covered") by the First Amendment, but that because the DMCA is targeting the "functional" aspect of that speech, it is "content neutral," and the intermediate scrutiny of *United States v. O'Brien* (1968), applies. The Court concluded that the DMCA survives this scrutiny, and also rejected prior restraint, overbreadth, and vagueness challenges. . . .

Discussion
I. Narrow Construction to Avoid Constitutional Doubt

The Appellants first argue that, because their constitutional arguments are at least substantial, we should interpret the statute narrowly so as to avoid constitutional problems. They identify three different instances of alleged ambiguity in the statute that they claim provide an opportunity for such a narrow interpretation.

First, they contend that subsection 1201(c)(1), which provides that "[n]othing in this section shall affect rights, remedies, limitations or defenses to copyright infringement, including fair use, under this title," can be read to allow the circumvention of encryption technology protecting copyrighted material when the material will be put to "fair uses" exempt from copyright liability. We disagree that subsection 1201(c)(1) permits such a reading. Instead, it simply clarifies that the DMCA targets the *circumvention* of digital walls guarding copyrighted material (and trafficking in circumvention tools), but does not concern itself with the *use* of those materials after circumvention has occurred. Subsection 1201(c)(1) ensures that the DMCA is not read to prohibit the "fair use" of information just because that information was obtained in a manner made illegal by the DMCA. The Appellants' much more expansive interpretation of subsection 1201(c)(1) is not only outside the range of plausible readings of the provision, but is also clearly refuted by the statute's legislative history.[13]

Second, the Appellants urge a narrow construction of the DMCA because of subsection 1201(c)(4), which provides that "[n]othing in this section shall enlarge or diminish any rights of free speech or the press for activities using consumer electronics, telecommunications, or computing products." This language is clearly precatory: Congress could not "diminish" constitutional rights of free speech even if it wished to, and the fact that Congress also expressed a reluctance to "enlarge" those rights cuts against the Appellants' effort to infer a narrowing construction of the Act from this provision.

Third, the Appellants argue that an individual who buys a DVD has the "authority of the copyright owner" to view the DVD, and therefore is exempted from the DMCA pursuant to subsection 1201(a)(3)(A) when the buyer circumvents an encryption technology in order to view the DVD on a competing platform (such as Linux). The basic flaw in this argument is that it misreads subsection 1201(a)(3)(A). That provision exempts from liability those who would "decrypt" an encrypted DVD with the authority of a copyright owner, not those who would "view" a DVD with the authority of a copyright owner. In any event, the Defendants offered no evidence that the Plaintiffs have either explicitly or implicitly authorized DVD buyers to circumvent encryption technology to support use on multiple platforms.[15]

---

[13] The legislative history of the enacted bill makes quite clear that Congress intended to adopt a "balanced" approach to accommodating both piracy and fair use concerns, eschewing the quick fix of simply exempting from the statute all circumventions for fair use. It sought to achieve this goal principally through the use of what it called a "fail-safe" provision in the statute, authorizing the Librarian of Congress to exempt certain users from the anti-circumvention provision when it becomes evident that in practice, the statute is adversely affecting certain kinds of fair use. Congress also sought to implement a balanced approach through statutory provisions that leave limited areas of breathing space for fair use. A good example is subsection 1201(d), which allows a library or educational institution to circumvent a digital wall in order to determine whether it wishes legitimately to obtain the material behind the wall. It would be strange for Congress to open small, carefully limited windows for circumvention to permit fair use in subsection 1201(d) if it then meant to exempt in subsection 1201(c)(1) *any* circumvention necessary for fair use.

[15] Even if the Defendants had been able to offer such evidence, and even if they could have demonstrated that DeCSS was "primarily designed . . . for the purpose of" playing DVDs on multiple platforms (and therefore not for the purpose of "circumventing a technological measure"), a proposition questioned by Judge Kaplan, the Defendants would defeat liability only under subsection 1201(a)(2)(A). They would still be

We conclude that the anti-trafficking and anti-circumvention provisions of the DMCA are not susceptible to the narrow interpretations urged by the Appellants. We therefore proceed to consider the Appellants' constitutional claims.

II. Constitutional Challenge Based on the Copyright Clause

In a footnote to their brief, the Appellants appear to contend that the DMCA, as construed by the District Court, exceeds the constitutional authority of Congress to grant authors copyrights for a "limited time," U.S. Const. art. I, § 8, cl. 8, because it "empower[s] copyright owners to effectively secure perpetual protection by mixing public domain works with copyrighted materials, then locking both up with technological protection measures." This argument is elaborated in the *amici curiae* brief filed by Prof. Julie E. Cohen on behalf of herself and 45 other intellectual property law professors. For two reasons, the argument provides no basis for disturbing the judgment of the District Court.

First, we have repeatedly ruled that arguments presented to us only in a footnote are not entitled to appellate consideration. Although an *amicus* brief can be helpful in elaborating issues properly presented by the parties, it is normally not a method for injecting new issues into an appeal, at least in cases where the parties are competently represented by counsel.

Second, to whatever extent the argument might have merit at some future time in a case with a properly developed record, the argument is entirely premature and speculative at this time on this record. There is not even a claim, much less evidence, that any Plaintiff has sought to prevent copying of public domain works, or that the injunction prevents the Defendants from copying such works. As Judge Kaplan noted, the possibility that encryption would preclude access to public domain works "does not yet appear to be a problem, although it may emerge as one in the future."

III. Constitutional Challenges Based on the First Amendment
A. Applicable Principles

Last year, in one of our Court's first forays into First Amendment law in the digital age, we took an "evolutionary" approach to the task of tailoring familiar constitutional rules to novel technological circumstances, favoring "narrow" holdings that would permit the law to mature on a "case-by-case" basis. In that spirit, we proceed, with appropriate caution, to consider the Appellants' First Amendment challenges by analyzing a series of preliminary issues the resolution of which provides a basis for adjudicating the specific objections to the DMCA and its application to DeCSS. These issues, which we consider only to the extent necessary to resolve the pending appeal, are whether computer code is speech, whether computer programs are speech, the scope of First Amendment protection for computer code, and the scope of First Amendment protection for decryption code. . . .

1. Code as Speech

Communication does not lose constitutional protection as "speech" simply because it is expressed in the language of computer code. Mathematical formulae and musical scores are written in "code," *i.e.,* symbolic notations not comprehensible to the uninitiated, and yet both are covered by the First Amendment. If someone chose to write a novel entirely in computer object code by using strings of 1's and 0's for each letter of each word, the resulting work would be no different for constitutional purposes than if it had been written in English. The "object code" version would be incomprehensible to readers outside the programming community (and tedious to read even for most within the

---

vulnerable to liability under subsection 1201(a)(2)(C), because they "marketed" DeCSS for the copying of DVDs, not just for the playing of DVDs on multiple platforms.

community), but it would be no more incomprehensible than a work written in Sanskrit for those unversed in that language. The undisputed evidence reveals that even pure object code can be, and often is, read and understood by experienced programmers. And source code (in any of its various levels of complexity) can be read by many more. Ultimately, however, the ease with which a work is comprehended is irrelevant to the constitutional inquiry. If computer code is distinguishable from conventional speech for First Amendment purposes, it is not because it is written in an obscure language.

2. Computer Programs as Speech

Of course, computer code is not likely to be the language in which a work of literature is written. Instead, it is primarily the language for programs executable by a computer. These programs are essentially instructions to a computer. In general, programs may give instructions either to perform a task or series of tasks when initiated by a single (or double) click of a mouse or, once a program is operational ("launched"), to manipulate data that the user enters into the computer. Whether computer code that gives a computer instructions is "speech" within the meaning of the First Amendment requires consideration of the scope of the Constitution's protection of speech.

The First Amendment provides that "Congress shall make no law . . . abridging the freedom of speech. . . ." U.S. Const. amend. I. "Speech" is an elusive term, and judges and scholars have debated its bounds for two centuries. Some would confine First Amendment protection to political speech. Others would extend it further to artistic expression.

Whatever might be the merits of these and other approaches, the law has not been so limited. Even dry information, devoid of advocacy, political relevance, or artistic expression, has been accorded First Amendment protection.

Thus, for example, courts have subjected to First Amendment scrutiny restrictions on the dissemination of technical scientific information and scientific research, and attempts to regulate the publication of instructions, see, e.g., United States v. Raymond (7th Cir. 2000) (First Amendment does not protect instructions for violating the tax laws); Herceg v. Hustler Magazine, Inc. (5th Cir. 1987) (First Amendment protects instructions for engaging in a dangerous sex act); United States v. Featherston (5th Cir. 1972) (First Amendment does not protect instructions for building an explosive device).

Computer programs are not exempted from the category of First Amendment speech simply because their instructions require use of a computer. A recipe is no less "speech" because it calls for the use of an oven, and a musical score is no less "speech" because it specifies performance on an electric guitar. Arguably distinguishing computer programs from conventional language instructions is the fact that programs are executable on a computer. But the fact that a program has the capacity to direct the functioning of a computer does not mean that it lacks the additional capacity to convey information, and it is the conveying of information that renders instructions "speech" for purposes of the First Amendment. The information conveyed by most "instructions" is how to perform a task.

Instructions such as computer code, which are intended to be executable by a computer, will often convey information capable of comprehension and assessment by a human being. A programmer reading a program learns information about instructing a computer, and might use this information to improve personal programming skills and perhaps the craft of programming. Moreover, programmers communicating ideas to one another almost inevitably communicate in code, much as musicians use notes. Limiting First Amendment protection of programmers to descriptions of computer code (but not the code itself) would impede discourse among computer scholars, just as limiting protection for musicians to descriptions of musical scores (but not sequences of notes) would impede their exchange of ideas and expression. Instructions that communicate information comprehensible to a human qualify as speech whether the instructions are designed for execution by a computer or a human (or both). . . .

For all of these reasons, we join the other courts that have concluded that computer code, and computer programs constructed from code can merit First Amendment protection, although the scope of such protection remains to be determined.

3. The Scope of First Amendment Protection for Computer Code

Having concluded that computer code conveying information is "speech" within the meaning of the First Amendment, we next consider, to a limited extent, the scope of the protection that code enjoys. As the District Court recognized, the scope of protection for speech generally depends on whether the restriction is imposed because of the content of the speech. Content-based restrictions are permissible only if they serve compelling state interests and do so by the least restrictive means available. A content-neutral restriction is permissible if it serves a substantial governmental interest, the interest is unrelated to the suppression of free expression, and the regulation is narrowly tailored, which "in this context requires . . . that the means chosen do not 'burden substantially more speech than is necessary to further the government's legitimate interests.'" *Turner Broadcasting System, Inc. v. FCC* (1994).

"[G]overnment regulation of expressive activity is 'content neutral' if it is justified without reference to the content of regulated speech." *Hill v. Colorado* (2000). "The government's purpose is the controlling consideration. A regulation that serves purposes unrelated to the content of expression is deemed neutral, even if it has an incidental effect on some speakers or messages but not others." *Ward v. Rock Against Racism* (1989). The Supreme Court's approach to determining content-neutrality appears to be applicable whether what is regulated is expression, conduct, or any "activity" that can be said to combine speech and non-speech elements.

To determine whether regulation of computer code is content-neutral, the initial inquiry must be whether the regulated activity is "sufficiently imbued with elements of communication to fall within the scope of the First . . . Amendment[]." . . . Once a speech component is identified, the inquiry then proceeds to whether the regulation is "justified without reference to the content of regulated speech." *Hill.*

The Appellants vigorously reject the idea that computer code can be regulated according to any different standard than that applicable to pure speech, *i.e.,* speech that lacks a nonspeech component. Although recognizing that code is a series of instructions to a computer, they argue that code is no different, for First Amendment purposes, than blueprints that instruct an engineer or recipes that instruct a cook. We disagree. Unlike a blueprint or a recipe, which cannot yield any functional result without human comprehension of its content, human decision-making, and human action, computer code can instantly cause a computer to accomplish tasks and instantly render the results of those tasks available throughout the world via the Internet. The only human action required to achieve these results can be as limited and instantaneous as a single click of a mouse. These realities of what code is and what its normal functions are require a First Amendment analysis that treats code as combining nonspeech and speech elements, *i.e.,* functional and expressive elements.

We recognize, as did Judge Kaplan, that the functional capability of computer code cannot yield a result until a human being decides to insert the disk containing the code into a computer and causes it to perform its function (or programs a computer to cause the code to perform its function). Nevertheless, this momentary intercession of human action does not diminish the nonspeech component of code, nor render code entirely speech, like a blueprint or a recipe. Judge Kaplan, in a passage that merits extensive quotation, cogently explained why this is especially so with respect to decryption code:

[T]he focus on functionality in order to determine the level of scrutiny is not an inevitable consequence of the speech-conduct distinction. Conduct has immediate effects on the environment. Computer code, on the other hand, no matter how functional, causes a computer to perform the intended operations only if someone uses the code to do so. Hence, one commentator, in a thoughtful article, has maintained that functionality is really "a proxy for effects or harm" and that its adoption as a determinant of the level of scrutiny slides over questions of causation that intervene between the dissemination of a computer program and any harm caused by its use. The characterization of functionality as a proxy for the consequences of use is accurate. But the assumption that the chain of causation is too attenuated to justify the use of functionality to determine the level of scrutiny, at least in this context, is not. Society increasingly depends upon technological means of controlling access to digital files and systems, whether they are military computers, bank records, academic records, copyrighted works or something else entirely. There are far too many who, given any opportunity, will bypass security measures, some for the sheer joy of doing it, some for innocuous reasons, and others for more malevolent purposes. Given the virtually instantaneous and worldwide dissemination widely available via the Internet, the only rational assumption is that once a computer program capable of bypassing such an access control system is disseminated, it will be used. . . . There was a time when copyright infringement could be dealt with quite adequately by focusing on the infringing act. If someone wished to make and sell high quality but unauthorized copies of a copyrighted book, for example, the infringer needed a printing press. The copyright holder, once aware of the appearance of infringing copies, usually was able to trace the copies up the chain of distribution, find and prosecute the infringer, and shut off the infringement at the source. In principle, the digital world is very different. Once a decryption program like DeCSS is written, it quickly can be sent all over the world. Every recipient is capable not only of decrypting and perfectly copying plaintiffs' copyrighted DVDs, but also of retransmitting perfect copies of DeCSS and thus enabling every recipient to do the same. They likewise are capable of transmitting perfect copies of the decrypted DVD. The process potentially is exponential rather than linear. . . . These considerations drastically alter consideration of the causal link between dissemination of computer programs such as this and their illicit use. Causation in the law ultimately involves practical policy judgments. Here, dissemination itself carries very substantial risk of imminent harm because the mechanism is so unusual by which dissemination of means of circumventing access controls to copyrighted works threatens to produce virtually unstoppable infringement of copyright. In consequence, the causal link between the dissemination of circumvention computer programs and their improper use is more than sufficiently close to warrant selection of a level of constitutional scrutiny based on the programs' functionality.

The functionality of computer code properly affects the scope of its First Amendment protection.

4. The Scope of First Amendment Protection for Decryption Code

In considering the scope of First Amendment protection for a decryption program like DeCSS, we must recognize that the essential purpose of encryption code is to prevent unauthorized access. Owners of all property rights are entitled to prohibit access to their property by unauthorized persons. Homeowners can install locks on the doors of their houses. Custodians of valuables can place them in safes. Stores can attach to products security devices that will activate alarms if the products are taken away without purchase. These and similar security devices can be circumvented. Burglars can use skeleton keys to open door locks. Thieves can obtain the combinations to safes. Product security devices can be neutralized.

Our case concerns a security device, CSS computer code, that prevents access by unauthorized persons to DVD movies. The CSS code is embedded in the DVD movie. Access to the movie cannot be obtained unless a person has a device, a licensed DVD player, equipped with computer code capable of decrypting the CSS encryption code. In its basic function, CSS is like a lock on a homeowner's door, a combination of a safe, or a security device attached to a store's products.

DeCSS is computer code that can decrypt CSS. In its basic function, it is like a skeleton key that can open a locked door, a combination that can open a safe, or a device that can neutralize the security device attached to a store's products.[27] DeCSS enables anyone to gain access to a DVD movie without using a DVD player.

The initial use of DeCSS to gain access to a DVD movie creates no loss to movie producers because the initial user must purchase the DVD. However, once the DVD is purchased, DeCSS enables the initial user to copy the movie in digital form and transmit it instantly in virtually limitless quantity, thereby depriving the movie producer of sales. The advent of the Internet creates the potential for instantaneous worldwide distribution of the copied material.

At first glance, one might think that Congress has as much authority to regulate the distribution of computer code to decrypt DVD movies as it has to regulate distribution of skeleton keys, combinations to safes, or devices to neutralize store product security devices. However, despite the evident legitimacy of protection against unauthorized access to DVD movies, just like any other property, regulation of decryption code like DeCSS is challenged in this case because DeCSS differs from a skeleton key in one important respect: it not only is capable of performing the function of unlocking the encrypted DVD movie, it also is a form of communication, albeit written in a language not understood by the general public. As a communication, the DeCSS code has a claim to being "speech," and as "speech," it has a claim to being protected by the First Amendment. But just as the realities of what any computer code can accomplish must inform the scope of its constitutional protection, so the capacity of a decryption program like DeCSS to accomplish unauthorized—indeed, unlawful—access to materials in which the Plaintiffs have intellectual property rights must inform and limit the scope of its First Amendment protection. . . .

B. First Amendment Challenge

The District Court's injunction applies the DMCA to the Defendants by imposing two types of prohibition, both grounded on the anti-trafficking provisions of the DMCA. The first prohibits posting DeCSS or any other technology for circumventing CSS on any Internet web site. The second prohibits knowingly linking any Internet web site to any other web site containing DeCSS. . . .

1. Posting

. . . As a content-neutral regulation with an incidental effect on a speech com-

---

[27] More dramatically, the Government calls DeCSS "a digital crowbar."

ponent, the regulation must serve a substantial governmental interest, the interest must be unrelated to the suppression of free expression, and the incidental restriction on speech must not burden substantially more speech than is necessary to further that interest. The Government's interest in preventing unauthorized access to encrypted copyrighted material is unquestionably substantial, and the regulation of DeCSS by the posting prohibition plainly serves that interest. Moreover, that interest is unrelated to the suppression of free expression. The injunction regulates the posting of DeCSS, regardless of whether DeCSS code contains any information comprehensible by human beings that would qualify as speech. Whether the incidental regulation on speech burdens substantially more speech than is necessary to further the interest in preventing unauthorized access to copyrighted materials requires some elaboration.

Posting DeCSS on the Appellants' web site makes it instantly available at the click of a mouse to any person in the world with access to the Internet, and such person can then instantly transmit DeCSS to anyone else with Internet access. Although the prohibition on posting prevents the Appellants from conveying to others the speech component of DeCSS, the Appellants have not suggested, much less shown, any technique for barring them from making this instantaneous worldwide distribution of a decryption code that makes a lesser restriction on the code's speech component. It is true that the Government has alternative means of prohibiting unauthorized access to copyrighted materials. For example, it can create criminal and civil liability for those who gain unauthorized access, and thus it can be argued that the restriction on posting DeCSS is not absolutely necessary to preventing unauthorized access to copyrighted materials. But a content-neutral regulation need not employ the least restrictive means of accomplishing the governmental objective. It need only avoid burdening "substantially more speech than is necessary to further the government's legitimate interests." The prohibition on the Defendants' posting of DeCSS satisfies that standard.

2. Linking

In considering linking, we need to clarify the sense in which the injunction prohibits such activity. . . . [T]he injunction . . . does not define "linking." Nevertheless, it is evident from the District Court's opinion that it is concerned with "hyperlinks." . . . The hyperlink can appear on a screen (window) as text, such as the Internet address ("URL") of the web page being called up or a word or phrase that identifies the web page to be called up, for example, "DeCSS web site." Or the hyperlink can appear as an image, for example, an icon depicting a person sitting at a computer watching a DVD movie and text stating "click here to access DeCSS and see DVD movies for free!" The code for the web page containing the hyperlink includes a computer instruction that associates the link with the URL of the web page to be accessed, such that clicking on the hyperlink instructs the computer to enter the URL of the desired web page and thereby access that page. With a hyperlink on a web page, the linked web site is just one click away.

In applying the DMCA to linking (via hyperlinks), Judge Kaplan recognized, as he had with DeCSS code, that a hyperlink has both a speech and a nonspeech component. It conveys information, the Internet address of the linked web page, and has the functional capacity to bring the content of the linked web page to the user's computer screen (or, as Judge Kaplan put it, to "take one almost instantaneously to the desired destination."). As he had ruled with respect to DeCSS code, he ruled that application of the DMCA to the Defendants' linking to web sites containing DeCSS is content-neutral. . . . The linking prohibition is justified solely by the functional capability of the hyperlink. . . .

Applying the *O'Brien/Ward/Turner Broadcasting* requirements for content-neutral regulation, Judge Kaplan then ruled that the DMCA, as applied to the Defendants' linking, served substantial governmental interests and was unrelated to the suppression of free expression. We agree. He then carefully considered the "closer call," as to whether a linking prohibition would satisfy the narrow tailoring requirement. In an especially carefully considered portion of his opinion, he observed that strict liability for linking to web sites containing DeCSS would risk two impairments of free expression. Web site operators would be inhibited from displaying links to various web pages for fear that a linked page might contain DeCSS, and a prohibition on linking to a web site containing DeCSS would curtail access to whatever other information was contained at the accessed site.

To avoid applying the DMCA in a manner that would "burden substantially more speech than is necessary to further the government's legitimate interests," Judge Kaplan adapted the standards of *New York Times Co. v. Sullivan* (1964), to fashion a limited prohibition against linking to web sites containing DeCSS. He required clear and convincing evidence

> that those responsible for the link (a) know at the relevant time that the offending material is on the linked-to site, (b) know that it is circumvention technology that may not lawfully be offered, and (c) create or maintain the link for the purpose of disseminating that technology.

He then found that the evidence satisfied his three-part test by his required standard of proof. . . .

Mindful of the cautious approach to First Amendment claims involving computer technology expressed in *Name.Space*, we see no need on this appeal to determine whether a test as rigorous as Judge Kaplan's is required to respond to First Amendment objections to the linking provision of the injunction that he issued. It suffices to reject the Appellants' contention that an intent to cause harm is required and that linking can be enjoined only under circumstances applicable to a print medium. As they have throughout their arguments, the Appellants ignore the reality of the functional capacity of decryption computer code and hyperlinks to facilitate instantaneous unauthorized access to copyrighted materials by anyone anywhere in the world. Under the circumstances amply shown by the record, the injunction's linking prohibition validly regulates the Appellants' opportunity instantly to enable anyone anywhere to gain unauthorized access to copyrighted movies on DVDs.

At oral argument, we asked the Government whether its undoubted power to punish the distribution of obscene materials would permit an injunction prohibiting a newspaper from printing addresses of bookstore locations carrying such materials. In a properly cautious response, the Government stated that the answer would depend on the circumstances of the publication. The Appellants' supplemental papers enthusiastically embraced the arguable analogy between printing bookstore addresses and displaying on a web page links to web sites at which DeCSS may be accessed. They confidently asserted that publication of bookstore locations carrying obscene material cannot be enjoined consistent with the First Amendment, and that a prohibition against linking to web sites containing DeCSS is similarly invalid.

Like many analogies posited to illuminate legal issues, the bookstore analogy is helpful primarily in identifying characteristics that *distinguish* it from the context of the pending dispute. If a bookstore proprietor is knowingly selling obscene materials, the evil of distributing such materials can be prevented by injunctive relief against the unlawful distribution (and similar distribution by others can be deterred by punishment of the distributor). . . . The digital world, however, creates a very different problem. If obscene materials are posted on one web site and other sites post hyperlinks to the first site, the materials are available for instantaneous worldwide distribution before any preventive measures can be effectively taken.

This reality obliges courts considering First Amendment claims in the context of the pending case to choose between two unattractive alternatives: either tolerate some impairment of communication in order to permit Congress to prohibit decryption that may lawfully be prevented, or tolerate some decryption in order to avoid some impairment of communication. . . .

In facing this choice, we are mindful that it is not for us to resolve the issues of public policy implicated by the choice we have identified. Those issues are for Congress. Our task is to determine whether the legislative solution adopted by Congress, as applied to the Appellants by the District Court's injunction, is consistent with the limitations of the First Amendment, and we are satisfied that it is.

IV. Constitutional Challenge Based on Claimed Restriction of Fair Use

Asserting that fair use "is rooted in and required by both the Copyright Clause and the First Amendment," the Appellants contend that the DMCA, as applied by the District Court, unconstitutionally "*eliminates* fair use" of copyrighted materials (emphasis added). We reject this extravagant claim.

Preliminarily, we note that the Supreme Court has never held that fair use is constitutionally required, although some isolated statements in its opinions might arguably be enlisted for such a requirement. . . .

We need not explore the extent to which fair use might have constitutional protection, grounded on either the First Amendment or the Copyright Clause, because whatever validity a constitutional claim might have as to an application of the DMCA that impairs fair use of copyrighted materials, such matters are far beyond the scope of this lawsuit for several reasons. In the first place, the Appellants do not claim to be making fair use of any copyrighted materials, and nothing in the injunction prohibits them from making such fair use. They are barred from trafficking in a decryption code that enables unauthorized access to copyrighted materials.

Second, as the District Court properly noted, to whatever extent the anti-trafficking provisions of the DMCA might prevent others from copying portions of DVD movies in order to make fair use of them, "the evidence as to the impact of the anti-trafficking provision[s] of the DMCA on prospective fair users is scanty and fails adequately to address the issues."

Third, the Appellants have provided no support for their premise that fair use of DVD movies is constitutionally required to be made by copying the original work in its original format. Their examples of the fair uses that they believe others will be prevented from making all involve copying in a digital format those portions of a DVD movie amenable to fair use, a copying that would enable the fair user to manipulate the digitally copied portions. One example is that of a school child who wishes to copy images from a DVD movie to insert into the student's documentary film. We know of no authority for the proposition that fair use, as protected by the Copyright Act, much less the Constitution, guarantees copying by the optimum method or in the identical format of the original. Although the Appellants insisted at oral argument that they should not be relegated to a "horse and buggy" technique in making fair use of DVD movies,[35] the DMCA does not impose even an arguable limitation on the opportunity to make a variety of traditional fair uses of DVD movies, such as commenting on their content, quoting excerpts from their

---

[35] In their supplemental papers, the Appellants contend, rather hyperbolically, that a prohibition on using copying machines to assist in making fair use of texts could not validly be upheld by the availability of "monks to scribe the relevant passages."

screenplays, and even recording portions of the video images and sounds on film or tape by pointing a camera, a camcorder, or a microphone at a monitor as it displays the DVD movie. The fact that the resulting copy will not be as perfect or as manipulable as a digital copy obtained by having direct access to the DVD movie in its digital form, provides no basis for a claim of unconstitutional limitation of fair use. . . . Fair use has never been held to be a guarantee of access to copyrighted material in order to copy it by the fair user's preferred technique or in the format of the original.

Conclusion

We have considered all the other arguments of the Appellants and conclude that they provide no basis for disturbing the District Court's judgment. Accordingly, the judgment is affirmed.

Questions:

1.) Why are Norwegian teenagers so good at hacking encryption systems? Long winter nights?

2.) Are you convinced that code is speech? If so, do you agree with the court's analysis of the First Amendment claim? If not, why not?

3.) What do you think of the Court's analysis of whether the DMCA unconstitutionally abridges fair use? If you were Corley's attorney, how would you have presented the argument? What if you were the attorney for Universal?

4.) How does the court reconcile its interpretation of 1201(a) with 1201(c)'s statement that "[n]othing in this section shall affect rights, remedies, limitations, or defenses to copyright infringement, including fair use, under this title"? Do you agree?

5.) The court did not reach the Constitutional argument that Section 1201 violates the IP clause's requirement that rights must be for "limited times." Why? Do you think there is an argument here? What if I add my copyrighted introduction to Shakespeare's sonnets and then (logically enough) encrypt the full eBook, so that circumventing in order to excerpt the public domain sonnets would run afoul of 1201(a); does this scenario raise constitutional concerns about "perpetual" copyright, or just involve matters of convenience and preferred format (anyone who wants the public domain sonnets should just buy another physical copy of them)? What if we reach the point when no one uses physical books anymore, and everything is only available on DRM-protected eBooks?

2.) Anti-Circumvention, Competition, and Consumer Choice

Chamberlain v. Skylink
381 F.3d 1178 (Fed. Cir. 2004)

GAJARSA, Circuit Judge.

Background

Chamberlain sued Skylink, alleging violations of the patent and copyright laws. . . . The matter on appeal involves only Chamberlain's allegation that Skylink is violating the DMCA, specifically the anti-trafficking provision of § 1201(a)(2). . . .

The technology at issue involves Garage Door Openers (GDOs). A GDO typically consists of a hand-held portable transmitter and a garage door opening device mounted in a homeowner's garage. The opening device, in turn, includes both a receiver with associated signal processing software and a motor to open or close the garage door. In order to open or close the garage door, a user must activate the transmitter, which sends a radio frequency (RF) signal to the receiver located on the opening device. Once the opener receives a recognized signal, the signal processing software directs the motor to open or close the garage door.

When a homeowner purchases a GDO system, the manufacturer provides both an opener and a transmitter. Homeowners who desire replacement or spare transmitters can purchase them in the aftermarket. Aftermarket consumers have long been able to purchase "universal transmitters" that they can program to interoperate with their GDO system regardless of make or model. Skylink and Chamberlain are the only significant distributors of universal GDO transmitters. . . .

Skylink's Model 39 universal transmitter

This dispute involves Chamberlain's Security+ line of GDOs and Skylink's Model 39 universal transmitter. Chamberlain's Security+ GDOs incorporate a copyrighted "rolling code" computer program that constantly changes the transmitter signal needed to open the garage door. Skylink's Model 39 transmitter, which does not incorporate rolling code, nevertheless allows users to operate Security+ openers. Chamberlain alleges that Skylink's transmitter renders the Security+ insecure by allowing unauthorized users to circumvent the security inherent in rolling codes. Of greater legal significance, however, Chamberlain contends that because of this property of the Model 39, Skylink is in violation of the anti-trafficking clause of the DMCA's anti-circumvention provisions, specifically § 1201(a)(2). . . .

Access and Protection

Congress crafted the new anti-circumvention and anti-trafficking provisions here at issue to help bring copyright law into the information age. Advances in digital technology over the past few decades have stripped copyright owners of much of the technological and economic protection to which they had grown accustomed. Whereas large-scale copying and distribution of copyrighted material used to be difficult and expensive, it is now easy and inexpensive. The *Reimerdes* court [*Reimerdes* is the District Court decision in *Corley*] correctly noted both the economic impact of these advances and their consequent potential impact on innovation. Congress therefore crafted legislation restricting some, but not all, technological measures designed either to access a work protected by copyright, § 1201(a), or to infringe a right of a copyright owner, § 1201(b).

Though as noted, circumvention *is not* a new form of infringement but rather a new violation prohibiting actions or products that facilitate infringement, it is significant that virtually every clause of § 1201 that mentions "access" links "access" to "protection." The import of that linkage may be less than obvious. Perhaps the best way to appreciate the necessity of this linkage—and the disposition of this case—is to consider three interrelated questions inherent in the DMCA's structure: What does § 1201(a)(2) prohibit above and beyond the prohibitions of § 1201(b)? What is the relationship between the sorts of "access" prohibited under § 1201(a) and the rights "protected" under the Copyright Act? and What is the relationship between anti-circumvention liability under § 1201(a)(1) and anti-trafficking liability under § 1201(a)(2)? The relationships among the new liabilities that these three provisions, §§ 1201(a)(1), (a)(2), (b), create circumscribe the DMCA's scope—and therefore allow us to determine whether or not Chamberlain's claim falls within its purview. And the key to disentangling these relationships lies in understanding the linkage between access and protection.

Chamberlain urges us to read the DMCA as if Congress simply created a new protection for copyrighted works without any reference at all either to the protections that copyright owners already possess or to the rights that the Copyright Act grants to the public. Chamberlain has not alleged that Skylink's Model 39 infringes its copyrights, nor has it alleged that the Model 39 contributes to third-party infringement of its copyrights. Chamberlain's allegation is considerably more straightforward: The only way for the Model 39 to interoperate with a Security+ GDO is by "accessing" copyrighted software. Skylink has therefore committed a *per se* violation of the DMCA. Chamberlain urges us to conclude that no necessary connection exists between access and *copyrights*. Congress could not have intended such a broad reading of the DMCA.

Chamberlain derives its strongest claimed support for its proposed construction from the trial court's opinion in *Reimerdes*, [the earlier name for *Corley*] a case involving the same statutory provision. Though Chamberlain is correct in considering some of the *Reimerdes* language supportive, it is the differences between the cases, rather than their similarities, that is most instructive in demonstrating precisely what the DMCA permits and what it prohibits.

The facts here differ greatly from those in *Reimerdes*. There, a group of movie studios sought an injunction under the DMCA to prohibit illegal copying of digital versatile discs (DVDs). The plaintiffs presented evidence that each motion picture DVD includes a content scrambling system (CSS) that permits the film to be played, but not copied, using DVD players that incorporate the plaintiffs' licensed decryption technology. The defendant provided a link on his website that allowed an individual to download DeCSS, a program that allows the user to circumvent the CSS protective system and to view *or to copy* a motion picture from a DVD, whether or not the user has a DVD player with the licensed technology. The defendant proudly trumpeted his actions as "electronic civil disobedience." The court found that the defendant had violated 17 U.S.C. § 1201(a)(2)(A) because DeCSS had only one purpose: to decrypt CSS.

Chamberlain's proposed construction of the DMCA ignores the significant differences between defendants whose accused products enable copying and those, like Skylink, whose accused products enable only legitimate uses of copyrighted software . . . Many of Chamberlain's assertions in its brief to this court conflate the property right of copyright with the liability that the anti-circumvention provisions impose.

Chamberlain relies upon the DMCA's prohibition of "fair uses . . . as well as foul," *Reimerdes*, to argue that the enactment of the DMCA eliminated all existing consumer expectations about the public's rights to use purchased products because those products might include technological measures controlling access to a copyrighted work. But Chamberlain appears to have overlooked the obvious. The possibility that § 1201 might prohibit some otherwise noninfringing public uses of copyrighted material, arises simply because the Congressional decision to create liability and consequent damages for making, using, or selling a "key" that essentially enables a *trespass* upon intellectual property need not be identical in scope to the liabilities and compensable damages for *infringing* that property; it is, instead, a rebalancing of interests that "attempt[s] to deal with special problems created by the so-called digital revolution."

Though *Reimerdes* is not the only case that Chamberlain cites for support, none of its other citations are any more helpful to its cause. In three other cases, *Lexmark International, Inc. v. Static Control Components, Inc.* (E.D. Ky. 2003), *Sony Computer Entertainment America, Inc. v. Gamemasters* (N.D. Cal. 1999), and *RealNetworks* (2000), the trial courts did grant preliminary injunctions under the DMCA using language supportive of Chamberlain's proposed construction. None of these cases, however, is on point. In *Lexmark*, the trial court ruled that the defendant's conduct constituted copyright infringement. In *Sony*, the plaintiff's allegations included both trademark and copyright infringement, and the defendant conceded that its product made "temporary modifications" to the plaintiff's copyrighted computer program. In *RealNetworks*, the defendant's product allegedly disabled RealNetworks' "copy switch," RealNetworks' technological measure designed to let the owner of copyrighted material being streamed over RealNetworks' media player either enable or disable copying upon streaming. The court stated explicitly that the avoidance of the copy switch appeared to have little commercial value other than circumvention and the consequent infringement that it enabled. In short, the access alleged in all three cases was intertwined with a protected right. None of these cases can support a construction as broad as the one that Chamberlain urges us to adopt, even as persuasive authority.

Furthermore, though the severance of access from protection appears plausible taken out of context, it would also introduce a number of irreconcilable problems in statutory construction. The seeming plausibility arises because the statute's structure could be seen to suggest that § 1201(b) strengthens a copyright owner's abilities to protect its recognized *rights*, while § 1201(a) strengthens a copyright owner's abilities to protect *access* to its work without regard to the legitimacy (or illegitimacy) of the actions that the accused access enables. Such an interpretation is consistent with the Second Circuit's description: "[T]he focus of subsection 1201(a)(2) is circumvention of technologies designed to *prevent access* to a work, and the focus of subsection 1201(b)(1) is circumvention of technologies designed to *permit access* to a work but *prevent copying* of the work or some other act that infringes a copyright." *Corley*.

It is unlikely, however, that the Second Circuit meant to imply anything as drastic as wresting the concept of "access" from its context within the Copyright Act, as Chamberlain would now have us do. Were § 1201(a) to allow copyright owners to use technological measures to block *all* access to their copyrighted works, it would effectively create two distinct copyright regimes. In the first regime, the owners of a typical work protected by copyright would possess only the rights enumerated in 17 U.S.C. § 106, subject to the additions, exceptions, and limitations outlined throughout the rest of the Copyright Act—notably but not solely the fair use provisions of § 107.[14] Owners who feel that technology has put those rights at risk, and who incorporate technological measures to protect those rights from technological encroachment, gain the additional ability to hold traffickers in circumvention devices liable under § 1201(b) for putting their rights back at

---

[14] We do not reach the relationship between § 107 fair use and violations of § 1201. The District Court in *Reimerdes* rejected the DeCSS defendants' argument that fair use was a *necessary* defense to § 1201(a); because any access enables some fair uses, *any* act of circumvention would embody its own defense. We leave open the question as to when § 107 might serve as an affirmative defense to a prima facie violation of § 1201. For the moment, we note only that though the traditional fair use doctrine of § 107 remains unchanged as a defense to copyright infringement under § 1201(c)(1), circumvention is not infringement.

risk by enabling circumventors who use these devices to infringe.

Under the second regime that Chamberlain's proposed construction implies, the owners of a work protected by *both* copyright *and* a technological measure that effectively controls access to that work per § 1201(a) would possess *unlimited* rights to hold circumventors liable under § 1201(a) *merely for accessing that work*, even if that access enabled *only* rights that the Copyright Act grants to the public. This second implied regime would be problematic for a number of reasons. First, as the Supreme Court recently explained, "Congress' exercise of its Copyright Clause authority must be rational." *Eldred v. Ashcroft* (2003). In determining whether a particular aspect of the Copyright Act "is a rational exercise of the legislative authority conferred by the Copyright Clause . . . we defer substantially to Congress. It is Congress that has been assigned the task of defining the scope of the limited monopoly that should be granted to authors . . . *in order to give the public appropriate access* to their work product." Chamberlain's proposed construction of § 1201(a) implies that in enacting the DMCA, Congress attempted to "give the public appropriate access" to copyrighted works by allowing copyright owners to deny all access to the public. Even under the substantial deference due Congress, such a redefinition borders on the irrational.

That apparent irrationality, however, is not the most significant problem that this second regime implies. Such a regime would be hard to reconcile with the DMCA's statutory prescription that "[n]othing in this section shall affect rights, remedies, limitations, or defenses to copyright infringement, including fair use, under this title." 17 U.S.C. § 1201(c)(1). A provision that prohibited access without regard to the rest of the Copyright Act would clearly affect rights and limitations, if not remedies and defenses. Justice Souter has remarked that "[n]o canon of statutory construction familiar to me specifically addresses the situation in which two simultaneously enacted provisions of the same statute flatly contradict one another. We are, of course, bound to avoid such a dilemma if we can, by glimpsing some uncontradicted meaning for each provision." *Reno v. American-Arab Anti-Discrimination Comm.* (1999) (Souter, J., dissenting). Chamberlain's proposed construction of § 1201(a) would flatly contradict § 1201(c)(1)—a simultaneously enacted provision of the same statute. We are therefore bound, if we can, to obtain an alternative construction that leads to no such contradiction.

Chamberlain's proposed severance of "access" from "protection" in § 1201(a) creates numerous other problems. Beyond suggesting that Congress enacted *by implication* a new, highly protective alternative regime for copyrighted works; contradicting other provisions of the same statute including § 1201(c)(1); and ignoring the explicit immunization of interoperability from anti-circumvention liability under § 1201(f); the broad policy implications of considering "access" in a vacuum devoid of "protection" are both absurd and disastrous. Under Chamberlain's proposed construction, explicated at oral argument, disabling a burglar alarm to gain "access" to a home containing copyrighted books, music, art, and periodicals would violate the DMCA; anyone who did so would unquestionably have "circumvent[ed] a technological measure that effectively controls access to a work protected under [the Copyright Act]." § 1201(a)(1). The appropriate deterrents to this type of behavior lie in tort law and criminal law, *not* in copyright law. Yet, were we to read the statute's "plain language" as Chamberlain urges, disabling a burglar alarm would be a per se violation of the DMCA.

In a similar vein, Chamberlain's proposed construction would allow any manufacturer of any product to add a single copyrighted sentence or software fragment to its product, wrap the copyrighted material in a trivial "encryption" scheme, and thereby gain the right to restrict consumers' rights to use its products in conjunction with competing products. In other words, Chamberlain's construction of the DMCA would allow virtually any company to attempt to leverage its sales into aftermarket monopolies—a practice that both the antitrust laws, and the doctrine of copyright misuse, normally prohibit.

Even were we to assume *arguendo* that the DMCA's anti-circumvention provisions created a new property right, Chamberlain's attempt to infer such an exemption from copyright misuse and antitrust liability would *still* be wrong. We have noted numerous times that as a matter of Federal Circuit law, "[i]ntellectual property rights do not confer a privilege to violate the antitrust laws. But it is also correct that the antitrust laws do not negate [a] patentee's right to exclude others from patent property." *CSU, L.L.C. v. Xerox Corp.* (Fed. Cir. 2000). In what we previously termed "the most extensive analysis of the effect of a unilateral refusal to license copyrighted expression," among our sister Circuits, the First Circuit explained that: "[T]he Copyright Act does not explicitly purport to limit the scope of the Sherman Act. . . . [W]e must harmonize the two [Acts] as best we can." *Data Gen. Corp. v. Grumman Sys. Support Corp.* (1st Cir. 1994).

Because nothing in Seventh Circuit law contradicts *Data General*, we similarly conclude that it is the standard that the Seventh Circuit would most likely follow. The DMCA, as part of the Copyright Act, does not limit the scope of the antitrust laws, either explicitly or implicitly. The Supreme Court

> has considered the issue of implied repeal of the antitrust laws in the context of a variety of regulatory schemes and procedures. Certain axioms of construction are now clearly established. Repeal of the antitrust laws by implication is not favored and not casually to be allowed. Only where there is a plain repugnancy between the antitrust and regulatory provisions will repeal be implied.

Gordon v. N.Y. Stock Exch., Inc. (1975). . . .

Finally, the requisite "authorization," on which the District Court granted Skylink summary judgment, points to yet another inconsistency in Chamberlain's proposed construction. . . . Underlying Chamberlain's argument on appeal that it has not granted such authorization lies the necessary assumption that Chamberlain is entitled to prohibit legitimate purchasers of its embedded software from "accessing" the software by using it. Such an entitlement, however, would go far beyond the idea that the DMCA allows copy‑right owner to prohibit "fair uses . . . as well as foul." Chamberlain's proposed con‑struc‑tion would allow copyright owners to prohibit *exclusively fair* uses even in the absence of any feared foul use. It would therefore allow any copyright owner, through a combination of contractual terms and technological measures, to repeal the fair use doctrine with respect to an individual copyrighted work—or even selected copies of that copyrighted work. Again, this implication contradicts § 1201(c)(1) directly. Copyright law itself authorizes the public to make certain uses of copyrighted materials. Consumers who purchase a product containing a copy of embedded software have the inherent legal right to use that copy of the software. What the law authorizes, Chamberlain cannot revoke.[17]

Chamberlain's proposed severance of "access" from "protection" is entirely inconsistent with the context defined by the total statutory structure of the Copyright Act, other simultaneously enacted provisions of the DMCA, and clear Congressional intent. It "would lead to a result so bizarre that Congress could not have intended it." The

---

[17] It is not clear whether a consumer who circumvents a technological measure controlling access to a copyrighted work in a manner that enables uses permitted under the Copyright Act but prohibited by contract can be subject to liability under the DMCA. Because Chamberlain did not attempt to limit its customers' use of its product by contract, however, we do not reach this issue.

statutory structure and the legislative history both make it clear that the DMCA granted copyright holders additional legal protections, but neither rescinded the basic bargain granting the public noninfringing and fair uses of copyrighted materials, § 1201(c), nor prohibited various beneficial uses of circumvention technology, such as those exempted under §§ 1201(d),(f),(g),(j).

We therefore reject Chamberlain's proposed construction in its entirety. We conclude that 17 U.S.C. § 1201 prohibits only forms of access that bear a reasonable relationship to the protections that the Copyright Act otherwise affords copyright owners. While such a rule of reason may create some uncertainty and consume some judicial resources, it is the only meaningful reading of the statute. Congress attempted to balance the legitimate interests of copyright owners with those of consumers of copyrighted products. . . .

Congress chose words consistent with its stated intent to balance two sets of concerns pushing in opposite directions. The statute lays out broad categories of liability and broad exemptions from liability. It also instructs the courts explicitly *not* to construe the anti-circumvention provisions in ways that would effectively repeal longstanding principles of copyright law. *See* § 1201(c). The courts must decide where the balance between the rights of copyright owners and those of the broad public tilts subject to a fact-specific rule of reason. Here, Chamberlain can point to no protected property right that Skylink imperils. The DMCA cannot allow Chamberlain to retract the most fundamental right that the Copyright Act grants consumers: the right to use the copy of Chamberlain's embedded software that they purchased.

Chamberlain's DMCA Claim

The proper construction of § 1201(a)(2) therefore makes it clear that Chamberlain cannot prevail. A plaintiff alleging a violation of § 1201(a)(2) must prove: (1) ownership of a valid copyright on a work, (2) effectively controlled by a technological measure, which has been circumvented, (3) that third parties can now access (4) without authorization, in a manner that (5) infringes or facilitates infringing a right protected by the Copyright Act, because of a product that (6) the defendant either (i) designed or produced primarily for circumvention; (ii) made available despite only limited commercial significance other than circumvention; or (iii) marketed for use in circumvention of the controlling technological measure. A plaintiff incapable of establishing any one of elements (1) through (5) will have failed to prove a prima facie case. A plaintiff capable of proving elements (1) through (5) need prove only one of (6)(i), (ii), or (iii) to shift the burden back to the defendant. At that point, the various affirmative defenses enumerated throughout § 1201 become relevant. . . .

Questions:

1.) Is *Skylink* consistent with *Corley*? Why or why not?

2.) Do you agree with the *Skylink* court's "nexus" requirement? Explain its reasoning. Are there other grounds on which the court could have ruled for Skylink?

3.) If *Skylink*'s interpretation of § 1201 is correct, can you provide an example of a violation of § 1201(a)(2) that is not also a violation of § 1201(b)? What would the *Skylink* court say is the purpose of having *both* anti-trafficking provisions?

PROBLEM 15-1

Look back at Problem 12-1. If you recall, a neighborhood bookstore had on display a mint-condition, unopened copy of Madonna's 1992 book *Sex*, which was sealed with a paper band. On the paper band was an announcement that breaking the band constituted a promise to buy, and that doing so without paying constituted copyright infringement. James broke the band, peeked inside the book, and left the store without buying it. Did James infringe copyright?

Now a few years have passed and James is raising tweenage girls who are huge fans of Miley Cyrus and Lady Gaga. He has become increasingly disturbed by the provocative behavior of these recording artists and how it is influencing his daughters. He concludes that overt sexuality in female recording stars can be traced back to a single source—Madonna's book. He decides that the most effective way of de-twerking popular culture is to create a powerful parody of this book. James finds an eBook version of *Sex* on the internet, but it is encrypted, and he cannot get an access code without paying for it. He refuses to support such depravity financially. Instead, he uses Jennifer's "FairXTract" program to decrypt the eBook and extract a small amount of text and imagery for his parody.

FairXTract is a popular open source program that can convert DRM encrypted text and image files into more open formats that can be freely read, copied or edited without restriction. The program is made available freely online and lists a number of possible uses: "Make backup copies of your e-library! Don't be locked in to your obsolete e-reader! Annotate and comment on your favorite literature. Create excerpts for your English class. FairXTract is the key to FairXUse!" James's parody, "(Im)material Girl," portrays Madonna's musings on sexuality as the cynical objectification of female sexuality in the service of profit. He posts it on his blog, "Family Values—A Return to Decency." Assume that his parody would be considered a fair use under § 107.

Has James violated the DMCA? Has Jennifer? If so, what provisions have they violated? How would the *Corley* court hold? What about the *Skylink* court?

3.) The Interaction between Copyright, Contracts, and the DMCA

MDY Industries, LLC v. Blizzard Entertainment, Inc.
629 F.3d 928 (9th Cir. 2010)

CALLAHAN, Circuit Judge.

Blizzard Entertainment, Inc. ("Blizzard") is the creator of World of Warcraft ("WoW"), a popular multiplayer online role-playing game in which players interact in a virtual world while advancing through the game's 70 levels. MDY Industries, LLC and its sole member Michael Donnelly ("Donnelly") (. . . "MDY") developed and sold Glider, a software program that automatically plays the early levels of WoW for players.

MDY brought this action for a declaratory judgment to establish that its Glider sales do not infringe Blizzard's copyright or other rights, and Blizzard asserted counterclaims under the Digital Millennium Copyright Act ("DMCA"), 17 U.S.C. § 1201 *et seq.*, and for tortious interference with contract under Arizona law. The district court found MDY and Donnelly liable for secondary copyright infringement, violations of DMCA §§ 1201(a)(2) and (b)(1), and tortious interference with contract. We reverse the district court except as to MDY's liability for violation of DMCA § 1201(a)(2) and remand for trial on Blizzard's claim for tortious interference with contract.

I.

A. World of Warcraft

In November 2004, Blizzard created WoW, a "massively multiplayer online role-playing game" in which players interact in a virtual world. WoW has ten million subscribers, of which two and a half million are in North America. The WoW software has two components: (1) the game client software that a player installs on the computer; and (2) the game server software, which the player accesses on a subscription basis by connecting to WoW's online servers. WoW does not have single-player or offline modes.

WoW players roleplay different characters, such as humans, elves, and dwarves. A player's central objective is to advance the character through the game's 70 levels by participating in quests and engaging in battles with monsters. As a player advances, the character collects rewards such as ingame currency, weapons, and armor. WoW's virtual world has its own economy, in which characters use their virtual currency to buy and sell items directly from each other, through vendors, or using auction houses. Some players also utilize WoW's chat capabilities to interact with others.

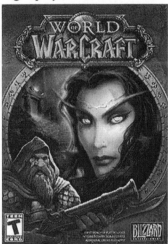

Image information available at https://en.wikipedia.org/wiki/World _of_Warcraft#/media/File:WoW_ Box_Art1.jpg.

B. Blizzard's use agreements

Each WoW player must read and accept Blizzard's End User License Agreement ("EULA") and Terms of Use ("ToU") on multiple occasions. The EULA pertains to the game client, so a player agrees to it both before installing the game client and upon first running it. The ToU pertains to the online service, so a player agrees to it both when creating an account and upon first connecting to the online service. Players who do not accept both the EULA and the ToU may return the game client for a refund.

C. Development of Glider and Warden

Donnelly is a WoW player and software programmer. In March 2005, he developed Glider, a software "bot" (short for robot) that automates play of WoW's early levels, for his personal use. A user need not be at the computer while Glider is running. As explained in the Frequently Asked Questions ("FAQ") on MDY's website for Glider:

> Glider . . . moves the mouse around and pushes keys on the keyboard. You tell it about your character, where you want to kill things, and when you want to kill. Then it kills for you, automatically. You can do something else, like eat dinner or go to a movie, and when you return, you'll have a lot more experience and loot.

Glider does not alter or copy WoW's game client software, does not allow a player to avoid paying monthly subscription dues to Blizzard, and has no commercial use independent of WoW. Glider was not initially designed to avoid detection by Blizzard.

The parties dispute Glider's impact on the WoW experience. Blizzard contends that Glider disrupts WoW's environment for non-Glider players by enabling Glider users to advance quickly and unfairly through the game and to amass additional game assets. MDY contends that Glider has a minimal effect on non-Glider players, enhances the WoW experience for Glider users, and facilitates disabled players' access to WoW by auto-playing the game for them.

In summer 2005, Donnelly began selling Glider through MDY's website for fifteen to twenty-five dollars per license. . . . In September 2005, Blizzard launched Warden, a technology that it developed to prevent its players who use unauthorized third-party software, including bots, from connecting to WoW's servers. Warden was able to detect Glider, and Blizzard immediately used Warden to ban most Glider users. MDY responded by modifying Glider to avoid detection and promoting its new anti-detection features on its website's FAQ. It added a subscription service, Glider Elite, which offered "additional protection from game detection software" for five dollars a month.

Thus, by late 2005, MDY was aware that Blizzard was prohibiting bots. MDY modified its website to indicate that using Glider violated Blizzard's ToU. In November 2005, Donnelly wrote in an email interview, "Avoiding detection is rather exciting, to be sure. Since Blizzard does not want bots running at all, it's a violation to use them." Following MDY's anti-detection modifications, Warden only occasionally detected Glider. As of September 2008, MDY had gross revenues of $3.5 million based on 120,000 Glider license sales.

D. Financial and practical impact of Glider

Blizzard claims that from December 2004 to March 2008, it received 465,000 complaints about WoW bots, several thousand of which named Glider. Blizzard spends $940,000 annually to respond to these complaints, and the parties have stipulated that Glider is the principal bot used by WoW players. Blizzard introduced evidence that it may have lost monthly subscription fees from Glider users, who were able to reach WoW's highest levels in fewer weeks than players playing manually. Donnelly acknowledged in a November 2005 email that MDY's business strategy was to make Blizzard's anti-bot detection attempts financially prohibitive. . . .

E. Pre-litigation contact between MDY and Blizzard

In August 2006, Blizzard sent MDY a cease-and-desist letter alleging that MDY's website hosted WoW screenshots and a Glider install file, all of which infringed Blizzard's copyrights. Donnelly removed the screenshots and requested Blizzard to clarify why the install file was infringing, but Blizzard did not respond. In October 2006, Blizzard's counsel visited Donnelly's home, threatening suit unless MDY immediately ceased selling Glider and remitted all profits to Blizzard. MDY immediately commenced this action.

II.

On December 1, 2006, MDY filed an amended complaint seeking a declaration that Glider does not infringe Blizzard's copyright or other rights. In February 2007, Blizzard filed counterclaims and third-party claims against MDY and Donnelly for, *inter alia*, contributory and vicarious copyright infringement, violation of DMCA §§ 1201(a)(2) and (b)(1), and tortious interference with contract.

In July 2008, the district court granted Blizzard partial summary judgment, finding that MDY's Glider sales contributorily and vicariously infringed Blizzard's copyrights and tortiously interfered with Blizzard's contracts. The district court also granted MDY partial summary judgment, finding that MDY did not violate DMCA § 1201(a)(2) with respect to accessing the game software's source code.

In September 2008, the parties stipulated to entry of a $6 million judgment against MDY for the copyright infringement and tortious interference with contract claims. They further stipulated that Donnelly would be personally liable for the same amount if found personally liable at trial. After a January 2009 bench trial, the district court held MDY liable under DMCA §§ 1201(a)(2) and (b)(1). It also held Donnelly personally liable for MDY's copyright infringement, DMCA violations, and tortious interference with contract.

. . . The district court permanently enjoined MDY from distributing Glider. MDY's efforts to stay injunctive relief pending appeal were unsuccessful. On April 29, 2009, MDY timely filed this appeal. On May 12, 2009, Blizzard timely cross-appealed the district court's holding that MDY did not violate DMCA §§ 1201(a)(2) and (b)(1) as to the game software's source code. . . .

IV.

We first consider whether MDY committed contributory or vicarious infringement (collectively, "secondary infringement") of Blizzard's copyright by selling Glider to WoW players. *See ProCD, Inc. v. Zeidenberg* (7th Cir. 1996) ("A copyright is a right against the world. Contracts, by contrast, generally affect only their parties."). To establish secondary infringement, Blizzard must first demonstrate direct infringement. To establish direct infringement, Blizzard must demonstrate copyright ownership and violation of one of its exclusive rights by Glider users. MDY is liable for contributory infringement if it has "intentionally induc[ed] or encourag[ed] direct infringement" by Glider users. *MGM Studios Inc. v. Grokster, Ltd.* (2005). MDY is liable for vicarious infringement if it (1) has the right and ability to control Glider users' putatively infringing activity and (2) derives a direct financial benefit from their activity. If Glider users directly infringe, MDY does not dispute that it satisfies the other elements of contributory and vicarious infringement.

As a copyright owner, Blizzard possesses the exclusive right to reproduce its work. 17 U.S.C. § 106(1). The parties agree that when playing WoW, a player's computer creates a copy of the game's software in the computer's random access memory ("RAM"), a form of temporary memory used by computers to run software programs. This copy potentially infringes unless the player (1) is a licensee whose use of the software is within the scope of the license or (2) owns the copy of the software. 17 U.S.C. § 117(a). As to the scope of the license, ToU § 4(B), "Limitations on Your Use of the Service," provides:

> You agree that you will not . . . (ii) create or use cheats, bots, "mods," and/or hacks, or any other third-party software designed to modify the World of Warcraft experience; or (iii) use any third-party software that intercepts, "mines," or otherwise collects information from or through the Program or Service.

By contrast, if the player owns the copy of the software, the "essential step" defense provides that the player does not infringe by making a copy of the computer program where the copy is created and used solely "as an essential step in the utilization of the computer program in conjunction with a machine." 17 U.S.C. § 117(a)(1).

A. Essential step defense

We consider whether WoW players, including Glider users, are owners or licensees of their copies of WoW software. If WoW players own their copies, as MDY contends, then Glider users do not infringe by reproducing WoW software in RAM while playing, and MDY is not secondarily liable for copyright infringement.

In *Vernor v. Autodesk, Inc.*, we recently distinguished between "owners" and "licensees" of copies for purposes of the essential step defense. In *Vernor*, we held "that a software user is a licensee rather than an owner of a copy where the copyright owner (1) specifies that the user is granted a license; (2) significantly restricts the user's ability to transfer the software; and (3) imposes notable use" restrictions.

Applying *Vernor*, we hold that WoW players are licensees of WoW's game client software. Blizzard reserves title in the software and grants players a non-exclusive, limited license. Blizzard also imposes transfer restrictions if a player seeks to transfer the license: the player must (1) transfer all original packaging and documentation; (2) permanently delete all of the copies and installation of the game client; and (3) transfer only to a recipient who accepts the EULA. A player may not sell or give away the account.

Blizzard also imposes a variety of use restrictions. The game must be used only for non-commercial entertainment purposes and may not be used in cyber cafes and computer gaming centers without Blizzard's permission. Players may not concurrently use unauthorized third-party programs. Also, Blizzard may alter the game client itself remotely without a player's knowledge or permission, and may terminate the EULA and ToU if players violate their terms. Termination ends a player's license to access and play WoW. Following termination, players must immediately destroy their copies of the game and uninstall the game client from their computers, but need not return the software to Blizzard.

Since WoW players, including Glider users, do not own their copies of the software, Glider users may not claim the essential step defense. Thus, when their computers copy WoW software into RAM, the players may infringe unless their usage is within the scope of Blizzard's limited license.

B. Contractual covenants vs. license conditions

"A copyright owner who grants a nonexclusive, limited license ordinarily waives the right to sue licensees for copyright infringement, and it may sue only for breach of contract." However, if the licensee acts outside the scope of the license, the licensor may sue for copyright infringement. Enforcing a copyright license "raises issues that lie at the intersection of copyright and contract law."

We refer to contractual terms that limit a license's scope as "conditions," the breach of which constitute copyright infringement. We refer to all other license terms as "covenants," the breach of which is actionable only under contract law. We distinguish between conditions and covenants according to state contract law, to the extent consistent with federal copyright law and policy.

A Glider user commits copyright infringement by playing WoW while violating a ToU term that is a license condition. To establish copyright infringement, then, Blizzard must demonstrate that the violated term—ToU § 4(B)—is a condition rather than a covenant. Blizzard's EULAs and ToUs provide that they are to be interpreted according to Delaware law. Accordingly, we first construe them under Delaware law, and then evaluate whether that construction is consistent with federal copyright law and policy.

A covenant is a contractual promise, i.e., a manifestation of intention to act or re-frain from acting in a particular way, such that the promisee is justified in understanding that the promisor has made a commitment. A condition precedent is an act or event that must occur before a duty to perform a promise arises. Conditions precedent are disfav-ored because they tend to work forfeitures. Wherever possible, equity construes ambig-uous contract provisions as covenants rather than conditions. However, if the contract is unambiguous, the court construes it according to its terms.

Applying these principles, ToU § 4(B)(ii) and (iii)'s prohibitions against bots and unauthorized third-party software are covenants rather than copyright-enforceable conditions. Although ToU § 4 is titled, "Limitations on Your Use of the Service," nothing in that section conditions Blizzard's grant of a limited license on players' compliance with ToU § 4's restrictions. To the extent that the title introduces any ambiguity, under Delaware law, ToU § 4(B) is not a condition, but is a contractual covenant.

To recover for copyright infringement based on breach of a license agreement, (1) the copying must exceed the scope of the defendant's license and (2) the copyright owner's complaint must be grounded in an exclusive right of copyright (e.g., unlawful reproduction or distribution). Contractual rights, however, can be much broader:

> [C]onsider a license in which the copyright owner grants a person the right to make one and only one copy of a book with the caveat that the licensee may not read the last ten pages. Obviously, a licensee who made a hundred copies of the book would be liable for copyright infringement because the copying would violate the Copyright Act's prohibition on reproduction and would exceed the scope of the license. Alternatively, if the licensee made a single copy of the book, but read the last ten pages, the only cause of action would be for breach of contract, because reading a book does not violate any right protected by copyright law.

Storage Tech. Corp. v. Custom Hardware Eng'g & Consulting, Inc. (Fed. Cir. 2005). Consistent with this approach, we have held that the potential for infringement exists only where the licensee's action (1) exceeds the license's scope (2) in a manner that implicates one of the licensor's exclusive statutory rights.

Here, ToU § 4 contains certain restrictions that are grounded in Blizzard's exclusive rights of copyright and other restrictions that are not. For instance, ToU § 4(D) forbids creation of derivative works based on WoW without Blizzard's consent. A player who violates this prohibition would exceed the scope of her license and violate one of Blizzard's exclusive rights under the Copyright Act. In contrast, ToU § 4(C)(ii) prohibits a player's disruption of another player's game experience. A player might violate this prohibition while playing the game by harassing another player with unsolicited instant messages. Although this conduct may violate the contractual covenants with Blizzard, it would not violate any of Blizzard's exclusive rights of copyright. The antibot provisions at issue in this case, ToU § 4(B)(ii) and (iii), are similarly covenants rather than conditions. A Glider user violates the covenants with Blizzard, but does not thereby commit copyright infringement because Glider does not infringe any of Blizzard's exclusive rights. For instance, the use does not alter or copy WoW software.

Were we to hold otherwise, Blizzard—or any software copyright holder—could designate any disfavored conduct during software use as copyright infringement, by purporting to condition the license on the player's abstention from the disfavored conduct. The rationale would be that because the conduct occurs while the player's computer is copying the software code into RAM in order for it to run, the violation is copyright infringement. This would allow software copyright owners far greater rights than Congress has generally conferred on copyright owners.[3]

We conclude that for a licensee's violation of a contract to constitute copyright infringement, there must be a nexus between the condition and the licensor's exclusive rights of copyright.[4] Here, WoW players do not commit copyright infringement by using

---

[3] A copyright holder may wish to enforce violations of license agreements as copyright infringements for several reasons. First, breach of contract damages are generally limited to the value of the actual loss caused by the breach. In contrast, copyright damages include the copyright owner's actual damages and the infringer's actual profits, or statutory damages of up to $150,000 per work. 17 U.S.C. § 504. Second, copyright law offers injunctive relief, seizure of infringing articles, and awards of costs and attorneys' fees. 17 U.S.C. §§ 502–03, 505. Third, . . . copyright law allows copyright owners a remedy against "downstream" infringers with whom they are not in privity of contract.

[4] A licensee arguably may commit copyright infringement by continuing to use the licensed work while failing to make required payments, even though a failure to make payments otherwise lacks a nexus to the

Glider in violation of the ToU. MDY is thus not liable for secondary copyright infringement, which requires the existence of direct copyright infringement.

It follows that because MDY does not infringe Blizzard's copyrights, we need not resolve MDY's contention that Blizzard commits copyright misuse. Copyright misuse is an equitable defense to copyright infringement, the contours of which are still being defined. The remedy for copyright misuse is to deny the copyright holder the right to enforce its copyright during the period of misuse. Since MDY does not infringe, we do not consider whether Blizzard committed copyright misuse.

We thus reverse the district court's grant of summary judgment to Blizzard on its secondary copyright infringement claims. . . .

V.

After MDY began selling Glider, Blizzard launched Warden, its technology designed to prevent players who used bots from connecting to the WoW servers. Blizzard used Warden to ban most Glider users in September 2005. Blizzard claims that MDY is liable under DMCA §§ 1201(a)(2) and (b)(1) because it thereafter programmed Glider to avoid detection by Warden.

A. The Warden technology

Warden has two components. The first is a software module called "scan.dll," which scans a computer's RAM prior to allowing the player to connect to WoW's servers. If scan.dll detects that a bot is running, such as Glider, it will not allow the player to connect and play. After Blizzard launched Warden, MDY reconfigured Glider to circumvent scan.dll by not loading itself until after scan.dll completed its check. Warden's second component is a "resident" component that runs periodically in the background on a player's computer when it is connected to WoW's servers. It asks the computer to report portions of the WoW code running in RAM, and it looks for patterns of code associated with known bots or cheats. If it detects a bot or cheat, it boots the player from the game, which halts the computer's copying of copyrighted code into RAM.

B. The Digital Millennium Copyright Act

. . . The first provision, 17 U.S.C. § 1201(a)(1)(A), is a general prohibition against "circumventing a technological measure that effectively controls access to a work protected under [the Copyright Act]." The second prohibits trafficking in technology that circumvents a technological measure that "effectively controls access" to a copyrighted work. 17 U.S.C. § 1201(a)(2). The third prohibits trafficking in technology that circumvents a technological measure that "effectively protects" a copyright owner's right. 17 U.S.C. § 1201(b)(1).

C. The district court's decision

The district court assessed whether MDY violated DMCA §§ 1201(a)(2) and (b)(1) with respect to three WoW components. First, the district court considered the game client software's **literal elements**: the source code stored on players' hard drives. Second, the district court considered the game client software's **individual non-literal elements**: the 400,000+ discrete visual and audible components of the game, such as a visual image of a monster or its audible roar. Finally, it considered the game's **dynamic non-literal elements**: that is, the "real-time experience of traveling through different worlds, hearing their sounds, viewing their structures, encountering their inhabitants and monsters, and

---

licensor's exclusive statutory rights. We view payment as sui generis, however, because of the distinct nexus between payment and all commercial copyright licenses, not just those concerning software.

encountering other players."

The district court granted MDY partial summary judgment as to Blizzard's § 1201(a)(2) claim with respect to WoW's literal elements. The district court reasoned that Warden does not effectively control access to the literal elements because WoW players can access the literal elements without connecting to a game server and encountering Warden; they need only install the game client software on their computers. The district court also ruled for MDY following trial as to Blizzard's § 1201(a)(2) claim with respect to WoW's individual non-literal elements, reasoning that these elements could also be accessed on a player's hard drive without encountering Warden. . . . The district court, however, ruled for Blizzard following trial as to its §§ 1201(a)(2) and (b)(1) claims with respect to WoW's dynamic non-literal elements, or the "real-time experience" of playing WoW. . . .

We turn to consider whether Glider violates DMCA §§ 1201(a)(2) and (b)(1) by allowing users to circumvent Warden to access WoW's various elements. MDY contends that Warden's scan.dll and resident components are separate, and only scan.dll should be considered as a potential access control measure under § 1201(a)(2). However, in our view, an access control measure can both (1) attempt to block initial access and (2) revoke access if a secondary check determines that access was unauthorized. Our analysis considers Warden's scan.dll and resident components together because the two components have the same purpose: to prevent players using detectable bots from continuing to access WoW software.

D. Construction of § 1201

One of the issues raised by this appeal is whether certain provisions of § 1201 prohibit circumvention of access controls when access does not constitute copyright infringement. To answer this question and others presented by this appeal, we address the nature and interrelationship of the various provisions of § 1201 in the overall context of the Copyright Act.

We begin by considering the scope of DMCA § 1201's three operative provisions, §§ 1201(a)(1), 1201(a)(2), and 1201(b)(1). We consider them side-by-side, because "[w]e do not . . . construe statutory phrases in isolation; we read statutes as a whole. Thus, the [term to be construed] must be read in light of the immediately following phrase. . . ."

1. Text of the operative provisions

"We begin, as always, with the text of the statute." Section 1201(a)(1)(A) prohibits "circumvent[ing] a technological measure that effectively controls access to a work protected under this title." Sections 1201(a)(2) and (b)(1) provide that "[n]o person shall manufacture, import, offer to the public, provide, or otherwise traffic in any technology, product, service, device, component, or part thereof, that—

§ 1201(a)(2)	§ 1201(b)(1)
(A)	(A)
is primarily designed or produced for the purpose of **circumventing a technological measure**	is primarily designed or produced for the purpose of **circumventing protection afforded by a technological measure**
that effectively controls access to **a work protected under this title;**	that effectively protects **a right of a copyright owner;**
(B)	(B)
has only limited commercially significant purpose or use other than to circumvent a technological measure	has only limited commercially significant purpose or use other than to circumvent protection afforded by a technological measure

that effectively controls access to a work protected under this title;	that effectively protects a right of a copyright owner under this title in a work or portion thereof;
(C) is marketed by a person or another acting in concert with that person with that person's knowledge for use in circumventing a technological measure that effectively controls access to a work protected under this title.	(C) is marketed by that person or another acting in concert with that person with that person's knowledge for use in circumventing protection afforded by a technological measure that effectively protects a right of a copyright owner under this title in a portion or work thereof."

(emphasis added).

2. Our harmonization of the DMCA's operative provisions

For the reasons set forth below, we believe that § 1201 is best understood to create two distinct types of claims. First, § 1201(a) prohibits the circumvention of any technological measure that effectively controls access to a protected work and grants copyright owners the right to enforce that prohibition. *Cf. Corley* ("[T]he focus of subsection 1201(a)(2) is circumvention of technologies designed to prevent access to a work"). Second, and in contrast to § 1201(a), § 1201(b)(1) prohibits trafficking in technologies that circumvent technological measures that effectively protect "a right of a copyright owner." Section 1201(b)(1)'s prohibition is thus aimed at circumventions of measures that protect the copyright itself: it entitles copyright owners to protect their existing exclusive rights under the Copyright Act. Those exclusive rights are reproduction, distribution, public performance, public display, and creation of derivative works. 17 U.S.C. § 106. Historically speaking, preventing "access" to a protected work in itself has not been a right of a copyright owner arising from the Copyright Act.

Our construction of § 1201 is compelled by the four significant textual differences between §§ 1201(a) and (b). First, § 1201(a)(2) prohibits the circumvention of a measure that "effectively controls access to *a work protected under this title,*" whereas § 1201(b)(1) concerns a measure that "effectively protects *a right of a copyright owner under this title in a work or portion thereof.*" We read § 1201(b)(1)'s language—"right of a copyright owner under this title"—to reinforce copyright owners' traditional exclusive rights under § 106 by granting them an additional cause of action against those who traffic in circumventing devices that facilitate infringement. Sections 1201(a)(1) and (a)(2), however, use the term "work protected under this title." Neither of these two subsections explicitly refers to traditional copyright infringement under § 106. Accordingly, we read this term as extending a new form of protection, i.e., the right to prevent circumvention of access controls, broadly to works protected under Title 17, i.e., copyrighted works.

Second, as used in § 1201(a), to "circumvent a technological measure" means "to descramble a scrambled work, to decrypt an encrypted work, or otherwise to avoid, bypass, remove, deactivate, or impair a technological measure, without the authority of the copyright owner." 17 U.S.C. § 1201(a)(3)(A). These two specific examples of unlawful circumvention under § 1201(a)—descrambling a scrambled work and decrypting an encrypted work—are acts that do not necessarily infringe or facilitate infringement of a copyright. Descrambling or decrypting only enables someone to watch or listen to a work without authorization, which is not necessarily an infringement of a copyright owner's traditional exclusive rights under § 106. Put differently, descrambling and decrypting do not necessarily result in someone's reproducing, distributing, publicly performing, or publicly displaying the copyrighted work, or creating derivative works based on the copyrighted work.

The third significant difference between the subsections is that § 1201(a)(1)(A) prohibits circumventing an effective access control measure, whereas § 1201(b) prohibits trafficking in circumventing devices, but does not prohibit circumvention itself because such conduct was already outlawed as copyright infringement. . . . This difference reinforces our reading of § 1201(b) as strengthening copyright owners' traditional rights against copyright infringement and of § 1201(a) as granting copyright owners a new anti-circumvention right.

Fourth, in § 1201(a)(1)(B)–(D), Congress directs the Library of Congress ("Library") to identify classes of copyrighted works for which "noninfringing uses by persons who are users of a copyrighted work are, or are likely to be, adversely affected, and the [anti-circumvention] prohibition contained in [§ 1201(a)(1)(A)] shall not apply to such users with respect to such classes of works for the ensuing 3-year period." There is no analogous provision in § 1201(b). We impute this lack of symmetry to Congress' need to balance copyright owners' new anti-circumvention right with the public's right to access the work. . . . [T]he Library is only entitled to moderate the new anti-circumvention right created by, and hence subject to the limitations in, DMCA § 1201(a)(1).

Our reading of §§ 1201(a) and (b) ensures that neither section is rendered superfluous. A violation of § 1201(a)(1)(A), which prohibits circumvention itself, will not be a violation of § 1201(b), which does not contain an analogous prohibition on circumvention. A violation of § 1201(a)(2), which prohibits trafficking in devices that facilitate circumvention of *access* control measures, will not always be a violation of § 1201(b)(1), which prohibits trafficking in devices that facilitate circumvention of measures that protect against *copyright infringement*. Of course, if a copyright owner puts in place an effective measure that both (1) controls access and (2) protects against copyright infringement, a defendant who traffics in a device that circumvents that measure could be liable under both §§ 1201(a) and (b). Nonetheless, we read the differences in structure between §§ 1201(a) and (b) as reflecting Congress's intent to address distinct concerns by creating different rights with different elements.

3. Our construction of the DMCA is consistent with the legislative history

Although the text suffices to resolve the issues before us, we also consider the legislative history in order to address the parties' arguments concerning it. Our review of that history supports the view that Congress created a new anti-circumvention right in § 1201(a)(2) independent of traditional copyright infringement and granted copyright owners a new weapon against copyright infringement in § 1201(b)(1). For instance, the Senate Judiciary Committee report explains that §§ 1201(a)(2) and (b)(1) are "not interchangeable": they were "designed to protect two distinct rights and to target two distinct classes of devices," and "many devices will be subject to challenge only under one of the subsections." That is, § 1201(a)(2) "is designed to protect access to a copyrighted work," while § 1201(b)(1) "is designed to protect the traditional copyright rights of the copyright owner." Thus, the Senate Judiciary Committee understood § 1201 to create the following regime:

> [I]f an effective technological protection measure does nothing to prevent access to the plain text of the work, but is designed to prevent that work from being copied, then a potential cause of action against the manufacturer of a device designed to circumvent the measure lies under § 1201(b)(1), but not under § 1201(a)(2). Conversely, if an effective technological protection measure limits access to the plain text of a work only to those with authorized access, but provides no additional

protection against copying, displaying, performing or distributing the
work, then a potential cause of action against the manufacturer of a
device designed to circumvent the measure lies under § 1201(a)(2), but
not under § 1201(b).

The Senate Judiciary Committee proffered an example of § 1201(a) liability with no
nexus to infringement, stating that if an owner effectively protected access to a
copyrighted work by use of a password, it would violate § 1201(a)(2)(A)

[T]o defeat or bypass the password and to make the means to do so, as
long as the primary purpose of the means was to perform this kind of
act. This is roughly analogous to making it illegal to break into a house
using a tool, the primary purpose of which is to break into houses.

The House Judiciary Committee similarly states of § 1201(a)(2), "The act of
circumventing a technological protection measure put in place by a copyright owner to
control access to a copyrighted work is the electronic equivalent of breaking into a locked
room in order to obtain a copy of a book." We note that bypassing a password and
breaking into a locked room in order to read or view a copyrighted work would not
infringe on any of the copyright owner's exclusive rights under § 106.

We read this legislative history as confirming Congress's intent, in light of the
current digital age, to grant copyright owners an independent right to enforce the
prohibition against circumvention of effective technological access controls. In
§ 1201(a), Congress was particularly concerned with encouraging copyright owners to
make their works available in digital formats such as "on-demand" or "pay-per-view,"
which allow consumers effectively to "borrow" a copy of the work for a limited time or
a limited number of uses. As the House Commerce Committee explained:

[A]n increasing number of intellectual property works are being
distributed using a "client-server" model, where the work is effectively
"borrowed" by the user (e.g., infrequent users of expensive software
purchase a certain number of uses, or viewers watch a movie on a pay-
per-view basis). To operate in this environment, content providers will
need both the technology to make new uses possible and the legal
framework to ensure they can protect their work from piracy.

Our review of the legislative history supports our reading of § 1201: that section
(a) creates a new anti-circumvention right distinct from copyright infringement, while
section (b) strengthens the traditional prohibition against copyright infringement. We
now review the decisions of the Federal Circuit that have interpreted § 1201 differently.

4. The Federal Circuit's decisions

The Federal Circuit has adopted a different approach to the DMCA. In essence, it
requires § 1201(a) plaintiffs to demonstrate that the circumventing technology infringes or
facilitates infringement of the plaintiff's copyright (an "infringement nexus requirement").

The seminal decision is *Chamberlain* (Fed. Cir. 2004). In *Chamberlain*, the
plaintiff sold garage door openers ("GDOs") with a "rolling code" security system that
purportedly reduced the risk of crime by constantly changing the transmitter signal
necessary to open the door. Customers used the GDOs' transmitters to send the changing
signal, which in turn opened or closed their garage doors.

Plaintiff sued the defendant, who sold "universal" GDO transmitters for use with
plaintiff's GDOs, under § 1201(a)(2). The plaintiff alleged that its GDOs and transmitters
both contained copyrighted computer programs and that its rolling code security system
was a technological measure that controlled access to those programs. Accordingly,
plaintiff alleged that the defendant—by selling GDO transmitters that were compatible

with plaintiff's GDOs—had trafficked in a technology that was primarily used for the circumvention of a technological measure (the rolling code security system) that effectively controlled access to plaintiff's copyrighted works.

The Federal Circuit rejected the plaintiff's claim, holding that the defendant did not violate § 1201(a)(2) because, *inter alia*, the defendant's universal GDO transmitters did not infringe or facilitate infringement of the plaintiff's copyrighted computer programs. The linchpin of the *Chamberlain* court's analysis is its conclusion that DMCA coverage is limited to a copyright owner's rights under the Copyright Act as set forth in § 106 of the Copyright Act. Thus, it held that § 1201(a) did not grant copyright owners a new anti-circumvention right, but instead, established new causes of action for a defendant's unauthorized access of copyrighted material when it infringes upon a copyright owner's rights under § 106. Accordingly, a § 1201(a)(2) plaintiff was required to demonstrate a nexus to infringement—i.e., that the defendant's trafficking in circumventing technology had a "reasonable relationship" to the protections that the Copyright Act affords copyright owners. The Federal Circuit explained:

> Defendants who traffic in devices that circumvent access controls in ways that facilitate infringement may be subject to liability under § 1201(a)(2). Defendants who use such devices may be subject to liability under § 1201(a)(1) whether they infringe or not. Because all defendants who traffic in devices that circumvent rights controls necessarily facilitate infringement, they may be subject to liability under § 1201(b). Defendants who use such devices may be subject to liability for copyright infringement. *And finally, defendants whose circumvention devices do not facilitate infringement are not subject to § 1201 liability.*

Chamberlain concluded that § 1201(a) created a new cause of action linked to copyright infringement, rather than a new anti-circumvention right separate from copyright infringement, for six reasons.

First, *Chamberlain* reasoned that Congress enacted the DMCA to balance the interests of copyright owners and information users, and an infringement nexus requirement was necessary to create an anti-circumvention right that truly achieved that balance. Second, *Chamberlain* feared that copyright owners could use an access control right to prohibit exclusively fair uses of their material even absent feared foul use. Third, *Chamberlain* feared that § 1201(a) would allow companies to leverage their sales into aftermarket monopolies, in potential violation of antitrust law and the doctrine of copyright misuse. Fourth, *Chamberlain* viewed an infringement nexus requirement as necessary to prevent "absurd and disastrous results," such as the existence of DMCA liability for disabling a burglary alarm to gain access to a home containing copyrighted materials.

Fifth, *Chamberlain* stated that an infringement nexus requirement might be necessary to render Congress's exercise of its Copyright Clause authority rational. The Copyright Clause gives Congress "the task of defining the scope of the limited monopoly that should be granted to authors . . . in order to give the public appropriate access to their work product." Without an infringement nexus requirement, Congress arguably would have allowed copyright owners in § 1201(a) to deny all access to the public by putting an effective access control measure in place that the public was not allowed to circumvent.

Finally, the *Chamberlain* court viewed an infringement nexus requirement as necessary for the Copyright Act to be internally consistent. It reasoned that § 1201(c)(1), enacted simultaneously, provides that "nothing in this section shall affect rights, remedies, limitations, or defenses to copyright infringement, including fair use, under this title." The *Chamberlain* court opined that if § 1201(a) creates liability for access without regard to the remainder of the Copyright Act, it "would clearly affect rights and limitations, if not remedies and defenses."

Accordingly, the Federal Circuit held that a DMCA § 1201(a)(2) action was foreclosed to the extent that the defendant trafficked in a device that did not facilitate copyright infringement.

5. We decline to adopt an infringement nexus requirement

While we appreciate the policy considerations expressed by the Federal Circuit in Chamberlain, we are unable to follow its approach because it is contrary to the plain language of the statute. In addition, the Federal Circuit failed to recognize the rationale for the statutory construction that we have proffered. Also, its approach is based on policy concerns that are best directed to Congress in the first instance, or for which there appear to be other reasons that do not require such a convoluted construction of the statute's language.

i. Statutory inconsistencies

Were we to follow Chamberlain in imposing an infringement nexus requirement, we would have to disregard the plain language of the statute. Moreover, there is significant textual evidence showing Congress's intent to create a new anti-circumvention right in § 1201(a) distinct from infringement. As set forth *supra*, this evidence includes: (1) Congress's choice to link only § 1201(b)(1) explicitly to infringement; (2) Congress's provision in § 1201(a)(3)(A) that descrambling and decrypting devices can lead to § 1201(a) liability, even though descrambling and decrypting devices may only enable non-infringing access to a copyrighted work; and (3) Congress's creation of a mechanism in § 1201(a)(1)(B)–(D) to exempt certain non-infringing behavior from § 1201(a)(1) liability, a mechanism that would be unnecessary if an infringement nexus requirement existed. . . .

The Chamberlain court reasoned that if § 1201(a) creates liability for access without regard to the remainder of the Copyright Act, it "would clearly affect rights and limitations, if not remedies and defenses." This perceived tension is relieved by our recognition that § 1201(a) creates a new anti-circumvention right distinct from the traditional exclusive rights of a copyright owner. It follows that § 1201(a) does not limit the traditional framework of exclusive rights created by § 106, or defenses to those rights such as fair use.[12] We are thus unpersuaded by Chamberlain's reading of the DMCA's text and structure.

ii. Additional interpretive considerations

. . . *Chamberlain* relied heavily on policy considerations to support its reading of § 1201(a). . . . *Chamberlain* feared that § 1201(a) would allow companies to leverage their sales into aftermarket monopolies, in tension with antitrust law and the doctrine of copyright misuse. Concerning antitrust law, we note that there is no clear issue of anti-competitive behavior in this case because Blizzard does not seek to put a direct competitor who offers a competing role-playing game out of business and the parties have not argued this issue. If a § 1201(a)(2) defendant in a future case claims that a plaintiff is attempting to enforce its DMCA anti-circumvention right in a manner that violates antitrust law, we will then consider the interplay between this new anti-circumvention right and antitrust law.

Chamberlain also viewed an infringement nexus requirement as necessary to prevent "absurd and disastrous results," such as the existence of DMCA liability for

---

[12] Like the *Chamberlain* court, we need not and do not reach the relationship between fair use under § 107 of the Copyright Act and violations of § 1201. MDY has not claimed that Glider use is a "fair use" of WoW's dynamic non-literal elements. Accordingly, we too leave open the question whether fair use might serve as an affirmative defense to a *prima facie* violation of § 1201.

disabling a burglary alarm to gain access to a home containing copyrighted materials. In addition, the Federal Circuit was concerned that, without an infringement nexus requirement, § 1201(a) would allow copyright owners to deny all access to the public by putting an effective access control measure in place that the public is not allowed to circumvent. Both concerns appear to be overstated, but even accepting them, arguendo, as legitimate concerns, they do not permit reading the statute as requiring the imposition of an infringement nexus. As § 1201(a) creates a distinct right, it does not disturb the balance between public rights and the traditional rights of owners of copyright under the Copyright Act. Moreover, § 1201(a)(1)(B)–(D) allows the Library of Congress to create exceptions to the § 1201(a) anti-circumvention right in the public's interest. If greater protection of the public's ability to access copyrighted works is required, Congress can provide such protection by amending the statute.

In sum, we conclude that a fair reading of the statute (supported by legislative history) indicates that Congress created a distinct anti-circumvention right under § 1201(a) without an infringement nexus requirement. Thus, even accepting the validity of the concerns expressed in Chamberlain, those concerns do not authorize us to override congressional intent and add a non-textual element to the statute. Accordingly, we reject the imposition of an infringement nexus requirement. We now consider whether MDY has violated §§ 1201(a)(2) and (b)(1).

E. Blizzard's § 1201(a)(2) claim

1. WoW's literal elements and individual non-literal elements

We agree with the district court that MDY's Glider does not violate DMCA § 1201(a)(2) with respect to WoW's literal elements and individual non-literal elements, because Warden does not effectively control access to these WoW elements. First, Warden does not control access to WoW's literal elements because these elements—the game client's software code—are available on a player's hard drive once the game client software is installed. Second, as the district court found:

> [WoW's] individual nonliteral components may be accessed by a user without signing on to the server. As was demonstrated during trial, an owner of the game client software may use independently purchased computer programs to call up the visual images or the recorded sounds within the game client software. For instance, a user may call up and listen to the roar a particular monster makes within the game. Or the user may call up a virtual image of that monster.

Since a player need not encounter Warden to access WoW's individual non-literal elements, Warden does not effectively control access to those elements.

Our conclusion is in accord with the Sixth Circuit's decision in *Lexmark International v. Static Control Components* (6th Cir. 2004). In *Lexmark*, the plaintiff sold laser printers equipped with an authentication sequence, verified by the printer's copyrighted software, that ensured that only plaintiff's own toner cartridges could be inserted into the printers. The defendant sold microchips capable of generating an authentication sequence that rendered other manufacturers' cartridges compatible with plaintiff's printers.

The Sixth Circuit held that plaintiff's § 1201(a)(2) claim failed because its authentication sequence did not effectively control access to its copyrighted computer program. Rather, the mere purchase of one of plaintiff's printers allowed "access" to the copyrighted program. Any purchaser could read the program code directly from the printer memory without encountering the authentication sequence. The authentication sequence thus blocked only one form of access: the ability to make use of the printer.

However, it left intact another form of access: the review and use of the computer program's literal code. The Sixth Circuit explained:

> Just as one would not say that a lock on the back door of a house "controls access" to a house whose front door does not contain a lock and just as one would not say that a lock on any door of a house "controls access" to the house after its purchaser receives the key to the lock, it does not make sense to say that this provision of the DMCA applies to otherwise-readily-accessible copyrighted works. Add to this the fact that the DMCA not only requires the technological measure to "control access" but requires the measure to control that access "effectively," 17 U.S.C. § 1201(a)(2), and it seems clear that this provision does not naturally extend to a technological measure that restricts one form of access but leaves another route wide open.

Here, a player's purchase of the WoW game client allows access to the game's literal elements and individual non-literal elements. Warden blocks one form of access to these elements: the ability to access them while connected to a WoW server. However, analogously to the situation in *Lexmark*, Warden leaves open the ability to access these elements directly via the user's computer. We conclude that Warden is not an effective access control measure with respect to WoW's literal elements and individual non-literal elements, and therefore, that MDY does not violate § 1201(a)(2) with respect to these elements.

2. WoW's dynamic non-literal elements

We conclude that MDY meets each of the six textual elements for violating § 1201(a)(2) with respect to WoW's dynamic non-literal elements. That is, MDY (1) traffics in (2) a technology or part thereof (3) that is primarily designed, produced, or marketed for, or has limited commercially significant use other than (4) circumventing a technological measure (5) that effectively controls access (6) to a copyrighted work.

The first two elements are met because MDY "traffics in a technology or part thereof"—that is, it sells Glider. The third and fourth elements are met because Blizzard has established that MDY *markets* Glider for use in circumventing Warden, thus satisfying the requirement of § 1201(a)(2)(C).[16] . . . The sixth element is met because, as the district court held, WoW's dynamic non-literal elements constitute a copyrighted work.

The fifth element is met because Warden is an effective access control measure. To "effectively control access to a work," a technological measure must "in the ordinary course of its operation, require[ ] the application of information, or a process or a treatment, with the authority of the copyright owner, to gain access to the work." Both of Warden's two components "require[ ] the application of information, or a process or a treatment . . . to gain access to the work." For a player to connect to Blizzard's servers

---

[16] To "circumvent a technological measure" under § 1201(a) means to "descramble a scrambled work, to decrypt an encrypted work, or otherwise to avoid, bypass, remove, deactivate, or impair a technological measure, *without the authority of the copyright owner.*" A circuit split exists with respect to the meaning of the phrase "without the authority of the copyright owner." The Federal Circuit has concluded that this definition imposes an additional requirement on a § 1201(a)(2) plaintiff: to show that the defendant's circumventing device enables third parties to access the copyrighted work without the copyright owner's authorization. *See Chamberlain.* The Second Circuit has adopted a different view, explaining that § 1201(a)(3)(A) plainly exempts from § 1201(a) liability those whom a copyright owner authorizes to circumvent an access control measure, not those whom a copyright owner authorizes to access the work. *Corley.* We find the Second Circuit's view to be the sounder construction . . . and conclude that § 1201(a)(2) does not require a plaintiff to show that the accused device enables third parties to access the work without the copyright owner's authorization. Thus, Blizzard has satisfied the "circumvention" element of a § 1201(a)(2) claim, because Blizzard has demonstrated that it did not authorize MDY to circumvent Warden.

which provide access to WoW's dynamic non-literal elements, scan.dll must scan the player's computer RAM and confirm the absence of any bots or cheats. The resident component also requires a "process" in order for the user to continue accessing the work: the user's computer must report portions of WoW code running in RAM to the server. Moreover, Warden's provisions were put into place by Blizzard, and thus, function "with the authority of the copyright owner." Accordingly, Warden effectively controls access to WoW's dynamic non-literal elements. We hold that MDY is liable under § 1201(a)(2) with respect to WoW's dynamic non-literal elements. . . .

F. Blizzard's § 1201(b)(1) claim

Blizzard may prevail under § 1201(b)(1) only if Warden "effectively protect[s] a right" of Blizzard under the Copyright Act. Blizzard contends that Warden protects its reproduction right against unauthorized copying. We disagree.

First, although WoW players copy the software code into RAM while playing the game, Blizzard's EULA and ToU authorize all licensed WoW players to do so. We have explained that ToU § 4(B)'s bot prohibition is a license covenant rather than a condition. Thus, a Glider user who violates this covenant does not infringe by continuing to copy code into RAM. Accordingly, MDY does not violate § 1201(b)(1) by enabling Glider users to avoid Warden's interruption of their *authorized* copying into RAM.

Second, although WoW players can theoretically record game play by taking screen shots, there is no evidence that Warden detects or prevents such allegedly infringing copying. This is logical, because Warden was designed to reduce the presence of cheats and bots, not to protect WoW's dynamic non-literal elements against copying. We conclude that Warden does not effectively protect any of Blizzard's rights under the Copyright Act, and MDY is not liable under § 1201(b)(1) for Glider's circumvention of Warden. . . .

VII.

. . . [W]e determine that MDY is not liable for secondary copyright infringement and is liable under the DMCA only for violation of § 1201(a)(2) with respect to WoW's dynamic non-literal elements. . . .

Questions:

1.) What is the significance of *MAI v. Peak*'s holding that RAM copies are "fixed" for purposes of copyright infringement to the *MDY* case? Put another way, if *MAI* were decided the other way, and RAM copies were too fleeting to infringe, how would this have changed the analysis in *MDY*?

2.) What is the difference between a covenant and condition? Why does it matter in this case?

3.) Have you ever read any Terms of Use agreements before clicking "I Agree"? Does it (should it) inform your analysis of *MDY* if you found that, in a related context, privacy scholars have estimated that an average user might access about 1450 websites per year that have privacy policies—note, not Terms of Use—and that it would take 244 hours a year to read those privacy policies?[1] It should be stressed that many other digital encounters—including those with games, phones and so on—*also* require assent to terms of use that are not captured in the study of *websites*. On the other hand, one does not have

---

[1] Aleecia M. McDonald & Lorrie Faith Cranor, *The Cost of Reading Privacy Policies*, *available at* https://kb.osu.edu/bitstream/handle/1811/72839/ISJLP_V4N3_543.pdf.

to assent to privacy policies to use many websites but at least formal assent to Terms of Use is necessary to use many services.

4.) "Were we to hold otherwise, Blizzard—or any software copyright holder—could designate any disfavored conduct during software use as copyright infringement, by purporting to condition the license on the player's abstention from the disfavored conduct. . . . This would allow software copyright owners far greater rights than Congress has generally conferred on copyright owners." Focus on the court's analysis of whether a violation of the Terms of Use is a condition or a covenant. The court rejects the formalistic argument suggested by *MAI* and § 106 that the code has been *copied* into RAM under an agreement and therefore that *any* violation of that agreement is a violation of copyright law. Instead, it focuses only on those violations of the TOU that have a nexus to the traditional rights of the copyright holder. Now compare this reasoning to the court's analysis of whether the copyright owner can impose through *digital* fences and watchdogs, requirements unrelated to copyright's traditional rights, and then label any attempt to get around them a violation of § 1201. **Why impose a "nexus to copyright infringement" requirement in one setting and then reject it for the other?** Why permit "rights-creep" by *code*, but not by *contract*? Is Judge Callahan a legal realist when it comes to § 106 but a formalist when it comes to § 1201? Is there some other explanation?

5.) This book is under a Creative Commons Attribution, Noncommercial, Sharealike license. You can find the license here: https://creativecommons.org/licenses/by-nc-sa/3.0/. You should look at the full terms of the license, available from that link, but the license deed (a human-friendly summary) is as follows:

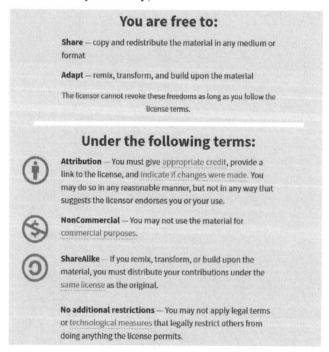

You are free to:

Share — copy and redistribute the material in any medium or format

Adapt — remix, transform, and build upon the material

The licensor cannot revoke these freedoms as long as you follow the license terms.

Under the following terms:

Attribution — You must give appropriate credit, provide a link to the license, and indicate if changes were made. You may do so in any reasonable manner, but not in any way that suggests the licensor endorses you or your use.

NonCommercial — You may not use the material for commercial purposes.

ShareAlike — If you remix, transform, or build upon the material, you must distribute your contributions under the same license as the original.

No additional restrictions — You may not apply legal terms or technological measures that legally restrict others from doing anything the license permits.

Your use of this book is subject to the terms of the license. You can copy it, send copies by email, put it on your website, adapt it for your own course by cutting and editing it. But you must comply with the listed terms. Use the analysis supplied in *MDY*. Are these conditions? Covenants? Answer the following questions.

a.) Joe is a law student who wants to go into business for himself. He finds the digital version of this book before his classmates realize they can download it freely. Joe offers to sell them digital versions for $10 each. Later, on Spring break, Joe's friends have their electronics stolen. Fearing professorial wrath, they are frantic to do their Intellectual Property reading. Joe has the only remaining iPad and he has a copy of the original pdf of this book on it. Ever the entrepreneur, Joe offers to let them read it on his device: $1 a minute.

b.) Joan is a professor who wants to impress her Dean with her productivity. She prints out a copy of the book, but simply removes the title page and replaces it with one naming her as the author.

c.) Jonathan, another professor, likes the book—except all the stuff about "framing" and "baselines." He removes that chapter and adds some of his own material, including a chapter on patent law's doctrine of equivalents. Jonathan really likes his version and does not want people meddling with it. He posts it on his own website for free download, but he uses the in-built restrictions in Microsoft Word to "freeze" the document. Editing is disabled.

d.) Jeremy gets an advance copy of the book and includes a lengthy review of the book in his Kindle Single "What's Wrong With Law Schools!"—a small ebook that he sells for $1.99. Jeremy is harshly critical of the book's approach and illustrates it with many quotations.

Have Joe, Joan, Jonathan or Jeremy violated the license? Exactly how? Be precise about the rights involved and the ways they were violated. Condition or covenant? What are the consequences if they have? Boyle and Jenkins get a lucrative offer from Aspen to sell the book commercially and decide to give up "all the hippy dippy open courseware stuff." They start sending DMCA takedown notices to anyone who posts a copy of the book. Sound? Are Boyle and Jenkins allowed to post a DRM-limited version of the book? (Think about this one carefully. Are they subject to the license?)

6.) Compare *MDY*'s and *Skylink*'s analyses of the reach of section 1201—which is more faithful to the language of the statute and the legislative history? What about the relevant policy arguments?

7.) "[I]n our view, an access control measure can both (1) attempt to block initial access and (2) revoke access if a secondary check determines that access was unauthorized." Should the court find a violation of a "technological measure" under 1201 only in circumvention of one that controls initial access to a work, or circumvention of any measure that can interfere with access after it has been lawfully gained? What are the implications of extending 1201(a) to the latter? Could Microsoft, for example, terminate Word if it finds you have a competing word processor on your laptop, or Apple shut down your phone if you have any disfavored app on it, and then label it a violation of Federal law were you to resist? Or does the language "if *access* was unauthorized" constrain the reach of this holding adequately? Is violation of the Terms of Use *as you are using your phone* enough to make your "access" "unauthorized"?

8.) What does *MDY* decide about the relationship of fair use to 1201? What does *Skylink* decide on the same issue? *Corley*? One court has ruled on this issue and two have declined to reach it. If they had to, what would they say?

PROBLEM 15-2

Google has decided to expand its search offerings to the "code" of that most powerful operating system of all, US law. Their lead engineer, John "Call me Von" Neumann has announced that researching Federal Law "should be as easy as Googling" and Google has initiated a secret project called Malomar to achieve this goal. (Assume that Neumann's activities are imputed to Google.) Malomar attempts to replicate the success of the Google Books project, but to do so with Federal cases and statutes. Google has determined that it would be "inefficient" simply to scan all of those materials from paper books. Instead, it purchased a high level subscription to Westlaw and started a program of downloading all of the Federal cases and statutes through that service. The Malomar program logs onto Westlaw, downloads the cases, removes West's proprietary head notes and Key Numbers—all without a human being ever seeing the document.

Malomar was proceeding brilliantly until it hit a snag. Google had exceeded the maximum allowable number of downloads from its Westlaw account, which was terminated as a result. Foreseeing an endless game of cat and mouse, Neumann took a different approach. Westlaw offers access in two ways, through a simple browser interface and through a customized "client" program that resides on the user's computer and offers more features. Neumann had his software engineers decompile the Westlaw client software he had received with Google's first authorized account. (To get this account, he had to click "assent" to the Westlaw License. Had he read it, he would have found that the license forbids in its Terms of Service, *inter alia*, decompiling the licensed copy of the Westlaw client, exceeding download limits, falsifying passwords or usernames, and extracting material from the Westlaw database in order to compete commercially with West.) From this decompiled software he was able to deduce the mathematical characteristics of the usernames and passwords generated by the Westlaw system—the underlying equation that generates a pattern of letters and numbers making up an authorized username and password. While these were not in fact authorized accounts, the Westlaw system would recognize them as valid. Neumann kept meticulous records of each "account" used and every month sent Westlaw a check for the amount he would have been charged for a valid account.

Having "cracked the code" of the client software, Neumann had no further use for it. Instead, the Malomar program would log on as a newly created "user" through the browser interface, download a large number of cases and statutes—automatically redacting them as described earlier. Malomar downloads no materials other than Federal cases and statutes (all public domain material under § 105). It then repeats the process with a different username and password, all without human intervention at any point. Westlaw does have an online system that terminates the sessions of users who exceed download limits, but since Malomar constantly changes identities it is not affected by that system.

What is the potential liability of Neumann himself, and of the Malomar program, under DMCA 1201? What are the technological measures in play? Refer back to the specific statutory provisions and definitions, as well as the analysis in the three cases that you have read in this chapter. Does it matter that Malomar is ultimately only downloading public domain material? What about its removal of headnotes and Key Numbers? Does the possible breach of the Westlaw License also constitute copyright infringement?

Note: A Copyright Checklist

The next page contains a checklist that goes back over all the material we have covered in copyright law. We suggest that you use the flow charts and checklists as bookends in your review of the material, two different ways to impose structure on the legal questions that we have covered, and to make sure you have not skipped over some portion of the analysis.

The checklist identifies legal questions and points you to the cases or statutory sections we used to answer those questions. The digital version of the book has an added feature—hyperlinks that will take you directly to the material discussing the issue. As before, please use this checklist with caution. Our analysis went much deeper than any two page list can reveal. In particular, the tensions in precedent, policy and statutory interpretation that are so central to our analysis are always going to be poorly represented in any summary form, be it chart or checklist. Nevertheless, students have told us they appreciate the structure they provide.

COPYRIGHT CHECKLIST
(Use this to review copyright law and to test your understanding.)

Does the plaintiff have a valid copyright?

- Identify the copyrighted work(s). Be specific. For example, in a video game there are copyrights over the underlying computer code as well as the audiovisual work on the screen.
- Is it **original** and **creative**? *Feist, West*
- Is it **fixed** in a tangible medium of expression? § 101 definition
- Is it within a category in § 102(a), and not excluded by one of the categories in § 102(b)?
- Is it **expression**, as opposed to **facts** or **ideas**? *Nichols*
- Even if it is expression, is there **merger** of expression and idea (or of expression and other unprotectable material)? *Selden, Kalpakian, Morrissey, Kregos* (note that *Selden* contains an early discussion of idea/expression, merger, and copyright not extending to useful arts)
- Is it a **compilation** of otherwise unprotectable material? If so, is the **selection** and/or **arrangement** copyrightable? If so, is there only minimal creativity, so that the compilation has "**thin**" copyright? *Feist, West, Kregos*
- Is it a **method of operation**? *Lotus* (note that in *Google v. Oracle* the Supreme Court declined to reach the subject matter question on APIs and methods of operation)
- More generally, with **software**, there will be a large amount of material that is not copyrightable—extending far beyond methods of operation. This will include issues of functionality, merger, material taken from the public domain, etc. Much of this will be dealt with in the infringement analysis. *Computer Associates*
- For pictorial graphic and sculptural works, is it the "design of a **useful article**"? If so, is it separable from the "utilitarian aspects of the article"? *Star Athletica*
- Is it a **character?** *Anderson*
- Should it be excluded in the infringement analysis as "*scènes à faire*"? See the discussion after *Computer Associates*
- Is it in another unprotectable category: titles, names, slogans, short phrases, **government works**? § 105, *West, A Natural Experiment, Public.Resource.Org*
- Note on **fixation**: computers, and the world wide web, create a multitude of arguably "fixed" copies. *MAI* But implementing a system that automatically creates temporary copies without human intervention may not be direct infringement. *Netcom*, § 512

Was there direct infringement?

- Did the defendant's activity implicate one of the **exclusive rights in § 106**—reproduction, preparing derivative works, distribution, public performance, public display?
- Was it **literal or non-literal copying**? For analyses of non-literal copying, see *Nichols* (patterns of increasing generality and idea/expression) and *Computer Associates* (for computer programs, abstraction-filtration-comparison).
- Apply the **two-part test** from *Arnstein*: 1) factual copying (access and probative similarity) and 2) unlawful appropriation (substantial similarity). Who should decide part 2, the ordinary/lay observer or intended audience? *Dawson* What standard should they use?
- **Exclude *unprotectable* material**—unoriginal material, facts, ideas, § 102(b), merger, scènes à faire, unoriginal selection/arrangement, useful articles without separability, unfixed material, government works. *Computer Associates*; see subject matter section above. If the only material used by the defendant was a character, think about whether the character was copyrightable. *Nichols, Anderson*
- Was the copying merely **de minimis**? *Newton*

Was the use a non-infringing "fair use"?

- Go through § 107, including its four factors listed below. Under each factor is a general spectrum from weighs against fair use to ⇔ weighs in favor of fair use
  1) the **purpose and character of the use**
     commercial; duplicative ⇔ nonprofit; educational; *transformative* (even if commercial)
  2) the **nature of the copyrighted work**
     more creative; unpublished ⇔ more factual; published
  3) the **amount and substantiality of the portion used**
     large amount; heart of the work ⇔ small amount; insignificant portion, only that which was needed for privileged or progress-promoting purpose
  4) the **effect of the use upon the potential market**
     market substitute ⇔ limited impact or non-cognizable market harm
- Apply relevant analysis from the cases you have read: *Sony, Harper & Row, Campbell, SunTrust, Sega, Perfect 10, Authors Guild, Oracle, MDS,* notes on *Cariou, Warhol, ComicMix*

Was there secondary liability?

- Is there direct liability? If not, there is no secondary liability.
- If so, what kind(s) of secondary liability apply? **Contributory** (knowledge + material contribution), **vicarious** (right and ability to control + direct financial benefit), or **inducement** (*Grokster*)? *Sony, Napster, Grokster*
- Does the *Sony* safe harbor apply? *Sony, Napster*

Does the DMCA § 512 safe harbor apply?

- Is the defendant a qualifying service provider? § 512(k), § 512(i)
- Do its activities fit within the relevant § 512 safe harbor—e.g. § 512(a) mere conduit? § 512(b) caching? § 512(c) storage at the direction of a user? § 512(d) information location tool?
- Did the defendant comply with the statutory requirements in the relevant section? § 512, *Viacom*

Is there a DMCA § 1201 violation?

- Is there a "technological measure"? If so, is it an access control or rights control? § 1201
- Was the technological measure circumvented? Was there a tool that enabled the circumvention? What is the copyrighted work covered by that measure? Determine whether the defendant violated § 1201(a)(1), § 1201(a)(2), and/or § 1201(b)(1). § 1201, *Corley, Skylink, Blizzard*
- If circumvention of an access control is for fair use or other non-infringing activity, do you follow *Corley/Blizzard* or *Skylink*?

Is there a violation of a contractual or license term that covers a copyrighted work?

- The intersection of copyright and licensing is a complex question that goes far beyond the space available in this book. We focused particularly on some of the basic questions brought up by software—where *using* the copyrighted work may also result in creating a *copy* of the copyrighted work, potentially allowing the copyright owner to impose licensing terms that go far beyond what copyright law itself would require.
- If the copyrighted work is software, is the defendant an owner protected by § 117(a)?
- If the defendant is not an owner but a licensee, does violation of the term = copyright infringement? *Blizzard* (No, if the term is a covenant, Yes, if it is a condition with a nexus to copyright)

CHAPTER SIXTEEN

Copyright & State Misappropriation Law: Preemption

Art. 6 cl. 2, U.S. Constitution:
This Constitution, and the laws of the United States which shall be made in pursuance thereof; and all treaties made, or which shall be made, under the authority of the United States, shall be the supreme law of the land; and the judges in every state shall be bound thereby, any thing in the Constitution or laws of any state to the contrary notwithstanding.

Introduction

As we mentioned in the Trademark section of this book, Federal law often coexists with state law that protects similar, or even identical, types of intellectual property. State trademark law is the most obvious example of this. Trade secrecy, which now has both Federal and state protection, is another. (Chapter 22 will explore whether preemption restricts the possible reach of rights under trade secrecy.)

What limits are there on this happy coexistence in the realm of copyright? When does Federal copyright law preempt state law? That is the subject of this chapter. More specifically, here we return to the law of misappropriation that we first met in *INS v. AP* in Chapter 1, and use that doctrinal area to explore some of the knottier issues in copyright preemption.

The Supreme Court has stressed that preemption turns largely on Congressional intent. Did Congress mean for this labeling requirement for cigarettes, or pesticides, or this automobile safety rule to preempt state laws that deal with roughly the same subject matter? Where Congress is silent, the courts will generally assume that its intent was *not* to preempt state law—at least in traditional areas of state regulation. (Preemption is often discussed with respect to state statutory schemes but it is important to remember that it can also include preemption of common law actions—for example, in tort law.) There are, however, at least two areas where intention takes a back seat—or is implied from the context. In "field preemption cases," where Federal law has effectively seized the entire field of activity, state regulatory action may be prohibited altogether. (Defining what counts as "the field," however, is often problematic, as recent cases on immigration have shown.) In "conflict preemption cases," it is impossible to comply both with the Federal and the state law. In that case, the Supremacy Clause governs and the state law is without effect.

Enter copyright.

State intellectual property law and Federal copyright law have had a tangled relationship from the beginning. The *Eldred* case features an extended wrangle among the Justices about how to understand the first Federal copyright statute, which largely replaced state schemes mainly rooted in the common law. But state "common law copyright" continued to exist until the 1976 Act, and the common law copyrights over sound recordings dating from the 1970's are still being litigated today.

Section 301 of the 1976 Copyright Act contains Congress's explicit instructions about preemption.

§ 301.—Preemption with respect to other laws

(a) On and after January 1, 1978, all legal or equitable rights that are equivalent to any of the exclusive rights within the general scope of copyright as specified by section 106 in works of authorship that are fixed in a tangible medium of expression and come within the subject matter of copyright as specified by sections 102 and 103, whether created before or after that date and whether published or unpublished, are governed exclusively by this title. Thereafter, no person is entitled to any such right or equivalent right in any such work under the common law or statutes of any State.

(b) Nothing in this title annuls or limits any rights or remedies under the common law or statutes of any State with respect to—

(1) subject matter that does not come within the subject matter of copyright as specified by sections 102 and 103, including works of authorship not fixed in any tangible medium of expression; or

(2) any cause of action arising from undertakings commenced before January 1, 1978;

(3) activities violating legal or equitable rights that are not equivalent to any of the exclusive rights within the general scope of copyright as specified by section 106; or

(4) State and local landmarks, historic preservation, zoning, or building codes, relating to architectural works protected under section 102(a)(8).

(c) With respect to sound recordings fixed before February 15, 1972, any rights or remedies under the common law or statutes of any State shall not be annulled or limited by this title until February 15, 2067. The preemptive provisions of subsection (a) shall apply to any such rights and remedies pertaining to any cause of action arising from undertakings commenced on and after February 15, 2067. Notwithstanding the provisions of section 303, no sound recording fixed before February 15, 1972, shall be subject to copyright under this title before, on, or after February 15, 2067.

(d) Nothing in this title annuls or limits any rights or remedies under any other Federal statute.

(e) The scope of Federal preemption under this section is not affected by the adherence of the United States to the Berne Convention or the satisfaction of obligations of the United States thereunder.

(f)(1) On or after the effective date set forth in section 610(a) of the Visual Artists Rights Act of 1990, all legal or equitable rights that are equivalent to any of the rights conferred by section 106A with respect to works of visual art to which the rights conferred by section 106A apply are governed exclusively by section 106A and section 113(d) and the provisions of this title relating to such sections. Thereafter, no person is entitled to any such right or equivalent right in any work of visual art under the common law or statutes of any State.

(2) Nothing in paragraph (1) annuls or limits any rights or remedies under the common law or statutes of any State with respect to—

(A) any cause of action from undertakings commenced

**before the effective date set forth in section 610(a) of the
Visual Artists Rights Act of 1990;
(B) activities violating legal or equitable rights that are not
equivalent to any of the rights conferred by section 106A
with respect to works of visual art; or
(C) activities violating legal or equitable rights which extend beyond the life of the author.**

The broad structure of § 301 depends on two limitations: general scope and subject matter. It preempts "all legal or equitable rights **that are equivalent to any of the exclusive rights within the general scope of copyright as specified by section 106 in works of authorship** that are **fixed in a tangible medium** of expression **and** come within the **subject matter of copyright as specified by sections 102 and 103**." Subsection b.) effectively restates this point in the negative—by saying that if the legal or equitable rights are not within the general scope of copyright or if they are over subject matter that copyright does not cover, then they are not preempted.

But therein lies a problem. As we have stressed in this casebook, intellectual property is defined as much by that which it excludes as that which it includes. To come back to the discussion of *Sony* in *The Public Domain*, "the holes matter as much as the cheese." The *exclusion* of ideas, facts and unoriginal material from copyright is as central to the Federal copyright scheme, as is the *inclusion* of original expression, fixed in material form. That is the essence of copyright. Yet, read literally, § 301 seems to say that states are entirely free to make law over all the things excluded from copyright. For example, § 102 says "[i]n no case does copyright protection for an original work of authorship extend to any idea, procedure, process, system, method of operation, concept, principle, or discovery." Those things are outside the subject matter of copyright. Does that mean that we could have 50 different state systems, in some of which ideas, unoriginal compilations of fact, methods of operation and so on, were subject to exclusive rights under state law? Might the white pages telephone directory from *Feist v. Rural*, the method of doing accountancy from *Baker v. Selden*, the menu structure from *Lotus v. Borland*—might all of these be protected under the laws of some state or other? Could someone in California be granted an exclusive right over the *idea* of a chase scene? Could someone in New York be given an exclusive right over the *facts* of the atomic weights of the elements?

What about scope? § 106 conveys only a limited number of exclusive rights. Can the states add to those without limit? Might reading a book without permission count as a violation of the law in Rhode Island, singing a song in the shower be a tort in South Dakota? § 107 explicitly limits the exclusive rights of § 106. If it is a fair use, it is not a violation of the § 106 exclusive rights. *A fortiori* this would seem to mean that fair uses are outside the general scope of copyright. Does this mean, then, that states are free to make all fair uses illegal? Could parodies be prohibited in Pennsylvania, and quotations in a critical review be a tort in Connecticut? Certainly the First Amendment would have something to say about those questions, but what about copyright law? Can it really be—as a literal reading of § 301 suggests—that none of these state rules would be preempted?

Thankfully, the answer is no—common sense still has an occasional role in statutory construction, and § 301 does not exhaust all of the indications to be grasped from the Copyright Act about those things which Congress must be assumed to want to preempt. (If intent is truly the touchstone here, as the courts always insist, then one has to say that Congress needs a lot of judicial speech-therapy to articulate those intentions.) But that still leaves the courts struggling to come up with a coherent idea of copyright preemption. Their problem is, effectively, a double-sided slippery slope. If they follow the literal language of

§ 301, then the states are allowed to make nonsense of Federal copyright policy by creating rights that negate all of its deliberate limitations and exceptions—whether in subject matter or scope. In other words, if only copyright's "inclusions"—in scope and subject matter—are preempted, then copyright's "exclusions" are fair game and that seems absurd. But on the other side, if we say that—for the purpose of preemption—copyright's empire consists of all the stuff that it covers *and all the stuff it excludes*, then preemption reaches very far indeed. What would *not* be preempted under such a standard? Copyright law gives no rights against defamation or trespass. Does that mean that defamation and trespass are preempted? And if they are not—as they clearly are not—then why can there not be state rights in ideas and unoriginal collections of facts, or state rights to prevent parodies and prohibit quotation? After all, those things are also outside of copyright's ambit.

What lies between these two slippery slopes? We will explore that question in the context of a single tort—misappropriation, the first intellectual property issue we covered in this book. But the implications of the discussion apply far beyond misappropriation, to give you a sense of how courts would deal with copyright-based preemption in any area of law.

PROBLEM 16-1
FRAMING AND PREEMPTION.

You have recently acquired a new client, HotNews.com, based in Manhattan. HotNews is a company whose sole product is an extremely popular internet site and whose sole revenue comes from advertisers who wish to place their messages on its site. The site is so popular because it offers, in the words of the HotNews slogan, "Your one-stop choice for Web News." HotNews does not gather news of its own. Instead it uses a process called "framing" to offer visitors to its page simultaneous access to the websites of a variety of news sources on the Web, including *The New York Times*, *The Washington Post*, and *Sports Illustrated*. A visitor to the HotNews page sees a screen divided into a number of partitions, like the frames of a picture (hence the name). Inside each of these frames will be shown the front page of a particular news-site, such as *The New York Times*, carefully identified as such. Since HotNews is, in effect, showing the newspapers' own sites, the viewer will see the familiar mastheads of each paper or magazine.

Describing the operation of their service to interested journalists, the HotNews management has been insistent that HotNews merely offers a set of useful instructions to the computers of its users; it is the user's computer that then fetches the different news sites and displays them side-by-side on the user's screen. In effect, the HotNews website tells the visitor's web-browsing program:

> "Divide your screen up into three frames. In number one, fetch and display http://www.nytimes.com, in number 2, fetch and display http://www.washingtonpost.com and in number 3, fetch and display http://www.sportsillustrated.com. In the spaces between and around these three frames, show HotNews' advertisements."

The HotNews site's most important feature is called deep-linking. Each day, HotNews' news analysts identify all the stories on a particular topic from different newspapers. Thus, for example, all the stories on Iraq or the search for the missing mass in the universe, would be indexed—whatever their source. The index would "deep link" the viewer directly to the story—bypassing the task of navigating through the newspaper's own screens and menus, and in the process avoiding some of the newspaper's advertising. What is more, the resultant stories would each be displayed in the "frame" for that publication. Thus a viewer could compare coverage given by the *Post* and *Times* to the same story; articles would appear literally side-by-side. Visitors to HotNews can then click through the various screens and stories in the different sites, all without ever moving out of the HotNews frames. HotNews claims that this is a significant convenience to its customers, and the number of people using the site (more than one million per day) seems to bear this claim out.

The New York Times and other featured newspapers and magazines do not see the process in such a benevolent light. Their reason is that the HotNews frames fit over, and replace, many of the banner advertisements carried at the top of their pages. Thus, a person viewing *The New York Times* at the HotNews site sees exactly the page they would get were they to go directly to http://www.nytimes.com, with one crucial exception: the advertisements at the tops and sides of the page will be those that HotNews has been paid to display, not those that *The New York Times* has been paid to display. Ads that are included inside the four corners of the article's dimensions will be shown, but these command a lower advertising fee than the prestigious banner position atop an article. *The New York Times* and the other likely plaintiffs are upset about this because it lowers their advertising revenue from Web-based news services.

All of the publications to which HotNews links offer a limited number of free articles to casual browsers. Once that limit—10 articles a month in the case of *The New York Times*—has been reached, the site will not show more stories unless the user purchases a digital subscription. (In practice, this nag-wall is easily circumvented if the user simply clears cookies from her machine.) HotNews does not disturb the nag screens or article limits in any way. If a user has gone over their limit, they see the same warning that they need to purchase a subscription in the relevant window on their desktop. However, the news sites believe that, precisely by offering *so many news sites*, HotNews might enable users to get their daily news without going over the relevant article limit. HotNews argues instead that it will drive more users to their sites, leading to more subscribers.

At present web journalism is struggling. The market for print is all but dead. Some mixture of paywalls and online advertising is the future. Thus newspapers are particularly touchy about aggregators. HotNews has come to believe it will soon be sued and has turned to you for legal advice.

Your mission: Using only the materials for today's assignment, you need to research whether the news organizations have a cause of action for "hot news misappropriation" against HotNews.com under New York State law, and whether that cause of action can be stated in such a way as to avoid preemption by Federal copyright law. [Hint: what are the § 106 exclusive rights potentially implicated here? You might want to look beyond the obvious and reread the discussion of the display right, and of fair use, in *Perfect 10*.] Bonus question: does Article 1, § 8, cl. 8 play a role in your *preemption* analysis? Should it? If so, how?

International News Service v. The Associated Press
28 U.S. 215 (1918)

Please re-read *INS* from Chapter 1, page 26.

• • • • • • • • • •

1.) Subject Matter and General Scope: Extra Elements

National Basketball Assoc. v. Motorola, Inc.
105 F.3d 841 (2d Cir. 1997)

WINTER, Circuit Judge.

Motorola, Inc. and Sports Team Analysis and Tracking Systems ("STATS") appeal from a permanent injunction. The injunction concerns a handheld pager sold by Motorola and marketed under the name "SportsTrax," which displays updated information of professional basketball games in progress. The injunction prohibits appellants, absent authorization from the National Basketball Association and NBA Properties, Inc. (collectively the "NBA"), from transmitting scores or other data about NBA games in progress via the pagers, STATS's site on America On-Line's computer dial-up service, or "any equivalent means."

The crux of the dispute concerns the extent to which a state law "hot-news" misappropriation claim based on *International News Service v. Associated Press* (1918) ("*INS*"), survives preemption by the federal Copyright Act and whether the NBA's claim fits within the surviving *INS*-type claims. We hold that a narrow "hot-news" exception does survive preemption. However, we also hold that appellants' transmission of "real-time" NBA game scores and information tabulated from television and radio broadcasts of games in progress does not constitute a misappropriation of "hot news" that is the property of the NBA.

I. BACKGROUND

The facts are largely undisputed. Motorola manufactures and markets the SportsTrax paging device while STATS supplies the game information that is transmitted to the pagers. The product became available to the public in January 1996, at a retail price of about $200. SportsTrax's pager has an inch-and-a-half by inch-and-a-half screen and operates in four basic modes: "current," "statistics," "final scores" and "demonstration." It is the "current" mode that gives rise to the present dispute. In that mode, SportsTrax displays the following information on NBA games in progress: (i) the teams playing; (ii) score changes; (iii) the team in possession of the ball; (iv) whether the team is in the free-throw bonus; (v) the quarter of the game; and (vi) time remaining in the quarter. The information is updated every two to three minutes, with more frequent updates near the end of the first half and the end of the game. There is a lag of approximately two or three minutes between events in the game itself and when the information appears on the pager screen.

SportsTrax's operation relies on a "data feed" supplied by STATS reporters who watch the games on television or listen to them on the radio. The reporters key into a personal computer changes in the score and other information such as successful and missed shots, fouls, and clock updates. The information is relayed by modem to STATS's host computer, which compiles, analyzes, and formats the data for retransmission. The information is then sent to a common carrier, which then sends it via satellite to various local FM radio networks that in turn emit the signal received by the individual SportsTrax pagers.

Finding Motorola and STATS liable for misappropriation, Judge Preska entered the permanent injunction, reserved the calculation of damages for subsequent proceedings, and stayed execution of the injunction pending appeal. Motorola and STATS appeal from the injunction.

II. THE STATE LAW MISAPPROPRIATION CLAIM

A. Summary of Ruling

Because our disposition of the state law misappropriation claim rests in large part on preemption by the Copyright Act, our discussion necessarily goes beyond the elements of a misappropriation claim under New York law, and a summary of our ruling here will perhaps render that discussion—or at least the need for it—more understandable.

The issues before us are ones that have arisen in various forms over the course of this century as technology has steadily increased the speed and quantity of information transmission. Today, individuals at home, at work, or elsewhere, can use a computer, pager, or other device to obtain highly selective kinds of information virtually at will. *INS* was one of the first cases to address the issues raised by these technological advances, although the technology involved in that case was primitive by contemporary standards. *INS* involved two wire services, the Associated Press ("AP") and International News Service ("INS"), that transmitted news stories by wire to member newspapers. INS would lift factual stories from AP bulletins and send them by wire to INS papers. INS would also take factual stories from east coast AP papers and wire them to INS papers on the west coast that had yet to publish because of time differentials. The Supreme Court held that INS's conduct was a common-law misappropriation of AP's property.

With the advance of technology, radio stations began "live" broadcasts of events such as baseball games and operas, and various entrepreneurs began to use the transmissions of others in one way or another for their own profit. In response, New York courts created a body of misappropriation law, loosely based on *INS*, that sought to apply ethical standards to the use by one party of another's transmissions of events.

Federal copyright law played little active role in this area until 1976. Before then, it appears to have been the general understanding—there being no caselaw of consequence—that live events such as baseball games were not copyrightable. Moreover, doubt existed even as to whether a recorded broadcast or videotape of such an event was copyrightable. In 1976, however, Congress passed legislation expressly affording copyright protection to simultaneously-recorded broadcasts of live performances such as sports events. Such protection was not extended to the underlying events.

The 1976 amendments also contained provisions preempting state law claims that enforced rights "equivalent" to exclusive copyright protections when the work to which the state claim was being applied fell within the area of copyright protection. *See* 17 U.S.C. § 301. Based on legislative history of the 1976 Amendments, it is generally agreed that a "hot-news" *INS*-like claim survives preemption. H.R. No. 94-1476 at 132 (1976). However, much of New York misappropriation law after *INS* goes well beyond "hot-news" claims and is preempted.

B. Copyrights in Events or Broadcasts of Events

The NBA asserted copyright infringement claims with regard both to the underlying games and to their broadcasts. The district court dismissed these claims, and the NBA does not appeal from their dismissal. Nevertheless, discussion of the infringement claims is necessary to provide the framework for analyzing the viability of the NBA's state law misappropriation claim in light of the Copyright Act's preemptive effect.

1. Infringement of a Copyright in the Underlying Games

In our view, the underlying basketball games do not fall within the subject matter of federal copyright protection because they do not constitute "original works of authorship" under 17 U.S.C. § 102(a). Sports events are not "authored" in any common sense of the word. There is, of course, at least at the professional level, considerable preparation for a game. However, the preparation is as much an expression of hope or faith as a determination of what will actually happen. Unlike movies, plays, television programs, or operas, athletic events are competitive and have no underlying script. Preparation may even cause mistakes to succeed, like the broken play in football that gains yardage because the opposition could not expect it. Athletic events may also result in wholly unanticipated occurrences, the most notable recent event being in a championship baseball game in which interference with a fly ball caused an umpire to signal erroneously a home run.

What "authorship" there is in a sports event, moreover, must be open to copying by competitors if fans are to be attracted. If the inventor of the T-formation in football had been able to copyright it, the sport might have come to an end instead of prospering. Even where athletic preparation most resembles authorship—figure skating, gymnastics, and, some would uncharitably say, professional wrestling—a performer who conceives and executes a particularly graceful and difficult—or, in the case of wrestling, seemingly painful—acrobatic feat cannot copyright it without impairing the underlying competition in the future. A claim of being the only athlete to perform a feat doesn't mean much if no one else is allowed to try.

For many of these reasons, Nimmer on Copyright concludes that the "far more reasonable" position is that athletic events are not copyrightable. Nimmer notes that, among other problems, the number of joint copyright owners would arguably include the league, the teams, the athletes, umpires, stadium workers and even fans, who all contribute to the "work."

Concededly, caselaw is scarce on the issue of whether organized events themselves are copyrightable, but what there is indicates that they are not. In claiming a copyright in the underlying games, the NBA relied in part on a footnote in *Baltimore Orioles, Inc. v. Major League Baseball Players Assn.* (7th Cir. 1986), which stated that the "players' performances" contain the "Modest Creativity Required for Copyrightability." However, the Court went on to state, "moreover, even if the players' performances were not sufficiently creative, the players agree that the cameramen and director contribute creative labor to the telecasts." This last sentence indicates that the court was considering the copyrightability of telecasts—not the underlying games, which obviously can be played without cameras.

We believe that the lack of caselaw is attributable to a general understanding that athletic events were, and are, uncopyrightable. Indeed, prior to 1976, there was even doubt that broadcasts describing or depicting such events, which have a far stronger case for copyrightability than the events themselves, were entitled to copyright protection. Indeed, as described in the next subsection of this opinion, Congress found it necessary to extend such protection to recorded broadcasts of live events. The fact that Congress did not extend such protection to the events themselves confirms our view that the district court correctly held that appellants were not infringing a copyright in the NBA games.

2. Infringement of a Copyright in the Broadcasts of NBA Games

As noted, recorded broadcasts of NBA games—as opposed to the games themselves—are now entitled to copyright protection. The Copyright Act was amended in 1976 specifically to insure that simultaneously-recorded transmissions of live performances and sporting events would meet the Act's requirement that the original work of authorship be "fixed in any tangible medium of expression." 17 U.S.C. § 102(a). Accordingly, Section 101 of the Act, containing definitions, was amended to read:

> A work consisting of sounds, images, or both, that are being transmitted, is "fixed" for purposes of this title if a fixation of the work is being made simultaneously with its transmission.

Congress specifically had sporting events in mind:

> [T]he bill seeks to resolve, through the definition of "fixation" in section 101, the status of live broadcasts—sports, news coverage, live performances of music, etc.—that are reaching the public in unfixed form but that are simultaneously being recorded.

The House Report also makes clear that it is the broadcast, not the underlying game, that is the subject of copyright protection. In explaining how game broadcasts meet the Act's requirement that the subject matter be an "original work[ ] of authorship," the House Report stated:

> When a football game is being covered by four television cameras, with a director guiding the activities of the four cameramen and choosing which of their electronic images are sent out to the public and in what order, there is little doubt that what the cameramen and the director are doing constitutes "authorship."

Although the broadcasts are protected under copyright law, the district court correctly held that Motorola and STATS did not infringe NBA's copyright because they reproduced only facts from the broadcasts, not the expression or description of the game that constitutes the broadcast. The "fact/expression dichotomy" is a bedrock principle of copyright law that "limits severely the scope of protection in fact-based works." *Feist Publications, Inc. v. Rural Tel. Service Co.* (1991). "No author may copyright facts or ideas. The copyright is limited to those aspects of the work—termed 'expression'—that display the stamp of the author's originality."

We agree with the district court that the "defendants provide purely factual information which any patron of an NBA game could acquire from the arena without any involvement from the director, cameramen, or others who contribute to the originality of a broadcast." Because the SportsTrax device and AOL site reproduce only factual information culled from the broadcasts and none of the copyrightable expression of the games, appellants did not infringe the copyright of the broadcasts.

C. The State-Law Misappropriation Claim

The district court's injunction was based on its conclusion that, under New York law, defendants had unlawfully misappropriated the NBA's property rights in its games. The district court reached this conclusion by holding: (i) that the NBA's misappropriation claim relating to the underlying games was not preempted by Section 301 of the Copyright Act; and (ii) that, under New York common law, defendants had engaged in unlawful misappropriation. We disagree.

1. Preemption Under the Copyright Act

a) Summary

When Congress amended the Copyright Act in 1976, it provided for the preemption of state law claims that are interrelated with copyright claims in certain ways. Under 17 U.S.C. § 301, a state law claim is preempted when: (i) the state law claim seeks to vindicate "legal or equitable rights that are equivalent" to one of the bundle of exclusive rights already protected by copyright law under 17 U.S.C. § 106—styled the "general scope requirement"; and (ii) the particular work to which the state law claim is being applied falls within the type of works protected by the Copyright Act under Sections 102 and 103—styled the "subject matter requirement."

The district court concluded that the NBA's misappropriation claim was not preempted because, with respect to the underlying games, as opposed to the broadcasts, the subject matter requirement was not met. The court dubbed as "partial preemption" its separate analysis of misappropriation claims relating to the underlying games and misappropriation claims relating to broadcasts of those games. The district court then relied on a series of older New York misappropriation cases involving radio broadcasts that considerably broadened *INS*. We hold that where the challenged copying or misappropriation relates in part to the copyrighted broadcasts of the games, the subject matter requirement is met as to both the broadcasts and the games. We therefore reject the partial preemption doctrine and its anomalous consequence that "it is possible for a plaintiff to assert claims both for infringement of its copyright in a broadcast and misappropriation of its rights in the underlying event." We do find that a properly-narrowed INS "hot-news" misappropriation claim survives preemption because it fails the general scope requirement, but that the broader theory of the radio broadcast cases relied upon by the district court were preempted when Congress extended copyright protection to simultaneously-recorded broadcasts.

b) "Partial Preemption" and the Subject Matter Requirement

The subject matter requirement is met when the work of authorship being copied or misappropriated "falls within the ambit of copyright protection." We believe that the subject matter requirement is met in the instant matter and that the concept of "partial preemption" is not consistent with section 301 of the Copyright Act. Although game broadcasts are copyrightable while the underlying games are not, the Copyright Act should not be read to distinguish between the two when analyzing the preemption of a misappropriation claim based on copying or taking from the copyrightable work. We believe that:

> [O]nce a performance is reduced to tangible form, there is no distinction between the performance and the recording of the performance for the purposes of preemption under § 301(a). Thus, if a baseball game were not broadcast or were telecast without being recorded, the Players' performances similarly would not be fixed in tangible form and their rights of publicity would not be subject to preemption. By virtue of being videotaped, however, the Players' performances are fixed in tangible form, and any rights of publicity in their performances that are equivalent to the rights contained in the copyright of the telecast are preempted.

Baltimore Orioles.

Copyrightable material often contains uncopyrightable elements within it, but Section 301 preemption bars state law misappropriation claims with respect to uncopyrightable as well as copyrightable elements. In *Harper & Row* [the Second Circuit decision that was reversed by the Supreme Court regarding the issue of fair use, not preemption] for example, we held that state law claims based on the copying of excerpts from President Ford's memoirs were preempted even with respect to information that was purely factual and not copyrightable. We stated:

> The [Copyright] Act clearly embraces "works of authorship," including "literary works," as within its subject matter. The fact that portions of the

Ford memoirs may consist of uncopyrightable material . . . does not take the work as a whole outside the subject matter protected by the Act. Were this not so, states would be free to expand the perimeters of copyright protection to their own liking, on the theory that preemption would be no bar to state protection of material not meeting federal statutory standards.

The legislative history supports this understanding of Section 301(a)'s subject matter requirement. The House Report stated:

As long as a work fits within one of the general subject matter categories of sections 102 and 103, the bill prevents the States from protecting it even if it fails to achieve Federal statutory copyright because it is too minimal or lacking in originality to qualify, or because it has fallen into the public domain.

Adoption of a partial preemption doctrine—preemption of claims based on misappropriation of broadcasts but no preemption of claims based on misappropriation of underlying facts—would expand significantly the reach of state law claims and render the preemption intended by Congress unworkable. It is often difficult or impossible to separate the fixed copyrightable work from the underlying uncopyrightable events or facts. Moreover, Congress, in extending copyright protection only to the broadcasts and not to the underlying events, intended that the latter be in the public domain. Partial preemption turns that intent on its head by allowing state law to vest exclusive rights in material that Congress intended to be in the public domain and to make unlawful conduct that Congress intended to allow.

c) The General Scope Requirement

Under the general scope requirement, Section 301 "preempts only those state law rights that 'may be abridged by an act which, in and of itself, would infringe one of the exclusive rights' provided by federal copyright law." However, certain forms of commercial misappropriation otherwise within the general scope requirement will survive preemption if an "extra-element" test is met.

We turn, therefore, to the question of the extent to which a "hot-news" misappropriation claim based on *INS* involves extra elements and is not the equivalent of exclusive rights under a copyright. Courts are generally agreed that some form of such a claim survives preemption. This conclusion is based in part on the legislative history of the 1976 amendments. The House Report stated:

"Misappropriation" is not necessarily synonymous with copyright infringement, and thus a cause of action labeled as "misappropriation" is not preempted if it is in fact based neither on a right within the general scope of copyright as specified by section 106 nor on a right equivalent thereto. For example, state law should have the flexibility to afford a remedy (under traditional principles of equity) against a consistent pattern of unauthorized appropriation by a competitor of the facts (i.e., not the literary expression) constituting "hot" news, whether in the traditional mold of *International News Service v. Associated Press* (1918), or in the newer form of data updates from scientific, business, or financial data bases.

The crucial question, therefore, is the breadth of the "hot-news" claim that survives preemption.

In *INS*, the plaintiff AP and defendant INS were "wire services" that sold news items to client newspapers. AP brought suit to prevent INS from selling facts and information lifted from AP sources to INS-affiliated newspapers. One method by which INS was able to use AP's news was to lift facts from AP news bulletins. Another method was to sell facts taken from just-published east coast AP newspapers to west coast INS newspapers whose editions had yet to appear. The Supreme Court held (prior to *Erie R. Co. v. Tompkins*) that INS's use of AP's information was unlawful under federal common law. It characterized INS's conduct as

> amount[ing] to an unauthorized interference with the normal operation of complainant's legitimate business precisely at the point where the profit is to be reaped, in order to divert a material portion of the profit from those who have earned it to those who have not; with special advantage to defendant in the competition because of the fact that it is not burdened with any part of the expense of gathering the news.

The theory of the New York misappropriation cases relied upon by the district court is considerably broader than that of *INS*. For example, the district court quoted at length from *Metropolitan Opera Ass'n v. Wagner-Nichols Recorder Corp.* (N.Y. Sup. Ct. 1950). *Metropolitan Opera* described New York misappropriation law as standing for the "broader principle that property rights of commercial value are to be and will be protected from any form of commercial immorality"; that misappropriation law developed "to deal with business malpractices offensive to the ethics of [ ] society"; and that the doctrine is "broad and flexible."

However, we believe that *Metropolitan Opera*'s broad misappropriation doctrine based on amorphous concepts such as "commercial immorality" or society's "ethics" is preempted. Such concepts are virtually synonymous for wrongful copying and are in no meaningful fashion distinguishable from infringement of a copyright. The broad misappropriation doctrine relied upon by the district court is, therefore, the equivalent of exclusive rights in copyright law.

Most of the broadcast cases relied upon by the NBA are simply not good law. Those cases were decided at a time when simultaneously-recorded broadcasts were not protected under the Copyright Act and when the state law claims they fashioned were not subject to federal preemption. For example, *Metropolitan Opera* involved the unauthorized copying, marketing, and sale of opera radio broadcasts. As another example, in *Mutual Broadcasting System v. Muzak Corp.* (N.Y. Sup. Ct. 1941), the defendant simultaneously retransmitted the plaintiff's baseball radio broadcasts onto telephone lines. As discussed above, the 1976 amendments to the Copyright Act were specifically designed to afford copyright protection to simultaneously-recorded broadcasts, and *Metropolitan Opera* and *Muzak* could today be brought as copyright infringement cases. Moreover, we believe that they would have to be brought as copyright cases because the amendments affording broadcasts copyright protection also preempted the state law misappropriation claims under which they were decided.

Our conclusion, therefore, is that only a narrow "hot-news" misappropriation claim survives preemption for actions concerning material within the realm of copyright. In our view, the elements central to an *INS* claim are: (i) the plaintiff generates or collects information at some cost or expense, (ii) the value of the information is highly time-sensitive, (iii) the defendant's use of the information constitutes free-riding on the plaintiff's costly efforts to generate or collect it; (iv) the defendant's use of the information is in direct competition with a product or service offered by the plaintiff, [and] (v) the ability of other parties to free-ride on the efforts of the plaintiff would so reduce the incentive to produce the product or service that its existence or quality would be substantially threatened.

INS is not about ethics; it is about the protection of property rights in time-sensitive information so that the information will be made available to the public by profit-seeking entrepreneurs. If services like AP were not assured of property rights in the news they pay to collect, they would cease to collect it. The ability of their competitors to appropriate their product at only nominal cost and thereby to disseminate a competing product at a lower price would destroy the incentive to collect news in the first place. The newspaper-reading public would suffer because no one would have an incentive to collect "hot news."

We therefore find the extra elements—those in addition to the elements of copyright infringement—that allow a "hot-news" claim to survive preemption are: (i) the time-sensitive value of factual information, (ii) the free-riding by a defendant, and (iii) the threat to the very existence of the product or service provided by the plaintiff.

2. The Legality of SportsTrax

We conclude that Motorola and STATS have not engaged in unlawful misappropriation under the "hot-news" test set out above. To be sure, some of the elements of a "hot-news" *INS*-claim are met. The information transmitted to SportsTrax is not precisely contemporaneous, but it is nevertheless time-sensitive. Also, the NBA does provide, or will shortly do so, information like that available through SportsTrax. It now offers a service called "Gamestats" that provides official play-by-play game sheets and half-time and final box scores within each arena. It also provides such information to the media in each arena. In the future, the NBA plans to enhance Gamestats so that it will be networked between the various arenas and will support a pager product analogous to SportsTrax. SportsTrax will of course directly compete with an enhanced Gamestats.

However, there are critical elements missing in the NBA's attempt to assert a "hot-news" *INS*-type claim. As framed by the NBA, their claim compresses and confuses three different informational products. The first product is generating the information by playing the games; the second product is transmitting live, full descriptions of those games; and the third product is collecting and retransmitting strictly factual information about the games. The first and second products are the NBA's primary business: producing basketball games for live attendance and licensing copyrighted broadcasts of those games. The collection and retransmission of strictly factual material about the games is a different product: e.g., box-scores in newspapers, summaries of statistics on television sports news, and real-time facts to be transmitted to pagers. In our view, the NBA has failed to show any competitive effect whatsoever from SportsTrax on the first and second products and a lack of any free-riding by SportsTrax on the third.

With regard to the NBA's primary products—producing basketball games with live attendance and licensing copyrighted broadcasts of those games—there is no evidence that anyone regards SportsTrax as a substitute for attending NBA games or watching them on television. In fact, Motorola markets SportsTrax as being designed "for those times when you cannot be at the arena, watch the game on TV, or listen to the radio. . . ."

The NBA argues that the pager market is also relevant to a "hot-news" *INS*-type claim and that SportsTrax's future competition with Gamestats satisfies any missing element. We agree that there is a separate market for the real-time transmission of factual information to pagers or similar devices. However, we disagree that SportsTrax is in any sense freeriding off Gamestats.

An indispensable element of an *INS* "hot-news" claim is free-riding by a defendant on a plaintiff's product, enabling the defendant to produce a directly competitive product for less money because it has lower costs. SportsTrax is not such a product. The use of pagers to transmit real-time information about NBA games requires: (i) the collecting of facts about the games; (ii) the transmission of these facts on a network; (iii) the assembling of them by the particular service; and (iv) the transmission of them to pagers or an on-line computer site. Appellants are in no way free-riding on Gamestats. Motorola and STATS expend their own resources to collect purely factual information generated in NBA games to transmit to SportsTrax pagers. They have their own network and assemble and transmit data themselves.

SportsTrax and Gamestats are each bearing their own costs of collecting factual information on NBA games, and, if one produces a product that is cheaper or otherwise superior to the other, that producer will prevail in the marketplace. This is obviously not the situation against which *INS* was intended to prevent: the potential lack of any such product or service because of the anticipation of free-riding.

For the foregoing reasons, the NBA has not shown any damage to any of its products based on free-riding by Motorola and STATS, and the NBA's misappropriation claim based on New York law is preempted.

IV. CONCLUSION

We vacate the injunction entered by the district court and order that the NBA's claim for misappropriation be dismissed.

Questions:

1.) Why are football games not copyrightable? (The game itself, not the live recording of it.) Is any sport copyrightable? If professional wrestling were to be entirely a sham sport, scripted in its entirety (which of course we know is untrue) would *it* be copyrightable? What would the copyright cover? The actual bout? The script for the bout? And how would it be classed? As choreography?

[Some of you will now be playing out all kinds of other copyright scenarios in your head. Is improvisational theater—in which characters are given general role guidelines, but no lines—copyrightable? Is a jazz jam session where all the musicians riff off each other's contributions copyrightable? Do you have a copyright over the awesomely destructive and unlikely path your character just took through World of Warcraft? This is a deadly serious editorial interjection: if you are indeed delightedly geeking out on this kind of stuff, you should consider a career as an intellectual property lawyer. Really. It is what makes it fun. Conversely, if all this strikes you as metaphysics for nerds (which it is) then intellectual property may not be for you.]

2.) Why are the live recordings of sporting events copyrightable? What is the original expression required by *Feist*? Who is the author? Does contemporaneous recording satisfy the constitutional fixation requirement?

3.) The District Court came up with the idea of partial preemption—that copyright would preempt giving a state right that covered the copyrightable elements of the broadcast, but not the non-copyrightable elements of the game (such as the game itself, the facts and so on). Why is this wrong? Isn't that what § 301 explicitly says?

4.) What are the requirements this case lays down for a state hot news misappropriation tort that survives Federal preemption?

5.) "[W]e believe that *Metropolitan Opera*'s broad misappropriation doctrine based on amorphous concepts such as "commercial immorality" or society's "ethics" is preempted. Such concepts are virtually synonymous for wrongful copying and are in no meaningful fashion distinguishable from infringement of a copyright." True? Are your favorite immoral or unethical ideas synonymous with wrongful copying? Even your best commercially immoral ideas? What does the court mean when it says this?

6.) This case is about preemption of one specific state tort—misappropriation. What can you glean from it about the reach of copyright-based preemption in, for example, the case of a state statute forbidding parodies, or giving an exclusive right to the compiler of white pages telephone directories? Would the specific extra elements the court mentioned here be relevant?

2.) Preemption, Misappropriation & the Fact/Expression Dichotomy

Barclays Capital Inc. v. Theflyonthewall.com, Inc.
650 F.3d 876 (2d Cir. 2011)

SACK, Circuit Judge.

The parties, the district court, and *amici* have raised a wide variety of interesting legal and policy issues during the course of this litigation. We need not address most of them. We conclude that under principles that are well established in this Circuit, the plaintiffs' claim against the defendant for "hot news" misappropriation of the plaintiff financial firms' recommendations to clients and prospective clients as to trading in corporate securities is preempted by federal copyright law. Based upon principles explained and applied in *National Basketball Association v. Motorola, Inc.* (2d Cir. 1997) (sometimes hereinafter "*NBA*"), we conclude that because the plaintiffs' claim falls within the "general scope" of copyright, 17 U.S.C. § 106, and involves the type of works protected by the Copyright Act, 17 U.S.C. §§ 102 and 103, and because the defendant's acts at issue do not meet the exceptions for a "hot news" misappropriation claim as recognized by *NBA*, the claim is preempted. We therefore reverse the judgment of the district court with respect to that claim.

The plaintiffs-appellees—Barclays Capital Inc. ("Barclays"); Merrill Lynch, Pierce, Fenner & Smith Inc. ("Merrill Lynch"); and Morgan Stanley & Co. Inc. ("Morgan Stanley") (collectively, the "Firms")—are major financial institutions that, among many other things, provide securities brokerage services to members of the public. Largely in that connection, they engage in extensive research about the business and prospects of publicly traded companies, the securities of those companies, and the industries in which those companies are engaged. The results of the research are summarized by the Firms in reports, which customarily contain recommendations as to the wisdom of purchasing, holding, or selling securities of the subject companies. Although the recommendations and the research underlying them in the reports are inextricably related, it is the alleged misappropriation of the recommendations, each typically contained in a single sentence, that is at the heart of the district court's decision and the appeal here.

Each morning before the principal U.S. securities markets open, each Firm circulates its reports and recommendations for that day to clients and prospective clients. The recipients thus gain an informational advantage over non-recipients with respect to possible trading in the securities of the subject companies both by learning before the world at large does the contents of the reports and, crucially for present purposes, the *fact* that the recommendations are being made by the Firm. The existence of that fact alone is likely to result in purchases or sales of the securities in question by client and non-client alike, and a corresponding short-term increase or decrease in the securities' market prices. The Firms and similar businesses, under their historic and present business models, profit from the preparation and circulation of the reports and recommendations principally insofar as they earn brokerage commissions when a recipient of a report and recommendation turns to the firm to execute a trade in the shares of the company being reported upon.

The defendant-appellant is the proprietor of a news service distributed electronically, for a price, to subscribers. In recent years and by various means, the defendant has obtained information about the Firms' recommendations before the Firms have purposely made them available to the general public and before exchanges for trading in those shares open for the day. Doing so tends to remove the informational and attendant trading advantage of the Firms' clients and prospective clients who are authorized recipients of the reports and recommendations. The recipients of the information are, in turn, less likely to buy or sell the securities using the brokerage services of the reporting and recommending Firms, thereby reducing the incentive for the Firms to create such reports and recommendations in the first place. This, the Firms assert, will destroy their business models and have a severely deleterious impact on their ability to engage in further research and to create further reports and recommendations. . . .

. . . The first of their two sets of claims against the defendant sounds in copyright and is based on allegations of verbatim copying and dissemination of portions of the Firms' reports by the defendant. The Firms have been entirely successful on these copyright claims. Although the extent to which the Firms' success on the copyright claims has alleviated their overall concerns is not clear, their victory on these claims is secure: Fly has not challenged the resulting injunction on appeal.

What remains before us, then, is the second set of claims by the Firms, alleging that Fly's early republication of the securities recommendations that the Firms create—their "hot news"—is tortious under the New York State law of misappropriation. The district court agreed and granted carefully measured injunctive relief. It is to the misappropriation cause of action that this appeal and therefore this opinion is devoted.

BACKGROUND

. . . This litigation concerns the trading "Recommendations," a term which the district court defined as "actionable reports," i.e., Firm research reports "likely to spur any investor into making an immediate trading decision. Recommendations upgrade or downgrade a security; begin research coverage of a company's security (an event known as an 'initiation'); or predict a change in the security's target price." The better known and more respected an analyst is, the more likely that a recommendation for which he or she is primarily responsible will significantly affect the market price of a security.

Most Recommendations are issued sometime between midnight and 7 a.m. Eastern Time, allowing stock purchases to be made on the market based on the reports and Recommendations upon the market opening at 9:30 a.m. Timely receipt of a Recommendations affords an investor the opportunity to execute a trade in the subject security before the market has absorbed and responded to it.

The Firms typically provide complimentary copies of the reports and Recommendations to their institutional and individual clients using a variety of methods.[6] The Firms then conduct an orchestrated sales campaign in which members of their sales

---

[6] . . . The universe of authorized report recipients is strikingly large. Morgan Stanley estimates that it distributes its research reports to 7,000 institutional clients and 100,000 individual investors. Each institutional client may in turn identify multiple employees to receive reports. Morgan Stanley estimates that in aggregate approximately 225,000 separate people are authorized to receive its reports.

forces contact the clients the Firms think most likely to execute a trade based upon the Recommendation, with the understanding that continued receipt of reports and Recommendations may be made contingent on the generation of a certain level of trading commissions paid to the Firm.

The Firms contend that clients are much more likely to place a trade with a Firm if they learn of the Recommendation directly from that Firm rather than elsewhere, and estimate that more than sixty percent of all trades result from Firm solicitations, including those highlighting Recommendations. It is from the commissions on those trades that Firms profit from the creation and dissemination of their reports and Recommendations. They assert that the timely, exclusive delivery of research and Recommendations therefore is a key to what they frequently refer to as their "business model."

Theflyonthewall.com

The defendant-appellant Theflyonthewall.com, Inc. ("Fly") is, among other things, a news "aggregator." For present purposes, "[a]n aggregator is a website that collects headlines and snippets of news stories from other websites. Examples include Google News and the Huffington Post."

Understanding that investors not authorized by the Firms to receive the reports and Recommendations are interested in and willing to pay for early access to the information contained in them—especially the Recommendations, which are particularly likely to affect securities prices—several aggregators compile securities-firm recommendations, including the Recommendations of the Firms, sometimes with the associated reports or summaries thereof, and timely provide the information to their own subscribers for a fee. Fly is one such company. It employs twenty-eight persons, about half of whom are devoted to content production. It does not itself provide brokerage, trading, or investment-advisory services beyond supplying that information.

Typical clients of the Firms are hedge funds, private equity firms, pension funds, endowments, and wealthy individual investors. By contrast, Fly's subscribers are predominately individual investors, institutional investors, brokers, and day traders. These customers purchase one of three content packages on Fly's website, paying between $25 and $50 monthly for unlimited access to the site.

In addition to maintaining its website, Fly distributes its content through third-party distributors and trading platforms, including some, such as Bloomberg and Thomson Reuters, that also separately provide authorized dissemination of the Firms' Recommendations. Fly has about 3,300 direct subscribers through its website, and another 2,000 subscribers who use third-party platforms to receive the service.

Fly characterizes itself as a source for breaking financial news, claiming to be the "fastest news feed on the web." It advertises that its "quick to the point news is a valuable resource for any investment decision." Fly has emphasized its access to analyst research, saying that its newsfeed is a "one-stop solution for accessing analyst comments," and brags that it posts "breaking analyst comments as they are being disseminated by Wall Street trading desks, consistently beating the news wires."

The cornerstone of Fly's offerings is its online newsfeed, which it continually updates between 5:00 a.m. and 7:00 p.m. during days on which the New York Stock Exchange is open. The newsfeed typically streams more than 600 headlines a day in ten different categories, including "hot stocks," "rumors," "technical analysis," and "earnings." One such category is "recommendations." There, Fly posts the recommendations (but not the underlying research reports or supporting analysis) produced by sixty-five investment firms' analysts, including those at the plaintiff Firms.

A typical Recommendation headline from 2009, for example, reads "EQIX: Equinox initiated with a Buy at BofA/Merrill. Target $110."

Fly's headlines, including those in the "recommendations" category, are searchable and sortable. Users can also subscribe to receive automated e-mail, pop-up, or audio alerts whenever Fly posts content relevant to preselected companies' securities.

Fly publishes most of its recommendation headlines before the New York Stock Exchange opens each business day at 9:30 a.m. Fly estimates that the Firms' Recommendation headlines currently comprise approximately 2.5% of Fly's total content, down from 7% in 2005.

According to Fly, over time it has changed the way in which it obtains information about recommendations. Some investment firms, such as Wells Fargo's investment services, will send Fly research reports directly as soon as they are released. Others, including the plaintiff Firms, do not. Until 2005, for recommendations of firms that do not, including the plaintiff Firms, Fly relied on employees at the investment firms (without the firms' authorization) to e-mail the research reports to Fly as they were released. Fly staff would summarize a recommendation as a headline (e.g., "EQIX initiated with a Buy at BofA/Merrill. Target $110."). Sometimes Fly would include in a published item an extended passage taken verbatim from the underlying report.

Fly maintains that because of threats of litigation in 2005, it no longer obtains recommendations directly from such investment firms. Instead, it gathers them using a combination of other news outlets, chat rooms, "blast IMs" sent by people in the investment community to hundreds of recipients, and conversations with traders, money managers, and its other contacts involved in the securities markets. Fly also represents that it no longer publishes excerpts from the research reports themselves, and now disseminates only the Recommendations, typically summarizing only the rating and price target for a particular stock.

The Firms' Response to the Threat Posed by Fly and Other Aggregators

Because the value of the reports and Recommendations to an investor with early access to a Recommendation is in significant part derived from the informational advantage an early recipient may have over others in the marketplace, most of the trading the Firms generate based on their reports and Recommendations occurs in the initial hours of trading after the principal U.S. securities markets have opened. Such sales activity typically slackens by midday. The Firms' ability to generate revenue from the reports and Recommendations therefore directly relates to the informational advantage they can provide to their clients. This in turn is related to the Firms' ability to control the distribution of the reports and Recommendations so that the Firms' clients have access to and can take action on the reports and Recommendations before the general public can.

The Firms have employed a variety of measures in an attempt to stem the early dissemination of Recommendations to non-clients. Most of them have either been instituted or augmented relatively recently in response to the increasing availability of Recommendations from Fly and competing aggregators and news services. . . .

DISCUSSION

III. Copyright Act Preemption

A. *National Basketball Association v. Motorola, Inc.*

. . . ii. Moral Dimensions

One source of confusion in addressing these misappropriation cases is that *INS v.*

AP itself was a case brought in equity to enjoin INS from copying AP's uncopyrightable news. In that context, the *INS* Court emphasized the unfairness of INS's practice of pirating AP's stories. It condemned, in what sounded biblical in tone, the defendant's "reap[ing] where it ha[d] not sown." . . .

The *NBA* court also noted that the district court whose decision it was reviewing had "described New York misappropriation law as standing for the 'broader principle that property rights of commercial value are to be and will be protected from any form of commercial immorality'; that misappropriation law developed 'to deal with business malpractices offensive to the ethics of [] society'; and that the doctrine is 'broad and flexible.'" But Judge Winter explicitly rejected the notion that "hot news" misappropriation cases based on the disapproval of the perceived unethical nature of a defendant's ostensibly piratical acts survive preemption. The Court concluded that "such concepts are virtually synonymous [with] wrongful copying and are in no meaningful fashion distinguishable from infringement of a copyright. The broad misappropriation doctrine relied upon by the district court is, therefore, the equivalent of exclusive rights in copyright law."

No matter how "unfair" Motorola's use of NBA facts and statistics may have been to the NBA—or Fly's use of the fact of the Firms' Recommendations may be to the Firms—then, such unfairness alone is immaterial to a determination whether a cause of action for misappropriation has been preempted by the Copyright Act. The adoption of new technology that injures or destroys present business models is commonplace. Whether fair or not,[29] that cannot, without more, be prevented by application of the misappropriation tort. Indeed, because the Copyright Act itself provides a remedy for wrongful copying, such unfairness may be seen as supporting a finding that the Act preempts the tort.

iii. Narrowness of the Preemption Exception

The *NBA* panel repeatedly emphasized the "narrowness" of the "hot news" tort exception from preemption. . . . This is a pressing concern when considering the "narrow" "hot news" misappropriation exemption from preemption. The broader the exemption, the greater the likelihood that protection of works within the "general scope" of the copyright and of the type of works protected by the Act will receive disparate treatment depending on where the alleged tort occurs and which state's law is found to be applicable.

The problem may be illustrated by reference to a recent case in the Southern District

---

[29] It is in the public interest to encourage and protect the Firms' continued incentive to research and report on enterprises whose securities are publicly traded, the businesses and industries in which they are engaged, and the value of their securities. But under the Firms' business models, that research is funded in part by commissions paid by authorized recipients of Recommendations trading not only with the benefit of the Firms' research, but on the bare *fact* that, for whatever reason, the Recommendation has been (or is about to be) issued. If construed broadly, the "hot news" misappropriation tort applied to the Recommendations alone could provide some measure of protection for the Firms' ability to engage in such research and reporting. But concomitantly, it would ensure that the authorized recipients of the Recommendations would in significant part be profiting because of their knowledge of the *fact* of a market-moving Recommendation before other traders learn of that fact. In that circumstance, the authorized recipient upon whose commissions the Firms depend to pay for their research activities would literally be profiting at the expense of persons from whom such knowledge has been withheld who also trade in the shares in question ignorant of the Recommendation.

None of this affects our analysis, nor do we offer a view of its legal implications, if any. We note nonetheless that the Firms seem to be asking us to use state tort law and judicial injunction to enable one class of traders to profit at the expense of another class based on their court-enforced unequal access to knowledge of a *fact*—the fact of the Firm's Recommendation.

of New York. In *Associated Press v. All Headline News Corp.*, the court sought to determine whether there was a difference between New York and Florida "hot news" misappropriation law in order for it to analyze, under choice-of-law principles, which state's law applied. Judge Castel observed that "[n]o authority has been cited to show that Florida recognizes a cause of action for hot news misappropriation. Then again, defendants have not persuasively demonstrated that Florida would not recognize such a claim."

It appears, then, that the alleged "hot news" misappropriation in *All Headline News Corp.* might have been permissible in New York but not in Florida. The same could have been said for the aggregation and publication of basketball statistics in *NBA*, and the same may be said as to the aggregation and publication of Recommendations in the case at bar. To the extent that "hot news" misappropriation causes of action are not preempted, the aggregators' actions may have different legal significance from state to state—permitted, at least to some extent, in some; prohibited, at least to some extent, in others. It is this sort of patchwork protection that the drafters of the Copyright Act preemption provisions sought to minimize, and that counsels in favor of locating only a "narrow" exception to Copyright Act preemption.

c. Three- and Five-Part "Tests"

Before concluding that the NBA's claim was preempted, the *NBA* panel set forth in its opinion—twice—a five-part "test" for identifying a non-preempted "hot news" misappropriation claim. The district court in this case, when applying *NBA*, structured its conclusions-of-law analysis around *NBA*'s first iteration of the "test". . . . But the [*NBA*] panel restated the five-part inquiry later in its opinion. . . .

Throughout this litigation the parties seem to have been in general agreement that the district court and we should employ a five-part analysis taken from the *NBA* opinion. It is understandable, of course, that counsel and the district court did in this case, and do in other comparable circumstances, attempt to follow our statements in precedential opinions as to what the law is—which we often state in terms of what we "hold." But that reading is not always either easy to make or technically correct. As Judge Friendly put it in colorful terms: "A judge's power to bind is limited to the issue that is before him; he cannot transmute dictum into decision by waving a wand and uttering the word 'hold.'" *United States v. Rubin* (2d Cir. 1979), *quoted in* Pierre N. Leval, *Judging Under the Constitution: Dicta about Dicta*, 81 N.Y.U. L. Rev. 1249, 1249 (2006). *See also generally* Leval ("A dictum [i.e., a conclusion or point of view in an opinion that is not a holding] is an assertion in a court's opinion of a proposition of law [that] does not explain why the court's judgment goes in favor of the winner.").

It is axiomatic that appellate judges cannot make law except insofar as they reach a conclusion based on the specific facts and circumstances presented to the court in a particular appeal. Subordinate courts and subsequent appellate panels are required to follow only these previous appellate legal "holdings." The *NBA* panel decided the case before it, and we think that the law it thus made regarding "hot news" preemption is, as we have tried to explain, determinative here. But the Court's various explanations of its five-part approach are not.[32]

Indeed, we do not see how they can be: The two five-part "tests" are not entirely

---

[32] Indeed, rather than identifying a set of required and specific "extra elements" essential to a non-preempted *INS*-like "hot news" claim, the Court in *NBA* was opining about the hypothetical set of circumstances—not present in that case—that might give rise to such a claim. Because the *NBA* court concluded that no such claim could be established on the facts of that case because of the absence of free-riding, its conjecture was descriptive and a helpful window into its reasoning, but could not bind subsequent courts. . . .

consistent, and are less consistent still with the three-"extra element" test, which also appears later in the opinion:

> We therefore find the extra elements—those in addition to the elements of copyright infringement—that allow a "hot-news" claim to survive preemption are: (i) the time-sensitive value of factual information, (ii) the free-riding by a defendant, and (iii) the threat to the very existence of the product or service provided by the plaintiff.

For example, the fifth of the five factors in the first iteration of the test is that "the ability of other parties to free-ride on the efforts of the plaintiff or others would so reduce the incentive to produce the product or service that *its existence or quality* would be substantially threatened." (emphasis added). The second iteration is similar, but adds a quotation from *INS* which can be read to make the factor far more difficult to demonstrate: that the conduct "would render [the plaintiff's] publication profitless, or so little profitable *as in effect to cut off the service by rendering the cost prohibitive in comparison with the return.*'" (emphasis added). Then, in rehearsing the "extra elements" that may avoid preemption, the panel referred to "the threat to the *very existence* of the product or service provided by the plaintiff." (emphasis added).

The distinctions between these various statements of a multi-part test are substantial. Were we required to rule on the district court's findings of fact ourselves in light of these various versions of elements, we might well perceive no clear error in a finding that the existence *or quality* of the Firms' reports were placed in jeopardy by what the district court found to be "free riding." By contrast, we might otherwise conclude that there is insufficient record evidence to sustain a finding either that the alleged free-riding by Fly and similar aggregators "in effect . . . cut off the [Firms'] service by rendering the cost prohibitive in comparison with the return" or were a "threat to the very existence of the product or service provided by the plaintiff[s]." It seems to us that each of *NBA*'s three multi-element statements serves a somewhat different purpose. The first is a general introduction, by way of summary, of what the decision concludes. The second may be described as "stating the elements of the tort." And the third focuses on what "extra elements" are necessary to avoid preemption despite the conclusion that the "general scope requirement" and the "subject matter requirement" have been met.

In our view, the several *NBA* statements were sophisticated observations in aid of the Court's analysis of the difficult preemption issues presented to it. Inconsistent as they were, they could not all be equivalent to a statutory command to which we or the district court are expected to adhere. . . .

B. Preemption and This Appeal

We conclude that applying *NBA* and copyright preemption principles to the facts of this case, the Firms' claim for "hot news" misappropriation fails because it is preempted by the Copyright Act. First, the Firms' reports culminating with the Recommendations satisfy the "subject matter" requirement because they are all works "of a type covered by section[] 102," i.e., "original works of authorship fixed in a[] tangible medium of expression." As discussed above, it is not determinative for the Copyright Act preemption analysis that the facts of the Recommendations themselves are not copyrightable. Second, the reports together with the Recommendations fulfill the "general scope" requirement because the rights "may be abridged by an act which, in and of itself, would infringe one of the 'exclusive rights' provided by federal copyright law," i.e., "acts of reproduction, performance, distribution or display."

Third and finally, the Firms' claim is not a so-called *INS*-type non-preempted claim because Fly is not, under *NBA*'s analysis, "free-riding." It is collecting, collating and disseminating factual information—the *facts* that Firms and others in the securities business have made recommendations with respect to the value of and the wisdom of purchasing or selling securities—and attributing the information to its source. The Firms are making the news; Fly, despite the Firms' understandable desire to protect their business model, is breaking it. As the *INS* Court explained, long before it would have occurred to the Court to cite the First Amendment for the proposition:

> [T]he news element—the information respecting current events contained in the literary production—is not the creation of the writer, but is a report of matters that ordinarily are *publici juris*; it is the history of the day. It is not to be supposed that the framers of the Constitution, when they empowered Congress "to promote the progress of science and useful arts, by securing for limited times to authors and inventors the exclusive right to their respective writings and discoveries" (Const., Art. I, § 8, par. 8), intended to confer upon one who might happen to be the first to report a historic event the exclusive right for any period to spread the knowledge of it.

The use of the term "free-riding" in recent "hot news" misappropriation jurisprudence exacerbates difficulties in addressing these issues. Unfair use of another's "labor, skill, and money, and which is salable by complainant for money," *INS*, sounds like the very essence of "free-riding," and, the term "free-riding" in turn seems clearly to connote acts that are quintessentially unfair.

It must be recalled, however, that the term free-riding refers explicitly to a requirement for a cause of action as described by *INS*. As explained by the *NBA* court, "[a]n indispensable element of an *INS* 'hot news' claim is free-riding by a defendant on a plaintiff's product."

The practice of what *NBA* referred to as "free-riding" was further described by *INS*. The *INS* Court defined the "hot news" tort in part as "taking material that has been acquired by complainant as the result of organization and the expenditure of labor, skill, and money, and which is salable by complainant for money, and . . . appropriating it and selling it as [the defendant's] own. . . ." That definition fits the facts of *INS*: The defendant was taking news gathered and in the process of dissemination by the Associated Press and selling that news as though the defendant itself had gathered it. But it does not describe the practices of Fly. The Firms here may be "acquiring material" in the course of preparing their reports, but that is not the focus of this lawsuit. In pressing a "hot news" claim against Fly, the Firms seek only to protect their Recommendations, something they *create* using their expertise and experience rather than *acquire* through efforts akin to reporting.

Moreover, Fly, having obtained news of a Recommendation, is hardly selling the Recommendation "as its own." It is selling the information with specific attribution to the issuing Firm. Indeed, for Fly to sell, for example, a Morgan Stanley Recommendation "as its own," as INS sold the news it cribbed from AP to INS subscribers, would be of little value to either Fly or its customers. If, for example, Morgan Stanley were to issue a Recommendation of Boeing common stock changing it from a "hold" to a "sell," it hardly seems likely that Fly would profit significantly from disseminating an item reporting that "*Fly* has changed its rating of Boeing from a hold to a sell." It is not the identity of Fly and its reputation as a financial analyst that carries the authority and weight sufficient to affect the market. It is Fly's accurate attribution of the Recommendation to the creator that gives this news its value.

We do not perceive a meaningful difference between (a) Fly's taking material that a Firm has *created* (not "acquired") as the result of organization and the expenditure of labor, skill, and money, and which is (presumably) salable by a Firm for money, and selling it *by ascribing the material to its creator Firm* and author (not selling it as Fly's own), and (b) what appears to be unexceptional and easily recognized behavior by members of the traditional news media—to report on, say, winners of Tony Awards or, indeed, scores of NBA games with proper attribution of the material to its creator. *INS* did not purport to address either.

It is also noteworthy, if not determinative, that *INS* referred to INS's tortious behavior as "amount[ing] to an unauthorized interference with the normal operation of complainant's legitimate business *precisely at the point where the profit is to be reaped*, in order to *divert a material portion of the profit* from those who have earned it to those who have not. . . ." (emphases added). As we have seen, the point at which the Firms principally reap their profit is upon the execution of sales or purchases of securities. It is at least arguable that Fly's interference with the "normal operation" of the Firms' business is indeed at a "point" where the Firms' profits are reaped. But it is not at all clear that *that* profit is being in any substantial sense "diverted" to Fly by its publication of Recommendations news. The lost commissions are, we would think, diverted to whatever broker happens to execute a trade placed by the recipient of news of the Recommendation from Fly.

To be sure, as the district court pointed out, "Fly [has made efforts], which have met with *some* success, to link its subscribers to discount brokerage services." (emphasis added). The court viewed these steps as "reflect[ing] the final stage in [Fly's] direct competition with the Firms by leveraging its access to their Recommendations and driving away their commission revenue[s]."

But we see nothing in the district court's opinion or in the record to indicate that the so-called "final stage" has in fact matured to a point where a significant portion of the diversion of profits to which the Firms object is lost to brokers in league with Fly or its competitors. Firm clients are, moreover, free to employ their authorized knowledge of a Recommendation to make a trade with a discount broker for a smaller fee. And, as we understand the record, the Firms channel fees to their brokerage operations using a good deal more than their Recommendations alone. A non-public Firm report, quite apart from the attached Recommendation—by virtue of the otherwise non-public information the report contains, including general news about the state of the markets, securities, and economic conditions—seems likely to play a substantial part in the Firms' ability to obtain trading business through their research efforts. It is difficult on this record for us to characterize Fly's publication of Recommendations as an unauthorized interference with the normal operation of Firms' legitimate business precisely at the point where the profit is to be reaped which, directly or indirectly, diverts a material portion of the Firms' profits from the Firms to Fly and others engaged in similar practices.

We do not mean to be parsing the language of *INS* as though it were a statement of law the applicability of which determines the outcome of this appeal. As we have explained, the law that *INS* itself established was overruled many years ago. But in talking about a "'hot-news' *INS*-like claim," as we did in *NBA*, or "the *INS* tort," as the district court did in this case, we are mindful that the *INS* Court's concern was tightly focused on the practices of the parties to the suit before it: news, data, and the like, gathered and disseminated by one organization as a significant part of its business, taken by another entity and published as the latter's own in competition with the former. The language chosen by the *INS* Court seems to us to make clear the substantial distance between that case and this one.

Here, like the defendants in *NBA* and unlike the defendant in *INS*, Fly "[has its] own network and assemble[s] and transmit[s] data [it] sel[f]." *NBA*. In *NBA*, Motorola and STATS employees watched basketball games, compiled the statistics, scores, and other information from the games, and sold the resulting package of data to their subscribers. We could perceive no non-preempted "hot news" tort. Here, analogous to the defendant's in *NBA*, Fly's employees are engaged in the financial-industry equivalent of observing and summarizing facts about basketball games and selling those packaged facts to consumers; it is simply the content of the facts at issue that is different.

And, according to our decision in *NBA*: "An indispensable element of a [non-pre-empted] *INS* 'hot-news' claim is free-riding by a defendant on a plaintiff's product, enabling the defendant to produce a directly competitive product for less money because it has lower costs." In *NBA*, we concluded that the defendant's SportsTrax service was not such a product, in part because it was "bearing [its] own costs of collecting factual information on NBA games." In this case, as the district court found, approximately half of Fly's twenty-eight employees are involved on the collection of the Firms' Recommendations and production of the newsfeed on which summaries of the Recommendations are posted. Fly is reporting financial news—factual information on Firm Recommendations—through a substantial organizational effort. Therefore, Fly's service—which collects, summarizes, and disseminates the news of the Firms' Recommendations—is not the "*INS*-like" product that could support a non-preempted cause of action for misappropriation.

By way of comparison, we might, as the *NBA* court did, speculate about a product a Firm *might* produce which *might* indeed give rise to a non-preempted "hot-news" misappropriation claim. If a Firm were to collect and disseminate to some portion of the public facts about securities recommendations in the brokerage industry (including, perhaps, such facts it generated itself—its own Recommendations), and were Fly to copy the facts contained in the Firm's hypothetical service, it might be liable to the Firm on a "hot-news" misappropriation theory. That would appear to be an *INS*-type claim and might survive preemption.[40] But the Firms have no such product and make no such claim. On the facts of this case, they do not have an "*INS*-like" non-preempted "hot news" misappropriation cause of action against Fly.

C. Judge Raggi's Concurrence

Judge Raggi would reach the same outcome as do we, but "would apply the *NBA* test to this case and reverse on the ground that the Firms failed to satisfy its direct competition requirement for a non-preempted claim." We express no opinion as to whether there is or was direct competition between the Firms and Fly with regard to the Recommendations because we are bound by the holding of *NBA*. On the facts of that case, the plaintiff's cause of action was preempted by the copyright law because the defendants did not "free ride" on the plaintiff's work product. The *NBA* panel did not decide the case before it on the basis of the presence or absence of direct competition, which it thought to be an element of the preemption inquiry but did not depend upon in its analysis. We think that the *NBA* panel's decision that the absence of "free riding" was fatal to the plaintiff's claim in that case is binding upon us on the facts presented here. In other words, even were we to conclude, hypothetically and contrary to Judge Raggi's views, that there *was indeed* direct competition between the Firms and Fly with respect to the Recommendations, we would nonetheless be

---

[40] Judge Raggi writes that by distinguishing between those who make the news and those who break it, we "foreclose the possibility of a 'hot news' claim by a party who disseminates news it happens to create." That issue is simply not before us. We therefore do not address it, let alone suggest or imply that such a claim would necessarily be foreclosed.

bound to reverse the judgment of the district court based on our reading of *NBA*. The presence or absence of direct competition is thus not determinative and is therefore a matter we are not called upon to decide here.

CONCLUSION

We conclude that in this case, a Firm's ability to make news—by issuing a Recommendation that is likely to affect the market price of a security—does not give rise to a right for it to control who breaks that news and how. We therefore reverse the judgment of the district court to that extent and remand with instructions to dismiss the Firms' misappropriation claim.

REENA RAGGI, Circuit Judge, concurring.

I join the court in reversing the judgment in favor of the Firms on their state law claims of "hot news" misappropriation on the ground that such claims are preempted by federal copyright law. Unlike my colleagues in the majority, I do not reject the five-part test enunciated in *National Basketball Association v. Motorola, Inc.* (2d Cir. 1997) ("*NBA*"), to reach this result. Whatever reservations I may have about that test as a means for identifying non-preempted "hot news" claims, I do not think it can be dismissed as *dictum*. Accordingly, I write separately to explain why I conclude that the Firms failed to satisfy the "direct competition" requirement of *NBA*'s test. . . .

b. *NBA*'s Test Is Not Dictum

Despite my reservations regarding *NBA*'s test, I think it controls our resolution of this appeal. My colleagues in the majority are of a different view. They conclude that *NBA* "held" only that the facts presented could not establish a non-preempted "hot news" claim. They dismiss *NBA*'s five-part test as an unnecessary discussion of hypothetical circumstances giving rise to a "hot news" claim, which, as dictum, we need not follow. I am not convinced.

In holding that the *NBA* plaintiff failed to assert a non-preempted "hot news" claim, the court was required to determine the "breadth of the 'hot news' claim that survives preemption." To answer that "crucial question," the court identified five factors required to state a non-preempted "hot news" claim, applied them to the facts presented, and concluded that plaintiff's claim failed. Because the test was thus necessary to the opinion's result, it is not dictum. . . .

Thus, I would apply the *NBA* test to this case and reverse on the ground that the Firms failed to satisfy its direct competition requirement for a non-preempted claim.

c. *The Firms Failed To Establish Direct Competition Between Their Recommendations and Fly's Substantially Different Aggregate Product*

In concluding that the Firms failed to establish a non-preempted "hot news" claim under the test identified in *NBA*, I rely on facts emphasized by the majority, namely, that Fly produces an aggregate product reporting many Firms' Recommendations among other financial news, and attributing each Recommendation to its source, while the Firms each disseminate only their own Recommendations to clients who engage in a particular level of trading with the Firms. The majority, however, uses these facts to draw a bright line distinguishing between the Firms, who generate news, and Fly and other news aggregators, who "break" the news, with the former falling outside of hot-news protection. I am not convinced that this distinction is determinative here because the Firms appear to play both roles. Not only do they generate their Recommendations, they then disseminate them, recouping the cost of generation through trading revenue. I am not prepared to foreclose the possibility of a "hot news" claim by a party who disseminates news it happens to create.

I conclude simply that the facts emphasized by the majority preclude the Firms from stating a non-preempted "hot news" claim for a different reason derived from *NBA*: the Firms' product and Fly's newsfeed do not directly compete.

Although *NBA* turned on the plaintiff's failure to show free riding on and a sufficient threat to its services, the court there discussed the direct competition element in noting that the plaintiff had "compresse[d] and confuse[d] three different informational products." Separating the NBA's dissemination of live basketball games and copyrighted broadcasts from its collection and transmission of factual material about the games through a pager service, the court determined that only the latter might directly compete with the defendant's product, another pager service providing facts about live games. In other words, only products in the "keenest" of competition satisfy the direct competition requirement for a non-preempted claim. *INS v. AP* (stating that plaintiff and defendant newspaper companies were "in the keenest competition" in gathering and publishing news throughout United States). . . .

It bears noting that, like the district court, I view Fly's conduct as strong evidence of free-riding, or worse depending on how it came into possession of the Recommendations. Although Fly expends some effort to gather and aggregate the Recommendations, Fly is usurping the substantial efforts and expenses of the Firms to make a profit without expending any time or cost to conduct research of its own. I cannot celebrate such practices, which allow Fly "to reap where it has not sown." As the majority notes, however, such apparent unfairness does not control preemption analysis. Although Fly free-rides on the Firms' efforts, Fly's attribution of aggregate Recommendations demonstrates the crucial difference between the businesses: while the Firms disseminate only their own Recommendations to select clients most likely to follow the advice and place trades with the Firms, Fly aggregates and disseminates sixty-five firms' Recommendations and other financial information to anyone willing to pay for it without regard to whether clients accept or trade on particular Recommendations.

An example illustrates the distinction. Two firms might disseminate opposing Recommendations on the same stock. These two firms directly compete in attempting to convince clients to follow their Recommendation and place a trade. Fly, on the other hand, would presumably report both opinions (as well as scores of others) to its readers without regard to whether they trade on the information. Some investors may place a particular value on learning all Recommendations, and some people may have a general interest in learning such news even without wishing to invest. Thus, Fly's product may directly compete with that of other financial news outlets, such as Dow Jones, that also seek to provide all Recommendations to anyone interested in such news. But Fly's aggregate subscription product is sufficiently distinct from the Firms' business model, which cannot be divorced from the trading market it targets, to preclude a finding of the direct competition required by *NBA*'s test. . . .

Questions:

1.) "It is understandable, of course, that counsel and the district court did in this case, and do in other comparable circumstances, attempt to follow our statements in precedential opinions as to what the law is—which we often state in terms of what we "hold." But that reading is not always either easy to make or technically correct. As Judge Friendly put it in colorful terms: "A judge's power to bind is limited to the issue that is before him; he cannot transmute dictum into decision by waving a wand and uttering the word 'hold.'" " So now we cannot trust judges about what they "hold" their own holding to be? Say *what*?

2.) Joking aside: this is a careful and thoughtful opinion, building law on top of the thoughtful *NBA* decision. As we pointed out at the beginning of this chapter, the *NBA* court was faced with a double-sided slippery slope—either everything is preempted or states can completely negate all of the limitations in copyright law. The *NBA* decision tries to avoid the problems it saw in the District Court's idea of partial preemption. What is this court trying to avoid in *NBA*'s "holding"? What *is* the holding of *NBA v. Motorola* according to this court? Why?

3.) Did the *NBA* court say that *the five part test* was necessary to survive preemption for hot news misappropriation? Or did it say that hot news misappropriation in New York could survive preemption if, *in* that five part test, there were three "extra elements"—the keys to surviving preemption? What does this court say?

4.) What law could New York draft which would a.) survive preemption and b.) stop news aggregators from spreading "facts" about brokerage recommendations?

5.) Final question: You are clerking in the 2d Circuit. Your judge tosses the two opinions you have just read at you and says—"My office, ten minutes. Tell me which is more important for copyright preemption, subject matter or scope?" Your answer?

CHAPTER SEVENTEEN

Patents: Hopes, Fears, History & Doctrine

1.) Hopes and Fears

For many people, patent law represents everything that is necessary, inspiring and worrying about intellectual property.

Necessary because there are lots of areas in which the monopolies granted by patent law seem to *work*: they get us innovations—innovations that save, change or enrich lives. Anyone reading this who has a friend or loved one who is alive—or functional—now because of a patented drug can explain what this means. Let us pause to contemplate this fact, a particularly luminous one in the time of a pandemic. Social institutions that work, even episodically, are to be cherished. A lot of things in life, perhaps most, do not work. Functionality should not be taken for granted.

Inspiring because the patent system represents an ideal that is deep in the Anglo-American psyche: It is not just the idea of the inventor in the garage—the little guy with an innovative idea who can change the world and give up his or her day job to work on other innovations. While that is an appealing vision, it is one that is increasingly a marginal part of the patent system, which is dominated by corporate research and development. It is the idea that we can couple the essential force of state funded research—basic science—with that of decentralized innovation through a market. The authors of this book admit to being believers in this idea. They understand it can be—and is frequently—misused. They realize that much innovation will happen without the inducement of patents—driven by ego, prestige economies, altruism, serendipity and good old fashioned competition. They know that the ideal of decentralized innovation hardly represents what happens in a company defensively patenting obvious technological steps, or a "non-practicing entity" (popularly known as a patent troll), wielding dubious patents to the innovators. They admit it will play no role in overcoming the difficulties in getting the global poor access to essential medicines—we need other tools for that. And this ideal bears little resemblance to the contortions that drug companies go through to "evergreen" their patents through trivial improvements. But they still think the patent system can be a vital part of our society's toolkit for the pursuit of innovation. Not everyone does.

Worrying for several reasons. First, Macaulay's reasons—elaborated in Chapter 10. "I believe, Sir, that I may safely take it for granted that the effect of monopoly generally is to make articles scarce, to make them dear, and to make them bad."

We talked in Chapter 1 about the losses imposed by intellectual property. The passive losses are represented by the people who would pay above marginal cost but who are priced out of the market when the intellectual property right gives the owner the ability to set a (constrained) monopoly price. (Constrained because, if ibuprofen is under patent and clearly is the best drug for me, there is still a price point at which I will buy aspirin or acetaminophen instead.) But the patent allows its owner to charge far above marginal cost and *that is not a bug, it is a feature*. The people who would have paid above marginal cost, but who cannot afford the price charged by the patent holder, are priced out of the market. Access-to-medicines activist Jamie Love, of Knowledge Ecology International, has a particularly powerful presentation in which he puts up the standard monopoly price graph, with its grey shaded triangle of social loss in the center. "In economics" he says, "we call this 'dead weight social loss.' With essential medicines we call it 'dead people.'" That point, too, is particularly luminous in the time of a pandemic,

Love's point is deliberately inflammatory but it is worth thinking about because it cuts both ways. Without the patent, it is quite possible we would not have the medicine *at all*—think about what that means for *all* those who might be saved by it. But the patent scheme—which accepts a limited-duration ability to charge above marginal cost as the social price for incentivizing the innovation in the first place—imposes a heavy burden, one that is measured in human as well as dollar terms. Where the passive loss involves not getting the cool feature on your new phone or the best material for your 3D printer until it goes off-patent, perhaps we can live with it. But as the drug example shows, patent law has consequences, both good and bad, that mean that policy makers, judges and citizens think about its costs differently than they do with copyright. And let us be clear here, these are the costs (and benefits) of the patent system *if legislated and implemented perfectly*. The passive or static losses caused by the patent monopoly are part of the design of the system. If the patent system is properly implemented, those losses are more than made up for by the innovations society receives, innovations it would otherwise not get. This critique does not speak to an *imperfect* patent system, in which poor patents are granted or patent holders are able to game the system or extend the lifetime of the patent beyond its correct term. The losses imposed by that system have no such compensating social gain.

Those are the passive losses. The active or dynamic losses are those imposed on *future* innovation. Here the problem is not that consumers are priced out of the market for goods for which they would pay above marginal cost. The question is the effect of existing patents on the *next* innovator. First, again assume that the patent system is operating perfectly—only truly novel, non-obvious and useful innovations are granted patents, the patents are clear, the required disclosure in the patents is adequate to understand the technology and the boundaries of the right that has been granted over the technology are well understood. In such a situation subsequent innovators can easily draw on the abstract knowledge contained in the patents, while avoiding trespassing on the actual patent—unless they choose to license it, which we presume they can do in an efficient and relatively friction-free market. In this world, there is a dynamic cost to patents but it is more than outweighed by the patent system's dynamic gains.

For simplicity's sake, imagine a patent system with only one technology—windscreen wipers—and one patent. Mr. First has patented the variable speed windscreen wiper. Since rain varies in intensity, this is truly a useful innovation. Mr. Second is inspired by this invention. He reads First's—statutorily required—disclosures of how the variable speed wiper works. (Note that the promise of the patent, and its 20 years of exclusivity, has made First abandon the trade secret regime, on which he might have relied, and instead has forced him to explain his innovation to the world.) But Second believes that the American driver should not have to engage in the massive labor of turning a dial to select what speed the wipers move at. His idea is to couple the variable speed wiper with a water sensor that would automatically detect the level of rain and adjust wiper speed accordingly. Let us assume for the moment that this counts as both novel and non-obvious. One of patent law's interesting features is that Second can patent his compound invention without First's approval. Now both patents sit in the system. Second cannot market, or license, his innovation without First's approval—First's patent would block that. But neither can First arrogate to himself Second's marginal improvements. The patent system sets up an incentive for them to bargain together in order to allow the commercialization of this new, compound, innovation.

What were the dynamic losses? Was a cost to Second (and to society) imposed by First's patent? Yes, in the obvious sense that Second will need to license First's patent and this will increase the marginal cost of the compound innovation. But—assuming again that the patent system is operating properly—without First's patent we would not have had Second's innovation to begin with. The dynamic benefits are greater than the costs. The design of the system—requiring disclosure and not requiring "permission" to create subsequent compound innovations, though permission would be required to practice them—is set up precisely with that in mind.

Now let us introduce some reality into the model. What if the system is not operating properly? What if the second innovator finds that, rather than "standing on the shoulders of giants," he is being sucked into a quicksand of patent claims? Does his research and development budget get eaten up trying to deal with vague, poorly drafted and improperly granted patents that block the road to the next innovation? What data do we have on how the patent system is functioning? Unfortunately, much of the recent empirical studies of the patent system provide a worrying picture. In some areas of technology, far from being an encouragement to progress, patents actually seem to be imposing a drag on innovation.

> During the past five years, academic researchers have published more than two dozen empirical studies on patent litigation and its economic impacts. These studies have been conducted by researchers with diverse views and using different methodologies. The preponderant economic picture presented is that patent litigation now imposes substantial costs, particularly on small and innovative firms, and that these costs have tended overall to reduce research and development, venture capital investment and firm startups. By most tallies, the majority of lawsuits are now filed by so-called "patent assertion entities," popularly known as "patent trolls." Estimates based on surveys of Form 10-K filings and stock prices find that patent litigation has been costing firms tens of billions of dollars per year since 2007. Startups and venture-backed firms, especially, report significant operational impacts from "PAE" lawsuits in survey-based studies. One analysis finds that the more R&D a firm performs, the more likely it is to be hit with a patent lawsuit. Another study associates lawsuits from PAEs with a decline of billions of dollars of venture capital investment; another found that costly lawsuits caused publicly listed defendant firms to substantially curtail R&D spending.[1]

Empirical scholarship,[2] and a great deal of practical experience, seems to suggest that in some areas of strongly cumulative innovation over particular types of technologies—software, for example—this is exactly what is happening. We tend to think about technological development as involving a limited number of "inputs" that can be clearly defined in advance—the innovator has to decide whether or not the new kind of spring patented by another inventor is worth licensing for use in his next-generation mousetrap. But with developments in complex technologies, the reality is much more complicated. Estimates for how many patents "read on"—that is, are potentially implicated by—a smart

---

[1] James Bessen & Michael J. Meurer, *A Third of the Economy Is at Stake and Patent Trolls Are to Blame*, WASHINGTON POST, Nov. 18, 2015, https://www.washingtonpost.com/news/in-theory/wp/2015/11/18/patent-trolls-are-costing-us-billions-they-must-be-stopped/.

[2] For example see, James Bessen & Michael J. Meurer, *Patent Failure: How Judges, Bureaucrats, and Lawyers Put Innovators at Risk* (2008); Adam Jaffe and Josh Lerner, *Innovation and Its Discontents: How Our Broken Patent System is Endangering Innovation and Progress, and What To Do About It* (2004).

phone, range from thousands to tens of thousands. Everything from the touchscreen, to the interface, to the software, to the hardware, to the way it works with networks may be covered by hundreds, even thousands of patents. And critics argue that those patents are *vague* and many of them are *bad*—meaning they are patents that should not have been granted; the technology is not truly novel or non-obvious. Imagine wandering through a minefield whose mines were painted by an impressionist—their boundaries are vague and overlapping and many of them should not be there in the first place.

In this situation it may be impossible to know what property rights your new technology is infringing, and which of those property rights would be upheld in a trial. Instead, firms have two options. First, they can "defensively" patent—going beyond genuine innovations to claims that their lawyers secretly think are pretty weak. Having accumulated their own war-chest of good and not so good patents, they can cross-license with their competitors. I agree to license my arsenal of good and dubious patents to you, if you will license your similar arsenal to me. Second, if cross-licensing does not work, they can use their arsenal for so-called "Mutual Assured Destruction." The patents are both so many and so vague that all parties know they are infringing at least some patents held by a competitor. As in the cold war, the threat of mutual destruction is supposed to hold back the missiles, or in this case, the lawsuits. Sometimes, of course, the threat is not enough and a controversy breaks out anyway—as in the smartphone patent wars—setting off an orgy of lawsuits which is excellent for future patent lawyers but of dubious social value otherwise.

The problems in such a system are obvious. The need for a huge arsenal of defensive patents will be a serious barrier to entry; IBM and Dell can cross-license. What of the upstart innovator? Legal costs will be high—both offensively and defensively. The "picket fences of the mind" will be poorly drawn, leading to under-development of technologies, or over-investment in legal precautions. And the threat of mutual assured destruction only works against genuine competitors—the troll (or "non-practicing entity") need not fear retaliatory suit, because it produces *nothing*. It is not infringing any patents because its only industrial outputs are the threatening letter and the lawsuit. But—just to be clear—these are costs that occur only when the patent system malfunctions. If patentable subject matter is appropriately delineated, if patents are only granted for genuinely novel, nonobvious and useful technological innovations that we would not get otherwise, if they are clearly drafted and defined and if all parties in a marketplace have the ability easily to license the ones they need, then these problems—unlike the problem of pricing people out of the market—can be avoided.

Our sense of the current patent system is that some parts of it—for example, patents over small molecule drugs—have fewer problems with vague and bad patents. That does not mean they are free from abuse. The issues of "ever-greening" patents, of vexatiously suing, or buying off the manufacturers of generic drugs, are well known. Still, the person patenting Tagamet and the person patenting Viagra both get a patent over something pretty clearly defined. They know what they have, they know what would infringe it and they do not need thousands of possibly patentable inputs to create their innovation. But patents over software, complex biotechnology or technologies such as smartphones may represent a very different reality. Thus, the problems we have just described are not evenly distributed throughout the patent system. If I am applying for a patent over a drug, the standards for patentability seem relatively well-defined, if subject to gamesmanship. The boundaries of the resulting patent are also clear. With the smartphone patents we mentioned earlier, the opposite is true.

Correspondingly, patent litigation is not evenly spread out. To be sure the question of how to classify patents is subject to dispute. Nevertheless, a substantial number of patent scholars agree that software and business method patents are far more likely to produce litigation than any other kind, perhaps because of their vague boundaries and unclear claims or perhaps because they were acquired with the goal of extracting a toll from companies that are making and doing things. Or both. Of course, it *could* be that this assessment is wrong and that there are many more business method pirates and software patent violators out there relative to those who would violate drug or chemical patents. Yet this seems unlikely and when we get to the discussion of patentable subject matter, you will see that several members of the Supreme Court believe there is cause for concern.

How do these very general comments about the necessary, inspiring and worrying aspects of patents bear on the actual doctrines of patent law? Just as the bounds, exceptions and limitations of trademark law and copyright law were built around our goals, hopes and fears in each of those fields, so too with patent. The patent term is short as compared to copyright and trademark—20 years rather than life plus 70, or perpetuity for trademark, so long as the mark continues to be used. The passive and dynamic losses are thus limited in time. The public domain awaits. The patent system explicitly allows follow-on innovators to build on the contributions of existing patent holders (though it denies them the right to practice that compound innovation without mutual consent). Patents are subject to—supposedly rigorous—examination procedures. Unlike a copyright which exists as soon as the original expression is fixed in material form, to get a patent one must satisfy a patent examiner that the innovation is worthy of a patent. It is on the last feature that we will concentrate in this book. We will look at four such architectural features of the patent system, four hurdles that someone seeking a patent must clear.

- The limitations on patentable subject matter: what can and cannot be patented
- The requirement of utility—that patents must be over useful innovations
- The requirement of novelty
- The requirement of non-obviousness.

Each of these limitations is designed to help minimize some of the concerns about patent law, while maximizing its social benefits. In a properly functioning patent system, goes the hope, we will grant patents that are over technologies that are important but not so fundamental as to give a monopoly over an abstract idea or law or product of nature in a way that would impede subsequent innovation. (Subject matter.) We try to make sure that the innovator has actually given society an invention that is usable *now* rather than trying to patent a line of research that has not yet been reduced to practice. (Utility.) We try to make sure that these innovations do not exist somewhere already. (Novelty.) If they do, then society does not need to pay the monopoly price for them, nor do subsequent innovators need to labor to get around the patent. Finally, we require that patentable innovations be non-obvious. If this is the next step in a mundane march of technology, then society likely would have received the innovation without paying the monopoly price. (Non-obviousness.) Thus the limitations we will explore in the next four chapters are, in a very real sense, our society's attempt to maximize the benefits and minimize the active and dynamic losses imposed by patents. Whether in their daily application they actually do so is another question.

Finally, what about costs? It is hard to estimate both public and private costs. The data is hard to come by. One often needs to use indirect studies that rely on effects on stock market prices and the like. One 2013 study, which only reaches data until 2009[3],

---

[3] James Bessen, Peter Neuhäusler, John L. Turner, Jonathan Williams, *The Costs and Benefits of United States Patents* (June 2013), Boston Univ. School of Law, Law and Economics Research Paper No. 13-24. Available at http://www.bu.edu/law/workingpapers-archive/documents/turnerjbessenjneuhauslerpwilliamsj061213.pdf.

attempted to measure private costs of patents (for example, of litigating a patent if one was sued), and to set those against the benefits provided to the patent holder by patent "rents"—the return to the patent holder provided by the statutory monopoly. The worrying aspect of this data is the way that litigation costs outpace patent "rents." The cost of litigation appears to be dwarfing the amount derived from the patent. What if the total return to all patent holders is less than the costs being imposed on all others by dealing with the patent system? Are we getting enough incentive "bang" for our administrative and litigation "buck"? Let us assume rational actors, who would rather license a patent if they believe they are legally required to and that a court would so hold. Yet in a world full of vague or bad patents, those actors would be unable to make those rational decisions accurately. Is the inventive stimulus of those patent rents being swallowed up by the costs imposed on outsiders by the system?

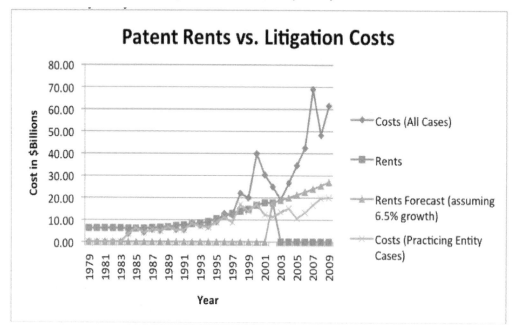

Notice a number of things. Patent litigation costs increased sharply. The proportion of those costs imposed by practicing entities has only a mild upward trend. In other words, the costs being imposed by those who do *not* use the technologies they are attempting to license, "patent trolls" is the common term, have increased dramatically. As of 2009, the study showed total patent litigation costs far outweighing the rents received by patent holders. This is a system in which patent *lawyers* will be well compensated. It is unlikely it is one that is *socially* desirable.

However there is some reason to believe that things may be changing. The chart above ends in 2009. On the following page is a more up to date chart of cases filed in district courts over copyright, patent and trademark issues. We have highlighted on the time axis the dates of some of the legislative interventions and landmark cases that we will discuss later.

Patent cases start at about 1800 a year in 1996, but start to accelerate steadily, surging between 2002–2006 and 2011–2014. Then filings begin to decline. It is hard to determine the exact causes for the drop, but they could include:

i.) The America Invents Act of 2011, which introduced a number of reforms, including the possibility of lower cost, post-grant patent challenges;

Figure 1: **U.S. District Courts--Intellectual Property Cases Filed, by Type, 1996 - 2018**

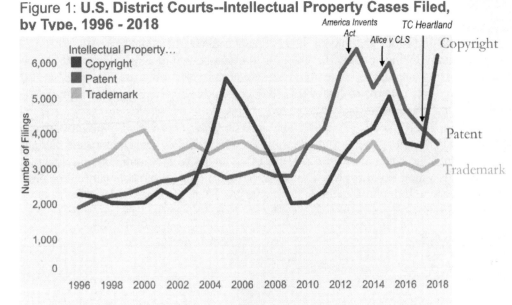

Source: U.S. Courts, Statistical Tables for the Federal Judiciary. Table C-7, 12-Month Periods Ending December 31, 1996 through 2018.

ii.) *Alice v. CLS*, a 2014 Supreme Court decision which raised patentable subject matter standards over abstract ideas implemented by a generic computer. That decision did not, as we will see later, cut down on the issuance of software patents, indeed they now amount to over 60% of all patents issued! It may however—at least temporarily—have curtailed some vexatious litigation.

iii.) *T.C. Heartland v. Kraft Foods*, a 2017 Supreme Court decision which clarified the patent venue rules in a way that denied many patent plaintiffs their favored venue: the Eastern District of Texas, which had accounted for up to third of all patent cases. The Eastern District's pro patent judges and its "rocket docket" were particularly popular with "non practicing entities," or NPE's, less affectionately referred to as patent trolls. (In fact, it was *so* popular that Samsung built a community ice skating rink next to the town where the court is located, arguably to curry favor with potential local jurors.) The problems have not been solved however, and cases have started to edge up again. Ironically, the Western District of Texas is now a preferred destination. The troll phenomenon is not confined to patents. The surge in copyright cases in recent years is partly fueled by so-called copyright trolls.[4]

2.) History

As with copyright law, our patent law has its roots in England, and in particular, in the effort to curtail monopolies. In response to the Crown's use of royal privileges or "letters patents" to grant monopolies over certain industries, the English Parliament passed

---

[4] To quote one court's definition, a troll is a plaintiff who is "more focused on the business of litigation than on selling a product or service or licensing their copyrights to third parties. A copyright troll plays a numbers game in which it targets hundreds or thousands of defendants seeking quick settlements priced just low enough that it is less expensive for the defendant to pay the troll rather than defend the claim." *Wisser v. Vox Media Inc.* (S.D.N.Y. 2020.) One law firm alone filed 1900 copyright cases between 2016 and 2019, a substantial proportion of the total.

the Statute of Monopolies in 1624. This law nullified "all monopolies," and restricted "any letters patents and grants of privilege" to a "term of fourteen years or under, hereafter to be made, of the sole working or making of any manner of new manufactures within this realm to the true and first inventor and inventors of such manufactures." In other words, patents could only be granted for novel inventions, for a term of no more than 14 years.

Acting under its Intellectual Property Clause power, Congress passed the first US patent law in 1790. It was titled "An Act to promote the progress of useful Arts." The term of protection was 14 years. The first patent was granted to Samuel Hopkins for "making Pot ash and Pearl ash by a new Apparatus and Process." (Potash was an industrial chemical derived from potassium carbonate used to make glass, soap, dyes, and other products.) An image of this patent is below. It is signed by George Washington, Thomas Jefferson, and Attorney General Edmund Randolph.

You have already read Thomas Jefferson's writings about patent law in Chapter 2 of *The Public Domain*. Under the 1790 law, Jefferson (as Secretary of State) was one of the three government officials tasked with deciding whether or not to grant patents. This proved unworkable, and the Patent Act of 1793 did away with this early patent examination process and made it easier to receive a patent. This led to patents over inventions that were not necessarily novel or useful, and increased patent litigation. The Patent Act of 1836 then reinstated a formal examination procedure by creating an official Patent Office and providing funding for professional patent examiners. The basis for current patent law—and the focus of this casebook—is the Patent Act of 1952, along with recent amendments made by the 2011 America Invents Act (discussed below).

In 1982, Congress created the United States Court of Appeals for the Federal Circuit, which has exclusive jurisdiction over patent-related appeals. Most commentators have seen the Federal Circuit as a more pro-patent court than the diverse Circuit Courts whose jurisdiction it assumed. (This of course might be no bad thing if prior courts had been under-protecting patent holders). Early empirical work showed that the Federal Circuit was considerably more likely to find patents valid. See John R. Allison and Mark A. Lemley,

Empirical Evidence on the Validity of Litigated Patents, 26 American Intellectual Property Law Association Quarterly Journal 185 (1998). Henry & Turner's work on the effects of the Federal Circuit's strong presumption of patent validity reinforced that finding 8 years later. Matthew Henry & John Turner, *The Court of Appeals for the Federal Circuit's Impact on Patent Litigation*, 35 Journal of Legal Studies 85 (2006). Scholars have also focused on the insularity of the Federal Circuit and the way in which its tight connections to the patent bar, and its lack of exposure to the views of competing Circuit courts, may reinforce a protectionist mindset. Our colleagues Arti Rai and Stuart Benjamin found, in a nice piece of understatement, that "[t]he behavior of the Federal Circuit was arguably consistent with standard accounts of capture of regulatory processes by well-represented interest groups." Stuart Minor Benjamin & Arti K. Rai, *Fixing Innovation Policy: A Structural Perspective*, 77 Geo. Wash. L. Rev 1, 17 (2008). Landes and Posner's fascinating review and extension of the statistical literature on the Federal Circuit tends to confirm these findings, suggesting that the court's rulings have led to a proliferation of weak and vague patents, the litigation outcome of which is uncertain. William M. Landes & Richard A. Posner, THE ECONOMIC STRUCTURE OF INTELLECTUAL PROPERTY LAW 335-353 (2003). Whether or not that result is in the interests of the patent bar, and we tend to be skeptical of the more overt forms of capture-theory, it is socially problematic. Others have argued that the Federal Circuit's jurisprudence is not only pro-patent but increasingly formalist, disconnected from the constitutional purposes the patent system is supposed to serve. John R. Thomas, *Formalism at the Federal Circuit*, 52 Am. U. L. Rev. 771 (2003). The books cited earlier by Bessen and Lerner collect many other examples.

Both the number of patents issued and the number of patent cases filed has more than tripled in recent decades. Earlier we included a graph that showed the rise in patent cases filed in District Courts from 1,165 in 1990 to 5,163 in 2012. In 2013, a private data source suggests, the number of cases rose 25 percent to a record high of 6,500, and the number of patents granted rose 7 percent to almost 300,000 patents. Pricewaterhouse-Coopers, *Patent Litigation Study* (July 2014). The role of corporate ownership has also expanded. As we mentioned at the beginning of the chapter, over time, patents have gone from the realm of the "lone workshop tinkerer" to that of "large-scale corporate R&D": "in 1885, only 12 percent of patents were issued to corporations. Slightly more than one hundred years later, the proportions had completely reversed: by 1998, only 12.5 percent of patents were issued to independent inventors." Robert P. Merges, *One Hundred Years of Solicitude: Intellectual Property Law*, 1900–2000, 88 Cal. L. Rev. 2187 (2000).

3.) Patent Basics

You have already learned a great deal about trademarks and copyrights. Patents are distinct in a number of ways. First, they are more difficult to obtain. Inventors can only secure a patent through a prosecution process before the United States Patent and Trademark Office (PTO), during which they need to convince the patent examiners that they have met the many requirements for patentability (summarized above). This process can be time-consuming and expensive. While times vary considerably depending on the subject matter and complexity of the application, studies have shown that the average duration of the examination process is between 2 and 3 years. *See* the USPTO *Performance and Accountability Report: Fiscal Year 2013* (showing an improvement of total pendency to 29.1 months); John R. Allison and Mark A. Lemley, *Who's Patenting What? An Empirical Exploration of Patent Prosecution*, 53 Vand. L. Rev. 2099 (2000) (showing an average of 2.77 years). As students entering patent practice will discover, patent application costs can be significant. After a patent is issued, however, the patent holder enjoys a broad right to exclude others from making, using, offering for sale, selling, or importing the invention. In contrast to copyright law, there is no need to prove that the defendant "copied," and independently creating or reverse engineering the invention is no defense.

On the other hand, the patent term is much shorter than that of copyright (life of the author plus 70 years) or trademark (potentially perpetual as long as the mark is continually used in commerce and paperwork is filed). Until 1995, the patent term lasted 17 years from the date that the patent was *granted*. The current patent term is 20 years from the date the application was *filed*. However, the current law tries to ensure that the patent holder will enjoy at least 17 years of post-grant protection by adding 1 day to the term for each day that it remains in prosecution after 3 years, as long as the delay is the fault of the PTO. § 154(b).

As we mentioned a moment ago, to obtain a patent, an invention must meet several requirements. It must consist of patentable subject matter, and be novel, non-obvious, and useful. §§ 101–103. The chapters that follow explore these requirements in detail. The additional requirement of *disclosure* is worth highlighting here. § 112. Patent protection not only provides incentives to innovate; its promise of exclusivity provides incentives to disclose valuable knowledge, rather than keeping it secret. A patent must describe the invention sufficiently well that any person skilled in the relevant art will be able to recreate and use it. This is a fundamental part of the patent bargain: in return for a broad 20-year grant of exclusive rights, the patent holder must disclose her technology so that others can benefit from it. This "promotes the progress" by ensuring that future inventors can build upon what came before them. The American Inventor's Protection Act of 1999 added to the store of public information by requiring the publication of *pending* applications 18 months after the filing date, so that the knowledge in long-pending applications would not remain secret. § 122(b). (This requirement was introduced partly because other countries had a similar 18-month disclosure requirement, and it was thought to be beneficial. Applicants in the United States, however, have several exemptions from the disclosure requirement—for example, they can request secrecy if they are not intending to file in any countries or under any multilateral agreements that require publication after 18 months.)

3 a.) The America Invents Act

In 2011, Congress passed the America Invents Act (AIA). Its key provisions went into effect on September 16, 2012 and March 16, 2013. Thus, you are studying patent law during a transitional period in which you will have to deal with patents granted under both systems. That said, in those areas where the AIA did not change the law, Congress sought to maintain much of the pre-AIA statutory language so that existing case law would continue to offer guidance. The full provisions of the AIA are beyond the scope of this introduction, but two of its key changes are summarized below.

"Who's on first?" One of the most sweeping changes in the AIA is a fundamental shift in how novelty and priority are determined.

Before the AIA, we had a first-to-invent system. Your invention was novel—that is, eligible for patent protection as the *first* such innovation—only if it was *invented* before anyone else invented the same thing. § 102(a)(pre-AIA). However, this provision was subject to an important caveat: even if you invented first, you could nevertheless lose "the right to patent" if you delayed too long before filing the application. § 102(b)(pre-AIA). (This is the statutory bar that disqualified inventions if they were already described in a printed publication, sold, or in public use for over a year before the application date.) Therefore, under pre-AIA law, novelty and priority initially turned on the date of *invention*, but patent eligibility could then be defeated based on the date of *filing*.

After the AIA, the key date across the board is the filing date. For all applications filed on or after March 16, 2013, the AIA implements a first-inventor-to-file system. Priority is now based on who filed first rather than who invented first. § 102(a)(post-AIA). However, that statement is subject to a vital limitation. The AIA did not repeal the requirement of novelty. You still are unable to patent an item that has been described in a printed publication, been on sale or available to the public. If on the day you file the patent application, none of those things is true, then your invention is considered novel *vis a vis* the prior art. This is subject to a 1-year grace period before the filing date during which a disclosure by the inventor (or a third party "who obtained the subject matter disclosed directly or indirectly from the inventor") will not count against the claimed invention as prior art. § 102(b)(post-AIA). (This is a highly simplified description of the AIA's new provisions, please refer to the full language for complete details. Of course, the language is not always entirely clear—there is already a difference of opinion among patent experts about the scope of the 1-year grace period.)

[margin note: After AIA, first-inventor-to-file system]

The second set of key changes involves expanded procedures for reviewing patents. As an example, under the AIA's "post-grant review" provision, anyone can challenge the validity of a patent (or its claims) within nine month of its issue. § 321. The goal is to improve patent quality by providing better mechanisms to invalidate "bad" patents that should not have been granted.

[margin note: AIA expanded procedures for reviewing patents]

3 b.) The PTO Application Process

An applicant can either begin by filing a complete application or a "provisional" application. § 111(b). The provisional route allows the applicant to file much simpler paperwork (it does not need to include a formal patent claim or an oath or declaration) and claim the earlier date as the effective filing date, so long as a full application follows within a year. It also allows the inventor to use the term "patent pending."

It takes an average of over a year for a patent examiner to begin reviewing an application. (Like customer service calls, patent applications are processed in the order in which they are received.) The examiner will often raise objections based on prior art and a lack of meeting the patentability requirements. The inventor can then contest the objections or *amend* to application.

Patent applications are not set in stone. In addition to amending the application, an inventor who wants to make significant changes can file a new "continuation-in-part" application; the material carried over from the original "parent" application maintains its earlier (preferable) filing date, while newly added material is subject to the later filing date of the continuation. (As you might expect, both provisional applications and continuations are subject to strategic use by patent attorneys.) If an application covers more than one independent and distinct invention, then the PTO may require that a "divisional application" be filed. § 121. If the material in the divisional application can be properly traced back to the description in the original application, then it can maintain the earlier filing date.

After a patent is granted, it is published in the Patent Gazette, and enjoys a (rebuttable) presumption of validity. (There is no eventual incontestability, as there is in trademark law.) If errors were made in the patent, it can be "reissued" with corrections, though claims can only be enlarged within two years after the initial grant of the patent. § 251.

3 c.) Reading a Sample Patent

The best way to appreciate the "art" of patent drafting is to review one in detail. A sample patent is on the upcoming pages. It is one of many inventions by Stanford professor and serial inventor Alan Adler, the man who developed the Aerobie flying disc (the rubber and plastic ring that can fly a really long way). The patent is over the AeroPress, a coffee maker that attracts fanatical support as brewing the best cup of coffee of any available technology.

Look at the information on the first page. The name and address of the inventor provide notice of who to contact about the invention. Unlike copyright law, which allows employers to be considered "authors" if a work was "made for hire," patent law does not substitute the employer for inventor. Even if the employer is by explicit assignment the patent holder, only the person who actually invented can be named as such in the application.

Next, notice the series of dates. See if you can tell how long the examination process took and when the patent will expire. As you can see, the inventor is required to list relevant "prior art" to help the examiner—and potential competitors—judge if the invention is truly novel and non-obvious.

Now look at the invention. Patent applications must contain a "specification"—a written description of the invention—and drawings, as relevant. (You can see a drawing on the first page, the other drawings have been omitted.) As you read through the upcoming chapters, think about whether you think this coffee press is novel and non-obvious. The specification is supposed to allow later inventors to build on the invention, or competitors to invent around it. Together with the claims, which we will discuss in a moment, the specification performs some of the same functions as the fixation requirement—it helps to fix the boundaries of the statutory monopoly. But as you can see, patent law requires far greater detail; its aim is greater precision in defining the limits of the right. As we will see later, this goal is not always achieved.

Now look at the actual patent claims on pages 2–3 of the patent. Claims provide an even more detailed delineation of the metes and bounds of the exclusive right. Patent drafters will try to make them as broad as possible, without sacrificing their validity to obviousness, or straying beyond patentable subject matter—which we will discuss in the next chapter. Claims 1, 12, and 14–16 are "independent" claims for various versions of the coffee or tea filtering press. These are deliberately broad. Read claim 1—what exactly does it describe? The other claims are "dependent" claims that refer back to the independent claims. These are narrower and will survive if the independent claim is invalidated, for example, for lack of novelty or for obviousness. Note that the claims use the term "comprising." This is a deliberately "open" term of art meaning the patentee is claiming something novel, and that another coffee maker might infringe this patent even if it has additional features not present in the claims. The alternative "closed" term would be "consisting of"—this would mean that the patentee is only claiming the exact listed elements. In that case, another coffee maker with additional features would not infringe.

US007849784B2

(12) **United States Patent**

Adler

(10) **Patent No.:**   **US 7,849,784 B2**

(45) **Date of Patent:**   **Dec. 14, 2010**

(54) **COFFEE OR TEA FILTERING PRESS**

(76) Inventor: **Alan J. Adler**, 446 Raquel La., Los
                  Altos, CA (US) 94022

(*) Notice: Subject to any disclaimer, the term of
              this patent is extended or adjusted under
              35 U.S.C. 154(b) by 744 days.

(21) Appl. No.: **11/132,500**

(22) Filed: **May 18, 2005**

(65)   **Prior Publication Data**

US 2006/0260471 A1 Nov. 23, 2006

(51) **Intl. Cl.**
     A47J 31/18   (2006.01)
     A47J 31/20   (2006.01)

(52) **U.S. Cl.** .... 99/297; 99/287; 99/302 P;
                                                    99/322

(58) **Field of Classification Search** 99/297,
              99/287, 302P, 306, 322, 210/473, 474, 477
      See application file for complete search history.

(56)   **References Cited**

U.S. PATENT DOCUMENTS

211,236 A * 1/1879 Hartman, Jr. 99/286

802,378	A	*	10/1905	Ellis	99/305
955,616	A		4/1910	Tava	
1,499,281	A	*	6/1924	Altieri	99/306
1,751,397	A	*	3/1930	Delsuc	99/306
2,529,395	A	*	11/1950	Hummel	99/302 P
2,601,821	A	*	7/1952	Johnson	99/287
3,120,170	A	*	2/1964	Garte	99/287
3,596,806	A		8/1971	Harschel	
3,657,993	A	*	4/1972	Close	99/297
3,695,168	A	*	10/1972	Van Brunt	99/306
5,312,637	A	*	5/1994	Midden	426/433
5,478,586	A		12/1995	Connor	
5,942,143	A		8/1999	Hartman et al.	
6,298,771	A	*	10/2001	Calvento	99/323

*cited by examiner

Primary Examiner— Reginald L. Alexander
(74) *Attorney, Agent or Firm*—Townsend and Townsend
and Crew LLP

(57)   **ABSTRACT**

A coffee or tea filtering press includes a hollow cylinder
having top and bottom openings, a perforated removable cap
which encloses the bottom opening, a removable piston
which is inserted into said top opening and pressed
downward to force liquid in the cylinder through the
perforated cap, and a support to hold the press above the
mouth of an open vessel.

17 Claims, 3 Drawing Sheets

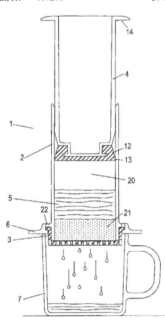

US 7,849,784 B2

1

COFFEE OR TEA FILTERING PRESS

BACKGROUND OF THE INVENTION

The present invention relates generally to beverage makers and more specifically to a press for making coffee or tea.

SUMMARY OF THE INVENTION

According to an aspect of the present invention, a coffee or tea filtering press comprises a hollow cylinder having top and bottom openings, a removable perforated cap which encloses the bottom opening, a removable piston which is inserted into the top opening and pressed downward to force liquid in the cylinder through the perforated cap, and a support to hold said press above the mouth of an open vessel. The support may extend radially outward from the hollow cylinder, or it may extend radially outward from the perforated cap. In the latter instance, the support has an upper cavity to collect liquid which leaks between the cylinder and the cap.

In some embodiments, the support is shaped to permit air to pass readily out of the open vessel when said press is resting on top of the vessel. The piston may be capped with a flexible seal to engage the inside of said hollow cylinder.

A further understanding of the nature and advantages of the present invention may be realized by reference to the remaining portions of the specification and the drawings.

BRIEF DESCRIPTION OF THE DRAWINGS

FIG. 1 illustrates a coffee or tea press according to a embodiment of the invention resting on a cup with the mixing paddle deployed during the initial mixing stage;

FIG. 2 illustrates the press with the piston deployed during the pressing stage; and

FIG. 3 illustrates an alternative version with the support extending radially outward from the perforated cap.

DESCRIPTION OF SPECIFIC EMBODIMENTS

FIGS. 1 and 2 show a coffee or tea filtering press 1 according to a specific embodiment of the invention. Press 1 includes a hollow cylinder 2 having top and bottom openings. A perforated removable cap 3 encloses the bottom opening. A removable piston 4 is inserted into the top opening and pressed downward to force liquid 5 in the cylinder through the perforated cap. The press has a support 6 to hold it on the mouth of an open vessel 7.

A filter 8 may be captured between the cap 3 and the cylinder 2 to strain particles from the liquid. As an alternative, the filter can be integrated into the cap structure.

FIG. 1 show a stirring paddle 9 having an upper stop 10 and a length, measured from its lower extremity 11 to stop 10, which is slightly less than the length of cylinder 2. The stop prevents the tip 11 of the paddle from touching the cap 3 or the filter 8 during stirring.

In operation, the press 1 is placed on an open vessel 7. Ground coffee or tea is put into the cylinder 2. Hot water is added and the mixture is stirred with paddle 9. The paddle is then removed and piston 4 is inserted into the top opening and pressed downward to force the liquid 5 through the filter and perforated cap and into the vessel. The piston pressurizes the air 20, above the liquid and it is this pressurized air which forces the liquid 5 through the cap. When the liquid is expelled, the press is then lifted off the vessel and the cap 3 is removed. Finally piston 4 is pressed farther to eject the spent puck 21 of coffee or tea into a waste receptacle.

2

The piston 4 is capped with a flexible seal 12 to engage the inside of the cylinder. The seal preferably has its maximum diameter 13 at its lowest point in order to wipe clean the inside of the cylinder when the maximum diameter is pushed fully through the cylinder with the cap removed during ejection of the spent puck.

The piston 4 has a stop 14 which limits the maximum travel of the piston but permits the maximum diameter 13 of the seal to extend beyond the bottom opening of the cylinder with the cap removed to eject the spent puck.

The perforated cap 3 has multiple drain holes 15, adjacent to and radially external to a perimeter line defined by the outer circumference of the bottom of cylinder 2. These drain holes relieve pressure between the outer wall of the cylinder and the inner wall of the cap and prevent leakage out of the top edge of the cap.

In FIGS. 1 and 2, perforated cap 3 is attached to cylinder 2 with a twist-lock 16.

FIG. 3 illustrates and alternative version of the invention with the support 6A extending radially outward from the perforated cap 3A. This figure also illustrates an alternative attachment method in which the perforated cap is attached to the cylinder with a screw thread 17. Yet another alternative would be to secure the perforated cap to the cylinder with a latch.

The figures illustrate a central bottom step 18 which extends below the rim of the open vessel in order to keep the press from slipping off the vessel. In FIGS. 1 and 2, this bottom step is the lower portion of cap 3. In FIG. 3, bottom step 18 is an extension below the lower surface of cap 3A.

The alternative cap and support of FIG. 3 also has an upper cavity 19 to collect liquid which leaks between the cylinder 2 and the cap 3A.

Supports 6 and 6A are shaped to permit air to pass readily out of the open vessel when the press is resting on top of the vessel and liquid is entering the vessel. The twist lock 16 of FIG. 1 and FIG. 2 has through-holes 22 which achieve this. In the alternative of FIG. 3, the bottom surface of support 6A is roughened or grooved to achieve this same result.

While the cylinder 2 may be made from a wide range of materials, the preferred materials are transparent so that the user can observe the pressing process. Glass and transparent plastics are suitable.

While a wide range of dimension are feasible for the invention, a cylinder having an inside diameter of approximately 2.25 inches and a length of approximately 5 inches has been found to perform very well.

While the above is a complete description of specific embodiments of the invention, the above description should not be taken as limiting the scope of the invention as defined by the claims.

What is claimed is:

1. A coffee or tea filtering press comprising:
   a constant-diameter hollow cylinder having full-diameter top and bottom openings;
   a removable perforated cap that encloses said bottom opening;
   a removable air-tight piston that has an upper portion configured to be engaged by a user so that said piston, when inserted into said top opening and pressed with direct downward pressure exerted by the user, forces liquid in said hollow cylinder through said perforated cap;
   and a support to hold said press above the mouth of an open vessel.

2. The press of claim 1 wherein said support extends radially outward from said hollow cylinder.

US 7,849,784 B2

| 3 | 4 |

3. The press of claim **1** wherein said support extends radially outward from said perforated cap.

4. The press of claim **3** wherein said support has an upper cavity to collect liquid which leaks between said hollow cylinder and said perforated cap.

5. The press of claim **1** wherein said support is shaped to permit air to pass readily out of said open vessel when said press is resting on top of said vessel.

6. The press of claim **1** wherein:

said piston is capped with a flexible seal to engage the inside of said hollow cylinder; and

said seal has its maximum diameter at its lowest point in order to wipe clean the inside of said cylinder when said maximum diameter is pushed fully through said hollow cylinder with the cap removed.

7. The press of claim **6** wherein said piston has a stop which limits the maximum travel of said piston but permits the maximum diameter of said seal to extend beyond the bottom opening of said hollow cylinder with the cap removed.

8. The press of claim **1** wherein said perforated cap has multiple drain holes, adjacent to and radially external to a perimeter line defined by the outer circumference of the bottom of said hollow cylinder.

9. The press of claim **1** wherein said hollow cylinder is transparent.

10. The press of claim **1** which has a central bottom step which extends below the rim of said open vessel in order to keep said press from slipping off said vessel.

11. The press of claim **1** wherein said hollow cylinder has an inside diameter of approximately 2.25 inches and a length of approximately 5 inches.

12. A coffee or tea filtering press comprising:

a constant-diameter hollow cylinder having full-diameter top and bottom openings;

a removable perforated cap that, when engaged with said cylinder, encloses said bottom opening;

a removable air-tight piston that has an upper portion configured to be engaged by a user so that said piston, when inserted into said top opening and pressed with direct downward pressure exerted by the user, forces liquid in said hollow cylinder through said perforated cap wherein said piston is capped with a flexible seal to engage the inside of said hollow cylinder; and

said piston having a sufficient range of travel that allows a maximum diameter portion of said seal to extend beyond

said bottom opening and wipe clean the inside of said cylinder when said cap is removed.

13. The press of claim **12**, and further comprising a support to hold said press above the mouth of an open vessel.

14. A coffee or tea filtering press comprising:

a constant-diameter hollow cylinder having full-diameter top and bottom openings;

a removable perforated cap that encloses said bottom opening wherein said perforated cap and said hollow cylinder are formed to allow said perforated cap to be attached to said hollow cylinder with a twist-lock;

a removable air-tight piston that is inserted into said top opening and pressed downward to force liquid in said hollow cylinder through said perforated cap; and

a support to hold said press above the mouth of an open vessel.

15. A coffee or tea filtering press comprising:

a constant-diameter hollow cylinder having full-diameter top and bottom openings;

a removable perforated cap that encloses said bottom opening wherein said perforated cap and said hollow cylinder are formed to allow said perforated cap to be attached to said hollow cylinder with a screw thread;

a removable air-tight piston that is inserted into said top opening and pressed downward to force liquid in said hollow cylinder through said perforated cap; and

a support to hold said press above the mouth of an open vessel.

16. A coffee or tea filtering press comprising:

a hollow cylinder having top and bottom openings;

a removable perforated cap that encloses said bottom opening;

a removable piston that is inserted into said top opening and pressed downward to force liquid in said hollow cylinder through said perforated cap; and

a stirring paddle, said paddle having an upper stop and a length, measured from its lower extremity to said stop, which is slightly less than the length of said hollow cylinder, such that said stop prevents the lower extremity of said paddle from touching said perforated cap during stirring.

17. The press of claim **16**, and further comprising a support to hold said press above the mouth of an open vessel.

* * * * *

3 d.) International Patent Law

Like trademark law, patent law is territorial. Inventors must file for patents in all countries where they seek protection, and those patents will be governed by domestic laws. However, there are a number of international agreements that seek to harmonize international rules and streamline the application process. The key international agreements are the Paris Convention for the Protection of Industrial Property or "Paris Convention" (1883), the Trade Related Aspects of Intellectual Property Agreement or "TRIPS Agreement" (1994)—negotiated as part of the Uruguay Round of the General Agreement on Tariffs and Trade (GATT), and the Patent Cooperation Treaty (1970).

The Paris Convention provides for "national treatment," meaning that participating countries must offer the same protection to patent owners from other signatories as they give to their nationals (if I patent my invention in Germany, they must give me the same rights as they give to a German inventor who patents there). In addition, the Paris Convention allows inventors to claim the initial filing date in one country as the priority date in all participating countries, as long as they file the other applications within a year. Like the Paris Convention, the TRIPS Agreement provides for national treatment and common priority dates, but it also establishes "minimum standards" for patent protection. Many of the features of our current patent law were added in order to comply with TRIPS. These include the current patent term of 20 years from the filing date, the ability to file "provisional" applications, and the exclusive rights of "offering for sale" and importation, among other provisions. The Patent Cooperation Treaty focuses on the *application* process, and has a series of procedures for streamlining the filing and prosecution of patent applications in multiple countries.

Before the passage of the America Invents Act, the United States was one of the few countries with a first-to-invent system. While not directly required by international treaties, our recent shift to a first-to-file system brings us into line with the predominant international standard. That said, there are still noteworthy differences between the patent laws of different nations. For example, in many other countries, inventors must file patent applications before publishing their inventions; there is no one-year "grace period" after disclosure as we have in § 102(b).

3 e.) Miscellanea

We will close with three final notes about subjects not covered in this casebook.

- **Design patents and plant patents:** The readings in this book focus on "utility patents," but there are also two additional kinds of patents that are subject to different rules. *Design patents* can issue to "whoever invents any new, original, and ornamental design for an article of manufacture." The invention must be *ornamental* rather than functional. Design patents have been granted for ornamental characteristics of items such as shoes and furniture, and they last for 15 years. §§ 171–173. *Plant patents* are another category that may be granted to "whoever invents or discovers and asexually reproduces any distinct and new variety of plant." §§ 161–164. (A law outside of the scope of patent law called the Plant Variety Protection Act covers sexually reproduced plants.)

- **Government patents & the Bayh-Dole Act:** In the copyright context, works of the US government go into the public domain under § 105. No such limitation obtains in patent law. The Federal government owns thousands of patents. The Bayh-Dole Act, however, allows certain private entities to keep ownership of the patents stemming from Federally-funded research. The Act was prompted by the (empirically contestable) belief that this will be a greater spur to both innovation and licensing.

- **Infringement and defenses:** The law of patent infringement and defenses is beyond the scope of this book. The bases of patent infringement are in § 271. As you read in *Sony v. Universal*, unlike in copyright law, the patent statute spells out both direct and contributory infringement. Among the defenses to patent infringement are prior commercial use, including exhaustion or "first sale" (once a patented product is sold, it can be resold and repaired) § 273, patent misuse (a common law doctrine that patents will not be enforced when they have been misused by the patentee, subject to limitations in § 271(d)), and inequitable conduct. Patent has no doctrine that is equivalent to copyright's broad and protean doctrine of fair use. For example, there was an extremely limited exception for experimental use, but its already minuscule protections were effectively rendered inconsequential by *Madey v. Duke* (Fed. Cir. 2002).

Note: A Patent Eligibility Flow Chart

On the next page you will find a flow chart laying out the requirements for patent-ability—patentable subject matter, utility, novelty and non-obviousness.

Once again, please use it in two ways; as a map of what you will be learning and a tool to help you in your analysis of the Problems.

We have stressed throughout the book that, while we think you will find the flow charts and checklists helpful, you need to understand their limitations. That warning is particularly needed in the patent section. Our book only covers the requirements for patent eligibility, leaving much of patent law unexplored. Still, even with that caveat, we hope you will find it useful.

REQUIREMENTS FOR PATENT PROTECTION
(This is a (highly) simplified preview of what you will learn and
a tool to use in the problems.)

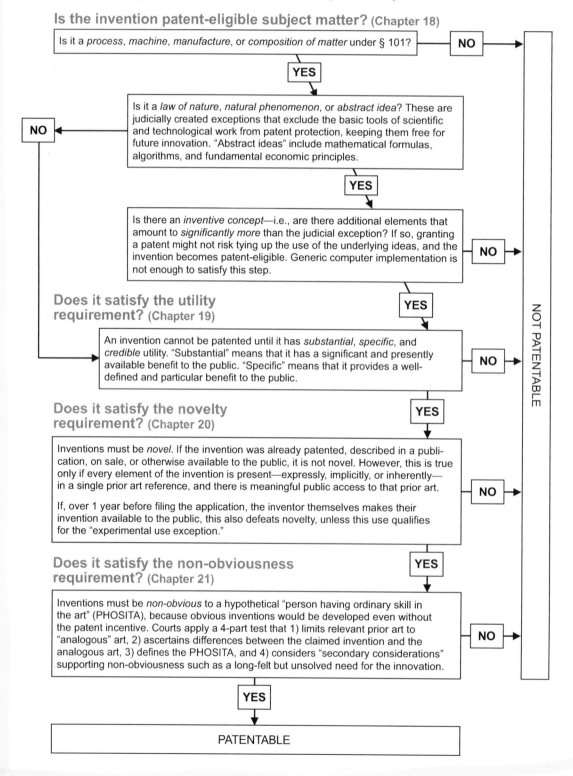

Is the invention patent-eligible subject matter? (Chapter 18)

Is it a *process*, *machine*, *manufacture*, or *composition of matter* under § 101? — **NO** →

YES ↓

Is it a *law of nature*, *natural phenomenon*, or *abstract idea*? These are judicially created exceptions that exclude the basic tools of scientific and technological work from patent protection, keeping them free for future innovation. "Abstract ideas" include mathematical formulas, algorithms, and fundamental economic principles. ← **NO**

YES ↓

Is there an *inventive concept*—i.e., are there additional elements that amount to *significantly more* than the judicial exception? If so, granting a patent might not risk tying up the use of the underlying ideas, and the invention becomes patent-eligible. Generic computer implementation is not enough to satisfy this step. — **NO** →

YES ↓

Does it satisfy the utility requirement? (Chapter 19)

An invention cannot be patented until it has *substantial*, *specific*, and *credible* utility. "Substantial" means that it has a significant and presently available benefit to the public. "Specific" means that it provides a well-defined and particular benefit to the public. — **NO** →

YES ↓

Does it satisfy the novelty requirement? (Chapter 20)

Inventions must be *novel*. If the invention was already patented, described in a publication, on sale, or otherwise available to the public, it is not novel. However, this is true only if every element of the invention is present—expressly, implicitly, or inherently—in a single prior art reference, and there is meaningful public access to that prior art.

If, over 1 year before filing the application, the inventor themselves makes their invention available to the public, this also defeats novelty, unless this use qualifies for the "experimental use exception." — **NO** →

YES ↓

Does it satisfy the non-obviousness requirement? (Chapter 21)

Inventions must be *non-obvious* to a hypothetical "person having ordinary skill in the art" (PHOSITA), because obvious inventions would be developed even without the patent incentive. Courts apply a 4-part test that 1) limits relevant prior art to "analogous" art, 2) ascertains differences between the claimed invention and the analogous art, 3) defines the PHOSITA, and 4) considers "secondary considerations" supporting non-obviousness such as a long-felt but unsolved need for the innovation. — **NO** →

YES ↓

PATENTABLE

NOT PATENTABLE

CHAPTER EIGHTEEN

Patentable Subject Matter

§ 101 of the Patent Act lays out, in very broad terms, the scope of patentable subject matter. Unlike the Copyright Act, the Patent Act has no simple and clear statutory description of the *exclusions* from that subject matter.

§ 101

Whoever invents or discovers any new and useful process, machine, manufacture, or composition of matter, or any new and useful improvement thereof, may obtain a patent therefor. . . .

Patentable subject
matter
☆

But these apparently broad terms come with a common law set of limitations. As the Supreme Court recently noted:

> We have "long held that this provision contains an important implicit exception[:] Laws of nature, natural phenomena, and abstract ideas are not patentable." Rather, "'they are the basic tools of scientific and technological work'" that lie beyond the domain of patent protection. . . . [W]ithout this exception, there would be considerable danger that the grant of patents would "tie up" the use of such tools and thereby "inhibit future innovation premised upon them." This would be at odds with the very point of patents, which exist to promote creation. The rule against patents on naturally occurring things is not without limits, however, for "all inventions at some level embody, use, reflect, rest upon, or apply laws of nature, natural phenomena, or abstract ideas," and "too broad an interpretation of this exclusionary principle could eviscerate patent law." As we have recognized before, patent protection strikes a delicate balance between creating "incentives that lead to creation, invention, and discovery" and "imped[ing] the flow of information that might permit, indeed spur, invention."[†]

In this chapter we will explore these limitations on patentable subject matter, consider how the courts have struggled to elaborate them in the context of new technologies, and search for the rationale—or rationales—behind them.

1.) Laws of Nature and Natural Phenomena

Diamond v. Chakrabarty
447 U.S. 303 (1980)

Mr. Chief Justice BURGER delivered the opinion of the Court.

We granted certiorari to determine whether a live, human-made micro-organism is patentable subject matter under 35 U.S.C. 101.

[†] *Association for Molecular Pathology v. Myriad Genetics, Inc.* (2013).

I

In 1972, respondent Chakrabarty, a microbiologist, filed a patent application, assigned to the General Electric Co. The application asserted 36 claims related to Chakrabarty's invention of "a bacterium from the genus Pseudomonas containing therein at least two stable energy-generating plasmids, each of said plasmids providing a separate hydrocarbon degradative pathway." This human-made, genetically engineered bacterium is capable of breaking down multiple components of crude oil. Because of this property, which is possessed by no naturally occurring bacteria, Chakrabarty's invention is believed to have significant value for the treatment of oil spills.

Chakrabarty's patent claims were of three types: first, process claims for the method of producing the bacteria; second, claims for an inoculum comprised of a carrier material floating on water, such as straw, and the new bacteria; and third, claims to the bacteria themselves. The patent examiner allowed the claims falling into the first two categories, but rejected claims for the bacteria. His decision rested on two grounds: (1) that micro-organisms are "products of nature," and (2) that as living things they are not patentable subject matter under 35 U.S.C. 101.

Chakrabarty appealed the rejection of these claims to the Patent Office Board of Appeals, and the Board affirmed the examiner on the second ground. Relying on the legislative history of the 1930 Plant Patent Act, in which Congress extended patent protection to certain asexually reproduced plants, the Board concluded that 101 was not intended to cover living things such as these laboratory created micro-organisms.

The Court of Customs and Patent Appeals, by a divided vote, reversed on the authority of its prior decision in *In re Bergy* (1977), which held that "the fact that microorganisms . . . are alive . . . [is] without legal significance" for purposes of the patent law. . . .

II

The Constitution grants Congress broad power to legislate to "promote the Progress of Science and useful Arts, by securing for limited Times to Authors and Inventors the exclusive Right to their respective Writings and Discoveries." Art. I, § 8, cl. 8. . . .

The question before us in this case is a narrow one of statutory interpretation requiring us to construe 35 U.S.C. 101, which provides:

> "Whoever invents or discovers any new and useful process, machine, manufacture, or composition of matter, or any new and useful improvement thereof, may obtain a patent therefor, subject to the conditions and requirements of this title."

Specifically, we must determine whether respondent's micro-organism constitutes a "manufacture" or "composition of matter" within the meaning of the statute.

III

In cases of statutory construction we begin, of course, with the language of the statute. . . . [T]his Court has read the term "manufacture" in 101 in accordance with its dictionary definition to mean "the production of articles for use from raw or prepared materials by giving to these materials new forms, qualities, properties, or combinations, whether by hand-labor or by machinery." *American Fruit Growers, Inc. v. Brogdex Co.* (1931). Similarly, "composition of matter" has been construed consistent with its common usage to include "all compositions of two or more substances and . . . all composite articles, whether they be the results of chemical union, or of mechanical mixture, or whether they be gases, fluids, powders or solids." *Shell Development Co. v. Watson* (D.D.C. 1957) (citing A. Deller, 1 Walker on Patents 14, p. 55 (1st ed. 1937)). In choosing such expansive terms as "manufacture" and "composition of matter," modified by the comprehensive "any," Congress plainly contemplated that the patent laws would be given wide scope.

The relevant legislative history also supports a broad construction. The Patent Act of 1793, authored by Thomas Jefferson, defined statutory subject matter as "any new and useful art, machine, manufacture, or composition of matter, or any new or useful improvement [thereof]." Act of Feb. 21, 1793, 1, 1 Stat. 319. The Act embodied Jefferson's philosophy that "ingenuity should receive a liberal encouragement." See *Graham v. John Deere Co.* (1966). Subsequent patent statutes in 1836, 1870 and 1874 employed this same broad language. In 1952, when the patent laws were recodified, Congress replaced the word "art" with "process," but otherwise left Jefferson's language intact. The Committee Reports accompanying the 1952 Act inform us that Congress intended statutory subject matter to "include anything under the sun that is made by man." S. Rep. No. 1979, 82d Cong., 2d Sess., 5 (1952); H. R. Rep. No. 1923, 82d Cong., 2d Sess., 6 (1952).[6]

This is not to suggest that 101 has no limits or that it embraces every discovery. The laws of nature, physical phenomena, and abstract ideas have been held not patentable. Thus, a new mineral discovered in the earth or a new plant found in the wild is not patentable subject matter. Likewise, Einstein could not patent his celebrated law that $E=mc^2$; nor could Newton have patented the law of gravity. Such discoveries are "manifestations of . . . nature, free to all men and reserved exclusively to none."

Judged in this light, respondent's micro-organism plainly qualifies as patentable subject matter. His claim is not to a hitherto unknown natural phenomenon, but to a non-naturally occurring manufacture or composition of matter—a product of human ingenuity "having a distinctive name, character [and] use." *Hartranft v. Wiegmann* (1887). The point is underscored dramatically by comparison of the invention here with that in *Funk*. There, the patentee had discovered that there existed in nature certain species of root-nodule bacteria which did not exert a mutually inhibitive effect on each other. He used that discovery to produce a mixed culture capable of inoculating the seeds of leguminous plants. Concluding that the patentee had discovered "only some of the handiwork of nature," the Court ruled the product nonpatentable:

> "Each of the species of root-nodule bacteria contained in the package infects the same group of leguminous plants which it always infected. No species acquires a different use. The combination of species produces no new bacteria, no change in the six species of bacteria, and no enlargement of the range of their utility. Each species has the same effect it always had. The bacteria perform in their natural way. Their use in combination does not improve in any way their natural functioning. They serve the ends nature originally provided and act quite independently of any effort of the patentee."

Here, by contrast, the patentee has produced a new bacterium with markedly different characteristics from any found in nature and one having the potential for significant utility. His discovery is not nature's handiwork, but his own; accordingly it is patentable subject matter under 101.

---

[6] This same language was employed by P. J. Federico, a principal draftsman of the 1952 recodification, in his testimony regarding that legislation: "[U]nder section 101 a person may have invented a machine or a manufacture, which may include anything under the sun that is made by man. . . ." Hearings on H. R. 3760 before Subcommittee No. 3 of the House Committee on the Judiciary, 82d Cong., 1st Sess., 37 (1951).

IV

Two contrary arguments are advanced, neither of which we find persuasive.

(A)

The petitioner's first argument rests on the enactment of the 1930 Plant Patent Act, which afforded patent protection to certain asexually reproduced plants, and the 1970 Plant Variety Protection Act, which authorized protection for certain sexually reproduced plants but excluded bacteria from its protection. In the petitioner's view, the passage of these Acts evidences congressional understanding that the terms "manufacture" or "composition of matter" do not include living things; if they did, the petitioner argues, neither Act would have been necessary.

We reject this argument. Prior to 1930, two factors were thought to remove plants from patent protection. The first was the belief that plants, even those artificially bred, were products of nature for purposes of the patent law. . . . The second obstacle to patent protection for plants was the fact that plants were thought not amenable to the "written description" requirement of the patent law. . . . Because new plants may differ from old only in color or perfume, differentiation by written description was often impossible.

In enacting the Plant Patent Act, Congress addressed both of these concerns. It explained at length its belief that the work of the plant breeder "in aid of nature" was patentable invention. And it relaxed the written description requirement in favor of "a description . . . as complete as is reasonably possible." No Committee or Member of Congress, however, expressed the broader view, now urged by the petitioner, that the terms "manufacture" or "composition of matter" exclude living things. . . . The [Senate] Reports observe:

> "There is a clear and logical distinction between the discovery of a new variety of plant and of certain inanimate things, such, for example, as a new and useful natural mineral. The mineral is created wholly by nature unassisted by man. . . . On the other hand, a plant discovery resulting from cultivation is unique, isolated, and is not repeated by nature, nor can it be reproduced by nature unaided by man. . . ."

Congress thus recognized that the relevant distinction was not between living and inanimate things, but between products of nature, whether living or not, and human-made inventions. Here, respondent's micro-organism is the result of human ingenuity and research. . . .

(B)

The petitioner's second argument is that micro-organisms cannot qualify as patentable subject matter until Congress expressly authorizes such protection. His position rests on the fact that genetic technology was unforeseen when Congress enacted 101. . . . The legislative process, the petitioner argues, is best equipped to weigh the competing economic, social, and scientific considerations involved, and to determine whether living organisms produced by genetic engineering should receive patent protection. In support of this position, the petitioner relies on our recent holding in *Parker v. Flook* (1978), and the statement that the judiciary "must proceed cautiously when . . . asked to extend patent rights into areas wholly unforeseen by Congress."

It is, of course, correct that Congress, not the courts, must define the limits of patentability; but it is equally true that once Congress has spoken it is "the province and duty of the judicial department to say what the law is." *Marbury v. Madison* (1803). Congress has performed its constitutional role in defining patentable subject matter in 101; we perform ours in construing the language Congress has employed. In so doing, our obligation is to take statutes as we find them, guided, if ambiguity appears, by the legislative history and statutory purpose. Here, we perceive no ambiguity. The subject-matter provisions of the patent law have been cast in broad terms to fulfill the constitutional and statutory goal of promoting "the Progress of Science and the useful Arts" with all that means for the social and economic benefits envisioned by Jefferson. Broad general language is not necessarily ambiguous when congressional objectives require broad terms.

Nothing in *Flook* is to the contrary. That case applied our prior precedents to determine that a "claim for an improved method of calculation, even when tied to a specific end use, is unpatentable subject matter under 101." The Court carefully scrutinized the claim at issue to determine whether it was precluded from patent protection under "the principles underlying the prohibition against patents for 'ideas' or phenomena of nature." We have done that here. *Flook* did not announce a new principle that inventions in areas not contemplated by Congress when the patent laws were enacted are unpatentable *per se*.

. . . A rule that unanticipated inventions are without protection would conflict with the core concept of the patent law that anticipation undermines patentability. Mr. Justice Douglas reminded that the inventions most benefiting mankind are those that "push back the frontiers of chemistry, physics, and the like." *Great A. & P. Tea Co. v. Supermarket Corp.* (1950) (concurring opinion). Congress employed broad general language in drafting 101 precisely because such inventions are often unforeseeable.

To buttress his argument, the petitioner, with the support of *amicus*, points to grave risks that may be generated by research endeavors such as respondent's. The briefs present a gruesome parade of horribles. Scientists, among them Nobel laureates, are quoted suggesting that genetic research may pose a serious threat to the human race, or, at the very least, that the dangers are far too substantial to permit such research to proceed apace at this time. We are told that genetic research and related technological developments may spread pollution and disease, that it may result in a loss of genetic diversity, and that its practice may tend to depreciate the value of human life. These arguments are forcefully, even passionately, presented; they remind us that, at times, human ingenuity seems unable to control fully the forces it creates—that, with Hamlet, it is sometimes better "to bear those ills we have than fly to others that we know not of."

It is argued that this Court should weigh these potential hazards in considering whether respondent's invention is patentable subject matter under 101. We disagree. The grant or denial of patents on micro-organisms is not likely to put an end to genetic research or to its attendant risks. The large amount of research that has already occurred when no researcher had sure knowledge that patent protection would be available suggests that legislative or judicial *fiat* as to patentability will not deter the scientific mind from probing into the unknown any more than Canute could command the tides. Whether respondent's claims are patentable may determine whether research efforts are accelerated by the hope of reward or slowed by want of incentives, but that is all.

What is more important is that we are without competence to entertain these arguments—either to brush them aside as fantasies generated by fear of the unknown, or to act on them. The choice we are urged to make is a matter of high policy for resolution within the legislative process after the kind of investigation, examination, and study that legislative bodies can provide and courts cannot. That process involves the balancing of competing values and interests, which in our democratic system is the business of elected representatives. Whatever their validity, the contentions now pressed on us should be addressed to the political branches of the Government, the Congress and the Executive, and not to the courts.

. . . Congress is free to amend 101 so as to exclude from patent protection organisms produced by genetic engineering. Cf. 42 U.S.C. 2181(a), exempting from patent protection inventions "useful solely in the utilization of special nuclear material or atomic energy in

*Lives/human-
made
microorganism
is
patentable
subject matter*

an atomic weapon." Or it may choose to craft a statute specifically designed for such living things. But, until Congress takes such action, this Court must construe the language of 101 as it is. The language of that section fairly embraces respondent's invention.

Accordingly, the judgment of the Court of Customs and Patent Appeals is Affirmed.

Dissent of Mr. Justice BRENNAN, with whom Mr. Justice WHITE, Mr. Justice MARSHALL, and Mr. Justice POWELL join. [Omitted.]

Questions:

1.) *Why* can one not patent naturally occurring material? After all, the Intellectual Property Clause speaks of "inventions and *discoveries*." Is it a theistic argument that nature has a divine "inventor" and that He does not like others taking credit for His work? Is it a Lockean argument that there should be enough and as good left over for others and thus a part of nature can never be removed from the common heritage of humankind? Or is it an implicit theory about how best to balance property-based incentives and the broad accessibility of a public domain on which others can build? If the latter, why is *nature* the right place to draw that line?

2.) The Court argues that, even if there are knotty ethical and environmental issues involved in patenting living things, they should not be dealt with in patent law. Do you agree?

3.) What were the key arguments against granting this patent? Why was the court not convinced?

4.) In 1987, in its normal rousing prose, the Patent and Trademark Office announced that it would not allow patent applications over human beings,

> A claim directed to or including within its scope a human being will not be considered to be patentable subject matter under 35 U.S.C. 101. The grant of a limited, but exclusive property right in a human being is prohibited by the Constitution. *Accordingly, it is suggested that any claim directed to a non-plant multicellular organism which would include a human being within its scope include the limitation "non-human" to avoid this ground of rejection.* The use of a negative limitation to define the metes and bounds of the claimed subject matter is a permissable [sic] form of expression.[3]

What lines does this limitation leave undrawn? Are those lines of patentable subject matter? Constitutional analysis? Both?

5.) The 2011 America Invents Act specifically addressed the question, taking the matter out of the hands of the PTO.

> § 33 (a) LIMITATION. Notwithstanding any other provision of law, no patent may issue on a claim directed to or encompassing a human organism.

What does it mean by "a human organism"?

---

[3] 1077 *Official Gazette Patent Office* 24 (April 7, 1987).

Mayo Collaborative v. Prometheus Labs

566 U.S. 66 (2012)

Justice BREYER delivered the opinion of the Court.

Section 101 of the Patent Act defines patentable subject matter. It says:

"Whoever invents or discovers any new and useful process, machine, manufacture, or composition of matter, or any new and useful improvement thereof, may obtain a patent therefor, subject to the conditions and requirements of this title." 35 U.S.C. § 101.

The Court has long held that this provision contains an important implicit exception. "[L]aws of nature, natural phenomena, and abstract ideas" are not patentable. *Diamond v. Diehr* (1981). Thus, the Court has written that "a new mineral discovered in the earth or a new plant found in the wild is not patentable subject matter. Likewise, Einstein could not patent his celebrated law that E=mc^2; nor could Newton have patented the law of gravity. Such discoveries are 'manifestations of . . . nature, free to all men and reserved exclusively to none.'" *Chakrabarty* (quoting *Funk Brothers Seed Co. v. Kalo Inoculant Co.* (1948)).

"Phenomena of nature, though just discovered, mental processes, and abstract intellectual concepts are not patentable, as they are the basic tools of scientific and technological work." *Gottschalk v. Benson* (1972). And monopolization of those tools through the grant of a patent might tend to impede innovation more than it would tend to promote it.

The Court has recognized, however, that too broad an interpretation of this exclusionary principle could eviscerate patent law. For all inventions at some level embody, use, reflect, rest upon, or apply laws of nature, natural phenomena, or abstract ideas. Thus, in *Diehr* the Court pointed out that "'a process is not unpatentable simply because it contains a law of nature or a mathematical algorithm.'" It added that "an application of a law of nature or mathematical formula to a known structure or process may well be deserving of patent protection." *Diehr*. And it emphasized Justice Stone's similar observation in *Mackay Radio & Telegraph Co. v. Radio Corp. of America* (1939):

"'While a scientific truth, or the mathematical expression of it, is not a patentable invention, a novel and useful structure created with the aid of knowledge of scientific truth may be.'"

Still, as the Court has also made clear, to transform an unpatentable law of nature into a patent-eligible application of such a law, one must do more than simply state the law of nature while adding the words "apply it."

The case before us lies at the intersection of these basic principles. It concerns patent claims covering processes that help doctors who use thiopurine drugs to treat patients with autoimmune diseases determine whether a given dosage level is too low or too high. The claims purport to apply natural laws describing the relationships between the concentration in the blood of certain thiopurine metabolites and the likelihood that the drug dosage will be ineffective or induce harmful side-effects. We must determine whether the claimed processes have transformed these unpatentable natural laws into patent-eligible applications of those laws. We conclude that they have not done so and that therefore the processes are not patentable.

Our conclusion rests upon an examination of the particular claims before us in light of the Court's precedents. Those cases warn us against interpreting patent statutes in ways that make patent eligibility "depend simply on the draftsman's art" without reference to the "principles underlying the prohibition against patents for [natural laws]." *Flook*. They warn us against upholding patents that claim processes that too broadly preempt the use of a natural law. And they insist that a process that focuses upon the use of a natural law also contain other elements or a combination of elements, sometimes referred to as an "inventive concept," sufficient to ensure that the patent in practice amounts to significantly more than a patent upon the natural law itself.

We find that the process claims at issue here do not satisfy these conditions. In particular, the steps in the claimed processes (apart from the natural laws themselves) involve well-understood, routine, conventional activity previously engaged in by researchers in the field. At the same time, upholding the patents would risk disproportionately tying up the use of the underlying natural laws, inhibiting their use in the making of further discoveries.

[handwritten margin note: Must add upon/ transform natural phenomena or law to make something patentable]

If a law of nature is not patentable, then neither is a process reciting a law of nature, unless that process has additional features that provide practical assurance that the process is more than a drafting effort designed to monopolize the law of nature itself. A patent, for example, could not simply recite a law of nature and then add the instruction "apply the law." Einstein, we assume, could not have patented his famous law by claiming a process consisting of simply telling linear accelerator operators to refer to the law to determine how much energy an amount of mass has produced (or vice versa). Nor could Archimedes have secured a patent for his famous principle of flotation by claiming a process consisting of simply telling boat builders to refer to that principle in order to determine whether an object will float.

A more detailed consideration of the controlling precedents reinforces our conclusion. The cases most directly on point are *Diehr* and *Flook*, two cases in which the Court reached opposite conclusions about the patent eligibility of processes that embodied the equivalent of natural laws. The *Diehr* process (held patent eligible) set forth a method for molding raw, uncured rubber into various cured, molded products. The process used a known mathematical equation, the Arrhenius equation, to determine when (depending upon the temperature inside the mold, the time the rubber had been in the mold, and the thickness of the rubber) to open the press. It consisted in effect of the steps of: (1) continuously monitoring the temperature on the inside of the mold, (2) feeding the resulting numbers into a computer, which would use the Arrhenius equation to continuously recalculate the mold-opening time, and (3) configuring the computer so that at the appropriate moment it would signal "a device" to open the press.

The Court pointed out that the basic mathematical equation, like a law of nature, was not patentable. But it found the overall process patent eligible because of the way the additional steps of the process integrated the equation into the process as a whole. Those steps included "installing rubber in a press, closing the mold, constantly determining the temperature of the mold, constantly recalculating the appropriate cure time through the use of the formula and a digital computer, and automatically opening the press at the proper time." It nowhere suggested that all these steps, or at least the combination of those steps, were in context obvious, already in use, or purely conventional. And so the patentees did not "seek to pre-empt the use of [the] equation," but sought "only to foreclose from others the use of that equation in conjunction with all of the other steps in their claimed process." These other steps apparently added to the formula something that in terms of patent law's objectives had significance—they transformed the process into an inventive application of the formula. . . .

For these reasons, we conclude that the patent claims at issue here effectively claim the underlying laws of nature themselves. The claims are consequently invalid. And the Federal Circuit's judgment is reversed.

It is so ordered.

Question:

1.) *Mayo* puts forward a theory of the role of the public domain of unpatentable ideas in the process of innovation. How is that theory supposed to aid a court in defining the natural laws that are excluded from patentable subject matter?

Ass'n for Molecular Pathology v. Myriad Genetics, Inc.
569 U.S. 576 (2013)

Justice THOMAS delivered the opinion of the Court.

Respondent Myriad Genetics, Inc. (Myriad), discovered the precise location and sequence of two human genes, mutations of which can substantially increase the risks of breast and ovarian cancer. Myriad obtained a number of patents based upon its discovery. This case involves claims from three of them and requires us to resolve whether a naturally occurring segment of deoxyribonucleic acid (DNA) is patent eligible under 35 U.S.C. § 101 by virtue of its isolation from the rest of the human genome. We also address the patent eligibility of synthetically created DNA known as complementary DNA (cDNA), which contains the same protein-coding information found in a segment of natural DNA but omits portions within the DNA segment that do not code for proteins. For the reasons that follow, we hold that a naturally occurring DNA segment is a product of nature and not patent eligible merely because it has been isolated, but that cDNA is patent eligible because it is not naturally occurring. We, therefore, affirm in part and reverse in part the decision of the United States Court of Appeals for the Federal Circuit.

I

A

Genes form the basis for hereditary traits in living organisms. The human genome consists of approximately 22,000 genes packed into 23 pairs of chromosomes. Each gene is encoded as DNA, which takes the shape of the familiar "double helix" that Doctors James Watson and Francis Crick first described in 1953. Each "cross-bar" in the DNA helix consists of two chemically joined nucleotides. The possible nucleotides are adenine (A), thymine (T), cytosine (C), and guanine (G), each of which binds naturally with another nucleotide: A pairs with T; C pairs with G. The nucleotide cross-bars are chemically connected to a sugar-phosphate backbone that forms the outside framework of the DNA helix. Sequences of DNA nucleotides contain the information necessary to create strings of amino acids, which in turn are used in the body to build proteins. Only some DNA nucleotides, however, code for amino acids; these nucleotides are known as "exons." Nucleotides that do not code for amino acids, in contrast, are known as "introns."

Creation of proteins from DNA involves two principal steps, known as transcription and translation. In transcription, the bonds between DNA nucleotides separate, and the DNA helix unwinds into two single strands. A single strand is used as a template to create a complementary ribonucleic acid (RNA) strand. The nucleotides on the DNA strand pair naturally with their counterparts, with the exception that RNA uses the nucleotide base uracil (U) instead of thymine (T). Transcription results in a single strand RNA molecule, known as pre-RNA, whose nucleotides form an inverse image of the DNA strand from which it was created. Pre-RNA still contains nucleotides corresponding to both the exons and introns in the DNA molecule. The pre-RNA is then naturally "spliced" by the physical removal of the introns. The resulting product is a strand of RNA that contains nucleotides corresponding only to the exons from the original DNA strand. The exons-only strand is known as messenger RNA (mRNA), which creates amino acids through translation. In translation, cellular structures known as ribosomes read each set of three nucleotides, known as codons, in the mRNA. Each codon either tells the ribosomes which of the 20 possible amino acids to synthesize or provides a stop signal that ends amino acid production.

DNA's informational sequences and the processes that create mRNA, amino acids, and proteins occur naturally within cells. Scientists can, however, extract DNA from cells using well known laboratory methods. These methods allow scientists to isolate specific segments of DNA—for instance, a particular gene or part of a gene—which can then be further studied, manipulated, or used. It is also possible to create DNA synthetically through processes similarly well known in the field of genetics. One such method begins with an mRNA molecule and uses the natural bonding properties of nucleotides to create a new, synthetic DNA molecule. The result is the inverse of the mRNA's inverse image of the original DNA, with one important distinction: Because the natural creation of mRNA involves splicing that removes introns, the synthetic DNA created from mRNA also contains only the exon sequences. This synthetic DNA created in the laboratory from mRNA is known as complementary DNA (cDNA).

Changes in the genetic sequence are called mutations. Mutations can be as small as the alteration of a single nucleotide—a change affecting only one letter in the genetic code. Such small-scale changes can produce an entirely different amino acid or can end protein production altogether. Large changes, involving the deletion, rearrangement, or duplication of hundreds or even millions of nucleotides, can result in the elimination, misplacement, or duplication of entire genes. Some mutations are harmless, but others can cause disease or increase the risk of disease. As a result, the study of genetics can lead to valuable medical breakthroughs.

B

This case involves patents filed by Myriad after it made one such medical breakthrough. Myriad discovered the precise location and sequence of what are now known as the BRCA1 and BRCA2 genes. Mutations in these genes can dramatically increase an individual's risk of developing breast and ovarian cancer. The average American woman has a 12- to 13-percent risk of developing breast cancer, but for women with certain genetic mutations, the risk can range between 50 and 80 percent for breast cancer and between 20 and 50 percent for ovarian cancer. Before Myriad's discovery of the BRCA1 and BRCA2 genes, scientists knew that heredity played a role in establishing a woman's risk of developing breast and ovarian cancer, but they did not know which genes were associated with those cancers.

Myriad identified the exact location of the BRCA1 and BRCA2 genes on chromosomes 17 and 13. Chromosome 17 has approximately 80 million nucleotides, and chromosome 13 has approximately 114 million. Within those chromosomes, the BRCA1 and BRCA2 genes are each about 80,000 nucleotides long. If just exons are counted, the BRCA1 gene is only about 5,500 nucleotides long; for the BRCA2 gene, that number is about 10,200. Knowledge of the location of the BRCA1 and BRCA2 genes allowed Myriad to determine their typical nucleotide sequence. That information, in turn, enabled Myriad to develop medical tests that are useful for detecting mutations in a patient's BRCA1 and BRCA2 genes and thereby assessing whether the patient has an increased risk of cancer.

Once it found the location and sequence of the BRCA1 and BRCA2 genes, Myriad sought and obtained a number of patents. Nine composition claims from three of those patents are at issue in this case.

C

Myriad's patents would, if valid, give it the exclusive right to isolate an individual's BRCA1 and BRCA2 genes (or any strand of 15 or more nucleotides within the genes) by breaking the covalent bonds that connect the DNA to the rest of the individual's genome. The patents would also give Myriad the exclusive right to synthetically create BRCA cDNA. In Myriad's view, manipulating BRCA DNA in either of these fashions triggers its "right to exclude others from making" its patented composition of matter under the Patent Act. 35 U.S.C. § 154(a)(1); see also § 271(a) ("[W]hoever without authority makes . . . any patented invention . . . infringes the patent").

But isolation is necessary to conduct genetic testing, and Myriad was not the only entity to offer BRCA testing after it discovered the genes. The University of Pennsylvania's Genetic Diagnostic Laboratory (GDL) and others provided genetic testing services to women. Petitioner Dr. Harry Ostrer, then a researcher at New York University School of Medicine, routinely sent his patients' DNA samples to GDL for testing. After learning of GDL's testing and Ostrer's activities, Myriad sent letters to them asserting that the genetic testing infringed Myriad's patents. In response, GDL agreed to stop testing and informed Ostrer that it would no longer accept patient samples. Myriad also filed patent infringement suits against other entities that performed BRCA testing, resulting in settlements in which the defendants agreed to cease all allegedly infringing activity. Myriad, thus, solidified its position as the only entity providing BRCA testing.

Some years later, petitioner Ostrer, along with medical patients, advocacy groups, and other doctors, filed this lawsuit seeking a declaration that Myriad's patents are invalid under 35 U.S.C. § 101. . . . The District Court . . . granted summary judgment to petitioners on the composition claims at issue in this case based on its conclusion that Myriad's claims, including claims related to cDNA, were invalid because they covered products of nature. The Federal Circuit reversed. *Association for Molecular Pathology v. United States Patent and Trademark Office* (2011), and this Court granted the petition for certiorari, vacated the judgment, and remanded the case in light of *Mayo Collaborative Services v. Prometheus Laboratories, Inc.* (2012).

On remand, the Federal Circuit affirmed the District Court in part and reversed in part, with each member of the panel writing separately. All three judges agreed that only petitioner Ostrer had standing. They reasoned that Myriad's actions against him and his stated ability and willingness to begin BRCA1 and BRCA2 testing if Myriad's patents were invalidated were sufficient for Article III standing.

With respect to the merits, the court held that both isolated DNA and cDNA were patent eligible under § 101. The central dispute among the panel members was whether the act of isolating DNA—separating a specific gene or sequence of nucleotides from the rest of the chromosome—is an inventive act that entitles the individual who first isolates it to a patent. Each of the judges on the panel had a different view on that question. Judges Lourie and Moore agreed that Myriad's claims were patent eligible under § 101 but disagreed on the rationale. Judge Lourie relied on the fact that the entire DNA molecule is held together by chemical bonds and that the covalent bonds at both ends of the segment must be severed in order to isolate segments of DNA. This process technically creates new molecules with unique chemical compositions. ("Isolated DNA . . . is a free-standing portion of a larger, natural DNA molecule. Isolated DNA has been cleaved (i.e., had covalent bonds in its backbone chemically severed) or synthesized to consist of just a fraction of a naturally occurring DNA molecule"). Judge Lourie found this chemical alteration to be dispositive, because isolating a particular strand of DNA creates a nonnaturally occurring molecule, even though the chemical alteration does not change the information-transmitting quality of the DNA. ("The claimed isolated DNA molecules are distinct from their natural existence as portions of larger entities, and their informational content is irrelevant to that fact. We recognize that biologists may think of molecules in terms of their uses, but genes are in fact materials having a chemical nature"). Accordingly, he rejected petitioners' argument that isolated DNA was ineligible for patent protection as a product of nature.

Judge Moore concurred in part but did not rely exclusively on Judge Lourie's conclusion that chemically breaking covalent bonds was sufficient to render isolated DNA patent eligible. ("To the extent the majority rests its conclusion on the chemical differences between [naturally occurring] and isolated DNA (breaking the covalent bonds), I cannot agree that this is sufficient to hold that the claims to human genes are directed to patentable subject matter"). Instead, Judge Moore also relied on the United States Patent and Trademark Office's (PTO) practice of granting such patents and on the reliance interests of patent holders. However, she acknowledged that her vote might have come out differently if she "were deciding this case on a blank canvas."

Finally, Judge Bryson concurred in part and dissented in part, concluding that isolated DNA is not patent eligible. As an initial matter, he emphasized that the breaking of chemical bonds was not dispositive: "[T]here is no magic to a chemical bond that requires us to recognize a new product when a chemical bond is created or broken." Instead, he relied on the fact that "[t]he nucleotide sequences of the claimed molecules are the same as the nucleotide sequences found in naturally occurring human genes." Judge Bryson then concluded that genetic "structural similarity dwarfs the significance of the structural differences between isolated DNA and naturally occurring DNA, especially where the structural differences are merely ancillary to the breaking of covalent bonds, a process that is itself not inventive." Moreover, Judge Bryson gave no weight to the PTO's position on patentability because of the Federal Circuit's position that "the PTO lacks substantive rulemaking authority as to issues such as patentability."

Although the judges expressed different views concerning the patentability of isolated DNA, all three agreed that patent claims relating to cDNA met the patent eligibility requirements of § 101. We granted *certiorari*.

II

A

Section 101 of the Patent Act provides:

"Whoever invents or discovers any new and useful . . . composition of matter, or any new and useful improvement thereof, may obtain a patent therefor, subject to the conditions and requirements of this title." 35 U.S.C. § 101.

We have "long held that this provision contains an important implicit exception[:] Laws of nature, natural phenomena, and abstract ideas are not patentable." *Mayo*. Rather, "'they are the basic tools of scientific and technological work'" that lie beyond the domain of patent protection. As the Court has explained, without this exception, there would be considerable danger that the grant of patents would "tie up" the use of such tools and thereby "inhibit future innovation premised upon them." This would be at odds with the very point of patents, which exist to promote creation. *Diamond v. Chakrabarty*

(1980) (Products of nature are not created, and "'manifestations . . . of nature [are] free to all men and reserved exclusively to none'").

The rule against patents on naturally occurring things is not without limits, however, for "all inventions at some level embody, use, reflect, rest upon, or apply laws of nature, natural phenomena, or abstract ideas," and "too broad an interpretation of this exclusionary principle could eviscerate patent law." As we have recognized before, patent protection strikes a delicate balance between creating "incentives that lead to creation, invention, and discovery" and "imped[ing] the flow of information that might permit, indeed spur, invention." We must apply this well-established standard to determine whether Myriad's patents claim any "new and useful . . . composition of matter," § 101, or instead claim naturally occurring phenomena.

B

It is undisputed that Myriad did not create or alter any of the genetic information encoded in the BRCA1 and BRCA2 genes. The location and order of the nucleotides existed in nature before Myriad found them. Nor did Myriad create or alter the genetic structure of DNA. Instead, Myriad's principal contribution was uncovering the precise location and genetic sequence of the BRCA1 and BRCA2 genes within chromosomes 17 and 13. The question is whether this renders the genes patentable.

Myriad recognizes that our decision in *Chakrabarty* is central to this inquiry. In *Chakrabarty*, scientists added four plasmids to a bacterium, which enabled it to break down various components of crude oil. The Court held that the modified bacterium was patentable. It explained that the patent claim was "not to a hitherto unknown natural phenomenon, but to a nonnaturally occurring manufacture or composition of matter—a product of human ingenuity 'having a distinctive name, character [and] use.'" The *Chakrabarty* bacterium was new "with markedly different characteristics from any found in nature," due to the additional plasmids and resultant "capacity for degrading oil." In this case, by contrast, Myriad did not create anything. To be sure, it found an important and useful gene, but separating that gene from its surrounding genetic material is not an act of invention.

Groundbreaking, innovative, or even brilliant discovery does not by itself satisfy the § 101 inquiry. In *Funk Brothers Seed Co. v. Kalo Inoculant Co.* (1948), this Court considered a composition patent that claimed a mixture of naturally occurring strains of bacteria that helped leguminous plants take nitrogen from the air and fix it in the soil. The ability of the bacteria to fix nitrogen was well known, and farmers commonly "inoculated" their crops with them to improve soil nitrogen levels. But farmers could not use the same inoculant for all crops, both because plants use different bacteria and because certain bacteria inhibit each other. Upon learning that several nitrogen-fixing bacteria did not inhibit each other, however, the patent applicant combined them into a single inoculant and obtained a patent. The Court held that the composition was not patent eligible because the patent holder did not alter the bacteria in any way. ("There is no way in which we could call [the bacteria mixture a product of invention] unless we borrowed invention from the discovery of the natural principle itself.") His patent claim thus fell squarely within the law of nature exception. So do Myriad's. Myriad found the location of the BRCA1 and BRCA2 genes, but that discovery, by itself, does not render the BRCA genes "new . . . composition[s] of matter," § 101, that are patent eligible.

Indeed, Myriad's patent descriptions highlight the problem with its claims. For example, a section of the '282 patent's Detailed Description of the Invention indicates that Myriad found the location of a gene associated with increased risk of breast cancer and identified mutations of that gene that increase the risk. In subsequent language

Myriad explains that the location of the gene was unknown until Myriad found it among the approximately eight million nucleotide pairs contained in a subpart of chromosome 17. The '473 and '492 patents contain similar language as well. Many of Myriad's patent descriptions simply detail the "iterative process" of discovery by which Myriad narrowed the possible locations for the gene sequences that it sought. Myriad seeks to import these extensive research efforts into the § 101 patent-eligibility inquiry. But extensive effort alone is insufficient to satisfy the demands of § 101.

Nor are Myriad's claims saved by the fact that isolating DNA from the human genome severs chemical bonds and thereby creates a nonnaturally occurring molecule. Myriad's claims are simply not expressed in terms of chemical composition, nor do they rely in any way on the chemical changes that result from the isolation of a particular section of DNA. Instead, the claims understandably focus on the genetic information encoded in the BRCA1 and BRCA2 genes. If the patents depended upon the creation of a unique molecule, then a would-be infringer could arguably avoid at least Myriad's patent claims on entire genes (such as claims 1 and 2 of the '282 patent) by isolating a DNA sequence that included both the BRCA1 or BRCA2 gene and one additional nucleotide pair. Such a molecule would not be chemically identical to the molecule "invented" by Myriad. But Myriad obviously would resist that outcome because its claim is concerned primarily with the information contained in the genetic sequence, not with the specific chemical composition of a particular molecule.

Finally, Myriad argues that the PTO's past practice of awarding gene patents is entitled to deference. . . . In this case . . . Congress has not endorsed the views of the PTO in subsequent legislation. While Myriad relies on Judge Moore's view that Congress endorsed the PTO's position in a single sentence in the Consolidated Appropriations Act of 2004, that Act does not even mention genes, much less isolated DNA. § 634, 118Stat. 101 ("None of the funds appropriated or otherwise made available under this Act may be used to issue patents on claims directed to or encompassing a human organism").

Further undercutting the PTO's practice, the United States argued in the Federal Circuit and in this Court that isolated DNA was not patent eligible under § 101, and that the PTO's practice was not "a sufficient reason to hold that isolated DNA is patent-eligible." These concessions weigh against deferring to the PTO's determination.

C

cDNA does not present the same obstacles to patentability as naturally occurring, isolated DNA segments. As already explained, creation of a cDNA sequence from mRNA results in an exons-only molecule that is not naturally occurring. Petitioners concede that cDNA differs from natural DNA in that "the non-coding regions have been removed." They nevertheless argue that cDNA is not patent eligible because "[t]he nucleotide sequence of cDNA is dictated by nature, not by the lab technician." That may be so, but the lab technician unquestionably creates something new when cDNA is made. cDNA retains the naturally occurring exons of DNA, but it is distinct from the DNA from which it was derived. As a result, cDNA is not a "product of nature" and is patent eligible under § 101, except insofar as very short series of DNA may have no intervening introns to remove when creating cDNA. In that situation, a short strand of cDNA may be indistinguishable from natural DNA.[9]

---

[9] We express no opinion whether cDNA satisfies the other statutory requirements of patentability. See, e.g., 35 U.S.C. §§ 102, 103, and 112.

III

It is important to note what is not implicated by this decision. First, there are no method claims before this Court. Had Myriad created an innovative method of manipulating genes while searching for the BRCA1 and BRCA2 genes, it could possibly have sought a method patent. But the processes used by Myriad to isolate DNA were well understood by geneticists at the time of Myriad's patents "were well understood, widely used, and fairly uniform insofar as any scientist engaged in the search for a gene would likely have utilized a similar approach," and are not at issue in this case.

Similarly, this case does not involve patents on new applications of knowledge about the BRCA1 and BRCA2 genes. Judge Bryson aptly noted that, "[a]s the first party with knowledge of the [BRCA1 and BRCA2] sequences, Myriad was in an excellent position to claim applications of that knowledge. Many of its unchallenged claims are limited to such applications."

Nor do we consider the patentability of DNA in which the order of the naturally oc-curring nucleotides has been altered. Scientific alteration of the genetic code presents a dif-ferent inquiry, and we express no opinion about the application of § 101 to such endeavors. We merely hold that genes and the information they encode are not patent eligible under § 101 simply because they have been isolated from the surrounding genetic material.
* * *

For the foregoing reasons, the judgment of the Federal Circuit is affirmed in part and reversed in part.

It is so ordered.

Concurrence

Justice SCALIA, concurring in part and concurring in the judgment.

I join the judgment of the Court, and all of its opinion except Part I–A and some portions of the rest of the opinion going into fine details of molecular biology. I am unable to affirm those details on my own knowledge or even my own belief. It suffices for me to affirm, having studied the opinions below and the expert briefs presented here, that the portion of DNA isolated from its natural state sought to be patented is identical to that portion of the DNA in its natural state; and that complementary DNA (cDNA) is a synthetic creation not normally present in nature.

Questions:

1.) As the Court explains, cDNA, or complementary DNA is—effectively—a purified ("exon only") form of DNA with all of the portions ("introns") that do not code for proteins spliced out. If you have a bad case of *biotechnologophobia*, or the inherent fear of biotechnology jargon, you could use a couple of analogies to understand this. When you get a new program for your computer, it will have all kinds of junk in it—help files, font libraries, flying paperclip animations. But there will also be a file that is the heart of the program's functions—the thing that makes the computer *work*; the ".exe file," in older Windows computers, for example. cDNA is the biological equivalent of that. For those who fear both the digital *and* the biotech world (are you perhaps in the wrong class?) think of DNA as your house key. It has a plastic tab on it to spare your fingers, it is emblazoned with a trademark of the lock company, and it sits on a keyring festooned with mini flashlights and supermarket loyalty cards—all things unconnected to opening the door. cDNA is the notched part of the key that opens the door—nothing else. What line does the court draw here in terms of patenting human genes and patenting cDNA sequences? Why? Does this distinction satisfy you? Why do we not ban all gene patents of any kind on the ground that the underlying raw material is "natural"?

2.) The court says that the purified sequences in cDNA are found nowhere in nature and are thus patentable subject matter. Extremely pure 24 karat gold is found nowhere in nature. Is it therefore patentable subject matter?

3.) Think back to Judge Boudin in *Lotus v. Borland*. He talked of the error costs of defining copyrightable subject matter too broadly or too narrowly. What potential error costs on either side does the *Myriad* court see when considering the question of patentable subject matter?

4.) What is the strongest argument you can think of that we should define patentable subject matter as broadly as we can and exclude as few subjects as possible? What is the strongest argument in favor of limiting patentable subject matter and making sure there cannot be patents on the most basic building blocks of knowledge? How should a court choose between those two arguments?

5.) This case is about patents over diagnostics—the key *utility* here is a.) identifying a particular gene sequence and b.) through epidemiological studies, showing that this gene sequence is correlated with a greater or lesser propensity to some health outcome. Does this not consist of simply correlating two, unpatentable, statements of fact or statistical probability?

2.) Abstract Ideas, Business Methods and Computer Programs

James Boyle, The Public Domain
pp. 168–169

U.S. patent law had drawn a firm line between patentable invention and unpatentable idea, formula, or algorithm. The mousetrap could be patented, but not the formula used to calculate the speed at which it would snap shut. Ideas, algorithms, and formulae were in the public domain—as were "business methods." Or so we thought.

The line between idea or algorithm on the one hand and patentable machine on the other looks nice and easy. But put that algorithm—that series of steps capable of being specified in the way described by the Turing machine—onto a computer, and things begin to look more complex. Say, for example, that algorithm was the process for converting miles into kilometers and vice versa. "Take the first number. If it is followed by the word miles, then multiply by 8/5. If it is followed by the word kilometers, multiply by 5/8 . . ." and so on. In the abstract, this is classic public domain stuff—no more patentable than $E=mc^2$ or F=ma. What about when those steps are put onto the tape of the Turing machine, onto a program running on the hard drive of a computer?

The Court of Appeals for the Federal Circuit (the United States's leading patent court) seems to believe that computers can turn unpatentable ideas into patentable machines. In fact, in this conception, the computer sitting on your desk becomes multiple patentable machines—a word processing machine, an e-mail machine, a machine running the program to calculate the tensile strength of steel. I want to stress that the other bars to patentability remain. My example of mile-to-kilometer conversion would be patentable subject matter but, we hope, no patent would be granted because the algorithm is not novel and is obvious. (Sadly, the Patent and Trademark Office seems determined to undermine this hope by granting patents on the most mundane and obvious applications.) But the concern here is not limited to the idea that without a subject matter bar, too many obvious patents will be granted by an overworked and badly incentivized patent office. It is that the patent was supposed to be granted at the very end of a process of investigation and scientific and engineering innovation. The formulae, algorithms, and scientific discoveries on which the patented invention was based remained in the public domain for all to use. It was only when we got to the very end of the process, with a concrete innovation ready to go to market, that the patent was to be given. Yet the ability to couple the abstract algorithm with the concept of a Turing machine undermines this conception. Suddenly the patents are available at the very beginning of the process, even to people who are merely specifying—in the abstract—the idea of a computer running a particular series of algorithmic activities.

The words "by means of a computer" are—in the eyes of the Federal Circuit—an incantation of magical power, able to transubstantiate the ideas and formulae of the public domain into private property. And, like the breaking of a minor taboo that presages a Victorian literary character's slide into debauchery, once that first wall protecting the public domain was breached, the court found it easier and easier to breach still others. If one could turn an algorithm into a patentable machine simply by adding "by means of a computer," then one could turn a business method into something patentable by specifying the organizational or information technology structure through which the business method is to be implemented.

If you still remember the first chapters of this book, you might wonder why we would want to patent business methods. Intellectual property rights are supposed to be handed out only when necessary to produce incentives to supply some public good, incentives that otherwise would be lacking. Yet there are already plenty of incentives to come up with new business methods. (Greed and fear are the most obvious.) There is no evidence to suggest that we need a state-backed monopoly to encourage the development of new business methods. In fact, we want people to copy the businesses of others, lowering prices as a result. The process of copying business methods is called "competition" and it is the basis of a free-market economy. Yet patent law would prohibit it for twenty years. So why introduce patents? Brushing aside such minor objections with ease, the Court of Appeals for the Federal Circuit declared business methods to be patentable. Was this what Jefferson had in mind when he said "I know well the difficulty of drawing a line between the things which are worth to the public the embarrassment of an exclusive patent, and those which are not"? I doubt it.

Bilski v. Kappos
561 U.S. 593 (2010)

Justice KENNEDY delivered the opinion of the Court, except as to Parts II–B–2 and II–C–2.* ROBERTS, C.J., and THOMAS and ALITO, JJ., joined the opinion in full, and SCALIA, J., joined except for Parts II–B–2 and II–C–2. STEVENS, J., filed an opinion concurring in the judgment, in which GINSBURG, BREYER, and SOTOMAYOR, JJ., joined. BREYER, J., filed an opinion concurring in the judgment, in which SCALIA, J., joined as to Part II.

---

* Justice SCALIA does not join Parts II–B–2 and II–C–2.

The question in this case turns on whether a patent can be issued for a claimed invention designed for the business world. The patent application claims a procedure for instructing buyers and sellers how to protect against the risk of price fluctuations in a discrete section of the economy. Three arguments are advanced for the proposition that the claimed invention is outside the scope of patent law: (1) it is not tied to a machine and does not transform an article; (2) it involves a method of conducting business; and (3) it is merely an abstract idea. The Court of Appeals ruled that the first mentioned of these, the so-called machine-or-transformation test, was the sole test to be used for determining the patentability of a "process" under the Patent Act, 35 U.S.C. § 101.

I

Petitioners' application seeks patent protection for a claimed invention that explains how buyers and sellers of commodities in the energy market can protect, or hedge, against the risk of price changes. The key claims are claims 1 and 4. Claim 1 describes a series of steps instructing how to hedge risk. Claim 4 puts the concept articulated in claim 1 into a simple mathematical formula. Claim 1 consists of the following steps:

> "(a) initiating a series of transactions between said commodity provider and consumers of said commodity wherein said consumers purchase said commodity at a fixed rate based upon historical averages, said fixed rate corresponding to a risk position of said consumers;
>
> "(b) identifying market participants for said commodity having a counter-risk position to said consumers; and
>
> "(c) initiating a series of transactions between said commodity provider and said market participants at a second fixed rate such that said series of market participant transactions balances the risk position of said series of consumer transactions."

The remaining claims explain how claims 1 and 4 can be applied to allow energy suppliers and consumers to minimize the risks resulting from fluctuations in market demand for energy. For example, claim 2 claims "[t]he method of claim 1 wherein said commodity is energy and said market participants are transmission distributors." Some of these claims also suggest familiar statistical approaches to determine the inputs to use in claim 4's equation. For example, claim 7 advises using well-known random analysis techniques to determine how much a seller will gain "from each transaction under each historical weather pattern."

The patent examiner rejected petitioners' application, explaining that it "'is not implemented on a specific apparatus and merely manipulates [an] abstract idea and solves a purely mathematical problem without any limitation to a practical application, therefore, the invention is not directed to the technological arts.'" The Board of Patent Appeals and Interferences affirmed, concluding that the application involved only mental steps that do not transform physical matter and was directed to an abstract idea.

The United States Court of Appeals for the Federal Circuit heard the case en banc and affirmed. The case produced five different opinions. Students of patent law would be well advised to study these scholarly opinions.

Chief Judge Michel wrote the opinion of the court. The court rejected its prior test for determining whether a claimed invention was a patentable "process" under § 101— whether it produces a "'useful, concrete, and tangible result'"—as articulated in *State Street Bank & Trust Co. v. Signature Financial Group, Inc.* (1998), and *AT&T Corp. v. Excel*

Communications, Inc. (1999). The court held that "[a] claimed process is surely patent eligible under § 101 if: (1) it is tied to a particular machine or apparatus, or (2) it transforms a particular article into a different state or thing." The court concluded this "machine-or-transformation test" is "the sole test governing § 101 analyses," and thus the "test for determining patent eligibility of a process under § 101." Applying the machine-or-transformation test, the court held that petitioners' application was not patent eligible. Judge Dyk wrote a separate concurring opinion, providing historical support for the court's approach.

Three judges wrote dissenting opinions. Judge Mayer argued that petitioners' application was "not eligible for patent protection because it is directed to a method of conducting business." He urged the adoption of a "technological standard for patentability." Judge Rader would have found petitioners' claims were an unpatentable abstract idea. Only Judge Newman disagreed with the court's conclusion that petitioners' application was outside of the reach of § 101. She did not say that the application should have been granted but only that the issue should be remanded for further proceedings to determine whether the application qualified as patentable under other provisions.

II
A

Section 101 defines the subject matter that may be patented under the Patent Act:
> "Whoever invents or discovers any new and useful process, machine, manufacture, or composition of matter, or any new and useful improvement thereof, may obtain a patent therefor, subject to the conditions and requirements of this title."

Section 101 thus specifies four independent categories of inventions or discoveries that are eligible for protection: processes, machines, manufactures, and compositions of matter. "In choosing such expansive terms . . . modified by the comprehensive 'any,' Congress plainly contemplated that the patent laws would be given wide scope." *Diamond v. Chakrabarty* (1980). Congress took this permissive approach to patent eligibility to ensure that "'ingenuity should receive a liberal encouragement.'" [*Chakrabarty*] (quoting 5 Writings of Thomas Jefferson 75–76).

The Court's precedents provide three specific exceptions to § 101's broad patent-eligibility principles: "laws of nature, physical phenomena, and abstract ideas." *Chakrabarty*. While these exceptions are not required by the statutory text, they are consistent with the notion that a patentable process must be "new and useful." And, in any case, these exceptions have defined the reach of the statute as a matter of statutory *stare decisis* going back 150 years. The concepts covered by these exceptions are "part of the storehouse of knowledge of all men . . . free to all men and reserved exclusively to none." *Funk Brothers Seed Co. v. Kalo Inoculant Co.* (1948).

The § 101 patent-eligibility inquiry is only a threshold test. Even if an invention qualifies as a process, machine, manufacture, or composition of matter, in order to receive the Patent Act's protection the claimed invention must also satisfy "the conditions and requirements of this title." § 101. Those requirements include that the invention be novel, see § 102, nonobvious, see § 103, and fully and particularly described, see § 112.

The present case involves an invention that is claimed to be a "process" under § 101. Section 100(b) defines "process" as:
> "process, art or method, and includes a new use of a known process, machine, manufacture, composition of matter, or material."

The Court first considers two proposed categorical limitations on "process" patents under

§ 101 that would, if adopted, bar petitioners' application in the present case: the machine-or-transformation test and the categorical exclusion of business method patents.

B

1

Under the Court of Appeals' formulation, an invention is a "process" only if: "(1) it is tied to a particular machine or apparatus, or (2) it transforms a particular article into a different state or thing." This Court has "more than once cautioned that courts 'should not read into the patent laws limitations and conditions which the legislature has not expressed.'" *Diamond v. Diehr* (1981). Any suggestion in this Court's case law that the Patent Act's terms deviate from their ordinary meaning has only been an explanation for the exceptions for laws of nature, physical phenomena, and abstract ideas. See *Parker v. Flook* (1978). This Court has not indicated that the existence of these well-established exceptions gives the Judiciary *carte blanche* to impose other limitations that are inconsistent with the text and the statute's purpose and design.

Adopting the machine-or-transformation test as the sole test for what constitutes a "process" (as opposed to just an important and useful clue) violates these statutory interpretation principles. Section 100(b) provides that "[t]he term 'process' means process, art or method, and includes a new use of a known process, machine, manufacture, composition of matter, or material." The Court is unaware of any "'ordinary, contemporary, common meaning,'" *Diehr*, of the definitional terms "process, art or method" that would require these terms to be tied to a machine or to transform an article.

The Court of Appeals incorrectly concluded that this Court has endorsed the machine-or-transformation test as the exclusive test. . . .

This Court's precedents establish that the machine-or-transformation test is a useful and important clue, an investigative tool, for determining whether some claimed inventions are processes under § 101. The machine-or-transformation test is not the sole test for deciding whether an invention is a patent-eligible "process."

2

It is true that patents for inventions that did not satisfy the machine-or-transformation test were rarely granted in earlier eras, especially in the Industrial Age, as explained by Judge Dyk's thoughtful historical review. But times change. Technology and other innovations progress in unexpected ways. For example, it was once forcefully argued that until recent times, "well-established principles of patent law probably would have prevented the issuance of a valid patent on almost any conceivable computer program." *Diehr* (STEVENS, J., dissenting). But this fact does not mean that unforeseen innovations such as computer programs are always unpatentable. [*Diehr*] (majority opinion) (holding a procedure for molding rubber that included a computer program is within patentable subject matter). Section 101 is a "dynamic provision designed to encompass new and unforeseen inventions." *J.E.M. Ag Supply, Inc. v. Pioneer Hi-Bred Int'l, Inc.* (2001). A categorical rule denying patent protection for "inventions in areas not contemplated by Congress . . . would frustrate the purposes of the patent law." *Chakrabarty*.

The machine-or-transformation test may well provide a sufficient basis for evaluating processes similar to those in the Industrial Age—for example, inventions grounded in a physical or other tangible form. But there are reasons to doubt whether the test should be the sole criterion for determining the patentability of inventions in the Information Age. As numerous *amicus* briefs argue, the machine-or-transformation test would create uncertainty as to the patentability of software, advanced diagnostic medicine techniques, and inventions based on linear programming, data compression, and the manipulation of digital signals.

It is important to emphasize that the Court today is not commenting on the patentability of any particular invention, let alone holding that any of the above-mentioned technologies from the Information Age should or should not receive patent protection. This Age puts the possibility of innovation in the hands of more people and raises new difficulties for the patent law. With ever more people trying to innovate and thus seeking patent protections for their inventions, the patent law faces a great challenge in striking the balance between protecting inventors and not granting monopolies over procedures that others would discover by independent, creative application of general principles. Nothing in this opinion should be read to take a position on where that balance ought to be struck.

C
1

Section 101 similarly precludes the broad contention that the term "process" categorically excludes business methods. The term "method," which is within § 100(b)'s definition of "process," at least as a textual matter and before consulting other limitations in the Patent Act and this Court's precedents, may include at least some methods of doing business. See, *e.g.,* Webster's New International Dictionary 1548 (2d ed. 1954) (defining "method" as "[a]n orderly procedure or process . . . regular way or manner of doing anything; hence, a set form of procedure adopted in investigation or instruction"). The Court is unaware of any argument that the "'ordinary, contemporary, common meaning,'" *Diehr*, of "method" excludes business methods. Nor is it clear how far a prohibition on business method patents would reach, and whether it would exclude technologies for conducting a business more efficiently. See, *e.g.,* Hall, Business and Financial Method Patents, Innovation, and Policy, 56 Scottish J. Pol. Econ. 443, 445 (2009) ("There is no precise definition of . . . business method patents").

The argument that business methods are categorically outside of § 101's scope is further undermined by the fact that federal law explicitly contemplates the existence of at least some business method patents. Under 35 U.S.C. § 273(b)(1), if a patent-holder claims infringement based on "a method in [a] patent," the alleged infringer can assert a defense of prior use. For purposes of this defense alone, "method" is defined as "a method of doing or conducting business." § 273(a)(3). In other words, by allowing this defense the statute itself acknowledges that there may be business method patents. Section 273's definition of "method," to be sure, cannot change the meaning of a prior-enacted statute. But what § 273 does is clarify the understanding that a business method is simply one kind of "method" that is, at least in some circumstances, eligible for patenting under § 101.

A conclusion that business methods are not patentable in any circumstances would render § 273 meaningless. This would violate the canon against interpreting any statutory provision in a manner that would render another provision superfluous. Finally, while § 273 appears to leave open the possibility of some business method patents, it does not suggest broad patentability of such claimed inventions.

2

Interpreting § 101 to exclude all business methods simply because business method patents were rarely issued until modern times revives many of the previously discussed difficulties. At the same time, some business method patents raise special problems in terms of vagueness and suspect validity. See *eBay Inc. v. MercExchange, L.L.C.* (2006) (KENNEDY, J., concurring). The Information Age empowers people with new capacities to perform statistical analyses and mathematical calculations with a speed and sophistication that enable the design of protocols for more efficient performance of a vast number of business tasks. If a high enough bar is not set when considering patent applications of this sort, patent examiners and courts could be flooded with claims that would put a chill on creative endeavor and dynamic change.

In searching for a limiting principle, this Court's precedents on the unpatentability of abstract ideas provide useful tools. Indeed, if the Court of Appeals were to succeed in defining a narrower category or class of patent applications that claim to instruct how business should be conducted, and then rule that the category is unpatentable because, for instance, it represents an attempt to patent abstract ideas, this conclusion might well be in accord with controlling precedent. But beyond this or some other limitation consistent with the statutory text, the Patent Act leaves open the possibility that there are at least some processes that can be fairly described as business methods that are within patentable subject matter under § 101.

Finally, even if a particular business method fits into the statutory definition of a "process," that does not mean that the application claiming that method should be granted. In order to receive patent protection, any claimed invention must be novel, § 102, nonobvious, § 103, and fully and particularly described, § 112. These limitations serve a critical role in adjusting the tension, ever present in patent law, between stimulating innovation by protecting inventors and impeding progress by granting patents when not justified by the statutory design.

III

Even though petitioners' application is not categorically outside of § 101 under the two broad and atextual approaches the Court rejects today, that does not mean it is a "process" under § 101. Petitioners seek to patent both the concept of hedging risk and the application of that concept to energy markets. Rather than adopting categorical rules that might have wide-ranging and unforeseen impacts, the Court resolves this case narrowly on the basis of this Court's decisions in *Benson*, *Flook*, and *Diehr*, which show that petitioners' claims are not patentable processes because they are attempts to patent abstract ideas. Indeed, all members of the Court agree that the patent application at issue here falls outside of § 101 because it claims an abstract idea. In *Benson*, the Court considered whether a patent application for an algorithm to convert binary-coded decimal numerals into pure binary code was a "process" under § 101. The Court first explained that "'[a] principle, in the abstract, is a fundamental truth; an original cause; a motive; these cannot be patented, as no one can claim in either of them an exclusive right.'" The Court then held the application at issue was not a "process," but an unpatentable abstract idea. "It is conceded that one may not patent an idea. But in practical effect that would be the result if the formula for converting . . . numerals to pure binary numerals were patented in this case." A contrary holding "would wholly pre-empt the mathematical formula and in practical effect would be a patent on the algorithm itself."

In *Flook*, the Court considered the next logical step after *Benson*. The applicant there attempted to patent a procedure for monitoring the conditions during the catalytic conversion process in the petrochemical and oil-refining industries. The application's only innovation was reliance on a mathematical algorithm. *Flook* held the invention was not a patentable "process." The Court conceded the invention at issue, unlike the algorithm in *Benson*, had been limited so that it could still be freely used outside the petrochemical and oil-refining industries. Nevertheless, *Flook* rejected "[t]he notion that post-solution activity, no matter how conventional or obvious in itself, can transform an unpatentable principle into a patentable process." The Court concluded that the process at issue there was "unpatentable under § 101, not because it contain[ed] a mathematical algorithm as one component, but because once that algorithm [wa]s assumed to be within the prior art, the application, considered as a whole, contain[ed] no patentable invention." As the Court later explained, *Flook* stands for the proposition that the prohibition against patenting abstract ideas "cannot be circumvented by attempting to limit the use of the formula to a particular technological environment" or adding "insignificant postsolution activity." *Diehr*.

Finally, in *Diehr*, the Court established a limitation on the principles articulated in *Benson* and *Flook*. The application in *Diehr* claimed a previously unknown method for "molding raw, uncured synthetic rubber into cured precision products," using a mathematical formula to complete some of its several steps by way of a computer. *Diehr* explained that while an abstract idea, law of nature, or mathematical formula could not be patented, "an *application* of a law of nature or mathematical formula to a known structure or process may well be deserving of patent protection." *Diehr* emphasized the need to consider the invention as a whole, rather than "dissect[ing] the claims into old and new elements and then . . . ignor[ing] the presence of the old elements in the analysis." Finally, the Court concluded that because the claim was not "an attempt to patent a mathematical formula, but rather [was] an industrial process for the molding of rubber products," it fell within§ 101's patentable subject matter.

In light of these precedents, it is clear that petitioners' application is not a patentable "process." Claims 1 and 4 in petitioners' application explain the basic concept of hedging, or protecting against risk: "Hedging is a fundamental economic practice long prevalent in our system of commerce and taught in any introductory finance class." The concept of hedging, described in claim 1 and reduced to a mathematical formula in claim 4, is an unpatentable abstract idea, just like the algorithms at issue in *Benson* and *Flook*. . . . Allowing petitioners to patent risk hedging would preempt use of this approach in all fields, and would effectively grant a monopoly over an abstract idea. . . .

* * *

Today, the Court once again declines to impose limitations on the Patent Act that are inconsistent with the Act's text. The patent application here can be rejected under our precedents on the unpatentability of abstract ideas. The Court, therefore, need not define further what constitutes a patentable "process," beyond pointing to the definition of that term provided in § 100(b) and looking to the guideposts in *Benson*, *Flook*, and *Diehr*.

And nothing in today's opinion should be read as endorsing interpretations of § 101 that the Court of Appeals for the Federal Circuit has used in the past. See, *e.g., State Street*; *AT&T Corp.* It may be that the Court of Appeals thought it needed to make the machine-or-transformation test exclusive precisely because its case law had not adequately identified less extreme means of restricting business method patents, including (but not limited to) application of our opinions in *Benson*, *Flook*, and *Diehr*. In disapproving an exclusive machine-or-transformation test, we by no means foreclose the Federal Circuit's development of other limiting criteria that further the purposes of the Patent Act and are not inconsistent with its text.

The judgment of the Court of Appeals is affirmed.

It is so ordered.

Justice STEVENS, with whom Justice GINSBURG, Justice BREYER, and Justice SOTOMAYOR join, concurring in the judgment.

In the area of patents, it is especially important that the law remain stable and clear. The only question presented in this case is whether the so-called machine-or-transformation test is the exclusive test for what constitutes a patentable "process" under

35 U.S.C. § 101. It would be possible to answer that question simply by holding, as the entire Court agrees, that although the machine-or-transformation test is reliable in most cases, it is not the *exclusive* test.

I agree with the Court that, in light of the uncertainty that currently pervades this field, it is prudent to provide further guidance. But I would take a different approach. Rather than making any broad statements about how to define the term "process" in § 101 or tinkering with the bounds of the category of unpatentable, abstract ideas, I would restore patent law to its historical and constitutional moorings.

For centuries, it was considered well established that a series of steps for conducting business was not, in itself, patentable. In the late 1990's, the Federal Circuit and others called this proposition into question. Congress quickly responded to a Federal Circuit decision with a stopgap measure designed to limit a potentially significant new problem for the business community. It passed the First Inventors Defense Act of 1999 (1999 Act) (codified at 35 U.S.C. § 273), which provides a limited defense to claims of patent infringement, see § 273(b), for "method[s] of doing or conducting business," § 273(a)(3). Following several more years of confusion, the Federal Circuit changed course, overruling recent decisions and holding that a series of steps may constitute a patentable process only if it is tied to a machine or transforms an article into a different state or thing. This "machine-or-transformation test" excluded general methods of doing business as well as, potentially, a variety of other subjects that could be called processes.

The Court correctly holds that the machine-or-transformation test is not the sole test for what constitutes a patentable process; rather, it is a critical clue. But the Court is quite wrong, in my view, to suggest that any series of steps that is not itself an abstract idea or law of nature may constitute a "process" within the meaning of § 101. The language in the Court's opinion to this effect can only cause mischief. The wiser course would have been to hold that petitioners' method is not a "process" because it describes only a general method of engaging in business transactions—and business methods are not patentable. More precisely, although a process is not patent-ineligible simply because it is useful for conducting business, a claim that merely describes a method of doing business does not qualify as a "process" under § 101. . . .

II

Before explaining in more detail how I would decide this case, I will comment briefly on the Court's opinion. . . .

First, the Court suggests that the terms in the Patent Act must be read as lay speakers use those terms, and not as they have traditionally been understood in the context of patent law. See, *e.g.*, *ante*, at 6 (terms in § 101 must be viewed in light of their "'ordinary, contemporary, common meaning'"); *ante*, at 10 (patentable "method" is any "orderly procedure or process," "regular way or manner of doing anything," or "set form of procedure adopted in investigation or instruction"). As I will explain at more length in Part III, if this portion of the Court's opinion were taken literally, the results would be absurd: Anything that constitutes a series of steps would be patentable so long as it is novel, nonobvious, and described with specificity. But the opinion cannot be taken literally on this point. The Court makes this clear when it accepts that the "atextual" machine-or-transformation test is "useful and important," even though it "violates" the stated "statutory interpretation principles"; and when the Court excludes processes that tend to pre-empt commonly used ideas.

Second, in the process of addressing the sole issue presented to us, the opinion uses some language that seems inconsistent with our centuries-old reliance on the machine-or-transformation criteria as clues to patentability. Most notably, the opinion for a plurality suggests that these criteria may operate differently when addressing technologies of a recent vintage.... Notwithstanding this internal tension, I understand the Court's opinion to hold only that the machine-or-transformation test remains an important test for patentability. Few, if any, processes cannot effectively be evaluated using these criteria.

Third, in its discussion of an issue not contained in the questions presented—whether the particular series of steps in petitioners' application is an abstract idea—the Court uses language that could suggest a shift in our approach to that issue. Although I happen to agree that petitioners seek to patent an abstract idea, the Court does not show how this conclusion follows "clear[ly]" from our case law. The patent now before us is not for "[a] principle, in the abstract," or a "fundamental truth." *Parker v. Flook* (1978). Nor does it claim the sort of phenomenon of nature or abstract idea that was embodied by the mathematical formula at issue in *Gottschalk v. Benson*, and in *Flook*.

The Court construes petitioners' claims on processes for pricing as claims on "the basic concept of hedging, or protecting against risk," and thus discounts the application's discussion of what sorts of data to use, and how to analyze those data, as mere "token postsolution components." In other words, the Court artificially limits petitioners' claims to hedging, and then concludes that hedging is an abstract idea rather than a term that describes a category of processes including petitioners' claims. Why the Court does this is never made clear. One might think that the Court's analysis means that any process that utilizes an abstract idea is *itself* an unpatentable, abstract idea. But we have never suggested any such rule, which would undermine a host of patentable processes....

The Court, in sum, never provides a satisfying account of what constitutes an unpatentable abstract idea. Indeed, the Court does not even explain if it is using the machine-or-transformation criteria. The Court essentially asserts its conclusion that petitioners' application claims an abstract idea. This mode of analysis (or lack thereof) may have led to the correct outcome in this case, but it also means that the Court's musings on this issue stand for very little.

III

Pursuant to its power "[t]o promote the Progress of . . . useful Arts, by securing for limited Times to . . . Inventors the exclusive Right to their . . . Discoveries," U.S. Const., Art. I, § 8, cl. 8, Congress has passed a series of patent laws that grant certain exclusive rights over certain inventions and discoveries as a means of encouraging innovation. In the latest iteration, the Patent Act of 1952 (1952 Act), Congress has provided that "[w]hoever invents or discovers any new and useful process, machine, manufacture, or composition of matter, or any new and useful improvement thereof, may obtain a patent therefor, subject to the conditions and requirements of this title," 35 U.S.C. § 101, which include that the patent also be novel, § 102, and nonobvious, § 103. The statute thus authorizes four categories of subject matter that may be patented: processes, machines, manufactures, and compositions of matter. Section 101 imposes a threshold condition. "[N]o patent is available for a discovery, however useful, novel, and nonobvious, unless it falls within one of the express categories of patentable subject matter." *Kewanee Oil Co. v. Bicron Corp.*

Section 101 undoubtedly defines in "expansive terms" the subject matter eligible for patent protection, as the statute was meant to ensure that "'ingenuit[ies] receive a liberal encouragement.'" *Diamond v. Chakrabarty* (1980). Nonetheless, not every new invention or discovery may be patented. Certain things are "free for all to use." *Bonito Boats, Inc. v.*

Thunder Craft Boats, Inc. (1989).

The text of the Patent Act does not on its face give much guidance about what constitutes a patentable process. The statute defines the term "process" as a "process, art or method [that] includes a new use of a known process, machine, manufacture, composition of matter, or material." § 100(b). But, this definition is not especially helpful, given that it also uses the term "process" and is therefore somewhat circular.

As lay speakers use the word "process," it constitutes any series of steps. But it has always been clear that, as used in § 101, the term does not refer to a "'process' in the ordinary sense of the word," *Flook*; see also *Corning v. Burden* (1854) ("[T]he term process is often used in a more vague sense, in which it cannot be the subject of a patent"). Rather, as discussed in some detail in Part IV, the term "process" (along with the definitions given to that term) has long accumulated a distinctive meaning in patent law. . . .

. . . Specifically, the Government submits, we may infer "that the term 'process' is limited to technological and industrial methods." The Court rejects this submission categorically, on the ground that "§ 100(b) already explicitly defines the term 'process.'" . . . In my view, the answer lies in between the Government's and the Court's positions: The terms adjacent to "process" in § 101 provide a clue as to its meaning, although not a very strong clue. . . .

The Court makes a more serious interpretive error. As briefly discussed in Part II, the Court at points appears to reject the well-settled proposition that the term "process" in § 101 is not a "'process' in the ordinary sense of the word," *Flook*. Instead, the Court posits that the word "process" must be understood in light of its "ordinary, contemporary, common meaning." Although this is a fine approach to statutory interpretation in general, it is a deeply flawed approach to a statute that relies on complex terms of art developed against a particular historical background.[4] Indeed, the approach would render § 101 almost comical. A process for training a dog, a series of dance steps, a method of shooting a basketball, maybe even words, stories, or songs if framed as the steps of typing letters or uttering sounds—all would be patent-eligible. I am confident that the term "process" in § 101 is not nearly so capacious.[5]

So is the Court, perhaps. What is particularly incredible about the Court's stated method of interpreting § 101 (other than that the method itself may be patent-eligible under the Court's theory of § 101) is that the Court deviates from its own professed commitment to "ordinary, contemporary, common meaning." As noted earlier, the Court accepts a role for the "a textual" machine-or-transformation "clue." The Court also accepts that we have "foreclose[d] a purely literal reading of § 101," *Flook*, by holding that claims that are close to "laws of nature, natural phenomena, and abstract ideas," *Diamond v. Diehr* (1981), do not count as "processes" under § 101, even if they can be colloquially described as such. The Court attempts to justify this latter exception to § 101 as "a matter of statutory *stare decisis*." But it is strange to think that the very same term must be interpreted literally on some occasions, and in light of its historical usage on others.

---

[4] For example, if this Court were to interpret the Sherman Act according to the Act's plain text, it could prohibit "the entire body of private contract," *National Soc. of Professional Engineers v. United States* (1978).

[5] The Court attempts to avoid such absurd results by stating that these "[c]oncerns" "can be met by making sure that the claim meets the requirements of § 101." Because the only limitation on the plain meaning of "process" that the Court acknowledges explicitly is the bar on abstract ideas, laws of nature, and the like, it is presumably this limitation that is left to stand between all conceivable human activity and patent monopolies. But many processes that would make for absurd patents are not abstract ideas. Nor can the requirements of novelty, nonobviousness, and particular description pick up the slack. A great deal of human activity was at some time novel and nonobvious.

In fact, the Court's understanding of § 101 is even more remarkable because its willingness to *exclude* general principles from the provision's reach is in tension with its apparent willingness to *include* steps for conducting business. The history of patent law contains strong norms against patenting these two categories of subject matter. Both norms were presumably incorporated by Congress into the Patent Act in 1952.

IV

Because the text of § 101 does not on its face convey the scope of patentable processes, it is necessary, in my view, to review the history of our patent law in some detail. . . . It is . . . significant that when Congress enacted the latest Patent Act, it did so against the background of a well-settled understanding that a series of steps for conducting business cannot be patented. These considerations ought to guide our analysis. As Justice HOLMES noted long ago, sometimes, "a page of history is worth a volume of logic."

English Backdrop

The Constitution's Patent Clause was written against the "backdrop" of English patent practices, *Graham v. John Deere Co. of Kansas City* (1966), and early American patent law was "largely based on and incorporated" features of the English patent system. The governing English law, the Statute of Monopolies, responded to abuses whereby the Crown would issue letters patent, "granting monopolies to court favorites in goods or businesses which had long before been enjoyed by the public." *Graham*. The statute generally prohibited the Crown from granting such exclusive rights, but it contained exceptions that, *inter alia*, permitted grants of exclusive rights to the "working or making of any manner of new Manufacture." . . .

Although it is difficult to derive a precise understanding of what sorts of methods were patentable under English law, there is no basis in the text of the Statute of Monopolies, nor in pre-1790 English precedent, to infer that business methods could qualify. There was some debate throughout the relevant time period about what processes could be patented. But it does not appear that anyone seriously believed that one could patent "a method for organizing human activity." . . .

Also noteworthy is what was *not* patented under the English system. During the 17th and 18th centuries, Great Britain saw innovations in business organization, business models, management techniques, and novel solutions to the challenges of operating global firms in which subordinate managers could be reached only by a long sea voyage. Few if any of these methods of conducting business were patented.

Early American Patent Law

At the Constitutional Convention, the Founders decided to give Congress a patent power so that it might "promote the Progress of . . . useful Arts." Art. I, § 8, cl. 8. There is little known history of that Clause. We do know that the Clause passed without objection or debate. This is striking because other proposed powers, such as a power to grant charters of incorporation, generated discussion about the fear that they might breed "monopolies." Indeed, at the ratification conventions, some States recommended amendments that would have prohibited Congress from granting "'exclusive advantages of commerce.'" If the original understanding of the Patent Clause included the authority to patent methods of doing business, it might not have passed so quietly. . . .

Thus, fields such as business and finance were not generally considered part of the "useful arts" in the founding Era. See, *e.g.,* The Federalist No. 8, p. 69 (C. Rossiter ed. 1961) (A. Hamilton) (distinguishing between "the arts of industry, and the science of finance"). Indeed, the same delegate to the Constitutional Convention who gave an address in which he listed triumphs in the useful arts distinguished between those arts and the conduct of business. He explained that investors were now attracted to the "manufactures and the useful arts," much as they had long invested in "commerce, navigation, stocks, banks, and insurance companies." T. Coxe, A Statement of the Arts and Manufactures of the United States of America for the Year 1810.

Some scholars have remarked, as did Thomas Jefferson, that early patent statutes neither included nor reflected any serious debate about the precise scope of patentable subject matter. See, *e.g.*, *Graham* (discussing Thomas Jefferson's observations). It has been suggested, however, that "[p]erhaps this was in part a function of an understanding—shared widely among legislators, courts, patent office officials, and inventors—about what patents were meant to protect. Everyone knew that manufactures and machines were at the core of the patent system." Merges, Property Rights for Business Concepts and Patent System Reform, 14 Berkeley Tech. L. J. 577, 585 (1999) (hereinafter Merges). Thus, although certain processes, such as those related to the technology of the time, might have been considered patentable, it is possible that "[a]gainst this background, it would have been seen as absurd for an entrepreneur to file a patent" on methods of conducting business.

Development of American Patent Law

During the first years of the patent system, no patents were issued on methods of doing business. Indeed, for some time, there were serious doubts as to "the patentability of processes per se," as distinct from the physical end product or the tools used to perform a process.

Thomas Jefferson was the "'first administrator of our patent system'" and "the author of the 1793 Patent Act." *Graham*. We have said that his "conclusions as to conditions of patentability . . . are worthy of note." During his time administering the system, Jefferson "saw clearly the difficulty" of deciding what should be patentable. He drafted the 1793 Act, and, years later, explained that in that Act "'the whole was turned over to the judiciary, to be matured into a system, under which every one might know when his actions were safe and lawful.'" As the Court has explained, "Congress agreed with Jefferson . . . that the courts should develop additional conditions for patentability." *Graham*.

Although courts occasionally struggled with defining what was a patentable "art" during those 160 years, they consistently rejected patents on methods of doing business. The rationales for those decisions sometimes varied. But there was an overarching theme, at least in dicta: Business methods are not patentable arts. . . . Between 1790 and 1952, this Court never addressed the patentability of business methods. But we consistently focused the inquiry on whether an "art" was connected to a machine or physical transformation, an inquiry that would have excluded methods of doing business.

By the early 20th century, it was widely understood that a series of steps for conducting business could not be patented. A leading treatise, for example, listed "'systems' of business" as an "unpatentable subjec[t]." 1 A. Deller, Walker on Patents § 18, p. 62 (1937). . . . Indeed, "[u]ntil recently" it was still "considered well established that [business] methods were non-statutory." 1 R. Moy, Walker on Patents § 5:28, p. 5-104 (4th ed. 2009).

Modern American Patent Law

. . . As discussed above . . . courts had consistently construed the term "art" to exclude methods of doing business. The 1952 Act likely captured that same meaning. Indeed, Judge Rich, the main drafter of the 1952 Act, later explained that "the invention of a more effective organization of the materials in, and the techniques of teaching a course in physics, chemistry, or Russian is not a patentable invention because it is outside of the enumerated categories of 'process, machine, manufacture, or composition of matter, or any new and useful improvement thereof.'" "Also outside that group," he added, was a process for doing business: "the greatest inventio[n] of our times, the diaper service."[40]

"Anything Under the Sun"

Despite strong evidence that Congress has consistently authorized patents for a limited class of subject matter and that the 1952 Act did not alter the nature of the then-existing limits, petitioners and their *amici* emphasize a single phrase in the Act's legislative history, which suggests that the statutory subject matter "'include[s] anything under the sun that is made by man.'" Similarly, the Court relies on language from our opinion in *Chakrabarty* that was based in part on this piece of legislative history.

This reliance is misplaced. We have never understood that piece of legislative history to mean that any series of steps is a patentable process. . . .

Since at least the days of Assyrian merchants, people have devised better and better ways to conduct business. Yet it appears that neither the Patent Clause, nor early patent law, nor the current § 101 contemplated or was publicly understood to mean that such innovations are patentable. Although it may be difficult to define with precision what is a patentable "process" under § 101, the historical clues converge on one conclusion: A business method is not a "process." . . .

V

Despite the strong historical evidence that a method of doing business does not constitute a "process" under § 101, petitioners nonetheless argue—and the Court suggests in dicta—that a subsequent law, the First Inventor Defense Act of 1999, "must be read together" with § 101 to make business methods patentable. This argument utilizes a flawed method of statutory interpretation and ignores the motivation for the 1999 Act.

In 1999, following a Federal Circuit decision that intimated business methods could be patented, see *State Street*, Congress moved quickly to limit the potential fallout. Congress passed the 1999 Act, codified at 35 U.S.C. § 273, which provides a limited defense to claims of patent infringement, see § 273(b), regarding certain "method[s] of doing or conducting business," § 273(a)(3).

It is apparent, both from the content and history of the Act, that Congress did not in any way ratify *State Street* (or, as petitioners contend, the broadest possible reading of *State Street*). The Act merely limited one potential effect of that decision: that businesses might suddenly find themselves liable for innocently using methods they assumed could not be patented. Particularly because petitioners' reading of the 1999 Act would expand § 101 to cover a category of processes that have not "historically been eligible" for patents, *Diehr*, we should be loath to conclude that Congress effectively amended § 101 without saying so clearly. We generally presume that Congress "does not, one might say, hide elephants in mouseholes." . . .

VI

The constitutionally mandated purpose and function of the patent laws bolster the conclusion that methods of doing business are not "processes" under § 101.

---

[40] Forty years later, Judge Rich authored the *State Street* opinion that some have understood to make business methods patentable. But *State Street* dealt with whether a piece of software could be patented and addressed only claims directed at machines, not processes. His opinion may therefore be better understood merely as holding that an otherwise patentable process is not unpatentable simply because it is directed toward the conduct of doing business—an issue the Court has no occasion to address today.

The Constitution allows Congress to issue patents "[t]o promote the Progress of . . . useful Arts," Art. I, § 8, cl. 8. This clause "is both a grant of power and a limitation." *Graham*. It "reflects a balance between the need to encourage innovation and the avoidance of monopolies which stifle competition without any concomitant advance in the 'Progress of Science and useful Arts.'" *Bonito Boats*. "This is the standard expressed in the Constitution and it may not be ignored. And it is in this light that patent validity 'requires reference to [the] standard written into the Constitution.'" *Graham*.[44]

Thus, although it is for Congress to "implement the stated purpose of the Framers by selecting the policy which in its judgment best effectuates the constitutional aim," *Graham*, we interpret ambiguous patent laws as a set of rules that "wee[d] out those inventions which would not be disclosed or devised but for the inducement of a patent," and that "embod[y]" the "careful balance between the need to promote innovation and the recognition that imitation and refinement through imitation are both necessary to invention itself and the very lifeblood of a competitive economy," *Bonito Boats*.

Without any legislative guidance to the contrary, there is a real concern that patents on business methods would press on the limits of the "standard expressed in the Constitution," *Graham*, more likely stifling progress than "promot[ing]" it. U.S. Const., Art. I, § 8, cl. 8. I recognize that not all methods of doing business are the same, and that therefore the constitutional "balance," *Bonito Boats*, may vary within this category. Nevertheless, I think that this balance generally supports the historic understanding of the term "process" as excluding business methods. And a categorical analysis fits with the purpose, as Thomas Jefferson explained, of ensuring that "'every one might know when his actions were safe and lawful,'" *Graham*. ("The monopoly is a property right; and like any property right, its boundaries should be clear. This clarity is essential to promote progress"); *Diehr* (STEVENS, J., dissenting) (it is necessary to have "rules that enable a conscientious patent lawyer to determine with a fair degree of accuracy" what is patentable).

On one side of the balance is whether a patent monopoly is necessary to "motivate the innovation." Although there is certainly disagreement about the need for patents, scholars generally agree that when innovation is expensive, risky, and easily copied, inventors are less likely to undertake the guaranteed costs of innovation in order to obtain the mere possibility of an invention that others can copy. Both common sense and recent economic scholarship suggest that these dynamics of cost, risk, and reward vary by the type of thing being patented. And the functional case that patents promote progress generally is stronger for subject matter that has "historically been eligible to receive the protection of our patent laws," *Diehr*, than for methods of doing business.

Many have expressed serious doubts about whether patents are necessary to encourage business innovation. Despite the fact that we have long assumed business methods could not be patented, it has been remarked that "the chief business of the American people, is business." Federal Express developed an overnight delivery service and a variety of specific methods (including shipping through a central hub and online package tracking) without a patent. Although counterfactuals are a dubious form of analysis, I find it hard to believe that many of our entrepreneurs forwent business innovation because they could not claim a patent on their new methods.

---

[44] See also *Quanta Computer, Inc. v. LG Electronics, Inc.* (2008) ("'[T]he primary purpose of our patent laws is not the creation of private fortunes for the owners of patents but is "to promote the progress of science and useful arts"'" (quoting *Motion Picture Patents Co. v. Universal Film Mfg. Co.* (1917))); *Pfaff v. Wells Electronics, Inc.* (1998) ("[T]he patent system represents a carefully crafted bargain that encourages both the creation and the public disclosure of new and useful advances in technology").

"[C]ompanies have ample incentives to develop business methods even without patent protection, because the competitive marketplace rewards companies that use more efficient business methods." Burk & Lemley 1618. Innovators often capture advantages from new business methods notwithstanding the risk of others copying their innovation. Some business methods occur in secret and therefore can be protected with trade secrecy. And for those methods that occur in public, firms that innovate often capture long-term benefits from doing so, thanks to various first mover advantages, including lockins, branding, and networking effects. Business innovation, moreover, generally does not entail the same kinds of risk as does more traditional, technological innovation. It generally does not require the same "enormous costs in terms of time, research, and development," and thus does not require the same kind of "compensation to [innovators] for their labor, toil, and expense."

Nor, in many cases, would patents on business methods promote progress by encouraging "public disclosure." Many business methods are practiced in public, and therefore a patent does not necessarily encourage the dissemination of anything not already known. And for the methods practiced in private, the benefits of disclosure may be small: Many such methods are distributive, not productive—that is, they do not generate any efficiency but only provide a means for competitors to one-up each other in a battle for pieces of the pie. And as the Court has explained, "it is hard to see how the public would be benefited by disclosure" of certain business tools, since the nondisclosure of these tools "encourages businesses to initiate new and individualized plans of operation," which "in turn, leads to a greater variety of business methods." *Bicron*.

In any event, even if patents on business methods were useful for encouraging innovation and disclosure, it would still be questionable whether they would, on balance, facilitate or impede the progress of American business. For even when patents encourage innovation and disclosure, "*too much* patent protection can impede rather than 'promote the Progress of . . . useful Arts.'" *Laboratory Corp. of America Holdings v. Metabolite Laboratories, Inc.* (2006) (BREYER, J., dissenting from dismissal of certiorari). Patents "can discourage research by impeding the free exchange of information," for example, by forcing people to "avoid the use of potentially patented ideas, by leading them to conduct costly and time-consuming searches of existing or pending patents, by requiring complex licensing arrangements, and by raising the costs of using the patented" methods. Although "[e]very patent is the grant of a privilege of exacting tolls from the public," *Great Atlantic* (DOUGLAS, J., concurring), the tolls of patents on business methods may be especially high.

The primary concern is that patents on business methods may prohibit a wide swath of legitimate competition and innovation. As one scholar explains, "it is useful to conceptualize knowledge as a pyramid: the big ideas are on top; specific applications are at the bottom." Dreyfuss 275. The higher up a patent is on the pyramid, the greater the social cost and the greater the hindrance to further innovation.[53] Thus, this Court stated in *Benson* that "[p]henomena of nature . . . mental processes, and abstract intellectual concepts are not patentable, as they are the basic tools of scientific and technological work." Business methods are similarly often closer to "big ideas," as they are the basic tools of *commercial* work. They are also, in many cases, the basic tools of further business innovation: Innovation in business methods is often a sequential and complementary process in which imitation may be a "*spur* to innovation" and patents may "become an *impediment*."

---

[53] See Dreyfuss 276; Merges & Nelson, On the Complex Economics of Patent Scope, 90 Colum. L. Rev. 839, 873–878 (1990).

Bessen & Maskin, Sequential Innovation, Patents, and Imitation, 40 RAND J. Econ. 611, 613 (2009).[54] "Think how the airline industry might now be structured if the first company to offer frequent flyer miles had enjoyed the sole right to award them." Dreyfuss 264. "[I]mitation and refinement through imitation are both necessary to invention itself and the very lifeblood of a competitive economy." *Bonito Boats.*

If business methods could be patented, then many business decisions, no matter how small, could be *potential* patent violations. Businesses would either live in constant fear of litigation or would need to undertake the costs of searching through patents that describe methods of doing business, attempting to decide whether their innovation is one that remains in the public domain. See Long, Information Costs in Patent and Copyright, 90 Va. L. Rev. 465, 487–488 (2004) (hereinafter Long).

These effects are magnified by the "potential vagueness" of business method patents, *eBay Inc.* (KENNEDY, J., concurring). When it comes to patents, "clarity is essential to promote progress." *Festo Corp.* Yet patents on methods of conducting business generally are composed largely or entirely of intangible steps. Compared to "the kinds of goods . . . around which patent rules historically developed," it thus tends to be more costly and time consuming to search through, and to negotiate licenses for, patents on business methods. See Long.

The breadth of business methods, their omnipresence in our society, and their potential vagueness also invite a particularly pernicious use of patents that we have long criticized.

These many costs of business method patents not only may stifle innovation, but they are also likely to "stifle competition," *Bonito Boats.* Even if a business method patent is ultimately held invalid, patent holders may be able to use it to threaten litigation and to bully competitors, especially those that cannot bear the costs of a drawn out, fact-intensive patent litigation. . . .

* * *

VII

The Constitution grants to Congress an important power to promote innovation. In its exercise of that power, Congress has established an intricate system of intellectual property. The scope of patentable subject matter under that system is broad. But it is not endless. In the absence of any clear guidance from Congress, we have only limited textual, historical, and functional clues on which to rely. Those clues all point toward the same conclusion: that petitioners' claim is not a "process" within the meaning of § 101 because methods of doing business are not, in themselves, covered by the statute. In my view, acknowledging as much would be a far more sensible and restrained way to resolve this case. Accordingly, while I concur in the judgment, I strongly disagree with the Court's disposition of this case.

Justice BREYER, with whom Justice SCALIA joins as to Part II, concurring in the judgment.

I

I agree with Justice STEVENS that a "general method of engaging in business transactions" is not a patentable "process" within the meaning of 35 U.S.C. § 101. This

---

[54] See also Raskind, The *State Street Bank* Decision, The Bad Business of Unlimited Patent Protection for Methods of Doing Business, 10 Fordham Intell. Prop. Media & Ent. L.J. 61, 102 (1999) ("Interactive emulation more than innovation is the driving force of business method changes").

Court has never before held that so-called "business methods" are patentable, and, in my view, the text, history, and purposes of the Patent Act make clear that they are not. I would therefore decide this case on that ground, and I join Justice STEVENS' opinion in full.

I write separately, however, in order to highlight the substantial *agreement* among many Members of the Court on many of the fundamental issues of patent law raised by this case. In light of the need for clarity and settled law in this highly technical area, I think it appropriate to do so.

II

In addition to the Court's unanimous agreement that the claims at issue here are unpatentable abstract ideas, it is my view that the following four points are consistent with both the opinion of the Court and Justice STEVENS' opinion concurring in the judgment:

First, although the text of § 101 is broad, it is not without limit. "[T]he underlying policy of the patent system [is] that 'the things which are worth to the public the embarrassment of an exclusive patent,' . . . must outweigh the restrictive effect of the limited patent monopoly." *Graham v. John Deere Co. of Kansas City* (1966) (quoting Letter from Thomas Jefferson to Isaac McPherson (Aug. 13, 1813)). The Court has thus been careful in interpreting the Patent Act to "determine not only what is protected, but also what is free for all to use." *Bonito Boats, Inc. v. Thunder Craft Boats, Inc.* (1989). In particular, the Court has long held that "[p]henomena of nature, though just discovered, mental processes, and abstract intellectual concepts are not patentable" under § 101, since allowing individuals to patent these fundamental principles would "wholly pre-empt" the public's access to the "basic tools of scientific and technological work." *Gottschalk v. Benson* (1972).

Second, in a series of cases that extend back over a century, the Court has stated that "[t]ransformation and reduction of an article to a different state or thing is *the clue* to the patentability of a process claim that does not include particular machines." *Diehr*. Application of this test, the so-called "machine-or-transformation test," has thus repeatedly helped the Court to determine what is "a patentable 'process.'" *Flook*.

Third, while the machine-or-transformation test has always been a "useful and important clue," it has never been the "sole test" for determining patentability. *Benson* (rejecting the argument that "no process patent could ever qualify" for protection under § 101 "if it did not meet the [machine-or-transformation] requirements"). Rather, the Court has emphasized that a process claim meets the requirements of § 101 when, "considered as a whole," it "is performing a function which the patent laws were designed to protect (*e.g.,* transforming or reducing an article to a different state or thing)." *Diehr*. The machine-or-transformation test is thus an *important example* of how a court can determine patentability under § 101, but the Federal Circuit erred in this case by treating it as the *exclusive test*.

Fourth, although the machine-or-transformation test is not the only test for patentability, this by no means indicates that anything which produces a "'useful, concrete, and tangible result,'" *State Street Bank & Trust Co. v. Signature Financial Group, Inc.* (1998), is patentable. "[T]his Court has never made such a statement and, if taken literally, the statement would cover instances where this Court has held the contrary." *Laboratory Corp. of America Holdings v. Metabolite Laboratories, Inc.* (2006) (BREYER, J., dissenting from dismissal of certiorari as improvidently granted). Indeed, the introduction of the "useful, concrete, and tangible result" approach to patentability, associated with the Federal Circuit's *State Street* decision, preceded the granting of patents that "ranged from the somewhat ridiculous to the truly absurd." *In re Bilski* (Fed. Cir. 2008) (Mayer, J., dissenting) (citing patents on, *inter alia*, a "method of training janitors to dust and vacuum using video displays," a "system for toilet reservations," and a "method of using color-coded bracelets to designate dating status in order to limit 'the embarrassment of rejection'"). To the extent that the Federal Circuit's decision in this case rejected that approach, nothing in today's decision should be taken as disapproving of that determination.

In sum, it is my view that, in reemphasizing that the "machine-or-transformation" test is not necessarily the *sole* test of patentability, the Court intends neither to deemphasize the test's usefulness nor to suggest that many patentable processes lie beyond its reach.

III

With these observations, I concur in the Court's judgment.

Questions:

1.) What is the actual *holding* of this case?

2.) Why is a business method not an abstract idea and thus unpatentable?

3.) Do we need patents on business methods in order to incentivize the production of new business methods? Is the answer to that question relevant to whether they are statutory subject matter as far as the Court is concerned? If it is, what countervailing factors does the Court see that mitigate against a *per se* rule excluding business method patents from statutory subject matter?

4.) Look back at the graphs on patent filing and litigation and the current state of the patent system in Chapter 17. To what extent do those concerns motivate the opinions in this case? Which Justices in particular? Is there a countervailing fear of harms that might come about if the requirements for patentable subject matter were more narrowly drawn?

PROBLEM 18-1

For the purposes of this problem we are taking today's jurisprudence on patentable subject matter back to the 1950s. Assume for these purposes Ray Kroc, who made McDonald's the success it is, is the first to realize that the Eisenhower freeways will transform America. People will be moving at high speed, in unfamiliar terrain, on a highway that separates them physically from the normal cognitive cues one gets about the type or quality of a restaurant. Kroc lays out a master plan that involves highly franchised restaurants serving food that will taste exactly the same anywhere in the country, thus freeing drivers from the fear of culinary regret (or surprised delight). He applies the logic of the industrial assembly line to the food preparation process, speeding it up. He pioneers the use of huge, colorful billboards that can easily be recognized at 60mph. Assume that these are the key innovations that go into "fast food."

As a matter of patentable subject matter, can Kroc patent the fast food business method described above?

Alice Corp. v. CLS Bank Intern'l
573 U.S. 208 (2014)

THOMAS, J., delivered the opinion for a unanimous Court. SOTOMAYOR, J., filed a concurring opinion, in which GINSBURG and BREYER, JJ., joined.

Justice THOMAS, delivered the opinion of the Court.

The patents at issue in this case disclose a computer-implemented scheme for mitigating "settlement risk" (*i.e.*, the risk that only one party to a financial transaction will pay what it owes) by using a third-party intermediary. The question presented is whether these claims are patent eligible under 35 U.S.C. § 101, or are instead drawn to a patent-ineligible abstract idea. We hold that the claims at issue are drawn to the abstract idea of intermediated settlement, and that merely requiring generic computer implementation fails to transform that abstract idea into a patent-eligible invention. We therefore affirm the judgment of the United States Court of Appeals for the Federal Circuit.

I
A

Petitioner Alice Corporation is the assignee of several patents that disclose schemes to manage certain forms of financial risk. According to the specification largely shared by the patents, the invention "enabl[es] the management of risk relating to specified, yet unknown, future events." The specification further explains that the "invention relates to methods and apparatus, including electrical computers and data processing systems applied to financial matters and risk management."

The claims at issue relate to a computerized scheme for mitigating "settlement risk"—*i.e.*, the risk that only one party to an agreed-upon financial exchange will satisfy its obligation. In particular, the claims are designed to facilitate the exchange of financial obligations between two parties by using a computer system as a third-party intermediary. The intermediary creates "shadow" credit and debit records (*i.e.*, account ledgers) that mirror the balances in the parties' real-world accounts at "exchange institutions" (*e.g.*, banks). The intermediary updates the shadow records in real time as transactions are entered, allowing "only those transactions for which the parties' updated shadow records indicate sufficient resources to satisfy their mutual obligations." At the end of the day, the intermediary instructs the relevant financial institutions to carry out the "permitted" transactions in accordance with the updated shadow records, thus mitigating the risk that only one party will perform the agreed-upon exchange.

In sum, the patents in suit claim (1) the foregoing method for exchanging obligations (the method claims), (2) a computer system configured to carry out the method for exchanging obligations (the system claims), and (3) a computer-readable medium containing program code for performing the method of exchanging obligations (the media claims). All of the claims are implemented using a computer; the system and media claims expressly recite a computer, and the parties have stipulated that the method claims require a computer as well.

B

Respondents CLS Bank International and CLS Services Ltd. (together, CLS Bank) operate a global network that facilitates currency transactions. In 2007, CLS Bank filed suit against petitioner, seeking a declaratory judgment that the claims at issue are invalid, unenforceable, or not infringed. Petitioner counterclaimed, alleging infringement. Following this Court's decision in *Bilski v. Kappos*, the parties filed cross-motions for summary judgment on whether the asserted claims are eligible for patent protection under 35 U.S.C. § 101. The District Court held that all of the claims are patent ineligible because they are directed to the abstract idea of "employing a neutral intermediary to facilitate simultaneous exchange of obligations in order to minimize risk."

A divided panel of the United States Court of Appeals for the Federal Circuit reversed, holding that it was not "manifestly evident" that petitioner's claims are directed to an abstract idea. The Federal Circuit granted rehearing en banc, vacated the panel opinion, and affirmed the judgment of the District Court in a one-paragraph *per curiam* opinion. Seven of the ten participating judges agreed that petitioner's method and media claims are patent ineligible. With respect to petitioner's system claims, the en banc Federal Circuit affirmed the District Court's judgment by an equally divided vote.

Writing for a five-member plurality, Judge Lourie concluded that all of the claims at issue are patent ineligible. In the plurality's view, under this Court's decision in *Mayo Collaborative Services v. Prometheus Laboratories, Inc.* (2012), a court must first "identif[y] the abstract idea represented in the claim," and then determine "whether the balance of the claim adds 'significantly more.'" The plurality concluded that petitioner's claims "draw on the abstract idea of reducing settlement risk by effecting trades through a third-party intermediary," and that the use of a computer to maintain, adjust, and reconcile shadow accounts added nothing of substance to that abstract idea.

Chief Judge Rader concurred in part and dissented in part. In a part of the opinion joined only by Judge Moore, Chief Judge Rader agreed with the plurality that petitioner's method and media claims are drawn to an abstract idea. In a part of the opinion joined by Judges Linn, Moore, and O'Malley, Chief Judge Rader would have held that the system claims are patent eligible because they involve computer "hardware" that is "specifically programmed to solve a complex problem." Judge Moore wrote a separate opinion dissenting in part, arguing that the system claims are patent eligible. Judge Newman filed an opinion concurring in part and dissenting in part, arguing that all of petitioner's claims are patent eligible. Judges Linn and O'Malley filed a separate dissenting opinion reaching that same conclusion.

We granted certiorari, and now affirm.

II

Section 101 of the Patent Act defines the subject matter eligible for patent protection. It provides:

> "Whoever invents or discovers any new and useful process, machine, manufacture, or composition of matter, or any new and useful improvement thereof, may obtain a patent therefor, subject to the conditions and requirements of this title."

"We have long held that this provision contains an important implicit exception: Laws of nature, natural phenomena, and abstract ideas are not patentable." We have interpreted § 101 and its predecessors in light of this exception for more than 150 years.

We have described the concern that drives this exclusionary principle as one of pre-emption. Laws of nature, natural phenomena, and abstract ideas are "the basic tools of scientific and technological work." "[M]onopolization of those tools through the grant of a patent might tend to impede innovation more than it would tend to promote it," thereby thwarting the primary object of the patent laws. We have "repeatedly emphasized this . . . concern that patent law not inhibit further discovery by improperly tying up the future use of" these building blocks of human ingenuity.

At the same time, we tread carefully in construing this exclusionary principle lest it swallow all of patent law. At some level, "all inventions . . . embody, use, reflect, rest upon, or apply laws of nature, natural phenomena, or abstract ideas." Thus, an invention is not rendered ineligible for patent simply because it involves an abstract concept. "[A]pplication[s]" of such concepts "'to a new and useful end,'" we have said, remain eligible for patent protection.

Accordingly, in applying the § 101 exception, we must distinguish between patents that claim the "'buildin[g] block[s]'" of human ingenuity and those that integrate the building blocks into something more, thereby "transform[ing]" them into a patent-eligible invention. The former "would risk disproportionately tying up the use of the underlying" ideas, and are therefore ineligible for patent protection. The latter pose no comparable risk of pre-emption, and therefore remain eligible for the monopoly granted under our patent laws.

III

In *Mayo Collaborative Services v. Prometheus Laboratories, Inc.*, we set forth a framework for distinguishing patents that claim laws of nature, natural phenomena, and abstract ideas from those that claim patent-eligible applications of those concepts. First, we determine whether the claims at issue are directed to one of those patent-ineligible concepts. If so, we then ask, "[w]hat else is there in the claims before us?" To answer that question, we consider the elements of each claim both individually and "as an ordered combination" to determine whether the additional elements "transform the nature of the claim" into a patent-eligible application. We have described step two of this analysis as a search for an "'inventive concept'"—*i.e.,* an element or combination of elements that is "sufficient to ensure that the patent in practice amounts to significantly more than a patent upon the [ineligible concept] itself."

A

We must first determine whether the claims at issue are directed to a patent-ineligible concept. We conclude that they are: These claims are drawn to the abstract idea of intermediated settlement.

The "abstract ideas" category embodies "the longstanding rule that '[a]n idea of itself is not patentable.'" In *Benson*, for example, this Court rejected as ineligible patent claims involving an algorithm for converting binary-coded decimal numerals into pure binary form, holding that the claimed patent was "in practical effect . . . a patent on the algorithm itself." And in *Parker v. Flook*, we held that a mathematical formula for computing "alarm limits" in a catalytic conversion process was also a patent-ineligible abstract idea.

We most recently addressed the category of abstract ideas in *Bilski v. Kappos* (2010). The claims at issue in *Bilski* described a method for hedging against the financial risk of price fluctuations. Claim 1 recited a series of steps for hedging risk, including: (1) initiating a series of financial transactions between providers and consumers of a commodity; (2) identifying market participants that have a counterrisk for the same commodity; and (3) initiating a series of transactions between those market participants and the commodity provider to balance the risk position of the first series of consumer transactions. Claim 4 "pu[t] the concept articulated in claim 1 into a simple mathematical formula." The remaining claims were drawn to examples of hedging in commodities and energy markets.

"[A]ll members of the Court agree[d]" that the patent at issue in *Bilski* claimed an "abstract idea." Specifically, the claims described "the basic concept of hedging, or protecting against risk." The Court explained that "'[h]edging is a fundamental economic practice long prevalent in our system of commerce and taught in any introductory finance class.'" "The concept of hedging" as recited by the claims in suit was therefore a patent-ineligible "abstract idea, just like the algorithms at issue in *Benson* and *Flook*."

It follows from our prior cases, and *Bilski* in particular, that the claims at issue here are directed to an abstract idea. Petitioner's claims involve a method of exchanging financial obligations between two parties using a third-party intermediary to mitigate settlement risk. The intermediary creates and updates "shadow" records to reflect the value of each party's actual accounts held at "exchange institutions," thereby permitting only those transactions for which the parties have sufficient resources. At the end of each day, the intermediary issues irrevocable instructions to the exchange institutions to carry out the permitted transactions.

On their face, the claims before us are drawn to the concept of intermediated settlement, *i.e.,* the use of a third party to mitigate settlement risk. Like the risk hedging in *Bilski*, the concept of intermediated settlement is "'a fundamental economic practice long prevalent in our system of commerce.'" The use of a third-party intermediary (or "clearing house") is also a building block of the modern economy. Thus, intermediated settlement, like hedging, is an "abstract idea" beyond the scope of § 101.

Petitioner acknowledges that its claims describe intermediated settlement, but rejects the conclusion that its claims recite an "abstract idea." Drawing on the presence of mathematical formulas in some of our abstract-ideas precedents, petitioner contends that the abstract-ideas category is confined to "preexisting, fundamental truth[s]" that "'exis[t] in principle apart from any human action.'"

Bilski belies petitioner's assertion. The concept of risk hedging we identified as an abstract idea in that case cannot be described as a "preexisting, fundamental truth." The patent in *Bilski* simply involved a "series of steps instructing how to hedge risk." Although hedging is a longstanding commercial practice, it is a method of organizing human activity, not a "truth" about the natural world "'that has always existed.'" One of the claims in *Bilski* reduced hedging to a mathematical formula, but the Court did not assign any special significance to that fact, much less the sort of talismanic significance petitioner claims. Instead, the Court grounded its conclusion that all of the claims at issue were abstract ideas in the understanding that risk hedging was a "'fundamental economic practice.'"

In any event, we need not labor to delimit the precise contours of the "abstract ideas" category in this case. It is enough to recognize that there is no meaningful distinction between the concept of risk hedging in *Bilski* and the concept of intermediated settlement at issue here. Both are squarely within the realm of "abstract ideas" as we have used that term.

B

Because the claims at issue are directed to the abstract idea of intermediated settlement, we turn to the second step in *Mayo*'s framework. We conclude that the method claims, which merely require generic computer implementation, fail to transform that abstract idea into a patent-eligible invention.

1

At *Mayo* step two, we must examine the elements of the claim to determine whether it contains an "'inventive concept'" sufficient to "transform" the claimed abstract idea into a patent-eligible application. A claim that recites an abstract idea must include "additional features" to ensure "that the [claim] is more than a drafting effort designed to monopolize the [abstract idea]." *Mayo* made clear that transformation into a patent-eligible application requires "more than simply stat[ing] the [abstract idea] while adding the words 'apply it.'"

Mayo itself is instructive. The patents at issue in *Mayo* claimed a method for measuring metabolites in the bloodstream in order to calibrate the appropriate dosage of thiopurine drugs in the treatment of autoimmune diseases. The respondent in that case contended that the claimed method was a patent-eligible application of natural laws that describe the relationship between the concentration of certain metabolites and the likelihood that the drug dosage will be harmful or ineffective. But methods for determining metabolite levels were already "well known in the art," and the process at issue amounted to "nothing significantly more than an instruction to doctors to apply the applicable laws when treating their patients." "Simply appending conventional steps, specified at a high level of generality," was not "*enough*" to supply an "'inventive concept.'"

The introduction of a computer into the claims does not alter the analysis at *Mayo* step two. In *Benson*, for example, we considered a patent that claimed an algorithm implemented on "a general-purpose digital computer." Because the algorithm was an abstract idea, the claim had to supply a "'new and useful'" application of the idea in order to be patent eligible. But the computer implementation did not supply the necessary inventive concept; the process could be "carried out in existing computers long in use." We accordingly "held that simply implementing a mathematical principle on a physical machine, namely a computer, [i]s not a patentable application of that principle."

Flook is to the same effect. There, we examined a computerized method for using a mathematical formula to adjust alarm limits for certain operating conditions (*e.g.,* temperature and pressure) that could signal inefficiency or danger in a catalytic conversion process. Once again, the formula itself was an abstract idea, and the computer implementation was purely conventional. In holding that the process was patent ineligible, we rejected the argument that "implement[ing] a principle in some specific fashion" will "automatically fal[l] within the patentable subject matter of § 101." Thus, "*Flook* stands for the proposition that the prohibition against patenting abstract ideas cannot be circumvented by attempting to limit the use of [the idea] to a particular technological environment." *Bilski*.

In *Diehr*, by contrast, we held that a computer-implemented process for curing rubber was patent eligible, but not because it involved a computer. The claim employed a "well-known" mathematical equation, but it used that equation in a process designed to solve a technological problem in "conventional industry practice." The invention in *Diehr* used a "thermocouple" to record constant temperature measurements inside the rubber mold—something "the industry ha[d] not been able to obtain." The temperature measurements were then fed into a computer, which repeatedly recalculated the remaining cure time by using the mathematical equation. These additional steps, we recently explained, "transformed the process into an inventive application of the formula." *Mayo*. In other words, the claims in *Diehr* were patent eligible because they improved an existing technological process, not because they were implemented on a computer.

These cases demonstrate that the mere recitation of a generic computer cannot transform a patent-ineligible abstract idea into a patent-eligible invention. Stating an abstract idea "while adding the words 'apply it'" is not enough for patent eligibility. *Mayo*. Nor is limiting the use of an abstract idea "'to a particular technological environment.'" *Bilski*. Stating an abstract idea while adding the words "apply it with a computer" simply combines those two steps, with the same deficient result. Thus, if a patent's recitation of a computer amounts to a mere instruction to "implemen[t]" an abstract idea "on . . . a computer," *Mayo*, that addition cannot impart patent eligibility. This conclusion accords with the preemption concern that undergirds our § 101 jurisprudence. Given the ubiquity of computers, wholly generic computer implementation is not generally the sort of "additional featur[e]" that provides any "practical assurance that the process is more than a drafting effort designed to monopolize the [abstract idea] itself." *Mayo.*

The fact that a computer "necessarily exist[s] in the physical, rather than purely conceptual, realm" is beside the point. There is no dispute that a computer is a tangible system (in § 101 terms, a "machine"), or that many computer-implemented claims are formally addressed to patent-eligible subject matter. But if that were the end of the § 101 inquiry, an applicant could claim any principle of the physical or social sciences by reciting a computer system configured to implement the relevant concept. Such a result would make the determination of patent eligibility "depend simply on the draftsman's art," *Flook*, thereby eviscerating the rule that "'[l]aws of nature, natural phenomena, and abstract ideas are not patentable,'" *Ass'n for Molecular Pathology v. Myriad* (2013).

2

The representative method claim in this case recites the following steps: (1) "creating" shadow records for each counterparty to a transaction; (2) "obtaining" start-of-day balances based on the parties' real-world accounts at exchange institutions; (3) "adjusting" the shadow records as transactions are entered, allowing only those transactions for which the parties have sufficient resources; and (4) issuing irrevocable end-of-day instructions to the exchange institutions to carry out the permitted transactions. Petitioner principally contends that the claims are patent eligible because these steps "require a substantial and meaningful role for the computer." As stipulated, the claimed method requires the use of a computer to create electronic records, track multiple transactions, and issue simultaneous instructions; in other words, "[t]he computer is itself the intermediary."

In light of the foregoing, the relevant question is whether the claims here do more than simply instruct the practitioner to implement the abstract idea of intermediated settlement on a generic computer. They do not.

Taking the claim elements separately, the function performed by the computer at each step of the process is "[p]urely conventional." *Mayo.* Using a computer to create and maintain "shadow" accounts amounts to electronic recordkeeping—one of the most basic functions of a computer. The same is true with respect to the use of a computer to obtain data, adjust account balances, and issue automated instructions; all of these computer functions are "well-understood, routine, conventional activit[ies]" previously known to the industry. *Mayo.* In short, each step does no more than require a generic computer to perform generic computer functions.

Considered "as an ordered combination," the computer components of petitioner's method "ad[d] nothing . . . that is not already present when the steps are considered separately." Viewed as a whole, petitioner's method claims simply recite the concept of intermediated settlement as performed by a generic computer. The method claims do not, for example, purport to improve the functioning of the computer itself. Nor do they effect an improvement in any other technology or technical field. Instead, the claims at issue amount to "nothing significantly more" than an instruction to apply the abstract idea of intermediated settlement using some unspecified, generic computer. *Mayo.* Under our precedents, that is not "*enough*" to transform an abstract idea into a patent-eligible invention.

C

Petitioner's claims to a computer system and a computer-readable medium fail for substantially the same reasons. Petitioner conceded below that its media claims rise or fall with its method claims. As to its system claims, petitioner emphasizes that those claims recite "specific hardware" configured to perform "specific computerized functions." But what petitioner characterizes as specific hardware—a "data processing system" with a "communications controller" and "data storage unit," for example—is purely functional and generic. Nearly every computer will include a "communications controller" and "data storage unit" capable of performing the basic calculation, storage, and transmission functions required by the method claims. As a result, none of the hardware recited by the system claims "offers a meaningful limitation beyond generally linking 'the use of the [method] to a particular technological environment,' that is, implementation via computers."

Put another way, the system claims are no different from the method claims in substance. The method claims recite the abstract idea implemented on a generic computer; the system claims recite a handful of generic computer components configured to implement the same idea. This Court has long "warn[ed] . . . against" interpreting § 101 "in ways that make patent eligibility 'depend simply on the draftsman's art.'" *Mayo*. Holding that the system claims are patent eligible would have exactly that result.

Because petitioner's system and media claims add nothing of substance to the underlying abstract idea, we hold that they too are patent ineligible under § 101.

For the foregoing reasons, the judgment of the Court of Appeals for the Federal Circuit is affirmed.

It is so ordered.

Concurrence

Justice SOTOMAYOR, with whom Justice GINSBURG and Justice BREYER join, concurring.

I adhere to the view that any "claim that merely describes a method of doing business does not qualify as a 'process' under § 101." *Bilski v. Kappos* (2010) (Stevens, J., concurring in judgment). As in *Bilski*, however, I further believe that the method claims at issue are drawn to an abstract idea. I therefore join the opinion of the Court.

Questions:

1.) The Court in *Alice* provides a very clear outline of the framework for determining patentable subject matter laid down in another recent case we read—*Mayo Collaborative Services v. Prometheus Laboratories*. What is that framework?

2.) Earlier, Boyle argued that "[t]he Court of Appeals for the Federal Circuit (the United States's leading patent court) seems to believe that computers can turn unpatentable ideas into patentable machines" and he went on to criticize this tendency. Those words were written before the *Alice* case. Does *Alice* clearly hold that one cannot use a computer to turn an unpatentable idea into a patentable machine?

3.) Is *Alice* an exception to the "machine or transformation" test? An application of it?

4.) Is *Alice* likely to ameliorate the concerns raised about software patents in Chapter 17? Why or why not? Read on for some empirical hints.

Note: "Can you still get everything you want at *Alice*'s restaurant?"

Some students come away from *Alice* with the impression that both business methods implemented through software and software itself are now unpatentable. Nothing could be further from the truth. In 2019, 6 years after the *Alice* decision, 61.8% of all utility patents issued by the PTO were software-related, a 20% increase from the previous year.[1] In other words, if one took the universe of patents over all kinds of inventions from mousetraps and coffee makers to vaccines and electronics, more than 6 in 10 were software-related—well over 200,000 annually. So an area where the patent system is experiencing problems—with the boundaries of the patent being more vague, the standards for patentable subject matter more contested and a very high preponderance of suits by NPE's—is also the area in which the most patents are granted. That does not imply software does not deserve or require patent protection. This is, after all, an information age and the machines of the 21st century are frequently built from binary code. Still, it should give one pause.

What about business methods? Here is a chart showing the *allowance* of business method patents by the USPTO as a percentage of business method patents filed, with the cases and regulations we have discussed layered onto the chart. What does this imply about the effect of SCOTUS's subject matter decisions? On the ability of lawyers to work around them, or of patent examiners or USPTO guidance documents to minimize (critics would say "ameliorate") their effect?

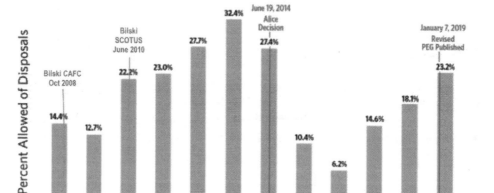

Business Methods Allowance Rate

Source: USPTO Data

As indicated on the chart, in January 2019, the PTO released its *Revised Patent Subject Matter Eligibility Guidance*, citing the need to "increase clarity and consistency" in the area. While this guidance "does not constitute substantive rulemaking and does not have the force and effect of law," it does "set[] out agency policy with respect to the USPTO's interpretation of the subject matter eligibility requirements," so it is important for anyone seeking a patent. This guidance has since been incorporated into the *Manual of Patent Examination Procedure* (MPEP). The Eligibility Guidance was widely seen as making examiners less likely to refuse on subject matter grounds, continuing the trend that you can see in the above chart.

Notably, under these new guidelines, the PTO added a prong to the first step of the *Mayo* test. If the claim recites a judicial exception, and is "integrated into a practical

---

[1] Raymond Millen, *Six Years After* Alice*: 61.8% of U.S. Patents Issued in 2019 Were 'Software-Related'— up 21.6% from 2018*. IP Watchdog, 17 Feb., 2020. https://www.ipwatchdog.com/2020/02/17/six-years-alice-61-8-u-s-patents-issued-2019-software-related-21-6-2018/id=118986/. The classification of a patent as being software-related is, of course, subjective—even when using the PTO's own classification system, but even if one accepts a degree of indeterminacy, the result is still striking.

application," then it is patent-eligible and the PTO does not proceed to *Mayo*'s second step. For many kinds of subject matter, therefore, this alters the *Mayo* test: one could argue that what would normally be relevant to the "inventive concept" under step 2 is now interpolated into step 1.

If a claim *is* directed to a judicial exception (and fails to integrate it into a practical application), then the PTO will proceed to evaluate whether it provides an "inventive concept" by asking whether there are additional elements that:

- "add a specific limitation or combination of limitations that are not well-understood, routine, conventional activity in the field, which is indicative that an inventive concept may be present

- or simply append well-understood, routine, conventional activities previously known to the industry, specified at a high level of generality, to the judicial exception, which is indicative that an inventive concept may not be present."

Is the excerpted guidance consistent with the case law that you have read?

***Alice*'s sequel:** Here is a summary of some of the early post-*Alice* case law. In *Amdocs v. Openet* (Fed. Cir. 2016), the Federal Circuit declined to define "abstract idea," opting instead for a flexible approach: "The problem with articulating a single, universal definition of 'abstract idea' is that it is difficult to fashion a workable definition to be applied to as-yet-unknown cases with as-yet-unknown inventions. . . . Instead of a definition, then, the decisional mechanism courts now apply is to examine earlier cases in which a similar or parallel descriptive nature can be seen—what prior cases were about, and which way they were decided. That is the classic common law methodology for creating law when a single governing definitional context is not available."

With this in mind, here is a list compiled by the PTO of subject matter that the Supreme Court and Federal Circuit have deemed "abstract ideas." (You are already familiar with most of the Supreme Court examples.)

> Mitigating settlement risk (*Alice*), hedging (*Bilski*), creating a contractual relationship (*buySAFE v. Google*), using advertising as an exchange or currency (*Ultramercial v. Hulu*), processing information through a clearinghouse (*Dealertrack v. Huber*), comparing new and stored information and using rules to identify options (*SmartGene v. Advanced Biological Labs*), using categories to organize, store and transmit information (*Cyberfone v. CNN*), organizing information through mathematical correlations (*Digitech Image Tech. v. Electronics for Imaging*), managing a game of bingo (*Planet Bingo v. VKGS*), the Arrhenius equation for calculating the cure time of rubber (*Diehr*), a formula for updating alarm limits (*Flook*), a mathematical formula relating to standing wave phenomena (*Mackay Radio v. Radio Corp*), and a mathematical procedure for converting one form of numerical representation to another (*Benson*).

☆ Abstract ideas

From the case law, the PTO has distilled the category of "abstract ideas" into the following three groups:

- **Mathematical concepts**—mathematical relationships, mathematical formulas or equations, mathematical calculations;
- **Certain methods of organizing human activity**—fundamental economic principles or practices (including hedging, insurance, mitigating risk); commercial or legal interactions (including agreements in the form of contracts;

legal obligations; advertising, marketing or sales activities or behaviors; business relations); managing personal behavior or relationships or interactions between people (including social activities, teaching, and following rules or instructions);

- **Mental processes**—concepts performed in the human mind (including an observation, evaluation, judgment, opinion).

After *Bilski* and *Alice*, what specific type of patents will be allowed or rejected? Here are two illustrative post-*Alice* cases from the Federal Circuit that deal with whether business practices conducted "over the Internet" (as compared to using a "generic computer")—arguably abstract ideas—are patent-eligible subject matter.

Ultramercial v. Hulu (Fed. Cir. 2014) addressed a "patent directed to a method for distributing copyrighted media products over the Internet where the consumer receives a copyrighted media product at no cost in exchange for viewing an advertisement, and the advertiser pays for the copyrighted content." (Sound familiar?) First, while noting that "we do not purport to state that all claims in all software-based patents will necessarily be directed to an abstract idea," the Federal Circuit held that "the process of receiving copyrighted media, selecting an ad, offering the media in exchange for watching the selected ad, displaying the ad, allowing the consumer access to the media, and receiving payment from the sponsor of the ad all describe an abstract idea, devoid of a concrete or tangible application." Turning to the question of whether there was any "inventive concept," the court explained that "'additional features' must be more than 'well-understood, routine, conventional activity' . . . [a]dding routine additional steps such as updating an activity log, requiring a request from the consumer to view the ad, restrictions on public access, and use of the Internet does not transform an otherwise abstract idea into patent-eligible subject matter." In a concurrence, Judge Mayer offered an alternative basis for rejecting the patent: "Because the purported inventive concept in Ultramercial's asserted claims is an entrepreneurial rather than a technological one, they fall outside 101."

Compare *Ultramercial* with *DDR Holdings v. Hotels.com* (Fed. Cir. 2014), which involved a system that allowed websites to retain viewers after they clicked on third-party ads by linking the viewers to a new composite webpage showing both the "look and feel" of the original site and the advertiser's product information. The Federal Circuit distinguished this invention from the one in *Ultramercial* by explaining that there was an "inventive concept" sufficient for patentability. While cautioning that "not all claims purporting to address Internet-centric challenges are eligible for patent," the court explained that "these claims stand apart because they do not merely recite the performance of some business practice known from the pre-Internet world along with the requirement to perform it on the Internet. Instead, the claimed solution is necessarily rooted in computer technology in order to overcome a problem specifically arising in the realm of computer networks." Thus, the invention was "not merely the routine or conventional use of the Internet." Do you agree with the distinction the Federal Circuit is drawing with its earlier case?

Citing *DDR Holdings*, the Federal Circuit has found other technological solutions to computer system problems to be patent-eligible subject matter. In *Amdocs v. Openet* (Fed. Cir. 2016) (the case cited above), the patents at issue covered "parts of a system designed to solve an accounting and billing problem faced by network service providers." Even assuming the patents were directed to an abstract idea, the court found a sufficient inventive concept in "an unconventional technological solution (enhancing data in a distributed fashion) to a technological problem (massive record flows which previously required massive databases)." And in *Bascom v. AT&T* (Fed. Cir. 2016), the court held that a customizable system for filtering objectionable Internet content was patent-eligible. Here the inventive concept was "the installation of a filtering tool at a specific location, remote from the end-users, with customizable filtering features specific to each end user." The court reasoned that this was not merely "conventional or generic," but rather "a technology-based solution . . . that overcomes existing problems with other Internet filtering systems."

The USPTO maintains a site with updated guidance on subject matter eligibility at https://www.uspto.gov/patent/laws-and-regulations/examination-policy/subject-matter-eligibility. Please visit this site for summaries of additional post-*Alice* case law and new reference guides.

One final note about terminology: As discussed at length in this chapter, judicially recognized exceptions to patentable subject matter hold "laws of nature," "natural phenomena," and "abstract ideas" to be unpatentable. Students should be aware that courts or examiners may also use other terminology, including (as noted by the PTO's *Manual of Patent Examining Procedure*) "physical phenomena," "scientific principles," "systems that depend on human intelligence alone," "disembodied concepts," "mental processes" and "disembodied mathematical algorithms and formulas." The breadth, and ambiguity, of these latter formulations may be of use in considering some of the problems we pose here.

Some industries have been very dissatisfied with the Supreme Court's subject matter jurisprudence and have lobbied extensively to encourage Congress to change the law in order to cut back on its limitations. Senators Tillis and Coons released a draft bill which contained the following language: "[N]o implicit or other judicially created exceptions to subject matter eligibility, including 'abstract ideas,' 'laws of nature,' or 'natural phenomena,' shall be used to determine patent eligibility under section 101, and all cases establishing or interpreting those exceptions to eligibility are hereby abrogated." Would the passage of this Bill be a good idea? Constitutional? Why?

PROBLEM 18-2

a.) Your client is Dr. Ender, a brilliant young biologist. Dr. Ender has developed a method of performing computational operations using biological materials rather than electrical circuits. Just as an electronic computer passes a reader over electromagnetic storage and registers either the presence or absence of a charge, a "1" or a "0," so Dr. Ender's system passes a biological probe over a genetic sequence and detects the presence or absence of a particular protein as a "1" or a "0." The computer can also "write" back to electromagnetic storage, again expressing itself in either 1's or 0's, the presence or absence of charge. Similarly Dr. Ender's system can "write" or not write the protein sequence on a biological medium, and this will later be "read" as a "1" or a "0." A computer uses this simple binary choice to build complex algorithms, each of which can be broken back down to a set of "off" or "on," "0" or "1," choices. This allows it to express some of the most basic algebraic or logical statements with which we are all familiar. ("If X, then Y." "If Not-X, then Z," for example.) To give a concrete example, if one were creating a simple computer program which converted miles into kilometers or kilometers into miles, the computer might register a request for a kilometers into miles conversion as a "0," and a request for a miles into kilometers conversion as a "1." If the computer registered a 1, then it would multiply whatever number of miles was entered by 1.6 to get the number of kilometers. If it registered a 0, then it would divide by 1.6.

These basic algebraic statements—"if, then" "if not, then" and so on—are the foundation for much of logic, computer science and indeed of thought itself. Dr. Ender wishes to patent the process of using a biological system to perform them. He claims he is the first to think of "using a biological system to go through the process electronic computers go through" and argues that, when fully developed, these systems will be both smaller and faster than their electronic equivalents. Dr. Ender wishes to file for two patents. The first claim is over the biological mechanism by which the presence or absence of the protein string, corresponding to 1 or 0, would be "written" and "read," "for the purpose of enabling the development of biological binary computation." The second claim is over some of the most basic algebraic or logical functions such as "if, then" and "if not, then" performed "by means of a biological computational device" in order "to solve problems of all kinds." Dr. Ender's original lawyer had a nervous breakdown and he is uncertain of the quality of legal advice he has received so far. He has come to you to ask you to assess the likelihood of success of his proposed patent claims.

Do Dr. Ender's patents meet the subject matter requirements for patentability? What—if any—facts would you need to know in order to answer the question?

b.) In a parallel universe, Dr. Craig Venture has completed the first draft of the human genome, decisively beating scientists from NIH who were struggling to do the same thing. The achievement is a notable one.

> During the 1980s, the importance of genes was obvious, but determining their location on chromosomes or their sequence of DNA nucleotides was laborious. Early studies of the genome were technically challenging and slow. Reagents were expensive, and the conditions for performing many reactions were temperamental. It therefore took several years to sequence single genes, and most genes were only partially cloned and described. Scientists had already reached the milestone of fully sequencing their first genome—that of the FX174 bacteriophage, whose 5,375 nucleotides had been determined in 1977 (Sanger et al., 1977b)—but this endeavor proved much easier than sequencing the genomes of more complex life forms. Indeed, the prospect of sequencing the 1 million base pairs of the E. coli genome or the 3 billion nucleotides of the human genome seemed close to impossible. For example, an article published in the New York Times in 1987 noted that only 500 human genes had been sequenced (Kanigel, 1987). At the time, that was thought to be about 1% of the total, and given the pace of discovery, it was believed that complete sequencing of the human genome would take at least 100 years.[‡]

Venture's innovation here was in the methods he used.

i.) Using high throughput genetic sequencers, he manages to speed up the process of discovery. First he uses machines to decode long genetic sequences (although he does not at this point know where in these sequences a gene is to be found).

ii.) Next, using a public domain library of cDNA,[§] he searches within those long sequences for a distinctive snippet identical to the cDNA sequence. Because he knows that cDNA codes for proteins, and that it is likely to be found somewhere in the gene (which includes both coding and non-coding sequences and which itself is hard to

---

[‡] J. Adams, *Sequencing human genome: the contributions of Francis Collins and Craig Venter*, 1 NATURE EDUCATION 133 (2008).

[§] See the explanation of complementary DNA in *Myriad*.

locate on the chromosome), it makes it much more likely that he will be able to find the needle of the gene in the haystack of the larger sequence. (The process here is the genetic equivalent of "Control F"—the way that you might use a distinctive line of text you remember from an ebook to find a particular passage.)

iii.) Once the gene is identified, he can focus attention on decoding *its* sequence alone, finding the exact sequence of A's C's, G's and T's that constitutes the gene. This is a process that is much faster than trying to sequence the entire chromosome.

Finally, having done this for all human genes, he has his first draft of the human genome. He comes to you in great excitement.

As a matter of patentable subject matter, can Venture get patents over his *draft of the genome*? (Can he *copyright* the genome?) Can he patent *the individual genes* he identifies? Can he patent the *three-step process of genetic discovery* described above? (Not the machines or the software used to achieve it, but the process itself?)[**]

[**] History has been modified and scientific facts simplified considerably for the purposes of this hypothetical.

CHAPTER NINETEEN
Requirements for Patent Protection: Utility

Utility, like patentable subject matter, is a component of patent eligibility that has recently received considerably more attention because of a series of technological changes. Patentable subject matter was once a sleepy area of patent doctrine, lightly touched on before beginning the real work of the requirements for prosecuting a patent. As we saw in the last chapter, then came the networked computer—which challenged the dividing line between patentable process and unpatentable idea or algorithm. At almost the same time we saw the arrival of the technology of genetic engineering, which disrupted the line between nature and invention.

Utility, beyond a few old cases dealing with immoral or pointless technologies, seemed to have little bite on real patent practice. It was also not clear why we would care about utility. Say we give a person a patent over something that is *not* useful. Who cares? It is not useful—so why would we want it, or care if its price or availability are affected by an incorrectly granted patent? The answer to all of these questions lies in the importance of multi-stage research efforts. A scientist discovers something that raises a question or a technological potential. Then she investigates it further, learning more and more about it. At what stage do her investigations merit a patent? At what stage have they become "useful" to the larger society? Of course, in some senses *all* knowledge is useful. But is that what we mean when we talk about satisfying the utility requirement for patentability?

1.) 'Research Intermediaries' and Hunting Licenses

Brenner v. Manson
383 U.S. 519 (1966)

Mr. Justice FORTAS delivered the opinion of the Court.

This case presents [a] question[] of importance to the administration of the patent laws: . . . whether the practical utility of the compound produced by a chemical process is an essential element in establishing a prima facie case for the patentability of the process. . . .

In December 1957, Howard Ringold and George Rosenkranz applied for a patent on an allegedly novel process for making certain known steroids. . . . In January 1960, respondent Manson, a chemist engaged in steroid research, filed an application to patent precisely the same process described by Ringold and Rosenkranz. He asserted that it was he who had discovered the process, and that he had done so before December 17, 1956. Accordingly, he requested that an "interference" be declared in order to try out the issue of priority between his claim and that of Ringold and Rosenkranz.

A Patent Office examiner denied Manson's application, and the denial was affirmed by the Board of Appeals within the Patent Office. The ground for rejection was the failure "to disclose any utility for" the chemical compound produced by the process. This omission was not cured, in the opinion of the Patent Office, by Manson's reference to an article in the November 1956 issue of the Journal of Organic Chemistry which revealed that steroids of a class which included the compound in question were undergoing screening for possible tumor-inhibiting effects in mice, and that a homologue adjacent to Manson's steroid had proven effective in that role. Said the Board of Appeals, "It is our view that the statutory requirement of usefulness of a product cannot be presumed merely because it happens to be closely related to another compound which is known to be useful."

The Court of Customs and Patent Appeals (hereinafter CCPA) reversed, Chief Judge Worley dissenting. The court held that Manson was entitled to a declaration of interference since "where a claimed process produces a known product it is not necessary to show utility for the product," so long as the product "is not alleged to be detrimental to the public interest." *Certiorari* was granted, to resolve this running dispute over what constitutes "utility" in chemical process claims. . . .

II.

Our starting point is the proposition, neither disputed nor disputable, that one may patent only that which is "useful." In *Graham v. John Deere Co.*, we have reviewed the history of the requisites of patentability, and it need not be repeated here. Suffice it to say that the concept of utility has maintained a central place in all of our patent legislation, beginning with the first patent law in 1790 and culminating in the present law's provision that

> Whoever invents or discovers any new and useful process, machine, manufacture, or composition of matter, or any new and useful improvement thereof, may obtain a patent therefor, subject to the conditions and requirements of this title.

As is so often the case, however, a simple, everyday word can be pregnant with ambiguity when applied to the facts of life. That this is so is demonstrated by the present conflict between the Patent Office and the CCPA over how the test is to be applied to a chemical process which yields an already known product whose utility—other than as a possible object of scientific inquiry—has not yet been evidenced. It was not long ago that agency and court seemed of one mind on the question. In *Application of Bremner*, the court affirmed rejection by the Patent Office of both process and product claims. It noted that "no use for the products claimed to be developed by the processes had been shown in the specification." It held that "It was never intended that a patent be granted upon a product, or a process producing a product, unless such product be useful." Nor was this new doctrine in the court.

The Patent Office has remained steadfast in this view. The CCPA, however, has moved sharply away from *Bremner*. The trend began in *Application of Nelson*. There, the court reversed the Patent Office's rejection of a claim on a process yielding chemical intermediates "useful to chemists doing research on steroids," despite the absence of evidence that any of the steroids thus ultimately produced were themselves "useful." The trend has accelerated, culminating in the present case where the court held it sufficient that a process produces the result intended and is not "detrimental to the public interest."

It is not remarkable that differences arise as to how the test of usefulness is to be applied to chemical processes. Even if we knew precisely what Congress meant in 1790 when it devised the "new and useful" phraseology and in subsequent re-enactments of the test, we should have difficulty in applying it in the context of contemporary chemistry where research is as comprehensive as man's grasp and where little or nothing is wholly beyond the pale of "utility"—if that word is given its broadest reach.

Respondent does not—at least in the first instance—rest upon the extreme proposition, advanced by the court below, that a novel chemical process is patentable so long as it yields the intended product and so long as the product is not itself "detrimental." Nor does he commit the outcome of his claim to the slightly more conventional proposition that any process is "useful" within the meaning of § 101 if it produces a compound whose potential usefulness is under investigation by serious scientific researchers, although he urges this position, too, as an alternative basis for affirming the decision of the CCPA. Rather, he begins with the much more orthodox argument that his process has a specific utility which would entitle him to a declaration of interference even under the Patent Office's reading of § 101. The claim is that the supporting affidavits filed pursuant to Rule 204 (b), by reference to Ringold's 1956 article, reveal that an adjacent homologue of the steroid yielded by his process has been demonstrated to have tumor-inhibiting effects in mice, and that this discloses the requisite utility. We do not accept any of these theories as an adequate basis for overriding the determination of the Patent Office that the "utility" requirement has not been met.

Even on the assumption that the process would be patentable were respondent to show that the steroid produced had a tumor-inhibiting effect in mice, we would not overrule the Patent Office finding that respondent has not made such a showing. The Patent Office held that, despite the reference to the adjacent homologue, respondent's papers did not disclose a sufficient likelihood that the steroid yielded by his process would have similar tumor-inhibiting characteristics. Indeed, respondent himself recognized that the presumption that adjacent homologues have the same utility has been challenged in the steroid field because of "a greater known unpredictability of compounds in that field." In these circumstances and in this technical area, we would not overturn the finding of the Primary Examiner, affirmed by the Board of Appeals and not challenged by the CCPA.

The second and third points of respondent's argument present issues of much importance. Is a chemical process "useful" within the meaning of § 101 either (1) because it works—i.e., produces the intended product? or (2) because the compound yielded belongs to a class of compounds now the subject of serious scientific investigation? These contentions present the basic problem for our adjudication. Since we find no specific assistance in the legislative materials underlying § 101, we are remitted to an analysis of the problem in light of the general intent of Congress, the purposes of the patent system, and the implications of a decision one way or the other.

In support of his plea that we attenuate the requirement of "utility," respondent relies upon Justice Story's well-known statement that a "useful" invention is one "which may be applied to a beneficial use in society, in contradistinction to an invention injurious to the morals, health, or good order of society, or frivolous and insignificant"—and upon the assertion that to do so would encourage inventors of new processes to publicize the event for the benefit of the entire scientific community, thus widening the search for uses and increasing the fund of scientific knowledge. Justice Story's language sheds little light on our subject. Narrowly read, it does no more than compel us to decide whether the invention in question is "frivolous and insignificant"—a query no easier of application than the one built into the statute. Read more broadly, so as to allow the patenting of any invention not positively harmful to society, it places such a special meaning on the word "useful" that we cannot accept it in the absence of evidence that Congress so intended. There are, after all, many things in this world which may not be considered "useful" but which, nevertheless, are totally without a capacity for harm.

It is true, of course, that one of the purposes of the patent system is to encourage dissemination of information concerning discoveries and inventions. And it may be that inability to patent a process to some extent discourages disclosure and leads to greater secrecy than would otherwise be the case. The inventor of the process, or the corporate organization by which he is employed, has some incentive to keep the invention secret while uses for the product are searched out. However, in light of the highly developed art of drafting patent claims so that they disclose as little useful information as possible—while broadening the scope of the claim as widely as possible—the argument based upon the virtue of disclosure must be warily evaluated. Moreover, the pressure for secrecy is easily exaggerated, for if the inventor of a process cannot himself ascertain a "use" for that which his process yields, he has every incentive to make his invention known to those able to do so. Finally, how likely is disclosure of a patented process to spur research by others into the uses to which the product may be put? To the extent that the patentee has power to enforce his patent, there is little incentive for others to undertake a search for uses.

Whatever weight is attached to the value of encouraging disclosure and of inhibiting secrecy, we believe a more compelling consideration is that a process patent in the chemical field, which has not been developed and pointed to the degree of specific utility, creates a monopoly of knowledge which should be granted only if clearly commanded by the statute. Until the process claim has been reduced to production of a product shown to be useful, the metes and bounds of that monopoly are not capable of precise delineation. It may engross a vast, unknown, and perhaps unknowable area. Such a patent may confer power to block off whole areas of scientific development, without compensating benefit to the public. The basic *quid pro quo* contemplated by the Constitution and the Congress for granting a patent monopoly is the benefit derived by the public from an invention with substantial utility. Unless and until a process is refined and developed to this point—where specific benefit exists in currently available form—there is insufficient justification for permitting an applicant to engross what may prove to be a broad field.

These arguments for and against the patentability of a process which either has no known use or is useful only in the sense that it may be an object of scientific research would apply equally to the patenting of the product produced by the process. Respondent appears to concede that with respect to a product, as opposed to a process, Congress has struck the balance on the side of non-patentability unless "utility" is shown. Indeed, the decisions of the CCPA are in accord with the view that a product may not be patented absent a showing of utility greater than any adduced in the present case. We find absolutely no warrant for the proposition that although Congress intended that no patent be granted on a chemical compound whose sole "utility" consists of its potential role as an object of use-testing, a different set of rules was meant to apply to the process which yielded the unpatentable product. That proposition seems to us little more than an attempt to evade the impact of the rules which concededly govern patentability of the product itself.

This is not to say that we mean to disparage the importance of contributions to the fund of scientific information short of the invention of something "useful," or that we are blind to the prospect that what now seems without "use" may tomorrow command the grateful attention of the public. But a patent is not a hunting license. It is not a reward for the search, but compensation for its successful conclusion. "[A] patent system must be related to the world of commerce rather than to the realm of philosophy. * * *"

The judgment of the CCPA is

Reversed.

Dissent

Mr. Justice DOUGLAS, while acquiescing in Part I of the Court's opinion, dissents on the merits of the controversy for substantially the reasons stated by Mr. Justice HARLAN.

Dissent

Mr. Justice HARLAN, concurring in part and dissenting in part.

While I join the Court's opinion on the issue of *certiorari* jurisdiction, I cannot agree with its resolution of the important question of patentability.

Respondent has contended that a workable chemical process, which is both new and sufficiently nonobvious to satisfy the patent statute, is by its existence alone a contribution to chemistry and "useful" as the statute employs that term. Certainly this reading of "useful" in the statute is within the scope of the constitutional grant, which states only that "[t]o promote the Progress of Science and useful Arts," the exclusive right to "Writings and Discoveries" may be secured for limited times to those who produce them. Art. I, § 8.[cl. 8] Yet the patent statute is somewhat differently worded and is on its face open both to respondent's construction and to the contrary reading given it by the Court. In the absence of legislative history on this issue, we are thrown back on policy and practice. Because I believe that the Court's policy arguments are not convincing and that past practice favors the respondent, I would reject the narrow definition of "useful" and uphold the judgment of the Court of Customs and Patent Appeals (hereafter CCPA).

The Court's opinion sets out about half a dozen reasons in support of its interpretation. Several of these arguments seem to me to have almost no force. For instance, it is suggested that "[u]ntil the process claim has been reduced to production of a product shown to be useful, the metes and bounds of that monopoly are not capable of precise delineation" and "[i]t may engross a vast, unknown, and perhaps unknowable area." I fail to see the relevance of these assertions; process claims are not disallowed because the products they produce may be of "vast" importance nor, in any event, does advance knowledge of a specific product use provide much safeguard on this score or fix "metes and bounds" precisely since a hundred more uses may be found after a patent is granted and greatly enhance its value.

The further argument that an established product use is part of "[t]he basic *quid pro quo*" for the patent or is the requisite "successful conclusion" of the inventor's search appears to beg the very question whether the process is "useful" simply because it facilitates further research into possible product uses. The same infirmity seems to inhere in the Court's argument that chemical products lacking immediate utility cannot be distinguished for present purposes from the processes which create them, that respondent appears to concede and the CCPA holds that the products are nonpatentable, and that therefore the processes are nonpatentable. Assuming that the two classes cannot be distinguished, a point not adequately considered in the briefs, and assuming further that the CCPA has firmly held such products nonpatentable, this permits us to conclude only that the CCPA is wrong either as to the products or as to the processes and affords no basis for deciding whether both or neither should be patentable absent a specific product use.

More to the point, I think, are the Court's remaining, prudential arguments against patentability: namely, that disclosure induced by allowing a patent is partly undercut by patent-application drafting techniques, that disclosure may occur without granting a patent, and that a patent will discourage others from inventing uses for the product. How far opaque drafting may lessen the public benefits resulting from the issuance of a patent is not shown by any evidence in this case but, more important, the argument operates against all patents and gives no reason for singling out the class involved here. The thought that these inventions may be more likely than most to be disclosed even if patents are not allowed may have more force; but while empirical study of the industry might reveal that chemical researchers would behave in this fashion, the abstractly logical choice for them seems to me to maintain secrecy until a product use can be discovered. As to discouraging the search by others for product uses, there is no doubt this risk exists but the price paid for any patent is that research on other uses or improvements may be hampered because the original patentee will reap much of the reward. From the standpoint of the public interest the Constitution seems to have resolved that choice in favor of patentability.

What I find most troubling about the result reached by the Court is the impact it may have on chemical research. Chemistry is a highly interrelated field and a tangible benefit for society may be the outcome of a number of different discoveries, one discovery building upon the next. To encourage one chemist or research facility to invent and disseminate new processes and products may be vital to progress, although the product or process be without "utility" as the Court defines the term, because that discovery permits someone else to take a further but perhaps less difficult step leading to a commercially useful item. In my view, our awareness in this age of the importance of achieving and publicizing basic research should lead this Court to resolve uncertainties in its favor and uphold the respondent's position in this case. . . .

Fully recognizing that there is ample room for disagreement on this problem when, as here, it is reviewed in the abstract, I believe the decision below should be affirmed.

Questions:

1.) "[A] patent is not a hunting license." This is one of the most quoted lines in patent law. What does it *mean*? Is this the patent version of *Pierson v. Post*—you do not own the fox until you have completed the chase and the capture?

2.) The Court acknowledges that this development of a method of synthesizing a new class of steroids may turn out to be useful. And it acknowledges that if patents cannot be obtained for "research intermediaries"—promising targets for future clinical research— there may be some danger of greater secrecy. Why does the Court nevertheless rule against patents on research intermediaries?

3.) Test tubes, reagents, agar jelly and many other objects are mainly used to perform other experiments—that is, they are a means to an experimental end, not the end itself. Does that mean that one could not get a patent over any of those? What is the distinguishing principle from this case?

4.) Justice Harlan says

> What I find most troubling about the result reached by the Court is the impact it may have on chemical research. Chemistry is a highly interrelated field and a tangible benefit for society may be the outcome of a number of different discoveries, one discovery building upon the next. To encourage one chemist or research facility to invent and disseminate new processes and products may be vital to progress, although the product or process be without "utility" as the Court defines the term, because that discovery permits someone else to take a further but perhaps less difficult step leading to a commercially useful item.

Why is the majority unpersuaded by this, apparently powerful, point? Is there any limiting principle on the idea? Does it imply abolishing the utility requirement altogether?

5.) Justice Harlan is unconvinced by the majority's claim that a more limited utility requirement will help us in defining the limits of the patent's reach. The majority had argued that "[u]ntil the process claim has been reduced to production of a product shown to be useful, the metes and bounds of that monopoly are not capable of precise delineation." With whom do you agree?

6.) Harlan goes on to say "nor . . . does advance knowledge of a specific product use provide much safeguard on this score or fix 'metes and bounds' precisely since a hundred more uses may be found after a patent is granted and greatly enhance its value." In saying this, he is restating hornbook law. The utility requirement requires the patent applicant to state *one* credible utility. After that, he or she has the right to exclude others from making, using, offering for sale or importing the patented item *for any purpose or function* whatsoever. The person to invent the laser probably did not foresee its use to detect speeders or scan barcodes. Nevertheless, if it were still in force, a laser patent would preclude the use of the laser for all of those purposes (at least without a license from the patentee). On the other hand, the person who later comes up with a novel and non-obvious way to *use* the patented invention—for example, to remove unwanted body hair come swimsuit season—would be able to patent *those* methods or processes. (All subject to the consent—and probably the requirement to pay—the initial patent holder.) Is this good policy? Why should we not confine the monopoly profits of the patent holder to the precise utility that he or she has identified? To foreseeable or proximate utility?

2.) Genetic Engineering & Utility

Brenner proved to be a prescient case. The genetic revolution produced some remarkable situations involving similar facts. In 1991 and 1992, Dr. Craig Venter, a prominent biotechnology researcher then working with NIH, filed patent applications on behalf of NIH on approximately 2700 partial cDNA sequences. As you may remember from our discussion of patentable subject matter, cDNA, or complementary DNA is—effectively—a purified ("exon only") form of DNA with all of the portions ("introns") that do not code for proteins spliced out. So what did Venter know? At the time the patent applications were filed, Venter and NIH knew that this was the cDNA—it coded for proteins. It *did something*. That is a significant finding—about 97–98% of human DNA does not code for proteins. (This DNA is sometimes dismissively described as "junk DNA." Of course, it turns out that it may well have many important functions.) But what did the cDNA do? What was the function of these proteins? Did this affect eye color, fast twitch muscle proportion, or propensity to get early onset Alzheimer's disease? That, the researchers did not know. They had—quite brilliantly—found 2700 keys scattered in an immense field, but they did not know which locks they opened. The PTO rejected the claims for lack of utility. (A correct application of *Brenner*?)

Realizing that utility would become a common ground of battle in early-stage biotech patents, the PTO issued revised Utility Examination Guidelines in 2001. It has since amended them to take account of the America Invents Act. Remember, "these Guidelines do not constitute substantive rulemaking and hence do not have the force and effect of law. Rejections will be based upon the substantive law, and it is these rejections which are appealable." Having said that, the Guidelines are extremely important in at least two ways. First, these are the internal rules that the examiners will be trying to follow. Second, they represent a snapshot of the PTO's own cultural understanding of its role in interpreting the concept of "utility."

USPTO Utility Examination Guidelines[1]

The following Guidelines establish the policies and procedures to be followed by Office personnel in the evaluation of any patent application for compliance with the utility requirements of 35 U.S.C. 101 and 35 U.S.C. 112(a), or pre-AIA 35 U.S.C. 112, first paragraph. These Guidelines have been promulgated to assist Office personnel in their review of applications for compliance with the utility requirement. The Guidelines do not alter the substantive requirements of 35 U.S.C. 101 and 35 U.S.C. 112, nor are they designed to obviate the examiner's review of applications for compliance with all other statutory requirements for patentability. The Guidelines do not constitute substantive rulemaking and hence do not have the force and effect of law. Rejections will be based upon the substantive law, and it is these rejections which are appealable. Consequently, any perceived failure by Office personnel to follow these Guidelines is neither appealable nor petitionable. . . .

Office personnel are to adhere to the following procedures when reviewing patent applications for compliance with the "useful invention" ("utility") requirement of 35 U.S.C. 101 and 35 U.S.C. 112(a) or pre-AIA 35 U.S.C. 112, first paragraph.

(A) Read the claims and the supporting written description.

(1) Determine what the applicant has claimed, noting any specific embodiments of the invention.

(2) Ensure that the claims define statutory subject matter (i.e., a process, machine, manufacture, composition of matter, or improvement thereof).

(3) If at any time during the examination, it becomes readily apparent that the claimed invention has a well-established utility, do not impose a rejection based on lack of utility. An invention has a well-established utility if (i) a person of ordinary skill in the art would immediately appreciate why the invention is useful based on the characteristics of the invention (e.g., properties or applications of a product or process), and (ii) the utility is specific, substantial, and credible.

(B) Review the claims and the supporting written description to determine if the applicant has asserted for the claimed invention any specific and substantial utility that is credible:

(1) If the applicant has asserted that the claimed invention is useful for any particular practical purpose (i.e., it has a "specific and substantial utility") and the assertion would be considered credible by a person of ordinary skill in the art, do not impose a rejection based on lack of utility.

(i) A claimed invention must have a specific and substantial utility. This requirement excludes "throw-away," "insubstantial," or "nonspecific" utilities, such as the use of a complex invention as landfill, as a way of satisfying the utility requirement of 35 U.S.C. 101.

(ii) Credibility is assessed from the perspective of one of

ordinary skill in the art in view of the disclosure and any other evidence of record (e.g., test data, affidavits or declarations from experts in the art, patents or printed publications) that is probative of the applicant's assertions. An applicant need only provide one credible assertion of specific and substantial utility for each claimed invention to satisfy the utility requirement.

(2) If no assertion of specific and substantial utility for the claimed invention made by the applicant is credible, and the claimed invention does not have a readily apparent well-established utility, reject the claim(s) under 35 U.S.C. 101 on the grounds that the invention as claimed lacks utility. Also reject the claims under 35 U.S.C. 112(a) or pre-AIA 35 U.S.C. 112, first paragraph, on the basis that the disclosure fails to teach how to use the invention as claimed. The 35 U.S.C. 112(a) or pre-AIA 35 U.S.C. 112, first paragraph, rejection imposed in conjunction with a 35 U.S.C. 101 rejection should incorporate by reference the grounds of the corresponding 35 U.S.C. 101 rejection.

(3) If the applicant has not asserted any specific and substantial utility for the claimed invention and it does not have a readily apparent well-established utility, impose a rejection under 35 U.S.C. 101, emphasizing that the applicant has not disclosed a specific and substantial utility for the invention. Also impose a separate rejection under 35 U.S.C. 112(a) or pre-AIA 35 U.S.C. 112, first paragraph, on the basis that the applicant has not disclosed how to use the invention due to the lack of a specific and substantial utility. The 35 U.S.C. 101 and 35 U.S.C. 112 rejections shift the burden of coming forward with evidence to the applicant to:

(i) Explicitly identify a specific and substantial utility for the claimed invention; and

(ii) Provide evidence that one of ordinary skill in the art would have recognized that the identified specific and substantial utility was well-established at the time of filing. The examiner should review any subsequently submitted evidence of utility using the criteria outlined above. The examiner should also ensure that there is an adequate nexus between the evidence and the properties of the now claimed subject matter as disclosed in the application as filed. That is, the applicant has the burden to establish a probative relation between the submitted evidence and the originally disclosed properties of the claimed invention.

(C) Any rejection based on lack of utility should include a detailed explanation why the claimed invention has no specific and substantial credible utility. Whenever possible, the examiner should provide documentary evidence regardless of publication date (e.g., scientific or technical journals, excerpts from treatises or books, or U.S. or foreign patents) to support the factual basis for the *prima facie* showing of no specific and substantial credible utility. If documentary evidence is not available, the examiner should specifically explain the scientific basis for his or her factual conclusions.

(1) Where the asserted utility is not specific or substantial, a *prima*

facie showing must establish that it is more likely than not that a person of ordinary skill in the art would not consider that any utility asserted by the applicant would be specific and substantial. . . .

(2) Where the asserted specific and substantial utility is not credible, a *prima facie* showing of no specific and substantial credible utility must establish that it is more likely than not that a person skilled in the art would not consider credible any specific and substantial utility asserted by the applicant for the claimed invention. . . .

(3) Where no specific and substantial utility is disclosed or is well-established, a *prima facie* showing of no specific and substantial utility need only establish that applicant has not asserted a utility and that, on the record before the examiner, there is no known well-established utility.

. . . Office personnel are reminded that they must treat as true a statement of fact made by an applicant in relation to an asserted utility, unless countervailing evidence can be provided that shows that one of ordinary skill in the art would have a legitimate basis to doubt the credibility of such a statement. . . .

Questions:

1.) On whom does the burden of proof on utility lie in a patent application? What is that burden of proof, precisely? If I assert that basketball shoes made out of "flubber" will allow anyone to dunk, should the examiner accept that? What if I say they will allow the average athlete to jump between .75 and 1.3 inches higher during a standing leap?

2.) Your client believes he has finally developed cold fusion—i.e. fusion at room temperatures and pressures. His device looks like a beaker of water with two different electrodes in it. You explain that the PTO might be skeptical. He suggests that the patent instead specify "making decorative bubbles in a beaker of liquid" as the utility. Patentable? If it were to be patentable, and the device was later shown to produce unlimited fusion power, would your client's patent cover that use?

3.) Justice Harlan and the Guidelines both reiterated the point that, once any specific and substantial utility is shown, the patent is valid for *all* uses. Are there particular dangers to this doctrine in the genetic realm? Benefits?

3.) Utility in the Court of Appeals for the Federal Circuit

In re Fisher
421 F.3d 1365 (Fed. Cir. 2005)

MICHEL, Chief Judge.

Dane K. Fisher and Raghunath Lalgudi appeal from the decision of the U.S. Patent and Trademark Office ("PTO") Board of Patent Appeals and Interferences ("Board") affirming the examiner's final rejection of . . . application Serial No. 09/619,643 (the "'643 application"), entitled "Nucleic Acid Molecules and Other Molecules Associated with Plants," as unpatentable for lack of utility under 35 U.S.C. § 101. . . . Because we conclude that substantial evidence supports the Board's findings that the claimed invention lacks a specific and substantial utility and that the '643 application does not enable one of ordinary skill in the art to use the invention, we affirm.

I. BACKGROUND

A. Molecular Genetics and ESTs

The claimed invention relates to five purified nucleic acid sequences that encode proteins and protein fragments in maize plants. The claimed sequences are commonly referred to as "expressed sequence tags" or "ESTs." Before delving into the specifics of this case, it is important to understand more about the basic principles of molecular genetics and the role of ESTs.

Genes are located on chromosomes in the nucleus of a cell and are made of deoxyribonucleic acid ("DNA"). DNA is composed of two strands of nucleotides in double helix formation. The nucleotides contain one of four bases, adenine ("A"), guanine ("G"), cytosine ("C"), and thymine ("T"), that are linked by hydrogen bonds to form complementary base pairs (i.e., A–T and G–C).

When a gene is expressed in a cell, the relevant double-stranded DNA sequence is transcribed into a single strand of messenger ribonucleic acid ("mRNA"). Messenger RNA contains three of the same bases as DNA (A, G, and C), but contains uracil ("U") instead of thymine. mRNA is released from the nucleus of a cell and used by ribosomes found in the cytoplasm to produce proteins.

Complementary DNA ("cDNA") is produced synthetically by reverse transcribing mRNA. cDNA, like naturally occurring DNA, is composed of nucleotides containing the four nitrogenous bases, A, T, G, and C. Scientists routinely compile cDNA into libraries to study the kinds of genes expressed in a certain tissue at a particular point in time. One of the goals of this research is to learn what genes and downstream proteins are expressed in a cell so as to regulate gene expression and control protein synthesis.

An EST is a short nucleotide sequence that represents a fragment of a cDNA clone. It is typically generated by isolating a cDNA clone and sequencing a small number of nucleotides located at the end of one of the two cDNA strands. When an EST is introduced into a sample containing a mixture of DNA, the EST may hybridize with a portion of DNA. Such binding shows that the gene corresponding to the EST was being expressed at the time of mRNA extraction. . . .

The '643 application generally discloses that the five claimed ESTs may be used in a variety of ways, including: (1) serving as a molecular marker for mapping the entire maize genome, which consists of ten chromosomes that collectively encompass roughly 50,000 genes; (2) measuring the level of mRNA in a tissue sample via microarray technology to provide information about gene expression; (3) providing a source for primers for use in the polymerase chain reaction ("PCR") process to enable rapid and inexpensive duplication of specific genes; (4) identifying the presence or absence of a polymorphism; (5) isolating promoters via chromosome walking; (6) controlling protein expression; and (7) locating genetic molecules of other plants and organisms.

B. Final Rejection

In a final rejection, dated September 6, 2001, the examiner rejected claim 1 for lack of utility under § 101. The examiner found that the claimed ESTs were not supported by a specific and substantial utility. She concluded that the disclosed uses were not specific to the claimed ESTs, but instead were generally applicable to any EST. For example, the examiner noted that any EST may serve as a molecular tag to isolate genetic regions. She also concluded that the claimed ESTs lacked a substantial utility because there was no known use for the proteins produced as final products resulting from processes involving the claimed ESTs. The examiner stated: "Utilities that require or constitute carrying out further research to identify or reasonably confirm a 'real world' context of use are not substantial utilities."

C. Board Proceedings

The Board ... concluded that using the claimed ESTs to isolate nucleic acid molecules of other plants and organisms, which themselves had no known utility, is not a substantial utility. . . .

. . . The Board analogized the facts to those in *Brenner v. Manson* (1966), in which an applicant claimed a process of making a compound having no known use. In that case, the Supreme Court affirmed the rejection of the application on § 101 grounds. Here, the Board reasoned: "Just as the process in *Brenner* lacked utility because the specification did not disclose how to use the end-product, the products claimed here lack utility, because even if used in gene expression assays, the specification does not disclose how to use . . . specific gene expression data." . . .

II. DISCUSSION

Whether an application discloses a utility for a claimed invention is a question of fact. . . .

A. Utility

1.

Fisher asserts that the Board unilaterally applied a heightened standard for utility in the case of ESTs, conditioning patentability upon "some undefined 'spectrum' of knowledge concerning the corresponding gene function." Fisher contends that the standard is not so high and that Congress intended the language of § 101 to be given broad construction. In particular, Fisher contends that § 101 requires only that the claimed invention "not be frivolous, or injurious to the well-being, good policy, or good morals of society," essentially adopting Justice Story's view of a useful invention from *Lowell v. Lewis* (C.C.D. Mass. 1817). Under the correct application of the law, Fisher argues, the record shows that the claimed ESTs provide seven specific and substantial uses, regardless whether the functions of the genes corresponding to the claimed ESTs are known. Fisher claims that the Board's attempt to equate the claimed ESTs with the chemical compositions in Brenner was misplaced. . . . Fisher likewise argues that the general commercial success of ESTs in the marketplace confirms the utility of the claimed ESTs. Hence, Fisher avers that the Board's decision was not supported by substantial evidence and should be reversed.

The government agrees with Fisher that the utility threshold is not high, but disagrees with Fisher's allegation that the Board applied a heightened utility standard. The government contends that a patent applicant need disclose only a single specific and substantial utility pursuant to Brenner, the very standard articulated in the PTO's "Utility Examination Guidelines" ("Utility Guidelines") and followed here when examining the '643 application. It argues that Fisher failed to meet that standard because Fisher's alleged uses are so general as to be meaningless. What is more, the government asserts that the same generic uses could apply not only to the five claimed ESTs but also to any EST derived from any organism. It thus argues that the seven utilities alleged by Fisher are merely starting points for further research, not the end point of any research effort. It further disputes the importance of the commercial success of ESTs in the marketplace, pointing out that Fisher's evidence involved only databases, clone sets, and microarrays, not the five claimed ESTs. Therefore, the government contends that we should affirm the Board's decision.

Several academic institutions and biotechnology and pharmaceutical companies write as *amici curiae* in support of the government. Like the government, they assert that Fisher's claimed uses are nothing more than a "laundry list" of research plans, each general and speculative, none providing a specific and substantial benefit in currently available form. The *amici* also advocate that the claimed ESTs are the objects of further research aimed at identifying what genes of unknown function are expressed during anthesis and what proteins of unknown function are encoded for by those genes. Until the corresponding genes and proteins have a known function, the *amici* argue, the claimed ESTs lack utility under § 101 and are not patentable.

We agree with both the government and the *amici* that none of Fisher's seven asserted uses meets the utility requirement of § 101. Section 101 provides: "Whoever invents ... any new and *useful* ... composition of matter ... may obtain a patent therefor. ..." (Emphasis added). In *Brenner*, the Supreme Court explained what is required to establish the usefulness of a new invention, noting at the outset that "a simple, everyday word ["useful," as found in § 101] can be pregnant with ambiguity when applied to the facts of life." Contrary to Fisher's argument that § 101 only requires an invention that is not "frivolous, injurious to the well-being, good policy, or good morals of society," the Supreme Court appeared to reject Justice Story's *de minimis* view of utility. The Supreme Court observed that Justice Story's definition "sheds little light on our subject," on the one hand framing the relevant inquiry as "whether the invention in question is 'frivolous and insignificant'" if narrowly read, while on the other hand "allowing the patenting of any invention not positively harmful to society" if more broadly read. In its place, the Supreme Court announced a more rigorous test, stating:

> The basic quid pro quo contemplated by the Constitution and the Congress for granting a patent monopoly is the benefit derived by the public from an invention with substantial utility. Unless and until a process is refined and developed to this point—where specific benefit exists in currently available form—there is insufficient justification for permitting an applicant to engross what may prove to be a broad field. ...

The Supreme Court has not defined what the terms "specific" and "substantial" mean *per se*. Nevertheless, together with the Court of Customs and Patent Appeals, we have offered guidance as to the uses which would meet the utility standard of § 101. From this, we can discern the kind of disclosure an application must contain to establish a specific and substantial utility for the claimed invention.

Courts have used the labels "practical utility" and "real world" utility interchangeably in determining whether an invention offers a "substantial" utility. Indeed, the Court of Customs and Patent Appeals stated that "'[p]ractical utility' is a shorthand way of attributing 'real-world' value to claimed subject matter. In other words, one skilled in the art can use a claimed discovery in a manner which provides some immediate benefit to the public." *Nelson*. It thus is clear that an application must show that an invention is useful to the public as disclosed in its current form, not that it may prove useful at some future date after further research. Simply put, to satisfy the "substantial" utility requirement, an asserted use must show that that claimed invention has a significant and presently available benefit to the public.

Turning to the "specific" utility requirement, an application must disclose a use which is not so vague as to be meaningless. Indeed, one of our predecessor courts has observed "that the nebulous expressions 'biological activity' or 'biological properties' appearing in the specification convey no more explicit indication of the usefulness of the compounds and how to use them than did the equally obscure expression 'useful for technical and pharmaceutical purposes' unsuccessfully relied upon by the appellant in *In re Diedrich* [(1963)]." Thus, in addition to providing a "substantial" utility, an asserted use must also show that that claimed invention can be used to provide a well-defined and particular benefit to the public.

In 2001, partially in response to questions about the patentability of ESTs, the PTO issued Utility Guidelines governing its internal practice for determining whether a claimed invention satisfies § 101. See Utility Examination Guidelines, 66 Fed.Reg. 1092 (Jan. 5, 2001). The PTO incorporated these guidelines into the Manual of Patent Examining Procedure ("MPEP"). The MPEP and Guidelines "are not binding on this court, but may be given judicial notice to the extent they do not conflict with the statute." *Enzo Biochem v. Gen-Probe* (Fed. Cir. 2002) (citing *Molins PLC v. Textron, Inc.* (Fed. Cir. 1995)). According to the Utility Guidelines, a specific utility is particular to the subject matter claimed and would not be applicable to a broad class of invention. Manual of Patent Examining Procedure § 2107.01. The Utility Guidelines also explain that a substantial utility defines a "real world" use. In particular, "[u]tilities that require or constitute carrying out further research to identify or reasonably confirm a 'real world' context of use are not substantial utilities." Further, the Utility Guidelines discuss "research tools," a term often given to inventions used to conduct research. The PTO particularly cautions that

> [a]n assessment that focuses on whether an invention is useful only in a research setting thus does not address whether the invention is in fact "useful" in a patent sense. [The PTO] must distinguish between inventions that have a specifically identified substantial utility and inventions whose asserted utility requires further research to identify or reasonably confirm.

The PTO's standards for assessing whether a claimed invention has a specific and substantial utility comport with this court's interpretation of the utility requirement of § 101.

Here, granting a patent to Fisher for its five claimed ESTs would amount to a hunting license because the claimed ESTs can be used only to gain further information about the underlying genes and the proteins encoded for by those genes. The claimed ESTs themselves are not an end of Fisher's research effort, but only tools to be used along the way in the search for a practical utility. Thus, while Fisher's claimed ESTs may add a noteworthy contribution to biotechnology research, our precedent dictates that the '643 application does not meet the utility requirement of § 101 because Fisher does not identify the function for the underlying protein-encoding genes. Absent such identification, we hold that the claimed ESTs have not been researched and understood to the point of providing an immediate, well-defined, real world benefit to the public meriting the grant of a patent.

2.

Fisher's reliance on *Jolles*, *Nelson*, and *Cross*, cases which found utility in certain claimed pharmaceutical compounds, is misplaced. In *Jolles*, the applicant filed an application claiming naphthacene compounds useful in treating acute myloblastic leukemia. To support the asserted utility, the applicant presented *in vivo* data showing eight of the claimed compounds effectively treated tumors in a mouse model. Our predecessor court reversed the Board's affirmance of the final rejection for lack of utility, finding that the structural similarity between the compounds tested *in vivo* and the remaining claimed compounds was sufficient to establish utility for the remaining claimed compounds. *Jolles*.

In *Nelson*, decided by the Court of Customs and Patent Appeals in the same year as *Jolles*, *Nelson* claimed prostaglandin compounds. . . . The issue before the Board was whether *Nelson* had established utility for the claimed prostaglandins as smooth muscle stimulants and blood pressure modulators via *in vivo* [tests on living organisms] and *in vitro* [laboratory tests literally "in glass,"] data, specifically, an *in vivo* rat blood pressure test and an *in vitro* gerbil colon smooth muscle stimulation test. The Board declined to award priority to *Nelson*, characterizing *Nelson*'s tests as "rough screens, uncorrelated with actual utility [in humans]." Our predecessor court reversed, concluding that "tests evidencing pharmacological activity may manifest a practical utility even though they may not establish a specific therapeutic use." *Nelson*.

In *Cross*, decided by the Federal Circuit five years after *Jolles* and *Nelson*, Iizuka filed an application claiming thromboxane synthetase inhibitors, alleged to be useful in treating inflammation, asthma, hypertension, and other ailments. The Board concluded that it offered a sufficient disclosure based upon *in vitro* data showing strong inhibitory action for thromboxane synthetase for structurally-similar compounds in human or bovine platelet microsomes. We affirmed, reasoning:

> Opinions of our predecessor court have recognized the fact that pharma-cological testing of animals is a screening procedure for testing new drugs for practical utility. This *in vivo* testing is but an intermediate link in a screening chain which may eventually lead to the use of the drug as a therapeutic agent in humans. We perceive no insurmountable difficulty, under appropriate circumstances, in finding that the first link in the screening chain, *in vitro* testing, may establish a practical utility for the compound in question. Successful *in vitro* testing will marshal resources and direct the expenditure of effort to further *in vivo* testing of the most potent compounds, thereby providing an immediate benefit to the public, analogous to the benefit provided by the showing of an *in vivo* utility.

The facts in these three cases are readily distinguishable from the facts here. In *Jolles*, *Nelson*, and *Cross*, the applicants disclosed specific pharmaceutical uses in humans for the claimed compounds and supported those uses with specific animal test data, *in vitro*, *in vivo*, or both. In contrast, Fisher disclosed a variety of asserted uses for the claimed ESTs, but failed to present any evidence—test data, declaration, deposition testimony, or otherwise—to support those uses as presently beneficial and hence practical. Fisher did not show that even one of the claimed ESTs had been tested and successfully aided in identifying a polymorphism in the maize genome or in isolating a single promoter that could give clues about protein expression. Adopting the language of the *Cross* court, the alleged uses in *Jolles*, *Nelson*, and *Cross* were not "nebulous expressions, such as 'biological activity' or 'biological properties' [alleged in the application in *Kirk*]," that "convey little explicit indication regarding the utility of a compound." *Cross*. Instead, the alleged uses in those cases gave a firm indication of the precise uses to which the claimed compounds could be put. For example, in *Nelson*, the claimed prostaglandins could be used to stimulate smooth muscle or modulate blood pressure in humans as shown by both *in vivo* and *in vitro* animal data. Hence, the *Jolles*, *Nelson*, and *Cross* courts concluded that the claimed pharmaceutical compounds satisfied the specific and substantial utility requirements of § 101. We cannot reach that same conclusion here. Fisher's laundry list of uses, like the terms "biological activity" or "biological properties" alleged in Kirk, are nebulous, especially in the absence of any data demonstrating that the claimed ESTs were actually put to the alleged uses.

Fisher's reliance on the commercial success of general EST databases is also misplaced because such general reliance does not relate to the ESTs at issue in this case. Fisher did not present any evidence showing that agricultural companies have purchased or even expressed any interest in the claimed ESTs. And, it is entirely unclear from the record whether such business entities ever will. Accordingly, while commercial success may support the utility of an invention, it does not do so in this case. See *Raytheon Co. v. Roper Corp.* (Fed. Cir. 1983) (stating that proof of a utility may be supported when a claimed invention meets with commercial success).

3.

As a final matter, we observe that the government and its *amici* express concern that allowing EST patents without proof of utility would discourage research, delay scientific discovery, and thwart progress in the "useful Arts" and "Science." See U.S. Const. art. I, § 8, cl. 8. The government and its *amici* point out that allowing EST claims like Fisher's would give rise to multiple patents, likely owned by several different companies, relating to the same underlying gene and expressed protein. Such a situation, the government and *amici* predict, would result in an unnecessarily convoluted licensing environment for those interested in researching that gene and/or protein.

The concerns of the government and *amici*, which may or may not be valid, are not ones that should be considered in deciding whether the application for the claimed ESTs meets the utility requirement of § 101. The same may be said for the resource and managerial problems that the PTO potentially would face if applicants present the PTO with an onslaught of patent applications directed to particular ESTs. Congress did not intend for these practical implications to affect the determination of whether an invention satisfies the requirements set forth in 35 U.S.C. §§ 101, 102, 103, and 112. They are public policy considerations which are more appropriately directed to Congress as the legislative branch of government, rather than this court as a judicial body responsible simply for interpreting and applying statutory law. Under Title 35, an applicant is entitled to a patent if his invention is new, useful, nonobvious, and his application adequately describes the claimed invention, teaches others how to make and use the claimed invention, and discloses the best mode for practicing the claimed invention. What is more, when Congress enacted § 101, it indicated that "anything under the sun that is made by man" constitutes potential subject matter for a patent. S.Rep. No. 82-1979, at 7 (1952), U.S. Code Cong. & Admin. News at 2394, 2399. Policy reasons aside, because we conclude that the utility requirement of § 101 is not met, we hold that Fisher is not entitled to a patent for the five claimed ESTs.

Questions:

1.) Why is the court inclined to look favorably on *in vitro* and *in vivo* animal studies as evidence of utility, but skeptical of Fisher's claims? Is this a modification of *Brenner* or simply an application of its tenets in the world of clinical trials on human beings, where there are no easy and safe alternatives?

2.) What role does commercial success have in showing utility? Why? What if a patent is being challenged for failing the utility requirement, and the patent holder uses her large licensing fee revenue as proof of utility? Do you see a problem? Have we met it before?

3.) Does *Fisher* implicitly say that the PTO got it right when it reframed the Utility Examination Guidelines?

PROBLEM 19-1

a.) Target, the store, has conducted extensive research over the susceptibility to advertising of its potential customers. It finds that store loyalty is very "sticky." People are unlikely to change stores except at significant life-change moments, such as the birth of a child. But it also finds that those who have just had children are too busy to pay attention to advertising. The key is to identify women who are about to give birth and advertise to them heavily before the baby is born. Target's demographers and statisticians conduct an extensive research program and find that pregnant women show distinct purchasing patterns—they tend to shift to cosmetic products with fewer fragrances, they purchase bland crackers and so on. Target develops a predictive statistical formula that identifies these women in its customer base, and produces a software application that employs the formula to "tag" their customer IDs with a particular probability of pregnancy. The application proves to be extremely accurate, sometimes even identifying women as potentially pregnant before they know it themselves. The CEO of Target is excited by the software and believes he can market it to advertisers across the United States.

i.) (A quick review of the last chapter.) Is the software patentable subject matter?

ii.) You are shown the current draft of the patent application. It states as the utility "a program accurately to identify women who may be particularly good advertising targets." Does this satisfy the utility requirement? Do you have suggested drafting changes?

b.) The Senate Judiciary Committee is disturbed by the number of times the Supreme Court has recently reversed the Court of Appeals for the Federal Circuit. You work for a Senator who wonders if the Senate should be asking better questions about judicial philosophy during the confirmation process. She tells you to take a look at this passage from *In re Fisher* and to give her your assessment of whether the nation's premier patent court is unduly formalistic.

> [W]e observe that the government and its *amici* express concern that allowing EST patents without proof of utility would discourage research, delay scientific discovery, and thwart progress in the "useful Arts" and "Science." See U.S. Const. art. I, § 8, cl. 8. The government and its *amici* point out that allowing EST claims like Fisher's would give rise to multiple patents, likely owned by several different companies, relating to the same underlying gene and expressed protein. Such a situation, the government and *amici* predict, would result in an unnecessarily convoluted licensing environment for those interested in researching that gene and/or protein. . . . The concerns of the government and *amici*, which may or may not be valid, are not ones that should be considered in deciding whether the application for the claimed ESTs meets the utility requirement of § 101. . . . Congress did not intend for these practical implications to affect the determination of

whether an invention satisfies the requirements set forth in 35 U.S.C. §§ 101, 102, 103, and 112. They are public policy considerations which are more appropriately directed to Congress as the legislative branch of government, rather than this court as a judicial body responsible simply for interpreting and applying statutory law.

Is this a good or bad way for the court to determine what utility *means*? Is attention to the practical effect of a definition of utility on a particular technology, patent law, or the "promote the progress" clause a non-judicial consideration? How does this fit with the attitude towards such "definitions" in the copyright field? (*Lotus, Sega, Computer Associates* and so on.) How does it fit with the Federal Circuit's own decision in the *Skylink* case interpreting § 1201 of the DMCA? What are its benefits—both in terms of fidelity to judicial role and in terms of practical effect? Does it support or refute the claim by some scholars, as discussed in Chapter 17, that the Federal Circuit is relatively formalistic?

c.) 23 & Me, a genetic research company, provides genetic testing kits. Individuals swab their mouths, send in their kits and receive back in the mail a lengthy printout of the probabilities they have of various negative health outcomes—senility, predisposition towards obesity, diabetes and so on.

i.) How would you state the utility of tests such as these in a patent application?

ii.) One of the most highly touted features of the tests is that they "let you know what to watch for in your health." Is this a utility that is distinguishable from *Brenner* and if so, how?

CHAPTER TWENTY

Requirements for Patent Protection: Novelty

 Novelty

35 U.S.C. 102 Conditions for patentability; novelty.
[Editor's Note: Applicable to any patent application subject to the first inventor to file provisions of the AIA. See 35 U.S.C. 102 (pre-AIA) for the law otherwise applicable.]

(a) Novelty; Prior Art.—A person shall be entitled to a patent unless—

(1) the claimed invention was patented, described in a printed publication, or in public use, on sale, or otherwise available to the public before the effective filing date of the claimed invention; or

(2) the claimed invention was described in a patent issued under section 151, or in an application for patent published or deemed published under section 122(b), in which the patent or application, as the case may be, names another inventor and was effectively filed before the effective filing date of the claimed invention.

(b) Exceptions.—

(1) **Disclosures Made 1 Year or Less Before the Effective Filing Date of the Claimed Invention.**—A disclosure made 1 year or less before the effective filing date of a claimed invention shall not be prior art to the claimed invention under subsection (a)(1) if—

(A) the disclosure was made by the inventor or joint inventor or by another who obtained the subject matter disclosed directly or indirectly from the inventor or a joint inventor; or

(B) the subject matter disclosed had, before such disclosure, been publicly disclosed by the inventor or a joint inventor or another who obtained the subject matter disclosed directly or indirectly from the inventor or a joint inventor.

(2) **Disclosures Appearing in Applications and Patents.**—A disclosure shall not be prior art to a claimed invention under subsection (a)(2) if—

(A) the subject matter disclosed was obtained directly or indirectly from the inventor or a joint inventor;

(B) the subject matter disclosed had, before such subject matter was effectively filed under subsection (a)(2), been publicly disclosed by the inventor or a joint inventor or another who obtained the subject matter disclosed directly or indirectly from the inventor or a joint inventor; or

(C) the subject matter disclosed and the claimed invention, not later than the effective filing date of the claimed invention, were owned by the same person or subject to an obligation of assignment to the same person.

(c) Common Ownership under Joint Research Agreements.—Subject

matter disclosed and a claimed invention shall be deemed to have been owned by the same person or subject to an obligation of assignment to the same person in applying the provisions of subsection (b)(2)(C) if—

> **(1) the subject matter disclosed was developed and the claimed invention was made by, or on behalf of, 1 or more parties to a joint research agreement that was in effect on or before the effective filing date of the claimed invention;**
>
> **(2) the claimed invention was made as a result of activities undertaken within the scope of the joint research agreement; and**
>
> **(3) the application for patent for the claimed invention discloses or is amended to disclose the names of the parties to the joint research agreement. . . .[1]**

Introduction

Editors of intellectual property casebooks generally begin the section on novelty by saying that the law involved is not a model of clarity. They are right. The Patent Act jumbles together provisions on novelty and statutory bars to patentability. The section on non-obviousness, which we will deal with in the next chapter, is not limpidly clear either. And then, into this existing fog, came the America Invents Act, which dramatically changed the United States from a first-to-invent, to a first-to-file system. Joy.

But there is a simple set of ideas to get into one's head that makes the whole thing a lot easier to understand.

- Novelty and statutory bar are both provisions that bar patentability because the public already "has" the invention and so we do not need—and should not grant—the statutory monopoly of the patent.

- The fundamental question in *novelty* is whether *someone else* has already invented the thing you are trying to patent and has either patented it, sold it, offered it to the public or described it in a printed publication. If *they* have then *you* do not get the patent.

- The fundamental question in *statutory bar* is whether *you* have done something to reveal the details of *your own* invention and have done it long enough ago and publicly enough, that the public already has access to the invention. If *you* have then *you* do not get the patent.

- Both provisions are subject to limitations—some statutory and some common law—that aim to make sure we do not punish inventors for doing things we want them to do, like experimenting with their inventions to make sure they work, or publishing their work less than a year in advance of the patent, or collaborating with other inventors who are under a joint research agreement.

Not so hard, really?

Onto this basic frame we add the America Invents Act and the move to first to file. In the statutory supplement there appears—courtesy of the USPTO—an annotated set of the statutory provisions applicable to pre-AIA and post-AIA patents. We are not going to

---

[1] **[USPTO] Note:** "The provisions of 35 U.S.C. 102(g), as in effect on March 15, 2013, shall also apply to each claim of an application for patent, and any patent issued thereon, for which the first inventor to file provisions of the AIA apply (see 35 U.S.C. 100 (note)), if such application or patent contains or contained at any time a claim to a claimed invention which is not subject to the first inventor to file provisions of the AIA." This is not the entire text of § 102. You can find that in your statutory supplement.

recapitulate all that here. Two larger points bear mentioning, however.

First, it is possible to overstate the changes produced by the AIA. Yes, the AIA fundamentally changes the patent law of the United States, particularly the rules of *priority*—what times matter in determining who gets the patent. But the novelty defense to patentability applies both to patents filed before and after the AIA. (Though the versions of the section governing novelty, § 102, are different, as we noted above.) Pre-AIA, if Joe has invented something and started selling it and Fred tries to file for a patent on the same invention, novelty bars the patent. Post-AIA? Fred gets to the USPTO first. Joe has been out there for a couple of years selling his invention, but has never bothered to file? Novelty bars the patent. There are differences to be sure, huge ones. For example, in cases where someone else has invented and not yet made the invention public or sold it, and is scooped by the quicker filer. Or in the dates applicable to determining priority, or the point at which we tell the person filing that prior art discovered after their filing will not defeat the patent. But both before and after the AIA, if an invention is truly non-novel (and we will learn what that means) then it cannot be patented. (Bonus question: is that fundamental result constitutionally required?)

Second, while the AIA certainly changed some fundamental aspects of the patent system, it was careful to retain a lot of the old statutory language. This means that courts (and inventors) can continue to rely on the body of case law that has elucidated that language.

1.) Novelty: Basics

Gayler v. Wilder
51 U.S. 477 (1850)

Mr. Chief Justice TANEY delivered the opinion of the court.

Three objections have been taken to the instructions given by the Circuit Court at the trial, and neither of them is, perhaps, entirely free from difficulty. . . .

The [third] question is upon the validity of the patent on which the suit was brought.

It appears that James Conner, who carried on the business of a stereotype founder in the city of New York, made a safe for his own use between the years 1829 and 1832, for the protection of his papers against fire; and continued to use it until 1838, when it passed into other hands. It was kept in his counting-room and known to the persons engaged in the foundery; and after it passed out of his hands, he used others of a different construction.

It does not appear what became of this safe afterwards. And there is nothing in the testimony from which it can be inferred that its mode of construction was known to the person into whose possession it fell, or that any value was attached to it as a place of security for papers against fire; or that it was ever used for that purpose.

Upon these facts the court instructed the jury, "that if Conner had not made his discovery public, but had used it simply for his own private purpose, and it had been finally forgotten or abandoned, such a discovery and use would be no obstacle to the taking out of a patent by Fitzgerald or those claiming under him, if he be an original, though not the first, inventor or discoverer."

The instruction assumes that the jury might find from the evidence that Conner's safe was substantially the same with that of Fitzgerald, and also prior in time. And if the fact was so, the question then was whether the patentee was "the original and first inventor or discoverer," within the meaning of the act of Congress.

The act of 1836, ch. 357, § 6, authorizes a patent where the party has discovered or invented a new and useful improvement, "not known or used by others before his discovery or invention." And the 15th section provides that, if it appears on the trial of an action brought for the infringement of a patent that the patentee "was not the original and first inventor or discoverer of the thing patented," the verdict shall be for the defendant.

Upon a literal construction of these particular words, the patentee in this case certainly was not the original and first inventor or discoverer, if the Conner safe was the same with his, and preceded his discovery.

But we do not think that this construction would carry into effect the intention of the legislature. It is not by detached words and phrases that a statute ought to be expounded. The whole act must be taken together, and a fair interpretation given to it, neither extending nor restricting it beyond the legitimate import of its language, and its obvious policy and object. And in the 15th section, after making the provision above mentioned, there is a further provision, that, if it shall appear that the patentee at the time of his application for the patent believed himself to be the first inventor, the patent shall not be void on account of the invention or discovery having been known or used in any foreign country, it not appearing that it had been before patented or described in any printed publication.

In the case thus provided for, the party who invents is not strictly speaking the first and original inventor. The law assumes that the improvement may have been known and used before his discovery. Yet his patent is valid if he discovered it by the efforts of his own genius, and believed himself to be the original inventor. The clause in question qualifies the words before used, and shows that by knowledge and use the legislature meant knowledge and use existing in a manner accessible to the public. If the foreign invention had been printed or patented, it was already given to the world and open to the people of this country, as well as of others, upon reasonable inquiry. They would therefore derive no advantage from the invention here. It would confer no benefit upon the community, and the inventor therefore is not considered to be entitled to the reward. But if the foreign discovery is not patented, nor described in any printed publication, it might be known and used in remote places for ages, and the people of this country be unable to profit by it. The means of obtaining knowledge would not be within their reach; and, as far as their interest is concerned, it would be the same thing as if the improvement had never been discovered. It is the inventor here that brings it to them, and places it in their possession. And as he does this by the effort of his own genius, the law regards him as the first and original inventor, and protects his patent, although the improvement had in fact been invented before, and used by others.

So, too, as to the lost arts. It is well known that centuries ago discoveries were made in certain arts the fruits of which have come down to us, but the means by which the work was accomplished are at this day unknown. The knowledge has been lost for ages. Yet it would hardly be doubted, if any one now discovered an art thus lost, and it was a useful improvement, that, upon a fair construction of the act of Congress, he would be entitled to a patent. Yet he would not literally be the first and original inventor. But he would be the first to confer on the public the benefit of the invention. He would discover what is unknown, and communicate knowledge which the public had not the means of obtaining without his invention.

Upon the same principle and upon the same rule of construction, we think that Fitzgerald must be regarded as the first and original inventor of the safe in question. The case as to this point admits, that, although Conner's safe had been kept and used for years, yet no test had been applied to it, and its capacity for resisting heat was not known; there was no evidence to show that any particular value was attached to it after it passed from his possession, or that it was ever afterwards used as a place of security for papers; and it appeared that he himself did not attempt to make another like the one he is supposed to have invented, but used a different one. And upon this state of the evidence the court put it to the jury to say, whether this safe had been finally forgotten or abandoned before Fitzgerald's invention, and whether he was the original inventor of the safe for which he obtained the patent; directing them, if they found these two facts, that their verdict must be for the plaintiff. We think there is no error in this instruction. For if the Conner safe had passed away from the memory of Conner himself, and of those who had seen it, and the safe itself had disappeared, the knowledge of the improvement was as completely lost as if it had never been discovered. The public could derive no benefit from it until it was discovered by another inventor. And if Fitzgerald made his discovery by his own efforts, without any knowledge of Conner's, he invented an improvement that was then new, and at that time unknown; and it was not the less new and unknown because Conner's safe was recalled to his memory by the success of Fitzgerald's.

We do not understand the Circuit Court to have said that the omission of Conner to try the value of his safe by proper tests would deprive it of its priority; nor his omission to bring it into public use. He might have omitted both, and also abandoned its use, and been ignorant of the extent of its value; yet, if it was the same with Fitzgerald's, the latter would not upon such grounds be entitled to a patent, provided Conner's safe and its mode of construction were still in the memory of Conner before they were recalled by Fitzgerald's patent.

The circumstances above mentioned, referred to in the opinion of the Circuit Court, appear to have been introduced as evidence tending to prove that the Conner safe might have been finally forgotten, and upon which this hypothetical instruction was given. Whether this evidence was sufficient for that purpose or not, was a question for the jury, and the court left it to them. And if the jury found the fact to be so, and that Fitzgerald again discovered it, we regard him as standing upon the same ground with the discoverer of a lost art, or an unpatented and unpublished foreign invention, and like him entitled to a patent. For there was no existing and living knowledge of this improvement, or of its former use, at the time he made the discovery. And whatever benefit any individual may derive from it in the safety of his papers, he owes entirely to the genius and exertions of Fitzgerald.

Upon the whole, therefore, we think there is no error in the opinion of the Circuit Court, and the judgment is therefore affirmed.

Mr. Justice McLEAN, dissenting. [Omitted.]

Questions:

1.) We invite you to muse on the business of a "stereotype founder."

2.) In one of its key passages, the opinion says:
> For if the Conner safe had passed away from the memory of Conner himself, and of those who had seen it, and the safe itself had disappeared, the knowledge of the improvement was as completely lost as if it had never been discovered. The public could derive no benefit from it until it was discovered by another inventor. And if Fitzgerald made his discovery by his own efforts, without any knowledge of Conner's, he invented an improvement that was then new, and at that time unknown; and it was not the less new and unknown because Conner's safe was recalled to his memory by the success of Fitzgerald's.

What does this tell you about the basic concept of novelty? Is it a metaphysical question of true priority in invention—in the sense that if we discovered a hidden stash of papers showing that someone had developed calculus 100 years before Leibniz and Newton, we would say they were the "true inventor of calculus"? Or is it a question of meaningful public access? If the latter, how does that square with the wording of the Intellectual Property Clause?

2.) Novelty: Novel to whom?

Gayler has the following interesting clause:

> And if the jury found the fact to be so, and that Fitzgerald again discovered it, we regard him as standing upon the same ground with the discoverer of a lost art, *or an unpatented and unpublished foreign invention*, and like him entitled to a patent.

With those words, it indicates the thrust of U.S. novelty doctrine—patents are defeated if there is already meaningful access for the American public and American inventors. *Gayler* assumes, reasonably in 1850, that unpatented and unpublished foreign inventions are, for all practical purposes, unavailable to American consumers and inventors. That idea was later given statutory form. The pre-AIA version of § 102 contained these words:

> A person shall be entitled to a patent unless—
> (a) the invention was known or used by others in this country, or patented or described in a printed publication in this or a foreign country, before the invention thereof by the applicant for patent, or
> (b) the invention was patented or described in a printed publication in this or a foreign country or in public use or on sale in this country, more than one year prior to the date of the application for patent in the United States. . . .

What of an invention that was being sold in Bulgaria, but had not been patented there, nor described in a printed publication, nor been made known to, or sold to the American public? Could that same invention be patented in the United States? The answer is yes.

> After the AIA, the section was amended to read as follows:
> (1) the claimed invention was patented, described in a printed publication, or in public use, on sale, or otherwise available to the public before the effective filing date of the claimed invention

There will still be questions of interpretation for the courts to flesh out. What does "available to the public" mean? What if it is on a Bulgarian e-commerce site? In a local neighborhood store in the countryside? But clearly some of the distinctions between foreign and domestic have been removed.

Questions:

1.) What role do search costs have in the analysis of novelty? Why remove the sharp distinction between foreign and domestic uses? How does the Internet change our assumptions about what information, and what products, are available to American inventors and consumers?

2.) How should the courts interpret "printed publication" in the online world? What about a prestigious scientific journal that is only made available online? A Russian physicist's blog?

3.) Novelty: Anticipation of Every Element

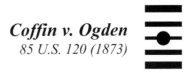

Coffin v. Ogden
85 U.S. 120 (1873)

Mr. Justice SWAYNE stated the case, recited the evidence, and delivered the opinion of the court.

The appellant was the complainant in the court below, and filed this bill to enjoin the defendants from infringing the patent upon which the bill is founded. The patent is for a door lock with a latch reversible, so that the lock can be applied to doors opening either to the right or the left hand. It was granted originally on the 11th of June, 1861, to Charles R. Miller, assignee of William S. Kirkham, and reissued to Miller on the 27th of January, 1863. On the 10th of June, 1864, Miller assigned the entire patent to the complainant. No question is raised as to the complainant's title, nor as to the alleged infringement by the defendants. The answer alleges that the thing patented, or a material and substantial part thereof, had been, prior to the supposed invention thereof by Kirkham, known and used by divers persons in the United States, and that among them were Barthol Erbe, residing at Birmingham, near Pittsburg, and Andrew Patterson, Henry Masta, and Bernard Brossi, residing at Pittsburg, and that all these persons had such knowledge at Pittsburg. The appellees insist that Erbe was the prior inventor, and that this priority is fatal to the patent. This proposition, in its aspects of fact and of law, is the only one which we have found it necessary to consider.

Kirkham made his invention in March, 1861. This is clearly shown by the testimony, and there is no controversy between the parties on the subject.

It is equally clear that Erbe made his invention not later than January 1st, 1861. This was not controverted by the counsel for the appellant; but it was insisted that the facts touching that invention were not such as to make it available to the appellees, as against the later invention of Kirkham and the patent founded upon it. This renders it necessary to examine carefully the testimony upon the subject.

Erbe's deposition was taken at Pittsburg upon interrogatories agreed upon by the parties and sent out from New York. He made the lock marked H.E. He made the first lock like it in the latter part of the year 1860. He made three such before he made the exhibit lock. The first he gave to Jones, Wallingford & Co. The second he sent to Washington, when he applied for a patent. The third he made for a friend of Jones. He thinks the lock he gave to Jones, Wallingford & Co. was applied to a door, but is not certain.

Brossi. In 1860 he was engaged in lockmaking for the Jones and Nimmick Manufacturing Company. He had known Erbe about seventeen years. In 1860 Erbe was foreman in the lock shop of Jones, Wallingford & Co., at Pittsburg. In that year, and before the 1st of January, 1861, he went to Erbe's house. Erbe there showed him a lock, and how it worked, so that it could be used right or left. He says: "He (Erbe) showed me the follower made in two pieces. One piece you take out when you take the knob away. The other part— the main part of the follower—slides forward in the case of the lock with the latch, so you can take the square part of the latch and turn it around left or right, whichever way a person wants to." He had then been a lockmaker eight years. He examined the lock carefully. He had never seen a reversible lock before. He has examined the exhibit lock. It is the same in construction. The only difference is, that the original lock was made of rough wrought iron. It was a complete lock, and capable of working. Erbe thought it a great thing. . . .

Masta. In 1860 he was a patternmaker for Jones, Wallingford & Co. Had known

Erbe fourteen or fifteen years. Erbe showed him his improvement in reversible locks New Year's day, 1861. He examined the lock with the case open. "You had to pull out the spindle, and the hub was fitted so that it would slide between the spindle and the plate and let the latch forward." . . . "The whole hub was made of three pieces. One part was solid to the spindle or hub shanks, and then the hub that slides between the plate and case, and a washer at the other side of the spindle." "There is not a particle of difference between the exhibit and the original lock. It is all the same." He identifies the time by the facts that he commenced building a house in 1861, and that year is marked on the water conductor under the roof. . . .

The case arose while the Patent Act of 1836 was in force, and must be decided under its provisions. The sixth section of that act requires that to entitle the applicant to a patent, his invention or discovery must be one "not known or used by others before his invention or discovery thereof." The fifteenth section allowed a party sued for infringement to prove, among other defences, that the patentee "was not the original and first inventor of the thing patented, or of a substantial and material part thereof claimed to be new."

The whole act is to be taken together and construed in the light of the context. The meaning of these sections must be sought in the import of their language, and in the object and policy of the legislature in enacting them. The invention or discovery relied upon as a defence, must have been complete, and capable of producing the result sought to be accomplished; and this must be shown by the defendant. The burden of proof rests upon him, and every reasonable doubt should be resolved against him. If the thing were embryotic or inchoate; if it rested in speculation or experiment; if the process pursued for its development had failed to reach the point of consummation, it cannot avail to defeat a patent founded upon a discovery or invention which was completed, while in the other case there was only progress, however near that progress may have approximated to the end in view. The law requires not conjecture, but certainty. If the question relate to a machine, the conception must have been clothed in substantial forms which demonstrate at once its practical efficacy and utility. The prior knowledge and use by a single person is sufficient. The number is immaterial. Until his work is done, the inventor has given nothing to the public. In *Gayler v. Wilder* the views of this court upon the subject were thus expressed: "We do not understand the Circuit Court to have said that the omission of Conner to try his safe by the proper tests would deprive it of its priority; nor his omission to bring it into public use. He might have omitted both, and also abandoned its use and been ignorant of the extent of its value; yet if it was the same with Fitzgerald's, the latter would not, upon such grounds, be entitled to a patent; provided Conner's safe and its mode of construction were still in the memory of Conner before they were recalled by Fitzgerald's patent." Whether the proposition expressed by the proviso in the last sentence is a sound one, it is not necessary in this case to consider.

Here it is abundantly proved that the lock originally made by Erbe "was complete and capable of working." The priority of Erbe's invention is clearly shown. It was known at the time to at least five persons, including Jones, and probably to many others in the shop where Erbe worked; and the lock was put in use, being applied to a door, as proved by Brossi. It was thus tested and shown to be successful. These facts bring the case made by the appellees within the severest legal tests which can be applied to them. The defence relied upon is fully made out.

DECREE AFFIRMED.

Question:

1.) To prove that an invention was not novel (or to prove "anticipation," in the language of patent law) one has to show that *every element of the innovation* was present *in a single prior art reference*. (Students sometimes mistakenly think a "prior art reference" has to be an article in a scholarly publication, or some highly technical piece of knowledge possessed by a scientist. In this case, the "prior art reference" was the latch.)

> The invention or discovery relied upon as a defence, must have been complete, and capable of producing the result sought to be accomplished; and this must be shown by the defendant. The burden of proof rests upon him, and every reasonable doubt should be resolved against him. If the thing were embryotic or inchoate; if it rested in speculation or experiment; if the process pursued for its development had failed to reach the point of consummation, it cannot avail to defeat a patent founded upon a discovery or invention which was completed, while in the other case there was only progress, however near that progress may have approximated to the end in view. The law requires not conjecture, but certainty.

Why require every element to be present?

Verdegaal Brothers, Inc. v. Union Oil Co. of California
814 F.2d 628 (Fed. Cir. 1987)

NIES, Circuit Judge.

. . . Verdegaal brought suit against Union Oil in the United States District Court for the Eastern District of California charging that certain processes employed by Union Oil for making liquid fertilizer products infringed all claims of its '343 patent. Union Oil defended on the grounds of non-infringement and patent invalidity under 35 U.S.C. §§ 102, 103. The action was tried before a jury which returned a verdict consisting of answers to five questions. Pertinent here are its answers that the '343 patent was "valid" over the prior art, and that certain of Union Oil's processes infringed claims 1, 2, and 4 of the patent. None were found to infringe claims 3 or 5. Based on the jury's verdict, the district court entered judgment in favor of Verdegaal.

Having unsuccessfully moved for a directed verdict under Fed.R.Civ.P. 50(a), Union Oil timely filed a motion under Rule 50(b) for JNOV seeking a judgment that the claims of the '343 patent were invalid under sections 102 and 103. The district court denied the motion without opinion.

II
ISSUE PRESENTED

Did the district court err in denying Union Oil's motion for JNOV with respect to the validity of claims 1, 2, and 4 of the '343 patent?

III

Our precedent holds that the presumption of validity afforded a U.S. patent by 35 U.S.C. § 282 requires that the party challenging validity prove the facts establishing invalidity by clear and convincing evidence. Thus, the precise question to be resolved in this case is whether Union Oil's evidence is so clear and convincing that reasonable jurors could only conclude that the claims in issue were invalid.

Anticipation

A claim is anticipated only if each and every element as set forth in the claim is found, either expressly or inherently described, in a single prior art reference. See, e.g., *Structural Rubber Prods. Co. v. Park Rubber Co.* (Fed. Cir. 1984); *Connell*; *Kalman v. Kimberly-Clark Corp.* (Fed. Cir. 1983), *cert. denied*, 465 U.S. 1026 (1984). Union Oil asserts that the subject claims of the '343 patent are anticipated under 35 U.S.C. § 102(e)[1] by the teachings found in the original application for U.S. Patent No. 4,315,763 to Stoller, which the jury was instructed was prior art.

From the jury's verdict of patent validity, we must presume that the jury concluded that Union Oil failed to prove by clear and convincing evidence that claims 1, 2, and 4 were anticipated by the Stoller patent. Under the instructions of this case, this conclusion could have been reached only if the jury found that the Stoller patent did not disclose each and every element of the claimed inventions. Having reviewed the evidence, we conclude that substantial evidence does not support the jury's verdict, and, therefore, Union Oil's motion for JNOV on the grounds that the claims were anticipated should have been granted.

The Stoller patent discloses processes for making both urea-phosphoric acid and urea-sulfuric acid fertilizers. Example 8 of Stoller specifically details a process for making 30-0-0-10 urea-sulfuric acid products. There is no dispute that Example 8 meets elements b, c, and d of claim 1, specifically the steps of adding water in an amount not greater than 15% of the product, urea in an amount of at least 50% of the product, and concentrated sulfuric acid in an amount of at least 10% of the product. Verdegaal disputes that Stoller teaches element a, the step of claim 1 of "providing a non-reactive, nutritive heat sink." As set forth in claim 2, the heat sink is recycled fertilizer.

The Stoller specification, beginning at column 7, line 30, discloses:

> Once a batch of liquid product has been made, it can be used as a base for further manufacture. This is done by placing the liquid in a stirred vessel of appropriate size, adding urea in sufficient quantity to double the size of the finished batch, adding any water required for the formulation, and slowly adding the sulfuric acid while stirring. Leaving a heel of liquid in the vessel permits further manufacture to be conducted in a stirred fluid mass.

This portion of the Stoller specification explicitly teaches that urea and sulfuric acid can be added to recycled fertilizer, i.e., a heel or base of previously-made product. Dr. Young, Union Oil's expert, so testified. Verdegaal presented no evidence to the contrary.

Verdegaal first argues that Stoller does not anticipate because in Stoller's method sulfuric acid is added slowly, whereas the claimed process allows for rapid addition. However, there is no limitation in the subject claims with respect to the rate at which sulfuric acid is added, and, therefore, it is inappropriate for Verdegaal to rely on that distinction. See *SSIH*. It must be assumed that slow addition would not change the claimed process in any respect including the function of the recycled material as a heat sink.

Verdegaal next argues that the testimony of Union Oil's experts with respect to what Stoller teaches could well have been discounted by the jury for bias. Discarding that testimony does not eliminate the reference itself as evidence or its uncontradicted disclosure that a base of recycled fertilizer in a process may be used to make more of the product.

Verdegaal raises several variations of an argument, all of which focus on the failure of Stoller to explicitly identify the heel in his process as a "heat sink." In essence, Verdegaal maintains that because Stoller did not recognize the "inventive concept" that the heel functioned as a heat sink, Stoller's process cannot anticipate. This argument is wrong as a matter of fact and law. Verdegaal's own expert, Dr. Bahme, admitted that Stoller discussed the problem of high temperature caused by the exothermic reaction, and that the heel could function as a heat sink. In any event, Union Oil's burden of proof was limited to establishing that Stoller disclosed the same process. It did not have the additional burden of proving that Stoller recognized the heat sink capabilities of using a heel. Even assuming Stoller did not recognize that the heel of his process functioned as a heat sink, that property was inherently possessed by the heel in his disclosed process, and, thus, his process anticipates the claimed invention. The pertinent issues are whether Stoller discloses the process of adding urea and sulfuric acid to a previously-made batch of product, and whether that base would in fact act as a heat sink. On the entirety of the record, these issues could only be resolved in the affirmative. . . .

After considering the record taken as a whole, we are convinced that Union Oil established anticipation of claims 1, 2, and 4 by clear and convincing evidence and that no reasonable juror could find otherwise. Consequently, the jury's verdict on validity is unsupported by substantial evidence and cannot stand. Thus, the district court's denial of Union Oil's motion for JNOV must be reversed.

Conclusion

Because the issues discussed above are dispositive of this case, we do not find it necessary to reach the other issues raised by Union Oil. In accordance with this opinion, we reverse the portion of the judgment entered on the jury verdict upholding claims 1, 2, and 4 of the '343 patent as valid under section 102(e) and infringed.
REVERSED.

Questions:

1.) This case provides a succinct statement of the "every element" test.

> A claim is anticipated only if each and every element as set forth in the claim is found, either expressly or inherently described, in a single prior art reference.

What does the court interpret that to mean? For example, must the prior art reference (in this case the patent) match exactly word for word with the proposed innovation? What kinds of differences do not matter?

2.) Returning to a question posed at the end of *Coffin*, why require that every element be present in order to prove anticipation? When we turn to non-obviousness, we will find that multiple references can be combined to make an innovation "obvious" and thus unpatentable.

4.) Novelty: Inherency

In re Cruciferous Sprout Litigation
301 F.3d 1343 (Fed. Cir. 2002)

PROST, Circuit Judge.

Brassica Protection Products LLC and Johns Hopkins University (collectively "Brassica") appeal from the decision of the United States District Court for the District of Maryland granting summary judgment that U.S. Patent Nos. 5,725,895 ("the '895 patent"), 5,968,567 ("the '567 patent"), and 5,968,505 ("the '505 patent") are invalid as anticipated by the prior art. We affirm the district court's ruling.

BACKGROUND

The three patents-in-suit relate to growing and eating sprouts to reduce the level of carcinogens in animals, thereby reducing the risk of developing cancer. Specifically, the patents describe methods of preparing food products that contain high levels of substances that induce Phase 2 enzymes. These enzymes are part of the human body's mechanism for detoxifying potential carcinogens. Thus, they have a chemoprotective effect against cancer. Foods that are rich in glucosinolates, such as certain cruciferous sprouts, have high Phase 2 enzyme-inducing potential. The inventors of the patents-in-suit recognized that the Phase 2 enzyme-inducing agents (or their glucosinolate precursors) are far more concentrated in certain sprouts (such as broccoli and cauliflower but not cabbage, cress, mustard or radish) that are harvested before the two-leaf stage than in corresponding adult plants. However, glucosinolate levels in cruciferous plants can be highly variable. According to the inventors, it is therefore desirable to select the seeds of those cruciferous plants which, when germinated and harvested before the two-leaf stage, produce sprouts that contain high levels of the desired enzyme-inducing potential.

The '895 patent was filed on September 15, 1995, and claims, *inter alia*, "A method of preparing a food product rich in glucosinolates, comprising germinated cruciferous seeds, with the exception of cabbage, cress, mustard and radish seeds, and harvesting sprouts prior to the 2-leaf stage, to form a food product comprising a plurality of sprouts." The '567 patent is a continuation of the '895 application and it claims a "method of preparing a human food product" from sprouts. The '505 patent is a divisional of the '895 application and it claims a "method of increasing the chemoprotective amount of Phase 2 enzymes in a mammal," as well as a "method of reducing the level of carcinogens in a mammal," by creating a "food product" from sprouts and then "administering said food product" to a mammal.

The three patents-in-suit are owned by Johns Hopkins University and exclusively licensed to Brassica Protection Products LLC. Johns Hopkins and Brassica sued [multiple "defendants"] in various district courts. Pursuant to 28 U.S.C. § 1407, the Judicial Panel on Multidistrict Litigation consolidated the various cases in the District of Maryland for pretrial proceedings. On June 7, 2001, the defendants filed a joint motion for partial summary judgment of invalidity, arguing that the patents were anticipated by prior art references disclosing growing and eating sprouts. Brassica filed a cross-motion for summary judgment that the patents are not invalid. On July 23, 2001, the district court held a *Markman* hearing to address claim construction issues and the parties' motions for summary judgment.

On August 10, 2001, the court granted defendants' motion for summary judgment of invalidity and denied Brassica's cross-motion for summary judgment. . . . Brassica appeals the judgment of invalidity, arguing that the district court failed to properly construe the claims and did not apply the properly construed claims to the prior art when determining that the claims are anticipated under 35 U.S.C. § 102(b).

DISCUSSION
I.

Brassica contends that the district court erroneously construed the claims by failing to treat the preamble of claim 1 of the '895 patent as a limitation of the claims. . . .

No litmus test defines when a preamble limits claim scope. Whether to treat a preamble as a limitation is a determination "resolved only on review of the entirety of the patent to gain an understanding of what the inventors actually invented and intended to encompass by the claim." In general, a preamble limits the claimed invention if it recites essential structure or steps, or if it is "necessary to give life, meaning, and vitality" to the claim. Clear reliance on the preamble during prosecution to distinguish the claimed invention from the prior art may indicate that the preamble is a claim limitation because the preamble is used to define the claimed invention.

In this case, both the specification and prosecution history indicate that the phrase "rich in glucosinolates" helps to define the claimed invention and is, therefore, a limitation of claim 1 of the '895 patent. The specification, for example, states that "this invention relates to the production and consumption of foods which are rich in cancer chemoprotective compounds." A stated object of the invention is "to provide food products and food additives that are rich in cancer chemoprotective compounds." The specification therefore indicates that the inventors believed their invention to be making food products that are rich in chemoprotective compounds, or, in other words, food products "rich in glucosinolates." In addition, during reexamination of the '895 patent the patentee argued as follows:

> Claim 1 of the patent, for example, is directed to "[a] method of preparing a food product rich in glucosinolates, . . . and harvesting sprouts prior to the 2-leaf stage, to form a food product comprising a plurality of sprouts."
> . . . Although "rich in glucosinolates" is recited in the preamble of the claim, the pertinent case law holds that the preamble is given weight if it breathes life and meaning into the claim. . . . Accordingly, the cited prior art does not anticipate the claims because it does not explicitly teach a method of preparing a food product comprising cruciferous sprouts that are rich in glucosinolates or contain high levels of Phase 2 inducer activity.

This language shows a clear reliance by the patentee on the preamble to persuade the Patent Office that the claimed invention is not anticipated by the prior art. As such, the preamble is a limitation of the claims. . . .

II.

Having construed the claim limitations at issue, we now compare the claims to the prior art to determine if the prior art anticipates those claims. In order to prove that a claim is anticipated under 35 U.S.C. § 102(b), defendants must present clear and convincing evidence that a single prior art reference discloses, either expressly or inherently, each limitation of the claim.

Brassica argues that the prior art does not expressly or inherently disclose the claim limitations of "preparing a food product rich in glucosinolates" (claims 1 and 9 of the '895 patent), or "identifying seeds which produce cruciferous sprouts . . . containing high Phase 2 enzyme-inducing potential" (claims 1 and 16 of the '505 patent, claim 1 of the '567 patent). According to Brassica, the prior art merely discusses growing and eating sprouts without mention of any glucosinolates or Phase 2 enzyme-inducing potential, and without specifying that particular sprouts having these beneficial characteristics should be assembled into a "food product." Moreover, Brassica argues, the prior art does not inherently disclose these limitations because "at most, one following the prior art would have a possibility or probability of producing a food product high in Phase 2 enzyme-inducing potential" and the "fact that one following the prior art might have selected seeds meeting the limitations of the claims is not sufficient to establish inherent anticipation."

It is well settled that a prior art reference may anticipate when the claim limitations not expressly found in that reference are nonetheless inherent in it. *See, e.g., Atlas Powder Co. v. Ireco Inc.* (Fed. Cir. 1999); *Titanium Metals Corp. v. Banner* (Fed. Cir. 1985). "Under the principles of inherency, if the prior art necessarily functions in accordance with, or includes, the claimed limitations, it anticipates." *MEHL/Biophile Int'l Corp. v. Milgraum* (Fed. Cir. 1999) (finding anticipation of a method of hair depilation by an article teaching a method of skin treatment but recognizing the disruption of hair follicles). "Inherency is not necessarily coterminous with the knowledge of those of ordinary skill in the art. Artisans of ordinary skill may not recognize the inherent characteristics or functioning of the prior art." *MEHL/Biophile.*

Brassica does not claim to have invented a new kind of sprout, or a new way of growing or harvesting sprouts. Rather, Brassica recognized that some sprouts are rich in glucosinolates and high in Phase 2 enzyme-inducing activity while other sprouts are not. *See* '895 patent, col. 10, ll. 28–42 ("Sprouts suitable as sources of cancer chemoprotectants are generally cruciferous sprouts, with the exception of cabbage (*Brassica olecracea capitata*), cress (*Lepidiumsativum*), mustard (*Sinapis alba* and *S. niger*) and radish (*Raphanus sativus*) sprouts."). But the glucosinolate content and Phase 2 enzyme-inducing potential of sprouts necessarily have existed as long as sprouts themselves, which is certainly more than one year before the date of application at issue here. *See, e.g.,* Karen Cross Whyte, *The Complete Sprouting Cookbook* 4 (1973) (noting that in "2939 B.C., the Emperor of China recorded the use of health giving sprouts"). Stated differently, a sprout's glucosinolate content and Phase 2 enzyme-inducing potential are inherent characteristics of the sprout. *Cf.* Brian R. Clement, *Hippocrates Health Program* 8 (1989) (referring to "[i]nherent enzyme inhibitors, phytates (natural insecticides), oxalates, etc., present in every seed"). It matters not that those of ordinary skill heretofore may not have recognized these inherent characteristics of the sprouts.

Titanium Metals Corp. v. Banner is particularly instructive in this regard. In that case, the claim at issue recited:

> A titanium base alloy consisting essentially by weight of about 0.6% to 0.9% nickel, 0.2% to 0.4% molybdenum, up to 0.2% maximum iron, balance titanium, said alloy being characterized by good corrosion resistance in hot brine environments.

Titanium Metals. The prior art disclosed a titanium base alloy having the recited components of the claim, but the prior art did not disclose that such an alloy was "characterized by good corrosion resistance in hot brine environments." We nevertheless held that the claim was anticipated by the prior art, because "it is immaterial, on the issue of their novelty, what inherent properties the alloys have or whether these applicants discovered certain inherent properties." *Titanium Metals* explained the rationale behind this common sense conclusion:

> The basic provision of Title 35 applicable here is § 101, providing in relevant part: "Whoever invents or discovers any *new* . . . composition

of matter, or any *new* ... improvement thereof, may obtain a patent therefor, subject to the conditions and requirements of this title."

... [C]ounsel never came to grips with the real issues: (1) what do the claims cover and (2) is what they cover new? Under the laws Congress wrote, they must be considered. Congress has not seen fit to permit the patenting of an old alloy, known to others through a printed publication, by one who has discovered its corrosion resistance or other useful properties, or has found out to what extent one can modify the composition of the alloy without losing such properties.

Brassica has done nothing more than recognize properties inherent in certain prior art sprouts, just like the corrosion resistance properties inherent to the prior art alloy in *Titanium Metals*. While Brassica may have recognized something quite interesting about those sprouts, it simply has not invented anything new.

Brassica nevertheless argues that its claims are not anticipated because the prior art does not disclose selecting the particular seeds that will germinate as sprouts rich in glucosinolates and high in Phase 2 enzyme-inducing potential (as opposed to selecting other kinds of seeds to sprout) in order to form a food product. We disagree. The prior art teaches sprouting and harvesting the very same seeds that the patents recognize as producing sprouts rich in glucosinolates and having high Phase 2 enzyme-inducing potential. According to the patents, examples of suitable sprouts are

typically from the family *Cruciferea*, of the tribe *Brassiceae*, and of the subtribe *Brassicinae*. Preferably the sprouts are *Brassica oleracea* selected from the group of varieties consisting of *acephala* (kale, collards, wild cabbage, curly kale), *medullosa* (marrowstem kale), *ramosa* (thousand head kale), *alboglabra* (Chinese kale), *botrytis* (cauliflower, sprouting broccoli), *costata* (Portuguese kale), *gemmifera* (Brussels sprouts), *gongylodes* (kohlrabi), *italica* (broccoli), *palmifolia* (Jersey kale), *sabauda* (savoy cabbage), *sabellica* (collards), and *selensia* (borecole), among others.

Numerous prior art references identify these same sprouts as suitable for eating. *See, e.g.*, Stephen Facciola, *Cornucopia: A Source Book of Edible Plants* 47 (1990) (listing "*Brassica oleracea Botrytis* Group Cauliflower ... Sprouted seeds are eaten"), Esther Munroe, *Sprouts to Grow and Eat* 9–14 (1974) (identifying "Broccoli, Brussels sprouts, Cabbage, Cauliflower, Collards and Kale"). These references therefore meet the claim limitation of identifying seeds to use in order to have sprouts with the inherent properties of glucosinolates and high Phase 2 enzyme-inducing activity. Despite the patents' admissions about the suitability of particular plant species found in these prior art references, Brassica argues that only specific cultivars of these plant species are rich in glucosinolates and high in Phase 2 enzyme-inducing activity. Thus, according to Brassica, the prior art fails to meet the "identifying" steps of the claims because it does not specify which cultivars should be sprouted. However, all of the appropriate cultivars that are identified in Brassica's patent are in the public domain. Brassica cannot credibly maintain that no one has heretofore grown and eaten one of the many suitable cultivars identified by its patents. It is unnecessary for purposes of anticipation for the persons sprouting these particular cultivars to have realized that they were sprouting something rich in glucosinolates and high in Phase 2 enzyme-inducing potential. *Atlas Powder* ("The public remains free to make, use, or sell prior art compositions or processes, regardless of whether or not they understand their complete makeup [or] the underlying scientific principles which allow them to operate."). ...

In summary, the prior art inherently contains the claim limitations that Brassica relies upon to distinguish its claims from the prior art. While Brassica may have recognized something about sprouts that was not known before, Brassica's claims do not describe a new method.

CONCLUSION

For the foregoing reasons, we affirm the district court's summary judgment that the claims at issue are anticipated by the prior art. The prior art indisputably includes growing, harvesting and eating particular sprouts which Brassica has recognized as being rich in glucosinolates and high in Phase 2 enzyme-inducing potential. But the glucosinolate content and Phase 2 enzyme-inducing potential of these sprouts are inherent properties of the sprouts put there by nature, not by Brassica. Brassica simply has not claimed anything that is new and its claims are therefore invalid.
AFFIRMED.

Questions:

1.) We admit to putting this case in the book partly because we love its name but it also raises some fascinating questions about novelty. The crux with novelty is whether the public had access to the benefit provided by the innovation. Did they here? Yes, they had sprouts. And yes, if they ate sprouts, at the right moment in their development, then they got the benefit of the anti-carcinogens. But they did not *know* that eating sprouts at that stage provided those benefits. So why claim that the claims were anticipated, that is, that they were not novel?

2.) Does this passage, approvingly quoted from another case, suggest some of the court's concerns?

> "The public remains free to make, use, or sell prior art compositions or processes, regardless of whether or not they understand their complete makeup or the underlying scientific principles which allow them to operate."

3.) What is the concept of "inherency" and how is it used here?

5.) Statutory Bar: Public Use

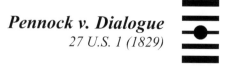

Pennock v. Dialogue
27 U.S. 1 (1829)

This case was brought before the Court, on a writ of error to the circuit court for the eastern district of Pennsylvania.

In that court, the plaintiffs in error had instituted their suit against the defendants, for an infringement of a patent right, for 'an improvement in the art of making tubes or hose for conveying air, water, and other fluids.' The invention claimed by the patentees, was in the mode of making the hose so that the parts so joined together would be tight, and as capable of resisting the pressure as any other part of the machine.

The bill of exceptions, which came up with the record, contained the whole evidence given in the trial of the cause in the circuit court. The invention, for which the patent right was claimed, was completed in 1811; and the letters patent were obtained in 1818. In this interval, upwards of *thirteen thousand feet of hose*, constructed according to the invention of the patentees, had been made and sold in the city of Philadelphia. One Samuel Jenkins, by the permission of, and under an agreement between the plaintiffs as to the price; had made and sold the hose invented by the plaintiffs, and supplied several hose companies in the city of Philadelphia with the same. Jenkins, during much of the time, was in the service of the plaintiffs, and had been instructed by them in the art of making the hose. There was no positive evidence, that the agreement between Jenkins and the plaintiffs in error was known to, or concealed from the public. The plaintiffs, on the trial, did not allege or offer evidence to prove that they had delayed making application for a patent, for the purpose of improving their invention; or that from 1811 to 1818, any important modifications or alterations had been made in their riveted hose. The plaintiffs claimed before the jury, that all the hose which had been made and sold to the public, prior to their patent, had been constructed and vended by Jenkins under their permission.

Upon the whole evidence in the case, the circuit court charged the jury:

> 'We are clearly of opinion that if an inventor makes his discovery public, looks on and permits others freely to use it, without objection or assertion of claim to the invention, of which the public might take notice; he abandons the inchoate right to the exclusive use of the invention, to which a patent would have entitled him, had it been applied for before such use. And we think it makes no difference in the principle, that the article so publicly used, and afterwards patented, was made by a particular individual, who did so by the private permission of the inventor. As long as an inventor keeps to himself the subject of his discovery, the public cannot be injured: and even if it be made public, but accompanied by an assertion of the inventor's claim to the discovery, those who should make or use the subject of the invention would at least be put upon their guard. But if the public, with the knowledge and the tacit consent of the inventor, is permitted to use the invention without opposition, it is a fraud upon the public afterwards to take out a patent. It is possible that the inventor may not have intended to give the benefit of his discovery to the public; and may have supposed that by giving permission to a particular individual to construct for others the thing patented, he could not be presumed to have done so. But it is not a question of intention, which is involved in the principle which we have laid down; but of legal inference, resulting from the conduct of the inventor, and affecting the interests of the public. It is for the jury to say, whether the evidence brings this case within the principle which has been stated. If it does, the court is of opinion that the plaintiffs are not entitled to a verdict.'

To this charge the plaintiffs excepted, and the jury gave a verdict for the defendant.

Mr. Justice STORY delivered the opinion of the Court.

. . . The single question then is, whether the charge of the court was correct in point of law. It has not been, and indeed cannot be denied, that an inventor may abandon his invention, and surrender or dedicate it to the public. This inchoate right, thus once gone, cannot afterwards be resumed at his pleasure; for, where gifts are once made to the public in this way, they become absolute. Thus, if a man dedicates a way, or other easement to the public, it is supposed to carry with it a permanent right of user. The question which generally arises at trials, is a question of fact, rather than of law; whether the acts or acquiescence of the party furnish in the given case, satisfactory proof of an abandonment or dedication of the invention to the public. But when all the facts are given, there does not seem any reason why the court may not state the legal conclusion deducible from them. In this view of the matter, the only question would be, whether, upon general principles, the facts stated by the court would justify the conclusion.

In the case at bar; it is unnecessary to consider whether the facts stated in the charge of the court would, upon general principles, warrant the conclusion drawn by the court, independently of any statutory provisions; because, we are of opinion, that the proper answer depends upon the true exposition of the act of congress, under which the present patent was obtained. The constitution of the United States has declared, that congress shall have power "to promote the progress of science and useful arts, by securing for limited times, to authors and inventors, the exclusive right to their respective writings and discoveries." It contemplates, therefore, that this exclusive right shall exist but for a limited period, and that the period shall be subject to the discretion of congress. The patent act, of the 21st of February, 1793, ch. 11, prescribes the terms and conditions and manner of obtaining patents for inventions; and proof of a strict compliance with them lies at the foundation of the title acquired by the patentee. The first section provides, "that when any person or persons, being a citizen or citizens of the United States, shall allege that he or they have invented any new or useful art, machine, manufacture, or composition of matter, or any new or useful improvement on any art, machine, or composition of matter, not known or used before the application; and shall present a petition to the secretary of state, signifying a desire of obtaining an exclusive property in the same, and praying that a patent may be granted therefor; it shall and may be lawful for the said secretary of state, to cause letters patent to be made out in the name of the United States, bearing *teste* [the ablative of *testis*, 'to bear witness'] by the President of the United States, reciting the allegations and suggestions of the said petition, and giving a short description of the said invention or discovery, and thereupon, granting to the said petitioner, &c. for a term not exceeding fourteen years, the full and exclusive right and liberty of making, constructing, using, and vending to others to be used, the said invention or discovery, &c." The third section provides, "that every inventor, before he can receive a patent, shall swear, or affirm, that he does verily believe that he is the true inventor or discoverer of the art, machine, or improvement for which he solicits a patent." The sixth section provides that the defendant shall be permitted to give in defence, to any action brought against him for an infringement of the patent, among other things, "that the thing thus secured by patent was not originally discovered by the patentee, but had been in use, or had been described in some public work, anterior to the supposed discovery of the patentee."

These are the only material clauses bearing upon the question now before the court; and upon the construction of them, there has been no inconsiderable diversity of opinion entertained among the profession, in cases heretofore litigated.

It is obvious to the careful inquirer, that many of the provisions of our patent act are derived from the principles and practice which have prevailed in the construction of that of England. It is doubtless true, as has been suggested at the bar, that where English statutes, such for instance, as the statute of frauds, and the statute of limitations; have been adopted into our own legislation; the known and settled construction of those statutes by courts of law, has been considered as silently incorporated into the acts, or has been received with all the weight of authority. Strictly speaking, that is not the case in respect to the English statute of monopolies; which contains an exception on which the grants of patents for inventions have issued in that country. The language of that clause of the statute is not, as we shall presently see, identical with ours; but the construction of it adopted by the English courts, and the principles and practice which have long regulated the grants of their patents, as they must have been known and are tacitly referred to in some of the provisions of our own statute, afford materials to illustrate it.

By the very terms of the first section of our statute, the secretary of state is authorised to grant a patent to any citizen applying for the same, who shall allege that he has invented a new and useful art, machine, &c. "not known or used before the application?" The authority is a limited one, and the party must bring himself within the terms, before he can derive any title to demand, or to hold a patent. What then is the true meaning of the words "not known or used before the application?" They cannot mean that the thing invented was not known or used before the application by the inventor himself, for that would be to prohibit him from the only means of obtaining a patent. The use, as well as the knowledge of his invention, must be indispensable to enable him to ascertain its competency to the end proposed, as well as to perfect its component parts. The words then, to have any rational interpretation, must mean, not known or used by others, before the application. But how known or used? If it were necessary, as it well might be, to employ others to assist in the original structure or use by the inventor himself; or if before his application for a patent his invention should be pirated by another, or used without his consent; it can scarcely be supposed, that the legislature had within its contemplation such knowledge or use.

We think, then, the true meaning must be, not known or used by the public, before the application. And, thus construed, there is much reason for the limitation thus imposed by the act. While one great object was, by holding out a reasonable reward to inventors, and giving them an exclusive right to their inventions for a limited period, to stimulate the efforts of genius; the main object was "to promote the progress of science and useful arts;" and this could be done best, by giving the public at large a right to make, construct, use, and vend the thing invented, at as early a period as possible; having a due regard to the rights of the inventor. If an inventor should be permitted to hold back from the knowledge of the public the secrets of his invention; if he should for a long period of years retain the monopoly, and make, and sell his invention publicly, and thus gather the whole profits of it, relying upon his superior skill and knowledge of the structure; and then, and then only, when the danger of competition should force him to secure the exclusive right, he should be allowed to take out a patent, and thus exclude the public from any farther use than what should be derived under it during his fourteen years; it would materially retard the progress of science and the useful arts, and give a premium to those who should be least prompt to communicate their discoveries.

A provision, therefore, that should withhold from an inventor the privilege of an exclusive right, unless he should, as early as he should allow the public use, put the public in possession of his secret, and commence the running of the period, that should limit that right; would not be deemed unreasonable. It might be expected to find a place in a wise prospective legislation on such a subject. If it was already found in the jurisprudence of the mother country, and had not been considered inconvenient there; it would not be unnatural that it should find a place in our own.

Now, in point of fact, the statute of 21 Jac., ch. 3, commonly called the statute of monopolies, does contain exactly such a provision. That act, after prohibiting monopolies generally, contains, in the sixth section, an exception in favour of "letters patent and grants of privileges for fourteen years or under, of the sole working or making of any manner of new manufactures within this realm, to the true and first inventor and inventors of such manufactures, which others, at the time of making such letters patent and grants, shall not use." Lord Coke, in his commentary upon this clause or proviso, (3 Inst. 184,) says that the letters patent "must be of such manufactures, which any other at the time of making such letters patent did not use; for albeit it were newly invented, yet if any other did use it at the making of the letters patent, or grant of the privilege, it is declared and enacted to be void by this act." The use here referred to has always been understood to be a public use, and not a private or surreptitious use in fraud of the inventor.

In the case of *Wood vs. Zimmer*, this doctrine was fully recognised by lord chief justice Gibbs. There the inventor had suffered the thing invented to be sold, and go into public use for four months before the grant of his patent; and it was held by the court, that on this account the patent was utterly void. Lord chief justice Gibbs said, "To entitle a man to a patent, the invention must be new to the world. The public sale of that which is afterwards made the subject of a patent, though sold by the inventor only, makes the patent void." By "invention," the learned judge undoubtedly meant, as the context abundantly shows, not the abstract discovery, but the thing invented; not the new secret principle, but the manufacture resulting from it.

The words of our statute are not identical with those of the statute of James, but it can scarcely admit of doubt, that they must have been within the contemplation of those by whom it was framed, as well as the construction which had been put upon them by Lord Coke. But if there were no such illustrative comment, it is difficult to conceive how any other interpretation could fairly be put upon these words. We are not at liberty to reject words which are sensible in the place where they occur, merely because they may be thought, in some cases, to import a hardship, or tie up beneficial rights within very close limits. . . .

It is admitted that the subject is not wholly free from difficulties; but upon most deliberate consideration we are all of opinion, that the true construction of the act is, that the first inventor cannot acquire a good title to a patent; if he suffers the thing invented to go into public use, or to be publicly sold for use, before he makes application for a patent. His voluntary act or acquiescence in the public sale and use is an abandonment of his right; or rather creates a disability to comply with the terms and conditions on which alone the secretary of state is authorized to grant him a patent.

The opinion of the circuit court was therefore perfectly correct; and the judgment is affirmed with costs. . . .

Questions:

1.) List all of the reasons Justice Story gives for applying a bar of public use.

2.) What relevance has the availability of secrecy as an alternative method of protecting an innovation? The possible combinations of secrecy and patent law?

3.) Would it have mattered if the inventor had told Jenkins to keep their agreement secret? Would it have mattered if the nature of the invention could not be gleaned from its use? For example, what if I invent a fryer with a secret feature that produces perfect doughnuts, but only the doughnuts and not the fryer are made available to the public. May I use the fryer for years, keeping its details secret, and *then* patent it?

6.) Statutory Bar: The Experimental Use Exception

City of Elizabeth v. Pavement Co.
97 U.S. 126 (1877)

Mr. Justice BRADLEY delivered the opinion of the court.

This suit was brought by the American Nicholson Pavement Company against the city of Elizabeth, N.J., George W. Tubbs, and the New Jersey Wood-Paving Company, a corporation of New Jersey, upon a patent issued to Samuel Nicholson, dated Aug. 20, 1867, for a new and improved wooden pavement, being a second reissue of a patent issued to said Nicholson Aug. 8, 1854. The reissued patent was extended in 1868 for a further term of seven years. A copy of it is appended to the bill; and, in the specification, it is declared that the nature and object of the invention consists in providing a process or mode of constructing wooden block pavements upon a foundation along a street or roadway with facility, cheapness, and accuracy, and also in the creation and construction of such a wooden pavement as shall be comparatively permanent and durable, by so uniting and combining all its parts, both superstructure and foundation, as to provide against the slipping of the horses' feet, against noise, against unequal wear, and against rot and consequent sinking away from below. Two plans of making this pavement are specified. Both require a proper foundation on which to lay the blocks, consisting of tarred-paper or hydraulic cement covering the surface of the road-bed to the depth of about two inches, or of a flooring of boards or plank, also covered with tar, or other preventive of moisture. On this foundation, one plan is to set square blocks on end arranged like a checker-board, the alternate rows being shorter than the others, so as to leave narrow grooves or channel-ways to be filled with small broken stone or gravel, and then pouring over the whole melted tar or pitch, whereby the cavities are all filled and cemented together. The other plan is, to arrange the blocks in rows transversely across the street, separated a small space (of about an inch) by strips of board at the bottom, which serve to keep the blocks at a uniform distance apart, and then filling these spaces with the same material as before. The blocks forming the pavement are about eight inches high. The alternate rows of short blocks in the first plan and the strips of board in the second plan should not be higher than four inches. . . .

The bill charges that the defendants infringed this patent by laying down wooden pavements in the city of Elizabeth, N.J., constructed in substantial conformity with the process patented, and prays an account of profits, and an injunction. . . .

[The defendants] averred that the alleged invention of Nicholson was in public use, with his consent and allowance, for six years before he applied for a patent, on a certain avenue in Boston called the Mill-dam; and contended that said public use worked an abandonment of the pretended invention. . . .

The next question to be considered is, whether Nicholson's invention was in public use or on sale, with his consent and allowance, for more than two years prior to his application for a patent, within the meaning of the sixth, seventh, and fifteenth sections of the act of 1836, as qualified by the seventh section of the act of 1839, which were the acts in force in 1854, when he obtained his patent. It is contended by the appellants that the pavement which Nicholson put down by way of experiment, on Mill-dam Avenue in Boston, in 1848, was publicly used for the space of six years before his application for a patent, and that this was a public use within the meaning of the law.

To determine this question, it is necessary to examine the circumstances under which this pavement was put down, and the object and purpose that Nicholson had in view. It is perfectly clear from the evidence that he did not intend to abandon his right to a patent. He had filed a caveat in August, 1847, and he constructed the pavement in question by way of experiment, for the purpose of testing its qualities. The road in which it was put down, though a public road, belonged to the Boston and Roxbury Mill Corporation, which received toll for its use; and Nicholson was a stockholder and treasurer of the corporation. The pavement in question was about seventy-five feet in length, and was laid adjoining to the toll-gate and in front of the toll-house. It was constructed by Nicholson at his own expense, and was placed by him where it was, in order to see the effect upon it of heavily loaded wagons, and of varied and constant use; and also to ascertain its durability, and liability to decay. Joseph L. Lang, who was toll-collector for many years, commencing in 1849, familiar with the road before that time, and with this pavement from the time of its origin, testified as follows: "Mr. Nicholson was there almost daily, and when he came he would examine the pavement, would often walk over it, cane in hand, striking it with his cane, and making particular examination of its condition. He asked me very often how people liked it, and asked me a great many questions about it. I have heard him say a number of times that this was his first experiment with this pavement, and he thought that it was wearing very well. The circumstances that made this locality desirable for the purpose of obtaining a satisfactory test of the durability and value of the pavement were: that there would be a better chance to lay it there; he would have more room and a better chance than in the city; and, besides, it was a place where most everybody went over it, rich and poor. It was a great thoroughfare out of Boston. It was frequently travelled by teams having a load of five or six tons, and some larger. As these teams usually stopped at the toll-house, and started again, the stopping and starting would make as severe a trial to the pavement as it could be put to."

This evidence is corroborated by that of several other witnesses in the cause; the result of the whole being that Nicholson merely intended this piece of pavement as an experiment, to test its usefulness and durability. Was this a public use, within the meaning of the law?

An abandonment of an invention to the public may be evinced by the conduct of the inventor at any time, even within the two years named in the law. The effect of the law is, that no such consequence will necessarily follow from the invention being in public use or on sale, with the inventor's consent and allowance, at any time within two years before his application; but that, if the invention is in public use or on sale prior to that time, it will be conclusive evidence of abandonment, and the patent will be void.

But, in this case, it becomes important to inquire what is such a public use as will have the effect referred to. That the use of the pavement in question was public in one sense cannot be disputed. But can it be said that the invention was in public use? The use of an invention by the inventor himself, or of any other person under his direction, by way of experiment, and in order to bring the invention to perfection, has never been regarded as such a use. Curtis, Patents, sect. 381; *Shaw v. Cooper.*

Now, the nature of a street pavement is such that it cannot be experimented upon satisfactorily except on a highway, which is always public.

When the subject of invention is a machine, it may be tested and tried in a building, either with or without closed doors. In either case, such use is not a public use, within the meaning of the statute, so long as the inventor is engaged, in good faith, in testing its operation. He may see cause to alter it and improve it, or not. His experiments will reveal the fact whether any and what alterations may be necessary. If durability is one of the qualities to be attained, a long period, perhaps years, may be necessary to enable the inventor to discover whether his purpose is accomplished. And though, during all that period, he may not find that any changes are necessary, yet he may be justly said to be using his machine only by way of experiment; and no one would say that such a use, pursued with a bona fide intent of testing the qualities of the machine, would be a public use, within the meaning of the statute. So long as he does not voluntarily allow others to make it and use it, and so long as it is not on sale for general use, he keeps the invention under his own control, and does not lose his title to a patent.

It would not be necessary, in such a case, that the machine should be put up and used only in the inventor's own shop or premises. He may have it put up and used in the premises of another, and the use may inure to the benefit of the owner of the establishment. Still, if used under the surveillance of the inventor, and for the purpose of enabling him to test the machine, and ascertain whether it will answer the purpose intended, and make such alterations and improvements as experience demonstrates to be necessary, it will still be a mere experimental use, and not a public use, within the meaning of the statute.

Whilst the supposed machine is in such experimental use, the public may be incidentally deriving a benefit from it. If it be a grist-mill, or a carding-machine, customers from the surrounding country may enjoy the use of it by having their grain made into flour, or their wool into rolls, and still it will not be in public use, within the meaning of the law.

But if the inventor allows his machine to be used by other persons generally, either with or without compensation, or if it is, with his consent, put on sale for such use, then it will be in public use and on public sale, within the meaning of the law.

If, now, we apply the same principles to this case, the analogy will be seen at once. Nicholson wished to experiment on his pavement. He believed it to be a good thing, but he was not sure; and the only mode in which he could test it was to place a specimen of it in a public roadway. He did this at his own expense, and with the consent of the owners of the road. Durability was one of the qualities to be attained. He wanted to know whether his pavement would stand, and whether it would resist decay. Its character for durability could not be ascertained without its being subjected to use for a considerable time. He subjected it to such use, in good faith, for the simple purpose of ascertaining whether it was what he claimed it to be. Did he do any thing more than the inventor of the supposed machine might do, in testing his invention? The public had the incidental use of the pavement, it is true; but was the invention in public use, within the meaning of the statute? We think not. The proprietors of the road alone used the invention, and used it at Nicholson's request, by way of experiment. The only way in which they could use it was by allowing the public to pass over the pavement.

Had the city of Boston, or other parties, used the invention, by laying down the pavement in other streets and places, with Nicholson's consent and allowance, then, indeed, the invention itself would have been in public use, within the meaning of the law; but this was not the case. Nicholson did not sell it, nor allow others to use it or sell it. He did not let it go beyond his control. He did nothing that indicated any intent to do so. He kept it under his own eyes, and never for a moment abandoned the intent to obtain a patent for it. . . .

It is sometimes said that an inventor acquires an undue advantage over the public by delaying to take out a patent, inasmuch as he thereby preserves the monopoly to himself for a longer period than is allowed by the policy of the law; but this cannot be said with justice when the delay is occasioned by a *bona fide* effort to bring his invention to perfection, or to ascertain whether it will answer the purpose intended. His monopoly only continues for the allotted period, in any event; and it is the interest of the public, as well as himself, that the invention should be perfect and properly tested, before a patent is granted for it. Any attempt to use it for a profit, and not by way of experiment, for a longer period than two years before the application, would deprive the inventor of his right to a patent. . . .

We think there is no error in the decree of the Circuit Court, except in making the city of Elizabeth and George W. Tubbs accountable for the profits. As to them a decree for injunction only to prevent them from constructing the pavement during the term of the patent, should have been rendered; which, of course, cannot now be made. As to the New Jersey Wood-Paving Company, the decree was in all respects correct. . . .

Questions:

1.) The court here discussed the two-year grace period an inventor is allowed after a disclosure before filing a patent. How long is that period now? (In other words, how long does an inventor have after his first disclosure to file a patent?)

2.) How can a road that is being used by the public for six years be said not to be disclosed to the public? Distinguish the "use" here from that in *Pennock*.

3.) "So long as he does not voluntarily allow others to make it and use it, and so long as it is not on sale for general use, he keeps the invention under his own control, and does not lose his title to a patent." Explain why the court here rules that the public had no more than incidental use of the road.

4.) "Any attempt to use it for a profit, and not by way of experiment, for a longer period than two years before the application, would deprive the inventor of his right to a patent." Why does it matter that the inventor not use the invention for a profit?

Note:

Today's courts still apply the standards in City of Elizabeth, but they also put considerable stress on such things as the nature of control exercised by the inventor and the extent of any confidentiality agreement covering the use. The Federal Circuit has listed thirteen factors potentially relevant in assessing experimental use: (1) the necessity for public testing, (2) the amount of control over the experiment retained by the inventor, (3) the nature of the invention, (4) the length of the test period, (5) whether payment was made, (6) whether there was a secrecy obligation, (7) whether records of the experiment were kept, (8) who conducted the experiment, (9) the degree of commercial exploitation during testing, (10) whether the invention reasonably requires evaluation under actual conditions of use, (11) whether testing was systematically performed, (12) whether the inventor continually monitored the invention during testing, and (13) the nature of contacts made with potential customers.

PROBLEM 20-1

a.) In June of 2013, Google released an experimental, "beta" version of their Ngram viewer. Ngrams are an offshoot of the Google Books project that you read about in the copyright section of this book. Google has scanned the words in a representative sample of books in English from 1800 to the present day. The original Ngram viewer allowed you to search for the frequency with which words appeared over that time. Thus, for example, you could look at the frequency with which the word "feminism" or the phrase "public domain" appeared. You could track the rise and fall of words such as "awesome," "gnarly" or "swive." The new viewer is called "Zeitgeist." Zeitgeist allows you to do much more contextual searches. For example you can do "most likely to be found with" searches, which indicate which words are most likely to be found with other words at any moment in history. (For example, "nattering" was once likely to be accompanied by "nabobs of negativism.") Zeitgeist has an emotion-coding device, which assigns emotional "heat" to contexts and can as a result give you a sense of whether a word tends to be associated with strong emotions.

It is common in the software industry to release so called "beta-test" versions of software in order to test them. Zeitgeist is prominently marked "Experimental beta test version." The user does not install any software, simply queries a typical Google search form on the Zeitgeist web page. The interface is clean: there are no terms of use or advertisements to be seen. **In August 2014, Google asks you if they can patent the Zeitgeist software. Assume that Zeitgeist is patentable subject matter and that it is otherwise novel and non-obvious. Your answer?**

b.) Aspirin has long been in the public domain. Bayer, aspirin's original inventor, has just discovered that taking a baby aspirin every other day reduces the risk of heart attack or stroke. Aspirin has side effects however, often causing gastric upset. Bayer does further experimentation and finds that taking aspirin with milk or food helps to avoid those side effects. It wishes to patent "a method for lowering risk of heart attack and strokes by the use of acetylsalicylic acid [aspirin's ingredient] in certain doses combined with various gastric protective measures." For purposes of this hypothetical assume that no-one has ever detected the correlation between aspirin and heart-health before. **Is Bayer's method novel? Does it pass the patentable subject matter test?**

c.) **What are the differences between the requirement of novelty (and, later, non-obviousness) described here in the context of patents and the requirement of originality explained in the copyright context in *Feist*? Are there constitutional differences?**

CHAPTER TWENTY-ONE
Non-Obviousness

Introduction

Non-obviousness is in many ways the heart of the patent system, the place where we draw the most important line between sub-patentable and patentable innovation. As you learned in the previous chapter, lack of novelty—or "anticipation"—is a complete bar to patentability. Yet as we saw in that chapter, for an invention to be anticipated, every element of it needs to be present in a single prior art reference. The person alleging anticipation is effectively saying "we've already got it" and the "it" is a single thing.

Obviousness is different. The person alleging that an invention is obvious is not necessarily saying it already exists. She is saying that it consists of a trivial recombination of elements of the prior art, that a Person Having Ordinary Skill in The Art (or PHOSITA) would have been able to make the leap from those prior art references to come up with the new invention. This is an inherently synthetic task. It requires us to consider a counterfactual—to put ourselves in the shoes of an imaginary PHOSITA before the new invention, to consider all the resources in the art that would have been available to that person, as well as the nature of the problem to be solved, and then to ask the question "was this combination of elements obvious"?

> **§ 103 Conditions for patentability; non-obvious subject matter.**[1]
> **A patent for a claimed invention may not be obtained, notwithstanding that the claimed invention is not identically disclosed as set forth in section 102, if the differences between the claimed invention and the prior art are such that the claimed invention as a whole would have been obvious before the effective filing date of the claimed invention to a person having ordinary skill in the art to which the claimed invention pertains. Patentability shall not be negated by the manner in which the invention was made.**

[handwritten margin note: Patentability requires nonobviousness]

The story of the non-obviousness statutory requirement is rooted in some wrangling between the courts and Congress. The courts, led by the Supreme Court, had set out tests for what counted as a patentable invention that many believed to be too high. Some referred to them as requiring "a flash of genius." Congress responded by passing the predecessor of § 103. It was the interpretation of that section, and the analysis of whether it trammeled on constitutionally forbidden territory, that was at stake in a case you have read before, *Graham v. John Deere*. We will be interested to see if your reaction to that case is different when you read it in the specific context of non-obviousness.

---

[1] **[USPTO Editor's Note:** Applicable to any patent application subject to the first inventor to file provisions of the AIA (see 35 U.S.C. 100 (note)). See 35 U.S.C. 103 (pre-AIA) for the law otherwise applicable.]

Graham v. John Deere Co.
383 U.S. 1 (1966)

Mr. Justice CLARK delivered the opinion of the Court.

After a lapse of 15 years, the Court again focuses its attention on the patentability of inventions under the standard of Art. I, § 8, cl. 8, of the Constitution and under the conditions prescribed by the laws of the United States. Since our last expression on patent validity, *Great A.&P. Tea Co. v. Supermarket Equipment Corp.* (1950), the Congress has for the first time expressly added a third statutory dimension to the two requirements of novelty and utility that had been the sole statutory test since the Patent Act of 1793. This is the test of obviousness, i.e., whether 'the subject matter sought to be patented and the prior art are such that the subject matter as a whole would have been obvious at the time the invention was made to a person having ordinary skill in the art to which said subject matter pertains. Patentability shall not be negatived by the manner in which the invention was made.' 35 U.S.C. § 103.

The questions, involved in each of the companion cases before us, are what effect the 1952 Act had upon traditional statutory and judicial tests of patentability and what definitive tests are now required. We have concluded that the 1952 Act was intended to codify judicial precedents embracing the principle long ago announced by this Court in *Hotchkiss v. Greenwood* (1851) and that, while the clear language of § 103 places emphasis on an inquiry into obviousness, the general level of innovation necessary to sustain patentability remains the same.

I.

The Cases.

(a). No. 11, *Graham v. John Deere Co.*, an infringement suit by petitioners, presents a conflict between two Circuits over the validity of a single patent on a 'Clamp for vibrating Shank Plows.' The invention, a combination of old mechanical elements, involves a device designed to absorb shock from plow shanks as they plow through rocky soil and thus to prevent damage to the plow. In 1955, the Fifth Circuit had held the patent valid under its rule that when a combination produces an 'old result in a cheaper and otherwise more advan-

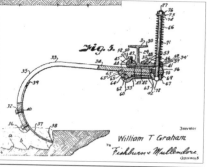

An image from Graham's patent

tageous way,' it is patentable. *Jeoffroy Mfg., Inc. v. Graham*. In 1964, the Eighth Circuit held, in the case at bar, that there was no new result in the patented combination and that the patent was, therefore, not valid. We granted certiorari. Although we have determined that neither Circuit applied the correct test, we conclude that the patent is invalid under § 103 and, therefore, we affirm the judgment of the Eighth Circuit. . . .

II.

At the outset it must be remembered that the federal patent power stems from a specific constitutional provision which authorizes the Congress 'To promote the Progress of * * * useful Arts, by securing for limited Times to * * * Inventors the exclusive Right to their * * * Discoveries.' Art. I, s 8, cl. 8. The clause is both a grant of power and a limitation. This qualified authority, unlike the power often exercised in the sixteenth and seventeenth centuries by the English Crown, is limited to the promotion of advances in the 'useful arts.' It was written against the backdrop of the practices—eventually curtailed by the Statute of

Monopolies—of the Crown in granting monopolies to court favorites in goods or businesses which had long before been enjoyed by the public. The Congress in the exercise of the patent power may not overreach the restraints imposed by the stated constitutional purpose. Nor may it enlarge the patent monopoly without regard to the innovation, advancement or social benefit gained thereby. Moreover, Congress may not authorize the issuance of patents whose effects are to remove existent knowledge from the public domain, or to restrict free access to materials already available. Innovation, advancement, and things which add to the sum of useful knowledge are inherent requisites in a patent system which, by constitutional command, must "promote the Progress of * * * useful Arts." This is the *standard* expressed in the Constitution, and it may not be ignored. And it is in this light that patent validity "requires reference to a standard written into the Constitution."

Within the limits of the constitutional grant, the Congress may, of course, implement the stated purpose of the Framers by selecting the policy which, in its judgment, best effectuates the constitutional aim. This is but a corollary to the grant to Congress of any Article I power. Within the scope established by the Constitution, Congress may set out conditions and tests for patentability. It is the duty of the Commissioner of Patents and of the courts in the administration of the patent system to give effect to the constitutional standard by appropriate application, in each case, of the statutory scheme of the Congress.

Congress quickly responded to the bidding of the Constitution by enacting the Patent Act of 1790 during the second session of the First Congress. It created an agency in the Department of State headed by the Secretary of State, the Secretary of the Department of War and the Attorney General, any two of whom could issue a patent for a period not exceeding 14 years to any petitioner that 'hath * * * invented or discovered any useful art, manufacture, * * * or device, or any improvement therein not before known or used' if the board found that 'the invention or discovery (was) sufficiently useful and important. * * *' 1 Stat. 110. This group, whose members administered the patent system along with their other public duties, was known by its own designation as 'Commissioners for the Promotion of Useful Arts.'

Thomas Jefferson, who as Secretary of State was a member of the group, was its moving spirit and might well be called the 'first administrator of our patent system.' See Federico 238 (1936). He was not only an administrator of the patent system under the 1790 Act, but was also the author of the 1793 Patent Act. In addition, Jefferson was himself an inventor of great note. His unpatented improvements on plows, to mention but one line of his inventions, won acclaim and recognition on both sides of the Atlantic. Because of his active interest and influence in the early development of the patent system, Jefferson's views on the general nature of the limited patent monopoly under the Constitution, as well as his conclusions as to conditions for patentability under the statutory scheme, are worthy of note.

Jefferson, like other Americans, had an instinctive aversion to monopolies. It was a monopoly on tea that sparked the Revolution and Jefferson certainly did not favor an equivalent form of monopoly under the new government. His abhorrence of monopoly extended initially to patents as well. From France, he wrote to Madison (July 1788) urging a Bill of Rights provision restricting monopoly, and as against the argument that limited monopoly might serve to incite 'ingenuity,' he argued forcefully that 'the benefit even of limited monopolies is too doubtful to be opposed to that of their general suppression.'

His views ripened, however, and in another letter to Madison (Aug. 1789) after the drafting of the Bill of Rights, Jefferson stated that he would have been pleased by an express provision in this form: 'Art. 9. Monopolies may be allowed to persons for their own productions in literature, & their own inventions in the arts, for a term not exceeding __ years, but for no longer term & no other purpose.' And he later wrote: 'Certainly an inventor ought to be allowed a right to the benefit of his invention for some certain time. * * * Nobody wishes more than I do that ingenuity should receive a liberal encouragement.'

Jefferson's philosophy on the nature and purpose of the patent monopoly is expressed in a letter to Isaac McPherson, a portion of which we set out in the margin.[2] He rejected a natural rights theory in intellectual property rights and clearly recognized the social and economic rationale of the patent system. The patent monopoly was not designed to secure to the inventor his natural right in his discoveries. Rather, it was a reward, an inducement, to bring forth new knowledge. The grant of an exclusive right to an invention was the creation of society—at odds with the inherent free nature of disclosed ideas—and was not to be freely given. Only inventions and discoveries which furthered human knowledge, and were new and useful, justified the special inducement of a limited private monopoly. Jefferson did not believe in granting patents for small details, obvious improvements, or frivolous devices. His writings evidence his insistence upon a high level of patentability.

As a member of the patent board for several years, Jefferson saw clearly the difficulty in 'drawing a line between the things which are worth to the public the embarrassment of an exclusive patent, and those which are not.' The board on which he served sought to draw such a line and formulated several rules which are preserved in Jefferson's correspondence. Despite the board's efforts, Jefferson saw 'with what slow progress a system of general rules could be matured.' Because of the 'abundance' of cases and the fact that the investigations occupied 'more time of the members of the board than they could spare from higher duties, the whole was turned over to the judiciary, to be matured into a system, under which every one might know when his actions were safe and lawful.' Letter to McPherson. Apparently Congress agreed with Jefferson and the board that the courts should develop additional conditions for patentability. Although the Patent Act was amended, revised or codified some 50 times between 1790 and 1950, Congress steered clear of a statutory set of requirements other than the bare novelty and utility tests reformulated in Jefferson's draft of the 1793 Patent Act.

III.

The difficulty of formulating conditions for patentability was heightened by the generality of the constitutional grant and the statutes implementing it, together with the underlying policy of the patent system that 'the things which are worth to the public the embarrassment of an exclusive patent,' as Jefferson put it, must outweigh the restrictive effect of the limited patent monopoly. The inherent problem was to develop some means of weeding out those inventions which would not be disclosed or devised but for the inducement of a patent.

---

[2] "Stable ownership is the gift of social law, and is given late in the progress of society. It would be curious, then, if an idea, the fugitive fermentation of an individual brain, could, of natural right, be claimed in exclusive and stable property. If nature has made anyone thing less susceptible than all others of exclusive property, it is the action of the thinking power called an idea, which an individual may exclusively possess as long as he keeps it to himself; but the moment it is divulged, it forces itself into the possession of everyone, and the receiver cannot dispossess himself of it. Its peculiar character, too, is that no one possesses the less because every other possesses the whole of it. He who receives an idea from me receives instruction himself without lessening mine, as he who lights his taper at mine, receives light without darkening me. That ideas should freely spread from one to another over the globe, for the moral and mutual instruction of man and improvement of his condition, seems to have been peculiarly and benevolently designed by nature when she made them, like fire, expansible over all space, without lessening their density in any point, and, like the air in which we breathe, move, and have our physical being, incapable of confinement or exclusive appropriation. Inventions then cannot, in nature, be a subject of property. Society may give an exclusive right to the profits arising from them, as an encouragement to men to pursue ideas which may produce utility, but this may or may not be done according to the will and convenience of the society, without claim or complaint from anybody." VI Writings of Thomas Jefferson at 180–181 (Washington ed.).

This Court formulated a general condition of patentability in 1851 in *Hotchkiss v. Greenwood*. The patent involved a mere substitution of materials—porcelain or clay for wood or metal in doorknobs—and the Court condemned it, holding:

'(U)nless more ingenuity and skill * * * were required * * * than were possessed by an ordinary mechanic acquainted with the business, there was an absence of that degree of skill and ingenuity which constitute essential elements of every invention. In other words, the improvement is the work of the skilful mechanic, not that of the inventor.'

... The *Hotchkiss* test laid the cornerstone of the judicial evolution suggested by Jefferson and left to the courts by Congress. The language in the case, and in those which followed, gave birth to 'invention' as a word of legal art signifying patentable inventions. ... The *Hotchkiss* formulation, however, lies not in any label, but in its functional approach to questions of patentability. In practice, *Hotchkiss* has required a comparison between the subject matter of the patent, or patent application, and the background skill of the calling. It has been from this comparison that patentability was in each case determined.

IV.

The 1952 Patent Act.

The Act sets out the conditions of patentability in three sections. An analysis of the structure of these three sections indicates that patentability is dependent upon three explicit conditions: novelty and utility, as articulated and defined in § 101 and § 102, and nonobviousness, the new statutory formulation, as set out in § 103. The first two sections, which trace closely the 1874 codification, express the "new and useful" tests which have always existed in the statutory scheme and, for our purposes here, need no clarification. The pivotal section around which the present controversy centers is § 103. It provides:

"§ 103. Conditions for patentability; non-obvious subject matter" "A patent may not be obtained though the invention is not identically disclosed or described as set forth in section 102 of this title, if the differences between the subject matter sought to be patented and the prior art are such that the subject matter as a whole would have been obvious at the time the invention was made to a person having ordinary skill in the art to which said subject matter pertains. Patentability shall not be negatived by the manner in which the invention was made."

The section is cast in relatively unambiguous terms. Patentability is to depend, in addition to novelty and utility, upon the "non-obvious" nature of the "subject matter sought to be patented" to a person having ordinary skill in the pertinent art.

The first sentence of this section is strongly reminiscent of the language in *Hotchkiss*. Both formulations place emphasis on the pertinent art existing at the time the invention was made, and both are implicitly tied to advances in that art. The major distinction is that Congress has emphasized "nonobviousness" as the operative test of the section, rather than the less definite "invention" language of *Hotchkiss* that Congress thought had led to "a large variety" of expressions in decisions and writings. In the title itself, the Congress used the phrase "Conditions for patentability; *non-obvious subject matter*" (italics added), thus focusing upon "nonobviousness," rather than "invention." The Senate and House Reports reflect this emphasis in these terms:

"Section 103, for the first time in our statute, provides a condition which exists in the law and has existed for more than 100 years, but only by reason of decisions of the courts. An invention which has been made, and which is new in the sense that the same thing has not been made before, may still not be patentable if the difference between the new thing and what was known before is not considered sufficiently great to warrant a patent. That has been expressed in a large variety of ways in decisions of the courts and in writings. Section 103 states this requirement in the title. It refers to the difference between the subject matter sought to be patented and the prior art, meaning what was known before as described in section 102. If this difference is such that the subject matter as a whole would have been obvious at the time to a person skilled in the art, then the subject matter cannot be patented.

That provision paraphrases language which has often been used in decisions of the courts, and the section is added to the statute for uniformity and definiteness. This section should have a stabilizing effect and minimize great departures which have appeared in some cases."

It is undisputed that this section was, for the first time, a statutory expression of an additional requirement for patentability, originally expressed in *Hotchkiss*. It also seems apparent that Congress intended by the last sentence of § 103 to abolish the test it believed this Court announced in the controversial phrase 'flash of creative genius,' used in *Cuno Engineering Corp. v. Automatic Devices Corp.* (1941).

It is contended, however, by some of the parties and by several of the amici that the first sentence of § 103 was intended to sweep away judicial precedents and to lower the level of patentability. Others contend that the Congress intended to codify the essential purpose reflected in existing judicial precedents—the rejection of insignificant variations and innovations of a commonplace sort—and also to focus inquiries under § 103 upon nonobviousness, rather than upon 'invention,' as a means of achieving more stability and predictability in determining patentability and validity.

The Reviser's Note to this section, with apparent reference to *Hotchkiss*, recognizes that judicial requirements as to 'lack of patentable novelty (have) been followed since at least as early as 1850.' The note indicates that the section was inserted because it 'may have some stabilizing effect, and also to serve as a basis for the addition at a later time of some criteria which may be worked out.' To this same effect are the reports of both Houses, which state that the first sentence of the section 'paraphrases language which has often been used in decisions of the courts, and the section is added to the statute for uniformity and definiteness.'

We believe that this legislative history, as well as other sources, shows that the revision was not intended by Congress to change the general level of patentable invention. We conclude that the section was intended merely as a codification of judicial precedents embracing the *Hotchkiss* condition, with congressional directions that inquiries into the obviousness of the subject matter sought to be patented are a prerequisite to patentability.

V.

Approached in this light, the § 103 additional condition, when followed realistically, will permit a more practical test of patentability. The emphasis on nonobviousness is one of inquiry, not quality, and, as such, comports with the constitutional strictures.

While the ultimate question of patent validity is one of law, the § 103 condition, which is but one of three conditions, each of which must be satisfied, lends itself to several basic factual inquiries. Under § 103, the scope and content of the prior art are to be determined; differences between the prior art and the claims at issue are to be ascertained; and the level of ordinary skill in the pertinent art resolved. Against this background, the obviousness or nonobviousness of the subject matter is determined. Such secondary considerations as commercial success, long felt but unsolved needs, failure of others, etc., might be utilized to give light to the circumstances surrounding the origin of the subject matter sought to be patented. As indicia of obviousness or nonobviousness, these inquiries may have relevancy.

This is not to say, however, that there will not be difficulties in applying the nonobviousness test. What is obvious is not a question upon which there is likely to be uniformity of thought in every given factual context. The difficulties, however, are comparable to those encountered daily by the courts in such frames of reference as negligence and *scienter*, and should be amenable to a case-by-case development. We believe that strict observance of the requirements laid down here will result in that uniformity and definiteness which Congress called for in the 1952 Act.

While we have focused attention on the appropriate standard to be applied by the courts, it must be remembered that the primary responsibility for sifting out unpatentable material lies in the Patent Office. To await litigation is—for all practical purposes—to debilitate the patent system. We have observed a notorious difference between the standards applied by the Patent Office and by the courts. While many reasons can be adduced to explain the discrepancy, one may well be the free rein often exercised by Examiners in their use of the concept of "invention." In this connection we note that the Patent Office is confronted with a most difficult task. Almost 100,000 applications for patents are filed each year. Of these, about 50,000 are granted and the backlog now runs well over 200,000. *1965 Annual Report of the Commissioner of Patents*. This is itself a compelling reason for the Commissioner to strictly adhere to the 1952 Act as interpreted here. This would, we believe, not only expedite disposition but bring about a closer concurrence between administrative and judicial precedent.

Although we conclude here that the inquiry which the Patent Office and the courts must make as to patentability must be beamed with greater intensity on the requirements of § 103, it bears repeating that we find no change in the general strictness with which the overall test is to be applied. We have been urged to find in § 103 a relaxed standard, supposedly a congressional reaction to the "increased standard" applied by this Court in its decisions over the last 20 or 30 years. The standard has remained invariable in this Court. Technology, however, has advanced—and with remarkable rapidity in the last 50 years. Moreover, the ambit of applicable art in given fields of science has widened by disciplines unheard of a half century ago. It is but an evenhanded application to require that those persons granted the benefit of a patent monopoly be charged with an awareness of these changed conditions. The same is true of the less technical, but still useful arts. He who seeks to build a better mousetrap today has a long path to tread before reaching the Patent Office. . . .

Questions:

1.) As we saw in Chapter 2, in the context of copyright law the Supreme Court has taken a very deferential approach towards Congress's interpretation of its powers under the Intellectual Property Clause. *Golan*, for example, appeared to set no limits on Congress's ability to withdraw material from the public domain and place it back under copyright. In other words, the *Golan* court allowed Congress to do the very thing the *Graham* court says can never be done.

> The Congress in the exercise of the patent power may not overreach the restraints imposed by the stated constitutional purpose. Nor may it enlarge the patent monopoly without regard to the innovation, advancement or social benefit gained thereby. **Moreover, Congress may not authorize the issuance of patents whose effects are to remove existent knowledge from the public domain, or to restrict free access to materials already available.**

Is *Graham* still good law, at least in the context of Congress's ability to make *patent* as opposed to copyright law? Why might we think the two areas would receive different levels of scrutiny or deference from the courts?

2.) How is the non-obviousness requirement (and for that matter the requirement of novelty) implicated by the bolded sentence above? How does it set boundaries on the statutory definitions of novelty and non-obviousness that Congress may set forth? Without an adequate definition of novelty or non-obviousness, what knowledge could otherwise be withdrawn from the public domain, what access impeded to materials already available? The answer seems relatively clear when it comes to the limits of Congress's powers with respect to *novelty*. If the thing already exists and the public has access to it, then putting it under patent is exactly what *Graham* says Congress cannot authorize and thus, presumably, the courts and the PTO cannot do. But what about *non-obviousness*? What knowledge is being removed from the public domain? What free access to material already available is being restricted? Is the court presuming that the public domain consists not merely of discrete objects of knowledge, but of the *connections* that could be made between those objects by any reasonably skilled practitioner of the art?

3.) Question 2 leads to the question whether the Intellectual Property Clause—as interpreted by *Graham*—requires something *at least as rigorous* as the current standard for non-obviousness. Nearly as rigorous? What are the constitutional limits? Imagine Congress had rewritten § 103 to read

> **A patent for a claimed invention may not be obtained, notwithstanding that the claimed invention is not identically disclosed as set forth in section 102, unless the inventor thought fairly hard about his work. (The courts should not construe this to require any kind of rocket scientist stuff, but the inventor has to make a mild effort to look beyond the blatantly obvious.) Patentability shall not be negated by the manner in which the invention was made.**

Is this constitutional under *Graham*'s standard?

4.) As we will see in a moment, *Graham*'s four part analysis of obviousness is central to the doctrine in this area. Beyond that does *Graham*'s constitutional analysis give courts any guidance about *how* to conduct that inquiry?

1.) A Four Step Test for Obviousness

Graham laid down the basic structure under which analysis of obviousness proceeds to this day.

> 1.) **"The scope and content of the prior art are to be determined."**
> 2.) **"Differences between the prior art and the claims at issue are to be ascertained"**
> 3.) **"and the level of ordinary skill in the pertinent art resolved."**
> 4.) **"Such secondary considerations as commercial success, long felt but unsolved needs, failure of others, etc., might be utilized to give light to the circumstances surrounding the origin of the subject matter sought to be patented."**

Reciprocal Definitions? The alert amongst you will have noticed that some of these inquiries are mutually dependent. How do I know what the scope and content of the prior art is, unless I know who the PHOSITA is and *vice versa*? If most people working in the field of developing new cryptographic software tools are mathematics PhDs with extensive knowledge of prior cryptographic schemes, then the "scope of the prior art" will include much more than if they are computer scientists who dabble in cryptography. But conversely, the relevant art literally defines the field in which the PHOSITA can be described.

Hindsight Bias? *Graham* describes one danger for patent law—that too lax a standard for inventions will give us a patent system that withdraws material from the public domain and conveys statutory monopolies for mere tinkering. But there is an opposing danger: the psychological literature strongly confirms the existence of a bias that is conventionally referred to as 20/20 hindsight vision. In retrospect, *everything* looks obvious. How do we "de-bias" our decisions about whether an innovation *was* obvious or not?

One answer is the *Graham* structure itself. By formalizing the steps of the analysis, forcing the examiner, or the court, to "show their work," we might hope that we would avoid hindsight bias. A second answer is provided by the "secondary considerations." While courts have put varying weights on them, secondary considerations force one to consider the counterfactual. If this was so obvious, and yet everyone in the industry wanted it, why did no one do it before? If it was so obvious, why did others fail repeatedly? If it was so obvious—to use another secondary consideration not mentioned here—why is it that many firms are willing to *license* the technology, apparently in the belief the patent is sound?

The rest of the chapter proceeds as follows. We will start with a case that goes through all of the *Graham* steps *en route* to a decision on obviousness. Then we will turn to a few instructive cases fleshing out some of the individual steps of the *Graham* inquiry. What is the scope and content of the prior art? Who bears the burden of proof on obviousness? Is an invention obvious if there are thousands of possible solutions to a problem and the PHOSITA would know to try them, one after another? How do we define the PHOSITA?

Note: In *KSR v. Teleflex* (2007), the Supreme Court affirmed the *Graham v. Deere* framework for assessing obviousness and endorsed an "expansive and flexible" approach to the inquiry, rejecting the Federal Circuit's overly "rigid" application of its "'teaching, suggestion, or motivation' (TSM) test, under which a patent claim is only proved obvious if the prior art, the problem's nature, or the knowledge of a person having ordinary skill in the art reveals some motivation or suggestion to combine the prior art teachings."

Stratoflex, Inc. v. Aeroquip Corp.
713 F.2d 1530 (Fed. Cir. 1983)

MARKEY, Chief Judge.

II. Background
A. The Technology

Stratoflex and Aeroquip manufacture electrically conductive polytetrafluoroethylene (PTFE) [also referred to as "Teflon"] tubing used in the aircraft and missile industry to convey pressurized fuel, lubricants, and other fluids.

PTFE has replaced organic and synthetic rubbers and plastic in fuel hoses because it has a number of superior characteristics. Though pure PTFE is dielectric (nonconductive), it can be made with fillers to make it conductive, though the "filled" tubing is more susceptible to leakage when voids form between the PTFE and filler particles.

B. The Invention

The Slade invention relates to a composite PTFE tubing, formed of an inner layer of electrically conductive PTFE having particles such as carbon black uniformly distributed in it and an outer layer of essentially pure non-conductive PTFE. Claims 1 and 7 are representative:

> 1. A tubular extrudate formed of attached concentric tubular extrusions, the inner tubular extrusion comprising associated particles of unsintered tetrafluoroethylene polymer and pulverulent, inert, electrically conductive particles, and the outer tubular extrusion comprising associated particles of unsintered tetrafluoroethylene polymer.
>
> 7. A tube of polytetrafluoroethylene and the like for conducting fluids under pressure and including means for discharge of internal static electricity to the ends of the tube and grounding the same from the tube interior at said ends in order to maintain the polytetrafluoroethylene tubing performance characteristics, said tubing having an integral polytetrafluoroethylene wall structure with an interior liner portion of a substantially annular conformation from end to end and having a uniform dispersion of electrically conductive particles embedded therein, the major portion of said tubing wall completely surrounding said liner portion exteriorly and being relatively nonconductive in character, said surrounding portion together with said liner containing fluid under pressures uniformly within said tubing. . . .

The particles in the inner layer of the claimed tubing dissipate electrostatic charges built up on the inner surface of the tubing, conducting them lengthwise of the tubing to grounded metal fittings at the ends of a hose assembly of which the tubing is part, to prevent arcing or discharging through the tubing wall to the surrounding metal braid. Arcing causes "pin holes" through which fuel can leak. The outer layer is coextruded or bonded around the inner layer to contain any fuel leaking through the inner layer. The composite tubing has excellent conductivity, while retaining the desirable characteristics of PTFE tubing.

C. Events Leading to the '087 Patent

Pure PTFE tubing had been used successfully in aircraft engines since at least 1956. In 1959, with the introduction of hydrocarbon jet fuels, leaks were noticed. Aeroquip assigned two staff engineers, Abbey and Upham, to determine the cause. They found the problem to be the arcing of electrostatic charges through the wall of the pure dielectric PTFE tubing to create "pin holes" as described above.

Abbey and Upham found the "pin hole" phenomenon exhibited by all three types of PTFE (White-Titeflex; Pink/Red-Aeroquip; Black-Goodrich) used in aircraft engines. The black tubing appeared superior because the carbon black it contained gave it an intermittent conductivity. The carbon black took the form of discontinuous strings and arcing across the spaces between string ends conveyed charges to the ends of the tubing. Electrical erosion of the strings, however, widened the spaces, destroying conductivity and leading to the "pin hole" phenomenon. Abbey and Upham concluded that susceptibility of PTFE tubing to "pin holing" was proportional to its conductivity, and that carbon black increased the conductivity of PTFE tubing.

In early 1960, having determined the cause of leaking, Aeroquip approached Raybestos-Manhattan (Raybestos), a PTFE hose manufacturer, for a solution. Aeroquip later purchased the hose section of Raybestos, obtaining the Slade patent by mesne assignment.

Raybestos assigned the project to the inventor, Winton Slade, who prepared several samples of conductive PTFE tubing (powdered lead, copper, chemically etched, and carbon black) and sent them for testing to Aeroquip in the summer of 1960. In the Fall, Aeroquip ordered a small production quantity of carbon black tubing. That tubing was not a composite and the carbon black was not uniformly distributed in it.

Slade conceived of the composite tube of the invention as early as August 5, 1960 and reduced it to practice in November of 1961. He filed a patent application on May 22, 1962, with claims directed to the composite tubing and also to various processes for making it. . . .

. . . Slade's original application issued with its product claims as the '087 patent on October 1, 1969.

D. Stratoflex Actions

From 1962 to 1970, Stratoflex purchased PTFE tubing containing carbon black from B.F. Goodrich. When Goodrich ceased production, Stratoflex purchased conductive PTFE tubing made by Titeflex under its license. Stratoflex then began manufacturing and selling its own "124" and "127" composite tubing having an inner layer with conductive carbon black uniformly dispersed throughout, and an outer layer that is essentially non-conductive, though that outer layer includes a small amount of carbon black to color the tubing and to aid extrusion.

On December 8, 1978, Aeroquip charged that Stratoflex's unauthorized manufacture and sale of "124" and "127" tubing infringed its rights under the '087 patent.

E. Trial and Opinion

Trial was held on December 15, 16, 18, 19 and 22, 1980. Stratoflex alleged that the '087 patent was invalid as anticipated under 35 U.S.C. § 102, as having been in public use or on sale, 35 U.S.C. § 102(b); for obviousness, 35 U.S.C. § 103; or because the claims were indefinite, 35 U.S.C. § 112. Judge Boyle[*] decided the validity issue on 35 U.S.C. § 103, and the appeal concerns only that Section.

I. VALIDITY

... (B) Obviousness

The declaration that claims 1, 3, 4, 6, and 7 of the '087 patent are invalid was based on a conclusion that the inventions set forth in those claims would have been obvious under 35 U.S.C. § 103, in the light of facts found in the course of following the guidelines set forth in *Graham v. John Deere Co.* (1966). Aeroquip contends that error occurred in findings on the scope and content of the prior art, level of ordinary skill, and differences between the prior art and the claimed invention, and in the legal conclusion of obviousness based on those findings.

Scope and Content of the Prior Art

Aeroquip contends that the scope of the relevant prior art excludes rubber hose because PTFE is a unique material, possessing properties that differ significantly from rubber, and that, because the claims are limited to PTFE, the rubber hose art could at most be peripherally relevant as background information.

The scope of the prior art has been defined as that "reasonably pertinent to the particular problem with which the inventor was involved." *In re Wood* (Cust. & Pat. App. 1979). The problem confronting Slade was preventing electrostatic buildup in PTFE

---

[*] [Casebook Editors' comment: No relation.]

tubing caused by hydrocarbon fuel flow while precluding leakage of fuel. None of the unique properties of PTFE would change the nature of that problem. Nor would anything of record indicate that one skilled in the art would not include the rubber hose art in his search for a solution to that problem.

Indeed, Slade himself referred to a standard textbook on conductive carbon black in rubber when he began his search for a solution. Judge Boyle correctly found Slade's act an acknowledgement by the problem solver of what he considered relevant prior art.

The examiner cited two prior art references in the rubber hose art, one disclosing the problem of electrostatic buildup caused by fuel flow. The Abbey-Upham report, though concerned with PTFE, included a conductivity comparison with carbon black filled rubber hose, and its bibliography listed several articles on electrostatic buildup in rubber. The record reflects that PTFE and rubber are used by the same hose manufacturers to make hoses and that the same and similar problems have been experienced with both. There is no basis for finding that a solution found for a problem experienced with one material would not be looked to when facing a problem with the other. The finding that the rubber hose art is relevant and thus within the scope of the art was not clearly erroneous.

The content of the prior art included the Abbey-Upham Report and several patents relating to conductive and composite rubber hose and to PTFE tubing.

The Abbey-Upham Report, as above indicated, discloses the cause of PTFE tubing "pin holes" as the arcing of electrostatic charges laterally through the non-conductive PTFE tubing wall to the surrounding metal braid, that carbon black increases conductivity of PTFE, and that susceptibility of PTFE tubing to "pinholing" is directly proportional to its conductivity. Judge Boyle correctly found the report to have disclosed the basic concepts underlying the claimed invention, but not that of forming PTFE tubing as a composite having a conductive inner layer and a nonconductive outer layer.

United States Patent No. 2,341,360 ('360 patent) teaches composite tubing having carbon black in one layer to make it electrically conductive for dissipation of static electricity.

U.S. Patent No. 2,632,205 ('205 patent) teaches a rubber or plastic composite tubing for conveying fluids and having powdered metal or other conductive materials embedded along the inner wall to conduct electric charges lengthwise of the tubing.

U.S. Patent No. 3,070,132 teaches extrusion of carbon black mixed with plastic to form a continuous conductive stripe in a normally dielectric tubing to prevent accumulation of electrostatic charges. It teaches that electrostatic discharge causes leaks through the wall of the tubing and explosions when inflammable materials are conveyed. It mentions rubber tubing.

U.S. Patent No. 2,108,759 discloses an "antistatic" fuel nozzle. It teaches dissipation of electrostatic charges caused by hydrocarbon fuel flow, before those charges can arc, by employing conductive materials like synthetic rubber in an inner layer of the nozzle.

U.S. Patent No. 2,781,288 ('288 patent) teaches a composite rubber hose with each layer arranged to take advantage of its particular properties. It suggests carbon black as a filler, but not as a conductor.

U.S. Patent No. 2,645,249 ('249 patent) and U.S. Patent No. 2,501,690 ('690 patent) teach composite tubing with each layer containing different fillers to impart varying characteristics to the inner and outer layers.

U.S. Patent No. 2,863,174, U.S. Patent No. 2,685,707, and U.S. Patent No. 2,752,637 disclose the use of carbon black as an extrusion aid in forming PTFE.

U.S. Patent No. 2,945,265 ('265 patent) teaches coextrusion of PTFE with different fillers, carbon black being used as a coloring agent.

Aeroquip's attack on the content-of-the-prior-art findings is limited to its argument that rubber hose should be excluded. That argument having been found wanting, the findings on the content of the prior art cannot be viewed as clearly erroneous.

Consideration of the scope and content of the prior art tilts the scales of decision toward a conclusion of obviousness. Thus the Abbey-Upham report teaches use of carbon black to increase conductivity of PTFE tubing to reduce the chance of electrostatic buildup on the tubing wall. It would appear to have been obvious to one skilled in the art to place the conductive material in the wall where the electrostatic buildup occurs (here the inner wall subjected to electrostatic buildup by fuel flow) as suggested by the '360 and '205 patents. It would appear to have been obvious from the '288, '249, and '690 patents to form a composite tubing with layers arranged to take advantage of their physical and chemical properties. On this record, consideration of the prior art as a whole, and in the absence of evidence that any special problem in following its teachings was created by the unique properties of PTFE, it would appear to have been obvious to place a conductive PTFE layer inside an essentially non-conductive outer PTFE layer to prevent fuel seepage associated with the conductive layer.

Differences Between the Claimed Invention and the Prior Art

. . . Aeroquip concedes that pure PTFE had been known to be dielectric, that carbon black was known to be conductive, and that PTFE had been made into tubing containing at least a small amount of carbon black. It alleges that the prior art does not show the composite tubing set forth in the claims, specifically a composite PTFE tubing with its inner layer formed of uniformly distributed carbon black and PTFE, to provide conductivity sufficient to dissipate electrostatic buildup, and an outer layer of relatively pure PTFE that prevents fuel leakage. It is true that no single reference shows all elements of the claims, but the holding here is one of invalidity for obviousness, not for anticipation. The question, therefore, is whether the inventions set forth in claims 1, 3, 4, 6 and 7, each as a whole, would have been obvious to one of ordinary skill in the art when they were made, in view of the teachings of the prior art as a whole.

Though findings on the "differences" from the prior art are suggested by *Graham v. John Deere*, the question under 35 U.S.C. § 103 is not whether the differences *themselves* would have been obvious. Consideration of differences, like each of the findings set forth in *Graham*, is but an aid in reaching the ultimate determination of whether the claimed invention *as a whole* would have been obvious.

Judge Boyle found that the differences between the claimed invention and the prior art were use of *PTFE* in concentric tubes and the "salt and pepper" process of forming the inner layer. The first difference would indicate a mere change of material. The second difference is, of course, irrelevant as stated, the claimed inventions having nothing to do with the process of making the inner layer. The finding may have been meant to indicate that the second difference lay in the structural *result* of the "salt and pepper" process, namely a uniform dispersion of carbon black particles in the inner layer (a limitation appearing only in claim 7).

With respect to use of a different material, the problem (leakage) and the cause ("pin holes" from electrostatic charges) were known with respect to that material (PTFE). A solution for the electrostatic charge problems, i.e., dissipation of charges lengthwise of the tubing, was known. Nothing in the first difference found would indicate that it would have been nonobvious to transfer that solution from tubing formed of other materials to tubing formed of PTFE. As above indicated, no special problem needed to be or was overcome in substituting a different material (PTFE) for the materials (rubber and plastics) of the prior art.

Similarly, with respect to uniform dispersion of conductive particles, it was known that spaces between carbon black areas in tubing permit arcing. Nothing of record establishes that use of uniform dispersion to limit or eliminate such spaces would not have been obvious. The same is true respecting use of a nonconductive outer layer to contain leakage from the inner conductive layer.

Aeroquip challenges the finding that the Abbey-Upham report does not teach away from use of carbon black in PTFE tubing, citing this language in the report: "The possibility of establishing continuous longitudinal strings of carbon particles during extrusion, especially in view of the relatively small percentage of carbon black used in Teflon hose seemed remote." . . .

In the sentence following that cited to us by Aeroquip, the Abbey-Upham report describes uneven spacing between carbon black particles as a possible cause of intermittent conductivity. Far from "teaching away," therefore, the report may be viewed as pointing in the direction of uniform dispersion of such particles, as set forth in claim 7, to produce less intermittent conductivity.

The findings that the differences here were use of a different material and uniform dispersion of carbon black particles were not clearly erroneous. Those differences do not tilt the scales toward a conclusion of nonobviousness of the invention as a whole in light of all prior art teachings summarized above.

Level of Ordinary Skill

The district court found the level of ordinary skill to be that of a chemical engineer or equivalent, having substantial experience in the extrusion arts. Aeroquip says that was too high, suggesting that of an engineer or technician in the PTFE art, as described by its expert, Townsend Beaman. The suggestion is but another effort to limit the prior art to PTFE tubing and avoid inclusion of the art of making fuel hoses of other materials.

The level of ordinary skill may be determined from several factors. Slade had the level of skill set by the district court. Stratoflex witness Linger was a mechanical engineer with years of experience in the rubber and PTFE hose art. Mr. Beaman was patent counsel for Aeroquip. Judge Boyle correctly viewed Beaman as an observer of, not a worker in, the relevant art.

The statute, 35 U.S.C. § 103, requires that a claim be declared invalid only when the invention set forth in that claim can be said to have been obvious "to one of *ordinary* skill in the art." (Emphasis added.) As an aid in determining obviousness, that requirement precludes consideration of whether the invention would have been obvious (as a whole and just before it was made) to the rare genius in the art, or to a judge or other layman after learning all about the invention.

Aeroquip has not shown the finding on the level of ordinary skill in the art to have been erroneous here.

Secondary Considerations

It is jurisprudentially inappropriate to disregard any relevant evidence on any issue in any case, patent cases included. Thus evidence rising out of the so-called "secondary considerations" must always when present be considered en route to a determination of obviousness. Indeed, evidence of secondary considerations may often be the most probative and cogent evidence in the record. It may often establish that an invention appearing to have been obvious in light of the prior art was not. It is to be considered as part of all the evidence, not just when the decisionmaker remains in doubt after reviewing the art.

Judge Boyle made findings on secondary considerations, but said she did not include them in her analysis because she believed the claimed inventions were plainly obvious and "those matters without invention will not make patentability" and should be considered only in a close case. That was error. . . .

A nexus is required between the merits of the claimed invention and the evidence offered, if that evidence is to be given substantial weight enroute to conclusion on the obviousness issue.

Aeroquip says commercial success is shown because: the "entire industry" makes the tubing claimed in the '087 patent; only Stratoflex is not licensed under the '087 patent; Curtiss-Wright retrofitted 10,000 engines with conductive tubing; and military specifications for conductive tubing are met only by tubing claimed in the '087 patent. We are not persuaded.

Recognition and acceptance of the patent by competitors who take licenses under it to avail themselves of the merits of the invention is evidence of nonobviousness. Here, however, Aeroquip does not delineate the make-up of the "entire industry." The record reflects only two manufacturers, Titeflex and Resistoflex, in addition to the parties. Titeflex has a royalty-free license, resulting from the interference settling agreement described above. Resistoflex has a license that includes several other patents and the right to use the trademark "HI-PAC" for complete hose assemblies. Aeroquip has shown neither a nexus between the merits of the invention and the licenses of record, nor that those licenses arose out of recognition and acceptance of the patent.

No evidence of record establishes that tubing covered by the claims of the '087 patent was used in the Curtiss-Wright retrofit. It cannot therefore be given weight in respect of commercial success.

The military specifications were promulgated after the claimed invention was known. Thus the invention did not meet a long-felt but unfilled need expressed in the specifications. Moreover, the record does not support Aeroquip's assertion that the specifications can be met only by tubing covered by the claims of the '087 patent. The nexus required to establish commercial success is therefore not present with respect to the military specifications.

Nor is there evidence that others skilled in the art tried and failed to find a solution for the problem. Aeroquip cites Abbey and Upham, but their effort was limited to investigation of the problem and its cause, and was not directed to its solution.

Upon full consideration of the evidence respecting the secondary considerations in this case, and of Aeroquip's arguments, we are persuaded that nonobviousness is not established by that evidence. Judge Boyle's error in refusing to include that evidence in her analysis was therefore in this case harmless.

"Synergism" and "Combination Patents"

Judge Boyle said "synergism" is "a symbolic reminder of what constitutes nonobviousness when a combination patent is at issue," and that under "either standard (*Graham* analysis or synergism) the combination . . . simply lacks the unique essence of authentic contribution to the Teflon art which is the heart of invention."

A requirement for "synergism" or a "synergistic effect" is nowhere found in the statute, 35 U.S.C. When present, for example in a chemical case, synergism may point toward nonobviousness, but its absence has no place in evaluating the evidence on obviousness. The more objective findings suggested in *Graham*, are drawn from the language of the statute and are fully adequate guides for evaluating the evidence relating to compliance with 35 U.S.C. § 103. Judge Boyle treated synergism as an alternative consideration. Hence the error of its analytical inclusion is harmless in view of Judge Boyle's employment of the *Graham* aids.

The reference to a "combination patent" is equally without support in the statute.

There is no warrant for judicial classification of patents, whether into "combination" patents and some other unnamed and undefined class or otherwise. Nor is there warrant for differing treatment or consideration of patents based on a judicially devised label. Reference to "combination" patents is, moreover, meaningless. Virtually *all* patents are "combination patents," if by that label one intends to describe patents having claims to inventions formed of a combination of elements. It is difficult to visualize, at least in the mechanical-structural arts, a "non-combination" invention, i.e., an invention consisting of a *single* element. Such inventions, if they exist, are rare indeed. Again, however, Judge Boyle's inclusion in her analysis of a reference to the '087 patent as a "combination" patent was harmless in view of her application of *Graham* guidelines.

Similarly, Judge Boyle's reference to "the heart of invention" was here a harmless fall-back to the fruitless search for an inherently amorphous concept that was rendered unnecessary by the statute, 35 U.S.C. The *Graham* analysis here applied properly looked to *patentability*, not to "invention."

We sit to review judgments, not opinions. The analysis reflected in an opinion filed with the judgment appealed from may on occasion be so flawed, however, as to obfuscate the true basis for the judgment or to establish that the judgment was erroneously based. Such might have here been the case if the judgment had not been accompanied by the alternative and proper analysis under *Graham* described above. In light of that alternative analysis, in which we see no error, we affirm the judgment declaring claims 1, 3, 4, 6, and 7 invalid for obviousness.

Questions:

1.) How would you draft the opinion to come out the other way? In other words, how would you characterize the facts on each of the factors the court discusses in order to find that the invention was non-obvious and thus patentable?

2.) Ordinary skill in the art:

> The district court found the level of ordinary skill to be that of a chemical engineer or equivalent, having substantial experience in the extrusion arts. Aeroquip says that was too high. . . . The statute, 35 U.S.C. § 103, requires that a claim be declared invalid only when the invention set forth in that claim can be said to have been obvious "to one of *ordinary* skill in the art." As an aid in determining obviousness, that requirement precludes consideration of whether the invention would have been obvious (as a whole and just before it was made) to the rare genius in the art, or to a judge or other layman after learning all about the invention.

How does one determine what "the art" is or what "ordinary skill" is? This is not a rhetorical question. What factual information would you look to? The level of education and experience typical in someone assigned to this task by a competitor? The qualifications that firms typically look for in hiring decisions? The qualifications of inventors who have made similar inventions? The person you think would be acceptable for such a task? (Also, "substantial experience in the extrusion arts"? Nice.)

3.) What was your gut feeling on this case as you read it? How did you think it was going to come out? If your prediction differed from the actual result, why the difference—either in your view or the court's?

4.) "Teaching Away:" Prior art references do not always render a new innovation more obvious. They may make it less obvious by "teaching away" from the solution found—

suggesting implicitly that this is the wrong line of development to pursue. Why does the court reject "teaching away" in this case?

2.) The Scope of Prior Art

In re Carl D. Clay
966 F.2d 656 (Fed. Cir. 1992)

LOURIE, Circuit Judge.

Carl D. Clay appeals the decision of the United States Patent and Trademark Office, Board of Patent Appeals and Interferences, affirming the rejection of claims 1–11 and 13 as being unpatentable under 35 U.S.C. § 103. These are all the remaining claims in application Serial No. 245,083, filed April 28, 1987, entitled "Storage of a Refined Liquid Hydrocarbon Product." We reverse.

BACKGROUND

Clay's invention, assigned to Marathon Oil Company, is a process for storing refined liquid hydrocarbon product in a storage tank having a dead volume between the tank bottom and its outlet port. The process involves preparing a gelation solution which gels after it is placed in the tank's dead volume; the gel can easily be removed by adding to the tank a gel-degrading agent such as hydrogen peroxide. Claims 1, 8, and 11 are illustrative of the claims on appeal:

Image from Clay's patent

1. A process for storing a refined hydrocarbon product in a storage tank having a dead volume between the bottom of said tank and an outlet port in said tank, said process comprising:

- preparing a gelation solution comprising an aqueous liquid solvent, an acrylamide polymer and a crosslinking agent containing a polyvalent metal cation selected from the group consisting of aluminum, chromium and mixtures thereof, said gelation solution capable of forming a rigid crosslinked polymer gel which is substantially insoluble and inert in said refined liquid hydrocarbon product;
- placing said solution in said dead volume;
- gelling said solution substantially to completion in said dead volume to produce said rigid gel which substantially fills said dead volume; and
- storing said refined liquid hydrocarbon product in said storage tank in contact with said gel without substantially contaminating said product with said gel and without substantially degrading said gel.

8. The process of claim 1 further comprising removing said rigid gel from said dead volume by contacting said gel with a chemical agent which substantially degrades said gel to a flowing solution.

11. The process of claim 1 wherein said gelation solution further comprises an aqueous liquid contaminant present in said dead volume which dissolves in said solution when said solution is placed in said dead volume.

Two prior art references were applied against the claims on appeal. They were U.S. Patent 4,664,294 (Hetherington), which discloses an apparatus for displacing dead space liquid using impervious bladders, or large bags, formed with flexible membranes; and U.S. Patent 4,683,949 (Sydansk), also assigned to Clay's assignee, Marathon Oil Company, which discloses a process for reducing the permeability of hydrocarbon-bearing formations and thus improving oil production, using a gel similar to that in Clay's invention.

The Board agreed with the examiner that, although neither reference alone describes Clay's invention, Hetherington and Sydansk combined support a conclusion of obviousness. It held that one skilled in the art would glean from Hetherington that Clay's invention "was appreciated in the prior art and solutions to that problem generally involved filling the dead space with *something*."

The Board also held that Sydansk would have provided one skilled in the art with information that a gelation system would have been impervious to hydrocarbons once the system gelled. The Board combined the references, finding that the "cavities" filled by Sydansk are sufficiently similar to the "volume or void space" being filled by Hetherington for one of ordinary skill to have recognized the applicability of the gel to Hetherington.

DISCUSSION

The issue presented in this appeal is whether the Board's conclusion was correct that Clay's invention would have been obvious from the combined teachings of Hetherington and Sydansk. Although this conclusion is one of law, such determinations are made against a background of several factual inquiries, one of which is the scope and content of the prior art. *Graham v. John Deere Co.* (1966).

A prerequisite to making this finding is determining what is "prior art," in order to consider whether "the differences between the subject matter sought to be patented and the prior art are such that the subject matter as a whole would have been obvious at the time the invention was made to a person having ordinary skill in the art." 35 U.S.C. § 103. Although § 103 does not, by its terms, define the "art to which [the] subject matter [sought to be patented] pertains," this determination is frequently couched in terms of whether the art is analogous or not, i.e., whether the art is "too remote to be treated as prior art." *In re Sovish* (Fed. Cir. 1985).

Clay argues that the claims at issue were improperly rejected over Hetherington and Sydansk, because Sydansk is nonanalogous art. Whether a reference in the prior art is "analogous" is a fact question. Thus, we review the Board's decision on this point under the clearly erroneous standard.

Two criteria have evolved for determining whether prior art is analogous: (1) whether the art is from the same field of endeavor, regardless of the problem addressed, and (2) if the reference is not within the field of the inventor's endeavor, whether the reference still is reasonably pertinent to the particular problem with which the inventor is involved.

The Board found Sydansk to be within the field of Clay's endeavor because, as the Examiner stated, "one of ordinary skill in the art would certainly glean from [Sydansk] that the rigid gel as taught therein would have a number of applications within the manipulation of the storage and processing of hydrocarbon liquids . . . [and that] the gel as taught in Sydansk would be expected to function in a similar manner as the bladders in the Hetherington patent." These findings are clearly erroneous.

The PTO argues that Sydansk and Clay's inventions are part of a common endeavor—

"maximizing withdrawal of petroleum stored in petroleum reservoirs." However, Sydansk cannot be considered to be within Clay's field of endeavor merely because both relate to the petroleum industry. Sydansk teaches the use of a gel in unconfined and irregular volumes within generally underground natural oil-bearing formations to channel flow in a desired direction; Clay teaches the introduction of gel to the confined dead volume of a man-made storage tank. The Sydansk process operates in extreme conditions, with petroleum formation temperatures as high as 115°C and at significant well bore pressures; Clay's process apparently operates at ambient temperature and atmospheric pressure. Clay's field of endeavor is the storage of refined liquid hydrocarbons. The field of endeavor of Sydansk's invention, on the other hand, is the extraction of crude petroleum. The Board clearly erred in considering Sydansk to be within the same field of endeavor as Clay's.

Even though the art disclosed in Sydansk is not within Clay's field of endeavor, the reference may still properly be combined with Hetherington if it is reasonably pertinent to the problem Clay attempts to solve. A reference is reasonably pertinent if, even though it may be in a different field from that of the inventor's endeavor, it is one which, because of the matter with which it deals, logically would have commended itself to an inventor's attention in considering his problem. Thus, the purposes of both the invention and the prior art are important in determining whether the reference is reasonably pertinent to the problem the invention attempts to solve. If a reference disclosure has the same purpose as the claimed invention, the reference relates to the same problem, and that fact supports use of that reference in an obviousness rejection. An inventor may well have been motivated to consider the reference when making his invention. If it is directed to a different purpose, the inventor would accordingly have had less motivation or occasion to consider it.

Sydansk's gel treatment of underground formations functions to fill anomalies so as to improve flow profiles and sweep efficiencies of injection and production fluids through a formation, while Clay's gel functions to displace liquid product from the dead volume of a storage tank. Sydansk is concerned with plugging formation anomalies so that fluid is subsequently diverted by the gel into the formation matrix, thereby forcing bypassed oil contained in the matrix toward a production well. Sydansk is faced with the problem of recovering oil from rock, i.e., from a matrix which is porous, permeable sedimentary rock of a subterranean formation where water has channeled through formation anomalies and bypassed oil present in the matrix. Such a problem is not reasonably pertinent to the particular problem with which Clay was involved—preventing loss of stored product to tank dead volume while preventing contamination of such product. Moreover, the subterranean formation of Sydansk is not structurally similar to, does not operate under the same temperature and pressure as, and does not function like Clay's storage tanks. See *In re Ellis* (CCPA 1973) ("the similarities and differences in structure and function of the invention disclosed in the references . . . carry far greater weight [in determining analogy]").

A person having ordinary skill in the art would not reasonably have expected to solve the problem of dead volume in tanks for storing refined petroleum by considering a reference dealing with plugging underground formation anomalies. The Board's finding to the contrary is clearly erroneous. Since Sydansk is non-analogous art, the rejection over Hetherington in view of Sydansk cannot be sustained.

CONCLUSION

For the foregoing reasons, the decision of the Board is
REVERSED.

Questions:

1.) Why does the court find this non-analogous prior art? What are the key differences on which it focuses? Are those absolute (that is, depending on differences in physical phenomena such as temperature and pressure) or relative to a particular specialty and the typical learning of that specialty? Both?

2.) When may references that are outside the PHOSITA's "field of endeavor" nevertheless be relevant for the purposes of obviousness?

3.) Burden of Proof and "Obvious to Try"

In re Bell
991 F.2d 781 (Fed. Cir. 1993)

LOURIE, Circuit Judge.

Applicants Graeme I. Bell, Leslie B. Rall, and James P. Merryweather (Bell) appeal from the March 10, 1992 decision of the U.S. Patent and Trademark Office (PTO) Board of Patent Appeals and Interferences, Appeal No. 91-1124, affirming the examiner's final rejection of claims 25–46 of application Serial No. 065,673, entitled "Preproinsulin-Like Growth Factors I and II," as unpatentable on the ground of obviousness under 35 U.S.C. § 103 (1988). Because the Board erred in concluding that the claimed nucleic acid molecules would have been obvious in light of the cited prior art, we reverse.

BACKGROUND

The claims of the application at issue are directed to nucleic acid molecules (DNA and RNA) containing human sequences which code for human insulin-like growth factors I and II(IGF), single chain serum proteins that play a role in the mediation of somatic cell growth following the administration of growth hormones.

The relevant prior art consists of two publications by Rinderknecht disclosing amino acid sequences for IGF-I and -II and U.S. Patent 4,394,443 to Weissman et al., entitled "Method for Cloning Genes." Weissman describes a general method for isolating a gene for which at least a short amino acid sequence of the encoded protein is known. The method involves preparing a nucleotide probe corresponding to the known amino acid sequence and using that probe to isolate the gene of interest. It teaches that it is advantageous to design a probe based on amino acids specified by unique codons. The Weissman patent specifically describes the isolation of a gene which codes for human histocompatibility antigen, a protein unrelated to IGF. It describes the design of the probe employed, stating that it was based on amino acids specified by unique codons.

The examiner rejected the claims as obvious over the combined teachings of Rinderknecht and Weissman. She determined that it would have been obvious, "albeit tedious," from the teachings of Weissman to prepare probes based on the Rinderknecht amino acid sequences to obtain the claimed nucleic acid molecules. According to the examiner, "it is clear from [Weissman] that the ordinary artisan knows how to find the nucleic acid when the amino acid sequence is known" and that "the claimed sequences and hosts would have been readily determinable by and obvious to those of ordinary skill in the art at the time the invention was made."

The Board affirmed the examiner's rejection, holding that the examiner had established a prima facie case of obviousness for the claimed sequences "despite the lack of conventional indicia of obviousness, e.g., structural similarity between the DNA which codes for IGF-I and the amino acid sequence of the polypeptide which constitues [sic] IGF-I." The Board reasoned that "although a protein and its DNA are not structurally similar, they are correspondently linked via the genetic code." In view of Weissman, the Board concluded that there was no evidence "that one skilled in the art, knowing the amino acid sequences of the desired proteins, would not have been able to predictably clone the desired DNA sequences without undue experimentation."

The issue before us is whether the Board correctly determined that the amino acid sequence of a protein in conjunction with a reference indicating a general method of cloning renders the gene prima facie obvious.

DISCUSSION

We review an obviousness determination by the Board *de novo*. Bell argues that the PTO has not shown how the prior art references, either alone or in combination, teach or suggest the claimed invention, and thus that it has failed to establish a prima facie case of obviousness.

We agree. The PTO bears the burden of establishing a case of prima facie obviousness. "A prima facie case of obviousness is established when the teachings from the prior art itself would appear to have suggested the claimed subject matter to a person of ordinary skill in the art." *In re Rinehart* (CCPA 1976).

The Board supported the examiner's view that the "correspondent link" between a gene and its encoded protein via the genetic code renders the gene obvious when the amino acid sequence is known. In effect, this amounts to a rejection based on the Rinderknecht references alone. Implicit in that conclusion is the proposition that, just as closely related homologs, analogs, and isomers in chemistry may create a prima facie case, see *In re Dillon* (Fed. Cir. 1990) (en banc), *cert. denied*, 111 S. Ct. 1682, (1991), the established relationship in the genetic code between a nucleic acid and the protein it encodes also makes a gene prima facie obvious over its correspondent protein.

We do not accept this proposition. It may be true that, knowing the structure of the protein, one can use the genetic code to hypothesize possible structures for the corresponding gene and that one thus has the potential for obtaining that gene. However, because of the degeneracy of the genetic code, there are a vast number of nucleotide sequences that might code for a specific protein. In the case of IGF, Bell has argued without contradiction that the Rinderknecht amino acid sequences could be coded for by more than 10^{36} different nucleotide sequences, only a few of which are the human sequences that Bell now claims.[3] Therefore, given the nearly infinite number of possibilities suggested by the

---

[3] [Casebook Editor's Note: Many sources, and at least two prominent casebooks, print this number as "1036." Readers of the actual case will see that it is in fact 10^{36}—10 followed by 35 zeroes. For magnitude comparison, the distance from our house to Houston is a little over 1036 miles. The distance to the sun in miles is a little less than 10 followed by 7 zeroes. (28 more zeroes to go.) It's the difference between going to Houston and getting a frequent flier account to the stars. The magnitude of the number seemed to be very important to the Federal Circuit. Whether the CAFC is *right* that that is the relevant number is a separate question. Many biologists would say the CAFC was wrong, that they based their assessment of the obviousness of biotech procedures on an outdated perception of arcane difficulty in what was routine, if tedious bench work. Nevertheless, knowing what magnitude of task they *thought* the inventors were facing here is important.]

prior art, and the failure of the cited prior art to suggest which of those possibilities is the human sequence, the claimed sequences would not have been obvious.

Bell does not claim all of the 10^{36} nucleic acids that might potentially code for IGF. Neither does Bell claim all nucleic acids coding for a protein having the biological activity of IGF. Rather, Bell claims only the human nucleic acid sequences coding for IGF. Absent anything in the cited prior art suggesting which of the 10^{36} possible sequences suggested by Rinderknecht corresponds to the IGF gene, the PTO has not met its burden of establishing that the prior art would have suggested the claimed sequences.

This is not to say that a gene is never rendered obvious when the amino acid sequence of its coded protein is known. Bell concedes that in a case in which a known amino acid sequence is specified exclusively by unique codons, the gene might have been obvious. Such a case is not before us. Here, where Rinderknecht suggests a vast number of possible nucleic acid sequences, we conclude that the claimed human sequences would not have been obvious.

Combining Rinderknecht with Weissman does not fill the gap. Obviousness "'cannot be established by combining the teachings of the prior art to produce the claimed invention, absent some teaching or suggestion supporting the combination.'" *In re Fine*. What a reference teaches and whether it teaches toward or away from the claimed invention are questions of fact.

While Weissman discloses a general method for isolating genes, he appears to teach away from the claimed invention by emphasizing the importance of unique codons for the amino acids. Weissman suggests that it is generally advantageous to design a probe based on an amino acid sequence specified by unique codons, and also teaches that it is "counterproductive" to use a primer having more than 14–16 nucleotides unless the known amino acid sequence has 4–5 amino acids coded for by unique codons. Bell, in contrast, used a probe having 23 nucleotides based on a sequence of eight amino acids, none of which were unique. Weissman therefore tends to teach away from the claimed sequences since Rinderknecht shows that IGF-I has only a single amino acid with a unique codon and IGF-II has none.

The PTO, in urging us to affirm the Board, points to the suggestion in Weissman that the disclosed method can "easily" be applied to isolate genes for an array of proteins including peptide hormones. The PTO thus argues that in view of Weissman, a gene is rendered obvious once the amino acid sequence of its translated protein is known. We decline to afford that broad a scope to the teachings of Weissman. While "a reference must be considered not only for what it expressly teaches, but also for what it fairly suggests," *In re Burckel* (CCPA 1979), we cannot say that Weissman "fairly suggests" that its teachings should be combined with those of Rinderknecht, since it nowhere suggests how to apply its teachings to amino acid sequences without unique codons.

We conclude that the Board clearly erred in determining that Weissman teaches toward, rather than away from, the claimed sequences. Therefore, the requisite teaching or suggestion to combine the teachings of the cited prior art references is absent and the PTO has not established that the claimed sequences would have been obvious over the combination of Rinderknecht and Weissman.

Finally, the PTO emphasizes the similarities between the method by which Bell made the claimed sequences and the method taught by Weissman. The PTO's focus on Bell's method is misplaced. Bell does not claim a method. Bell claims compositions, and the issue is the obviousness of the claimed compositions, not of the method by which they are made. See *In re Thorpe* (Fed. Cir. 1985) ("The patentability of a product does not depend on its method of production.").

CONCLUSION

Because we conclude that the combination of prior art references does not render the claimed invention obvious, we reverse the Board's decision affirming the examiner's rejection of claims.

REVERSED.

1.) *Bell* hints at, but never quite resolves, a fundamental question. What happens when the PHOSITA would look at a problem and say "Yes, that's a hard one but solvable. I'd try the following 1200 obvious and standard approaches and find out which one works. One of them surely will. Come back in 9 months." Does that defeat obviousness? What about the final clause of § 103? "Patentability shall not be negated by the manner in which the invention was made." Does it have any significance here?

2.) Who has the burden of proof on obviousness? Why?

3.) Teaching away: what significance does it have here?

4.) 'These Are Not the PHOSITA's you've been looking for. . . .'

Kimberly-Clark v. Johnson & Johnson
745 F.2d 1437 (Fed. Cir. 1984)

RICH, Circuit Judge.

This appeal is from the February 4, 1983, March 15, 1983 (219 USPQ 214), and April 5, 1983, 573 F. Supp. 1179, judgments of the United States District Court for the Northern District of Illinois, Eastern Division, sitting without a jury, holding that Kimberly-Clark Corporation's Roeder patent No. 3,672,371 ('371) issued June 27, 1972, for "Sanitary Napkin with Improved Adhesive Fastening Means" was not infringed, "unenforceable" because of "fraud on the PTO," and invalid under 35 U.S.C. § 103. We affirm the holding of non-infringement, reverse the holdings of obviousness and fraud, and remand. . . .

A. Who Is Presumed To Know The Prior Art

. . . Since January 1, 1953, the effective date of the 1952 Patent Act, the implementation of that social policy has not required courts to use the legal fiction that an inventor must be presumed to know the "prior art." The inventor, for the purposes of legal reasoning, has been replaced, as some courts have discovered, by the statutory hypothetical "person having ordinary skill in the art" who has been provided by 35 U.S.C. § 103. Since that date, there has been no need to presume that the inventor knows anything about the prior art.

Since we believe that progress in legal thinking is not only possible but highly desirable when it simplifies such thinking, we believe the time has come to discontinue this particular fiction of the patent law. Congress has given us in § 103 a substitute for the former "requirement for invention," which gave rise to the presumption, and that substitute, being statutory, should be used exclusively. We hereby declare the presumption that the inventor has knowledge of all material prior art to be dead.

What controls the patentability of the fruits of the inventor's labors are the statutory conditions of novelty, utility, and unobviousness "to a person having ordinary skill in the art to which said subject matter pertains" as stated in § 103. It should be clear that that hypothetical person is not the inventor, but an imaginary being possessing "ordinary skill in the art" created by Congress to provide a standard of patentability, a descendant of the "ordinary mechanic acquainted with the business" of *Hotchkiss v. Greenwood*. Realistically, courts never have judged patentability by what the real inventor/applicant/patentee could or would do. Real inventors, as a class, vary in their capacities from ignorant geniuses to Nobel laureates; the courts have always applied a standard based on an imaginary worker of their own devising whom they have equated with the inventor.

Dan L. Burk and Mark A. Lemley, "Is Patent Law Technology-Specific?"
17 BERKELEY TECH. L.J. 1155 (2002)

Fundamental shifts in technology and in the economic landscape are rapidly making the current system of intellectual property rights unworkable and ineffective. Designed more than 100 years ago to meet the simpler needs of an industrial era, it is an undifferentiated, one-size-fits-all system. . . . In theory, then, we have a unified patent system that provides technology-neutral protection to all kinds of technologies.

Of late, however, we have noticed an increasing divergence between the rules themselves and the application of the rules to different industries. The best examples are biotechnology and computer software. In biotechnology cases, the Federal Circuit has bent over backwards to find biotechnological inventions nonobvious, even if the prior art demonstrates a clear plan for producing the invention. On the other hand, the court has imposed stringent enablement and written description requirements on biotechnology patents that do not show up in other disciplines. In computer software cases, the situation is reversed. The Federal Circuit has essentially excused software inventions from compliance with the enablement and best mode requirements, but has done so in a way that raises serious questions about how stringently it will read the nonobviousness requirements. As a practical matter, it appears that while patent law is technology-neutral in theory, it is technology-specific in application. . . .

Much of the variance in patent standards is attributable to the use of a legal construct, the "person having ordinary skill in the art" (PHOSITA), to determine obviousness and enablement. The more skill those in the art have, the less information an applicant has to disclose in order to meet the enablement requirement—but the harder it is to meet the nonobviousness requirement. The level of skill in the art affects not just patent validity, but also patent scope. Because both claim construction and the doctrine of equivalents turn on the understanding of the PHOSITA in certain circumstances, judgments the court makes about ordinary skill in an industry affect the scope of patents that issue.

One reading of the biotechnology and computer software cases is that the Federal Circuit believes computer programmers are extremely skilled, while biotechnology experts know very little about their art. This implication is closely tied to the Federal Circuit's designation of some technologies as belonging to the "unpredictable arts"; the court treats biotechnology as if the results obtained in that art are somehow outside the control of those of skill in the art, whereas computer science is treated as if those of skill in the art have their outcomes well in hand.

We do not challenge the idea that the standards in each industry should vary with the level of skill in that industry. We think the use of the PHOSITA provides needed flexibility for patent law, permitting it to adapt to new technologies without losing its essential character. We fear, however, that the Federal Circuit has not applied that standard properly in either the biotechnology or computer software fields. The court has a perception of both fields that was set in earlier cases but which does not reflect the modern realities of either industry. The changes in an industry over time present significant structural problems for patent law, both because law is necessarily backward-looking and precedent-bound, and because applying different standards to similar inventions raises concerns about horizontal equity. Nonetheless, we believe the courts must take more care than they currently do to ensure that their assessments of patent validity are rooted in understandings of the technology that were accurate at the time the invention was made.

Questions:

1.) Lemley and Burk revisited their findings in 2011 and found them largely unchanged. In light of their argument, how should we proceed? Lemley and Burk embrace the idea that judges should be sensitive to the average level of learning in a field. Is it also appropriate for judges to adjust the sophistication level of the PHOSITA deliberately to regulate the number and breadth of patents in a given area of technology? For example, could they do so if there were strong network effects that might magnify the effect of borderline patents? Did judges in software copyright cases do something similar when they defined methods of operation, fair use in the context of decompilation, or what counted as infringement? Or does this cross a line?

2.) At the beginning of the course we pointed out that the Federal intellectual property system had only three pigeon holes—trademark, copyright and patent. As you look back now, would you say that we actually have technologically specific law in the following three areas: domain names in trademark, software in copyright and—if Burk and Lemley are correct—software and genetic technology in patent?

PROBLEM 21-1

a.) Our friend Mr. Turning, the software developer who had a tiff with Facebook, is back in your office. He has developed some new software. It proudly bears the legend "Quis Custodiet Ipsos Custodes?" or "who guards the guardians?" It allows system operators, or users, to test the security of a particular online service and to see if its password services are vulnerable to a series of the most common techniques used by hackers, but also to some new ones that Mr. Turning developed himself. In the process, Custodes will generate "test passwords" which the system administrators or legitimate users can use to validate Custodes' findings, but which the unscrupulous could use to gain unauthorized entry to any vulnerable service. Custodes has indeed spawned a huge reaction; users have been furious to find that their private data was protected only by insecure passwords, content companies (particularly Netflix and Apple's iTunes) have been furious to find that their material is now accessible and being illegally downloaded in massive quantities, and malicious hackers and the NSA have been furious to find this vulnerability revealed so publicly, since they had been quietly benefitting from it. The release of Custodes has prompted a wave of changes to make password systems more secure. Turning wants your advice on the possibility of patenting some of the innovations that he came up with during the process of development of Custodes.

The first thing that Turning wants to patent is a process, or algorithm, called Houdini, that can generate valid passwords far faster than normal "brute force" attacks in which every possible permutation is tried until success is achieved. The algorithm allows one to generalize from the shared characteristics of failed attempts and to "learn" from a very small number of failures, so that an entire class of passwords (e.g. those with initial capital letters) are eliminated based on "statistical hunches" and the user can move on to more promising password types. While this process does not guarantee success (the algorithm's early "hunch" may be wrong), Houdini has been shown to be, on average, 5 times faster than a simple brute force attack. In addition, Turning wishes to patent the Custodes password-cracking program itself. It automates the process of running the Houdini algorithm and applying it to a defined web service. In your research, you find the following information.

- An industry insider tells you of a rumor that a Hungarian mathematician called von Neumann has been privately working on an identical algorithm. The project—which is shrouded in secrecy—was apparently almost entirely complete in 2011, but von Neumann has put it aside because of rapidly proliferating health problems.
- A 1993 article in the New Zealand Journal of Epidemiology reveals the possibility of statistically diagnosing underlying diseases that cause symptoms in large populations who then report those symptoms to their doctors. It does so by generalizing from small numbers of failed diagnoses, eliminating entire classes of hypothetical disease causes based on epidemiological "hunches," and instead focusing on more promising potential diagnoses. The statistical method is similar but not identical to that employed in Houdini.
- A 2009 article in the Arizona Journal of Cryptography outlines the possibility of a computer program that "used a variety of statistical and mathematical methods" to test the security of password systems. The methods suggested were not fully described because the authors were concerned

about their possible use for criminal activity.

- Russian news reports from 2011 suggest that Russian criminal hackers use techniques that are similar but cruder than Custodes to break into secure financial systems. Because their activities are illegal, their tools are not widely available.

Can Turning patent Custodes and Houdini? In particular, are they patentable subject matter? Are they useful? Are they novel? Are they non-obvious?

b.) Your boss on the Senate Judiciary Committee wants another report. She likes "efficiency" and she wants to know why we need the novelty requirement if we have the non-obviousness requirement. One of her campaign contributors has been pressuring her on this. She forwarded you his email. It reads, "I mean, if it already *exists*, then it's *obvious*, duh! So everything that is non-novel is, by definition, also obvious. The set of all obvious inventions includes the entire set of non-novel inventions (and a lot more). We can abolish the novelty requirement as unnecessary." She has asked for you to draft a response listing all the reasons why we have both the non-obviousness and the novelty requirements and the reasons the two categories, while overlapping in part, are different.

Note: A Patentability Checklist

The next page contains the final checklist in the book. It goes back over all the material we have covered on patent eligibility. As before, we suggest that you use the flow charts and checklists as bookends in your review of the material, two different ways to impose structure on the legal questions that we have covered, and to make sure you have not skipped over some portion of the analysis.

The checklist identifies legal questions and points you to the cases or statutory sections we used to answer those questions. The digital version of the book has an added feature—hyperlinks that will take you directly to the material discussing the issue. As before, please use this checklist with caution. Our analysis went much deeper than any two page list can reveal. Nevertheless, we hope you find it useful.

PATENTABILITY CHECKLIST

(Use this to review our coverage of patentability and to test your understanding.)

Nota Bene: This is merely an *introduction* to intellectual property law. In the book we chose to spend our limited space on the basic requirements for patentability. Patent law goes far beyond these issues and is the subject of separate specialized classes.

1) Subject matter eligibility under § 101 and judicial exceptions

- Is the claimed invention a process, machine, manufacture, or composition of matter?
- Is it directed to a *judicial exception*—law of nature, natural phenomenon, abstract idea? *Mayo* step 1
- If so, is there an *inventive concept*: does the claim recite additional elements that amount to *significantly more* than the judicial exception? *Mayo* step 2. Generic computer implementation is not enough to satisfy this step. *Alice*
- Look at the case law for guidance on what is naturally or non-naturally occurring, what constitutes an abstract idea, and what kinds of inventions include an inventive concept sufficient for patentability.
  - Patent eligible: *Chakrabarty* (genetically modified bacteria), *Myriad* (cDNA), *Diehr* (industrial process of operating a rubber-molding press), *DDR Holdings* (e-commerce outsourcing system/generating a composite web page)
  - Patent ineligible: *Mayo* (process for determining drug dosage), *Myriad* (isolated DNA), *Bilski* (method for hedging risk), *Alice* (generic computer implementation of intermediated settlement), note new cases such as *Ultramercial* (ad supported content delivery) and older cases *Funk Brothers*, *Benson*, *Flook* (see citations within cases)
- Consider special issues associated with business method, software, and biotech patents

2) Utility § 101

- Does the asserted use show that the invention has *substantial, specific, credible* utility?
- *Brenner*: no patents over research intermediaries, "a patent is not a hunting license"
- *See Fisher* for definitions of substantial and specific utility and application to ESTs

3) Novelty § 102

- Is the invention novel? Or is it anticipated by prior art?
- There must be meaningful public access to the prior art (*Gayler*), and to anticipate, every element must be present in a single prior art reference (*Coffin*), but the elements can be expressly, implicitly (*Verdegaal*), or inherently (*Cruciferous Sprout*) described.
- Statutory bar: if, more than 1 year before filing the application, the inventor makes the invention available, the invention is not novel (§ 102(a), *Pennock*), unless the experimental use exception applies (*City of Elizabeth, Allen Engineering*).

4) Non-obviousness § 103

- Is the invention non-obvious to a PHOSITA? Apply the 4-part test from *Deere*. 1.) "the scope and content of the prior art are to be determined"; 2.) "differences between the prior art and the claims at issue are to be ascertained"; 3.) "and the level of ordinary skill in the pertinent art resolved"; 4.) "Such secondary considerations as commercial success, long felt but unsolved needs, failure of others, etc., might be utilized to give light to the circumstances surrounding the origin of the subject matter sought to be patented."

- We illuminated that test through the following cases: *Stratoflex* (all 4 factors are analyzed), *Clay* (analogous art is in the same field of endeavor or reasonably pertinent to the problem), *Bell* (obvious to try only defeats patentability when the inventor is choosing from a finite number of identified, predictable solutions). NB the PHOSITA is a hypothetical, imaginary being. *Kimberly-Clark*.

CHAPTER TWENTY-TWO

Trade Secrecy & Preemption

Introduction

The oldest form of protection for valuable information or innovation is secrecy. If I have a new method of making steel or lacquering violins or I have developed obstetrical forceps that are dramatically safer than the alternative, or a list of all the people in Pennsylvania who buy barrels, I can simply keep the information to myself. By itself, secrecy is a factual, not a legal protection. Of course, the law is involved to the extent that some of my existing legally protected interests make it easier to keep the secret. My property rights over land make it illegal for you to trespass in my factory to spy on my steel-making. My legally protected interests in bodily security and the rules of criminal law mean you are not allowed to kidnap or torture me to try and find out my secrets. But those legally protected interests are independent, not intended to promote the goals of intellectual property.

In this chapter we ask whether the law does and should go further. (For the impatient, the answers are respectively "Yes and maybe.") Should there be a free-standing protection for trade secrets? If so, what conduct should it protect against? A patent would allow me to exclude the person who independently invents the steel making method or the forceps. Should trade secrecy? What about if I carelessly leave the blueprints on the bus, and a stranger finds them? *Why* should the law help me protect the secret? We return to the very first chapter and our discussion of competing theories of intellectual property law. Is this to incentivize innovation and the collection of valuable information? Is it a reward for hard work? A way of policing bad behavior and the "commercial immorality" of snoops and cheats? Finally, how does trade secrecy interact with our other three intellectual property schemes: copyright, trademark and patent? Do those Federal schemes ever preempt state trade secrecy protections, just as we saw that copyright law sometimes preempts unfair competition protections? In this chapter we will try to answer all of those questions.

The Restatement, Uniform Trade Secrets Act, and Defend Trade Secrets Act

Until 2016, the civil law of trade secrecy was a matter of state law. The main sources of that law were the Restatement (First) of Torts (1939) (the provisions of which were later included in the Restatement (Third) of Unfair Competition), and the Uniform Trade Secrets Act ("UTSA"), the most recently amended version of which dates from 1985.[1] In turn, states relied on those two basic frameworks in creating their own law of trade secrecy, both by statute and in the courts. Most states (New York and Massachusetts are exceptions) adopted some version of the UTSA, with their own amendments.[2] In May of 2016, Congress passed the Defend Trade Secrets Act ("DTSA"), adding a new Federal civil cause of action to the existing Federal criminal prohibitions against Economic

---

[1] The Economic Espionage Act of 1996 added severe criminal penalties for the misappropriation of trade secrets with knowledge or intent that it would benefit a foreign power or harm the owner of the trade secret used in a product for interstate or international commerce.

[2] In the Statutory Supplement we include California's adoption of the Uniform Trade Secrets Act, noting the places where the California legislation makes changes.

Espionage.[3] Just as the Lanham Act does not preempt state trademark law, the DTSA does not preempt state trade secrecy protections. The Restatement, the UTSA and the DTSA rest on broadly similar foundations but, as we will see, there are some differences. As you read through the definitions offered below, note the central features of trade secrecy.

- The basic form of the protection is that it provides legal backing to the existing "factual" secrecy we described earlier. If you take reasonable efforts to protect your secret, the law of trade secrecy aids you by forbidding certain methods of uncovering that secret—such as by spying, or bribing one of your employees to violate a duty of confidentiality.

- Trade secrecy is much more expansive and less demanding in its criteria than patentable subject matter. It can also extend to material that is outside of copyright's subject matter—such as an unoriginal compilation of facts.

- The criteria for what counts as a trade secret are mixed—they go to the value of the information, the cost of developing it and the care taken in maintaining the secrecy. The Restatement attempted to distinguish "single shot" secrets (the amount of an individual bid, not eligible for protection) with those that have a continued importance to the operation of the business (a database of all bids made over time, correlated by the factors predicting their success, eligible for protection). The UTSA and DTSA lower the bar, protecting any type of secret information so long as it has "actual or potential" value based on its secrecy.

- The protection is not absolute. The trade secret can be uncovered through reverse engineering, or lost through publication, independent discovery or carelessness. In other words, only certain types of behavior—which we call, with some degree of circularity, "misappropriation"—can violate a trade secret.

- Information may be shared without losing its legal protection as a trade secret so long as it travels with a duty of confidentiality on those with whom it is shared. (What policy reasons would there be for us to want to allow secrets to be shared and yet to retain their protection?)

- The protection is not the kind of strict liability property system we saw in copyright and in patent. If I innocently acquire a trade secret without knowing or having reason to know that the person from whom I receive it disclosed it without authorization, I am not liable to the owner for my use of the information. (Though my informant may well be.)

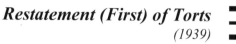

Restatement (First) of Torts
(1939)

SECTION 757. LIABILITY FOR DISCLOSURE OR USE OF ANOTHER'S TRADE SECRET

GENERAL PRINCIPLE. One who discloses or uses another's trade secret, without a privilege to do so, is liable to the other if
    (a) he discovered the secret by improper means, or
    (b) his disclosure or use constitutes a breach of confidence reposed in

---

[3] The DTSA was passed as a series of amendments to the Economic Espionage Act ("EEA"). The Statutory Supplement contains both the EEA, as amended, and the DTSA.

him by the other in disclosing the secret to him, or

(c) he learned the secret from a third person with notice of the facts that it was a secret and that the third person discovered it by improper means or that the third person's disclosure of it was otherwise a breach of his duty to the other, or

(d) he learned the secret with notice of the facts that it was a secret and that its disclosure was made to him by mistake.

Comment b. Definition of Trade Secret.

A trade secret may consist of any formula, pattern, device or compilation of information which is used in one's business, and which gives him an opportunity to obtain an advantage over competitors who do not know or use it. It may be a formula for a chemical compound, a process of manufacturing, treating or preserving materials, a pattern for a machine or other device, or a list of customers. It differs from other secret information in a business . . . in that it is not simply information as to single or ephemeral events in the conduct of the business, as, for example, the amount or other terms of a secret bid for a contract or the salary of certain employees, or the security investments made or contemplated, or the date fixed for the announcement of a new policy or for bringing out a new model or the like. A trade secret is a process or device for continuous use in the operation of the business. Generally it relates to the production of goods, as, for example, a machine or formula for the production of an article. It may, however, relate to the sale of goods or to other operations in the business, such as a code for determining discounts, rebates or other concessions in a price list or catalogue, or a list of specialized customers, or a method of bookkeeping or other office management.

The subject matter of a trade secret must be secret. Matters of public knowledge or of general knowledge in an industry cannot be appropriated by one as his secret. Matters which are completely disclosed by the goods which one markets cannot be his secret. Substantially, a trade secret is known only in the particular business in which it is used. It is not requisite that only the proprietor of the business know it. He may, without losing his protection, communicate it to employees involved in its use. He may likewise communicate it to others pledged to secrecy. Others may also know of it independently, as, for example, when they have discovered the process or formula by independent invention and are keeping it secret. Nevertheless, a substantial element of secrecy must exist, so that, except by the use of improper means, there would be difficulty in acquiring the information. An exact definition of a trade secret is not possible. Some factors to be considered in determining whether given information is one's trade secret are:

- the extent to which the information is known outside of his business;
- the extent to which it is known by employees and others involved in his business;
- the extent of measures taken by him to guard the secrecy of the information;
- the value of the information to him and to his competitors;
- the amount of effort or money expended by him in developing the information;
- the ease or difficulty with which the information could be properly acquired or duplicated by others.

Uniform Trade Secrets Act
With 1985 Amendments

SECTION 1. DEFINITIONS. As used in this [Act], unless the context requires otherwise:

(1) "Improper means" includes theft, bribery, misrepresentation, breach or inducement of a breach of a duty to maintain secrecy, or espionage through electronic or other means;

(2) "Misappropriation" means:

(i) acquisition of a trade secret of another by a person who knows or has reason to know that the trade secret was acquired by improper means; or

(ii) disclosure or use of a trade secret of another without express or implied consent by a person who

(A) used improper means to acquire knowledge of the trade secret; or

(B) at the time of disclosure or use, knew or had reason to know that his knowledge of the trade secret was

(I) derived from or through a person who had utilized improper means to acquire it;

(II) acquired under circumstances giving rise to a duty to maintain its secrecy or limit its use; or

(III) derived from or through a person who owed a duty to the person seeking relief to maintain its secrecy or limit its use; or

(C) before a material change of his [or her] position, knew or had reason to know that it was a trade secret and that knowledge of it had been acquired by accident or mistake. . . .

(4) "Trade secret" means information, including a formula, pattern, compilation, program, device, method, technique, or process, that:

(i) derives independent economic value, actual or potential, from not being generally known to, and not being readily ascertainable by proper means by, other persons who can obtain economic value from its disclosure or use, and

(ii) is the subject of efforts that are reasonable under the circumstances to maintain its secrecy.

COMMENT

. . . "A complete catalogue of improper means is not possible," but Section 1(1) includes a partial listing.

Proper means include:

1. Discovery by independent invention;

2. Discovery by "reverse engineering", that is, by starting with the known product and working backward to find the method by which it was developed. The acquisition of the known product must, of course, also be by a fair and honest means, such as purchase of the item on the open market for reverse engineering to be lawful;

3. Discovery under a license from the owner of the trade secret;

4. Observation of the item in public use or on public display;

5. Obtaining the trade secret from published literature.

Because the trade secret can be destroyed through public knowledge, the unauthorized disclosure of a trade secret is also a misappropriation.

Defend Trade Secrets Act of 2016

§ 1836 (b)(1) In general.—An owner of a trade secret that is misappropriated may bring a civil action under this subsection if the trade secret is related to a product or service used in, or intended for use in, interstate or foreign commerce.

[The DTSA largely takes its definition of trade secrecy from the (broad) existing definition in the Economic Espionage Act (§ 1839), which it amends.]

§ 1839 (3) [T]he term "trade secret" means all forms and types of financial, business, scientific, technical, economic, or engineering information, including patterns, plans, compilations, program devices, formulas, designs, prototypes, methods, techniques, processes, procedures, programs, or codes, whether tangible or intangible, and whether or how stored, compiled, or memorialized physically, electronically, graphically, photographically, or in writing if

> **(A) the owner thereof has taken reasonable measures to keep such information secret; and**
>
> **(B) the information derives independent economic value, actual or potential, from not being generally known to, and not being readily ascertainable through proper means by, another person who can obtain economic value from the disclosure or use of the information.**

[The original § 1839 had read "not being generally known to, and not being readily ascertainable through proper means by, *the public*." The amended version now tracks the UTSA: "by another person who can obtain economic value from the disclosure or use of the information." The DTSA also mirrors the UTSA's definition of "misappropriation" given on the previous page and reiterates its description of improper means, while specifically clarifying conduct that is *not* improper, in a manner similar to the California version of the UTSA.]

§ 1839 (6) the term 'improper means'

> **(A) includes theft, bribery, misrepresentation, breach or inducement of a breach of a duty to maintain secrecy, or espionage through electronic or other means; and (B) does not include reverse engineering, independent derivation, or any other lawful means of acquisition. . . .**

Despite the similarities between the DTSA and the state trade secrecy schemes built on the foundation of the UTSA, there are also differences.

- **Federal Cause of Action**: Most obviously, for the first time this provides a cause of action in the Federal courts. Plaintiffs can now use Federal courts to assert both Federal and state trade secrecy causes of action, though not *vice versa*. Alternatively, they may bring separate Federal and state actions.
- **Whistleblower Immunity**: The DTSA provides civil and criminal immunity to individuals who disclose trade secrets to Federal or state governments or to an

attorney in order to report a violation of the law. It also allows for disclosures, under seal, in certain court filings and disclosures in the case of anti-retaliation suits. No such immunity is explicitly given in most state trade secrecy regimes. Notably, employers *must* notify employees of the existence of this whistleblower immunity in order to keep their full range of rights under the DTSA (though that notification may be buried in a larger policy document).

- ***Ex Parte* Civil Seizure**: A large portion of the DTSA is taken up with a significant new remedy for plaintiffs. From § 1836 (b): "[T]he court may, upon *ex parte* application but only in extraordinary circumstances, issue an order providing for the seizure of property necessary to prevent the propagation or dissemination of the trade secret that is the subject of the action." *Ex parte* applications, that is applications made by one party without the other party's participation, are obviously subject to few of the restraints of a full hearing. The application must satisfy the judge that the plaintiff is likely to win at trial (that is, that it is a trade secret, it has been misappropriated and so on) and will suffer irreparable injury if the order is not granted, and that the benefit caused by the order will outweigh harms to the defendant and "substantially outweigh" harms to third parties. Even with these limitations and the possibility of a suit in the case of misuse, this gives plaintiffs a powerful right which can be triggered before the judge has heard the defendant's side of the story. It is a right that many scholars,[4] including the authors of this casebook, fear may end up being abused for anti-competitive ends.

- **Compatibility with Labor Mobility**: Some states, most notably California, generally reject on public policy grounds injunctions that would prevent employees from changing employers. By contrast the DTSA forbids only injunctions that "prevent a person from accepting an offer of employment under conditions that avoid actual or threatened misappropriation."

Question:

1.) What differences in emphasis do you see between the Restatement, the UTSA and the DTSA? What policy choices do they represent?

Preemption

In Chapter 16 we considered the question of when Federal Copyright law preempts state causes of action, such as unfair competition protection of "hot news." Similarly, Federal Copyright Law presumably imposes *some* limits on state trade secrecy laws. Not on the core concept. Trade secrecy allows for protection of at least certain kinds of "facts." Copyright does not. Yet, *Theflyonthewall.com* notwithstanding, trade secrecy rights would surely survive a preemption challenge, largely because of the narrowness of the right and the commercial circumstances in which it arises. The DTSA signals Congress's clear belief that basic state trade secrecy rights are not inconsistent with existing Federal intellectual property law, for it explicitly allows those state rights to continue to exist. Yet could California amend its trade secrecy law to say that publicly distributed movies were "trade secrets" and thus that it was illegal ever to reproduce or screen them, even after the

---

[4] Eric Goldman, *Ex Parte Seizures and the DTSA*, 72 WASH. & LEE LAW REV. ONLINE 284 (2015).

copyright term had expired? We think not. There's no magic in the phrase "trade secrecy." Merely *labeling* something a "trade secrecy right" does not thereby make it immune from preemption challenge.

What about patent law? The Patent Act lacks the Copyright Act's explicit statutory section outlining its preemptive reach. The courts, therefore, must turn to logic and purpose to guide them. In so doing, they produce some of the most extensive discussions of the nature and function of the patent system and of the state rights which might conflict with that system—including, but by no means limited to, trade secrecy. In doing so, they cast further light on our earlier discussion of preemption and copyright.

Sears, Roebuck & Co. v. Stiffel Co.
376 U.S. 225 (1964)

Mr. Justice BLACK delivered the opinion of the Court.

The question in this case is whether a State's unfair competition law can, consistently with the federal patent laws, impose liability for or prohibit the copying of an article which is protected by neither a federal patent nor a copyright. . . .

Sears has been held liable here for unfair competition because of a finding of likelihood of confusion based only on the fact that Sears' lamp was copied from Stiffel's unpatented lamp and that consequently the two looked exactly alike. Of course there could be "confusion" as to who had manufactured these nearly identical articles. But mere inability of the public to tell two identical articles apart is not enough to support an injunction against copying or an award of damages for copying that which the federal patent laws permit to be copied. Doubtless a State may, in appropriate circumstances, require that goods, whether patented or unpatented, be labeled or that other precautionary steps be taken to prevent customers from being misled as to the source, just as it may protect businesses in the use of their trademarks, labels, or distinctive dress in the packaging of goods so as to prevent others, by imitating such markings, from misleading purchasers as to the source of the goods. But because of the federal patent laws a State may not, when the article is unpatented and uncopyrighted, prohibit the copying of the article itself or award damages for such copying. The judgment below did both and in so doing gave Stiffel the equivalent of a patent monopoly on its unpatented lamp. That was error, and Sears is entitled to a judgment in its favor.

Reversed.

Kewanee Oil Co. v. Bicron Corp.
416 U.S. 470 (1974)

Mr. Chief Justice BURGER delivered the opinion of the Court.

We granted certiorari to resolve a question on which there is a conflict in the courts of appeals: whether state trade secret protection is pre-empted by operation of the federal patent law. . . .

II

The protection accorded the trade secret holder is against the disclosure or unauthorized use of the trade secret by those to whom the secret has been confided under the express or implied restriction of nondisclosure or nonuse. The law also protects the holder of a trade secret against disclosure or use when the knowledge is gained, not by the owner's volition, but by some "improper means," Restatement of Torts § 757 (a), which may include theft, wiretapping, or even aerial reconnaissance. A trade secret law, however, does not offer protection against discovery by fair and honest means, such as by independent invention, accidental disclosure, or by so-called reverse engineering, that is by starting with the known product and working backward to divine the process which aided in its development or manufacture.

IV

The question of whether the trade secret law of Ohio is void under the Supremacy Clause involves a consideration of whether that law "stands as an obstacle to the accomplishment and execution of the full purposes and objectives of Congress." The laws which the Court of Appeals in this case held to be in conflict with the Ohio law of trade secrets were the patent laws passed by the Congress in the unchallenged exercise of its clear power under Art. I, § 8, cl. 8, of the Constitution. The patent law does not explicitly endorse or forbid the operation of trade secret law. However, as we have noted, if the scheme of protection developed by Ohio respecting trade secrets "clashes with the objectives of the federal patent laws," *Sears, Roebuck & Co. v. Stiffel Co.*, then the state law must fall. To determine whether the Ohio law "clashes" with the federal law it is helpful to examine the objectives of both the patent and trade secret laws.

The stated objective of the Constitution in granting the power to Congress to legislate in the area of intellectual property is to "promote the Progress of Science and useful Arts." The patent laws promote this progress by offering a right of exclusion for a limited period as an incentive to inventors to risk the often enormous costs in terms of time, research, and development. The productive effort thereby fostered will have a positive effect on society through the introduction of new products and processes of manufacture into the economy, and the emanations by way of increased employment and better lives for our citizens. In return for the right of exclusion—this "reward for inventions"—the patent laws impose upon the inventor a requirement of disclosure. To insure [sic] adequate and full disclosure so that upon the expiration of the 17-year period "the knowledge of the invention enures to the people, who are thus enabled without restriction to practice it and profit by its use," the patent laws require that the patent application shall include a full and clear description of the invention and "of the manner and process of making and using it" so that any person skilled in the art may make and use the invention. 35 U.S.C. § 112. When a patent is granted and the information contained in it is circulated to the general public and those especially skilled in the trade, such additions to the general store of knowledge are of such importance to the public weal that the Federal Government is willing to pay the high price of 17 years of exclusive use for its disclosure, which disclosure, it is assumed, will stimulate ideas and the eventual development of further significant advances in the art. The Court has also articulated another policy of the patent law: that which is in the public domain cannot be removed there from by action of the States. "[F]ederal law requires that all ideas in general circulation be dedicated to the common good unless they are protected by a valid patent." *Lear, Inc. v. Adkins.*

The maintenance of standards of commercial ethics and the encouragement of invention are the broadly stated policies behind trade secret law. "The necessity of good faith and honest, fair dealing, is the very life and spirit of the commercial world." In *A. O.*

Smith Corp. v. Petroleum Iron Works Co., the Court emphasized that even though a discovery may not be patentable, that does not "destroy the value of the discovery to one who makes it, or advantage the competitor who by unfair means, or as the beneficiary of a broken faith, obtains the desired knowledge without himself paying the price in labor, money, or machines expended by the discoverer."

In *Wexler v. Greenberg* (1960), the Pennsylvania Supreme Court noted the importance of trade secret protection to the subsidization of research and development and to increased economic efficiency within large companies through the dispersion of responsibilities for creative developments.

Having now in mind the objectives of both the patent and trade secret law, we turn to an examination of the interaction of these systems of protection of intellectual property—one established by the Congress and the other by a State—to determine whether and under what circumstances the latter might constitute "too great an encroachment on the federal patent system to be tolerated."

As we noted earlier, trade secret law protects items which would not be proper subjects for consideration for patent protection under 35 U.S.C. § 101.

Since no patent is available for a discovery, however useful, novel, and nonobvious, unless it falls within one of the express categories of patentable subject matter of 35 U.S.C. § 101, the holder of such a discovery would have no reason to apply for a patent whether trade secret protection existed or not. Abolition of trade secret protection would, therefore, not result in increased disclosure to the public of discoveries in the area of nonpatentable subject matter. . . . The question remains whether those items which are proper subjects for consideration for a patent may also have available the alternative protection accorded by trade secret law.

Certainly the patent policy of encouraging invention is not disturbed by the existence of another form of incentive to invention. In this respect the two systems are not and never would be in conflict. Similarly, the policy that matter once in the public domain must remain in the public domain is not incompatible with the existence of trade secret protection. By definition a trade secret has not been placed in the public domain.

The more difficult objective of the patent law to reconcile with trade secret law is that of disclosure, the *quid pro quo* of the right to exclude. We are helped in this stage of the analysis by Judge Henry Friendly's opinion in *Painton & Co. v. Bourns, Inc.* (2d Cir. 1971). There the Court of Appeals thought it useful, in determining whether inventors will refrain because of the existence of trade secret law from applying for patents, thereby depriving the public from learning of the invention, to distinguish between three categories of trade secrets: "(1) the trade secret believed by its owner to constitute a validly patentable invention; (2) the trade secret known to its owner not to be so patentable; and (3) the trade secret whose valid patentability is considered dubious."

As to the trade secret known not to meet the standards of patentability, very little in the way of disclosure would be accomplished by abolishing trade secret protection. With trade secrets of nonpatentable subject matter, the patent alternative would not reasonably be available to the inventor.

Even as the extension of trade secret protection to patentable subject matter that the owner knows will not meet the standards of patentability will not conflict with the patent policy of disclosure, it will have a decidedly beneficial effect on society. Trade secret law will encourage invention in areas where patent law does not reach, and will prompt the independent innovator to proceed with the discovery and exploitation of his invention. Competition is fostered and the public is not deprived of the use of valuable, if not quite patentable, invention.

Even if trade secret protection against the faithless employee were abolished, inventive and exploitive effort in the area of patentable subject matter that did not meet the standards of patentability would continue, although at a reduced level. Alternatively with the effort that remained, however, would come an increase in the amount of self-help that innovative companies would employ. Knowledge would be widely dispersed among the employees of those still active in research. As a result, organized scientific and technological research could become fragmented, and society, as a whole, would suffer.

Another problem that would arise if state trade secret protection were precluded is in the area of licensing others to exploit secret processes. The holder of a trade secret would not likely share his secret with a manufacturer who cannot be placed under binding legal obligation to pay a license fee or to protect the secret. The result would be to hoard rather than disseminate knowledge. Instead, then, of licensing others to use his invention and making the most efficient use of existing manufacturing and marketing structures within the industry, the trade secret holder would tend either to limit his utilization of the invention, thereby depriving the public of the maximum benefit of its use, or engage in the time-consuming and economically wasteful enterprise of constructing duplicative manufacturing and marketing mechanisms for the exploitation of the invention. The detrimental misallocation of resources and economic waste that would thus take place if trade secret protection were abolished with respect to employees or licensees cannot be justified by reference to any policy that the federal patent law seeks to advance.

Nothing in the patent law requires that States refrain from action to prevent industrial espionage. In addition to the increased costs for protection from burglary, wiretapping, bribery, and the other means used to misappropriate trade secrets, there is the inevitable cost to the basic decency of society when one firm steals from another. A most fundamental human right, that of privacy, is threatened when industrial espionage is condoned or is made profitable; the state interest in denying profit to such illegal ventures is unchallengeable.

The next category of patentable subject matter to deal with is the invention whose holder has a legitimate doubt as to its patentability. The risk of eventual patent invalidity by the courts and the costs associated with that risk may well impel some with a good-faith doubt as to patentability not to take the trouble to seek to obtain and defend patent protection for their discoveries, regardless of the existence of trade secret protection. Trade secret protection would assist those inventors in the more efficient exploitation of their discoveries and not conflict with the patent law. In most cases of genuine doubt as to patent validity the potential rewards of patent protection are so far superior to those accruing to holders of trade secrets, that the holders of such inventions will seek patent protection, ignoring the trade secret route. For those inventors "on the line" as to whether to seek patent protection, the abolition of trade secret protection might encourage some to apply for a patent who otherwise would not have done so.

The point is that those who might be encouraged to file for patents by the absence of trade secret law will include inventors possessing the chaff as well as the wheat. Some of the chaff—the nonpatentable discoveries—will be thrown out by the Patent Office, but in the meantime society will have been deprived of use of those discoveries through trade secret-protected licensing. Some of the chaff may not be thrown out. This Court has noted the difference between the standards used by the Patent Office and the courts to determine patentability. *Graham v. John Deere Co.* (1966). In *Lear, Inc. v. Adkins* (1969), the Court thought that an invalid patent was so serious a threat to the free use of ideas already in the public domain that the Court permitted licensees of the patent holder to challenge the validity of the patent. Better had the invalid patent never been issued. More of those patents would likely issue if trade secret law were abolished. Eliminating trade secret law for the doubtfully patentable invention is thus likely to have deleterious effects on society and patent policy which we cannot say are balanced out by the speculative gain which might result from the encouragement of some inventors with doubtfully patentable inventions which deserve patent protection to come forward and apply for patents. There is no conflict, then, between trade secret law and the patent law policy of disclosure, at least insofar as the first two categories of patentable subject matter are concerned.

The final category of patentable subject matter to deal with is the clearly patentable invention, i.e., that invention which the owner believes to meet the standards of patentability. It is here that the federal interest in disclosure is at its peak; these inventions, novel, useful and nonobvious, are "'the things which are worth to the public the embarrassment of an exclusive patent.'" *Graham v. John Deere Co.* (quoting Thomas Jefferson). The interest of the public is that the bargain of 17 years of exclusive use in return for disclosure be accepted. If a State, through a system of protection, were to cause a substantial risk that holders of patentable inventions would not seek patents, but rather would rely on the state protection, we would be compelled to hold that such a system could not constitutionally continue to exist. In the case of trade secret law no reasonable risk of deterrence from patent application by those who can reasonably expect to be granted patents exists.

Trade secret law provides far weaker protection in many respects than the patent law. While trade secret law does not forbid the discovery of the trade secret by fair and honest means, e. g., independent creation or reverse engineering, patent law operates "against the world," forbidding any use of the invention for whatever purpose for a significant length of time. The holder of a trade secret also takes a substantial risk that the secret will be passed on to his competitors, by theft or by breach of a confidential relationship, in a manner not easily susceptible of discovery or proof. Where patent law acts as a barrier, trade secret law functions relatively as a sieve. The possibility that an inventor who believes his invention meets the standards of patentability will sit back, rely on trade secret law, and after one year of use forfeit any right to patent protection, 35 U.S.C. § 102 (b), is remote indeed.

Nor does society face much risk that scientific or technological progress will be impeded by the rare inventor with a patentable invention who chooses trade secret protection over patent protection. The ripeness-of-time concept of invention, developed from the study of the many independent multiple discoveries in history, predicts that if a particular individual had not made a particular discovery others would have, and in probably a relatively short period of time. If something is to be discovered at all very likely it will be discovered by more than one person.

We conclude that the extension of trade secret protection to clearly patentable inventions does not conflict with the patent policy of disclosure. Perhaps because trade secret law does not produce any positive effects in the area of clearly patentable inventions, as opposed to the beneficial effects resulting from trade secret protection in the areas of the doubtfully patentable and the clearly unpatentable inventions, it has been suggested that partial pre-emption may be appropriate, and that courts should refuse to apply trade secret protection to inventions which the holder should have patented, and which would have been, thereby, disclosed. However, since there is no real possibility that trade secret law will conflict with the federal policy favoring disclosure of clearly patentable inventions partial pre-emption is inappropriate.

Partial pre-emption, furthermore, could well create serious problems for state courts in the administration of trade secret law. As a preliminary matter in trade secret actions, state courts would be obliged to distinguish between what a reasonable inventor would and would not correctly consider to be clearly patentable, with the holder of the trade secret arguing that the invention was not patentable and the misappropriator of the trade secret arguing its undoubted novelty, utility, and nonobviousness. Federal courts have a difficult enough time trying to determine whether an invention . . . is patentable. . . . [I]t would be undesirable to impose the almost impossible burden on state courts to determine the patentability—in fact and in the mind of a reasonable inventor—of a discovery which has not been patented and remains entirely uncircumscribed by expert analysis in the administrative process. Neither complete nor partial pre-emption of state trade secret law is justified.

Trade secret law and patent law have co-existed in this country for over one hundred years. Each has its particular role to play, and the operation of one does not take away from the need for the other. Trade secret law encourages the development and exploitation of those items of lesser or different invention than might be accorded protection under the patent laws, but which items still have an important part to play in the technological and scientific advancement of the Nation. Trade secret law promotes the sharing of knowledge, and the efficient operation of industry; it permits the individual inventor to reap the rewards of his labor by contracting with a company large enough to develop and exploit it. Congress, by its silence over these many years, has seen the wisdom of allowing the States to enforce trade secret protection. Until Congress takes affirmative action to the contrary, States should be free to grant protection to trade secrets.

Since we hold that Ohio trade secret law is not preempted by the federal patent law, the judgment of the Court of Appeals for the Sixth Circuit is reversed, and the case is remanded to the Court of Appeals with directions to reinstate the judgment of the District Court.

Bonito Boats, Inc. v. Thunder Craft Boats, Inc.
489 U.S. 141 (1989)

JUSTICE O'CONNOR delivered the opinion of the Court.

We must decide today what limits the operation of the federal patent system places on the States' ability to offer substantial protection to utilitarian and design ideas which the patent laws leave otherwise unprotected. In *Interpart Corp. v. Italia* (Fed. Cir. 1985), the Court of Appeals for the Federal Circuit concluded that a California law prohibiting the use of the "direct molding process" to duplicate unpatented articles posed no threat to the policies behind the federal patent laws. In this case, the Florida Supreme Court came to a contrary conclusion. It struck down a Florida statute which prohibits the use of the direct molding process to duplicate unpatented boat hulls, finding that the protection offered by the Florida law conflicted with the balance struck by Congress in the federal patent statute between the encouragement of invention and free competition in unpatented ideas. We granted certiorari to resolve the conflict and we now affirm the judgment of the Florida Supreme Court. . . .

. . . [I]n *Kewanee Oil Co. v. Bicron Corp.* (1974), we held that state protection of trade secrets did not operate to frustrate the achievement of the congressional objectives served by the patent laws. Despite the fact that state law protection was available for ideas which clearly fell within the subject matter of patent, the Court concluded that the nature and degree of state protection did not conflict with the federal policies of encouragement of patentable invention and the prompt disclosure of such innovations.

Several factors were critical to this conclusion. First, because the public awareness of a trade secret is by definition limited, the Court noted that "the policy that matter once in the public domain must remain in the public domain is not incompatible with the existence of trade secret protection." Second, the *Kewanee* Court emphasized that "[t]rade secret law provides far weaker protection in many respects than the patent law." This point was central to the Court's conclusion that trade secret protection did not conflict with either the encouragement or disclosure policies of the federal patent law. The public at large remained free to discover and exploit the trade secret through reverse engineering of products in the public domain or by independent creation. Thus, the possibility that trade secret protection would divert inventors from the creative effort necessary to satisfy the rigorous demands of patent protection was remote indeed. Finally, certain aspects of trade secret law operated to protect noneconomic interests outside the sphere of congressional concern in the patent laws. As the Court noted, "[A] most fundamental human right, that of privacy, is threatened when industrial espionage is condoned or is made profitable." There was no indication that Congress had considered this interest in the balance struck by the patent laws, or that state protection for it would interfere with the policies behind the patent system. . . .

At the heart of *Sears* and *Compco* [a similar case about design protection and unfair competition] is the conclusion that the efficient operation of the federal patent system depends upon substantially free trade in publicly known, unpatented design and utilitarian conceptions. In *Sears*, the state law offered "the equivalent of a patent monopoly," in the functional aspects of a product which had been placed in public commerce absent the protection of a valid patent. While, as noted above, our decisions since Sears have taken a decidedly less rigid view of the scope of federal pre-emption under the patent laws, we believe that the *Sears* Court correctly concluded that the States may not offer patent-like protection to intellectual creations which would otherwise remain unprotected as a matter of federal law. Both the novelty and the nonobviousness requirements of federal patent law are grounded in the notion that concepts within the public grasp, or those so obvious that they readily could be, are the tools of creation available to all. They provide the baseline of free competition upon which the patent system's incentive to creative effort depends. A state law that substantially interferes with the enjoyment of an unpatented utilitarian or design conception which has been freely disclosed by its author to the public at large impermissibly contravenes the ultimate goal of public disclosure and use which is the centerpiece of federal patent policy. Moreover, through the creation of patent-like rights, the States could essentially redirect inventive efforts away from the careful criteria of patentability developed by Congress over the last 200 years. We understand this to be the reasoning at the core of our decisions in *Sears* and *Compco*, and we reaffirm that reasoning today.

Questions:

1.) In *Kewanee* the Court says: "Certainly the patent policy of encouraging invention is not disturbed by the existence of another form of incentive to invention. In this respect the two systems are not and never would be in conflict." Do you agree? Is this consistent with the holding of the *Sears* case? The *Bonito Boats* case? With the holdings of the courts in the copyright preemption cases *NBA v. Motorola* or *Barclays v. Theflyonthewall.com*? How might adding new forms of protection for innovation change the balance set up by the Federal patent scheme? Does the passage of the DTSA strengthen the Court's argument?

2.) The *Kewanee* Court discusses the effect of trade secret protection on three classes of innovations; those that are clearly unpatentable, those that are clearly patentable, and those of dubious patentability. In each case, it finds that trade secret law does not effectively deprive the public of the type of disclosure promised by the patent system. Do you agree? Does the fact that the patent system focuses so much on promoting disclosure indicate that it was a Congressional response to the possibility of factual or legal secrecy by offering a different set of incentives that would encourage inventors to relinquish that secrecy?

3.) The *Bonito Boats* case struck down as preempted a state law protecting boat hull designs from direct mold copying, and only that form of copying. In that case the Court had to reconcile its *Sears* and *Kewanee* decisions. It stressed three arguments made by the *Kewanee* Court: i.) By definition, trade secrets are not in the public domain—unlike the unpatentable design of a good already on sale—thus the public is deprived of nothing; ii.) Trade secret law is far weaker than patent protection; iii.) Trade secret law protects additional non-economic values beyond the promotion of innovation—in this case the "fundamental human right of privacy." Is a ban that goes only to boat designs copied by direct molding far weaker than patent protection? Do unfair competition actions—such as that involved in the *Sears* case—involve non-economic values beyond the promotion of innovation? That leads us to consider the very reasonable idea that trade secrets, by definition, are not in the public domain. The next case provides us with an intriguing fact situation to test what we mean by "facts available to the public."

Improper Means

E.I. du Pont de Nemours & Co. v. Christopher
431 F.2d 1012 (5th Cir. 1970)

GOLDBERG, Circuit Judge:

    This is a case of industrial espionage in which an airplane is the cloak and a camera the dagger. The defendants-appellants, Rolfe and Gary Christopher, are photographers in Beaumont, Texas. The Christophers were hired by an unknown third party to take aerial photographs of new construction at the Beaumont plant of E. I. DuPont de Nemours & Company, Inc. Sixteen photographs of the DuPont facility were taken from the air on March 19, 1969, and these photographs were later developed and delivered to the third party.

    DuPont subsequently filed suit against the Christophers, alleging that the Christophers had wrongfully obtained photographs revealing DuPont's trade secrets which they then sold to the undisclosed third party. DuPont contended that it had developed a highly secret but unpatented process for producing methanol, a process which gave DuPont a competitive advantage over other producers. This process, DuPont alleged, was a trade secret developed after much expensive and time-consuming research, and a secret which the company had taken special precautions to safeguard. The area photographed by the Christophers was the plant designed to produce methanol by this secret process, and because the plant was still under construction parts of the process were exposed to view from directly above the construction area. Photographs of that area, DuPont alleged, would enable a skilled person to deduce the secret process for making methanol. DuPont thus contended that the Christophers had wrongfully appropriated DuPont trade secrets by taking the photographs and delivering them to the undisclosed third party. In its suit DuPont asked for damages to cover the loss it had already sustained as a result of the wrongful disclosure of the trade secret and sought temporary and permanent injunctions prohibiting any further circulation of the photographs already taken and prohibiting any additional photographing of the methanol plant.

The Christophers argued both at trial and before this court that they committed no "actionable wrong" in photographing the DuPont facility and passing these photographs on to their client because they conducted all of their activities in public airspace, violated no government aviation standard, did not breach any confidential relation, and did not engage in any fraudulent or illegal conduct. In short, the Christophers argue that for an appropriation of trade secrets to be wrongful there must be a trespass, other illegal conduct, or breach of a confidential relationship. We disagree.

It is true, as the Christophers assert, that the previous trade secret cases have contained one or more of these elements. However, we do not think that the Texas courts would limit the trade secret protection exclusively to these elements. On the contrary, in *Hyde Corporation v. Huffines* (1958), the Texas Supreme Court specifically adopted the rule found in the Restatement of Torts which provides:

"One who discloses or uses another's trade secret, without a privilege to
do so, is liable to the other if

(a) he discovered the secret by improper means, or

(b) his disclosure or use constitutes a breach of confidence reposed
in him by the other in disclosing the secret to him * * *."

Restatement of Torts § 757 (1939).

Thus, although the previous cases have dealt with a breach of a confidential relationship, a trespass, or other illegal conduct, the rule is much broader than the cases heretofore encountered. Not limiting itself to specific wrongs, Texas adopted subsection (a) of the Restatement which recognizes a cause of action for the discovery of a trade secret by any "improper" means.

The question remaining, therefore, is whether aerial photography of plant construction is an improper means of obtaining another's trade secret. We conclude that it is and that the Texas courts would so hold. The Supreme Court of that state has declared that "the undoubted tendency of the law has been to recognize and enforce higher standards of commercial morality in the business world." *Hyde Corporation v. Huffines.* That court has quoted with approval articles indicating that the proper means of gaining possession of a competitor's secret process is "through inspection and analysis" of the product in order to create a duplicate. *K & G Tool & Service Co. v. G & G Fishing Tool Service.* Later another Texas court explained:

"The means by which the discovery is made may be obvious, and the
experimentation leading from known factors to presently unknown
results may be simple and lying in the public domain. But these facts do
not destroy the value of the discovery and will not advantage a
competitor who by unfair means obtains the knowledge *without paying
the price expended by the discoverer.*" *Brown v. Fowler* (emphasis
added).

We think, therefore, that the Texas rule is clear. One may use his competitor's secret process if he discovers the process by reverse engineering applied to the finished product; one may use a competitor's process if he discovers it by his own independent research; but one may not avoid these labors by taking the process from the discoverer without his permission at a time when he is taking reasonable precautions to maintain its secrecy. To obtain knowledge of a process without spending the time and money to discover it independently is improper unless the holder voluntarily discloses it or fails to take reasonable precautions to ensure its secrecy.

In the instant case the Christophers deliberately flew over the DuPont plant to get pictures of a process which DuPont had attempted to keep secret. The Christophers delivered their pictures to a third party who was certainly aware of the means by which they had been acquired and who may be planning to use the information contained therein to manufacture methanol by the DuPont process. The third party has a right to use this process only if he obtains this knowledge through his own research efforts, but thus far all information indicates that the third party has gained this knowledge solely by taking it from DuPont at a time when DuPont was making reasonable efforts to preserve its secrecy. In such a situation DuPont has a valid cause of action to prohibit the Christophers from improperly discovering its trade secret and to prohibit the undisclosed third party from using the improperly obtained information.

In taking this position we realize that industrial espionage of the sort here perpetrated has become a popular sport in some segments of our industrial community. However, our devotion to free wheeling industrial competition must not force us into accepting the law of the jungle as the standard of morality expected in our commercial relations. Our tolerance of the espionage game must cease when the protections required to prevent another's spying cost so much that the spirit of inventiveness is dampened. Commercial privacy must be protected from espionage which could not have been reasonably anticipated or prevented. We do not mean to imply, however, that everything not in plain view is within the protected vale, nor that all information obtained through every extra optical extension is forbidden. Indeed, for our industrial competition to remain healthy there must be breathing room for observing a competing industrialist. A competitor can and must shop his competition for pricing and examine his products for quality, components, and methods of manufacture. Perhaps ordinary fences and roofs must be built to shut out incursive eyes, but we need not require the discoverer of a trade secret to guard against the unanticipated, the undetectable, or the unpreventable methods of espionage now available.

In the instant case DuPont was in the midst of constructing a plant. Although after construction the finished plant would have protected much of the process from view, during the period of construction the trade secret was exposed to view from the air. To require DuPont to put a roof over the unfinished plant to guard its secret would impose an enormous expense to prevent nothing more than a school boy's trick. We introduce here no new or radical ethic since our ethos has never given moral sanction to piracy. The marketplace must not deviate far from our *mores*. We should not require a person or corporation to take unreasonable precautions to prevent another from doing that which he ought not do in the first place. Reasonable precautions against predatory eyes we may require, but an impenetrable fortress is an unreasonable requirement, and we are not disposed to burden industrial inventors with such a duty in order to protect the fruits of their efforts. "Improper" will always be a word of many nuances, determined by time, place, and circumstances. We therefore need not proclaim a catalogue of commercial improprieties. Clearly, however, one of its commandments does say "thou shall not appropriate a trade secret through deviousness under circumstances in which countervailing defenses are not reasonably available."

Having concluded that aerial photography, from whatever altitude, is an improper method of discovering the trade secrets exposed during construction of the DuPont plant, we need not worry about whether the flight pattern chosen by the Christophers violated any federal aviation regulations. Regardless of whether the flight was legal or illegal in that sense, the espionage was an improper means of discovering DuPont's trade secret.

The decision of the trial court is affirmed and the case remanded to that court for proceedings on the merits.

Questions:

1.) **Improper Means:** The Comments to the UTSA endorse *Christopher*. Why is this conduct "improper under the circumstances"?

2.) **Holding:** Does *Christopher* hold that trade secrets may only be legally discovered through reverse engineering? Through methods that cost the discoverer as much as the initial secret cost its owner to develop? Through conventional methods that the trade secret owner had already thought about and countered? Some other possibility?

3.) **Baselines & Positive Externalities**: One of the rationales the court offers for its decision is a moral one. "We introduce here no new or radical ethic since our ethos has never given moral sanction to piracy. The market place must not deviate far from our *mores. We should not require a person or corporation to take unreasonable precautions to prevent another from doing that which he ought not do in the first place.*" (Emphasis added.) How would Pitney respond? Brandeis? Is there a tension between this reasoning and the preemption analysis in the *NBA v. Motorola* or *Barclays v. Theflyonthewall.com* cases?

4.) **Incentives**: The court's other main rationale could be expressed in terms of efficient incentives for secrecy. "To require DuPont to put a roof over the unfinished plant to guard its secret would impose an enormous expense to prevent nothing more than a school boy's trick. . . ." Does this mean that as new technologies make old techniques of secrecy less effective and countermeasures more expensive, the use of those new technologies is thus *prima facie* illegal?

5.) **Framing**: The court here frames the defendant's conduct in the first line of the decision. "This is a case of industrial espionage in which an airplane is the cloak and a camera the dagger." How would you frame the issue if you were the Christophers' lawyer?

Reasonable Efforts to Preserve Secrecy

To establish that something is a trade secret, you first have to show that it is a secret at all. Trade secrecy law thus exists on a knife-edge. On the one hand, its very existence suggests that sometimes even vigorous attempts to preserve secrecy will fail—otherwise the legal protection would not be needed. On the other hand, how does one distinguish a lack of security that negates the claim to legal protection from the act of infringing the trade secret itself? As always, the common law answers that question by turning to the concept of "reasonableness"—in this case reasonable efforts to preserve secrecy. And who better to explore the concept of the reasonably secret man, or at least his economically-minded brother, than Judge Posner?

Rockwell Graphic Systems, Inc. v. DEV Industries, Inc.

925 F.2d 174 (7th Cir. 1991)

POSNER, Circuit Judge.

This is a suit for misappropriation of trade secrets. Rockwell Graphic Systems, a manufacturer of printing presses used by newspapers, and of parts for those presses, brought the suit against DEV Industries, a competing manufacturer, and against the president of DEV, who used to be employed by Rockwell. The case is in federal court by virtue of the RICO ("Racketeer Influenced and Corrupt Organizations") statute. The predicate acts required for liability under RICO are acts of misappropriation (and related misconduct, such as alleged breaches of fiduciary duty) committed by the individual defendant, Fleck, and by another former employee of Rockwell and present employee of DEV, Peloso. These acts are alleged to violate Illinois law, and in pendent counts Rockwell seeks to impose liability for them directly under that law as well as indirectly under RICO. The district judge granted summary judgment for the defendants upon the recommendation of a magistrate who concluded that Rockwell had no trade secrets because it had failed to take reasonable precautions to maintain secrecy. Therefore there had been no misappropriation, which in turn was the foundation for the predicate acts; so the RICO count had to be dismissed. With the federal claim out of the case, the district judge relinquished jurisdiction over the pendent counts, resulting in a dismissal of the entire case.

When we said that Rockwell manufactures both printing presses and replacement parts for its presses—"wear parts" or "piece parts," they are called—we were speaking approximately. Rockwell does not always manufacture the parts itself. Sometimes when an owner of one of Rockwell's presses needs a particular part, or when Rockwell anticipates demand for the part, it will subcontract the manufacture of it to an independent machine shop, called a "vendor" by the parties. When it does this it must give the vendor a "piece part drawing" indicating materials, dimensions, tolerances, and methods of manufacture. Without that information the vendor could not manufacture the part. Rockwell has not tried to patent the piece parts. It believes that the purchaser cannot, either by inspection or by "reverse engineering" discover how to manufacture the part; to do that you need the piece part drawing, which contains much information concerning methods of manufacture, alloys, tolerances, etc. that cannot be gleaned from the part itself. So Rockwell tries—whether hard enough is the central issue in the case—to keep the piece part drawings secret, though not of course from the vendors; they could not manufacture the parts for Rockwell without the drawings.

Rockwell employed Fleck and Peloso in responsible positions that gave them access to piece part drawings. Fleck left Rockwell in 1975 and three years later joined DEV as its president. Peloso joined DEV the following year after being fired by Rockwell when a security guard caught him removing piece part drawings from Rockwell's plant. This suit was brought in 1984, and pretrial discovery by Rockwell turned up 600 piece part drawings in DEV's possession, of which 100 were Rockwell's. DEV claimed to have obtained them lawfully, either from customers of Rockwell or from Rockwell vendors, contrary to Rockwell's claim that either Fleck and Peloso stole them when they were employed by it or DEV obtained them in some other unlawful manner, perhaps from a vendor who violated his confidentiality agreement with Rockwell. Thus far in the litigation DEV has not been able to show which customers or vendors lawfully supplied it with Rockwell's piece part drawings.

The mere fact that Rockwell gave piece part drawings to vendors—that is, disclosed its trade secrets to "a limited number of outsiders for a particular purpose"—did not forfeit trade secret protection. On the contrary, such disclosure, which is often necessary to the efficient exploitation of a trade secret, imposes a duty of confidentiality on the part of the person to whom the disclosure is made. But with 200 engineers checking out piece part drawings and making copies of them to work from, and numerous vendors receiving copies of piece part drawings and copying them, tens of thousands of copies of these drawings are floating around outside Rockwell's vault, and many of these outside the company altogether. Not only did Rockwell not limit copying of those drawings or insist that copies be returned; it did not segregate the piece part drawings from the assembly drawings and institute more secure procedures for the former. So Rockwell could have done more to maintain the confidentiality of its piece part drawings than it did, and we must decide whether its failure to do more was so plain a breach of the obligation of a trade secret owner to make reasonable efforts to maintain secrecy as to justify the entry of summary judgment for the defendants.

The requirement of reasonable efforts has both evidentiary and remedial significance, and this regardless of which of the two different conceptions of trade secret protection prevails. The first and more common merely gives a remedy to a firm deprived of a competitively valuable secret as the result of an independent legal wrong, which might be conversion or other trespass or the breach of an employment contract or of a confidentiality agreement. Under this approach, because the secret must be taken by improper means for the taking to give rise to liability, the only significance of trade secrecy is that it allows the victim of wrongful appropriation to obtain damages based on the competitive value of the information taken. The second conception of trade secrecy, illustrated by *E.I. du Pont de Nemours & Co. v. Christopher* is that "trade secret" picks out a class of socially valuable information that the law should protect even against nontrespassory or other lawful conduct—in *Christopher*, photographing a competitor's roofless plant from the air while not flying directly overhead and hence not trespassing or committing any other wrong independent of the appropriation of the trade secret itself.

Since, however, the opinion in *Christopher* describes the means used by the defendant as "improper," which is also the key to liability under the first, more conventional conception of trade secret protection, it is unclear how distinct the two conceptions really are. It is not as if *Christopher* proscribes all efforts to unmask a trade secret. It specifically mentions reverse engineering as a proper means of doing so. This difference in treatment is not explained, but it may rest on the twofold idea that reverse engineering involves the use of technical skills that we want to encourage, and that anyone should have the right to take apart and to study a product that he has bought.

It should be apparent that the two different conceptions of trade secret protection are better described as different emphases. The first emphasizes the desirability of deterring efforts that have as their sole purpose and effect the redistribution of wealth from one firm to another. The second emphasizes the desirability of encouraging inventive activity by protecting its fruits from efforts at appropriation that are, indeed, sterile wealth-redistributive—not productive—activities. The approaches differ, if at all, only in that the second does not limit the class of improper means to those that fit a preexisting pigeonhole in the law of tort or contract or fiduciary duty—and it is by no means clear that the first approach assumes a closed class of wrongful acts, either.

Under the first approach, at least if narrowly interpreted so that it does not merge with the second, the plaintiff must prove that the defendant obtained the plaintiff's trade secret by a wrongful act, illustrated here by the alleged acts of Fleck and Peloso in removing piece part drawings from Rockwell's premises without authorization, in violation of their employment contracts and confidentiality agreements. Rockwell is unable to prove directly that the 100 piece part drawings it got from DEV in discovery were stolen by Fleck and Peloso or obtained by other improper means. But if it can show that the probability that DEV could have obtained them otherwise—that is, without engaging in wrongdoing—is slight, then it will have taken a giant step toward proving what it must prove in order to recover under the first theory of trade secret protection. The greater the precautions that Rockwell took to maintain the secrecy of the piece part drawings, the lower the probability that DEV obtained them properly and the higher the probability that it obtained them through a wrongful act.

Under the second theory of trade secret protection, the owner's precautions still have evidentiary significance, but now primarily as evidence that the secret has real value. For the precise means by which the defendant acquired it is less important under the second theory, though not completely unimportant; remember that even the second theory allows the unmasking of a trade secret by some means, such as reverse engineering. If Rockwell expended only paltry resources on preventing its piece part drawings from falling into the hands of competitors such as DEV, why should the law, whose machinery is far from costless, bother to provide Rockwell with a remedy? The information contained in the drawings cannot have been worth much if Rockwell did not think it worthwhile to make serious efforts to keep the information secret.

The remedial significance of such efforts lies in the fact that if the plaintiff has allowed his trade secret to fall into the public domain, he would enjoy a windfall if permitted to recover damages merely because the defendant took the secret from him, rather than from the public domain as it could have done with impunity. It would be like punishing a person for stealing property that he believes is owned by another but that actually is abandoned property. If it were true, as apparently it is not, that Rockwell had given the piece part drawings at issue to customers, and it had done so without requiring the customers to hold them in confidence, DEV could have obtained the drawings from the customers without committing any wrong. The harm to Rockwell would have been the same as if DEV had stolen the drawings from it, but it would have had no remedy, having parted with its rights to the trade secret. This is true whether the trade secret is regarded as property protected only against wrongdoers or (the logical extreme of the second conception, although no case—not even *Christopher*—has yet embraced it and the patent statute might preempt it) as property protected against the world. In the first case, a defendant is perfectly entitled to obtain the property by lawful conduct if he can, and he can if the property is in the hands of persons who themselves committed no wrong to get it. In the second case the defendant is perfectly entitled to obtain the property if the plaintiff has abandoned it by giving it away without restrictions.

It is easy to understand therefore why the law of trade secrets requires a plaintiff to show that he took reasonable precautions to keep the secret a secret. If analogies are needed, one that springs to mind is the duty of the holder of a trademark to take reasonable efforts to police infringements of his mark, failing which the mark is likely to be deemed abandoned, or to become generic or descriptive (and in either event be unprotectable).

But only in an extreme case can what is a "reasonable" precaution be determined on a motion for summary judgment, because the answer depends on a balancing of costs and benefits that will vary from case to case and so require estimation and measurement by persons knowledgeable in the particular field of endeavor involved. On the one hand, the more the owner of the trade secret spends on preventing the secret from leaking out, the more he demonstrates that the secret has real value deserving of legal protection, that he really was hurt as a result of the misappropriation of it, and that there really was misappropriation. On the other hand, the more he spends, the higher his costs. The costs can be indirect as well as direct. The more Rockwell restricts access to its drawings, either by its engineers or by the vendors, the harder it will be for either group to do the work expected of it. Suppose Rockwell forbids any copying of its drawings. Then a team of engineers would have to share a single drawing, perhaps by passing it around or by working in the same room, huddled over the drawing. And how would a vendor be able to make a piece part—would Rockwell have to bring all that work in house? Such reconfigurations of patterns of work and production are far from costless; and therefore perfect security is not optimum security.

There are contested factual issues here. Obviously Rockwell took some precautions, both physical (the vault security, the security guards—one of whom apprehended Peloso *in flagrante delicto*) and contractual, to maintain the confidentiality of its piece part drawings. Obviously it could have taken more precautions. But at a cost, and the question is whether the additional benefit in security would have exceeded that cost. We do not suggest that the question can be answered with the same precision with which it can be posed, but neither can we say that no reasonable jury could find that Rockwell had done enough and could then go on to infer misappropriation from a combination of the precautions Rockwell took and DEV's inability to establish the existence of a lawful source of the Rockwell piece part drawings in its possession.

This is an important case because trade secret protection is an important part of intellectual property, a form of property that is of growing importance to the competitiveness of American industry. Patent protection is at once costly and temporary, and therefore cannot be regarded as a perfect substitute. If trade secrets are protected only if their owners take extravagant, productivity-impairing measures to maintain their secrecy, the incentive to invest resources in discovering more efficient methods of production will be reduced, and with it the amount of invention. And given the importance of the case we must record our concern at the brevity of the district court's opinion granting summary judgment (one and a half printed pages). Brevity is the soul of wit, and all that, and the district judge did have the benefit of a magistrate's opinion; but it is vital that commercial litigation not appear to be treated as a stepchild in the federal courts. The future of the nation depends in no small part on the efficiency of industry, and the efficiency of industry depends in no small part on the protection of intellectual property.

The judgment is reversed and the case remanded to the district court for further proceedings consistent with this opinion (including reinstatement of the pendent counts). REVERSED AND REMANDED.

Questions:

1.) What are the two views of trade secrecy that Posner outlines? What role does evidence of the adequacy of secrecy play in each one? With which does he agree?

2.) "This is true whether the trade secret is regarded as property protected only against wrongdoers or (the logical extreme of the second conception, although no case—not even *Christopher*—has yet embraced it and the patent statute might preempt it) as property protected against the world." Why does Posner think that Federal law would preempt trade secrecy rights if they were treated as property protected against the world? Does the *Bonito Boats* Court agree?

"Are Trade Secrets 'Property'?" Why Do You Ask, Pray Tell?

Definitions are part and parcel of the lawyer's craft, but searching for answers by defining the supposed essence of an activity *in the abstract* leads to sterile, purposeless conceptualism. This general point is illustrated with great clarity in a confused and confusing debate over the question of whether trade secrets are *really* property. The most useful answer comes by first asking "what do you mean by property, and why do you want to know?" When lawyers ask "is this property?" they may mean many things.

- Is this a physical, tangible thing?
- Is this a right protected by a property rule (for example, your right to refuse to sell your modest house to Donald Trump at any price) or a liability rule (for example, the right of the cement company in *Boomer v. Atlantic Cement* to go on causing a nuisance to a neighbor's property so long as it pays "actual damages")? If the homeowner in *Boomer* can get an injunction against nuisance, it is a property rule. If he must accept the damages, it is a liability rule.
- Is this a right that is "good against the world" and protected by strict liability— such as the right of the owner of the copyright to sue anyone who copies their work, even in good faith, for damages? This is a characteristic we associate with "property rights." Or is it a right that goes only against the person who has committed the wrongful act—the initial tortfeasor, or the person who violates the contract or the license?
- Is this a right, which if substantially extinguished by the state, will trigger the protections of the US Constitution against "takings" of property?
- Is it pragmatically *useful* (in terms of analogies, policies, precedents that can be used) to place this legally protected interest in the conceptual box we call "property" or should we instead think about it as part of a set of relationship-based obligations, such as fiduciary duties?

And so on. When posed this way, we can see that the answers to these questions with regard to trade secrecy present a fascinating pattern. Trade secrecy is protected by injunctions as well as damages. Yet it is not a right good against the world, protected by strict liability penalties even against the innocent acquirer. (Indeed, Judge Posner suggested in *Rockwell* that such a right—because of its breadth—would probably be preempted.) Trade secrecy is relational and conduct-based. If I find out your trade secret by reverse engineering and as a result, cause great harm to your profits, I commit no legal wrong. If I "misappropriate" the exact same information, causing the same harm, I violate your trade secret. In other words, the answer to the question "are trade secrets property?" is "It depends. What do you mean and why are you asking?" In fact, you might usefully think of the definitional inquiry as a slightly confused way to pose a different question. Why do we have trade secrecy? For reasons of morality? Efficiency? Innovation? And against what behavior, by individuals, companies and states, *should* we defend it?

E.I. du Pont de Nemours Powder Co. et al. v. Masland et al.
244 U.S. 100 (1917)

Mr. Justice HOLMES delivered the opinion of the court.

The case has been considered as presenting a conflict between a right of property and a right to make a full defence, and it is said that if the disclosure is forbidden to one who denies that there is a trade secret, the merits of his defence are adjudged against him before he has a chance to be heard or to prove his case. We approach the question somewhat differently. The word property as applied to trade-marks and trade secrets is an unanalyzed expression of certain secondary consequences of the primary fact that the law makes some rudimentary requirements of good faith. Whether the plaintiffs have any valuable secret or not the defendant knows the facts, whatever they are, through a special confidence that he accepted. The property may be denied but the confidence cannot be. Therefore the starting point for the present matter is not property or due process of law, but that the defendant stood in confidential relations with the plaintiffs, or one of them. These have given place to hostility, and the first thing to be made sure of is that the defendant shall not fraudulently abuse the trust reposed in him. It is the usual incident of confidential relations. If there is any disadvantage in the fact that he knew the plaintiffs' secrets he must take the burden with the good.

Ruckelshaus v. Monsanto Co.
467 U.S. 986 (1984)

Justice BLACKMUN delivered the opinion of the Court.

In this case, we are asked to review a United States District Court's determination that several provisions of the Federal Insecticide, Fungicide, and Rodenticide Act (FIFRA), are unconstitutional. The provisions at issue authorize the Environmental Protection Agency (EPA) to use data submitted by an applicant for registration of a pesticide in evaluating the application of a subsequent applicant, and to disclose publicly some of the submitted data.

This Court never has squarely addressed the applicability of the protections of the Taking Clause of the Fifth Amendment to commercial data of the kind involved in this case. In answering the question now, we are mindful of the basic axiom that "'[p]roperty interests ... are not created by the Constitution. Rather, they are created and their dimensions are defined by existing rules or understandings that stem from an independent source such as state law.'"

Monsanto asserts that the health, safety, and environmental data it has submitted to EPA are property under Missouri law, which recognizes trade secrets, as defined in § 757, Comment b, of the Restatement of Torts, as property.... And the parties have stipulated that much of the information, research, and test data that Monsanto has submitted under FIFRA to EPA "contains or relates to trade secrets as defined by the Restatement of Torts."

Because of the intangible nature of a trade secret, the extent of the property right therein is defined by the extent to which the owner of the secret protects his interest from disclosure to others. Information that is public knowledge or that is generally known in an industry cannot be a trade secret. If an individual discloses his trade secret to others who are under no obligation to protect the confidentiality of the information, or otherwise publicly discloses the secret, his property right is extinguished.

Trade secrets have many of the characteristics of more tangible forms of property. A trade secret is assignable. A trade secret can form the res of a trust, and it passes to a trustee in bankruptcy.

Even the manner in which Congress referred to trade secrets in the legislative history of FIFRA supports the general perception of their property-like nature. In discussing the 1978 amendments to FIFRA, Congress recognized that data developers like Monsanto have a "proprietary interest" in their data. Further, Congress reasoned that submitters of data are "entitled" to "compensation" because they "have legal ownership of the data." This general perception of trade secrets as property is consonant with a notion of "property" that extends beyond land and tangible goods and includes the products of an individual's "labour and invention." 2 W. Blackstone, Commentaries 405; see generally J. Locke, The Second Treatise of Civil Government.

Although this Court never has squarely addressed the question whether a person can have a property interest in a trade secret, which is admittedly intangible, the Court has found other kinds of intangible interests to be property for purposes of the Fifth Amendment's Taking Clause. See, *e. g., Armstrong v. United States* (1960) (material-man's lien provided for under Maine law protected by Taking Clause); *Louisville Joint Stock Land Bank v. Radford* (1935) (real estate lien protected); *Lynch v. United States* (1934) (valid contracts are property within meaning of the Taking Clause). That intangible property rights protected by state law are deserving of the protection of the Taking Clause has long been implicit in the thinking of this Court.

We therefore hold that to the extent that Monsanto has an interest in its health, safety, and environmental data cognizable as a trade-secret property right under Missouri law, that property right is protected by the Taking Clause of the Fifth Amendment.

Questions:

1.) "The word property as applied to trade-marks and trade secrets is an unanalyzed expression of certain secondary consequences of the primary fact that the law makes some rudimentary requirements of good faith." What does Holmes mean? How does this relate to his comment in *INS v. AP*? "Property, a creation of law, does not arise from value, although exchangeable—a matter of fact. . . . Property depends upon exclusion by law from interference, and a person is not excluded from using any combination of words merely because someone has used it before, even if it took labor and genius to make it. If a given person is to be prohibited from making the use of words that his neighbors are free to make some other ground must be found." What ground is Holmes suggesting trade secrecy rests upon?

2.) Do you agree with the Supreme Court's decision in *Ruckelshaus*? Why? Why not? Note, by the way, that among the other rights the court says are protected from takings of *property*, are valid *contracts*, further proof of the importance of the "what do you mean" question posed at the beginning of this section. (*Ruckelshaus* did not leave the government powerless. The court also held "a voluntary submission of data by an applicant in exchange for the economic advantages of a registration can hardly be called a taking." In this case, Monsanto had received guarantees of confidentiality.)

PROBLEM 22-1
TRADE SECRETS, MISAPPROPRIATION & PREEMPTION

CJ Jones Jr., the legendary and innovative CEO behind the Agora supermarket chain, has pioneered a data-driven approach towards the placement of his stores. Early in his career, he realized that his best performing branches had certain things in common—not the obvious ones like population density or amount of competition but more subtle features. For example, successful stores were no more than ¾ mile from a freeway exit, were no more than 4 minutes from the nearest public school and 6 minutes to the nearest gas station and so on. At first, his insight was more art than science, but over the years—investing millions in data gathering—he refined it into a massive database. All of these statistics were, in time, compiled into the "CJ Index" which Agora internal documents describe as "the crown jewel" of the Agora Empire. The CJ Index is used by Agora to choose where to place branches in new locations. Superior branch placement decisions—together with fine ingredients, excellent customer service and competitive pricing—have enabled Agora to earn profits well above the industry average. The actual algorithm behind the Index is disclosed only to the board and top executive team of Agora, all of whom sign confidentiality agreements. The Index itself, as well as the database on which it relies, is encrypted, marked as "Highly Confidential" and kept on a password-protected computer in a room guarded by security personnel.

Larry Lessig, a hot-shot freelance programmer, was being recruited by Agora for a top executive position. Lessig was interested but bridled when he was told a non-disclosure agreement would be part of the deal. "Is this something that will restrict my ability to work with other supermarket companies in the future?" Lessig asked. "No," said the Vice President in charge of his recruitment, "It simply covers things proprietary to Agora, like how we use data to place our stores, for example." Lessig, a deep believer in "open data," declined the position and did not sign the agreement. Going home, he fired up his laptop, pulled up Google Maps' "Satellite View" and in half an hour wrote a simple multiple regression program that would scan Google Maps looking for commonalities in the placement of Agora stores. Google Maps makes the location of businesses publicly available—a service Agora is delighted to have, since it sends more customers their way. Lessig's program looked for statistically significant "clusters" on those maps. When a common feature on the map was found for three or four stores—proximity to a swimming pool, a fire station or a school, for example—the program automatically checked to see if those features explained the placement of a wider number of stores. Lessig set it to run, and headed out to dinner. By the time he got home, the program had identified the common features of the Agora supermarkets. The insight behind the CJ Index was his. Lessig emailed the CEO of Whole Paycheck Stores—a pricy competitor to Agora—and offered to sell "the results of a program I've run, analyzing the common features of the legendarily successful Agora stores." John Mack, the CEO of Whole Paycheck, had long been jealous of Agora's success and was eager to peddle his kale chips, yoga magazines and quinoa salads to a wider audience. Anything that would increase customer satisfaction sounded good to him. "Is this data completely kosher?" he asked Lessig. "Yes" Lessig replied, "I compiled it from public data drawn from Google Maps." "Done," said Mack, sending him a check for $20,000.

Lessig lives in the State of Confusion, which borders Florida and Georgia.

Confusion has not formally adopted either the Restatement or the UTSA, but its courts have relied on both in prior trade secret cases. In addition, Confusion has a wide-reaching tort of "misappropriation and commercially unfair competition by copying" which aims "to raise the standard of commercial morality in our businesses." Confusion's judges have embraced this task with fervor, often using in their decisions the Biblical injunction against "reaping where you have not sown" and the courts have used that tort to supplement trade secrecy.

Getting wind of Lessig's activities, Agora has sued Lessig and Whole Paycheck for i.) violation of the DTSA ii.) violations of Confusion state trade secrecy protection and iii.) for "commercially unfair competition by copying." Agora's suit asks for damages and for an injunction that would prevent both Lessig and Whole Paycheck from ever using or revealing the patterns in Agora's store placement. Agora has also invoked the DTSA's civil seizure provisions, making an *ex parte* application to the court for seizure of Lessig's computers and his data, before any hearing is held. Discuss the likelihood of success of these causes of action against each plaintiff, including the arguments that might persuade a court either way. Be specific about the language from the DTSA, the Restatement, the UTSA and court decisions on which you are resting your analysis. (We recommend in particular that you look at the requirements for trade secrecy and the varying definitions of a trade secret and of misappropriation. You should also look at the DTSA's requirements for invoking *ex parte* seizure in § 1836.) In your answer, be sure to discuss whether either of Agora's state law claims would be preempted by Federal intellectual property law. You would be wise to look back at the *Motorola* and *Theflyonthewall.com* cases as well as the cases in this chapter.

CHAPTER TWENTY-THREE

A Creative Commons?
Summary and Conclusion

We hope you have gleaned a number of things from this book. The first is the remarkable power of both rhetorical framing and moral and economic baselines in the debates we have been describing. If you understand them, it is like having a map of the entire area rather than tediously memorizing directions. Take trademark law. Earlier we summed up the two dominant visions of trademark.

One vision of the scope of a trademark confines it tightly to the semantic interaction between *this* good or service, *this* mark, *this* consumer and *this* manufacturer. Dove for soap does not infringe Dove for chocolate. The rationale for the right is to maintain stable meaning of the symbols that producers use and consumers rely on. The key *market* is the one the trademark owner is already in, with perhaps a small room for expansion to closely related markets (Levi designer jeans not Levi Jeep interiors). The key *person* whose confusion is relevant is the purchaser (and thus labels that explicitly disclaim connection to another producer are very strong evidence that consumers will not be likely to be confused). The key *moment* is the moment of sale. Confusion before the moment of sale (as with the person who clicks on a Google advertisement served up by her search for "Coach bags," only to be shown Kate Spade bags that she ends up preferring to Coach) is irrelevant. Confusion *after* the moment of sale (as when the Chrysler 300 is seen on the street and mistaken for a Bentley, when the driver knows very well it is not) is irrelevant. Wherever the narrow reach of the right does not extend, competition—including competition built on deliberately copying non-trademarked features of another product—is to be welcomed.

The second, broader, vision of the scope of a trademark right views it partly as a device to avoid (current) consumer confusion and diminution of the utility of trademark symbols. In that it agrees with the narrower view. But it goes beyond that to see the trademark right as rooted in broader themes of unfair competition law, protecting acquired goodwill which can be leveraged into new markets whenever the producer wants, and preventing other producers from "reaping where they have not sown" even if the *consumer* is not at all confused. The right is no longer confined tightly to the semantic interaction between this consumer, this mark, this good and this producer. It is extended to cover possible *future* markets. It is as if, by having the mark, I have planted a semantic claim stake on the empty range next door. The relevant *moment* is expanded both before and after the point of sale, to cover initial interest confusion and post point of sale confusion. If the consumer was interested initially in my mark, I deserve to get that consumer, even if they come to prefer the goods of my rival. The person whose likelihood of confusion is relevant is not merely the actual consumer, but the bystander and possible future purchaser. This vision of the right protects a larger swath of time, reaches a larger swath of markets and protects against (as a legal realist, Cohen would say 'judicially creates') "harms" that the first vision simply does not reach.

These two views of trademark law are of great importance in the doctrine. Compare genericide, *WalMart v. Samara* and the defense of fair or nominative use with *PETA*, initial interest confusion and anti-dilution law. Can you see the differing baselines of Pitney, Brandeis or Holmes here? Do you notice assumptions about whether positive externalities "naturally" (or efficiently) belong to the originator? See the way that the frames of competition and information-flow in the first view shade into the framing of property and entitlement in the second?

Our point is that these themes come up not just in trademark, but *throughout* intellectual property law. In some sense, we fight the same battles again and again—it would be nice to know that we are doing it, to understand the other side, to be a better advocate but also a better counselor and advisor.

Is computer code speech or property? Musical score or digital crowbar? Is an algorithm an invention running on a computer—and thus in the world of property? Or is it an idea, part of the great public domain of science, belonging in the world of free expression and interchange? Should we see the reverse engineering of a game-cartridge as the facilitating of competition by allowing interoperability? Or should we see it as a case of shamelessly copying, reaping where you have not sown? Is digitally restricting fair use just a property rights issue, like locking your diary in the safe, or is it an attempt to use copyright's monopoly to restrict protected speech? Should trade secrets be protected only against acts that are illegal on other grounds, such as breach of confidentiality agreements? Or should the owner be protected even from legal actions, such as an airplane overflight that might gather valuable information, either because we think that it is immoral or because it leads to inefficient precautions? Yes, economic analysis can tell us much about these issues, but it too begins from implicit frames and baselines.

The second theme was the effect of constitutional law—both the Intellectual Property clause and the First Amendment—on intellectual property. To summarize, we see a wild divergence between deference to Congress in copyright (*Eldred, Golan*) and—if *Graham* is still good law—a firmer hand in applying the Constitution's limits to patent. We see that the Court is reluctant to strike down legislative provisions outright, but will do so if they seem flagrantly unconstitutional (*Tam, Brunetti*). But we also see a willingness to be guided by constitutional purposes and the First Amendment's strictures in *applying* intellectual property law. The constitution may exert its greatest sway on intellectual property interstitially.

The third theme was the adaptation of law to technological change. We had three main case studies: trademark law's attempt to deal with domain names, copyright law's attempts to deal with software, and patent law's attempts to deal with genetic engineering on the one hand and the networked computer on the other. Each domain was presented with a *methodological* choice—does one formalistically apply the old rules to a reality that the technology has changed? Or does one focus on the purposive and utilitarian *goals* of the system and interpret the law accordingly—often using the old pigeon-holes of the law in new and surprising ways? The *PETA* decision in trademark, the *MAI* decision in copyright and—to a lesser extent—the CAFC's disdain for "policy arguments" in the *Fisher* decision on utility standards in genetic patents represent the first tendency. By contrast, the *Playboy v. Welles* decision about nominative use and search engines in trademark, the *Lotus, Perfect 10* and *Google Books* cases in copyright and *some* aspects of the

Alice case in patent represent the second. You should be able to come up with many others. We tried to present the arguments for both approaches. While admitting its difficulties, we are proponents of the second approach. You should make up your own mind.

The fourth theme was that the limitations on and exceptions to intellectual property are as important as the rights themselves. "The holes matter as much as the cheese" to quote the discussion of *Sony*. In each field of intellectual property we saw the attempt to balance those things that should be in the realm of property and private right, and those that should be in the public domain, free for all to use. This balance is the recurrent *motif* of intellectual property policy. But how to *strike* that balance?

Again in each field, two tendencies manifested themselves. One sees strong rights as necessary and vital incentives. It views attempts to limit or constrain those rights as inherently problematic, a loss or "taking" from the property owner and a threat to innovation and economy. If X level of protection gives us Y level of innovation, then 2X will give us 2Y and so on. The norm is property. The best example of this was the discussion of "The Internet Threat" in copyright policy and the idea that rights should vary inversely with the cost of copying. Costless copying will require nearly perfect—digitally enabled—control.

The other vision sees rights as "necessary evils"—Macaulay and Jefferson were its most articulate proponents. The right is a limited monopoly that has to be created to produce some social good: it should be held to the minimum scope, duration and extent necessary to achieve that goal. The norm is freedom, and the goal of intellectual property law is the crafting of limitations and exceptions to make sure the losses are as small as possible and the gains as great. The fair use cases presented many examples of this theme. How powerful is it? Well, if one looks at *Congressional* action—for example the repeated retrospective extensions of copyright—one has to say that it faces an uphill struggle. Will the fact that copyright law now directly affects citizens in a way it did not before change that fact? We do not know.

There is much that the book did not cover—though we wish we had time to do so. There has been very little here about the issues of distributive justice in intellectual property. Our patent system will never produce drugs that treat the diseases of the global poor. If one assesses value by ability and willingness to pay, as some but not all economic analysis does, obesity and hair loss treatments are more valuable than malaria vaccines. Most people find that result outrageous, correctly, but respond—wrongly in our view—by blaming pharmaceutical companies for it. We are the ones who set the system up that way. If we want drugs (and other inventions) that respond to the needs of the global poor, then other systems of incentives will be needed.

There *are* such systems—ranging from "prize funds" to cost-plus contracts to crowd-sourced innovation (though that last one will be of little help for the truly enormous problems of pharmaceutical development). Meanwhile the Access to Knowledge or A2K movement has stressed the role of liberal copyright policies in securing access to educational and cultural materials. These are deep and important issues and we invite you to read further on them.[1]

But what of the future? In our final reading, we offer one last perspective on the changes that the internet may yet wreak on our assumptions about incentives, sharing and creativity.

---

[1] *See* Knowledge Ecology International http://keionline.org/vectors (visited July 20, 2018); Amy Kapczynski, *The Access to Knowledge Mobilization and the New Politics of Intellectual Property*, 117 YALE L.J. 804 (2008); Madhavi Sunder, *From Goods to a Good Life: Intellectual Property and Global Justice* (2012).

James Boyle, A Creative Commons
The Public Domain, *pp. 179–181, 183–200*

If you go to the familiar Google search page and click the intimidating link marked "advanced search," you come to a page that gives you more fine-grained control over the framing of your query. Nestled among the choices that allow you to pick your desired language, or exclude raunchy content, is an option that says "usage rights." Click "free to use or share" and then search for "physics textbook" and you can download a 1,200-page physics textbook, copy it, or even print it out and hand it to your students. Search for "Down and Out in the Magic Kingdom" and you will find Cory Doctorow's fabulous science fiction novel, online, in full, for free. His other novels are there too—with the willing connivance of his commercial publisher. Search for "David Byrne, My Fair Lady" and you will be able to download Byrne's song and make copies for your friends. You'll find songs from Gilberto Gil and the Beastie Boys on the same page. No need to pay iTunes or worry about breaking the law.

Go to the "advanced" page on Flickr, the popular photo sharing site, and you will find a similar choice marked "Creative Commons License." Check that box and then search for "Duke Chapel" and you will get a selection of beautiful photos of the lovely piece of faux Gothic architecture that sits about three hundred yards from the office where I am writing these words. You can copy those photos, and 66 million others on different subjects, share them with your friends, print them for your wall, and, in some cases, even use them commercially. The same basic tools can be found on a range of specialized search engines with names like OWL Music Search, BlipTV, SpinExpress, and OERCommons. Searching those sites, or just sticking with the advanced options on Google or Yahoo, will get you courses in music theory, moral philosophy, and C++ programming from famous universities; a full-length movie called Teach by Oscar-winning director Davis Guggenheim; and free architectural drawings that can be used to build low-cost housing. At the Wellcome Library, you will find two thousand years of medical images that can be shared freely. Searching for "skeleton" is particularly fun. You can even go to your favorite search engine, type in the title of this book, find a site that will allow you to download it, and send the PDF to a hundred friends, warmly anticipating their rapturous enjoyment. (Better ask them first.)

All this copying and sharing and printing sounds illegal, but it is not (at least if you went through the steps I described). And the things you can do with this content do not stop with simply reproducing it, printing it on paper, or sending it by e-mail. Much of it can be changed, customized, remixed—you could rewrite the module of the class and insert your own illustrations, animate the graphs showing calculus in action, morph the photo into something new. If you search for a musician with the unpromising name "Brad Sucks," you will find a Web site bearing the modest subtitle "A one man band with no fans." Brad, it turns out, does not suck and has many fans. What makes him particularly interesting is that he allows those fans, or anyone else for that matter, to remix his music and post their creations online. I am particularly fond of the Matterovermind remix of "Making Me Nervous," but it may not be to your taste. Go to a site called ccMixter and you will find that musicians, famous and obscure, are inviting you to sample and remix their music.

On December 15, 2002, in San Francisco, a charitable organization called Creative Commons was launched. (Full disclosure: I have been a proud board member of Creative Commons since its creation.) Creative Commons was the brainchild of Larry Lessig, Hal Abelson, and Eric Eldred. All the works I have just described—and this book itself—are under Creative Commons licenses. The authors and creators of those works have chosen to share it with the world, with you, under generous terms, while reserving certain rights for themselves. They may have allowed you to copy it, but not to alter it—to make derivative works. Or they may have allowed you to use it as you wish, so long as you do so noncommercially. Or they may have given you complete freedom, provided only that you attribute them as the owner of the work. There are a few simple choices and a limited menu of permutations.

What makes these licenses unusual is that they can be read by two groups that normal licenses exclude—human beings (rather than just lawyers) and computers. The textbooks, photos, films, and songs have a tasteful little emblem on them marked with a "cc" which, if you click on it, links to a "Commons Deed," a simple one-page explanation of the freedoms you have. There are even icons—a dollar with a slash through it, for example—that make things even clearer. Better still, the reason the search engines could find this material is that the licenses also "tell" search engines exactly what freedoms have been given. Simple "metadata" (a fancy word for tags that computers can read) mark the material with its particular level of freedoms. This is not digital rights management. The license will not try to control your computer, install itself on your hard drive, or break your TV. It is just an expression of the terms under which the author has chosen to release the work. That means that if you search Google or Flickr for "works I am free to share, even commercially," you know you can go into business selling those textbooks, or printing those photos on mugs and T-shirts, so long as you give the author attribution. If you search for "show me works I can build on," you know you are allowed to make what copyright lawyers call "derivative works."

. . .

From one perspective, Creative Commons looks like a simple device for enabling exercise of authorial control, remarkable only for the extremely large number of authors making that choice and the simplicity with which they can do so. From another, it can be seen as re-creating, by private choice and automated licenses, the world of creativity before law had permeated to the finest, most atomic level of science and culture—the world of folk music or 1950s jazz, of jokes and slang and recipes, of Ray Charles's "rewording" of gospel songs, or of Isaac Newton describing himself as "standing on the shoulders of giants" (and not having to pay them royalties). Remember, that is not a world without intellectual property. The cookbook might be copyrighted even if the recipe was not. Folk music makes it to the popular scene and is sold as a copyrighted product. The jazz musician "freezes" a particular version of the improvisation on a communally shared set of musical motifs, records it, and sometimes even claims ownership of it. Newton himself was famously touchy about precedence and attribution, even if not about legal ownership of his ideas. But it is a world in which creativity and innovation proceed on the basis of an extremely large "commons" of material into which it was never imagined that property rights could permeate.

For many of us, Creative Commons was conceived of as a second-best solution created by private agreement because the best solution could not be obtained through public law. The best solution would be a return of the formality requirement—a requirement that one at least write the words "James Boyle copyright 2008," for example, in order to get more than 100 years of legal protection backed by "strict liability" and federal criminal law. Those who did not wish to have the legal monopoly could omit the phrase and the work would pass into the public domain. . . .

[But actually] Creative Commons licenses or the tools of free and open source software—to which I will turn in a moment—represent something more than merely a second-best solution to a poorly chosen rule. They represent a visible example of a type of creativity, of innovation, which has been around for a very long time, but which has reached new salience on the Internet—distributed creativity based around a shared commons of material.

Free and Open Source Software

In 2007, Clay Shirky, an incisive commentator on networked culture, gave a speech which anyone but a Net aficionado might have found simultaneously romantic and impenetrable. He started by telling the story of a Shinto shrine that has been painstakingly rebuilt to exactly the same plan many times over its 1,300-year life—and which was denied certification as a historic building as a result. Shirky's point? What was remarkable was not the building. It was a community that would continue to build and rebuild the thing for more than a millennium.

From there, Shirky shifted to a discussion of his attempt to get AT&T to adopt the high-level programming language Perl—which is released as free and open source software under the General Public License. From its initial creation by Larry Wall in 1987, Perl has been adapted, modified, and developed by an extraordinary range of talented programmers, becoming more powerful and flexible in the process. As Shirky recounts the story, when the AT&T representatives asked "where do you get your support?" Shirky responded, "'we get our support from a community'—which to them sounded a bit like 'we get our Thursdays from a banana.'" Shirky concluded the speech thus:

> We have always loved one another. We're human. It's something we're good at. But up until recently, the radius and half-life of that affection has been quite limited. With love alone, you can plan a birthday party. Add coordinating tools and you can write an operating system. In the past, we would do little things for love, but big things required money. Now we can do big things for love.

There are a few people out there for whom "operating systems" and "love" could plausibly coexist in a sentence not constructed by an infinite number of monkeys. For most though, the question is, what could he possibly have meant?

The arguments in this book so far have taken as a given the incentives and collective action problems to which intellectual property is a response. Think of Chapter 1 and the economic explanation of "public goods." The fact that it is expensive to do the research to find the right drug, but cheap to manufacture it once it is identified provides a reason to create a legal right of exclusion. In those realms where the innovation would not have happened anyway, the legal right of exclusion gives a power to price above cost, which in turn gives incentives to creators and distributors. So goes the theory. I have discussed the extent to which the logic of enclosure works for the commons of the mind as well as it did for the arable commons, taking into account the effects of an information society and a global Internet. What I have not done is asked whether a global network actually transforms some of our assumptions about how creation happens in a way that reshapes the debate about the need for incentives, at least in certain areas. This, however, is exactly the question that needs to be asked.

For anyone interested in the way that networks can enable new collaborative methods of production, the free software movement, and the broader but less political movement that goes under the name of open source software, provide interesting case studies. Open source software is released under a series of licenses, the most important being the General Public License (GPL). The GPL specifies that anyone may copy the software, provided the license remains attached and the source code for the software always remains available. Users may add to or modify the code, may build on it and incorporate it into their own work, but if they do so, then the new program created is also covered by the GPL. Some people refer to this as the "viral" nature of the license; others find the term offensive. The point, however, is that the open quality of the creative enterprise spreads. It is not simply a donation of a program or a work to the public domain, but a continual accretion in which all gain the benefits of the program on pain of agreeing to give their additions and innovations back to the communal project.

For the whole structure to work without large-scale centralized coordination, the creation process has to be modular, with units of different sizes and complexities, each requiring slightly different expertise, all of which can be added together to make a grand whole. I can work on the sendmail program, you on the search algorithms. More likely, lots of people try, their efforts are judged by the community, and the best ones are adopted. Under these conditions, this curious mix of Kropotkin and Adam Smith, Richard Dawkins and Richard Stallman, we get distributed production without having to rely on the proprietary exclusion model. The whole enterprise will be much, much, much greater than the sum of the parts.

What's more, and this is a truly fascinating twist, when the production process does need more centralized coordination, some governance that guides how the sticky modular bits are put together, it is at least theoretically possible that we can come up with the control system in exactly the same way. In this sense, distributed production is potentially recursive. Governance processes, too, can be assembled through distributed methods on a global network, by people with widely varying motivations, skills, and reserve prices. . . .

What is remarkable is not merely that the software works technically, but that it is an example of widespread, continued, high-quality innovation. The really remarkable thing is that it works socially, as a continuing system, sustained by a network consisting both of volunteers and of individuals employed by companies such as IBM and Google whose software "output" is nevertheless released into the commons.

Here, it seems, we have a classic public good: code that can be copied freely and sold or redistributed without paying the creator or creators. This sounds like a tragedy of the commons of the kind that I described in the first three chapters of the book. Obviously, with a nonrival, nonexcludable good like software, this method of production cannot be sustained; there are inadequate incentives to ensure continued production. *E pur si muove*, as Galileo is apocryphally supposed to have said in the face of Cardinal Bellarmine's certainties: "And yet it moves." Or, as Clay Shirky put it, "we get our support from a community."

For a fair amount of time, most economists looked at open source software and threw up their hands. From their point of view, "we get our support from a community" did indeed sound like "we get our Thursdays from a banana." There is an old economics joke about the impossibility of finding a twenty-dollar bill lying on a sidewalk. In an efficient market, the money would already have been picked up. (Do not wait for a punch line.) When economists looked at open source software they saw not a single twenty-dollar bill lying implausibly on the sidewalk, but whole bushels of them. Why would anyone work on a project the fruits of which could be appropriated by anyone? Since copyright adheres on fixation—since the computer programmer already has the legal power to exclude others—why would he or she choose to take the extra step of adopting a license that undermined that exclusion? Why would anyone choose to allow others to use and modify the results of their hard work? Why would they care whether the newcomers, in turn, released their contributions back into the commons?

. . .

Yochai Benkler and I would argue that these questions are fun to debate but ultimately irrelevant. Assume a random distribution of incentive structures in different people, a global network—transmission, information sharing, and copying costs that approach zero—and a modular creation process. With these assumptions, it just does not matter why they do it. In lots of cases, they will do it. One person works for love of the species, another in the hope of a better job, a third for the joy of solving puzzles, and a fourth because he has to solve a particular problem anyway for his own job and loses nothing by making his hack available for all. Each person has their own reserve price, the point at which they say, "Now I will turn off Survivor and go and create something." But on a global network, there are a lot of people, and with numbers that big and information overhead that small, even relatively hard projects will attract motivated and skilled people whose particular reserve price has been crossed.

More conventionally, many people write free software because they are paid to do so. Amazingly, IBM now earns more from what it calls "Linux-related revenues" than it does from traditional patent licensing, and IBM is the largest patent holder in the world. . . .

Why on earth should we care? People have come up with a surprising way to create software. So what? There are at least three reasons we might care. First, it teaches us something about the limitations of conventional economics and the counterintuitive business methods that thrive on networks. Second, it might offer a new tool in our attempt to solve a variety of social problems. Third, and most speculative, it hints at the way that a global communications network can sometimes help move the line between work and play, professional and amateur, individual and community creation, rote production and compensated "hobby."

We should pay attention to open source software because it shows us something about business methods in the digital world—indeed in the entire world of "information-based" products, which is coming to include biotechnology. The scale of your network matters. The larger the number of people who use your operating system, make programs for your type of computer, create new levels for your game, or use your device, the better off you are. A single fax machine is a paperweight. Two make up a communications link. Ten million and you have a ubiquitous communications network into which your "paperweight" is now a hugely valuable doorway.

This is the strange characteristic of networked goods. The actions of strangers dramatically increase or decrease the usefulness of your good. At each stage the decision of someone else to buy a fax machine increases the value of mine. If I am eating an apple, I am indifferent about whether you are too. But if I have a fax machine then my welfare is actually improved by the decisions of strangers to buy one. The same process works in reverse. Buy a word processing program that becomes unpopular, get "locked in" to using it, and find yourself unable to exchange your work easily with others. Networks matter and increasing the size of the networks continues to add benefits to the individual members. . . .

I write a column for the Financial Times, but I lack the fervor of the true enthusiast in the "Great Game of Markets." By themselves, counterintuitive business methods do not make my antennae tingle. But as Larry Lessig and Yochai Benkler have argued, this is something more than just another business method. They point us to the dramatic role that openness—whether in network architecture, software, or content—has had in the success of the Internet. What is going on here is actually a remarkable corrective to the simplistic notion of the tragedy of the commons, a corrective to the Internet Threat storyline and to the dynamics of the second enclosure movement. This commons creates and sustains value, and allows firms and individuals to benefit from it, without depleting the value already created. To appropriate a phrase from Carol Rose, open source teaches us about the *comedy of the commons*, a way of arranging markets and production that we, with our experience rooted in physical property and its typical characteristics, at first find counterintuitive and bizarre. Which brings us to the next question for open source. Can we use its techniques to solve problems beyond the world of software production?

In the language of computer programmers, the issue here is "does it scale?" Can we generalize anything from this limited example? How many types of production, innovation, and research fit into the model I have just described? After all, for many innovations and inventions one needs hardware, capital investment, and large-scale, real-world data collection—stuff, in its infinite recalcitrance and facticity. Maybe the open source model provides a workaround to the individual incentives problem, but that is not the *only* problem. And how many types of innovation or cultural production are as modular as software? Is open source software a paradigm case of collective innovation that helps us to understand open source software and not much else?

Again, I think this is a good question, but it may be the wrong one. My own guess is that an open source method of production is far more common than we realize. "Even before the Internet" (as some of my students have taken to saying portentously), science, law, education, and musical genres all developed in ways that are markedly similar to the model I have described. The marketplace of ideas, the continuous roiling development in thought and norms that our political culture spawns, owes much more to the distributed, nonproprietary model than it does to the special case of commodified innovation that we think about in copyright and patent. Not that copyright and patent are unimportant in the process, but they may well be the exception rather than the norm. Commons-based production of ideas is hardly unfamiliar, after all. . . .

. . . I have given my guesses about the future of the distributed model of innovation. My own utopia has it flourishing alongside a scaled-down, but still powerful, intellectual property regime. Equally plausible scenarios see it as a dead end or as the inevitable victor in the war of productive processes. These are all guesses, however. At the very least, there is some possibility, even hope, that we could have a world in which much more of intellectual and inventive production is free. "'Free' as in 'free speech,'" Richard Stallman says, not "free as in 'free beer.'" But we could hope that much of it would be both free of centralized control and low- or no-cost. When the marginal cost of reproduction is zero, the marginal cost of transmission and storage approaches zero, the process of creation is additive, and much of the labor doesn't charge, the world looks a little different. This is at least a possible future, or part of a possible future, and one that we should not foreclose without thinking twice.

The point is, then, that there is a chance that a new (or old, but under-recognized) method of production could flourish in ways that seem truly valuable—valuable to free speech, innovation, scientific discovery, the wallets of consumers, to what William Fisher calls "semiotic democracy," and, perhaps, valuable to the balance between joyful creation and drudgery for hire. True, it is only a chance. True, this theory's scope of operation and sustainability are uncertain. But why would we want to foreclose it?

Learning from the Sharing Economy

Lesson number one comes from nonprofit activities—everything from Wikipedia to Web sites created by enthusiasts. People like to create and wish to share. In many cases they will do so without financial reward. A surprising amount of useful, creative, or expressive activity is generated without any financial incentive at all.

Should this cause us to throw out the economic case for copyrights? No. But it should lead us to reassess it. As I explained in Chapter 1, copyright provides an incentive for two distinct activities. First, it offers an incentive to create the work in the first place. The author of *Windows for Dummies* or *Harry Potter* gets a right to exclude others from copying the work, a right that he or she can sell in the marketplace. The goal is to offer a financial reason to devote time to this particular creative activity. It is this incentive that is most often cited when attempting to persuade policy makers to expand protection. Second, it offers an incentive to distribute the work—to typeset and print large quantities of the work and to sell it to bookstores, or to broadcast it, or put it on movie screens.

Each medium is economically different, of course. The economics of the feature film are different from those of the book, the magazine, or the operating system. Thus, we have never had very good figures on the relative importance of these incentives. We can only guess at how much of the incentive from copyright goes to encouraging creation and how much to distribution. Until recently, most types of distribution demanded higher levels of capital. The industry structure that resulted often consisted of creators who worked as wage or contract labor for distributors—either never acquiring copyright in their work in the first place or immediately transferring that copyright to their employers. Because distribution was expensive, our experience with material generated for fun or out of a love of sharing was an essentially private and local one. You might have a neighbor's photocopied sheet of baking recipes that worked well at high altitudes, or of fishing techniques that worked well on a particular lake, a song that a friend created for a special occasion, or a short story you wrote for your kids—and then typed up for them to tell to theirs. Financial incentives were not needed to encourage the creation of the work, but the cost of distribution dramatically limited its dissemination.

The single most dramatic thing that the Web has done by lowering the cost of communication and distribution, at the same moment that other electronic tools lowered the cost of production, is to make this local and private activity a global and public one. Someone, somewhere, will have written the guide to fishing on that lake, baking at that altitude, washing windows, or treating stings from Portuguese man-of-war jellyfish. Someone will have taken a photo of the Duke Chapel or explained the history, economics, and chemistry of shoe polish or distilling. Someone might even have created a great class on music theory or C++ programming. Someone will have written a handy little program to manage DNS requests on a local network. . . .

True, much of the material on the Web is inane or insane, confused, badly written, tendentious, and inaccurate. (It should be noted that this is hardly a problem confined to the Web or volunteer-generated material. Personally, I would not want *People* magazine or Fox News in a time capsule to represent my civilization. But some of the material on the Web is clearly worse.) Yes, Wikipedia is occasionally inaccurate—though in one test in *Nature* it stacked up well against the Encyclopedia Britannica, and it is obviously much more encyclopedic in its coverage. But all of this misses the point. . . .

These examples are not the end of the process. Our methods of sorting, ranking, and verifying the material generated are still evolving. They may improve even beyond this point. We are only [twenty] years into this particular experiment, after all. And a huge amount of this material is produced by our fellow citizens without the profit motive.

Does this mean that we no longer need copyright or patent protection to encourage the production and distribution of creative work? No. The fishing tips are great, but I still might buy a handsomely illustrated guide to take on the lake with me or, even better, just stay at home and read *A River Runs Through It. The New Yorker*, and not a sheaf of printouts from the Web, still sits on my coffee table, though much of the high-quality content I read